international encyclopedia of economic sociology

The *International Encyclopedia of Economic Sociology* is the first encyclopedia in the field and a timely response to the surge of interest in economic sociology over the last 30 years.

Economic sociology deals with the multiple and complex relations between economy and society. In particular, it focuses on the impact of social, political and cultural factors on economic behaviour. The encyclopedia gives comprehensive and accessible coverage of the wide range of areas and subjects covered by the field, including, amongst many others, such major topics as consumption, corruption, democracy and economy, ecology, embeddedness, gender and economy, globalization, industrial relations, law and economy, markets, organization theory, political economy, religion and economic life, social capital, the sociology of money, state and economy, trust, and work.

The *International Encyclopedia of Economic Sociology* is a much-needed major reference work on one of the richest areas of development in the social sciences in recent years. It is an extremely valuable new resource for students and researchers in sociology, economics, political science, and business, organization and management studies.

Entries are cross-referenced and carry compact bibliographies. There is a full index.

Jens Beckert is Director, Max Plank Institute for the Study of Societies, Köln, Germany.

Milan Zafirovski is Associate Professor, Department of Sociology, University of North Texas, USA.

international encyclopedia of economic sociology

edited by

jens beckert

milan zafirovski

Routledge
Taylor & Francis Group

LONDON AND NEW YORK

First published 2006
by Routledge
2 Park Square, Milton Park, Abingdon, Oxon OX14 4RN

Simultaneously published in the USA and Canada
by Routledge
270 Madison Ave, New York, NY 10016, USA

Routledge is an imprint of the Taylor and Francis Group

© 2006 Routledge

Typeset in Bembo and Helvetica by Taylor & Francis Books
Printed and bound in Great Britain by MPG Books Ltd, Bodmin

British Library Cataloguing in Publication Data
A catalogue record for this book is available from the British Library

Library of Congress Cataloging in Publication Data
A catalog record for this book has been requested

ISBN10: 0-415-28673-5
ISBN13: 9-78-0-415-28673-2

Taylor & Francis Group is the Academic Division of T&F Informa plc.

contents

illustrations

figures

tables

advisors

introduction

The analysis of the economy has been a core concern of sociological scholarship ever since the institutionalization of sociology as an academic discipline. For 'classical' sociologists like Emile Durkheim, Max Weber, Karl Marx, Georg Simmel, Vilfredo Pareto and others, the understanding of the economy, its social and political constitution, and its effects on society were main areas of their scholarship. Many of their writings stand close to the institutionalist traditions in economics. During the post World War II period the focus on the economy in sociological scholarship receded. Over the last twenty-five years, however, economic sociology has experienced a dramatic revival of interest. This shows in the many anthologies and journal articles that have been published on the subject, in newly founded journals and in a growing number of monographs in the field.

Despite this great interest in scholarship in economic sociology, no publication has been available so far that gives a comprehensive overview of the core concepts, terms, substantial subfields and main contributors of economic sociology. It is this gap that the *International Encyclopedia of Economic Sociology* attempts to close. The Encyclopedia assembles about 250 articles by more than 160 different authors who are well-known experts on their topics. The chosen entries and the authors were selected by the editors together with the editorial board of twelve internationally leading economic sociologists.

We strove for the production of a volume that is broad, integrative and interdisciplinary. To this end we included central concepts, terms and authors from economic sociology but also from adjacent disciplines like economics, anthropology, political science and organization studies to the extent they are relevant for current research in economic sociology. The goal was to provide a comprehensive resource that gives an easily accessible overview over the expanding field of economic sociology.

The articles are structured in a specific way. Authors define their topic and its relevance at the beginning of their articles. The main part of the entries is devoted to the core debates, schools, concepts and developments of the topic, followed by a conclusion and outlook. Entries communicate the historical aspects of the subject, outlining traditional and contemporary developments and reflect in many cases country-specific aspects of the relevant debate. A broad international perspective has also been encouraged by choosing authors from a great number of countries. Cross-references, marked in **bold**, help the reader to find entries related to the topic. The bibliography at the end of each article leads the reader to crucial further publications on the issue.

The encyclopedia aims at all scholars, students and members of the general public wishing to explore the sociological perspective on the economy. They can be sociologists, economists, political scientists, anthropologists or scholars from business studies and organization studies, as well as students and researchers from other disciplines. The book will give students and researchers a systematic up-to-date picture of the extent and range of work in economic sociology. In addition, the Encyclopedia is also of interest for research-oriented policy and business consultants, economic institutions, foundations and the like. To support this broad interest authors were asked to write in a reader-friendly though technically precise manner. Since the Encyclopedia encompasses a far broader range of subjects compared to existing readers in the field of economic sociology, it will be an important companion to research and scholarship upon which undergraduates, graduates, professors and researchers can draw. We hope that the reader will find the Encyclopedia a clear and concise guide to economic sociology and its particular topics which also provides a springboard for further exploration, analysis and thought. The editors would like to thank the members of the editorial board for their many valuable suggestions, especially at the early stages of the development of the Encyclopedia. We would also like to thank the authors who wrote this large book in a collective effort that none of us could have accomplished alone. Special thanks go to Aileen Harvey, the Development Editor at Routledge, for her effective work in helping us with the organizational tasks that come with coordinating so many articles written by so many different authors. We also thank Gerard Greenway, the Commissioning Editor at Routledge, for entrusting us with this important and demanding project. Finally, Jens Beckert would like to thank Barbara Temps for her secretarial help.

Jens Beckert
Milan Zafirovski

contributors

Mitchel Y. Abolafia
University at Albany, New York, USA

Ruth V. Aguilera
University of Illinois, Urbana-Champaign, USA

Arthur S. Alderson
Indiana University, USA

Penney Alldredge
University of California, Davis, USA

Patrik Aspers
Stockholm University, Sweden, and Max Planck Institute for the Study of Societies, Cologne, Germany

Mie Augier
Stanford University, USA

Reinhard Bachmann
Birkbeck College, University of London, UK

Roger E. Backhouse
University of Birmingham, UK

Jesse Barba
University of Massachusetts, USA

Jack Barbalet
University of Leicester, UK

Filippo Barbera
University of Turin, Italy

Kimberly P. Barton
St. Cloud University, USA

Thomas D. Beamish
University of California, Davis, USA

Giacomo Becattini
University of Florence, Italy

Jens Beckert
Max Planck Institute for the Study of Societies, Cologne, Germany

Marco Bellandi
University of Florence, Italy

Johannes Berger
University of Mannheim, Germany

Thomas Beschorner
University of Montreal, Canada

Yanjie Bian
Hong Kong University of Science and Techonology

Nicole Woolsey Biggart
University of California, Davis, USA

Jim Bingen
Michigan State University, USA

Judith R. Blau
University of North Carolina, USA

Fred Block
University of California, Davis, USA

Terry Boswell
Emory University, USA

Robert Boyer
L'Ecole des Hautes Etudes en Sciences Sociales, France

Peter D. Brandon
University of Massachusetts, Amherst, USA

Ronald L. Breiger
University of Arizona, USA

Benjamin D. Brewer
Johns Hopkins University, USA

Richard L. Brinkman
Portland State University, USA

Mary C. Brinton
Harvard University, USA

Daniel W. Bromley
University of Wisconsin-Madison, USA

Michelle J. Budig
University of Massachusetts, USA

Thomas J. Burns
University of Oklahoma, USA

Lawrence Busch
Michigan State University, USA

Alain Caillé
University of Paris 10, Nanterre, France

Charles Camic
University of Wisconsin-Madison, USA

John L. Campbell
Dartmouth College, USA

Bruce G. Carruthers
Northwestern University, USA

Ha-Joon Chang
University of Cambridge, UK

Christopher Chase-Dunn
University of California, Riverside, USA

Eve Chiapello
Groupe HEC, France

Simon Clarke
University of Warwick, UK

William Coleman
Australian National University, Canberra

Karen S. Cook
Stanford University, USA

Edward Crenshaw
Ohio State University, USA

Colin Crouch
European University Institute, Italy

Harry F. Dahms
University of Tennessee, Knoxville, USA

Gerald Davis
University of Michigan, USA

John B. Davis
University of Amsterdam, The Netherlands and Marquette Univerity, USA

David Dequech
University of Campinas, São Paulo, Brazil

Christoph Deutschmann
University of Tübingen, Germany

Frank Dobbin
Harvard University, USA

Stanislav D. Dobrev
University of Chicago, USA

Wilfred Dolfsma
Erasmus University, Rotterdam, and Maastricht University, The Netherlands

Jonathan Eastwood
Boston University, USA

David Ellerman
University of California, Riverside, USA

Amitai Etzioni
George Washington University, Washington DC, USA

Susan Brown Eve
University of North Texas, USA

Thomas J. Fararo
University of Pittsburgh, USA

Robert Faulkner
University of Massachusetts, Amherst, USA

Michael Faust
Sociological Research Institute at Göttingen University, Germany

Adrian Favell
University of California, Los Angeles, USA

Michel Ferrary
CERAM Sophia Antipolis Business School, France

Marion Fourcade-Gourinchas
University of California, Berkeley, USA

Robert H. Frank
Cornell University, USA

Melissa Fugiero
University of Massachusetts, Amherst, USA

Simon Gächter
University of Nottingham, UK

Joseph Galaskiewicz
University of Arizona, USA

Markus Gangl
University of Mannheim, Germany

Heiner Ganssmann
Freie Universität Berlin, Germany

Roberto Garvía
Carlos III University, Madrid, Spain

Philipp Genschel
International University Bremen, Germany

Alexandra Gerbasi
Stanford University, USA

Elisabeth Göbel
University of Trier, Germany

Heidi Gottfried
Wayne State University, Michigan, USA

Liah Greenfeld
Boston University, USA

Reiner Grundmann
Aston University, UK

Mauro F. Guillén
University of Pennsylvania, USA

Aldo Haesler
Université de Caen Basse-Normandie, France

Jerald Hage
University of Maryland, USA

Charles N. Halaby
University of Wisconsin-Madison, USA

Kieran Healy
University of Arizona, USA

Peter Hedström
Nuffield College, Oxford, UK

Alexander Hicks
Emory University, USA

Geoffrey M. Hodgson
University of Hertfordshire, UK

Randy Hodson
Ohio State University, Columbus, USA

Michael Hölscher
Institute for Higher Education Research, Wittenberg, Germany

Martin Höpner
Max Planck Institute for the Study of Societies, Germany

Geoffrey Ingham
University of Cambridge, UK

Søren Jagd
Roskilde University, Denmark

LuAnne R. Johnson
University of Minnesota, USA

Yukio Kawano
Daito-Bunka University, Japan

Lisa A. Keister
Ohio State University, USA

John R. Kelly
University of Illinois, Urbana-Champaign, USA

Lane Kenworthy
Emory University, USA

Edgar Kiser
University of Washington, Seattle, USA

David Knoke
University of Minnesota, USA

Karin Knorr Cetina
Universität Konstanz, Germany, and University of Chicago, USA

Bruce Kogut
INSEAD, France

Sabine T. Koeszegi
University of Vienna, Austria

Richard N. Langlois
University of Connecticut, USA

Magali Sarfatti Larson
Temple University, Philadelphia, USA

Frédéric Lebaron
Maison des Sciences de l'Homme, Paris, France

Barry B. Levine
Florida International University, USA

Nan Lin
Duke University, USA

Siegwart Lindenberg
University of Groningen, Netherlands

April Linton
University of California, San Diego, USA

Michael Lounsbury
University of Alberta, Canada

Loren Lutzenhiser
Washington State University, USA

Michael W. Maher
University of California, Davis, USA

George Marcus
Rice University, USA

Barry Markovsky
University of South Carolina, USA

Christopher Marquis
Harvard University, USA

Peter V. Marsden
Harvard University, USA

Alberto Martinelli
Università degli studi di Milano, Italy

Steffen Mau
University of Bremen, Germany

Patrick McGuire
University of Toledo, Ohio, USA

Andrea Mennicken
London School of Economics, UK

Enzo Mingione
Università di Milano-Bicocca, Italy

Joya Misra
University of Massachusetts, Amherst, USA

Mark S. Mizruchi
University of Michigan, USA

Stephanie Moller
University of North Carolina, Charlotte, USA

Mark Moritz
Western Oregon University, USA

Bert Mosselmans
Roosevelt Academy, The Netherlands

Richard Münch
University of Bamberg, Germany

Fabian Muniesa
Ecole des Mines de Paris, France

Victor Nee
Cornell University, USA

Claus Offe
Humboldt University of Berlin, Germany

Anton Oleinik
Memorial University of Newfoundland, Canada

Sonja Opper
University of Tübingen, Germany

Robert J. Oxoby
University of Calgary, Canada

Donald Palmer
University of California, Davis, USA

Christian Papilloud
University of Bielefeld, Germany

Axel T. Paul
Albert-Ludwigs-Universtität Freiburg, Germany

Valina Petrova
Emory University, USA

Geny Piotti
Max Planck Institute for the Study of Societies, Cologne, Germany

Reinhard Pirker
Vienna University of Economics, Austria

Joel M. Podolny
Harvard University, USA

Melvin Pollner
University of California, Los Angeles, USA

Stephen Pratten
King's College, University of London, UK

Harland Prechel
Texas A&M University, USA

Christopher Prendergast
Illinois Wesleyan University, USA

Hermann Rauchenschwandtner
Vienna University, Austria

Marino Regini
Università degli studi di Milano, Italy

David Reisman
Nanyang Technological University, Singapore

Norbert Reuter
Technische Universität Aachen,
Germany

Steven Revard
University of Toledo, Ohio, USA

George Ritzer
University of Maryland, USA

Daniel G. Rodeheaver
University of North Texas, USA

Susan Rose-Ackerman
Yale University, USA

Jörg Rössel
University of Leipzig, Germany

William G. Roy
University of California, Los Angeles, USA

Warren Samuels
Michigan State University, USA

Scott Sawyer
Washington State University, USA

A. Allan Schmid
Michigan State University, USA

Juliet Schor
Boston College, USA

Michael Schwartz
State University of New York,
Stony Brook, USA

Chris Matthew Sciabarra
New York University, USA

Rudy Ray Seward
University of North Texas, USA

Darren E. Sherkat
Southern Illinois University, USA

Hwa Ji Shin
State University of New York,
Stony Brook, USA

Leslie Sklair
London School of Economics, UK

Charles W. Smith
Queens College and The Graduate Center,
City University of New York, USA

Michael R. Smith
McGill University, Montreal, Canada

Laurel Smith-Doerr
Boston University, USA

Sarah Busse Spencer
Drew University, USA

Andrew Spicer
University of South Carolina, USA

James Ronald Stanfield
Colorado State University, USA

Jacqueline Bloom Stanfield
University of Northern Colorado, USA

Nico Stehr
Zeppelin University, Friedrichshafen,
Germany

Philippe Steiner
Université Charles-de-Gaulle Lille 3,
France

Jeffrey Stepnisky
University of Maryland, USA

Wolfgang Streeck
Max Planck Institute for the Study of
Societies, Cologne, Germany

Teresa A. Sullivan
University of Texas, Austin

Richard Swedberg
Cornell University, USA

Joerg Sydow
Freie Universität Berlin, Germany

Laurent Thévenot
Ecole des Hautes Etudes en Sciences
Sociales (EHESS), Paris, France

A. Javier Treviño
Wheaton College-Massachusetts USA

Carlo Trigilia
Universita di Firenze, Italy

Bryan Turner
University of Cambridge, UK

Eric Tymoigne
University of Missouri-Kansas City, USA

Lars Udehn
Stockholm University, Sweden

Olav Velthuis
University of Constance, Germany

Rudolf Vetschera
University of Vienna, Austria

Thomas Voss
University of Leipzig, Germany

Löic Wacquant
University of California, Berkeley, USA and Chercheur, Centre de sociologie européenne, Paris, France

David Weakliem
University of Connecticut, USA

Arnold Windeler
Technische Universität Berlin, Germany

Erik Olin Wright
University of Wisconsin, USA

Dale E. Yeatts
University of North Texas, USA

Milan Zafirovski
University of North Texas, USA

Min Zhou
University of California, Los Angeles, USA

Sharon Zukin
Brooklyn College, USA

list of entries

A

ACCOUNTING, SOCIOLOGY OF

Accounting systems have come to play a key role in the organization of modern economies and societies. Organizational activities are structured around cost–benefit analyses, balanced score cards, costing procedures, cash flow analyses, risk calculations and many other numerical forms of organizational representation and economic measurement. The sociology of accounting is concerned with the study of the ways in which accounting shapes, and in turn is shaped by, the social, organizational and institutional contexts in which it operates. Attention is drawn to the complex interrelations that exist between accounting, calculative practices, organizational structures, and the wider social and institutional contexts in which accounting systems are embedded. A body of explicitly sociologically oriented accounting research began to take shape in the late 1980s. Interestingly, this research strand emerged largely outside the discipline of sociology itself. Although the founding fathers of economic sociology – **Weber**, **Sombart** and **Marx** – pointed out the pivotal role that double-entry bookkeeping and capital accounting played in the emergence of capitalist modes of production, studies that appeared in connection with the formation of the new **economic sociology**, with a few exceptions, remained largely silent on this topic.

The initial research programme

While in the 1960s and 1970s sociologically oriented accounting research was still dominated by micro-oriented studies of budgeting and management control systems, in the 1980s first attempts were undertaken to move accounting research beyond the boundaries of management and organizational research. An important platform for the new strand of sociological accounting studies provided, and still provides, the journals *Accounting, Organizations and Society* (founded in 1976) and *Critical Perspectives on Accounting* (founded in 1990). Initial steps to formulate and institutionalize the new research programme were undertaken by Hopwood, in his article 'On Trying to Study Accounting in the Contexts in Which It Operates' (1983), and Burchell *et al.*, in their study of 'The Roles of Accounting in Organizations and Society' (1980). Both articles outlined a research programme that was aimed at the study of the wider social and political aspects of accounting practices. Hopwood and Burchell *et al.* argued for the need to link micro- and macro-research levels and opened up research agendas for questions related to the different economic, social and political roles that accounting plays in organizations and society. In this context, particular emphasis was placed on the constituting – rather than mirroring – roles that accounting plays in economic life. The authors assumed that accounting practices actively create, rather than merely reflect, economic realities.

Hopwood and Burchell *et al.* criticized technical perspectives on accounting that take the rationality and functionality of calculative techniques for granted. Their aim was to move away from normative research questions of how accounting systems can be improved to an analysis of how accounting systems actually work in practice. Hopwood, in particular, wanted accounting research to become engaged with the following questions: how does accounting get implicated in the creation of particular organizational conceptions? How and when do accountings of organizational performance provide an incentive for action? How does accounting achieve and maintain the position of organizational significance?

The body of sociological accounting literature that emerged subsequent to Hopwood and Burchell *et al.*'s articles does not represent a coherent, clearly identifiable strand of research. Sociological accounting research is built on a multiplicity of different, often conflicting, sociological theories and methodologies. Sociological accounting studies have been influenced in particular by the following four theoretical approaches: new institutionalism (see **institutionalism, old and new**); Foucauldian studies of governmentality; **political economy** approaches; and interactionist perspectives.

Accounting and new institutionalism

In accordance with a neo-institutionalist analytical framework that, for example, has been formulated in Powell and DiMaggio's book *The New Institutionalism in Organizational Analysis* (1991), neo-institutionalist accounting research emphasizes both the rationalizing and symbolic qualities of accounting systems. Accounting systems are seen as symbolically codified institutions, which serve as important vehicles of organizational self-representation justifying and

legitimizing organizational action. Neo-institutionalist accounting researchers stress the importance of the wider environment in the determination and expansion of accounting work (see Meyer 1986). It is assumed that accounting elements are primarily incorporated into organizational structures on the basis of institutional pressures that are exercised by the accounting profession, the state, consultancy firms and other agencies. Important research themes around which neo-institutionalist accounting research has evolved are: the ceremonial and symbolic functions of auditing and accounting; the organizational and regulatory fields surrounding accounting activities (see **organizational fields**); the emergence, expansion and institutionalization of new accounting techniques; and histories of professionalization (see **professions**).

In his study of *The Audit Society* (1999), Michael Power examined ideological bases of auditing practices. He showed that the legitimacy-providing function of auditing procedures is not grounded in the formal rationality of the procedures themselves, but rather in the auditing procedures underlying generally accepted norms and standards, which are part of an established community of specialists. Covaleski and Dirsmith developed 'An Institutional Perspective on the Rise, Social Transformation, and Fall of a University Budget Category' (1988) and showed how societal expectations are mapped into the budgeting practices of a university. Burchell *et al.* traced in their article 'Accounting in Its Social Context: Towards a History of Value Added in the United Kingdom' (1985) the different institutional agencies and agendas involved in the establishment of value-added accounting in the UK.

Accounting and studies of governance

Another important line of thinking that influenced sociological accounting research consists in Foucauldian studies of governmentality. Here, accounting is understood as a disciplining technology that plays a central role in the governance of economic life. Accounting practices are seen as a technology producing calculability and thereby allowing for 'action at a distance'. It is assumed that accounting techniques provide a mechanism for aligning economic, social and personal conduct. Miller and Rose, for example, argued in their seminal article 'Governing Economic Life' (1990) that accounting technologies provide a relay between macroeconomic politics and microeconomic action. In his article 'Accounting Innovation Beyond the Enterprise' (1991), Miller showed that the development and spread of discounted cash flow accounting, in the UK, was closely linked to the neo-liberal re-orientation of the government's economic policy. In a similar vein, Hoskin and Macve examined in their study of 'The Genesis of Accountability' (1988) how the emergence of US-American managerialism in the nineteenth century was connected to shifts in power–knowledge relations.

But Foucauldian accounting studies draw our attention not only to the entrenchment of calculative practices in politics; they also deliver important insights into the multiplicity of activities, actors and instruments that are involved in the formation of specific 'accounting constellations'. Drawing on actor-network approaches, which were primarily developed within the sociology of science and technology, Foulcauldian accounting research focuses on the network of social relations, practices and technical devices through which particular types of accounting practice and other calculative regimes emerge. Accounting is seen as a historically contingent phenomenon and it has become one of the central tasks of Foucauldian accounting research to analyse the conditions on the basis of which accounting change occurs.

The political economy of accounting

Parallel to neo-institutionalist and Foucauldian research frameworks, since the 1980s, also political economy approaches began to influence sociological accounting research. Political economy approaches focus on the roles that **class** and other sectional interests play in the development and employment of accounting techniques. Accounting systems are seen as a means of capitalist control and domination. Their working is analysed with reference to the general order of capitalist relations of production. How is accounting able to exercise control over **industrial relations**? In what way does accounting provide a mechanism for the reinforcement of class interests? How are accounting systems embedded in structures of social stratification? These and other questions are frequently posed by critical accounting researchers.

Political economy perspectives on accounting draw on a variety of different theoretical traditions. Major reference points constitute the labour process debate, the writings of Marx and critical theory (Frankfurt School). For example, in his study 'The History of Accounting and the Transition to Capitalism in England', Bryer emphasizes the relevance of **historical materialism** for an understanding of accounting practices (2000). A labour process perspective on accounting was adopted by Hopper et al. (1986). In their study of the National Coal Board, Hopper et al. pointed out the importance of class relationships for an understanding of the organization of financial control in the declining British coal mining industry. And Puxty et al., in their study of 'Modes of Regulation in Advanced Capitalism' (1987), employed a critical theory perspective to explain international variety in accounting regulation.

Interactionist perspectives on accounting

A fourth and rather different sociological perspective on accounting provides interactionist or ethnographic studies of accounting. Ethnographic studies of accounting are concerned with the analysis of calculative practices within local settings. Attention is drawn to particular situations of interaction and the experience of individual actors. Ethnographic studies of accounting examine how formalized mechanisms of calculation actually work. How are accounting systems embedded in the day-to-day activities of financial managers? What meanings do accounting techniques unfold in a certain context? Ethnographic accounting research is structured around detailed, rich case studies. Its major aim is to describe and understand the different cultures, activities and people shaping and constituting calculative action.

Ahrens, for example, used an ethnographic approach in his study of management accounting practices in English and German beer brewers (1997). Peters analyses micro-structures of budgeting processes in her article 'When Reform Comes Into Play' (2001). And Dent, in his study 'Accounting and Organizational Cultures' (1991), explores the relationship between accounting and organizational meaning structures in a major British railway company.

Ethnographic accounting research adds to our understanding of the relationship between calculative practices and often idealized, formalized systems of financial control. It provides important insight into how economic representations are produced, and thereby helps us understand how different economic orders are achieved on the micro level of economic life.

Conclusion

The sociology of accounting poses many interesting and challenging questions, which economic sociologists could use as a starting point for entering into a dialogue with a discipline that they have neglected for so many years. Although sociological accounting studies have accumulated a great deal of knowledge about the history, functioning and change of systems of formalized calculation, there are still many open questions, which are in need of further exploration. For example, there is need for more research into questions of how systems of calculation and computation are related to different forms of formal organization. What impact do accounting systems have on the ways in which economic life is organized? There is also the need to link studies in accounting more systematically to topics that are more typical for economic sociology, such as the study of money or **markets**. One could also imagine interesting comparative research into the roles that accounting plays in the constitution of different economic systems. For example, what role does accounting play in phases of **economic development** and transition? In what ways are accounting systems involved in the creation of new economic orders? Sociologically oriented accounting research has set the scene for the exploration of such questions; economic sociology can contribute to the expansion and deepening of this research field.

References and further reading

Ahrens, T. (1997) 'Talking Accounting: An Ethnography of Management Knowledge in British and German Brewers', *Accounting, Organizations and Society*, 22: 617–37.

Bryer, R. A. (2000) 'The History of Accounting and the Transition to Capitalism in England', *Accounting, Organizations and Society*, 25(2): 131–62.

Burchell, S., Clubb, C., Hopwood, A., Hughes, J. and Nahapiet, J. (1980) 'The Roles of Accounting in Organizations and Society', *Accounting, Organizations and Society*, 6(1): 5–27.

Burchell, S., Clubb, C. and Hopwood, A. (1985) 'Accounting in Its Social Context: Towards a History of Value Added in the

United Kingdom', *Accounting, Organizations and Society*, 10(4): 381–413.

Cooper, David and Hopper, Trevor (eds) (1990) *Critical Accounts*, London: Macmillan.

Covaleski, M. and Dirsmith, M. (1988) 'An Institutional Perspective on the Rise, Social Transformation, and Fall of a University Budget Category', *Administrative Science Quarterly*, 33: 562–87.

Dent, J. F. (1991) 'Accounting and Organizational Cultures: A Field Study of the Emergence of a New Organizational Reality', *Accounting, Organizations and Society*, 16(8): 705–32.

Hopper, T., Cooper, D., Capps, T., Lowe, E. A. and Mouritsen, J. (1986) 'Management Control and Worker Resistance in the National Coal Board', in D. Knights and H. Willmott (eds), *Managing the Labour Process*, Aldershot, UK: Gower, pp. 109–41.

Hopwood, A. (1983) 'On Trying to Study Accounting in the Contexts in Which It Operates', *Accounting, Organizations and Society*, 8: 287–305.

Hopwood, A. and Miller, P. (eds) (1994) *Accounting as Social and Institutional Practice*, Cambridge: Cambridge University Press.

Hoskin, K. and Macve, R. (1988) 'The Genesis of Accountability', *Accounting, Organizations and Society*, 13(1): 37–73.

Meyer, J. W. (1986) 'Social Environments and Organizational Accounting', *Accounting, Organizations and Society*, 11: 345–56.

Miller, P. (1991) 'Accounting and Objectivity: The Invention of Calculating Selves and Calculable Spaces', *Annals of Scholarship*, 9: 61–86.

—— (1991) 'Accounting Innovation Beyond the Enterprise', *Accounting, Organizations and Society*, 16(8): 733–62.

Miller, P. and Rose, N. (1990) 'Governing Economic Life', *Economy and Society*, 19: 1–27.

Peters, K. (2001) 'When Reform Comes Into Play: Budgeting as Negotiations between Administrations', *Accounting, Organizations and Society*, 26(6): 521–39.

Powell, W. W. and DiMaggio, P. J. (1991) *The New Institutionalism in Organizational Analysis*, Chicago: University of Chicago.

Power, M. (1999) *The Audit Society*, Oxford: Oxford University Press.

Puxty, A. G., Willmott, H. C., Cooper, D. and Lowe, E. A. (1987) 'Modes of Regulation in Advanced Capitalism', *Accounting, Organizations and Society*, 12(3): 273–91

Vollmer, Hendrik (2003) 'Bookkeeping, Accounting, Calculative Practice: The Sociological Suspense of Calculation', *Critical Perspectives on Accounting*, 14: 353–81.

ANDREA MENNICKEN

ADAPTATION See: functional imperatives; systems approach to economic sociology

ADVERTISING

Advertising can be defined as a set of means and activities that aim at making products publicly visible and attractive. Usually related to commodities and to the use of publicity techniques in markets and **mass consumption**, this notion also applies to publicity in a wider sense (as in, for instance, political campaigns). Advertising is intimately linked to communication media and, in spite of the fact that it can embrace a wide variety of material forms, it is usually associated to visual culture.

Advertising has been analysed from many angles within the sociological tradition and in related disciplines such as anthropology, semiotics, media studies or economics as well. It has been considered, for instance, as a manipulation of symbols, as an instrument for **capitalism** or as a complex know-how and a professional activity.

Semiotics, structuralism and psychoanalysis have played a major role in the analysis of the symbolic capacity of advertising (Barthes 1957). Within such perspective, advertising is predominantly regarded as a combination of signs that refer to (and act upon) an often unconscious and socially structured desire. This kind of analysis often limits its scope to the visual manifestation of advertisements (which constitutes only one facet of advertising). Images, slogans and promotional texts are then predominantly analysed in the terms of their latent contents (gender stereotypes, bourgeois leitmotivs, etc.).

This vision connects to some extent to another angle of advertising: its socially situated purpose. Advertising is then treated

5

as a tool for capitalistic endeavour, i.e. for selling. In a rather critical perspective, that usually focuses on the birth and development of mass consumption in North American society, advertising is presented as a set of persuasion techniques used in order to spread ideological messages (that of consumption equals freedom) with the purpose of creating a market for a supply-driven economy. Therefore, the effect of advertising on consumer behaviour (and its prediction) becomes a crucial question, a concern shared by both social scientists and marketing practitioners. The controversial character of this question in the social sciences can be exemplified through debates such as the one opposing Ewen's critical position to Schudson's realism (Ewen 1977; Schudson 1986).

More concrete approaches to advertising practices show how this technique cannot be disconnected from a complex set of economic practices (marketing, strategic management, industrial design, merchandising, photography and cinematography, etc.). Conversely, on the consumer side, advertising faces an entangled world of desires and concerns that is far from straightforward. Within this perspective, advertising is closer to an exploratory mediation between products and consumers than to a simple matter of persuasion (Hennion and Méadel 1989; McFall 2004).

References and further reading

Barthes, Roland (1957) *Mythologies*, Paris: Seuil.
Ewen, Stuart (1977) *Captains of Consciousness: Advertising and the Social Roots of the Consumer Culture*, New York: McGraw-Hill.
Hennion, Antoine and Méadel, Cécile (1989) 'The Artisans of Desire: The Mediation of Advertising Between the Product and the Consumer', *Sociological Theory*, 7(2): 191–209.
McFall, Liz (2004) *Advertising: A Cultural Economy*, London: Sage.
Schudson, Michael (1986) *Advertising: The Uneasy Persuasion. Its Dubious Impact in American Society*, New York: Basic Books.

FABIAN MUNIESA

AGENCY THEORY

Agency theory is used to model situations in which a principal delegates authority to an agent to act on the principal's behalf. It can be used to study relationships between patients and doctors, clients and lawyers, voters and politicians, politicians and bureaucrats, employers and employees, and stockholders and managers (in each case the former is the principal and the latter the agent). Delegating authority does not ensure that an agent will always act in the interests of the principal, so the principal must find ways to control the behaviour of the agent. The goal of the principal is to create a situation in which the agent's actions conform to the principal's objectives, by choosing particular types of agent, and developing mechanisms to monitor and sanction the agent's actions.

The classical roots of agency theory are found in the work of Max **Weber**. The core of his political sociology is agency relations within the **state**: rulers must delegate authority to state officials in order to implement any of their policies. They have problems controlling these agents, due to the conflicting interests of principals and agents, and informational asymmetries (see **asymmetrical information**) favouring agents. Weber's ideal types of forms of state organization (patrimonialism, bureaucracy) can best be understood as an attempt to model agency problems in different structural contexts.

Contemporary agency theory emerged as part of **institutional economics**. Prior to this, the firm remained a 'black box' in neoclassical economic models, as economic organizations were reduced to 'production functions' managed by an entrepreneur who maximized profits in an environment in which all contracts were perfectly and costlessly monitored and enforced. This left neoclassical economics with no theory of the relationship between **incentives** and performance within firms.

The new institutionalism in economics began to open up the black box of the firm, with a focus on **property** rights, transaction costs and agency problems. Agency theory in economics focuses on three main things: (1) the way risk preferences affect contract choice (the more risk averse agents are, the more they want fixed salaries); (2) the effects of different monetary incentive schemes on performance; and (3) the effects of hiring different types of agents. Because employment contracts allocate risk between principals and agents, it is important to understand the effects of variations in risk aversion across different types of actors. Risk averse agents essentially purchase insurance by accepting fixed salary contracts with lower total value but less variation. Therefore, taking risk into account allows economists to explain the existence of 'inefficient' contracts (more precisely, contracts that would be inefficient if all actors were risk neutral).

Jensen and Meckling (1976) have further developed the role of incentive structures in the model, and apply it to the agency problem between stockholders and managers of firms, the problem sociologists often refer to as the separation of ownership and control. Their analysis provides a theoretical foundation for paying managers in stock, since this aligns their interests with those of stockholders. Sociological work has broadened the concept of incentives to include providing high status to agents who perform well.

The selection of agents is also important in economic models of agency relations, since one of the things stressed by several analyses is that there are 'types' of agents that differ in their general levels of ability, effort and honesty. These differences are better known to agents than to principals, another aspect of the information asymmetry between the two. Certain types of contracts tend to attract certain types of agents. For example, piece rate systems tend to attract hard-working agents, whereas fixed salaries attract agents interested in providing lower effort (the latter problem is called 'adverse selection'). More socio-logical work on agency theory has attempted to endogenize agent type by looking for the structural and cultural sources of hard-working and honest agents. For example, agents who are dependent on principals (due to the high opportunity costs of alternative employment) or those from groups that socialize actors to be honest or that provide separate monitoring of their honesty (called 'third party' enforcement; some religious groups provide a good example) will be more trustworthy than others.

Work on agency relations in politics has concentrated on the difficulties faced by politicians in controlling bureaucrats. The focus has been on the general issue of 'bureaucratic drift' – the tendency for the actions of a bureaucratic agency to 'drift away' from the goals of the politicians trying to control them. Echoing Weber, they argue that one of the main threats to contemporary democracy is that elected politicians are losing power relative to appointed bureaucrats. They begin with the assumption that bureaucrats want to maximize the budget of the agency they control. Bureaucrats are often able to do this, in spite of the fact that it is contrary to the interests of politicians, because they have better information than politicians or voters do about what budget level is necessary for their bureaucratic agency to adequately carry out their mission. Because bureaucrats are often successful in getting budgets that are larger than necessary, the state is growing larger and more expensive than either politicians or voters want it to be.

One of the main problems with the current literature on agency relations is its strong disciplinary orientation. Economists use formal mathematical models to study firms, political scientists use looser versions of these models to analyse states, and sociologists focus on the structural conditions within which agency relations are embedded in a wide variety of institutional contexts. However, because of their differences in theoretical style and substantive orientation, scholars working on agency problems in these different disciplines generally ignore each other. Agency theory will only reach its full potential when these disciplinary barriers are transcended.

References and further reading

Jensen, Michael and Meckling, William (1976) 'Theory of the Firm: Managerial Behavior, Agency Costs, and Ownership Structure', *Journal of Financial Economics*, 3: 305–60.

Kiser, Edgar (1999) 'Comparing Varieties of Agency Theory in Economics, Political Science, and Sociology: An Illustration from State Policy Implementation', *Sociological Theory*, 17(2): 146–70.

Weber, Max ([1922]1968) *Economy and Society*, Berkeley, CA: University of California Press.

EDGAR KISER

AGIL MODEL

See: functional imperatives; systems approach to economic sociology

ALIENATION

Alienation involves a social and psychological separation between oneself and one's life experiences and is a concept most often applied to work and work settings. Theories of alienation start with the writings of **Marx**, who identified the capacity for self-directed *creative activity* as the core distinction between humans and animals. If workers cannot express their *species being* (their creativity), they are reduced to the status of animals or machines.

Marx argued that, under **capitalism**, workers lose creative control over their work and, as a consequence, are alienated in at least four ways. First, they are alienated from the *products* of their labour. They no longer determine what is to be made, nor how to dispose of it. Work becomes a means to an end – a means to acquire money to buy the material neces-

sities of life. Second, workers are alienated from the *process* of work. Someone else controls the pace, pattern, tools and techniques of their work. Third, because workers are separated from their activity, they become alienated from *themselves*. Non-alienated work, in contrast, would allow the same enthusiastic absorption and self-realization as hobbies or leisure pursuits. Fourth, alienated labour is an isolated endeavour, not part of a collectively planned effort to meet a group need. Workers, consequently, are alienated from *others* as well as from themselves. These four components of alienation reach their peak under industrial capitalism. Alienated work is inherently dissatisfying and will naturally produce in workers a desire to change the existing system. Alienation, in Marx's view, would thus lead to social revolution.

The study of alienation has probably inspired more writing and research in the social sciences than any other single topic. Today, the core of that research has moved away from the social philosophical approach of Marx, based on projecting a future that *could be*, and towards a more empirical study of the causes and consequences of alienation within the world of work as it *actually exists*. Although less sweeping than Marx's original vision, this approach has produced insights that are largely consistent with his views. The contemporary approach substitutes measures of job satisfaction for Marx's more expansive conception of alienation. Job autonomy and freedom from oppressive supervision (see **management**) have been identified as among the most important determinants of experiencing satisfaction in one's work. Other causes of job satisfaction have also been identified. These include positive foundations, such as perceptions of justice at work and supportive co-workers, and corrosive factors, such as large organizational size, bureaucracy and control of local operations by remote corporate entities. Job satisfaction, in turn, has been linked to reduced employee turnover and increased effort, commitment and creativity at work.

Alienation, as a concept, focuses on the characteristics and organization of work. Yet the absence of work can also generate a sense of alienation because one has no useful role in society. High levels of unemployment have been empirically linked with increased depression, higher rates of illness and even suicide. **Globalization** has contributed to job loss for many workers around the world, displaced by those who either use better technology or accept lower pay. Work that is inadequate in terms of providing a livelihood or utilizing one's skills can also be alienating. Insecure employment, even if the work is otherwise good, can also be alienating and may be on the increase due to global competition. Finally, overwork can produce feelings of alienation and dissociation from oneself and one's social setting. The Japanese have coined the term *karoshi* (death from overwork) to capture the negative consequences of extreme overwork.

Job insecurity and overwork have become leading intellectual frontiers in the study of alienation. Ruth Milkman's *Farewell to the Factory* (1997) explores the consequences of downsizing in an automobile factory and the distress and anger resulting from abuse, lack of control and chronic job insecurity. Richard Sennett's *The Corrosion of Character* (1998) explores more broadly the consequences of work lives that are increasingly insecure because of globalization and corporate layoffs. Sennett argues that insecurity and short-term horizons erode the sense of a sustainable self that is necessary for the development of human character, particularly the aspects of character that bind society together into a cooperative whole.

For those who have good work, overwork and the experience of feeling chronically rushed have become increasingly common. Professional workers, whose salaries generally provide both basic needs and some luxuries, frequently express a preference for less work. In spite of widespread overwork, however, Hochschild observes in *The Time Bind* (1997) that workers sometimes prefer work over family and **leisure** activities, further contributing to overwork and even *workaholism*. At least some work in modern society may compete well with alternative activities. If workers prefer work to family and leisure, does this imply that alienation from work has ended? Or does it simply suggest that the roles of community and family are fading as these assume a smaller and smaller place in people's lives, and that people are choosing work and career as a last, best refuge for a sustainable sense of self? These changes, if true, present a challenge to traditional alienation theory as it struggles to understand the increasingly diverse experience of work.

Theories of alienation, as scientific explorations of the causes of job satisfaction, serve a pivotal function in moving us beyond workplace practices that destroy human motivation and towards practices that liberate human creativity. Theories of alienation, as exercises in social philosophy, help to keep alive questions about the future of society by envisioning possible alternatives that do not yet exist. Such exercises are necessary if the social sciences are to retain a transformative potential beyond the tyranny of *what is* and towards *what could be.*

References and further reading

Geyer, Felix and Heinz, Walter R. (eds) (1992) *Alienation, Society, and the Individual*, New Brunswick, NJ: Transaction Books.

Hochschild, Arlie (1997) *The Time Bind: When Work Becomes Home and Home Becomes Work*, New York: Metropolitan Books.

Hodson, Randy (2001) *Dignity at Work*, New York: Cambridge University Press.

Milkman, Ruth (1997) *Farewell to the Factory: Auto Workers in the Late Twentieth Century*, Berkeley, CA: University of California.

Sennett, Richard (1998) *The Corrosion of Character: The Personal Consequences of Work in the New Capitalism*, New York: W. W. Norton.

RANDY HODSON

ALTRUISM

There is no agreed definition of what constitutes altruistic behaviour. At one extreme, there are those who limit the definition to actions that benefit others but require significant sacrifices on the part of the actor. For example, Howard Margolis views an act as altruistic only if 'the actor could have done better for himself had he chosen to ignore the effect of his choice on others' (quoted in Piliavin and Charng 1990: 29). At the opposite extreme, there are those who view altruistic behaviour as any act that is basically pro-social – volunteer work, helping an elderly person across the street, etc. – regardless of the costs or benefits. (Katherine Renwick Monroe (1994: 863), who subscribes to the first definition, characterizes pro-social acts that benefit both the actor and the recipient as 'collective welfare' rather than altruism.) Hence, depending on the definition of the term, one might conclude that altruistic acts are either very rare or quite common.

These definitions also point to different understandings of the conditions under which altruistic acts arise and what motivates them. According to the narrow, heroic definition, these are acts of exceptional individuals, to be explained largely by their unusual psychological attributes. For instance, early studies of those who risked their lives to save Jews during the Holocaust focused primarily on what some have called the 'altruistic personality' (Berger *et al.* 1998: 268). In contrast, wider definitions lead one to more sociological explanations. According to these definitions, certain behaviours, such as making donations to a charity, are expected by a particular group of which the person under study is a member in good standing (or seeks to become one) and are instilled in group members through socialization (Piliavin and Charng 1990: 37).

Until the 1980s, there was a strong tendency among social scientists to explain altruistic behaviour as a reflection of self-interest, in one form or another, or as part of the quest to gain pleasure and avoid pain. Many of these texts in effect debunk altruism, scoffing at the naive public who do not see what these social scientists reveal: people are not nearly as virtuous as they claim to be. All such writings reflect a general assumption that people seek to maximize their self-interest, an assumption widely shared by major bodies of economic literature and branches of psychology and sociology. Specifically, these social scientists argue that people perform altruistic acts because they have been socialized to understand that they are likely to receive a reward for such action. For instance, those who give money to charity are said to be motivated by tax deductions or a desire to impress their friends. Elliot Sober and David Sloane Wilson provide a catch-all explanation of altruism, claiming that all altruistic acts can always be explained by the 'internal rewards' that are received by those who act altruistically, such as the avoidance of guilt or the warm feeling that such actions may give a person (Brunero 2002: 413).

Amitai Etzioni argues that introspection reveals a clear distinction between acting out of self-interest and acting out of regard for others, for instance if one compares the sense one has when risking one's life to save a drowning child versus lying on a sunny beach to enjoy a vacation day. Moreover, a mountain of behavioural data shows that people do act in selfless ways, such as spouses who stay with their partners when they are afflicted with Alzheimer's for years on end. Finally, Etzioni argues that theories that maintain that there is no difference between altruistic and selfish behaviour serve to undermine altruistic behaviour (Etzioni 1988: 52).

In recent years, the tendency has been to explain altruistic behaviour as a reflection of human nature, as the result of either an altruistic gene or changes in evolutionary biology. Some sociobiologists, for instance, argue that altruism is an evolutionary genetic trait which developed and spread due to the importance of cooperation for the survival of social groups – known as the group selection hypothesis (Monroe 1994: 870). Similarly, Herbert Gintis and his colleagues have found 'strong reciprocity' to be a predisposition of human behaviour that trumps self-interest in several empirical studies. For instance, subjects will often punish people who do not contribute to the good of the group even if it involves a cost to themselves (Gintis *et al.* 2003).

Biological interpretations raise their own problems, as biology changes slowly while altruistic behaviour ebbs and flows much more rapidly as moral cultures and social conditions change. Sociobiologists respond by arguing that culture can act to dampen or accentuate biological predispositions. Hence one must, at best, view sociobiological explanations of altruism as partial ones.

References and further reading

Batson, C. D. (1991) *The Altruism Question: Toward a Socio-Psychological Answer*, Hillsdale, NJ: Lawrence Erlbaum Associates.

Berger, R. J., Green, III, C. S. and Krieser, K. (1998) 'Altruism Amidst the Holocaust: An Integrated Social Theory', *Perspectives on Social Problems*, 10: 267–91.

Brunero, J. S. (2002) 'Evolution, Altruism and "Internal Reward" Explanations', *The Philosophical Forum*, 33(4): 413–24.

Etzioni, A. (1988) *The Moral Dimension*, New York: Free Press.

Gintis, H., Bowles, S., Boyd, R. and Fehr, E. (2003) 'Explaining Altruistic Behavior in Humans', *Evolution and Human Behavior*, 24: 153–72.

Margolis, H. (1982) *Selfishness, Altruism, and Rationality*, Cambridge: Cambridge University Press.

Monroe, K. R. (1994) 'A Fat Lady in a Corset: Altruism and Social Theory', *American Journal of Political Science*, 38(4): 861–93.

Oliner, S. P. and Oliner, P. M. (1988) *The Altruistic Personality: Rescuers of Jews in Nazi Europe*, New York: Free Press.

Phelps, E. S. (ed.) (1975) *Altruism, Morality, and Economic Theory*, New York: Sage.

Piliavin, J. A. and Charng, H. (1990) 'Altruism: A Review of Recent Theory and Research', *Annual Review of Sociology*, 16: 27–65.

Sober, E. and Wilson, D. S. (1998) *Unto Others: The Evolution and Psychology of Unselfish Behavior*, Cambridge, MA: Harvard University Press.

Wilson, E. O. (1975) *Sociobiology: The New Synthesis*. Cambridge, MA: Belknap Press.

AMITAI ETZIONI

AMERICAN INSTITUTIONALISM

See: institutional economics; Institutionalism; Veblen

ANOMIE See: See: Durkheim; norms and values; solidarity

ART AND ECONOMY

Art and economy have long been interpreted as two antithetical fields, spheres or domains. This antithesis can be regarded as a manifestation of a more general division between the **sacred** and the profane, which Emile **Durkheim** studied in the *Elementary Forms of Religious Life*. In the humanities this division has been invoked when art critics and art historians argued that the world of art is elevated above 'the stream of life', or that artists need to withdraw themselves from 'the markets of capitalism'. Others, such as Frankfurter Schule philosopher Theodor Adorno, used the derogatory term of 'culture industry' to point out the contaminating effect which the economy has on art: *quid pro quo* market exchange would degrade the value of art, critical faculties would be stifled, whereas the artist would alienate from his work, his labour, as well as his public.

Art's identity has in other words been partially defined in terms of the economy, albeit negatively. Thus, dominant strands within the humanities, conservative as well as critical, have subscribed to what economic sociologist Viviana Zelizer has called a 'hostile worlds' perspective. Studying the world of art, neoclassical economists have countered such a perspective by arguing that producers and consumers are no less motivated by self-interest than other economic agents; that the market allocates scarce resources within the art world, such as talent, efficiently; and that aesthetic or artistic value is neutrally and perfectly reflected by market prices.

Both perspectives may be considered 'disembedded' (see **embeddedness**), to use a concept out of economic sociology, as far as they disregard the social and cultural context in which art is produced, distributed and consumed. This disembedded perspective is countered within the sociology of art as far as it deals with art's economic aspects, and also within economic sociology. Indeed, it is noteworthy that a number of frequent contributors within economic sociology, such as Harrison White, Paul DiMaggio, Pierre Bourdieu, Paul Hirsch, Brian Uzzi and Jens Beckert, have included the arts in their research. A number of different, but interrelated, contributions can be distinguished.

First of all, historical patterns in the production, distribution and consumption of art have been accounted for. To give some examples: from a Marxist perspective, Arnold Hauser has argued how, in the seventeenth century, the commission-based system, with a strong, direct interference of the maecenas, made way for the 'free', anonymous market for art. Harrison and Cynthia White have argued how, in nineteenth-century France, appreciation of art shifted from single canvases to artists' careers; simultaneously, the support system for artists drifted away from the art academies and was adopted by the concerted efforts of the art dealer and the art critic.

Second, the so-called 'production of culture' perspective can be credited with putting art, including its economic aspects, on the sociological research agenda. Initi-

ated by Richard Peterson in the 1970s, sociologists using this approach analysed the way in which structures and processes within the cultural industries have both enabled and constrained the production of cultural goods, thus codetermining their content. More recently, Peterson has shown that consumption patterns within the arts are more 'omnivorous' than common wisdom about elite taste accounts for.

Third, Pierre **Bourdieu** has grounded the market for symbolic goods like art in the field of power. This means that the conflict between different aesthetics within the market is a transfiguration of a conflict between different social classes. Also, the negation of the economy, which prevails in some of these markets, is in effect a means to accumulate symbolic capital. This form of capital consists in being able to 'make a name for oneself' and having the power to consecrate cultural goods; in the long run it can be converted into economic capital.

A fourth contribution has been the application of a social constructionist and institutionalist perspective to the intersecting fields of art and economy. This contribution recognizes first of all that art and economy are socially constructed categories in themselves (see **social construction of the economy**), and second that the field of art and the field of economy operate according to different institutional logics: the logic of the arts, as it emerged from the nineteenth century onwards, is a qualitative logic and centres around the creation of symbolic, expressive or imaginative goods; the logic of the (capitalist) economy is a quantitative logic, directed at the accumulation, measurement and commodification of human activity. It is therefore not surprising that markets for art, where the logics of both fields intersect, give rise to institutional conflicts. However, unlike the perspective presupposed by the 'hostile world', this does not mean that 'contamination' is inevitable. Instead, Raymonde Moulin, Stuart Plattner and Olav

Velthuis, among others, have focused in their ethnographic studies of the art market on the mediating role which art dealers and other intermediaries manage to perform when marketing art. In doing so, these studies show how artistic as well as economic value is constructed simultaneously on the intersection of both fields.

Recent developments have further questioned the antithetical relation between art and economy. On the one hand, due to a range of factors among which are the expansion of cultural industries, contemporary artists taking up the economy as a theme in their work, and a corrosion of the distinction between high and low art, economic models and viewpoints within the arts have gained in legitimacy. On the other hand, the 'commercialization' of the arts, which has long preoccupied the humanities, has found a counterpart in a 'cultural turn' within the economy. Authors like Jeremy Rifkin have argued that the postmodern economy operates according to a qualitative rather than a quantitative logic; producing cultural experiences, this postmodern economy relies on theatrical metaphors and considers creative and innovative business cultures to be its prime asset. Open to debate is if these developments are here to stay, what repercussions they have on an institutional and organizational level, and how they recast the modern antithesis between art and economy.

References and further reading

Bourdieu, Pierre (1993) *The Field of Cultural Production. Essays on Art and Literature*, Cambridge: Polity Press.

Moulin, Raymonde ([1967]1987) *The French Art Market. A Sociological View*, trans. Arthur Goldhammer, New Brunswick, NJ: Rutgers University Press.

White, Harrison C. and White, Cynthia A. (1965) *Canvases and Careers: Institutional Change in the French Painting World*, New York: John Wiley and Sons.

OLAV VELTHUIS

ASYMMETRICAL INFORMATION

To neoclassical economics, the market is completely transparent. This means that at any given moment, all market participants have at their disposal all the necessary information free of charge and can process it to create perfect contracts. All 'transaction costs', in particular the costs and problems encountered in the search for and processing of information, are ignored.

These assumptions were criticized as being unrealistic, and new theories, such as **institutional economics** and **information** economics, were developed which took information problems into account. In particular **agency theory**, a branch of institutional economics, is concerned with asymmetrical information. Asymmetrical information means that there are differences in the amount of information available to the principal and the agent. In agency theory models, it is normally assumed that the agent has more information at her disposal regarding the market transaction than the principal. A seller (agent) knows more about the quality of the sold product than the customer (principal). An employee (agent) is better informed about her knowledge and skills than the employer (principal). Problems arise from this information lead if the agent acts purely out of self-interest and pursues goals which are contrary to those of the principal. Some typical examples: if the employer cannot judge with certainty how hardworking his employees are, shirking is to be expected. Or: the seller of a second-hand car will try to exploit the ignorance of the purchaser regarding the true quality of the car and ask for an excessive price.

It is assumed that the principal will endeavour to protect himself from the negative consequences of such asymmetrical information. For example, he will carefully monitor to obtain more information. Or he will make contracts such that the agent will receive a monetary reward only if the principal achieves his aims. But the agent may also have an interest in eliminating the asymmetry of information. For example, sellers can obtain a reasonable price on goods of above-average quality only if they can give proof of the quality of the goods by means of credible signals.

Repeated or longer-term relationships between the same market participants reduce information asymmetry through experience. This may be one important reason why market participants prefer known transaction partners to unknown ones.

The introduction of asymmetrical information into economic models has led to many new insights, and has brought economics a big step closer to more realistic models. But there is also criticism. The information lead of the principal as against the agent is often neglected. In fact, it is not only the employee who can deceive the employer but also vice versa. The employee may be persuaded to accept lower wages on the principal's allegation that profits are declining. There is also criticism of the negative picture that agency theory holds of the behaviour of people. Because of this pessimistic view, asymmetric information is presented solely as a threat to the principal. However, the fact that the agent knows more than the principal in some respects also constitutes her value.

References and further reading

Akerlof, George (1970) 'The Market for Lemons', *Quarterly Journal of Economics*, August: 488–500.

Pratt, John W. and Zeckhauser, Richard J. (1984) 'Principals and Agents: An Overview', in John W. Pratt and Richard J. Zeckhauser (eds), *Principals and Agents: The Structure of Business*, Boston MA: Harvard Business School Press, pp. 1–35.

ELISABETH GÖBEL

AUCTIONS

Auctions are a family of social practices for allocating items by means of a variety of competitive bidding processes. Individual auctions take various forms depending upon the type of bidding system used, types of items allocated, participation restrictions, use of minimum/reserve prices and other rules governing collaboration, guarantees, commissions and so forth. The entire process is generally supervised by an auctioneer who solicits bids from potential buyers, designates who has the bid at any particular time, determines when the bidding is ended and designates the winning bid. Most auctions rely on public outcry or visual bids, though it is not uncommon for buyers to signal their bids silently. Some auctions rely on written bids, with each bidder sometimes allowed only a single bid while at other times multiple bids are allowed. Some charity auctions also rely on written bids and are commonly referred to as silent auctions.

Offered bids generally begin low and move incrementally higher – the term 'auction' is derived from the Latin word *auctio*, to increase – until no further bids are made; such auctions are generally called English auctions. In what are commonly referred to as Dutch auctions, the first asking bid is set above the expected final price and incrementally reduced. The first buyer to accept the asking bid as it drops is declared the winner. This format is usually employed in 'preference and choice' auctions where multiples of similar items are being auctioned. The first winning bidder selects those specific items he or she wants and the requested bid continues to drop, with second, third and so on winning bids making their selections until all the items have been sold. In other auctions, buyers, and sometimes sellers, simultaneously ask for and offer different bids. Such auctions are sometimes referred to as Japanese auctions, since this practice is followed in

Japanese fish auctions. It is also the system used on most financial – stocks, bonds, options and futures – exchanges.

The price paid for the item being auctioned is usually the same as the highest bid tendered plus a commission that can range from a few per cent to over 20 per cent, depending on the type of auction. A few auctions have experimented with a second highest price, or Vickrey, method, in setting the sale price. In these auctions, the highest bid wins, but the final price is equal to the next highest bid. The rationale for this system, which is grounded in theoretical auction modelling, is fairly complex, but, in effect, the goal is to allocate the item to the bidder valuing it the highest but at a price that theoretically is Pareto optimal. While other more esoteric auction systems are utilized in particular situations, the systems described above constitute the great majority of ongoing auctions.

From the early 1990s, onwards with the growth of global **markets**, **financial markets** and Internet markets, auctions have become more numerous and salient; they have also come to play a more significant role in the growing dialogue among and between economists and sociologists regarding the nature of economic behaviour. While mathematical auction models continue to embody central aspects of the neoclassical economic paradigm such as **rationality**, individualism and utility maximization, and **game theory** auction models explore behavioural/psychological economic alternatives, sociologically/anthropologically grounded ethnographic studies by highlighting the emotional, collective and constructivist qualities suggest dramatically different interpretations of these fascinating allocation processes.

Practically every sort of goods or service can be and has been auctioned at some time or another. From a neoclassical economic perspective this is not surprising since the auction format, whether framed in game theory terms or Walras' *auctioneer tatônnment*

idea, is seen as the purest form of a rational, voluntary price-setting economic exchange. The fact that auctions are generally relied upon when there is a high degree of ambiguity regarding the proper price to be paid, however, indicates that auctions also serve an important definitional function (Smith 1989). The earliest auctions recorded, Babylonian bride auctions noted by Herodotus, Roman war booty auctions known as *sub hasta* auctions and seventeenth- and eighteenth-century seaport auctions, for example, all dealt with objects where questionable provenance and legitimacy created not only ambiguity in determining economic value, but also a good deal of moral criticism of the entire auction process. Nevertheless, auctions became sufficiently established by the end of the sixteenth century that the *Oxford English Dictionary* contains a 1595 reference to the term, and by the middle of the eighteenth century the auction houses of Sotheby's and Christie's were established.

In modern times, auctions have continued to be used most extensively where considerable ambiguity exists regarding the proper economic value of items, such as agricultural goods, used goods, one-of-a-kind rare items and works of art. Whereas the ambiguity regarding agricultural goods reflects uncertainties (see **risk and uncertainty**) regarding supply and demand of highly perishable goods, rare antiques and works of art require putting a price on such ephemeral things as artistic genius, provenance and cultural tastes. Used goods generate their own value uncertainties.

While auctions are generally open to all, participation in some auctions, particularly wholesale and exchange auctions, tend to be restricted to members. The New England Fish Exchange, major financial exchanges, commodity exchanges and tobacco auctions, for example, are closed. The decision to restrict participation, like most other auction rules, is determined by the specific purposes and conditions relevant to each auction, be it a commodity auction, a charity auction, a racehorse auction, a book-rights auction, a jewellery auction, a foreclosure auction, or any of the dozens of other auctions that occur daily. The growth of the web and e-commerce in recent years has given rise not only to numerous new web-based auctions such as those sponsored on eBay and Yahoo, but also many new business-to-business auctions in which companies both buy and sell supplies and merchandise to each other.

During the last quarter of the twentieth century, with the world economy becoming more market oriented, the volume of goods auctioned has grown significantly, as has the public visibility of auctions. Seeing them as embodying free-market principles in their purest form, western capitalist governments, particularly the United States, have supported their use in allocating resources, including previously owned government resources. This greater use of auctions has also been fostered by the growth of e-commerce and the Internet, which enable otherwise separated individuals to interact directly with each other electronically. As these various types of markets have grown, so have the debates regarding their long-term value and equity and their susceptibility to fraud as compared to more controlled and monitored exchange systems. It is likely that economic sociologists will play a larger role in these future debates than they have historically.

References and further reading

Cassady, Ralph, Jr (1967) *Auctions and Auctioneering*, Berkeley and Los Angeles, CA: University of California Press.

Smith, Charles W. (1989/1990) *Auctions: The Social Construction of Value*, New York: Free Press (1989) and Berkeley, CA: University of California Press (1990).

—— (1993) 'Auctions: From Walras to the Real World' in Richard Swedberg (ed.) *Explorations in Economic Sociology*, New York: Russell Sage Foundation.

Vickrey, William (1961) 'Counterspeculation, Auctions and Competitive Sealed Tenders', *Journal of Finance*, 16: 8–37.

CHARLES W. SMITH

AUSTRIAN ECONOMICS

The term 'Austrian economics' refers to a set of positions in economic theory, methodology and public policy first adopted by Carl Menger (1840–1921), founder of the school, and developed further by talented collaborators and successors at the University of Vienna, including Friedrich von Wieser and Eugen Böhm von Bawerk in the second generation, and Joseph Schumpeter, Ludwig von Mises and Friedrich A. Hayek in the third generation. Eight positions lie at the core of Austrian economics: a subjective theory of value based on economizing actors' estimates of the marginal utilities involved in economic choices; the use of simple ordinal measures for ranking actors' economic preferences (thereby rejecting the use of the infinitesimal calculus in marginal utility analysis); sensitivity to issues of time and process in the study of entrepreneurship, production and business cycles; methodological individualism (a term coined by Schumpeter in 1908); the compositive method (building up the edifice of economic theory from simple models of economizing action and exchange); a strongly aprioristic conception of the basic concepts and laws of economics; a conception of ideal social organization as a 'spontaneous order' arising from voluntary exchange transactions; and a libertarian, anti-interventionist stance in economic policy. (Wieser and Schumpeter must be exempted from the last two positions.) A contemporary, fourth generation of Austrian economists explores issues of time, uncertainty and expectations in market processes while undertaking historical, polemical and epistemological studies of the school's theoretical and methodological positions.

For decades Carl Menger was hailed, along with Léon Walras in Switzerland and Stanley Jevons in England, as one of three independent discoverers of the concept of marginal utility. (It is now recognized that at least a dozen economists independently developed the marginal concept under various names going back to 1752; see **utility**.) The term 'Austrian school of economics' was originally used derisively during the bitter **Methodenstreit** ('struggle over methods') that Menger initiated in 1883, in defence of economics as an 'exact', nomological-deductive science. That debate, and the label, crystallized the identity of the school. During the 1920s, Mises resolved to secure the school's core positions against any possible criticism. His efforts resulted in a new a priori inquiry, praxeology, based the concept of *homo agens* (acting man, the intentional – and therefore rational – agent) (Mises 1949). Its identity secured, Austrian economics lost its theoretical edge. By 1930 its star had been eclipsed by the rapid theoretical consolidation of the Jevons–Walras wing of the marginalist revolution, which is today called 'neoclassical economics.'

The impact of Austrian economics on economic sociology has been indirect, mediated by methodological considerations and hard to disentangle from other influences. The two sociologists closest to the school, Max **Weber** and Alfred Schutz, identified economic theory with Austrian marginalism and considered the methodological positions above to be appropriate for the study of economizing action, though they wished to refine them in certain respects. Weber, considered a 'champion of the Austrian school' at Heidelberg (Swedberg 1998: 185), felt that Menger 'proposed excellent views even if they were not methodologically finished' (Weber 1975: 33n). He rejected the remnants of psychologism in the subjective theory of value and of epistemological certainty in Austrian apriorism. So did Schutz. Schutz, who had many friends among the third generation of

Austrian economists from his participation in Mises' private seminar on methodology, used phenomenological analysis to revamp Weber's concepts of social action, understanding and the **ideal type**. He then showed how Austrian apriorism – its insistence that the basic concepts and laws of economics were self-evident truths confirmed by introspection and valid everywhere and always – could be placed on a more secure foundation. Discarding the naive rationalism of Menger and Mises, he interpreted the basic concepts and laws of economics as ideal types that had been formalized and generalized to 'anyone' from the economizing actions of 'contemporaries' by theorists who were simultaneously defining the very subject matter of economics (Schutz 1967: 241–9). Schutz's subtle historicization and conventionalization of the a priori was rejected by Mises, but embraced by other Austrians embarrassed by the proclaimed indubitability of Menger's 'principles of human economy'.

Many economic sociologists follow **Veblen** (1961: 171) in considering the Austrian school to be 'scarcely distinguishable from the neoclassical'. In fact, Austrian marginalism resisted the emerging neoclassical synthesis since the 1880s. Its view of human nature is *homo agens*, not Bentham's calculating hedonist. In place of the perfect knowledge assumption, contemporary Austrians develop explanations based on rational-but-fallible agents equipped with imperfect knowledge. They focus theoretical attention on the disequilibria produced when agents act on false beliefs about prices and the goods-character of things, and attribute equilibria to actors' subsequent learning of pragmatic, market-specific knowledge.

References and further reading

Caldwell, B. J. (ed.) (1990) *Carl Menger and His Legacy in Economics*, Durham, NC: Duke University Press.

Mises, L. von (1949) *Human Action: A Treatise on Economics*, New Haven, CT: Yale University Press.

Pribram, K. (1983) *A History of Economic Reasoning*, Baltimore, MD: Johns Hopkins University Press.

Schutz, A. (1967) *The Phenomenology of the Social World*, Evanston, IL: Northwestern University Press.

Swedberg, R. (1998) *Max Weber and the Idea of Economic Sociology*, Princeton, NJ: Princeton University Press.

Veblen, T. (1961) *The Place of Science in Modern Civilization and Other Essays*, New York: Russell and Russell.

Weber, M. (1975) 'Marginal Utility Theory and "The Fundamental Law of Psychophysics"', *Social Science Quarterly*, 56: 21–36.

CHRISTOPHER PRENDERGAST

AUTHORITY See: legitimacy

AUTOPOIESIS See: Luhmann, systems approach to economic sociology

B

BANKRUPTCY

Every society must find a way to regulate the relationship between creditors and those debtors who are unable to pay their debts. The Twelve Tables in Rome permitted creditors to divide the debtor's body into pieces, pro rata, an idea that reappears in Shakespeare's *The Merchant of Venice* as a pound of flesh that is owed to the creditor. Debt slavery, debtors' prison, and debtors' colonies are three methods that were used from time to time by European countries. In Italy, artisans would break the workbench of a fellow artisan who was unable to repay debts. This *banca rota* – broken bench – gave us the word 'bankruptcy'.

Debtors whose assets exceed their debts are termed insolvent. An insolvent person who does not declare bankruptcy may instead struggle to repay or flee the creditors. Bankruptcy is a legal action undertaken to settle the unpayable debts of a business or of an individual. Bankrupt debtors, who are usually but not always insolvent, invoke a legal procedure that triggers some relief, limits the behaviour of both creditors and debtors, and ensures similar treatment for creditors who are similarly situated. Bankruptcy actions may be initiated by the debtor, termed a voluntary bankruptcy, or by the creditors, termed an involuntary bankruptcy. Because businesses and other entities may borrow money, there are provisions for bankruptcy by businesses as well as by individuals.

In the United States, the most common form of bankruptcy is a liquidation, called a Chapter 7. State law determines what assets of the debtor are exempt from claims of the creditors. Exempt assets are typically personal effects and sometimes the home or part of the equity in the home. All non-exempt assets in a Chapter 7 will be sold and distributed pro rata to the creditors. Not all creditors are equal in bankruptcy; creditors with a security interest are entitled to take collateral. Some creditors receive priority treatment for public policy reasons; for example, unpaid employees or children awarded child support take priority over credit card companies. In the United States, most individual bankruptcy cases in Chapter 7 result in no distribution to creditors because the debtor has so few assets. After the asset surrender, if any, remaining debts are discharged – that is, forgiven.

In the United States and increasingly in the other advanced industrial countries, there is an alternative bankruptcy form that involves an administered repayment programme from the debtor's earnings. Called Chapter 13 in the United States, this form of bankruptcy requires debtors to have a plan approved by the court to repay all or part of their debts from their current incomes for up to sixty months. At the end of the plan any remaining debt is discharged. About one-third of all bankruptcies are filed in Chapter 13, and about one-third of these bankruptcies are successful in completing the plan.

By regulating the repayment demands of many creditors, bankruptcy attempts to treat all creditors fairly. In the absence of bankruptcy, individual creditors may aggressively seek other remedies, including state law legal judgments against the debtor, garnished wages, foreclosures, repossessions and evictions. In some European countries, however, directors of bankrupt companies may be subject to criminal penalties. Bankruptcy may remain on a credit record for ten years, and an individual may not receive a second discharge of debt for seven years.

In the early 2000s the number of bankruptcies filed in the United States exceeded 1.5 million annually. Bankruptcy rates were also rising in Canada, Great Britain and Israel, among other countries, but the relative levels were much lower.

Empirical studies in the United States have indicated that most individual debtors declare bankruptcy following a job loss. Other important causes of bankruptcy are illness or injury in the family, divorce or other family disorganization, and overextension of debt, especially credit cards and to a lesser extent home mortgages. Credit cards are of particular interest because the high interest rates and escalating penalty fees accelerate the growth of the debt. The worldwide penetration of credit cards appears to be associated with increased bankruptcy rates. On the other hand, the provision of a social safety net with unemployment compensation and universal health care has contributed to the generally lower levels of bankruptcy in Canada and Europe, compared with the United States.

References and further reading

Niemi-Kiesilainen, J., Ramsay, I. and Whitford, W. C. (eds) (2003) *Consumer Bankruptcy in Global Perspective*, Oxford: Hart Publishing.

Sullivan, T. A., Warren, E. and Westbrook, J. L. (2000) *The Fragile Middle Class: Americans in Debt*, New Haven, CT: Yale University Press.

TERESA A. SULLIVAN

BANKS

The traditional function of banks has been to hold customer deposits and issue loans, but banks have recently expanded into many other financial businesses, including securities, mutual funds, investment banking and insurance. Sociologists who have studied banking have recently turned their attention to these changes. Historically, however, sociologists have also documented the prominent role of banks in national business communities, and the degree of banks' economic and political power has been the source of considerable debate. In this essay we examine the place of banks in historical perspective. Because of the enormous cross-national variation in banking systems and laws, our focus will be on the United States. We do include comparisons with the German and Japanese banking systems, however.

Banking in the US developed in a decentralized manner. Banks that were national in scope had already developed in the early nineteenth century. By the Civil War, however, public fear of consolidated financial power led to a series of governmental actions, most notably the National Banking Acts of 1863 and 1864 that eliminated national banks and branch banking. This resulted in banks being generally confined to the state of their headquarters, and in many cases limited to a single office (Roe 1994). In contrast with the US, concerns about consolidated financial power were less widespread in Germany and Japan, and banking thus developed in a more concentrated fashion in those countries. By the early twentieth century, a limited number of German and Japanese banks came to dominate their respective economies, typically by acting as the central funding source for a network of connected businesses. Although the American banking system was generally decentralized, it is important to note that large US banks were still able to achieve consolidated power through mechanisms such as **interlocking directorates**. This concentrated power subsided, however, after the Clayton Act of 1914, which limited interlocks among competitors, and the Glass–Steagall Act of 1933, which separated commercial and investment banking. The US banking industry continued to include a number of powerful 'money centre' commercial banks, based mostly in New York, for much of the twentieth century. On the whole, however, banks were primarily locally based, and most banks maintained close ties to their communities. Beginning in the 1980s, many of the earlier geographic constraints and restrictions on function began to fall. US banks began to branch out nationally, and they developed increasingly into financial conglomerates. The Glass–Steagall Act, which had forced the separation of commercial from investment banking, was repealed in 1999.

The implications of these historical changes for the social role of banks have been a source of continuing controversy among sociologists. For decades, sociologists debated the extent to which banks held disproportionate power, both in the business community and the larger society. In one influential study, Mintz and Schwartz (1985) argued that because of their control of a universal resource – capital – banks have been the most powerful members of the corporate communities in developed capitalist societies. The continuing centrality of banks in networks of interlocking directorates was viewed by many sociologists as consistent with this argument (Mizruchi 1996). As alternative forms of financing emerged during the 1980s, however, nonfinancial corporations began to borrow less from banks, and banks found it necessary to move away from cor-

porate lending toward more fee-based strategies. By the 1990s, perhaps as a result of these changes, banks were no longer the most central firms in the national interlock network (Davis and Mizruchi 1999), although they do remain central in many local interlock networks. The situation in Germany and Japan remains considerably different from that in the US. Banks in Germany and Japan are permitted to directly hold equity in firms, and nonfinancial firms in both countries are more likely than in the US to raise capital through the use of credit rather than the capital market. This may explain why banks appear to be more active in setting firm policies in both Germany and Japan than in the US.

The significant transformation of the banking industry since the 1980s has raised questions about the future of banks as an institutional form. Many banking firms in the US have evolved into full service financial corporations, similar to the 'universal banks' that exist in Germany and Japan. The 1998 merger that created the financial services company Citigroup combined into a single firm the extensive commercial banking operation of the former Citibank, the Travelers insurance company, and the retail brokerage and investment banking businesses of Salomon Smith Barney. Banks have also expanded geographically, resulting in a new organizational form – the super-regional. To take one example, as of 2003, Bank of America had over 4,000 branch locations in twenty-one states. Only twenty years earlier, its precursor, NCNB, was a small regional bank in Charlotte, North Carolina. Some investigators have suggested that the rise of alternative sources of financing has led to a decline in bank power, both economic and political. The consolidation of the financial industry across both function and geography indicates that banks, in their new form, will continue to be important. Banks' traditional source of power – their control

21

of capital – may be less significant at the turn of the twenty-first century than it was in earlier years. The massive size and scope of these new banking organizations suggests that they will continue to exercise influence, both economically and politically.

References and further reading

Davis, Gerald F. and Mizruchi, Mark. S. (1999) 'The Money Center Cannot Hold: Commercial Banks in the US System of Corporate Governance', *Administrative Science Quarterly*, 44: 215–39.

Mintz, Beth and Schwartz, Michael (1985) *The Power Structure of American Business*, Chicago: University of Chicago Press.

Mizruchi, Mark S. (1996) 'What Do Interlocks Do? An Analysis, Critique, and Assessment of Research on Interlocking Directorates', *Annual Review of Sociology*. 22: 271–98.

Roe, Mark J. (1994) *Strong Managers, Weak Owners: The Political Roots of American Corporate Finance*, Princeton, NJ: Princeton University Press.

Stearns, Linda Brewster and Mizruchi, Mark S. (2004) 'Banking and Financial Markets', in Neil J. Smelser and Richard Swedberg (eds), *The Handbook of Economic Sociology*, second edition, Princeton, NJ: Princeton University Press.

CHRISTOPHER MARQUIS
MARK S. MIZRUCHI

BARGAINING THEORY

Neoclassical economic theory effectively explains the workings of markets, i.e. the determination of prices and quantities, when many want goods and many are willing to supply them. Under these conditions, trading is efficient and complete. Despite the elegance of neoclassical economic theory, its orthodoxy left the bargaining problem indeterminate. So, traditionally, neoclassical economic theory assumed that the division of the surplus (the core) of bilateral monopoly bargaining depended on the parties' bargaining skills, about which it had little to say. The brilliant contributions of John Forbes Nash Jr to bargaining theory, published in two papers in 1950 and 1953,

alongside two other seminal papers on non-cooperative games published in 1950 and 1951, radically broke with this tradition and forever changed the course of economic thinking.

The 20-year-old Nash started his graduate studies in the Department of Mathematics at Princeton University in September 1948. Prior to commencing graduate studies at Princeton, the undergraduate Nash had already completed an important paper on bargaining while enrolled in an elective course in international economics at the Carnegie Institute of Technology in Pittsburgh, Pennsylvania. His former undergraduate advisors in Pittsburgh, who considered Nash a genius, were undoubtedly unsurprised to learn that Nash's completed thesis was accepted by the Mathematics Department in May of 1950, a mere twenty months after arriving at Princeton. From the thesis he tailored his 1950 publication for *Econometrica* entitled 'The Bargaining Problem'. In this paper, he presented a bargaining solution that was completely unanticipated in the literature. Breaking with the past, he used a simple yet path-breaking axiomatic approach and a non-cooperative model of games to derive a bargaining solution between two rational persons. This axiomatic approach aimed to identify the common characteristics of bargaining and its solutions rather than describe the processes involved in bargaining. In a second, 1953, publication on bargaining theory entitled 'Two-Person Cooperative Games', which was also based upon his thesis and also published in *Econometrica*, Nash stated: 'One states as axioms several properties that it would seem natural for the solution to have and then one discovers that the axioms actually determine the solution uniquely' (Nash 1953: 129).

Nash's bargaining theory specified four axioms that the bargaining solution should obey. One axiom was invariance of **utility** functions, i.e. the solution to the bargaining problem was independent of the units measuring utility. A second axiom was Pareto-efficiency, i.e. the bargaining solution was Pareto optimal so that not both players could be made better off. A third axiom was called the independence of irrelevant alternatives. This third axiom stated that the feasible options not chosen, (i.e. irrelevant), had no impact on the final bargaining solution. And a fourth axiom was called symmetry, which meant that individuals in bargaining situations had completely symmetric roles. Thus, the bargaining solution was independent of the unobserved attributes of each individual; essentially, each individual was interchangeable. Together, the four axioms implied a unique solution to any bargaining situation and maximized the possible gains to the bargainers.

The solution to the bargaining problem proposed by Nash initially spread slowly, but once the significance of his solution was comprehended, referring to it became simply inescapable. Recognition of Nash's work did not necessarily mean embracing it, however. In fact, Nash's solution to the bargaining problem has not been immune from challenges or refinements. For example, a major criticism of Nash's work has centred upon the independence of irrelevant alternatives axiom. Critics have argued that numerous situations exist in which non-chosen alternatives affect the final bargaining solution. Other detractors have claimed the symmetry and efficiency axioms are unrealistic because many bargains struck between persons have reasonable but inefficient outcomes or reasonable asymmetric outcomes. But, according to Nash's formulations, the bargaining outcome results from unspecified processes of negotiation or strategizing by the individual bargainers acting rationally. He argued that his aim was to sift through the complex details of the bargaining process, not elaborate them. Nonetheless, the static nature of Nash's bargaining solution and scepticism about the axioms' applicability to many economic situations has motivated his successors to formalize the actual bargaining process. By doing so, the non-cooperative approach to bargaining theory was given crucial impetus.

An influential contribution to explicating the steps of negotiation and formalizing the dynamism of bargaining was Ariel Rubinstein's paper 'Perfect Equilibrium in a Bargaining Model' published in *Econometrica* in 1982. Rubinstein's solution to the bargaining problem used non-cooperative bargaining theory and assumed a process of sequential offers that the bargainers either accepted or rejected. But delay was costly for both parties to different degrees, and the longer taken to reach agreement, the smaller the size of the 'pie' left to share. In an ingenious exposition, Rubinstein showed that the bargaining parties considered the degree of impatience of one another and made an optimal offer that took account of relative impatience. Ultimately, the bargaining outcome is immediate, efficient and unique, and depends on for whom delay is more costly.

The specifics may differ, but Rubinstein's 1982 paper and Nash's 1950 and 1953 papers have both suffered from the same general criticism: the proposed solutions to the bargaining problem are unrealistic. Many in **game theory**, such as Kreps (1990) and Sutton (1986), have complained that bargaining outcomes are not always immediate, (such as in the Rubinstein case), efficient, conflict free, without outside options, or conducted with perfect information. Thus, the heirs to Nash and Rubinstein's contributions have continued to expand and redefine the boundaries of bargaining theory, especially by examining contingent-specific bargaining models that analyse the effect of information on bargaining outcomes. Nash's re-introduction and analysis of the indeterminacy problem was a turning point in modern economic thinking and gave social scientists a valuable tool for understanding bargaining behaviour which is at the core of the human condition.

References and further reading

Kreps, David (1990) *Game Theory and Economic Modelling*, New York: Oxford University Press.

Nash, John (1950) 'The Bargaining Problem', *Econometrica*, 18: 155–62.

—— (1953) 'Two-Person Cooperative Games', *Econometrica*, 21: 128–40.

Rubinsten, Ariel (1982) 'Perfect Equilibrium in a Bargaining Model', *Econometrica*, 50: 97–109.

Sutton, John (1986) 'Non-Cooperative Bargaining Theory: An Introduction', *Review of Economics and Statistics*, 53(5), 176: 709–24.

PETER D. BRANDON

BARTER

Barter is the exchange of goods, services or things in the absence of money: that is, in the absence of a system for the calculation of standardized value in economic transactions. Many writers have associated barter with the most primitive form of organized economic activity on a scale of social evolution leading from the primitive to the civilized, from the traditional to the modern, from the underdeveloped to the developed. In fact, this view is erroneous. An important contribution of anthropology has been to establish and document the existence through human history of complex systems of exchange and reciprocity in the tribal and aboriginal societies that preceded and then coexisted with empires, industrial, and now post-industrial societies. All of these traditional systems of exchange have had means of calculating value, approximate to modern systems of money. So-called primitive 'monies' are actually categories of valuables that determine elaborate patterns of exchange in traditional societies and are often associated with rituals and sacred contexts of meaning. Examples would be the *tambua*, or polished whale teeth, of Fiji; ceramics, beads and brasswares in Borneo; and the prototypical case of kula valuables – shell discs and armlets – among the Trobriand islanders. Sometimes goods or commodities are swapped in such societies in terms of another commodity that serves as a common standard of value. Thus, in Fiji, the *tambua* might be a standard of value for assessing routine exchanges of non-ritual commodities like pigs for canoes.

Strictly construed, barter exists when parties to exchange do not have a given means to calculate value, and they thus must negotiate situationally the terms of exchange. Such exchange occurs under the following two general conditions: at the points of first or infrequent contact between members of two very different societies, where the monetary system of calculating value common to one party is alien to the other; and when the rules of an economic system have broken down because of war or natural disasters, or when they do not apply under special circumstances to a particular population, for example, as in the case of prisoners. Under each of these conditions, parties to an exchange must work out directly the value of one item in terms of another. Even in these cases, however, barter is an unstable condition of economic activity, and with the passage of time and the frequency of contacts, norms or conventions of calculating value in exchanges will arise – for example, so many beaver pelts for an iron pot in early European/Native American contact, so many cigarettes for taxi rides in the broken economy of the Soviet Union before its collapse, or so much narcotics for protection in a prison population. In the context of modern international trade, even industrial nations sometimes barter exports among themselves for a period of time, when pricing structures have broken down. Barter is thus a marginal means of exchange when the rules of calculation in any society are, for whatever reason, absent.

References and further reading

Gregory, Chris (1982) *Gifts and Commodities*, London: Academic Press.
Mauss, Marcel ([1925]1967) *The Gift: Forms and Functions of Exchange in Archaic Societies*, New York: W. W. Norton.
Sahlins. Marshall D. (1972) *Stone-Age Economics*, New York: Aldine.

GEORGE MARCUS

BEHAVIOURAL ECONOMICS

Behavioural economics (BE) is an integration of psychology into economics. It is a growing field that has entered mainstream economics. This is a rather new development. For decades economics was mostly separated from the other social sciences. This was not always so. From Adam **Smith** to John M. **Keynes**, economists regularly used psychological arguments in their economic explanations. In post-war economics, theorists aimed at developing a pure economic theory based on methodological individualism and without any recourse to psychological or sociological ideas. This approach has led to an impressive development of economic theory in numerous areas of economics. The main advantage is that it provides economists with a unified (formal) language and conceptual framework for undertaking economic analysis. This also holds for BE. BE would probably not exist in its present form without the great advances of modern economic theory. The goal of BE is not to disprove economic theory, but to improve economic analysis by resting it on psychologically plausible assumptions about economic behaviour.

The progress of BE is to a large degree due to (1) pinpointing problems in basic economic assumptions by providing empirical evidence from the field and tightly controlled laboratory experiments; and (2) new theoretical developments. I will therefore structure my discussion along the canonical economic model. Elements of it can be found in almost all economic models. In this model, agents are modelled as decision-makers who maximize their (discounted stream of future) utility, given their constraints and their information about uncertain events. To make it workable, the following assumptions have been typically made:

1. *Selfishness*: the agent only cares about his or her own consumption.
2. *Expected utility maximization*: the agent's preferences over risky choice alternatives obey the axioms of expected utility theory.
3. *Exponential discounting*: future utilities are discounted at a constant rate.
4. *Bayesian rationality*: information processing and probability judgements obey the probability axioms and Bayes' rule.
5. *Maximization*: agents optimize.

Research in BE has attacked all assumptions. The remainder of this article looks at these five topics. In addition to field studies, tightly controlled, and often replicated laboratory experiments, where participants are paid according to their decisions, have been very instrumental for BE.

My approach will be necessarily selective. Camerer *et al.* (2004) is a useful comprehensive reader on seminal contributions to the field of BE.

Social preferences

In contrast to the often-made assumption of selfishness, many people take the well-being of others into account in their decision-making. Experiments have unambiguously established this fact, by showing that many people are motivated by fairness and reciprocity. The results have also led to new theoretical developments (e.g. Fehr and Schmidt 1999).

A highly influential game has been the ultimatum game. This is a two-person game, where player 1 is endowed with €10. He has to make a proposal $0 \leq y \leq 10$ to player 2, who can only reject or accept the offer. If she accepts, she gets y and player 1 gets $10 - y$. If she rejects, both get nothing. A selfish player 2 should accept everything and therefore player 1 should offer the smallest money unit. Yet this is not what typically happens. Participants in the role of player 2 tend to reject offers below 50 per cent with an increasing probability the lower the offer is. Player 1s typically make offers of 40 to 50 per cent. This result has been replicated hundreds of times and in different cultures.

The behaviour of player 2s in the ultimatum game illustrates 'negative reciprocity'. People are often willing to forgo money in order to punish behaviour that is perceived as unfair. Negative reciprocity can also be observed in other games: for instance, in cooperation games that permit punishment cooperators typically punish the defectors. There is also substantial evidence from various games for 'positive reciprocity', i.e. people are willing to reward behaviour that is perceived as kind.

These results are important for understanding a variety of economic issues, like wage formation, the provision of **incentives** and limits to free riding (Fehr and Gächter 2000).

Loss aversion and reference-dependent (risk) preferences

The dominant theory of behaviour under risk is expected utility theory. Yet, very early on, experiments have demonstrated violations even in very simple lotteries.

Kahneman and Tversky (1979) found that people evaluate changes in wealth rather than absolute wealth. Choices depend on a reference point, which defines gains and losses. Many people are loss averse. Loss aversion means that people dislike losses more than they enjoy equal-sized gains. This leads to risk aversion in the

gain domain and risk seeking in the loss domain. Prospect theory formally models these observations and further assumes that people weigh probabilities non-linearly, overweighting small probabilities and underweighting mid-range probabilities.

Prospect theory is a prime example for BE, because it is based on careful experimentation. It is meant to be a descriptive, psychologically based theory of behaviour under risk. It has been highly influential in many fields.

Loss aversion is not restricted to risky choices. It can explain, for instance, why there is a status quo bias in many decisions.

Hyperbolic discounting

Many decisions concern future gains or losses. According to the dominant model, people discount future utilities at a constant discount rate, i.e. the discount rate is independent of the time delay. If someone prefers €100 today over €120 in one year, he or she should also prefer €100 over €120 if these amounts are due in one and two years, respectively. Yet, in contrast to this, many people experience a preference reversal as time passes. People are impatient in the short run and prefer €100 today over €120 one year hence. But when €100 is due in one year and €120 in two years, people are willing to wait another year to get €120. A large body of evidence supports the conclusion that people are impatient in the short run and patient in the long run (Frederick *et al.* 2002). This pattern of discounting is called 'hyperbolic discounting'.

The observation that many people's long-run intentions and their short-run actions are in conflict has profound implications. It leads people to save too little for their retirement, because the short-run gratification of immediate **consumption** overrides the long-run benefits of a better pension provision. Similarly, people often intend to lead a healthier life, but short-run temptations often undermine the good intentions. This divergence creates a demand for commitment. For instance, people save in illiquid assets and the state forces people to save for retirement by automatically deducting the pension contributions from their wages.

Heuristics and biases

Many economic decisions require the judgement of probabilities. In standard economic models people process probabilistic information according to the probability axioms and Bayes' law. Yet, as the hugely influential 'heuristics and biases' approach by Tversky and Kahneman (1974) has shown, people often use heuristics, i.e. decision short-cuts and rules of thumb, to make judgements. While heuristics are generally useful, they can sometimes lead people astray.

One important short-cut in making judgements is the 'representativeness heuristic'. For instance, when people have to judge the probability that event X belongs to set Y they often make their judgement on the basis of how *similar* X is to the stereotype of Y and thereby disregard the a priori probability of X. If someone looks like a librarian, people overestimate the likelihood that he or she actually is a librarian because they ignore the fact that only a small fraction of the population are librarians. For a similar reason people tend to overgeneralize from small samples.

Another useful heuristic is 'anchoring'. A quantity is estimated by starting from a salient anchor and then adjusted in the appropriate direction. Yet adjustments are typically insufficient. For instance, when people are asked to estimate the confidence interval of the Dow Jones index on some particular date in the future, they take the current value as an anchor and adjust their estimates up and down. Typically this leads to much too narrow confidence intervals, i.e. people's judgement displays 'overconfidence'. This phenomenon and obser-

vations on related heuristics and biases have sparked a lot of research in behavioural finance. For instance, overconfidence can explain 'excessive trading' observed in **financial markets**.

Bounded rationality

Taken literally, the canonical model assumes that people maximize the utility function outlined above, using the tools of optimization theory. Herbert Simon, who pioneered research on bounded **rationality**, was the first to point out the implausibility of optimization. Instead of general-purpose algorithm like optimization, people use domain-specific heuristics from an 'adaptive toolbox' (Gigerenzer and Selten 2001). This toolbox comprises search rules, stopping rules and decision rules. Search rules describe how to search for alternatives and how to evaluate them. Stopping rules describe when to stop the search. For instance, the search may be stopped after an alternative has met a certain aspiration level. Once the search has stopped a decision rule describes how a decision or inference is made.

Research in this field has made a lot of progress. It turned out that rather simple heuristics, like 'Take the Best', which only looks for a few cues and then takes the best alternative, are quite successful and beat more complicated rules that take more information into account. This will surely be a fertile area of research in the years to come.

Conclusion

Making progress in science often requires a dual process of 'destruction' and 'reconstruction'. Understanding the validity and scope of assumptions with the help of careful experimentation and interdisciplinary research (most recently in neuroscience) is one thing; being able to better explain core economic phenomena is another one. BE has made progress on this 'reconstructive' front as well. First, research in BE has led to theoretical alternatives to the standard assumptions outlined above. Prospect theory, hyperbolic discounting and models of social preferences are prime examples. Second, inspired by the new theories, empirical researchers have taken fresh looks on well-known phenomena in many subfields of economics. Research on social preferences, learning and heuristics has led to a field called 'behavioural game theory' (Camerer 2003), which aims at explaining human strategic behaviour. The field of 'behavioural macroeconomics' is influenced by research on consumption and savings decisions, but also by the insight that fairness, for instance, might contribute to the phenomenon of wage rigidity, which is a long-standing macroeconomic issue. Prospect theory and the 'heuristics and biases' programme have helped forming the field of 'behavioural finance', but have also influenced decision sciences and created the field of 'behavioural law and economics'. The interested reader should consult Camerer *et al.* (2004), which contains many interesting applications. And many more applications are sure to come.

References and further reading

Camerer, Colin (2003) *Behavioral Game Theory*, Princeton, NJ: Princeton University Press.

Camerer, Colin, Loewenstein, George and Rabin, Matthew (2004) *Advances in Behavioral Economics*, Princeton, NJ: Princeton University Press.

Fehr, Ernst and Gächter, Simon (2000) 'Fairness and Retaliation. The Economics of Reciprocity', *Journal of Economic Perspectives*, 14: 159–81.

Fehr, Ernst and Schmidt, Klaus (1999) 'A Theory of Fairness, Competition and Cooperation', *Quarterly Journal of Economics*, 117: 817–68.

Frederick, Shane, Loewenstein, George and O'Donoghue, Ted (2002) 'Time Discounting and Time Preferences: A Critical Review', *Journal of Economic Literature*, 40: 351–401.

Gigerenzer, Gerd and Selten, Reinhard (2001) *Bounded Rationality. The Adaptive Toolbox*, Cambridge, MA: MIT Press.

Kahneman, Daniel and Tversky, Amos (1979) 'Prospect Theory: An Analysis of Decisions Under Risk', *Econometrica*, 47: 313–27.

Tversky, Amos and Kahneman, Daniel (1974) 'Judgment under Uncertainty: Heuristics and Biases', *Science*, 185: 1124–31.

SIMON GÄCHTER

BELIEFS

In general a belief is defined as a proposition a social actor holds to be true. In order to explain the behaviour or the economic action of a person we usually need to know the situational restrictions shaping the feasible set of actions for her, her desires and preferences and her beliefs about the causal structure of the situation. Here we have to differentiate between two types of beliefs: first, the actor's beliefs about the structure of the external situation, e.g. her perception about the development of the occupational structure with regard to her own educational decisions, or her assessment of the impact of globalization on living standards and social security which may be important for her electoral behaviour and the stances of political parties with respect to economic policy. There is quite a lot of survey evidence showing that huge differences exist between the beliefs of the general public and of professional economists on economic issues (Caplan 2002). Second, based on their beliefs about the structure of the objective situations, actors develop a subjective estimate of their own capability to reach certain goals. Here one could also speak of 'perceived behavioural control'. Especially in occupational and educational status attainment processes there is strong evidence for the causal effect of class and gender differences in the subjective beliefs about the probability of success in certain areas of education and the occupational structure. Therefore, persons with a working-class background are likely to underestimate their chances for educational and occupational success, a fact that leads to the continuing reproduction of class differences in education. Also, women tend to have a rather low subjective perception of their probability of success in usually higher-paying male-dominated occupations, and thus tend to choose occupations that are designated as female.

In basic versions of **rational choice theory** and neoclassical economics it is generally assumed that actors decide on the basis of having full **information**. Therefore, rational beliefs, relying on sufficient empirical evidence, are a necessary condition for rational deliberation of alternative courses of action. In the context of real-world decisions, this heroic assumption cannot be sustained: usually social actors will collect a suboptimal amount of information because of search costs; they often use information selectively, do not conform to the usual guidelines of statistical reasoning, depend on information which is easily activated from memory and are very dependent on the cultural framing of the respective situation. Especially social psychology has shown that, rather than an evaluation of the actual structure or rational beliefs, easily activated attitudes and beliefs often determine behaviour in a spontaneous way. Only when actors are motivated to control their behaviour and to decide rationally, and furthermore have the opportunity to do so, will this type of automatic processing give way to a more deliberate and rational approach to behavioural decisions (Fazio and Towles-Schwen 1995). Even processes of deliberate reasoning are often influenced by automatically activated attitudes so that the selection and evaluation of information will be congruent with the preceding beliefs.

Thus, the analysis of the structure and formation of beliefs is of utmost importance for the sociology of economics, because individual economic behaviour and even economic policy decisions are based on beliefs that sometimes are false, incorrect or weakly supported. The process of belief formation is therefore an important field of research for sociology. Its roots are going back to **Marx**'s analysis of class consciousness, **Durkheim**'s study on the development of religion and Karl Mannheim's sociology of knowledge. Whereas the sociological classics focused on the analysis of collective beliefs, contemporary research is predominantly concerned with the individual mechanisms of belief formation, like different types of heuristics in social psychology. Raymond Boudon, for example, tries to show that even reasonable actors will often form false or weakly supported beliefs, due, first, to their cognitive dispositions in the interpretation of situations and, second, to their social positions and ensuing perspectives on social phenomena. The theoretical explanation of beliefs has necessarily to rely on these individual-level mechanisms. But phenomena like the ebb and flow of specific economic theories in public policy, e.g. the demise of Keynesianism and the universal spread of monetarist economic philosophy, the importance of different economic beliefs in the transformation of state-socialist into market economies and the myths about globalization in the advanced capitalist countries, show that the macrosociological conditions for the diffusion and predominance of certain economic beliefs have to be analysed more closely. Research on cultural differences in economic beliefs is still an emerging field. With respect to the formerly state-socialist European countries, for instance, Hölscher shows the complex shaping of current economic beliefs and values of publics in Eastern Europe through the legacies of the state-socialist regimes and religious traditions, which lead on the one hand to a stronger reliance on the state for economic security, but on the other hand to a much stronger belief in the importance of competition and achievement compared to the capitalist societies in Western Europe (Hölscher 2004).

Furthermore, research on the conditions for the diffusion of certain economic beliefs and theories is a very important desiderate. There is still a lot of room to discover and to analyse the interplay between actors and institutions struggling for the power to define the public and professional agenda on economic issues, which are very important preconditions for sometimes far-reaching political decisions with respect to economic matters.

See also: economic action; embeddedness; emotions and the economy

References and further reading

Caplan, Bryan (2002) 'Systematically Biased Beliefs about Economics: Robust Evidence on Judgemental Anomalies from the Survey of Americans and Economists on the Economy', *The Economic Journal*, 112: 433–58.
Fazio, Russel and Towles-Schwen, Tamara (1995) 'The MODE-Model of Attitude–Behavior Processes', in Shelly Chaiken and Yaacov Trope (eds), *Dual-Process Theories in Social Psychology*, New York and London: Guilford Press.
Hölscher, Michael (2004) 'Wirtschaftskulturen in Europa' [Economic Cultures in Europe], dissertation thesis, University of Leipzig.

JÖRG RÖSSEL
MICHAEL HÖLSCHER

BOUNDED RATIONALITY See: satisficing; Carnegie School

BOURDIEU, PIERRE

Pierre Bourdieu's interest in economic issues is obvious in his first work on Algeria (Bourdieu 1958). But from that time onwards, Bourdieu has never stopped using and discussing economic theories or models, especially the rational-choice model (Bourdieu 1974, 1977, 1980, 1994). Neither did he stop contributing to the empirical exploration of various economic realities, like the field of economic power, the market for private housing, the French publishers, etc. The publication in 2000 of

Les Structures sociales de l'économie stands in continuity to this earlier work.

His various investigations of the economic sphere rest on a coherent view of the economy and economics, aiming at integrating the analysis of economic behaviour and institutions into a general vision of social practice, a 'general economy of practice', as he wrote in *Le Sens pratique* (1980). This programme was developed in two directions. First, Bourdieu stressed the symbolic aspect of economic life, which relates his sociology directly to both the Weberian and the Durkheimian traditions, but he also concentrates on symbolic domination and struggles, which connects him with Marx. Second, Bourdieu elaborates an original anthropological critique of the dominant economic theory (that is to say neoclassical theory), which he puts at the centre of the theoretical construction and of his scientific method, especially through a 'dispositional' definition of action.

The symbolic genesis of economic life

In Bourdieu's view, the distinction between 'material' and 'symbolic' dimensions of reality leads to fallacies. The most common of these is the opposition between the economic 'infrastructure' and the intellectual 'superstructure' of social reality, which causes a disastrous division of labour between economists (interested in wealth, production, wages, etc.) and other social scientists (more devoted to cultural, psychological or intellectual issues). Following **Durkheim**, Bourdieu thinks there is no ontological heterogeneity between the sphere of 'representations' and 'beliefs' and the sphere of economic interests, institutions and actions. He refuses the idea that economic life should escape from sociological understanding because it has been developed historically as an autonomous sphere of reality (Bourdieu 2000). One therefore needs 'to abandon the economic/ non-economic dichotomy which makes it impossible to see the science of 'economic' practices – including those that are experienced as disinterested or gratuitous, and therefore freed from the 'economy' – as economic practices aimed at maximizing material or symbolic profit' (Bourdieu 1980/1990: 122).

Bourdieu first considers the economic order as a symbolic order. We can speak of an 'economic' order, because a specific kind of social belief and interest has been differentiated and made autonomous from social reality, leading social agents to refer more and more to 'economic' criteria and to leave aside other kinds of social criteria, at least in some parts of their practice. The invention of a particular *illusio* (close to *investment in a game* and also *libido*, Bourdieu 1994) is at the origin of the existence of an 'autonomous' economic order. The economic field is a specific type of field. '[The] fundamental laws [of the fields] are often tautologies. That of the economic field, which has been elaborated by utilitarian philosophers [is] "business is business" ' (Bourdieu 1994/1998: 83).

The history of this field is the history of a process of increasing autonomy, and of expansion, because the law of this field tends to determine the whole of social life, even though it is limited by the existence of other fields (religious field, bureaucratic field, fields of cultural production). This argument has its roots in Bourdieu's 'Algerian period' and in his analysis of the construction of a particular capitalist *cosmos* (Bourdieu 1963, 1977). In his works on Algeria, Bourdieu pointed out the existence of an 'anti-economic' behaviour (from a 'rational' point of view), rooted in 'traditional' dispositions, for which calculation, anticipation and also monetary accumulation were not really defined and systematically constituted as legitimate practices. The systematic introduction of money contributes to the generalization as well as the intensification of exchanges, and the related development of a 'capitalist

mind', which is nothing other than the *economic illusio*. This 'rationalization' process presupposes that certain economic and social conditions are fulfilled. The *'sousprolétaires'* are precisely those who fail to project themselves in the future, either by adhering to revolutionary goals or by *interiorizing* the laws of the capitalist cosmos.

Economic domination, essentially analysed as 'exploitation' in the Marxist tradition, is considered by Bourdieu as a particular case of symbolic domination (Bourdieu 1989). In his conception of domination, the dominated actively participate in their domination: they perceive the world through the eyes of the dominating groups, and their behaviour is profoundly determined by the relation of domination in which they take part (Bourdieu 1998). Bourdieu describes the decline of a group like the small farmers from Béarn as the result of their incapacity to adopt the dispositions (including matrimonial strategies) necessary to compete in a more global market. 'The socially exalted relationship between brothers can in [the case of] Béarn, serve as a mask and a justification for economic exploitation, with a younger brother often being an acknowledged "unpaid servant", often condemned to celibacy' (Bourdieu, 1980/1990: 16).

An imaginary anthropology

In Bourdieu's view, neoclassical theory, especially in its anthropological dimension, is a particular case of the scholastic fallacy. It is a theory which confuses the things of logic and the logic of things, and makes ordinary economic agents reason like pure theoreticians.

> Denying the pretension of economic agents to possess adequate knowledge of economic mechanisms, the academic economist claims for himself a monopoly on the total point of view and declares

31

himself capable of transcending the partial, particular viewpoints of particular groups.

(Bourdieu 1980/1990: 28)

In this sense, Bourdieu describes neoclassical theory as an 'imaginary anthropology' which oscillates between the subjectivism of 'free, conscious choice' and a quasi-mechanical objectivism (because there is often only one rational solution to a problem) (1980/1990: 46–7, 2000). Similarly, neoclassical theory reduces markets to an idealized vision which is far distant from the social reality of empirical markets.

The hegemony of rational actor theory in economics, and its success in sociology, are founded on scholastic bias. But they also proceed from the increasing autonomy of the economic field in the sense that they can be seen as a formalization of this process. 'Rational actor' theory, which seeks the 'origin' of action, strictly economic or not, in an 'intention' or 'consciousness', is often associated with a narrow conception of the 'rationality' of practices, an economism which regards as rational those practices that are consciously oriented by the pursuit of maximum (economic) profit at a minimum (economic) cost which is presented as a 'pure theory' of this field (Bourdieu, 1980/1990: 50). The most radical neoclassical economists try to generalize this economic *illusio* to the whole social reality, most of the time in contradiction to the results of the other social sciences. Bourdieu's general economy of practice is the precise opposite of this attempt, showing the specificity of the fields of cultural production where a particular economy takes place on the refusal of economic criteria (Bourdieu 1994). Bourdieu's original use of 'economic metaphors' is an attempt to understand today's economic practices as particular cases of a far more general economy of practices, a general theory of social value.

The mathematical formalization of economics allows neoclassical economists to separate the economic logic still further from the social and historical conditions in which it is embedded. The use of simple models and the practice of hypothesis testing simulate the experimental method without any chance of obtaining universal conclusions. The simplified models of economics are mostly very distant from the ethnographic or sociological observations of the underlying realities.

Bourdieu has therefore made an intensive use of geometric data analysis methods. These methods help to *reveal* structural homologies, for example between the social space and the fields of production, which permit an understanding of the social process of fit between supply and demand in a market. The perspective of the theory of fields appears more structural than can be any kind of 'network analysis', which tends to reduce relations between agents to very particular links inside a network, while it ignores the related *social properties* that are at stake (Bourdieu 1971).

References and further reading

Bourdieu, Pierre (1958) *Sociologie de l'Algérie*, Paris: PUF.

—— (1963) *Travail et travailleurs en Algérie*, Paris and The Hague: Mouton.

—— (1971) 'Une interprétation de la théorie de la religion selon Max Weber', *Archives européennes de sociologie*, XII, 1: 7–26.

—— (1974) 'Avenir de classe et causalité du probable', *Revue Française de Sociologie*, 15(1): 3–42.

—— (1977) *Algérie 60: structures économiques et structures temporelles*, Paris: Minuit.

—— (1980) *Le Sens pratique*, Paris: Minuit (English translation: *The Logic of Practice*, Cambridge: Polity, 1990).

—— (1984) 'Espace social et genèse des "classes"', *Actes de la Recherche en Sciences Sociales*, 52–3: 3–17.

—— (1989) 'Reproduction interdite: les dimensions symboliques de la domination économique', *Etudes Rurales*, 113–14: 15–36.

—— (ed.) (1990) 'L'Economie de la maison', *Actes de la Recherche en Sciences Sociales*, 81–2: 86–96.

—— (1994) *Raisons pratiques*. Paris: Le Seuil (English translation: *Practical Reasons*, Cambridge: Polity, 1998).

—— (1998) *La Domination masculine*, Paris: Le Seuil.

—— (2000) *Les Structures sociales de l'économie*, Paris: Le Seuil.

Bourdieu, Pierre and colleagues (1993) *La Misère du monde*, Paris: Seuil.

FRÉDÉRIC LEBARON

BUDGETS See: Public Budget

BUREAUCRACY See: organization theory; Weber

BUSINESS ASSOCIATIONS

There are two kinds of business associations. Employer associations represent business interests in the labour market whereas trade associations represent firms as producers. In some countries and sectors, labour market-related 'social' and product market-related 'economic' interests are represented by the same organizations. Business associations exist at national, sectoral and local, and increasingly also at supranational, level. Some are federations that organize and coordinate lower-level associations; others are direct membership associations; and some are both, organizing associations as well as (large) firms.

Modern business associations emerged in reaction to trade unionism on the one hand and increasing state interventionism on the other. Most of them date back to the late nineteenth century. Initially they tried to suppress **trade unions** and took sides in contemporary conflicts between sectors and countries over free trade and protectionism. Like trusts and cartels they also engaged in price-fixing and limiting market access. In the two world wars they became deeply involved in the management of the respective war economies.

After 1945, especially in the neocorporatist countries of the European continent, employer associations turned into 'social partners' of increasingly firmly established trade unions with whom they engaged in joint regulation of the labour market (Windmuller and Gladstone 1984). Likewise, trade associations came to accept a wide range of quasi-public responsibilities, from the enforcement of quality, safety and environmental standards to the delivery of public policies, for example in support of small firms. This holds in particular for associations with obligatory membership, such as chambers of commerce and industry. Whereas in countries with corporatist traditions (see **corporatism**) economic governance came to rely heavily on business associations, turning these into 'private interest governments' (Streeck and Schmitter 1985), in liberal political systems business associations became confined to lobbying the bureaucracy and the legislature. Similarly, in more voluntaristic **industrial relations** systems, where unions are weak and collective bargaining is decentralized, employer associations remained ephemeral or never came to exist.

Business associations face problems of **collective action** different from those of trade unions. That there are far fewer firms than employees would seem to give business a natural advantage over labour. Still, organizational density rates of business associations differ widely between countries and sectors. Firms tend to be well resourced and often prefer to pursue their interests individually. They also tend to be rational actors willing to free ride on the collective goods procured by associations. Business associations have therefore early on emphasized 'outside inducements' to membership, especially services that can be withheld from non-members. Often, however, these fail to neutralize the disorganizing effect of market relations among potential members. Competition for workers in tight labour markets, but in particular competition in product markets and price pressure in supplier relations between small and large firms, often causes conflict and mutual suspicion.

Encompassing organization of business is therefore difficult. This tends to move the

33

coordination of business interests to relations between rather than within associations. The number of business associations exceeds the number of trade unions by far. One study of the 1980s investigating fifty-six sectors in nine countries found on average more than sixteen business associations to one trade union (Streeck 1991). As firms are involved in more product than labour markets, trade associations tend to be even more fragmented than employer associations.

Business associations are often divided, not just by sector and region, but also by firm size. Big firms find it easier to defend their economic interests on their own. But they also often seek protection against trade union demands in employer associations that include small firms. Size differences between firms are taken into account by business associations linking membership dues to employment or turnover, and voting rights to dues paid. Equal voting rights are found mainly in business associations with obligatory membership, such as the Austrian *Wirtschaftskammer*. Outside Austria, obligatory membership in business associations is largely confined to the small business sector.

Business associations are changing under current processes of internationalization, liberalization of market economies, and the restructuring of the post-war nation-state. Supranational political arenas offer less supportive opportunity structures to them than most traditional nation-states (Greenwood 1997). As large firms turn multinational, they outgrow national politics and associations. In supranational settings they tend to rely on their superior resources and pursue their interests independently. Alternatively they enter into loose alliances with other large firms, like American-style 'business roundtables'.

Within national systems, widespread decentralization of collective bargaining constrains employer associations to find a new role, e.g. in delivering external support to firms negotiating terms of employment directly with their workforces. In economic policy, governments increasingly allow large firms to bypass associations while the latter find it harder to aggregate more specific individual interests into collective positions. Public subsidies to industry are being cut back, the battle over free trade is largely decided, and government intervention in the economy is being transferred to depoliticized regulatory agencies, limiting the space for collective political exchange between business and the state.

References and further reading

Coleman, William D. (1988) *Business and Politics: A Study of Collective Action*, Montreal: McGill-Queen's University Press.

Grant, Wyn (1993) *Business and Politics in Britain*, second edition, London: Macmillan.

Greenwood, J. (1997) *Representing Interests in the European Union*, New York: St Martin's Press.

Martinelli, Alberto (ed.) (1991) *International and Global Firms: A Comparative Study of Organized Firms in the Chemical Industry*, London: Sage.

Olson, M. (1982) *The Rise and Decline of Nations: Economic Growth, Stagflation, and Social Rigidities*, New Haven, CT: Yale University Press.

Schmitter, P. C. and Streeck, W. ([1981]1999) *The Organisation of Business Interests: Studying the Associative Action of Business in Advanced Industrial Societies, Discussion Paper 99/1*, Cologne: Max Planck Institute for the Study of Societies.

Streeck, W. (1991) 'Interest Heterogeneity and Organizing Capacity: Two Class Logics of Collective Action?' in Roland M. Czada and Adrienne Windhoff-Héritier (eds), *Political Choice: Institutions, Rules, and the Limits of Rationality*, Boulder, CO: Westview Press, pp. 161–98.

Streeck, W. and Schmitter, P. C. (eds.) (1985) *Private Interest Government. Beyond Market and State*, London: Sage.

Traxler, Franz (1995) 'Two Logics of Collective Action?' in Colin Crouch and Franz Traxler (eds), *Organized Industrial Relations in Europe: What Future?* Aldershot, UK: Avenbury.

Windmuller, John P. and Gladstone, Alan (eds) (1984) *Employers Associations and Industrial Relations*, Oxford: Clarendon Press.

WOLFGANG STREECK

BUSINESS GROUPS See: Enterprise Groups

C

CALCULATION See: rational choice theory; rationality

CAPITAL See: capitalism; Marx, social capital

CAPITALISM

The concept of capitalism was forged during the nineteenth century. The word 'capitalism' seems to have been penned for the first time in 1850 by the French socialist Louis Blanc in his treatise *Organisation du travail*. But the word was in fact seldom used in the nineteenth century. Proudhon used it very little. **Marx** hardly seems to have known the term, although F. Engels used it, and the German economist Alfred Schäffle used the word *Kapitalismus* as early as 1870 (Braudel 1981). It was only at the turn of the twentieth century that the word 'took off' on the intellectual and political scenes. In fact, it was Werner Sombart who popularized the term, in his 1902 work *Der moderne Kapitalismus*. The word was then incorporated into the Marxist vocabulary.

The idea of 'capitalism' is thus a recent one, even though the phenomenon described by the concept is considered to predate it. F. Braudel considers that its story essentially began in the fifteenth century, but this does not prevent him from making several references to thirteenth-century Italy. Following a familiar pattern, once the concept had been formed based on observation and theorization of the present, previous centuries were re-examined in search of the origins. Since it was **Sombart** who popularized the term, we shall take his definition as our starting point, before going back to look at the concept's eventful history.

A definition of capitalism

According to Sombart (2001: 4–5), 'Capitalism designates an economic system significantly characterized by the predominance of capital', an 'economic system' being a concept which 'enables us to classify the fundamental characteristics of economic life of a particular time, to distinguish it from the economic organization of other periods' (p. 5). It is 'a formative conception not derived from empirical observation' which enables economic science 'to arrange its material in systems' (pp. 4–5).

'Capitalism' thus functions as a Weberian **ideal type**, a theoretical construct used to identify relevant elements of the world and analyse them by differentiation from the typical model. It is clearly a concept of economic sociology, since in its description of the economy, the economy is seen primarily as a set of social institutions and relationships.

Indeed Sombart goes on to define an economic system as 'a mode of providing for material wants' comprising three aspects: (1) a mental attitude or spirit; (2) a form of organization; (3) a technique.

In relation to capitalism, these three aspects are described as follows:

1. Mental attitude or spirit

> The spirit of capitalism is dominated by three ideas: acquisition, competition and rationality ... The aim of all economic activity is not referred back to the living person. An abstraction, the stock of material things, occupies the center of the economic stage ... There are no limits to acquisition, and the system exercises a psychological compulsion to boundless extension.
>
> (Sombart 2001: 6–7)

2. Form of organization

> It is a system based upon private initiative and exchange. There is a regular cooperation of two groups of the population, the owners of the means of production and the propertyless workers, all of whom are brought into relation through the market.
>
> (Sombart, quoted by Parsons 1928: 647)

The 'high capitalism' period (from 1850 to 1914) is also marked by the autonomous existence of the company.

> By the combination of all simultaneous and successive business transactions into a conceptual whole, an independent economic organism is created over and above the individuals who constitute it. This entity appears then as the agent in each of these transactions and leads, as it were, a life of its own, which often exceeds in length that of its human members.
>
> (Sombart 2001: 13)

3. Technique

> Capitalist technology must ensure a high degree of productivity ... The compensation of wage earners, which is limited to the amount needed for subsistence, can, with increased productivity be produced in a shorter time, and a larger proportion of the total working time remains therefore for the production of profits.
>
> (Sombart 2001: 12)

The various characteristics described above have since been taken up by the sociological tradition that has chosen to discuss capitalism. Authors belonging to this tradition stress certain aspects of the social system: the existence of an economic process oriented towards unlimited accumulation of capital, the importance of the firm as an agent of the system, private ownership of production resources, 'free' wage labour, free enterprise and competition, involvement of science in the process and increasing rationalization of economic activity.

The emergence of the notion of capitalism

The word 'capitalism' is much more recent than the root word 'capital' on which it has been constructed. 'Capital' was used in an economic sense in Italy in a Florentine accounting ledger dating from 1211. The term then appears to have spread from Italy throughout Europe with the expansion of Italian commerce and banking. From the late eighteenth century, the emerging discipline of economics took the word 'capital' and gave it new acceptations. Thus, the birth of the term 'capitalism' would not have been possible without the prior birth of economic thinking that had given theoretical value to the term of 'capital', already part of the language of commerce and banking. The question is what need of thought was met by the conceptual creation of the idea of capitalism.

After the double revolution (the industrial revolution and the French revolution), the rising importance in the nineteenth century of characteristics indicated by the idea of capitalism made it an obvious area for study by the emerging discipline of sociology. At the time the two revolutions were considered cataclysms, although today there is a tendency to bury their identity in analyses of long-term developments. A new world had been born where discontinuity was more striking than continuity, and nineteenth-century thinkers set out to understand this major transformation from the point of view of various moral judgements. The idea of 'capitalism' arose from thinking inspired by a critical assessment of the new society, concerned primarily with new economic inequalities and the poverty of the working class (other critical assessments sensitive to other aspects of the new society also developed over the same period but are not relevant here).

Being a critical concept, connected to the heritage of the socialist writers which made it a deeply divisive concept, the term 'capitalism' was studiously avoided by some in the sociological tradition (Raymond Aron, for instance, preferred to talk about the 'industrial society'). In fact it was only fairly recently, and mainly in the United States, that the term 'capitalism' came to carry positive connotations and appeared in pro-capitalist work, a typical example being the free-market economist Milton Friedman's book *Capitalism and Freedom* (1962). The success of socialist ideas spread by the labour movement, so warmly welcomed in the Soviet Union, stimulated thinking and comparison of the advantages and disadvantages of the two systems (for example by Schumpeter in *Capitalism, Socialism and Democracy* (1942)). Following a classic dynamic in the history of ideas, criticism led to defence and justification. The pro-capitalist discourses of the twentieth century are above all a response to the same period's anti-capitalist discourses.

The significance of Marx's analyses

Although Marx scarcely used the term 'capitalism', tending instead to use 'capitalist system' or 'capitalist production', it was Marx who, as Sombart says, 'virtually discovered the phenomenon'. Analyses of capitalism thus are all developed from, and must position themselves in relation to,

Marxian theory. What are the characteristics of capitalism according to Marx?

The first important aspect is the M–C–M' formula to describe accumulation of capital. Capital is any money thrown into the sphere of circulation for the purpose of being recovered with a surplus, and this cycle is seen as endless. This limitless accumulation, found at the heart of Sombart's spirit of capitalism, is also central to Marx's definition, but for Marx it is first and foremost a material process, while for Sombart it is a way of viewing the world and giving purpose to one's actions (even though there would no longer be any need for a spirit once businesses have become autonomous and turned into 'material monsters', as the logic of the system would be imposed on all). The capitalist is forever insatiably throwing new capital into circulation, with the aim of increasing the abstract wealth formed by circulating capital. This places him in opposition to the miser, who accumulates a stock of money by removing it from circulation.

The second key aspect of Marxian theory is his theory of exploitation, which in his opinion explains the origin of the increase in value between M and M' that is the purpose of the capitalist process. There can only be capital if there is a surplus value. Marx found the origins of it in the consumption by the capitalist of a specific merchandise – labour – that by nature creates value when consumed. The surplus value that is the hidden origin of capitalist profit lies in the fact that the wage paid to workers is lower than the value they contribute to productions, which is pocketed by the capitalist when he puts new products on the market. And so for money to be transformed into capital, the existence of a wage-earning class is necessary for the capitalist to extract the surplus value that justifies his activities. A class conflict between the proletariat and the capitalists, inherent to the capitalist system, is born out of the wage relationship and tends to become exacerbated over time, producing the historical dynamics.

Responses to Marx and new ways

Marx's theory of exploitation has been heavily criticized, with analysts pointing out that while profits could come from payment of insufficient wages to workers, they could also have other origins that Marx refused to see. The most virulent critics on this question were the economists, who finally rejected the notion of labour value the Marxian system is built on. Marx's various predictions concerning the eventual condemnation of the capitalist system have also been re-examined many times, since history has so far failed to vindicate him.

Marx thought that he could establish laws for economics as precise as laws for the natural sciences; he also thought that sociocultural and political factors belonged to the superstructure, while historical movement is mainly produced by deeper structural determinations relating to economic factors, the main one being the wage relationship, and therefore the class struggle. These are the points that Sombart and Weber's economic sociology was to criticize, leaving criticism of labour value theory and the thorny question of justification of profit to the economists.

Unlike Marx, Sombart gives priority in his analyses to the role of the spirit of capitalism rather than to the role of the class struggle in describing the historical process. In Sombart's own words: 'It is a fundamental contention of this work that at different times different attitudes toward economic life have prevailed and that it is the spirit which has created a suitable form for itself and has thus created economic organization' (*Der moderne Kapitalismus*, quoted by Parsons 1928: 644). Its original aim was to complete the Marxian perspective by adding a socio-psychological and sociocultural dimension to the analysis.

This dimension was to be taken up by Max Weber in his famous essay *The Protestant Ethic and the Spirit of Capitalism* (1904/1920). As he explains,

the question of the motive forces in the expansion of modern capitalism is not in the first instance a question of the origin of the capital sums [as Marx thought] which were available for capitalistic uses, but, above all, of the development of the spirit of capitalism. Where it appears and is able to work itself out, it produces its own capital and monetary supplies as the means to its end, but the reverse is not true.
(Weber, quoted by Swedberg 1999: 67)

But Weber never intended 'to replace a one-sided "materialist" with an equally one-sided "spiritualist" causal account of culture and history. Both are equally possible' (Weber, quoted by Löwith 1982: 103). Weber left these issues for the analysis of empirical materials, refusing to take sides in any generalization.

The major distinctive feature of Max Weber's thinking on capitalism is that he places it in the much broader history of the modern West, which for him is characterized by a process of increasing rationalization that applies to a sphere wider than production and exchange. Encompassing the whole of western existence, this process can be seen at work in the arts, the sciences, and law or economic and social affairs. Weber was in fact only interested in what he called the 'modern rational' form of capitalism. The less openly politically committed nature of Weber's work (he methodologically seeks to separate the scientific from the political in his life), his own political choices and his very broad theoretical perspective have all contributed to make him a typical representative of the bourgeois sociology held in such contempt by Marxists. All the same, it cannot be said of Weber that he did not in his way cast a scathing critical eye over capitalist modernity.

In Weber's opinion, rationalization, initially a force for progress vital in liberating people from traditional ways of life, ended up as a stronger, longer-lasting source of tyranny. Weber endeavours to show that what was gradually emerging from the rationalization process was something deeply irrational. For example, while earning money in order to live is a rational, intelligible activity, the rational capitalist activity of insatiably seeking profit for profit's sake is perfectly irrational.

> This reversal marks the whole of modern civilization, whose arrangements, institutions and activities are so 'rationalized' that whereas humanity once established itself within them, now it is they which enclose and determine humanity like an 'iron cage'. Human conduct, from which these institutions originally arose, must now in turn adapt to its own creation which has escaped the control of its creator.
>
> (Löwith 1982: 48)

The variety of economic systems

The idea of capitalism was immediately associated with that of the existence of a variety of possible economic systems. Capitalism was first considered in opposition to other very different systems, whether they were its historical predecessors (slave economy or the feudalism in the classic Marxian analysis), or alternatives in the political debate (socialism).

Also from the outset, the idea was put forward that capitalism could take different forms in history, and that there was thus a historical variety of different capitalisms. The German historical school in economics played a vital role in this (see **historical school**). This school was to produce a theory of stages, identifying various periods and their related economic systems. This was at the origin of the idea of capitalism as an epoch of history, but also of the idea that there were separate identifiable periods within capitalism itself. In keeping with this tradition, Sombart, in *Der Moderne Kapitalismus* (1916–28), identified three stages in the development of capitalism: early capitalism (from 1200 to 1750), high capitalism

(from 1750 to 1914) and late capitalism (since 1914).

Other types of division have been proposed since, for example by I. Wallerstein in his work *The Modern World System* (1974). The World System is focused around central regions surrounded by various spaces defined in hierarchical order (core, semi-periphery, periphery, external) and linked by an international division of labour. The development of the modern world economy lasted centuries, during which time different regions changed their relative position within the system (see **world-systems approach to economic sociology**).

For the most recent period in the history of capitalism, an approach concentrating mainly on economic transformation factors is the **régulation school**, which is at the centre of a debate on Fordism as a new model for accumulation following the Second World War, and its apparent crisis point in the 1970s before its eventual evolution into post-Fordism. Taking an approach closer to the tradition of Sombart and Weber, Boltanski and Chiapello (2005) have proposed a system of phases based on changes in the spirit of capitalism, i.e. the normative systems accompanying capitalism. They identify three successive spirits of capitalism covering the twentieth century, the second of which corresponds approximately to the Fordist period.

The fact that several capitalisms exist, not in an orderly history but simultaneously in different countries, is an idea that has attracted attention mostly since the 1990s (see **capitalism, varieties of**). This interest was largely stimulated by Reagan and Thatcher's conservative revolutions in the USA and the UK, which exacerbated the differences between continental European capitalism and Anglo-American capitalism, but also by the fall of the Soviet empire. Today, it is clear that competition between economic systems concerns different capitalist systems. This field of research uses the term 'capitalism' in a much more axiologically neutral way, since judgement now concerns its variant forms rather than its own order.

See also: accounting, sociology of; class; economic sociology; political economy.

References and further reading

Boltanski and Chiapello, E. (2005) *The New Spirit of Capitalism*, London: Verso.

Braudel, Fernand (1981) *Civilization and Capitalism*, three volumes, New York: Harper and Row.

Löwith, Karl (1982) *Max Weber and Karl Marx*, London: George Allen and Unwin.

Marx, Karl (1990) *Capital. Volume 1. A Critique of Political Economy*, London: Penguin Classics and New Left Review.

Parsons, Talcott (1928) '"Capitalism" in Recent German Literature: Sombart and Weber', *Journal of Political Economy*, 36(6): 641–61 (and also (1929) 37(1): 31–51)).

Sombart, Werner (2001) 'Capitalism', in Nico Stehr and Reiner Grundmann (eds), *Werner Sombart. Economic Life in the Modern Age*, New Brunswick, NJ, and London: Transaction Books, pp. 3–29 (reprinted from Edwin. R. Seligman and Alvin Johnson (eds), *Encyclopedia of the Social Sciences*, New York: Macmillan, 1930).

Weber, M. (1930). *The Protestant Ethic and the Spirit of Capitalism*, London: Allen and Unwin.

EVE CHIAPELLO

CAPITALISM, VARIETIES OF

The term 'Varieties of Capitalism' (VoC) refers to the research field that compares institutional forms of modern capitalism. The scope of this subfield of comparative **political economy** can be defined in two different ways, one encompassing both diachronic and synchronic perspectives, the other concerning only a particular research field about sectoral, regional and national forms of capitalism.

In the broad sense, the VoC approach studies origins, structures and functions of capitalist institutions, comparing national forms and, in particular, distinguishing between different phases of capitalism. Since the 1920s, political economists have discussed the transformation of capitalism into a more planned and organized, and therefore market-restricting, system. The behaviour of firms was thus increasingly determined by non-market institutions, and firms' microeconomic rationality was more and more supplemented by societal, 'post-capitalist' perspectives. In the American context, such debates followed upon theories of managerialism, developed in the 1940s by scholars like Berle and Means and Burnham (see **managerial revolution**). In the 1960s and beyond, Galbraith, for example, argued that capitalism was no longer driven by competition and pecuniary reward. Rather, firms were governed by the 'techno structure', which was constituted by a managerial elite that aimed at economic planning, scientific business management and the application of sophisticated technology as an end in itself. In Germany, theoretical concepts about the emergence of a new institutional form of capitalism were often advanced by scholars with Marxist or Social Democratic backgrounds. Examples from the 1920s to the 1940s are Hilferding's 'organized capitalism', **Sombart**'s 'modern capitalism' and Pollock's 'state capitalism'.

Shonfield's 1965 book *Modern Capitalism* belongs to the same literature cluster, as he did not refer to a variety of capitalism in the narrow sense, but to the transition of the economies of such different countries as France, Germany and the USA into a more planned, organized phase, in which firms adopted features of public bureaucracies and in which competition was complemented by coordination. Since the 1970s, the French **régulation school** combines research on phases and national varieties of capitalism. Scholars like Aglietta, Lipietz and Boyer analyse changes in capitalist accumulation regimes. The focus of the French *régulation* school is therefore on change over time, for example regarding the transition from Fordism to post-Fordism; beyond that, this approach has also been used for the identification of sectoral, regional and national varieties of capitalism.

In the narrow sense, VoC has developed since the late 1980s, especially since the breakdown of socialist regimes in Eastern Europe, and is defined as the discussion over different national, sometimes regional and sectoral institutional foundations of capitalism. After the heydays of the debate over neo-corporatism in the late 1970s and early 1980s, literature clusters emerged that analysed different sectoral forms of economic governance, national specifics of production regimes, mechanisms of coordination between companies and interaction effects between institutions. VoC emerged by combining these discussions. Especially, it originated from analyses of capitalist varieties such as Japan and Germany. Some of the features that the earlier literature about phases of capitalism had identified as elements of 'modern', 'organized' capitalism re-emerged as features of specific national varieties of capitalism.

VoC cannot be identified with a single theory, but refers to a rich cluster of different approaches. However, VoC scholars mostly share some – though not necessarily all – of the following six interrelated premises and perspectives.

1. *Firms*: according to VoC, firms are the crucial actors in production regimes and the targets of regulation. Their role in regulation itself is a matter of debate. VoC scholars argue that companies have at least a certain influence on the stability and change of production regime institutions. Politicians anticipate a part of the firms' needs for policies that support their coordination.

2. *Modes of governance*: different varieties of capitalism are characterized by the modes in which managements coordinate their actions with stakeholders, other firms and societal entities. These relationships can rely on different norms and rules that constitute institutions. Markets, hierarchies, associations, communities and networks can be distinguished as basic modes of governance.

3. *Institutional domains*: the economic behaviour of firms is influenced by a multitude of institutions. These institutions form clusters referred to as institutional domains. Relevant domains are: industrial relations, **corporate governance**, rules of internal company decision-making, product standardization, skill formation; in the wider sense also welfare regime, competition policy, currency regime.

4. *Complementarity*: VoC scholars share the assumption that production regimes are not shaped by cumulated effects of isolated institutions but primarily by the interaction of institutions from the same or from different domains. The concept of institutional complementarity is central to this part of the debate. Complementarity refers to a situation in which the functionality of an institutional form is conditioned by the existence of other institutional forms. Therefore, VoC perceives the search for 'one best way' of organizing industrial relations, corporate governance, etc., as misleading. Institutional analysis, following VoC, has to focus on the interaction of a given institution with other institutions, i.e. the coherence of an institutional configuration as a whole. A given institution might fit coherently into one configuration but might undermine the functionality of another country's configuration.

5. *Different varieties of capitalism*: institutional configurations of production regimes differ not only over time and sectorally but – above all –

41

internationally and can be associated with country clusters. At least two such clusters with different internal logics can be distinguished. The Anglo-American countries, in which the institutional domains rely to a large extent on coordination by markets, form a relatively homogenous country cluster (described as the group of 'Liberal Market Economies' or LMEs by Hall and Soskice). In contrast, the country cluster referred to as 'Coordinated Market Economies' (CMEs) – sometimes also labelled 'nonliberal' or 'organized' economies – is more heterogeneous. For example, Amable distinguishes a continental European, a Social Democratic, an Asian and a Mediterranean subcluster.

6. *Comparative advantage and congenial institutional environment*: VoC scholars discuss whether different institutional configurations can be associated with different comparative advantages in the international division of labour. Following this, institutional capacities of Anglo-American countries support radical product innovation, while strategic coordination in the continental European country cluster supports incremental innovation in production sectors such as automobiles and mechanical engineering.

Since the late 1980s and early 1990s, the systematic combination of these assumptions has led to new perspectives on different research questions in political economy. For example, VoC provides reasons for scepticism about the idea that increased competition results in institutional convergence. VoC scholars discuss whether internationalization might even lead to increased orientation towards the respective national comparative advantages and, ultimately, to increased international diversity of capitalist institutional configurations.

VoC brings forward a strong argument against the neoclassical mainstream and its focus on a market-driven 'one best way'. Furthermore, implications also concern theories on political power resources, particularly in the context of debates over welfare state retrenchment. VoC emphasizes welfare states' contributions to the comparative advantages of the respective national economies and raises doubts about the assumption of class theory that firms behave antagonistically against every form of welfare policy and social protection.

Especially since the late 1990s, research on institutional forms of capitalism has generated great interest in and beyond political economy. One reason is the multitude of research fields that VoC brings together. VoC relies on research by a large number of scholars with diverse theoretical backgrounds and methodological approaches. However, the introduction of Hall and Soskice's edited volume *Varieties of Capitalism*, due to its programmatic formulation, has often been used as a point of reference. A large number of debate issues belong to the VoC research field; by and large, four groups can be distinguished.

1. *Economic performance*: one debate concerns the economic outcomes of different varieties of capitalism. In a sense, VoC focuses on the 'coordinated', 'organized' form of capitalism, as its imaginary reader is a neoclassical mainstream thinker and its main purpose is to explain the functioning of continental Europe's institutions which seem to be, in the purely neoclassical view, deficiently designed. In an early account of the concept, Soskice described VoC as a reinterpretation of neo-corporatism that provided a better explanation for the superior economic performance of countries like Japan, Germany and Switzerland. During the 1990s, the idea of the superiority of CMEs gave

way to the alternative concept of – at least – two different ways to good macroeconomic performance, one relying on a coherent set of coordinating, the other relying on market enforcing institutions. Hall and Gingerich show empirically that such coherent configurations, compared to mixed types, achieved higher growth rates between the early 1970s and the late 1990s. Comparative policy research shows that causal links between institutional variables and performance measures are often heavily dependent on observed time periods. However, some differences in the performance of national varieties of capitalism – for example, concerning innovation patterns and distributional consequences of industrial relations and welfare state institutions – are undisputed.

2. *Divergence and convergence*: another discussion concerns the future of institutional diversity in the context of internationalization of production and finance, European integration, and the growth of the service sector. Some scholars raise doubt about the stability of continental Europe's CMEs, as their industrial relations and corporate governance systems have been subject to increasing liberalization since the 1980s. However, it is controversial whether this liberalization actually alters the main logics of the respective production regimes, or whether the outcome will be more flexible but still basically coordinated capitalist varieties.

3. *Theory and empirics of complementarity*: the existence of a complementary interplay of different institutions and its significance for the functionality of institutional configurations are less disputed than the sources of complementarity. One debate concerns the question whether complementarity originates from structurally similar institutions, or whether it is more likely to be developed in the context of heterogeneous modes of interaction. Furthermore, authors in the tradition of the French *régulation* school link the idea of complementarity to the concept of institutional hierarchy and argue that dominant institutions impose their internal logic to neighbouring institutions; changes in institutional hierarchy therefore lead to cyclical changes in the main logic of accumulation regimes. Key aspects of empirical debates concern the interaction of skill formation and welfare regimes; of industrial relations and corporate governance; of industrial relations and welfare regimes. In addition, a part of the VoC debate concerns the question whether complementarity also exists between features of political systems and domains of production regimes.

4. *Origins and functionality*: yet another debate concerns the origins of the different varieties of capitalism. Especially, it is controversial whether the functionality of institutional configurations explains their origins. The contributors to the volume *The Origins of Nonliberal Capitalism*, edited by Streeck and Yamamura, describe the origins of Japan's and of Germany's production regime institution as an outcome of the steering capacity of political elites in extraordinary historical moments, driven by hybridization and experimentation in the context of uncertainty about the way in which institutions – for example, competition policy and co-determination – would interact after institution-building. However, it is also undisputed that the functionality of a configuration is one – though certainly not the only – source of institutional change.

In addition to these debates, it has been shown that both Anglo–American and continental European production regimes have been subject to parallel changes since the 1980s. Examples for this are the growth of pension funds, technological changes in the **financial markets**, and the growth of the service sector. This reminds us that, besides national varieties, there still exist phases of capitalism. Comparative political economy has to be able to describe both diachronic and synchronic differences in the institutional order of capitalism. However, so far, an accomplished combination of theories on phases and on sectoral, regional and national varieties of capitalism has not been developed. Important contributions come from the French *régulation* school.

References and further reading

Amable, B. (2003) *The Diversity of Modern Capitalism*, Oxford: Oxford University Press.

Aoki, M. (1994) 'The Contingent Governance of Teams: Analysis of Institutional Complementarity', *International Economic Review*, 35: 657–76.

Boyer, R. (1990) *The Régulation School: A Critical Introduction*, New York: Columbia University Press.

Hall, P. A. and Gingerich, D. W. (2004) *Varieties of Capitalism and Institutional Complementarities in the Macroeconomy*, MPIfG Discussion Paper 2004–5, Cologne: Max Planck Institute for the Study of Societies.

Hall, P. A. and Soskice, D. (eds) (2001) *Varieties of Capitalism. The Institutional Foundations of Comparative Advantage*, Oxford: Oxford University Press.

Hollingsworth, J. R. and Boyer, R. (eds) (1997) *Contemporary Capitalism. The Embeddedness of Institutions*, Cambridge: Cambridge University Press.

Shonfield, A. (1965) *Modern Capitalism*, London: Oxford University Press.

Soskice, D. (1990) 'Reinterpreting Corporatism and Explaining Unemployment: Co-ordinated and Non-coordinated Market Economies', in R. Brunetta and C. Dell'Aringa (eds), *Labour Relations and Economic Performance*, London: Macmillan, pp. 170–211.

Streeck, W. (1991) 'On the Institutional Conditions of Diversified Quality Production', in E. Matzner and W. Streeck (eds), *Beyond Keynesianism. The Socio-Economics of Production and Full Employment*, Aldershot, UK: Edward Elgar, pp. 21–61.

Streeck, W. and Yamamura, K. (eds) (2001) *The Origins of Nonliberal Capitalism: Germany and Japan in Comparison*, Ithaca, NY: Cornell University Press.

MARTIN HÖPNER

CAPITALIST CLASS, TRANSNATIONAL
See: Transnational Capitalist Class

CARE AND HEALTH

Health of the population of a society and the economic structure of the society are reciprocally related. Societal economic policies affect the health of the population, and the health of the population affects the economy. The reciprocal effects of health and the economy will be discussed in three specific areas of medical sociology: (1) social stratification and health; (2) globalization and health; and (3) the structure of the health care system.

Social stratification and health

Critical social theorists going back to Marx and Engels have observed that social stratification and health are inversely linked. Beginning with Michael Marmot's (Marmot and Theorell 1997) classic study of the British civil service in the 1970s, which demonstrated the link between the occupational status hierarchy and death rates from coronary heart disease, research on the effect of social stratification on health has burgeoned. Marmot and his colleagues found that there was a steep and steady increase in the death rate due to coronary heart disease over a ten-year period as occupational status within the civil service decreased.

This finding of the link between social status and health is robust and has been found for people of all ages across the life course, and in all nations, including developed and developing nations, nations of the north and of the south, and rich and poor nations (Diderichsen *et al.* 2001). Social status has generally been measured using income, occupational status or education. Measures of health have included general measures, such as life expectancy and death rates; subjective assessments of health; and disease specific mortality and morbidity rates. Historical studies have found that the relationship also holds across time. More recently, Wilkinson (1999) discovered that income inequality – i.e. the gap between the rich and poor – both between and within countries also affects health. Populations of countries or geographical subareas within countries, such as counties or provinces, that rate high on income inequality also have lower life expectancies and higher death rates than those countries or subareas with relatively low rates of income inequality.

Link and Phelan (2000) maintain that socio-economic status is the fundamental cause of social disparities in health. Higher socio-economic status is associated with greater resources, such as knowledge, money, power and prestige, which can be used to prevent risk of disease and death, or to cope with disease or the threat of death when it occurs. Diderichsen and his colleagues (2001) argue that social status positions are differentially exposed to health threats and, because of differences in resources, have differential vulnerability to health threats, resulting in differential health consequences. Negative health consequences, in turn, have negative social consequences such as decreased employment capabilities or impoverishment due to health care debts which affect not only the patient but the patient's family, further decreasing their social position. Widespread prevalence of disabling illness may also overwhelm the society, as in sub-Saharan African countries where high rates of HIV/AIDS have devastated the economy through high disability and death rates of adults in their prime working years, leaving behind high numbers of impoverished orphaned children.

Diderichsen *et al.* argue that government economic policies can significantly affect the link between social status and health inequalities. First, the effects of social stratification itself can be minimized through social welfare policies that support education, labour and families. Second, vulnerability can be decreased through risk reduction campaigns that target the most disadvantaged members of the population in culturally appropriate ways. Finally, the consequences of disease and death can be ameliorated by equitable, universal health care financing and safety-net welfare programmes to protect the sick and their families from impoverishment.

Globalization and health

Ulrich Beck (1992) argues that reflexive modernity in industrial countries and globalization have created risks and consequences that pose irreversible threats to health of all people of the world. Risks may at first affect those in the lower socio-economic classes but will eventually affect all members of society, although those with higher social status continue to have more resources to cope with risk. Economic decisions in industrial nations to relocate hazardous industries to poorer countries, where the labour is cheaper and less regulated, environmental laws are less stringent, and the safety regulations are more lax, are creating new health inequalities between rich and poor nations. These decisions lead to health catastrophes which may occur more often in the poor countries (e.g. the Bhopal incident in India), but risks can also cross borders (e.g. smog, pesticides in food imported from poor to rich countries).

Economic globalization has produced both convergence and divergence in patterns of morbidity and mortality (Zielinski Gutierrez and Kendall 2000). With improvements in agriculture and the resulting

45

increased standard of living in developed nations during the twentieth century, those countries began to pass through the 'epidemiological transition': that is, mortality rates from infectious diseases, particularly for children, decreased, and mortality rates from chronic diseases, particularly among older adults, increased. This transition has also been occurring in developing nations. However, the transition is still a matter of degree; infectious diseases account for the majority of deaths in developing countries, and for a substantial minority of deaths in developed nations. In both developed and developing nations infectious diseases tend to have the greatest effect on the lower socio-economic classes. Migration of people from developing to developed nations increases the risk of contracting infectious diseases in developed nations, while the marketing and export of life-style products, such as tobacco products and fast food, from the developed nations is increasing morbidity and mortality rates from chronic diseases in the developing countries.

Effect of economy on structure of the health care system

Pescosolido et al. (2000) argue that economics has been the primary force shaping the health care delivery system in all nations by mobilizing market resources to pay for the elements of the structure: for example, training of specialized health care providers, building hospitals and clinics, developing technology and pharmaceuticals, etc. In the developed nations, private philanthropy and/or governments provided the capital to develop the systems and therefore determined the structure. The wealthy industrialists provided the philanthropic funds to finance the building of large public hospitals as the foundation of the American health care system. In European countries, the government tended to be the major holder of wealth (compared to the US model) and therefore supported the emergence of 'sci-

entific medicine' and the structure to support it through general and employer taxes. In developing countries, even today, the lack of financial resources from either the government or the wealthy elites have prohibited these countries from training the personnel and developing the infrastructure needed to develop a modern health care system. Gallagher et al. (2000) maintain that lack of income will continue to be a barrier to the development of a western-style system.

In the area of comparative health care research, Whiteford and LaCivita Nixon (2000) argue that the work of pioneers like Milton Roemer in the modern period was focused primarily on developing a scheme for classifying the different health care delivery systems. These models assumed that modernization and industrialization would produce a convergence of delivery systems. In the postmodern era, researchers have used the 'mosaic' concept to examine the development of different systems in response to particular social, political and historical factors within a given society. Even given the diversity of health care delivery models, globalization of the economy has produced pressures towards convergence in the health care systems of developed nations in particular. With the development of increasing sophisticated medical technologies and pharmaceuticals, the cost of health care has increased dramatically, creating a crisis for those entities that pay for the care, including especially governments, employers and employees. This economic crisis is occurring simultaneously with the demographic shift of the populations of the developed countries from relatively young populations to aging populations, who are more likely to need and use health care. Money spent on health care cannot be spent on other social welfare programmes, including education, housing, transportation and social services. Therefore, these nations have been moving towards changes to limit the costs of their systems. These changes include (1) cost containment strategies, such as managed care systems and prospective payment systems; (2) privatization of health care; and (3) decentralization and devolution of government responsibility for health care costs.

In developing countries, Gallagher *et al.* (2000) maintain that, while citizens are aware of modern medicine and want it when they are sick, the models developed in the developed countries may not be culturally appropriate for developing countries, much less affordable. Models that incorporate respect for existing cultural, social and religious practices might be more appropriate, as well as affordable.

References and further reading

Beck., U. (1992) *Risk Society: Towards a New Modernity*, Thousand Oaks, CA: Sage.

Diderichsen, F., Evans, T. and Whitehead, M. (2001) 'The Social Basis of Disparities in Health', in T. Evans, M. Whitehead, F. Diderichsen, A. Bhuiya and M. Wirth (eds), *Challenging Inequities in Health: From Ethics to Action*, New York: Oxford University Press, pp. 12–23.

Gallagher, E. B., Stewart, T. J. and Stratton, T. D. (2000) 'The Sociology of Health in Developing Countries', in C. E. Bird, P. Conrad and A. M. Fremont (eds), *Handbook of Medical Sociology*, fifth edition, Upper Saddle Rover, NJ: Prentice Hall, pp. 389–97.

Link, B. G. and Phelan, J. C. (2000) 'Evaluating the Fundamental Cause Explanation for Social Disparities in Health', in C. E. Bird, P. Conrad and A. M. Fremont (eds), *Handbook of Medical Sociology*, fifth edition, Upper Saddle Rover, NJ: Prentice Hall, pp. 33–46.

Marmot, M. and Theorell, T. (1997) 'Social Class and Coronary Heart Disease: The Contribution of Work', in P. Conrad (ed.), *The Sociology of Health and Illness: Critical Perspective*, fifth edition, New York: St Martin's Press, pp. 93–105.

Pescosolido, B. A., McLeod, J. and Alegria, M. (2000) 'Confronting the Second Social Contract: The Place of Medical Sociology in Research and Policy in the Twenty-First Century', in C. E. Bird, P. Conrad and A. M. Fremont (eds), *Handbook of Medical Sociology*, fifth edition, Upper Saddle Rover, NJ: Prentice Hall, pp. 411–26.

Whiteford, L. M. and LaCivita Nixon, L. (2000) 'Comparative Health Systems: Emerging Convergences and Globalization', in G. L. Albrecht, R. Fitzpatrick and S. C. Scrimshaw (eds), *The Handbook of Social Studies in Health and Medicine*, Thousand Oaks, CA: Sage, pp. 440–53.

Wilkinson, R. G. (1999) 'Income Distribution and Life Expectancy', in I. Kawachi, R. G. Wilkinson and B. P. Kennedy (eds), *The Society and Population Health Reader: Income Inequality and Health*, New York: New Press, pp. 28–35.

Zielinski Gutierrez, E. C. and Kendall, C. (2000) 'The Globalization of Health and Disease: The Health Transition and Global Change', in G. L. Albrecht, R. Fitzpatrick and S. C. Scrimshaw (eds), *The Handbook of Social Studies in Health and Medicine*, Thousand Oaks, CA: Sage, pp. 84–99.

SUSAN BROWN EVE

CARNEGIE SCHOOL

History and scope

The 'Carnegie School' is often identified with the pioneering work in **behavioural economics** done by Herbert Simon, James G. March and Richard Cyert in the 1950s and 1960s (Earl 1988). The Carnegie behaviouralists are known for their interest in understanding how individuals and organizations act and make decisions in the real world, and their challenges to the neoclassical theory of optimization and maximization in decision-making and organizations. Concepts such as bounded **rationality** and **satisficing** were developed to describe individuals and organizations acting in the face of 'the uncertainties and ambiguities of life' (March and Simon 1958: 2). Many of these concepts were first discussed in the book *Organizations* (March and Simon 1958), and none of them has lost currency. They prove their usefulness whenever actual behaviour departs from the tenets of rationality (for instance, when action is rule-based rather than consequence-based; or when it conflicts with statistically informed strategies as

47

described in the prospect theory of Tversky and Kahneman).

The background for the Carnegie School was the Ford Foundation's mission to establish a broad and interdisciplinary behavioural social science in the late 1940s and early 1950s, and much of their efforts were directed at supporting the early setup of the Graduate School of Industrial Administration (GSIA) at Carnegie Mellon University (originally Carnegie Institute of Technology), where Simon, March and Cyert worked. The Carnegie Institute of Technology had been founded in 1912 by Andrew Carnegie and had established itself as one of the better engineering schools in the country. The early president Robert Doherty, who had come from Yale, wanted Carnegie Tech to be a leader in research and, hence, to break with the traditional mechanical engineering view of business education and include broader social and interdisciplinary aspects. As a result of his ambitions, the first dean of what came to be known as the Graduate School of Industrial Administration (GSIA), George Leland Bach, was hired. Bach wanted to staff his department with economists who combined intellectual skills and experience in applying theory to real world situations and he wanted to put Carnegie at the forefront of US business schools. Simon, March and Cyert all came to Carnegie to help develop this view.

Business education at that time wasn't much oriented towards research, but Simon, Cyert and March wanted to be different. They wanted to do research. They wanted their research to be relevant for business leaders, while at the same time emphasizing the tools of good science. Early core courses in the programme included 'quantitative control and business' (consisting of basically accounting and statistics), a sequence of micro- and macroeconomics, and **organization theory**. The vision they had was reflected in an emphasis on creating a new behavioural science which was broad enough to accommodate disciplines such as economics, sociology and social psychology, yet precise enough to reflect the rigour and technical sophistication of mathematical models. In the end, their implementation of this vision produced significant contributions to areas such as **behavioural economics**, operations research, experimental economics and theories of the firm (Day and Sunder 1996). It also created a model for business schools that was widely adopted across the United States and (later) Europe.

The behavioural group at Carnegie was embedded in a larger group of scholars, which included innovative economists such as Franco Modigliani, John Muth, Charles Holt and Merton Miller. The spirit at Carnegie was that everybody interacted with everybody else; discussed each other's research and discussed science, so collaborative teams worked together as well as across each other's projects. Consisting of different people with different interests, these teams always worked together in a friendly way, despite different disciplines and despite varying degrees of admiration for the idea of rationality. It was an environment in which people were united by their deep and intense interest for doing science. And it was a unique environment where joy from work was present more than anywhere else. Several Nobel prize-winners were fostered during the golden years at Carnegie: Robert Lucas, Franco Modigliani, Merton Miller and Herbert Simon, and Carnegie had outstanding records on other accounts as well (Simon 1991).

The Carnegie School tried to develop the rudiments of process-oriented understandings of how economic organization and decision-making take place. They did so in an interdisciplinary way, linking economics to organization theory, cognitive science, sociology and psychology, and centring around concepts such as uncertainty, ambiguity, norms, routines, learning and satisficing. They used ideas from social science more broadly to advance understanding of economics and, in the process, contributed to the strands that came to be called behavioural economics (Day and Sunder 1996). The ideas initiated by the Carnegie School helped to establish a foundation for modern ideas on bounded rationality, adaptive and evolutionary economics, and transaction cost theory, among other areas.

Key ideas and theories

The behavioural research of Simon, Cyert and March aimed at making understandable how individuals make decisions and behave in the real world. They found that neoclassical economics gave too little attention to the institutional and cognitive constraints on economic and organizational behaviour and on individual decisions, and too little room for human mistakes, foolishness, the complications of limited attention and other results of bounded rationality. As a result, they proposed to include the whole range of limitations on human knowledge and human computation that prevent organizations and individuals in the real world from behaving in ways that approximate the predictions of neoclassical theory. For example, decision-makers are sometimes confronted by the need to optimize several, sometimes incommensurable, goals (Cyert and March 1963). Furthermore, instead of assuming a fixed set of alternatives among which a decision-maker chooses, the Carnegie School postulated a process for generating search and alternatives and analysing decision processes through the idea of aspiration levels (March and Simon 1958), a process that is regulated in part by variations in organizational slack (Cyert and March 1963). Finally, individuals and organizations often rely on routines or rules of thumb learned from experience or from others, rather than seek to calculate the consequences of alternatives.

One of the first major results of the Carnegie School's work was a propositional inventory of organization theory, involving Herbert Simon, James March and Harold Guetzkow, which led to the book *Organizations* (March and Simon 1958). The book was intended to provide the inventory of knowledge of the (then almost non-existing) field of organization theory, and also a more proactive role in defining the field. Results and insights from studies of organizations in political science, sociology, economics and social psychology were summarized and codified. The book expanded and elaborated ideas on behavioural decision-making, search and aspiration levels and elaborated the idea of the significance of organizations as social institutions in society.

> The basic features of organization structure and function [March and Simon wrote] derive from the characteristics of rational human choice. Because of the limits of human intellective capacities in comparison with the complexities of the problems that individuals and organizations face, rational behavior calls for simplified models that capture the main features of a problem without capturing al its complexities.
>
> (March and Simon 1958: 151)

March and Simon also wanted to unite empirical data-gathering research with rigorous theorizing in order to create a rigorous empirical theory that could organize and so give meaning to empirical facts with legitimate theory. Science, they believed, was the product of the organization of empirical facts into conceptual schemes, and the progress of science was based on the development of more sophisticated and elegant theoretical systems, but not necessarily the discovery of new facts.

The Ford Foundation also supported a larger project on behavioural theories of organizations which was carried out by Richard Cyert and James March (along with their students, including Julian Feldman, Edward Feigenbaum, William Starbuck and Oliver Williamson). This project originated in the works of Cyert and March to develop improved models of oligoploy pricing by using organization theory. The research on the behavioural theory of the firm aimed at investigating how the characteristics of business firms as organizations affect important business decisions. Integrating theories of organizations with existing (mostly economic) theories of the firm; they developed an empirical theory rather than a normative one; and focused on classical problems in economics (such as pricing, resource allocation, and capital investment) to deal with the processes for making decisions in organizations.

At the centre of *A Behavioral Theory of the Firm* is the idea of the firm as an adaptive political coalition (Cyert and March 1963), a coalition between different individuals and groups of individuals in the firm, each having different goals, and hence the possibility of conflict of interest. Said Cyert and March:

> Since the existence of unresolved conflict is a conspicuous feature of organizations, it is exceedingly difficult to construct a useful positive theory of organizational decision-making if we insist on internal goal consistency. As a result, recent theories of organizational objectives describe goals as the result of a continuous bargaining-learning process. Such a process will not necessarily produce consistent goals.
> (Cyert and March 1992: 28)

The firm is therefore seen as an adaptive system that through learning and experimentation adapts to its environment. The experience of the firm is embodied in a number of standard operating procedures (for instance, solutions that have served the firm well in the past will be included in the organizational repertoire and will be easily reactivated in the face of similar problems in the future). As time passes and experience changes, so do standard operating

procedures change through processes of search and learning. In other words, the firm is not an unchangeable entity – it is a system of rules, driven to change by current aspirations and targets reflecting experienced or anticipated dissatisfaction.

This view of the firm was important to modern developments such as evolutionary theory (see **evolutionary economics**) and **transaction cost economics** which both bear intellectual debts to the ideas in the behavioural theory of the firm. For example, the idea of bounded rationality and conflict of interest are now standard in the transaction cost theory of especially Oliver Williamson (1985, 1996); elements of the thoughts of the firm as an adaptive political coalition can be found in both the theory of teams (Marschak and Radner 1972) and **game theory**, and the view of the firm as a system of rules which adapt to its changing environment is important in the evolutionary theory put forward by Richard Nelson and Sidney Winter (1982).

See also: rationality.

References and further reading

Augier, M. and March, J. G. (2002) 'A Model Scholar', *Journal of Economic Behavior and Organization*, 49: 1–17.

Cyert, R. and March, J. G. ([1963]1992) *A Behavioural Theory of the Firm*, second edition, Oxford: Blackwell.

Day, R. and Sunder, S. (1996) 'Ideas and Work of Richard M. Cyert', *Journal of Economic Behavior and Organization*, 31: 139–48.

Earl, P. (ed.) (1988) *Behavioural Economics*, Aldershot, UK: Edward Elgar.

March, J. G. and Simon, H. A. ([1958]1993) *Organizations*, second edition, Oxford: Blackwell.

Marschak, J. and Radner, R. (1972) *Economic Theory of Teams*, New Haven, CT: Oxford University Press.

Nelson, R. and Winter, S. (1982) *An Evolutionary Theory of Economic Change*, Cambridge, MA: Belknap Press.

Simon, H. A. (1955) 'A Behavioral Model of Rational Choice', *Quarterly Journal of Economics*, 69: 99–118.

—— (1991) *Models of My Life*, Cambridge, MA: MIT Press.

Williamson, O. E. (1985) *The Economic Institutions of Capitalism*, New York: Free Press.

—— (1996) 'Transaction Cost Economics and the Carnegie Connection', *Journal of Economic Behavior and Organization*, 31: 149–55.

—— (2002) 'Empirical Microeconomics: Another Perspective', in M. Augier and J. G. March (eds), *The Economics of Choice, Change and Organization: Essays in Memory of Richard M. Cyert*, Cheltenham, UK: Edward Elgar.

MIE AUGIER

CATALLACTIC (MARKET) EXCHANGE

See: exchange, markets

CHANDLER, ALFRED DUPONT

Alfred Dupont Chandler is widely recognized as the most important and influential business historian of the twentieth century. His theory of the managerial revolution bridged the theories of institutional economists such as Ronald Coase and sociologists such as Talcott Parsons; his work almost single-handedly shifted the agenda over the rise of big business from a moralistic debate over 'robber barons' vs 'captains of industry' to search for social and economic factors behind the rise of managerial hierarchies. Large firms came to be seen as qualitatively different from other firms, less because of their market power or accumulation of wealth than for the structure of organization and forms of management. Attention was drawn away from the motives of the men who created corporate giants towards the exogenous conditions, especially technological change, that made managerial hierarchies and new organizational forms rational and efficient. While debate has continued about whether his accounts provide the best explanation (Roy 1997), there is no doubt that Chandler is the standard against which virtually all scholarship on the rise of big business is measured. His prodigious and prolific career over the last half-century has earned him a unique

place in American business history and related social science disciplines.

Chandler's major insight, and the issue that has shaped the scholarly agenda, is that the managerial form of large scale firms has a major effect on efficiency and effectiveness (see **economic organizations**). More particularly, top managers in the early twentieth century responded to changes in the technology of production and the scale of markets by developing new business strategies with new organizational forms, most notably the multidivisional form (see **rationalization**). In the multidivisional form, perfected by Alfred Sloan at General Motors, the home office acts as a financial and strategic coordinator of various divisions (Chevrolet, Pontiac and the other name brands for GM), which operate semi-autonomously. Such a system can find the optimal balance between economies of scale and scope and flexible response to changing conditions.

Chandler was born in 1918 to an old New England family and educated at Phillips Exeter Academy, Harvard College, the University of North Carolina, and once again Harvard, where he earned a PhD in history. His career has included conventional political history, including editing the presidential papers of Theodore Roosevelt and Dwight D. Eisenhower. In graduate school, his most influential teacher was Talcott Parsons, who introduced him to Weber, **Durkheim** and structural functional theory. 'In one way or other, for the next forty years, Parsonian and especially Weberian sociology informed the corpus of nearly all of Chandler's studies' (McCraw 1991). This, even though he came of intellectual age in a period in which disciplinary boundaries divided sociology and history into rarely bridged islands.

His business history studies began with a dissertation on his great-grandfather, Henry Varnum Poor, one of the first compilers of stock market data and an influential advocate of rationalizing the turbulent railroad industry. The study, published as *Henry Varnum Poor: Business Editor, Analyst and*

Reformer (Chandler 1956), gave Chandler access to his ancestor's encyclopedic data on virtually all major American railroads during the maturation of what he would later call 'America's First Big Business'. While academically respected, the book had only portents of what was to come. The work that established Chandler as a major figure and that changed the way we understand large scale enterprise was *Strategy and Structure* (Chandler 1962). With case studies of DuPont, General Motors, Standard Oil and Sears, Roebuck, the book recounted the conditions to which managers were responding in adopting the multi-divisional form, along with a survey of the seventy largest American industrial firms. The emphasis on entrepreneurs in American business was replaced with a focus on managers. The attention to the uniqueness of case studies gave way to generalization and the implications for theory.

Strategy and Structure established Chandler's reputation in business history. His next major book, *The Visible Hand* (Chandler 1977) changed all the disciplines that made business history a topic, especially economic sociology. The thesis is simple, profound and paradigm-rocking: the large modern business firm, by its scale and scope, has replaced the 'invisible hand' of the market as the primary mechanism of economic coordination, vaunting capitalism into a new epoch: managerial capitalism. Sparked by advancing technology, especially the lowered cost of transportation and communication and the standardization of mass production, it became rational for large-scale enterprise to consolidate different steps of production (vertical integration) and formerly competing firms (horizontal integration) under a single management. He emphasized that the role of the firm is less to manipulate demand or prices than to coordinate the complex functions of production and distribution. This line of reasoning is extended in *Scale and Scope: The Dynamics of Industrial Capit-*

alism (Chandler 1990), which employs comparative analysis to explain the relative vitality and stamina of national business systems. The adoption of appropriate managerial forms, he argues, explains the dominance of the German economy before World War I, the relative decline of the British and the robustness of the American.

Chandler has been extremely influential in economic sociology both as inspiration and as foil. Before the 1970s economic sociology was dominated by Parsonian functionalism (see **functional imperatives/ prerequisites (AGIL)**), on which Chandler based his theoretical reasoning, but focused more on the meaning of **economic action** and the differences between economy and society than the institutional dimension emphasized by Chandler. However, the revitalization of economic sociology in recent decades, springing out of organizational sociology, has turned again to the nature of the firm, especially large-scale enterprise. The market has become seen as an alternative means of coordination and governance. But Chandler has also been seen as the primary representative of 'efficiency theory', the notion that economic forms exist and thrive because they are more efficient than other forms. Economic sociologists have criticized his reliance on Parsonian functionalism, his inattention to politics and power, his benign view of capitalism, and his inattention to national cultural differences. But no business historian is in the same league for influencing economic sociology.

See also: corporate governance; economics, history of; firms; managerial revolution; Parsons, Talcott; technological change.

References and further reading

Chandler, Alfred D. Jr (1956) *Henry Varnum Poor: Business Editor, Analyst, and Reformer*, Cambridge, MA: Harvard University Press.

—— (1962) *Strategy and Structure: Chapters in the History of the Industrial Enterprise*, Cambridge, MA: MIT Press.

—— (1977) *The Visible Hand: The Managerial Revolution in American Business*, Cambridge, MA: Belknap Press.

—— (1990) *Scale and Scope: The Dynamics of Industrial Capitalism*, Cambridge, MA: Belknap Press.

McCraw, Thomas (1991) *The Essential Alfred Chandler: Essays Toward a Historical Theory of Big Business*, Boston: Harvard Business School Press.

Roy, William G. (1997) *Socializing Capital: The Rise of the Large Industrial Corporation in America*, Princeton, NJ: Princeton University Press.

WILLIAM G. ROY

CHARISMA

Charisma, in sociological terms, refers to the collective attribution of extraordinary abilities or characteristics to a person (see Bendix 1962). This differs markedly from the way 'charisma' is used in everyday language, where simply an aura of 'specialness' or having a 'magnetic personality' indicates charisma. In contrast, Max Weber used the term 'charisma' in a way that is far more restrictive (see Biggart 1989).

According to Weber, an individual endowed with charisma is set apart from ordinary persons and is treated as if in possession of exceptional qualities that are not available to ordinary persons. On the basis of being perceived to have these powers, the individual is treated as a leader (Bendix 1962: 88, n. 15).

The rare quality or 'gift of grace' that is believed to reside in a charismatic individual manifests as 'supernatural, superhuman, or at least specifically exceptional qualities', an endowment 'regarded as of divine origin or as exemplary' (see Weber 1947: 358–9 in Biggart 1989: 130–1). The social 'roles' of charismatic individuals are of heroes, messiahs, oracles and shamans. Individuals who are powerful and well known are not necessarily charismatic in this 'pure' sense.

The essential 'proof' of charisma is the presence of a following. Once followers recognize a leader's claim as valid, they are morally obligated to submit to the leader's direction. Followers must repudiate their former lives and assume new selves, becoming devotees or converts. To maintain their position as charismatics, leaders must periodically demonstrate the 'extraordinary abilities' that they are believed to have. These demonstrations may be miracles, the continued success of a particular mission, or other proofs that are judged to be valid. Religious and political figures such as Jesus Christ, Mahatma Ghandi and Martin Luther King were all charismatic in the Weberian sense, but despotic figures such as Adolf Hitler may also qualify as charismatics. It is the fact of a following that confirms a charismatic, not the nature of the mission.

Charismatic authority breaks with the accepted 'order' out of which it emerges (Giddens 1994: 161). Charisma is a driving force that cuts through the established authority of an existing order; it is an irrational phenomenon and not subject to routines but rather to the pronouncements of the charismatic, which may be idiosyncratic. In contrast to traditional or rational-legal authority, charismatic authority is not attached to a position or office, but to a person. Because it is not an incremental force for transformation, but rather a revolutionary one that springs from the person of a figure, charisma has been one of the primary forces for social revolution and change over the course of history.

In his sociology of law, Weber does not identify all positive change with charisma and all negative forces with routinization (Bendix 1962: 327). As charismatic authority is gradually supplanted by other forces, new legal norms are also created. In this way, innovating activity can come through routinization, and not only through charismatic leadership. For example, while Jesus Christ led a charismatic movement with himself at its centre, over time the Roman Catholic Church institutionalized and routinized his charisma where it is now found in the office of the Pope. Institutionalized charisma, while not the pure type, may be attached to important religious and political offices; whoever is the incumbent is endowed with a measure of charismatic influence. Even as charisma recedes in overt importance as it is supplanted by other forms of authority, it remains an important element of social structure (Gerth and Mills 1946: 262).

In organizations based on charismatic leadership, a leader's interactions are 'based on an emotional form of communal relationship' (Wilson 1975: 360–1). These leaders are followed by disciples or aides who have withdrawn from the everyday world in order to serve the mission. Devotees may give up jobs, possessions, their homes and their individuality. For them, the mission of the charismatic movement is critical and all else secondary, including the economic and material aspects of life. Disciples of charismatics often survive on supporter donations of food and other forms of sustenance, allowing the closest disciples to turn their efforts towards the charismatic mission.

This type of charismatic organization is, first, rare and, second, difficult to maintain in its original state. Though Weber saw the 'decline of charisma' as a distinct historical tendency (being increasingly supplanted by traditional and rational-legal authority structures), he also perceived it to be an ever-recurrent phenomenon. Bureaucracy and charisma are not necessarily incompatible. In fact, the cycle of emerging charismatic leadership and its routinization are possible during any phase of history (Bendix 1962: 327).

While it may seem that charismatic organizations are limited in type to those that are religious, as Richard Swedberg discusses in *Max Weber and the Idea of Economic Sociology*, many, if not all, economic systems (including rational capitalism) have charismatic elements (Swedberg 1998: 50).

For example, in *Charismatic Capitalism* (1989), Nicole Biggart describes network direct-selling organizations that, while not strictly charismatic in the 'pure' sense outlined by Weber, are in a 'weakened' sense charismatic in the manner described by Weber scholar Wolfgang Schluchter. This weakened type of institutionalized charisma can come about when as few as one, or as many as all, of the critical elements of charisma outlined by Weber are met. For example, in some direct-selling organizations, charismatic figures may describe the selling of products as having a 'higher' purpose, such as promoting health or social welfare, and the economic success of the organization can be interpreted as 'proof' of the power of the mission. Salespeople may come to see themselves as disciples of the leader, and their selling behaviour as acting towards a social and moral good.

Modern capitalism is largely based on the rational and calculating quest of gain and methodical organization in the pursuit of profit, but there are forms of capitalist enterprise that have significant charismatic elements. These forms, called 'booty' and 'adventure' capitalism, are typically associated with great risk of capital and even social and physical danger in the search for gain. 'Colonial exploitation, risky financial transactions, private financing of military ventures, and slave trade, or piracy are all forms of "booty capitalism", in which the stakes are enormous and success frequently depends upon the spellbinding leadership of some individual' (Bendix 1962: 306).

Start-up organizations may have charismatic elements where early employees devote their work lives to the success of an individual and his or her business ideas and see their efforts as having a missionary character. Risky exploration for new biotechnology substances, gas and minerals, or spectacular financial gains through novel investment vehicles may all infuse charismatic elements into capitalist enterprise. Each may be organized around the efforts of scientific or business leaders able to galvanize the emotional attachment and dedication of employee-followers who work tirelessly to promote the entrepreneurial vision.

Charisma is a powerful force for change but it cannot endure in its most pure forms, eventually including either or both of traditional or bureaucratic-rational elements. The reasons for this weakening result from the need eventually to solve two problems that all charismatic organizations must face. First, the charismatic leader needs eventually to be replaced as illness, infirmity or death demands a successor. Successors may assume the post through heredity or through the assumption of an office according to some sort of principled selection process. In charismatic business enterprises, this often is the moment when the capabilities of the entrepreneur are strained and the demand for routinized business practices become undeniable.

Second, charismatic organization is eventually required to deal with the material needs of its organization; its anti-economic stance is no longer tenable as the material needs and interests of its participants weigh on the daily operation of the mission. Disciples and followers seek to stabilize their lives through assured income streams or salaries, and economic routines become established. Often, one or both of these challenges are not met and the charismatic movement disbands.

Charisma, as a social force, has been a crucial means for social and economic revolution, overturning traditional regimes and, with its appeal to the emotions and larger aspirations, attracting followers away from the routines of a bureaucratically organized existence. However, charisma is an extremely unstable form of organization, and if successful, eventually incorporates traditional and routinized elements of organization.

References and further reading

Bendix, Reinhard (1962) *Max Weber: An Intellectual Portrait*, Garden City, NY: Doubleday Anchor.

Gerth, H. and Wright Mills, C. (1946) *From Max Weber: Essays in Sociology*, New York: Oxford University Press.

Giddens, Anthony (1994) *Capitalism and Modern Social Theory: An Analysis of the Writings of Marx, Durkheim, and Max Weber*, Cambridge: Cambridge University Press.

Swedberg, Richard (1998) *Max Weber and the Idea of Economic Sociology*, Princeton, NJ: Princeton University Press.

Weber, Max (1947) *The Theory of Social and Economic Organization*, edited by Talcott Parsons, New York: Free Press.

—— (1978) *Economy and Society*, edited by Guenther Roth and Claus Wittich, Berkeley, CA: University of California Press.

Wilson, Bryan (1975) *The Noble Savages: The Primitive Origins of Charisma and its Contemporary Survival*, Berkeley, CA: University of California Press.

PENNEY ALLDREDGE
NICOLE WOOLSEY BIGGART

CHILDREN AND ECONOMIC LIFE

Childhood as the initial distinct stage in the life cycle has not been universally recognized. In western countries before the sixteenth century, youngsters mixed with adults and performed adult activities as soon as they were capable of doing without their mothers (Elkin and Handel 1984). Even after children began to have separate activities and were viewed as distinct from adults, the parameters of childhood varied a great deal. Up until the eighteenth century, infants were often 'put out' to wet nurses and families took in others' offspring to supplement their finances. Childrearing was not the parents' top priority and children were expected to help meet the family's survival needs. Childhood was considered to be over by at least age 14, when youngsters were often sent out to other families to receive proper discipline, learn a trade, work as servants, or in rare cases attend school. By the end of the eighteenth century, parents had become more indulgent and a growing number gave older children the freedom to work outside the home or go to school. Temporarily leaving home was replaced by a pattern of longer residence with parents, but increasingly children spent more of their daily lives away from adults in specialized age-segregated institutions like schools. By the end of the nineteenth century, childhood was defined as a special life stage with unique developmental needs, and the traditional productive roles for children in families were rapidly disappearing. In the early twentieth century, interaction between parents and children became more intimate, but older children were being given more freedom from direct parental supervision and their behaviour was becoming more heavily influenced by peers.

Children in developing countries today are still primarily considered economic assets, an investment in the family's future, and birth rates tend to be high. Children can be extra workers who can contribute to the family's income by working either at home or outside, providing geriatric care for elderly parents, and carrying on the family farm or business.

Although child labour has been banned and obligatory schooling introduced and gradually extended as nations have industrialized, children often perform income-earning labour in the developing world. Child labour allows poor families to increase their income or productivity. But the stereotype of children doing **sweatshop labour** ignores the diverse forms of child labour and incorrectly assumes that child labour is a substitute for adult labour. Many forms of child labour are more appropriately regarded as apprenticeships, and others would or could not be done by adults (e.g. low productivity agriculture jobs).

In developed countries, children are primarily considered economic liabilities, objects of parental affection in need of proper nurturing, and birth rates tend to be low. Children incur cost for care, housing, food, clothing and schooling, and are not expected, nor allowed before a specified age, to contribute to the family's income. Costs for job-related education often extend into early adulthood. In addition, indirect costs are incurred that encompass unpaid care and services within the family and the lost opportunity costs for parents. The latter include forgoing earnings due to employment interruptions or working time reductions, the depreciation of human capital, lower pay upon re-entering employment after interruptions, lost pension rights, and economic risks of divorce for a partner who has invested more time in child care. Parents have the primary obligation to pay these costs, with mothers bearing most of the indirect costs. Some governments and employers provide benefits that cover some of these costs (e.g. paid parental leave, child allowances), especially in northern Europe.

Children's contributions to the indirect costs have become minimal. Children only occasionally perform **housework**, although variation by the type of chores and the child's gender, age and family structure have been found. More time is devoted to chores such as babysitting or pet care than adult chores. Girls devote more time than boys, teens do more chores than younger children, and children in larger and single-parent families do the most.

Gary S. Becker (1991) has applied economic theory, including rational choice (see **rational choice theory**), to the status of children. Becker infers that increases in family income may lead to increased investment in children that may reduce the number of children per family. Reductions in fertility are due to underlying economic and social conditions rather than to improved birth control techniques. As women expect greater participation in the labour force, they will invest more in market-oriented human capital-like education that further increases their earning power and participation, and further reduces fertility. Critics have challenged Becker's assumptions that free markets are family friendly and households act as small factories, but the alternative family decision-making models proposed tend to be less tractable than Becker's, and often the implications of these models can be generated just as well from Becker's model (Carlin 1993: 526–7).

Children's economic status has always varied a great deal by the social **class** standing of parents, but some recent concerns in the United States are as follows. Divorce usually lowers children's status as a consequence of the immediate costs, the diminished employment opportunities for custodial parents (usually mothers) and the non-payment or underpayment of child support by non-custodial parents (usually fathers). Some negative outcomes for children have been found when mothers are employed, but this is often offset by the advantages related to the increases in family income. The more children parents have, the fewer the resources that are available for investment in the children's human capital.

References and further reading

Becker, Gary S. (1991) *A Treatise on the Family*, enlarged edition, Cambridge, MA: Harvard University Press.
Carlin, Paul S. (1999) 'Economics and the Family', in Marvin Sussman, Suzanne K. Steinmetz and Gary W. Peterson (eds), *Handbook of Marriage and the Family*, second edition, New York: Plenum Press, pp. 525–52.
Elkin, Stanley and Handel, Gerald (1984) *The Child and Society: The Process of Socialization*, fourth edition, New York: Random House.

RUDY RAY SEWARD

CHOICE See: economic action, economics; history of; rational choice theory

CIRCUITS OF COMMERCE

'Circuits of commerce' is a relatively new concept within economic sociology. Randall Collins first spoke of 'Zelizer circuits' to refer to the dense, meaningful exchange patterns studied by economic sociologist Viviana Zelizer (Collins 2000). Zelizer herself later renamed the term 'circuits of commerce'. Commerce here has the classical connotation of 'conversation, interchange, intercourse, and mutual shaping' (Zelizer 2004). More specifically, the term draws attention to the fact that exchange is invariably conducted in particularized social and cultural settings.

Circuits of commerce consist of networks that include some social actors (be it individuals, households or organizations) and exclude others. These networks have, in other words, boundaries that are to a greater or lesser degree stable and identifiable. However, 'circuits of commerce' does not address the structural features of these networks, but what may be called their cultural content: particular forms of exchange are accompanied by specified morals, manners, symbols and rituals, which, in turn, have shared meanings for people within a circuit.

Social ties are not uniform within these circuits, but are instead subject to differentiation. People may, for instance, mark the manifold exchange relationships they engage in, whether intimate or relatively impersonal, by means of special names, the use of particular media of exchange, or the giving of gifts. The implication is that the transfer of goods and services within a circuit is not restricted to either market or gift exchange, but often involves a combination of both.

Apart from social relationships, seemingly homogeneous or generalized entities such as money or price are subject to differentiation within circuits of commerce. This means that actors within circuits make distinctions between different types of money, or prices that not only differ in quantitative, but also in qualitative respects (see **money, sociology of**). Indeed, circuits of commerce may be characterized by the use of special media of exchange; apart from money, these may include merchandise coupons, local currencies, different types of vouchers, or commodities like cigarettes which go to replace legal tender under certain circumstances. These different 'monies', in turn, undo the commensurating effect of monetization and market exchange to some extent.

In terms of conception of human action, circuits of commerce imply that economic actors have goals that are more encompassing than utility maximization, and permanently seek to make sense of economic life. In doing so, their action is not universally rational, but only locally so within the circuits that they inhabit. Methodologically, circuits of commerce call for thick descriptions, detailed historical analyses and rich cross-cultural comparisons.

Apart from Zelizer's own work on subjects such as the emergence of life insurance in the nineteenth century, the changing valuation of children or the economy of intimacy, examples of circuits of commerce include diverse fields such as non-western bazaars, where bargaining rituals are subject to moral values (Geertz 1979); home care work in New England, where the boundaries between paid bodily care and unpaid, friendship-like personal attention blur (Stone 1999); foreign currency markets, where traders establish microstructures on a global scale and do each other favours by exchanging strategic information (Knorr Cetina and Bruegger 2002); or art markets, where prices convey a wide range of social and cultural meanings to exchange partners (Velthuis 2003) (see **art and economy**). Thus the concept of circuits of commerce brings together a wide range of culturally sensitive approaches within economic sociology, similar to the way **embeddedness** has brought social structural approaches under a common denominator. In doing so, it promises to be a powerful alternative within economic sociology to the reductive, parsimonious notion of exchange that prevails in neoclassical economics.

References and further reading

Collins, Randall (2000) 'Situational Stratification: A Micro-Macro Theory of Inequality', *Sociological Theory*, 18(1): 17–43.

Geertz, Clifford (1979) 'Suq: The Bazaar Economy in Sefrou', in Clifford Geertz, Hildred Geertz and Lawrence Rosen (eds), *Meaning and Order in Moroccan Society*, Cambridge, Cambridge University Press, pp. 123–225.

Knorr Cetina, Karin and Bruegger, Urs (2002) 'Global Microstructures: The Virtual Societies of Financial Markets', *American Journal of Sociology*, 107(4): 905–50.

Stone, Deborah (1999) 'Care and Trembling', *The American Prospect*, 43: 61–7.

Velthuis, Olav (2003) 'Symbolic Meanings of Prices. Constructing the Value of Contemporary Art in Amsterdam and New York Galleries', *Theory and Society*, 31: 181–215.

Zelizer, Viviana A. (2004) 'Circuits of Commerce', in Jeffrey Alexander, Gary T. Marx and Christine Williams (eds), *Self, Social Structure, and Beliefs. Explorations in the Sociological Thought of Neil Smelser*, Berkeley, CA: University of California Press.

—— (forthcoming) 'Circuits within Capitalism', in Victor Nee and Richard Swedberg (eds) *The Economic Sociology of Capitalism*, Princeton, NJ, Princeton University Press.

OLAV VELTHUIS

CITIZENSHIP

Introduction: dimensions of citizenship

Citizenship, the rights and duties of members of a nation-state, is a juridical status that confers a sociopolitical identity, and determines how economic resources are redistributed within society. There are broadly two versions of the **social rights** that constitute citizenship. In the strong version, citizenship is an important element in distributive justice, because it involves a contributory principle in which there must be some balance between contributions, typically through work, military service and parenting, and rewards such as welfare, education and subsidies. The central idea behind active citizenship is that the democratic state is an association, where membership and its rewards are ultimately dependent on individual contributions to the public good. For example, old age pensions were historically conceived as a reward for services to society during the lifetime of the recipient. In the weak version of welfare rights, entitlements are related to needs rather than to qualifying behaviour, individual merit or status. For example, provision for handicapped children is a benefice rather than a reward for contributions. In addition to social rights, citizenship is also a component of liberal democracy, because civil and political rights are an important part of citizen status.

Historical development of citizenship and the welfare state

A citizen was originally the denizen of a city, and citizenship can be traced historically back to the classical world of Rome and Greece via the Renaissance cities of northern Italy, but modern citizenship is the product of revolutions, especially the French revolution, and industrialization (Turner 1986). In the process of nation-building, nineteenth-century citizenship incorporated the urban working class into **capitalism** through welfare institutions (Mann 1987). Welfare states achieved the pacification of working-class radicalism with relatively little concession to basic inequalities of class, wealth and power. Citizenship ameliorated but did not undermine the system of social stratification. While welfare capitalism avoided the revolutionary conflicts that were predicted by Karl **Marx**, there were significant variations between capitalist regimes in terms of their relationship to democracy and authoritarianism. In Germany, Otto von Bismarck was the reluctant founder of the modern welfare state, and social citizenship was developed with few firm provisions for civil and political rights. This authoritarian

welfare system remained in place until the First World War. In Japan, the Meiji Restoration of 1868 used the emperor system as a legitimating principle in its strategy of conservative modernization, and promoted citizenship as an exclusionary principle of loyalty and hierarchy. Japanese modernization was undertaken without a bourgeois revolution and hence citizenship was a tool of bureaucratic state control rather than a basis of civil liberties. Russia was in the long run unsuccessful in developing a strategy to retain power and modernize the regime. It embraced repression and exclusion, combined with periods of ineffective reform. The absence of elementary citizen rights, agrarian backwardness, rapid industrialization and heavy military expenditure created the prerequisites for violent revolutionary change (Weber 1995). These authoritarian regimes, with the possible exception of Germany, did not develop social citizenship, and civil rights were periodically expunged by arbitrary political power.

In Britain, welfare institutions expanded in response to working-class pressure on the state to protect workers from unemployment and sickness, but war and preparation for war were important contributory factors. Nineteenth-century imperial wars often served to illustrate the poor health of the British working class. Evidence from medical examinations of British army recruits demonstrated a significant depth of disability, and health statistics were important in the development of the national efficiency movement that promoted discipline and health through physical training, temperance and military service. The welfare state often appears as an aspect of social reconstruction that according to William Beveridge (1944) existed to remove the five giant evils of want, disease, ignorance, squalor and idleness (see **welfare state and the economy**). The state would intervene to limit the negative consequences of the free market where individuals and families were often unable to respond to the contingencies of unemployment, illness and old age. In reality, social citizenship was more an unintended consequence of wartime mobilization and strategies to rebuild post-war Britain (Titmuss 1958).

T. H. Marshall (1950) argued that citizenship was composed of three sets of rights. Civil rights emerged in the seventeenth and eighteenth centuries, and were institutionalized in common law, habeas corpus and the jury system. Nineteenth-century political rights were inscribed in the parliamentary system, and social rights were built into the twentieth-century welfare state. The sociological theories of Beveridge, Marshall and Titmuss were somewhat parallel to the economic ideas of John Maynard **Keynes** (1936), who argued that state intervention to invest in utilities would stimulate demand and mitigate the negative effects of the business cycle. In short, the development of social citizenship in Britain was not so much the consequence of a specific social strategy, but a general unintended effect of social Keynesianism, which was a set of policies to preserve capitalism rather than to advance welfare socialism.

Social Keynesianism has been resisted in the United States, which retained a greater emphasis on individual responsibility for welfare and reliance on local community initiatives to solve collective problems. Citizenship in America remains indebted to Alexis de Tocqueville's theory of associational democracy. In *Democracy in America* Tocqueville (2003) argued in Volume I in 1835 that the lack of centralized, bureaucratic administration had encouraged individual initiative, and voluntary associations and community groups rather than state intervention had flourished to address social and political problems. Sociological research has found that Americans are often alienated from formal politics, but their political commitments are expressed through a multitude of local and informal associations (Bellah *et al.* 1985). However, **social capital** – participation in churches, voluntary associations and clubs – has decline continuously through the post-war period, resulting in a decline of trust, political participation and interest in politics (Putnam 2000). Modern Americans watch more television, read fewer newspapers and undertake less voluntary service, producing an erosion of active citizenship (Turner 2001). There is evidence that the decline in civic engagement in America reflects a general decline in volunteering in modern societies (Brown *et al.* 2000).

Neo-liberalism and consumer citizenship

Citizenship and welfare have been profoundly altered by the neo-liberal revolution of the late 1970s, which created a political environment in which governments were no longer committed to the universalistic principles of social citizenship, a comprehensive welfare state and full employment. These economic changes – reduction of state intervention, deregulation of the labour and **financial markets**, implementation of free trade, reduction in personal taxation, fiscal regulation of state expenditure – were a reflection of the New Right doctrines of F. A. Hayek, Karl Popper and Milton Friedman. New Right theorists argued that the spontaneous order of the market must not be regulated by the state, and that judgements about human needs should be left to the operation of the market. The neo-liberal revolution has converted the citizen into a passive member of consumer society, where conservative governments understand 'active citizenship' to be a method of regulating the efficiency of public utilities such as the railways. An active citizen is somebody who complains about poor services.

References and further reading

Bellah, R. N, Madsen, R., Sullivan, W. M., Swidler, A. and Tipton, S. M. (1985) *Habits of the Heart. Individualism and Commitment in American Life*, Berkeley, CA: University of California Press.

Beveridge, W. H. (1944) *Full Employment in a Free Society*, London: Allen and Unwin.

Brown, K., Kenny, S. and Turner, B. S. (2000) *Rhetorics of Welfare. Uncertainty, Choice and Voluntary Associations*, Basingstoke, UK: Macmillan.

Keynes, J. M. (1936) *The General Theory of Employment, Interest and Money*, London: Macmillan.

Mann, M. (1987) 'Ruling Class Strategies and Citizenship', *Sociology*, 21(3): 339–54.

Marshall, T. H. (1950) *Citizenship and Social Class and Other Essays*, Cambridge: Cambridge University Press.

Putnam, R. (2000) *Bowling Alone. The Collapse and Revival of American Community*, New York: Simon and Schuster.

Titmuss, R. (1958) *Essays in 'the Welfare State'*, London: Allen and Unwin.

Tocqueville, A. de (2003) *Democracy in America*, London: Penguin Books.

Turner, B. S. (1986) *Citizenship and Capitalism. The Debate over Reformism*, London: Allen and Unwin.

—— (2001) 'The Erosion of Citizenship', *British Journal of Sociology*, 52(2): 189–209.

Weber, M. (1995) *The Russian Revolutions*, Cambridge: Polity Press.

BRYAN TURNER

CLASS

While class is one of the core themes in economic sociology, there is no general consensus among sociologists about how best to define this concept or about the broader theoretical framework within which it should be studied. Any elaboration of the concept of class, therefore, must simultaneously be an explication of the central differences in alternative conceptualizations of class.

In what follows we will begin by mapping out what might be termed the common terrain of class analysis – the inventory of interconnected concepts that are present in most approaches to the study of class. This will be followed by a detailed discussion of the concept of class in the Weberian and Marxist traditions of sociology.

A conceptual inventory

In ordinary language the word 'class' is most often used as a noun, as in expressions like 'the working class' and 'the middle class'. In sociology, in contrast, the most analytically rigorous use of the concept appears mainly as an adjective, as in expressions like 'class location', 'class relations', 'class structure', 'class struggle' and so on. To map out the conceptual space of class analysis, therefore, we must begin by defining the core elements of this inventory.

Class relations

Any economic system requires the deployment of a range of resources in production: tools, machines, land, raw materials, labour power, skills, and so forth. This deployment can be described in technical terms as a production function – so many inputs of different kinds are combined in a specific process to produce an output of a specific kind. The deployment can also be described in social relational terms: the individual actors that participate in production have different kinds of rights and powers over the use of the inputs and over the results of their use. 'Powers' refers to the effective capacity of people to control the use of means of production, including the capacity to appropriate the results of that use; 'rights' refers to the legal enforcement by third parties of those powers. Rights and powers over resources, of course, are attributes of social relations, not descriptions of the relationship of people to things as such: to have rights and powers with respect to land, for example, defines one's social relationship to other people with respect to the use of the land and the appropriation of the products of using the land productively.

When the rights and powers of people over productive resources are unequally distributed these relations can be described as class relations. Both Marx and Weber understand class relations in this way for capitalist societies, where the core class relation is between owners of means of production and owners of labour power, since 'owning' is a description of rights and powers with respect to a resource deployed in production.

It is important to be quite precise here: The rights and powers in question are not defined with respect to the ownership or control of things in general, but only of resources or assets insofar as they are deployed in production. A capitalist is not someone who owns machines, but someone who owns machines, deploys those machines in a production process, hires owners of labour power to use them and appropriates the profits from the use of those machines. A collector of machines is not, by virtue of owning those machines, a capitalist.

Class location

'Class location' is a micro-level concept referring to the location of individuals (and sometimes families) within class relations. Class relations are thus analytically prior to locations. Just as the location 'husband' and 'wife' within a family can only be defined within the social relations we call 'marriage', so the definition of specific class locations presupposes a definition of the social relations that bind them together.

In these terms, to say that someone is 'in' a working-class class location is to claim that they are embedded in a set of micro-level interactions within capitalist class relations in which, to gain access to means of production and subsistence, they must engage in an exchange activity with an employer and then obey the commands of a boss within a labour process. To say someone is 'in' a managerial class location is

to claim that they are embedded in a set of interactions in which they are empowered to give various kinds of commands either directly to their subordinates or indirectly via their control over production decisions.

Class structure

'Class structure' is a more macro-level concept than the concepts of class locations and class relations. It designates the overall organization of class relations within some macro-unit of analysis. One can therefore describe the class structure of a firm as the organized set of all the class relations within a firm, or the class structure of a region or a country or perhaps even the world as the organized set of class relations within these increasingly larger units of analysis.

Class interests

By virtue of their location within class relations, and by virtue of the broader class structure of which those class relations are a part, individuals have available different strategies for securing and improving their material interests. Owning considerable wealth means a person faces different alternatives and trade-offs from a person who simply owns labour power. 'Class interests' refers to the interests actors have by virtue of these class-determined strategic alternatives.

Class consciousness

'Class consciousness' refers to the **beliefs** actors hold about class relations, class structure and their own class interests. Insofar as actors may have faulty beliefs about the nature of the class structure in which they live, about their location within that structure and the strategies which would best advance their class interests, then one can speak of their class consciousness being 'false'. But, more broadly, the concept of class consciousness is not mainly about the truth-content of the beliefs people hold but about their class character.

Class practices and class struggle

'Class practices' are the activities actors engage in pursuit of their class interests on the basis of their understanding of class relations. Insofar as the interests of classes exist in antagonistic relation to each other, then class practices typically involve 'class struggle', i.e. the pursuit of interests *against* those of another class.

Class formation

'Class formation' refers to the formation of collectively organized actors in pursuit of class interests. When employers form a chamber of commerce or workers form a trade union or labour party to advance their respective class interests, they have constructed a particular kind of class formation. Class formations vary in many ways: in the extent to which they are encompassing or fractional; in the extent to which they challenge the institutions that define strategic alternatives they face or accept those institutions; in the extent to which they involve coalitions across different kinds of class locations. What renders all of these variations as instances of *class* formation is that they contribute to the organized capacity of actors to pursue class-based interests.

Taken together, this inventory of concepts provides a rich conceptual space in which to conduct class analysis. The space include micro-level concepts centring on the lives, conditions and experiences of individuals (class location, class interests, class consciousness, class practices), macro-level concepts mapping the contexts in which those micro-level processes operate (class structure, class formation, class struggle), and the concept of class relations which bridges the micro and macro levels of analysis: class locations are defined within class relations; class structures are made up of class relations.

The pivotal concept within this inventory is 'class relations', for it is this concept that gives the adjective 'class' its content in all of the elements. This is also the concept which best reveals the central difference in the theoretical apparatus of the two principal traditions of class analysis – Marxist and Weberian.

Class in Weber and Marx

The concepts of class in the Marxist and Weberian theoretical traditions share much in common: they both reject simple gradational definitions of class; they are both anchored in the social relations which link people to economic resources of various sorts; they both see these social relations as affecting the material interests of actors, and, accordingly, they see class relations as the potential basis for solidarities and conflict. Yet they also differ in certain fundamental ways. The core of the difference is captured by the favourite buzzwords of each theoretical tradition: 'life chances' for Weberians, and 'exploitation' for Marxists.

The Weberian concept: class as market-determined life chances

The intuition behind Weber's idea of life chances is straightforward: the kind and quantity of resources you own affects your opportunities for income in market exchanges (Weber [1922]1978). 'Opportunity' is a description of the feasible set individuals face, the trade-offs they encounter in deciding what to do. Owning means of production (the capitalist class) gives a person different alternatives from owning skills and credentials (the 'middle' class), and both of these are different from simply owning unskilled labour power (the working class). Furthermore, in a market economy, access to market-derived income affects the broader array of life experiences

63

and opportunities for oneself and one's children. The study of the life chances of children based on parents' market capacity is thus an integral part of the Weberian agenda of class analysis.

The Marxist concept: class as exploitation

Within a Marxist framework, the feature of the relationship of people to economic resources that is at the core of class analysis is 'exploitation'. Both 'exploitation' and 'life chances' identify inequalities in material well-being that are generated by inequalities in access to resources of various sorts. Thus both of these concepts point to conflicts of interest over the *distribution* of the assets themselves. What exploitation adds to this is a claim that conflicts of interest between classes are generated not simply by what people *have*, but also by what people *do with what they have*. The concept of exploitation points our attention to conflicts within *production*, not simply conflicts in the *market*.

Exploitation is a complex and challenging concept. In classical Marxism this concept was elaborated in terms of a specific technical framework for understanding capitalist economies, the 'labour theory of value'. In terms of sociological theory and research, however, the labour theory of value has never figured very prominently, even among sociologists working in the Marxist tradition. And in any case, the concept of exploitation and its relevance for class analysis does not depend on the labour theory of value.

The concept of exploitation designates a particular form of interdependence of the material interests of people, namely a situation that satisfies three criteria:

1. *The inverse interdependent welfare principle*: the material welfare of exploiters causally depends upon the material deprivations of the exploited.

2. *The exclusion principle*: this inverse interdependence of welfares of exploiters and exploited depends upon the exclusion of the exploited from access to certain productive resources.

3. *The appropriation principle*: exclusion generates material advantage to exploiters because it enables them to appropriate the labour effort of the exploited.

Exploitation is thus a diagnosis of the process through which the inequalities in incomes are generated by inequalities in rights and powers over productive resources: the inequalities occur, in part at least, through the ways in which exploiters, by virtue of their exclusionary rights and powers over resources, are able to appropriate surplus generated by the effort of the exploited. If the first two of these principles are present, but not the third, economic oppression may exist, but not exploitation. The crucial difference is that in *non-exploitative* economic oppression, the privileged social category does not itself *need* the excluded category. While their welfare does depend upon exclusion, there is no ongoing interdependence of their activities. In the case of exploitation, the exploiters actively need the exploited: exploiters depend upon the effort of the exploited for their own welfare.

This conceptualization of exploitation underwrites an essentially polarized conception of class relations in which, in capitalist societies, the two fundamental classes are capitalists and workers. The Marxist tradition of class analysis, however, also contains a variety of strategies for elaborating more concrete class concepts, which allow for much more complex maps of class structures in which managers, professionals and the self-employed are structurally differentiated from capitalists and workers. Wright (1997), for example, argues that managers in capitalist firms constitute a type of 'contradictory location within class relations' in the sense of having the relational properties of both capitalists and workers.

The two traditions compared

Both Marxist and Weberian class analyses differ sharply from simple gradational accounts of class in which class is itself directly identified within inequalities in income, since both begin with the problem of the social relations that determine the access of people to economic resources. In a sense, therefore, Marxist and Weberian definitions of class in capitalist society share much the same *operational* criteria for class structure within capitalist societies. Where they differ is in the theoretical elaboration and specification of the implications of this common set of criteria: the Marxist model sees two causal paths being systematically generated by these relations – one operating through market exchanges and the other through the process of production itself – whereas the Weberian model traces only one causal path; and the Marxist model elaborates the mechanisms of these causal paths in terms of exploitation as well as bargaining capacity within exchange, whereas the Weberian model only deals with the latter of these. In a sense, then, the Weberian strategy of class analysis is contained within the Marxist model.

This difference between Marx's and Weber's treatments of the causal mechanisms linked to class relations is itself derived from the broader theoretical agendas in which their specific conceptualizations of class are located. In Weber, the concept of class is deeply connected to his preoccupation with the theoretical and historical problem of rationalization of social relations. Running throughout Weber's work is a threefold distinction in the sources of power that individuals use to accomplish their goals: social honour, material resources and authority. Each of these, in turn, can be organized within social interactions

in highly rationalized forms or in relatively non-rationalized forms. Class, in these terms, designates highly rationalized social relations that govern the way people get access to and use material resources. It is thus contrasted, on one hand, with non-rationalized ways of governing access to resources, especially ascriptively based **consumption** groups, and on the other hand, with rationalized forms of social relations involving other sources of social power.

Weber's definition of class relations in terms of market exchanges is intimately connected to the problem of rationalization. When people meet to make an exchange in a market, they rationally calculate the costs and benefits of alternatives on the basis of the prices they face in the market. These prices provide the kind of information required for people to make rational calculations, and the constraints of market interactions force them to make decisions on the basis of these calculations in a more or less rational manner. Weber is, fundamentally, less interested in the problem of the material deprivations and advantages of different categories of people as such, or in the collective struggles that might spring from those advantages and disadvantages, than he is in the underlying normative order and cognitive practices – instrumental rationality – that are embodied in the social interactions that generates these life chances. This is precisely what his market-centred conceptualization of class relations accomplishes.

For Marx, in contrast, class is embedded in a theoretical agenda revolving around the problem of understanding the historical possibilities for human emancipation. Class plays a central role in answering the question, 'What sorts of transformations are needed to eliminate economic oppression and exploitation within capitalist societies?' This is a complex, and contentious, question for it implies not simply an explanatory agenda about the mechanisms that explain forms of **economic action** and generate economic inequalities, but a normative judgement about those inequalities – they are forms of oppression and exploitation – and a normative vision of the transformation of those inequalities. It suggests a concept of class which is not simply defined in terms of the social relations to economic resources, but which also figures centrally in a political project of emancipatory social change. Marx's conceptualization of class relations in terms of both exchange and exploitation accomplishes this.

While the Marxist concept of class may be particularly suited to the distinctively Marxist question about emancipatory transformations, is it still sociologically useful if one rejects that question? There are a number of reasons why elaborating the concept of class in terms of exploitation has theoretical payoffs beyond the specific normative agenda of Marxist class analysis itself:

1. *Linking exchange and production*: the Marxist logic of class analysis affirms the intimate link between the way in which social relations are organized within exchange and within production. This is a substantive, not definitional, point: the social relations which organize the rights and powers of individuals with respect to productive resources systematically shapes their location both within exchange relations and within the process of production itself.

2. *Conflict*: conflict is a prominent feature of both Marxist and Weberian views of class. The distinctive feature of the Marxist account of class relations in these terms is not simply that it gives prominence to class conflict, but that by identifying the antagonism of material interests generated by the exploitative character of capitalist class relations it understands conflict as generated by *inherent properties* of

those relations rather than simply contingent factors.

3. *Power*: the concept of exploitation draws attention to the ways in which class conflicts do not simply reflect conflicting interests over the distribution of a pie. Rather, to characterize class relations as exploitative emphasizes the ways in which exploiting classes are *dependent upon* the exploited class for their own economic well-being, and because of this dependency, the ways in which exploited classes have *capacities for resistance* that are organic to class relations. Because workers always retain some control over the expenditure of effort and diligence, they have a capacity to resist their exploitation; and because capitalists need workers, there are constraints on the strategies available to capitalists to counter this resistance. Exploitation thus entails a specific kind of duality: conflicting material interests plus a real capacity for resistance. This duality has implications for the way we think about both the individual and collective power of workers: As individuals, the power of workers depends both on the scarcity of the kind of labour power they have to offer in the labour market (and thus their ability to extract individual 'skill rents' through the sale of their labour power) and on their ability to control the expenditure of their individual effort within the labour process; as a collectivity, workers' power depends on their ability to collectively regulate the terms of exchange on the labour market (typically through unions) and their ability to control the organization of work, surveillance and sanctions within production.

4. *Coercion and consent*: the extraction of labour effort in systems of exploitation is costly for exploiting classes

because of the inherent capacity of people to resist their own exploitation. Purely coercively backed systems of exploitation will often be suboptimal since it is frequently too easy for workers to withhold diligent performance of labour effort. Exploiting classes will therefore have a tendency to seek ways of reducing those costs. One of the ways of reducing the overhead costs of extracting labour effort is to do things that elicit the active consent of the exploited. These range from the development of internal labour markets which strengthen the identification and loyalty of workers to the firms in which they work to the support for ideological positions which proclaim the practical and moral desirability of capitalist institutions. Such consent-producing practices, however, also have costs attached to them, and thus systems of exploitation can be seen as always involving trade-offs between coercion and consent as mechanisms for extracting labour effort.

References and further reading

Bourdieu, Pierre (1984) *Distinction*, Cambridge, MA: Harvard University Press.

Giddens, Anthony (1981) *The Class Structure of the Advanced Societies*, second edition, New York: Harper and Row.

Goldthorpe, John H. (2000) 'Social Class and the Differentiation of Employment Contracts', in John H. Goldthorpe, *On Sociology*, Oxford: Oxford University Press.

Pakulski, Jan and Waters, Malcolm (1996) *The Death of Class*, London: Sage.

Scott, John (1996) *Stratification and Power*, Cambridge: Polity Press.

Weber, Max ([1922]1978) *Economy and Society*, edited by G. Roth and C Wittich, Berkeley, CA: University of California Press.

Wright, Erik Olin (1989) *The Debate on Classes*, London: Verso.

—— (1997) *Class Counts: Comparative Studies in Class Analysis*, Cambridge: Cambridge University Press.

—— (2003) 'The Shadow of Exploitation in Weber's Class Analysis', *American Sociological Review*, 67, December: 832–53.

—— (2004) 'Social Class', in George Ritzer (ed.), *Encyclopedia of Social Theory*, New York: Sage.

ERIK OLIN WRIGHT

CLASSIFICATION

In the natural sciences, the assignment of objects and beings to classes was long thought to be a simple function of the characteristics of the things themselves. The broad genus and the narrower species were taken to be given by nature. Mammals were grouped by nature on the basis of lactation, apes on the basis of upright posture. Classification did not seem to be a sociological process.

Emile **Durkheim**'s *The Elementary Forms of the Religious Life* (1961) challenged this view, showing that classification systems vary significantly. The classification systems of Pacific islanders made no sense to a European. A category might include animals, plants and a human tribe that shared certain spiritual qualities.

Whereas neoclassical economists found self-interest at the core of the human psyche, Durkheim found meaning-making through classification. To make sense of the world, all tribes, aboriginal and modern, develop classificatory systems. Cosmologies depend on classifications, because cosmologies provide frameworks for understanding the relationships among classes of things.

Durkheim's revelation was that the totem (frog, bat or butterfly) is at once the group's deity and its flag. Totem and tribe are classified together, with the totem representing the notion that there is something divine in social life. The totem locates that thing outside of society. This idea is the kernel of the social constructionist theory of cosmology. For Durkheim, ancestor-worshipping tribes trace social customs to an exogenous spirit world. Religious societies trace social customs to an exogenous deity.

Rationalized societies likewise trace customs to something outside of society – to universal laws of nature and economics. It is those laws, people believe, that define the various classes of things – monkey and human in biology, or buyer and seller in economics. Social constructionists argue that cognitive structures come to reflect customs and the laws that modern societies define as underlying them (Berger and Luckmann 1966). For them, the classifications we make reflect the surrounding social order.

In addition to classifying things and beings, we classify behaviours and their utility for pursuing particular goals. **Hirschman** (1977) shows that only recently have human societies classified human behaviour as, by nature, interest-driven. Even after the Enlightenment, Europeans classified human behaviour as driven by diverse passions – greed or lust or hunger. We now tend see all of human behaviour, historical and contemporary, as self-interested at heart. Historical studies, such as the economist Avner Greif's (1993) analysis of early trading patterns, classify economic behaviour well back into antiquity as driven by innate self-interest.

Economic sociologists tend, instead, to think that the classifications produced by early societies are themselves important objects of study. It is certainly the case, as Weber (1978) and Swedberg (2002) argue, that elements of self-interest can be found in early modern Europe, but anthropological studies consistently show that aboriginal societies did not classify behaviour as self-interested (Smelser 1995)

For economic sociologists, one of the most interesting aspects of modern classification is the process by which individuals and groups succeed in classifying certain economic conventions as rational. Marx (1972) was particularly intrigued by how capitalists could succeed in classifying the state institutions they had designed as rational for society at large.

For cultural analysts of economic behaviour, classifications are the building blocks of cultural schemas. Erving Goffman (1974) referred to these as frames for understanding the world. Ann Swidler calls them cultural tool kits (Swidler 1986). Frames or tool kits express causal relationships among objects and beings, and thus they depend on widely shared classifications that identify actors, intentions and processes.

For instance, organizational sociologists find that prescriptions for how an organization should behave depend on how it is classified. DiMaggio and Powell (1983) noted that, within industries, peripheral firms copy leaders. Changes in industry classification lead to changes in the models organizations copy. Scott et al. (2000) find that as the classification 'hospital' became subdivided into specialized categories, particular organizations chose new management models to follow.

Economic classifications do not necessarily become more fine-grained with time. Industry classifications, for management purposes, have become broader (Meyer 1994). Organizations now model themselves on other organizations in entirely different sectors of the economy. The leaders of social service agencies are increasingly likely to be called CEOs and to have MBAs rather than degrees in social work. Understanding economic behaviour depends very much on understanding the social construction of such classifications.

References and further reading

Berger, Peter and Luckmann, Thomas (1966) *The Social Construction of Reality: A Treatise on the Sociology of Knowledge*, Garden City, NJ: Doubleday.

DiMaggio, Paul J. and Powell, Walter W. (1983) 'The Iron Cage Revisited: Institutionalized Isomorphism and Collective Rationality in Organizational Fields', *American Sociological Review*, 48: 147–60.

Goffman, Erving (1974) *Frame Analysis*, Cambridge, MA: Harvard University Press.

Greif, Avner (1993) 'Contract Enforceability and Economic Institutions in Early Trade: The Maghribi Traders' Coalition', *American Economic Review*, 83(3): 525–48.

Hirschman, Albert O. (1977) *The Passions and the Interests: Political Arguments for Capitalism before its Triumph*, Princeton, NJ: Princeton University Press.

Marx, Karl (1972) 'The Germany Ideology', in *The Marx-Engels Reader*, edited by Robert Tucker, New York: Norton.

Meyer, John W. (1994) 'Rationalized Environments', in W. Richard Scott and John W. Meyer (eds), *Institutional Environments and Organizations: Structural Complexity and Individualism*, Thousand Oaks, CA: Sage, pp. 28–54.

Scott, W. Richard, Ruef, Martin, Mendel, Peter J. and Caronna, Carol (2000) *Institutional Change and Healthcare Organizations: From Professional Dominance to Managed Care*, Chicago: University of Chicago Press.

Smelser, Neil (1995) *Economic Rationality as a Religious System*, in Robert Wuthnow (ed.), *Rethinking Materialism: Perspectives on the Spiritual Dimension of Economic Behavior*, Grand Rapids, MI: William B. Eerdmans Publishing, pp. 73–92.

Swedberg, Richard (2002) 'The Case for an Economic Sociology of Law', *Theory and Society*, 32: 1–37.

Swidler, Ann (1986) 'Culture in Action: Symbols and Strategies', *American Sociological Review*, 51: 273–86.

Weber, Max (1978) *Economy and Society*, two volumes, edited by Guenther Roth and Claus Wittich, Berkeley, CA: University of California Press.

FRANK DOBBIN

CLIQUES See: network analysis

CLUSTERS See: network analysis

COGNITION See: mental models

COLEMAN, JAMES S.

James S. Coleman (1926–95) was a highly influential sociologist of the late twentieth century. A leading scholar in several social science fields – including education, inequality and stratification, mathematical sociology, methodology, organizational analysis, social policy and social theory – Coleman led the research team responsible for a 1966 report on inequality in educational opportunity that had a broad impact on United States educational policy. A prolific author, Coleman advocated a rational choice approach for the discipline of sociology in *Foundations of Social Theory* (1990).

This account concentrates on elements of Coleman's scholarship most relevant for economic sociology (see also Swedberg 1996). He regarded explanation of social system-level phenomena as the central intellectual problem for sociological theory, taking an approach much influenced by economic analysis. Coleman embraced a broadly conceived methodological individualism, assuming simple micro-foundations: purposive actors pursuing interests. He especially appreciated the economic approach for its capacity to address the micro-to-macro problem: accounting for collective or macro-level phenomena as sometimes unintended outcomes of interdependent actions of micro-level actors. The determination of an equilibrium market price based on a balancing of supply and demand was an exemplar.

To Coleman, the major limitation of standard economic approaches was their neglect of social structure. He asserted that action occurs within social networks that can limit the flow of information and the formation of exchange relations, generate interdependencies among interests, enforce norms and produce trust. He argued that features of social organization affect the efficiency of organizational practices. The New York City wholesale diamond market, which requires a high level of trustworthiness due to its highly valued merchandise, exemplifies conditions in which the impersonal devices of Weberian bureaucracy are inefficient. Kinship, religious and community ties among merchants were seen as efficient sources of trust rather than as nepotistic vestiges.

Coleman proposed that social phenomena including collective decisions and norms could be understood as resultants of interdependent rational actions. Norms, for example, would be produced when a set of actors demand control over a target action because of its positive or negative effects on them; when simple exchanges or market mechanisms cannot yield control over the target action; and when social organization is sufficient to supply effective sanctions enforcing conformity to a behavioural standard.

In one of his most influential works, Coleman (1988) conceptualized **social capital** as those aspects of social structures that facilitate action. Social capital could be found in both formal and informal organizations, residing in relationships within and around families, schools, communities, firms and other social groups. Of special interest to Coleman was social capital that could produce trust or support norms specifying cooperative instead of selfish actions. His theoretical work demonstrated that dense, closed social structures support effective norms. He thus suggested that some differences in achievement and other outcomes of schooling can be traced to variations in the density of relations within and among families.

Coleman observed that social capital is not a fully generalized social resource: structures that enable some actions might be detrimental for others. While social density can engender effective norms and trust, for example, it simultaneously can limit innovation and the diffusion of information. Moreover, individual actors lack full control over social capital because of its location in social relationships, and social capital often benefits actors other than those who produce it. Hence, Coleman asserts, direct **incentives** to produce informal social capital are often insufficient. He calls attention to 'appropriable social organization' – social structures that can be redirected towards purposes distinct from those for which they were created – as an important source of social capital.

On a broader scale, Coleman (1992) described a 'Great Transformation', a shift from 'primordial' family-related social organization towards 'constructed' social organization. A key element in this was the 'social invention' of the corporate actor (Coleman 1974): a deliberately designed, special-purpose social structure having legal standing. Encouraged by such legal devices as the notions of 'juristic persons' and limited liability, corporate actors offered new means through which individual persons could combine resources to pursue interests. Corporate actors could be greater in size, complexity, flexibility, mobility and longevity than primordial organizational forms.

Individual persons act as agents of corporate actors. Both corporate actors and agents may pursue their own interests, however, distinct from those of owners or principals – the individual persons whose resources are vested in the corporate actor. In Coleman's view, the appropriate criterion for evaluating the performance of a form of social organization was its effect on the welfare of individual persons. He was keenly concerned with social problems attendant to the shift from primordial groups to corporate actors. Among these were a drift of power towards corporate actors, potential irresponsibility on the part of agents, and providing for persons – such as youth and the aged – not closely tied to powerful corporate actors.

Coleman believed that constructed social organization could better serve the interests of individual persons than do spontaneous organizational forms. In keeping with his view that social theory should inform social policy, he advocated social research oriented towards designing better-performing corporate actors, and offered many proposals for increasing their responsiveness. Some, such as increasing the liability of agents, would change the internal structure of corporate actors. Others, including the introduction and maintenance of competition among corporate actors, would instead alter their environments.

See also: free rider; network analysis; norms and values; organization theory; public goods; rational choice theory; social capital.

References and further reading

Coleman, James S. (1974) *Power and the Structure of Society*, New York: W. W. Norton.
—— (1988) 'Social Capital in the Creation of Human Capital', *American Journal of Sociology*, 94: S95–S120.
—— (1990) *Foundations of Social Theory*, Cambridge, MA: Harvard University Press.
—— (1992) 'The Rational Reconstruction of Society: 1992 Presidential Address', *American Sociological Review*, 58: 1–15.
Swedberg, Richard (1996) 'Analyzing the Economy: On the Contribution of James S. Coleman', in Jon Clark (ed.), *James S. Coleman*, London: Falmer Press, pp. 313–28.

PETER V. MARSDEN

COLLECTIVE ACTION

Collective action involves cooperation among social actors to achieve shared goals and interests in goods and services or public policies. The participants may be natural persons, but are usually organizations such as **firms** and trade associations. These **inter-firm relations** may create enduring organizations, inter-organizational networks, and formal institutions that coordinate continuing efforts to affect communal outcomes. Collective action may aim to produce direct mutual benefits for the participants and to influence governmental policy decisions affecting economic conditions. Fundamental research issues include the conditions and **incentives** generating diverse forms of economic collective action, recruiting new participants and reducing turnover, acquiring and allocating joint resources, creating **trust**, resolving **conflict**s over collective action decisions, distributing benefits among contributors and noncontributors,

and the consequences of collective action for both participants and the **political economy**. Researchers can apply theories and methods developed for investigating collective action in such non-economic settings as social movements, political institutions and cultural change.

Four major forms of economic collective action are strategic alliances, business groups, trade associations and lobbying coalitions. In addition to differing modes of participation, they vary in governance and administrative structures, mechanisms for coordinating and safeguarding their participants' resource contributions, and the division of rewards resulting from cooperative activities. Strategic alliances are typically short-term agreements between corporations to pool knowledge and expertise on a specific research, product development or marketing project. Alliance governance forms range from joint ventures in which the partners create a new company, to joint equity investments in a third enterprise, to less formalized cartels and relational contracting arrangements. Business groups, such as Japanese *keiretsu* and Korean *chaebol*, are more durable federations of independent companies governed by a dominant entrepreneur, family or company. Organizations form alliances and business groups for many objectives, including: speeding entry into new product or geographic markets; accelerating cycle times for developing or commercializing new products; improving product or service quality; gaining technical skills, tacit knowledge and competencies; sharing production costs; spreading risks and uncertainties; and monitoring environmental changes in the political economy.

Trade associations provide diverse direct services to member firms within a specific industry, such as exchanging technical information, establishing commercial standards, and facilitating social and business contacts. They may also initiate and coordinate member efforts to influence public policy decisions affecting their industry's economic conditions. A few peak associations – such as the Chamber of Commerce of the United States, the National Association of Manufacturers, and the Business Roundtable (an association of CEOs of the largest corporations) – claim to speak for the economic and political interests of broader business sectors. Although most trade associations are formally governed by member-elected boards of directors, many are actually oligarchies controlled by a few large organizational contributors. Lobbying coalitions involve coordinated actions by firms and trade associations attempting to influence governmental or judicial institutions to change the market allocation system. In contrast to neoclassical economic theory, which assumes that utility-maximizing actors redistribute resources through the efficient pricing mechanism of perfectly competitive markets, lobbying coalitions collectively pressure the state to provide participants with economic advantages by intervening in market exchanges.

Three prominent theories attempt to explain the formation, development and impacts of collective action. **Transaction cost economics** pinpoints where efficient boundaries fall between an organization (hierarchy) and its environment (market). Hybrid forms, such as inter-organizational alliances and networks, arise when specialized investments would lose their value if transferred to a market exchange partner. The conditions favouring collaborative agreements include highly uncertain demand coupled with stable supply, asset-specific exchanges creating dependencies, complex tasks performed under intense time pressures, and frequent exchanges among network members. Resource dependence theories emphasize intrinsic tensions between resource-procurement needs and organizational desires to preserve autonomy and power. Inter-organizational collaborations arise from interdependencies and constraints when one firm controls critical resources – such as money, information, patents, intellectual property, production facilities, distribution skills, entry into foreign markets, and governmental influence – that another firm needs to achieve its objectives. Strategic alliances, business groups and lobbying coalitions enable partners to benefit through mutual access to one another's social capital, information, knowledge, financial and political resources. Institutionalist theories emphasize how social norms constrain acceptable forms of collective action. Firms and associations gain public legitimacy by imitating the formal structures and strategies predominant within their industry, especially where inter-organizational environments are experiencing accelerating changes from technological innovations, global competition and political intervention. Governmental regulations may also coercively compel organizational isomorphism (convergence towards similar forms).

An important research objective is to identify the relative importance of theoretically hypothesized influences on organizational decisions to initiate collective action. For example, resource dependence principles appear more relevant than transaction costs for understanding strategic alliance formation. Resource dependencies drove collaborations between start-up biotechnology companies and large corporations that exchanged technical expertise for financial support (Smith-Doerr *et al.* 1999). The small, innovative R&D laboratories typically lacked funds, public legitimacy and in-house capability to market their products and manoeuvre through the federal government's regulatory maze. Therefore, they teamed up with resource-rich pharmaceutical, chemical and agricultural firms which provided sustaining resources. In turn, these established firms entered alliances to acquire tacit knowledge and learn new technological skills from their smaller partners.

The creation of trade associations involves exchanges between entrepreneurial leaders, who invest their social and economic capital to offer benefits to potential participants, and firms that obtain those benefits by paying dues and participating in association affairs. Many benefits are material goods and services either unavailable or more costly to non-members, thus enticing potential participants to join the association. Mancur Olson (1965) asserted the irrationality of contributing resources to any collective action organization seeking only pure public goods, i.e. indivisible benefits from which eligible recipients cannot be excluded, such as crop subsidies or tariffs. Utility-maximizing firms would take a 'free ride' on collective political advocacy efforts, refusing to fund its efforts to influence public policies from which they could benefit despite their non-contributions. Olson deduced that organizations would fail to mobilize optimum support by relying solely on public goods to attract resources. Therefore, trade associations must offer 'selective incentives,' i.e. private goods that prospective members could receive only by contributing towards organizational lobbying for public goods. These incentives include magazine subscriptions, group insurance, social gatherings, certification and training programmes, and similar benefits from which non-members could be effectively excluded. The free-rider conundrum transforms recruitment and resource mobilization strategies from emphasizing collective goals to satisfying members' and supporters' preferences for personal material and social benefits. Organizational leaders obtain resources to wage public policy battles as a 'by-product' of providing selective incentives to politically disinterested members, opening a gap between members' interests and organizational goals. Although Olson's by-product explanation is theoretically elegant, some investigations cast doubt on its empirical accuracy (Marwell and Oliver 1993).

US business lobbying coalitions were stimulated by institutional changes in electing officials, legislating and regulating public affairs that made the policy-influence game more complicated and costly to play. By the end of the twentieth century, an escalating number of corporations either created government affairs offices in Washington or hired specialists to represent their interests in public policy issues. Firms deployed diverse tactics to pressure policymakers, ranging from formal and informal contacts to mobilizing grassroots constituencies. Both transaction cost and principal-agent theories propose that organizations make cost–benefit calculations when deciding whether to: invest resources in developing governmental affairs staff; contract with outside lobbying specialists; join in lobbying coalitions with other firms and industry trade associations; or follow mixed strategies to influence policy outcomes. Successful lobbyists deploy diverse advocacy tactics to accomplish three primary functions: 'getting attention, communicating with contacts about mutual information needs, and reinforcing for lobbying targets the value of their continuing to give the lobbies attention' (Browne 1998: 81).

Lobbying coalitions are central collective actors in an organizational state model of public policy domains characterized by multiple inter-organizational networks (Laumann and Knoke 1987). Each policy domain consists of interest groups (business associations, corporations, labour unions, public interest groups), state and local government associations, executive agencies and ministries, and legislative committees that engage in setting agendas, formulating policies, gaining access, advocating positions, organizing collective action campaigns and selecting among proposals concerned with delimited substantive policy problems, such as national defence, education, agriculture or welfare. In every domain, some organizations participate in dozens of legislative, executive and judicial policy events, while others pursue narrower objectives. Given their divergent organizational interests and fragmented attention spans, no organization can control or even dominate a domain's policy-making. Rather, most policy struggles involve short-term lobbying coalitions assembled to fight collectively to influence public policy decisions.

A comparative study of the US, German, and Japanese labour policy domains found that organizations more centrally located in both communication networks (measured by policy information exchanges) and support networks (measured by resource exchanges) had higher reputations as especially influential players (Knoke *et al.* 1996). Similarly, greater centrality in both networks led to participation in more political influence activities across numerous legislative events, including joining coalitions with other organizations. In the US and German cases, the communication centrality effect was much stronger than the support centrality effect on both organizational influence reputations and political activities, while the pattern in Japan was just the reverse. Detailed analyses of specific legislative decisions showed that most national labour policy fights were conducted by relatively small organizational coalitions that: held the same preferred event outcome (passage or failure of a bill); communicated directly or indirectly with one another about policy affairs; and consciously coordinated their policy influence activities. **Business associations** and labour unions were primary coalition leaders in all three nations, frequently taking opposing positions on legislative bills and almost never collaborating on rare occasions when they preferred the same policy outcome. After public officials made their policy decision, lobbying coalitions broke apart as subsequent events gave rise to new constellations of organized interest groups. The resulting patterns were fluid, continually changing network structures. Yet, despite this micro-level flux, national policy domains remainedrelatively stable, socially constructed macro-systems whose boundaries and constituents persisted over long periods.

Research remains inconclusive about the extent to which collective actions actually influence public policy decisions. Electoral campaign donations, organizational resources and lobbying coalition activities are just three factors in complex political calculations by legislators, which also include politicians' party affiliations, personal ideologies, perceived constituency preferences and instincts for self-preservation. By assisting public officials to craft the details of legislative and regulatory proposals, lobbying coalitions reap the fruits planted by their campaign funds. The capacity of political money to open doors was evident in two controversial bills considered by the US House Ways and Means and the Agriculture Committees in 1985 (Wright 1990). Committee votes were best explained, not by political action committee donations, but by numbers of contacts that legislators had with advocates of opposing sides. 'Consistent with the popular notion that money "buys" access but not votes, campaign contributions influenced voting decisions indirectly through lobbying' (Wright 1990: 433–4). Similarly, interest groups achieved greater subjective success in influencing federal agency rule-making through formal procedures, for example by commenting on proposed rules and testifying at public hearings. Future research should seek to assess the impacts of collective **economic actions** across a broader range of public policy-making contexts.

References and further reading

Browne, William P. (1998) *Groups, Interests, and US Public Policy*, Washington, DC: Georgetown University Press.

Knoke, David, Pappi, Franz Urban, Broadbent, Jeffrey and Tsujinaka, Yutaka (1996) *Comparing Policy Networks: Labor Politics in the US,*

Germany, and Japan, New York: Cambridge University Press.

Laumann, Edward O. and Knoke, David (1987) *The Organizational State: Social Choice in National Policy Domains*, Madison, WI: University of Wisconsin Press.

Marwell, Gerald and Oliver, Pamela (1993) *The Critical Mass in Collective Action: A Micro-Social Theory*, Cambridge: Cambridge University Press.

Olson, Mancur (1965) *The Logic of Collective Action: Public Goods and the Theory of Groups*, Cambridge, MA: Harvard University Press.

Smith-Doerr, Laurel, Owen-Smith, Jason, Koput, Kenneth W. and Powell, Walter W. (1999) 'Networks and Knowledge Production: Collaboration and Patenting in Biotechnology', in R. T. A. J. Leenders and S. Gabbay (eds), *Corporate Social Capital*, Boston: Kluwer Academic Publishers, pp. 390–408.

Wright, John R. (1990) 'Contributions, Lobbying, and Committee Voting in the US House of Representatives', *American Political Science Review*, 84: 417–38.

DAVID KNOKE

COLLECTIVE GOODS

See: public goods

COLLECTIVE REPRESENTATION

A representation is a mental construct that shapes our way of defining, interpreting and evaluating various aspects of reality, and also the way we behave and communicate. A "collective" representation is one shared by the members of a particular group, who through this representation construct a consensual vision of reality. Empirically, collective representations are relatively easy to identify: they are found in discourses, carried in words and conveyed though various media; they also find concrete form in material and spatial arrangements.

The notion of a "collective representation" relates to a cluster of concepts not always easily distinguishable from each other: beliefs, ideology, values, mentalities, spirit (of a people, of capitalism), common sense, etc. Although no current of sociology has omitted to include cognitive process factors in its conceptualization of society, E. **Durkheim** is indisputably the inventor of the actual concept of "collective representations".

In the definition he provides at the end of *The Elementary Forms of Religious Life* (1912), he contrasts collective and individual representations from two angles. Firstly, "collective representations are more stable than individual ones; for while the individual is sensitive to even slight changes in his internal or external environment, only quite weighty events can succeed in changing the mental equilibrium of society."; then, although the representations may be common to an entire social group, this does not mean they "are a simple average of the corresponding individual representations; if they were that, they would be of poorer intellectual content (...) they correspond to the way in which the special being that is society thinks about the things of its own experience. (...) They add to what our personal experience can teach us all the wisdom and science that the collectivity has amassed over centuries."

Collective representations are one of the categories of social facts which Durkheim believes sociology is there to explain by relating them to each other. In his *Rules of Sociological Method* (1895), he defines social facts as "ways of acting, thinking, and feeling that present the noteworthy property of existing outside the individual consciousness. These types of conduct or thought are not only external to the individual but are, moreover, endowed with coercive power, by virtue of which they impose themselves upon him, independent of his individual will". The substratum of collective representations is not the individual but society itself, which through socialisation instils them in individuals. As Durkheim says, "it is to be found in each part because it exists in the whole, rather than in the whole because it exists in the parts" (ibid.).

Therefore, in its original form, the notion of collective representation was restricted to shared cognitive productions that pre-exist and are imposed on individuals. Durkheim did not examine one aspect of representations studied by later sociologists, that of the social process by which new collective representations are forged. The term "social representation", often preferred today, can more easily encompass both senses of the individual-representation relationship, i.e. collective representation imposed on individuals, and individuals constructing collective representations together. The expression "social representation" leaves open the possibility that something individual can become "social", whereas this is not possible in the traditional view (Moscovici, 1993).

From the outset, the Durkheimian origins of the concept of collective representation place it in opposition to individualist or utilitarian approaches. For Durkheim, social facts are not reducible; society is not merely the product of interaction between parties, even if only because the categories of individual thought are social in origin. Economic sociology is thus faithful to Durkheim when, for instance, it tries to show that trade interactions and contracts "only" hold because the protagonists share collective representations and conventions that are imposed on them and govern their interactions.

In her book *How institutions think* (1986), in the Durkheimian tradition, anthropologist Mary Douglas explains that the meeting of individual preferences is insufficient to explain the formation of the social bond, as both the thinkable and the desirable are always pre-modeled by the institutions within which we live, or to put it another way, that in our thinking and choice-making we are tri-butaries of the institutions which in the main do the job of thinking and choosing for us. What differentiates our society from the primitive societies that the anthropologist likes to cite as an example is the fact that our institutions are different from theirs.

Sociological analysis can use the concept of collective representation to describe micro-sociological situations, such as a study of a specific market (e.g. art auctions), which can be shown to operate smoothly only because the protagonists hold in common, for instance, the main criteria for valuation of the goods exchanged there. It can also be used to understand a general state or a trend in society as a whole. Max **Weber**'s essay *The Protestant Ethic and the Spirit of Capitalism* (1920) belongs to this second category. For Weber, certain collective representations, in this case deriving from religion, contributed to the emergence of capitalism in that they led to a new representation that conferred a more positive image on the search for profit. This contributed to a change in behavior as it transformed both employers and wage earners' "psychological motivations", influencing them to look favorably on capitalist accumulation.

Finally, the question remains of the relationship between collective representations and social institutions, and between collective representations and social action. There is hardly any disagreement when it comes to explaining a situation of stability and permanence: representations and institutions are mutually reinforcing and the action is a reproductive action, reaffirming previous institutions and representations. In contrast, social theorists' opinions are divided over the crucial question of how social change, and change in society's institutions, comes about, because this requires identification of the principal engine for historical change (e.g. ideas, interests, systemic breakdown, etc.) and explanation of the relationship between human beings and collective representations, which become less externally imposed as they produce new ones of their own.

See also: Beliefs; Cognition; Convention School; Cultural Embeddedness; Culture and Economy; Customs; Education and the Economy; Habits; Holism; Ideology; Norms and Values; Religion and Economic Life; Rules; Spirit of capitalism; Values

Selected references

Douglas, Mary (1986) *How institutions think.* Syracuse, NY, Syracuse University Press.
Durkheim, Emile (1974) *Sociology and Philosophy.* New York, Free Press.
Durkheim, Emile (1995) *The Elementary Forms of Religious Life.* New York, Free Press.
Moscovici, Serge (1993) 'Des représentations collectives aux représentations sociales'. D. Jodelet (ed.) *Les représentations sociales.* Paris, PUF, pp. 64–86.

EVE CHIAPELLO

COLONIALISM

Colonialism can be seen as essentially a collection of practices or as an idea or constellation of ideas (themselves, of course, bound to a set of practices). Definitions of the phenomenon have generally fallen into one of these two categories. Illustrating the former, Charles Verlinden (1970: xii, xv) understood modern colonialism as 'the creation and putting to use by a metropolis with an advanced technology of overseas settlements in zones where economic and particularly technological development has been slower', or, alternatively, as 'conquest followed by exploitation'. Given this broad definition, it is not surprising that Verlinden found colonialism to have been practised throughout various historical periods. For such commentators, the study of colonialism would be something like the study of political domination itself: the study of something the presence of which is basically a sociological constant despite varia-

tions in form. So-called 'internal colonialism', an idea most famously developed by Michael Hechter, is also dependent upon the same unnecessarily broad definition of colonialism itself.

An alternative, and perhaps more fruitful, approach – one relying on the latter of the two styles of definition noted above – regards colonialism as an historically specific constellation of ideas which developed over the course of the eighteenth century (though they were not without antecedents as early as the fifteenth) and reached their realization in European foreign policy in the nineteenth and early twentieth centuries.

The term 'colonialism' derives, of course, from the word 'colony', with its origins in the Latin term *colonia*, which (like the later word 'culture') had its roots in the idea of cultivation of the earth (being a derivation of *colonus*, meaning farmer). The primary meaning of *colonia* for the Romans was 'a settlement or colony of citizens sent from Rome or the people composing it' (*Oxford Latin Dictionary*, 1982). More recently, colonies have come to be understood as political communities subjugated under the control of a foreign power (i.e. the colonial population is the subjected population; the 'colonials' are the indigenous rather than the occupiers). Yet this use is often anachronistically applied to sets of political arrangements not considered 'colonial' by the parties who participated in them. The so-called Spanish 'colonial' world is perhaps the best example: both American Spaniards and residents of the Iberian peninsula only began to consider the relationship properly 'colonial' in the mid-to-late eighteenth century, as reformist intellectuals influenced by French ideas began to see the overseas possessions of the Spanish Crown in these terms. The much-discussed Bourbon Reforms – which aimed to centralize, consolidate and secure political control of the American possessions, as well as to return them to previous levels of profitability – are perhaps best understood as a reflection of this changing perception of their place vis-à-vis the centre. The case of the English 'colonies' is somewhat different than the Spanish, though both share the common feature of being completely distinct from the pattern of nineteenth-century 'colonialism'. As Liah Greenfeld has argued, English 'colonials' in the Americas considered themselves equal members of the English or British nation from the beginning, and only began to regard themselves as unjustly subjugated to a 'foreign' power (what would be called a 'colonial' power in the nineteenth-century cases) as the privileges they believed themselves entitled to as Englishmen were withheld from them.

Not surprisingly, the concept of 'colonialism' has more recent origins. The *Oxford English Dictionary*'s first cited case of 'colonialism' dates from 1853, and the first that appears unequivocally consistent with our sense of the word dates from 1886 (*Oxford English Dictionary*, third edition). That is to say, the idea of 'colonialism' developed historically after the sorts of relationships that would come to be understood in terms of it. The very idea is best understood as a rationalization of a varied set of practices, most of which began with the pursuit of economic gain on the part of individuals or private companies (though sanctioned by home governments, Spanish, Portuguese, Dutch and English foreign ventures – later dubbed colonial – all began as essentially private **economic actions**, and later Dutch and English 'colonialism' remained in the private domain for a considerable period of time). As it was seen how profitable such ventures could be – not surprisingly – more participants got into the act. Over the course of the nineteenth century, overseas colonial possessions became a mark of international prestige: a nation was not a first-rate power unless it was a colonial power. It is important to note that conceptualizations of the colonial relationship were not static phenomena but were

being worked out all the time as massive projects of colonial acquisition and maintenance were taking place. Though highly paternalistic and often based on now-discredited premises of racial and/or cultural superiority/inferiority, a number of European colonial powers attempted to provide social and educational services to the subjugated populations. Colonialism, then, is best understood as a mentality of sorts, one that has largely been eclipsed and is now almost exclusively the object of revulsion. It is the presence of this mentality, as well as the pervasiveness of the phenomenon itself in its day, that distinguishes it from seeming similar practices in the Greek and Roman world.

'Colonialism' as we are considering it here has been the subject of a great deal of attention in recent academic discourse. This has been less true in sociology than in other fields, most probably because of sociology's traditional, if receding, preoccupation with 'modern' industrial societies in Europe and the United States. Despite colonialism's obvious relevance for economic sociologists, no major work of economic sociology has focused on it or on colonial relations, at least if we understand economic sociology, as the authors of a recent definitive statement of the field's scope and aims do, to be 'the study of the social organization of economic phenomena, including those related to production, trade, leisure, and consumption' (Guillén *et al.*, 2002: 6). Instead, a focus on colonialism has dominated the disciplines of anthropology, literary studies, the various fields of area studies and, to a lesser extent, history. Perhaps the most influential text in much of this work was Edward Said's *Orientalism*, which attempted to demonstrate that an integral part of colonial subjugation was the construction of an inferior 'other'. Whereas Said was fundamentally concerned with European intervention in the Middle East, other scholars have focused on how European colonial powers described the peoples indigenous to Africa and Asia. Indeed, part of the crisis of contemporary cultural and social anthropology has to do with the perception on the part of some anthropologists that their own field was born amidst and contributed to 'the colonial project'. In a characteristic pronouncement, Nicholas Dirks has written that 'If colonialism can be seen as a cultural formation, so also culture is a colonial formation', thereby linking the central concept of the field to a past that was chequered at best (Dirks 1992: 3). There has been a great deal of ink spilled in recent years in an effort to expiate these disciplinary sins. Some would argue that this preoccupation has been so intense as to derail significant research. It is here that economic sociology (informed, of course, by cultural sociology) could make important contributions.

That economic sociology has not as of yet made important contributions to the study of colonialism (relatively little work has been done on how economic activity in colonial situations has been culturally organized) does not mean that the economic processes involved in colonialism have not received considerable attention. Indeed, many scholars have reduced colonial projects to economic motives and nothing more, suggesting that colonizers sought only control of raw materials, cheap labour and/or new markets for the **consumption** of goods produced in the centre. Leaving to the side the question of the precise relationship between colonialism and imperialism, we see that Lenin saw colonial projects as an inevitable part of the developing capitalist system, following on the emergence of monopoly capitalism and centred on the export of capital. Indeed, colonization, for Lenin, amounted to a sort of political monopoly linked to the emergence of a small number of monopolistic, capitalist firms. His essentially Marxist perspective has been carried on by Frank, Wallerstein and the *dependencia* school of Cardoso, though these latter thinkers have alleged that these economic processes lead

to the extended impoverishment of what was once called the Third World, and therefore they are seen by their authors and proponents as modifications of the traditional Marxist approach to these questions. Though there are variations between these theoretical approaches, all see colonialism as a more or less inevitable development in a capitalist world. These scholars tend to conflate colonialism with unequal economic relations – a society which produces primary products and which serves as a market for the manufactured goods and/or large-scale investment of a central economy is understood as a society suffering from colonialism or 'neo-colonialism', a term most often used to characterize relations between Latin America and the United States, precisely due to the fact that the United States has had very little involvement that could be characterized as colonial, properly speaking, in the region. Economic historians have done a considerable amount of work on the economics of colonialism. More recently, scholars have focused on the implications of styles of colonial rule (as well as the cultures transmitted through colonialism) for later post-colonial states. It would not be an exaggeration to claim that most of today's states passed through one or more periods of so-called colonial 'tutelage', and therefore understanding colonialism is truly central to understanding modern politics. The same is true of contemporary economic development.

See also: democracy and economy; economic development; economic imperialism; modernity.

References and further reading

Boswell, Terry (1989) 'Colonial Empires and the Capitalist World-Economy: A Time Series Analysis of Colonization, 1640–1960', *American Sociological Review*, 54: 180–96.

Dirks, Nicholas B. (1992) 'Introduction', in Nicholas B. Dirks (ed.), *Colonialism and Culture*, Ann Arbor, MI: University of Michigan Press.

Fieldhouse, D. K. (1984) *Economics and Empire, 1830–1914*, London: Macmillan.

Glare, P. G. W. (ed.) (1982) *Oxford Latin Dictionary*, Oxford: Clarendon Press.

Go, Julian and Foster, Ann (eds) (2003) *The American Colonial State in the Philippines: Global Perspectives*, Durham, NC: Duke University Press.

Guillén, Mauro F., Collins, Randall, England, Paula and Meyer, Marshall (2002) 'The Revival of Economic Sociology', in Mauro F. Guillén, Randall Collins, Paula England and Marshall Meyer (eds), *The New Economic Sociology: Developments in an Emerging Field*, New York: Russell Sage Foundation.

Hechter, Michael (1975) *Internal Colonialism: The Celtic Fringe in British National Development, 1536–1966*, Berkeley, CA: University of California Press.

Verlinden, Charles (1970) *The Beginnings of Modern Colonization*, translated by Yvonne Freccero, Ithaca, NY: Cornell University Press.

Young, Crawford (1994) *The African Colonial State in Comparative Perspective*, New Haven, CT: Yale University Press.

JONATHAN EASTWOOD

COMMODITIES See: goods/commodities

COMMUNISM See: Marx; Historical Materialism, Socialism

COMMUNITARIANISM

Communitarianism holds that societies ought to formulate a shared understanding of the good. It is frequently contrasted with philosophies that maintain that each individual should choose that which is good on their own. Communitarians study the process by which shared conceptions of the good (or values) are created, shared, justified and enforced. Hence, communitarians have an interest in social entities such as families, schools (especially character education), communities (and their norms) and voluntary associations, and in societies at large.

Communitarians pay much attention to the relationship between the self and the community. Political theorists depict the self as 'embedded', which implies that the self is constrained by the community. They stress that individuals who are well integrated into communities are better able to reason and act in responsible ways than isolated individuals, but add that if social pressure to conform rises to high levels, it will undermine the individual self.

Among scholars, communitarians often belong either to political science (and social philosophy) or sociology. Among the first group, those often cited are Michael Sandel (*Democracy's Discontent, Liberalism and Its Critics*), Charles Taylor (*The Malaise of Modernity, Sources of the Self: The Making of the Modern Identity*) and Michael Walzer (*Spheres of Justice* and *Thick and Thin: Moral Argument at Home and Abroad*). Alisdair MacIntyre (*After Virtue: A Study in Moral Theory*) is sometimes listed as a communitarian. None of these scholars use the term themselves, and MacIntyre explicitly disowned it.

Sociologists who studied communitarian issues (although they did not use the term either) include Ferdinand Tönnies and Emile Durkheim, who focused on the transition from a society that was centred around villages, and hence viable communities, to one that they saw as merely based on associations, in which people were atomized, losing much of their natural social fabric.

Although the term 'communitarian' was used only as of 1847, ideas that are communitarian were formed much earlier. They are found in the Bible, Catholic theology (for example, treatments of the Church as community and subsidiarity – the principle that the lowest level of authority capable of addressing an issue is the one best able to handle it), and more recently in socialist doctrine (especially in writings about the early commune and about workers' solidarity).

In the 1980s, Robert Bellah and his associates criticized the excessive individualism found in the United States and championed by President Ronald Reagan and in Britain by Prime Minister Margaret Thatcher. Alan Ehrenhalt, in his book *The*

Lost City: The Forgotten Virtues of Community in America, questioned the value of choice, achieved at the cost of maintaining community and authority. Robert Putnam in *Bowling Alone* referred to 'social capital' – the element of communities that forms affective bonds among people – and emphasized the value of 'bridging social capital': the bonds of connectedness formed *across* diverse communities, rather than those that make each social group stronger but also potentially antagonistic to other communities.

Amitai Etzioni defined a good communitarian society as one that is based on a carefully crafted balance between autonomy and social order, with a social order that is based as much as possible on moral suasion rather than coercion. His book *The Spirit of Community* provided a popular communitarian text and his *New Golden Rule: Community and Morality in a Democratic Society* an academic one. He and his colleagues, including William A. Galston, Mary Ann Glendon, Jean Bethke Elshtain and other figures from academia and politics, issued a platform endorsed by a wide range of leading Americans and started what has been often referred to as a communitarian social movement.

Criticism and responses

Critics of communitarians argue that the core concept of communitarianism, that of community, is very ill-defined. Robert Booth Fowler, in *The Dance With Community*, collected numerous definitions and showed that none of them is consistently used. Elizabeth Frazer, in her book *The Politics of Community*, argued that no social entity lives up to what communitarians call community. In *Community Studies*, Colin Bell and Howard Newby (1973: 15) asked, 'But what is community? ... [I]t will be seen that over ninety definitions of community have been analyzed and that the one common element in them all was man!'

In response, Amitai Etzioni noted that community can be defined with reasonable precision. Community has two characteristics: first, a web of affect-laden relationships among a group of individuals, relationships that often crisscross and reinforce one another (as opposed to one-on-one or chain-like individual relationships); and second, a measure of commitment to a set of shared values, norms and meanings, and a shared history and identity – in short, a particular culture. The second element, often overlooked by those who pay mind only to social bonds or social capital, has been flagged by David E. Pearson (1995: 47) who writes that

> To earn the appellation 'community', it seems to me, groups must be able to exert moral suasion and extract a measure of compliance from their members. That is, communities are necessarily, indeed, by definition, coercive as well as moral, threatening their members with the stick of sanctions if they stray, offering them the carrot of certainty and stability if they don't.

Other critics argued that communitarians ignore the darker side of traditional communities. Communities, critics write, use their moral voice to oppress people, are authoritarian by nature, and push people to conform. Amy Gutmann (1985: 319) writes that communitarians 'want us to live in Salem', a community of strong shared values that went so far as to accuse non-conformist members of witchcraft during the seventeenth century. Will Kymlicka claims that this oppression can entail the community prescribing roles of subordination, roles that limit people's individual potential and threaten their psychological well-being. Derek Phillips (1993: 195) adds:

> In their celebration of the ecstasy of belonging, communitarian writers exhibit a frightening forgetfulness about the past. They fail to acknowledge that the quest for community often involves domination for some and subordination for others.

In attacking post-Enlightenment liberalism and the politics of rights, communitarian theorists threaten to rob individuals of their most basic protections against abuses of power. In emphasizing the importance of community for people's everyday lives, communitarians fail to see that it is attachment rather than membership that is a general human value.

Communitarians respond that behind many of these criticisms lies an image of old, or total, communities, which are neither typical of modern society nor necessary for, or even compatible with, a communitarian society. Old communities (traditional villages) were geographically bounded and the only communities of which people were members. In effect, other than escaping into no-man's land, often bandit territories, individuals had few opportunities for choosing their social attachments. In short, old communities had monopolistic power over their members.

New communities are often limited in scope and reach. Members of one residential community are often also members of other communities – for example work, ethnic or religious ones. As a result, community members have multiple sources of attachments, and if one threatens to become overwhelming, individuals will tend to pull back and turn to another community for their attachments. Thus, for example, if a person finds herself under high moral pressure at work to contribute to the United Way, to give blood or to serve at a soup kitchen for the homeless, and these are lines of action she is not keen to follow, she may end up investing more of her energy in other communities – her writers' group, for instance, or her church. If a person who has recently been divorced is under severe censure by his church community, on the other hand, he may well take on extra hours at work. This multi-community membership protects the individuals from both moral oppression and

ostracism. However, incongruity between the values of a person's multiple communities may substantially weaken the moral voice, and thus the importance of the next-level moral community.

In short, the moral voice is most powerful when people are members of only one community, but it can be overwhelming in such cases. It is more moderated when individuals are members of several communities, but it still may suffice to undergird a good part of the social order, as long as the various communities share at least some core values.

For the same reason it is a valid criticism to argue that a total and monolithic community can drive people to conformism, if this means that such a community will push people to sacrifice large parts of their individual differences in order to follow shared values. But total communities are rare in contemporary societies, while multi-community attachments are much more common. To worry, in this context, about traditionalism is like worrying about the effects of excessive savings in an economy long plagued by debts and deficits and rather reluctant to mend its ways.

Critics also held that communities are authoritarian. Some mean by this that communities are totalistic, a point already covered. Others mean that they are dominated by power elites or have one group that forces others to abide by the values of those in power. Communitarians find that this criticism has merit, but it is misdirected. There are communities both past and present that have been or are authoritarian. The medieval phrase *Stadt luft macht frei* ('the air of the cities frees') captures what the farmers of traditional villages must have felt when they first moved into cities at the beginning of the industrial era. (Poor working conditions and slums aside, being away from the stricter social codes of their families and villages seems to have given them a sense of freedom, which in some cases led to anarchic behaviour.) Totalitarian communities exist in contemporary communities, such as North Korea. However, most contemporary communities, especially in communitarian societies, are not authoritarian even when they are defined by geography. Also, relative ease of mobility means that people often choose which community to join and within which to live. Agnostics will not move into a Hasidic community in Brooklyn, and prejudiced whites will not move into a neighbourhood dominated by the Nation of Islam.

Dominances by power elites and other forms of authoritarianism are not basic or inherent features of community, but reflections of the way it can be distorted. To be fully or even highly communitarian, communities require authentic commitment of most – if not all – of their members to a set of core values. To attain such a commitment, the values that are being fostered need to be truly accepted by the members and responsive to their underlying needs. If some members of the society are excluded from the moral dialogue, or are manipulated into abiding by the moral voice, or if their true needs are ignored, they will eventually react to the community's lack of responsiveness in an antisocial manner. In short, communities can be distorted by those in power, but then their moral order will be diminished, and they will either have to become more responsive to their members' true needs or transform into some other noncommunitarian social pattern.

Still other critics have accused communitarians not merely of ignoring the darker side of traditional communities, but of also seeking to revive these features. Thus Michael Taves (1988: 7–8) believes that the communitarian vision concerns itself mostly with 'reclaiming a reliance on traditional values and all that entails with regard to the family, sexual relations, religion, and the rejection of secularism'.

Early communitarians might be charged with being, in effect, social conservatives, if not authoritarians. However, many con-

temporary communitarians, especially those who define themselves as responsive (or new) communitarians, fully realize and often stress that they do *not* seek to return to traditional communities, with their authoritarian power structure, rigid stratification and discriminatory practices against minorities and women. These communitarians seek to build communities based on open participation, dialogue and truly shared values. R. Bruce Douglass (1994: 55) points out that 'Unlike conservatives, communitarians are aware that the days when the issues we face as a society could be settled on the basis of the **beliefs** of a privileged segment of the population have long since passed.'

Furthermore, communitarians observe that communities need to be embedded socially and morally in more encompassing entities if violent conflict among them is to be avoided. Society should not be viewed as composed of millions of individuals, but as pluralism (of communities) within unity (the society). The existence of subcultures does not undermine societal unity as long as there is a core of shared values and institutions.

References and further reading

Bell, C. and Newby, H. (1973) *Community Studies: An Introduction to the Sociology of the Local Community*, New York: Praeger.

Bell, D. A. (1993) *Communitarianism and Its Critics*, Oxford: Clarendon Press.

Bellah, R., Madsen, R., Sullivan, W. M., Swidler, A. and Tipton, S. M. (1985) *Habits of the Heart: Individualism and Commitment in American Life*, Berkeley, CA: University of California Press.

Douglass, R. B. (1994) 'The Renewal of Democracy and the Communitarian Prospect', *Responsive Community*, 4(3): 55–62.

Elshtain, J. B. (1997) *Real Politics: Politics and Everyday Life*, Baltimore: Johns Hopkins University Press.

Galston, W. A. (1991) *Liberal Purposes: Goods, Virtues, and Diversity in the Liberal State*, New York: Cambridge University Press.

Glendon, M. A. (1991) *Rights Talk: The Impoverishment of Political Discourse*, New York: Free Press.

Gutmann, A. (1985) 'Communitarian Critics of Liberalism', *Philosophy and Public Affairs*, 14: 308–22.

Pearson, D. E. (1995) 'Community and Sociology', *Society*, 32(5): 44–50.

Phillips, D. L. (1993) *Looking Backward: A Critical Appraisal of Communitarian Thought*, Princeton, NJ: Princeton University Press.

Taves, M. (1988) 'Roundtable on Communitarianism', *Telos*, 76: 7–8.

AMITAI ETZIONI

COMMUNITY AND ECONOMY

Introduction

Few concepts in sociology stimulate as much controversy as the one of community. For R. Nisbet (1966: 47), it is: 'the most fundamental and far-reaching of sociology's unit-ideas'. For G. Busino (1978), community does not have any value as a scientific concept.

Many of the critical remarks point to the fact that the concept is fuzzy, invoked as a catch-all term to cover very different phenomena. Others accuse it of being too much involved in utopian debates, closer to political philosophy as a normative discipline than to sociology as a scientific one. The concept of community was early introduced in classical and modern sociology, where it was equipped with a few fundamental meanings that we find also in contemporary sociology; despite this legacy it's not always acknowledged. In an important review of the uses of the concept of community, George A. Hillery Jr (1955) identified ninety-four definitions with very little area of agreement among them. Nonetheless, a majority of the definitions include three elements: local area, social ties or networks and social action and interaction (Bell and Newby 1971: 29; Bagnasco 1999). As I will point out, these three elements are indeed at the core of sociological meanings and uses of the concept. In the

following sections I will illustrate these uses, focusing especially on the application of community-derived analytical categories for the explanation of economic phenomena and for the clarification of the community–economy relationship.

The classical use

To begin with, Ferdinand Tönnies introduced the dichotomy community (*Gemeinschaft*) vs society (*Gesellschaft*) to illustrate the transition to modern society and disappearance of traditional forms of social relations. The traditional community was described as based upon personal intimacy, emotional depth (cf. **emotions and the economy**), **reciprocity** and social cohesion. In this vein, the opposition community–economy – as well as other classical concepts like status vs contract or mechanic solidarity vs organic solidarity – is an aspect of the romantic reaction against modernity of the early sociology. Community 'was thus used as a means of invidious comparison with contemporarily exemplified society' (Bell and Newby 1971: 22).

In the work of Max **Weber** this nostalgic nuance becomes much weaker, and a more analytic and scientific use of the concept is emerging. First of all, Weber wants to link the idea of community to his theory of action. In *Economy and Society* he makes a distinction between social relations based on *association* – where the meaning of one's action is based upon instrumental or value **rationality** – and social relations based on *community*, where the meaning refers to affects/emotions or traditions. Second, the interest of Weber in community-type relationships is embedded in a broader intellectual project devoted to establish a robust and specific scientific status for sociology. The concept of **ideal type** serves this purpose. Communitarian social relations have the status of an ideal type. They are never found as such in empirical reality, and it is not useful to characterize a whole society or to summarize an historical period as consisting of community relations. In fact, for Weber, it's possible to find dimensions of both community and society in all historical phases as well as in small villages and in modern cities.

The American sociologist Talcott **Parsons** elaborates on Weber's and Tönnies' distinctions in order to include their contributions in his AGIL model. For Parsons, every actor faces a choice between a set of four binary action orientations. Those alternatives together form the 'pattern variables' of Parson's system for the analysis of social action. As Parsons himself argued, the end of the continua of the polar opposition 'very closely characterize what in much sociological literature have been thought of as polar types of institutional structure, the best known version of which perhaps has been the *Gemeinschaft–Gesellschaft* dichotomy of Tönnies' (Parsons and Shils, 1952: 207–8). The polar oppositions are:

- affectivity vs affective neutrality: which refers to immediate self-gratification or its deferment;
- specificity vs diffuseness: which refers to the more or less broad scope of a relationship;
- universalism vs particularism: which refers to the presence of evaluation schemas more or less peculiar to the actors involved in the relationship;
- ascription vs achievement: which refers to the criteria used to evaluate or characterize other actors.

Community involves particularism, ascription, diffuseness and affectivity, while society includes affective neutrality, specificity, universalism and achievement. For instance, a social system where kinship is not an important dimension will be characterized by patterns of social action close to the society ideal type, rather than to the communitarian one.

Georg **Simmel** never used the word 'community' (Bagnasco 1999). Simmel, however, is also interested in exploring the effect of the transition to modernity on individual life. Simmel is particularly relevant for his attention on how the spatial organization of society can influence phenomena such as friendship, loyalty and **trust**: all elements usually associated with the idea of community. Modern life – especially through new forms of urban complexes, rationalization and over-stimulation of cognitive capabilities – creates a new form of individual that never existed before. 'The sophistication, anonymity and reserve of metropolitan life are given a kind of counterpoint relation to the simplicity, directness, and warmth of the traditional community' (Nisbet 1966: 99). The impersonality of economic **exchange** through money – compared to the personal exchange of pre-modern societies – represents one of the most well-known examples of this transition.

Finally, the spatial or area dimension of community has been widely used as a form of empirical research (in so-called 'community studies'), especially in the early American sociology.

The Chicago School and the book on *Middletown* by Robert and Helen Lynd are among the most important classic examples of this perspective. In both cases – as well as all other community studies – social phenomena cannot be understood if abstracted from their spatial and temporal location. Here the concept of community denotes a well-defined area with a distinct form of spatial organization or a definite local society in a well-identified spatial location. The very essence of the phenomena being studied relies on the particular spatial disposition of groups (e.g. suburbs, ghettos), localization of social practices and patterns of social phenomena (e.g. individual and area careers). Here the concept of community melds with the one of (local) society, and it denotes a small-scale but nevertheless complete society where face-to-face inter-action plays a crucial role in shaping social and economics outcomes.

The contemporary use of community in economic sociology

The three meanings of the concept of community – social relationships, social (inter)action and spatial organization of local areas – are widely used also in con-temporary sociology.

To begin with, the idea of social ties or social relationship – are at the core of two influential concepts, **economic sociology** network closure (James S. **Coleman**) and structural holes/weak ties (R. Burt, M. Granovetter). In both cases, it is shown how the transition to modern society and the growth of individualization did not under-mine the crucial role of social ties. The network closure perspective demonstrates – in Coleman's original contribution (1990: ch. 12) – the role of **social capital** in enabling individual actors to privately rea-lize their interest as well as the **public goods** dimension of social capital creation. Bypassing this distinction, it's possible to argue that network closure shows: (1) how a set of closed social relationship can affect the creation of social norms; (2) how social ties can enhance group identity; and (3) at what conditions networks are able to sti-mulate concerns for one's **reputation** in economic exchange.

The effects of this kind of social rela-tionship have been analysed for various social and economic phenomena: school achievements of kids, immigration deci-sions, **collective action** and social move-ments, among others. For instance, Coleman showed how families living in communities with closed social ties can be more successful in promoting their kids' education than families living in commu-nities without such a strong network clo-sure. He also argued that markets with a strong network closure can – also without

formal **contract** – facilitate risky economic transactions.

In the case of structural holes and/or weak ties a set of disconnected social relationships create opportunities for strate-gic behaviour; they give access to non-redundant **information** and they facilitate **entrepreneurship**, status attainment and individual achievement. The effect of structural holes has been also analysed for the study of elite behaviour in Renaissance Florence, showing how the de' Medici clan based their 'robust action' on the dis-connection existing between the social networks of the aristocracy and those of the 'new rich' (Padgett and Ansell 1993).

In a similar vein, Mark Granovetter's famous thesis about the 'strength of weak ties' – namely, where ties with acquain-tances give access to better information than ties with friends – highlights the role of a particular kind of social relationship for the explanation of economic phenomena like labour market dynamics, careers and work mobility. Granovetter also points out that an analytical focus on social networks may invite the use of a different model of social action relative to the one of neo-classical economics (Granovetter 2002). Horizontal and vertical relations – the argument goes on – promote social factors like trust, **norms and values**, power and compliance in a way far beyond the action view of economics. Following this line, the social relations dimension on commu-nity moves closer to the social action dimension.

Much of the sociological criticism against mainstream economics is really built around a different core of behavioural assumptions. Two themes are of special importance in the debate: cognitive limits (e.g. bounded rationality) and motivational assumptions like **altruism** or non-selfish behaviour of various kinds (e.g. values-driven action). This line constitutes the second con-temporary legacy of the classic use of the concept of community as a model of social action. For instance, the so-called **socio-economics** approach (Etzioni 1988) strongly argues for the irreducibility of moral behaviour to **utilitarianism** or hedonism, for the pervasive presence of a sense of **fairness** in human action and for a clear difference between morality and pleasure. This viewpoint is also committed to normative reasoning about the role of communitarian action in building the 'good society', as well as to a social ontology which denies that individual and self-consistent actors are the proper unit of analysis for sociological inquiry.

Apart from utopian considerations, the explanatory power of the assumption of mixed motives in social action is widely confirmed by other contemporary views. Experimental economics and laboratory **game theory**, among others, have convincingly shown the role of multiple types of 'players', not reducible to the rational egoist model. In this line, the action-based use of the concept of community points to a multidimensional model where cost–benefit considerations enter the picture along with moral, altruistic and commitment factors and both consequentialist and non-consequentialist motivations for human behaviour.

Finally, the third use of the concept is built around the idea of community as a form of spatial organization. For instance, the early research on **industrial districts** focused quite strongly on the effects of space on local development. The geographic closeness between rural and urban areas, along with others spatial factors, were included amid other key explanatory dimensions of industrial districts' development. Small and medium-sized enterprises, widespread entrepreneurship and good economic performance of particular local areas have been closely linked to 'communitarian' characteristics such as trust, reciprocity and a shared local identity. In the opinion of the main scholars of sociological industrial districts research in Italy, the spatial and institutional preconditions of these regions allowed for 'communitarian market behaviour' instead of individualism (for a review and the relevant literature see Barbera 2002). Spatial factors are also at the core of the contemporary debate on local development and local productions system: concepts like 'learning regions' and 'innovative milieux' point to the very importance of spatial organization of local economies (Crouch et al. 2001: ch. 1).

Conclusion

Despite these three common dimensions – social relations, social (inter)action and local area issues – the shift from the classical to the contemporary concept of community highlights some important differences. To begin with, the effect of communitarian dimensions on economic life is no longer seen as a residual category of the 'past'. In this vein – although utopian and normative considerations did not vanish completely – the contemporary use is much closer to Weber's ideal-type interpretation than to Tönnies essentialist one. If analytically decomposed into social relations, social action and spatial organization, the concept reveals the selective character of modernization: namely, that modernizing processes always include a selection of the elements of past societal organization.

Second, the contemporary use of the concept makes clear that its usefulness is strongly linked to the idea of middle-range theory: social networks, mixing-motives action and spatial features make sense only as models and mechanisms of recognizable causal patterns valid in a plurality of situations, but not everywhere. For instance, empirical research in the south of Italy has shown that particularistic and nepotistic social ties can both prevent and enhance **economic development**. More empirical inquiries into the scope and conditions of the **social mechanisms** standing behind such puzzling phenomena should be at the core of research on the community–economy relationship.

Finally, the contemporary use of the concept points to some major issues such as social identity, individualization, social capital, local development and trust. For instance, the so-called 'boundaryless' careers of managers highlight the crucial role of professional communities and social networks in promoting or preventing a career path. The issue of social capital would appear to be of particular importance for the discussion on community-related issues (e.g. Putnam 2000). As James S. Coleman argued, one of the challenges for modern societies is the replacement of primordial social capital (e.g. family and community) with the one of constructed social organization:

> What *does* constitute a substitute in the new social structure for the social capital that is eroding? A part of the answer lies in constructed social organization, narrow-purpose corporate bodies that cover some functions once served by family and local community: schools, medical insurers ... government agencies that provide old-age benefits or unemployment benefits.
>
> (Coleman 1990: 653)

This general idea – which is neither new nor particularly original – can nonetheless serve the purpose of creating concrete research questions if dissected into the three dimensions previously discussed. For instance: what kind of social relationships are important to connect primordial and constructed social capital? Can intrinsic motivation be at work also in modern welfare systems? How does the spatial organization of local societies make a difference in the global economy?

References and further reading

Abbot, A. (1997) 'Of Time and Space: The Contemporary Relevance of the Chicago School', *Social Forces*, 75(4): 1149–82.

Bagnasco, A. (1999) *Tracce di comunità*, Bologna: Il Mulino.

Barbera, F. (2002) 'Economic Sociology in Italy: Past and Present', *International Review of Sociology*, 12(1): 145–57.

Bell, C. and Newby, H. (1971) *Community Studies*, London: Unwin.

Busino, G. (1978) 'Comunità', in *Enciclopedia Einaudi*, vol. III, Torino: Einaudi.

Coleman, J. S. (1957) *Community Conflict*, London: Collier-Macmillan.

—— (1990) *Foundations of Social Theory*, Cambridge, MA: Belknap Press.

Crouch, Colin, Le Galès, Patrick, Trigilia, Carlo and Voelzkow, Helmut (2001) *Local Production Systems in Europe. Rise or Demise?* Oxford: Oxford University Press.

Etzioni, A. (1988) *The Moral Dimension. Toward a New Economics*, New York and London: Free Press.

—— (1993) *The Spirit of Community: Rights, Responsibilities and the Communitarian Agenda*, New York: Crown.

Granovetter, M. (2002) 'A Theoretical Agenda for Economic Sociology', in Mauro F. Guillén, Randall Collins, Paula England and Marshall Meyer (eds), *The New Economic Sociology: Developments in an Emerging Field*, New York: Russell Sage Foundation.

Hannerz, U. (1980) *Exploring the City. Inquiries Toward an Urban Anthropology*, New York: Columbia University Press.

Hillery, G. A., Jr (1955) 'Definitions of Community: Areas of Agreement', *Rural Sociology*, 20(2): 111–23.

Jahoda, M., Lazarsfeld, P. F. and Zeisel, H. Marienthal (1972) *The Sociography of an Unemployed Community*, London: Tavistock.

Nisbet, R. (1966) *The Sociological Tradition*, New York: Basic Books.

Padgett, J. F. and Ansell, C. (1993) 'Robust Action and the Rise of the Medici 1400–1434', *American Journal of Sociology*, 98: 1259–319.

Parsons, T. and Shils, E. (1952) *Toward a General Theory of Action*, New York and London: Harper Torchbook.

Putnam, R. (2000) *Bowling Alone: The Collapse and Revival of American Community*, New York, Simon and Schuster.

Storper. M. (1997) *The Regional World: Territorial Development in a Global Economy*, New York and London: Guilford Press.

FILIPPO BARBERA

COMPETITION See: capitalism; economic action, markets; Weber

COMPLEX ORGANIZATIONS

The formal study of complex organizations emerged around the mid twentieth century. Prior to this time, studies of organizations were focused on one or another element of the organization or on one or another type of organization rather than on the more general focus of the complex organization itself. Scott in *Organizations* (2003) provides an insightful review of the history of the study of complex organizations, some of which is summarized below.

There were many important works that led to the study of complex organizations. Weber in the *Theory of Social and Economic Organization* (1947) focused on a variety of topics related to the operations of organizations, including bureaucracy and authority. Marx focused on the ways in which work is carried out and how power is used within organizations. He spoke of control of the workers and of the organization as an instrument for control. **Durkheim** in the *Division of Labor in Society* (1933) focused on the factors that hold an organization together and discussed the concepts of *mechanical solidarity* – where the people have a common set of **beliefs** and sentiments that serve to encourage consensus and integration – and *organic solidarity* – where people depend on one another's different abilities in order to achieve their goals.

The emergence of the field of complex organizations might be roughly dated soon after the translation into English of Weber's work and to a lesser extent Michels' *Political Parties* (1949). At that time, Merton and his students at Columbia University (Merton *et al.* 1952) began outlining the boundaries of this new field by applying theoretical and empirical materials dealing with various aspects of organizations. This included Selznick's examination of the Tennessee Valley

Authority (1949) and Gouldner's study of a gypsum mine and factory (1954). Other studies of importance included Blau's study of a state employment agency and a federal law-enforcement agency (1955) and studies by Lipset (1956). At this point, sociologists were beginning to develop and test generalizations dealing with the structure and functioning of complex organizations.

Also important to the development of complex organizations was the work being done by industrial psychologists. Topics such as managerial activities, work processes and employee morale and turnover were receiving attention (Taylor 1911; Fayol 1949). However, these works did not concentrate on the general development of organizational theory but rather on 'prescriptive' concerns with how organizations 'should' be structured. This lack of focus on theory was overcome to some degree by the work of Simon (1946) and the interdisciplinary team that he brought together at the Carnegie Institute of Technology (now Carnegie-Mellon University) to develop a behaviourally oriented science of administration, including a focus on decision-making and choice within organizations that he more recently described in *Administrative Behavior* (1997). Soon after this development, economic models began being modified so that the view of organizations was expanded beyond a focus on the rational behaviour of organizations to the 'intendedly' rational behaviour. From this view, organizational behaviour was seen as less than rational because of the cognitive limitations of the organization's participants (March and Simon 1958) and because of the competing objectives of the participants (Cyert and March 1963). During this time, psychology and political science played a growing role in the understanding of organizational behaviour.

During and following these many developments, the concept of the 'complex organization' emerged. At this stage social scientists began to (1) make generalities and

89

propose theories that were at a level of abstraction that allowed for organizations of varying types to be viewed as being similar in form and function; and (2) develop methodologies for conducting empirical tests of these generalities or theories.

A focus on an organization's *technology* emerged as a means of understanding why organizations are structured as they are and behave and perform as they do. Technology was defined in a variety of ways but generally was viewed as the means, activities and knowledge used to transform materials and inputs into organizational outputs. Woodward in *Management and Technology* (1958) distinguished three types of core technologies and suggested that all organizations use one of these three types. Her typologies varied from simple craft work to complex ways of transforming inputs that cannot be easily broken down into discrete operations. She then examined how the technology used affected other characteristics of the organization and, in particular, the management structure. Blauner in *Alienation and Freedom* (1964) advanced these ideas by suggesting that the type of technology used is directly related to worker **alienation**. Low-level alienation was proposed to exist in simple craft technologies while high alienation existed in assembly-line technologies (viewed as moderately complex). Thompson in *Organizations in Action* (1967) also proposed technology to be the primary explanation for organizational structure and behaviour but categorized organizational technologies into three groups different from those offered by Woodward. And similarly, Perrow (1967) believed technology to be the explanation for organizational structure and behaviour but again offered different categories and suggested that there are two primary types: task variability and task analysability.

Trist (1981) and his associates at the Tavistock Institute agreed with the earlier suggestions that technology is extremely important to understanding complex orga-

nizations. However, they carried this work further by suggesting that it is a combination of the technological system and the organization's social system that determine an organization's structure, behaviour and performance. Their theoretical perspective has been referred to as 'socio-technical systems theory'. High organizational performance was viewed as an optimization of the relationship between the technologies used and the social and psychological needs of the workers.

A focus on the *environment* surrounding the organization was next to gain the attention of social scientists. Initially the environment was viewed as anything 'out there' of interest to the researcher. These researchers progressively began to catalogue things that we should look for 'out there'. The first step was the analysis of two or three interacting organizations, initially labelled 'inter-organizational analysis', with the emphasis on the effect of the other organizations on the focal organization. Then, the idea of a 'set' of organizations began to gain interest among researchers, and from there the idea of a network of organizations, focusing on the properties of the networks rather than any one organization within it. Advocates of the environmental perspective typically have focused on the complexity of an organization's environment, ranging from the organization's interaction with immediate customers and suppliers to systems of government, ecological systems, and cultural beliefs. It is explained that these varying complex environments can have crucial impacts on an organization's behaviour and performance.

Social scientists who have studied the environment often highlight the constant state of environmental change and the consequent impacts on the organization. Emery and Trist (1965) described a 'turbulent field' in which the environment is changing independently of organizational actions but in ways that are often threatening to organizational survival. On the other hand, Pasmore in *Designing Effective Organizations*

(1988) has noted that constant organizational change, resulting from environmental changes, can result in recurring opportunity for an organization to gain competitive advantage. This led some theorists to concentrate their research on how organizations change with turbulent environments and how environments change due to the manipulations of organizations. General Motors provides a good example of an organization responding to and, at the same time, manipulating its environment. It responded to international competition by changing its technologies and implementing new management practices to better match those of its competition. At the same time, it attempted to manipulate the environment by placing pressure on US legislators to establish tougher automobile import quotas. 'Contingency theory' grew out of the studies of the environment. This perspective suggests that the most effective organizational structure is 'contingent' on the type of environment surrounding an organization.

Toward the end of the twentieth century, Scott (1987) attempted to categorize the varying organizational theories and subsequently suggested that there were three major perspectives. Those adhering to the *rational system perspective* viewed organizations as collectivities oriented to the pursuit of relatively specific goals with formalized social structures. Those adhering to the *natural system perspective* viewed organizations as collectivities whereby the participants are less formally structured. The focus is on the informal activities of the participants. The third perspective was termed the *open system perspective* and viewed organizations in terms of competing groups of people within and outside the organization that attempt to influence the goals and direction of the organization.

Other social scientists have chosen to use existing sociological theories to explain the structure and behaviour of complex organizations. There have been at least three prominent theories that have been applied. Those who support a *structural functionalist view* explain complex organizations in terms of the functions performed and tend to focus on organizational stability and order. Parsons' concepts of adaptation, goal attainment, integration and latency – all a part of the structural functional view described in *Structure and Process in Modern Societies* (1960) – have been applied here. The *conflict perspective* is used to highlight existing conflicts between groups, power struggles, competition and the existence of continual change brought on by a variety of factors including differing political interests and differing cultures. The works of Karl Marx have been used to develop this view. The third theoretical approach, *symbolic interactionism*, uses a more micro-level view that focuses on individual behaviour to explain order and conflict. When applied to organizations, the theorist is concerned with how individuals interpret organizations and their place within them. Communication between people entails symbolic messages that may or may not have the same meaning for those involved in the communication.

The study of complex organizations in the future may take any or all of several directions. Social scientists are likely to continue using the three major perspectives noted by Scott as well as the three prominent sociological theories to explain organizational structure, behaviour and performance. Some organizational theorists have chosen to view organizations from a *postmodern perspective* and this view could become more widely accepted. The postmodern perspective suggests that the 'complex organization' only exists as a subjective concept. Complex organizations are viewed as subjective constructions based on images, language and rhetoric rather than actual, real entities unto themselves. As Jaffee showed in *Organization Theory* (2001), the essence and meaning of the complex organization is constantly shifting, depending on the perspective of the observer. So there is a focus on how the concept is defined and why it is defined as it is, with the implicit suggestion that the definer or social scientist has motives behind the selection of definition. At the other extreme are those who reify the organization and apply economic models to explain organizational behaviour. As Pfeffer explained in *New Directions for Organization Theory* (1977), this perspective relies on a *rational economic view* of the complex organization and may also gain in interest among social scientists. Still another perspective that has grown in interest is that of *organizational culture* and its influence on organizational behaviour and performance. Thus, there are many theoretical perspectives that have been or are being developed to explain the complex organization. While a single theoretical approach does not appear in sight, it is clear that the field is rich in theoretical development and progress is being made.

References and further reading

Cyert, R. and March, J. (1963) *A Behavioral Theory of the Firm*, Englewood Cliffs, NJ: Prentice Hall.

Emery, F. E. and Trist, E. (1965) 'The Causal Texture of Organizational Environments', *Human Relations*, 18: 21–32.

Fayol, H. (1949) *General and Industrial Management*, London: Sir Isaac Pitman and Sons.

Jaffee, D. (2001) *Organization Theory*, New York: McGraw-Hill.

March, J. G. and Simon, H. A. (1958) *Organizations*, New York: John Wiley and Sons.

Merton, R. K., Gray, A. P., Hockey, B., Selvin, H. C. and eds (1952) *Reader in Bureaucracy*, Glencoe, IL: Free Press.

Pasmore, W. (1988) *Designing Effective Organizations*, New York: John Wiley and Sons.

Perrow, C. (1967) 'A Framework for the Comparative Analysis of Organizations', *American Sociological Review*, 32: 194–208.

Pfeffer, J. (1977) *New Directions for Organization Theory*, New York: Oxford University Press.

Scott, W. R. (1987) 'The Adolescence of Institutional Theory', *Administrative Science Quarterly*, 32: 493–511.

—— (2003) *Organizations*, Englewood Cliffs, NJ: Prentice Hall.

Simon, H. A. (1997) *Administrative Behaviour*, New York: Free Press.

Taylor, F. W. (1911) *The Principles of Scientific Management*, New York: Harper.

Trist, E. L. (1981) 'The Evolution of Socio-technical Systems as a Conceptual Framework and as an Action Research Program', in A. Van de Ven and W. F. Joyce (eds), *Perspectives on Organization Design and Behavior*, New York: John Wiley and Sons, Wiley-Interscience.

DALE E. YEATTS

CONFLICT

Conflict can be defined as a structural relation between two or more individual or collective actors pursuing incompatible interests or intentions. Two general empirical conditions for the emergence of conflict can be identified: first, structural conditions like domination or stratification that shape incompatible interests regarding scarce resources or values; second, the distribution of power resources necessary for the undertaking of conflict between the concerned parties. Social conflict is much more likely to occur under conditions of equal power resources. In the definition of conflict, *latent and manifest conflicts* can be differentiated. Conflicts may remain latent when one of the involved actors does not follow his interests or when actors do not have the necessary power resources to pursue their goals. Thus, powerless actors often refrain from uttering their deprivations and will behave obediently. Furthermore, certain interests in society may be institutionally excluded from the decision-making process because of selectivity in political institutions and biases in media coverage. This phenomenon has been discussed as so-called *non-decisions* in political science. Latent conflict is typically associated with unequal distributions of resources, most importantly wealth and income, or with relations of exploitation.

Manifest or overt conflict results from two or more parties actually pursuing their conflicting interests or intentions. This rather wide concept also includes processes of peaceful bargaining, competition and **exchange**. It can be further differentiated according to the power resources used in conflict behaviour. When all parties concerned use *rewarding* resources to influence the other actors' course of action, the type of conflict can be labelled as *exchange or competition*. If some of the actors involved use *punishing* resources and the other parties bring in rewarding resources one can speak of *plunder*. In a final step we can define *manifest conflict* in a narrow sense, as a situation where all concerned actors resort to punishing moves.

We may define conflicts as related to the economy if the concerned parties pursue interests focusing on economic resources, such as the distribution of household incomes between members of a family, political struggles concerning government spending for different spheres of public life and war between states over the economic exploitation of natural resources. Generally speaking, these very different types of conflict may deal with economically related issues. However, these are usually topics of the sociology of the family, political sociology and political science. For economic sociology it is useful to focus directly on economic conflicts which are defined as happening between actors constituted in the economic sphere of society, like industrial conflicts between capital and labour, struggles between different management factions inside firms or bargaining between sellers and buyers in production markets. In the remainder of this article discussion focuses on examples of manifest conflict in the narrow sense and on exchange and competition as types of conflict in the economy. (See Figure 1.)

Importance of conflicts

From a sociological point of view, markets and firms are power structures constituting actors with adverse interests. Social and economic conflicts are important causes of social and economic change, but since manifest conflict depends on several preconditions history is full of long periods of stable domination, only punctuated by manifest or violent conflict. The importance of social conflict for the development and change of social institutions was underlined by Jack Knight (1992). He argues convincingly that institutions and their collective benefits emerge as by-products of social and economic conflicts over distributional issues.

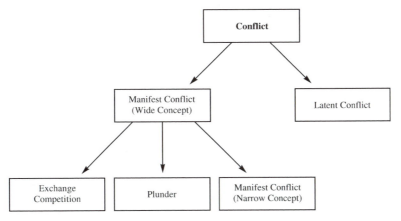

Figure 1. Definitions of conflict

Industrial conflict

The most important economic conflicts discussed in sociology are those between capital and labour. Karl **Marx** in particular established the sociological view that capitalist economies (see **capitalism**) have a basically asymmetric power structure with the working class subordinated to capital. Capital's control over the means of production is central to the livelihood of most citizens in contemporary societies, since it enables capital to hire labour and to establish a relationship of domination and exploitation in business organizations. Theoretical micro-foundations for this concept of asymmetric power structures in capitalist society between capital and labour have been developed in the theory of contested exchange. The structural asymmetry shapes contradicting interests for capital and labour not only in the distribution of economic gains and working conditions but in the long-term development of society. Therefore, it is the structural basis for the emergence of class conflict. This includes economic conflicts such as workplace unrest, strikes and lockouts, but also spills over into class-based political conflicts. From the classical Marxist perspective, the process of class formation and therefore the development of class conflicts is facilitated by the homogenization of the working class and its spatial concentration in large factories and cities.

Industrial conflict is the best analysed aspect of class conflicts in the economy. The macroeconomic, social and political determinants of strike development and frequency have been well researched. In developed capitalist nations the frequency of strikes is positively associated with employees' bargaining power (low unemployment), negatively influenced by political and economic repression against workers, furthered by unions mobilizing large numbers of employees and the institutional structure of industrial bargaining (Franzosi 1995). An exception to this pattern is found in countries with highly centralized, strong labour movements with stable political representation such as Sweden, where strike frequencies are low despite the existence of strong unions, low repression against workers and relatively high bargaining power of employees. The organizations of the labour movement in these countries have decided to shift class conflict from the economic arena, with its asymmetric power structure and therefore rather costly conflicts, to the symmetrically structured political sphere.

The focus on the determinants of the development of strike frequencies, however, is much too narrow, because it is limited to the macroeconomic surface of phenomena. Research on inter-industry and plant-level differences in industrial conflicts shows that groups of employees with higher workplace autonomy, higher social cohesion and strong horizontal social networks (furthered by the absence of racial, ethnic or religious cleavages, of socio-economic differentiation and sharp power differences), higher union organization and less powerful employers resort to strikes more often (Rössel 2000). Despite the fact that strikes are *economic* conflicts, their frequency and development can be explained with the same theoretical approaches as other social protests and movements.

Economic conflicts between capital and labour do not only influence the distribution of economic resources and the development of working conditions. From an economic point of view, the ensuing institutionalization of rules regulating the sequence and termination of industrial conflict is important to minimize costs for all parties involved in the conflict. Furthermore, it has effects on political development (political crises, the development of welfare states), the structure and organization of firms, the development of technology and machinery, and sometimes on the whole social structure of accumulation

(Franzosi 1995). Especially the great historical strike waves have contributed to wholesale changes in the social, economic and political structure of societies.

Intraorganizational struggle

Industrial conflicts, such as strikes and lockouts, are the most prominent and best-researched examples of manifest conflicts in the economy. In addition to industrial conflict, it is possible to identify conflicts among groups of employees of business organizations struggling for their own interests. Factions of management try to organize other branches of management and their subordinates in ways that further their own interests. In a study of large corporations Neil Fligstein (1990) showed that finance personnel and general management personnel increasingly came to control large firms in the United States. These internal and sometimes external power struggles shaped the development of organizational structures in the twentieth century. This thesis contrasts with economic approaches accounting for organizational changes by efficiency gains. However, there is much empirical evidence for a sociological perspective explaining organizational developments like vertical integration, the multidivisional form and different types of product diversification by relating them to social conflicts between actors trying to pursue strategies based on different power resources and conceptions of their respective organizational field (Fligstein 1990).

Other types of conflict: exchange and competition

Several types of manifest economic conflict in the narrow sense, such as strikes and power struggles between management factions, have proven to be important in contemporary societies. The conflict type of plunder is rather exceptional for modern capitalist economic systems based on peaceful and voluntary exchanges. It is more frequent in pre-modern types of predatory capitalism, based on colonial exploitation and piracy. Much more important for sociological thinking about contemporary economic systems are competition and exchange as types of conflict. Both forms of relationship between economic agents are examples of conflict according to the definition explicated above. They are both based on partially incompatible interests between actors and do not remain latent. Particularly, exchange processes can be seen as a compromise resulting from a preceding conflict between diverging interests concerning prices and product quality (Max **Weber**). The organization of exchange, however, differs between specific types of markets according to their power structures, forms of institutionalization and role structures.

In contrast to processes of exchange which are based on direct interaction between the parties concerned, *pure* competition excludes direct interaction between competing actors. Whereas in direct conflict one has to pursue one's interest against other actors' opposition, the achievement of objectives in competitive structures is based on parallel efforts of all actors directed towards an external goal, e.g. young men competing for the favour of a woman, swimmers racing side-by-side or several grocers competing for customers. Especially Georg **Simmel** has argued that competitive structures are typical for modern societies, allowing a businesslike struggle between persons abstaining from personal dislike or hate. Hence, competition is a special type of struggle that is also much less regulated by law and morality than other types of conflict. There are no accepted moral rules or legal provisions to prevent a person's economic and social existence being ruined by competition, which is obviously the case for direct assault on the same person. Society tolerates the brutality of competition because it leads to the more efficient production of collective benefits for large segments of the population.

According to the definition given above, economic conflict has many faces. The most well researched are industrial conflict and intraorganizational struggles. Exchange processes and structures of competition are less well recognized as situations of conflict, but are part of established definitions of conflict. It seems reasonable that, based on a conflict perspective, the significance of institutions, power and role structures on markets can be enlightened.

See also: collective action; trade unions.

References and further reading

Fligstein, N. (1990) *The Transformation of Corporate Control*, Cambridge, MA: Harvard University Press.

Franzosi, R. (1995) *The Puzzle of Strikes: Class and State Strategies in Post-war Italy*, Cambridge, MA: Cambridge University Press.

Knight, J. (1992) *Institutions and Social Conflict*, Cambridge, MA: Cambridge University Press.

Rössel, J. (2000) 'Mobilisierung und Streikverhalten. Eine Analyse des amerikanischen Stein- und Anthrazitkohlenbergbaus am Ende des 19. Jahrhunderts', *Berliner Journal für Soziologie*, 10: 403–22.

JÖRG RÖSSEL

CONSPICUOUS CONSUMPTION

See: Veblen, Thorstein; consumption

CONSULTANTS

Consulting is a pervasive phenomenon in modern societies. A wide range of different consultants offers services for individuals and organizations. Consultants address problems arising in different functional subsystems of society, from the economy, politics and health care to education, and they give advice regarding different aspects of everyday life, from career planning to marriage counselling. However, most commonly the term refers to management consulting performed by independent consulting firms, predominantly addressing the management of private industry organizations but increasingly also public and third-sector organizations.

The rise of consulting to managers goes back to the emergence of the large-scale managerial enterprise in the USA in late nineteenth century. With the development of 'scientific management', associated with the names of Frederick W. Taylor and some of his successors, consulting became a clearly recognizable business service. The focus of these early consulting firms, known as 'efficiency experts', was on shop-floor efficiency. Some of these firms expanded their services to Europe, especially to the United Kingdom. These companies had a considerable influence on the diffusion, further development and local translation of the ideas of scientific management. However, international comparison shows that there are functional equivalents to consulting firms for the diffusion of management ideas and concepts.

Although Frederick W. Taylor is often portrayed as the first management consultant, the dawn of 'modern management consulting' is better grasped looking at the emergence of a different type of consulting firm, addressing the overall performance, structure and strategy of the large-scale managerial corporation. Although the first consultancy, Arthur D. Little, was founded in 1886, the real take-off of modern management consulting began in the 1930s driven by institutional reforms of the US banking and securities regulation in the aftermath of the Great Depression. These reforms prohibited consulting activities of **banks** towards the non-banking sector and emancipated management consultants from their former subordination to the banks. The rapid growth and increasing complexity of corporations and the emerging 'managerial capitalism' became the seedbed for the advancement of modern management consulting in the US which has no parallel elsewhere. Culturally legitimated by the American model and the pervading 'American Management Mystique' (Locke), large US consulting firms started an exceptional international expansion after World War II. Following their customers to Europe, they expanded their services to European corporations, which tried to imitate the success of their US competitors by adopting the multidivisional form. It lay ground to the dominance of US-originated firms in the field persisting to this day. Among these firms was McKinsey & Co., perceived as the archetypal modern management consulting firm. It has become a truly transnational company, maintaining eighty-three offices all over the world and employing more than 6,000 consultants in 2000.

During the 1960s and 1970s the range of actors expanded and diversified. With few exceptions this phase was again dominated by US firms. Some of them, for instance the Boston Consulting Group, were split-offs from first generation companies, specializing in strategy consulting. During the 1980s and 1990s, large Anglo-American tax and audit companies, based on their established relations to multinational corporations, increasingly expanded their services to general management consulting, specializing in corporate strategy and finance and IT strategy and implementation. Since the 1980s, the boundaries between management consulting and more specialized IT-related expert services are being blurred, reflecting the changing emphasis of information technology as a strategic management issue.

From the 1980s onwards the management consulting industry was one of the fastest growing business sectors. While in 1980 world-wide turnover of the industry was approximately three billion dollars, it grew up to 60 billion dollars in 1999 (Clark and Fincham 2002). The consulting boom of this period co-evolved with the rise of the 'management guru' and the phenomenon of management fashions (Abrahamson 1996). Management consultants and gurus are at the core of the 'fashion-setting community' and the evolution of management fashions constantly produces new demands for consulting services.

The increasing significance of consulting in modern societies parallels the rise of the 'service-oriented society'. As an advice-giving activity, consulting has several characteristics in common with other services. Its product is intangible and results from a co-production between a service provider and a client organization encompassing both problem definition, identification of possible solutions and possibly implementation. As the consulting 'product' emerges from a process of co-production it can hardly be defined ex-ante. Because of the complex causal texture in which consulting projects are embedded their effects cannot be evaluated ex-post. Attribution of success and failure is inextricable. All the more, the authority of their advice is of significance. Consultants portray their advice as based on 'objective' and 'independent' expertise provided by specially trained and qualified persons. Such claims resemble those of professional business services like lawyers, auditors or IT specialists, some of them having achieved the status of a full profession. Although consultants rely on specialized expertise in a variety of fields, too, management consulting in general is not a profession because management in itself cannot be a profession (see **professions**). Authoritative management knowledge is bound to varying national institutions, associated with different and often competing academic disciplines and changes over time. Rather, claims of professionalism are embarked to enhance consultant authority and credibility. The authority of management consultants rests upon the reputation and the brand image of the individual consulting firm, and is not derived from a generally accepted body of professional knowledge. Instead, the emerging 'knowledge industry' (Kipping and Engwall 2002) and its 'merchants of meaning' themselves have a heavy impact on the accelerated development and 'commodification' of management knowledge. By doing so, management consultants have achieved the status of 'supra-experts' (Ernst and Kieser 2002) or even a 'new reflection elite' (Deutschmann 1993) with respect to their broader influence on political and societal change.

Beyond particular consulting projects they influence managerial agenda-setting and the definition of situations and problems whereby particularly promoted strategies and concepts come to be perceived as 'inevitable'. The influence of consultancies can be detected in almost all major management trends. Their contributions became widely recognized and had a considerable impact on organizational change in a variety of fields, e.g. the promotion of the M-Form, Overhead Value Analysis, Portfolio Analysis, Business Process Re-engineering; and the Shareholder Value Concept. Some of the propagated concepts can be found in standard academic textbooks, still showing the authorship of the branded consulting firms.

Based on the reputation of large consulting firms and the reference to fashionable concepts, the motives of managers to call in consultants expand beyond customary outsourcing motives, e.g. to utilize expert knowledge deemed to be too costly to be developed internally or needed only occasionally. Given an increasing uncertainty of organizational decision-making, hiring consultants is often motivated by the need to legitimate a course of action towards rival camps within organizations and towards external stakeholders. To pick up a fashionable concept with consultant help gives the initiating manager the aura of an innovator and is likely to boost his career while, in case of failure, it reduces the risk to become blamed for an organizational innovation which is not backed by alleged 'best practices'. Within particular projects consultants take on the role of a catalyst of organizational change, helping to forge coalitions of change and to overcome internal reluctance.

However, only large and highly reputed consultancies are likely to become fashion setters and to fulfil these roles. In the 1990s they have been gaining growing shares of the world-wide consulting market. Most other consultants do their business within emerging trends and are not capable to influence the development of management knowledge. The increasing significance of the consulting industry since the 1980s has propelled academic research within which neo-institutional approaches have gained some prominence. Although considerable progress has been made since then there are still controversial issues and unexplored fields. While the literature often deals with communicated images of consultant work, empirical in-depth studies are lacking, both on the translation of de-contextualized ideas on national, field and organizational levels and on consultant–client relationships grasping its interactive and micro-political nature and different consultant role models discussed in research literature.

Progress has been made in analysing the rhetoric and persuasion techniques of consultants and 'gurus', but too often the recipient managers have been portrayed as passive adopters or relatively powerless victims of management fashions and consultancy influence. A wider range of managerial and organizational responses has to be taken into account, by which concepts and consultancy influence are modified, revised or rejected, including cynical attitudes. On the other hand, the insecure nature of the consulting business itself has to be emphasized. Consulting firms are embedded actors and not autonomous manipulators of ideas. Furthermore, multinational consulting firms themselves are embedded in various institutional contexts which they have to reflect both in the construction of commodified concepts and in their local application.

Historical studies emphasize institutional and wider sociopolitical factors explaining the rise of the industry, and at the same time point to functional equivalents for consultant roles emerging in different institutional contexts. It cannot be excluded that the most recent, early twentieth-century stagnation of the industry going along with an increasing criticism of mainstream consulting indicates a new phase which will again call for explanations referring to institutional change.

References and further reading

Abrahamson, Eric (1996) 'Management Fashion', *Academy of Management Review*, 21: 254–85.
Clark, Timothy and Fincham, Robin (eds) (2002) *Critical Consulting. New Perspectives on the Management Advice Industry*, Oxford: Blackwell.
Deutschmann, Christoph (1993) 'Unternehmensberater – eine neue "Reflexionselite?"' in Walther Müller-Jentsch (ed.), *Profitable Ethik – effiziente Kultur: neue Sinnstiftung durch das Management?* Munich: Hampp, pp. 57–82.
Ernst, Berit and Kieser, Alfred (2002) 'In Search for Explanations for the Consulting Explosion', in Kerstin Sahlin-Andersson and Lars Engwall (eds), *The Expansion of Management Knowledge: Carriers, Ideas, and Sources*, Stanford: Stanford University Press, pp. 47–73.
Kipping, Matthias and Engwall, Lars (eds) (2002) *Management Consulting. Emergence and Dynamics of a Knowledge Industry*, Oxford: Oxford University Press.

MICHAEL FAUST

CONSUMER CULTURE

The term 'consumer culture' has been used in a variety of ways. Most contemporary usage relies on a broad definition of culture, following the contributions of Raymond Williams, Stuart Hall, Clifford Geertz and others to whom culture denotes the practices and meanings of social life. Consumer culture refers to practices, **beliefs** and activities that are oriented to the marketing, purchase and use of commodities. ('Commodities' are goods and services bought and sold on a market for final use by consumers.) In the West, when consumer culture has come to dominate, the acquisition and use of commodities has become key in the structuring and reproduction of social life and the production of meaning. The construction of personal identity, values, daily life practices and the reproduction of gender, race and social class all develop under the sway of consumer culture.

In the last twenty-five years the literature on consumer culture has become vast. Historians have studied the rise of 'consumer society' in early modern Europe and the eventual triumph of mass consumption. Anthropologists have taken account of the globalization of consumer culture, and its articulation with local cultures. In cultural studies, consumer culture has been a central preoccupation. Sociologists have analysed narcissism, celebrity, tourism, shopping and food, among other consumer topics.

For much of the twentieth century, sociological thinking about consumer culture was heavily influenced by Thorstein **Veblen**. Veblen focused on conspicuous **consumption** of a consensus set of status goods and a trickle-down theory of consumer culture, in which innovations were made by the wealthy and gradually made their way to lower income groups. In the 1970s, Pierre **Bourdieu** published *Distinction*, an influential account of how taste in consumer goods and culture is produced by class background and education, and how taste itself is central to the reproduction of **class** inequality. Soon after the publication of *Distinction*, however, this tradition came under attack. There has been considerable debate about the relevance of Bourdieu's approach to the United States by scholars who argued that class patterning was weak on account of a large middle class with common consumption patterns. Georg Simmel's work on fashion and money has also been important, and the latter underlies much work in the sociology of fashion (see **fashion, sociology of**).

Alternatives to class and status-based approaches came from post-structuralism and postmodernism, in particular the work of Jean Baudrillard, who put forward the view that consumer society is increasingly dominated by images and, relying on semiotic theory, of signs. Baudrillard argued that consumer culture has reached the era of 'simulation', in which reality comes to be constructed through media images, and goods become valuable not for their material realities, but for their meanings as signs. Baudrillard's view is that electronic media, **advertising**, fashion and culture industries drive contemporary consumer culture. Sociologists Mike Featherstone, George Ritzer and others have argued that this postmodern turn has resulted in the aestheticization of everyday life and a re-enchantment of consumers' experience through theme parks, entertainment and tourism. A related theme is that 'consumption' has come to dominate 'production', and a rejection of Marxism and other productivist approaches which relegated consumption to a minor role.

The literature on consumer culture has been preoccupied with the question of consumer agency. Classical liberal and neoclassical economic theory assumed that consumers are sovereign and drive market trends. Critics of consumer culture have argued otherwise. For example, the influential 1944 article by Frankfurt School members Theodor Adorno and Max Horkheimer took the view that the culture industries are able to 'dissect', 'manipulate' and dominate consumers, who retain little independence. Later works by critics of consumer culture such as John Kenneth Galbraith, Vance Packard and Betty Friedan made similar arguments. These views are now typically derided as elitist and inaccurate, because consumers are thought to have far more capacity for independent and creative approaches to consuming. Interestingly, postmodern treatments of consumer agency are split on these issues, and encompass those which see the consumer as dominated by media as well as those which emphasize her sovereignty and use of products to create identity and meaning. However, rather than seeing these issues in a purely theoretical light, as the literature has tended to do, Douglas Holt (2002) reminds us that the consumer critics need to be interpreted in their historical context. At the time they wrote, advertisers and marketers possessed an enormous cultural authority which has been eroded over time. As that authority declined, marketers have been forced to identify and validate reigning consumer values, in an ongoing, and in Holt's view, dialectic relationship.

Studies of subcultures, especially youth subcultures have also been a theoretically productive area, following the intellectual lead of Stuart Hall, Dick Hebdige, Paul Willis and Angela McRobbie, the so-called Birmingham School. These empirical studies of British youth rejected earlier Marxist views of consumption, and highlighted the ways in which goods and cultural forms created community and resistance to the dominant consumer culture. Maffesoli's work on community and what he called neo-tribalism has also been influential. Finally, sociologists have contributed to the thriving debate on the expansion of western consumer culture around the world – in particular, on its effects on local cultures and cultural diversity, on the forces which are causing this expansion, and on its impacts on local populations.

Looking forward, there is reason to be optimistic about the emergence of the field from the theoretical straitjackets of Marx and Veblen especially, and the growth of empirical studies of consumers. The waning influence of postmodern consumer accounts, which are theoretically one-dimensional and not empirically grounded, is also welcome. However, the study of consumer culture within sociology currently lacks a subdisciplinary home, and sits awkwardly between economic sociology and the sociology of culture. Resolving that awkwardness is an urgent task.

References and further reading

Holt, Douglas B. (2002) 'Why Do Brands Cause Trouble? A Dialectical Theory of Consumer Culture and Branding', *Journal of Consumer Research*, 29(1): 70–90.
Miller, Daniel (1995) *Acknowledging Consumption: A Review of New Studies*, London: Routledge.
Slater, Don (1997) *Consumer Culture and Modernity*, London: Polity Press.

JULIET SCHOR

CONSUMPTION

Consumption is the economic activity that depends most on social and cultural context and least on either formal rationality or complex technology. Although consumption initially referred to the use, and even the using up, of goods, its meaning expanded with the historical development of the hallmarks of modernity – the autonomy of the individual self, the programmatic responsiveness of the state to citizens' demands for welfare services, and both state and market acting as coordinators linking productive capacity to demand. In early modern times, before factories made mass production possible, consumption was assumed to respond directly to basic human needs, many of which – for food, clothing and shelter – were fulfilled at home by unpaid domestic labour. From the mid nineteenth century, however, industrialization in Europe and North America created unprecedented numbers and varieties of new products for sale in standardized forms. More sophisticated needs were fulfilled by complex, interrelated networks of production, transportation and information, which were located outside the home, often quite far away. Within a few decades, a major portion of consumption shifted from basic needs to socialized wants, with the building of an institutional field consisting

of big stores, especially in cities, corporate brands and an information infrastructure of **advertising**, illustrated magazines, market research and consumer guides. By the mid twentieth century, mass consumption of both goods and services had so thoroughly permeated the industrialized regions of the world that social critics termed these countries a consumer society. From that point, consumption was no longer only thought of as an indicator of a satisfactory standard of living. It became, paradoxically, both a creative expression of individual identity and a driving force towards a standardized, global culture.

Despite this schematic overview, it is not easy to date the origins of consumer society. Historians speak of a consumer revolution in England as early as the eighteenth century, when entrepreneurs such as the northern factory-owner Josiah Wedgwood used royal patronage, elegant London showrooms and market segmentation to develop his potteries into one of the most successful (and enduring) consumer products industries of all time. Also in the eighteenth century, North American British colonists relied on extensive credit and trading networks to expand their consumption of manufactured goods, mainly imported from England. But a mental readiness for consumption, as well as a middle class with the financial ability to purchase attractive goods, is also related to the technical ability to produce them. Changes in both printing technology and the cotton trade in fifteenth- and sixteenth-century England induced a passion for pictorial prints and a fashion for printed calicoes – suggesting that we trace the origins of consumer society to this time. Certainly, consumption becomes more intense, and more widespread, with the use of mass production technologies, money and credit, and cultural expectations of self-expression. Although consumers' activities – such as going shopping at the mall – retain many of their early social functions as collective rituals, they show the influence of larger institutional fields and markets.

Consumption spaces and modern institutional systems

Consumption is rooted as much in modern institutional systems, especially the economy and the state, as in individual human desires. Whether goods and services are provided by public subsidies or acquired privately in the market, their availability and distribution are to some degree determined by macroeconomic policy, which in turn reflects underlying power relations among groups of capitalists, labour and the state, and specific resolutions of **conflicts** over income, work and political power. The growth of mass consumption also depends on the buildup of productive capacity in basic industries as well as in those that create consumer goods, with the synergies of production and consumption expressed paradigmatically in early twentieth-century 'Fordism' (an adaptation of Antonio Gramsci's 'Americanism'). In this market-based system of social regulation, assembly-line production makes available many low-price consumer goods, such as Henry Ford's Model T car, which workers are able to save up for, and buy, because their corporate employers pay decent wages. But the apparent democracy of consumption, as well as the sanctification of wants over needs, breaks with previous culture and ideology – including most organized religion. New ideas and beliefs gradually justify 'getting and spending' for members of every social class.

Consumption requires, and fuels, a more intensive integration of markets. Since the late nineteenth century, national and local coalitions of industry, banking and political leaders in most regions of the world have encouraged men and women to buy goods, while magazines, supplemented by growing numbers of experts in advertising, marketing and public relations, present seductive images of, and information about, new products. Anticipatory socialization piques curiosity and stimulates the desire to try new things; family members, co-workers and friends establish the social nexus in which products are tried, discussed and compared. All this would not be possible without the periodic development of new distribution channels, from stores and roads to air freight and the Internet. In the 1870s, three new types of consumption space – the department store, five-and-dime store and mail order catalogue – set a model of quasi-industrial processing of information about consumer demand. Each established a paradigmatic social space in which consumer products were abundant, accessible and, for the most part, affordable. Supplemented by individual pedlars, corner stores and door-to-door salespeople, these spaces trained people in the totalizing experience of shopping. Men and women began to see themselves in the social role of consumers.

The choice of Keynesian macroeconomic policy in the United States, during the Great Depression, institutionalized the importance of consumption in maintaining economic growth. While the jobs policies of the New Deal tried to renew Americans' buying power, new governmental agencies represented consumers' interests at the bargaining table and extended federal regulation of product quality and prices. Partly these changes reflected government's willingness to support capitalism by managing demand. But they also responded to years of activism by housewives who wanted merchants to charge fair prices, to African-American boycotts of neighbourhood stores that refused to hire them, and to consumer economists and advocates who rejected the power of manufacturers and big stores to set prices and wages. Consumption offers not just a chance to buy, then, but also represents an opportunity for consumers' social activism.

Most attention nonetheless focuses on consumers' buying power. The 'reconversion' of the American economy after World War II offers the largest historical example of how states and markets stimulate consumption on a massive scale. Through preferential lending policies which favoured military veterans, especially white men, the federal government subsidized college tuitions, mortgages to buy homes and farms, and business start-ups – all of which increased disposable income and fostered a material base for upward social mobility. Big programmes of housing and highway construction, relying on partnerships between government and private developers, spread ownership of cars and homes to a growing middle class and more prosperous, unionized factory workers. Home ownership in turn stimulated the purchase of household appliances and furniture and also – with a generational turn to starting a family – TVs, clothing and toys. Post-war consumption fed the 'American dream': the presidential promise to put 'a chicken in every pot' during the Great Depression expanded to cover 'the little house with the white picket fence' and the two-car garage. Yet the general impression of achieving prosperity through mass consumption hid major social problems: the state's overwhelming support of private-sector providers, especially in the corporate sector, who had little interest in social welfare; a mainstream culture that sanctified the division of labour between women as consumers and men as producers, which put pressure on women to remain out of the job market, at home; diversion of investment from cities to suburbs; exclusion of ethnic minorities from consumption of suburban amenities; and low-income families' continued inability to own the mid twentieth-century necessities: a house and car.

Although problems of access to consumer goods remained acute among social classes and racial and ethnic groups, a specific set of problems expressed the need of all consumers for protection against the fraudulent practices or defective products of producers. Just as the state gradually assumed responsibility to support demand for consumer goods, so state agencies, from law courts to new regulatory organizations, enforced consumers' rights. They were pressed to do so by consumer organizations. During the early 1900s, such organizations had focused on both work conditions of those who produced consumer goods and the qualities of goods themselves; especially in northern England, these groups sometimes formed consumers' cooperatives. By the 1960s, however, new consumer advocacy groups confronted large manufacturers with evidence of false claims and dangerous products; they no longer protested on behalf of a company's workers, but on behalf of those who bought and used the products. Consumer organizations often made demands for new kinds of products, like organically grown food and fuel-saving cars, that would be safer for humans and also reduce damage to the natural environment. By opposing businesses' claims, urging the state to act, and setting out a moral agenda, consumer advocates helped to form a public consciousness around consumption, once again, as a space of social action.

If department stores represented key consumption spaces of the late nineteenth century, whose means of enchanting consumers included plate-glass windows, electric and neon lights, and lavish displays of abundant and exotic wares, shopping malls mobilized consumers' attention after World War II. The malls' plate-glass windows, artificial air and light, and hermetically enclosed circuit between anchor stores, speciality shops, food court and cinemas placed shoppers in 'neon cages'. This type of environment had developed gradually since the 1840s, when enclosed shopping galleries or 'arcades' began to mesmerize consumers in European and American cities with displays of luxury goods and imports. Their shop windows created the experience of consumption spaces as places of dreams, connecting the gaze of the mobile shopper with endless opportunities for fantasy, and channelling the desire to be a better, richer or more attractive person into the urge to buy specific commodities. Although men as well as women frequented the arcades, by the late nineteenth century astute department-store owners specifically targeted women shoppers. Shopping offered middle-class women a public space where they could legitimately appear unescorted, and women took advantage of the tearooms and other amenities department stores provided to make excursions into the public sphere. As both shoppers and sales clerks, women played a key role in making consumption a modern public sphere parallel to male-dominated production. This feminized public sphere became prominent in the residential suburbs after World War II without making a connection between shopping and social activism.

Consumption spaces do influence forms of sociality. Marketplaces in seventeenth-century England and eighteenth-century France – and public markets in nineteenth-century America – were raucous carnivals in which upper and lower classes mingled and social roles were not firmly fixed; they were sites for working out norms of early capitalist exchange as well as of liberal democracy. These forms of sociality changed with wider distribution networks and new technologies. In the twentieth century, cinemas and supermarkets helped to create a modern, mobile public, whose fleeting gaze sifts through goods as well as experiences ('Just browsing'). At the same time, shoppers who push their carts through the aisles of large, self-service stores – side-by-side and yet completely alone – develop a sense of 'autonomous presence' rather than of collectivity ('Bowling alone'). This kind of individualism is heightened by regional shopping malls and discount stores that are located at increasing distances from the home and require travel alone, or with the family, by

automobile. Since the 1990s, moreover, **electronic commerce** has intensified the abstraction of selecting goods without social interaction. Like fashion magazines and mail order catalogues, retail websites lay out a flat visual display of images and texts – a semiotics of consumption for an automated culture.

Over time, the building of consumption spaces in cities and suburbs creates new grids of profit and desire. Malls offer opportunities for shopping where native grasses and farms once stood. Fast food restaurants and theme parks connect the satisfaction of basic needs to ever rationalizing, continually expanding corporate providers. And discount chains, designer boutiques and branded stores enable us to move, on a daily basis, through our dreams. Discount stores bring us together in a dream of social equality. Designer boutiques respond to our dream of an ever-improving self. Branded stores encourage us to dream that buying a specific label leads to upward social mobility. At least in marketing theory, the aura of a Niketown or Ralph Lauren store – or the low prices of a Wal-Mart – overcomes consumers' anxieties about choice, the economy and the self.

The choosing self

Choice is emblematic of the individual's responsibility in consumer society. A growing availability of goods, and a wider variety of styles, models and labels, offers a huge range of self-expression through commodities – but consumers bear responsibility for making the right choices. When traditional bonds, such as family, religion, social class and community, weaken, men and women turn to commodities to express both their individuality and new collective identities. Since modern society offers the opportunity to develop multiple identities, commodities often become useful, if temporary, vehicles of connecting to larger social groups. Consumption then treats products as signs of group identity – an implicit but forceful method of imposing both difference and conformity, especially among young consumers.

If traditional authorities no longer set norms of consumption, consumers rely on lessons and rules promulgated by an increasing array of experts, models and honest brokers. Advertising is the oldest and broadest means of disseminating new rules of consumption. Exploiting, and developing, new sites and media for reaching consumers, advertisements provide lessons in words and images so consumers will learn how using commodities will help to construct a better self. Yet advertisements don't reduce consumers' anxiety; they focus on, and emphasize, likely sources of personal embarrassment – such as odour, fat, imperfect teeth and dressing out of fashion. Ads have always targeted the bodily anxieties of women, especially, in order to promote products of the clothing, cosmetics and fitness industries. But, although investment in appearance is usually associated with women, fashion and grooming advertisements also reach out to men. The recent introduction of new products such as men's fragrances and new media such as men's fashion magazines aim to expand consumption for self-improvement regardless of gender.

The choice of consumer goods also reflects the efforts of honest brokers who produce critiques of products and services. Connected with neither producers nor consumers, but representing a disinterested midpoint between them, honest brokers communicate objective norms for evaluating commodities in their own, subjective voice. Beginning in the 1920s in England, with reviews of classical music recordings in *Gramophone* magazine, and continuing with the founding of *Consumer Reports* in the 1930s in the United States, product reviews have formed a large literature of consumption, both stimulating interest in commodities in general and reducing consumers' anxiety about making the wrong choice. They are an important counterweight to advertising because they are assumed to rest on greater expertise and more willingness to take risks than an ordinary consumer can muster. Consumers **trust** reviewers because they believe in both their honesty and their ability to represent the consumers' concerns. Not only must reviewers appear to be independent of stores and manufacturers, their voice must also resonate with that of their reader (see **reputation**).

Regardless of who influences consumer choice, the selection of specific goods and services creates a sense of coherence and control in a fragmented social world. When consumers choose a certain movie or car, they achieve a desirable aesthetic unity in their lives. By choosing, they also assemble the signs of social solidarity – with a status group, an ethnic community or an inchoate public of likeminded consumers. These patterns of choice are amalgamated in the popular concepts of 'taste' and 'life style', which are systems of social and cultural practices through which individuals classify themselves by their **classification** of consumer goods. Examined by the French sociologist Pierre **Bourdieu**, taste is less a matter of individual choice than a collective expression of exclusive status or distinction. Knowing the status codes shows consumers' ability to discern good taste from bad – a key to association with the 'right' people. Although taste may be learned from advertisements and magazines, it is deeply rooted in relative access to economic, social and cultural capital and can only be demonstrated by the power to buy commodities.

The autonomy of the choosing self is superficial. Consumer society tethers individuals to a treadmill of continual consumption, which pushes people to express individuality but makes it less feasible for them to do so. Moreover, when former taboos against advertising certain products, like prescription drugs, either fall by the wayside or are eliminated by the state, consumers take on new responsibilities for choice when they may not be equipped to do so. Even worse, the idea of consumer choice has been taken as a model by neo-liberal societies, with political and social equality defined in terms of the right to select a candidate, policy or public or private provider without attention to their substantive rationality. This places responsibility for achieving social welfare on the shoulders of individual consumers rather than on the state. It also encourages men and women to displace their hopes for democracy, equality or upward social mobility into consumption choices.

Consumption as a moral issue

Consumption often tends to be associated with hedonism, with self-gratification interpreted as a weakening of moral fibre rather than a normal response to pervasive stimuli. Historically, tension between the assumed hedonism of the consumer and the assumed asceticism of the producer is endemic in much religious thought. But this tension is exaggerated during social campaigns for economic expansion, when leaders stress the need for labour discipline and capital accumulation. These issues were resolved in capitalist economies in the early 1900s by the growth of wages and leisure time and by easy access to consumer credit. Most socialist states did not address them until abandoning a command economy and introducing market mechanisms, in the 1990s. In all market societies, however, growth in consumption leads to sharp increases in individual and household debt and, although the overall standard of living may improve, to marked increases in social inequality. Despite political leaders' continued commitment to consumption, critics still believe that hedonistic consumers work less and lose their attachment to core social and cultural values – whether they are the

values of **capitalism**, **solidarity** or self-sacrifice for a common cause.

Periodically critics attack consumers who 'consume too much', During the consumer boom of the 1950s and 1960s, liberal critics invoked Thorstein **Veblen**'s critique of the waste economy and status consumption. In the latter 1960s, conservative critics accused the counterculture of unwillingness to defer gratification, on the one hand, while consuming forbidden drugs, on the other. During the 1990s, new consumer movements for 'slow food' and more modest levels of consumption emerged in North America and Europe; political leaders in Singapore and China criticized over-consumption as 'western' without severely limiting the licensing of multinational fast food franchises, discount superstores and blue jeans manufacturers.

Global economic and cultural integration depends on circuits, or commodity chains, of both production and consumption. When they generate social movements against **sweatshop labour**, environmentally harmful products and unfair conditions of trade, they show that consumption – no less than production – shapes a viable social morality.

Transitions to consumer society

Consumer society is a distinctive product of modernity – yet the timing of its development, and its social, cultural and economic forms, are not the same in all societies. It may be best to think of consumer society as being produced by coordinated shifts in social practices and mentality, which free the imagination, create new spaces of leisure and pleasure, and inspire individuals to seek novelty in new possessions. Almost all the institutions of consumption that we see around us today – including large stores, a huge advertising apparatus and integrated, but highly competitive, global markets for commodities – fit within this general frame. Regardless of when the transition to a full-fledged consumer society occurs, however, it suggests a loosening of state, religious or other normative controls over most material means of expression. It also corresponds to a concentration of markets and media in urban centres and a lot more disposable income in everybody's – or almost everybody's – hands. The satisfaction of a widespread demand for goods encourages the growth, first, of crafts and, then, of industrial production, which stimulates a take-off into a larger, more complex economy. With the efforts of a growing and global media infrastructure, the cultural rituals and expectations of mass consumption result in a world-wide consumer society.

References and further reading

Baudrillard, Jean (1998) *The Consumer Society (La societe de consommation)*, London and Thousand Oaks CA: Sage.

Bourdieu, Pierre (1984) *Distinction: A Social Critique of the Judgement of Taste (La distinction: Critique social du jugement)*, Cambridge, MA: Harvard University Press.

Cohen, Lizabeth (2003) *A Consumers' Republic: The Politics of Mass Consumption in Post-war America*, New York: Knopf.

Langman, Lauren (1992) 'Neon Cages: Shopping for Subjectivity', in Rob Shields (ed.), *Lifestyle Shopping: The Subject of Consumption*, London, Routledge, pp. 40–82.

Slater, Don (1997) *Consumer Culture and Modernity*, Cambridge: Polity.

Zukin, Sharon (2004) *Point of Purchase: How Shopping Changed American Culture*, New York: Routledge.

SHARON ZUKIN

CONSUMPTION MARKETS

See: consumption

CONTRACT

A contract is an agreement to exchange goods or services at some point in the future. Given a known probability distribution over all future states of the world, a contract could specify what each party would do under every possible condition. In most real situations, however, such knowledge is unattainable. For example, neither a worker nor an employer can anticipate all the problems that might come up on the job. Hence, it will be necessary to leave some issues open for future negotiation and to allow each party to make some decisions at their own discretion. Self-interested actors will engage in what Oliver Williamson calls 'opportunism': attempts to exploit their autonomy and private knowledge to their own benefit. The problem is the design of contracts to provide **incentives** which align the interests of the parties. A simple case would be when a contract includes penalties for non-fulfilment. Thus, the theory of contracts is closely related to principal-agent theory (see **principal and agent**).

In any given situation, many different contractual arrangements are possible. For example, a land-owner could hire farm workers, lease the land at a fixed rent, or lease it in return for a share of the crops. Moreover, many subtypes would be possible within each of these general categories. Each type of contract would have different implications for production and the distribution of risk. For example, the farmer has a stronger incentive to increase production under a fixed rent than under sharecropping. However, a fixed rent would mean that the farmer assumed all of the risk. Hence, risk-averse farmers might prefer sharecropping to a fixed rent. Alternatively, they might buy insurance from a third party. If individual farmers and landlords differ in their degree of risk aversion, some mix of different types of contracts might be found. The feasibility of a given contract also depends on other institutional conditions, such as the availability of insurance against the relevant risks or the extent to which it can be enforced by law.

There is a substantial theoretical literature in economics on the optimal design of contracts. Empirical studies, however, have found that actual contracts are simpler and less diverse than would be expected given theoretical considerations. Some contracts that would be attractive in principle are rarely or never found in practice, and often a standard form is dominant even when the diversity among individuals would be expected to produce a wide variety of contracts.

Another strand of the literature focuses on systems of governance rather than explicit contracts. This approach starts from the assumption that a comprehensive and unambiguous contract is impractical. As a substitute, the parties develop rules and customs to govern their interactions. Although they will try to interpret the rules to their own advantage, the need to consider future interactions will help to restrain opportunism. The best-known example of this approach is Williamson's transactions cost analysis (see **transaction cost economics**). More formal models of this kind can be found in the literature on 'implicit' and 'incomplete' contracts. One of the major objectives of this literature is to explain variation in institutional forms. Williamson, for example, argues that differences in the organization of firms can be explained by the nature of transactions costs. In fact, he argues that the very existence of firms can be attributed to transactions costs: since it would be costly to negotiate prices and conditions for every exchange, it is more efficient to give one party (the employer) the authority to direct the actions of the other (the employee).

One common feature of all economic approaches is that efficiency considerations are held to be the major determinant of contractual form. These approaches recognize the existence of differences of interest, but hold that they can be separated from efficiency issues. That is, both sides benefit from adopting the contractual arrangement that maximizes productivity. Given this arrangement, they will bargain over the distribution of the product, and power will be an important influence at this stage. The

weaker party may be able to capture only a small fraction of the gains from adopting the most efficient organization, but will still be better off than it would be under a less efficient alternative. In contrast, many sociological accounts hold that contractual relationships reflect power differences, and that a stronger party can impose unfavourable conditions on a weaker one.

Economic approaches provide an important service by observing that power and efficiency considerations may be separable. There are, however, some alternatives to efficiency-based explanations of contractual arrangements. One possibility is that contracts may be designed to reduce the potential for future shifts in power. This issue is particularly relevant to the employment relationship, since employers may attempt to reduce the chance that workers will organize in the future. The form of organization that minimizes the chance of successful organization is not necessarily the same as the form that maximizes efficiency. Another possibility is that contractual arrangements are shaped by prevailing ideas about fairness and authority. Despite their plausibility, such accounts have had difficulty in explaining why some cultural patterns persist, while others change dramatically over short periods of time. Recent work on the development and maintenance of conventions may help to shed light on this point.

With the exception of Williamson's work, the literature on contracts is not well known among sociologists. However, this work seems to be moving in an empirical direction and to be taking factors such as customs and norms more seriously. Hence, it is potentially of considerable interest to sociologists.

References and further reading

Chiappori, Pierre Andre and Salanie, Bernard (2003) 'Testing Contract Theory: A Survey of Some Recent Work', in Mathias Dewatripont, Lars Peter Hansen and Stephen J. Turnovsky (eds), *Advances in Economics and*

Econometrics, vol. 1, Cambridge: Cambridge University Press, pp. 115–49.

Williamson, Oliver (1986) *The Economic Institutions of Capitalism*, New York: Free Press.

Young, H. Peyton and Burke, Mary A. (2001) 'Competition and Custom in Economic Contracts: A Case Study of Illinois Agriculture', *American Economic Review*, 91: 555–73.

DAVID WEAKLIEM

CONTROL

The concept of control is central for the social sciences but it is used with a variety of different meanings. In general, control can be defined as a process where first, preferred states of affairs or goals are specified; second, existing structures and processes are monitored and evaluated according to these predetermined criteria; and third, adjusted, if necessary (Janowitz 1975: 85). In early American sociology the concept referred to the macrosociological self-regulation of society according to desired principles and values. Therefore, social control was central for the explanation of social order and collective social behaviour, whereas it was assumed that the individual utilitarian calculus is not sufficient to explain these phenomena. This usage of the concept of social control fits in rather nicely with the basic idea of a large part of the new sociology of economics, to show the social, political and cultural presuppositions of functioning markets and rational economic behaviour.

In the history of sociological thinking the meaning of control has shifted from this idea of societal self-regulation to a conception focusing more on power, enforcement of interests and the regulation of behaviour defined as deviant according to the preferred goals. Especially in social relations, institutions and networks that combine actors with opposing goals, powerful actors will regularly resort to strategies of control to enforce their interests. Especially three discussions in the sociology of economics

are important with respect to this facet of the concept of control:

1. Since the publication of Berle and Means' study *The Modern Corporation and Private Property* (1932) it is assumed that owner control of the modern corporation has given way to management control. The underlying assumption is that shareholding is widely dispersed so that the huge number of scattered owners are not able to enforce their interests and control the actual determination of company policies which now falls to the management. However, this idea has to be qualified in several ways: first, the dispersion of share ownership differs substantially between Anglo-Saxon and continental European countries, where family ownership and ownership concentration is much more pervasive (Windolf 2002). Second, even in countries with a widespread dispersion of ownership the largest shareholders are often able to enforce a form of minority control that does not allow a domination of the day-to-day working of the organization but of its general policies. Third, especially in the Anglo-Saxon countries there has been an reclaiming of authority by shareholders since the 1980s. This development was preceded in the 1970s by the normative claims of agency theory, that managers and corporations should obey the principles of shareholder value. Alongside this ideological preparation there were mainly two causes for the reclaiming of control by owners: first, the growing importance and power of institutional investors, and second, the increase of a market for corporate control characterized by waves of mergers, acquisitions and, above all, hostile takeovers. Both developments

have the effect of aligning management policies more strongly with shareholder interests.

2. Related to the discussion about the separation of ownership and control is the research on the external control of corporations and especially the concept of bank control. This notion was introduced by the Austrian economist Rudolf Hilferding (see **Austrian economics**) and means that in a strongly organized economy of interlocked big corporations the **banks** as providers of investment capital take up the commanding heights. In fact, banks have a central position in the networks of **interlocking directorates** and of capital shareholding. But whereas in the continental European countries the relationships of interlocking directorates and ownership often reinforce each other so that bank control in a meaningful sense is possible, investment banks in the Anglo-Saxon countries hold shares of a vast number of corporations on whose boards they are usually not represented. Therefore, bank control of the day-to-day operations of corporations is clearly impossible. However, given their concentrated control over investment capital, financial institutions are still able to structure economic decisions and even to intervene into **corporate governance** in situations of crisis, so that Mintz and Schwartz still speak of a financial hegemony in contemporary capitalist economies in their book *The Power Structure of American Business* (1985). In the research on the separation of ownership and control as well as on bank control, there should be a stronger focus on the economic consequences of structural linkages between shareholders, managers and banks, especially by comparative case studies on actual conflicts of interests and their outcomes to show the working of the process of economic control.

3. In capitalist economies business managers face the challenge of extracting work effort from their employees to keep the organization running and profitable. Therefore, control of the workforce is an essential management task, due to the conflicting interests of management and workforce (see **organization theory**). Especially Edwards (1979) has shown that modes of control in capitalist business organizations have historically evolved through the interplay of worker resistance, changing socio-economic conditions and management strategies from more direct forms of personal control to institutionalized forms of bureaucratic control relying on impersonal rules and regulations. The development of new forms of information technology, the incorporation of the workforce (teamwork, total quality management) and finally the manipulation of cultural symbols as a basis for moral discipline for some researchers seems to herald a new era of complete control. However, past experiences with then up-to-date management strategies show that even today empirical studies of organizational control should keep an eye on the strategies of employees to deal with and to resist new techniques of control.

See also: agency theory; conflict; corporate governance; network analysis; principal and agent.

References and further reading

Berle, A. and Means, G. (1932) *The Modern Corporation and Private Property*, New York: Macmillan.

Edwards, Richard (1979) *Contested Terrain. The Transformation of the Workplace in the Twentieth Century*, New York: Basic Books.

Janowitz, Morris (1975) 'Sociological Theory and Social Control', *American Journal of Sociology*, 81: 82–108.

Mintz, B. and Schwartz, M. (1985) *The Power Structure of American Business*, Chicago: University of Chicago Press.

Windolf, Paul (2002) *Corporate Networks in Europe and the United States*, New York: Oxford University Press.

JÖRG RÖSSEL

CONVENTION SCHOOL

Specifications and differences

Considering that economic and social worlds are made up of a plurality of modes of coordination, the research programme of the Convention School (CS) concentrates on the conventional forms which support the coordination of action (Dupuy *et al.* 1989).

It first pays attention to the plurality of the most legitimate constitutive conventions – market competition being only one among others – with the aim of decomposing organizations. It also explores a second type of conventions which differ according to their scope. These types offer a range of conventional formats of action that support coordination. They range from publicized to localized and personalized formats. Rather than stressing the tensions between social groups or strategic individuals, the Convention School takes into consideration the tensions between the different modes of coordination. This leads to unorthodox views on politics.

The programmatic of the Convention School differs from two already existing and contrasting views on coordination. The first was mainly developed in sociology and assumes that powerful collective forces determine coordination, either externally through fixed constraints, or internally through stable dispositions. The second view is more favoured by economists and opposes the collectivist thrust of the first approach. Building on Hume's legacy, it aims at reducing conventions to individual preferences, as exemplified by David Lewis' philosophical study of conventions. This view is in line with methodological individualism but rests on a disputed notion of 'common knowledge', defined as an infinite regress of reciprocal expectations (Dupuy in Dupuy *et al.* 1989). Contrary to the first view, the Convention School is primarily concerned with the uncertain, pluralist and dynamic production of coordination. From the second view it differs by paying much attention to the common forms of cognition and evaluation which support conventions of coordination and cannot be reduced to individual preferences.

Within a context of pervasive uncertainty with respect to the interpretation of actions and expectation of actors, conventions merely channel uncertainty through a conventional formatting of events. The idea is that the kind of cognitive relevance which channels uncertainty is specified by a specific form of evaluation. When persons grasp events as human actions in the perspective of coordination, they relate behaviours to some relevant good, the format of the good being highly variable. Constitutive conventions of great legitimacy involve forms of evaluation which rely on grammars of the public or of the common good.

Instead of downplaying **value**s to individual tastes or preferences, the Convention School takes side with political philosophy and its theories of justice, fairness and the common good. Contrary to these theories, however, the Convention School considers the sense of injustice as located in situations and in action. It thus investigates lower-level conventions which rest on more limited formats of the good, as do rule-like guidelines for standard actions. Interest is an example of a good with restricted scope, which still allows relatively distant coordination. By contrast, local and personal conveniences demand closer relationships i.e. familiar use. They govern close coordination which is not rule-governed.

When they are properly formatted, persons and things qualify for a certain mode of coordination. Whereas information economics states that unequal or asymmetric information about the quality of goods is the factor which jeopardizes competitive markets, the Convention School acknowledges the plurality of conventional qualifications of people and things and offers a more balanced and complex view on the composition of markets, firms and other organizational devices. In order to qualify for market competition, an object or a person's conventional quality differs from the standardized competence supporting the industrial convention of coordination, from the dedicated format which upholds **trust** coordination and is involved in the **informal economy**, and from the concern for **solidarity** and inequality in the economy which sustains the civic convention of coordination and is found in work ethics, **altruism** and egalitarianism.

The previous distinctions indicate the realist thrust of the Convention School, in the sense that the material arrangement of qualified objects makes an important contribution to coordination. The qualification which upholds anticipation is neither subjective nor idealist. It is put to the test of effective coordination, and leads to the dynamics of critical revision, innovation and creativity. Although cognition and evaluation are key issues for the Convention School, conventional forms differ from collective representations – or framing – since they rely on the actual shaping of the material environment of action. In contrast to many sociologists who rely on an over-socialized and over-symbolized reality, or to economists who naturalize goods, the Convention School investigates the various ways agents engage in the material environment, and display a sense of relevant reality which depends on the convention of coordination. The shape of marketable commodities, or that of efficient technologies, are different from the shape of objects formatted as signs. These objects support, on the ground of their conspicuity, a third convention of coordination based on signalling and the worth of common opinion. This last shaping of objects plays a significant role in the economy, in branding and corporate images, fashion, conspicuous **consumption** and **speculation**.

Cross-fertilization between sociology, economics and politics

In the same way as American Institutionalism was linked to philosophical and sociological **pragmatism**, the Convention School has developed from intense and enduring interaction between economists and sociologists who share a common concern in returning to the core issues of both disciplines, such as coordination, action, cognition and evaluation (Salais and Thévenot 1986). They do not aim at reducing all human interactions to an extended system of market coordination, nor at reducing the specificity of market exchange and industrial **production** to other social ties. The resulting research programme looks for possibilities of integration rather than mutual critical reduction (Dupuy et al. 1989; Orléan 1994).

On the sociological side, there is a long tradition of research on cognitive forms which contribute to the coordination of social action and produce understanding without directly determining collective behaviours. An influential lineage begins with the views of **Durkheim** and of **Mauss** on classifications, and subsequent research by Mary Douglas, Pierre **Bourdieu** and Luc Boltanski. Following studies on statistical categories by Desrosières, Salais and Thévenot, a further step led Boltanski and Thévenot to relating categorization to evaluation and to its material support. Conventional forms and cognitive formats which sustain economic and social coordination are supported by equipment which results from various types of 'investments in forms'. Such orientations are convergent with the cognitive turn which new institutionalism took for granted when insisting on classifications, representations, scripts and schemas. However, this last trend of research is more inclined to oppose, rather than to relate, cognition and evaluation. Regarding legitimate evaluation, **Weber**'s legitimate orders of domination offer a seminal answer, although purely relativist.

On the economists' side, limited cognition became more recently a debated issue and drew attention on modes of transaction which depart from market exchange. **Transaction cost economics** singles out different types of transactions, while maintaining the doubtful general equivalence of cost which allows for the agent's optimal choice of a particular transaction mode. **Agency theory** concentrates on the optimal design of contracts in order to cope with **asymmetrical information**, but still assumes a common format of information and unbounded capacities to optimize the contract ex ante, while the concept of bounded rationality is more open to the various limitations of human cognition. By differentiating **risk and uncertainty** Frank Knight drew attention on the distinction between radical uncertainty and measurable probability, and **Keynes**' research on probability pointed to the unequal relevance and weight of probable arguments depending on orders of similarity. The Convention School paid much attention to the necessity that agents tame radical uncertainty with the help of conventional formats of information on which they rely in their disputes. Conventions of quality are thus needed to coordinate actions through goods (Eymard-Duvernay in Dupuy *et al.* 1989, and in Orléan 1994) and to account for the variety of forms of evaluation on **labour markets**. In the case of **financial markets**, Keynes had pointed to the role played by the convention on the average opinion about the present state of the economy (Orléan in Dupuy *et al.* 1989, and in Orléan 1994).

Analytical tools and domains of research

The exploration of a plurality of legitimate conventions of coordination extends Albert **Hirschman**'s analysis of shifting involvement, since each of them implies a specific kind of commitment and expression of disagreement. A first line of Convention School research related them to systematic constructions which philosophers modelled as political grammars that govern action in reference to the common good. Each constitutive convention specifies the ways people and things qualify for coordination as worthy, according to different specification of the common good: market competition, industrial efficiency, public opinion, trust and **reputation** based on customs and traditions, civic solidarity and equality, creative inspiration (Boltanski and Thévenot 1991). But each qualification downplays the other and raises critical tensions with it. All of them satisfy a set of common requirements which capture the grounding of critiques and justifications on an everyday sense of justice, and can be paralleled to Rawls' second principle of justice, or Walzer's notion, taken from Pascal, of the tyrannical overlapping of one sphere of justice by another. This line of research penetrates **political economy**, **moral economy** and the relation between **democracy and economy**. It is not limited to **deliberation** but also pays much attention to the way material environments contribute to the coordination of action, and allows 'compromise' and the building of hybrids between conflicting worlds. It offers a dynamic picture of the composition of markets, organizations, institutions, and such transversal coordination devices as participative forums, intermediary institutions, standardization committees or authorities of regulation.

113

Differentiating conventions of coordination contributes to **organization theory** and to the analysis of the firm by contrasting forms of authority and hierarchy (industrial/domestic). Eymard-Duvernay identified three models of firms, each of them based on a predominant convention of qualification: standard goods qualifying for an industrial worth and following a logic of scale economics; branded goods qualifying for domestic worth and following a logic of tradition and reputation; renewable market goods qualifying for market competition worth and strongly oriented towards the customer (Eymard-Duvernay in Dupuy *et al.* 1989). Apart from outweighing convention of coordination, the firm is a complex organization of compromise between a plurality of conventions (Thévenot 2001). In a comparative perspective, Salais and Storper's analysis of possible 'worlds of production' shows the different combinations of conventions concerning market relations, on the one hand, and technology and organization on the other (Storper and Salais 1997). The distinction between several quality conventions allows the differentiation of types of markets (Favereau *et al.* 2002), in particular those which are far from being reducible to market competition, such as labour markets and **financial markets**. Mimetic processes involved in speculation lead to a convention of opinion which departs both from strict market competition and from the industrial qualification of the firm (Orléan 1994). An interpretative view on rules makes the link between conventions and organizational learning in the economy (Favereau in Orléan 1994). The analysis of the plurality of conventions of variable scope, and the concern with material arrangements which support them, brings new light on the dynamics of an 'equipped humanity' (Thévenot 2002).

The Convention School offers a fresh and critical view on politics and policies, while allowing the linking of micro and macro levels. At a macro level, it brings light on the emergence of new legitimate conventions, in terms of a connectionist order of worth indicating a 'new spirit of capitalism' (Boltanski and Chiapello 1999), or an order of information worth. It offers tools to analyse and criticize different types of power abuse, in particular the tyranny of an overwhelming worth. It helps to disclose the conventional forms of evaluation which are concealed under governance procedures and indicators pretending to value neutrality. This critical investigation addresses European Community politics and the relation between the state and the economy. Considering the interplay between different levels of convention, the macro–micro-flexibility of the tools used by the Convention School brings light on policies close to persons in terms of manpower, welfare and reintegration policies. The needed formatting for the public and for law enforcement creates tensions with care and close engagements. The analysis of such pressures leads to extend the critical notion of domination.

References and further reading

Boltanski, L. and Chiapello, E. (1999) *Le nouvel esprit du capitalisme*, Paris: Gallimard.

Boltanski, L. and Thévenot, L. (1991) *De la justification. Les économies de la grandeur*, Paris: Gallimard (on translation at Princeton University Press).

Dupuy, J.-P., Eymard-Duvernay, F., Favereau, O., Orléan, A., Salais, R. and Thévenot, L. (1989) *Revue économique*, numéro spécial 'L'économie des conventions', 2, mars.

Eymard-Duvernay, F. (2002) 'Conventionalist Approaches to Enterprise', in O. Favereau and E. Lazega (eds), *Conventions and Structures in Economic Organization: Markets, Networks and Hierarchies*, Cheltenham, UK: Edward Elgar, pp. 60–78.

Favereau, O., Biencourt, O. and Eymard-Duvernay, F. (2002) 'Where Do Markets Come From? From (Quality) Conventions!' in O. Favereau and E. Lazega (eds), *Conventions and Structures in Economic Organization:*

Markets, Networks and Hierarchies, Cheltenham, UK: Edward Elgar, pp. 213–52.

Orléan, A. (ed.) (1994) *Analyse économique des conventions*, Paris: PUF (revised edition published 2004).

Salais, R. and Thévenot, L. (eds) (1986) *Le Travail; marchés, règles, conventions*, Paris: INSEE-Economica.

Storper, M. and Salais, R. (1997) *Worlds of Production. The Action Frameworks of the Economy*, Cambridge MA: Harvard University Press.

Thévenot, L. (2001) 'Organized Complexity: Conventions of Coordination and the Composition of Economic Arrangements', *European Journal of Social Theory*, 4(4): 405–25.

—— (2002) 'Which Road to Follow? The Moral Complexity of an "Equipped" Humanity', in John Law and Annemarie Mol (eds), *Complexities: Social Studies of Knowledge Practices*, Durham, NC, and London: Duke University Press, pp. 53–87.

LAURENT THÉVENOT

COOPERATION

Two or more actors cooperate when they are engaged in the realization of a common enterprise, the outcome of which depends upon the commitment of each. Economic activities are not only characterized by competition. On the contrary, economic goals can often only be realized through processes of cooperation among economic actors. Efficient production requires a certain level of division of labour, so that actors control resources and are interested in resources controlled by others for their aims. However, improvements in economic performance also require the production or the safeguard of collective goods. In this case actors are interested in the benefits deriving from them but not in assuming the costs for their realization. Hence, those actors engaged in a process of cooperation are characterized by mutual dependency. Furthermore, cooperative processes stress the problem of the redistribution of risks and gains attendant on cooperation among the parties and of opportunistic behaviour and exploitation.

Game theory investigates how cooperation can occur among individuals pursuing their own self-interest without being constrained by means of authority or any previous knowledge of each other. According to the simple scheme of the Prisoner's Dilemma, defection is actually more rational than cooperation in one-shot interactions. In case of a known finite number of interactions, it is rational to cooperate until the next-to-last move. However, as defection is probable in the last move, cooperation is jeopardized in the preceding moves as well. As the individual goals are given, cooperation is due to an accidental complementarity of the actors' preferences. In the book *The Evolution of Cooperation* Robert Axelrod identifies TIT FOR TAT – 'starting with cooperation, and thereafter doing what the other player did on the previous move' (1984: viii) – as the strategy through which cooperation can spontaneously evolve and be strengthened. A precondition of this form of mutuality and reciprocity is a game characterized by an indefinite number of interactions, in which the actors remember the history of their transactions and put a relatively high value on future interactions compared to current ones. Interactions within small groups facilitate cooperation.

As far as the production of collective goods is concerned, Mancur Olson emphasizes in *The Logic of Collective Action* (1965) how opportunistic behaviour cannot be avoided unless monetary or non-monetary **incentives** are established, be they institutional, like contracts, or social, like social status and social acceptance. Incentives of the latter type are more likely to work in small groups than in larger ones.

Cooperation and reciprocity norms are usually associated with **trust** and **social capital** because of uncertainties about the behaviour of the other parties, **asymmetrical information** or dependency. In the game-theoretical and economic perspective, cooperation is mainly the result of a calculation by self-interested actors. As calculative trust is considered a contradiction in terms, cooperation is mainly explained through reputational mechanisms (see **reputation**). In the culturalist framework (non-calculative) trust and cooperation are considered as a product of culture, varying in different societies. Culture is determined by history and institutions and cannot be influenced by the actors, so that the possibilities of creating cooperation among individuals situated in low-trust contexts are presumably very low, while in more developed areas people seem to be part of a community of fate in which cooperation is an immutable natural fact (Putnam *et al.* 1993). On the other hand, cooperation and trust – forms of social capital – can also be considered the result of the interaction among individuals within a community, therefore they are something substantially negotiable. Sabel (1993) synthesizes both positions of game theory and the culturalist approach by referring to a concept of the individual both long-term-oriented and conditioned by self-interest, whose personality develops reflexively with community norms, norms that are ambiguous, hence constantly redefined. By reshaping norms actors can instigate loyalty and forbearance, redefine their goals and **beliefs**, reinterpret their collective past and draw new community boundaries in which trusting cooperation can emerge also from calculative cooperation. These processes can be encouraged by **deliberation** activities.

Cooperation is a very important aspect for economic exchanges and development processes. In more **traditional economies** development can also be favoured by the safeguard of (scarce or exhaustible) common-pool resources, which require a commitment by all the beneficiaries (Ostrom 1990). **Industrial districts** are an example of a mix between competition and cooperation among regionally concentrated firms. They were capable of providing a flexible response to the new market challenges of the 1970s and 1980s (Pyke *et al.* 1990). A similar form of organization can also account for the high economic perfor-

mance of Japan in the 1980s. Cooperation concerns not only supplier relationships but also the production of collective goods like common services or vocational training.

Cooperation is facilitated in community contexts and more generally by common traditions and values, but also depends on the capacity of the actors to create social cohesion around new values and economic ideas. Significant economic effects derived, for example, also from the action of virtual communities that contributed to the production and the improvement of free software, each of the members renouncing to the individual gain and contributing to expand market in the sector.

References and further reading

Axelrod, Robert (1984) *The Evolution of Cooperation*, New York: Basic Books.

Olson, Mancur (1965) *The Logic of Collective Action: Public Goods and the Theory of Groups*, Cambridge, MA: Harvard University Press.

Ostrom, Elinor (1990) *Governing the Commons: The Evolution of Institutions for Collective Action*, Cambridge: Cambridge University Press.

Putnam, Robert D., Leonardi, Robert and Nanetti, Raffaella (1993) *Making Democracy Work: Civic Traditions in Modern Italy*, Princeton, NJ: Princeton University Press.

Pyke, Frank, Becattini, Giacomo and Sengenberger, Werner (1990) *Industrial Districts and Inter-firm Co-operation in Italy*, Geneva: International Institute for Labour Studies.

Sabel, Charles (1993) 'Studied Trust: Building New Forms of Cooperation in a Volatile Economy', in Richard Swedberg (ed.), *Explorations in Economic Sociology*, New York: Russel Sage Foundation, pp. 104–44.

GENY PIOTTI

COORDINATION (MODES OF)

See: convention school

CORPORATE CRIME

Introduction

A plethora of theories have been offered to explain wrongdoing in and by corporations.

These theories have been differentiated along two dimensions. First, theories have been distinguished on the basis of whether they assume that wrongdoing is the result of organizational as opposed to individual behaviour. The former type of theory focuses on corporations, while the latter focuses on managers. Second, theories have been distinguished on the basis of whether they assume that wrongdoing is the result of historical structures as opposed to situational processes. The former type of theory focuses on structures that crystallize before the opportunity to engage in wrongdoing presents itself, while the later focuses on processes that unfold close to the time (and in some cases, in the moment) when wrongdoing is perpetrated.

We think that explanations of organizational wrongdoing can also be distinguished along a third dimension – on the basis of whether they assume that actors (individual or organizational) are autonomous as opposed to embedded in social relations (historical or situational). The former type of theory tends to assume that actors formulate their behaviour on the basis of rational cost–benefit analysis, while the later tends to assume that actors formulate their behaviour in reference to normative and cognitive frameworks and are influenced by inter-organizational and inter-personal bonds.

Below we briefly outline the four theoretical approaches to corporate wrongdoing implied by the widely accepted two-dimensional characterization of the literature. Then we briefly elaborate two specific theories representative of each general approach to corporate wrongdoing, one which views organizations and managers as isolated actors and the other which views organizations and managers as embedded in inter-organizational and social structures. We conclude by discussing the limitations of our characterization of existing theory of corporate wrongdoing.

A typology of theories of corporate wrongdoing

Organizational actors – historical structures

This type of theory focuses on organizational attributes and relations established before the opportunity to engage in wrongdoing presents itself.

Theories that focus on the market structure of the economy? Some theories of corporate wrongdoing focus on a firm's position in the market structure of the economy. Most theories of this type focus more specifically on the competitiveness of the industries in which firms produce. These theories are based on the assumption that firms producing in competitive industries have fewer legitimate means to secure survival and prosperity, and thus are more likely to use illegitimate means to attain these ends. Industry profit margins have been used to measure industry competitiveness (Staw and Szwajkowski 1975).

Theories that focus on the normative structure of the economy? Many theorists focus on the cultural milieus in which firms are embedded. The norms prevalent in a firm's industry can endorse wrongdoing. Alternatively, cognitive techniques available in a firm's industry can neutralize the effect of internalized norms that otherwise would block wrongdoing. These norms and techniques of neutralization might be produced by the market constraints discussed above. For example, some believe that the electrical equipment industry was plagued by cut-throat competition in the 1950s. Over time, the practice of cooperating in the allocation of contracts with municipal, state and federal government entities became a common practice. When new sales employees were hired, they found that price-fixing was expected of them by their superiors (Geis 1967).

Organizational actors – situational processes

This type of theory focuses on organizational attributes and relationships that evolve close to the time (and in the moment) that the opportunity to engage in wrongdoing presents itself.

Theories that focus on firm performance? Many theories focus on temporal variation in corporate performance. These theories generally assume that when firms suffer performance problems, they take risks that they would otherwise not take in an attempt to remain economically viable. Most variants of this theory contend that the decline in economic performance, sometimes referred to as the 'profit squeeze', leads to wrongdoing (Simpson 1986).

Theories that focus on inter-organizational relations? Some theories focus on the emergent inter-organizational relationships in which firms are embedded. These theories assume that firms experience uncertainty about which practices to pursue, and that inter-firm relationships help reduce this uncertainty by providing information about strategic options. For the most part, theorists have assumed that **inter-firm relations** stimulate the diffusion of legitimate organizational practices. However, researchers have begun to examine how inter-firm relations facilitate the diffusion of what might be considered deviant organizational practices, such as hostile acquisitions (Palmer and Barber 2001).

Individual actors – historical structures

This type of theory focuses on individual attributes and relationships established before the opportunity to engage in wrongdoing presents itself.

Theories that focus on corporate governance structures? Many theories focus on the organizational structures that monitor and control managerial behaviour. Foremost among these theories is **agency theory**. It assumes that managers (agents) are prone to opportunism, which involves the pursuit of individual self-interest with guile, at the expense of the organization's stockholders (principals). The extent to which organizational structures align the interests of principals and agents and provide principals the opportunity to monitor and control agents' behaviour explains variation in corporate wrongdoing. Most agency theory research focuses on a firm's ownership relationships and assumes that when managers do not own a substantial block of stock in the firms they command and when owners do not occupy positions in top management or the board, the firm will be more prone to illegal behaviour (Jensen 1993).

Theories that focus on the political-cultural context of the firm? Some theories focus on the political-cultural relations in which top managers are embedded. These theories assume that corporations are composed of competing coalitions with alternative conceptions of control and thus different strategic preferences. Political contests between these coalitions determine which coalition will be dominant, which conception of control will be operative, and which strategies will be pursued. For example, some think that top managers who rise to power through the finance function tend to focus on improving their firm's short-term stock market performance rather than its long-term survival and growth and that this short-term orientation gives rise to wrongdoing (Daboub *et al.* 1995).

Individual actors – situational structures and processes

This type of theory focuses on individual attributes and relationships that unfold close to the time (and in the moment) that the opportunity to engage in wrongdoing presents itself.

Theories that focus on individual incentive structures? Many theories focus on managerial perceptions of the costs and benefits associated with pursuing wrongful courses of actions. Rational choice theory is the most popular such theory. It assumes that people pursue wrongful courses of action when they think that the rewards associated with the course of action are great relative to the risks (Becker 1968). A person's estimation of expected returns takes into account his/her capacity to successfully pursue the wrongful course of action as well as the value that s/he places on the expected outcomes of the behaviour (including the value s/he places on being considered ethical or law-abiding by him/herself and/or others). A person's estimation of expected risks take into account the likelihood of being found out and the severity of any resulting punishment.

Theories that focus on social influence processes. While no one has yet explicitly done so, it is possible to formulate theories focusing on the social bonds that tie managers to one another in the workplace. Such theories could be based on the widely recognized fact that people often pursue courses of action without the benefit of thorough cost–benefit analyses and instead look to others for guidance regarding how to think and act. Some such theories, such as social comparison and role theory, assume that actors import the rationale for following a course of action from others in the course of engaging in the action, either because others serve as relevant models or because others convey relevant expectations. Other theories, such as commitment theory, assume that actors develop the rationale for pursuing a course of action after the fact. Finally, other theories, such as theories about formal authority, assume that actors sometimes never establish a rationale for pursuing a course of action. We think future theory construction in this area could be extremely fruitful.

Discussion

Limitations of our typology of corporate wrongdoing

Our characterization of theories of corporate wrongdoing is limited in two important respects. First, like all typologies, our typology oversimplifies reality. The distinction between organizational and individual actors is often blurred in practice. All organizational behaviour is ultimately the result of individual behaviour. Further, the location of managers and subordinates in their organization shape their interests and capacities. Indeed, the interests of top managers often coincide with the interests of their organizations. Thus, theories that explain how individuals come to violate fundamental ethical principles and/or legal codes can often help explain wrongdoing that appears to be primarily the result of organizational-level dynamics and vice versa.

Further, the distinction between historical structures and situational processes also is often blurred in practice. Historical structures conducive to wrongdoing are sometimes only recognized by individual and organizational actors long after they have unfolded, thus appearing to them (and the researchers who study them) as characteristics of the situation. Further, crimes that are intentionally planned in advance often run into road blocks and must be re-rationalized and improvised. Finally, crimes that develop incrementally and that are rationalized after the fact can become standardized and formalized, sometimes as the result of reactions to labelling agents (e.g. law enforcement agencies). Thus, theories that explain how historical structures shape individual and organizational behaviour can sometimes help explain wrongdoing that appears to be primarily the result of situational processes and vice versa.

Finally, the distinction between autonomous rational actors and embedded social ones is also often blurred in practice. For example, managers who attempt to weigh the risks and rewards associated with pursuing a particular wrongful action will become more inclined to pursue that behaviour if embedded in social networks that can provide information that improve the chances of success or reduce the chance of detection. Similarly, the development of socially acceptable rationalizations for wrongdoing may determine whether or not employees act on risk/reward calculations that reveal wrongdoing to be a rational course of behaviour. Thus, theories that explain how autonomous rational action shapes corporate or individual wrongful action can sometimes help explain wrongdoing that appears to be primarily the result of embedded normative action and vice versa.

Second, our typology does not take into account the role the state plays in creating corporate wrongdoing. The line between right and wrong is drawn in the course of a social process. In the advanced societies, that line is drawn by a functionally and structurally differentiated state, composed of law-makers (e.g. legislators), enforcers (e.g. the police) and adjudicators (e.g. the courts). We have completely ignored the way in which state action determines which firms and individuals are labelled wrongdoers.

References and further reading

Becker, Gary (1968) 'Crime and Punishment: An Economic Approach', *Journal of Political Economy*, 76: 169–217.

Daboub, A. J., Rasheed, A. M. S., Priem, R. L. and Gray, D. A. (1995) 'Top Management Team Characteristics and Corporate Illegal Activity', *Academy of Management Review*, 20: 138–70.

Geis, Gilbert (1967) 'White Collar Crime: The Heavy Electrical Equipment Antitrust Case of 1961', in Marshall B. Clinard and Richard Quinney (eds), *Criminal Behavior Systems: A Typology*, New York: Holt, Rinehart and Winston.

Jensen, Michael C. (1993) 'The Modern Industrial Revolution, Exit, and the Failure of Internal Control Systems', *Journal of Finance*, 48: 831–80.

Palmer, D. and Barber, B. (2001) 'Challengers, Elites, and Owning Families: A Social Class Theory of Corporate Acquisitions in the 1960s', *Administrative Science Quarterly*, 46(1): 87–120.

Simpson, Sally (1986) 'The Decomposition of Antitrust: Testing a Multi-Level, Longitudinal Model of Profit-Squeeze', *American Sociological Review*, 51: 859–75.

Staw, Barry and Szwajkowski, Eugene (1975) 'The Scarcity–Munificence Component of Organizational Environments and the Commission of Illegal Acts', *Administrative Science Quarterly*, 20: 345–54.

DONALD PALMER
ROBERT FAULKNER
MICHAEL W. MAHER

CORPORATE GOVERNANCE

Corporate governance is the study of the distribution of rights and responsibilities among different participants in the corporation, such as, managers, shareholders, the board of directors and other **stakeholders** (e.g. employees, suppliers and consumers). This area of inquiry is at the heart of economic sociology as it explores the social relations between organizational actors and institutions that often have conflicting interests. The concept of governing, or ruling with authority and control, is not recognized in neoclassical economic studies or in Adam Smith's invisible hand of the marketplace. Flourishing corporate governance studies have spurred on interdisciplinary research in sociology, economics, law and political science surrounding the relationships between power relations, **financial markets**, legal systems, political systems, and product and labour markets.

The study of corporate governance, that originally developed in the context of **agency theory** and was thus based on the premise of shareholder maximization, has been enriched by economic sociologists and other social scientists who developed two new theoretical and empirical dimensions.

First, these scholars have striven to shed light to the different stakeholders in the firm and their relationships. Second, historical and comparative studies have questioned the key factors leading to diverse national corporate governance systems around the world. I discuss each of them in turn.

The shareholder view of corporate governance

The agency theory perspective of corporate governance as exemplified by Michael Jensen and colleagues assumes that firms are dispersedly owned. This stands in line with Berle and Means' 1932 definition of the American 'modern' corporation. The main consequence of dispersedly owned firms is that there exits a separation between the owners of the firm (principals) and those who control the firm's daily operations (agents or managers). As a result, corporate governance is conceptualized around the corporate governance 'problem'. The problem is that principals who are risk-bearing shareholders, interested in maximizing their investments, must monitor agents because these might be shirking or working towards enhancing their individual interests. Thus, as Shleifer and Vishny (1997) state, agency theorists aim to understand how investors get the managers to give them back their money (p.738) and hence minimize agency costs.

In sum, agency theory research has devoted a lot of effort to outline the incentives of managers and owners and to identify market mechanisms to minimize potential agency costs. Particularly salient within the management dimension are studies of the role of the Chief Executive Officer, often related to his/her incentives within the firm (e.g. performance-related behaviour) and in the labour market more generally (e.g. career mobility). Finally, agency theory scholars have also paid a great deal of attention to uncover the role

of the third point in their conceptualization of the corporate governance triangle: the board of directors. Boards are the intermediary governance body between shareholders and management. In principle, directors' interests are aligned with those of owners as they are elected by shareholders to represent their collective interests in their monitoring of management. Studies of boards of directors in the context of corporate governance examine to what degree different board characteristics such as board composition (insiders/outsiders directors, board subcommittees and dual leadership) or **interlocking directorates** will minimize agency costs. For example, an insider director might be more likely to pursue managerial interests such as empire-building if her compensation is tied to firm revenues.

From the sociological perspective, the agency theory accounts of corporate governance are viewed as *undersocialized* for three main reasons. First, the **principal and agent** relationship and the assumption of dispersed ownership overlook the diverse identities of stakeholders within the firm, particularly in the case where the owners are blockholders such as families, institutional investors or industrial **banks** with socially constructed interests. Second, its focus on bilateral contracts discounts the important interdependencies with other firm stakeholders. Finally, corporate governance needs to be understood in an institutional context wider than shareholder rights so that we can better capture the institutional complexity. Hence, social relations and institutional embeddedness, also described as actorcentred institutionalism, should be the fundamental unit of analysis in examining corporate governance (Aguilera and Jackson 2003).

The stakeholder view of corporate governance

The stakeholder view of the firm based on systems theory has expanded the firm's boundaries by defining firms as 'open systems', where firm external links are part of every organization. A key factor of this perspective is the recognition of stakeholders (e.g. employees, suppliers, customers among others) and their relationships (e.g. employee ownership). According to this view, firms are not always driven solely by shareholder value maximization because managers may be altruistic about employee empowerment, owners may be concerned about the survival of the firm as in the case of family businesses, and market pressures for profitability are more long term due to the existence of patient capital and the underdevelopment of capital markets. While discussions about suppliers and consumers within the corporate governance equation are scarce, significant contributions exist regarding the role of employees, as exemplified by the important work of Margaret Blair, Mary O'Sullivan and Mark Roe.

An important contribution to the corporate governance literature is the interaction effects among the different stakeholders competing for limited firm resources. Aguilera and Jackson (2003) discuss three main interactions between owners, managers and employees: **class** conflict, insider–outsider conflict and accountability conflicts. *Class* conflict may arise when the interests of owners and management oppose the interests of employees, particularly regarding distributional issues, e.g. wages. Where owners and management pursue mostly shareholder maximizing interests, such as in the USA, conflict is likely to arise around tradeoffs between wages and profits, capital reinvestments and paying out dividends, or levels of employment and shareholder returns. Management may often use employee ownership or contingent pay as a means to align employee interests with owners, and minimize governance conflicts. *Insider–outsider* conflicts may arise when the interests of employees and management (insiders) oppose the interests of owners (outsiders).

Insiders may favour internal diversification ('empire-building'), block efforts at restructuring or erect takeover defences to reduce the threat of external takeovers. Insider–outsider conflicts are often acute in Japan due to the intense commitment of capital to specific firms, strong internal participation of core employees, and highly committed management. Insiders' interests conflict with minority shareholders' interests in greater liquidity and financial returns, as well as the interests of certain employees, e.g. mobile professionals and noncore employees. Finally, *accountability* conflicts concern the common interests of owners and labour vis-à-vis management. Shareholders and employees may form coalitions to remove poorly performing management or to demand higher corporate transparency. Here managerial accountability to different stakeholders is not a zero-sum relationship. In Germany, strong labour participation in the supervisory board complements committed blockholders in actively monitoring management. But where the interests of owners and employees diverge too sharply, such coalitions may break down and give management increasing autonomy to pursue its own agenda and thereby damage accountability.

Historical and comparative research in corporate governance

Corporate governance is best conceptualized when stressing the interplay of institutions and firmlevel actors where the underlying assumption is that firms are embedded in multiple institutional settings, yet corporate stakeholders and their coalitions also have the capacity to influence firmlevel outcomes (Aguilera and Jackson 2003). The work of Nicole W. Biggart, Gerald Davis, Frank Dobbin, Neil Fligstein and Mauro Guillén are excellent examples of this theoretical setting.

Historical and comparative research in corporate governance sharpens our understanding of the rights and responsibilities between the parties with a stake in the firm because it systematically identifies the patterns of change over time and it uncovers the idiosyncrasies of each national system. In doing so, it also reinforces the importance of different institutional contexts where corporations are embedded, as has been illustrated by Peter Hall and David Soskice's (2001) edited volume on the 'varieties of capitalism', Richard Whitley's (2001) 'business systems', and Wolfang Streeck and Kozo Yamamura's (2001) edited volume on the political foundations of institutional complementarities.

The institutional effects on corporate governance are well researched. Institutions including labour markets, financial markets, product markets, capital markets, education and training, and so on, are not viewed as selfstanding but rather as *complementary* to each other and mutually reinforcing the corporate governance outcomes. For instance, the traditional lifetime employment in Japan and firmspecific skills could only be sustained because Japan had generally speaking a closed labour market, enterprise unionism and financial reciprocity among the firms in a *kieretsu*. If one of the institutions in the constellation were to change, Japanese high employee involvement would transform.

Historical research relies on analysis of path-dependency as corporate governance change is often incremental as opposed to radical. For example, studies contrasting corporate governance transformations in Central and Eastern Europe from the planned economy period to market economies are an excellent social laboratory to explore corporate governance change.

The internationalization of markets in the 1980s and 1990s triggered an immense and vibrant amount of *comparative* interdisciplinary research on corporate governance systems around the world and their respective effectiveness. The initial comparative studies contrast the distinctive traits of two main corporate governance systems: the AngloAmerican (labelled as outsider, common-law, marketoriented, shareholdercentred or liberal) and the continental European (also labelled as insider, civil-law, blockholder, bankoriented, stakeholdercentred, coordinated or 'Rhineland') models.

The AngloAmerican system is stylized as dispersed ownership expecting short-term returns, strong shareholder rights, arm's-length creditors financing through equity, active markets for corporate control, and flexible labour markets. Conversely, the continental system exemplified by Germany relies on longterm debt finance, ownership by large blockholders, weak markets for corporate control, and rigid labour markets. This classification only partially fits Japan and other East Asian countries, characterized by different configurations of business groups, or the variations within continental Europe, as illustrated by empirical studies describing the pyramidal familyowned firms and weak industry–bank relationships in Italy versus the strong state, bank and foreign capital interventionism in Spain. Despite the rich description found in the existing research literature, the challenge remains in uncovering the key factors explaining national differences.

Hence, comparative corporate governance scholars continue to inquire why corporate governance systems differ quite substantially around the world, and particularly when it comes to two ownership patterns: ownership type (who owns corporations: families, state, banks, floating individuals, institutional investors, etc.) and how much they own (majority or dispersed ownership). Several explanatory paradigms have been offered, drawing from different disciplinary fields. For example, scholars from the *legal paradigm* (or Quality of Corporate Law in protecting minority shareholders), represented mostly by La Porta and colleagues, argue that national legal differences, namely common-law versus civil-law legal traditions, are strongly associated with corporate governance outcomes. Other scholars, Mark Roe being its main advocate, focus on the *political paradigm*. It is believed that national political forces such as party systems or employee job security explain a large part of corporate governance models' variance in advanced industrialized countries. A main finding is that strong social democracy is highly correlated with weak shareholder rights and ownership dispersion. Finally, other scholars have stressed the role of different types of *financial systems* and their capacity to provide external finance to firms. The work of John Zysman is a good example of this paradigm. Other variables that tend to be included in the corporate governance equation are degree of state intervention, employee influence, and economic openness.

Conclusion

Initial debates on whether **globalization** triggered convergence of corporate governance systems have migrated to questions on the degree of change in corporate governance systems and where the new adopted practices come from. There is a great deal of interest on the hybridization of corporate governance models and the diffusion of practices across national borders. Other areas of corporate governance research that need further attention are the relationship between corporate governance and innovation systems leading to increased competitiveness, the influence of codes of **good governance** in light of needs for further corporate transparency, corporate accountability, corporate social responsibility, and the dynamics of corporate governance within multinational firms.

References and further reading

Aguilera, Ruth V. and Jackson, Gregory (2003) 'The Cross-National Diversity of Corporate Governance: Dimensions and Determinants', *Academy of Management Review*, 28(3): 447–65.

Berle, Adolf and Means, Gardiner (1932) *The Modern Corporation and Private Property*, New York: Macmillan.

Federowicz, Michal and Aguilera, Ruth V. (2004) *Corporate Governance in a Changing Economic and Political Environment. Trajectories of Institutional Change on the European Continent*, London: Palgrave Macmillan.

Hall, Peter A. and Soskice, David (2001) *Varieties of Capitalism: The Institutional Foundations of Comparative Advantage*, Oxford: Oxford University Press.

Shleifer, Andrei and Vishny, Robert W. (1997) 'A Survey of Corporate Governance', *Journal of Finance*, 2: 737–83.

Streeck, Wolfang and Yamamura, Kozo (2001) *The Origins of Nonliberal Capitalism: Germany and Japan in Comparison*, Ithaca, NY: Cornell University Press.

Whitley, Richard (ed.) (1992) *European Business Systems. Firms and Markets in their National Contexts*, London: Sage.

RUTH V. AGUILERA

CORPORATE SOCIAL RESPONSIBILITY

See: Social responsibility of firms

CORPORATISM

Corporatism, or corporatist concertation, refers to a mode of policy-making in which organized interest groups – most notably, encompassing, concentrated and centralized business and labour confederations – participate in the decision-making process. It is frequently counterposed to 'pluralism', in which interest groups' role is limited to lobbying.

Broad overviews of corporatism are provided in Berger (1981); Goldthorpe (1984); Lehmbruch and Schmitter (1982); Molina and Rhodes (2002); Schmitter and Lehmbruch (1979); Streeck and Kenworthy (2004); Streeck and Schmitter (1985). I focus here on corporatism's impact on economic outcomes, which has been one of the central concerns of researchers. The study of modern, democratic corporatism originated in the late 1970s and early 1980s after the wave of worker militancy in the late 1960s and the economic downturn beginning in 1973. Cross-country research has explored whether, and if so why, corporatist countries have performed better economically than countries with more fragmented interest groups and policy-making arrangements. Analysts have focused in particular on the effects of centralized or coordinated wage setting on unemployment and inflation.

Three causal mechanisms have been hypothesized. First, centralized or coordinated wage setting may yield low unemployment or inflation by engendering wage restraint. If employees bargain aggressively for high wage increases, employers can do five main things in response: raise productivity, raise prices, reduce profits paid out to investors, reduce investment, and/or reduce the number of employees. Where wages are bargained separately for individual firms, none of these responses will necessarily have an adverse short-term effect on employment or inflation-adjusted wages, which are the principal concerns of union negotiators. For instance, if a firm raises prices, this is likely to have little impact on the living standard of its workers. Even if the firm chooses to reduce employment, those laid off should be able to find work elsewhere as long as wage increases and layoffs are not generalized throughout the economy. Thus, where bargaining is decentralized and uncoordinated, there is an incentive for unions to pursue a strategy of wage militancy.

By contrast, if wage negotiations cover a large share of the workforce, union bargainers can be reasonably sure that a large wage increase will have an adverse impact on their members. When firms representing a sizable share of the economy raise prices, the resulting inflation offsets or nullifies the wage gains of most workers.

Similarly, if layoffs are economy-wide, employment opportunities will diminish. Centralized or coordinated wage-setting thus generates an incentive for wage moderation, as interest groups are forced by their size and structure to internalize the negative impact of aggressive bargaining.

Many researchers have assumed a linear relationship between wage-setting centralization or coordination and wage restraint. However, some have proposed that the effect is parabolic, with high and low levels of centralization best at generating wage restraint. Others contend that corporatist wage-setting yields superior performance outcomes only in combination with particular types or levels of central bank independence, left government, unionization or public sector unionization. Still others hypothesize that the effect is both hump-shaped and interactive with central bank independence or the monetary regime.

One glaring weakness of research in this area is the dearth of empirical investigation of the assumed causal mechanism. Only a handful of studies have actually examined the relationship between wage-setting and wage developments. Most have looked only at the statistical correlation between wage-setting and macroeconomic performance and have simply presumed that the link between wage-setting and wage restraint, and also between wage restraint and performance outcomes, is as hypothesized.

A second potential link between corporatist wage-setting and unemployment is economic growth. One of the outcomes of centralized or coordinated wage determination, achieved either informally or explicitly in corporatist pacts, may be greater investment, which in turn tends to spur more rapid growth of economic output. Faster growth, in turn, increases employment.

A third hypothesized link is government policy. Policy orientations are seen as a key determinant of cross-country differences in unemployment. Policy-makers in countries with centralized or coordinated wage-setting are likely to feel more confident than their counterparts in countries with fragmented bargaining that wage increases will be moderate. Thus, they should tend to worry less about wage-push inflation. This may increase their willingness to adopt an expansive monetary or fiscal policy, an active labour market policy, or other policies that reduce unemployment. By contrast, policy-makers in nations with less coordinated wage arrangements may feel compelled to resort to higher levels of unemployment in order to keep inflation in check.

Although there are some dissenting findings, most analyses have discovered an association between corporatist wage setting and low unemployment or inflation in the 1970s and 1980s (see Flanagan 1999 for an overview). Interest in national incomes policies surged in the 1990s in the context of efforts by European governments to bring down persistent unemployment and meet the strict criteria for accession to the European Monetary Union. In countries such as the Netherlands, Ireland, Italy and Belgium, national employment and stability pacts were proposed and negotiated that aimed to bring union wage-setting behaviour in line with the imperatives of a monetarist macroeconomic policy and the need to consolidate government budgets. Unlike in the 1970s, neither encompassing and centralized union movements nor governments of the left seemed necessary to the creation or success of such pacts. However, restrictive monetary policy coupled with growing employer leverage also led to substantial wage restraint in the 1990s in countries with neither regularized nor temporary wage pacts, such as Canada, France, the United Kingdom and the United States. Consequently, there appears to have been little or no difference between corporatist and noncorporatist countries in wage developments and macroeconomic performance in the 1990s (Kenworthy 2002).

While most of the research on corporatism's economic impact centres on wage-

setting, some studies have examined the effects of union participation in broader economic policy making (i.e. not confined to wages). Unions desire low unemployment. The more input unions have in economic policy decisions, the more likely it would seem that government policies will give priority to fighting unemployment. To the extent that such policies are effective, the result should be lower rates of joblessness. Empirical findings have tended to be favourable, even into the 1990s (e.g. Compston 1997; Kenworthy 2002).

The bulk of research on the effects of corporatism has dealt with macroeconomic performance, but a number of studies suggest that its impact may be no less important, and perhaps more so, for the distribution and redistribution of income. Unions tend to prefer smaller pay differentials, and centralized or coordinated wage-setting increases unions' leverage over the wage structure. Since differentials are more transparent if wages are set simultaneously and collectively for a large share of the workforce, centralization may reinforce union preferences for pay compression. Furthermore, pay compression may be one of the things unions request from employers in exchange for pay restraint. Empirical findings have tended to yield strong support for the hypothesis that corporatist wage-setting is associated with lower pay inequality (e.g. Wallerstein 1999). There also is reason to expect a link between corporatism and the redistributive efforts of government. Unions may demand more generous redistributive programmes in exchange for wage moderation, and regularized participation by unions in the policy-making process may heighten their influence. Here, too, there is empirical support in the literature (e.g. Hicks 1999), though it is difficult to disentangle the impact of corporatism from that of related factors such as social democratic government.

The future of corporatism is bound up with ongoing transformations of social structure and of the nation-state. With heightened **globalization**, the decline of Fordist industrial organization and Keynesian economic policy, and the growing prominence of the service sector, workers and employers have become less cohesive and more difficult to organize into centralized, monopolistic and hierarchical associations. In addition, other groups with distinct political interests have emerged, such as women and immigrants, who are not well represented within traditional corporatist arrangements. Where national governments lose control to international markets, their ability to underwrite tripartite bargains diminishes. And globalization heightens pressures for competitiveness and openness of national economies. Partly as a result, many governments have embarked on a strategy of liberalizing their economies. Liberalization implies a greater role for markets and regulatory authorities, at the expense of both discretionary state intervention and corporatist bargaining.

At the same time, various observers have expressed scepticism about the degree to which globalization is likely to alter national institutional structures and policy choices. Non-market institutions can offer competitive advantages to firms that may outweigh their costs. Where governments can no longer keep capital captive, they may depend to an increasing extent on organized groups to create institutional conditions and infrastructures attractive to investors. Also, countries that come under international pressure to balance their budgets, like the member states of the European Union, may need the cooperation of still-powerful unions for institutional reform and wage restraint.

In a recent study, Traxler *et al.* (2001) find little if any convergence in interest group organization, wage-setting arrangements, and interest group participation through the late 1990s. However, they do find evidence of a trend towards 'organized decentralization' of wage bargaining, whereby wages are set largely at the sectoral rather than the national level but coordinated informally across sectors. Meanwhile, as noted above, corporatist pacts dealing with issues such as wage restraint and labour market and social security reform have played a prominent role in the Netherlands and Ireland – two countries widely viewed as European economic success stories over the past decade. Similar pacts have been forged or renewed in Norway, Finland, Belgium and Italy.

References and further reading

Berger, Suzanne D. (ed.) (1981) *Organizing Interests in Western Europe*, Cambridge: Cambridge University Press.

Flanagan, Robert J. (1999) 'Macroeconomic Performance and Collective Bargaining: An International Perspective', *Journal of Economic Literature*, 37: 1150–75.

Goldthorpe, John H. (ed.) (1984) *Order and Conflict in Contemporary Capitalism*, Oxford: Clarendon Press.

Hicks, Alexander (1999) *Social Democracy and Welfare Capitalism*, Ithaca, NY: Cornell University Press.

Kenworthy, Lane (2002) 'Corporatism and Unemployment in the 1980s and 1990s', *American Sociological Review*, 67: 367–88.

Lehmbruch, Gerhard and Schmitter, Philippe C. (eds) (1982) *Patterns of Corporatist Policy-Making*, London: Sage.

Molina, Oscar and Rhodes, Martin (2002) 'Corporatism: The Past, Present, and Future of a Concept', *Annual Review of Political Science*, 5: 305–31.

Schmitter, Philippe C. and Lehmbruch, Gerhard (eds) (1979) *Trends Toward Corporatist Intermediation*, London: Sage.

Streeck, Wolfgang and Kenworthy, Lane (2004) 'Theories and Practices of Neo-Corporatism', in Thomas Janoski, Robert Alford, Alexander Hicks and Mildred A. Schwartz (eds), *Handbook of Political Sociology*, Cambridge: Cambridge University Press.

Streeck, Wolfgang and Schmitter, Philippe C. (eds) (1985) *Private Interest Government: Beyond Market and State*, London: Sage.

Traxler, Franz, Blaschke, Sabine and Kittel, Bernhard (2001) *National Labour Relations in Internationalized Markets*, Oxford: Oxford University Press.

Wallerstein, Michael (1999) 'Wage-Setting Institutions and Pay Inequality in Advanced Industrial Societies', *American Journal of Political Science*, 43: 649–80.

LANE KENWORTHY

CORRUPTION

Corruption is the misuse of public office for private or political gain. This definition leaves open the issue of what constitutes misuse, but it recognizes that sometimes public office can legitimately provide private benefits to politicians and bureaucrats. Narrowly targeted projects and special interest legislation are not corrupt. They result from the day-to-day operation of a representative political system.

This entry concentrates on corruption that involves a public official, either a politician or a bureaucrat. However, corrupt **incentives** can also arise in purely private interactions. Corruption is, in essence, a principal–agent problem. An agent violates the trust of his or her principal through self-enrichment or through illegally enriching a political party. A public official may take a bribe in return for a favourable decision or may simply steal from the state's coffers. Clearly, corporate managers can face similar incentives, and with the growing privatization of former state enterprises the locus of some forms of corruption will shift into the private sector.

This entry summarizes a large literature on the causes and consequences of public sector corruption. Readers who want to pursue these issues further should consult Rose-Ackerman (1978, 1999) and Bardhan (1997) which also include extensive references to the literature. To access current work, the World Bank Institute maintains a website [http://www.worldbank.org/wbi/governance] as do Transparency International (TI) an international nongovernmental organization committed to fighting international corruption [http://www.transparency.org] and the U4 Utstein Anti-Corruption Resource Centre [http://www.u4.no].

The government allocates scarce benefits and imposes costs. Individuals and firms may be willing to pay government agents to obtain the former and to avoid the latter. Opportunities for corruption arise whenever the officials exercise discretion and are impossible to monitor perfectly. The potential bribe revenues available to any individual politician or bureaucrat depend upon his or her monopoly power. If potential bribe payers have legal alternatives, bribes, if they are paid at all, will be low. If the chance of being caught and punished is high, corruption will be deterred. The mere existence of corrupt opportunities, however, says nothing about their welfare implications. The size of bribes is a poor measure of their social cost. Sometimes very small bribes have large consequences. Bribe may be low, not because the value of the quid pro quo is low, but because the bribe payer has bargaining power relative to the official. For example, if a majority-rule legislature with weak parties is bribed to approve a law favoured by a particular firm, no individual politician has much bargaining power; he or she can easily be replaced by another person formerly outside the corrupt coalition.

One might suppose that if a government has scarce benefits to distribute, say a number of import licences, then corruption will distribute them to those with the highest willingness-to-pay, and the winners will be the most efficient firms. There are several responses to this claim. First, corrupt markets are inefficient compared with the aboveboard sale of licences. Bribe-prices are secret, and entry may be blocked. Thus, the government could legally sell the scarce rights if its goal is to allocate the service to those who value it the most in money terms. Second, the basic purposes of some public programmes would be violated by sales to the highest bidders. For example, selling places in public universities and in subsidized housing would undermine the basic goals of those programmes. Third, toleration of corruption gives officials an incentive to engage in the creation of more scarce benefits in order to create more corrupt opportunities. For example, corrupt contracting officials have an incentive to support wasteful public projects designed to make payoffs easy to hide.

Consider bribes paid to avoid the imposition of costs. If a regulation is onerous and inefficient, then paying for an exemption seems efficient. However, permitting such individualized law compliance can be very harmful. Officials will seek to create even more restrictive rules so that they can be paid to decline to enforce them. Empirical work suggests that in countries where corruption is high, red tape is high, and managers spend considerable time dealing with public officials (e.g. Kaufmann 1997). Thus, even if each individual corrupt decision is rational for the bribing firm, the overall costs of doing business in society are high. Investment and entrepreneurship are discouraged.

The costs of corruption are not limited to its impact on the efficacy of public programmes taken one by one. In addition, endemic corruption has implications for the legitimacy of the state in the eyes of its citizens. In highly corrupt states, where both day-to-day interactions with officials and high-level deals are riddled with payoffs, people often express great cynicism about political life. This can lead to vicious spirals. The theoretical work on corruption has produced a number of multiple-equilibria models where both high corruption and low corruption solutions exist (Bardhan 1997, Rose-Ackerman 1999: 107–8, 124–5) and empirical work supports this observation.

Research on corruption is difficult because the perpetrators seek to keep their transactions secret. Nevertheless, scholars have begun to analyse and measure the impact of corruption on economic and political phenomena and to explain how political and economic conditions contribute to corruption. Cross-country research uses data that measure perceptions of corruption, such as the composite Transparency International index or the World Bank Institute's recalculation using similar data. The perceptions are mostly those of international business people and country experts. Studies using these data have found that high levels of corruption are associated with lower levels of investment and growth, and that capital inflows and foreign direct investment are discouraged (e.g. Graf Lambsdorff 2003). Highly corrupt countries tend to under-invest in human capital by spending less on education and to over-invest in public infrastructure relative to private investment (Mauro 1997; Tanzi and Davoodi 2002). Corrupt governments lack political legitimacy and hence tend to be smaller than more honest governments, everything else equal (Johnson *et al.* 2000). Corruption reduces the effectiveness of industrial policies and encourages business to operate in the unofficial sector in violation of tax and regulatory laws (Kaufmann 1997).

Turning the causal story around, recent research suggests that autocracies tend to be more corrupt than democracies, but that democracy is not a simple cure. Within the universe of democracies, corruption is facilitated by features of government structure such as presidentialism, closed-list proportional representation and federalism (Kunicova and Rose-Ackerman, 2005).

These are important findings, but they are limited by the aggregate nature of the data. Each country is treated as a single data point that is more or less 'corrupt'. This work shows that corruption is harmful but says little about the precise mechanisms. To counter this weakness, two new types of research are underway: detailed questionnaires that target households, businesses and public officials; and what might be called 'econometric case studies'. The questionnaires permit researchers to explore people's actual experiences. The case studies help one understand how corrupt sectors operate and how malfeasance might be controlled.

Several studies questioned businesses about the costs of corruption and red tape. Other researchers have used questionnaires and focus groups to examine household attitudes and behaviour. Researchers have studied countries as diverse as those in sub-Saharan Africa and in Central and Eastern Europe. Some of the most comprehensive are a study of four countries in Central and Eastern Europe by Miller *et al.* (2001) and work that focuses on the business environment in the same region by Johnson *et al.* (2000). This research complements the World Bank Institute's work on 'state capture' and administrative corruption in post-socialist countries (Hellman *et al.* 2003).

Sectoral studies are represented by work on how corruption limits the performance of the judiciary in Latin America, by estimates of the waste and corruption generated by China's two-price policy for basic raw materials, and research on the bench-marking of product prices in the hospital sector in Argentina that shows how monitoring and civil service pay reform can go hand in hand. As an example of research that can make a difference, Reinikka and Svensson (2004) documented the severe leakage of federal funds meant for local schools in Uganda. Their study led to a simple, information-based reform that had positive results.

These contributions use detailed data to understand both how corrupt systems operate and which policies have promise. Only if one looks at the fine structure of political and economic systems can one go beyond a showing that corruption is harmful to an understanding of the way it operates in different contexts. Given that knowledge, reform programmes can attack corruption where it has the worst effects.

Reform strategies attack the problem of corruption from several directions: programme redesign, law enforcement, improved government performance and accountability. If a country faces a vicious spiral of corruption, the government is in a dysfunctional low-level trap where piece-meal reform will be ineffective. The state needs a major overhaul in law enforcement and in the recruitment of personnel. However, a simple attempt to shrink the state will not be effective because it can create a chaotic situation in which a lawless free-for-all replaces the corruption that went before. A new kind of corruption and self-dealing may arise that is based on the attempt to establish some kind of certainty in a situation of fluidity and chaos.

If corruption can not be countered by single-minded efforts to limit the size of government, then one must consider ways to reform government from within and to limit the willingness of citizens and firms to pay bribes. Anti-corruption policies can increase the benefits of being honest, increase the probability of detection and the level of punishment, reduce the corrupt opportunities under the control of public officials, and increase the accountability of government to its citizens. The incentives for corruption are influenced by:

- the level of benefits and costs under the discretionary control of officials;
- the formal laws designed to combat corruption, bribery, and conflicts of interest, and to regulate campaign spending;
- the credibility of law enforcement against both those who pay and those who accept bribes;
- the conditions of civil service employment, and the performance incentives officials face;
- the extent of auditing and monitoring within government;
- the ability of citizens to learn about government activities, file complaints and obtain redress; and

• the level of press freedom and the freedom of individuals to form non-governmental organizations.

Corruption has a moral dimension, but it can be understood and combated through changing the institutional environment in which firms and citizens operate. A first step in the understanding of corruption is the documentation of the incentives for private gain built into political and bureaucratic processes. Next is an evaluation of the social costs when officials and private citizens succumb to these incentives. Part of the reform agenda involves documenting the social harm of corruption and trying to change a culture of tolerance both within government and in the citizenry and the business community. Moral suasion may work if backed up by concrete arguments for why corruption is harmful to society. The key point is to encourage people to look beyond the net gains from any particular corrupt deal to see how tolerance of corruption has negative systemic effects.

However, most people will not behave well simply because they are told that such actions are in the public interest. A change in behaviour needs to be in their interest as well. Reformers must go beyond documenting the costs of corruption to suggest ways to lower its incidence and impact. Although reforms in law enforcement and in internal monitoring are part of the story, one must consider the redesign of individual public programmes, on the one hand, and ways to increase government transparency and accountability, on the other. Such strategies both reduce the corrupt incentives facing bribe payers and recipients and facilitate effective public oversight by the population.

References and further reading

Bardhan, Pranab (1997) 'Corruption and Development: A Review of Issues', *Journal of Economic Literature*, 35: 1320–46.

Graf Lambsdorff, Johann (2003) 'How Corruption Affects Persistent Capital Flows', *Economics of Governance*, 4: 229–43.

Hellman, Joel S., Jones, Gereint and Kaufmann, Daniel (2003) '"Seize the State, Seize the Day": State Capture, Corruption, and Influence in Transition', *Journal of Comparative Economics*, 31: 751–73.

Johnson, Simon, Kaufmann, Daniel, McMillan, John and Woodruff, Christopher (2000) 'Why Do Firms Hide? Bribes and Unofficial Activity after Communism', *Journal of Public Economics*, 76: 495–520.

Kaufmann, Daniel (1997) 'The Missing Pillar of Growth: Strategy for Ukraine: Institutional and Policy Reforms for Private Sector Development', in Peter K. Cornelius and Patrick Lenain (eds), *Ukraine: Accelerating the Transition to Market*, Washington: International Monetary Fund, pp. 234–75.

Kunicova, Jana and Rose-Ackerman, Susan (2005) 'Electoral Rules as Constraints on Corruption', *British Journal of Political Science*, 35.

Mauro, Paolo (1997) 'The Effects of Corruption on Growth, Investment, and Government Expenditure: A Cross-Country Analysis', in Kimberly Ann Elliott (ed.), *Corruption and the Global Economy*, Washington, DC: Institute for International Economics, pp. 83–108.

Miller, William L., Grødeland, Åse and Koshechkina, Tatyana Y. (2001) *A Culture of Corruption: Coping with Government in Post-Communist Europe*, Budapest, Central European University Press.

Reinikka, Ritva and Svensson, Jakob (2004) 'Local Capture: Evidence from a Central Government Transfer Program in Uganda', *Quarterly Journal of Economics*, 119(2): 679–705.

Rose-Ackerman, Susan (1978) *Corruption: A Study in Political Economy*, New York: Academic Press.

—— (1999) *Corruption and Government: Causes, Consequences and Reform*, Cambridge: Cambridge University Press.

Tanzi, Vito and Davoodi, Hamid (2002) 'Corruption, Public Investment and Growth', in George T. Abed and Sanjeev Gupta (eds), *Governance, Corruption, and Economic Performance*, Washington, DC: International Monetary Fund, pp. 280–99.

SUSAN ROSE-ACKERMAN

CREATIVITY See: Schumpeter

CREDIT See : Banks; micro-credit

CRISIS, ECONOMIC

An economic crisis is a situation in which the reproduction of an economic unit is suddenly compromised, typically when it is unable to meet its contractual obligations. A crisis may be generalized from one unit to the system as a whole, with the crisis being transmitted through a breakdown of the financial system as one failure provokes others and undermines the confidence of investors.

For the economist, an economic crisis is essentially a subjective phenomenon, arising when rosy expectations of the future prove faulty. A general crisis is typically the culmination of an economic boom, during which agents are optimistic about the future and credit is cheap and easily available. Minor failures can be absorbed by the system, but a chain of failures may undermine optimism, leading to a withdrawal of credit and cuts in spending which provoke a generalized crisis and subsequent depression. In retrospect, the waves of optimism and pessimism underlying the business cycle seem irrational, but at the time the expectations of economic agents are self-fulfilling and so their mood appears entirely realistic. The economists' theory of crisis may be complemented by social psychological accounts of the swings of 'market psychology', but leaves little space for sociological explanation.

Sociological contributions to the theory of economic crisis have been almost entirely confined to the Marxist tradition, in which economic crisis has been seen not as an irrational eruption on the surface of capitalism, but as an expression of the inherent contradictions of the capitalist mode of production. While orthodox economists believe that competition ensures that supply and demand adjust smoothly to one another as capitalists adapt their production plans to expected market conditions, Marx and Engels believed that competition drives capitalists to expand the forces of production without limit, so that capitalism is marked by an inherent tendency to overproduction, which underlies the periodic economic crises through which production is brought back within the limits of the market. However, Marx's own writings on crisis are fragmentary and inconsistent so that the Marxist theory of crisis has been an area of intense debate, emphasizing now one and now another aspect of Marx's theory.

The traditional Marxist theory of crisis, propounded by Kautsky, derived from Engels and referred somewhat vaguely to the 'anarchy of the market', within the context of the secular tendency to overproduction, as the source of crises. This theory was challenged in the 1890s by Eduard Bernstein, who denied the necessity of crisis, arguing that cartels would overcome the anarchy of the market. Bernstein's arguments challenged the Marxist assumption of the necessity of socialism, so the theory of crisis became the lynchpin of Marxist orthodoxy. Against Bernstein, Rosa Luxemburg proposed an 'underconsumptionist' theory of crisis, while Rudolf Hilferding proposed a 'disproportionality' theory. Hilferding's theory was compromised because it seemed to imply that corporatist regulation could ensure the proportionality of the various branches of production, so 'underconsumptionism' became the dominant Marxist theory of crisis, endorsed by the ideologists of the Soviet Union. However, 'underconsumptionism' was compromised in its turn by the 'Keynesian revolution', which suggested that state fiscal regulation could overcome any threat of a crisis of underconsumption.

The post-Second World War boom appeared to vindicate the critics of Marxist crisis theory, because it seemed that Keynesian macroeconomic regulation was indeed able to secure sustained economic growth. Nevertheless, the recurrence of crisis tendencies and the failure of Keynesian regulation from the late 1960s provoked a renewed interest in the Marxist theory of crisis. One feature of the renewed crisis tendencies was a marked fall in the rate of profit in the metropolitan centres of capitalist accumulation and Marxist crisis theory now came to focus on the explanation of crisis as a result of this fall in the rate of profit. During the 1970s, Marxist debate raged between those who believed that the fall in the rate of profit was the result of the erosion of profits by rising wages and increasing state social expenditure, as an expression of the intensifying 'class struggle', and those who linked it to Marx's 'law of the tendency for the rate of profit to fall'. As capital came to prevail over labour in the struggle over wages and social spending during the 1970s, it was the 'law of the tendency for the rate of profit to fall' that emerged as the canonical Marxist theory of crisis, although this was more often invoked as a rhetorical device than as a systematic theory.

Before the 1970s, the 'law of the tendency for the rate of profit to fall' had not played a significant role in the explanation of economic crises in the Marxist tradition. If it played any role in Marxist theorizing, it was as a long-term secular tendency, which might make capitalism more vulnerable to a crisis but was not itself the cause of the crisis. The sharp fall in the rate of profit in a crisis was seen as the *result* of the crisis, not as its *cause*, which was found elsewhere. The Marxist debates in the 1970s and 1980s focused on the issue of whether and in what sense Marx established a necessary tendency for the rate of profit to fall, with much less attention being paid to the question of whether and why such a tendency should find its necessary expression in a crisis.

The theory of crisis has played a central ideological role within Marxism because the necessity of crisis supposedly establishes the inevitability of socialism. However, even if the necessity of crisis is established, this ideological role is undermined by two counter-arguments, which Marx and Engels themselves fully recognized. First, a crisis marks not so much the destruction of capitalism as the means of its regeneration. In the wake of the crisis, archaic production capacity is destroyed, while the surviving capitalists are able to force down wages and intensify labour, preparing the ground for a renewal of capitalist accumulation on the basis of an increased rate of profit. Second, the period of depression following a crisis is by no means conducive to the mobilization of the working class, so that an economic crisis will only provoke a revolutionary political crisis if the organized working class is already politically and ideologically prepared to take power.

References and further reading

Clarke, S. (1994) *Marx's Theory of Crisis*, Basingstoke, UK, and London: Macmillan, and New York: St Martin's.

Engels, F. (1987) 'Anti-Dühring', in K. Marx and F. Engels, *Collected Works*, vol. 25, London: Lawrence and Wishart.

Howard, M. C. and King, J. E. (1989/1992) *A History of Marxian Economics*, two volumes, Basingstoke, UK, and London: Macmillan, and New York: St Martin's.

SIMON CLARKE

CULTURAL EMBEDDEDNESS
See: embeddedness

CULTURE AND ECONOMY
See: economic sociology; classification; consumption; Weber

CUSTOMS See: habits

D

DECISION THEORY

Max **Weber** identified rational calculation as a crucial dimension of decision-making in profit-seeking enterprises because quantification is capable of determining 'the expected advantages of every projected course of economic action' (Weber 1978: 81–92). For Weber, rational calculation is historically contingent and occurs slowly 'in the absence of the objective need for it' (1978: 106, 89). During periods of declining **efficiency** and profit, corporations intensify their efforts to standardize decision-making and centralize authority by establishing incentives and shared interests for social action. However, there is no guarantee that the application of formal rationality results in substantive goal rationality.

In contrast to Weber's emphasis on centralization, contingency theorists (e.g. Woodward 1965; Perrow 1970) focus on organizational characteristics that decentralize decisions. This organizational theory maintains that uncertainty contributes to decentralization of decisions in three ways. First, if the relationship between means and ends is poorly understood, rules are not established to govern decisions and authority is delegated. Second, if problems are non-routine and unpredictable, solutions cannot be preprogrammed and personnel at lower levels in the organizational hierarchy have decision-making discretion. Third, in rapidly changing environments, decision-making authority is allocated to lower levels because rules cannot specify how to respond to unanticipated conditions and deferring decisions up the managerial hierarchy reduces organizational responsiveness and flexibility.

The centralization–decentralization thesis is a core concept in the **Carnegie School**, which stresses bounded rationality and the cognitive limits of individuals (March and Simon 1958). This perspective identifies several organizational mechanisms that affect decisions. First, centralizing the information sources available to decision-makers limits the possibility of contradictory information and differences of perception and cognition. Second, premise controls centralize control by limiting the content and flow of information, which limits the search for alternatives and restricts behaviour. Successfully implemented, premise controls restrict the range of stimuli used when making a decision (Simon 1957). Together, the specification of information sources, rules and premise controls limits the search for alternatives in order to maximize the probability of predictable consistent decisions. However, historically, premise controls were limited to non-routine decisions by professionals and operated at higher levels in the organizational hierarchy. Thus, complex tasks such as coordination were accomplished by decentralizing decisions. Bounded rationality is also a central concept in garbage-can theory, which suggests that decision-making is a symbol-driven activity whereby managers engage in **satisficing** behaviour by drawing from a repertoire of responses that provide satisfactory solutions to problems (Cohen *et al.* 1972).

Corporate transformation in the 1980s and 1990s resulted in a renewed interest in decision-making. Researchers agree that economic **globalization** and increased competition require the capability for instant data analysis to increase flexibility and product quality. However, disagreement exists on how restructuring affects decision-making. Some scholars suggest that corporations establish decentralized cooperative **work teams**, extend managerial freedom, weaken the boundaries between managers and workers, and emphasize informal networks that increased autonomy and participation (Piore and Sabel 1984). Others maintain that the managerial process became more centralized, autonomy declined and middle-managerial work was degraded (Burris 1993). Research evaluating these propositions shows that in response to inefficiencies caused by contradictions in the managerial process that increased cost and reduced product quality, operating decisions in manufacturing **firms** were restructured with increased emphasis on quantification in order to standardize decision-making. This neo-Fordist theory maintains that in late **capitalism**, decision-making and authority must be conceptualized as independent variables that are located in different parts of the corporation (Prechel 1994). Sophisticated computer technology allows experts (e.g. accountants, computer technicians, engineers) to separate conception from execution by relocating authority into a single office where they quantify information in order to create bureaucratic and premise controls. These controls are transmitted to the point of **production** on a need-to-know basis to operating managers who execute decisions. Limiting the source of

decision-making information also establishes unobtrusive controls by setting the cognitive premise underlying team decisions. This extension of formal **rationality** to the managerial process eliminates many decisions and routinizes others, which makes it possible to flatten the organizational hierarchy while increasing flexibility and product quality. Although these formal controls centralize authority, they are frequently associated with an **ideology** of decentralization (Smith 1990; Prechel 2000). Recent studies of manufacturing firms show that these expert-centred controls create new workplace **conflict**s and contradictions (Vallas 2003).

Contradictions exist in other decision-making arenas of the corporation. Research on strategic decisions in manufacturing firms shows that long-term structural **embeddedness** and resource dependence create decision-making barriers to migration, even when relocation would reduce production costs (Romo and Schwartz 1995). Network research that tests Granovetter's strength of weak ties and Burt's structural holes hypotheses shows that when uncertainty exists in **banks**, decision-makers are more likely to obtain information from their strong-tie associates than weak-tie associates (Mizruchi and Stearns 2001). However, strong-tie associates provide less information on how to improve a deal, which results in outcomes that are less attractive to corporate clients.

References and further reading

Burris, Beverly (1993) *Technocracy at Work*, Albany: State University of New York Press.

Cohen, Michael, March, James and Olsen, Johan (1972) 'A Garbage Can Model of Organizational Choice', *Administrative Science Quarterly*, 17: 1–25.

Galbraith, Jay (1977) *Organization Design*, Reading, PA: Addison-Wesley.

March, James and Simon, Herbert (1958) *Organizations*, New York: John Wiley and Sons.

Mizruchi, Mark and Stearns, Linda (2001) 'Getting Deals Done', *American Sociological Review*, 66: 647–71.

Perrow, Charles (1970) *Organizational Analysis*, Belmont, CA: Wadsworth.

Piore, Michael and Sabel, Charles (1984) *The Second Industrial Divide*, New York: Basic Books.

Prechel, Harland (1994) 'Economic Crisis and Centralization of Control over the Managerial Process', *American Sociological Review*, 59: 723–45.

—— (2000) *Big Business and the State*, Albany: State University of New York.

Romo, Frank and Schwartz, Michael (1995) 'The Structural Embeddedness of Business Decisions', *American Sociological Review*, 60: 874–907.

Simon, Herbert (1957) *Administrative Behavior*, second edition. New York: Macmillan.

Smith, Vicki (1990) *Managing in the Corporate Interest*, Berkeley, CA: University of California Press.

Vallas, Steven (2003) 'Why Teamwork Fails', *American Sociological Review*, 68: 223–50.

Weber, Max ([1921]1978) *Economy and Society*, Berkeley, CA: University of California Press.

Woodward, Joan (1965) *Industrial Organization*, London: Oxford University Press.

HARLAND PRECHEL

DEFLATION

Each month, the prices of several consumption goods and services (from raw materials like oil or steel to apples, haircuts and flight tickets) are computed in order to calculate indicators like the consumer price index or the GDP deflator. When the rate of growth of these price indexes is negative, the economy is said to be in a period of deflation. More precisely, deflation characterizes a period of *continuous* and *general* decrease in the prices of goods and services. Thus, if the decrease concerns only few commodities or if the general decrease is only temporary, there is no deflation. Deflation is thus the opposite of **inflation** and it must not be confused with disinflation: that is to say, a period of general and durable deceleration of price rise. The classical example of massive deflation hav-

ing huge international consequences for production and employment is the Great Depression that started in the USA. From 1929 to 1932, the basic commodity price decreased by 52 per cent in the USA, 38 per cent in France, 34 per cent in England.

Deflation has a double impact on the economy via its effects on the production and the distribution of wealth, its major effect being, contrary to inflation, on the first one (Keynes 1923). In order to understand why, it is necessary to remember that we live in what **Marx** and **Keynes** called a *monetary production economy*. The main actors of this kind of economy are entrepreneurs and the members of the financial community (bankers or actors in the financial markets). These actors are engaged in productive and speculative activities that induce them to borrow or to lend money today in expectation of future money inflows. This has two consequences: first, borrowers are committed to provide lenders with regular payments (debt services, dividends, rents, etc.) whatever their actual cash inflows; second, lenders depend, for their own activities, on the regular payments of borrowers (unless they can securitize their assets, which is more and more the case today for several assets like home and commercial mortgages, student loans, auto loans and many others). Thus each economic activity starts with money and ends with money. The financing is provided by lenders, and its amount depends on the value and quality of the collateral assets provided and on the convention existing inside the financial community. This convention determines creditworthiness and what is considered as a safe lending behaviour (normal ratio of liquidity, normal debt ratio, normal margins over the value of collateralized assets and so on).

One can see that there is an interlinkage of financial relations that rests on what entrepreneurs and the financial community think about the future: the income of lenders depends on the healthiness of borrowers' activities and the latter depends on the realization of expectations within an acceptable margin of error. What, then, are the effects of deflation, especially if its level is higher than expected? First, entrepreneurs and other borrowers are off their expected cash inflows by a large amount and, thus, may have problems to honour their financial commitments. They may then ask for a renegotiation of outstanding debts but, if lenders are themselves under pressure of their own creditors, lenders may refuse to accept to do this and, on the contrary, may demand the fulfilment of financial commitments. Borrowers have then only two solutions to avoid **bankruptcy**: to sell assets as fast as possible, or to decrease costs by laying off workers and/or demanding more productivity. This goes first via selling output at a lower and lower price, which, again, contributes to deflation, and, second, if not enough, by selling other assets (financial assets, machines, etc.). At the same time the laying-off of workers shrinks aggregate demand, which make things worse for entrepreneurs. On the other side, lenders, because of the decrease in value of collaterals and the incapacity to get money inflows in an amount large enough to pay back their own creditors (some of them being the new unemployed that have to rely more on their savings to survive), may cut loans and themselves start to liquidate assets. The financing of activities, and notably productive activities, then stops at a moment when borrowers crucially need money, which may lead to the bankruptcy of many activities. One may then end up with a situation called debt-deflation (Fisher 1933; Minsky 1986): deflation creates difficulties to service debts which themselves contribute to generate deflation, and so on.

One can see that deflation makes more difficult for borrowers to repay their debts because it increases the real value of debts. The borrowers thus end up paying back more than they expected, and this also contributes to make them reluctant to pursue their own activity. When this redistributive effect concerns entrepreneurs, employment and production suffer.

The sources of deflation are multiple. Orthodox economists agree that deflation is mainly explained by a decrease of the money supply, which decreases demand for goods and services and so generates deflation. This is the basic result of the quantity theory of money derived from a particular interpretation of the following identity:

$$MV \equiv PQ \Rightarrow P \equiv MV/Q$$

The general price level (P) depends on the money supply (M), the velocity of money (V that is supposed to be constant because of habits of payment), and Q the level of production (which is also constant because the economy is supposed to be at full employment). Thus, as soon as V and Q are constant, P can only move if M changes.

However, this explanation of general price level is criticized by many economists like Keynes and his followers (Minsky 1986). Their macroeconomic explanation of prices is based on national accounting:

$$PQ \equiv W + \Pi \Rightarrow P \equiv wN/Q + \Pi/Q$$
$$\Rightarrow P \equiv w/\mathrm{AP}_L + \Pi/Q$$

The income approach to the GDP identity shows us that the GDP deflator depends on several elements: the distribution of income in the society (wN/Q being the share of wage and Π/Q being the share of profit), the productivity of factors of production and notably of labour (AP_L: average productivity of labour). The explanation of deflation is not based mainly on money for those authors: class conflicts, innovation in the processes of production (better organization, better formation of workers, invention of new machines, etc.), are far more important to explain deflation (or inflation).

Another explanation of deflation, which is compatible with the preceding one, can be derived from the debt-deflation process described above. Deflation results from an excess of optimism by entrepreneurs and bankers that led them to implement activities that are more fragile financially (expectation of profits are more uncertain and more sensitive to external shocks like changes of monetary policy, temporary changes in the patterns of consumption, re-evaluation, increases in the price of raw materials, etc.). Here the deflation bias has its roots in an excessive monetary creation in the past! The total opposite to the orthodox macroeconomic explanation of prices!

Therefore, the usual explanation based on monetary sources of deflation is not sufficient and not general. Moreover, once the possibility of debt-deflation exists other questions become relevant: why should we not be concerned with the variation of prices other than consumption goods? Should not we include financial assets, real estates and other investment goods in the measure of deflation (or inflation)? A regulation of these assets, in addition to the current regulation of the prices of consumption goods, seems more than reasonable. This question is, however, very controversial among economists.

References and further reading

Fisher, I. (1933) 'The Debt Deflation Theory of Great Depressions', *Econometrica*, 1, October: 337–57.

Keynes, J. M. ([1923]1973) 'Social Consequences of Changes in the Value of Money', in *The Collected Writings of John Maynard Keynes*, vol. 9, London: Macmillan, pp. 59–75.

Minsky, H. P. (1986) *Stabilizing an Unstable Economy*, New Haven, CT: Yale University Press.

ERIC TYMOIGNE

DEINDUSTRIALIZATION

Deindustrialization has been one of the defining features of the world's most advanced economies for a number of decades. It is presently a topic of growing interest and concern in a number of newly industrializing countries as well. As a subject of academic and policy research and debate, deindustrialization is typically defined as involving the decline of manufacturing employment relative to employment in other sectors of the economy. By this definition, deindustrialization has been widespread, and often dramatic, across the global North in recent years. In the United States, for instance, manufacturing's share of employment declined from 26.4 per cent of civilian employment in 1970 to 14.7 per cent in 2000. In the United Kingdom, employment in manufacturing declined from 34.2 per cent to 17.1 per cent of civilian employment across the same period (OECD 2002).

The phenomenon of deindustrialization has given rise to a lively debate over its causes and consequences. It has often been viewed with considerable apprehension and has regularly been invoked as a leading 'suspect' in the twin 'mysteries' of rising income inequality in the USA and the UK and rising unemployment in continental Europe.

Accounts of the experience of the last third of the twentieth century vary widely. An early theme in the literature was that deindustrialization was the result of especially poor industrial performance; of poor product quality, spiralling labour costs, destructive conflicts between labour and management, poor corporate and government policy. This diagnosis appears to have originated in the literature devoted to dissecting the causes of the 'British disease' or 'Englanditis' of the 1960s and 1970s. It has re-emerged regularly since then in a number of other national literatures. In the 1990s, attention turned to the role of **glo-**

balization in deindustrialization. A number of analysts have linked rising international trade (especially North–South trade) and the growing international mobility of capital to the relative decline of manufacturing employment. This theme emerged in treatments of deindustrialization in the USA and has grown in prominence in tandem with the increasing scholarly and public interest in globalization.

Participants in this debate have not always fully appreciated that deindustrialization had in fact long been anticipated. Social scientists had predicted, well before Daniel Bell (1973), the future 'coming of post-industrial society'. For instance, the British economist Colin Clark ([1940]1957) expected a shift from manufacturing to services owing to two processes: first, with **economic development**, 'as real income per head rises ... the *relative* demand for agricultural products falls all the time, and ... the relative demand for manufacture first rises, and then falls in favour of services'; second, higher productivity in the manufacturing sector relative to services means that one should expect over time a '*decreasing* proportion of the labour force to be employed [in manufacturing]' (pp. 493–4, emphasis in original). Also in the 1940s, the French economist Jean Fourastié (1949) made similar arguments regarding the effects of productivity and demand differences across sectors of the economy on manufacturing's share of employment. These early treatments of deindustrialization suggest that as productivity grows and economies mature, one should expect manufacturing employment to contract (and service sector employment to expand) in the normal course of economic development. Interestingly, this generalization about long-run economic development was first made as long ago as 1691 by the proto-economist Sir William Petty (1899).

How then should we understand deindustrialization? An especially useful framework has been developed by Robert Rowthorn and his colleagues (e.g. Rowthorn and Wells 1987; Rowthorn and Ramaswamy 1998). This allows that deindustrialization has in fact had multiple causes. First, there is the *positive deindustrialization* noted by figures such as Clark and Fourastié. Such deindustrialization is a 'natural outcome' of successful economic development. It occurs as a consequence of the typically higher rate of productivity growth in manufacturing relative to services and of the systematic changes in demand that occur over the course of development (i.e. Engle's law). This deindustrialization is 'positive' because it is not a pathological phenomenon. It is a symptom of economic success and is associated with rising living standards. Second, there is the *negative deindustrialization* discussed in the context of the 'British disease' of the 1960s and 1970s and of the sharp recession of the early 1980s in the United States. This form of deindustrialization is a pathological phenomenon, a structural disequilibrium that prevents an economy from reaching its growth potential or a full employment of its resources, and is associated with stagnating real incomes and rising unemployment. Third, there are a set of *external sources* of deindustrialization, rooted in international specialization (1) between manufactured goods and other goods and services and (2) within manufacturing itself. Concerns about globalization, especially for the impact of North–South trade, can be framed in this context.

These differing forms of deindustrialization have operated concurrently; that is, the deindustrialization experienced by the advanced economies in recent decades has not solely been the result of any one 'form' of deindustrialization. Instead, the literature suggests that contemporary deindustrialization has been the result of a mix of 'positive', 'negative' and 'external' factors. Among these, 'positive' factors are typically described as being most important. Alderson (1999) finds evidence for all three forms

of deindustrialization in a cross-national analysis, but concludes that the net impact of
negative deindustrialization and of external
sources is considerably more modest than is
suggested in some alarmist treatments of
deindustrialization. Rowthorn and Ramaswamy (1998) show that the largest part of the
deindustrialization observed in their cross-
national analyses is positive deindustrialization. Among external sources of deindustrialization, globalization is regularly observed
to be a significant, if secondary, factor.
Alderson (1999) estimates that North–South
trade explains more than a quarter of the
deindustrialization in countries he studies.
Rowthorn and Ramaswamy (1998) find that
it explains less than a fifth of the deindustrialization they observe. Both of these estimates are notably smaller than the figure
suggested by Wood (1994), who attributes
more than half of the decline in manufacturing employment to trade globalization.

References and further reading

Alderson, Arthur S. (1999) 'Explaining Dein-
dustrialization: Globalization, Failure, or
Success?' *American Sociological Review*, 64:
701–21.
Bell, Daniel (1973) *The Coming of Post-Industrial
Society*, New York: Basic Books.
Bluestone, Barry and Harrison, Bennett (1982)
The Deindustrialization of America, New York:
Basic Books.
Clark, Colin ([1940]1957) *The Conditions of
Economic Progress*, third edition, London:
Macmillan.
Fourastié, Jean (1949) *Le Grand Espoir du XXème
siècle. Progrès technique, progrès économique, Pro-
grès Social* [The Great Hope of the Twentieth
Century], Paris: Presses Universitaires de
France.
OECD (2002) *OECD Historical Statistics, 1970–
2000*, Paris: OECD.
Petty, Sir William (1899) *The Economic Writings of
Sir William Petty*, vol. 1, edited by C. H. Hull,
Cambridge: Cambridge University Press.
Rowthorn, Robert E. and Ramaswamy,
Ramana (1998) *Growth, Trade, and Deindus-
trialization. Working Paper of the International
Monetary Fund 98/60*, Washington, DC:
International Monetary Fund.
Rowthorn, Robert E. and Wells, John R.
(1987) *De-Industrialization and Foreign Trade*,
Cambridge: Cambridge University Press.
Wood, Adrian (1994) *North–South Trade,
Employment, and Inequality*, Oxford: Oxford
University Press.

ARTHUR S. ALDERSON

DELIBERATION

The concept of deliberation finds its reference point in Jürgen Habermas's theory of
communicative action. A minimal definition according to Diego Gambetta is that of
'a conversation where individuals speak and
listen sequentially before making a collective decision' (1998: 19). So defined,
deliberation can be considered as synonymous with the discussion and exchange of
information in the context of decision-
making independent of the asymmetries
between the actors, their aims and motives,
be they interest, passion or reason. In this
broad definition, forms of communicative
decision-making like arguing and bargaining (see **bargaining theory**) are a constitutive part of the deliberative process. For
Jon Elster, deliberation includes 'decision-
making by means of arguments offered by
and to participants who are committed to
the value of rationality and impartiality'
(1998: 8). In this normatively oriented
definition the parties are equal; discussion is
normally on matters of principle with the
aim of changing the preferences of the
counterparts. Thus, according to Elster,
arguing is genuinely deliberative. Contrary
to this, it can be reasonably expected that
interest-oriented communication is based
on the exchange of threats and promises, in
which the actors' goals cannot be substantially changed. Hence, the case of bargaining, for instance, cannot be considered
as a form of deliberation.

Both positions, however, share the premises of what constitutes (good) deliberation and the positive consequences in terms

of outputs and outcomes of deliberative decision-making.

Deliberative conversations rely in fact on an elementary form of **cooperation** by the parties – at least their willingness to listen – that may differ according to the institutional setting and culture of different societies. Advantages of deliberation include the better allocation of information, Pareto-superior decisions (see **Pareto, Vilfredo**), fairer outcomes in terms of distributive justice, larger consensus and legitimacy for the decision, and better implementation. Other possible by-products are the improvement of the moral and intellectual qualities of the participants to the discussion through the dissemination of principles in public life and the creation of a culture of cooperation.

With respect to socio-economic processes, collective decision-making through deliberation is applied in the realm of welfare and economic policies, in the negotiation of work and wage conditions as well as to explain forms of development based on cooperation. Hall and Soskice underline how the success of coordinated market economies relies on redundant deliberative institutions 'that encourage the relevant actors to engage in collective discussion and to reach agreement with each other' (Hall and Soskice 2001: 11). Deliberation is important because it 'provides the actors with an opportunity to establish the risks and gains attendant on cooperation and to resolve the distributive issues associated with them' (Hall and Soskice 2001: 11). Shared **information** is a significant source of confidence and the institutionalization of conceptions and **beliefs** about distributive justice which facilitate agreements in subsequent exchanges. On the other hand, they can enhance the strategic capacities of the actors in situations of uncertainty related, for example, to external shocks. It has been argued historically that deliberative forms of decision-making have produced less conflict and better performance in fighting inflation in the 1970s, but also

better capacity of adaptation of the European national political economies to inflation and public debt called for in the processes of the European economic and monetary integration during the 1990s.

As already mentioned above, deliberation is also central to another important field explored by economic sociology, i.e. the processes of development through cooperation. According to Sabel 'the more deliberative the parties apply the general principle of cooperation to their particular activities, the more effective those activities will be' (1995: 139). Deliberation makes it possible to escape cultural fixations as well as to overcome the limits of **game theory** concerning the instigation of cooperation and **trust**. By making the parties interdependent, reciprocal monitoring is encouraged and deceit is discouraged. Furthermore, institutions that lend themselves to discursive processes 'transform transactions into discussions ... by which parties come to reinterpret themselves and their relations to each other by elaborating a common understanding of the world' (1995: 138). Deliberation thus helps in creating common identities that may become the foundation for economic cooperation. Deliberative cooperative relationships among economic actors can help to explain the success of both the industrial districts in the more traditional sectors and agglomerations of high-tech industry and services like Silicon Valley. Deliberative institutions were also important for development processes in Japan and in other late-comer economies. On the other hand, it has been argued that the lack of deliberative networks could account for incoherencies in the economic restructuring of the post-socialist countries (Stark and Bruszt 1998).

In both fields examined – concertation and economic development – associations are crucial actors either as parties in the negotiations or as promoters of cooperation among economic actors. However, authors like Sabel (1995) and Stark and Bruszt

(1998) point out some differences between organized interests and developmental associations of economic actors in terms of the deliberative processes they are able to instigate. While the former associations generally discuss contracts and are characterized by strong organizational identities and fixed interests that are not changed through their bargaining activities, developmental associations play a stronger role in shaping identities and goals of the economic actors. Similar to Elster, they are cautious about including bargaining in the framework of deliberation.

References and further reading

Elster, Jon (1998) 'Introduction', in Jon Elster (ed.), *Deliberative Democracy*, Cambridge: Cambridge University Press, pp. 1–18.

Gambetta, Diego (1998) '"Claro!": An Essay on Discursive Machism', in Jon Elster (ed.), *Deliberative Democracy*. Cambridge: Cambridge University Press, pp. 19–43.

Hall, Peter A. and Soskice, David (2001) 'An Introduction to Varieties of Capitalism', in Peter A. Hall and David Soskice (eds), *Varieties of Capitalism. The Institutional Foundations of Comparative Advantages*, Oxford: Oxford University Press, pp. 1–68.

Sabel, Charles (1995) 'Learning by Monitoring: The Institutions of Economic Development', in Neil J. Smelser and Richard Swedberg (eds), *The Handbook of Economic Sociology*, Princeton, NJ: Princeton University Press, pp. 137–65.

Stark, David and Bruszt, Lásló (1998) *Postsocialist Pathways: Transforming Politics and Property in East Central Europe*, Cambridge: Cambridge University Press.

GENY PIOTTI

DEMOCRACY AND ECONOMY

The topics of democracy and the economy have had a remarkably distorted relationship in modern times. Since the mid nineteenth century, democracy has been a near-universal norm for government at the national, local and municipal levels. The natural question is: what is the relationship of democracy to the economy – or, specifically, to the economic enterprises in a private property market economy?

One approach to this democracy-and-economy question is to evoke a 'public–private' distinction. Democracy is seen as a norm only in the 'public sphere'; the democratic germ is quarantined out of the 'private sphere' by the rights of **property**. The economic governance of the people working in an economic enterprise is seen as an attribute of property ('ownership of the means of production'), much as political governance was once seen as an attribute of land ownership – when the landlord was the 'Lord of the land'. As Marx put it in *Capital*:

> It is not because he is a leader of industry that a man is a capitalist; on the contrary, he is a leader of industry because he is a capitalist. The leadership of industry is an attribute of capital, just as in feudal times the functions of general and judge were attributes of landed property.
>
> (Vol. I, Ch. XIII: Co-operation)

Starting with this analysis of public democratic rights versus private property rights, there are at least three paths to extending democracy to the economy:

1. democratic socialism path: by moving the ownership of the means of production into the public sphere at the national, local, or municipal levels;
2. social democracy path: by attenuating the rights of private property without nationalization (e.g. co-determination); and
3. economic democracy path: by abolishing the employment relationship in favour of all workers becoming the legal members of their enterprises – after noting that the employer's governance over the employees never was an attribute of property (Marx was simply wrong) but is a consequence of the employment contract.

The practice of real existing socialism is a matter of historical record but, even in theory, 'democratic socialism' would not establish self-government in the workplace. The geographically defined political electorate extended far beyond the workers in any particular enterprise so the workers would at best be 'public employees' in a political democracy rather than self-governing members of a democratic work-community. Much social experimentation in the twentieth century was exploration of this dead-end path.

Perhaps the best recent example of a social democratic thinker is political scientist Robert Dahl, particularly in *A Preface to Economic Democracy* (1985). Dahl is a remarkable exception to one of the open intellectual scandals of our time, the 'disconnect' between the near-universal espousal of democracy in the midst of an economic system based on the renting, employing or hiring of human beings in the workplace that is not democratic even in theory. Dahl is not content to have democracy limited to the 'public sphere', but accepts the argument that the governance by the capitalist-employer is an attribute of private property. His response is to attenuate the rights of private property rather than nationalize them. The German system of works councils and co-determination represents a partial step in this direction.

The economic democracy path (as I will call it) rejects the argument that private property restricts democracy to the 'public sphere' by showing that the non-democratic governance of workers follows from the employment contract, not private property. It is remarkably simple to see that ownership of the means of production is neither necessary nor sufficient for the control rights in an economic enterprise in a private property market economy. It is not necessary since the employer could be renting or leasing but not owning the land, buildings and machinery. And it is not sufficient since the owner of that capital could be leasing them out to the employer. To be the legal party undertaking an enterprise, it is necessary and sufficient that the party own the services of the people (e.g. man-hours) and the services of all the means of production (e.g. machine-hours) that are used up in the enterprise. Ownership of the people and capital goods is not required, only the purchase of the services (not already owned) in rental, leasing or hiring contracts. In particular, the control over the people involved in the economic activities comes from employing them, i.e. buying their services, in the employer–employee contract (called the 'master–servant' contract up to nineteenth century).

Thus the economic democracy approach argues that democracy is not at war with private property at all, but that democracy is at war with the renting of human beings in the employment contract. Indeed, if property is to be founded on the principle of appropriating the (positive and negative) fruits of one's labour, then private property would actually entail economic democracy (i.e. people in an enterprise being the legal members of it). The fundamental juridical principle, e.g. used in civil or criminal trials, is to assign the legal responsibility to those who were in fact responsible. Assign de jure responsibility according to de facto responsibility. In an economic enterprise, all the people who work in the enterprise are jointly de facto responsible for using up the inputs (negative fruits of their labour) in the course of producing the outputs (positive fruits of their labour). Applying that justice principle to the workplace, they should have the de jure or legal responsibility for those input-liabilities (paid for as expenses) and those output-assets (sold as the revenues), i.e. they should be the legal members of the enterprise as a legal party. That is how the Jeffersonian family farms and family firms can be extended so that people are always jointly working for themselves in private enterprises of any size.

Whither the employment contract? Today, as Paul Samuelson put it in his primer *Economics*: 'Since slavery was abolished, human earning power is forbidden by law to be capitalized. A man is not even free to sell himself; he must *rent* himself at a wage' (1976: 52). But the employment contract for people renting themselves out, like the older self-sale contract, conflicts with the fact that people cannot voluntarily transfer or alienate de facto responsibility. The self-rental contract should join the self-sale contract in history's dustbin of invalid contracts. People would then always own or rent things (e.g. capital) instead of the owners of things renting people. To reconcile democracy and the economy, there is no need to nationalize the means of production or even to attenuate the actual rights of private property. But there is a need to legally recognize the invalidity of the employment contract – the contract that operates 'as if' de facto responsible human action could be voluntarily alienated and transferred. Then property would be refounded on the justice principle of inalienable responsibility.

We have so far approached democracy and the economy by starting with the alleged juxtaposition of democracy and property. We might also trace out the classical liberal approach which holds that democracy and the economy (i.e. the employment system) are perfectly compatible because both are based on voluntary contracts. In Milton Friedman's classic *Capitalism and Freedom* (1962), he poses the basic choice as being between consent or coercion.

Fundamentally, there are only two ways of coordinating the economic activities of millions. One is central direction involving the use of coercion – the technique of the army and of the modern totalitarian state. The other is voluntary cooperation of individuals – the technique of the marketplace (Friedman 1962: 13).

Democracy as 'government based on the consent of the governed' and 'capitalism' are both based on voluntary contracts – so they seem to be on the same side of the argument.

It is a remarkable fact of modern intellectual history that classical liberalism has been able to sell this consent-or-coercion approach as the correct framing of the question about democracy and capitalism. But there have been sophisticated arguments at least since the Middle Ages which grounded autocracies (non-democratic governments) on an implicit or explicit social contract of subjugation, the *pactum subjectionis*. There were always a few volunteer strawmen for classical liberalism who argued that the king's rulership was based not on consent but on Divine Right or, more plausibly, on the king's ultimate ownership of the land. But as the German legal historian Otto Gierke noted in his *Political Theories of the Middle Age* (1958: 88), 'Then, when the question about Ownership had been severed from that about Rulership, we may see coming to the front always more plainly the supposition of the State's origin in a Contract of Subjection made between People and Ruler.' In about 1310, according to Gierke, 'Engelbert of Volkersdorf is the first to declare in a general way that all *regna et principatus* originated in a *pactum subjectionis*' (1958: 146) We may then 'fast forward' through Thomas Hobbes' *Leviathan* (1651) to Harvard's late moral philosopher Robert Nozick, who argued on libertarian grounds in *Anarchy, State, and Utopia* (1974: 113) that people should be allowed to contract away their rights of self-government to a Hobbesian 'dominant protective association' and even that the self-sale contract should be revalidated. 'The comparable question about an individual is whether a free system will allow him to sell himself into slavery. I believe that it would' (1974: 331).

Classical liberalism's simplistic consent-or-coercion framework ignores the contractarian arguments for non-democratic government from Engelbert of Volkersdorf to Nozick of Harvard. The deeper debate was between two fundamentally different types of contract – between a social contract of subjugation alienating the right to self-government and a democratic constitution which secures that right. The democratic tradition argued contra Hobbes that the *pactum subjectionis* was naturally invalid and that the right to self-government was inalienable even with consent. That inalienability doctrine descended from Reformation argument for the inalienability of conscience, e.g. that one inextricably had to make one's own decision about religious **beliefs**. In Martin Luther's 'Concerning Secular Authority', he argued for the inalienability of this responsibility:

> Furthermore, every man is responsible for his own faith, and he must see it for himself that he believes rightly. As little as another can go to hell or heaven for me, so little can he believe or disbelieve for me; and as little as he can open or shut heaven or hell for me, so little can he drive me to faith or unbelief.
>
> ([1523]1942: 316)

During the Scottish Enlightenment, this argument was developed into a theory of inalienable rights by Francis Hutcheson and then was passed to Thomas Jefferson, who popularized it in the Declaration of Independence.

There is a good reason why classical liberalism ignores the democratic tradition of inalienable rights – so that democracy and the employment system ('capitalism') will seem to be on the same rather than opposite sides of the democratic argument. The employment contract that lies at the foundation of our economic civilization is a scaled-down workplace version of the *pactum subjectionis*. The employer is not the representative or delegate of the employees; the employees agree to alienate and transfer the rights of self-governance in the work-

place to the employer. Yet as Luther argued, one's de facto decision-making capacity is not transferable to another – neither the Pope nor one's employer. Agreeing to follow an injunction to believe X or an order to do Y is only another way of deciding to believe X or do Y.

Thus starting with the classical liberal approach to democracy and the economy, we have come around again to the employment contract. From the viewpoint of both responsible action and decision-making, the employment contract pretends to alienate that which is inalienable. Thus it is invalid, like the full-blown collective *pactum subjectionis* and the individual self-sale contract. That is how democracy comes to the economy.

References and further reading

Dahl, Robert (1985) *A Preface to Economic Democracy*, Berkeley, CA: University of California Press.

Ellerman, David (1992) *Property and Contract in Economics: The Case for Economic Democracy*, Cambridge MA: Blackwell (full text available at www.ellerman.org).

Friedman, Milton (1962) *Capitalism and Freedom*, Chicago: University of Chicago Press.

Gierke, Otto (1958) *Political Theories of the Middle Age*, translated and edited by F. W. Maitland, Boston: Cambridge University Press.

Greider, William (2003) *The Soul of Capitalism: Opening Paths to a Moral Economy*, New York: Simon and Schuster.

Luther, Martin ([1523]1942) 'Concerning Secular Authority', in Francis W. Coker (ed.), *Readings in Political Philosophy*, New York: Macmillan, pp. 306–29.

Nozick, Robert (1974) *Anarchy, State and Utopia*, New York: Basic Books.

Samuelson, Paul A. (1976) *Economics*, New York: McGraw-Hill.

DAVID ELLERMAN

DEMOGRAPHY OF DEVELOPMENT

Thomas Malthus' famous dictum that agricultural productivity increases arithmetically while population increases geometrically has convinced generations of social scientists that demography and development are antithetical social processes. Coale and Hoover (1958), for instance, theorized that rapid population growth forces families to consume savings, adversely affecting capital formation and resulting investment via lower national savings rates. In addition, high youth dependency ratios force nations to invest scarce capital in a game of 'catch-up' to provide education, jobs and infrastructure for a rapidly expanding labour force. This theory and others constitute the neo-Malthusian wisdom that rapid population growth and dense habitation lead to habitual poverty.

Nonetheless, Malthus' pessimism concerning the role of demography in development stands in sharp contrast to the views of other classical writers. A long pronatalist tradition typifies western philosophy, with many commentators of the ancient and medieval worlds considering population size and growth sure indicators of successful, expansionary social systems (e.g. Cicero, Plato, Machiavelli). Indeed, the founders of social science explicitly modelled population variables as (beneficial) catalysts in economic transformation (Smith, Spencer and **Durkheim**).

Given this conceptual history, it is no surprise that the neo-Malthusian orthodoxy has been giving way to a more balanced view of demography's role in economics. Owing to inconsistent research findings on the influence of population growth and **economic development**, as well as to a few persistent voices in the wilderness that insisted on the positive effects of population on economic institutions (e.g. Julian Simon), social scientists began to question neo-Malthusian orthodoxy by the 1980s. The alternative theory, well rooted in classical thinking, asserts that increasing population size and density encourage economic complexity, a dynamic Smith and Spencer attributed to market niche-formation and

Durkheim to competition. As individuals and groups struggle for scarce resources in heavily populated environments, they specialize and innovate to realize new opportunities and to reduce competition. Organizational specialization and technological development are therefore *emergent properties* springing from *population pressure*.

Three formative areas of the new demography of development focus on population growth/age structure, population density and population composition. The lion's share of this revisionist demographic literature points to age structure as the operative mechanism mediating population and economic growth. Put simply, some types of population growth contribute to economic activities while other types detract from it. As the major actors in any economy, working-age adults compete for resources, specialize to avoid competition, and engage in major consumption. Population growth rates among the very young and old, however, have far fewer immediate multipliers and some substantial costs (e.g. education, medical care) (Bloom and Freeman 1988; Kelley and Schmidt 1995). In short, working-age adults constitute every economy's cutting edge, while children are its *investment* in the future.

These countervailing demographic effects suggest *demographic windfalls* and *ratchets* (Crenshaw *et al.* 1997). That is, for countries undergoing demographic transition, as fertility falls adult population growth overshadows child population growth. Under such circumstances, a society will enjoy a demographic windfall – a generation-long boost in economic growth due to labour force growth sans the costs of children. Over time, of course, and *absent sufficient international immigration*, these relatively childless adult cohorts will retire, placing demands on a greatly diminished labour force. Undermanned labour markets enhance earnings and opportunities and may encourage earlier marriage and increased fertility (the Easterlin effect –

Easterlin 1968). In this scenario, the demographic engine of economic growth acts as a ratchet – rapid economic growth during baby busts followed by slower economic growth as societies reinvest via higher fertility. The simple terms for the other scenario, where a shrinking labour force does not encourage higher fertility, is social decline and eventual extinction, a fate that is only briefly postponed by immigration from countries that are themselves undergoing demographic transitions.

Population density is also an important variable in economic change, signalling historical differences in climates, disease regimes and social environments among contemporary societies, differences that suggest a continuum running from the *pre-modern* to the *modern* (Crenshaw and Oakey 1998; Burkett *et al.* 1999). *Proto-modern* societies, or societies where historical population pressures forced advanced agrarianism and institutional development, more easily transit into the club of developed societies. The link between pre-modern population density and current economic performance can be traced (in part) to plough agriculture, which produced the economic surplus that encouraged urbanization, written language, the invention of money to replace **barter**, complex occupational structures, government bureaucracy, and many other hallmarks of 'modernity' (Lenski and Nolan 1984). In short, historical population density (or demographic inheritance) is an unmistakable telltale of an evolutionary process that is crucial in contemporary economic development.

Diversity in ascribed status (e.g. ethnicity, race, language) is also an integral part of the new demography of development. In a nutshell, for every Cordoba in world history there is a Beirut; ethnic/racial competition generally challenges social cohesion. In theoretical terms, sociocultural diversity can interfere with social differentiation and interdependency, impeding the formation

of social capital (Temple and Johnson 1998) and institutional props such as contract law and public spending on infrastructure (Easterly and Levine 1997). Recent sociological research highlights the economic benefits of ethnicity-based *social capital*. The use of ascribed statuses as axes of organization provides the phenotypic markers, tight social interdependencies and common cultural understandings that create effective social organization and control (Hechter 1987: 176). Nevertheless, there may be a national price to pay for economic miracles dependent on 'bounded solidarity'. The downside of ethnic solidarity includes 'out-grouping', slower diffusion of technologies and norms, and often inter-ethnic violence, none of which maximize economic growth.

This brief sketch of the demographic causes of economic change points out the need for greater specifics in theoretical development. The influences of age structure, demographic inheritance and population composition on economic behaviour, organization and change are likely to be complex, but understanding them holds out the hope for a more complete human ecology of economic development.

References and further reading

Bloom, David E. and Freeman, Richard B. (1988) 'Economic Development and the Timing and Components of Populations Growth', *Journal of Policy Modeling*, 10: 57–81.

Burkett, John P., Humblet, Catherine and Putterman, Louis (1999) 'Preindustrial and Post-war Economic Development: Is There a Link?' *Economic Development and Cultural Change*, 47: 471–95.

Coale, A. J. and Hoover, E. M. (1958) *Population Growth and Economic Development in Low-Income Countries*, Princeton, NJ: Princeton University Press,

Crenshaw, Edward M. and Oakey, Doyle Ray (1998) 'Jump-Starting Development: Hyperurbanization as a Long-Term Economic Investment', *Sociological Focus*, 31: 321–40.

Crenshaw, Edward M., Ameen, Ansari and Christenson, Matthew (1997) 'Population Dynamics and Economic Development: The

Differential Effects of Age-Specific Population Growth Rates on Per Capita Economic Growth in Developing Countries, 1965 to 1990', *American Sociological Review*, 62: 974–84.

Easterlin, R. A. (1968) *Population, Labor Force, and Long Swings in Economic Growth: The American Experience*, New York: National Bureau of Economic Research.

Easterly, William and Levine, Ross (1997) 'Africa's Growth Tragedy: Policies and Ethnic Divisions', *Quarterly Journal of Economics*, 112: 1203–50.

Hechter, Michael (1987) *Principles of Social Solidarity*, Berkeley, CA: University of California Press.

Kelley, Allen C. and Schmidt, Robert M. (1995) 'Aggregate Population and Economic Growth Correlations: The Role of the Components of Demographic Change', *Demography*, 32: 543–55.

Lenski, Gerhard and Nolan, Patrick (1984) 'Trajectories of Development: A Test of Ecological Evolutionary Theory', *Social Forces*, 63: 1–23.

Temple, Jonathan and Johnson, Paul A. (1998) 'Social Capability and Economic Growth', *Quarterly Journal of Economics*, 113: 965–90.

EDWARD CRENSHAW

DEMOGRAPHY OF ORGANIZATIONS

See: organization theory

DIFFERENTIATION

See: Luhmann; Systems Approach to Economic Sociology; Weber

DISCRIMINATION

Discrimination is the act of distinguishing between two or more groups on the basis of perceived differences (real or not) and favouring or differentially treating an individual on the basis of his or her group membership. Economic sociologists recognize that individuals, organizations and social institutions can engage in discriminatory behaviour. Victims of discrimination are often members of relatively less economically powerful groups. Regardless of their relative numerical size, groups that experi-

ence discrimination are called minority groups while those that discriminate are referred to as dominant groups. In addition to individual and organizational agents engaging in discriminatory behaviour, economic institutions can have a less visible and often unintended infrastructure that produces unequal outcomes for minority groups. This essay first discusses agentic forms of discrimination and then turns to discriminatory aspects of economic institutions.

In the USA, under Title VII of Civil Rights Act of 1964, workplace discrimination is considered illegal if the criteria used to discriminate are not relevant to the performance of the job. As codified into law, discrimination falls into two basic categories: disparate treatment and disparate impact. In cases involving disparate treatment, plaintiffs must demonstrate that a work-related disparity in treatment between groups results from intentional discrimination. Disparate impact cases do not require proof of intentional discrimination by employers. The Supreme Court, in the 1971 decision *Griggs v. Duke Power Company*, ruled that any policy that has an adverse economic impact on a group protected by the Civil Rights Act can be ruled discriminatory, even if that policy appears at face value to be neutral, provided that the defendant cannot demonstrate that the policy in question is a business necessity or relevant to the job in question.

Social scientists differ in what they identify as the causes of and, thus, the solutions to discrimination. Neoclassical economists typically conceptualize discrimination as an anomaly of market capitalism. In this perspective, discrimination is generated by individual tastes and/or individual error. Discriminators can be individuals acting on their own behalf or on the behalf of an organization. Several economic explanations of discrimination are in interdisciplinary use.

One distinction is *taste discrimination*. Economist Gary Becker (1957) argues that individuals may have a taste for discrimination and may be willing to pay to indulge their taste. Individual tastes are considered to be unchanging, unmeasurable and exogenous to models of discrimination. It is not necessary that the taste for discrimination should come solely from within a company, as the tastes of a company's customer base may be sufficient to effect hiring practices. Employers that have a taste for discrimination should be at a competitive disadvantage to firms that do not, or at least have a lower taste for discrimination, due to lost productivity and opportunity. Firms with high tastes for discrimination, and the higher wage costs paid to indulge these tastes, should eventually be driven out of business. Note that this theory, with its characteristically economic emphasis on individual employers, may be unable to explain widely held prejudices that may be shared across employers and help mitigate the proposed penalty for discrimination. Additionally, if customers are willing, or given no other choice, to pay for the prices required to indulge their taste for discrimination, it is not necessarily the case that companies that engaged in discriminatory practices will be forced out of the market.

A second model of discrimination offered by economic theory is *statistical discrimination*. Statistical discrimination refers to discrimination that results from the inevitability of imperfect information that firms are faced with in making hiring decisions. The gathering of a given individual's information that is pertinent to a decision on employment (training, educational quality and credentials, work experience, productivity, etc.) for a large number of applicants is an expensive, and at times impossible, proposition for most employers. Given their de facto reliance on imperfect information about individual applicants, employers resort to a basis for decisions that relies heavily on differences in the *average* abilities between groups. Closely related to statistical discrimination is *error discrimination*. Error discrimination occurs when economic decisions are made on the basis of an employer's misestimation of the work-related traits of a given group on average, and thus are unwilling to hire from these groups. Most economic theory holds that error discrimination cannot be a persistent factor in contributing to economic inequality, as employers would inevitably correct errors in their calculations of average potential as their experience in hiring across social characteristics accumulates.

Neoclassical economic theory argues that discrimination will inevitably be eliminated by market competition due to the inefficiency of discrimination. To the extent discrimination increases labour costs relative to revenue, discriminating firms will be pushed out of business by more profitable non-discriminating firms.

In contrast to neoclassical economists, sociologists view discrimination not just as a result of individual actors, but also as a part of the social structure. Discriminatory practices can be codified into rules, social policy and social institutions. Institutional discrimination resides in the policies and practices that systematically disadvantage definable social groups. As a built-in feature of social structure, institutional discrimination is more difficult to notice and to solve. Individuals can unknowingly participate in institutional discrimination despite their individual intent to discriminate.

Organizations scholars argue that firms, in an effort to function harmoniously with the larger organizational and social environment, will mirror the hierarchies and inequities of society. An example of this is found Kanter's (1977) landmark study. Kanter's data show that the traditional gender division of labour in the family is reflected in firms so that some jobs are considered 'appropriate' for men (high-prestige professional and managerial work) and other jobs are considered 'appropriate' for women (low-prestige service and support work). The gendered division of labour is associated with gender segregated occupations throughout the economy. Feminists argue that occupational segregation, coupled with the devaluation of women's work, is an important factor behind the gender gap in pay. Even if jobs were not segregated by gender, feminists argue that the organization of work and jobs disadvantages women. For example, ideal employees are assumed to have few non-work distractions or competing demands for their time (the assumption is another person is available to take care of hearth and home). Promotions and pay frequently reward those with seniority, who work long hours and are available to take on additional assignments. This disadvantages women who, as a group, bear the bulk of responsibility for children, housework and other unpaid caring labour. Thus, apparently gender-neutral job structures can discriminate against women.

Some social theorists claim that discrimination lies at the heart of social and economic systems and through which dominant groups actively seek to preserve their competitive advantage. Marxist theorists argue that the perpetuation of inequality and discrimination is fundamental to maintaining and strengthening the economic interests of dominant groups. Discrimination thus has its roots in class conflict between capitalists and workers. Capital interests are served by dividing the working class along whatever discriminatory lines are convenient and exploitable (e.g. race and gender); this decreases the chance that workers will develop class-consciousness and ultimately revolt against capitalists. Dividing the working class has added bonus of depressing wages and increasing profit.

Marxist theory of working-class division along gender and racial lines finds its most clear expression in the *split labour market* theory of Edna Bonacich (1976). Split labour market theory provides a way to view inequality as having a functional role in maintaining the current class order. According to this theory, capitalists use

social categories of difference as a wedge to employ 'divide and conquer' tactics to suppress working-class solidarity and to artificially depress wages. By favouring a subset of workers with culturally valued ascribed characteristics (i.e. white and male) in hiring and pay practices, capitalists curry the favour of the more powerful members of the working class while simultaneously creating a 'reserve army of labour' of disfavoured workers. Women and men of colour are crowded into lower-paying occupations where competition for jobs further decreases the pay. Capitalists use the threat of employing these inexpensive workers to maintain control over the favoured workers. Split labour market theory finds empirical support employers' use of both Irish immigrants and African Americans as strikebreakers (or at least as a plausible threat of cheaper labour as a replacement) to disrupt unionization efforts and depress labour costs in the nineteenth century.

In contrast to individual-level theories of discrimination, institutional theories argue that discrimination can only be eliminated through the efforts of social movements, public policy and cultural change. The civil rights movement and two feminist movements of the twentieth century began the process of reducing discrimination resulting in such policies as affirmative action and comparable worth. However, Marxists argue that discrimination can only be ended by the elimination of the capitalist economic system.

References and further reading

Becker, Gary (1957) *The Economics of Discrimination*, Chicago: University of Chicago Press.
Bonacich, Edna (1976) 'Advanced Capitalism and Black/White Race Relations in the United States: A Split Labor Market Interpretation', *American Sociological Review*, 41(1): 34–51.
Kanter, Rosabeth Moss (1977) *Men and Women of the Corporation*, New York: Basic Books.

MICHELLE J. BUDIG
JESSE BARBA

DOUBLE CONTINGENCY

When we distinguish the social from the physical or biological realm, we refer to events that involve at least two actors. Social relations, structures, systems exist only if more than one actor participates, where actors are human beings capable of goal-oriented behaviour. Since the social realm starts with a minimum of two, it has appeared self-evident for social theorists to think about its constitution or emergence using models of a dyadic constellation: the mother–child dyad (R. Spitz) in psychoanalysis, bilateral exchange in economic theory, the problem of 'double contingency' (Parsons) in sociology. Such models openly or implicitly tell a story about how the social world has evolved or what its conditions of possibility are. They involve a hen–egg problem: to explain the origins of the social world, do we (but how can we?) presuppose actors sufficiently competent to engage in communication? In the mother–child dyad, one actor, the mother, is competent, the other not yet. In the economics of bilateral exchange, the question is how two competent actors can complete an exchange and thus determine a price for the goods that change hands. In sociology, however, it does not make sense to assume competent actors if the ambition is to model a stylized primordial social situation. Where should actors have learned how to communicate? At the same time, the problem of 'double contingency' only arises if two competent actors face each other. An *ego*, conscious of the freedom to make choices, to follow wishes, to define purposes, runs into another being who is not just *alter*, the other, but in whom he recognizes the very qualities he assumes for himself: *alter ego*. 'Double contingency' is a problem only if the freedom to choose exists on both sides of the elementary social relation and both sides know this. Such knowledge potentially leads to paralysis. Therefore, it is tempting to take such a stylized social constellation as a zero point for social analysis. Everything interesting happens once this paralysis is overcome. What happens depends on how it is overcome. But it is worthwhile to keep in mind that modelling a social zero point should not involve the assumption of competent actors. Such competence must be socially conditioned.

In what follows, the development of the notion of double contingency will be sketched starting from **game theory** via **Parsons** to end with **Luhmann**'s theory of social systems.

Game theory

In 1935, Oskar Morgenstern published a paper entitled 'Vollkommene Voraussicht und wirtschaftliches Gleichgewicht' (Perfect foresight and economic equilibrium). Referring to a Conan Doyle story in which Sherlock Holmes and Professor Moriarty try to outfox each other in a life-and-death game, Morgenstern demonstrated that the assumption of 'perfect foresight' in general equilibrium theory is inconsistent. For two strategically interacting actors, the possibilities of outguessing each other can be inexhaustible. Moriarty observes Holmes and Holmes observes Moriarty. But Holmes knows that he is observed by Moriarty and Moriarty knows that he is observed by Holmes. So Holmes tries to act in ways that are to influence Moriarty's expectations of what he is going to do and Moriarty tries to act in ways that are to influence Holmes' expectations of what he is going to do. Since both know that they are both extremely smart, they take into account these attempts to influence each other's expectations of expectations, etc.

This argument about the impossibility of perfect foresight in strategic interaction can be transported into economic theory starting with bilateral exchange. Two actors want something from each other and they are not locked into a single exit situation as in perfect competition. The standard treatment of bilateral exchange shows (see the usual Edgeworth box diagram in microeconomics) that the dual maximizing problem of bilateral exchange cannot be satisfactorily solved with traditional microeconomic tools. First, the indifference curve apparatus allows for the definition of a set of feasible exchanges: each actor wants to be at least as well or better off than with her current bundle of goods. Second, it allows for the determination of the contract curve as the locus of equilibrium trades: the points of tangency of indifference curves within the feasible set of exchanges define the results that fulfil the standard Pareto condition. Once a point on the contract curve is reached, none of the actors can improve his position without the other becoming worse off. We can safely assume that rational, utility maximizing actors will bargain until they reach a point on the contract curve, because as long as they are off the curve there will be possibilities of improvement for at least one of the two without damage to the other. But we do not know which point they will reach because we cannot know from which point in the feasible set they will start bargaining.

This indeterminacy can be understood as an implication of double contingency: if what I get depends on your choice and what you get depends on my choice, and if we are both free to choose, the result is uncertainty. It may be paralysing because we both want to influence the choice of the other but we do not know the most favourable way to accomplish this. If we cannot find ways of bridging uncertainty, we cannot trade. Morgenstern brought this problem into his cooperation with John von Neumann that resulted in the pioneering *Theory of Games and Economic Behavior* (1944). Their argument took off from the proposition that economic actors are neither Robinson Crusoes facing a nonsocial environment nor price-takers in perfect competition, but actors involved in

strategic interaction. The game theory apparatus they developed uses several possibilities to reduce the contingency involved in interaction: The rational actors facing each other have limited options by assuming that a set of alternative outcomes is known and evaluated in a shared way (as illustrated by a payoff matrix) and by introducing decision rules that ensure optimal outcomes relative to what the opponent does.

Parsons

When Talcott Parsons brought the concept of 'double contingency' into sociology, he was influenced by the new game theory. His definition of double contingency could easily pass for a description of bilateral exchange: 'there is a *double contingency* inherent in interaction. On the one hand, *ego*'s gratifications are contingent on his selection among available alternatives. But in turn, *alter*'s reaction will be contingent on *ego*'s selection and will result from a complementary selection on *alter*'s part' (Parsons *et al.* 1951: 16). Parsons went beyond the game theoretical argument by undoing the exclusive concern with rational action. He wanted to demonstrate that actors can overcome double contingency only by relying on shared values and norms. Double contingency implies that actors are uncertain about what others will do. To form expectations, they have to integrate each other into their meaning systems. These meaning systems have to be complementary.

> First, since the outcome of *ego*'s action (e.g. success in the attainment of a goal) is contingent on *alter*'s reaction to what *ego* does, *ego* becomes oriented not only to *alter*'s probable overt behavior but also to what *ego* interprets to be *alter*'s expectations relative to *ego*'s behavior, since *ego* expects that *alter*'s expectations will influence *alter*'s behavior. Second, in an integrated system, this orientation to the expectations of the other is reciprocal or complementary.
>
> (Parsons and Shils 1951: 105)

Such complementarity is possible only if 'actions, gestures, or symbols have more or less the same meaning for both *ego* and *alter*' (ibid.), which is the same thing as saying that 'a common culture exist[s] between them, through which their interaction is mediated' (ibid.). The common culture has normative force:

> The most important single condition of the integration of an interaction system is a shared basis of normative order ... It must guide action by establishing some distinctions between desirable and undesirable lines of action which can serve to stabilize interaction.
>
> (Parsons 1968: 437).

How do actors acquire the competence to follow the rules set by the normative order? 'The most basic condition of such compliance is the internalization of a society's values and norms by its members, for such socialization underlies the consensual basis of a societal community' (Parsons 1966: 14). It follows from this crucial role of socialization that Parsons does not use the problem of double contingency to model a social zero point: actors have become culturally competent in socialization before they run into each other and into the problem of double contingency. Thus, the hen–egg problem mentioned is avoided by a reference to socialization. The child learns from the mother who learned from her mother when she was a child. The constant in this process is culture. Transmitted by socialization, culture is to structure and constrain actions that would otherwise threaten order and stability.

Luhmann

Luhmann refers to double contingency in order to propose an **impossibility theorem**: 'Action cannot take place if *alter* makes his action dependent on how *ego* acts, and *ego* wants to connect his action to *alter*'s' (Luh-mann 1995: 103). However, instead of seeing actors as being drawn into n^{th}-order guessing games, which may again be paralysing, Luhmann attempts to view double contingency as something productive: It cannot be eliminated from interaction, but it induces self-observation and reflexivity which, in turn, reduce the improbability of communication.

> In this way an emergent order can arise that is conditioned by the complexity of the systems that make it possible but that does not depend on this complexity being calculated or controlled. We call this emergent order a social system.
>
> (Luhmann 1995: 110)

Double contingency stimulates the emergence of simple social systems if, in the two-communicators case, *ego* agrees with *alter ego*: 'I will do what you want if you do what I want.' However, this deceptively simple rule is based on the possibility of not agreeing, on the freedom to go away. Thus, the emerging social system stays unstable. To handle the problem of instability, Luhmann adds media of communication to his argument. They increase the probability that a communication is not only understood, but accepted: *ego* – appropriating the information given by *alter* – adopts it as the premise of her response.

While Luhmann convinces us that double contingency cannot be eliminated in social systems and that – instead of blocking communication – it can stimulate the emergence of stabilizing social constructions like media, the starting point of his argument where he treats double contingency as a sort of social zero point is misguided. Double contingency only is a problem once actors are competent communicators. But once they are competent communicators and can observe each other, the axiom holds: 'One cannot not communicate' (Watzlawick *et al.* 1967: 48).

Conclusion

The concept of double contingency implies a clear distinction between social and non-social phenomena. Neoclassical economics has neglected the social dimension of economic action and thus missed the problem of double contingency. Game theory offers a remedy within the rational choice framework by starting from the proposition that interaction involves uncertainty. The theory of social systems extends this framework to include norms and values as means to overcome double contingency (Parsons) and to emphasize that it is never overcome but remains a permanent and creative feature of social interaction (Luhmann).

Reference to double contingency allows for a precise definition of the subject matter of economic sociology: Social interaction, including the economic transactions of rational actors, generates uncertainty (see **risk and uncertainty**). The economy, its institutions and action patterns can only be fully understood if they are analysed as ways to cope with such uncertainty.

References and further reading

Luhmann, Niklas (1995) *Social Systems*, Stanford: Stanford University Press.

Morgenstern, Oskar (1935) 'Vollkommene Voraussicht und wirtschaftliches Gleichgewicht' [Perfect Foresight and Economic Equilibrium], *Zeitschrift für Nationalökonomie*, VI(3): 337–57.

Neumann, John von and Morgenstern, Oskar (1953) *Theory of Games and Economic Behavior*, Princeton, NJ: University of Princeton Press.

Parsons, Talcott (1966) *Societies*, Englewood Cliffs, NJ: Prentice Hall.

—— (1968) 'Social Interaction', in David L. Sills (ed.), *International Encyclopedia of the Social Sciences*, New York: Macmillan, vol. 7, pp. 429–41.

Parsons, Talcott and Shils, Edward (eds) (1951) *Toward a General Theory of Action*, Cambridge, MA: Harvard University Press.

Parsons, Talcott *et al.* (1951) 'Some Fundamental Categories of the Theory of Action: A General Statement', in Talcott Parsons and Edward A. Shils (eds), *Toward a General Theory of Action*, Cambridge: Harvard University Press, pp. 3–29.

Spitz, René A. (1957) *No and Yes. On the Beginning of Human Communication*, New York: International University Press.

Vanderstraeten, Raf (2002) 'Parsons, Luhmann, and the Theorem of Double Contingency', *Journal of Classical Sociology*, 2: 77–92.

Watzlawick, Paul, Bavelas, Janet B. and Jackson, Donald D. (1967) *Pragmatics of Human Communication*, New York: Norton.

HEINER GANSSMANN

DUALITY OF STRUCTURE

See: structuration theory

DURKHEIM, EMILE

Emile Durkheim (1858–1917), one of the founders of modern sociology, set out key arguments, concepts and theories that have had an enduring impact on later theory and research in the discipline. In one of his major works, *The Rules of Sociological Method* (1895), he set forth a conception of the subject matter of the field as analogous to that of other sciences that deal with emergent phenomena. Just as psychology deals with mental facts that emerge from associations among neurons, so sociology deals with social facts that emerge from associations among human beings. Modes of thinking, feeling and acting are instituted in any society and constitute the truly fundamental social facts that he called institutions.

He argued that institutions are collective entities that cannot be understood in terms of properties of individuals whose nature is conceived to be independent of social life. Hence, just as individual psychology is not sufficient for sociological explanation, neither is an individualistic economics. These disciplines have arisen in modern societies as one aspect of the rise of individualism with both its egoistic and its moral aspects, the latter defined by the value placed on individual rights and individual dignity in modern societies. Sociology, the new discipline

Durkheim attempted to define and advance, would focus on the social causation and social function of social facts.

In developing these ideas in his writings, Durkheim worked out a number of themes that we can interpret as his economic sociology. While Adam **Smith** had stressed the *economic* function of the division of labour in terms of productivity, in his first major work, *The Division of Labour in Society* (1893), Durkheim analysed the *social* function of the division of labour in terms of **solidarity**. Pre-modern societies with little division of labour bound the individual tightly to collective values and norms with little 'space' for individual choice, but with the advance of the division of labour, common values become more generalized and social norms allow for greater autonomy in their relevance to specialized activities. Yet the individual is more dependent on others. This has the potential to produce a new type of solidarity he calls 'organic' because the parts of the social system are not just different but also interdependent. Thus, the division of labour is not just an economic fact but also a social fact of enormous functional significance in terms of its consequences in regard to the mode of integration that characterizes modern societies.

Durkheim is not arguing that normative elements are not important in modern societies. On the contrary, social regulation of differentiated functions is a necessary aspect of an organic society, one towards which societies are moving but with turbulence arising from insufficient normative control along the way. In a forceful polemic against the notion of a society based on contractual relations set forth by the nineteenth-century sociologist Herbert Spencer, he argued that contractual agreements between individuals were based upon immediate interests and were hardly sufficient to produce enduring social bonds. Thus, a fully contractual society would be a sociological monstrosity lacking the moral foundations of social order. On the contrary, he noted, there is a non-contractual element in contracts. This is the institutional element involving societal norms and the values that undergird them, an argument that influenced later economic sociology, e.g. Talcott **Parsons**' analysis of contractual relationships.

To this argument he added some historical analyses and an enduring concept relating to a lack of social order. He argued that the industrializing societies of the nineteenth century were suffering from a condition he called anomie: insufficient normative regulation of the differentiated spheres of social life, particularly the economy. This moral condition, he argued in *Suicide* (1897) is one reason for the increasing suicide rates in that century. Earlier traditional social controls had become less effective with the rapid social change brought about by industrialization so that there was a lag in the development of new moral norms to guide individuals.

The implication of such an argument is that a fully organic type of society is one in which there is a societal equilibrium state characterized by an appropriate level of moral regulation of the division of labour. In this sense, the anomic type of division of labour is a disequilibrium state and as such, for Durkheim, 'abnormal'. In these terms, he takes note of a second type of abnormal division of labour that he calls 'forced'. In a society in the equilibrium state of organic solidarity, by contrast, there is a 'spontaneous' matching of individual aptitudes and the functions they perform. Without this condition, what we find coercion. This analysis is in broad agreement with **Marx**'s analysis as to the nature of labour in capitalist society.

There is a sense in which Durkheim is also saying that the division of labour has a religious consequence for society. In *Elementary Forms of the Religious Life* (1912), he defined religion in terms of a cultural distinction between the sacred and the profane with accompanying social practices in relation to the sacred that express a 'ritual attitude' of awe and respect for sacred things. He deliberately excluded any requirement that sacred things involve anything supernatural, thereby greatly generalizing the sociological conception of religion. Similarly, he used the term 'cult' in a non-negative way to denote a doctrine held in common in a community or society. In these terms, he argued that the shared religion of modern societies is 'the cult of the individual', the doctrine of individual dignity and rights that is expressed in constitutions and in other cultural and social forms.

Where does this cult come from? As later writers such as Randall Collins (1992) have emphasized, the answer in the Durkheimian tradition is that the cult of the individual is one manifestation of the general idea that religious ideas emerge and change with social change. They are reflections of the type of social structure. With the emergence of the highly differentiated modern type of society, then, ideas of what is sacred shift towards reflection of the social fact that individuals have more autonomy. In other words, the greater individualism of modern societies – a consequence of its extremely high division of labour – comes to be celebrated and sanctified in the common culture. It becomes the religion of modern society and people become morally outraged when individuals are not treated with due respect for their value as such.

The cult of the individual has a mixed impact in terms of solidarity. It can provide some level of cultural integration but it is hardly a substitute for the moral regulation of the economy that Durkheim's analysis of anomie highlighted as necessary to complete the transition to fully organic solidarity. Thus, Durkheim proposes that for the purpose of such needed social control, a modern society might well develop a modern form of the medieval guild. That is, legally empowered national collectivities might be formed that would deal with economic issues, such as wages and working conditions, in a mode that provided moral regulation of occupational activity. Whatever the merits of this proposal, which has stimulated a good deal of discussion among some sociologists, it is one more aspect of Durkheim's enduring focus on the moral element in relation to the economy and other sectors of social life. For excerpts from Durkheim's major works referred to in this article and for later applications of his ideas, see Emirbayer (2003).

References and further reading

Collins, Randall (1992) *Sociological Insight: An Introduction to Non-Obvious Sociology*, second edition, New York: Oxford University Press.

Emirbayer, Mustafa (ed.) (2003) *Emile Durkheim: Sociologist of Modernity*, Oxford: Blackwell.

THOMAS J. FARARO

E

EARNINGS

Why some earn more than others is a question that has preoccupied many great thinkers for at least three hundred years. As early as 1691, the English physician and political economist Sir William Petty theorized about the compensation individuals received for their labour. Late in the next century, Adam **Smith** in his celebrated book *The Wealth of Nations* introduced the idea of equalizing differentials. Smith argued that the wages received by workers should compensate them for differences in the conveniences and inconveniences associated with the work they performed. According to Smith's reasoning, if two workers with the same skills performed the same jobs, but one worked at a 'less advantageous' workplace than the other's workplace, then the worker at the more disagreeable workplace should receive more compensation than the worker at the less disagreeable workplace. If the compensation was not higher at the more disagreeable workplace, Smith argued, individuals would not supply their labour.

Numerous studies on earnings provide data that support Smith's conception of equalizing differentials. Milton Friedman and Simon Kuznets in an important 1954 publication, *Income from Independent Professional Practice* (New York: National Bureau of Economic Research), provided strong evidence showing earnings were related to workplace disamenities. Other notable labour economists have also corroborated Smith's predictions about compensating differentials. Robert Hall, for instance, reported in his influential 1979 article in *Industrial and Labor Relations Review* that earnings were positively associated with the risk of death on the job.

Importantly, Smith's writings on equalizing differentials laid the foundation for the present-day theory of human capital, which has been the leading theory advanced to explain earnings differentials among people. Seminal works on human capital theory and the distribution of earnings by Jacob Mincer, Gary Becker, and Theodore Schultz argued that earnings differentials are the expected outcomes of prior human capital investments. According to human capital theory, earnings should vary if some individuals choose to improve their productivity through investments in schooling, job training, job search or migration while others chose otherwise. Moreover, human capital theory offers at least two reasons why the distribution of earnings disproportionately favours the more educated, thereby generating inequality in the distribution of earnings. First, those making human capital investments to increase their life-time earnings are generally persons with higher ability. So, while lower-ability people work and their productivity remains relatively unchanged by investments, higher-ability

157

people improve their productively by investments. The interactions among ability, human capital accumulation and working will increase the earnings of the more adept and thereby tilt the dispersion towards the upper earnings levels. Second, ongoing human capital investments mean larger costs, yet fewer periods over a career-life to reap the returns on those investments. So, while there is a disincentive to keep investing, for those who choose to continue investing in human capital the rewards are substantial, which further skews the earnings distribution towards the upper earnings levels.

For some time, measurement problems and inadequate data prevented studying what human capital theory had to say about earnings. Jacob Mincer ended the impasse with his publications on returns to education and the estimation of statistical earnings functions. His ground-breaking empirical work provided the roadmap for evaluating human capital theory's predictions about earnings differentials. The 'Mincer earnings function' has been very successful across time and country at measuring earnings differentials and relating them to schooling, on-the-job training and levels of work experience interacted with levels of schooling. Nowadays compared with when human capital theory was first formalized, more is known about the effects of type of job, ability, time horizon, age, family background, location and union membership on earnings.

Despite applied human capital theory's success at relating earnings to schooling investments, critics argue the theory has failed to explain the substantial inequality in earnings according to the personal characteristics of workers that should be unrelated to productivity. Yet data show that there are considerable differences in earnings according to the personal traits of workers, e.g. gender, race, sexual orientation and disability status. The documented earnings differentials by personal characteristics have often been considered indicators

of **discrimination** against minorities, such as the disabled, or blacks in the United States, or women.

Earnings disparities between minority and non-minority groups and between men and women have caused widespread social concern about discrimination, its sources and potential policy responses. To redress differences in earnings, some countries have implemented 'comparable worth' policies, which are designed to pay disadvantaged groups the intrinsic value of their jobs. Notwithstanding, the more effective policy remedies have sought to first identify the source of the discrimination. Perhaps the source of discrimination lay with less access to productivity-enhancing schooling opportunities rather than an employer. Alternatively, given similar qualifications, a particular disadvantaged group might occupy less agreeable jobs than an advantaged group; or the disadvantaged group might receive lower pay for the same job compared with an advantaged group. Establishing whether differences in earnings between groups stem from labour-market discrimination or pre-market factors is crucial. While the identification of discrimination remains controversial, few disagree that earnings inequalities by gender are larger than those by race. Even after accounting for women's shorter job tenures and training experiences compared with men, women still earn less.

Earnings disparities by gender and race, and newly documented disparities by disability and sexual orientation, have generated new research. Contemporary research attempts to identify discrimination, incorporate culture, measure past parental influences, and model families' decisions about work and the division of labour within the household. Human capital theory provided important insights into the determinants of earnings, but not enough of them to explain the disparities that exist among groups. Now, sociological and psychological theories augment human capital theory to better explain the large unexplained variation in earnings.

References and further reading

Becker, Gary (1964) *Human Capital*, New York: Columbia University Press.

Bowles, Samuel, Gintis, Herbert and Osborne, Melissa (2001) 'The Determinants of Earnings: A Behavioral Approach', *Journal of Economic Literature*, 39: 1137–76.

Willis, Robert (1986) 'Wage Determinants: A Survey and Reinterpretation of Human Capital Earnings Functions,' in Orley Ashenfelter and Richard Layard (eds), *The Handbook of Labor Economics*, Vol. 1, Amsterdam: North Holland/Elsevier Science Publishers, pp. 525–602.

PETER D. BRANDON

ECOLOGICAL FIELDS

An ecological field consists of a population of separate bounded systems and non-systems such as networks, which are located in the same physical space within which they compete for space and resources and interact selectively with each other in order to obtain resources from or exchange resources with each other. All relationships and linkages found among the members of an ecological field are contingent and, thus, episodic.

Currently, the concept of system is used in the natural and social sciences to describe anything that is characterized by connections or contains a set of relationships. However, not all relationships qualify with respect to the characteristics of a system. This means that there exist organizational phenomena which are not systems. Ergo, the term 'system' as such is sociologically meaningless. So, how do we conceptually deal with the existence of 'non-systems'? The concept of the ecological field can liberate us from the limitations of systems theory and the concept system.

A system is defined primarily as an organization in which relationships are bonded (Bates and Harvey 1975; Bates 1997). The flow of goods, services and information are determined by a specific, internal set of relationships. The rules of exchange are self-determined and these organizations are fully independent, except for forces and conditions that influence their exchange with other autonomous systems. That is, systems are self-referential (Maturana and Varela 1980; Bates 1997).

The dilemma as how to define 'non-systems' and what to call them has been around for quite some time. In contrast to Parsons (1951) and Parsons and Shils (1951), Sorokin (1956) recognized this flaw when he defined social systems as sociocultural phenomena that are united logically and meaningfully by causal ties of interdependence, historical, and/or characterized by reflexive social change in that members are interdependent and, thus, change together. As an alternative to the concept of system, Sorokin (1956: 267) defined congeries as 'two or more sociocultural phenomena which do not belong to each other meaningfully and "causally"'. However, because ecological fields and networks are not random or meaningless collections of social systems and because they contain an ordered set of probabilistic and contingent relationships, Sorokin's notion of congeries could not be operationalized.

In terms of human populations, an ecological field refers to a form of sociopolitical organization which contains many separate human systems as operating elements but which as a total entity does not meet the requirements for being a system in and of itself. According to this definition, human communities of all orders of scale are to be regarded as ecological fields rather than as systems or mega-systems. Thus human communities, societies and so-called world-systems are defined as types of ecological fields rather than as social systems. Also, the parts of ecological fields which consist of networks of independent bounded systems are to be regarded as subfields: for example markets, political networks and various forms of specialized exchange networks.

In order to properly understand the notions of ecological fields versus systems, the nature of sociopolitical relationships must be defined. In short, there are two types of relationships involved in social, economic and political phenomena: bonded and contingent. Bonded relationships are characteristic of those found in systems. These relationships are mandatory in that the specific connections for exchange and the rules for exchange are mandated solely upon internal rules for behaviour established by the system itself. The rules of bonded relationships generally force cooperation among the specific parties to an exchange.

On the other hand, the rules that govern contingent relationships control the conflict inherent in these relationships. For example, the provider–client relationship involves a conflict of interests and the structure of such a group 'has the effect of preserving the boundaries of independent elemental groups and of supporting the internal independence of their structure as separate, bounded, self-referential systems' (Bates 1997: 191). As such, the relationships that characterize ecological fields and networks are contingent in that these relationships are contingent upon a set of conditions being in place at any given moment and in particular space.

For example, the economy and its markets are often described conventionally as a system of exchange relationships (Zafirovski 2003). Sociologically, Parsons (1951) defined the market as a subsystem within the larger social system (i.e. society). However, the market illustrates ecological fields and networks as more appropriately defined by a 'web' of contingent relationships since, by definition, the market is competitive and specifically dependent upon contingent relationships which offer alternatives. This means that there is choice, a characteristic that is not common to bonded relationships.

These exchange relationships arise out of an economic division of labour within an ecological subfield. Categories of specialized systems occupy niches and seek inputs or resources within this division of labour. This economic division of labour contains categories (i.e. other systems) of potential suppliers of these inputs upon which these specialized systems are functionally dependent (Bates 1997). Therefore, the expression 'market system' 'does not refer so much to a kind of "economic organism" or "machine" as it does to an organized or established method or procedure of accomplishing the goal of distributing the outputs' (Bates 1997: 170).

In sum, the concept ecological field provides a means of explaining organizational phenomena that exist at a level beyond that of a system. The key to understanding this concept lies in the nature of relationships. Some relationships are bonded and, in this sense, they are closed to alternative interactions; i.e. those found in systems. Others are contingent and, thus, are open to alternative and competing sets of interactions, i.e. those characteristic of ecological fields and networks. The economy and its market are examples of ecological fields and networks.

References and further reading

Bates, Frederick L. (1997) *Sociopolitical Ecology: Human Systems and Ecological Fields*, New York: Plenum Press.

Bates, Frederick L. and Harvey, Clyde (1975) *The Structure of Social Systems*, New York: Gardner Press.

Maturana, H. and Varela, F. (1980) *Autopoiesis and Cognition: The Realization of the Living*, Boston: Reidel.

Parsons, Talcott (1951) *The Social System*, Glencoe, IL: Free Press.

Parsons, Talcott and Shils, Edward A. (eds) (1951) *Toward a General Theory of Action*, Cambridge, MA: Harvard University Press.

Sorokin, Pitrim A. (1956) *Fads and Foibles in Modern Sociology and Related Sciences*, Chicago: Henry Regnery.

Zafirovski, Milan (2003) *Market and Society: Two Theoretical Frameworks*, Westport, CT: Praeger.

DANIEL G. RODEHEAVER

ECOLOGY AND ECONOMY

A house divided

Although economy and ecology share the same etymology ('eco-' from the Greek *oikos*, meaning 'house'), an inherent conflict between the two spheres has often been recognized. Natural scientists, as well as social scientists from many different fields (e.g. environmental history, human ecology, ecological economics, environmental sociology), share an understanding that ecosystems function as supply depots, waste repositories or recyclers, and living spaces for humans. Despite romanticized visions of our pre-industrial past as a time of harmony with nature, environmental historians have shown that human societies have always impacted (e.g. through the use of fire, deforestation, protecting certain species) the natural ecosystems that sustain them. The level of impact – the amount of material and energy withdrawn from ecosystems and the amount of waste and pollution added to ecosystems – is a function of the sizes of human populations, their cultural patterns, technologies and social organization (e.g. division of labour, economic and political systems). The relative sustainability of ecosystems and societies depends upon changes in these factors over time.

Given current unprecedented levels of economic production and material standards of living throughout the world, and the predicted growth of both, many scientists have expressed serious concern about the sustainability of contemporary societies. The situation is exacerbated by the fact that the analytic tools of mainstream economics were developed during an era when humans were relatively oblivious to their embeddedness within ecosystems. Proponents of new patterns of development and sympathetic environmental movements now attempt to describe possible transitions towards more sustainable societies. It falls, in turn, to economic sociology and ecological economics to try to reformulate an economics grounded in social and ecological realities.

The economy in environmental sociology: the treadmill of production

With a few exceptions, sociology paid little attention to the environment until 1980, when two important theoretical statements, William Catton's *Overshoot: The Ecological Basis of Revolutionary Change* and Alan Schnaiberg's *The Environment: From Surplus to Scarcity*, were published. Catton argued that technological developments have allowed societies to exceed the carrying capacities of their ecological bases, with inevitable negative long-term social consequences. Schnaiberg stressed an inherent conflict between an exchange value (commodified) conception of nature and the social and ecological use values of natural resources. His 'treadmill of production' thesis situated the society–environment relation within the context of globalizing capitalism. Over the past two decades, Schnaiberg and colleagues have elaborated and refined the treadmill of production model, characterizing the society–environment relation as an inexorable process in which economic actors (primarily corporations) use and degrade ecological resources in order to increase their accumulation of capital. Failure to do this would threaten profitability and the survival of firms (who are also driven to enhance profits by cutting labour costs and investing in capital-intensive technologies that, in turn, further increase the withdrawals of resources and energy from, and increase additions of waste and pollution to, ecosystems). Because corporate managers are constrained by the demand for expanding profits, there is persistent pressure to externalize true ecological and social costs. When corporations are prodded to account for these costs (e.g. by governments, social movement organizations, public opinion) they tend to use their considerable influence (e.g. political lobbying and campaign contributions) to resist change. At the same time, workers (in order to secure and maintain jobs) and governments (in order to provide for 'national development' and 'social security') are also dependent on the treadmill of production and, therefore, must work to facilitate its expansion. Since the treadmill of production is strongly anti-ecological and societies around the planet are caught up in its continued operation, Schnaiberg and colleagues foresee enduring conflict between the economy and the environment at all levels: international, national, regional, local and interpersonal (Schnaiberg and Gould 1994).

Ecological modernization and the triple bottom line

An alternative position has been advanced by advocates of 'ecological modernization' – part of a larger 'sustainable development' movement that advocates for more environmentally benign technologies of production and consumption (e.g. based on principles of 'radical resource productivity', 'biomimicry', 'product lifecycle design') and the integration of environmental concerns into the fabric of societal institutions. Sociologists with an eye towards these developments point to evidence of institutional change with the emergence of 'green purchasing', the membership of corporate executives in international 'Natural Step' networks, corporate environmental performance certification by the International Standards Organization (ISO), adoption of the 'precautionary principle' by firms (i.e. not waiting for positive proof of impacts before taking pro-environmental action), increased government incentives, regulation and direct investment in sustainability programmes, and a broader role in environmental governance by civil society actors. In the ecological modernization view, a combination of institutional, political, cultural, technical and economic

reforms can avert widespread environmental degradation, with 'significant environmental improvements in production and consumption [being] possible under different "relations of production"' (Mol and Spaargaren 2002: 37).

Mol and Spaargaren suggest that the treadmill of production and other neo-Marxist critiques offer only 'meager and utopian strategies' as solutions to environmental problems. From their point of view, substantive instances of ecological modernization can be observed across both for-profit and non-profit sectors where there are incipient movements to apply enlightened policy and technology changes to accrue 'triple bottom line' – economic prosperity, environmental quality and social justice – benefits. There are, in fact, a variety of reasons that firms might behave in this way. Some embrace environmental concerns and stewardship as basic organizational principles (e.g. sustainable products manufacturers and retailers). Some adjust along with, or ahead of, changing environmental and technological conditions (e.g. forward-looking petroleum and chemical companies). Others profit from new paradigms and the rethinking of business practices (e.g. green business and investment services). Some organizations respond to changing government, professional and movement-induced standards (e.g. ISO business performance standards, green building rating systems, the certification of organic food and fibre), and others respond to market pressures and opportunities (e.g. pollution trading schemes, demands for renewable power).

Treadmill of production proponents, on the other hand, suggest that many firms and governments respond only after coercion by regulators. Some businesses are oblivious and/or constrained (e.g. most small businesses), while others are resistant and work actively to block change (e.g. business lobby groups, trade associations). From the treadmill of production view, 'there is no compelling evidence that the environment has been emancipated from the economic in decision-making criteria' (Pellow *et al.* 2000: 111). In addition, presumably clear-cut cases of ecological modernization such as recycling may concentrate environmental hazards to workers – an instance of the more general unequal distribution of environmental harms and benefits that are rarely the focus of ecological modernization advocacy or analysis (Pellow *et al.* 2000). Another criticism is that 'dematerialization' – an ecological modernization goal that reduces the amount of raw materials required per unit of gross domestic product – may actually contribute to the expanded use of raw materials and an acceleration of the treadmill of production (York *et al.* 2003). The debate continues.

The visible hand of economics

Contemporary industrial societies have been built on 'a central belief that they can progress by conquering nature and expanding production' (Schnaiberg and Gould 1994: v), and formal modes of economic analysis have usually supported this belief. Ecological economists, offering a critique from within the discipline of economics, argue that the widespread influence of neoclassical economic analysis has resulted in the acceptance of fallacies of misplaced concreteness in concepts such as 'the market' (and in introducing 'externalities' as a way of correcting models), in limited measures of economic success (e.g. GDP as an adequate indicator of national welfare), and in an overemphasis on 'capital' and 'labour' as factors of production, while largely ignoring 'land' (a striking reduction of nature in its own right). Economic sociologists have also criticized key neoclassical economic premises, particularly that rational, self-interested actors know best how to allocate their time, energy and money, and that the interplay between actors leads to the optimal utilization of resources and the most efficient economy. In contrast, economic sociologists point out that economic behaviour (whether individual or organizational) is embedded in, and accomplished through, webs of social relations, with all that that entails in terms of the influence of norms, institutions and sociocultural dynamics.

It is unlikely that many economists now hold very strict neoclassical views of the market, economic indicators and *homo economicus*, given the prevalence of economic concepts such as transaction costs, market failures, incomplete information and a host of new (to economics) insights gleaned from psychologists and experiments in 'behavioural' economics. And resource economists, in particular, have expanded the neoclassical framework by introducing analysis of 'non-market values' and 'externalized environmental costs', and by proposing pollution trading regimes and other market-oriented approaches to environmental problems.

Historically there have been ecologically sound alternatives to neoclassical economics. Martinez-Alier (1987) makes the case that an economics based on the flow of energy and materials through the economy (i.e. an economics that 'internalized externalities') could have been established decades ago if the works of Frederick Soddy, Serhii Podolinsky, Eduard Sacher and others had been seriously considered by economists. Along the same lines, John Bellamy Foster (2001) argues that if **Marx**'s theory of a 'metabolic rift' (between society and environment) had not been largely overlooked until recently, a wider swathe of the social sciences could have been ecologically oriented at an earlier date.

The emerging field of ecological economics seeks to more firmly redress the imbalance within economics by taking issues of intergenerational, intragenerational and interspecies equity into account, and by more thoroughly valuing 'ecosystem services' (e.g. see work in the journal *Ecological Economics*). At the same time, the rapidly growing field of economic sociology offers insights that improve both undersocialized economic accounts and highly generalized environmental sociological accounts of markets, economic behaviour and the environment.

Filling the gaps

An unintended consequence of academic specialization is that sometimes the weaknesses of one field are the strengths of another. Thus, their integration offers considerable promise. In the case of ecology and economy, the strength of economic sociology (its conceptualization of actors, organizations and markets) balances out a key weakness in ecological economics (its lack of theorizing about social structures, culture and the development of markets). The strength of ecological economics (the valuation of ecosystems) balances a shortcoming in economic sociology (its lack of consideration of ecological factors). Both fields enhance and are enhanced by environmental sociology's insights about the changing nature of the society–environment relationship. And each contributes to actionable social, economic and policy agendas. For example, policies intended to encourage the ecological modernization of business would be aided by an understanding of the institutionalized conceptions and social conditions within which particular firms are embedded. The internal and external barriers to, and opportunities for, innovation that organizations face (i.e. what they could expect from governments and trade allies in terms of support or opposition) are thus made more apparent. Structural transformation and new conceptions of control are possible to the extent that businesses are able to marshal resources and devise new rules and understandings of how a sustainable business should operate. An empirical test of impacts on the natural environment,

both before and after particular changes are made – the type of analysis for which ecological economics is well suited – would indicate if businesses were actually accelerating or decelerating the treadmill of production. So a cross-pollination among fields in this domain is both possible and useful.

References and further reading

Catton, William R. (1980) *Overshoot: The Ecological Basis of Revolutionary Change*, Urbana, IL: University of Illinois Press.

Daly, Herman E. and Cobb, John B., Jr (1994) *For the Common Good: Redirecting the Economy Toward Community, the Environment, and a Sustainable Future*, Boston: Beacon Press.

Foster, John B. (2001) *Marx's Ecology: Materialism and Nature*, New York: Monthly Review Press.

Hawken, Paul, Lovins, Amory and Lovins, L. Hunter (1999) *Natural Capitalism: Creating the Next Industrial Revolution*, Boston: Little, Brown.

Martinez-Alier, Juan (with Klaus Schlupmann) (1987) *Ecological Economics: Energy, Environment and Society*, Oxford: Blackwell.

Mol, Arthur P. J. and Spaargaren, Gert (2002) 'Ecological Modernization and the Environmental State', *Research in Social Problems and Public Policy*, 10: 33–52.

National Research Council, Board on Sustainable Development (1999) *Our Common Journey: A Transition Toward Sustainability*, Washington, DC: National Academy Press.

Pellow, David N., Schnaiberg, Allan and Weinberg, Adam S. (2000) 'Putting the Ecological Modernization Thesis to the Test: The Promises and Performances of Urban Recycling', in Arthur P. J. Mol and David A. Sonnenfeld (eds), *Ecological Modernization Around the World: Perspectives and Critical Debates*, London: Frank Cass, pp. 109–37.

Schnaiberg, Allan (1980) *The Environment: From Surplus to Scarcity*, New York: Oxford University Press.

Schnaiberg, Allan and Gould, Kenneth Alan (1994) *Environment and Society: The Enduring Conflict*, New York: St Martin's Press.

York, Richard, Rosa, Eugene A. and Dietz, Thomas (2003) 'Footprints on the Earth: The Environmental Consequences of Modernity', *American Sociological Review*, 68: 279–300.

LOREN LUTZENHISER
SCOTT SAWYER

ECONOMIC ACTION

Economic action is one of the key categories of mainstream economics as well as **economic sociology**. However, some important differences in conceptualization exist between conventional economics and economic sociology, as illustrated below.

The idea of economic action as rational pursuit of materialistic ends arises or germinates in early economics or classical **political economy**. Adam **Smith** famously conceptualizes (in *The Wealth of Nations*) economic action in terms of 'truck, **barter** and exchange' primarily induced by material self-interest or gain, and only exceptionally by other, disinterested motivations (discussed in his earlier work *The Theory of Moral Sentiments*). David Ricardo adopts and reinforces Smith's view by treating economic action as the consistent and systematic seeking of profit in the sense of a monetary form of materialist motivation. Smith and Ricardo also harbour the alternative but cognate concept of economic action as the accumulation and investment of capital for the sake of profit, or simply as rational entrepreneurial activity. Parenthetically, an illustrious contemporary of Smith and Ricardo, Jeremy Bentham, conceives of all human behaviour, thus by implication its economic form, in terms of utility or pleasure as the principle 'which approves or disapproves of every action'. Notably, both Smith and Ricardo take entrepreneurship and production, i.e. (capitalist) entrepreneurs or producers, as the point of departure in conceptualizing rational economic action; and this holds true of classical political economy as a whole. As Ludwig von Mises comments, classical economics observes the rational economic actor or *homo economicus* 'only as a man engaged in business, not as a consumer of economic goods'. This is particularly manifest in Senior's conception of economic action in terms of 'abstinence' as the source of capital and profit, i.e. as 'the

conduct of a person who either abstains from the unproductive use of what he can command, or designedly prefers the production of the remote to that of immediate results'. Elaborating on Smith and Ricardo, John Stuart Mill conceives of economic action as the rational process of 'acquisition of wealth', so essentially summarizes and codifies the position of classical political economy. Mill suggests that economic action be regarded as 'flowing solely from the desire of wealth' and thus as consisting in 'acquiring and consuming wealth', while admitting that many such actions 'are really the result of a plurality of motives'. His rationale for this suggestion is implied in the assertion that every economic (and even human) action is either immediately or remotely influenced by the 'mere desire of wealth [as] the main and acknowledged end'. Mill's follower and perhaps the last classical economist, John Cairnes, largely adopts his concept of economic action by redefining it as the 'pursuit of wealth', whilst also conceding that the 'desires, passions and propensities' influencing actors in this process are 'almost infinite'.

Neoclassical economics or marginalism essentially retains the classical conception of economic action as the rational pursuit of material self-interest epitomized in profit and wealth. As a prominent marginalist, Francis Edgeworth, puts it, the 'first principle of Economics is that every agent is actuated only by self-interest'. However, in approaching economic action neoclassical economics purports to shift the emphasis from production/producers to consumption/consumers, or at least to strike a balance between the two, in an attempt to redress what was perceived to be an unduly (specifically, Ricardian) focus on the first. To indicate such a shift, one of the marginalist pioneers, William Jevons contends that economic theory must start with an 'exact theory of consumption' and redefines economics accordingly – i.e. as a 'science of human wants and their satisfaction' – in contrast with classical political economy's (especially Ricardo's) focus on production and distribution. So do other prominent marginalists like Knut Wicksell, Philip Wicksteed, etc. In turn, they regard the theory of consumption as the application of what Wicksteed calls the 'great psychological law of diminishing returns of satisfaction' or decreasing marginal utility.

Consequently, neoclassical economics observes economic action as consisting of the activities of producers and consumers alike, who are consequently both considered rational actors in the sense of *homo economicus* (as Mises suggests). Notably, in marginalism consumers' economic action constitutes a type of conduct in accordance with the operation of the 'law of diminishing returns of satisfaction' or the principle of decreasing marginal utility. Formally, in the sphere of consumption rational economic action becomes the process of maximization or optimization of utility, with the later being (mathematically) maximized at the point of the curve at which the marginal utilities of commodities to consumers are zero. By analogy, producers' or entrepreneurial economic action represents a kind of behaviour deployed according to this law as operating in the realm of production, viz. the principle of decreasing marginal productivity in reference to productive factors. In formal terms, in the field of production rational economic action is the procedure of entrepreneurial maximization of profits reaching a maximum when the marginal productivity of productive factors is zero. Early marginalism explicit (Walras, Jevons, Edgeworth) or implicit (Menger) formal notion of economic action as utility maximization – originating or anticipated in Bentham's principle of utility applied to 'every' human action – is adopted, reinforced and further formalized in modern mathematical economics as seen below.

Generally, marginalism, especially its utilitarian-hedonistic (neo-Benthamite) version particularly represented by Jevons and Edgeworth, observes economic (and all) action from the prisms of utility–disutility, pain–pleasure, happiness, and the like. Jevons argues that economic (and other human) action springs from the 'feelings of pleasure and pain', an argument his followers like Edgeworth embrace and develop. Following Jevons (and Bentham), Edgeworth states that the 'end of right action', economic and other, lies in the 'greatest possible sum-total of pleasure' or 'greatest happiness'. Another marginalist pioneer, Léon Walras, conceptualizes economic action in more implicit or pseudo utilitarian terms asserting that the 'law of economic relations' is 'Utile or Interest', so by implication the principle of marginal utility. In turn, Carl Menger, also a pioneer of marginalism, defines economic action as a 'provisional activity that aims at satisfaction' of human wants or a 'precautionary activity of humans directed toward covering material needs'. In his view, entrepreneurship is an essential form of economic action, with capital being the 'foundation for the means of subsistence' obtained by such activities guided by the 'scarcity' of objects and the 'urgency' of needs. Following Menger's stress on the relation between material scarcity and needs, Wieser proposes that the key function of economic action, especially its market mode, is the 'ideal adaptation of scarce means to competing wants', which suggests that Austrian marginalism anticipates Lionel Robbins' subsequent influential conception discussed below. Another prominent neoclassical economist, Alfred Marshall, describes economic action as the 'ordinary business of life', that part of 'individual and social existence' that involves the 'attainment and use of material requisites of well-being', thus those 'branches of behavior in which the force of motives chiefly concerned can be measured by money price', a description his disciples like Alfred Pigou and John Neville Keynes embrace. For example, Pigou suggests that economic action is that element of social action which seeks material welfare by satisfying those desires and satisfactions measured by the 'measuring rod of money'. Keynes proposes that economic action involves those activities which 'are determined by the desire for wealth'. However, in some sociological interpretation (**Parsons**), Marshall did not adopt the neoclassical (Mengerian) view that economic actions are only means to wealth acquisition or want satisfaction, but also viewed them as 'fields' for exercising human faculties and developing 'moral character'.

Contemporary mainstream economics follows and elaborates on both classical and neoclassical approaches to economic action. It essentially retains, with occasional qualifications, the classical concept of economic action as the rational pursuit of material interest epitomized by seeking monetary profit and acquiring wealth (especially) in modern capitalism. For example, Mises defines the concept as involving 'those actions which are conducted on the basis of monetary calculation' and Schumpeter suggests that 'economic action at least in capitalist society cannot be explained without taking into account money'.

Also, contemporary mainstream economics adopts or restates neoclassical explanations of economic action in terms of marginal utility and scarcity, including their Benthamite utilitarian-hedonist elements (as Schumpeter remarks about **welfare economics**) in Jevons *et al.*, formalized as the social utility function, hedonic functions, etc. The outcome is the probably prevalent contemporary conception of economic action as utility-seeking activity in the face of scarcity of resources as what Robbins describes as the 'almost ubiquitous condition of human behavior'. On the latter premise, he defines economic action as a rational form of human behaviour arising out of the 'scarcity of means' for achieving multiple ends – i.e. as 'disposing' with scarce resources – thus involving the 'conflict of choice' concerning means (with ends taken as given). Curiously, he sees this rational activity as having 'no economic ends, but only economic and non-economic ways of the attainment of given ends', a view also implicit in Hicks' description of economic action as the means to extraneous ends (freedom and justice) rather than to its own goals. Robbins' influential definition builds on early Austrian marginalism's emphasis on the scarcity of goods in relation to needs (Menger and Wieser), as does that of Mises, who describes economic action as consisting of attempts to 'satisfy wants insofar as the scarcity of means affords' and as being 'necessarily rational' (as is, in his view, all human behaviour) due to its 'basis of monetary calculation'. In a similar vein, Frank Knight contends that the defining element of economic action, so the first postulate of economics, constitutes the 'reality of economizing behavior' conditioned by resource scarcity.

Finally, modern mathematical economics has made explicit and further formalized the implicit formal concept of economic action as maximization of utility (and profit) in early marginalism. For illustration, contemporary leading mathematical economists define economic action as optimization, or the 'maximization (minimization) of some magnitude' (Samuelson 1983: 3), especially maximization of utility and profit by consumers and producers, respectively, given 'budget constraints' or scarcities. Simply, they treat economic action as maximizing or optimizing conduct – and economic actors as maximizers/optimizers – thus as perfectly rational, and 'explained in terms of preferences, which are in turn defined [revealed] only by behavior' (Samuelson 1983: 92). Moreover, some modern economists regard all social action, economic as well as non-economic, as a 'generalized calculus of utility maximizing behavior' (Stigler and Becker 1977), or briefly utility maximization (Becker and

Murphy 2000: 5). Despite alternative conceptions of economic (and social) action and actors as 'satisficing' and 'satisfiers' rather than optimizing and maximizers, such as bounded rationality theory (Simon 1982: 296–300), utility maximization remains paradigmatic for modern economics.

Economic action is also a prominent category of economic sociology, but the latter's conception differs from that in mainstream economics in several important respects. Early or classical economic sociology displays (as Parsons intimates) a sort of convergence on what Max Weber calls a 'sociological theory of economic action' that is critical of and transcends its version in orthodox economics. So does a fortiori the new economic sociology in virtue of its converging on the conception of social embeddedness as an alternative sociological paradigm of the phenomenon.

Within classical economic sociology, Weber's conception of economic action is especially important and rich (Swedberg 1998), though eclectic, viz. a mix of elements from Austrian marginalism and the German **historical school**. Weber proposes and outlines the 'sociology of economic action' focusing on the 'sociological categories of economic action'. Notably, he envisions that this discipline may need to create its own 'theoretical constructs' grounded in but distinct from those in conventional economics. Weber essentially treats economic action as a particular ideal type of social action or 'economically oriented social action'. For illustration, he observes that social action becomes economic or 'economically oriented' to the extent that it seeks, in accordance with its 'subjective meaning' for the actor, satisfaction of the desires for goods ('utilities'). Weber adds that economic action exists only if the satisfaction of such desires hinges, in actors' subjective judgements, on 'relatively scarce resources' in relation to wants and a 'limited number of possible actions'. He stresses that a decisive element

of economic action is that the scarcity of resource is 'subjectively presumed' and that conduct is oriented accordingly, thus echoing Menger's views and anticipating their modern versions. Notably, elaborating on the former and pre-formulating the latter, Weber states that the 'most essential aspect' of economic action is the 'prudent choice' between means (and ends) to the effect that such rational choices are 'oriented to the scarcity of the [available] means' relative to various ends or wants.

Generally, Weber sees economic processes and objects as characterized by the meaning they have for social action in their roles as 'ends, means, obstacles and by-products'. In turn, he warns that economic actions, including the prices and 'subjective valuations' of goods *à la* marginal utility, are not 'merely psychic phenomena', which implies some departure from Menger *et al.*, who tend to reduce all human behaviour to its economic form and conceive of the latter in pseudo-psychological terms. In virtue of describing economic action as generally (thought not invariably) rational – i.e. the 'rationally oriented' exercise of control over resources seeking via planning and calculation to attain 'economic ends' – Weber views it as a special case of instrumental or purposive-rational (*zweckrational*) actions distinguished from those value-rational (*wertrational*). He admonishes that one 'shall not consider every instrumental action as economic' on the ground that the former is a broader category incorporating economic as well as non-economic conduct and **rationality**. In particular, Weber warns that not every type of social action that is rational or efficient in its 'choice of means' represents rational economic conduct, a case in point being technological activities that also involve such choices, prompting him to suggest that the **economy** should be distinguished from technology.

Next, Weber distinguishes two types of economic action: first, satisfaction of wants in case of a 'scarcity of goods and services in relation to demand'; second, profit-seeking by the 'controlling and disposing of scarce goods' – i.e. between consumer and producer behaviour – which also echoes Menger's and adumbrates Robbins' emphasis on scarcity. More originally, Weber makes a distinction between the 'formal rationality' and 'substantive rationality' of economic action. He defines the formal rationality of economic action as the degree of potential and actual quantitative speculation or monetary accounting as an instrument of its 'calculatory orientation'. In turn, the substantive rationality of 'economically oriented social action' is defined by the extent to which it is undertaken under 'some criterion of ultimate values'. As defined, the formal and substantive rationality of economic action correspond to and express instrumentally rational and value-rational actions, respectively. Also, Weber insists on differentiating economic action from its political type, arguing that the use of force as the mark of the latter is 'strongly opposed to the [peaceful] spirit of economic acquisition' within modern capitalism. Still, while excluding the use of physical force or violence from the definition, Weber suggests that the 'sociological concept of economic action' should include the 'criterion of power of control and disposal', which signifies a significant break from pure economics exemplified by (Austrian) marginalism. The ground for such inclusion is that any economy, including its market type, comprises the de jure (legal) as well as 'de facto distribution of powers of control and disposal'. A case in point is what Weber denotes as 'domination by virtue of a constellation of interests' in the market, particularly 'by virtue of a position of monopoly'. He proposes that any form of economic domination can be converted and expanded into 'domination by virtue of authority' or the (political) 'power to command and the duty to obey', noting that this especially holds true of that type 'originally founded on a position of monopoly'.

In contrast to most Austrian and other marginal economists, Weber does not regard economic action as invariably rational in the sense of instrumental rationality. Moreover, he confines rational orientation to entrepreneurial activity or 'managerial action' and thus implicitly excludes consumer behaviour, which comes closer to classical political economy than neoclassical economics. Specifically, Weber allows that economic action can be the matter not only of 'goal-oriented rationality' but also of non- or pseudo-rational factors like ultimate values ('substantive rationality'), traditions and emotions. This suggests that, like all social action, economic behaviour can be instrumentally rational as well as value-rational, traditional and emotional in orientation. Weber identifies an historical exemplar of economic behaviour as (a mode of) value-rational action in the conduct of early Protestant entrepreneurs described as primarily motivated by transcendental values like 'otherworldly salvation' as the ultimate end to which wealth acquisition serves as a means, secondary and intermediate goal, or unintended effect. Also, Weber contends that even in situations in which economic action features a 'high degree of rationalization' or instrumental rationality, the 'element of traditional orientation remains considerable'. In addition, he suggests that economic action is often affected by emotions observing that even the most 'calculating and hard-headed' relationship, viz. between merchants and customers, may contain extra-economic elements like 'emotional values which transcend its utilitarian significance', which hints at the embeddedness of market transactions in social ties and networks. If so, such economic action, 'in Weber's fourfold classification of types of social action, has stronger elements of "affectual" or "habitual" than of purposive (zweckrational) action' (Granovetter 2001: 5).

The presence and salience of what Weber denotes 'non-rational elements of actual economic action' is indicated by that the latter, including its market mode, is induced either by 'ideal or material interests', a far cry from orthodox economics' near-exclusive focus on materialist ends. Further, he observes that the historical development of rational economic action 'has been to a large extent determined' by non-economic factors such as social structures influencing such actions. Notably, Weber observes that economic action is 'influenced by the autonomous structure of social action within which it exists', which also intimates modern economic sociology's embeddedness conception. The observed 'constant influence of non-economic factors on economic action' expresses what he terms the 'causal heteronomy' of the economy as opposed to its presumptive autonomy or independence in pure economics. Hence, Weber urges that a key task of economic sociology is to explore the 'degree of elective affinity' between concrete economic actions and 'structures of social action'. A case in point is his investigation of the 'elective affinity' between the spirit of capitalism and the ethic of Protestantism. In sum, Weber conceives economic action 'as only a special, if important, category of social action' (Granovetter 1990: 107–8). In particular, for Weber economic action 'makes little sense from a sociological viewpoint if it is divorced from the idea that the economy constitutes a major source of power in society' (Granovetter and Swedberg 1992: 8).

Despite a different theoretical tradition and methodological approach, **Durkheim**'s sociological theory of economic action appears congruent with Weber's. In turn, this congruence is a particular dimension of the (Parsonian) convergence between Weber and Durkheim on a 'voluntaristic' theory of social action, as both engage in the analysis of economic conduct from a sociological perspective. In Knight's words, Weber's sociological economics and Durkheim's *sociologie économique* are essentially

cognate endeavours in proposing an alternative social explanation of economic action. In other interpretations, Durkheim views economic action as 'always oriented toward and inspired by certain "collective representations"' (e.g. notion of monetary value as an example of a collective representation as well as a social construct of meaning in Weber's sense)' (Granovetter and Swedberg 1992: 8). For instance, the notion of monetary value as a collective representation is implicit in Durkheim's treatment of economic values as social constructs formed and changed within a societal, especially institutional, setting. He conceives of defines economic action as the sphere or mode of social action in which the 'desire for wealth [has] a preponderant role', which resembles Weber's definition (the 'desires for utilities'). Also, like Weber, Durkheim outlines the 'subject matter of economic sociology' as consisting of economic actions and institutions existing within a larger social-institutional milieu (though Durkheim, embracing Comte's sociological critique of orthodox economics, is more critical of the latter than is Weber). Alternatively, Durkheim argues that the assumption of orthodox economics that economic conduct is an autonomous sphere independent of society is not plausible, an argument similar to Weber's idea of the 'causal heteronomy' of the economy. Durkheim also complains that its subject matter involves 'not the realities given to immediate observations but merely conjectures that are the product of pure intellect', which evokes Weber's emphasis on orthodox economics' use of ideal types as intellectual constructs. In particular, Durkheim objects that what orthodox economics calls economic laws, including the fundamental law of supply and demand, are 'unworthy' of this description, because they are 'merely maxims for action, or practical precepts in disguise'. He describes these laws as possessing only logical necessity by enunciating the 'natural' means to attain certain 'hypothetical end' in economic action, but not the 'necessity that the true laws of nature present', so should not be designated as forms of natural law contrary to orthodox economics. Durkheim's view of the laws of economic action as the product of logic is similar, if not identical, to Weber's description of these as instances of ideal or 'scientifically formulated' pure types, with actual phenomena being 'only an approximation' to these types. Notably, Durkheim implies that economic action is 'embedded' in and affected by social relations and institutions by noting that, while its main incentive is private interest, human actors remain 'in relation with others' and their habits, ideas and other cultural factors 'can never be totally absent' in such actions.

Like Weber and Durkheim, Karl Marx conceives of economic actions as particular forms of social action. For instance, he describes producer behaviour (the process of material production) as a definite form and expression of the social 'mode of life' and the labour process as 'human action with a view to the production of use values'. Similarly, Marx considers the exchange of products, or (in **Polanyi**'s terms) the market form of economic action, a 'social transaction of a general character'. Focusing on modern capitalism, he observes that the economic activities of human agents (including both capitalists and workers) in the 'social process of production' become 'purely atomic', and consequently their relationships to each other in this process assume an objective material quality 'independent of their control and conscious individual action'. Their economic behaviour is increasingly 'objectified' or 'commodified' in the sense that, in actors' eyes, their 'social action takes the form of the action of objects' to the point of commodity 'fetishism'. For Marx, the economic actions of entrepreneurs as well as workers become a 'mere function of capital', with the operation of the law of supply and demand completing what he sees as the

'despotism of capital' over labour and even capitalists themselves.

In a vein akin to Weber, Georg Simmel conceives of economic action as a 'peculiarly interwoven form' of social interaction. In particular, Simmel characterizes economic competition as a 'sociological process', an 'incomparable sociological constellation', a 'web of a thousand sociological threads', etc. Similarly, he describes economic **exchange** as the 'purest and most developed kind' of social interaction, a 'sociological phenomenon *sui generis* and the original form and function of social life', the 'purest sociological occurrence', and the like, while specifying that interaction is the 'more comprehensive concept and exchange the narrower one'. For Simmel, exchange operates as a means of overcoming what he terms the 'purely subjective value significance' of a commodity into an 'objective, supra-personal relationship' between objects, which reflects the tendency of economic action to overcome (and establish) 'distances'. In particular, money as the 'autonomous manifestation' of economic action, especially exchange transactions, is, in his view, 'entirely a sociological phenomenon, a form of human interaction'. Simmel contends that exchange transactions are 'by no means simply an economic fact', since such facts that would be fully explained by economics do not really exist, suggesting that this form of economic action, 'just as legitimately', be treated as a sociological (socio-psychological) category. Further, he argues that even when deemed a category of economics, exchange and so, economic action becomes the subject of sociological analysis that explores its preconditions in extra-economic phenomena and its consequences for other social relationships. Finally, Simmel suggests that sociological analysis should approach economic action in terms of 'what really happens in the mind' of actors, which resembles Weber's method of understanding (*Verstehen*).

In contrast to Simmel (and Durkheim), economist-sociologist Vilfredo Pareto makes a sharp distinction between economic action and non-economic behaviour on the ground that the first is typically rational, and the second non-rational. Pareto describes as 'not too far removed from realities' the hypothesis that actors perform rational-logical economic acts – though like Weber he sees rational or logical action as (as Parsons remarks) 'explicitly broader' than the economic – in the aim of satisfying their wants or tastes. However, the alternative hypothesis that in their non-economic actions people derive logical inferences from 'residues' (sentiments) and so act rationally is, in his view, 'far removed from realities', which implies that a social science predicated on the assumption of 'rational choice' would be what he calls 'a sociology like a non-Euclidean geometry [with] little or no contact with reality'. Moreover, he contends that the 'greater part' of human behaviour is guided by non-rational rather than rational elements in virtue of originating 'not in logical reasoning but in sentiment', which further weakens the case for the hypothesis of universal rationality as the basis for general social theory. Still, Pareto retains the rational–non-rational distinction in his sociological works, holding that the hypothesis of non-rationality is 'principally true' for those social actions 'not motivated economically', while the opposite applies to their economic types. In Parsons' view, Pareto reaches the conviction that the utilitarian hypothesis of rationality (marginal utility theory) is inadequate for explaining even concrete economic action and that strictly confining pure economics to this hypothesis aims to construct a supplementary 'broader synthetic sociological theory'. Also, as a variation on his general convergence thesis, Parsons find it 'remarkable' that Pareto and Weber, while coming from different theoretical traditions – neoclassical and historical economics, respectively – reach an 'almost identical' conception of economic action or the 'place of the economic element' in social action.

Contemporary economic sociology mostly continues the classical treatment of economic action, which indicates essential continuities in the sociological theory of this subject. Thus, leading contemporary economic sociologists follow Weber by describing economic action as a special type of social action motivated by a variety of motives. Still, modern economic sociology makes important additions and contributions to this theory. The most important and best known is probably its reinvention, reformulation or reinforcement of the conception of the social **embeddedness** of economic action implicit or germinating in much of its classical version as well as economic anthropology. Moreover, the conception of social embeddedness has become paradigmatic for (the analysis of economic action within) the new economic sociology, even for the discipline as a whole. Perhaps the first explicit statement of the embeddedness conception of economic action can be credited to Polanyi, a heterodox economist as well as anthropologist influenced by classical sociologists like Durkheim, Weber and Marx. Polanyi states that economic action is 'embedded and enmeshed' in social relations and institutions, but this applies only or mostly to traditional societies. By contrast, he argues that in modern capitalism economic action is 'disembedded' from social relations and institutions which are instead 'embedded' in the economy, an argument the new economic sociology categorically rejects. (Also, Polanyi distinguishes market and non-market modes of economic action, viz. exchange from reciprocity and redistribution.)

Leading contemporary economic sociologists object that even in modern capitalist societies economic action 'is not "disembedded", as Polanyi thought [rather] embedded in a different way' (Granovetter and Swedberg 1992: 10). Hence, in contrast to Polanyi's version, the new economic sociology applies the embeddedness conception of economic action to both traditional and contemporary societies, with a focus on the latter (leaving the former to economic anthropology). Both building on and going beyond Polanyi's ideas, the new economic sociology posits that economic action, including its market mode, is 'embedded' in social relations and networks within modern society (Granovetter 1985: 481), or affected by actors' personal ties and the 'structure of the overall network of relations' (Granovetter 1990: 98). Generally, it assumes that economic action is a particular form of social action that is socially situated and influenced (Granovetter and Swedberg 1992: 6) in contrast to the 'undersocialized' conception in orthodox utilitarian economics (Granovetter 1990: 107–8). Consequently, what is treated as pure economic action in mainstream economics the new economic sociology considers to be complex 'social economic actions', thus adopting Weber's views (Swedberg 2003: 15). The two key features of the new economic sociology's conception of economic action are usually summarized as, first, its 'embeddedness' in networks of social relations, second, its 'intertwining' of materialist with non-material motivations (Granovetter 1992: 256). In regard with the second feature, the new economic sociology assumes that economic action is 'not only driven by economic interest [as assumed in pure economics] but by [values], tradition and emotions as well' (Swedberg 2003: 15), an assumption apparently derived from Weber's respective ideas. Another specific motivational assumption is that 'at all scales in economic action' actors often tend to comply with 'what they understand others want them to do' (Granovetter 2001: 8), which also evokes Weber's idea of the 'power to command and the duty to obey' or 'domination by virtue of authority' operating in or influencing the economy.

Conceptions of economic action in conventional economics and economic sociology can be compared and contrasted as follows (Smelser and Swedberg 1994). First, while economics limits itself to the type of economically rational action, economic sociology incorporates several alternative types (viz. in Weber's fourfold taxonomy), those driven by materialist ends as well as ideal values, traditions and emotions. Second, economics equates rational economic action with the efficient use of scarce resources or utility maximization in contrast to economic sociology's broader view in which efficiency or maximizing is (following Weber) designated formal or procedural rationality distinguished from substantive or value-laden rationality premised on other principles (Weberian 'ideal values'). Third, if mainstream economists treat rationality as an a priori assumption, constant or universal of economic action, economic sociologists see it as a variable subject to variation across societies and in history. Fourth, for economists the meaning of economic action is to be inferred from the relation between given preferences or stable tastes and the prices and quantity of goods, but economic sociologists see such meanings as culturally and historically 'constructed'. Finally, economics assumes that only tastes and resource scarcity (plus technology) constrain economic action and actors, whereas economic sociology considers a wide range of social, institutional and cultural constraints, notably the constraining influence of power.

References and further reading

Becker, Gary and Murphy, Kevin (2000) *Social Economics*, Cambridge, MA: Harvard University Press.

Beckert, Jens (2002) *Beyond the Market*, Princeton, NJ: Princeton University Press.

Etzioni, Amitai (1988) *The Moral Dimension*, New York: Free Press.

—— (1999) *Essays in Socio-Economics*, New York: Springer.

Fararo, Thomas (2001) *Social Action Systems*, Westport: Praeger.

Fligstein, Neil (2001) *The Architecture of Markets*, Princeton, NJ: Princeton University Press.

Granovetter, Mark (1985) 'Economic Action and Social Structure: The Problem of Embeddedness', *American Journal of Sociology*, 91: 481–510.

—— (1990) 'The Old and the New Economic Sociology: A History and an Agenda', in Roger Friedland and A. F. Robertson (eds), *Beyond the Marketplace*, New York: Aldine de Gruyter, pp. 89–112.

—— (1992) 'The Sociological and Economic Approaches to Labor Market Analysis: A Social Structural View', in Mark Granovetter and Richard Swedberg (eds), *The Sociology of Economic Life*, Boulder, CO: Westview Press, pp. 233–63.

—— (2001) 'A Theoretical Agenda for Economic Sociology. Economic Sociology at the Millennium', in Mauro Guillén, Randall Collins, Paula England and Marshall Meyer (eds), *The New Economic Sociology*, New York: Russell Sage Foundation.

Granovetter, Mark and Swedberg, Richard (eds) (1992) *The Sociology of Economic Life*, Boulder, CO: Westview Press.

Guillén, Mauro, Collins, Randall, England, Paula and Meyer, Marshall (eds) (2002) *The New Economic Sociology*, New York: Russell Sage Foundation.

Parsons, Talcott (1967) *The Structure of Social Action*, New York: Free Press.

Parsons, Talcott and Smelser, Neil (1956) *Economy and Society*, New York: Free Press.

Polanyi, Karl (1944) *The Great Transformation*, New York: Farrar and Rinehart.

Samuelson, Paul (1983) *Foundations of Economic Analysis*, Cambridge, MA: Harvard University Press.

Simon, Herbert (1982) *Models of Bounded Rationality*, Cambridge, MA: MIT Press.

Slater, Don and Tonkiss, Fran (2001) *Market Society*, London: Polity Press.

Smelser, Neil and Swedberg, Richard (eds) (1994) *The Handbook of Economic Sociology*, Princeton, NJ: Princeton University Press.

Stigler, George and Becker, Gary (1977) 'De Gustibus Non Est Disputandum', *American Economic Review*, 67(2): 76–90.

Swedberg, Richard (1998) *Max Weber and the Idea of Economic Sociology*, Princeton, NJ: Princeton University Press.

—— (2003) *Principles of Economic Sociology*, Princeton, NJ: Princeton University Press.

MILAN ZAFIROVSKI

ECONOMIC ANTHROPOLOGY

Economic anthropology is the study of economic institutions and behaviour using ethnographic methods (Plattner 1989). The ethnographic approach entails an in-depth, holistic and longitudinal study of one society, using multiple methods, including participant observation. This empirical approach to the study of the economy sets economic anthropology apart from economics. For most of its history, economic anthropologists defined themselves in relation to the other, more influential discipline (Wilk 1996), either using neoclassical theories and concepts in the study of **traditional economies**, or arguing that these were inadequate in explaining the economic behaviour of people in traditional societies. This was the key issue in the polemic debate between substantivists and formalists that dominated economic anthropology from the late 1950s to the early 1970s.

Bronislaw Malinowski was the first anthropologist to engage with the discipline of economics in his ethnography *Argonauts of the Western Pacific* (1922). Malinowski argued that Trobrianders did not fit economists' models, and described how Trobrianders' engagement in economic activities, like the ritual **kula exchange**, in which men from different islands traded shell valuables, was not motivated by their desire to satisfy material wants but to achieve social distinction. Malinowski also stressed the magical practices that were critical for Trobrianders in ensuring successful seafaring trading expeditions, thereby blurring the boundaries between the analysis of economic and religious domains and thus raising the issue of what constitutes the 'economy' in both traditional and capitalist societies.

Until the 1950s economic anthropology was primarily a descriptive field that covered one of the domains of traditional societies, in which economy essentially equalled technology. Some texts labelled all non-industrial economies as primitive economies, lumping Australian foragers together with Indian peasants and African pastoralists. Others classified economies by adaptive strategies, e.g. foraging, horticulture, agriculture, pastoralism, and studied the economy within a functionalist (Forde 1934) or cultural ecology framework (Steward 1955).

The emergence of economic anthropology as a separate field was signalled by the publication of Herskovitz' *Economic Anthropology* (1952) in which the author argued for the universality of economizing, i.e. the logic of rational choice in a situation of scarcity. This assumption was contested by the economic historian Karl **Polanyi**, who argued that there were two meanings of the economy: the substantive, which refers to a category of observable behaviour, e.g. production, consumption, distribution; and the formal, which refers to the logic of rational choice. Formalists (LeClair and Schneider 1968) assumed this logic universal, while substantivists (Polanyi *et al.* 1957) argued that rational choice is only 'instituted' in the sociocultural and political systems of capitalist societies, and that in other societies, principles such as reciprocity and redistribution guide economic behaviour, i.e. exchange. Marshall Sahlins (1972) later developed this typology of exchange systems and further distinguished between generalized, balanced, and negative reciprocity.

In the 1970s Marxists anthropologists moved away from typologies of societies based on exchange systems and instead focused on systems of production. Eric Wolf (1982) argued that the European capitalist expansion had transformed societies throughout the world and that the traditional economies studied by anthropologists were in part a product of this expansion. One of the implications was that anthropologists could no longer study traditional economies in isolation, but had to consider the capitalist world systems in their analysis. French Marxist anthropologists, like Meillassoux (1981), conducted detailed ethnographic studies of the process of articulation of modes of production in Africa in which the dominant capitalist mode of production developed further by extracting surplus production and labour from traditional modes of production. Marxists anthropologists in the USA primarily focused on inequalities within societies and the role of power and ideology herein (e.g. Donham 1990).

Most economic anthropologists are members of the Society for Economic Anthropology (SEA), which was formed in 1980 by anthropologists and archaeologists who reunited the discipline after the substantivist-formalist debate. Selected papers from the society's annual meetings are published as *Monographs in Economic Anthropology* (Volume 20 was published in 2004). Another important series of ethnographic, archaeological and historical papers is *Research in Economic Anthropology*, published by JAI Press.

In the last two decades, the boundaries between economics and economic anthropology have become fuzzier as anthropologists are increasingly studying western societies and the emergence of heterodox economics. This has coincided with a proliferation of monographs that combine social, cultural, institutional and economic analysis in the study of the interaction of the local and the global. New institutional analyses have been successfully used by anthropologists, for example in the study the emergence of markets in pastoral societies (Ensminger 1992), others have examined how processes of transnational capitalism shape and are shaped by local indigenous people in new and unexpected ways (e.g. Freeman 2000). The integration of different analyses, focus on interaction between structure and agency, and transnational ethnography have made economic anthropology one of the most dynamic fields within anthropology, such that today it is best defined as 'something that economic anthropologists do'.

References and further reading

Donham, Donald (1990) *History, Power, Ideology: Central Issues in Marxism and Anthropology*, Cambridge: Cambridge University Press.

Ensminger, Jean (1992) *Making a Market: The Institutional Transformation of an African Society*, Cambridge: Cambridge University Press.

Forde, Darryl C. (1934) *Habitat, Economy, and Society*, New York: Dutton.

Freeman, Carla (2000) *High Tech and High Heels in the Global Economy: Women, Work, and Pink-Collar Identities in the Caribbean*, Durham, NC: Duke University Press.

Herskovitz, Melville J. (1952) *Economic Anthropology: The Economic Life of Primitive Peoples*, New York: Norton.

LeClair, Edward, and Schneider, Harold (eds) (1968) *Economic Anthropology*, New York: Holt, Rinehart and Winston.

Malinowski, B (1922) *Argonauts of the Western Pacific*, London: Routledge.

Meillassoux, Claude (1981) *Maidens, Meal, and Money: Capitalism and the Domestic Community*, Cambridge: Cambridge University Press.

Plattner, Stuart (ed.) (1989) *Economic Anthropology*, Stanford: Stanford University Press.

Polanyi, Karl, Arensberg, Conrad and Pearson, Harry (eds) (1957) *Trade and Market in the Early Empires*, New York: Free Press.

Steward, Julian (1955) *The Theory of Culture Change*, Urbana, IL: University of Illinois.

Wilk, Richard R. (1996) *Economies and Cultures: Foundations of Economic Anthropology*, Boulder, CO: Westview Press.

Wolf, Eric (1982) *Europe and the People Without History*, Berkeley, CA: University of California Press.

MARK MORITZ

ECONOMIC DEVELOPMENT

Social factors of economic development

In the standard literature, economic development is often thought of as an essentially technological process, where we would find more effective ways (technologies) to combine various factors of production – capital, labour and land. Obviously if the world worked in this kind of way, all countries that have similar endowments of the factors of production and using the same technology (which, in the standard literature, is assumed to be equally available to all countries that are willing to pay for it) should be equally successful in economic development. That this is usually not the case is what makes us interested in less tangible, less quantifiable 'social' aspects of economic development.

The problem is that, while many would agree that social factors matter for economic development, there is little agreement on what these social factors are and, more importantly, how exactly they matter. Below, we examine three main groups of literature in which the role of social factors in economic development is emphasized, namely the literatures on culture, social capital and social conflict.

Culture

The most common way to conceptualize social factors in economic development has been to say that people's values, outlooks and attitudes – or 'culture' for a shorthand – affect the way they behave in the economic sphere and therefore play an important role in determining their society's ability to achieve economic development. There is of course no consensus on what the 'right' culture for economic development looks like, but it is usually supposed to encourage things like wealth accumulation, educational achievement, discipline and risk-taking.

The most important in this line of thinking is that of Max **Weber**'s thesis on the positive role of Protestantism in capitalist development in Western Europe, developed in *The Protestant Ethic and the Spirit of Capitalism*. Weber argued that the Protestant ethic based on the two principles of hard work as chief duty of life and limited enjoyment of its products led to rapid accumulation of capital because it exerted pressure on the believer to prove (but not earn – because it was supposed to be pre-ordained) his salvation.

Weber is often misinterpreted as having asserted the Hegelian position (also shared by some members of the German **historical school**, with which he had a close relationship) that it is the idea or the 'spirit' (or *Geist*) that drives history over the Marxist position that ideas are mere epiphenomena. However, Weber sided with neither of these positions, and saw the dominance of ideas over material (or economic) factors as something that is possible but not inevitable. He was also very critical of the neo-classical and Austrian views of human nature, both of which assumed individuals as acting on the basis of purely hedonistic rational calculation. Weber intended to show that rationality assumed to be universal by these approaches is historically specific to capitalism.

From the 1980s, following the 'miracle' in the East Asian economies, it has become popular to argue that Confucian culture is beneficial for economic development. Especially influential was the book *Why Has Japan Succeeded?* by the famous Japanese economist Michio Morishima, who saw himself as applying the Weberian perspective to the Japanese economic history. Morishima argued that Japan's economic success can be attributed to the special kind of Confucianism that Japan had – the kind that emphasizes group loyalty rather than personal edification like the Chinese or the Korean variety. Others emphasized other aspects of Confucianism that are supposed to help economic development, such as its emphasis on thrift, encouragement of capital accumulation, and emphasis on social discipline.

As a result, a series of arguments have been deployed in order to reaffirm the superiority of 'western' values over Confucianism. The American economist Paul Krugman argued that the collectivist cultures of the 'East' (which for him comprises both Eastern Europe and East Asia) are not capable of supporting economic growth driven by innovation, which is the exclusive domain of individualistic, entrepreneurial 'western' cultures. The economic historian David Landes argues in his recent controversial book, *The Wealth and Poverty of Nations*, that economic under-development can be explained by various cultures that are inimical to economic development. Some recent econometric studies have tried to establish links between 'cultural' factors like legal tradition and economic growth.

The problem with the literature is that 'cultural stereotypes' break down if we take a longer-term perspective. For example, the Muslim culture, whose allegedly irrationalism and otherworldliness have lead to economic failures, used to be the centre of science and commerce west of the Indian subcontinent until the fifteenth century or so. In fact, the Renaissance itself, which many regard as having laid the foundational stone for capitalist development in Western Europe, would not have happened if the Muslim world had not preserved the classical texts, many of which were destroyed by the Catholic Church. For another example, Confucian culture used to be blamed for economic stagnation of East Asia until the onset of economic 'miracles' in the region. People argued that its emphasis on classics education produced a scholastic attitude inimical to entrepreneurship, while the traditional social hierarchy that put artisans and merchants below peasants made able people avoid careers in engineering and business.

These examples, and many others, show that culture is how our notion of what is a good culture for economic development is based on a simplistic notion of culture. The point is that cultural traditions are complex and multifaceted. All of them contain both elements that are beneficial for economic development and elements that are not, and therefore it is up to human intervention to change the balance between different elements and harness it (or not) for economic development.

Social capital

During the last decade or so, **social capital** has been a popular concept among those who attempt to incorporate social factors into their analyses of economic development. The concept is thought to have been first used by two sociologists of very different theoretical persuasions. One is the French sociologist **Bourdieu**, for whom social capital is what people commonly call 'connections'. For him, like other forms of capital, it is an instrument of power and a means to reproduce social classes. The other is the American sociologist James **Coleman**, who used the term to describe shared information and trust among a group of people that help them lower transaction costs between themselves.

However, it was the American political scientist Robert Putnam who made the term fashionable and started building a new theoretical edifice different from those of Bourdieu and Coleman around the concept. In his study of the Italian and the American politics, Putnam advanced the thesis that a society with a higher level of 'civic engagement' or social capital (measured by things like newspaper readership or participation in voluntary associations) produces better 'governance' of the society. Thus, in contrast to Bourdieu and Coleman, for whom it was 'private' or 'group' property, Putnam sees social capital as a collective property of the whole society.

In the subsequent literature, attempts have been made to associate the level of social capital with various desirable outcomes, such as growth, political democracy and high-quality social services. Strongly influenced by this literature, the World Bank and other aid donors have started to pour a lot of money into projects that are meant to accelerate the accumulation of social capital in developing countries – especially by bypassing the 'untrustworthy' governments and channelling the money into NGOs, thus significantly changing the dynamics of development and poverty alleviation in many poor developing countries.

Despite its popularity, the mainstream social capital literature has some serious problems. First of all, many doubt the validity of the concept itself. Many question whether things like 'civic engagement' can be conceptualized as capital at all. In particular, Ben Fine in his *Social Capital versus Social Theory* argues that all forms of capital are 'social' and therefore the notion that there can be a separate category of social capital is unacceptable. Second, by making social capital a property of the whole society, Putnam and his followers have failed to see the 'dark side' of social capital, as the LSE political scientist James Putzel once pointed out. Trust-based relationship within an exclusive group can allow it to better exercise influence and power over other groups, possibly through criminal activities. Third, as John Harris put it in his book *Depoliticising Development*, the mainstream social capital literature has an unfortunate anti-politics bias. In this literature, social capital, or 'civic engagement', is portrayed as an alternative to organized politics, especially state intervention. However, in reality the very existence of civic engagement requires the existence of a civil society, which in turn presupposes an institutional framework put into place through the agency of a state. Therefore, portraying civic engagement and organized politics as two exclusive alternatives creates a false dichotomy, which is intended to discredit organized politics and the state.

Social conflict and economic development

Some economists have tried to explain international differences in economic performance in terms of the existence or otherwise of social conflicts. For example, many have argued that equal income distribution and ethnic homogeneity have contributed to East Asian 'miracle' by providing political stability that is necessary for long-term investment. In contrast, it is often argued that unequal income distribution in Latin America and ethnic heterogeneity in sub-Saharan Africa have contributed to sluggish economic growth by intensifying social conflicts, which reduces investment by shrinking investor horizon and/or encouraging redistributive demands.

It may sound uncontroversial to argue that a less conflict-ridden society will perform better than a more conflict-ridden one. However, the problem with this view is that the supposed causal mechanism through which income inequality and ethnic heterogeneity hurt economic growth is conceptualized in very simplistic ways. The role of ideologies that help people 'interpret' these 'objective' facts (including the very notions of ethnicity) is totally ignored, the political institutions that enable (or otherwise) people to 'translate' their grievances into political outcomes are not systematically incorporated into the analysis, and the history of conflicts is overlooked.

Unless these things are taken into account, how do we explain that Japan, an allegedly harmonious society characterized by highly equitable income distribution and ethnic homogeneity, had much higher incidences of industrial strikes than the UK or France in the 1950s, or that Sweden, another society with relatively high ethnic homogeneity and income inequality, in the 1920s had the highest incidence of industrial strikes in the world? For another example, why has ethnic heterogeneity in countries like Singapore or Switzerland not generated the intense conflicts that it is supposed to generate?

Despite these problems in the existing theories, there can be no doubt that how a country manages social conflict is very

important in determining its economic performance. The welfare state, which was adopted first by Germany in the late nineteenth century and adopted by other developed countries in the first half of the twentieth century, is the most obvious example of an institution that has helped economic growth and stability by reducing social conflict. In other countries, protection of disadvantaged groups and regions through tariffs, subsidies, quotas in education and jobs, and financial inducements to invest in particular areas have been used, with varying degrees of success, to manage social conflicts. Japan used an enterprise-level system that offers the workers lifetime employment, influence in management decisions, and profit-sharing at the enterprise level in return for industrial peace as a key to its conflict management.

Social implications of economic development

The interaction between social factors and economic development is, of course, not one-way. While many people theorize as if social factors are more or less given and therefore the challenge is to find out ways to 'work around' them (should they prove inimical to economic development), economic development transforms social factors, which in turn influence the path of economic development. In this section of the entry, I will illustrate this point by looking at three examples.

Family and community

Economic development leads to changes in the demographic profile, local community integration, the family structure and gender relationship, thus fundamentally affecting the way the society is organized.

In poor agrarian societies, people typically live in extended families situated in closely knit communities. In these societies, gender division of labour is more pronounced, if not necessarily more 'unequal', than in industrialized economies. With industrialization, families tend to become smaller, more mobile and more varied in structure, with a tendency towards the erosion of a clear-cut gender division of labour. With more mobile and varied families and more varied occupational structure, local communities tend to become less homogeneous and therefore less integrated.

In many ways, such changes in the structure of gender relations, family structure and community organization have fundamental effects on the nature of the individuals and the society that they make up. For example, take the case of the disintegration of the extended family. It means that children grow up with more intense interactions with fewer adults, thus fundamentally affecting their emotional development and the acquisition of their social skills. It makes families more mobile and communities less integrated, thereby changing the way we view other people. Greater labour mobility and the consequent disintegration of the traditional family means that people cannot expect their children to take care of them in their old age, thus changing the way people view the relationship between the parents and the children. The change in this relationship, in turn, puts pressure on the government to channel more resource into the care of the elderly, which can increase tax burden, which in turn changes the relationship between the state and the citizens.

The examples can go on, but they illustrate how economic development can change the basic social units like the family and the local community as well as the state–citizen relationship, thus fundamentally affecting the way we are formed as individuals and the way the society is organized.

Work

One important 'social' change that economic development brings about is the change in the nature of people's work, which in turn changes their outlook and attitude.

We frequently hear people from developed countries describing developing country people as 'lazy' and 'laid back' and trying to 'explain' their poverty in terms of such an attitude. However, what appears as a 'laid-back' outlook of life reflects at least partly, and in my view predominantly, the way work is organized in agrarian societies. In these societies, people work more in line with the rhythm of nature and do not require as much precise time-keeping as in industrial societies. In industrial activities, time-keeping and time-saving in workplaces is much more important for coordination and productivity than in agrarian societies. As a result, those who work and live in an industrialized societies have to develop a keener sense of time. It is only natural that to these people the agrarian attitude to life appears 'laid back', even though the inhabitants of poor agrarian societies may actually work harder, longer hours, and with much more physical strain than those who live in industrial societies do. To put it in another way, it is not that developing country people are poor because they are 'laid back' but that they are 'laid back' because they are poor.

This point can be confirmed by numerous historical examples where many peoples who now we think as diligent and efficient were once called 'laid back' and 'lazy' when they were poor agrarian nations.

For example, an Australian engineer who visited Japanese factories to advise on productivity improvement at the invitation of the Japanese government in 1915 said:

> My impression as to your cheap labour was soon disillusioned when I saw your people at work. No doubt they are lowly paid, but the return is equally so; to see your men at work made me feel that you are a very satisfied easy-going race who

reckon time is no object. When I spoke to some managers they informed me that it was impossible to change the habits of national heritage.

(Jagdish Bhagwati, quoted in Srinivasan 1984)

This is such a fundamentally different image of the Japanese workers from the one we have today, and illustrates how fundamentally economic development (together with conscious campaign for building 'good' work habits) has changed the Japanese 'habits of national heritage'. For another example, until the early nineteenth century the English frequently described the Germans as simplistic, emotional people. This is almost the polar opposite of what the English think of the Germans as these days, once again showing how the 'national character' that many people regard as immutable can change dramatically as a result of economic development.

Economic development and social conflict

In the first half of this entry, we discussed how social conflicts can affect economic development. However, the interaction between the two is not unidirectional. Economic development can affect the way social conflicts are generated, manifested and managed.

Technological innovation that characterizes the process of economic development inevitably leads to dislocation of productive factors, physical and human. With perfectly mobile factors of production, this should not cause a problem, as the owners of those productive assets (including human assets, such as skills) that need to find alternative employment will easily be able to switch to the next best option, whose return will be only marginally lower. This what is usually assumed in mainstream economics, where a perfectly competitive economy with perfect resource mobility is assumed.

However, in reality the mobility of many physical and human assets is limited, and therefore their owners face the prospect of obsolescence, which leads to unemployment and fall in incomes, if they accept the market outcome. Often, these people will take immediate non-market or political actions to redress the situation (e.g. workers striking against factories moving abroad, capitalists bribing government officials to grant them subsidies in order to avoid plant closure), which may lead to counteractions. Even when the action against market forces is not immediate, the discontents of those who are adversely affected are likely to accumulate to the point where they may manifest themselves in street riots and armed resurgences.

Given this inevitable conflicts that characterize the process of economic development, the ability of a society to manage the resulting conflicts becomes essential in sustaining economic development, as we discussed above.

References and further reading

Dore, R. (1987) *Taking Japan Seriously*, London: Athlone Press.
Fine, B. (2001) *Social Capital vs Social Theory*, London: Routledge.
Goldthorpe, J. (ed.) (1984) *Order and Conflict in Contemporary Capitalism*, Oxford: Oxford University Press.
Srinivasan, T. N. (1984) 'Comment on Lord Bauer's "Remembrance of Studies Past: Retracing First Steps"', in G. Meier and D. Seers (eds), *Pioneers in Development*, Oxford and New York: Oxford University Press.

HA-JOON CHANG

ECONOMIC GROWTH, SOCIOLOGY OF

Economic growth and attendant changes in social organization have always been central themes in social science. As an independent variable, economic growth has been linked to virtually every facet of 'modernization', linkages that justify an interdisciplinary interest in the topic.

Not surprisingly, research in development economics has evolved away from production functions that focus on capital, labour, material resources and technology. Besides typical economic variables such as investment rates and (more recently) human capital, geography/biophysical climates, institutional quality, government expenditures, age structure and the general health of populations have cropped up as predictors of economic growth, suggesting the need to go beyond formal economic models. The focus on institutions as transaction-cost minimizers by the 'new institutional economics' school also points to the increasing weight being given to non-economic determinants of economic growth.

Although economic sociology has many founders, current sociological work on economic change can be traced to **Durkheim**'s rejection of **utilitarianism** in *The Division of Labor in Society* and **Weber**'s counterpoint to **Marx**'s economic determinism in *The Protestant Ethic and the Spirit of Capitalism*. Contemporary economic sociology inherited two foci from these early works: (1) the notion that social psychology and 'culture' influence economic change; and (2) that social networks and social institutions shape and channel economic change. Underlying both is the implicit rejection of the view that markets and economic institutions emerge from the rational pursuits of atomized individuals. While the 'thin' account of social organization provided by **rational choice theory** has had its proponents within sociology (e.g. **Coleman**), most economic sociologists have sided with Durkheim in rejecting traditional economic accounts of change and growth.

Much of contemporary economic sociology can be placed under the broad umbrella of 'social capital.' While no complete consensus exists on the definition of social capital, Inkeles' (2000) defines the concept as non-economic 'community resources' that facilitate economic exchange. He notes four broad areas of empirical research: (1) institutional matrices; (2) modes of communication (e.g. networks and associations); (3) cultural patterns and **beliefs** (e.g. religious creeds and civic ethical systems); and (4) social psychologies (e.g. norms, generalized trust). Research on how social capital affects economic growth can therefore be dichotomized into structural and intersubjective components.

In general, both structural and normative accounts of social capital link it to economic growth via such mechanisms as heightened trust in government institutions and officials, reduced transaction costs given the lessened need for formal sanctions and regulation, and fewer problems with free-riders given stronger normative order (Knack and Keefer 1997). Structural social capital is simply the social organization surrounding and penetrating economic behaviour. Research in this area ranges from the study of how social networks (of individuals, firms and industries) shape market exchanges to the impact of political organization on economic performance. One primary goal of studying structural social capital is to introduce power dynamics into the study of markets (Lie 1997), which is seen as an important corrective to the undersocialized conception of human beings found in neoclassical economics. Essentially, most structural economic sociologists reject the notion that the pursuit of utility is the arbiter (or selection agent) of economic organization. Rather, economic organization is 'embedded' in broader social organization, and as such is influenced by power dynamics, political organization, stratification, and the myriad vicissitudes of social life (Granovetter 1985). Under such conditions, it is obvious (to most economic sociologists, at least) that the market alone cannot guarantee the greatest good for the greatest number (i.e. Smith's 'invisible hand'), and that understanding economics will require more sociology than economics.

Structural work relating social organization to economic growth is typically meso- or macrosocial. Some researchers see successful modernization as dependent on matching long-standing cultural and organization traits with global market-niches (Biggart and Guillén 1999), while others point to the transparency and effectiveness of government as the key to economic development (Evans and Rauch's (1999) work on Weberian bureaucratic forms and economic growth is noteworthy here). There is also a sizeable literature testing the influence of democracy on economic development (Kurzman *et al.* 2002). For impressive sweep, however, none employ the notion of social capital better than Fukuyama (1995). In his account, historical attempts to centralize power have devastated many sources of social capital in some societies (e.g. social networks and intermediating associations in Imperial China), leaving these populations only the most fundamental sources to fall back on. Essentially, the family becomes the sole foundation of these civil societies. This creates a 'bounded' social capital, thereby lowering generalized trust and crippling the potential for larger and more universal forms of economic organization. While this does not necessarily retard economic growth, Fukuyama insists that this dynamic forces these societies to rely on state-owned enterprise and foreign firms in lieu of large, private corporations. This industrial structure in turn determines a society's niche in the global economy and probably influences its subsequent potential for development.

Social psychological studies of social capital have been dominated by the idea of 'generalized trust' in a population as a predictor of economic growth. Another interesting area of cultural inquiry follows Weber's lead in seeing religion as an important economic engine. For instance, many contemporary analysts point to the Confucian emphasis on family obligations, the desirability of education, and the legitimacy of strong central government and elite decision-making as particularly compatible with capitalist development (Hofstede and Bond 1988), although empirical assessments have been mixed. Barro and McCleary (2003) provide a more generalized test of how religiosity and belief influence development; their results suggest that formal participation in religious worship negatively influences economic growth, while fundamental spiritual belief (e.g. belief in heaven and hell) boosts economic growth. This suggests that Weber's focus on the internal locus of control exerted by religious belief – the psychological mechanism that translates intersubjective theology into individualized behaviour – is apt to be correct, and that internalized norms are relatively more important than external social control.

The fact that economists and others are increasingly incorporating elements of sociological analysis into their investigations is encouraging. Like the concept of human capital, we can expect social capital (and social organization more broadly) to become a standard element in econometric analysis in the very near future.

References and further reading

Barro, Robert and McCleary, Rachel (2003) 'Religion and Economic Growth across Countries', *American Sociological Review*, 68: 760–81.

Biggart, Nicole Woolsey and Guillén, Mauro F. (1999) 'Developing Difference: Social Organization and the Rise of the Auto Industries of South Korea, Taiwan, Spain and Argentina', *American Sociological Review*, 64: 722–47.

Evans, Peter and Rauch, James E. (1999) 'Bureaucracy and Growth: A Cross-National Analysis of the Effects of "Weberian" State Structures on Economic Growth', *American Sociological Review*, 64: 748–65.

Fukuyama, Francis (1995) 'Social Capital and the Global Economy', *Foreign Affairs*, September/October: 89–103.

Granovetter, Mark (1985) 'Economic Action and Social Structure: The Problem of Embeddedness', *American Journal of Sociology*, 91: 481–510.

Hofstede, Geert and Bond, Michael H. (1988) 'The Confucian Connection: From Cultural Roots to Economic Growth', *Organizational Dynamics*, 16: 4–21.

Inkeles, Alex (2000) 'Measuring Social Capital and its Consequences', *Policy Sciences*, 33: 245–68.

Knack, Stephen and Keefer, Philip (1997) 'Does Social Capital have an Economic Payoff? A Cross-Country Investigation', *Quarterly Journal of Economics*, 112: 1251–88.

Kurzman, C., Werun, R. and Burkhart, R. E. (2002) 'Democracy's Effect on Economic Growth: A Pooled Time-Series Analysis, 1951–1980', *Studies in Comparative International Development*, 37: 3–33.

Lie, John (1997) 'Sociology of Markets', *Annual Review of Sociology*, 23: 341–60.

EDWARD CRENSHAW

ECONOMIC IMPERIALISM

Economic imperialism originally referred to a subtype of imperialism, or domination by one group over others by wielding economic power or influence. This usage still appears in contemporary economics in reference to the aggressive economic behaviour of nations or monopolistic firms. In the interaction of scholarly disciplines, economic imperialism refers to two trends: the application of economic analysis to topics not traditionally included in economics, and the expansion of an economic approach in other disciplines. The term was first used in this way in sociology by **Parsons**, who in 1934 encouraged sociologists to resist the expansionist tendency of economics.

The first trend is best exemplified in the work of Gary Becker, who applies the economic approach to human behaviour to topics as diverse as **discrimination**, immigration, crime, the family and the formation of preferences. The second trend appears in the rise of theories across disciplines which adopt economic assumptions, including **rationality**, goal-seeking or maximizing individuals, the tendency to equilibrium, stable preferences and the search for efficiency. **Rational choice theory**, in particular the work of James S. **Coleman**, exemplifies this type of economic imperialism; public/social choice theory and **game theory** are other examples.

Advocates of economic imperialism see the widespread adoption of the economic approach as a clear sign of success. For Lazear (2000), economics deserves to be imitated because of its rigour, parsimony, abstraction and adherence to scientific method. Lazear credits economic imperialism for the increased use of economics in management topics such as personnel economics and strategy, but also cites its influence in religion, law and health care.

Critics of economic imperialism object to its colonization of other disciplines. In Swedberg's interviews with key scholars in *Economics and Sociology* (1990), he asks them to discuss economic imperialism. Several scholars express open hostility, calling economic imperialism 'too simplistic', 'excessive', 'fundamentally misguided' or 'unrealistic' in its assumptions (Swedberg 1990: 326). Stinchcombe refers to the individual unit of analysis as a 'fundamental mistake' (Swedberg 1990: 295). Granovetter argues that the 'methodological and intellectual base of neoclassical economics is just too narrow' (Swedberg 1990: 105), echoing his rejection of the undersocialized conception of the economic agent in economics. In a separate critique, Zafirovski finds little theoretical foundation in classical economics for the 'universal economic approach employed by modern rational choice theorists and thus for economic imperialism' at all (2000: 467).

Economic imperialism also appears when concepts originating in economically inspired theories circulate more widely. For example, Coleman uses the term **social capital** in his rational choice framework, but even Bourdieu, openly opposed to that theoretical view, also utilizes the phrase despite its economistic implications. In *Social Capital Versus Social Theory* (2001), Ben Fine advocates avoiding the term 'social capital' in rejecting the economic imperialist project. This radical political economist joins scholars across disciplines who, like many sociologists, seek to reclaim their disciplines from the encroachment of economic imperialism in its many forms.

References and further reading

Fine, B. (2001) *Social Capital Versus Social Theory*, London: Routledge.

Lazear, Edward P. (2000) 'Economic Imperialism', *Quarterly Journal of Economics*, 115(1): 99–146.

Parsons, T. (1934) 'Some Reflections on "The Nature and Significance of Economics"', *Quarterly Journal of Economics*, 58: 511–45.

Swedberg, R. (1990) *Economics and Sociology, Redefining Their Boundaries: Conversations with Economists and Sociologists*, Princeton, NJ: Princeton University Press.

Zafirovski, Milan (2000) 'The Rational Choice Generalization of Neoclassical Economics Reconsidered: Any Theoretical Legitimation for Economic Imperialism?' *Sociological Theory*, 18(3): 448–71.

SARAH BUSSE SPENCER

ECONOMIC KNOWLEDGE, SOCIOLOGY OF

The sociology of knowledge deals with social processes that explain why, how and to what extent ideas are – or are not – produced and spread. Moreover, it is concerned with the social consequences of the diffusion of ideas. The centrality of the sociology of knowledge becomes obvious if one considers that **Durkheim** put social representations and common values at the core of his approach. Durkheim defined social events as 'ways of doing, *thinking* and *feeling*' – whereas **Weber** emphasized the role of values for the *meaningful* social actions that are at the root of comprehensive sociology.

Based on Durkheim, it is useful to make a general distinction between two forms of economic representations. On the one hand, there are economic representations which are produced by economic activity: a good example is **Marx**'s fetishism of money, according to which economic agents consider goods as things (instead of social relations between human beings through goods) and give to money a mystical power of command over goods (Marx [1867]1976: ch. 1). On the other hand, there exist economic representations resulting from a social construction: for example, one can consider the Weberian explanation of the spirit of capitalism as an unintended social construction stemming from the religious values of the Puritan sects. This approach is also followed by studies which focus on the social effects of economic or organizational teachings upon managers (Bendix 1974; Boltanski and Chiapello 1999), the high administration (Lebaron 2000) or the general public (Duval 2000). We shall focus here on this second kind of economic representations or economic knowledge, following Michel Callon's idea of the 'economic embeddedness of economic action'.

What is *economic* knowledge? Here is a first controversial issue since 'economy' is not simple to define: is the economy a substantive component of society, as Karl **Polanyi** (1944) advocated, or is it a formal view on human behaviour so that anything can be said to be economic that involves the use of scarce resources, including time? In order to simplify, we shall use 'economy' as a conventional word for market-oriented relations, so that we can both speak of a given social domain and consider a specific social behaviour. A second issue is related to what is considered as economic *knowledge*. According to a Weberian approach (Steiner 1998), there exist various forms of rational economic knowledge, or economic theories, dealing explicitly with the complex system of interactions involving a large number of actors and goods; Walras' general economic equilibrium approach is a well-known example of such rational economic knowledge. There are as well non-rational forms of economic knowledge. They are non-rational in that they do not deal with these systems of interaction and are limited to a given economic event (food shortage, unemployment in the local community, etc.) or their reasoning is dominated by pragmatic (business) interests, moral values, political principles and the like. It is important to stress that non-rational economic knowledge is not a weakened version of a given rational knowledge: it ranges from folk representations of the functioning of the economy to elaborated discourses on its ideal functioning. Furthermore, they are necessary elements of economic behaviour even for all those who have some training in economics.

These various forms of knowledge are at work simultaneously and thus there are numerous conflicts between them. First, there are conflicts between academic economists as to what they consider as 'correct' economic science: for example, **Keynes**'s approach was considered as *ad hoc* economics since, in his *General Theory*, Keynes explained that the labour market was not as flexible as a commodity market, as long as workers resist any reduction of their nominal income. Still in line with a Weberian approach, one can say that conflicts are always to be expected between formally rational economic knowledge, according to which economists should implement 'unflinchingly and relentlessly' the principles of maximizing behaviour, equilibrium and stable preferences (Becker 1976: 5), and materially rational economic knowledge which incorporates values for providing a better understanding of economic behaviour and systems. This was the case with Keynes and many others. Second, there exist also conflicts between rational and non-rational knowledge when a government implements an economic policy grounded on rational economic knowledge while laymen react against this policy

according to their economic representations and their interests, i.e. their conception of justice. As far as they encapsulate a moral dimension, that is to say a definition of what is considered just, economic representations are an important element for understanding how people are able to justify their position in a conflict and how they strive to convince other parties to reach an agreement around their own conception of (economic) justice (Boltanski and Thévenot 1992). Edward P. Thompson's (1971) study on the **moral economy** of eighteenth-century English crowd is a good example of such a situation of conflict, whereas Viviana Zelizer's study on life insurance provides another one in a less dramatic situation (1983).

Surveys show strong differences among people with regard to economic knowledge if evaluated according to the general consensus of (American) economists. Factual economic knowledge (e.g. knowledge on current economic figures such as the federal budget deficit or the rate of inflation over the last twelve months) is rather poor; institutional knowledge (e.g. what is a fiscal policy and who sets it) is somewhat better. Simple economic mechanisms (e.g. prices as a result of demand and supply) are rather well known by the general (American) public. Nevertheless, there are surprising results related to **money**, since a large number of people seem not to be aware that money does not keep its value in a period of inflation or that inflation is a good thing for those who have borrowed money at fixed rates; monetary illusion seems very common in the real world, as is also shown by the experiments of economic psychology (Shafir *et al.* 1997). One can notice as well that distribution and international trade are domains in which political (the rich versus the poor and economic nationalism) or pragmatic (merchants versus producers) interests are at work. In this respect, the sociology of economic knowledge has to consider how education and the media and everyday encounters with business produce these economic representations.

The sociology of economic knowledge has a special interest in agents whose formal or practical economic knowledge is high, as it is the case with people such as traders in **financial markets** (Abolafia 1996; Godechot 2001) or managers (Bendix 1974; Fligstein 1990; Boltanski and Chiapello 1999). This special interest can be explained by the strong emphasis that contemporary social sciences ascribe to knowledge and expertise (Giddens 1984) and, more specifically, by the fact that a small number of actors on financial markets may have a tremendously large impact on the economic life of a large number of people all over the world. Management literature is considered non-rational economic knowledge devoted to provide the managers with a vision of what they should do and what their (successful) life should be. Management literature is an interesting social data to be studied in order to gain an understanding of how markets function and evolve in terms of forms of competition and decision rules implemented by firms and public administrations (Fligstein 1990). It is also essential for understanding the making of the 'new spirit of capitalism': that is to say, the values that give to the managers a rationale for their behaviour and involvement in a new organizational world (Boltanski and Chiapello 1999). The representations and values provided by economic knowledge are also at work within the financial markets when traders distinguish between what is fair competitive legitimate profit-oriented behaviour and what is opportunism and non-legitimate aggressive behaviour (Abolafia 1996). Beyond this cultural element, economic knowledge is a major element in understanding the actual functioning of financial markets in which many traders know the complex mathematical economics of price setting. And many of those who are not able to actually master this formally rational

economic knowledge would find it quite manageable within their computers. Here it is as easily available as any other knowledge that materializes in software for the general public (Hutchins 1995; Godechot 2001).

Finally, one can consider the nature of the social institutions through which economic knowledge spreads or through which this resource is available to actors in a given context. As noticed above, economic education and media are decisive in this respect, but there are many other mechanisms that are quite important too. In certain contexts, knowledge is distributed among a set of actors and the issue is to relate to those who are relevant (i.e. they have the relevant knowledge or information). In this sense, Mark Granovetter's network approach is a study in the distribution of knowledge (not only information but knowledge about who can provide a given job and who is able to perform the job satisfactorily) on the labour market (Granovetter 1974). An empirical illustration of such situation is provided by Emmanuel Lazega's analysis of the functioning of a law firm (Lazega 2001). However, education, the media and networks are not the only institutions to be considered. Callon has rightly emphasized the role of knowledge which is buried within the machines – for example, computers – or within practical institutions such as jurisprudence, standardization rules and the like. In these cases, economic knowledge may structure economic actions even if actors are not in full command of the given knowledge: they just implement it through the material resources at hand.

References and further reading

Abolafia, Mitchel Y. (1996) *Making Markets. Opportunism and Restraint on Wall Street*, Harvard: Harvard University Press.
Becker, Gary (1976) *The Economic Approach to Human Behaviour*, Chicago: Chicago University Press.

Bendix, Reinhard (1974) *Work and Authority in Industry. Ideologies of Management in the Course of Industrialization*, Berkeley, CA: University of California Press.

Boltanski, Luc and Chiapello, Eve (1999) *Le nouvel esprit du capitalisme*, Paris: Gallimard.

Boltanski, Luc and Thévenot, Laurent (1992) *De la justification. Les économies de la grandeur*, Paris: Gallimard.

Callon, Michel (1998) 'The Economic Embeddedness of Economic Action', in Michel Callon (ed.), *The Laws of the Markets*, Cambridge: Blackwell, pp. 1–57.

Duval, Julien (2000) 'Concessions et conversions à l'économie. Le journalisme économique en France depuis 1980', *Actes de la recherche en sciences sociales*, 116–17: 3–32.

Fligstein, Neil (1990) *The Transformation of Corporate Control*, Cambridge, MA: Harvard University Press.

Giddens, Anthony (1984) *The Constitution of Society*, Cambridge: Polity Press.

Godechot, Olivier (2001) *Les Traders. Essai de sociologie des marchés financiers*, Paris: La Découverte.

Granovetter, Mark (1974) *Getting a Job. A Study of Contacts and Careers*, Chicago: University of Chicago Press.

Hutchins, E. (1995) *Cognition in the Wild*, Cambridge: MIT Press.

Lazega, Emmanuel (2001) *The Collegial Phenomenon. The Social Mechanisms of Cooperation among Peers in a Corporate Law Partnership*, Oxford: Oxford University Press.

Lebaron, Frédéric (2000) *La Croyance économique. Les économistes entre sciences et politique*, Paris: Seuil.

Marx, K. ([1867]1976) *Capital*, Vol. 1, London: Penguin Books.

Polanyi, K. (1944) *The Great Transformation*, New York: Rinehart.

Shafir, E., Diamond, P. and Tversky, A. (1997) 'Money Illusion', *Quarterly Journal of Economics*, 112(2): 341–74.

Steiner, Philippe (1998) *Sociologie de la connaissance économique. Essai sur les rationalisations de la pensée économique (1750–1850)*, Paris: Presses Universitaires de France.

Thompson, Edward P. (1971) 'The Moral Economy of English Crowd in the Eighteenth Century', *Past and Present*, 50: 76–136.

Zelizer, Viviana (1983) *Morals and Markets. The Development of Life Insurance in the United States*, New Brunswick: Transaction Books.

PHILIPPE STEINER

ECONOMIC ORGANIZATIONS

Organizational theory about the kinds of organizations began to appear in the period immediately after the Second World War when the translations of **Weber** became widespread. His **ideal type** model of rational-legal authority and of bureaucracy was applied in a number of studies, usually of public bureaucracies. Since then, one can easily distinguish three distinct and quite different literatures in the development of the thinking about the nature of the type of economic organizations. During the 1960s and 1970s, types were explained by the contingencies of the market and of the technology or changes in them (Lawrence and Lorsch 1967). Starting in the early 1980s, organizational ecology rejected the idea of contingencies, instead arguing that there were different forms for each kind of organizational population or industrial sector where the technology and the market are now defined in much more specific terms. Finally, during the 1990s, research on the inter-organizational relationship as a new kind of economic organization (Piore and Sabel 1984) developed quite rapidly. Again, a wide variety of forms has been generated. Neither the organizational ecology nor the inter-organizational literature has been related back to contingency theory.

The focus of this essay is to synthesize as much as it is possible these three disparate literatures about the types and forms of economic organizations around three issues: (1) outlining the development of contingency theory; (2) connecting this theory with organizational ecology; and (3) suggesting some ways in which specific kinds of inter-organizational relationships might be related to types of economic organization. Coherence is maintained by focusing on several dominant themes, specifically the role of knowledge and of innovation in explaining the dynamics of evolution in organizational populations and the relative importance of dyads, joint ventures, research consortia, etc.

Despite the above literatures emphasizing differences between either generic types or specific organizational forms or kinds of inter-organizational relationships, paradoxically much of the thinking about economic organizations in all the relevant disciplines focuses on one single type: the large, quasi-monopoly corporation that emerged during the industrial revolution in the United States and elsewhere in Western Europe (Chandler 1977). Structurally, this organization is highly centralized in its decision-making and relies upon bureaucratic mechanisms of control such as rules and regulations; it corresponds to Weber's ideal type of rational-legal bureaucracy.

The success of this form of economic organization has been built upon stability in both its technology and in market demand because of an acceptance of a standard design. Productivity increases occur because of strategies of worker deskilling, work routinization and large capital investments in fixed machines in the assembly line. The reduction of costs results an evolutionary process of concentration within the industrial sector with the less productive firms either disappearing or being absorbed via mergers. Chandler (1977) provides many examples of this type of economic organization, as does much of the organizational ecology literature.

Limits on concentration or economies of scale, as Chandler (1977) has observed, were set by the variety of tastes or the differentiation of market demand and by whether there is some standardized and stable technology for producing the product or providing the service. He argued these affected the capacity of the managers to coordinate and control the production and marketing processes. Hence, the major contingencies for this type of economic organization are a mass market and standardized production technology that changes little. But there is also a political

contingency, which is not frequently mentioned, and that is the presence of anti-trust laws that are enforced to prevent the creation of monopolies, which are the logical end result in this evolution of firms within the same sector.

Burns and Stalker (1961) were the first to recognize a new type of economic organization: the organic model. Their description of the structural and control characteristics in this model sharply contrasts with the previous one that they labelled the mechanical model. Decision-making is decentralized with a network of communication and of control. Leadership shifts depending upon the nature of the task and thus does not fit the rational-legal form of authority. The contingencies of this type are its capacity to be highly flexible and to rapidly adjust to changing technologies and market demands. The type is most appropriate for a small market that is highly dynamic and where competition is over innovation. Many of these firms build prototypes for larger firms rather than engage in any production themselves.

Building upon Burns and Stalker's (1961) distinction between these two opposing types, a number of authors in the organization and management literatures generated typologies build around the size of the market, the size of the knowledge base and the sophistication of the technology as represented by the emphasis on R&D (Hage 1980) and the stability in both the technology and market demand. This cross-classification generates four types, each with a different structure and strategy. The two other types have various names depending upon the author. The small craft organization produces for a limited and frequently local market. Product lives are quite short because fashion dominates tastes. As the name suggests, the workers tend to have technical and craft skills. The other form is the large science-based organization, which has a large industrial research laboratory engaged in basic research. Unlike the first type of organization, the large mechanical bureaucracy, this form continues to introduce new products into the marketplace. In fact, these companies spend a large percentage of the total industrial R&D dollars to produce semi-mass products or what Chandler calls economies of scope (Chandler 1977). Because of this some authors refer to this type as the mixed mechanical-organic, with the large research laboratory reflecting the organic type and the manufacturing representing the mechanical type. Another typology that is also quite similar is the competing values framework found in management.

The intent of this typology is not static but dynamic. It can be used to describe the differences that occur when an entire sector changes. One of the most dramatic examples of this is the automobile industry, which use to be a mass market and has over the last twenty years become much more of a science-based one, as indicated by the large increases in the proportion of the sales dollar spent on R&D. The opposite movement towards a mass market occurs as well, as we have seen with the PC and word and document processing.

At the same time, the dominant trend is towards a greater proportion of organic and mixed mechanical-organic types, for two reasons. Increasingly more and more firms are investing in R&D and globalization is largely eliminating the mechanical bureaucratic type. Furthermore, various kinds of networks are becoming attached to these types.

As we have observed, organizational ecology has proliferated a large number of forms, sometimes even several for each discrete organizational population defined by technological regime. The above typology of four basic kinds of economic organization is one way of grouping organizational populations. The specific market and technology of a population can be perceived to be variations on a basic theme.

The vast bulk of the research in organizational ecology has been in sectors where the mechanical bureaucracy type is located. In this group of sectors or of organizational populations, as Chandler (1977) observed in his classical study, organizational populations consolidate over time: that is, the number of organizations become less and less as a few organizations grow larger and larger.

In contrast, in the science-based sectors and especially in those sectors with organic firms, which are quite small, the organizational populations have differentiated over time as radically new products have created new markets and thus opportunities for new firms to be founded. In other words, the contingencies for predicting the structure of the economic organization can also be used to predict the general pattern in the evolution of the organizational populations across time.

Combinations of consolidation and of differentiation describe the craft industries, such as restaurants, and the large science-based industries, as found in electrical products. With the knowledge of the relative importance of each process, it would seem possible to predict average organizational age, average organizational size, the relative importance of a generalist vs specialist strategy and other properties that have been the focus of organizational ecologists. Research along these lines would then synthesize contingency theory with organizational population theory around the twin themes of type of economic organization and patterns of evolution across time.

Piore and Sabel (1984) observed in the middle of Italy that there was a quite different type of organization, one that is not captured in the typology nor has been described in organizational ecology. This form involves the combination of small firms into a network that is highly responsive to rapidly changing tastes in the marketplace. These inter-organizational networks of small firms also adopted new technologies such as flexible manufacturing more readily.

Since their groundbreaking work, a large number of studies have emerged describing a rich variety of different kinds of inter-organizational dyads and networks including research consortia. Space prevents a careful delineation of the various kinds, and as yet there is not a satisfactory typology for describing this variety. Instead, the focus here, as it was in the discussion of organizational ecology, is on the dynamics that push organizations into various kinds of cooperative inter-organizational relationships.

The inter-organizational literature largely concurs that the high cost of R&D, including risks associated with this and the need for various kinds of knowledge skills frequently located in other countries, explains many if not all the kinds of inter-organizational relationships between firms. One example of this kind of dynamic is the relationship between biotech or small high-tech firms and pharmaceutical companies or large science-based firms. The former does research on prototypes while the latter has the financial and knowledge resources to do clinical trials and to market the product.

Quite different are research consortia in which competitors band together to increase the knowledge base of their industry. In particular, this very special form of inter-organizational network is most typical in large science-based industries where the investments of R&D are quite high. International competitive pressures have forced national competitors to work together as a method for survival. A good example is the semiconductor industry in the USA.

In complex products with different organizations specializing in particular components and where product costs are also quite high, one finds the pattern of the inter-organizational network along the supply chain. Examples are the automobile and aircraft construction industries. These relationships are distinctive because they are enduring over long periods of time.

In contrast to these relatively enduring relationships are many of the strategic alliances that band together a combination of competitors and organizations with different kinds of expertise to develop a new product that will set a global standard. These alliances are typical in consumer electronics.

Although the supply chain pattern of inter-organizational relationships, which also includes dyads as well as networks and is one of those most frequently studied, a new form which is called the idea innovation network is also emerging.

Those large mechanical bureaucracies that have survived globalization have recognized that they also need skills. Some have developed commodity chains and moved much of their production overseas. Others have created joint ventures, another very common form, to have access to production and market skills in other countries.

Much more work and theory needs to be accomplished to develop a satisfactory theory about the types of economic organizations that recognizes these new intellectual developments in organizational ecology and in network analysis. Here the attempt has been made to indicate ways in which the old contingency theory can be updated and connected to these developments, by focusing on the themes of knowledge and of innovation that provide change dynamics including the differential patterns of evolution of organizational populations and the push for firms to develop cooperative relationships.

See also: capitalism, varieties of; network analysis.

References and further reading

Burns, T. and Stalker, G. M. (1961) *Managing Innovation*, London: Tavistock.

Chandler, A. (1977) *The Visible Hand: The Managerial Revolution in American Business*, Cambridge, MA: Harvard University Press.

Hage, J. (1980) *Theories of Organizations: Form, Process and Transformation*, New York: John Wiley and Sons.

Lawrence, P. and Lorsch, J. (1967) *Organizations and Environments*, Boston: Harvard Business School.

Pavitt, K. (1984) 'Sectorial Patterns of Technical Change. Towards a Taxonomy and a Theory', *Research Policy*, 13: 343–73.

Piore M. and Sabel, C. (1984) *The Second Industrial Divide: Possibilities for Prosperity*, New York: Basic Books.

JERALD HAGE

ECONOMIC SOCIOLOGY

Definition of economic sociology and differences with economics

As a first approximation, economic sociology can be defined as *a field of sociological studies aimed at analysing the links between economic and social phenomena*. The objective is to deal with questions such as the influence of religious ideas, public policies or social relations on the economic activities. But the focus is also on the consequences of economic phenomena on social and political life.

Max **Weber**, who made a crucial contribution to the scientific agenda of economic sociology at the beginning of the twentieth century, highlights the bi-directionality of sociological research on the economy. For him, economic sociology should analyse the interdependence between economic and social phenomena. While economics focuses on the 'technical-economic problems of prices formation and market in the modern exchange economy', the main aim of economic sociology is to shed light on 'economically relevant' and 'economically conditioned' phenomena (Weber [1904]1949: 64–6). The former concern the influence of non-economic institutions, such as religious or political institutions, on the functioning of the economy; the latter illustrate how not only political orientations, but also aspects of social life which

might seem very far removed from economic issues, such as aesthetic or religious phenomena, are in fact influenced by economic factors. In setting out his scientific agenda, Weber explicitly contrasted his views with those of **Marx**. In his polemics against the more naive and mechanistic variants of Marxism, he tried to show both that the influence of economic structures on the characteristics of a society could not be ignored, and that a crude materialistic interpretation had little scientific merit.

Looking at the interdependence between economy and society implies a particular conception of the economy, which distinguishes the perspective of economic sociology, and of other social sciences, from that of mainstream economics. Economic sociology, as well as economic history or anthropology, holds that economic activity is an institutionalized process. Unlike mainstream economics, these disciplines do not start from the isolated individual with utilitarian motivations, trying to reconstruct from his behaviour aggregate effects on the production and distribution of goods and services. They focus instead on the institutions which regulate economic activity: that is, on the social norms which orient and regulate behaviour and which are based on sanctions to provide compliance on the part of individuals. For example, in economic behaviour, there may be ethical standards in business which are based only on social approval, or else there may be norms which are based on formal sanctions (those of civil and labour law) which regulate the market exchange of goods and capital, or of labour. Other kinds of norms – no less important – define the aims of the actors rather than the ways in which they are pursued, as illustrated in the previous examples. In other words, they can involve the way in which labour is conceived or, more generally, the commitment to economic activities as opposed to those in other areas of activity, e.g. military activity (in traditional societies) or leisure and **consumption** (in contemporary societies).

The view shared by mainstream economists is based on the idea of economy as 'economizing', as a synonym of rational allocation of scarce resources in order to obtain the most from the means available. The conception shared by sociologists is more general. It concerns the set of activities which are usually carried out by members of a society in order to produce, distribute and exchange goods and services. In this framework, the satisfaction of needs and economic behaviour can be handled in different ways, depending on how society is organized. For example, in primitive societies economic activities are not distinct, but take place in the context of family and kinship relations, which regulate how goods are produced, distributed and exchanged. **Polanyi** (1977) points to 'reciprocity' as the main form of regulation of the economy in those settings (he used the concept of 'form of integration'). In the great empires of antiquity, the state played a very important role in the regulation of economic activity through the mechanisms of what Polanyi called 'redistribution'. In capitalist societies – based on the private ownership of the means of production – the economy has freed itself from social and political controls and is mainly regulated by the 'market trade'. Thus, the satisfaction of needs depends more on the functioning of 'self-regulating' markets, where resource allocation and price-setting are conditioned by relations of demand and supply. It is in this latter context that the definition of economy which is more widely shared by economists finds its historical roots.

By focusing on institutions, economic sociology tries to build up a bridge between economy and society. Economic phenomena are situated in a historical context – in a specific period of time and in a particular territory. Therefore, economic sociology does not study the economy in general, and does not confine itself to market economy, but instead analyses specific 'economic systems': for example, the economy of primitive societies, feudal economies or different types of capitalist economies. The concept of economic system is crucial in this perspective: it underlines the different ways, over space and time, in which institutions orient and regulate economic activities.

Differences between mainstream economics and economic sociology also involve the method of inquiry. While the former tends to prefer an analytical-deductive and normative method, economic sociology is more inductive, and is based on a historical-empirical and comparative approach.

The origins of economic sociology

A sociological perspective on the economy developed prior to the emergence of the discipline. One could say that economic sociology and economics were strictly linked in classical economics, especially in the work of Adam Smith. Only later, with the advent of the neoclassical economists did the disciplinary boundaries become clearer (see **economics, history of**). Economic studies concentrated on a more limited range of variables and thus radically distanced economics from the analysis of the institutional framework. While this allowed greater analytical precision and a higher degree of generalization for economics, it incurred the cost of losing adherence to historical-empirical reality. This 'economistic' turn took form with the 'marginalist revolution' in economics in the 1870s, which was promoted in different context by S. Jevons, L. Walras and L. Robbins.

Neoclassical economics, by abandoning the analysis of institutions, left greater space to sociology. This, however, was not occupied in Britain or in France, where sociology had already emerged with the work of Herbert Spencer and Auguste Comte. The foundation of economic sociology as autonomous discipline took place in Germany, in the work of Max Weber and Werner **Sombart**. The socio-cultural context of Germany was strongly influenced by idealistic philosophy, which, on the one hand, oriented the economic tradition towards historicism, and, on the other, distanced sociology from British and French positivism, and thus from the search for general laws of society. Max Weber played a crucial role in providing a methodological foundation to economic sociology as an independent discipline. At the beginning of the 1900s, he systematically engaged with economic historicism and the German idealistic philosophy, but he also tried to respond to the theoretical challenge posed by Marxism.

Weber (1904) agreed with the German philosophical criticism of sociology. According to this latter view, people, as conscious beings, forged social institutions and modified them continually through cultural development. It was thus not possible to construct generalizations that predicted the course of human action, because this does not have the regularities of natural phenomena. However, neither did this mean that it was not possible to carry out the scientific study of social phenomena. In this respect, a crucial instrument is the construction of **ideal types**.

This meant that sociology, to the extent that it studied behaviour as being influenced by social relations, could contribute to more effective knowledge when it examined specific activities. For example, by means of ideal types, it could seek to evaluate how economic activity was influenced by shared expectations of behaviour that oriented action, as in the Protestant ethic, or certain sorts of state organization: in other words, the formal or informal norms which constituted the institutions of a given society.

The twofold rejection of a general positivist sociology and of historicism opened the way to the affirmation of economic sociology as an independent discipline. The

'social-economic science' or 'economic sociology' (*Wirtschaftssoziologie*, as it was called by Weber in *Economy and Society* (1922) and Sombart in *Modern Capitalism* (1916)) took the reciprocal interaction of economic and sociocultural phenomena as its object of study. This was the reason for their research interest in western capitalism, its origins, functioning and prospects. Their economic sociology was intended as a theoretical contribution to historical knowledge and it developed as a sociology of modern capitalism.

The legacy of the classics

The founders of economic sociology gave their contribution between 1890 and 1940. Of special importance was the German context, with Sombart, Weber and **Schumpeter**. However, scholars with other intellectual linkages are to be included among the classics: **Durkheim** and **Veblen**, who were more influenced by positivism, and Polanyi with his own peculiar background. Obviously, any choice of founding fathers is somewhat arbitrary. Other authors could be considered (see, for instance, Gislain and Steiner 1995; Swedberg 2003). However, the above-mentioned scholars' contributions were exemplary in two senses. First, from the methodological point of view, they shared an institutional and historically oriented approach to the study of economic activities. Second, they applied this methodological perspective to the study of the origins and transformation of capitalism in developed western societies − a topic that was not analysed by mainstream economics. Rather than trying to summarize the individual contribution of the classics, it may be worth focusing on three aspects of their legacy which are part of the tradition of economic sociology: their view of the market, **economic development** and consumption.

Origins and operation of the market

In economic thought, it is generally held that market relations spread because of their efficiency as compared to other modalities of economic organization: that is, their capacity to satisfy the preferences of single actors at lower costs. At the centre of economic sociology's explanation is the notion of legitimacy. First of all, in order to establish itself as the main regulatory mechanism of the economy, the market must become socially accepted, but this is a difficult process without any definite outcomes. This perspective is central in the research carried out by Sombart (1916) and Weber, with reference to a particular historical period: the origins of capitalism in the West. They try to show the complex series of cultural and institutional factors that legitimized, encouraged and supported market relations, including religion, the state and the legal system, the city and modern science. As Weber showed in his comparison between West and East, this process was more difficult in other parts of the world, where culture and institutions opposed and resisted the market.

Other authors like Durkheim (1893), Veblen (1904), Schumpeter (1942), Polanyi (1944) were more interested in the consequences of the capitalist market. However, they share with Sombart and Weber the view that the market works better when problems of **fairness** and **trust** are successfully dealt with.

First, economic sociology is more interested in the problems of fairness in real markets, while economics focuses on problems of efficiency, taking it for granted that a fully competitive market will also resolve any problems of equity. If labour relations are particularly unbalanced, **conflict**s may emerge in bargaining relations, which risk endangering productive activities; or alternatively, workers may become less committed to their tasks, lowering productivity. In these cases, the institutions

representing the collective interest of workers and introducing political regulation into the **labour markets**, become important. Moreover, state intervention to regulate working conditions and to reduce social inequalities brought about by the market are also necessary precisely to have more efficient markets.

Second, individuals are not normally well informed or fully capable of rational calculation, and not everyone can be considered equally trustworthy. The lack of perfect information, together with the risk of moral hazard, makes market exchanges problematic, even where they have been legitimized. In addition, markets are not always fully competitive. In real societies, therefore, the market works better insofar as there are institutions that generate and reproduce trust through personal interactions (for example, those tied to families, kinship relations, local communities, etc.) or in an impersonal way, through formal institutions (such as legal sanctions applied to people who violate contracts). Therefore, what Durkheim called non-contractual conditions of the contract are crucial for the tradition of economic sociology. As Schumpeter ([1942]1961: 417) wrote: 'No social system can work which is based exclusively upon a network of free contracts.'

Economic development

Schumpeter points out that economic development – understood as the creation of new added resources – is not investigated by neoclassical economics. In the sociological perspective, in contrast, the behaviour of actors is variable and resources are not a given. The aim is to explain their growth over time. The basic question is: how does economic development occur? The classics would respond that economic innovation is fundamentally dependent on **entrepreneurship**: that is – as Schumpeter underlined – on the capacity to realize new things (new products, new processes and methods of organization of production, and new markets). When one innovates, one creates new relations, and one has to face even more uncertainty about the end results of action, as well as moral hazard. Therefore, Schumpeter emphasizes that the entrepreneur is characterized by particular qualities that allow him to tackle such problems more effectively: determination, capacity for vision, commitment, but also a desire for social success and recognition.

The explanation for these unusual qualities and their spread is not only psychological-individual. Rather, it involves the social context: that is, the presence of institutions that facilitate or hinder entrepreneurship. Following this perspective, Schumpeter's position is close to that of other classics, who underlined the importance of *normative factors* like religion (Weber), or exclusion from citizenship rights (Sombart, Simmel), for the emergence of economic entrepreneurship. In addition, some scholars, including Veblen, Sombart and Schumpeter, were well aware of the growing role that *cognitive resources* – the actors' knowledge, routines and know-how – play in the formation of entrepreneurship and in development in modern capitalist economies.

Consumption

The tradition of economic sociology also questions the atomism and **utilitarianism** of the neoclassical theory of action with regard to consumption. It is hard to find consumers that are independent from the influences of other actors, with stable preferences, adequate information and a capacity to make precise calculations about their utility in real societies. The interest of sociologists thus concentrates on the socio-cultural factors conditioning both preferences and the ways in which they are pursued. They point out that goods are desired and consumed, to a large extent, because of their symbolic and social value: that is, the meaning that they take on in social relations with others, functioning as signs of recognition for actors and social groups with whom consumers want to be identified, and as signs of differentiation from other groups.

Simmel (1911) was one of the first scholars to highlight the symbolic function of consumption in the competition to gain higher social status. In growing cities, in which the traditional institutions have even less influence, consumption functions as a means to get one recognized, to gain social status and to mark out an identity. It is in this context that fashion finds fertile terrain. According to Simmel, it serves a double goal: it allows individuals to identify with some social groups and distinguish themselves from others through the goods they consume.

For his part, Weber (1922) links consumer behaviour to the search for status typical of 'status groups,' groups which have a particular prestige. In modern society, status groups usually share a professional basis (the self-employed, intellectuals, soldiers, etc.) and are distinguished by a particular life style to which the quantity and quality of consumption contribute. However, it is above all Veblen (1899), with his analysis of 'conspicuous consumption', who linked consumption to the competition for social status. Veblen emphasized how growing access to mass consumption is an essential instrument for the integration of disadvantaged social groups.

There is, however, yet another aspect to be taken into consideration, as pointed out by economic sociologists. Flesh-and-blood consumers, even apart from the social pressures discussed above, are not well informed, and they have few resources to acquire the knowledge necessary to evaluate the quality of the offered goods. In modern capitalist economies, this tends to be consciously exploited by firms, which try to increase the symbolic value of goods and to control consumption behaviour through fashions. **Advertising** plays an increasing role in this respect.

The redefinition of the boundaries between economics and sociology

After the Second World War, the legacy of the classics became fragmented and economic sociology moved towards greater thematic and disciplinary specialization. New fields emerged, such as industrial and labour sociology, organizational studies, **industrial relations**. On the whole, however, there was a decline of economic sociology, which lasted until the 1970s.

Many factors have affected the process of fragmentation and disciplinary specialization, but it is worth drawing attention to two main reasons. The first concerns the consequences of intense economic growth and social and political stabilization. In other words, many of the worries about the difficult relationship between the economy and society in liberal capitalism – on which the founders of economic sociology had focused their attention – now seemed less important as a consequence of the 'great transformation' of capitalism. This occurred particularly in the more developed countries, where Keynesian policies and 'Fordist' forms of industrial organization became widespread.

The second reason involves the contemporary redefinition of the boundaries between economics and sociology. On the one hand, with the 'Keynesian revolution', economics proposed new effective instruments to interpret and guide this new and intense phase of economic growth. On the other, the institutionalization of sociology pushed scholars towards fields that were less studied by economists, and encouraged a more specific fragmentation and disciplinary specialization. The work of Talcott **Parsons** played a crucial role in the redefinition of the boundaries between economics and sociology.

Parsons (1937) criticized the atomistic individualism of neoclassical economics, because it presupposes that individuals define their ends independently of their mutual interaction. Social order instead requires a set of shared goals – of common **value**s that orient action. This is what forms the objective of sociology. Therefore, it was wrong to define both economics and sociology as empirical sciences and it was necessary to work on a different foundation for the two disciplines and their relations, which he called 'the analytical factor view'. Economics must be conceived as the analytical theory of a factor of action based on the rational pursuit of individual interest, a factor that is particularly present in concrete economic activities, although not only in these, and never in isolation. In this sense, neoclassical economics can maintain its own space undisturbed. For its part, sociology can be conceived as an abstract analytical theory of another factor of action, one linked to 'ultimate values'. An important effect of this influential view was to favour the academic insitutionalization of sociology in new fields not presided by economics, but at the same time this trend moved the interests of the sociological community away from economic sociology and towards other themes.

This latter tendency was not changed by the ambitious attempt Parsons later made, together with Neil Smelser, to work out a theoretical model of the relations between economy and society. According to this theory, society is viewed as a system of interdependent parts (structures) that must carry out some fundamental functions for maintaining social order. In *Economy and Society*, Parsons and Smelser (1956) used this framework pointing to the complex exchanges that occur between the economy and other structures. They highlighted, for example, the importance of the contribution of the 'latency system' (religion, family, school) to form motivations to work, but also of the economy, by means of income, to the reproduction of motivating structures, and in particular the family. Other important exchanges are to be found in the economic sphere, which provides important resources for the stability of state structures, which in turn, sustain economic growth through specific policies, for example through the regulation of credit. However, even though the effort to underline the interdependent relations between economy and society is of interest, it remained at a very high level of analytical abstraction and suffered from a complex conceptual framework, related to Parson's general theory of social systems. Therefore, instead of reviving economic sociology and contributing to a better integration between economic and sociological theory, *Economy and Society* remained an isolated work that neither excited the interest of economists, nor brought sociologists closer to tackling economic issues.

Economic sociology, the study of economic development and comparative political economy

After the decline of the classical tradition, in the post-war period, the re-emergence of a specific approach that is defined and recognized as 'new economic sociology' can be traced in the 1980s. However, in the previous decades, there were various fields of study and research that could be included in a wider conception of economic sociology, consistent with the classics' view, even though their protagonists did not define their work as economic sociology. In this perspective, it may be worth considering two branches of literature: studies of economic growth in developing countries and the 'new comparative political economy'.

Modernization and sociology of economic development

As we saw, after the Second World War the theme of **economic development**, which was at the centre of the classical tradition, became less important in the study of the more developed western countries. However, economic sociology's original

interest in the relation between institutions and economic development continued to flourish mainly in studies of under-developed areas and countries, where it found new fodder in the process of de-colonialization.

Some American scholars tried to emphasize the importance of cultural and institutional factors for the success of policies promoting economic development. In this way the *theory of modernization* first developed, in the 1950s and 1960s, under the influence of Parson's theory. Underlying this branch of studies is the idea that western modernity provides a challenge to less developed societies, which pushes them ineluctably towards social change. Especially at the beginning, scholars adopted an optimistic view in which the outcome of this change involved backward countries emulating the models provided by developed ones. However, as the gap between these expectations and the actual difficulties faced by the countries of the so-called Third World (Latin America, Africa and Asia) grew increasingly wide, a more critical approach to modernization began to gain ground, pointing to possible 'failures' and 'blockages'. A more radical criticism, strongly influenced by Marxism, was later developed by a new approach: the theory of dependency. Mainly drawing on the experiences of Latin American countries, the emphasis was placed on the economic constraints posed on backward countries by developed ones.

However, as the modernization processes began to take root in the different developing countries, this rather rigid and pessimistic framework was unable to account for the increasing divergences in how Third World countries were modernizing. At this point, another approach emerged focusing on the Asian countries, which exhibited remarkable economic dynamism. It may be dubbed *new comparative political economy*, since it concentrates on the role of political institutions in the process of modernization, also comparing Asian and Latin American countries (Gereffi and Wyman 1990, Evans 1995). In this perspective, the consequences of exogenous constraints are not predetermined but are mediated by the strategic capacity of the state to play a developmental role. This is in turn dependent on institutional traditions influencing the efficiency of the state bureaucracy, and on cultural traditions which may underpin the legitimacy of the leadership and its autonomy from social interests. In addition, peculiar forms of organization, based on weak firms and strong networks (family and community ties), seem at work in the 'Asian capitalism'. Therefore, the study of Asian capitalism leads beyond political economy to the role of different civilizations in shaping economic development (Hamilton 1994).

The comparative political economy of advanced countries

During the 1970s the analytical tools used in the Keynesian approach seemed to be less effective to adequately explain the new difficulties facing the economies of the more highly industrialized economies. These were simultaneously affected by high levels of unemployment and inflation, and by an unexpected harsh wave of social conflicts. Sociologists, industrial relations scholars and political scientists became more interested in the problems of economic development. They analysed the crisis of the 'Keynesian welfare state', and focused on the striking differences in the adjustments of various countries to the new challenges. Comparison between national cases was particularly useful to discuss how institutional factors influenced the emerging social and economic tensions, and the different responses. Among these factors, special importance was paid to the political dimension and especially to the influence of the system of interest representation on macroeconomic management and social policies. This led to

the emergence of a 'comparative political economy' – an approach similar to that used for backward countries.

Initially, the most important research problem involved the origins of **inflation**. Later on, this approach focused on the role of interest organization in the policy-making, with the comparison between pluralist and neo-corporatist countries (Schmitter and Lehmbruch 1979; Berger 1981; Goldthorpe 1984). Underlying this literature is the idea that better results in terms of control of economic and social tensions, namely, of the 'perverse effects' of the Keynesian welfare state, are associated with a system of interest representation and political decision-making based on neo-corporatist features: a model of political economy in which large interest organizations participate together with the government in a process of central 'concertation' of economic and social policies.

Subsequently, however, especially during the 1980s, research began to focus on the problem of competition among firms and on the dynamism inherent to the different capitalist systems. The objective of this literature was to define different models of national capitalism, characterized by a particular institutional context. There was an attempt at combining the results of comparative studies at the macro level with those brought about at the micro level by research on the changes in the organization of production. The first branch of literature mainly deals with changes in corporatist arrangements (see, for example, Soskice 1990; Crouch 1993; Regini 1995), and with the transformation of welfare state (see, for example, Esping-Andersen 1999; Pierson 1994). Research at the micro level concerns the crisis of Fordism and the emergence of 'flexible specialization' (Piore and Sabel 1984; Streeck 1992; and, with particular reference to Japan, Dore 1986), together with the growth of local systems of production and **industrial districts** (Becattini 1990; Crouch et al. 2001).

199

The new literature on the 'varieties of capitalism' (see **capitalism, varieties of**) tended initially to highlight the advantages of 'coordinated market economies'. These are based on a model of capitalism that is more organized and long-term oriented, as in the Japanese or German types, vis-à-vis the 'non-coordinated market economies', more short-term oriented, prevailing in Anglo-Saxon settings (Soskice 1990; Albert 1993; Dore 1986; Streeck 1992; Hollingsworth and Boyer 1997). However, since the end of the 1980s, these advantages have been questioned. This is because there have been signs of recovery and dynamism in the British and American economies, and, more generally, because of a need to account for the phenomenon of globalization. The growing interdependence and integration of economies at the global level seems to threaten the more organized models of the economy, where markets are restrained by other forms of regulation. A new debate has then opened on the possible impact of globalization on the different regulatory systems of economic activities: that is, on the national varieties of capitalism (Berger and Dore 1996; Crouch and Streeck 1997; Hall and Soskice 2002; Fliegstein 2001). In this discussion comparative political economy warns against accepting uncritically any hypothesis about a progressive institutional convergence induced by **globalization**. In following this path, this literature shares with the tradition of economic sociology a view that underlines the autonomous role of political institutions in orienting economic activities (Fliegstein 2001; Trigilia 2002).

The new economic sociology

Together with the research-driven studies above mentioned, another more theory-driven approach emerged since the 1980s: the 'new economic sociology'. In this case, sociologists were the protagonists of this trend, which marks a new explicit interest in economic sociology, mainly oriented to the micro level.

Two main factors have influenced this turn. First, there was a theoretical reaction to the attempts of a new economic neo-institutionalism to analyse the increasing variety of productive organization. Besides market and hierarchy (i.e. the firm functioning as the bureaucratic organization), a growing number of hybrid forms were developing, based on a more or less formalized collaboration between firms (joint ventures, alliances, cooperation agreements, etc.). Although transaction costs theory (Williamson 1985) tried to redefine the theory of action traditionally used by economists by taking into account aspects such as the 'bounded rationality' and 'opportunism', still this approach explains organizational choices in terms of a rational search for efficiency. Thus, it is not able to provide a satisfying explanation of economic actions under conditions of lack of information and uncertainty (see, for criticism from the economic sociology point of view, Beckert 2002). On the side of sociology, the development of neo-institutional economic theories triggered, in turn, new attempts to explain organizational variety that underlined the autonomous role of social networks, cultural factors and power relations.

This leads to a second factor. In the 1970s and early 1980s, there was a growing dissatisfaction in sociology with the theory of action developed by Talcott Parsons. The new economic sociology was influenced by the criticisms developed by ethno-methodology and phenomenology. Therefore, it shares a theory of action that is more constructivist, more contingent and open to direct social interactions. Drawing on the distinction proposed by Mark Granovetter (1985), it can be said that the criticism affects not only the 'undersocialized' conception of the actor typical of economics (including the neo-institutional approach), but also to the 'oversocialized' version of sociology developed by Parsons. The latter refers to models in which actors' behaviour is strongly conditioned by culture and norms interjected through the socialization process.

Different approaches converge in the new economic sociology. However, they differ from the 'old' economic sociology (Granovetter 1990), not only in the sense that they share a view of social action more open to social interaction, but also because they tend to trespass the traditional boundaries between economics and sociology. While new institutional economists try to explain economic institutions by using the traditional economic tools, economic sociologists tend now to analyse aspects of economic activities that were previously left to the economists, such as the operation of the market and the organization of production, or the choices of consumption.

The structural approach, social networks and social capital

For scholars of the structural approach, **economic action** is socially embedded: it is viewed in structural terms because it is assumed that action is fundamentally influenced by the variable location of single actors in social networks. Stable networks of social relations constitute structures that need to be reconstructed to evaluate the effects on economic behaviour. In this respect Mark Granovetter's work (1973, 1985). deserves particular attention.

The insertion of actors in stable networks of personal relations enables information to be spread and opportunism to be controlled, generating trust and rapidly isolating those who are not trustworthy. As a consequence of this approach, it is not reasonable to explain the various economic organizations as merely efficient responses to the problems of transaction costs by actors who rationally pursue their interests, as in the influential work by Williamson. According to Granovetter, this model tends to overestimate the capacities of hierarchy

and the firm to govern complex transactions, and to underestimate those of the market. Actually, empirical evidence shows that complex and potentially risky transactions can also be carried out through the market, if networks of trust relations linking the involved parties exist and thus lower transaction costs. Recourse to the market, hierarchy or to intermediate forms will thus be influenced autonomously by the existence and features of social networks.

The structural approach has been applied in different fields. First, the pioneering study by Granovetter (1974) on the influence of social networks on labour markets should be mentioned. In this research Granovetter not only demonstrates the importance of informal contacts as an instrument for getting jobs, but he also draws attention to the 'strength of weak ties' (Granovetter 1973). His contention is that subjects inserted into networks of weak social relations have more chances of access to a larger and more diversified (nonredundant) amount of information vis-à-vis those which are obtainable through 'strong' ties: that is, through family or kin ties and through close friends. Other significant applications of the structural approach can be found in the study of **business associations** and inter-firm relations, in new high-tech activities, such as bio-technologies, and in the stock market.

The contribution of the structural approach to the development of a 'sociology of markets' (Swedberg 1994) has been more limited to theoretical debate. Economic models usually hypothesize that firms are isolated and independent from each other, merely reacting to consumers' demand. Some network-oriented studies (White 1981, 1992) rather point to the influence exercised by all firms operating in a given market on the specific strategies of product differentiation, and on the search for a niche, followed by each of these firms. In this sense, markets are seen as *cliques* of producers who keep each other under strict surveillance in order to determine the most advantageous strategy in terms of the quality and price of goods offered. In this view, markets thus respond to a logic of producers' self-reproduction rather than of efficiency in terms of satisfaction of consumer demand at lower costs.

Other studies, particularly developed in the United States, concern the widespread attempt by firms to avoid competition or to keep it under control by developing networks of relations between them as a means of exercising power (Burt 1983). These involve not only forms of ownership control and shareholdings, but also the cross-participation of representatives on the boards of directors ('**interlocking directorates**').

The structural approach thus underlines the influence of social networks on various forms of economic organization. However, the consequences of social networks for economic activity are not always positive. They can also be an instrument to avoid or elude competition and can thus reduce efficiency by collusion between the actors. This opening up of the social networks leading to different economic outcomes is also entailed in the concept of **social capital**. Social capital can be considered as a set of social relations on which an individual (for instance, an entrepreneur or a worker) or a collective actor (either private or public) can rely at any given moment. Through the availability of this relational capital, cognitive resources (e.g. information) or normative resources (e.g. trust) allow actors to realize objectives which would not otherwise be realized, or which could only be obtained at a much higher cost. A specific entrepreneurial attitude can be exercised through the ability to bridge 'structural holes' as a means of creating social capital. This means acting as broker in relations between people otherwise disconnected in the social structure (Burt 1992).

Moving from the individual to the aggregate level, it may also be said that a particular territorial context is more or less rich with social capital depending on the extent to which individual or collective actors of the same area are involved in networks of relations. Social capital can be a crucial resource for economic development as far as its potential for collusion is checked by autonomous and efficient political institutions (Evans 1995; Trigilia 2001). It is to be stressed that this conception, drawn from Coleman and the structural approach, places a greater emphasis on social networks as the basis of social capital rather than on shared culture and civicness, as presented in the study by Putnam (1993).

The sociological neo-institutionalism and new studies of consumption

While for structuralists networks determine resources and constraints that condition the rational pursuit of interests by actors, for neo-institutionalists cultural factors contribute to defining the interests themselves and the procedures by which they may be pursued by actors. They draw attention not only to the structural (network-based) embeddedness of action, but also to cognitive, cultural and political embeddedness (Zukin and DiMaggio 1990).

The theory of action of neo-institutionalism is thus wider than that of the structuralists, and it is multi-dimensional. In this case, criticism of new institutional economics is accompanied by an interest in institutions as independent variables: a turn towards cognitive and cultural explanations (Powell and Di Maggio 1991). This leads to emphasizing the cognitive dimension of institutions as opposed to the normative one. In other words, the role played by routines – by informal rules of behaviour largely taken for granted – is now more carefully investigated; as are shared schemas and frames or rituals helping to define identities and individual interests, as well as the procedures for following them.

In this case, criticism of different forms of new institutional economics leads to underlining the legitimacy of organizational choices. Attention is drawn to the appropriateness of action with respect to prevailing frames. In other words, in the face of a lack of information and risks of transactions, it is hard for actors to follow a rigorous rational choice for the most efficient solutions. This perspective enables the inertia of organizational structures to be explained even when they lose economic efficiency.

A good example of the analytical consequences resulting from the neo-institutionalist approach is the work on 'isomorphism' by Powell and Di Maggio (1991). In empirical research, this approach has stimulated numerous contributions, especially in sectors that are not affected by market competition, such as non-profit and cultural organizations, as well as financial institutions and large accounting firms. Fliegstein's work (1990) on the productive diversification of large American firms provided an interesting application.

In the structural approach, the actor's location in the structure of social relations is crucial to understand his or her actions. This also explains why a strong contrast with the theory of rational choice is not perceived in the work by Granovetter (1985) or in the way in which social capital is conceived by Coleman (1990). The position of the neo-institutionalists in the new economic sociology is different from that of the structuralists, because they want instead to highlight the autonomous role played by cultural factors in motivating actors. Their framework is wider than that of the structuralists, who concentrate mainly on the role of social networks. However, it is also true that in concrete research practices, these differences in the new economic sociology become weaker. Both the structural approach and the sociological neo-institutionalism provide a view of the market as embedded in social structures, and try to explain the real action of economic actors in concrete markets. But in this way they do not take into account the role of states in the social construction of markets. This criticism leads Fliegstein (2001) to underline the importance of political embeddedness. His proposal of a 'political-cultural approach' is promising because it tries not only to contribute to a more integrated sociology of markets, but also to build a bridge between the microeconomic sociology and the macro-comparative political economy and the varieties of capitalism approach (see also, in the same perspective, Block 1990). Some studies of transition to market economy in Eastern Europe and in China provide useful insights in this respect.

The new economic sociology also includes studies of consumption. Recent research has also highlighted the influence of cultural factors on consumption behaviour. Even though this work is not directly connected to neo-institutionalism, it was largely inspired by the same background. Some of the authors involved come from sociology, but others are anthropologists or social historians. With respect to the tradition of economic sociology, more recent developments seem characterized by a twofold tendency. On the one hand, they are less influenced by the Veblenian model that closely linked consumption to competition for social status. On the other, they are also critical of those models that stress the passive subordination of consumers to the choices imposed by firms and supported by advertising and mass media. It may be useful, therefore, to distinguish between an approach which still emphasizes the search for social differentiation, and another that is more interested in the role of culture in shaping consumers' behaviour and economic activity. This latter is closer to the new economic sociology, especially through the work by Viviana Zelizer.

In Zelizer's view, the new sociology of consumption tries to distinguish itself from the conception of a 'boundless market': that is, from the idea of a progressive diffusion of utilitarian and individualistic values. For example, Zelizer has shown how in some markets for goods considered to be 'sacred' – linked to life and death – cultural factors play an important autonomous role in orienting consumers' behaviour and the value of the goods. She used this approach in her pioneering study of the life insurance market (Zelizer 1983), and in the study of the 'child market' (adoptions, insurance, 'sales', etc.) (Zelizer 1987). Moreover, cultural factors can be also seen in the use of money as a standardized means of exchange, utilized in different contexts according to different and specific rules, which reflect particular cultural frames, for example according to whether money is used for gifts, for domestic use, or for charity (Zelizer 1994).

A concluding remark

The review of contemporary developments has shown the variety and quality of studies that may be included in the new economic sociology, and has illustrated the growing interest in the discipline. Both the new economic sociology and the comparative political economy are part of a wider economic sociology. This approach is increasingly demanded to deal with the rapid changes and growing uncertainty which affect economic activities and human labour in a globalized world. Despite recent trends and efforts, it is unlikely that economics will be able to respond to the new questions in isolation from economic sociology. Economists strongly maintain their traditional preference for building analytical models that can be formalized and provide more general and parsimonious explanations. However, the advantages of these models face some clear shortcomings when the concrete variety of organizational forms is to be explained, and has to be taken into account to design more effective and fine-tuned policies.

Therefore, as in the past, there is a space to fill for economic sociology in the expla-nation of varieties and changes in economic activities. As Granovetter (1990: 106) underlines: 'outcomes can vary dramatically even for the *same* economic problems and technologies, if the social structure, institutional history, and collective action are different ... Less contingent arguments are cleaner, simpler and more elegant. But they fail to identify causal mechanisms.' Thus, there is not one best way of organizing the economy. However, there are two clear risks in this conception of economic sociology. One is that of falling into a too narrow and contingent historicism, and the other concerns the production of loose explanation. To avoid these dangers, it seems necessary to increase the interaction between theory and research and to strengthen comparative analysis through a better connection between the micro and macro level. If economic sociology is able to develop a more effective balance between the openness to the variety of economic action and the need for good theory, it will continue to contribute to a better understanding and a more reflexive construction of society.

References and further reading

Albert, M. (1993) *Capitalism against Capitalism*, London: Whurr.

Becattini, G. (1990) 'The Marshallian Industrial District as a Socio-Economic Notion', in F. Pyke, G. Becattini and W. Sengenberger (eds), *Industrial Districts and Inter-Firm Co-operation in Italy*, Geneva: ILO, pp. 37–51.

Beckert, J. (2002) *Beyond the Market. The Social Foundations of Economic Efficiency*, Princeton, NJ: Princeton University Press.

Berger, S. (1981) *Organizing Interests in Western Europe*, Cambridge: Cambridge University Press.

Berger, S. and Dore, R. (eds) (1996) *National Diversity and Global Capitalism*, Ithaca, NY: Cornell University Press.

Block, F. (1990) *Postindustrial Possibilities: A Critique of Economic Discourse*, Berkeley, CA: University of California Press.

Burt, R. (1983) *Corporate Profits and Cooptation*, New York: Academic Press.

—— (1992) *Structural Holes: The Social Structure of Competition*, Cambridge, MA: Harvard University Press.

Coleman, J. (1990) *Foundations of Social Theory*, Cambridge, MA: Harvard University Press.

Crouch, C. (1993) *Industrial Relations and European State Traditions*, Oxford: Clarendon Press.

Crouch, C. and Streeck, W. (1997) 'Introduction: The Future of Capitalist Diversity', in C. Crouch and W. Streeck (eds), *Political Economy of Modern Capitalism*, London: Sage, pp. 1–18.

Crouch, C., Le Galès, P., Trigilia, C. and Voelzkow H. (2001) *Local Production Systems in Europe: Rise or Demise?* Oxford: Oxford University Press.

Dore, R. (1986) *Flexible Rigidities*, Stanford, CA: Stanford University Press.

Durkheim, E. ([1893]1984) *The Division of Labor in Society*, translated by W. D. Halls, New York: Free Press.

Esping-Andersen, G. (1999) *Social Foundations of Postindustrial Economies*, Oxford: Oxford University Press.

Evans, P. (1995) *Embedded Autonomy. States and Industrial Transformation*, Princeton, NJ: Princeton University Press.

Fliegstein, N. (1990) *The Transformation of Corporate Control*, Cambridge, MA: Cambridge University Press.

—— (2001) *The Architecture of Markets. An Economic Sociology of Twenty-First-Century Capitalist Societies*, Princeton, NJ: Princeton University Press.

Gereffi, G. and Wyman, D. (1990) *Manufacturing Miracles. Paths of Industrialization in Latin America and East Asia*, Princeton, NJ: Princeton University Press.

Gislain, J. and Steiner, P. H. (1995) *La Sociologie economique 1890–1920*, Paris: Presses Universitaires de France.

Goldthorpe, J. (ed.) (1984) *Order and Conflict in Contemporary Capitalism*, Oxford: Clarendon Press.

Granovetter, M. (1973) 'The Strength of Weak Ties', *American Journal of Sociology*, 78: 1360–80.

—— (1974) *Getting a Job, A Study of Contacts and Careers*, Cambridge, MA: Harvard University Press.

—— (1985) 'Economic Action and Social Structure: The Problem of Embeddedness', *American Journal of Sociology*, 91: 481–510.

—— (1990) 'The Old and New Economic Sociology: A History and an Agenda', in R. Friedland and A. F. Robertson (eds), *Beyond the Marketplace. Rethinking Economy and Society*, New York: Aldine de Gruyter, pp. 89–112.

Hall, P. and Soskice, D. (2002) *Varieties of Capitalism. The Institutional Foundations of Comparative Advantage*, Oxford: Oxford University Press.

Hamilton, G. (1994) 'Civilizations and the Organization of the Economy', in N. Smelser and R. Swedberg (eds), *The Handbook of Economic Sociology*, Princeton, NJ: Princeton University Press, pp. 183–205.

Hollingsworth, R. and Boyer, R. (1997) *Contemporary Capitalism. The Embeddedness of Institutions*, Cambridge: Cambridge University Press.

Parsons, T. ([1937]1968). *The Structure of Social Action*, two volumes, New York: Free Press.

Parsons, T. and Smelser, N. (1956) *Economy and Society: A Study in the Integration of Economic and Social Theory*, Glencoe, IL: Free Press.

Pierson, P. (1994) *Dismantling the Welfare State?* Cambridge: Cambridge University Press.

Piore, M. and Sabel, C. (1984) *The Second Industrial Divide*, New York: Basic Books.

Polanyi, K. ([1944]1985) *The Great Transformation*, Boston: Beacon Press.

—— (1977) *The Livelihood of Man*, edited by Harry W. Pearson, New York: Academic Press.

Powell, W. and DiMaggio, P. (1991) 'Introduction', in W. Powell and P. DiMaggio (eds), *The New Institutionalism in Organizational Analysis*, Chicago: University of Chicago Press, pp. 1–38.

Putnam, R. (1993) *Making Democracy Work*, Princeton, NJ: Princeton University Press.

Regini, M. (1995) *Uncertain Boundaries: The Social and Political Construction of European Economies*, Cambridge: Cambridge University Press.

Schmitter, P. and Lehmbruch, G. (eds) (1979) *Trends Toward Corporatist Intermediation*, Beverly Hills, CA: Sage.

Schumpeter, J. ([1942]1961) *Capitalism, Socialism, and Democracy*, New York: Harper and Row.

Simmel, G. ([1911]1971) 'Fashion', in G. Simmel, *On Individuality and Social Forms. Selected Writings*, edited and with an introduction by Donald N. Levine, Chicago: University of Chicago Press, pp. 294–323.

Sombart, W. ([1916]1922) *Der moderne Kapitalismus*, two volumes, Berlin: Dunker and Humblot.

—— (1928) *Der moderne Kapitalismus*, vol. 3, Berlin: Dunker and Humblot.

Soskice, D. (1990) 'Reinterpreting Corporatism and Explaining Unemployment: Coordinated and Non-Coordinated Market Economies', in R. Brunetta and C. Dell'Aringa (eds), *Markets, Institutions and Corporations: Labour Relations and Economic Performance*, New York: New York University Press, pp. 170–211.

Streeck, W. (1992) *Social Institutions and Economic Performance*, London: Sage.

Swedberg, R. (1994) 'Markets as Social Structures', in N. Smelser and R. Swedberg (eds), *The Handbook of Economic Sociology*, Princeton, NJ: Princeton University Press, pp. 255–82.

—— (2003) *Principles of Economic Sociology*, Princeton, NJ: Princeton University Press.

Trigilia, C. (2001) 'Social Capital and Local Development', *European Journal of Social Theory*, 4(4): 427–42.

—— (2002) *Economic Sociology: State, Market and Society in Modern Capitalism*, Oxford: Blackwell.

Veblen, T. ([1899]1934) *The Theory of the Leisure Class: An Economic Study of the Evolution of Institutions*, New Brunswick, NJ: Transaction Books.

Weber, M. ([1904]1949) '"Objectivity" in Social Sciences and Social Policy', in M. Weber, *The Methodology of Social Sciences*, translated by E. A. Shils and H. A. Finch, New York: Free Press, pp. 49–112.

—— ([1922]1978) *Economy and Society: An Outline of Interpretive Sociology*, two volumes, edited by G. Roth and C. Wittich and translated by E. Fischoff, Berkeley, CA: University of California Press.

White, H. (1981) 'Where Do Markets Come From?' *American Journal of Sociology*, 87: 517–47.

—— (1992) *Identity and Control: A Structural Theory of Social Action*, Princeton, NJ: Princeton University Press.

Williamson, O. (1985) *The Economic Institutions of Capitalism*, New York: Free Press.

Zelizer, V. (1983) *Morals and Markets: The Development of Life Insurance in the United States*, New Brunswick, NJ: Transaction Books.

—— (1987) *Pricing the Priceless Child: The Changing Value of Children*, New York: Basic Books.

—— (1994) *The Social Meaning of Money*, New York: Basic Books.

Zukin, S. and DiMaggio, P. (1990) 'Introduction', in S. Zukin and P. DiMaggio (eds), *Structures of Capital*, Cambridge: Cambridge University Press, pp. 1–36.

CARLO TRIGILIA

ECONOMIC TRANSFORMATION IN POST-COMMUNIST SOCIETIES

In post-communist societies, economic transformation entails not simply the state changing the formal rules of the game to dismantle central planning, but fundamentally it involves a bottom-up realignment of interests of political and economic actors. First, the growth of markets opens new opportunity structures that enable and motivate private entrepreneurs to compete with state-owned firms which dominate the transition economy. Second, decentralized markets provide an alternative framework for the pursuit of interests, beyond the control of the state. Lastly, as actors adapt and compete in the emergent market economy, they institute new organizational practices and rules that enable their firms to survive and profit in competitive markets. In sum, the emergence of a market economy alters the incentives for economic actors in opening new pathways for mobility, which in turn causes a decline in the significance of political connections as a form of capital needed for socio-economic attainment.

A central task in the comparative analysis of economic transformation is to specify the role of institutions. Economic transformation entails the co-evolution of multiple pathways of transformation as firms and economic actors adapt and compete in an economy shifting to increased reliance on market mechanisms. Accordingly, the institutional environment of transition economies is best conceived as constituted of competing and overlapping institutional orders whose boundaries are defined by distinct property rights, organizational forms and governance structures. In the state-owned sector, for example, for-profit firms face powerful inertia forces that lock them into long-standing organizational routines and interests, limiting their ability to adapt and compete in the emergent market economy. By contrast new organizational forms – private enterprises and hybrids – are faster in adapting to and learning the new rules and approaches to competition and cooperation of an expanding market economy. Yet they are constrained by the privileged position of state- and collective-owned firms with respect to access to finance capital, raw materials and markets. In the transition economy, discrete governance structures of firms shape the principal–agent relationship and structure of incentives for economic agents. Variation in governance structures influence returns to investments in different forms of capital. In state-owned firms and public organizations, the old Communist Party-based networks persist as an entrenched interest group with privileged access to power and resources reserved for its members and leaders. Hence in the public sectors of the transition economy, political capital confers advantages based on positional power. However, the more private ownership rights and free markets shape the environment of firms, the less the power and privilege stemming from political connections and party membership (Opper *et al*. 2002). Private enterprise and hybrid firms foster organizational rules and routines that privilege other forms of capital – human, social and financial – not gained directly through political connections. Economics and economic sociology have contributed to the growing literature on economic transformation.

The early economic literature on transition economies often adopted a normative tone evident in its neo-liberal prescriptions on how best to change a centrally planned economy into a market economy. When western economists travelled to Eastern Europe and the former Soviet Union to advise reformers at the onset of market reforms, they consistently emphasized instituting capitalism by implementing sweeping changes in the formal rules governing property rights, capital and labour markets. The objective of establishing a western-style market economy was taken for granted and the necessary strategic elements for such an endeavour were distilled from the western economics literature (Sachs 1996). In this view, the objective of economic reform was to reduce the state's commanding control over the economy and pave the way for a rapid transition to a free enterprise-based market capitalism. Such emphasis on writing and legislating new rules of economic action overlooked the realities of power and interests vested in existing institutional arrangements and long-standing personal relationships of the political elite. By contrast, the trial-and-error approach taken by reformers in China has allowed for a more evolutionary approach to economic transition. China's greater success in economic transformation shows that institutional change is driven not so much by new formal rules but by bottom-up realignment of interests and power as new organizational forms, private property rights and new market institutions evolve in an economy shifting away from state control over economic activity. In China, changes in the formal rules governing the emerging market economy have tended to follow ex post changes in the informal economic practices, and the competitive environment in which firms compete and cooperate. A parallel process occurred in Eastern Europe and the former Soviet Union, where following failed attempts at designing capitalism in one fell swoop, more incremental bottom-up approach tacitly replaced the big-bang approach of top-down legal and regulatory changes as political and economic actors grappled step by step with the concrete problems of their emergent market economy.

The sociological literature on market transition has been motivated by a long-standing debate inspired by two competing approaches to explaining economic transformation. The first is a *political economy* approach advanced by market transition theorists. Market transition theory advances

207

three core arguments about the nature of institutional change in departures from state socialism: (1) that institutional innovations in economic reform are initiated and implemented by the state and the course of subsequent institutional change arises from the interaction between the revenue maximizing interests of political actors and constraints imposed on rulers by organizational and economic actors; (2) that instituting market exchange as the dominant coordinating mechanism for an economy involves a *deinstitutionalization* of core features of state socialist redistribution, contributing to a decline in the relative advantages of the political elite; and (3) that institutional change promoting reliance on the market mechanism alters the structure of incentives through changes in the informal and formal rules governing property rights and expanding payoff to market-oriented performance for economic agents and firms (Nee and Cao 1999).

Studies of the pattern of earnings attainment in discrete sectors of the transition economy indicate that the institutional environment is far from homogenous, and the structure of incentives differs across discrete sectors of the transition economy varying according to the extent the institutional logic of a market economy permeates and transforms the pre-existing framework. Nee and Cao (2004) examine the pattern of earnings inequality in urban China, confirming that three market-based causal mechanisms reshape the structure of incentives and hence the pattern of earnings inequality in the transitional period: (1) the higher marginal productivity of private enterprise relative to state-owned enterprises; (2) labour market competition by firms for skilled workers following the end of state monopoly on labour allocation; and (3) the expansion of merit-based reward systems in firms in response to increased competition between firms for market share and profits. All are market-driven mechanisms that contribute to relative decline in

the earnings payoff of political capital and increase in returns to human capital.

Market transition theory does not rule out an independent, ongoing, causal effect of the state in shaping the post-communist stratification order in urban China. Specifying a political economy approach that posits two sources of causal mechanisms shaping the stratification order in departures from state socialism, it claims 'as long as major productive assets are owned or controlled by the state, officials will pursue power-conversion the more political capital is diminished relative to the appreciation of economic capital' (Nee and Cao 1999: 806). Notwithstanding, market transition theorists tend to focus on mechanisms of transformative change that stem from the emergence of decentralized market exchange.

By contrast, *state-centred* theorists take a different tack from market transition theory's focus on the causal effects of market penetration and state intervention in departures from central planning. Evidence supporting the persistent reproduction of core features of the state socialist institutional order despite the collapse of central planning is interpreted as contradicting market transition theory's claim of decline in significance of political capital (Bian and Logan 1996; Zhou 2000). Walder (2004), for example, focuses solely on political variables centring on regime change (or not) and constraints (or not) on asset appropriation by the political elite to explain the course of market transitions in post-communist economies. Walder's state-centred approach provides a coherent set of predictions specifying only political variables determining the fate of the old regime political elite in market transition.

With respect to the broader economic transformation, however, the *political economy* approach favoured by market transition theorists emphasizing the interactions between market mechanisms and state intervention best explains the dynamics of institutional change. The practical dilemmas of instituting the rules of the game in a market economy require the state to remain involved (Nee 2000). In transition economies, institutional change (such as the creation of private property rights and free markets) does not rely on evolutionary processes but has to be built and coordinated by the state. In the absence of a working capitalist system, such endeavour moreover calls for a state with a strong government, where state actors take the role of the main architects of the new economic system.

To resolve practical dilemmas stemming from institutional change, direct relationships between state actors and firms provide the basis for deployment of strategic resources in transition economies. Not surprisingly, state–firm relations remain close and bargaining processes between the state and firms persist as path-dependent dimensions of the post-communist state–firm relations, though there is no doubt that the form and extent of intervention in business matters have changed dramatically when compared with the socialist era (Stark 1996). In post-communist economies, market transition theorists argue that hybrid capitalist systems are characterized by blurred boundaries between the state and bureaucracy on the one hand and economic actors on the other hand. State ownership of large equity holdings in key enterprises is a common power-preserving strategy for continuing direct interference of the political and bureaucratic elite. In addition, chances for continuing direct involvement at the micro level are secured by opaque market regulations that give leeway for discretionary interference by bureaucrats and politicians. Overall, the character and extensiveness of interaction between government and economic actors in post-communist economies differs from countries with a long tradition of free markets. For this reason, market transition theorists characterize the institutional order of post-communist economies as *politicized capitalism*, where state actors set the regulatory framework *and* remain directly involved in transactions

in large firms. Under politicized capitalism – distinct from western-style market economies – state actors remain directly involved in decision-making at the firm-level. Hence, the distinct feature of politicized capitalism is the absence of clearly defined state–firm boundaries and the significant overlap of the economic and political sphere in firms' decision-making.

The empirical evidence on economic performance effects of direct state intervention within politicized capitalism of transition economies is inconclusive. On one side of the debate on the role of the state, critics of close state–firm relations point to Russia's financial crisis in 1997 as ample evidence of the negative effect of the 'grabbing hand' of the state, embedded in 'crony capitalism'. On the other hand, proponents of an active, interventionist state refer to China's economic miracle of the last two decades and ascribe its positive development experience partially to a 'helping hand' of the Chinese party-state, where state actors enjoy abundant opportunities to directly interfere into private economic transactions. The suggested positive account of China's party-state is particularly puzzling as market liberalization has not been accompanied by the destruction of central instruments of state action of the socialist regime (official ideology, Communist Party, state security apparatus and the bureaucratic apparatus). Although the government's intent to shift to indirect economic tools is explicit in many policy statements, the Chinese constitution only imposes minimal constraints on the power of the state, allowing great latitude for politicians and bureaucrats to serve their political and personal objectives.

For modern corporations, political control of decision-making in China's firms is associated with two opposing effects. On the one hand, political control results in political costs when politicians use firms to serve political, social or individual objectives. On the other hand, political control may help prevent managers from serving their own personal objectives at the expense of firm performance. Political control may therefore help improve firm performance through the mitigation of agency costs. All these studies offer some evidence that political control is associated with reduced agency problems, but they indicate that – on balance – the existing level of political control is excessive and negatively correlated with overall firm performance.

References and further reading

Bian, Yanjie and John Logan (1996) 'Market Transition and the Persistence of Power: The Changing Stratification System in Urban China', *American Sociological Review*, 61: 739–58.

Nee, Victor (2000) 'The Role of the State in Making a Market Economy', *Journal of Institutional and Theoretical Economics*, 156: 64–88.

Nee, Victor and Yang Cao (1999) 'Path Dependent Societal Transformation: Stratification in Hybrid Mixed Economies', *Theory and Society*, 28: 799–834.

—— (2004) 'Market Transition and the Firm: Institutional Change and Income Inequality in Urban China', *Management and Organization Review*, 1(1): 23–56.

Opper, Sonja, Wong, Sonia M. L. and Hu Ruyin (2002) 'Party Power, Market and Private Power: CCP Persistence in China's Listed Companies', *Research in Social Stratification and Mobility*, 19: 103–36.

Sachs, Jeffrey D. (1996) 'The Transition at Mid-Decade', *American Economic Review, Papers and Proceedings*, 86(2): 128–33.

Stark, David (1996) 'Recombinant Property in East European Capitalism', *American Journal of Sociology*, 101(4): 993–1027.

Walder, Andrew (2004) 'Elite Opportunity in Transitional Economy', *American Sociological Review*, 68: 899–916.

Zhou, Xueguang (2000) 'Economic Transition and Income Inequality in Urban China: Evidence from a Panel Data', *American Journal of Sociology*, 105: 1135–74.

VICTOR NEE
SONJA OPPER

ECONOMICS, HISTORY OF

English classical political economy

Economics did not start with Adam **Smith** but for many English economists in the early nineteenth century it might as well have done. His book, *An Inquiry into the Nature and Causes of the Wealth of Nations* (1776), was taken as the virtual beginning of scientific political economy, a reading that was greatly helped by his failure to take seriously, or even cite, many of his contemporaries and predecessors. He made it easy for people to see the story of economics as proceeding from the fallacies of the mercantile system (illustrated by the writings of an English merchant, Thomas Mun, writing in the first half of the seventeenth century), through the 'system of agriculture' (François Quesnai) to the truth of his own system. Outside England, Smith's book provided the starting point for the most influential French economist of the early nineteenth century, Jean-Baptiste Say. It was also widely read, though not always so favourably, in Germany. His influence lasted throughout the nineteenth century: even around 1900 textbooks were still being written that approached economics in a Smithian way.

Though their influence never rivalled Smith's, Thomas Robert Malthus and David Ricardo contributed the theories of population growth, wages, rent and international trade on which much of classical political economy was based. Ricardo worked out a much more rigorous system, including a labour theory of value, but though his work was very influential, his influence never rivalled that of Smith. Classical economics was summed up by John Stuart Mill, whose *Principles of Political Economy and their Application to Social Philosophy* (1848) became the standard textbook on the subject till the 1890s. It was concerned with economic growth. The main cause of economic growth was division of labour made possible by capital accumulation. Population would expand in response to rising demand for labour. Policy was therefore dominated by the need to preserve the incentives to work and to save. Classical economics, as systematized by

Ricardo, provided the basis for the economics of Karl Marx. He took over Ricardo's labour theory of value, using it as the basis for a theory of exploitation. The organization of capitalist society, with production being organized by those who owned the means of production, resulted in exploitation of labour. This variation on classical economics was incorporated into a Hegelian view of history, historical materialism, providing the basis for an alternative tradition in economics. At times Marxist and non-Marxist economists clashed, whereas at other times they went their separate ways, exploring issues in which the other had no interest.

The professionalization of economics

Classical economics was produced by an educated class rather than by specialists, but by the end of the century economics (as it was increasingly called) had become an academic discipline. Its content changed too. In Germany, the dominant approach to economics was that of the German **historical school** of Gustav Schmoller at Berlin. Historical economics was also influential in other countries. There was a largely indigenous movement towards historical economics in Britain and historical economics was influential in the United States. Many American economists took doctorates in Germany. The leading figure of this generation was John Bates Clark; though he was a major figure in the development of marginal theories, he held an organic view of society that meant that other traditions could also look back to his work.

This period saw the rise of economics based on marginal **utility**, or marginalism, independently in three countries. Carl Menger, at Vienna, started the Austrian branch of marginalism, arguing that the value of a commodity was determined by the human needs that could be satisfied by having command over an additional unit of the commodity. Drawing on a French tradition that attached importance to demand for commodities, Léon Walras developed a mathematical theory in which demand for commodities depended on their marginal utility. He then showed how all prices in the economy could be determined simultaneously by supply and demand – general equilibrium. William Stanley Jevons, in Britain, started from Jeremy Bentham's **utilitarianism**.

The dominant figure around the turn of the century was Alfred Marshall, at Cambridge. Marshall combined marginalist ideas with an evolutionary analysis of human behaviour. Human behaviour changed in response to conditions of life. Firms also evolved. His was a realistic economics, taking account of time and uncertainty, that of necessity focused on one market at a time – partial equilibrium analysis. His *Principles of Economics* (1890) became the leading textbook for the first half of the twentieth century. For several decades Marshall's work defined much of the agenda for economics.

Thorstein **Veblen** also took up evolutionary ideas, but was a radical critic of American society. His *Theory of the Leisure Class* (1894) was the starting point in a critique of orthodox economics based on a distinction between business (making money) and industry (making goods). He lambasted economic orthodoxy, coining the phrase neoclassical economics to describe it. The marginalists shared the classical economists' deductive, individualistic, teleological, non-evolutionary approach. Veblen was primarily a critic but inspired others to develop what was, from 1919, termed 'American Institutionalism'. John Rogers Commons analysed the legal foundations of capitalism; Wesley Clair Mitchell engaged in painstaking empirical and statistical research, founding the influential National Bureau of Economic Research. Institutionalism represented a scientific approach to economics, according to the nineteenth-century conception of science in which being scientific meant being grounded in evidence rather than engaging in deductive speculation on the basis of abstract assumptions about human nature. It was secular in its orientation, breaking with the religious tradition that had previously been strong in American economics.

From pluralism to orthodoxy

Economics from the 1930s onwards was increasingly dominated by the United States. In part this was simply due to the size and resources of the American academic system. Political events in Europe were also important. There was the migration (partly forced and partly voluntary) of economists from Russia and Eastern Europe after the Bolshevik revolution. This was followed by the emigration of economists from Central and Western Europe after the Nazi rise to power. This weakened German economics and strengthening economics in the United States.

In the 1920s and 1930s, American economics was pluralistic. Neoclassical and institutional economists coexisted, with many economists doing work that defied classification. In the 1920s and 1930s the mathematization of the economics had barely begun, though there was important pioneering work being undertaken in mathematical economics that later generations would view as laying the foundations for their work. Marshallian economics was formalized, his somewhat elusive theory of value being developed, by Joan Robinson and Edward Chamberlin, into the theories of imperfect and monopolistic competition. These provided the geometric price theory that was to dominate post-war microeconomics textbooks and the foundations of post-war industrial economics, which sought to explain industries' performance in terms of industrial structure (factors such as product differentiation, the number of competitors, and so on).

There was also much work on the business cycle. Business cycle institutes were established in many countries in the 1920s, and the Great Depression further stimulated such work. There was a rich variety of theories; fluctuations were explained as the result of innovations, business confidence and monetary factors. The concepts of aggregate saving and investment, central to macroeconomics as it developed after the 1930s, were worked out. Income-expenditure analysis was developed by several authors as an alternative to the traditional quantity theory of money. There was a proliferation of empirical work, notably at the National Bureau in the United States. Economists, began to take an interest in stabilization policy, and implications of alternative monetary policy regimes were investigated. In the early 1930s the most noticeable debate was between Friedrich Hayek, who pursued the Austrian view that the Great Depression was the result of a decade of excessively expansionary policy, and John Maynard **Keynes**, who saw it as the result of deficient demand for which more expansionary fiscal or monetary policy was the remedy. With the publication of Keynes's *General Theory of Employment, Interest and Money* (1936), the Keynesian view triumphed in academic economics. Policy, however, was still strongly influenced by economists from the institutionalist tradition of Mitchell and Commons, such as Rexford Tugwell and (later) Alvin Hansen and Arthur Burns.

The turning point in twentieth-century economics was the Second World War. This was the economists' war. Economists were involved in economic planning. National income estimates produced by Simon Kuznets and Robert Nathan in the United States, and by James Meade and Richard Stone in Britain, were used for planning. Attempts were also made to estimate enemy capacity. Economists were involved more directly in military activity through what came to be known as 'operations research', a process in which economists (barely distinguishable from statisticians) solved detailed problems about the use of resources and the design of equipment. This work gave the subject many new techniques but, more important, it fostered a change in attitude. The prestige of economics was enhanced and it came to be seen more like engineering – developing a set of techniques that could be used to solve problems. This phase of the subject continued after the war, partly because governments set themselves more ambitious agendas for social reform and the role of government was greatly enlarged, but also because of the Cold War; economists held out the prospect of solving problems (even nuclear strategy) for which the US armed forces needed solutions.

After the war, economics became more technical. Theories were developed more formally, using algebra and geometry, and applied economics became more statistical. John Hicks popularized general equilibrium theory in *Value and Capital* (1939) and Paul Samuelson provided what was effectively a manual in how to do economics mathematically in *Foundations of Economic Analysis* (1947). An important focus of mathematical economics in the 1940s was the Cowles Commission, which set itself the task of combing mathematical economic theory and statistical methods, taking general equilibrium as its organizing framework. Keynesian economics also provided a stimulus to economics becoming more formal. Though Keynesian theory could be expressed without mathematics (or using very simple mathematics) it lent itself to quantitative analysis. The theory was formulated more rigorously on formal microeconomic foundations. National income statistics had been constructed around a Keynesian theoretical framework and, inspired by the earlier work of Jan Tinbergen for the League of Nations, members of the Cowles Commission and others (such as Lawrence Klein) turned to the task of

estimating macroeconomic models using an ever-expanding range of statistical methods.

By around 1960, there had emerged what Samuelson described as the 'neoclassical synthesis'. Microeconomics was based on models of optimizing agents operating in markets that were, in general competitive, and macroeconomics was largely Keynesian. The task of macroeconomic policy was to maintain full employment, and once that was done markets could normally allocate resources efficiently. There would be particular cases, such as public goods (goods that, if they were provided, had to be provided for everyone) and externalities (such as pollution) where government intervention might be required. At the level of theory, Kenneth Arrow and Gerard Debreu had provided an extremely general, rigorous proof that the general equilibrium model, on which most economic theory was believed to rest, was coherent in the sense that an equilibrium would exist. It was an era of great confidence in economics.

Trends in modern economics

This situation changed dramatically in the 1970s, for many reasons. Economic theorists had come up against fundamental problems with the general equilibrium programme, in that it had been proved that it was impossible to derive general proofs that equilibrium was stable and that there was in general no simple relationship between the behaviour of individual agents and demand and supply at the level of the market. **Game theory**, a branch of economics that the US military had promoted during the Cold War, was beginning to provide an alternative framework for microeconomic theory but had the characteristic that solutions depended very much on context; the search for very general results was pointless. However, the most dramatic disturbances were the macroeconomic shocks caused first by the

Vietnam War and then the OPEC price rises of 1973–4. **Inflation** rose alarmingly in most industrial countries and after 1973 so too did unemployment. This was a policy scenario for which Keynesian theory could provide no guidance, with the result that economists were forced to look elsewhere. Macroeconometric models, by then very large, some with thousands of equations, that had performed well up to 1973, failed to predict what was going on. They did not model the supply-side factors that had become important. It also became clear to economists that, whereas expectations of inflation could be neglected in the 1950s and 1960s when inflation was low and stable, inflationary expectations were vital to understanding inflation in the 1970s.

The theory to which much of the profession turned was monetarism. Milton Friedman had been arguing since the early 1950s that the quantity of money was the cause of inflation and that governments should pay more attention to monetary policy. He provided a theory that could explain rising inflation and unemployment. The path taken by macroeconomic theory, however, was influenced more by Robert Lucas. Drawing on earlier work by Edmund Phelps and others who had analysed the situations with limited information, Lucas developed a theory of the business cycle where all agents predicted the future as accurately as it was possible to predict it (rational expectations) and in which markets worked perfectly. Unemployment arose because workers failed to predict inflation correctly and supplied less labour than they had intended. This was the New Classical Macroeconomics. Lucas also provided an explanation of why Keynesian macroeconometric models had broken down. Lucas's belief that the cycle could be explained in terms of monetary shocks turned out to be wrong and alternative models were put forward, some (Real Business Cycle Theory) maintaining his assumptions about efficient markets and

others (New Keynesian Macroeconomics) finding reasons why labour markets would not work and workers might find themselves involuntarily unemployed.

Microeconomics was also transformed after the 1970s, for different reasons. Game theory began to take off, transforming various fields of economics, starting with industrial organization, later spreading to most fields of economics. By the end of the century, it could be argued that game theory had displaced general equilibrium theory (which could be portrayed as the equilibrium of a particular types of game) as the organizing framework for the subject. Nash equilibrium, formulated by the mathematician, John Nash in the 1950s, was widely used. Game theory provided a way to handle strategic interaction between agents that had been missing in earlier theories. The theory of international trade was transformed when Paul Krugman and Elhanan Helpman used formal models of imperfect competition to break away from the perfect competition framework. Joseph Stiglitz developed the economics of information, showing how markets where information was unevenly distributed would not behave in the standard way. Markets for information could not generally be efficient and where there was **asymmetrical information** it was entirely possible that firms might maximize profit at a price where supply and demand were not equal. This might explain why **banks** chose to ration credit or why firms might not wish to lower wages in the face of unemployment.

Economists also turned to experiments as a way to explore issues that theory could not settle. One stimulus to such work came from results that challenged economists traditional assumptions about rationality. For example, Daniel Kahneman and Amos Tversky found that a significant proportion of subjects, when choosing between two lotteries, would choose the one on which they placed the lowest monetary value.

Experimental methods led to the emergence of **behavioural economics**. Behavioural finance took off as a way of analysing aspects of **financial markets** that appeared irrational from the perspective of conventional theory. Economists became interested in bounded **rationality**, a concept developed by Herbert Simon in the 1950s. Oliver Williamson and others took up the idea of transactions costs. This was the 'new institutional economics', contrasted with the 'old' institutionalism of the interwar period. Drawing on ideas of Ronald Coase, transactions costs were used to analyse both the firm and situations where one person's action harmed someone else.

Economists applied their techniques to problems traditionally considered in the domain of other disciplines. Gary Becker initiated a literature that used standard optimizing models to explain social phenomena including crime, marriage and divorce. Public choice theory used the same model to tackle political processes, transforming the way economists viewed policy. Instead of being disinterested agents concerned with social welfare, policymakers became part of the process in which they were intervening, seeking to achieve their own ends. Endogenizing the policy-making process meant that rent-seeking – earning profits by lobbying for favourable treatment by the government – might be more profitable for individuals than productive investment.

These trends had two effects on economics. One was a blurring of the boundaries between economics, political science and sociology. Becker's work, for example, might be seen as either sociology or economics, public choice theory as economics or political science. The other was that it was no longer possible, as it might have been around 1960, to speak of an analytical framework that provided a common core to the subject. When general equilibrium theory no longer provided such a framework, economists moved in many direc-

tions. Game theory underlay much economic theory, but there were growing branches of theory that did not rely on it. It has been argued that virtually all that united economists working on these various approaches was a commitment to mathematical rigour.

The pursuit of more rigorous theories meant that economists who dissented felt excluded from the profession: journals were not open to their work and professional advancement was difficult. This feeling was particularly strong in the late 1960s and 1970s, when the insistence on rigour had increased but the proliferation of new approaches had yet to occur. For some, the trends in the profession also had political implications to which they objected. A number of groups organized and developed their own identities: radical economics, **Austrian economics**, **post Keynesianism** and others joined the list of heterodoxies of which Marxian economics had been the most significant example. Towards the end of the 1990s, feeling even more beleaguered, many of these groups appropriated the term 'Heterodox economics' as a banner under which they could coalesce, uniting on a plea for greater pluralism in economics. Ironically, this happened at the time when orthodoxy was, with the emergence of approaches such as the new institutional economics and behavioural economics, becoming more pluralistic than it had been in the 1960s and 1970s.

References and further reading

Backhouse, Roger E. (2002) *The Penguin History of Economics/The Ordinary Business of Life*, London: Penguin Books, and Princeton, NJ: Princeton University Press.

Coats, A. W. (1997) *The Post-1945 Internationalization of Economics*, Durham, NC: Duke University Press.

Mirowski, Philip (2002) *Machine Dreams: Economics Becomes a Cyborg Science*, Cambridge: Cambridge University Press.

Morgan, Mary S. (forthcoming) 'The Formation of "Modern" Economics: Engineering and

Ideology', in *The Cambridge History of Science*, vol. 7, *Modern Social and Behavioural Sciences*, Cambridge: Cambridge University Press.

Morgan, Mary S. and Rutherford, Malcolm (1998) *From Inter-war Pluralism to Post-war Neoclassicism*, Durham, NC: Duke University Press.

Perlman, Mark and McCann, Charles (1998) *The Pillars of Economic Understanding*, two volumes, Ann Arbor, MI: Michigan University Press.

ROGER E. BACKHOUSE

ECONOMICS, SOCIOLOGY OF

The history of economics has long been an academic specialization within economics itself. In recent years, however, a sociologically grounded analysis of the development and operation of economics as a science and as a profession has emerged, which has both expanded the domain of empirical investigation and brought new theoretical questions and analytical tools to bear on the study of economics. More importantly, it has also shown that this 'sociology of economics' has a distinctive role to play within economic sociology.

The history of economic thought tradition

Most of the scholarly research about economics comes from a subfield of the discipline called 'history of economic thought'. Partly because they share a firm and well-institutionalized sense of disciplinary hierarchies and boundaries, economists have always regarded the history of their science as an academic specialty in its own right. As a result, it has always been common practice among economists to contribute to the history of economic ideas and theories one way or another, either through exegesis, biography or intellectual history. The texts produced in this fashion – including textbooks, dictionaries, encyclopedias – constitute an eclectic yet extraordinary reservoir of facts and insights into the development of the discipline,

sometimes – in the most brilliant cases – combined with considerable historical erudition. Hence Schumpeter's *History of Economic Analysis* (1954) remains to this day one of the most compelling efforts at explaining the generation of economic ideas by referring to the larger intellectual and sociological context. Heckscher's *Mercantilism* (1931) masterfully interprets the history of nation-building in Europe from the sixteenth to the eighteenth century in light of the set of **beliefs** – the mercantilist doctrine – that inspired and sustained it.

Compared with other social scientists, economists have also been remarkably interested in the epistemological underpinnings of their discipline and in the philosophical assessment of its scientific status. Many prominent economic writers were involved in such exercises, which culminated in various efforts to reconstruct the history of economics in Popperian and Lakatosian terms after World War II. Witnessing the mathematization of the discipline, Popper himself celebrated its Newtonian revolution. Friedman's 'instrumentalist' position – or the notion that the scientific character of economics depends not on its assumptions, which can be unrealistic or even false, but solely on its ability to make predictions – seemed to successfully shelter economics from epistemological critique.

This intellectual landscape, however, started to break apart in the 1970s, both on the historical and on the methodological fronts. First, the history of economic thought was progressively purged out of leading American PhD programmes as economics became more formalized and technically oriented. This development, paradoxically, seems to have freed historians of economics from the conventions imposed by their role as gatekeepers of the canon, sometimes leading them to forge alliances with neighbouring disciplines in order to survive. From a valuable pastime carried out alongside many productive scientific careers, the history of economics turned into a full-time research enterprise, practised at the margins of mainstream economics (hence of top US departments). The new history of economic thought set out to contest traditional interpretations, unearth forgotten authors and texts and broaden its focus. It gave itself an influential medium with the review *History of Political Economy (HOPE)* and an international forum with the *History of Economics Society*. Stimulated by Coats' work on the professionalization of British and American economics (1993), historians of economics started to give increased prominence to sociological and institutional aspects in their work – a trend largely reflected in the evolution of *HOPE*, but also in a new generation of monographs (see Bernstein's (2001) fine study of the rise and fall of the American economics profession's public purpose during the twentieth century).

The second important development is that the positivist epistemological model came under attack from a variety of standpoints, both within and outside the philosophy of science. One of the most creative attempts in this area was the emergence of a research agenda centred on the rhetoric and style of argumentation in economics, showing that economic writing is carefully constructed to make a rather muddled research process look scientifically rational and objective. McCloskey's (1985) well-known study revealed that much of the standard literary forms found in economic papers (e.g. appeals to authority, analogies, hypothetical toy economics, experimental format) are all rhetorical tools that authors mobilize in order to persuade their readers. In a related vein, Mirowski (1989) showed that nineteenth-century neoclassical economics followed closely the evolution of paradigms within physics, mimicking the latter's intellectual procedures and representation of the world in order to gain scientific status. Finally, using interviews with graduate students at top economics pro-

grams, Klamer and Colander (1990) vividly exposed the distinctive scientific and political ideologies transmitted by each institution.

Economics through the lens of science studies

The maturity of the study of economics as a 'field' is also perceptible in the growing interest of historians and sociologists of science. To a certain extent, this transformation can be considered a remote – and long overdue – consequence of the revolution in science studies initiated by Kuhn's *Structure of Scientific Revolutions*. In Kuhn's view, which became the rallying point for the sociology of scientific knowledge (SSK), scientific production consists mainly of routine activities, which are shaped by a complex nexus of social experiences among the community of scientists.

The new science studies largely defined their agenda around a demystification of research procedures in the *natural* sciences, however, and did not pay much attention to the social sciences, economics among them (the one exception is Richard Whitley 1987). This situation is dramatically changing today, on both the historical (Porter and Ross 2003) and sociological (Callon 1998; MacKenzie and Millo 2003) fronts. Particularly remarkable as a successful attempt to reshape the history of economics from a history of science point of view is Philip Mirowski's 2002 opus on the emergence of **game theory**. Mirowski (himself an economist) applies to economics the increasingly influential view that cybernetic themes and models, actively engineered and financed by the US Department of Defense and its various spin-offs, came to shape the modern sciences in the wake of World War II and the Cold War. Drawing on a breathtaking wealth of archival evidence, Mirowski shows that the development of game theory (and even, to a certain extent, of modern general equilibrium analysis) in post-war

217

America is intimately intertwined with the rise of the US military itself.

The work of the Israeli sociologist Yuval Yonay (1998) provides perhaps one of the most explicit applications of SSK concepts and methodologies to the study of economics. Drawing on Bloor's principles of symmetry and impartiality to the history of economics, Yonay resuscitates institutionalism as a major intellectual player in interwar economics. His 1998 book on intellectual competition in American economics during the interwar offers a complex account of the relationship between the knowledge produced, its pretension to a 'scientific' status, and the strategies of the actors sustaining it. Relying on Latour and Callon's actor-network theory, Yonay uses published methodological statements to investigate the controversy between institutionalism and traditional neoclassical theory. The ultimate outcome of the episode (the dismissal of institutionalism and the rise of mathematical economics), he argues, did not inevitably follow from differences in the scientific objectivity of each school's productions, but from repeated 'trials of strength' in which each side sought to forge alliances and convince audiences that it better fit an accepted canon of science.

Breslau and Yonay's (1999) have recently pushed this constructivist line of analysis further. Ambitioning to transfer the model of laboratory studies to the analysis of article writing in economics in order to uncover the field's 'epistemic culture', they have shown that mathematical modelling is a not simply guided by rhetorical rules, but by embedded disciplinary rules that operate at the level of the field's social structure. After repeatedly interviewing economic authors about the process of article writing, they find that 'vaguely defined but generally accepted conventions regarding the movement from [economic] reality to models' (p. 41) constitute a discursive meta-structure, which effectively constrains the scientific process.

Fields, professions and networks

The above-mentioned body of research is fundamentally 'science-centred': it is concerned with the production, translation and diffusion of particular economic discourses and ideas. Yet, as Foucault insisted, knowledge wields power: the ability to name and define economic reality is inseparable from the ability to act upon this reality. As sociologist of science Michel Callon put it, the distinctiveness of economics as a science is its fundamentally 'performative' character: It is not so much that economists observe and describe how the economy functions. Rather, 'economics, in the broad sense of the term, performs, shapes and formats the economy' (1998: 2). Sociologists, then, should turn their attention towards the 'embeddedness of markets in economics' – and study how economic ideas routinely construct and transform economies.

The study of economics as a professional practice with transformative power was notably developed by institutionalist scholars within sociology and political science (e.g. John Campbell, Peter Hall, Theda Skocpol, Margaret Weir among others), who have shown (1) that administrative structures play a critical role in defining both the economists' academic and professional space, and their relationship with policy; and (2) that, conversely, economic ideas participate in the transformation of state structures and capacities by serving as an intellectual background for institutional change.

What is driving this scholarship, however, is more an interest in political institutions and the substantive conditions and mechanisms that allow for the diffusion of economic policy paradigms than a curiosity for 'economics' per se. Still, the research produced in this vein (e.g. see Hall 1989) has been of considerable importance in helping foster a body of scholarship that looked beyond the bounded world of disciplinary discourse and scientific production towards politics and administrative organization as mediating social structures. Building on this legacy, an 'externalist' perspective on the economics profession has emerged, which questions how economics itself is socially constructed by the broader social context.

The interesting question, in this perspective, is not so much how people write or do economics any more, but who is authorized to speak about, or act upon, the economy, and why. In other words, it has to do with the social bases of economics as a domain of practice. This, of course, is not to say that the substantive content of economic science has become irrelevant – merely that such 'internal' analysis is now subordinate to a broader understanding of the functioning of the field as a whole and its embeddedness in the larger society. This changed focus has brought to the fore three key contextual elements: institutions, field dynamics and interpersonal networks.

Comparative analysis constitutes a particularly fruitful way to demonstrate the profound inscription of knowledge in local culture and institutions. Fourcade-Gourinchas (forthcoming) shows that being an economist takes on different meanings across nations, as the practice of economics emerges out of different institutional systems. In the United States, a decentralized political culture has produced an economics profession that is market-oriented – both in form and content. The more statist French culture and institutional make-up, on the other hand, has given rise to a fragmented and institutionally weak profession, dominated by the technocratic sector. Finally, the traditional orientation of British elites towards public service helped shape a scientistic and hierarchical economics profession, which nonetheless freely communicates with the broader public through a host of civil society institutions and networks. Relying on the sociology of knowledge claim that discourse and jur-

isdiction are intimately intertwined, the author then argues that the same patterns also account for certain distinctive characteristics in the *intellectual* trajectory of economics in these countries.

While the comparative approach tends to focus on relatively stable differences *across* nations, what may be called the 'field' approach concentrates on power struggles *within* fields of economic knowledge – whether national or international ones. Best exemplified by the work of Lebaron (2000) and Dezalay and Garth (2002), it provides a powerful reminder that economics remains a contested intellectual and professional enterprise. The argument relies on a systematic mapping of the different segments involved in the quest for legitimacy, an analysis of the social logics behind intellectual positions, and a description of the dynamics that underlie historical transformations in the field's social and intellectual structure. Applying Bourdieusian field theory to the study of French economics, Lebaron (2000) sets out to reveal the sociological mechanisms that preside over the construction of a 'belief' in economics in modern societies. One way to achieve this is by showing that economics is eminently a science of power. Through detailed empirical study, Lebaron shows that the social characteristics of economists largely explain their position within the scientific space: occupational location and intellectual stance in economics are basically split along the two Bourdieusian dimensions of the volume and structure of capital, and both spaces are homologically related. Another way is by documenting extensively the progressive construction of a quasi-religious belief in markets, sanctified by the authority of science, and particularly noticeable in the neo-liberal evolution of French economics training, research and economic policy.

Dezalay and Garth (2002) similarly rely on field analysis – but translate it to the global level. Turning their scientific capital into politico-administrative capital, internationally trained economists, they argue, have entered Latin American public bureaucracies and political elites en masse since the 1970s, ultimately displacing the traditional supremacy of gentlemen-lawyers over economic governance. In part these changes were set in motion by developments within the North American academic field – including power struggles between different segments of the profession that were 'exported' and played out in the South, in a movement the authors dub the 'internationalization of palace wars'. These processes of transformation were highly uneven across countries, however, and largely shaped by domestic institutions (the authors examine closely the cases of Argentina, Chile, Mexico and Brazil).

Though she is more sensitive to the interaction between elite competition and the grassroots context, Babb (2001) conveys a similar point in her important study of the transformations of Mexican economics over the twentieth century (her main reference, however, is Abbott's model of professional competition, not Bourdieu's field dynamics). *Managing Mexico* describes the dramatic evolution of post-war Mexican economic ideology from 'developmentalism' to 'neo-liberalism' as a consequence of ideological struggles in the society at large and, in particular, the radicalization of Mexican student politics in the 1960s and 1970s. Babb shows that the financial side of the technocracy responded to these challenges by actively sponsoring conservative economics training programs and tightening its connections with American universities, thereby engineering the stock of expertise on which the neo-liberal transition would ultimately be built.

The question of transnational linkages and networks, omnipresent in these works, certainly constitutes one of the most exciting research avenues in the sociology of economics today. Yet beyond the fertile ground offered by Latin America the scholarly literature remains scant. A fine illustration of the challenges awaiting sociologists working on other world regions, nonetheless, is Bockman and Eyal's (2002) analysis of the intellectual roots of neo-liberal transitions in Eastern Europe. Their argument underlines the importance of antecedents such as the 1950s transnational debate about socialist economic calculation, and the Cold War era exchanges between economic reformers in Eastern Europe and libertarian social scientists in the United States and Britain. By stressing the role of long-term international networks in the socialist transition to the market, Bockman and Eyal dismiss easy explanations in terms of US-made intellectual exports.

The relevance of the sociology of economics to economic sociology

In these sociological accounts, economic ideas and theories are historically evolved, hybrid products that people use, translate and mobilize strategically in order to foster broader political or scientific purposes. Still, the question of the pervasiveness of such ideas remains unanswered. Callon's urgent injunction to study the performative power of economics goes, indeed, well beyond the influence of *economists* as scientists, experts, professionals or ideologues: It goes to the heart of a modernity – our modernity – which is itself *constituted by* economics. Understanding properly the relationship between economics and the economy – between scientific representations and the construction of economies – starts with the acknowledgement that the production of tools for apprehending and dealing with the world is intimately tied with the redefinition of the world through the tools themselves. The real power of economics, in other words, is ontological – it is the power to 'economicize' the material world through the imposition of a legitimate language and the proliferation of 'calculative agencies'.

In Callon's Polanyian framework, economics produces a world (an economy) in which calculability is a key cultural competence, thereby reinforcing the applicability and performative power of economics itself. Furthermore, this back-and-forth movement between economy and economics is itself constitutive of the stable economic objects that we call 'markets' or 'prices'. Empirical illustrations of such mechanisms can be found in Marie-France Garcia's (1986) analysis of the construction, by a former economics student, of a local strawberries market in France and in MacKenzie and Millo's (2003) study of how the Black–Scholes formula helped bring modern finance into being. The sociology of economics meets economic sociology through this systematic unravelling of the processes whereby particular forms of calculability, particular 'economic' behaviours, are engineered – and through the painful reconstruction of the way in which economic theory routinely creates and recreates *homo economicus* out of real flesh. From this perspective, the task of the sociology of economics has only begun.

References and further reading

Babb, Sarah (2001) *Managing Mexico: Mexican Economists from Nationalism to Neoliberalism*, Princeton, NJ: Princeton University Press.

Bernstein, Michael (2001) *A Perilous Progress: Economists and the Public Purpose in America*, Princeton, NJ: Princeton University Press.

Bockman, Johanna and Eyal, Gil (2002) 'Eastern Europe as a Laboratory for Economic Knowledge: The Transnational Roots of Neo-Liberalism', *American Journal of Sociology*, September, 108(2): 310–54.

Breslau, Daniel and Yonay, Yuval (1999) 'Beyond Metaphor: Mathematical Models in Economics as Empirical Research', *Science in Context*, 12(2): 317–32.

Callon, Michel (1998) 'The Embeddedness of Economic Markets in Economics', in M. Callon (ed.), *The Laws of the Markets*, Oxford: Blackwell, pp. 1–57.

Coats, A. W. Bob (1993) *The Sociology and Professionalization of Economics. British and American Economic Essays*, vol. II, London and New York: Routledge.

Dezalay, Y. and Garth, B. (2002) *The Internationalization of Palace Wars. Lawyers, Economists, and the Contest to Transform Latin American States*, Chicago: University of Chicago Press.

Fourcade-Gourinchas, Marion (forthcoming) *The National Trajectories of Economic Knowledge: Discipline and Profession in the United States, Great Britain and France*, Princeton, NJ: Princeton University Press.

Garcia, Marie-France (1986) 'La Construction sociale d'un marché parfait: le marché au cadran de Fontaines-en-Sologne', *Actes de la Recherche en Sciences Sociales*, 65: 2–13.

Hall, Peter A. (ed.) (1989) *The Political Power of Economic Ideas*, Princeton, NJ: Princeton University Press.

Klamer, Arjo and Colander, David (1990) *The Making of An Economist*, Boulder, CO: Westview Press.

Lebaron, Frédéric (2000) *La Croyance économique. Les économistes entre science et politique*, Paris: Seuil.

McCloskey, Donald N. (1985) *The Rhetoric of Economics*, Madison, WI: University of Wisconsin Press.

MacKenzie, Donald and Millo, Yval (2003) 'Constructing a Market, Performing Theory: The Historical Sociology of a Financial Derivatives Exchange', *American Journal of Sociology*, 109: 107–45.

Mirowski, Philip (1989) *More Heat than Light: Economics as Social Physics, Physics as Nature's Economics*, Cambridge and New York: Cambridge University Press.

—— (2002) *Machine Dreams. Economics Becomes a Cyborg Science*, Cambridge: Cambridge University Press.

Porter, Ted and Ross, Dorothy (eds) (2003) *The Cambridge History of Science: Volume 7, The Modern Social Sciences*, Cambridge: Cambridge University Press.

Whitley, Richard (1987) 'The Structure and Context of Economics as a Scientific Field', in *Research in the History of Economic Thought and Methodology*, volume 4, Amsterdam: Elsevier.

Yonay, Yuval P. (1998) *The Struggle over the Soul of Economics: Institutionalist and Neoclassical Economists in America between the Wars*, Princeton, NJ: Princeton University Press.

MARION FOURCADE-GOURINCHAS

ECONOMIZING See: efficiency

ECONOMY

An economy is an aspect of a wider system of human social behaviour. To the extent that a boundary between the economy and the non-economic aspects of that system can be drawn, we can say that the economy is a subsystem of the wider system and that it thereby has two kinds of environments. On the one hand, whatever is environment to the wider system is also environmental to the economy. On the other hand, any units or processes internal to that system that are not considered part of the economy comprise a kind of 'internal' environment of the economy.

Consider, for instance, 'the world economy'. Clearly, the biophysical units and processes on and around the planet Earth form a significant 'external' environment of the world economy while global political processes are part of the 'internal environment' of the world economy.

As a different example, consider the economy of a university department, treating the latter as the immediate wider system. Then, for instance, the other departments of the university, forming part of the environment of the department, are in the external environment of the specified departmental economy while that department's political processes – notably, the processes of departmental decision-making – are part of the internal environment. In each of these examples, events or actions that are non-economic as such may have important relationships to economic events or actions that are included in the economy.

Thus, several introductory conceptual points are indicated in these remarks. First, 'economy' is a general concept that applies to any system of human interaction at any scale. Second, there is no such thing as 'the economy' without an environment because an economy is always only an aspect of a more complex system. Third, the environment itself is complex, consisting of both internal and external units and processes. And, finally, there are significant relations between an economy and its environments.

The question of how the economy relates to society is one of the key themes in the history of sociological theory, both in its classical phase and in its post-classical and recent phases. There are three interrelated types of cognitive orientation that have been taken toward the problem of relating the economy to its internal and/or external environments: world-historical, critical and general-theoretical. Specific theorists or theories can be thought of as embodying weighted combinations of the three modes of orientation. The fundamental problem treated in the sociological literature from a world-historical standpoint has been the rise and development of capitalism, whether the capitalist system is conceptualized as embedded in a particular national society or as constituting a historically specific world system.

The general theoretical orientation takes a generalizing approach, as in the opening paragraph above, in that no particular economy and no particular wider system is stipulated. Rather, the problem is dealt with, at least at the outset, in all generality. The critical orientation adds a normative standpoint: whether one takes the historical or the generalizing orientation to the problem, from this standpoint, the ultimate aim of any such theorizing is to promote human freedom.

In the remainder of the present article, the emphasis is on the generalizing orientation and it will be referred to as the orientation of 'theoretical sociology'.

In the history of theoretical sociology, the problem of how to conceptualize and explain the relations of the economy to its environments, especially its internal environments, has been one of the main themes of major theorists. In the writings of **Marx** there are systematic and general ideas about these relations, especially the historical materialist basis-superstructure model (Cohen 1978). In the writings of **Weber**, we find an important emphasis on the role of cultural orientations – religious and ethical ideas and interests – in the interpretation of economic phenomena. In **Durkheim**'s writings, we find an important emphasis on institutionalized morality in relation to economic and other modes of conduct. His work is important for our topic in another respect, namely the generalization of the idea of division of labour along with a world-historical thesis of increasing social differentiation. In the later development of theoretical sociology, Talcott **Parsons** drew upon Weber, Durkheim and other sources to formulate the most elaborate and conceptually rigorous account of the economy in relation to its environments in a collaborative treatise that is based upon his AGIL scheme (Parsons and Smelser 1956).

From the latter point of view, an economy is a functional subsystem of a social system. An important distinction is implicit in this statement, namely between two types of social systems. One type is characterized by the variable property of solidarity with its potential for action-in-concert. For instance, firms and households have this property, enabling them to participate as producing and consuming actors in a differentiated social system, i.e. a society in which firms and households exist as distinct collective units. The other type of social system cannot be characterized in terms of solidarity: it has no potential for action in concert. An economy cannot act although it is defined in terms of exchange relations between actors, individual and collective. Within this second type, the existence of a *functional* subsystem of a social system is one that is defined in terms of its contribution to the meeting of a requirement for the existence and continuation of the social system. The AGIL scheme provides a model of four such functional requirements for any social system in terms of adaptation to the environment of the social system (A), definition and attainment of

collective goals for the social system (G), integration of the parts of the social system (I), and reproduction of the elements of normative culture that guide the actions of actors in their various roles in the social system (L).

Parsons and Smelser propose that the economy be treated as the adaptive subsystem of a social system. The basis for this correspondence may be understood in terms of the environments of the social system itself. The social system is embedded in a wider system of human action that includes instances of cultural systems (e.g. artistic styles, ethical doctrines), personality systems (e.g. motivational states of members of the social system), and behavioural systems (e.g. skills and capacities of members). From this analytical standpoint, the external environment includes the bodies of the members of the social system and the nature of the habitat in which they are collectively embedded. Thus the adaptation problem of the social system is one of gaining some degree of control, in the cybernetic sense, of these environmental states. For instance, human bodies have their own functional imperatives, such as adequate food, water and shelter. The habitat may enable but also constrain how these needs can be satisfied. Thus, provision of these primary needs in the given biophysical environment and of other needs of personalities that arise in and through action processes within a cultural tradition constitutes the functional imperative of the social system to which its economy is the ongoing solution, however adequate or inadequate from some normative point of view (e.g. there may be widespread hunger in a given society).

Given a differentiated social system, each of its functional imperatives has some ongoing form of solution in terms of a functional subsystem. Briefly, then, in addition to the economy, a differentiated social system will have three other primary functional subsystems that meet the other three functional requirements set out earlier:

a polity (G), a community or system of solidarities (I) and a fiduciary system (L).

An important principle about functional subsystems is that each member of the social system participates in each of the functional subsystems to some variable degree. For instance, even if the ordinary citizen does no more than vote, the exercise of that vote is a participation in the polity. In regard to the economy, as Parsons and Smelser (1956: 14) put it, 'The whole society is in one sense part of the economy, in that all of its units, individual and collective, *participate in* the economy ... But no concrete unit participates *only* in the economy. Hence, no concrete unit is "*purely* economic".' For instance, a school is not a firm: its functional specialization is fiduciary, not economic but it participates in the economy as a purchaser of needed facilities, services and supplies. Similarly, firms in a capitalist system contribute to the reproduction of capitalist values simply by hiring workers, making profits, distributing dividends, and the like, all of which contribute to retention of value orientations supportive of capitalism. As Weber noted, modern capitalism no longer requires religion for the reproduction of the spirit of capitalism.

Cultural templates that are institutionalized form the highest level of cybernetic control within a social system. Of course, they emerge from prior social interaction but once institutionalized they control lower levels of the generation of actions, including **economic actions**. Four types of units can be used to 'parse' such templates into components, according to Parsons: values, norms, collectivities and roles. For instance, any differentiated social system will have aspects that are economic values (e.g. 'the spirit of capitalism'), economic norms (e.g. efficiency), economic collectivities (e.g. firms) and economic roles (e.g. investor). Similarly, for instance, with respect to the fiduciary function that refers to some mode of responsibility for passing on the culture of the social system, the abstract

types are fiduciary values, fiduciary norms, fiduciary collectivities and fiduciary roles.

Given the above distinctions, it follows that the question of the relation to economy and its internal environments becomes: how is the economy of a differentiated social system related to the other three functional subsystems? Using the language of systems analysis along with analogies drawing upon macroeconomics, Parsons and Smelser construct a complex multi-level model of these relations. There is a kind of interstitial system connecting the economy and the polity, connecting the economy and the community and connecting the economy and the fiduciary system.

The general idea is that many of the interactions in a differentiated social system are functionally specialized exchanges of various sorts and that, in the aggregate, these produce market or market-like phenomena. For instance, the labour market connects the economy to the fiduciary system in that the latter produces actors who can take positions in some context of production that enables them to enact the corresponding roles in relation to others. At the micro level, two people may engage in an exchange process, one of whom is in a representative role for a firm while the other may be connected to a household as one of its employed members and whose income performs a significant function in the context of that social subsystem of the system under analysis. At the macro level, this is but one exchange among numerous others that together form what Parsons calls an 'interchange system' that connects the economy and the fiduciary system.

The cybernetic viewpoint leads to the idea that a hierarchy of control model might apply to these internal social system processes. Here the ideas are very much in need of greater rigour of formulation, but in their intuitive formulation that we find in the works of Parsons, the internal cybernetic hierarchy of the social system has a postulated order in which the higher order of control involves the fiduciary system, the next lower is the community as a system, followed by the polity and, at the lowest level of the social system, the economy. The reverse ordering characterizes the enabling but constraining aspects that connect the lower level to the higher level in each pair of control levels. For instance, the polity controls the economy in the sense that political decisions set parameters for the behaviour of producers. However, the state of the economy at any time will enable or limit the menu of feasible political decisions. A related cybernetic aspect of interchange systems is the mediation of exchanges by distinctive symbolic media. In the case of the economy and the fiduciary system, the interchange system involves two such media, money and generalized commitments. For instance, money goes to households as certain members commit to work for firms in exchange for wages. Exactly how the cybernetic control relation works in such relationships, however, remains rather obscure. Although the model proposed by Parsons and Smelser is of considerable value in addressing the question of how the economy relates to its social environments, issues relating to lack of clarity and rigour in the formulation of the model have limited its usefulness to other analysts of economy and society.

References and further reading

Parsons, Talcott and Smelser, Neil (1956) *Economy and Society*, New York: Free Press.
Stinchcombe, Arthur L. (1983) *Economic Sociology*, New York: Academic Press.
Weber, Max ([1922]1978) *Economy and Society*, edited by G. Roth and C. Wittich, Berkeley, CA: University of California Press.

THOMAS J. FARARO

EFFICIENCY

The relationship between efficiency and social organization is one of the most hotly contested issues in the social sciences. In his analysis of western rationalism, Max **Weber** maintained that the application of rational calculation to standardize social action and increase economic efficiency cannot be separated from social domination because 'the maximum of formal rationality in capital accounting is possible only where workers are subjected to domination by entrepreneurs' (1978: 138). Weber also maintained that although the application of formal **rationality** may be a more efficient means of control than previous forms of social organization, formally rational controls can be irrational when evaluated in relationship to substantive goals. Empirical research supporting Weber's framework shows that the application of formal rationality to establish domination efficiency in the Roman Empire took precedence over the substantive goal of wealth extraction. This irrationality between efficiency domination and wealth extraction remained undetected until the Empire was in decline because the ideology of cost efficiency legitimated the system and suppressed information about production inefficiency (Antonio 1979: 909–910).

Similarly, sociologists who examine corporate strategies and structures in the United States show that efficiency considerations were secondary to the goal of ensuring oligopolistic advantages by dominating markets (Perrow 1981; Roy 1997). In contrast to the domination thesis in sociology, business historian Alfred D. **Chandler** attributes the social organization of the corporation to the efficiency of professional management and innovative cost accounting techniques that increase administrative capabilities. The multidivisional form replaced previous corporate forms and persisted over time because it 'permitted greater productivity, lower costs, and higher profits than coordination by market mechanisms' (Chandler 1977: 6). Similarly, microeconomists maintain that organizations emerge and grow because they are more efficient than markets. Elaborating institutional economics, they maintain that the efficiency of internalizing transaction costs explains the emergence of managerial hierarchies in the multidivisional form. Specifically, this form emerged because, under certain conditions, markets are subject to bounded rationality and opportunism, 'a condition of self-interest seeking with guile,' that increase transaction costs (Williamson 1985: 30, 64). Thus, transaction cost analysis suggests that hierarchy replaces the market because its monitoring capabilities are more cost–efficient arenas for decision-making.

Some sociologists maintain that the narrow focus of **organization theory** on efficiency led to a neglect of Weber's emphasis on legitimacy and the institutional context that produce rationalized formal structures (Meyer and Rowan 1977). The new institutionalism suggests that organizational success is dependent on powerful social actors external to organizations and management adopts governance structures that are perceived to ensure survival. Comparative research on the rise of corporate structures in Japan, Taiwan and South Korea shows that 'organizational growth is best explained by market and cultural factors, but that authority patterns and legitimation strategies best explain organizational structure' (Hamilton and Biggart 1988: S87). Other new institutionalists reject the efficiency argument completely and suggest that **corporate governance** structures are derived from shifts in the 'conception of how the largest firms should operate to preserve their growth and profitability' (Fligstein 1990: 2). Quantitative research in this tradition confirms Chandler's argument that between the 1920s and 1970s the multidivisional form became the prevailing corporate form. However, the emergence and spread of this form were associated with diversification strategies caused by the Celler–Kefauver Act and managers' background in accounting and finance (Fligstein 1990). Other sociological analysis show that

network ties among business elites, dependence on resources, and efficiency explain predatory acquisition strategies by US corporations in the 1960s (Palmer et al. 1995).

Research on corporate change in the late twentieth century shows that formally rational controls in large divisions achieved efficiency domination, but this governance structure produced substantively irrational social action in relationship to corporate efficiency (i.e. costs) and effectiveness (i.e. profits) goals. In response to inefficiencies in the multidivisional form, corporations mobilized politically to transform their political-legal institutional arrangements in a way that made the multilayer-subsidiary form viable. Then, the most capital dependent and politically active corporations changed to this form. This multilayer-subsidiary form has a parent company at the top of the corporate hierarchy that operates as a financial management company, with two or more levels of legally separate subsidiary corporations embedded in it. By 1993, 65 per cent of the largest US industrial corporations were organized as the multilayer-subsidiary form: 'they had one or no divisions and multiple subsidiaries and layers of subsidiaries' (Prechel 2000: 244). Transforming large divisions into several smaller subsidiary corporations embeds operating units directly into the specific market in which they compete, which provides management with information (e.g. profits, stock values) on their capacity to compete in those markets (Prechel 2000). Subsequent analysis (Prechel 2003) shows that the **embeddedness** of the multilayer-subsidiary form in the new institutional arrangements permitted self-interest seeking with guile that resulted in widespread corporate fraud and malfeasance.

References and further reading

Antonio, Robert (1979) 'The Contradiction of Domination and Production in Bureaucracy', *American Sociological Review*, 44: 895–912.

Chandler, Alfred (1977) *The Visible Hand*, Cambridge, MA: Harvard University Press.

Fligstein, Neil (1990) *The Transformation of Corporate Control*, Cambridge, MA: Harvard University Press.

Hamilton, Gary and Biggart, Nicole Woolsey (1988) 'Market, Culture, and Authority', *American Journal of Sociology*, 94: S52–S94.

Meyer, John and Rowan, Brian (1977) 'Institutionalized Organizations', *American Journal of Sociology*, 83: 340–63.

Palmer, Donald, Barber, Brad and Zhou, Xueguang (1995) 'The Acquisition of Large US Corporations in the 1960s', *American Sociological Review*, 60: 469–99.

Perrow, Charles (1981) 'Markets, Hierarchy and Hegemony', in Andrew Van de Ven and William Joyce (eds), *Perspectives on Organization Design and Behavior*, New York: John Wiley and Sons, pp. 371–86.

Prechel, Harland (2000) *Big Business and the State*, Albany, NY: State University of New York Press.

—— (2003) 'Historical Contingency Theory, Policy Paradigm Shifts, and Corporate Malfeasance at the Turn to the 21st Century', in Betty Deboratz, Timothy Buzzell and Lisa Waldner (eds), *Research in Political Sociology*, Amsterdam: Elsevier Press.

Roy, William G. (1997) *Socializing Capital*, Princeton, NJ: Princeton University. Press.

Weber, Max ([1921]1978) *Economy and Society*, Berkeley, CA: University of California Press.

Williamson, Oliver (1985) *The Economic Institutions of Capitalism*, New York: Free Press.

HARLAND PRECHEL

EFFICIENCY WAGES

Neoclassical wage models produce two clear outcomes. First, workers with any particular skill level facing a given level of labour demand will be paid the same. Second, unemployment is only a matter of adjustment time. There is unemployment while job–seekers and employers acquire the information about each other necessary to make a suitable match. This is true whether an economy is in equilibrium, or an external shock has forced it into disequilibrium so that employers have to adjust to substantial changes in either the cost or demand structure they confront (as in real business cycle theory).

Evidence suggests substantial divergences from either of these outcomes. Within local labour markets there are significant wage differences between employees with similar skill levels. For example, large employers usually pay more than small employers. And, unemployment rates in some countries seem to be sufficiently, durably, high to suggest that something more than a straightforward adjustment and matching process is operating. Efficiency wage theory was created to explain these anomalies: specifically, why might employers choose to pay wages higher than those prevailing in a particular labour market for a particular skill?

1. In the Third World, the prevailing wage rate for unskilled labour may support a diet that is inadequate for sustained effort. If this is so, employers may generate higher revenue if they pay a wage that exceeds the prevailing wage rate because the extra effort made possible by an adequate caloric intake exceeds the extra wage cost.

2. Where employees have job-specific skills and/or where recruitment is costly, quits impose significant costs on employers. An employer who pays a wage above the prevailing rate deters quits by increasing the cost to an employee of quitting. The reduction in costs associated with quitting may exceed the extra wage cost.

3. Assume that there is disutility attached to effort. Employees will, then, shirk when they can. Employers can sometimes counter this by tying pay to output. But the output of most jobs is not easily counted. Or, employers can have work closely supervised. But supervision is costly, and difficult where work has team properties that prevent an inexpensive partitioning of responsibility for output. To prevent shirking, then,

employers may have to rely on the occasional opportunity to catch workers who are flagrantly shirking, and to dismiss them as an example to others. But if the wage of the employee is identical to what he or she would receive from another employer, the sanction associated with dismissal is negligible. Employers can, however, increase the cost of dismissal to the employee by paying a wage that exceeds the prevailing rate. Doing so may mean that the revenue gained from the extra output generated in the absence of shirking exceeds the extra wage cost.

4. The standard observable indicators of employee ability – like education – are imperfect. It is often hard for employers to gauge the relative capacities of job applicants who share similar *curricula vitae*. In fact, while the would-be employee has good information on his or her ability, the employer often does not. What, then, can an employer do to be sure to get a reasonable share of more capable job candidates? One method is to offer a wage that exceeds the standard market rate. Doing so ensures that the employer can select from a pool of candidates that includes *some* more able ones. Some of those who finally get hired will have above average abilities.

5. The final mechanism is labelled 'sociological'. Assume, again, that effort is difficult to monitor and that employee shirking is a risk. In this case, however, the solution is not to make coercion more effective. Instead, employers offer higher than market wages in order to engage the loyalty, trust, and commitment of their employees. There is a Maussian 'gift relationship'. Employers treat their employees well. Employees reciprocate by developing, and acting in accord with, norms of high performance.

There are, then, several reasons why employers might pay wages that exceed the market rate. What does this have to do with unemployment? The answer is that efficiency wages imply downward wage rigidity. In neoclassical economics markets clear because prices adjust. This is as true of the market for labour as of the market for widgets. Unemployment is impossible in such a context because the unemployed will be willing to accept a lower wage than those already employed. They will bid down the wage rate. But suppose the wage rate of the employed has been set according to any one of the mechanisms described above. In each case, the effect of a wage cut would be to reduce productivity by more than the reduction in wage costs. Efficiency wages, then, are downwardly inflexible wages. That is a source of unemployment.

Efficiency wage theory is interesting and plausible. But there are difficulties with it. Here are some examples. While there is abundant evidence of pay differences between employees with equivalent observable skills, that does not preclude the possibility that unobserved skill differences might explain those differences. If efficiency wages are a method for reducing shirking they should be more frequently applied to occupations where monitoring is a problem. In fact, within particular industries, all occupations seem to command about the same wage premium. Monitoring may be more difficult in large firms, and those firms do tend to pay higher wages. But large firms also have relatively long average employment tenures. Insofar as that is the case it raises a question about the credibility of the threat of dismissal – which is central to the coercive mechanism. Finally, even if some jobs command an efficiency wage, if a secondary sector exists in which wages are fully flexible, there need be no unemployment, since the secondary sector can mop up surplus labour.

References and further reading

Akerlof, George E. and Yellen, Janet L. (eds) (1986) *Efficiency Wage Models of the Labour Market*, Cambridge: Cambridge University Press.

Carmichael, Lorne (1990) 'Efficiency Wage Models of Unemployment: One View', *Economic Inquiry*, 28: 269–95.

MICHAEL R. SMITH

EGALITARIANISM See: equality

ELECTRONIC COMMERCE

Although the term 'electronic commerce' is widely used, there is no universally accepted definition. In very general terms, electronic commerce (e-commerce) refers to performing economic activities by using information technology. Existing definitions differ both in the scope of economic activities and technical media they consider. While extensive definitions include all activities along a value chain, both within a firm and between different economic actors, e-commerce in a narrow sense, as it is used here, refers only to transactions between independent economic actors. Electronic support of both internal and external activities is often referred to as e-business. On the technology dimension, e-commerce is sometimes defined only with respect to using the Internet, and sometimes as use of any information and communication technology.

Different types of e-commerce can be defined based on the actors involved, which can be businesses, consumers or government. Thus nine types of e-commerce transactions can be distinguished of which business-to-business (B2B) and business-to-consumer (B2C) are the most important.

An important issue in B2B e-commerce is the impact of information technology on the structure of buyer–supplier relationships. Based on arguments from **transaction cost economics**, Malone *et al.* (1994) developed the 'Move to the Market' hypothesis. Since external suppliers are specialized, their production costs are lower compared to internal production of components. Because of competition between suppliers, these cost advantages will be passed on to buyers. Usually, a firm's possibilities to outsource activities are limited by transaction costs, such as costs of searching for transaction partners, bargaining and monitoring their performance. The use of information and communication technology decreases transaction costs and thus enables firms to outsource a larger fraction of their activities to external suppliers and exploit their cost advantages.

The predictions of this hypothesis were only partially confirmed empirically. While firms do rely on external suppliers for an increasing part of their value creation, at the same time a drastic reduction in the actual number of suppliers was observed. A prominent example for this development is the car industry, where the number of suppliers was typically reduced by 50 per cent or more in the late 1990s.

These results led to the development of the 'Move to the Middle' hypothesis, introduced, among others, by Clemons *et al.* (1993). They argued that buyers limit the number of suppliers because of the high set-up costs of relationships and to create stronger incentives for suppliers to make the necessary non-contractible investments in product development or quality. While the developments of information and communications technology and especially of open standards have significantly reduced the technical difficulties and costs of interacting with suppliers, changes in the organization of business processes and the creation of mutual **trust** between closely linked business partners, who exchange sensitive information, still require significant effort. At the same time, these set-up costs are a significant barrier against frequent switching of suppliers. This increases a tendency towards long-term, highly integrated relationships with only few suppliers, who are closely linked via information technology. The resulting structure is called an 'electronic hierarchy', in which the traditional structure based on authority and work contracts is replaced by influences on the decision processes of nominally independent entities through information technology.

Developments in practice seem to confirm both the 'Move to the Market' and the 'Move to the Middle' hypotheses. While strong and close relationships between buyers and a relatively small number of selected suppliers exist in many industries, purchasing platforms and electronic marketplaces in which a large number of suppliers compete against each other for orders have also been established. The efficiency of the market mechanism in these platforms is frequently enhanced by the use of **auctions** to determine prices and allocate goods.

In the B2C (business to consumer) sector, the development of e-commerce has led to similar institutional changes. In traditional physical markets, intermediaries like wholesalers or retailers offer brokerage services to link different parts of the value chain and facilitate market transactions. Information technology enables direct trade between exchange partners without a need for intermediating agents. This has led to a 'disintermediation effect'. As in the B2B sector, disintermediated, directly market-based coordination takes place mainly for standardized goods of low specificity. Specialized goods or goods demanding tacit knowledge require a close interaction between buyer and seller and thus cannot be disintermediated easily (Picot *et al.* 1997).

The separation between the product flow and payment as well as the anonymity of transaction partners increases the problem of opportunism in electronic markets. Common risks associated with B2C e-commerce from a consumer's perspective include (1) the invasion of privacy through abuse of personal information; (2) financial fraud through illegal use of payment information; and (3) lack of performance by dishonest or irresponsible sellers.

To overcome these problems, new institutions and roles have emerged to replace or emulate traditional intermediary roles in physical markets. Electronic brokers (market makers) provide brokerage services and enable reintermediation. Apart from providing market platforms, which form the technological basis for market transactions, they contribute additional essential third-party services such as information aggregation, e.g. through electronic agents for online price comparison, yellow pages services, or negotiation services for more complex transactions. A major role of electronic brokers is to provide an appropriate institutional framework to overcome the problems of increased **risk and uncertainty** in the anonymous environment of e-commerce. By acting as a trusted third party, they provide several institutional arrangements fostering trust building of consumers. Important mechanisms include structural assurances like accreditation as well as positive and negative **reputation** systems to exclude fraudulent sellers from the marketplace, privacy protection and security seals, escrow services, or the provision of product inspection, as well as development of inspection and quality standards.

Despite these mechanisms, opportunistic behaviour cannot be fully precluded in e-commerce and leads to disputes and Internet fraud. Electronic mediation and arbitration services for dispute resolution have emerged to handle these cases. Often, market makers themselves offer alternative dispute resolution services or suggest independent state or private mediation services to facilitate confidence-building of their customers. As a signalling device, costs of alternative dispute resolution are in many cases covered by sellers.

References and further reading

Clemons, Eric K., Reddi, Sahidhar P. and Row, Michael C. (1993) 'The Impact of Information Technology on the Organization of Economic Activity: The "Move to the Middle" Hypothesis', *Journal of Management Information Systems*, 10: 9–35.

Malone, Thomas W., Yates, Joanne and Benjamin, Robert J. (1994) 'Electronic Markets and Electronic Hierarchies', in Thomas Allen and Michael S. Scott Morton (eds), *Information Technology and the Corporation of the 1990s*, New York: Oxford University Press, pp. 61–81.

Picot, Arnold, Bortenlänger, Christine and Röhrl, Heiner (1997) 'Organisation of Electronic Markets: Contributions from the New Institutional Economics', *The Information Society*, 13: 107–23.

SABINE T. KOESZEGI
RUDOLF VETSCHERA

EMBEDDEDNESS

The term delineates an interpretative and analytical approach based on the theoretical assumption that economic behaviour and decision-making cannot be understood as the utility function of atomized actors (as assumed within neoclassical economics) but instead as the product of actors interacting in different social contexts. Such contexts comprise networks of social interaction and social, political, cognitive and cultural institutions and their norms and habits. It is assumed, therefore, that **economic action** and the resulting modalities structuring economic life vary in different social conditions and diverse historic and cultural contexts.

The concept of embeddedness is a tool used both at the micro and macro level to identify the underling social diversity that characterizes economic behaviour. Today, approaches based on embeddedness are widely used not only within economic sociology and anthropology but also within institutional economics, the social sciences in general and the media. As it will be discussed, there are different ways of understanding the concept of embeddedness and, as a result, its methodological and epistemological debates are still open. In any case, the concept of embeddedness is currently a strong interpretative tool used to examine the variety of economic life in the presence of processes of vertical disintegration and de-standardization of the economy.

The original concept in Karl Polanyi: critical features

The idea of embeddedness stems from the fundamental contribution of Karl **Polanyi** (1944, 1957). For Polanyi,

> The human economy ... is embedded and enmeshed in institutions, economic and non economic. The inclusion of the non-economic is vital. For religion or government may be as important for the structure and functioning of the economy as monetary institutions or the availability of tools and machines themselves that lighten the toil of labor.
>
> (Polanyi 1957: 250)

In fact, the functioning of the substantive economy, as opposed to the abstract and formal conception of the economy used by neoclassical economists and marginalists, cannot be understood without considering the relations, rules and social institutions that characterize it. Polanyi identifies three distinct and pure patterns that orient in different ways the logic of economic exchanges: reciprocity, redistribution and market **exchange**.

Each of the three patterns contribute a different form of social integration that delineate the institutions of economic life and the configurations of embeddedness. These forms are ever present and may occur historically in different combinations. An epistemological problem arises as a result of a presumed incongruence of the three forms. While the patterns of reciprocity and redistribution express within their own logic of exchange different forms of social integration, market exchange in its abstract form, from which formal economics derives, is based on the absence of systematic social relations. Market exchange, governed by a logic of maximum efficiency where prices are fixed by competition, is based on occasional interactions between buyers and sellers not to be affected by particular and long-lasting social relations. While the patterns of reciprocity and redistribution express logics already embedded in forms of social integration, market exchange is logically disembedded.

Reciprocal exchanges cannot be understood without taking into account institutions and social groups that rely on communal solidarity, delayed restitution and economic benefits derived from membership in a specific social group (family, friends, acquaintances, ethnic groups, and so on). From a Weberian perspective, reciprocity therefore identifies community membership and the priority of group interests and well-being over the immediate interest of individual economic actors.

Redistributive exchanges cannot be understood without the existence of institutions and legitimate political relations that allow for economic resources to be extracted from some subjects in order to be redistributed to others according to socially constructed and approved logics that sanction the functioning of hierarchical structures of power, the maintenance of social order, savings and investment to activate **economic development** and the support of economically weak, but socially deserving subjects. Redistribution therefore indicates membership in a hierarchically organized society that defines the priority of communal welfare in opposition to the urgent interests of economic actors (adopting a Weberian terminology we may speak of **value** rationality versus instrumental rationality). The functioning and importance of logics of reciprocity and redistribution may vary culturally and

historically, yet the different meanings of rules and institutions that such logics express in terms of embeddedness are always clear (membership in small communal groups or in a wider and stratified social community characterized by shared social values). More complicated and controversial is the meaning of embeddedness and form of social integration that the market (with its spreading hegemonic logic) takes on in industrial societies.

Polanyi does not dwell theoretically on this issue. However, in his most important work, *The Great Transformation* (1944), the author offers interesting insight. He expresses a severe critique of the self-regulating capacity of the market and of liberalism. In this sense the diffusion of market economy, particularly the commodification of fictitious commodities, such as land and labour, turned out to have a devastating impact by tearing apart traditional social relations. Thus it should not be compatible with any form of social order. If we assume the logical disembeddedness of market exchange relations we cannot accept the idea of a self-regulating capacity of the market and the concomitant possible existence of a market society. Indeed, Polanyi asserts that even market exchange generates social institutions, for within substantive economies exchange could not occur without a favourable social context allowing for the systematic encounter of actors (firms, financial institutions, contracts, labour regulations, and so forth). Hence market exchange constitutes a form of social integration, and therefore is re-embedded in society (for a critique to this assumption of Polanyi and the elaboration of an alternative approach based exclusively on reciprocity and associative logics see Enzo Mingione 1991). The process of re-embeddedness of the market is not a mechanic self-regulating capacity deriving from the immediate advantages of atomized and punctual competition but rather an indirect process that builds the social institutions of cooperation necessary to make the diffusion of market relations compatible with the social order. This is an important point to be emphasized as the logic of mechanic self-regulation would be based on competitiveness and efficiency while the indirect logic of the social institutions of the market is, according to Polanyi, based on cooperation and regulation.

For Polanyi embeddedness is therefore a complex and variable interplay of the three different logics of social integration. *The Great Transformation* is a historical phase involving changing conditions of embeddedness. It is a turbulent phase in which the diffusion of market exchange redefines the institutions and the rules of economic life (with the double movement of dis-embedment and re-embeddedment). At the same time the logic of reciprocity and redistribution fail to disappear and actually express new and important areas of regulation of economic life. These areas include with regard to reciprocity, household economy, petty family production and friendship networks; and with regard to redistribution, nation-state regulations, the expansion of taxation and welfare programmes.

A hidden theory of embeddedness in Weber?

Although Max **Weber** does not use the term one may very well wonder whether his contribution does not contain theoretical insights that lead one to an interpretation based on the diversification of economic behaviour in accordance with the conditions of social insertion, and therefore with embeddedness. Weber identifies two different types of social interaction that have a different effect on economic behaviour: the first, when two or more actors are held together by a common sense of belonging (community); the second, when two or more actors share the same interest (association). There is here an obvious analogy between the Weberian

idea of communal relations and the Polanyian view of reciprocity. Noteworthy also in Weberian thought is the importance attributed to the tensions between the instrumental rationality and the value rationality. As earlier stated, while the former explicitly recalls market exchange, the latter can be considered the foundation of redistributive logics. The process of modernization is marked by the diffusion of rational economic behaviour across a variable and changing arena of tensions between the two different rational logics where values call for, above all else, regulations and economic planning and the priority of socially shared public welfare over the immediate benefits that the individual economic actor could accomplish.

From these brief reflections, it is evident that Weber did not believe the economic actor to be an atomized individual always maximizing the immediate utility of his/her actions, but rather saw this actor as a subject influenced by his/her communal networks, traditions, habits and by shared values and culture. The diversity of social contexts in which the economic actor is located, be it within networks and relations or be it in terms of values habits and culture, produce consistent variations in the 'interests of the actors as they themselves are aware of them' (Weber [1922]1978: 30). It is the latter and not immediate utility that informs the meaning of economic actions.

Furthermore *The Protestant Ethic and the Spirit of Capitalism* (Weber [1904–5]1958) can be considered a pioneer work on the sociocultural embeddedness of economic action. Weber insists on the fact that the typical economic behaviour of modern capitalism, the drive to profit and accumulation, the generalization of professional *beruf*, can be spread and consolidated, at least originally, only in a culturally favourable context generated by the Protestant ethic. It is not a matter of actions simply geared toward gain and personal success, but rather behaviour which transgresses traditional values with uncertain and risky outcomes, behaviour that requires a particular attitude and cultural climate. Beyond the specificity of Weber's work and the critical debate that the *Protestant Ethic* stimulated, there remains the belief that *homo economicus* is not autonomous from the cultural context, but in fact that different sociocultural configurations (family, ethnicity, locality, religion, social groups in which individuals are socialized) maintain a decisive influence in determining economic behaviour even when it is freed from traditional metaphysical and supernatural **beliefs**.

Mark Granovetter and the new economic sociology

In his 1985 article in the *American Journal of Sociology*, 'Economic Action and Social Structure: The Problem of Embeddedness', Mark Granovetter resumes the embedded approach as a central element of the new economic sociology. While in Polanyi's *The Great Transformation* the political aspect of embeddedness prevails over its methodological component, Granovetter, by contrast, asserts the rigorous epistemological and methodological nature of the concept.

> Much of the utilitarian tradition, including classical and neoclassical economics, assumes rational, self-interested behavior affected minimally by social relations, thus invoking an idealized state [based on the assumption that the economic actor is atomized] ... At the other extreme lies what I call the argument of 'embeddedness'; the arguments that the behaviour and institutions to be analyzed are so constrained by ongoing social relations that to construe them as independent is a grievous misunderstanding.
>
> (1985: 481–2)

At the centre of Granovetter's notion of embeddedness is the criticism of the 'assumption of "atomized" decisionmaking' both in the undersocialized economic version and in the oversocialized sociological and institutional version. In fact 'despite the apparent contrast between under- and oversocialized views, we should note an irony of great theoretical importance: both have in common a conception of action and decision carried out by atomized actors' (1985: 485).

Embeddedness then assumes a double meaning, theoretical and methodological, pointing to the crucial 'role of concrete personal relations and structures (or "networks") of such relations' (1985: 490) not only in shaping the orientations of empirical economic behaviour, in contrast to the utilitarian undersocialized approaches, but also in building the social and economic institutions of economic life, in contrast to the oversocialized views of functionalist sociology and institutionalism.

It is in this latter sense that Granovetter specifically critiques Oliver Williamson's argument discussed in *Markets and Hierarchies* (1975). According to Williamson the hierarchical organization of large firms is a pre-established institutional assumption of atomized economic actors and not, as Granovetter has argued, a variable behaviour depending on relations and networks in which social actors are embedded.

Granovetter's notion of embeddedness is based primarily on the variety of social networks in which economic actors are positioned ('network embeddedness' rather than 'political economy embeddedness', as could be defined in Polanyi's notion of this concept. As such it is a 'kind of umbrella under which a lot of different and more precise kinds of research could be done on the ways in which social networks affect the conduct of the economy, economic behaviour, economic actions, economic institutions' (Granovetter 1998: 88–9).

The notion of embeddedness in Granovetter's early articles stresses the methodological component but is limited by the lack of attention to cultural diversification and to issues regarding the political and institutional regulation of economic behaviour, which are in fact central in Polanyi's approach. In a recent contribution Granovetter (2000) acknowledges these limitations and re-examines in a more comprehensive and expansive manner his formulation of embeddedness.

His approach, however, remains decidedly oriented to micro-analysis. The link that explains how networks and systems of social relations turn into institutions and macro-social regulations of economic behaviour, is yet to be established. As Nee and Ingram (1998: 20) argue,

> without incorporating institutional effects, this network-embeddedness perspective is limited in its explanatory power ... A firmer basis for intellectual trade between economics and sociology results from understanding how institutions and network ties are linked. Specifying the social mechanisms through which institutions affect behaviour provides the missing link, integrating a choice-within-institutional-constraints approach with the network-embeddedness perspective.
>
> (Nee and Ingram 1998: 20)

To a certain extent, the network-embeddedness perspective evokes the notion of **social capital**, even though these two concepts have different bearings. On the one hand, the assumption is that the systems of social interaction are at the foundation of all economic behaviour and of all institutions regulating social life. On the other hand, there is the importance that network configurations founded upon solidarity and trust can take on in certain areas of economic choice, especially in the functioning of **labour markets**, **entrepreneurship** and the organization of **firms**.

The perspectives of embeddedness in a post-industrial global economy

Granovetter's contribution has triggered a fertile debate within economic sociology with reference to the modalities of embeddedness, centred on how the social, political, cultural and cognitive variety of the systems of social relations may guide in diversified ways the behaviour and the institutions of contemporary economic life.

Such debate takes place during a phase of deep economic transformation across industrialized countries, where **deindustrialization**, the vertical disintegration of large bureaucratic and industrial organizations, tertiarization, the diffusion of business networks and of increasingly complex forms of subcontracting, and the importance of information technology, are causing and proliferating the de-standardization of economic life. Considerable attention to the variety of social and cultural situations that condition the choices, the actions, the institutions and the regulations of economic life is therefore required. Embeddedness can become a powerful tool for understanding the diversification of economic life. To do so it must overcome a few of its limitations, namely those identified by Granovetter such as the oversocialized interpretation, where institutions, values and culture are preconditions attributed to the atomized economic actor. Attention should be focused on identifying the processes of the social construction of institutions, of culture and of cognitive structures, and how these, in turn, influence in interactive social modalities, the diverse economic preferences and the behaviours of actors inserted in different social networks.

One of the most interesting trajectories that has emerged in the unfolding of this debate rests on the intertwining between an approach based on embeddedness and the studies of the way cultural diversity affect economic behaviour. As Zelizer (1988) has pointed out, the exclusive emphasis on

235

social relations and networks tends to completely leave out cultural diversity and leads to 'social structural absolutism'. On the other hand, cultural studies tends to explain the variety of economic behaviour by means of cultural differences which lead to 'cultural absolutism'. A more mature cultural embeddedness approach should then 'plot a middle course between cultural and social structural absolutism' (Zelizer 1988: 629).

'Culture can either affect economic behaviour by influencing how actors define their interests (*constitutive* effects ...), by constraining their efforts on their own behalf (*regulatory* effects), or by shaping a group's capacity to mobilize or its goal in mobilizing' (DiMaggio 1994: 28). Along these lines, cultural differences constitute important factors of differentiation in economic behaviour. It is necessary, then, to identify which characteristics and which configurations of social relations (entrepreneurial behaviour, modes of consumption, organizational behaviour in business, work strategies and the building of trust networks) can be interpreted as variations of economic behaviour (as evident, for example, in the numerous studies on the Japanese economic model, on the Italian industrial districts and on ethnic entrepreneurship). It is in this direction, through approaches based on the notion of embeddedness, that the strong diversification of contemporary economic systems – including the importance of local economies, the systems of firm networks and the crucial role of different types of trust relations – can be better understood in order to examine the connection between cognitive and cultural factors (which may be both a constraint and a resource for the individual), and their relationship to economic action and networks of social relations characterizing the field of economic choice for actors positioned in highly diversified social and political contexts.

See also: markets, sociology of; rationality.

References and further reading

DiMaggio, Paul (1994) 'Culture and Economy', in N. Smelser and R. Swedberg (eds), *The Handbook of Economic Sociology*, New York and Princeton, NJ: Russell Sage Foundation and Princeton University Press, pp. 27–57.

Granovetter, Mark (1985) 'Economic Action and Social Structure: The Problem of Embeddedness', *American Journal of Sociology*, 91: 481–510.

—— (1998) 'NET Society: Mark Granovetter on Network, Embeddedness and Trust', *Sosiologi IDAG – Norway*, 4: 88–9.

—— (2000) *Le Marché autrement. Les Reseaux dans l'economie*, Paris: Desclée de Brouwer.

Mingione, Enzo (1991) *Fragmented Societies. A Sociology of Economic Life Beyond the Market*, Oxford: Blackwell.

Nee, V. and Ingram, P. (1998) 'Embeddedness and Beyond: Institutions, Exchange, and Social Structure', in M. Brinton and V. Nee (eds), *The New Institutionalism in Sociology*, New York: Russell Sage Foundation, pp. 19–45.

Polanyi, Karl (1944) *The Great Transformation*, Boston: Beacon.

—— (1957) 'The Economy as Institute Process', in Karl Polanyi, K. C. Arensberg and H. W. Pearson (eds), *Trade and Markets in the Early Empires*, Chicago: Regnery, pp. 243–69.

Swedberg, Richard (2003) *Principles of Economic Sociology*, Princeton, NJ: Princeton University Press.

Weber, Max ([1904–5]1958) *The Protestant Ethic and the Spirit of Capitalism*, New York: Charles Scribner's Sons.

—— ([1922]1978) *Economy and Society: An Outline of Interpretive Sociology*, two volumes, Berkeley, CA: University of California Press.

Williamson, Oliver (1975) *Markets and Hierarchies*, New York: Free Press.

Zelizer, Viviana (1988) 'Beyond the Polemics of the Market: Establishing a Theoretical and Empirical Agenda', *Sociological Forum*, 4: 614–34.

ENZO MINGIONE

EMOTIONS AND THE ECONOMY

Definition and scope

Early understandings of emotion in philosophy and psychology focused on the mental and physiological aspects of emotion, as feelings and as bodily sensations respectively. These conceptualizations support the view that emotions are involuntary and possibly disordering processes. They fail to appreciate, however, the role of social circumstances, expressive communication and actor intentions in emotional experience. More recent research has tended to emphasize instead the cognitive, motivational or dispositional, and evaluational functions of emotion. The understanding of emotions that results from this broader perspective has the consequence of undermining the view, characteristic of western thinking since at least the late seventeenth century, that emotions and rationality are necessarily opposed. If emotions underscore **value**s, interests and meanings in social life, then they are implicated in rational as well as irrational conduct and outlook. Thus Max **Weber**'s distinction, for instance, between rational action and affective action, loses its relevance when emotion is seen not to found only a particular type of action, such as a panic on the stock exchange, but to underlie all action. If there is an emotional dimension to all action, then the question is how particular emotions are implicated in distinct types of social interaction or process becomes the appropriate focus of research and interpretation.

In addition to the idea that emotions are necessarily opposed to reason or **rationality**, two other misleading notions concerning emotion have to be indicated before the importance of emotion to social and economic processes can be properly appreciated. Emotions are frequently regarded as phenomena of short duration, rapidly dissipating as a provoking stimulus passes. Some emotions may rise and fall within a short timeframe, but it is not a necessary characteristic of emotions. This image of emotions owes much to the methods and interests of experimental psychology, which in laboratory research predominantly studies reactive and highly

visceral emotions amenable to white-coat work and readily elicited from experimental subjects usually drawn from undergraduate populations. Many important emotions are not brief and episodic but enduring or ongoing. Envy in market relations, for example, endues meaning and purpose to actions that are patterned and organizing of particular types of long-term behaviour. Another misunderstanding is that those experiencing particular emotions are necessarily conscious of them. They need not be. Many emotions, including the most important for social processes, are experienced below the threshold of awareness. Indeed, self-knowledge may be attained as part of a process of becoming aware of the emotions that are responsible for disposition and inclinations to particular types of actions and orientations. Thomas Scheff, for instance, has shown that much social conformity can be explained in terms of shame of which the subject is not consciously aware (*American Sociological Review* 1988).

Rationality and emotions: economic interests

The supposed necessary opposition between emotion and reason or rationality is premised on the understanding of emotions as compulsive and labile, distracting those who experience them from their purposes. Acknowledging that if emotions distract persons from their purposes, they also establish afresh what their purposes are to be, leads to repair of the oppositional view of emotions and reason. Emotions may not oppose reason but give it direction. This was the eighteenth-century view of David Hume and Adam **Smith**, for instance, which has over the past two decades regained currency. The relevance of this perspective for an understanding of social and economic processes is in the realization that meanings and purposes are rooted in the emotions of the social actors who bear and express them. Values and interests, therefore, which most frequently have drawn sociological attention, are thus secondary to emotions, which therefore deserve closer attention than they typically receive. This is particularly clear in understanding economic 'interest'.

Economic rationality, in Weberian terminology, is formal not substantive. It refers to decision-making and not reasoning about the world and its investigation. Economic rationality entails at minimum a choice or decision based on a schedule of preferences operating within a matrix of alternative means related to distinct goals. In market societies the goals or ends are limited to maximizing the amount of money achieved as a result of choice, and choice therefore is predominantly concerned with calculating the means best suited to achieving that goal or end. This latter is characterized as the chooser's interest. According to this account, interests are objective and quantifiable in terms of money whereas individual preferences or tastes, which pertain to the realm of choice of means, is the locus of emotion to the degree that emotion might be found in economies or markets. History of the origins of market capitalism in the seventeenth and eighteenth centuries, however, shows that economic interest is itself essentially emotional. Albert **Hirschman** (1977), for instance, has shown that during the seventeenth century destructive passions leading to war were displaced by other passions to avert political dangers and achieve peace. In this transition avarice, the 'foulest passion', became domesticated into innocuous economic 'interest', displacing violence through pursuit of trade for economic gain or satisfaction of greed. In the language of current economic sociology, emotions are embedded in market institutions, including economic interest.

Consumption and emulation

In monetized societies, as Emile **Durkheim** and others have shown, value differentia-

tion tends to quantitative rather than qualitative distinction. Market behaviour, therefore, is directed to insatiable increases in consumption. While limits of means may constrain acquisitive emotions of **consumption** markets, the structure of consumption markets themselves encourage emotions of indulgence by **advertising**, that links personal identity with product brands and other symbolic values, and credit, that encourages feelings of security in purchases beyond means. **Fashion**, and the constancy of product change inherent in it, is one mechanism of market variety supporting continuous consumer demand. Georg **Simmel**, for instance, has shown that fashion draws on prior feelings of shame, and encourages feelings of imitation and envy. Indeed, envy is an emotion proscribed in small-scale societies in which market exchanges are disruptive of traditional relations but sponsored by ancillary institutions of national market economies.

The role of envy and associated emotions in societies in which differential spending is associated with prestige hierarchies has been highlighted in Thorstein **Veblen**'s discussion of the phenomenon of conspicuous **consumption** and pecuniary canons of taste (*The Theory of the Leisure Class*). These practices and outlooks are encouraged by positive social evaluation of symbolic displays, according to Veblen. The emotional impetus of invidious comparison, accordingly, is the basis of reputation, and the ensuing chain of resentment, envy, desire and market purchase consolidates a culture of consumerism.

Work and its loss

Labour markets are also arenas of the most diverse emotions. Emotions of self-evaluation and comparison with others as well as those associated with job satisfaction are the most obvious. Employment raises the prospect of unemployment and the fear of insecurity is therefore also a characteristic labour market emotion. Indeed, the fear of unemployment is more than fear of loss of work. This is because employment provides a link between the individual and a larger community beyond the labour market but accessed through labour market standing, which is also lost through unemployment. Unemployment is therefore not merely loss of employment but of a range of associations and capacities, some of which are ostensibly unconnected with employment. Indeed, Karl Mannheim describes how unemployment destroys an individual's 'life plan', and in doing so is much more likely to create 'apathy rather than rebellion in the minds of its victims' (*Man and Society* 1940). Also, the sources of advantage in labour markets may translate to aggravated disadvantage in unemployment. For instance, technologically skilled workers who suffer structural rather than cyclical unemployment may face longer periods of unemployment than less skilled and therefore more mobile workers. These and similar fundamental experiences necessarily contain compelling emotional dimensions. In summary, those who fail in labour markets, according to Robert Lane (1991: 170), following Marie Jahoda, 'learn externality, passivity, helplessness, the importance of luck, chance, and fate ... [and] many will learn self-blame, demoralization, and depression'.

Thinking of those emotions explained in a simple Kemperian model (Kemper, *A Social Interactional Theory of Emotions*, 1978), it can be expected that unemployment will typically generate fear, through an insufficiency of one's own power in labour market relations; shame, through an excess of status in terms of the ratio of market relevant qualities to market performance; depression, through an insufficiency of status in terms of the ratio of past standing to present standing; and anger, through an excess of the status of other's standing in labour markets, be they employers, managers, employed workers or whoever. This

is a simple and minimal set of probabilities, to which others must be added. Differential time frames impact on emotional experience, especially around the emotion of hopelessness. Resentment has been identified as a key emotion among declining groups in trade cycle movements. The likelihood of experience of moral indignation in those who are disadvantaged by a distributional system they regard as legitimate can also be mentioned in this context. Another emotion also typical of the condition of unemployment is boredom.

Investment and confidence

Rational actor models of economic behaviour in general assume that decision-makers orient to optimizing expected benefits. Expectation is thus central in consideration of **economic action** and institution. The basis of expectation is of considerable interest to economic sociology because of the unavoidable uncertainty of economic systems. Uncertainty is inherent in all systems of action as any given action changes the conditions of all future actions. Thus uncertainty is not overcome with time. In monetized economies uncertainty inheres in the possibility of conversion of assets to liquidity, for instance, the possibility of deferring investment options, and so forth. Thus an actor's expected benefits are in fact the balance of their hopes and fears in the face of an unknowable future.

Economic organizations function as means of holding the future accountable by increasing the predictability of events and processes. Organizations have varying but limited capacities to control and therefore regulate their members and their environments, and are ultimately unable to insulate themselves from the impact of changes in the environment that they cannot control or possibly foresee. Ultimately the future remains unknown and it is engaged not only with information or calculation but also necessarily with anticipatory emotions, including confidence, optimism and pessimism. The economist John Maynard **Keynes** (*The General Theory of Employment, Interest and Money*, 1936) has shown that the propensity to investment is largely a function of the state of confidence through which expectations of future returns on investment influence present investment practices. Keynes also appreciates the emotional nature of confidence.

The application of a sociological understanding of confidence as an emotion can be taken beyond the issue of the embeddedness of emotions in economic institutions to the macroscopic realm of relations between institutions in explanation of the investment process, as Jack Barbalet (1998: 94–101) has shown. The social basis of confidence is in the actor's acceptance in previous relationships and the resources to which such relationships have given access. Business confidence, represented as the affectively or emotionally constructed inclination to economic investment, is not therefore based simply on market opportunities but on the business community's relationship with other collective or institutional actors, including **trade unions**, the scientific and technological communities, and so on, but especially the political state. The level and direction of state expenditure, according to this account, is dependent on or a function of government acceptance and recognition of the needs of business. Thus the business community's relationship with the political state is a source of confidence that informs expectations regarding future returns on current expenditure.

References and further reading

Barbalet, J. M. (1998) *Emotion, Social Theory, and Social Structure: A Macrosociological Approach*, Cambridge: Cambridge University Press.

Frank, Robert H. (1988) *Passions within Reason: The Strategic Role of the Emotions*, New York: W. W. Norton.

Hirschman, Albert O. (1977) *The Passions and the Interests: Political Arguments for Capitalism before Its Triumph*, Princeton, NJ: Princeton University Press.

Lane, Robert E. (1991) *The Market Experience*, Cambridge: Cambridge University Press.

JACK BARBALET

ENTERPRISE GROUPS

Instead of operating as individual economic actors, firms may find it economically convenient to function in an organizational environment where they are capable of building different kinds of ties with other firms. Enterprise groups arise precisely from such a variety of formal and informal ties and relationships among firms. They may be large conglomerates, inter-firm networks, strategic rival alliances, joint ventures, subcontracting relations and so forth. A narrower definition of the term would exclude those firms that by means of systematic mergers and acquisitions have become one single corporation, and those that are bound together by short-term alliances (Granovetter 2001).

Since the late 1970s, the transition from mass production to more flexible forms of production has brought some remarkable changes. Firms have been more prompted to experiment new forms of economic organization, such as networked companies, resulting in a shift from vertical bureaucracies to horizontal corporations. Even large Fordist firms have began to adopt many of the organizational innovations (such as the outsourcing) that were though to be the domain of small and mid-sized enterprises. Moreover, as argued by Manuel Castells (1996), informational technologies have favoured the diffusion of network organizations, particularly in high-tech sectors.

Yet the sociological implication of the existence of enterprise groups has been far less examined than their mere economic significance. On the economic side scholars interpret the existence of enterprise groups in a functionalistic way: that is, as economic institutions created as responses to organizational or economic problems. This is the main argument of the new institutional economics, which is based on the assumption that transaction costs and concerns with efficiency may lead an enterprise either to form a hierarchically organized (i.e. vertically integrated) structure or to join a group. Others, such as the business historian Alfred **Chandler**, argue that the agglomeration of firms is a transitional modality of organization, which will eventually give way to more stable types of large integrated firms.

The sociological relevance of enterprise groups rests with the fact that these sets of firms are 'integrated neither completely nor barely in the middle range of coalitions and federations' (Granovetter 2001: 330). Below this level there stands the individual firm, above this level there stands the wider market and economic policies. New studies in economic sociology are approaching this middle level to understand not simply 'why' firms join one another, but 'how' they set up formal and informal structures, 'what' makes possible their agglomeration, and more broadly what their role is in shaping modern capitalism.

In this respect the empirical literature on social capital and trust has opened up new prospects for research. One important element is that in many culturally different settings reciprocity guides relations within enterprise groups. In the Korean *chaebol* kinship ties and managerial control of the firms are heavily intertwined. In the Japanese *keiretsu* (the modern form of the old *zaibatsu*) kinship bonds are still important, albeit less than in the family-dominated *zaibatsu*, and it is evident in the interlocking system of family-tied shareholders. Another example of enterprise groups is given by the innovative **industrial districts**, particularly in Italy (Piore and Sabel 1984). In this case it is the geographic contiguity and a homogeneous social context that create the conditions to develop trust in the networked

firms. What seems to characterize enterprise groups cross-culturally is the **embeddedness** of social relations. Key actors are bound together by personal and moral commitments that may transcend the expectation of mere business relations.

See also: inter-firm relations; social capital; transaction cost economics; trust.

References and further reading

Castells, Manuel (1996) *The Rise of Network Society*, vol. 1 of *The Information Age. Economy, Society and Culture*, Oxford: Blackwell.

Granovetter, Mark (2001) 'Coase Revisited: Business Groups in the Modern Economy', in Mark Granovetter and Richard Swedberg, *The Sociology of Economic Life*, second edition, Boulder, CO: Westview Press.

Piore, Michael and Sabel, Charles (1984) *The Second Industrial Divide: Possibilities for Prosperity*, New York: Basic Books.

Powell, Walter W. and Smith-Doerr, Laurel (1994) 'Networks and Economic Life', in N. Smelser and R. Swedberg (eds), *The Handbook of Economic Sociology*, Princeton, NJ, and New York: Princeton University Press and Russell Sage Foundation, pp. 368–402.

ENZO MINGIONE

ENTREPRENEURSHIP

Entrepreneurs are innovators who combine and transform the factors of production (labour, land and capital, but also knowledge and social capital) in order to produce value-added goods and services to be sold in a market. They bear the risks connected with their activities and enjoy a special status in capitalist market societies. Entrepreneurs predate capitalism and do exist in other economic systems, but are especially associated with market economies. The market would be a very poor social coordinator if it were, as it is sometimes naively conceived, a set of interactions in which people exchange surpluses for other more scarce goods. Markets need participants specialized in intermediary roles who take advantage of opportunities. Entrepreneurs are the intermediaries through which markets operate.

Entrepreneurship cannot be fully understood without making reference to the sociocultural and politico-institutional context where it arises and develops. The context influences entrepreneurial attitudes and motives, the resources that can be mobilized, the constraints and opportunities to starting and expanding a business, and the cultural climate that can either legitimize or hinder the entrepreneurial role.

Schumpeter as a starting point

Schumpeter is the scholar of entrepreneurship *par excellence*. He puts entrepreneurship at the centre of his theory of development and conceptualized it as innovation, i.e. the introduction of a new combination of the factors of production that is the engine of economic dynamics. The entrepreneur calls for a specific type of personality and conduct. Although orienting his conduct to rational values and taking advantage of rationally based components of his environment, such as money, science and individual freedom, he is not the average product of bourgeois culture, which defines rationality from the narrower viewpoint of calculating one's short-term advantage. The entrepreneur acts on the basis of an autonomous drive to conquest and struggle, to achieve and create for its own sake, and also to establish a family dynasty. This sets him apart from the routine manager. Entrepreneurship is the distinctive historical form that leadership assumes in capitalism, which rests on the premise of a separate economic sphere and is closely linked to the bourgeoisie. The bourgeoisie is the leading class in capitalism, because bourgeois families have performed the innovating and leadership role in the economy and because they acquire, consolidate and transfer prestige, power and wealth to future generations. Schumpeter's

identification of the fate of the nineteenth-century entrepreneur with that of the bourgeois class is largely responsible for his faulty prediction of the collapse of capitalism. He predicted that the routinization of innovation in large oligopolies would render the entrepreneurial function superfluous and undermine the basis for continued bourgeois dominance (1942). In reality, capitalism has proved capable of fundamental transformations – through that process of 'creative destruction' that Schumpeter clearly perceived, but underestimated. Several different brands of capitalism exist, which proved compatible with the existence of very large firms and with state intervention in the economy.

Schumpeter asked the relevant questions and provided useful insights. He paved the way to systematic research of the Harvard Center for Entrepreneurial History. But he was not very influential among mainstream economists who assume that entrepreneurial services are highly elastic and that failures in entrepreneurship are due to maladjustments to external market conditions and to the lack of economic incentives, disregarding the social and cultural complexity and the variety of different historical settings. Among the few notable exceptions, Kirzner analysed entrepreneurs as middlemen between markets and gap-fillers alert to new opportunities and entrepreneurial activity as a discovery procedure of profit opportunities (1973). Other social sciences studying economic phenomena – first of all **economic sociology** – consider entrepreneurship a more problematic phenomenon, deeply embedded in societies and cultures, and focus on the interaction between actor and context, and the mutual interplay among economic and non-economic factors – such as cultural norms and **beliefs**, bounded **solidarity** and **trust**, deviant behaviour and marginality status, **class** relations and **collective action**, organizational structures, state intervention and control.

The double embeddedness of entrepreneurship

The concept of double (or mixed) embeddedness is a useful way to give account of major sociological contributions to the study of entrepreneurship (Klooster-man *et al.* 1999). Embeddedness highlights the two major ways in which the context of entrepreneurship can be analysed: first, as the social and cultural environment of entrepreneurs, such as cultural attitudes favouring technological innovation and risk-taking (e.g. the deviant entrepreneur) or networks of social relations and **social capital**; second, as the politico-institutional context of market capitalism, such as types of markets (of factors of production and of goods and services), types of laws (fiscal, labour, anti-trust, etc.) and institutions of governance (Martinelli 2004).

A basic question addressed by sociologists has been whether entrepreneurs mostly belong to the privileged or marginal social groups. Studies of entrepreneurship in terms of deviance and marginality status have a long-standing tradition since **Sombart**. The creativity and the ability to break traditional values and patterns which characterize the capitalist entrepreneur can be found in all peoples, social groups and religions, but they are more frequent among the members of certain minorities, such as the heretics, the strangers and the Jews. These groups were not completely accepted in the societies where they belonged and could avoid more easily than others the traditional cultural restrictions which regulated economic behaviour in pre-modern Europe. Because of their minority status they developed specific skills in commercial and financial activities which they were allowed to practise; and because of their acute sense of diversity, they maintained a high degree of group solidarity which favoured trust and credit among the members of the group. More recent works on ethnic communities (Light and Rosenstein 1995; Rath 2000) and women (Goffee and Scase 1985) follow a similar 'positional' approach. Structural factors within the larger society, such as racism, sexism and credentialism, render people 'outsiders' through processes of exclusionary closure; such 'outsiders' often form 'feeder groups' from which new entrepreneurs emerge.

Sociological research on ethnic entrepreneurship shows how important for entrepreneurial success are bounded solidarity and enforceable trust as sources of social capital, which do not stem from shared value orientations, but from the position of the ethnic minorities within the wider social structure (see **ethnic economy**). Bounded solidarity is created among immigrant customers, workers and investors by being treated as foreigners and by a heightened awareness of the symbols of common nationhood. Bounded solidarity is accompanied by the existence of enforceable trust against malfeasance among prospective ethnic entrepreneurs. Trust is based on the ostracism of violators, cutting them off from sources of credit and opportunity in the ethnic economy. Citizens of China, Korea or Cuba do not display any exceptional bienfeasance and solidarity in economic transactions when they are in their native countries. Such benefits stem from their being the members of an identifiable social minority in the host country. The social capital represented by social networks within the ethnic community is important in acquiring the human and financial resources necessary for entrepreneurial activity and in creating specialized 'protected' markets for ethnic goods and services.

The social marginality approach has been challenged both by those who maintain that dominant classes in society can produce entrepreneurs more than marginal groups, because of their access to economic, political and social resources, and by those who argue for the importance of hegemonic societal values and see social approval as a requisite of entrepreneurship.

Classical studies of capitalist development, both in the Marxist and non-Marxist traditions, stressing social relations of production, state policies and political and social conflict, show the importance of core rather than marginal classes and status groups. **Marx**'s account of primitive capital accumulation, Pirenne's analysis of the role of merchants in the formation of the urban bourgeoisie, Dobb's thesis of the revolutionary role plaid by yeomen and independent artisans, are all instances of the key modernizing role played by social groups with well-established positions in the 'traditional' societies. Although in different ways, studies of modernization and world capitalist development show the importance of well-entrenched social classes in entrepreneurial formation and consolidation. Even in a much more open society like the United States, the contribution of immigrants and lower classes to the formation of entrepreneurship has been overstressed, since most of the business elite in the period of American industrialization (1870–1910) came from land-owners or entrepreneurial families. The importance of the upper and middle classes in the formation of entrepreneurship is shown by studies in social mobility and the class structure of contemporary western societies as well (Bottomore and Brym 1989). Key variables in this respect are the mechanisms and institutions of social reproduction of the business class, such as schools, marriage patterns and social networks.

The cultural environment of entrepreneurship

Weber's comparative analysis of religious ethics and **economic action** in the origins of capitalism provides the basis for studies focusing on cultural context variables. Studying the interplay between religious ethos and modern rationalization in the rise of capitalism, Weber argued that the advent of ascetic Protestantism provided an especially fruitful breeding ground for the mentality of economic rationality. Through a complex process, material success is a sign of ascetic realization. The entrepreneur is clearly distinguished from his historical predecessors in **traditional economies** by virtue of his 'instrumental rationality', the rational and systematic pursuit of economic gain, the reliance on calculation measured in relation to this economic criterion, the extension of trust through credit, and the subordination of consumption in the interest of accumulation.

Neo-Weberian research focuses on the way and the degree to which the forces of rationalization responsible for dislodging individuals from their embeddedness in nature, religion, and tradition continue to shape economic growth and social modernization. Scholars like Kellner and Berger (Berger 1991) analyse the typical cognitive style that distinguish modern consciousness, such as instrumental rationality and a pronounced propensity to combine and recombine various elements of its activities for the achievement of rationally calculated ends. Evidence for this approach is found in various empirical researches, like those studying the relation between basic aspects of the Chinese culture – such as Confucian ethic and family attitudes – and the entrepreneurial behaviour among overseas Chinese, or the role of Protestant sects in generating a dynamic process among segments of the urban poor in contemporary Latin American cities that fosters entrepreneurial activities.

Cultural interpretations have been charged of having little predictive power since they are invoked only after a particular group has demonstrated its economic prowess, and of being ultimately tautological. They can also be criticized for making no clear distinction between hegemonic culture and marginal groups' subcultures and for stretching the concept of culture so far as to include social interaction in general and all sorts of social networks, without paying attention to their structural dimension. Yet this approach can contribute to explaining why ethnic minorities having a similar marginal status show different levels of economic performance.

The institutional context of entrepreneurship

The other component of the double embeddedness of entrepreneurship is the institutional context of entrepreneurship. This can also claim a long-standing tradition of research, from the famous 'social attitudes' debate (Gerschenkron 1966) to the recent studies on the varieties of capitalism and the embeddedness of institutions. Entrepreneurship is basically defined by technological innovation in a competitive market. But both technology and competition require an extensive analysis oft the social organization of markets. Successful entrepreneurs are those who succeed in establishing stable relationships to their **stakeholder**s (i.e. to all those groups and individuals whose cooperation is needed for a successful business performance and who have claims, rights and interests at stake with the firm's activities). The ability to establish these relationships is itself dependent on the establishment of a stable and reliable legal and political environment. Government legislation and policies are necessary in the forms of patents, anti-monopolistic laws, consumers' protection laws, public spending to sustain aggregate demand, support for exporting firms, etc.). Entrepreneurship flourishes in a regulated context, where the confidence of customers, investors and employees is not shaken by predatory behaviour and illegal action.

There is not, however, one single appropriate institutional environment for entrepreneurial development. Different varieties of capitalism exist and evolve through time, with different laws and forms of government impinging on different competitive strategies and modes of corpo-

rate control. Studies on the institutional varieties of capitalism have shown how more complex institutional mixes of markets, states, hierarchical organizations, communities, clans and networks, and associations coordinate and regulate business activities. Each of these coordinating mechanisms has its own logic – i.e. its own organizational structure, rules of exchange, procedures for enforcing compliance, both individually and collectively; and it can be evaluated in terms of its efficiency, effectiveness in delivering private and collective goods, and its capability to meet the claims and expectations of the various stakeholders of the firm. No single best mix of institutional coordinating mechanisms can pretend universal validity, since a more complex mix of context-specific and continuously evolving institutional arrangements coordinate economic activity, combining individual self-interest with social obligation.

This richness of institutional context has not diminished because of **globalization**. Contrary to a widespread belief, globalization does not induce homogenization towards a single model but stimulates a variety of institutional responses which are rooted in the specific cultural codes and social relations of different countries and regions. Globalization imposes the recombination of economic institutions at various spatial levels, their complex intertwining at all levels of the world (nestedness), since the embeddedness of economic institutions at the level of the nation-state is progressively eroded both from above and from below.

To conclude, sociological studies of entrepreneurship challenge two central assumptions in neoclassical economics: the assumption of a general theory applicable to all societies at all times explaining how people allocate scarce resources to different ends, and the assumption of perfectly competitive markets which are based on profit maximization and perfect information. They maintain, on the contrary, that social relations and societal institutions are not exogenous to market capitalism, but endogenous elements as much as innovation and competition; and that they change over time and from place to place, and provide contingent solutions to specific economic crises and political conflicts.

References and further reading

Berger, B. (ed.) (1991) *The Culture of Entrepreneurship*, San Francisco: ICS Press.

Berger P., Berger, B. and Kellner, H. (1973) *The Homeless Mind: Modernization and Consciousness*, New York: Random House.

Bottomore, T. and Brym, R. J. (eds) (1989) *The Capitalist Class. An International Study*, New York: Harvester Wheatsheaf.

Gerschenkron, A. (1966) 'The Modernization of Entrepreneurship', in A. Gerschenkron, *Continuity in History and Other Essays*, Cambridge, MA: Belknap Press.

Goffee, R. and Scase, R. (1985) *Women in Charge: The Experiences of Female Entrepreneurs*, London: Allen and Unwin.

Hollingsworth J. R. and Boyer, R. (eds) (1997) *Contemporary Capitalism. The Embeddedness of Institutions*, New York: Cambridge University Press.

Kirzner I. M. (1973) *Competition and Entrepreneurship*, Chicago: University of Chicago.

Kloosterman, R., van der Leun, J. P. and Rath, J. (1999) 'Mixed Embeddedness, Migrant Entrepreneurs and Informal Economic Activities', *International Journal of Urban and Regional Research*, 14(5): 659–76.

Light, I. and Rosenstein, C. (1995) *Race, Ethnicity, and Entrepreneurship in Urban America*, New York: Aldine de Gruyter.

Martinelli, A. (2004) 'The Context of Entrepreneurship', in G. Corbetta, M. Huse and D. Ravasi (eds), *Crossroads of Entrepreneurship*, Amsterdam and London: Kluwer.

Rath J. (ed.) (2000) *Immigrant Businesses. The Economic, Political and Social Environment*, Houndmills: Macmillan.

Schumpeter J. (1942) *Capitalism, Socialism and Democracy*, New York: Harper and Row.

ALBERTO MARTINELLI

EQUALITY

The study of the processes that generate inequality in society is a central topic of sociology. Indeed, it has often been noted that, to the extent that sociology has a 'core', it lies in the study of the complex processes that generate inequalities of power, privilege and prestige in human societies. Many of the ideas that sociologists use to explain economic inequality between individuals and groups are plainly borrowed from other social sciences, especially economics. However, as Sørensen (1996: 1334) notes, sociologists have typically brought something distinctive to the study of economic inequality; namely, 'the idea that social structure is somehow relevant for the creation of inequality'. To understand what this means, it is useful to think in terms of a broad contrast with classical and neoclassical economics: where orthodox economists start from the assumption that economic inequality should be explainable in terms of the different **preferences** that people have – e.g. tastes for consumption versus investment or for work versus leisure – and in terms of their different individual characteristics – e.g. skill, experience, training – sociologists start from the idea that pre-existing patterns of social relations – the social structure that confronts the individual – may itself create opportunities and constraints that generate inequality.

What sociologists mean by the claim that 'social structure creates inequality' varies widely from one scholar to the next, as does the definition of 'social structure.' Sørensen (1996) discerns two broad themes. In the first, social structure affects inequality by leading people to adjust their effort, skills, etc., in ways that have consequences for their productivity and, ultimately, their income. So, for instance, two otherwise identical employees, faced with different incentive structures at work, may be led to invest to very different degrees in human capital and in effort at work, producing very different patterns of income and career mobility. This conception of the operation of social structure is common in research on **labour markets**. In the second, the properties of positions in social structure shape income, wealth and other rewards independently of the characteristics of their occupants. Sørensen identifies Marxist class theory as a model of this sort of sociological thinking on inequality: the advantages enjoyed by capitalists and the disadvantages experienced by workers in Marxist theory are viewed as independent of their individual behaviour and performance. To understand inequality, then, we must know something about the properties of the positions that people occupy.

While Marxist class theory provides an especially clear illustration of the distinct perspective that sociology brings to bear on thinking about economic inequality, there are numerous non-Marxist approaches within sociology that share similar meta-theoretical assumptions regarding the role of social structure in generating opportunities and constraints relevant for inequality: Blau's (1994) macro-structural theory demonstrates formally how the distribution of individuals across social positions and their nexus can shape life chances in dramatic ways. White's (1970) work on vacancy chains reveals how opportunities for social mobility, and thus distributional outcomes, can be determined by the movement of other individuals linked together structurally. Building on the Simmelian notion that 'form determines process', Kanter (1977) shows how highly skewed sex ratios in the workplace generate a set of perceptual phenomena that shape interpersonal dynamics between men and women and severely limit the range of interactional possibilities. Granovetter (1974) demonstrates how the matching of people to jobs is embedded in social relations that can alternatively facilitate or thwart the job search. The 'new structuralism' of the 1970s and 1980s in the sociology of labour markets reveals how 'work structures' such as occupation, industry, business organization, **class** and union can

combine to produce different job rewards for similar workers (Kalleberg 1988). Finally, as regards traditional class analysis, the refounded 'neo-Durkheimian' approach pursued by Grusky and his colleagues (e.g. Grusky and Sørensen 1998) suggests the operation of social closure processes at the occupational level that allow for skill-based exploitation and generate inequality.

The scholarly debate over 'pay equity' or 'comparable worth' nicely showcases the sociological focus on the social determinants of economic inequality. Why are workers in 'female-dominated' occupations paid less than workers in other occupations? Neoclassical theories of human capital and of compensating differentials suggest one ready answer. Female-dominated occupations pay less because they may involve less cognitive, physical or social skill and because the jobs dominated by men may be more unpleasant or hazardous than those dominated by women. Taking such factors into account should explain away most, if not all, of the wage penalty associated with location in a female-dominated job, as wage **discrimination** should be difficult to maintain in a competitive market. Research on comparable worth, however, finds that the proportion of females in an occupation has a substantively significant negative effect on pay even after controlling statistically for human capital and compensating differentials. Numerous explanations for this finding have been advanced. Kilbourne et al. (1994) stress the role of 'gendered valuation' in the pay gap. They argue that 'because women are devalued, social roles (including occupations) and skills that are associated with women are culturally devalued relative to those associated with men' (1994: 694). Thus the process that determines what occupations pay is not 'gender neutral'. Rather, it is strongly gendered. Occupations that have a higher proportion of females or that require the sorts of nurturant skills that are usually associated with women will pay less. Kilbourne et al.

(1994) go on to show evidence consistent with this interpretation and conclude that gendered valuation explains as much as 17 per cent of the pay gap. Remarkably, this is considerably larger than the effects of other occupational skill demands, of education and of compensating differentials. Only experience, which explains 21–24 per cent of the pay gap, has a larger effect.

Since the early 1990s, interest in the social determinants of economic inequality has grown across all of the social sciences, including economics. This has occurred for at least three reasons. First, there has been a good bit of cross-fertilization between 'new institutionalism' in sociology and the new institutionalism in economics and political science. Second, there is growing interest in contemporary 'new structuralisms' (not to be confused with that discussed above), new lines of structuralist thinking associated with social **network analysis**, contemporary institutional and organizational analysis, and the study of contentious politics. Finally, the force of events – the stagnation of wages and the remarkable upswing in income inequality in a number of countries since the early 1970s – have, after a considerable post-war hiatus, put the question of the distribution of wealth and income back on the agenda in economics and has led sociologists to address the same question more directly than they ever had before. The 'sociological approach' to economic inequality is presently becoming less distinctively sociological.

References and further reading

Blau, Peter (1994) *Structural Contexts of Opportunities*, Chicago: University of Chicago Press.

England, Paula (1992) *Comparable Worth: Theories and Evidence*, New York: Aldine de Gruyter.

Granovetter, Mark (1974) *Getting a Job*, Cambridge, MA: Harvard University Press.

Grusky, David B. and Sørensen, Jesper B. (1998) 'Can Class Analysis be Salvaged?' *American Journal of Sociology*, 103: 1187–234.

Kalleberg, Arne L. (1988) 'Comparative Perspectives on Work Structures and Inequality', *Annual Review of Sociology*, 14: 203–25.

Kanter, Rosabeth (1977) 'Some Effects of Proportions on Group Life: Skewed Sex Ratios and Responses to Token Women', *American Journal of Sociology*, 82: 965–90.

Kilbourne, Barbara Stanek, Farkas, George, Beron, Kurt, Weir, Dorothea and England, Paula (1994) 'Returns to Skill, Compensating Differentials, and Gender Bias: Effects of Occupational Characteristics on the Wages of White Women and Men', *American Journal of Sociology*, 100: 689–719.

Runciman, W. G. (1974) 'Towards a Theory of Social Stratification', in Frank Parkin (ed.), *The Social Analysis of Class Structure*, London: Tavistock, pp. 54–101.

Sørensen, Aage (1996) 'The Structural Basis of Social Inequality', *American Journal of Sociology*, 101: 1333–65.

White, Harrison C. (1970) *Chains of Opportunity: System Models of Mobility in Organizations*, Cambridge, MA: Harvard University Press.

ARTHUR S. ALDERSON

EQUILIBRIUM

The concept of equilibrium has a general meaning that has been specified to various contexts of theoretical analysis both in the natural sciences and in the social and behavioural sciences. Intuitively, a system in the world is thought of as in an equilibrium state if there is no inherent tendency for it to change apart from external disturbances. It is usually added that such a state is stable if, for a sufficiently small disturbance produced by some external cause, it tends to return to the equilibrium state. For instance, an egg can be made to stand still on one of its ends but such a position is an unstable equilibrium state. A system can have a multiplicity of equilibrium states, some stable, others unstable. In some scientific contexts, the concept is represented in mathematical terms, which greatly clarifies its meaning and its relationships to other concepts (e.g. 'state of system', comparative statics, dynamics). In what follows, the emphasis will be on a conception of 'general equilibrium', first in economic theory and then, more generally, in social theory.

In classical economics the idea of equilibrium was still only intuitive, associated with the impact of Adam **Smith**'s pioneering ideas. Analysts used the metaphor of the invisible hand that leads the competitive economy to an equilibrium state in which resources are efficiently allocated. In the neoclassical phase of economic theory, as in the 'scissors' consisting of intersecting supply and demand curves, the notion of equilibrium was specified in terms of the determination of a price that cleared the market. Mathematical functions and graphs yield a more mathematical treatment of equilibrium. This is partial equilibrium analysis, so called because it treats a single market in isolation from its environment of other, related markets. When a system of interdependent markets is treated, the economist refers to this as general equilibrium analysis. In both types of analysis, the behaviour of the economic actors is assumed to be rational.

In the standard type of general equilibrium theory, there are two populations of units, firms and households, and two types of markets, commodity markets and labour markets. In the aggregate, the behaviour of various firms generates the supply side of each commodity market, while the need for labour on the part of firms generates the demand side of each labour market. Similarly, the offer of services on the part of members of households generates the supply side of each labour market and their consumption behaviour generates the demand side of the commodities markets. An equilibrium state in such a complex system corresponds to a society with efficient markets both in terms of labour and commodities.

Much of sociological theory, both in its classical and its contemporary phases, has been characterized by attempts to generalize the economic approach to human behaviour and human society. The economist-turned-sociologist Vilfredo **Pareto** in his major work *Mind and Society* ([1916]1935) attempted to treat sociology as a kind of generalization of economics, favouring the construction of abstract models of social systems and employing the equilibrium concept – without, however, the mathematical rigour of neoclassical economic theory.

Talcott **Parsons**, also trained in economics, aimed to create a general social theory through a synthesis of core ideas drawn from the economic theorist Marshall and the three sociological writers whose theories he analysed, **Weber**, **Durkheim** and Pareto. In doing so, his conceptual discussion in *The Structure of Social Action* (1937) employed the equilibrium concept, as in 'the sociologistic theorem' that states that a necessary (but not sufficient) condition for a stable social equilibrium state of a social system is that the actors share a common value system. For instance, treating a social movement as a social action system, the theorem claims that shared values are necessary for a movement to form and persist but they are not sufficient (as indicated by the **free rider** problem). Although Parsons did not repudiate the rationality assumption of economic theory, he regarded it as scope-restricted to instrumental action at best and argued, following Weber and Pareto, that general social theory requires a model of human action that includes non-rational elements.

In Parsons' later functionalist type of theorizing, the treatment of equilibrium is conducted at a macro level. In *Economy and Society* (1956), Parsons and Smelser do not cite or discuss general equilibrium theory in economics as such. But their theoretical framework can be interpreted as treating it as a kind of partial equilibrium in its own right from the standpoint of the society as a complex system of functional subsystems, only one of which is the economy. For definiteness, Parsons employs a model with three other such systems in addition to the **economy**. The general equilibrium system discussed earlier in which there are two types of markets is embedded in this model. Firms are units in the economy while households are units in the 'fiduciary system' (that reproduces commitments to the common value system via socialization). The system of interdependent economic markets analysed in general equilibrium theory now corresponds to what Parsons calls 'double interchange'. It follows that there are five other such double interchanges, one for each pair of societal subsystems. Thus, a form of general social equilibrium analysis is defined in such a way as to capture the economist's general equilibrium theory as a special case.

As pointed out above, Parsons' form of general social equilibrium theory lacks both a formal representation and a clearly specified model of the behaviour of actors, which would generalize the rational choice model that provides the micro-foundation of general equilibrium theory in economics. As a consequence, the ideas lack the crispness of specification of assumptions and the derivation of logical consequences (theorems) that characterize the models constructed by economic theorists.

The theoretical programme of James S. **Coleman** set out in *Foundations of Social Theory* (1990) can be interpreted as an effort to overcome this dual deficiency in Parsons' general social equilibrium theory. The key theoretical strategy is to create a *formal* generalization of the economic theory that includes the retention of the rational choice principle of behaviour. The resulting theory is stated more abstractly so that the economic content is only one instantiation of it. For instance, households and firms are instances of *actors* while commodities and labour services are instances of *resources*. Two relations between these entities that generalize the economic instance are defined: each actor has some amount of *control* over each resource (generalizing

ownership) and each actor has some degree of *interest* in each resource (yielding preferences). The *power* of each actor is defined as the sum over all the resources controlled by the actor, where each resource is weighted by its exchange value in general social equilibrium. This generalizes the concept of wealth in economic theory. In turn, the *value* of a resource is a sum over all interest parameters, each weighted by the power of the actor with that level of interest. Coleman shows how an equilibrium state of the social action system arises as actors engage in the exchange of resources that they have as initial endowments.

A very important point arises here concerning the meaning of equilibrium in relation to the economics and sociology. 'When applied to markets, equilibrium denotes a situation in which, in the aggregate, buyers and sellers are satisfied with the current combination of prices and quantities bought or sold, and so are *under no incentive to change their present actions*' (Pearce 1986: 129, italics added). In a nutshell, this is a meaning of equilibrium that pervades economic thought: 'no incentive to change their present actions'. The same idea pervades game theoretic and related models that employ what is called the Nash equilibrium concept.

In sociology, George C. Homans (1958) employed a similar idea in his early paper on generalized exchange equilibrium in a small group context and this may have been one source of Coleman's move in this direction. Note how the conception of equilibrium reflects the specifically *action* system context. It is a meaning of equilibrium that flows directly out of the representation of actors as trying to do the best they can under the circumstances, i.e. as rational. No other type of theory in social science yields such an intuitively clear meaning of equilibrium. When economic theory is generalized, so long as it remains within the action framework, the study of equilibrium will retain this intuitively appealing meaning. The problem, of course, is that many social theorists, like Parsons, favour a theory of action that incorporates non-rational elements.

In short, the general social equilibrium theory that arises has four primitive concepts (actors, resources, control, interests) and two defined concepts, power and value. From this abstract social theory, Coleman can derive a social equilibrium, a state in which no actor has an incentive to change action. A social equilibrium state is associated with a notion of *social efficiency*, another generalization of the economic theory of general equilibrium. In addition, the theory is 'structurally extended' beyond the template derived from economics by introducing barriers to exchange, indivisible goods and other such factors.

This discussion has been limited to two major efforts by sociologists to produce a theory of general social equilibrium. Each theory has certain strengths but also some weak aspects. The functionalist theory is more clearly articulated to elements of culture and personality in a way that is not true of the more abstract rational choice theory. The latter has a deductive structure that is missing from the functionalist theory. One possibility for future efforts in the theory of general social equilibrium would be to envision and attempt to implement some sort of synthesis of the two approaches so as to retain their strengths and eliminate their weaknesses (Fararo 1993).

References and further reading

Fararo, Thomas J. (1993) 'General Social Equilibrium: Toward Theoretical Synthesis', *Sociological Theory*, 11: 291–313.

Homans, George C. (1958) 'Social Behavior as Exchange', *American Journal of Sociology*, 63: 597–606.

Pearce, David W. (ed.) (1986) *The MIT Dictionary of Modern Economics*, third edition, Cambridge, MA: MIT Press.

THOMAS J. FARARO

ETHNIC ECONOMY

The ethnic economy concept may be defined differently by social scientists. In layman's eye, however, it often refers to small-scaled economic activities conducted by ethnic or immigrant group members who are in marginal social positions of the mainstream society or are considered outsiders to the society's dominant group. Ethnic entrepreneurs often carry images of petty traders, merchants, dealers, shopkeepers and even pedlars and hucksters, and engage in such industries or businesses as restaurants, sweatshops, laundries, greengrocers, liquor stores, nail salons, newsstands, swap meets, taxicabs and so on. Indeed, few would think of Computer Associates International (a large public firm specialized in computer technology based in New York) and Watson Pharmaceuticals (a large public firm based in Los Angeles) as *ethnic* businesses and their founders, Charles B. Wang, an immigrant from China, and Allen Chao, an immigrant from Taiwan, as *ethnic* entrepreneurs. These immigrant or ethnic minority members appear to have successfully shed their ethnic distinctiveness and have incorporated their businesses into the core of the mainstream economy.

Ethnic economies have occupied a visible place in capitalist economies for a long time and have not reduced its significance in the wake of post-industrial economic developments. For example, in 1977, there were 561,395 minority-owned firms, 19 per cent with paid employees, yielding gross sales receipts of $26.4 billion, in the United States. Among these minority-owned, 42 per cent were black-owned, 39 per cent Hispanic-owned, and 19 per cent Asian-owned (US Bureau of the Census 1980). These figures changed drastically in twenty years, with Asian and Hispanic businesses growing at unprecedented rates. As of 1997, the number of minority-owned businesses rose to 3,039,033, a 441 per cent growth, with gross sales receipts of $591.3

billion. Among them, 40 per cent were Hispanic-owned, 30 per cent Asian-owned, and 27 per cent black-owned. Asian-owned firms grew at the fastest rate, increasing 768 per cent (from 105,158 in 1977 to 912,960) and had the largest gross sales receipts, at $306.9 billion; Hispanic-owned firms increased 447 per cent (from 219,255 in 1977 to 1,199,896) and had gross sales receipts of $186.2 billion; and black-owned firms increased 256 per cent (from 231,203 in 1977 to 823,4990 and had gross sales receipts of $71.2 billion. These figures indicate that there are approximately one co-ethnic-owned firm for every eleven Asians, one for every twenty-nine Hispanics, and one for every forty-two blacks in the United States (US Bureau of the Census 2001).

The growth of contemporary entrepreneurial activities among ethnic and immigrant groups has produced desirable mobility outcomes for group members. Scholarly research over the past few decades has developed, challenged, and revised many theories on the ethnic economy aiming at providing a fuller account of the phenomenon. This essay briefly revisits some major concepts and the controversies that have lingered around them and highlights the implications of ethnic entrepreneurship for social mobility.

Conceptualizing the ethnic economy

Entrepreneurs are simultaneously owners and managers or operators of their own businesses, including the self-employed (Aldrich and Waldinger, 1990). Ethnic entrepreneurs are those business owners whose group membership is tied to a common cultural heritage or origin and is known to out-group members as having such traits. Most importantly, ethnic entrepreneurs are intrinsically intertwined in particular social structures in which individual behaviour, social relations and economic transactions are constrained.

Existing research in this area has been vigorous while producing much controversy. Central to the controversy are theoretical debates on how ethnic economies should be conceptualized – in terms of the 'ethnic' or 'enclave' economy – and whether 'non-mainstream' economy activities provides a viable path to social mobility among disadvantaged group members. The sociologists Edna Bonacich, John Modell and Ivan Light are among the first to theoretically develop the ethnic economy concept and empirically test it with case studies. The ethnic economy is broadly conceptualized to include any immigrant or ethnic group's self-employed, employers and co-ethnic employees (Bonacich and Modell, 1980; Light 1972, 1979, 1984). The concept encompasses several major phenomena of ethnic economies, namely, middleman-minority entrepreneurship, ethnic niching and the enclave economy.

Middleman-minority entrepreneurship refers to the entrepreneurial activities that trade between a society's elite and the masses. Historically, middleman-minority entrepreneurs were sojourners, interested in making a quick profit from their portable and liquefiable businesses and then reinvesting their money elsewhere, often implying a return home. So they most commonly established business niches in poor minority neighbourhoods or immigrant ghettos in urban areas deserted by mainstream retail and service industries or by business owners of a society's dominant group. But in recent years, they have been found to open up businesses in affluent urban neighbourhoods and middle-class suburbs and show up in the both secondary and primary sectors of the host society's mainstream economy. The theory of middleman minorities explains why certain ethnic minorities have a higher propensity than others to engage in trade and commerce (Bonacich 1973).

Ethnic niching refers to special places, or economic specializations, in the labour market into which ethnic group members are channelled. Roger Waldinger operationalizes a niche as 'an industry, employing at least one thousand people, in which a group's representation is at least 150 per cent of its share of total employment' (Waldinger 1996: 95). According to Waldinger, three important features characterize an ethnic niche in addition to industrial or occupational clustering. First, an ethnic niche sets boundaries between in-group and out-group members, regardless of the ethnicity of owners and/or managers. Ethnic network ties serve as basic mechanism not only for sorting out workers into areas of concentration but also for maintaining a status quo. Second, heightened group identity among workers in a niche, for example, creates pressure for owners or managers to recognize the group's position relative to members of other groups. Such group pressures can produce easy access to jobs in the niche as well as more favourable treatment for group members. The implications are that ethnics employed in niches may do better than their co-ethnics in niches with low ethnic density and that niche employment may offer co-ethnics rewards comparable to those enjoyed by members of the dominant group with similar qualifications. Third, ethnic niching is a dynamic process, structured along the horizontal and vertical dimensions of specialization and rank. Not all niches are equal: some niches are more desirable, yielding better rewards and upward mobility opportunities than others. And not all niches are competitive: some niches have a greater tendency to overlap with other groups and thus a greater potential for intense inter-group competition than others while others are non-competitive. As is so defined, an ethnic niche can also be found in the public sector as in the case of African Americans.

The enclave economy is distinct from the other two phenomena in that it has a geographic dimension, referring to the concentration of ethnic businesses in an ethnically identifiable enclave bounded by both co-ethnicity and location. I will come back to this concept shortly.

It appears that the ethnic economy is an umbrella concept. Light and his colleagues have even pushed it to a higher level of generality (Gold and Light, 2000; Light and Gold 2000; Light and Rosenstein, 1995; Light et al. 1994). There are two key components in their reconceptualized ethnic economy: one is the ethnic-owned component, referring to an ethnic group's maintenance of 'a controlling ownership stake' as well as its co-ethnic labour force including unpaid family labour; and the other is the 'ethnic-controlled' component, whereby co-ethnic employment networks arise to channel co-ethnics into non-co-ethnic firms and even in the public sector in the general economy (Light and Karageorgis 1994: 648). The ethnic economy concept, with its dual aspects of co-ethnic ownership and employment networks, is thus a neutral designation for every enterprise that is either owned, or supervised, or staffed by racial/ethnic minority group members regardless of size, type and locational clustering. It is also agnostic about the intensity of ethnicity, neither requiring nor assuming 'an ethnic cultural ambience within the firm or among sellers and buyers' (Light and Karageorgis 1994: 649).

In sum, '[e]very middleman minority has an ethnic economy, but every ethnic economy does not betoken a middleman minority' (Light and Karageorgis 1994: 648). Similarly, every ethnic or immigrant group has an ethnic economy but only some has an ethnic enclave economy. Under this conception, the groups that are known to have higher than average rates of self-employment, such as the Jews, Japanese, Koreans, Chinese, Iranians and Cubans, have their respective ethnic economies; the groups that are known to have low self-employment rates but have control over recruitment networks in certain industries in non-co-ethnic firms and even in the public sector, such as blacks, Mexicans and Salvadorans, would also have their own ethnic economies. Such conception allows for two types of analyses: one is to account for variations in mobility outcomes among ethnic group members who create employment opportunities for themselves and their co-ethnic workers, and the other is to account for variations in the level of economic integration of group members who enter the general economy via co-ethnic employment networks. This conception also facilitates the comparison of mobility and economic integration of immigrant and ethnic minorities in different societal contexts. Moreover, it creates flexibility in operationalization, especially when using various sources of secondary data. For example, the ethnic economy is operationalized by either co-ethnicity of owners and co-workers or co-ethnicity of supervisors and co-workers. It can also be measured by industrial or occupational clustering.

The ethnic economy is considered an effective strategy for the disadvantaged to cope with employment discrimination in the host economy. Studies have show that the ethnic economy yields direct earnings benefits for the self-employed and for their co-ethnic employees despite relatively low wages as many workers in the ethnic economy face unemployment as their only other option. However, research has also yielded opposite findings – lack of benefit or lack of mobility opportunities – depending on how the ethnic economy is defined.

The enclave economy: a special case and an alternative conceptualization

The ethnic economy concept takes into consideration not simply job creation by ethnic entrepreneurs, but also access to existing jobs in the general economy by ethnic networks. It captures the dynamics of various forms of ethnic economic activ-

ities. However, when a concept is too broad, it risks weakening its explanatory power because substantive internal differences are so large. For example, co-ethnic businesses concentrated in an ethnic neighbourhood are very different from those dispersed in other non-coethnic neighbourhoods serving primarily non-coethnics, a situation more appropriately referred to as the middleman minority. Similarly, businesses that are owned and staffed by co-ethnics are very different from those that are owned by non-coethnics but staffed by supervisors and co-workers of the same ethnicity, a situation more appropriately referred to as ethnic industrial or occupational niching. Also, because of its generality, the ethnic economy concept is susceptible to invalid measurement. For example, middleman-minority and ethnic niching are two qualitatively different phenomena. When collapsing into one single measure, the findings are likely to be inconsistent and even misleading.

Furthermore, by extending ethnic economies beyond bounded ethnicity, the ethnic economy concept is decontextualized. Such a broad concept may be useful when examining individual outcomes, such as earnings outcomes or employment opportunities of the disadvantaged; but it is not of much use when examining processes of community building and social capital formation in poor neighbourhoods. For example, Korean entrepreneurs running businesses as middleman minorities in non-Korean neighbourhoods do not tend to invest in the social structures of the neighbourhoods they are serving, because they are not bounded by social relationships with local residents and because their businesses serve a singular function – trade or commerce – with little attachment to any significant social structures there. Quite the contrary: Korean entrepreneurs running businesses in Koreatown have a 'stake' in the community and are intertwined in multiple social relationships with co-ethnic residents and multiple ethnic social structures there. Thus, it is the variations in social **embeddedness** of ethnic economic activities, rather than the ethnic economy per se, that explain why social organization in neighbourhoods vary by ethnicity, why neighbourhood-based resources vary from neighbourhoods to neighbourhoods, and why access to neighbourhood-based resources vary from one group to another.

The enclave economy is a special case of the ethnic economy as well as an alternative conceptualization. The sociologist Alejandro Portes and his colleagues are among the first to develop this concept, drawing heavily on the dual labour market theory (Averitt 1968; Portes and Bach 1985; Wilson and Portes 1980). In Portes' conceptualization, the enclave economy has a structural and a cultural component. As a distinct ethnic economy, it consists of a wide range of economic activities that exceed the limits of small-scale trade and commerce and traditional mom-and-pop stores. It encompasses some of the businesses that offer competitive wages, job security and mobility prospects, resembling, to a varying degree, the key characteristics of the primary sector of the mainstream economy.

Unlike the ethnic economy concept that includes almost every business under an ethnic umbrella, the enclave economy has several distinct characters. First, the group that is involved has a sizeable entrepreneurial class. The presence of co-ethnic entrepreneurship in an ethnic community serves to shield the community from unemployment and social disorganization. Second, economic activities are not exclusively commercial, but include productive activities directed towards the general consumer market rather than towards co-ethnic or other ethnic minority consumer markets. Third, the clustering of ethnic businesses maintains a high level of diversity including economic activities that are in direct competition with those in the general economy such as professional services

and production and are not just limited to those niches shunned by natives. Fourth, co-ethnicity epitomizes the relationships between owners and workers and between patrons and clients to a lesser extent. Last and perhaps most importantly, the enclave economy requires a physical concentration within an ethnically identifiable neighbourhood with a minimum level of institutional completeness. That is, economic activities in the enclave are embedded in the ethnic community's social structure and are mediated by various ethnic institutions, such as merchant associations, chambers of commerce, informal credit associations, family/hometown associations, the ethnic media and other ethnic civic organizations. Especially in their early stages of development, ethnic businesses have a need for proximity to a co-ethnic clientele which they initially serve, a need for proximity to ethnic resources, including access to credit, information and other sources of support, and a need for ethnic labour supplies.

The enclave economy also has an integrated cultural component. Economic activities are governed by bounded solidarity and enforceable trust – mechanisms of support and control necessary for economic life in the community and for reinforcement of **norms and values** and sanctioning of socially disapproved behaviour (Portes and Zhou 1992). Relationships between co-ethnic owners and workers, as well as customers, generally transcend a contractual monetary bond and are based on a commonly accepted norm of reciprocity. My study of the garment workers in New York's Chinatown offers a concrete example. Immigrant Chinese women with little English and few job skills often find working in Chinatown a better option despite low wages, because the enclave enables them to fulfil their multiple roles more effectively as wage-earners, wives and mothers. In Chinatown, jobs are easier to find, working hours are more flexible, employers are more tolerant to children's presence, and private child care within close walking distance of work is more accessible and affordable (Zhou 1992). Such reciprocity is absent in the general secondary labour market, where co-ethnicity is not typical of owner–worker relationships, because there is no common ethnic community to enforce this norm. Likewise, ethnic employers who run businesses in non-coethnic neighbourhoods or employ non-coethnic workers can effectively evade the social control of the ethnicity community while causing unintended consequences of heavier social costs such as interethnic conflicts.

In the past, enclave entrepreneurs have typically operated businesses in socially isolated but self-sustaining immigrant enclaves where their own ethnic group members dominated and where they were themselves intertwined in an intricate system of ethnic social networks. At present times, as many ethnic enclaves evolve into multi-ethnic neighbourhoods and new ones develop in affluent middle-class suburbs, those who run businesses in a particular location may simultaneously play double roles – as middleman-minority and as enclave entrepreneurs. For example, a Chinese immigrant who runs a fast food takeout restaurant in a Latino neighbourhood is a middleman-minority entrepreneur, but he would become an enclave entrepreneur when he comes back to his other fast food takeout in Chinatown. In contrast, a Korean immigrant opens up his business in Los Angeles' Koreatown may be an enclave entrepreneur to his Korean co-ethnics who live there, but to the Latino residents who make up the majority of that neighbourhood he may just be one of many middleman-minority entrepreneurs.

In sum, the enclave economy is not any type of ethnic economies. The adjective 'enclave' is not just there to invoke the concept of 'ethnic economy' but refers to a specific phenomenon, one that is bounded by an identifiable ethnic community and embedded in a system of community-based co-ethnic social relations and observable institutions. The central argument of the enclave economy is that the enclave is more than a shelter for the disadvantaged who are forced to take on either self-employment or marginal wage work in small business but has the potential to develop a distinct structure of economic opportunities as an effective alternative path to group social mobility.

Conclusion: ethnic economies as a means to social mobility

Each of the concepts that I have just discussed approaches ethnic economic activities from different angles and captures some core aspects of the phenomenon. Despite disagreement on how ethnic economies should be best conceptualized, there is a strong consensus that these activities create opportunities for upward social mobility of ethnic group members who are disadvantaged by either minority status or immigrant status, or both. Ample empirical evidence has shown support for five major arguments about mobility outcomes. First, ethnic entrepreneurship creates job opportunities for the self-employed as well as for ethnic workers who would otherwise be excluded. Second, ethnic entrepreneurship relieves sources of potential competition with native-born workers by generating new employment opportunities rather than taking up jobs, or crowding out natives, in the existing labour market. Third, ethnic entrepreneurship not only fosters entrepreneurial spirit and sets up role models among co-ethnics but also trains prospective entrepreneurs. Fourth, ethnic entrepreneurship affects the economic prospects of group members as well as out-group members. Fifth, and perhaps most controversial, there is a significant earnings advantage of self-employment over other forms of employment net other observable human capital and demographic characteristics. Research regarding earnings benefits has yielded mixed results.

Much of the controversies are rooted in varied ways of conceptualization. In my view, the analytical distinctions of different type of ethnic economies are sociologically meaningful as economic transactions of ethnic entrepreneurs are conditioned by different social structures and social relations. For instance, the stone face of a Korean shop owner in a black neighbourhood is often misinterpreted as hostile and even racist, and the effect of that facial expression can be exacerbated by a lack of English proficiency, but the same face is taken matter-of-factly in Koreatown by co-ethnics, and a common language often eases potential anxiety. For investigating the social processes of community building and social capital formation among disadvantaged ethnic or immigrant minorities, the enclave economy concept is superior to the ethnic economy concept. It allows for a more focused and detailed examination of varied social contexts and their effects on mobility outcomes, hence enabling the unpacking of the ethnicity black box. A fuller account of the variations in social contexts can offer a better explanation of why the ethnicity variable has a positive effect on outcome for some groups but a negative effect for others in the same model. It also allows for the development of a theoretically conception to understand more precisely how social resources are produced and reproduced in the ethnic community.

References and further reading

Aldrich, Howard E. and Waldinger, Roger (1990) 'Ethnicity and Entrepreneurship', *Annual Review of Sociology*, 16: 111–35.

Averitt, Robert T. (1968) *The Dual Economy*, New York: Norton.

Bonacich, Edna (1973) 'A Theory of Middleman Minorities', *American Sociological Review*, 38: 583–94.

Bonacich, Edna and Modell, John (1980) *The Economic Basis of Ethnic Solidarity*, Berkeley, CA: University of California Press.

Gold, Steven J. and Light, Ivan (2000) 'Ethnic Economies and Social Policy', *Research in Social Movement, Conflict and Change*, 22: 165–91.

Light, Ivan (1972) *Ethnic Enterprise in America: Business and Welfare among Chinese, Japanese, and Blacks*, Berkeley, CA: University of California Press.

—— (1979) 'Disadvantaged Minorities in Self-Employment', *International Journal of Comparative Sociology*, 20: 31–45.

—— (1984) 'Immigrant and Ethnic Enterprise in North America', *Racial and Ethnic Studies*, 7(2): 195–216.

Light, Ivan and Gold, Steven J. (2000) *Ethnic Economies*, San Diego, CA: Academic Press.

Light, Ivan and Karageorgis, Stavros (1994) 'The Ethnic Economy', in Neil J. Smelser and Richard Swedberg (eds), *The Handbook of Economic Sociology*, Princeton, NJ: Princeton University Press, pp. 647–69.

Light, Ivan and Rosenstein, Carolyn (1995) 'Why Entrepreneurs Still Matter', in Ivan Light and Carolyn Rosenstein (eds), *Race, Ethnicity, and Entrepreneurship in Urban America*, New York: Aldine de Gruyter, pp. 1–29.

Light, Ivan, Sabagh, Georges, Bozorgnehr, Mehdi and Der-Martirosian, Claudia (1994) 'Beyond the Ethnic Enclave Economy', *Social Problems*, 41: 65–80.

Portes, Alejandro and Bach, Robert L. (1985) *The Latin Journey: Cuban and Mexican Immigrants in the United States*, Berkeley, CA: University of California Press.

Portes, Alejandro and Zhou, Min (1992) 'Gaining the Upper Hand: Economic Mobility among Immigrant and Domestic Minorities', *Ethnic and Racial Studies*, 15: 491–522.

US Bureau of the Census (1980) *1977 Survey of Minority-Owned Business Enterprises*. Washington, DC: US Government Printing Office.

—— (2001) *1997 Economic Census: Survey of Minority-Owned Business Enterprises*, Washington, DC: US Government Printing Office.

Waldinger, Roger (1996) *Still the Promised City? African-American and New Immigrants in Post-industrial New York*, Cambridge, MA: Harvard University Press.

Wilson, Kenneth and Portes, Alejandro (1980). 'Immigrant Enclaves: An Analysis of the Labor Market Experience of Cubans in Miami', *American Journal of Sociology*, 86: 295–319.

Zhou, Min (1992) *Chinatown: The Socioeconomic Potential of an Urban Enclave*, Philadelphia: Temple University Press.

MIN ZHOU

ETHNOGRAPHY

See: economic anthropology

EUROPEAN MARKET

European Union (EU) – the impressive emergence in the decades since World War II of a virtually borderless internal market across the states of Europe – is a subject largely overlooked by economic sociology. This is curious given that the EU is both a huge natural experiment in the political construction of a market, and the most highly evolved example of an international governance structure in the global economy today. If we define **globalization** as the emergence of increasingly integrated markets over ever larger territories, the European market represents the fullest example of regional economic integration, unified around specific rules, a range of novel political and economic institutions, and an extraordinarily high degree of regional economic interdependence.

Despite all this, sociological contributions to the study of the EU have been thin on the ground. Major economic sociologists have been absent from a growing body of academic work led by scholars in law, political science, IR, economics and history. Their work charts the evolution of an ever more integrated European market, out of post-war reconstruction and a variety of intra-European free-trade arrangements, through various stages of customs union, single (common) market and a single currency. Today, the European market is the single largest in the world, with comparable GDP and a larger population than the USA. A predominantly economic rationale lies behind the process of European Union, but it has accrued diffuse political power

through the supranational institutions of the European Commission (the EU's main administrative body) and European Parliament, which are central to policy-making in conjunction with the member-state governments. Its laws are enforced by the European Court of Justice, which administers a body of international law which holds supremacy over the national law of all member-states. The merger of what were otherwise fragmented national markets has created opportunities for European industries to develop and compete on the global stage, as well as the liberalization of European economies (Rodríguez-Pose 2002), but it has been notably slower in areas of non-economic political cooperation, such as defence and foreign policy. The most impressive data concerns the marked shift of member-states' national economies from external to internal markets in the post-war decades, a fact that underlines the pragmatic economic rationale reinforcing a project initially rooted in the idealism of a generation determined to avoid the disastrous military conflicts of the recent past. Beyond the economy, European Union can also be read (controversially) as a vast social experiment in postnational society.

Macro-dimensions of European Union

Within a global economy marked by unprecedented levels of economic interpenetration, and a political context in which there have been several attempts to institutionalize international instruments of economic governance (WTO, NAFTA, World Bank, etc.), the European Union stands out as the most advanced such example. The initial treaties relating the coal and steel sectors first bound a small group of six European nation-states devastated by World War II. It was expanded in the landmark Treaty of Rome of 1957, to incorporate all sectors of the economy, and instituting the 'four freedoms' of a nascent European common market: freedom of movement of goods, capital, services and persons. Membership of the Union expanded from six to fifteen by the mid 1990s, following early expansion of powers during the boom years of the 1950s and 1960s, a long period of stagnation in the 1970s, and a new push towards the completion of a single market, with further treaties in 1986, 1992 and 1997, and the introduction of a single currency (the euro) in 2001. The progressive deepening of the Union, across all kinds of policy sectors, has also set the stage for the declaration of a constitution, and the long-negotiated enlargement of the EU to the countries of the former Soviet bloc in 2004. The economic unit has expanded to twenty-five nation-states, a population of nearly half a billion, and about 20 per cent of the world's import and export trade. Moreover, the European market represents a form of capitalism quite distinct from American and Asian varieties of neo-liberalism (see **capitalism, varieties of**).

The theory of regional economic integration developed by Balassa (1961) best captures the economic logic behind the expansionary widening and deepening of a territorially integrated market, and why political actors might enter into supranational economic agreements that ostensibly reduce their control ('sovereignty') over the economy. The theory accounts for degrees of economic integration, moving from a free-trade area, which removes internal tariffs and barriers, through a customs union, which harmonizes external trade and sets up internal regulatory institutions. A common market completes this process with the removal of all non-tariff barriers to free factor mobility (i.e. allowing complete free movement of labour and business across borders), and finally, economic union, in which members harmonize their economic policies into a monetary union, creating a common currency. Steps towards political union go beyond the final degree of economic integration. On this, Scharpf (1986) points to a

canonical distinction between the negative integration of the early days, in which the market-building functions of European Union were driven principally by deregulation and the removal of barriers to trade, and latter stages of positive integration, in which member-states and EU institutions have more self-consciously worried about creating new instruments of integration – such as coordinated policy, harmonized directives, law, constitution, currency and so on. The elaboration of rules of trade and exchange through European law, and the highly progressive tendency of the EU to intervene to protect workers, firms and consumers from the operation of an 'unfettered' market, all point towards the positive construction of a socialized economy distinct on the global stage.

Establishing a typology of stages of integration is an easier task than establishing a theoretically satisfactory explanation for the actual historical forms that European Union has taken. Debates on European integration have centred on archetypal IR preoccupations about realism versus idealism in the motivations of national political actors. They ask why such actors would commit themselves to such an extensive and binding range of international agreements and institutions. Liberal intergovernmentalists have stressed the ultimately convergent national interests behind this construction, while neo-functionalists and institutionalists point towards the unpredicted or unexpected dynamics in integration. Neo-functionalists argue that 'spillover' occurs of certain functions of economic cooperation into non-economic areas, while institutionalists underline the emergence of effective autonomous actors in both European law and the European Commission and its orbit in Brussels (home of the main European institutions). The alleged *sui generis* nature of the European project, and hence its non-generalizability to other regional integration projects, has led to much characteristically post-hoc theorizing in the literature, which is often better on commentary than explanation.

Despite this fertile territory for macrosociology in general, and any economic sociologist interested in the global political economy in particular, sociologists have not contributed to the literature on the common market and European Union. Only one major figure, Neil Fligstein, has attempted to apply the theoretical tools and sensibilities of contemporary economic sociology to this important empirical topic. In a series of both solo and co-authored papers (1996, 2003), he has argued for a sociological reading of evidence about the EU's emergence, that emphasizes the deliberate political construction of this market: in terms of property rights, governance structures, rules of exchange and conceptions of control. Fligstein thereby portrays the European Union in classic economic sociology terms, looking at how markets emerge, stabilize and are transformed. This kind of theory offers a great advance on many of the specialist Europeanist accounts. It portrays the emergence of a European market as parallel to the history of economic organization that could be found in any of the major European nations, and which he, in particular, has traced in the USA; only here it is a process taking place at supra-national level, and absent of many of the features of national political integration that gave this task nation-centred form and coherence in the past.

In the case of the EU, the emergence of complex regulation and a body of European law, has enabled a market based on the free movement of goods, capital, services and persons comparable only to the federal United States of America. The EU has removed trade barriers and tariffs; eased competition across national borders over products and services that used to be protected and/or subsidized nationally; developed rules of exchange about common standards, insurance, liability, ownership across borders, as well as health and safety

standards, and standards of employment practices and workers' rights; and promoted a convergence on more open, liberal ideas of economy, the liberalizing of business practices, and the transformation of economic organizations along less hierarchical lines. To these ends, the Commission has been able to successfully mobilize state and business actors in specific sectors (especially export-oriented industries, such as food, transportation, pharmaceuticals, chemicals) where competition and more open markets were desirable, and ground this in a cultural project legitimized by both political idealism about a unified Europe, and the neo-liberal agenda of multinational corporations. Fligstein substantiates the corporate influence on the EU, charting the highly proactive lobbying and consultation role of major multinational business interests from the early decades onwards, and tracing the impact of various business ideas on deregulation, standardization and modernization. Much of the building of a European market has indeed been about the opening of Europe for global firms, enabling the implantation of American and Japanese firms. Yet this self-evident facet of globalization is complicated by the fact that many of the EU's stated positions on corporate takeovers, **social rights**, the environment, privacy, and so on, differ sharply from the norms promoted by successive US administrations. Notably, too, the EU has not got directly involved in the reform of national European welfare systems – that remain the bedrock of European economic exceptionalism – except indirectly through rules on government debt and spending imposed on those who signed up to the single currency.

These aspects point towards the somewhat paradoxical outcomes of European Union. Despite its remarkable supranational dimensions, European Union has not so much undermined member-state sovereignty as reinforced it, by enabling a far greater degree of collective national control over the economy than might be the case in a wholly US-dominated global economy. At the same time, the building of the internal market has both reinforced certain 'neo-liberal' conceptions of the market, and yet has also broken many of these rules, via substantial welfare redistribution at a supra-national level – through its policy on regional development, and the common agricultural policy, for example.

Micro-dimensions in the sociology of Europe

Another fertile area for research on European integration would be the move towards disaggregating sociologically (and spatially) the measurements of the actual transactions and flows that (presumably) constitute the macroeconomic data about, say, trade or GDP by which by which market integration is typically reckoned. Beyond postmodern speculation, there has been precious little exploration of the sociology of **globalization** in this sense, and the lack of sociology of European Union is even more striking. Some fine ethnography of cross-national **labour markets** and other forms of mobility have been made, and economic geographers have produced interesting work on regional development, spatial inequalities across the Union, and commodity chains within Europe. But, as ever, the sociological vision of these inherently transnational topics seems hampered by the discipline's tendencies to methodological nationalism.

The micro-level challenge is to put a human face on the economic flows and transactions behind macro-data sets. Studies of European identity are one way this has been operationalized (often using data produced to this end by the European institutions), but new qualitative research is needed on the novel social/spatial trajectories experienced by a new generation of European citizens. These economic actors are now living out their lives in a different conceptual space: pursuing studies, careers, consumption patterns (as tourists, retirees, cross-border shoppers), and perhaps even relationships and family lives across national borders, that would have once defined the norms and outer limits of their social worlds and social mobility. A remarkable growth in personal mobility across borders has accompanied the increased business interactions. Both phenomena underline how individuals are willing to personally transcend the still often sharp sense of national distinction which most European societies continue to preserve, indeed embellish, with their domestic media, and cultural or political preoccupations. Yet it is less clear that such mobility is leading to more migration (i.e. movement plus resettlement). In fact, the long-term stability of Europe's internal migration figures, and only equivocal evidence on increased intermarriage and naturalization, suggest the opposite. The localistic, regionally rooted notions of 'home' and 'belonging' held by most Europeans point to a longer-standing historical reluctance to move among Europeans. This rootedness perhaps lies behind the stable affluence of the numerous mid-sized cities that make up the central swathe of the wealthiest parts of Europe, from northern Italy to the North Sea. In this respect, not much has changed in the economic geography of the continent since the Renaissance.

What has changed has been the populations of lower-class workers who provide the dynamo for these economies. The majority of West European nations now have predominantly middle-class populations, and a disappearing working class, less willing than ever to take menial, lower-end employment. Moreover, European's high rates of female workforce participation have also created many openings in the service sector. The solution as elsewhere has been immigration, but the migrants on the labour market have changed. Whereas once positions would have been filled with workers from the south of Europe, these flows have largely dried up, as economic differences between north and south evened out, and more generous welfare regimes were extended to even the poorest parts of the Mediterranean Europe. Migrants in Europe, nowadays, are typically non-European immigrants, from all over the planet, many of which are undocumented (see **ethnic economy**). Europe's wealth, in fact, rests now on an informal economic dynamo, and structural reliance on the black economy in agriculture, manufacturing and service sectors, comparable to the extraordinarily open North American economy. This is the case even in countries such as Denmark or the Netherlands with far more ostensibly regulated social regimes – although there is an economic clash here that is leading to great political tensions. The demographics of migration are also linked to the chronic aging of the European population, and the apparent long-term non-sustainability of its post-war welfare regimes, that are perhaps the most distinctive claim there is to there being a distinctive version of 'European modernity' (Therborn 1995). It is not yet clear how enlargement will affect all this, although it seems most likely that the likes of Poland, Hungary, Lithuania, or even Bulgaria and Romania, will follow the formerly backward economies of previous accession states like Portugal, Greece, Spain and Ireland, into the ranks of the wealthier in Europe.

These dimensions of the European economy point to real concerns about the compatibility of elements of neo-liberal dynamism and openness, to the somewhat distinct forms of capitalism found historically, albeit unevenly, across all of Europe. As it is, Europe's own exceptionalisms – its welfarist conception of capitalism, commitment to redistribution, high levels of social benefits, corporatist union–government relations, conceptions of participatory citizenship, and the rejection of extremes of income inequality that have been settled on in the USA and elsewhere in the developing world – continue to offer a reminder of the diversity of forms of capitalism possible in the world today.

References and further reading

Balassa, Bela (1961) *The Theory of Economic Integration*, London: Allen and Unwin.

Fligstein, Neil and Mara-Drita, Iona (1996) 'How to Make a Market: Reflections on the Attempt to Create a Single Market in the European Union', *American Journal of Sociology*, 102(1): 1–33.

—— (2003) 'The Political and Economic Sociology of International Economic Arrangements', in Neil Smelser and Richard Swedberg (eds), *Handbook of Economic Sociology*, second edition, Princeton, NJ: Princeton University Press.

Rodríguez-Pose, Andres (2002) *The European Union: Economy, Society, and Polity*, Oxford: Oxford University Press.

Scharpf, Fritz (1986) 'Negative and Positive Integration in the Political Economy of European Welfare States', in Gary Marks, Fritz Scharpf, Philippe Schmitter and Wolfgang Streeck (eds), *Governance in the European Union*, Sage: London.

Therborn, Göran (1995) *European Modernity and Beyond: The Trajectory of European Societies, 1945–2000*, Thousand Oaks, CA: Sage.

ADRIAN FAVELL

EVOLUTION

See: evolutionary economics

EVOLUTIONARY ECONOMICS

The term 'evolutionary economics' is currently applied to a wide variety of approaches within the subject. Several main uses of the phrase can be identified:

- More than a century ago Thorstein **Veblen** (1899, 1919) argued for an 'evolutionary' and 'post-Darwinian' economics. 'Old' institutionalists frequently describe their approach as 'evolutionary economics', as exemplified in the titles of the (USA) Association for Evolutionary Economics and the European Association for Evolutionary Political Economy.
- Joseph **Schumpeter** (1942) famously described capitalist development as an

'evolutionary process'. Work influenced by Schumpeter is also described as 'evolutionary economics' as evidenced by the title of the *Journal of Evolutionary Economics*, published by the International Joseph Schumpeter Association.

- The approach of the Austrian school of economists is often described as 'evolutionary', as portrayed in Carl Menger's theory of the evolution of money and other institutions, and by the extensive use of an evolutionary metaphor from biology in the later works of Friedrich Hayek, especially in relation to his concept of spontaneous order.

- There is a related tradition in evolutionary economics that emphasizes processes of spontaneous self-organization and the emergence of novelty and complexity (Foster 1997; Witt, 1997), particularly taking inspiration from Prigogine and Stengers (1984), Kauffman (1993) and others.

- In addition, the economics of assorted writers such as Adam **Smith**, Karl **Marx**, Alfred **Marshall** and others is also sometimes described as 'evolutionary' in character.

- Evolutionary **game theory** is a prominent recent development in mathematical economics and has been inspired by related mathematical work in theoretical biology.

- The word 'evolutionary' is sometimes attached to 'complexity theory', such as developed by the Santa Fe Institute in the United States. This involves chaos theory, replicator dynamics, genetic algorithms, genetic programming and various types of computer simulation.

Today, the use of the word 'evolutionary' in economics seems very much to be a matter of fashion. However, in the social sciences as a whole, the term 'evolution' fell out of favour between the two world wars. The word 'evolution' became more widespread in economics after the publication of Richard Nelson and Sidney Winter's classic (1982) work *An Evolutionary Theory of Economic Change*. By the late 1980s, work in 'evolutionary economics' had been broadened and accelerated by the growth in both America and Europe of various institutional, Austrian and Schumpeterian approaches to economics.

There have been notable and fruitful applications of these ideas, particularly in the sphere of **technological change**. Evolutionary economics has already established an impressive research programme and has had a major impact on economic policy, particularly in the areas of technology policy, corporate strategy and national systems of innovation (Dosi *et al.* 1988).

Nevertheless, there is still no established consensus on what 'evolutionary economics' might mean. A curious aspect of 'evolutionary economics' is that many people use the term as if it required little further explanation and that everyone knows what it means. It is a serious mistake to take the meaning of the concept of economic evolution for granted. It is important both to sort out the different meanings of the term and to consider carefully its conceptual history.

Novelty and change

Several authors have proposed that variety and its replenishment through novelty and creativity should be central themes of 'evolutionary economics'. Accordingly, Ulrich Witt (1992: 3) writes: 'for a proper notion of socio-economic evolution, an appreciation of the crucial role of novelty, its emergence, and its dissemination, is indispensable'. Likewise, Nicolai Foss (1994) argues forcefully for an ontological characterization of the divergence between evolutionary and neoclassical thinking in economics. He argues that evolutionary economics of the type developed by Dosi, Nelson, Winter, Witt and others is concerned with 'the transformation of already existing structures and the emergence and possible spread of novelties' (p. 21).

However, there is less detailed exploration of the nature and source of novelty. One possible avenue is to use insights from chaos theory and complexity theory. Chaos theory suggests that even if events in the world are determined, many are unpredictable and seemingly indeterministic. Even if novelty is caused, it may appear as entirely spontaneous and free. We can never know for sure if any event is caused or uncaused, but chaos theory suggests that we have to treat non-linear systems as if they were indeterministic. The chaos literature blurs the boundary between randomness and determinism.

Even if chaos theory makes indeterminacy deterministic, it does so by undermining the possibility of a reductionist or full causal explanation and by instating the concept of emergence (Hodgson 2004). A property can be said to be emergent if there is a sense by which it depends upon lower-level elements in a system, but is not predictable in terms of those elements, or reducible to them. Emergent properties are not capable of full, reductive explanation in terms of other elements. There is a long tradition of linking emergent properties with evolution (Blitz 1992).

In his studies of **economic development**, Schumpeter repeatedly emphasized the sources of change from within. Likewise, Witt defines evolution as 'the transformation of a system over time through endogenously generated change' (Witt 1991: 87, emphasis removed). Similarly, Esben Sloth Andersen (1994: 1) regards an 'evolving' as a 'self-transforming' economic system. However, it is difficult to find a justification for this one-sided emphasis on endogenous change. In biology, neither individuals nor species nor even ecosystems are entirely 'self-transforming'. Evolution

takes place within *open* systems involving *both* exogenous and endogenous change.

Evolutionary economists that emphasize endogenous change also typically emphasize self-organization, or the spontaneous development of order (Foster 1997; Witt 1997). Here the central idea is that endogenous interactions can give rise to novelty and complex organization. This is an important insight, and there is much to learn from this literature, but it neglects the additional processes of creativity through interaction with the environment and selection pressure.

Instead of the one-sided emphasis on endogenous change in evolutionary economics, it would be better if more use was made of the concept of an 'open system'. Ludwig von Bertalanffy first made the distinction between an open and a closed system in 1950. The term has been taken up and emphasized by institutional economists such as K. William Kapp (1976). National economic systems export and import, and even the world economic system extrudes waste and is dependent on energy flows from the sun.

The significance of novelty and creativity in an evolutionary framework is that they are a major source of variety within evolving socio-economic systems (Andersen 1994; Metcalfe 1988; Nelson 1991). By such novelties and innovations, variety is replenished. Ongoing variety means that a population of entities cannot be represented by a few distinct characteristics that represent their essence. Such 'typological essentialism' is rejected in favour of 'population thinking'. In population thinking, species are described in terms of a distribution of characteristics. Whereas in typological thinking novelty and variation are classificatory nuisances, in population thinking they are of supreme interest because it is precisely the variety of the system that provides fuel for the evolutionary process (Foss 1994; Hodgson 1993; Mayr 1985).

Darwinism and evolutionary economics

The relationship between evolutionary economics and Darwinism has yet to be adequately resolved. But it should be made clear at the outset that the word 'evolution' was used long before Charles Darwin, when it was applied systematically to natural phenomena by the German biologist Albrecht von Haller in 1744. There is nothing in the etymology or usage of the words 'evolution' or 'evolutionary' that necessarily connotes Darwinism. 'Evolution' is a term of wide meaning.

The question is then raised of the relationship between Darwinism and evolutionary economics (Hodgson 2002). Clearly, the former is a subset of the latter. But to what extent is Darwinism evident in the evolutionary economics literature? The most explicit and sustained use of Darwinism is in the writings of Veblen (1899, 1919). Subsequently, Darwinian analogies involving mechanisms of variation, selection and replication were used rarely, until the appearance of Nelson and Winter (1982).

A significant feature of these milestone cases is that, while Darwinian analogies are used, there is no attempt to reduce economic evolution to biological terms. Darwinian principles are instead applied to *socio-economic* units, such as *institutions* (Veblen) or *routines* (Nelson and Winter). These anti-reductionist approaches contrast with attempts elsewhere to reduce economic explanations to biological terms (Becker 1976; Hirshleifer 1977; Tullock 1979).

Instead of biological reductionism, what is suggested here is the possibility that Darwinian principles themselves may have a wider application than to biology alone. Darwin (1859: 422–3; 1871, vol. 1: 59–61, 106) himself proposed that they might apply to the evolution of language, as well as to biological organisms. This possibility of a 'generalized' or 'universal' Darwinism (which does not necessarily involve biological reductionism) has been recognized periodically by a range of authors (Bagehot 1872; Ritchie 1896; Veblen 1899, 1919; Campbell 1965; Dawkins 1983).

Exploration of this possibility has only just begun among evolutionary economists, and many of the details remain to be clarified (Hodgson 2003, 2004). What must first be elucidated, if this work is to begin to bear fruit, is the very meaning of the generalized concepts of selection and replication in the socio-economic domain, as well as the detailed mechanisms involved. While generalized Darwinian principles may apply, it is clear that the detailed mechanisms in society and nature are very different. Darwinism thus provides a meta-theoretical framework, within which specific, detailed explanations must be placed (Blute 1997; Hodgson 2001). Darwinism, as such, cannot provide all the answers.

References and further reading

Andersen, Esben Sloth (1994) *Evolutionary Economics: Post-Schumpeterian Contributions*, Pinter: London.

Bagehot, Walter (1872) *Physics and Politics, or, Thoughts on the Application of the Principles of "Natural Selection" and "Inheritance" to Political Society*, London: Henry King.

Becker, Gary S. (1976) 'Altruism, Egoism, and Genetic Fitness: Economics and Sociobiology', *Journal of Economic Literature*, 14(2), December: 817–26.

Blitz, David (1992) *Emergent Evolution: Qualitative Novelty and the Levels of Reality*, Dordrecht: Kluwer.

Blute, Marion (1997) 'History Versus Science: The Evolutionary Solution', *Canadian Journal of Sociology*, 22(3): 345–64.

Campbell, Donald T. (1965) 'Variation, Selection and Retention in Sociocultural Evolution', in H. R. Barringer, G. I. Blanksten and R. W. Mack (eds), *Social Change in Developing Areas: A Reinterpretation of Evolutionary Theory*, Cambridge, MA: Schenkman, pp. 19–49. Reprinted (1969) in *General Systems*, 14: 69–85.

Darwin, Charles R. (1859) *On the Origin of Species by Means of Natural Selection, or the Preservation of Favoured Races in the Struggle for Life*, first edition, London: John Murray.

—— (1871) *The Descent of Man, and Selection in Relation to Sex*, first edition, two volumes, London: John Murray, and New York: Hill.

Dawkins, Richard (1983) 'Universal Darwinism', in D. S. Bendall (ed.), *Evolution from Molecules to Man*, Cambridge: Cambridge University Press, pp. 403–25.

Dosi, Giovanni, Freeman, Christopher, Nelson, Richard, Silverberg, Gerald and Soete, Luc L. G. (eds) (1988) *Technical Change and Economic Theory*, London: Pinter.

Foss, Nicolai Juul (1994) 'Realism and Evolutionary Economics', *Journal of Social and Evolutionary Systems*, 17(1): 21–40.

Foster, John (1997) 'The Analytical Foundations of Evolutionary Economics: From Biological Analogy to Economic Self-Organisation', *Structural Change and Economic Dynamics*, 8: 427–51.

Hirshleifer, Jack (1977) 'Economics from a Biological Viewpoint', *Journal of Law and Economics*, 20(1), April: 1–52.

Hodgson, Geoffrey M. (1993) *Economics and Evolution: Bringing Life Back into Economics*, Cambridge, UK and Ann Arbor, MI: Polity Press and University of Michigan Press.

—— (2001) *How Economics Forgot History: The Problem of Historical Specificity in Social Science*, London and New York: Routledge.

—— (2002) 'Darwinism in Economics: From Analogy to Ontology', *Journal of Evolutionary Economics*, 12(2), June: 259–81.

—— (2003) 'The Mystery of the Routine: The Darwinian Destiny of *An Evolutionary Theory of Economic Change*', *Revue Economique*, 54(2), March: 355–84.

—— (2004) *The Evolution of Institutional Economics: Agency, Structure and Darwinism in American Institutionalism*, London and New York: Routledge.

Kapp, K. William (1976) 'The Nature and Significance of Institutional Economics', *Kyklos*, 29(2): 209–32.

Kauffman, Stuart A. (1993) *The Origins of Order: Self-Organization and Selection in Evolution*, Oxford and New York: Oxford University Press.

Mayr, Ernst (1985) 'How Biology Differs from the Physical Sciences', in David J. Depew and Bruce H. Weber (eds), *Evolution at a Crossroads: The New Biology and the New Philosophy of Science*, Cambridge, MA: MIT Press, pp. 43–63.

Metcalfe, J. Stanley (1988) 'Evolution and Economic Change', in Aubrey Silberston (ed.), *Technology and Economic Progress*, Basingstoke, UK: Macmillan, pp. 54–85.

Nelson, Richard R. (1991) 'Why Do Firms Differ, and How Does it Matter?' *Strategic Management Journal*, 12, Special Issue, Winter: 61–74.

Nelson, Richard R. and Winter, Sidney G. (1982) *An Evolutionary Theory of Economic Change*, Cambridge, MA: Harvard University Press.

Prigogine, Ilya and Stengers, Isabelle (1984) *Order Out of Chaos: Man's New Dialogue with Nature*, London: Heinemann.

Ritchie, David G. (1896) 'Social Evolution', *International Journal of Ethics*, 6(2): 165–81. Reprinted in David G. Ritchie, *Studies in Political and Social Ethics*, London and New York: Swan Sonnenschein and Macmillan, 1902.

Schumpeter, Joseph A. (1942) *Capitalism, Socialism and Democracy*, first edition, London: George Allen and Unwin.

Tullock, Gordon (1979) 'Sociobiology and Economics', *Atlantic Economic Journal*, September: 1–10.

Veblen, Thorstein B. (1899) *The Theory of the Leisure Class: An Economic Study in the Evolution of Institutions*, New York: Macmillan.

—— (1919) *The Place of Science in Modern Civilisation and Other Essays*, New York: Huebsch.

Witt, Ulrich (1991) 'Reflections on the Present State of Evolutionary Economic Theory', in Geoffrey M. Hodgson and Ernesto Screpanti (eds), *Rethinking Economics: Markets, Technology and Economic Evolution*, Aldershot, UK: Edward Elgar, pp. 83–102.

—— (ed.) (1992) *Explaining Process and Change: Approaches to Evolutionary Economics*, Ann Arbor, MI: University of Michigan Press.

—— (1997) 'Self-Organisation and Economics – What is New?' *Structural Change and Economic Dynamics*, 8: 489–507.

GEOFFREY M. HODGSON

EXCHANGE

Superficially, exchange is a simple notion: A gives something to B, and in return B gives something else to A. For the purposes of developing theories and conducting research in the social and behavioural sciences, however, we require a working definition that is both more general and more precise: an exchange is a contingent transfer of valued objects and/or valued acts between actors. Some theories treat exchange as a cause, others treat it as an effect. Theories of the latter type are concerned with factors that affect the way exchanges transpire, and what actors actually gain or lose in exchanges. Theories that treat exchange as a causal factor may consider the impact of exchanges on the individual actors involved, for example, on their accumulated wealth, emotional reactions or subsequent exchanges. Such theories also may examine the impact of exchange on the involved actors' relationship with each other, on the larger social structure, or on any of a variety of other phenomena of interest.

The precise meaning of the foregoing definition of exchange hinges upon the meanings of its terms. Therefore some of those terms warrant further discussion. Actors are the parties involved in exchange and may be individual people or collectivities such as groups or organizations. An object is any identifiable entity, and an act is any identifiable behaviour. For the purposes of exchange, actors are interested in a relatively small subset of all possible objects and acts: those that are of some **value** in the exchange context. A positively valued object or act is one that an actor desires to receive, possess and/or control, thereby providing benefits to the actor. A negatively valued object or act is one that an actor desires to relinquish or avoid, thus incurring costs for the actor when not relinquished or avoided.

The specific kinds of valued objects or acts under consideration will depend upon the purposes of the theorist or researcher, the context of the exchange, the kinds of actors participating in the exchange, and other factors. For example, a micro-economist may be interested solely in the interpersonal exchange of money for goods; a criminologist in the exchange of prison terms for criminal acts; a social psychologist in the exchange of praise for role-appropriate behaviours in a task setting. In every case, there is a sense in which objects and acts are transferred between actors. That is, there is a physical or symbolic movement of objects from one actor to another, or mutual enactments of behaviours among parties to the exchange.

Finally, to say that exchange is contingent means that transfers of objects or acts are not independent of one another. Rather, they must be linked (or at least perceived to be linked) such that, at minimum, one transfer occurs in anticipation of another, in response to another, or both.

Elements, processes and contexts of exchange

Different theoretical perspectives attend to different elements, processes and contexts of exchange. Early sociologists addressed fundamental problems of social order: for example, 'What is the "glue" that binds together all of society's components?' Some early solutions to these problems began with neoclassical economic assumptions, e.g. that rational actors with full information about their options seek to maximize their own profits by exchanging in competitive markets. In so doing, the argument goes, actors become bound and organized through systems of mutually beneficial exchanges. (See **rationality** and **utilitarianism**.)

Subsequent alterations and elaborations have been developed for every one of the basic exchange elements. Furthermore, many aspects of exchange processes and exchange contexts have been dissected and examined in different ways by theorists and researchers in various academic disciplines. The paragraphs to follow illustrate just some of the different ways that exchange has been conceptualized as a consequence of employing different variations on the original economic themes. (See **exchange theory** for further discussion of particular theoretical approaches.)

Actors

Properties of the actors participating in an exchange profoundly affect how the exchange transpires. The social and behavioural sciences have devoted a great deal of attention to identifying and exploring these properties. Among exchange approaches that focus exclusively on individuals, some offer assumptions about what values they possess and how they translate these values into specific preferences and actions, and about whether or not actors can explore different strategies to improve their outcomes. Some offer assumptions about how actors use their insights about future exchanges, how they learn from past exchanges, whether they may seek alternative exchange partners, and whether they have the capacity to threaten and administer punishment as well as to offer reward. Different conceptualizations of actors have ranged from 'minimalist' to 'omniscient'. For example, some approaches assume only that actors know what they want and can make greater-than/less-than comparisons among options. Others assume that actors possess full and accurate information about their own and others' values and holdings and employ all of this information in choosing their courses of action. Most exchange approaches lie somewhere between these two extremes.

In addition to assumptions about actors' information-processing capacities, conceptualizations also have varied along an abstract–concrete dimension. At one extreme, for example, some mathematical approaches such as **game theory** build actor models that are highly abstract and artificial. Such models may provide insight into what choices would maximize outcomes in a given situation. In contrast, an anthropologist may develop a unique, detailed and realistic description of members of one particular culture and their methods of exchanging with one another for food, clothing and shelter. Each approach is useful for certain purposes.

Operant psychology inspired some early and seminal exchange theories in social psychology. Its principles assume that organisms repeat behaviours that are associated with rewards from any source, as long as they continue to be associated with those behaviours. The behaviours diminish if they go unrewarded or if satiation begins to set in, and behaviours that are associated with punishment are avoided. Social psychologists attempted to generalize these principles by treating actors as sources for one another's rewards and punishments.

Other approaches focused on actors' motivations to fulfil psychological needs and desires, rather than assuming automatic responding to rewards and punishments or a single-minded pursuit of material interests. For example, actors may exchange in order to establish relationships that they find emotionally satisfying. In larger contexts, the interpersonal bonds thus formed may be viewed as the social glue that integrates disparate actors into cohesive groups, and disparate groups into unitary societies. At least implicitly – and often explicitly – attention to the larger system entails taking into account indirect exchanges. That is, whatever A gives to B in exchange most likely came to A from prior exchanges with others. (See **kula exchange**.) Analyses of patterns of the flow of resources through networks of actors offers a perspective on group solidarity that is not available when focusing on individuals or pairs.

Game theory may be characterized by the assumption that actors are strategic and their exchange outcomes are highly contingent upon mutual acts and responses. Actors' strategies guide their responses to the acts of others, especially when others' strategies and the rules of the game produce contingencies that are complex and uncertain.

In the examples above, exchanging actors usually are individual people. Exchange approaches also have applied when the actors are sets of individuals acting as one. Groups-as-actors may emerge as a consequence of exchange processes, or may be defined *a priori* in terms of their differential access to valued objects such as wealth or education. Stratification theorists, including Karl **Marx** with his analysis of relationships between capitalist and proletarian classes, have found it useful to collapse multiple individuals into groups that act as individual agents in inter-class exchange relationships. Peter Blau provides another theory that accommodated groups as parties in exchange. He claimed that groups differentiate according to their relative power to shift the terms of exchange, generating forces towards both group solidarity and group conflict. Blau also identified institutionalization as a property of macro-level exchange structures that simply does not exist at the level of human dyads.

Objects and acts

Just as the properties of actors vary across different exchange approaches, so do the objects and acts that are the media of exchange. Early anthropological work focused on the fundamental objects needed for survival. They soon expanded their purview, however, in recognition that every culture identifies its unique array of significant objects and acts, thereby imbuing them with exchange value. Cattle, chickens, corn, sons and daughters, trinkets, favours, services, even symbolic gestures may be exchanged for real or symbolic profits.

As implied in the previous section, different assumptions about actors may entail different exchange media. With their focus on utilitarian actors, economic theories usually regard money and goods as the objects of exchange, and labour as a fundamental act. Microeconomics looks at choices made by individual actors with regard to these interests; macroeconomics applies at the level of organizations, markets or institutions.

Sociological approaches have a wider latitude than economics when it comes to objects and acts of potential value to exchange parties. Georg **Simmel**'s philosophy of money is an early example of a sociological take on economic activities. It attempted, among other things, to explain how money affects social relations and how social interaction affects economic exchange. Later theories such as George Homans' recognized that, even in the work setting, valued rewards may go beyond money, taking the form of words or other symbolic gestures that become sought after in their own right. James **Coleman** theorized about 'rights to act' as a valued exchange commodity. For example, rights to act are exchanged when voters elect candidates into office, thereby granting authority to those who will ply their expertise on the voters' behalf.

Contingencies and contexts

Actors and objects in exchange transactions may be the most obvious targets for theory and research, but arguably they are no more important than the forces that establish and govern exchanges, and the contexts that imbue them with meaning and purpose for those involved. If we could enter into an exchange relationship taking nothing for granted, the underlying richness and complexity of the situation at once would become apparent. In most cases, participants import a great deal of shared, tacit knowledge: who the actors are, what they want, what they do not want, how to communicate appropriately, and so on. They also may have **beliefs** about their relative abilities as negotiators, their social identities and their entitlements. They may guide or limit their actions according to rules mandated by law or by social convention. For example, distributive justice theory and research emphasizes the application of norms such as reciprocity, need, equity or equality to the outcomes of exchange; procedural justice theory considers how actors evaluate the **fairness** of the procedures that lead up to allocation of outcomes in exchange settings. In the absence of shared knowledge and expectations on the part of all participating actors, completing mutually beneficial exchanges becomes a chancier prospect.

Exchange theorists have taken into account the effects of prior and ongoing exchange relationships, the timing of exchanges in multi-actor settings, and the independent effects stemming from the pattern of exchange relationships that may exist among members of a group or network. For instance, some exchange relationships are characterized by repeated, explicit negotiations while other times negotiations are implicit, perhaps signalled by symbolic gestures or prior outcomes. Such gestures and outcomes may be meaningless outside of the unique histories of particular exchange contexts. Such histories may include the evolution of generalized exchange cycles in which actors give valued objects to one set of others, and receive their benefits from a different set of others. In short, exchange can be regarded as a simple phenomenon for some theoretical purposes. For other purposes, however, it is essential to build in additional factors as needed to capture natural complexities and extend our understanding of the phenomenon.

References and further reading

Cook, Karen S. (2000) 'Social Exchange Theory', in E. Borgatta and R. J. V. Montgomery (eds), *Encyclopedia of Sociology*, revised edition, New York: Macmillan, pp. 2669–76.

Turner, Jonathan H. (2003) *The Structure of Sociological Theory*, seventh edition, Belmont, CA: Wadsworth.

Zafirovski, Milan (2001) *Exchange, Action and Social Structure: Elements of Economic Sociology*, Westport, CT: Greenwood Press.

BARRY MARKOVSKY

EXCHANGE THEORY

Exchange theory is a multidisciplinary collection of ideas and explanations pertaining to the nature, causes and consequences of transactions among individuals and collectivities. It is characterized by many different approaches and focal issues, thus it is a misnomer to refer to it as a singular 'theory'. It is more useful to speak of an exchange perspective that incorporates a variety of formulations ranging from nebulous and undeveloped conjectures to rigorous axiomatic theories. With few exceptions, distinct theories within the tradition have not benefited from programmes of sustained, rigorous empirical testing. As a consequence, when older exchange theories diminish in their direct impact on current research, usually it is not because they have been falsified or improved upon, but rather it is because their adherents have passed away, retired or moved on to other matters.

The paragraphs that follow review some of the basic ideas that are common to the various formulations, and a selection of the more frequently cited lines of work. First, however, a useful working definition: an exchange is a contingent transfer of valued objects and/or valued acts between actors. (See **exchange** for elaborations of the various parts of this definition.) Implicitly or explicitly, all exchange theories employ some version of this conceptualization. Interpretations of its terms vary widely in the exchange literature, however, depending upon theoretical and empirical purposes. Valued objects and acts range from basic life necessities to symbolic gestures. Examples of actors include specific individuals at particular times and places, or computer-simulated groups with vast numbers of interacting members. The contingencies may be the simple rules of a trading game in an experimental setting, or a complex array of statutes and norms governing economic exchanges between industrialized nations.

Exchange theories also vary insofar as the particular assumptions they employ in their explanations. For instance, some presume that decisions and choices are guided by some kind of learning process that takes into account prior actions and outcomes. Others assume **rationality** – that actors calculate the future costs, benefits and contingencies associated with different options. Despite their differences, however, exchange theories also share certain themes or presuppositions. For instance, they presume that exchanges cannot occur unless each party has control over something of value to the other. Furthermore, what one stands to gain from exchanging with a particular partner must exceed what one stands to gain from exchanging with alternative partners or from not exchanging at all.

Beyond such basic notions, over time the various lines of exchange theoretic work have not intersected a great deal, probably to the detriment of the field. Theories progress more rapidly when we theorists can identify competing predictions that may be adjudicated by empirical testing. More concerted efforts may then be focused on only the most promising theories. This does not happen often in the area of exchange theory, and so most exchange formulations have developed little beyond their original statements.

Theories

The roots of the modern exchange perspective in sociology can be traced to economics, anthropology and behavioural psychology. Economic approaches generally adopted a utilitarian stance, assuming that actors pursue their personal interests when buying, selling and trading in markets (see **markets, sociology of**; **utilitarianism**). For the most part, anthropologists focused on the survival and solidarity functions of exchange, for instance **gift** exchange and the fulfilment of social obligations. Early psychological approaches highlighted sti-

mulus–response relationships that form in social contexts, applying theories developed for animal behaviour.

Karl **Marx** and Georg **Simmel** were among several theorists to bring exchange-theoretic ideas to the fore in sociology, primarily out of dissatisfaction with approaches used in other disciplines. Marx's dialectical conflict theory, for example, examined the relationship between capitalists and the working class: Working-class labour is exchanged for material rewards from the capitalist class. Each group depends upon the other, but the balance of power shifts toward the capitalists when there is a surplus of available labour. Marx emphasized that the working class can shift the balance towards its own advantage through various forms of **collective action** including the formation of labour organizations and, if necessary, full-scale revolution.

Marx's analysis was aimed at the dynamics of capitalist–worker exchange. Simmel responded via his 1907 book *The Philosophy of Money*, offering a theory that was in certain respects both more focused and more general than Marx's. To address how money affects society, Simmel identified factors that lead people into social contact with one another. He assumed that individuals have unique constellations of **value**s, determined jointly by the particular objects they want or need to have, and by how available they are. Greater need and greater scarcity create greater value, and a concomitant increase in the likelihood that the actor will search for satisfaction by establishing exchange relationships with those from whom those valued objects are obtainable. The cost of attaching high value to another's resources is the relinquishment of power. This disadvantage is mitigated if one's resources are highly fungible – that is, in a form that is of potential use or value to many others. Money satisfies this criterion in modern societies, hence it is an important source of power in its own right. Simmel further argued that tension and conflict always are latent in exchange relations because actors have an interest in mis-representing their needs and their resource holdings in order to shift the balance of power towards their own advantage. Monetary forms of exchange thus are a natural outgrowth of the evolution of more complex social systems, but also play a role in transforming social relationships and society more generally.

In the 1960s the exchange perspective began to come into its own as a viable, widely adopted approach to understanding broad areas of social behaviour. With their 1959 book *The Social Psychology of Groups*, John W. Thibaut and Harold H. Kelley used reinforcement theory as the founda-tion for decades of work on exchange and interdependence in small groups. They offered an explicit model for behaviour that was applicable in a wide array of social interaction contexts. The model showed how the rewards and costs stemming from different behavioural options are con-tingent not only on the actor's behavioural choice, but also on choices made by others. Thibaut and Kelley assumed that actors discover these contingencies through the process of exploring their behavioural options, and that over time they compare their outcomes with those that they believe are obtainable from alternative relationships. The authors further identified particular reward/cost contingencies that would result in one actor having the power to control the behaviours and/or outcomes of another.

At about the same time that Thibaut and Kelley's work became prominent, Harvard social psychologist George C. Homans made his own mark on exchange theory. His approach – most clearly articulated in the 1974 book *Social Behavior: Its Elementary Forms* (first published in 1961) – also pre-dicated social phenomena on explicit psy-chological principles. His strategy was to ground the utilitarian approach of eco-nomics in the behaviourist approach from psychology, providing a theoretical basis for both economic and non-economic exchange. A set of propositions linked action to prior rewards for similar actions, to the anticipated value and likelihood of the rewards, and to the absence of satiation for the rewards. Other propositions asserted that positive versus negative emotions, and approving versus aggressive behaviour, fol-low from the satisfaction or non-satisfaction of reward expectations. In addition to using these propositions to explain individual and dyadic exchange behaviour, Homans used them to interpret the macro-level behaviour of social groups and societies: for example, how groups make decisions about what public goods to offer in order to satisfy the needs of their individual members.

In the 1964 book *Exchange and Power in Social Life*, Peter M. Blau began with an approach similar to Homans'. Blau empha-sized the roles of reciprocity and **fairness** norms in building long-term exchange relationships in larger social systems and institutional settings. At the same time, he recognized the potential for conflicts and strains that can emerge when actors attempt to balance multiple relationships. Violations of reciprocity and fair exchange norms create such conflicts, as do feelings of deprivation among the disadvantaged. As the disadvantaged become increasingly cognizant of their condition, their group solidarity increases and opposition to the more advantaged and powerful rises. Blau identified similarities between micro and macro exchange, but also recognized that there are forces at work in exchanges between groups, organizations, classes, institutions, etc., which differ from those affecting exchange at the interpersonal level. For instance, macro exchange may involve historical circumstances, regulations and social structures that transcend all of the individuals involved in the sense that none of the participants were present when the exchange structures and rules were estab-lished. Rather than being fuelled by inter-personal attraction or self-interest, macro-exchange systems require shared values across group members and the political regulation of organizations within the larger system.

Richard M. Emerson is best known for his power-dependence theory, another approach that employs the principles of operant psychology to explain micro-level exchange. The theory assumes that an actor has power over another to the extent that the other depends on the actor for valued rewards; that power is unbalanced when one actor is more dependent than the other; and that disadvantaged actors can restore balance by reducing the extent to which they value rewards controlled by others, or by finding alternative exchange sources. Emerson further argued that these principles apply as well to groups in exchange relationships as they do to individuals. The real innovation of Emerson's work, however, was his analysis of how power phenomena are affected by interaction in larger networks. Most prior work on exchange applied only to dyadic relations. Emerson and his colleagues were the first to develop and test a mathematical model that showed how the shape of an exchange network could affect power and exchange outcomes. Some predictions and findings were counter-intuitive, as when the most centrally located network positions turned out to be disadvantaged in certain networks under certain contingencies.

Similar to several other exchange theories with a basis in utilitarian principles, David Willer's 'elementary theory' is distinguished by its explicit and rigorous approach to structural and macro-level phenomena, and by its extensive body of systematic empirical evidence. In 1981 his book *Networks, Exchange and Coercion* offered theoretical models for individual choices, for simple exchange systems, and for structures of economic exchange and coercion at the macro level. It reported on supportive research from laboratory experiments, comparative-historical analysis, institutional analysis and ethnographic case studies. Willer's 1987 book, *Theory and the Experimental Investigation of Social Structures*, reported a series of laboratory experiments investigating structural conditions for exchange and coercion. They demonstrated how power differences are produced by mobility in exchange hierarchies, and by exclusion processes in exchange structures. In 1999, *Network Exchange Theory* reviewed and extended fifteen years of progress in the exchange network branch of the elementary theory. The network exchange theory provided the most parsimonious and thoroughly tested model for predicting, among other things, resource distributions for each position in exchange networks of any shape and size.

Game theory offers a toolbox of mathematical solutions that are used to determine optimal behavioural strategies under a wide range of multi-actor contingencies. It has diverse applications in a number of disciplines, including exchange in dyads and networks. Some of these models of have been applied to social exchange contexts, with varying degrees of success. Applications to exchange networks have not fared so well as alternative approaches when the goal has been to predict long-run exchange profits based on the network structure. More promising are iterative applications of game theoretic models whereby, given a set of ongoing exchange relationships, contingencies are analysed in step-by-step fashion, in essence simulating the series of games expected to confront each actor in the dyad or network at each point in time.

James S. **Coleman**'s *Foundations of Social Theory* was one of the more ambitious attempts to build models of society on utilitarian, micro-exchange premises. Each actor is assumed to control an array of resources, to have interests in an array of resources, and to act so as to maximize the realization of their interests. Most often, claims Coleman, this entails exchanging control over resources or events, or exchanging rights to such control. With a degree of theoretical rigour not present in most other attempts at 'grand theorizing', Coleman extended his basic ideas to address numerous topics such as collective behaviour, norm formation, the modernization of society, authority relations, organizations and families.

Conclusion

This brief review covers the major statements in exchange theory. Absent due to space limitations, however, are critical analyses, evaluations of evidence, or reviews of much recent and ongoing research. As for critical analysis, it may suffice to say that there is no consensus on fundamental assumptions. That is, we cannot yet say whether or under what conditions exchanges are driven by rational calculation, gut feelings, learning from the past, or a variety of other mechanisms that have been suggested. It is laudable that some theories have been extended in order to permit interpretations of macro phenomena, but those theories remain tentative until they have been carefully tested against one another, and until their ostensive underlying processes are supported empirically. Despite such unresolved issues at its core, recent and current research lines show just why the exchange perspective remains vibrant: The range of applications is vast. They include the emotional consequences of exchange, justice evaluations, job turnover, close relationships, family dynamics, political power, organizational, networks, international exchange, and many others.

References and further reading

Cook, Karen S. (2000) 'Social Exchange Theory', in E. Borgatta and R. J. V. Montgomery (eds), *Encyclopedia of Sociology*, revised edition, New York: Macmillan, pp. 2669–76.

Turner, Jonathan H. (2003) *The Structure of Sociological Theory*, seventh edition, Belmont, CA: Wadsworth.

Zafirovski, Milan (2001) *Exchange, Action and Social Structure: Elements of Economic Sociology*, Westport, CT: Greenwood Press.

BARRY MARKOVSKY

EXPLOITATION
See: class, Marx

F

FAIRNESS

The term 'fairness' explicitly refers to fair returns to producers ('fair trade'), but more generally refers to a broad vision of justice in the global economy that stresses sustainable ecosystems and communities, good labour practices, respect for human rights, and universal access to education, health and social services. The United Nations, UNESCO as well as participants in the World Social Forum (Social Watch 2003) embrace this vision; economists such as Amartya Sen have helped to advance and disseminate these ideas; and International Nongovernmental Organizations (INGOs) have worked to implement these practices. Advocating fair practices in global economic transactions is a way of countering the neoliberal orthodoxy that has stressed private ownership, minimum regulations, private ownership and investment, and, more generally, market logic and market mechanisms.

A growing coalition, as especially evident at the UN's Millennium Development Summit, shapes programmatic goals to promote fairness in the global economy, and is also evident in shifts in the policies of the World Bank and International Monetary Fund. These goals stress that people's lives as well as economic activities are highly interdependent and that interdependencies require more in the way of international agreements, multilateral institutions and coalitions around human development goals (United Nations Development Programme, annual). Through its emphasis on the 'Social Compact' the United Nations has created a framework for fairness in the exchanges and transactions involving private goods, along with a conception of fairness in providing public goods (Kaul *et al.* 2003). Critics of neoliberal orthodoxy advocate regulation of markets, protections for emerging economies, social safety nets, taxes on 'hot money' and, more generally, mechanisms that would collectivize the risks that vulnerable populations incur (Blau 2001).

Fairness is also used in a very specific way to refer to 'fair trade', namely direct or largely direct transactions involving producers, sellers and buyers. The most successful transactions of this sort involve products that require few processing steps. Consumers in economically developed nations can buy fair trade products such as coffee, chocolate, honey and handicrafts. Producers and sellers provide certain guarantees including, for example, that production is carried out under conditions that uphold labour and environmental standards and promote community sustainability goals. Fair trade campaigns are expanding to include products that require more complex processing steps and more complex linkages, such as using seeds from indigenous crops rather than those that are genetically engineered. Thus, the practices of localized producers and localized consumers, though remote from one another, become connected, and also mirror emerging practices at macro levels in ways that reinforce fairness.

References and further reading

Blau, J. R. (2001) 'Bringing in Codependence', in J. R. Blau (ed.), *The Blackwell Companion to Sociology*, Malden, MA: Blackwell, pp. 58–70.

Kaul, I., Conceição, P., Goulvein, K. L. and Mendoza, R. U. (2003) *Providing Public Goods: Managing Globalization*, New York: United Nations Development Programme.

Ransom, D. (2001) *The No-Nonsense Guide to Fair Trade*, Oxford: New Internationalist Press.

Sen, A. (1999) *Development as Freedom*, New York: Knopf.

Social Watch (2003) *The Social Impact of Globalization in the World*, Montevideo, Uruguay: The Third World Institute.

UN Development Programme (annual) *Human Development Report*, New York: UNDP.

JUDITH R. BLAU

FAMILY AND ECONOMY See: children and economic life; housework

FASHION, SOCIOLOGY OF

Fashion has not been a major topic for economic sociology. In developed societies, however, where cultural objects become central in production and consumption, fashion must be included into the analysis to understand a large number of markets, and the economy at large.

Fashion as a phenomenon may reach back to the dawn of social life, but became common with the emergence of consumer society. Social scientist showed interest in fashion in the late nineteenth century. A broad sociological definition of fashion is 'being first with the latest'. This means that fashion trends undulate, and that an object, style or activity is popular among a clique of people, and that others view this clique as having the status to set the fashion. Once a phenomenon is too common, it is no longer in fashion. By being viewed as set-ting fashion trends, individuals may secure their status positions, and fashion is in this way linked to social structure. Though fashion initially concerned clothes, this definition reflects the fact that analysis of fashion can and has been made on a vast variety of social objects, and not just *haute couture*. Having said this, clothes are still the main objects of analysis. The sociological approach ultimately grounds the explanation of fashion in social relations and meaning of the objects. Fashion is not identical with fads, which lack a history of undulations, and can be analysed as other processes of diffusion. In addition to the sociological approach to fashion, there is the semiotic approach used by for example art-historians, which sees clothes as text, possible to analyse as language. Finally, there is also anthropological, psychological and economic literature on fashion.

Simmel was the first sociologist to carefully study fashion (1904), and his work constitutes the natural starting point for sociologists approaching the subject. At the time when he wrote, many social scientists saw fashion as the epitome of irrationality. But according to Simmel, fashion is set by the upper class as a means of making distinctions. His treatment of fashion is an example of individualism versus collectivism (the group), and Simmel takes it for granted that fashion is a process that spreads from the upper class to the lower segments of society through adaptation. When fashion diffuses down to the middle class, the upper class has to come up with a new style to uphold the social distinctions. Simmel thinks that this exemplifies the idea of the cyclic change of fashion: There is a fixed need among the people in the upper classes to change their clothing to distinguish themselves from ordinary people. Simmel also states that outside the western hemisphere, customs are stronger and status is fixed by social structure like castes. Much has happened since Simmel wrote on fashion, though the consumer side of fashion still is what occupies most social scientists, being the focus of the sociology of **consumption** literature. Today, the idea to correlate the length of skirts with business cycles, which was common around World War II, is completely outmoded.

Though fashion is a way of displaying difference and a way of study inequality, every individual has some power to affect the current fashion. However, some individuals and groups have more influence than others. To this one must add that subgroups, of cultural or ethnic derivation, may have different reference groups, and that there are local, regional and national variations of fashion. The so-called Cultural Study approach has analysed this. Simmel's idea that fashion mainly is a western phenomenon began to change in the 1970s and many developing countries have since then been included in the logic of fashion. This means that people in many corners of the world take part in the process of affecting, in many cases through production, and being affected by fashion, though the leading European fashion designers dominate.

The production side of fashion is sometimes neglected. Production refers to creation of fashion, designer labels, marketing and similar topics. Relatively few studies have analysed fashion as an important dimension in economic life, despite the fact that the garment industry is one of the largest in the world. Paul Hirsch (1972) developed a framework for analysing products that are not sold for their utility function, but rather for their aesthetic or expressive value. Hirsch shows that industries producing things that are subject to the vagaries of fashion are organized to cope with the uncertainty firms face.

The next step in the development of the scientific knowledge of fashion is made by, among others, Pierre **Bourdieu**, who integrates the consumer and producer sides of fashion. Bourdieu finds that the rate of investment in fashion, both in terms of how one keeps up with fashion by reading fash-

ion magazines, and to what degree one buys clothes through mail order catalogues or in popular stores, is connected to the composition of capital of the individual. This is related to the symbolic value of designer labels. Cultural production, including fashion, is an important aspect in economies of modern and postmodern societies. This means that both the producers and the consumers of objects in many cases must be accounted for in a sociological analysis of fashion (Aspers 2001).

In sum, Simmel's 'trickle down' theory of fashion has step by step been replaced with a model that accounts also for bottom-up effects and for horizontal differentiation; this process has taken place simultaneously with an increased pace of undulations of fashion. Fashion is not merely relevant for the consumption economy, it is also important for generating and recreation of social structure. Finally, it is a social phenomenon that is deeply embedded in the economy, both on the consumption and on the production side.

References and further reading

Aspers, Patrik (2001) *Markets in Fashion, A Phenomenological Approach*, Stockholm: City University Press.

Hirsch, Paul (1972) 'Processing Fads and Fashions: An Organization-Set Analysis of Cultural Industry System', *American Journal of Sociology*, 77: 639–59.

Simmel, Georg (1904/1971) 'Fashion', in Donald Levine (ed.), *Georg Simmel on Individuality and Social Forms*, Chicago: Chicago University Press, pp. 294–323.

PATRIK ASPERS

FIELD See: organizational fields

FINANCIAL MARKETS

Financial markets can be said to lie at the heart of the capitalist system in the sense that they provide much of the capital raised by firms. These markets supply financing for industry, agriculture, home mortgages and government debt. They typically exhibit a large number of buyers and sellers exchanging standardized instruments such as stocks, bonds, futures and options contracts. Since the automation of price quotes by the ticker in the nineteenth century, prices have been transparent to all participants. These characteristics bring financial markets close to the perfectly competitive market idealized in economic theory and make them an exemplar for the process of price determination. Both their central function in capitalism and their similarity to the economic ideal make financial markets an important area of research for economic sociologists.

Financial markets are sociologically different from producer markets such as steel, cars, food and clothing markets in terms of their role structures. In a producer market the seller produces a product for someone who is going to consume it, the buyer. Buyer and seller are separate roles. In most of the activity on financial markets, the buyers are also sellers. This activity occurs in what are called secondary markets. The roles here are those of investors and speculators. Investors are those who buy an instrument, such as a corporate bond, and hold it with the expectation that its value will increase because of underlying economic conditions. They eventually become sellers of that same instrument. Speculators buy expecting a short-term profit and sell as quickly as possible. In the primary market, the roles consist of the original issuer of the instrument, usually a firm or government agency, and the first buyer of the instrument who eventually passes it off into the much larger secondary market. The primary market more closely resembles a production market sociologically and will not be dealt with here (see **production**).

Financial markets are currently undergoing a major redefinition of 'place'. Since at least the end of the seventeenth century, when stock markets were located in coffee houses (Carruthers 1996), financial markets

have been face-to-face affairs. The early New York Stock Exchange met on the street under a buttonwood tree. For most of their subsequent history, financial markets resembled, in one fashion or another, a crowd. The telegraph and telephone allowed external participants to be connected to this crowd (centralized marketplace) from all over the world. Most recently, the computer has obviated the need for a physical marketplace. Trades can be matched in a central computer or traders can become part of a global computer network that operates twenty-four hours a day.

The structure of financial markets

In the economic sub-field of finance, markets are generally understood to consist of autonomous, atomized individuals who engage in the auction of some standardized financial instrument thereby determining its price. While most economists would admit that this is an idealized version of reality, it does, nevertheless, underlie their models. Sociologists tend to be sceptical of idealized models. Our preference for getting as close to empirical reality as possible results in messier, empirically based models of financial markets. Our concern is to understand both how markets work and how they deviate from the idealized model.

Economics and sociology both understand the basic unit of the financial market to be the transaction, the exchange between buyer and seller. When economists model the price determination process, they treat markets as an aggregation of these separate transactions. Sociologists focus on the social relations, culture and institutions within which these transactions are embedded (see **embeddedness**). Baker (1984) examined the network of social relations in which traders at a Chicago options exchange were embedded. He varied two key assumptions from the idealized model. He said that actors are subject to bounded **rationality**, i.e. that they can neither assimilate nor transmit all the information available, and that some actors behave opportunistically. In markets with a large number of actors, these constraints were found to generate differentiated networks of traders. Instead of the market being one large crowd, there were multiple sub-groups present. The consequence was that these large markets had higher price volatility than smaller markets, which is the reverse of what the idealized model would predict.

Another approach to understanding the embeddedness of trades in financial markets was developed by Abolafia (1996). He questioned the assumption that coordination in financial markets was automatic and asocial. He observed that the apparent anarchy in futures pits around the world is really quite structured. Coordination is accomplished through the routinization of transaction. The market is not simply the tumult in the trading pit. Every transaction follows a fixed path from the customer to the Commission House, which actually becomes the principal in the trade, from the Commission House to the pit where buyer and seller meet, and from the pit to the Clearing House where trades are matched and verified, the clearing house assuming responsibility for fulfilment of all contracts. From this perspective, a futures market may be understood as a highly institutionalized sorting, control and governance mechanism. The financial market is not just the crowd of buyers and sellers, but is a set of institutional arrangements for the reproduction of trustworthy and efficient transactions.

As exchange-based trading, such as we might expect to see on the New York Stock Exchange or Chicago Board of Trade, has declined in importance, sociologists have turned their attention to the screen-based networks that are replacing stock and futures exchanges. Knorr Cetina and Bruegger (2002) describe the production of a 'global microstructure' in which a world-wide financial market is enacted without face-to-face interaction. Starting at the level of the dyadic relationship, they show how screens can bring traders into each other's presence. Although these traders are not spatially coordinated, they are coordinated by being members of a community in time. Their connection through computers and their shared orientation to the same market events creates a unique form of social integration, a new form of virtual market structure.

Knowledge and its performance

Michel Callon has observed that 'economics, in the broad sense of the term, performs, shapes, and formats the economy' (1998: 2). This seems to be especially true of financial markets. Ideas and ideologies permeate the financial markets. Charles Smith (1999) studied the ideology of stock market professionals. He identified six interpretive schema that Wall Street natives used to make sense of the price determination process in these markets. Cadres of true believers use fundamentalist, cyclist, efficient markets, and other ideologies to make either speculative or investment decisions. Brokers (salespeople), who are rarely true believers, use the same interpretive schemas to sell the market to their customers. Such schemas are used to warrant the accuracy and predictive validity of their recommendations. The existence of so many models of the price determination process, used so promiscuously by market professionals, suggests both the centrality and limits of knowledge about price trends.

Although current ideas and ideologies in financial markets are transmitted as fact, they often bear closer resemblance to fads and fashions. The socially constructed nature of financial knowledge becomes clear when viewed in an historical perspective. In the eighteenth century, financial markets were still thought of as pernicious gambling dens by the broader public. Alex Preda (2000) shows that over the course of the nineteenth century not only was financial knowledge disseminated through middle-class manuals and journals, but even the word 'market' went from referring to a place to referring to a set of activities, price movements and events. This continuous reframing has made possible the popularization of financial markets. Today's disseminators of financial knowledge have come to include securities analysts who have assumed enormous power in the determination of a firm's identity and a security's success in the market (Zuckerman 1999).

In his study of the automation of the Paris Bourse, Fabian Muniesa (2000) illustrates how economic knowledge is used to perform or format new financial markets. Muniesa describes how market architects developed a call auction algorithm for the daily close of the market. The algorithm was a solution to the problem of manipulation at the close. The algorithm basically freezes the market at a single equilibrium price. Muniesa pointed out that this solution for 'performing price' was not neutral, but rather the result of negotiations over volatility, rationality and transparency and thus linked to networks of people, resources, constraints and interests.

Perhaps the most striking example of the direct application of economics in the creation of a financial market has been the creation of the Chicago Board Options Exchange (CBOE). In their historical analysis of the CBOE, MacKenzie and Millo (2003) illustrate how the Black–Scholes–Merton option pricing model was used by traders to set options prices. The market was literally brought in line with the theory as market participants began to price options as the model said they should. But instead of finding atomistic, amoral *homines economici*, MacKenzie and Millo found that the market was both a moral community and an arena for political action (Abolafia 1996; Fligstein 2001). A network of economists, politicians and market professionals mobilized to promote and defend the Exchange.

Panics, scandals and regulation

Economic theory generally sees panics and scandals as irrational deviations in the history of financial markets. Regulation has often been treated as deleterious and even dangerous to the efficiency of these markets. Sociologists tend to see all three of these phenomena as intrinsic to the market. Panics and scandals grow out of hypercompetitive action that is counternormative, but not irrational. Regulation is part the system of constraints that organizes that competition and maintains the arena (see **Polanyi, Karl**; **regulation of the market**). By varying their assumptions about rationality and the nature of competition, economic sociologists have drawn dramatically different conclusions than economists about the organization and disorganization of financial markets.

In his examination of the American stock market and securities law, James Burk (1988) argues against the economic argument that financial markets are self-regulating. The economic argument is that markets create their own moral order because people will be attentive to others' needs and desires in order to insure that their own desires will be met. Burk argues instead that people organize politically and deploy group power to modify the operations of the market to obtain their goals. These groups' ability to influence the government and government's own influence on market operation is far more extensive than the economic paradigm considers. Ultimately, Burk believes that financial regulation fails because of the power of special interests. An alternative position has been taken by McCaffrey and Hart (1998) and Faerman *et al.* (2001). They argue that self-regulation in these markets works and that Wall Street 'polices itself'. In a study of the regulation of financial innovation, McCaffrey and his colleagues found that large financial firms were able to collaborate successfully with federal regulatory agencies to create rules for the derivatives market The authors note that the government is relying on cooperation to engage good-faith compliance.

Important new work in behavioural finance by psychologists Kahneman and Tversky, and others suggests that markets are not immune to irrational behaviour (see **behavioural economics**). In contrast to the efficient markets hypothesis, these theorists believe that manias and speculative bubbles are to be expected. Investors are found to overreact to recent information and to weight losses more strongly than they weight gains. Although such irrationalities are clearly influential in manias and panics, economic sociologists have suggested that attention needs to be kept on the market manipulations that encouraged investor overreaction in the first place. In his studies of a speculative bubble in futures in the late 1970s and the scandal in junk bonds in the late 1980s, Abolafia (1996) found that financial bubbles are often precipitated by the actions of deviant innovators, challengers to the status quo, who alter some aspect of the normative structure. Initial success encourages escalating challenges that often blind the innovators to the power of the established elite whose interests have been threatened. This suggests a theory of action for speculative bubbles that is missed by those looking only for irrationalities.

Conclusion

In two decades of work, economic sociologists have only scratched the surface of financial markets. The research discussed above suggests that much can be learned from a closer examination of the following questions: how do rules organize and legitimate financial markets? How do networks of social relations affect the price determination process? What are the meanings of time and space in these markets and how do they shape behaviour? What role does technology play in constructing price? How does local rationality vary from market to market? Why do bubbles occur? These and other questions hint at the enormous potential of the economic sociology of financial markets.

References and further reading

Abolafia, Mitchel Y. (1996) *Making Markets: Opportunism and Restraint on Wall Street*, Cambridge, MA: Harvard University Press.

Baker, Wayne (1984) 'The Social Structure of a National Securities Market', *American Journal of Sociology*, 89: 775–811.

Burk, James (1988) *Values in the Marketplace*, New York: Aldine de Gruyter.

Callon, Michel (1998) 'Introduction: The Embeddedness of Economic Markets in Economics', in Michel Callon (ed.), *The Laws of Markets*, Oxford: Blackwell.

Carruthers, Bruce (1996) *City of Capital*, Princeton, NJ: Princeton University Press.

Faerman, Sue, McCaffrey, David and Van Slyke, David (2001) 'Understanding Interorganizational Cooperation: Public–Private Collaboration in Regulating Financial Market Innovation', *Organizational Science*, 12(3): 372–88.

Fligstein, Neil (2001) *The Architecture of Markets*, Princeton, NJ: Princeton University Press.

Knorr Cetina, Karin and Bruegger, Urs (2002) 'Global Microstructures: The Virtual Societies of Financial Markets', *American Journal of Sociology*, 107: 905–50.

McCaffrey, David and Hart, David (1998) *Wall Street Polices Itself*, New York: Oxford University Press.

Mackenzie, Donald and Millo, Yuval (2003) 'Constructing a Market, Performing a Theory: A Historical Sociology of a Financial Derivatives Exchange', *American Journal of Sociology*, 109: 107–45.

Muniesa, Fabian (2000) 'Performing Prices: The Case of Price Discovery Automation in the Financial Markets', in H. Kaltoff, R. Rottenburg and H. Wagener (eds), *Facts and Figures: Economic Representations and Practices*, Marburg, Germany: Metropolis.

Preda, Alex (2000) 'Financial Knowledge and the "Science of the Market" in England and France in the 19th Century', in Ökonomie und Gesellschaft, 16, Marburg, Germany: Metropolis.

Smith, Charles (1999) *Success and Survival on Wall Street*, Lanham, MD: Rowman and Littlefield.

Zuckerman, Ezra (1999) 'The Categorical Imperative: Securities, Analysts and the Illegitimacy Discount', *American Journal of Sociology*, 104: 1398–438.

MITCHEL Y. ABOLAFIA

FIRMS

Generally, firms are approached through **organization theory** which seeks to identify maximum efficiency in relation to historical and **technological change**. Economic sociology offers a different perspective and can be summarized in the following four points addressing areas overlooked or dismissed by organization theory.

1. Firms are specific types of organizations in which the goal of making a profit (and the analysis of costs and price) is tied to the capacity to promote stable forms of social cooperation between actors with different interests (entrepreneurs, potential shareholders, managers and bureaucrats, employees with varying skills and professional qualifications).
2. The socially variable configurations of firms do not solely depend upon internal relations, but also upon a whole series of fundamentally social and not just economic external interactions, such as relations with clients, the state and local government or ecological, political and social awareness.
3. These ties elicit a wide range of enterprise forms, from the small family-run firm to the large multinational corporation, from the immigrant firm to different networks of firms (held together by subcontracting and franchising agreements) which have become increasingly popular since the 1970s.
4. As social institutions firms 'can be described as distinct constellations of interests and social relations, which are backed up by the legal machinery' (Swedberg 2003: 74).

While firms have benefited from more in-depth study in organization theory, sociology has made a few important contributions, which allow for the articulation of the four points mentioned above. This sociological perspective stems from both social theory (such as Weber's theory of capitalism and bureaucracy, and some approaches to **embeddedness** theory) and from empirical case studies (such as the research on human relations, on the systems of small enterprises and on the immigrant firms).

The Weberian approach: the rational firm and beyond

We owe to **Weber** at least two central contributions for the sociological comprehension of the modern firm. The first is the social, historical and institutional framework that has characterized the diffusion of firms in the industrial era, a period that marks the creation of rationally organized profit-making institutions. Weber's second fundamental contribution refers to the identification of the diverse interests that social actors exhibit when engaged in the management (expressed in different modalities) of these organizations.

The modern profit-making firm is based upon a few social assumptions that historically came into being in Western Europe between the eighteenth and the nineteenth century. Eventually these assumptions became widespread notions underlying the very existence of the contemporary capitalist enterprise. The first notion is that workers must be free to sell their own labour to an entrepreneur/employer, and therefore to voluntarily associate with the enterprise even though their interests and that of the entrepreneur may not coincide. The second is the use of book-keeping as a method for calculating the best cost/revenue ratios in order to estimate the profit margin. The third is the presence of a political (the state and state policies) and a legal (contracts and regulations) system that allows firms to operate in an efficient and predictable way (for example, by making possible the sale of goods to anybody willing to buy them at a set price; or by allowing for the purchase of raw material and machinery at the market price from anybody willing to offer them). Only when all of the aforementioned conditions are adequately met can a rational capitalist enterprise exist. Yet the conditions of its existence in society are always complicated by the presence of social relations among actors (which is the cause for various kinds of irrational behaviour, and for the tensions between value rationality and instrumental rationality). Even though Weber does not carefully examine this issue because he overlooks the importance of informal relations pervading the social life of a firm, his theory does offer insights into the modalities and the social meanings of firm.

The Weberian rational firm is, by definition, a free association of cooperation among individuals with different interests. How such difference is then reconciled through the constitution of various forms of efficient organization is one of the aspects the sociological investigation needs to explain. In this respect Weber puts forth the notion of bureaucracy as the most efficient form of administration and envisages its inescapable expansion foreseeing a 'bureaucratization of capitalism' (Weber [1922]1978: 999). In reality Weber's ideal type of bureaucracy is complicated by the presence of a number of 'imperfections'. The expansion of the rational firm must occur with the development of an organizational knowledge geared to maximize efficiency, based on a formal body of rules and on a hierarchical structure of authority. This last element should be able to produce a coherent order and mediate between the entrepreneurial interest in profit and the employee's interest in carrying out his/her own *beruf* and improving his/her standard of living. The interest of managers/bureaucrats in organizing the enterprise activity by means of their technical organizational knowledge is legitimated through the economic growth of the firm, which is the ultimate goal of the firm and thus supersedes the individual interests at stake. Weber's major preoccupation, however, was that bureaucratization would stifle the innovative character of **entrepreneurship** as well as the individual and collective initiatives of employees. Unlike the Tayloristic view of scientific management which aims at providing the best way to administer a firm, for Weber the transformations proposed by scientific management are not an issue of concern. He focuses on bureaucratization, as an administrative form based on formal rationality in the efficient pursuit of economic goals, a long process, albeit contrasting and contradictory, that accompanies the growth of the firm and the progressive expansion of capitalism.

Informal social relations, trust and transaction costs

The Weberian view of capitalist enterprise emphasizes the importance of formal social relationships emerging from the process of rationalization; however, it does not deny the persistence of other forms of social relations. This is evident in organizations such as the family firm, where economic calculation is not sophisticated, and profit goals are limited by family interests. The labour is directed toward the well-being of the family, and formal internal rules and bureaucratic norms are not needed, resulting in the persistence of a more traditional patriarchal and paternalistic organization. New forms of enterprise provide another example. Product innovation and new forms of production are generated by an innovative entrepreneurial spirit which prevails over formal internal rules and bureaucratic norms.

The emphasis on formal relations of organization undermines the importance of the informal aspects of social relations, both within and outside the firm, typical of any kind of enterprise. As Blumer argues in his introduction to an edited volume on the human relations perspective: 'In viewing industrial organization as a machine-like coordination of separate industrial tasks there is always a danger of failing to see clearly or appreciate fully the social structure in which this coordination becomes embedded' (1951: v).

The well-known Hawthorne experiments, at the Western Electric Company – which contributed to develop the so-called human relations perspective – were very influential in suggesting that more attention be paid to the influence of informal social relations within firms. During the experiments employee productivity invariably increased both in the division where labour conditions had been improved substantially, and in the control work-group of another division of the plant. The study showed that apparently the attention given to the work-groups by the researchers was more influential on productivity than any improvement in working conditions. What can be inferred from the study is the significance of a whole series of social relations in firms of different types and sizes, and their influence on the organization of labour, such as the formation of highly cooperative small groups and the formation of reciprocal bonds of interactions and sentiments based mainly on **trust** (Homans 1950). The social life of a firm and its ability to implement effective forms of cooperation do not depend only on the efficiency of formal norms, but also on the presence of cooperative interactions based on interpersonal relations of trust and loyalty. The subsequent investigation of successful industrial models, such as the Japanese, the Italian **industrial districts**,

the thriving entrepreneurship within particular ethnic enclaves have confirmed the importance of the notion of trust and loyalty not only in the organization of the firm, but also in the firm's embeddedness in the social context in which it operates (relations with suppliers, clients, local and national public institutions, to name but a few).

The importance of interpersonal relations of trust and loyalty in economic cooperation, inside and outside the firm, is also evident in the transaction cost theory of the neo-institutionalist approach in economics. As explained by Williamson (1994: 103) these are

> ex ante costs of drafting, negotiating, and *safeguarding* an agreement and, more especially, the ex post costs of maladaptation and adjustment that arise when contract execution is misaligned as a result of gaps, errors, omissions, and unanticipated disturbance, the costs of running the economic system.

It is evident that informal situations occurring in conditions of social homogeneity, trust, and interpersonal loyalty tend to lower transaction costs. This is the case in small family-run businesses and immigrant firms, which are competitive, beyond formalized models of accounting, precisely because they are able to create internal cohesion, through shared values and culture. This situation cannot be easily reproduced by the rigidity of formal regulations in business organizations nor by the norms regulating contractual relationships.

Recent trends: interpreting the social heterogeneity of firms

With the expansion of mass production the organization of firms became larger and more bureaucratized, as Weber predicted, but in the 1970s the situation started to change radically. Tertiarization, vertical disintegration, the diffusion of diversified networks of firms connected by means of different kinds of co-operational agreement (Piore and Sabel 1984), the rise of the informational economy and globalization, have been producing new and diversified forms of business enterprises (Castells 1996). As the social characteristics of companies change, new interpretive problems arise, thus calling for new explanations and answers.

This new social context offers a wide range of organizational options and produces blurred demarcations between what pertains to the inner structure of a firm and its relation with the (external) environment, as well as between the social profiles and the interests of the actors involved in the firm. Franchising, contracting-out and other forms of vertical dis-integrated production in sectors like researching, marketing and cleaning are examples.

New and more unstable forms of work redefine the notion of embeddedness. These are often found in knowledge-based professions, in high-tech communication, and in the networks of relatively autonomous firms. In general these forms of work weaken the stability and the loyalty of cooperative interpersonal relations in favour of a more complex interplay between personal interest and social responsibility.

At the centre of this transformation sociology, and economic sociology in particular, is challenged to move beyond the study of efficient organizational models to discover the logic of embeddedness in the social context of the firm, a context increasingly heterogeneous, complex and open. Such a challenge raises a whole series of issues.

The narrow definition of modern firms as profit-driven organizations may be, at least in part, sociologically overcome. In fact, new social enterprises are emerging (such as firms involved in service provision, especially in the areas of health care and education) that are destabilizing the apparent relationship between efficiency and profit.

Higher profits do not necessarily determine the stability and efficiency of a firm, which in many instances has to do with product quality and good client/consumer relations. There is also the issue of the complex functioning of the dense network of interconnected firms. Some firms within a network may be highly efficient and profitable, while others may be less so. Another complex matter refers to the separation of ownership, financial investment and management as the most blatant example of how the firm is becoming a repository of highly heterogeneous and divergent economic and social interests.

The multifarious interests at stake within and outside the contemporary firm increasingly escape the control exerted by formal regulations and by bureaucracy. In addition they cannot entirely fit any longer in trust-based models of formal cooperation characterized by steady and homogeneous interpersonal relationships, because the level of homogeneity and stability is lessening. The growing attention towards systems of governance seeks to come to terms with this complexity even in business organization, by identifying the interplay of increasingly heterogeneous interests and the modalities through which they are mediated. This problem encompasses all of the typologies of firms that are usually studied. In family firms, for example, paternalism is less effective; first because of the demographic transformations that are changing roles and family composition; second because of the development of information technology, as it modifies the social organization of work within the firm. In large factories and in large bureaucratized companies operating in the service sector the interface between formal rules and steady interpersonal relations is no longer sufficient to maintain the efficient cooperation among actors with individual and heterogeneous professional interests. Consider, for example, the expansion of various professions such as business consultants, and the growing importance of information technology and the Internet as new powerful resources for the firm.

References and further reading

Blumer, H. (1951) 'Introduction', in R. Dubin (ed.), *Human Relations in Administration. The Sociology of Organization, with Readings and Cases*, New York: Prentice Hall, pp. v–vi.

Castells, Manuel (1996) *The Rise of Network Society*, vol. 1 of *The Information Age. Economy, Society and Culture*, Oxford: Blackwell.

Homans, George C. (1950) *The Human Group*, New York and Burlingame: Harcourt, Brace, and World.

Nohria, Nitin and Gulati, Ranjay (1994) 'Firms and their Environments', in N. Smelser and R. Swedberg (eds), *The Handbook of Economic Sociology*, Princeton, NJ, and New York: Princeton University Press and Russell Sage Foundation, pp. 529–55.

Piore, Michael and Sabel, Charles (1984) *The Second Industrial Divide: Possibilities for Prosperity*, New York: Basic Books.

Swedberg, Richard (2003) *Principles of Economic Sociology*, Princeton, NJ: Princeton University Press.

Weber, Max ([1922]1978) *Economy and Society: An Outline of Interpretive Sociology*, two volumes, Berkeley, CA: University of California Press.

Williamson, O. (1994) 'Transaction Cost Economics and Organization Theory', in N. Smelser and R. Swedberg (eds), *The Handbook of Economic Sociology*, Princeton, NJ and New York: Princeton University Press and Russell Sage Foundation, pp. 77–107.

ENZO MINGIONE

FISCAL SOCIOLOGY

Fiscal sociology is the study of how taxes and state expenditures (i.e. public finances) are determined and affect society. Many public finance economists argue that decisions about public finances are made by politicians in response to market failures. These economists are also especially concerned with studying how fiscal policy

affects revenue flows, income distributions, economic performance, and the like. Fiscal sociology is concerned with these things but also with how non-economic causes and consequences are involved that are at least as important as those discussed by economists.

Rudolf Goldscheid is credited with coining the phrase fiscal sociology in 1917. Following Goldscheid, Joseph **Schumpeter**, an economist, believed that the importance of fiscal sociology stemmed from the fact that in most historical periods state finances explained a great deal not only about the development of the economy but about all aspects of its culture. For this reason he maintained that 'the public finances are one of the best starting points for an investigation of society, especially though not exclusively of its political life' (Schumpeter 1954: 7). In fact, public finances have proven to be an *increasingly* appropriate starting point for such an investigation because the levels of taxation and state expenditures increased in many countries during the twentieth century. For instance, by 1998 in the advanced capitalist countries taxes and spending rose to about 29 per cent and 30 per cent of gross domestic product, respectively. In some cases, notably Scandinavia, these levels were even higher (World Bank 2001: 236).

Fiscal sociology remained in its infancy until about 1970 when Daniel Bell, James O'Connor and others began to look more carefully at how state finances reflected broader forces in society. This literature developed in two directions. Some scholars focused on state expenditures while others looked at taxation. Often they tried to explain historical and cross-national variation in the levels and structure of state expenditures and taxation.

State expenditures

Much of the literature on state expenditures is concerned primarily with spending on social programs like unemployment compensation, social insurance, health care, and the like (see **welfare state and the economy**). It emerged in three stages. First, was the so-called logic of industrialism view, which argued that states increase their levels of spending to help citizens cope with the social and economic dislocations associated with industrialization and urbanization. Modern states must address the demands of citizens for public help, social security and other public services. For instance, families forced to migrate from rural to urban locations due to the mechanization of agriculture can no longer rely on their community and kin for aid and so must turn to the state instead. In a related vein, some scholars suggested that while industrialization is a key determinant of rising public expenditures, differences in national values explain why some countries, such as Germany, adopted social policies earlier during industrialization than others, such as the United States. In this case, liberalism is said to have permeated US politics, thereby delaying the adoption of social security and other expenditures while in Germany a Christian social ethic led to a much earlier adoption of social policies. The work of Harold Wilensky and Gaston Rimlinger are important examples of this tradition.

Second, critics of the industrialization thesis argued that it neglects how political struggles shape state expenditures. Although a variety of social groups were identified in this literature, class politics received much attention and it was often argued that the relative political strength of farmers, industrial workers and the business community shape expenditures and that as this balance of power shifts, so too does the level and structure of state spending. For example, some argued that social expenditures will be high in countries with strong labour unions or where farmers and industrial workers join into formidable political alliances. Important cross-national and historical work in this tradition has been done by Gøsta Esping-Andersen, Walter Korpi and John Stephens.

Finally, some scholars suggested that this perspective neglects how the organization of political institutions and the interests of political actors within these institutions influence expenditures in ways that are independent of the effects of industrialization, urbanization and the politics of social groups and classes outside of the state. Most notably, Theda Skocpol argued that expenditures for social programmes vary significantly according to the organization of political party competition, the relative bureaucratic insulation of policy-makers from external pressure groups, the level of fragmentation among state administrative agencies, constitutional differences and other institutional aspects of states and politics.

Taxes

Similar debates mark the literature on taxation. To begin with, scholars argued that as economies grow and especially as they become more engaged in international trade the level of taxation rises in order to finance programmes that are necessary to guard citizens from the volatility of international economic conditions. O'Connor and other Marxists added that although states are forced to increase spending for these and other programmes, concerns about preserving political legitimacy and avoiding the possibility of capital flight prevent states from increasing tax levels enough to cover higher levels of expenditures. The result is a tendency for capitalist states to incur budget deficits and experience fiscal crisis. As with the literature on state expenditures, some scholars held that variation in a country's political culture will affect its tax system. For example, countries whose culture privileges the individual over central political authority tend to have lower taxes than others.

Goldscheid maintained that tax struggles are among the oldest forms of class struggle. Indeed, many researchers have shown that the political power of social classes and other interest groups are important determinants of tax systems. In particular, much work has been done investigating how business interests have influenced corporate income taxes. Less work has been done to determine how other social groups affect taxation but rational choice theorists like Margaret Levi and James Buchanan theorized that political elites seek to maximize tax revenues but are constrained in doing so by well-organized social groups who resist higher taxes.

Of course, how social groups are organized is determined partly by the systems of political representation in which they operate and the state institutions that they confront. For instance, Sven Steinmo and others showed that in parliamentary democracies with several political parties and proportional representation, policy-making tends to be based on consensus. As a result, taxes tend to be higher and more progressive than in countries with different political institutions. Taxes are also often higher in countries that tend to be dominated by labour or social democratic governments. Public choice theorists have argued that electoral politics matter insofar as incumbent politicians lower taxes to obtain votes as elections approach, but then raise them afterwards. However, there is much research that suggests that electoral cycles have little effect on taxes and that policy-makers generally adjust taxes in only incremental ways for fear of upsetting voters at any time with radical tax reforms. Scholars have also argued that in situations, like the United States, where political institutions are permeable to interest groups who can lobby for special tax deductions, loopholes and other forms of tax expenditures, tax burdens tend to be lighter. The system of tax expenditures is sometimes referred to as a 'hidden welfare state'.

Finally, sociologists, such as Charles Tilly and Michael Mann, have shown that states raise taxes in response to war. Virtually everyone agrees that this is because political leaders need more revenues to defend the country. Beyond that, however, public choice theorists argue that taxes rise because citizens are more tolerant of tax increases during war. Marxists suggest that taxes rise because the threat of capital flight – a constraint on tax increases during peace time – is reduced when profits are to be made from increased military spending during war. Rational choice theorists claim that states raise taxes during war because political elites are primarily interested in preserving their power and, as a result, are willing to discount the importance of other pressures that militate against raising taxes during peace time. Geopolitical factors figure more prominently into research on taxation than into research on state expenditures.

Effects of fiscal policy

It is generally agreed that fiscal policies have important influences on many aspects of society. The economic ones are the most commonly discussed. Scholars agree that both taxation and state spending affect income inequality, poverty levels and a variety of factors associated with economic performance, such as growth, inflation, unemployment, productivity, investment and international competitiveness. Debate rages over how fiscal policies affect these things and whether these effects are good or bad. But scholars have also examined how fiscal policies affect things beyond the economy per se. For instance, there is a vast literature on how various types of state expenditures, notably social policies, affect rates of divorce, marriage, out-of-wedlock child birth, teenage pregnancy and the social development and career prospects of children in single-parent households. Much has also been written about how taxation has affected political rebellion and revolution, state-building, labour force participation and philanthropy. Debate over these issues continues and much remains to be learned about how taxation and spending affect these and other aspects of society. Nevertheless, it is clear from this brief list that fiscal sociology bears directly on many important policy questions. Some of these relate directly to increasing levels of international economic activity.

Globalization and fiscal sociology

Since 1970 the levels of trade, foreign direct investment, currency speculation and other forms of international economic activity have increased significantly. Similarly, the development of international trading zones, such as the European Union, the North American Free Trade Agreement and Mercosur, have facilitated easier cross-border economic activity. Many observers have referred to this as a process of **globalization** and suggest that it is having important consequences on taxation and state expenditures around the world. Broadly speaking, there are two schools of thought on this. On the one hand, following earlier arguments about the problems of capital flight, some have suggested that as investment capital becomes increasingly mobile internationally, it will seek national locations that have comparatively low taxes. As a result, in order to attract investment, states will have to compete against each other by lowering taxes on capital that, in turn, will reduce revenues and create fiscal pressure to reduce spending as well. The result will be a 'race to the bottom' where states all experience downward pressure on revenues and expenditures and converge on a common fiscal system with generally low rates of taxation and spending. On the other hand, some scholars reject this view and argue that a variety of domestic political and institutional pressures, many of which are discussed above,

will prevent states from engaging in the race to the bottom.

Debates about how globalization affects state finances are of great importance, not only for fiscal sociology but also for policymakers. Several questions loom large here. To what extent does capital actually favour moving to other states that offer lower tax rates? To what extent are states really concerned about the threat of capital flight and take it into consideration when making decisions about taxation and spending? To what extent do states alter their fiscal systems in order to attract capital from elsewhere? To what extent is there evidence of a race to the bottom in taxation and spending or at least a shift in tax burdens away from investors to other groups in society? These sorts of questions should provide an important impetus for new research in fiscal sociology.

References and further reading

Campbell, John L. (1993) 'The State and Fiscal Sociology', *Annual Review of Sociology*, 19: 163–85.

Garrett, Geoffrey (1998) *Partisan Politics in the Global Economy*, New York: Cambridge University Press.

Schumpeter Joseph (1954) 'The Crisis of the Tax State', in Alan Peacock, Wolfgang Stolper, Ralph Turvey and Elisabeth Henderson (eds), *International Economic Papers*, No. 4, New York: Macmillan, pp. 5–38.

Skocpol, Theda (1992) 'State Formation and Social Policy in the United States', *American Behavioral Scientist*, 35: 559–84.

Steinmo, Sven (1993) *Taxation and Democracy*, New Haven, CT: Yale University Press.

World Bank (2001) *World Development Indicators*, Washington, DC: World Bank.

JOHN L. CAMPBELL

FLEXIBILIZATION

The concept of flexibilization has dual meanings within classical studies of political economy and contemporary economic sociology: one refers to a process immanent within capitalist development, and the other to an ensemble of practices and discourses within the workplace. This first roots flexibilization in the social productive forces of labour and can be detected implicitly in the works of Marx, Lenin and Gramsci. These late nineteenth-century and early twentieth-century theorists derive their understanding of flexibilization from analyses of the historical shift from domestic production to large-scale manufacturing, culminating in the application of Fordist production methods. The second focuses on strategic practices and discourses, which are increasingly the hallmark of post-Fordist work organizations, labour processes and corporate structures in late twentieth-century capitalism. This entry views the genealogy of flexibilization as theoretical articulations in response to the shift from the triumph of Fordism to the uncertainty of post-Fordism.

Implicit reference to flexibilization both as a feature and as a consequence of the capital accumulation process appears in Marx's *Capital*, Volume 1. Marx (1977) addresses the topic in terms of the transition from formal subsumption of labour to capital to real subsumption. This formal versus real distinction turns on a deconstruction of production technology as an 'autonomous' force. More specifically, the development of machinery and large-scale industry foster the possibility for a multifold development freeing individual workers from a lifetime bound to a single profession. Marx argues that: 'This large-scale industry, by its very nature, necessitates variation of labor, fluidity of functions, and mobility of the worker in all directions' (617). In Marx, flexibilization implies both a potential for labour's opposition to capital and a means for capital's control over labour.

With an eye towards its practical as well as its theoretical import, Lenin (1975) engages the topic of flexibilization in relationship to Taylorism and the assembly line (449). To Lenin, Taylorism may realize

flexibilization as a result of its technological prowess and superior work and accounting methods.

> The Taylor system, the last word of capitalism in this respect, like all capitalist progress, is a combination of the refined brutality of bourgeois exploitation and a number of the greatest scientific achievements in the field of analyzing mechanical motions during work, the elimination of superfluous and awkward motion, the elaboration of correct methods of work, the introduction of the best system of accounting and control, etc.
>
> (448–9)

An uncritical faith in the potential benefits of the Taylor system permeates Lenin's later writings where he reflects on the urgency for raising labour's productivity.

Around the same time that Lenin extols the virtues of new mass production techniques, Gramsci (1978) notes the contradictory nature of Fordism, and by extension flexibilization. Hints of Gramsci's thinking about flexibilization materialize in his evocation of the cultural and political landscape of American Fordism. Gramsci frames his analysis of flexibilization around the birth of hegemony in Detroit's factories, both as a symbolic and a genesis site of Fordism. His analysis opposes breakdown theories in favour of an argument that emphasizes the complex capacity for adjustment of capitalism as a system of decentralized decision-making. 'Hegemony ... requires for its exercise only a minute quantity of professional political and ideological intermediaries' (Gramsci 1978: 285). Gramsci's focus on ideological and political elements prefigures the second sense of flexibilization as a set of strategic practices inhabiting the ways people think and act.

During the 1970s, flexibilization gained wide currency as a way to characterize the organizing logic of late capitalism and to represent Fordism in the process of transition. No single source can be credited with minting these new applications of the concept. Rather, by the mid-to-late 1980s and throughout the 1990s, diffuse meanings circulated signifying diverse and broad institutional reconfiguration and employment adjustments. In these latest usages, flexibilization explicitly references forms of functional and numerical changes in the social organization of production.

One bold foray by Piore and Sabel (1984) lays out a template for understanding the history of industrialization which they reinterpret in terms of the struggle between two alternative configurations: one predicated on diversity of consumption patterns and adaptability of skills and production techniques in flexible specialization; and the other on highly standardized mass production employing low-skilled, blue-collar workers. In moving from hierarchical, mass-production systems to flatter work systems better suited to respond quickly to innovation and change, flexible specialization entails the social reorganization of work, promises a new artisanal system for workers in small-scale craft production, provides expanded opportunities for developing skills and discretion on-the-job, and operates through networked relationships between firms.

Following up on themes raised by both Marx and Gramsci, the French Regulation perspective views flexibilization as both immanent to and a specific strategy developed for the purpose of social control and expanded capital accumulation in a new phase of post- or neo-Fordism (Boyer 1988). Aglietta (1979) coins the term neo-Fordism to define the application of Fordist methods of production to welfare services and leisure activities and as a reorganization of the labour process to increase the intensity of work by means of new information technology, automatic control of production and semi-autonomous **work teams**. Neo-Fordism delimits an ensemble of institutions and social relationships that originate in, and extend, Fordist produc-

tion and consumption principles but that embody emergent flexible forms (Gottfried 2000).

A variant of the Regulation approach examines the political meanings of flexibilization in the context of welfare state retrenchment and deregulation. Flexibilization articulates a political project around an ascendant neo-liberal discourse. It represents a retreat from former obligations and rights embodied in the expansionary welfare state of the post-war period. In this sense, flexibilization can be understood as a set of reflexive practices as well as a theoretical representation of post-Fordism.

New staffing trends point to a numerical form of flexibility. Numerical flexibility alters employment relationships by diversifying locations of work, working time patterns and working conditions through contractual adjustments. Functional flexibility changes work organization by removing demarcations between jobs.

Contemporary forms of flexibilization affect increasing lines of segmentation both *within* (segmented internal labour markets into core and periphery) and *between* firms (externalization of labour through outsourcing and subcontracting). Segmentation results in a reconfiguration of the social division of labour as some workers learn new skills and as a growing number of workers are employed on a non-standard basis (e.g. part-time, temporary, casual labour). Such changing fault lines raise questions about the formation of class and gender relations.

References and further reading

Aglietta, Michel (1979) *A Theory of Capitalist Regulation*, London: New Left Books.
Boyer, Robert (1988) *The Search for Labour Market Flexibility: The European Economies in Transition*, Oxford: Clarendon Press.
Gottfried, Heidi (2000) 'Compromising Positions: Emergent Neo-Fordisms and Embedded Gender Contracts', *British Journal of Sociology*, 52(2): 235–59.

Gramsci, Antonio (1978) 'Americanism and Fordism', in Q. Hoare and N. Smith (eds), *Selections from the Prison Notebooks of Antonio Gramsci*, New York: International Publishers, pp. 277–318.

Lenin, I. V. (1975) *The Lenin Anthology*, edited by Robert Tucker, New York: W. W. Norton.

Marx, Karl (1977) *Capital*, vol. 1, translated by Ben Fowkes, New York: Vintage Books.

Piore, Michael and Sabel, Charles (1984) *The Second Industrial Divide*, New York: Basic Books.

Standing, Guy (1999) 'Global Feminization Through Flexible Labor: A Theme Revisited', *World Development*, 27(3): 583–602.

HEIDI GOTTFRIED

FRAMING See: classification; game theory; social rationality

FREE RIDER

A 'free rider' is someone who reaps the fruits of other people's labour in some kind of collective undertaking or, more precisely, who enjoys the benefits of some collective good without contributing to the costs of its production. Examples of free riding are when someone shirks from cleaning up after a party, does less than his or her share in some teamwork, evades taxes or enjoy television without paying a fee for the right to do so.

Even though the term does not occur in it, the idea of 'free riding' gained currency with the publication of Mancur Olson's book *The Logic of Collective Action* (1965, second edition 1971). In this book, Olson took issue with the prevailing sociological theory of groups, which assumed that individuals always act in their common interest. Instead, he suggested an economic approach implying that rational and self-interested individuals will not engage in **collective action** unless the group is small, or there is some 'selective incentive' added to the benefit derived from the collective good. This is the reason taxes are coercive and labour unions use both coercion and private benefits, such as insurances and jour-

nals, to attract members. According to Olson, pressure groups emerge as by-products of organizations originally created for the provision of some private good.

There are several reasons why rational egoists will decide not to participate in collective action, but the most important is the possibility of free riding. If the group is large and if there are no selective incentives, the rational thing to do for a self-interested individual is to free ride on the contributions of others. The result is that collective action will fail or, at least, that the provision of collective goods will be suboptimal. Free riding gives rise to a situation that is the obverse of Adam **Smith**'s invisible hand. Individual rationality leads to collective irrationality. This is the problem of collective action.

Free riding occurs only in collective action for a common purpose and is closely related to some defining features of collective goods. According to the classic definition, collective, or public, goods are characterized above all by indivisibility, or jointness of supply. The utility an individual derives from a public good does not diminish as it is consumed also by other individuals. The paradigmatic example of a public good is a lighthouse, which serves many boats equally well. The important point for Olson, however, is not jointness, but non-excludability. It is because of the impossibility, or difficulty, of excluding people from consuming a public good, that free riding becomes a possible course of action.

After the publication of Olson's book, the logic of collective action was increasingly analysed with the help of non-cooperative **game theory**. At first, the collective action problem was interpreted as an N-person Prisoner's Dilemma, but it was soon recognized that free riding is possible also in other games where self-interest suggests a strategy of defection. It was also recognized that there might be a collective action problem even in the absence of an incentive to free ride. If there are several, equally good, alternatives, or multiple equilibria, to choose between, there is a problem of coordination, which might be equally severe as the problem of cooperation created by free riding.

Originally, game theory was static. This was a serious shortcoming in the analysis of social life, which is evidently dynamic. A remedy was found in the development of iterated games, or super-games. If people meet again an indefinite number of times, even rational egoists may be led to cooperate. The best strategy in the iterated Prisoner's Dilemma is 'tit-for-tat', which means that people cooperate as long as other people cooperate. The most famous version of this argument can be found in Robert Axelrod's *The Evolution of Cooperation* (1984), where rational choice is replaced by an evolutionary theory explaining cooperation in terms of the emergence of a 'norm of reciprocity'. The importance attached to Axelrod's result was due to the implied prospect of cooperation in the absence of a centralized agency of coercion.

The economic theory of collective action predicts free riding and little, or no, collective action at all in large groups. This prediction is contradicted by ordinary experience, which suggests that people do cooperate for many purposes, even when self-interest dictates free riding. Mancur Olson's explanation of this fact was in terms of selective incentives, but this explanation has its problems. One problem is that it invites *ad hoc* explanations in terms of whatever motivates an individual to engage in collective action. There is thus a risk that the theory becomes empty of content. Another problem befalls the common explanation of collective action in terms of negative sanctions. To suggest that people cooperate because of a threat of punishment is no solution, since sanctions are also collective goods. This explanation, then, gives rise to a second-order collective action problem and, ultimately, to an infinite regress.

The idea of free riding was developed in the context of the economic approach to human behaviour and is closely related to some of its basic assumptions: that individuals are isolated, homogeneous and self-interested. From the point of view of a sociological approach, where individuals are assumed to interact, occupy positions in social structures and follow social norms, cooperation seems less problematic. Free riding is the behaviour to be expected of *homo economicus*, but not of *homo sociologicus*. Its prevalence, therefore, provides a crucial test of the fertility of the respective models of human beings. What is the evidence?

There have been many attempts to test the assumption of free riding in a scientific way, including lots of experiments. A conspicuous finding, which might be more than a mere curiosity, is that economics students tend to free ride more than other students. A more significant finding is that free riding becomes less frequent when people are allowed to communicate with one another. Why? One suggestion is that communication gives rise to a collective identity, which somehow motivates individuals to cooperate. Another suggestion is that communication elicits norms of cooperation and against free riding.

References and further reading

Elster, Jon (1989) *The Cement of Society. A Study of Social Order*, Cambridge: Cambridge University Press.

Hardin, Russell (1982) *Collective Action*, Baltimore, MD: Johns Hopkins University Press.

Taylor, Michael (1987) *The Possibility of Cooperation*, Cambridge: Cambridge University Press.

LARS UDEHN

FUNCTIONAL IMPERATIVES/ PREREQUISITES (AGIL)

The concept of functional imperatives (or requisites) – that societies have certain basic needs that must be met – is central to functional analysis, a theoretical approach in sociology and anthropology that had its beginnings in the nineteenth-century writings of thinkers such as Herbert Spencer and Emile **Durkheim**. These theorists posed two main questions about society. First, what is the 'function', or positive contribution, that a particular social institution or cultural pattern makes to society as a whole? Second, and related, what are those social needs that institutions and patterns must fulfil in order for a society to 'survive' – that is, to maintain itself in some form of recognizable continuity? The functional analysts further reasoned that if these requirements, which are said to be fundamental to all societies, are not satisfied, the society in question would experience social dysfunctions, or negative consequences, in the form of extinction, disequilibrium, disintegration, and so on.

Several sociologists and anthropologists have attempted to identify and inventory the functional imperatives of all societies. For example, Spencer postulated three: (1) the need to secure and circulate resources; (2) the need to produce usable substances; and (3) the need to regulate, control, and administer activities. Similar to Durkheim, the British anthropologist A. R. Radcliffe-Brown, who focused on the 'necessary conditions of existence', postulated only 'social integration' as the essential functional requirement of societies. By contrast, Bronislaw Malinowski identified a number of distinctive biological, cultural and social needs, all of which he regarded as indispensable. He identified the four basic social needs as: (1) production and distribution; (2) social control and regulation; (3) education and socialization; and (4) organization and integration.

During the 1950s, particularly in the United States, several sociologists believed that if they could produce a list of the main functional imperatives, they would then know the basic survival requirements of any society and thus be able to discover how these requirements were actually

being met in a particular society. The most explicit analytical attempt at formulating such a list was made by D. F. Aberle and his colleagues in a paper they published in 1950. Here they argued that in order to avoid the conditions that can terminate its existence, it is imperative that a society perform the following functions: (1) it must adapt to, manipulate and alter its environment; (2) it must differentiate between and assign certain essential roles; (3) it must provide effective means of communication; (4) it must have shared points of view; (5) it must have a shared, clear set of goals; (6) it must regulate the means for attaining the goals; (7) it must foster, structure and restrict the expression of emotions; (8) it must provide adequate socialization; (9) it must engage in the effective control of disruptive behaviour.

In order to address the issue of social change, Marion J. Levy, Jr, in his 1952 book, *The Structure of Society,* standardized the concept of functional *prerequisites,* which refer to the conditions necessary for a society, not to maintain its continuing existence, but *to come into existence.* Levy also introduced *structural* prerequisites, which consider which 'structures' (or patterns of action, as opposed to 'functions,' or generalized conditions) must be present if a particular society is to come into being in a particular setting.

Two main problems that have long plagued functional-requisite analysis are those of 'tautology' and 'illegitimate teleology'. The problem of tautology, or circular reasoning, occurs when functional analysts claim that if a society is to survive then certain needs, such as social integration, have to be met. Following this they then say that a society survives because it has met the need of social integration. Such argumentation implies that 'integration' is inherent in the analyst's conception of society; as such there is no true cause-and-effect explanation. Illegitimate teleology, or the idea that the existence of something can be explained in terms of its need, is also problematic. To assert that functional imperatives exist because they are necessary is to imply that society must continue to exist because it is necessary. Scientifically speaking, nothing can be alleged to exist because it is necessary. Thus, there is no explanation in terms of causes.

In his attempt at codifying the concepts of functional analysis, Robert K. Merton argued against the assumption of 'functional indispensability' – that certain specialized social institutions or cultural patterns are necessary in addressing the functional imperatives. Instead, Merton proposed the idea of 'functional alternatives' – that different and equally appropriate institutions and patterns can fulfil any particular functional imperative.

The conceptualization of functional imperatives attained its most systematic and rigorous formulation in the work of Talcott **Parsons**, who focused not so much on concrete societies, but on analytic *social systems*. Derived in part from Robert F. Bales' experiments of small groups, as well as from Malinowski's list of social needs, Parsons' set of functional imperatives were devised in reference to the four basic 'problems' which all social systems must continually confront and solve in order to operate effectively and remain viable. Parsons' formulation, which was first elaborated and applied in a 1956 volume coauthored with Neil J. Smelser, *Economy and Society*, became known as the AGIL model in accordance to the acronym of the first letter of the names for these four functional imperatives. The 'A' function, adaptation, involves the securing and distributing of environmental resources. The 'G' function, goal-attainment, has to do with mobilizing resources for achieving goals. The 'I' function, integration, is involved in coordinating system components. Lastly, the 'L' function, latency, manages tensions and motivates appropriate behaviour.

Another criticism levelled against the conceptualization of functional imperatives has to do with its hypostatization of 'system' and 'needs'. British sociologist Anthony Giddens has suggested that the idea of 'system needs' always presupposes the existence of 'interests'. And since social systems, unlike biological organisms, cannot have any interest in their own survival, the idea is false if it is not acknowledged that system needs presuppose individual's interests.

During the 1980s, in a revised and updated version of functionalism, called 'neofunctionalism', American sociologist Jeffrey C. Alexander endeavoured to deal with the criticisms of tautology, illegitimate teleology and hypostatization by downplaying the conceptualization of functional imperatives. Instead, neofunctionalism focuses on other, less controversial matters such as social differentiation and social change.

Functional analysts of the twenty-first century, however, have not abandoned the idea of functional imperatives. Indeed, in the same vein as previous functionalist theorists, but moving away from macro-structural considerations and towards an examination of the micro-processes that motivate social interaction, Jonathan H. Turner has considered 'transactional needs'. These are states of being that all individuals in all social encounters must realize if they are to avoid negative emotions – such as feeling deprived, anxious, fearful or potentially angry – that would disrupt and breach the interaction.

References and further reading

Aberle, D. F., Cohen, A. K., Davis, A. K., Levy, M. J., Jr and Sutton, F. X. (1950) 'The Functional Prerequisites of a Society', *Ethics*, 60: 100–111.

Levy, Marion J. (1952) *The Structure of Society*, New Haven, CT: Yale University Press.

Parsons, Talcott, and Smelser, Neil J. (1956) *Economy and Society*, New York: Free Press.

A. JAVIER TREVIÑO

G

GAME THEORY

Game theory studies social interactions among two or more rational actors who want to maximize their interests. It is a branch of the general theory of rational behaviour (or **rational choice theory**) that deals with strategic interactions. Strategic interactions are situations in which the outcomes of rational decisions of agent A are not only determined by A's choices but also by the choices of A's interaction partners B, C, ... Since most situations which are of interest to social scientists involve strategic interactions, it is not surprising that game theoretic ideas are dominating rational choice analyses within many fields, in particular in economics and its subdisciplines such as organizational economics, in political science, law and sociology.

Historical background

Based on von Neumann's earlier mathematical work, the first major systematic treatment on game theory was published by John von Neumann and Oskar Morgenstern in 1944. It focuses on two-person zero-sum games (with completely antagonistic interests among the players), and on multi-person games in which the players are able to form coalitions. Another set of seminal ideas is related to the axiomatic treatment of rational decision-making under risk. If an agent's preferences among risky alternatives are consistent and satisfy some further reasonable assumptions, the agent is acting as if she maximized her expected utility. Payoffs of a game standardly are assumed to fulfil requirements of cardinal utilities in von Neumann–Morgenstern's sense. In the early 1950s, John Nash proposed the distinction between cooperative and non-cooperative games. In a cooperative game, the players can make fully binding or enforceable commitments. Non-cooperative games, on the other hand, are defined by the absence of binding agreements. Though cooperative games are important, in particular in certain fields of economics and political science, the bulk of applications and basic research since the 1970s has been on non-cooperative games. This is because models of non-cooperative games may correspond to social situations in which cooperation among the actors is efficient (that is, optimal from the point of view of the agents), but albeit problematic to achieve. Some social situations of this kind are called 'social dilemmas'. Careful analysis of non-cooperative games can illuminate the conditions such that the agents themselves enforce an agreement on mutual cooperation. Furthermore, according to the so-called Nash-programme, cooperative games should finally be reduced to non-cooperative games: that is, it should be an aim of an analysis of non-cooperative games to demonstrate that cooperative games are an outcome of appropriately specified non-cooperative games.

Non-cooperative games and equilibrium points

Social situations with two or more actors who cannot bindingly agree on commitments and whose interests, at least partially, overlap, are best analysed by non-cooperative non-zero sum games. A game contains at least the following components: (1) there are two or more *players*, who (2) choose among a set alternatives which are called *strategies*; a strategy is a rule that unequivocally specifies how a player acts under any circumstance that is (logically) possible within a game. (3) After every player has chosen his or her strategy, an *outcome* is realized and each player is assigned a payoff. The *payoff* functions are usually interpreted in terms of cardinal utilities. (4) The players are provided with *information* about basic features of the game. Classical game theory assumes *complete* information about the parameters (1), (2) and (3). In other words, each player is assumed to know the set of strategies and payoff functions of each participant of the game. Nash discovered in 1950 that almost every game of this kind has an *equilibrium* point. This concept is commonly called 'Nash equilibrium'. A Nash equilibrium is defined as a profile of strategies s = $(s_1, s_2, \ldots, s_n)$ with the property that no player has a positive incentive to *unilaterally* deviate from the equilibrium, given the strategies of the other players. Denote u_i the payoff of player i, and denote $s_{-i} := (s_1, s_2, \ldots, s_{i-1}, s_{i+1}, \ldots, s_n)$. Then a profile s is a Nash equilibrium, if and only if $u_i(s) \geqslant u_i(s_i^*, s_{-i})$ for each player i and for every strategy s_i^* that is distinct from s_i. Note that an equilibrium does not necessarily exist within the set of pure strategies but may require mixed strategies such that strategies are not realized with certainty but with a positive probability. Nash equilibria are the most important *solution* concepts for non-cooperative games. Substantively, Nash equilibria can be interpreted as self-enforcing (tacit or explicit) agreements among the players. They are self-enforcing because no player will have an incentive to deviate unilaterally. That rational actors will necessarily choose a Nash equilibrium can be deduced from certain *rationality postulates* of classical game theory. Game theory is thus a *normative* theory of rational behaviour from which one can derive prescriptions for choosing a strategy: 'If you accept certain rationality postulates, you should choose X in a situation S.' However, in the social sciences, equilibria are generally treated as *empirical predictions* (or as elements of an explanation) which can be submitted to an empirical test.

Sequential games

Consider the following simple sequential (or dynamic) game: Player 1 (e.g. an employer) can choose among two contracts, A and B, a contract which he offers to player 2. Player 2 (e.g. a worker) can accept or reject the proposed contract. Assume that player 1 has the first move. Thereafter, player 2 decides whether to reject or accept. If player 2 rejects, both receive payoffs of 0. If contract A is realized, player 1 receives a payoff of 1, and player 2 receives 5. If B is realized, this yields 5 to player 1 and 1 to player 2. Consider the pair of strategies: (player 1: propose contract A; player 2: accept, if contract A; otherwise reject). This profile is clearly a Nash equilibrium. It is, however, not sensible. Player 2's strategy uses a *threat* to reject an offer that is unfavourable to him. This threat is not *credible*, because player 2 would have a positive incentive to deviate from the action which this threat requires: If, out-of-equilibrium, player 1 offers contract B, player 2's *best reply* is to accept. This means that player 2 has no incentive to reject because by this he would, so to speak, punish himself (by yielding him the lowest payoff of 0) and not only punish the other player. Reinhard Selten's formal concept of *subgame perfection* is a refinement or extension of the Nash equilibrium that covers *dynamic* games in which the players *sequentially* choose among moves that are possible in certain histories of a game. Intuitively, subgame perfection means that an equilibrium should only imply threats or promises which are credible.

Games of incomplete information

Many real-world social situations do not provide the participants with complete information on all basic parameters of the game. For instance, some agents may not be completely selfish but have internalized standards of fairness such that their payoff functions assign some value to their partner's outcomes. It may be unreasonable to assume complete transparency with respect to these preferences. John C. Harsanyi's path-breaking *Bayesian approach* to games of *incomplete information* rests on the idea to apply Bayesian **decision theory** in a game theoretic context. This requires a quantification of the uncertainties of a game by assuming common prior probability distributions. For example, the players may lack information about whether another player is of a specific type (e.g. endowed with certain preferences), but they have common knowledge about the probabilities of player types in the population. Using this information, the players decide on actions that are best replies and hence equilibria which maximize expected subjective utilities. This approach leads to still other refinements of the Nash equilibrium concept (Bayesian equilibria, perfect Bayesian equilibria, sequential equilibria, etc.). There are numerous applications and extensions of this Bayesian approach to information asymmetries in principal–agent relationships. Another idea related to information asymmetries is *signalling*. Players with pri-

vate information about certain parameters of a game (e.g. knowledge about their own preferences) may choose actions which are messages about their player type. Other players who receive these messages may use this data to update their **beliefs** with regard to the sender's player type. Michael Spence pioneered the idea of signalling with respect to labour markets. Besides applications in information economics, sociological applications abound: Camerer (1988) argues that 'gifts' in social exchange relations may be signals of trustworthiness. An informal theory of social norms (Eric Posner) uses the idea that conformity to certain norms of etiquette signals cooperativeness with respect to other, more fundamental interactions in social life.

Repeated games

Real-world social situations often involve interactions which are repeated among the same participants several times. Social exchange relations and interpersonal relationships in groups and neighbourhoods are cases in point. Economic sociologists have argued that economic transactions are 'embedded' in repeated interactions which correspond to social networks of various kinds. Models of repeated games are suitable analytic tools to represent these intuitions. Since the 1950s, the game theory community shared knowledge about theorems (called 'folk-theorems') which state that (indefinitely) repeated interactions enable the existence of efficient Nash equilibria with payoffs that are Pareto-improvements in comparison to the one-shot game. It took a couple of decades until general folk-theorems were formally proved and published (James Friedman; Drew Fudenberg and Eric Maskin). The Prisoner's Dilemma, for example, has a unique equilibrium of mutual defection that is suboptimal (inefficient). The infinitely repeated Prisoner's Dilemma, in contrast, has multiple equilibria. If the 'shadow of the future' (Axelrod) is large, there exist many equilibria yielding cooperation. This is so because in the case of a repeated game the players may employ strategies of *conditional cooperation* which punish the partner's defection by defecting themselves. Many social scientists and game theorists argue that repeated games provide the bases of social order among rational egoists (Binmore 1998). The repeated games approach has been useful to explain the emergence of informal social norms. It can be extended to analyse effects of social networks via multilateral reputation (see, e.g. Buskens 2002). In organizational economics, repeated games are used to explain outcomes of relational contracting, for instance between a focal firm and its suppliers. An obstacle to the usefulness of repeated games is the *equilibrium selection* problem that is implied by the existence of multiple Nash equilibria. Greif (1994) coined the term 'cultural beliefs' to point out the fact that real-life repeated interactions are embedded in a set of shared cultural rules which serve to coordinate the players' expectations on specific equilibrium points. Given this, it is not surprising that *path-dependent* outcomes are commonly observed in social situations that are similar to repeated games.

Adaptive rationality and evolutionary games

A branch of game theory that was discovered by John Maynard Smith and other biologists dispenses with the assumption of individual rationality. *Evolutionary game theory* adopts the population thinking of modern evolutionary theory to study interactions among strategies which are reproduced in proportion to their relative success. Darwinian selection forces generate equilibrium outcomes that are called *evolutionary stable strategies* (ESS). An ESS is a special case of a Nash equilibrium. Robert Axelrod's (1984) simulation studies on

cooperation used an approach that is close to evolutionary game theory (but albeit different). It inspired much subsequent work in the social sciences. Since the 1990s game theorists increasingly investigate outcomes of long run evolutionary processes that may lead to stable equilibria. H. Peyton Young, Larry Samuelson and others model assumptions of *adaptive* or *bounded rationality* in a large population of interacting individuals by means of stochastic dynamic systems (that is, mathematical tools borrowed from statistical physics). Young (1998) demonstrates that *social conventions* are the long run equilibria of cultural evolution in coordination games. Remarkably, this evolutionary approach does not depend on Darwinian premises with regard to the selection of strategies but is consistent with purposive, boundedly rational action.

References and further reading

Axelrod, Robert (1984) *The Evolution of Cooperation*, New York: Basic Books.

Binmore, Ken (1998) *Game Theory and the Social Contract, Volume 2, Just Playing*, Cambridge, MA: MIT Press.

Buskens, Vincent (2002) *Social Networks and Trust*, Dordrecht: Kluwer.

Camerer, Colin (1988) 'Gifts as Economic Signals and Social Symbols', *American Journal of Sociology*, 94 (Supplement): S180–S214.

—— (2003) *Behavioral Game Theory*, Princeton, NJ: Princeton University Press.

Dixit, Avinash and Skeath, Susan (1999) *Games of Strategy*, New York: Norton

Gintis, Herbert (2000) *Game Theory Evolving*, Princeton, NJ: Princeton University Press.

Greif, Avner (1994) 'Cultural Beliefs and the Organization of Society', *Journal of Political Economy*, 102: 912–50.

Osborne, Martin J. (2004) *An Introduction to Game Theory*, Oxford: Oxford University Press.

Young, H. Peyton (1998) *Individual Strategy and Social Structure*, Princeton, NJ: Princeton University Press.

THOMAS VOSS

GENDER AND ECONOMY

The study of gender and the economy is concerned with the division of labour between men and women in the spheres of paid labour (the market) and unpaid labour (the household), and with the differential rewards men and women receive for their labour. The area is termed gender stratification or gender inequality. Beginning in the 1970s and accelerating in the 1980s, research on gender inequality in **labour markets** and households proliferated in sociology, with a parallel stream of work produced in economics as well. One of the most striking aspects of the field of gender inequality is that a number of concepts have been considered key to the measurement of inequality, and the literature demonstrates strong trends in the attention given to different concepts over the past thirty years as the field has matured.

Beginning in the late 1960s, status attainment researchers in sociology produced a large volume of research on the process of educational and occupational attainment and the influence of parents' socio-economic background on these outcomes. Research initially focused on the intergenerational transmission of educational and occupational status to sons, but by the mid 1970s scholars began to pay more attention to the status transmission process for women as well. Status-attainment researchers found that the process through which parental educational and occupational background is transmitted to daughters is very similar to that for sons, and also that the mean and variance of women's occupational status is very similar to that for men. But it quickly became clear that occupational prestige was an inadequate measure of socio-economic attainment for the purpose of gender comparisons. Paula England demonstrated in a 1979 article that men and women are essentially distributed on two separate occupational ladders, each of which has occupations that span the range of occupational prestige. This makes it theoretically possible for men's and women's *average* occupational prestige scores to be identical even in the presence of nearly complete occupational sex segregation. Likewise, it is possible for the process of occupational attainment to operate very similarly for men and women even though the two sexes cluster in very different occupations, i.e. higher education leads to more prestigious occupational outcomes for each sex, although men may become physicians while women become nurses.

As researchers noted that men and women were distributed differently across the range of occupations in the economy and also that a gender wage gap has persisted across time and appears to be related to occupational sex segregation, the field of gender inequality began to develop at a rapid pace. The political tenor of the 1970s was not an insignificant element in this, as the women's movement called greater attention to **discrimination** against women in the workplace and in educational institutions. Studies of occupational sex segregation proliferated in the 1980s, with researchers focusing on a number of themes: (1) the comparison of occupational sex segregation across industrial societies; (2) the trend in occupational sex segregation across time within a specific country; (3) the sources of occupational sex segregation; and (4) the relationship between women's concentration in 'female-dominated' occupations (defined as those comprised mainly, e.g. 70 per cent, by women) and the gender gap in pay. While sociologists' energies were spread across these varied purposes, labour economists tended to focus on the latter two – the causes of occupational sex segregation and the implications of segregation for the male–female wage gap.

Economists and sociologists have had somewhat different theoretical predilections as to the causes of occupational sex segregation, with economists in general favouring theories emphasizing the choices and preferences of men and women for different occupations and sociologists favouring theories that emphasize constraints on the labour demand (employer) side. As occupational sex segregation became more broadly recognized and both sociologists and labour economists turned their attention to it in the late 1970s and 1980s, the human capital theorist Solomon Polachek argued in a series of papers that women tend to choose occupations in which they will suffer the least skill atrophy and wage depreciation, thereby making it easier to leave the labour force during childrearing and to re-enter the labour force later on. Sociologists examined the underlying assumptions and predictions of this argument and found little empirical substantiation. Jerry Jacobs demonstrated that many women move between female-dominated, male-dominated and mixed-sex occupations over time rather than starting out in one sex-type of occupation and remaining in it. Paula England found no evidence for the assertion of differential wage depreciation by sex-type of occupation. Nor do female-dominated occupations have higher starting wages than men's in order to compensate for a more gradual age-earnings curve, another assertion of Polachek's argument. The thesis that women cluster into occupations that are 'family-friendly' has also received little empirical support; this is a thesis tested by Jennifer Glass in a series of publications.

Other explanations for occupational sex segregation place greater emphasis on the demand side, and generally invoke 'pure discrimination' and/or 'statistical discrimination' as important causes of the segregation of men and women into different occupations. Pure discrimination refers to biases and prejudices against individuals with certain ascriptive characteristics (e.g. African Americans, females) whereas statistical discrimination refers to employers' belief, whether founded on empirical observation or not, that certain ascriptively based groups (e.g. by sex or ethnicity) have lower average productivity than others. This leads to a bias against hiring individuals with these ascriptive traits. Both types of discrimination can involve the preferences and judgements of clients, customers and co-workers as well as employers and managers. Gary Becker postulated that discrimination is economically irrational and that discriminatory employers will eventually be driven out of the market by non-discriminatory employers, as the latter can draw from a larger labour pool and can thus offer lower wages. Sociologists' response is that many social forces keep discriminatory behaviour in place. Cass Sunstein, a legal scholar, presents logical arguments for why market forces might not naturally eradicate discrimination. A number of these arguments invoke feedback effects from employers' or customers' discriminatory behaviour to the preferences and behaviours of individual workers, who may crowd into a smaller set of occupations and thereby inadvertently depress wages. These arguments apply to minorities as well as women (see **inclusion and exclusion**).

Much greater agreement exists between economists and sociologists on the dominant trends over time in occupational sex segregation. In the USA, the level of occupational sex segregation remained virtually constant throughout the twentieth century until 1970; the index of segregation hovered around 70 (signifying that 70 per cent of either men or women would have to switch occupations in order for the two sexes to be evenly distributed across the occupational structure). The level of sex segregation fell by more than ten percentage points in the USA after 1970.

Coterminous with the decline in sex segregation in the USA was a significant decline in the wage gap between male and female workers. Even so, the female/male wage ratio in the USA is only around 76 per cent. The ratio varies widely among western post-industrial economies, ranging from 65 to 90 per cent. Francine Blau and Lawrence Kahn have argued that countries with centralized wage-setting mechanisms and more compressed wage structures tend to have a lower female–male wage gap. These include the Northern European countries and some Western European economies.

Both economists and sociologists have produced numerous studies attempting to measure the association between occupational sex segregation and the gender wage gap, based on the widely verified social fact that jobs in which women are concentrated generally pay less than those with high proportions of men. Estimates of the proportion of the wage gap explained by occupational sex segregation range from about 20 to 40 per cent across studies, depending upon the level of detail at which occupation is measured. Because much sex segregation is job- rather than occupation-based, studies that use very detailed occupational classifications explain more of the gender wage gap than those that use broader classifications. This is especially true in contexts where job hierarchies exist within occupations. One of the dominant examples is managerial occupations, where men typically become more predominant the higher one goes in the level of job prestige (and pay).

While industrial and post-industrial societies vary in the level of occupational sex segregation they evidence, the finding that occupations with high concentrations of female incumbents pay lower wages on average appears to be universal across societies. This has led gender inequality researchers to assert that once occupations or jobs become labelled as 'women's work', they become culturally devalued and wages tend to stagnate. This has been documented both in studies of change over time in the sex composition of given occupations and in comparative studies where given occu-

pations tend to be male-dominated in some countries and female-dominated in others.

The cultural devaluation of women's work has also been a recent sociological theme in the study of the household division of labour (see **housework**). Household labour became an area of interest in labour economics in the 1970s and 1980s via the work of human capital economists such as Gary Becker, Robert Michael, Theodore Schultz and Robert Willis at the University of Chicago. The field quickly became known as the 'new home economics'. These economists made an analogy between the firm and the household, arguing for the analytical utility of the concept of a 'household production function'. As Theodore Schultz wrote in an early volume in this area,

> In terms of economic analysis, the family as a decision-making unit with respect to household production is here viewed as an application of [sic] the theory of the firm in traditional economic theory. In this view of the family, the assumption is made that the welfare of each member of the family is normally integrated into a unified family welfare function.
>
> (1974: 8)

The new household economics postulated an altruistic household head who orchestrated the division of household members' labour between the market and the household so as to maximize members' joint utility.

Many sociologists and feminist economists voiced considerable misgivings about the concepts of a unified family welfare function and an altruistic household head. Some have pointed out that experimental social psychological evidence as well as evidence from economies where resources and food are scarce generally indicate that women behave more altruistically than men vis-à-vis others, casting doubt on the viability of the assumption of an altruistic household head (usually a male) who maximizes the joint utility of household members. Additionally, sociologists have argued that economists' emphasis on household efficiency and the ability of the household division of labour to adapt to changing circumstances such as a husband's unemployment or a wife's wage increase are not only misplaced but fundamentally mistaken. They point instead to the stability of the household division of labour (with wives contributing more non-market labour than husbands) across time and across cultures in the face of significant increases in married women's labour force participation and, in some countries, increases in women's wages as well. Sociological arguments counterposed to the new household economics stress instead the cultural devaluation of work within the home and its classification as feminine, which may lead men to shun such work at almost all cost. This is related to arguments that as married women have entered the labour force in increasing numbers since the 1970s, they have increasingly come to work a 'second shift', taking care of household members and the domestic domain in addition to participating in full-time labour force activity.

While the amount of research on gender and the economy in industrial and post-industrial societies as summarized above is voluminous, a parallel line of research concerns women's status and roles in predominantly agricultural or 'less developed' economies. This research exists in a largely separate tradition. While overlap exists in the area of household labour, many of the other theoretical issues are quite distinct given the different nature of work in settings that are dominated by a combination of agriculture and small-scale production and retail enterprises. Ester Boserup's classic work on women and **economic development** argued that women's economic status often declines as an economy moves from being primarily based on agricultural production to one based on industrial produc-

tion. As production moves outside the home and into the market, traditional skills are devalued and education becomes more important. If education is allocated differently betweens sons and daughters, men acquire a distinct earning advantage. Moreover, employers in developing industries may prefer young female workers who will work up until the point of marriage and then quit or be fired; this constitutes a renewable and cheap source of labour. Married women in industrializing economies often work in small family-run businesses and are categorized as 'family enterprise workers' rather than as paid employees. Their economic status is thereby more closely dependent upon their husband's income than is the case if they hold a paid job independent of the family business.

Consistent with Boserup's early work, the economist Claudia Goldin has provided empirical substantiation of a U-shaped relationship between economic development and women's labour force participation, with married women's participation declining in the early stages of industrialization and increasing as the economy matures and more jobs are concentrated in the service sector. This appears to be a cultural universal, although traditionally patriarchal societies such as some in East Asia, Southern Europe, the Middle East and Latin America show lower participation rates at comparable levels of economic development.

References and further reading

England, Paula and Folbre, Nancy (2005) 'Gender and the Economy', in Neil J. Smelser and Richard Swedberg (eds), *The Handbook of Economic Sociology*, second edition, New York: Russell Sage Foundation.

Goldin, Claudia (1995) 'The U-Shaped Female Labor Force Participation Function in Economic Development and Economic History', in T. Paul Schultz (ed.), *Investment in Women's Human Capital*, Chicago: University of Chicago Press, pp. 61–90.

Petersen, Trond and Morgan, Laurie A. (1995) 'Separate and Unequal: Occupation-Establishment Sex Segregation and the Gender Wage Gap', *American Journal of Sociology*, 101: 329–65.

Reskin, Barbara (1993) 'Sex Segregation in the Workplace', *Annual Review of Sociology*, 19: 241–70.

Schultz, Theodore W. (1974) *Economics of the Family: Marriage, Children, and Human Capital*, Chicago: University of Chicago Press.

MARY C. BRINTON

GERMAN HISTORICAL SCHOOL

See: Historical school

GIFT

Since 1923–4, with the publication in *L'Année sociologique* of *L' Essai sur le don* by Marcel **Mauss** – **Durkheim**'s nephew and intellectual heir – enquiries on the practices of ceremonial gift have been central in the work of ethnologists. But it would be a great mistake to believe that gift practices are relevant only for savage societies and have disappeared in ours. The obligation to give – or, better, the triple obligation to give, take and return – which embodies the basic social rule in at least a certain amount of savage and archaic societies (Pierre Clastres), as Mauss shows, is just the concrete face of the principle of reciprocity. This principle of reciprocity erected by Claude Lévi-Strauss as the basic anthropological principle and set by Karl **Polanyi** in sharp contrast with market and redistribution. If economic sociology shall thrive, it will necessarily be through asking, for each case of economic practice today, which role the logics of market, redistributive hierarchy or reciprocal gift respectively play. Beyond the special case of economic sociology, one can argue that the theory of gift relation is indispensable to general sociological theory.

Mauss' essential discovery is that in what one can call the first society (this generalization is mine: Mauss is more cautious; A. C.) the social bond is not built on the basis of contract, **barter** or market exchange, but through obeying the obligation of rivalry through displayed generosity. Savage gift indeed has nothing to do with Christian charity. Pervaded with aggression and ambivalence, it is an agonistic gift. It is not through economizing but in spending and even dilapidating or in accepting to lose his most precious goods that one can make his name grow and acquire prestige. This discovery represents, of course, a huge challenge to the central postulates of economic theory and of rational–actor theory, since it shows that '*homo economicus* is not before but after us'. He entirely lacks the naturality which economists attribute to him. The goods which are so given, taken and returned (counter-given) generally have no utilitarian value at all. They are valued only as symbols of the social relation they allow to create and feed through activating the unending circulation of a debt, which can be inverted but never liquidated. Gifts are symbols, and they are reciprocal. The gifts which circulate are not only positive ones, benefits, but as well negative ones, misdeeds, insults, injuries, retaliations or bewitchings. The most famous illustrations of this type of gift are the **potlatch** of the Kwakiutl Indians (NW of Canada's coast) and the kula of the Trobrianders.

What remains today of this primitive universe of the gift apart from Christmas or birthday gifts? Apparently not a great many things, and anyway our conception of gift has been altered and reshaped by 2,000 years of Christianity (all great religions, moreover, must be construed as the results of a universalistic transformation of the primary system of archaic gift). Yet, if one looks closer at it, it appears that a large amount of goods and services still circulate through the gift principle. Since Titmuss' *The Gift Relationship*, the best-known illustration is the case of bloodgivers. Jacques T. Godbout shows that the genuine specificity of modern gift is that it can become a gift to strangers. More generally, it is possible to hypothesize that the obligation to give remains the fundamental rule of primary sociality, i.e. of the face-to-face relationships. And even in the sphere of secondary sociality – impersonal on principle – the obligation to give, receive and reciprocate still matters. It is subordinated to market and hierarchy but its role is often nonetheless decisive.

The connection between Mauss's discovery of the gift and the new economic sociology is clearly visible. As Mark Granovetter explains, the key to the understanding of social action must not be looked for in an overarching holistic rule nor in individual rationality, but in the networks or, more precisely, in the trust which the participants to the network share. All this is true, but it must be added that networks are created by gifts and that it is through the renewal of those gifts that networks are nourished. Network relationships are gift relationships (the first large network ever studied was the kula ring described by B. Malinovski).

But we can go a step further. A possible and even obligatory step if we believe the M.A.U.S.S. group and the *Revue du MAUSS* (Anti-Utilitarian Movement in Social Science, www.revuedumauss.com, founded by Alain Caillé and J. T. Godbout among others). This group advances the idea that the specificity of sociology, as compared to economics, lies in an anti-utilitarian way of thinking shared by Durkheim, Weber, Marx and even Pareto. 'This principled anti-utilitarianism, however, can make full sense only on the basis of Mauss's discovery of the gift and in taking seriously what A. Caillé calls the paradigm of the gift. What Mauss shows, through his enquiry on archaic gift, is that social action is not shaped only by the individual and rational self-interest stressed by rational-actor theory but also by a primary logic of sympathy (called *aimance* by Caillé), and that this tension between self-interest and sympathy is crossed by another tension between obligation and freedom. The obligation to give is a paradoxical obligation to be free and to oblige others to be free too. Social bond is constructed neither starting from rational interest or from an overarching and eternal law. It can be correctly construed neither on an individualistic or a holistic paradigm. It is built through a logic of alliance and association. Maussian gift is a political gift. It was long thought and enacted through religion. Today, the democratic ideal represents its most advanced form.

References and further reading

Caillé Alain (2000) *Anthropologie du don. Le tiers paradigme*, Paris: Desclée de Brouwer.

Godbout Jacques T. (with Alain Caillé) (1998) *The World of the Gift*, Montreal: MacGill/Queen's University Press

Mauss, Marcel (1950) 'Essai sur le don (1923–24)', in Marcel Mauss, *Sociologie et Anthropologie*, Paris: PUF. (English translation: *The Gift*, with an introduction by Mary Douglas, London: Routledge, 1990.)

ALAIN CAILLÉ

GLOBALIZATION

Globalization is one of the most controversial topics in the social sciences. The existing theoretical and empirical debates refer to a wide variety of issues, involving not only its associated causes, processes and effects but also the very definition of what it is and the timing of its origins and development. The controversy has also been enhanced by the large number and variety of thinkers and writers who have been attracted to it, including historians, economists, sociologists, political scientists, geographers, demographers, anthropologists, philosophers, military strategists, diplomats, politicians, labour leaders, grassroots activists and **consultants**, among many others. Similarly, organizations of various sorts have become deeply involved in globalization debates, including states, multilateral organizations, grassroots groups, labour unions and multinational firms.

What is globalization? What are its causes?

An important reason for the confusion and diversity of views in the literature on globalization is the lack of a widely accepted definition of the term. Part of the problem lies in that some people think of globalization as an end-state, as the result of an inexorable force leading in one pre-determined direction towards a specific destination (with no agreement as exactly what it is). Globalization, however, is a *process*, not an outcome or a state of affairs, one not necessarily carrying with it a specific teleological thrust. Another definitional problem has to do with the lack of agreement as to whether the causes and the effects of globalization can be disentangled theoretically and empirically. Lastly, writers and commentators on globalization differ in the extent to which they take into consideration the various economic, financial, cultural, geographical, political and social aspects of the process.

Defining globalization in theoretically and empirically meaningful terms requires the consideration of several important points. An appropriate point of departure is to recognize that globalization is a process fuelled by, and resulting in, increasing flows of goods, services, money, people, information and culture across the world that do not observe national borders or other kinds of barriers (Held *et al.* 1999: 16). Social scientists such as Anthony Giddens, David Harvey and Roland Robertson have specifically pointed out three important dimensions of globalization (Guillén 2001a). First, it entails a 'decoupling' between space and time, i.e. a 'compression' or 'shrinking' of the world. Second, it produces both more interdependence, and perhaps coordination, between or among actors, organizations and aggregate entities situated in hitherto unrelated parts of the world. And third, it enhances our consciousness of the world as one big place, thus producing

increasing mutual awareness. I propose to combine these dimensions and define globalization as a process of intensified exchange leading to greater interdependence and mutual awareness among economic, political and social units in the world, and among actors in general (Guillén 2001a; Held *et al.* 1999: 429–31; Waters 1995: 63).

Aside from a process making us more aware of each other, globalization is an *ideology*, one with multiple meanings and lineages. Sometimes it appears loosely associated with neo-liberalism and with technocratic solutions to economic development and market-oriented reforms (Evans 1997). The term also appears linked to cross-border advocacy networks and organizations defending human rights, the environment, women's rights or world peace (Keck and Sikkink 1998). The environmental movement, in particular, has raised the banner of globalism in its struggle for a clean planet (Held *et al.* 1999: 376–413. Thus, globalization is often constructed as an impersonal and inevitable force in order to justify certain policies or behaviours, however praiseworthy some of them might be. In a broader historical sense, some globalization scholars cogently argue that not only capitalism or advocacy movements but also Christianity, Islam, and Marxism have made global claims and harboured global pretensions.

The timing of globalization is also a contested issue, one with key definitional implications (Held *et al.* 1999). Most of the debate has been framed in empirical terms. Some argue that globalization begins with the dawn of history. The bulk of the literature, however, has tended to date the start of globalization more recently, and often in the experience of the West. At one end of the spectrum, historians have noted the importance of the first circumnavigation of the earth in 1519–21. World-system theorists maintain that the expansion of European capitalism in the sixteenth century marks the start of globalization (Waters

1995: 2–4). Some economic historians point to the turn of the century as the heyday of international trade and investment before the convulsions of World War I and the Great Depression threw the world into spiralling protectionism. Scholars like Ronald Robertson argue that globalization 'took off' between 1875 and 1925 with the establishment of global time zones, the international dateline, the spread of the Gregorian calendar, and standard telegraphic and signalling codes. Other scholars start the analysis of globalization at the end of World War II, with the coming of the nuclear age, the emancipation of colonies, the renewed expansion of trade and investment, and the economic rise of northeast Asia. There is also justification to tell the story of globalization beginning with the unravelling of *pax americana* in the early 1970s or with the rise of neo-liberal ideology in the late 1970s and early 1980s. Thus, there seems to be no agreement as to whether it was with Magellan and Mercator, James Watt and Captain Cook, Truman and Stalin, Nixon and Kissinger or Thatcher and Reagan that globalization started or, to be more precise, that the narrative of globalization ought to begin.

The difficult and momentous issue of timing is unlikely to be satisfactorily resolved on empirical grounds alone. One needs to tackle the problem in a more theoretically informed way. Several social scientists highlight that the process of globalization has changed in a qualitative sense since about 1980, one with direct implications for the intensification of global awareness. About two decades ago, globalization became not a phenomenon driven by the interaction of nation-states but rather one that transcends them because of its network properties, the rising importance of information flows, and the enhanced ability of organizations and individuals to partake in it (see Held *et al.* 1999 and Guillén 2001a for reviews). Thus, globalization has acquired a more democratic

and individualized character, and its effects have multiplied in myriad unexpected ways, well beyond what can be captured by measuring trade, investment or money flows. Martin Albrow has perhaps advanced this line of reasoning most forcefully when arguing that globalization is a 'transformation, not a culmination', and a 'transition to a new era rather than the apogee of the old'. He proposes a stark distinction between *modernity* as the imposition of practical rationality upon the rest of the world through the agency of the state and the mechanism of the market, the generation of universal ideas to encompass the diversity of the world', and *globality* as restoring 'the boundlessness of culture and promot[ing] the endless renewability and diversification of cultural expression rather than homogenization or hybridization' (Albrow 1997: 4, 33, 95–101, 144).

The effects of globalization

Equally contested is the debate over the consequences of globalization, in part driven by the lack of consensus as to its definition, timing and main causes. Four possible effects are of especial relevance to economic sociologists: namely, the extent to which globalization produces convergence in organizational or economic practices and outcomes, inequality, an erosion in the authority of the nation-state, and the rise of a global culture.

Convergence

A central tenet in economic sociology is that technology or efficiency do not necessarily produce convergence or uniformity in economic behaviour or outcomes. Most famously expressed in modernization theory, the spread of markets and technology is predicted to cause societies to converge from their pre-industrial past, although total homogeneity is deemed unlikely. This line of thinking was advanced during the

307

1950s and 1960s by both economists and sociologists (Guillén 2001b; Waters 1995: 13–15; Albrow 1997: 49). Contemporary support for the convergence thesis comes from the 'world-society' approach in sociology, which argues that the expansion of rationalized state activities has acquired a momentum of its own, largely unaffected by cross-national differences in political structure or economic growth rates. Rather, the diffusion of rationalized systems follows the imperative of global social organization and results in increasing structural similarities of form among societies although not necessarily of outcomes (Meyer *et al.* 1997). While world-society scholars have empirically documented an increasing degree of organizational similarity in the world, political scientists have noted that there is scope for national peculiarity in institution-building and policy-making in spite of globalization (see Guillén 2001a for a review). Comparative organizational sociologists have also offered qualitative and quantitative evidence to the effect that firms pursue different modes of **economic action** and adopt different organizational forms depending on the institutional and social structures of their home countries even as globalization intensifies (Guillén 2001b).

Inequality

Perhaps the most controversial effect of globalization is its alleged impact on inequality, both across and within countries. The evidence seems to indicate that there is today *more* inequality across countries than ten, twenty, fifty or even one hundred years ago. Stunningly, the gap in per capita income between rich and developing countries has grown fivefold between 1870 and 1990. Only a handful of developing countries have managed to close the gap significantly. During the 1990s, however, China and India – two large countries – have grown very rapidly, thus arresting the increase in cross-national

inequality in the world as a whole. By contrast to inequality from country to country, it is not clear whether increased foreign trade and investment during the last twenty years have resulted in substantially higher wage inequality or unemployment *within* countries. Wage inequality has certainly risen in most advanced countries during the last three decades, but it is not clear that it is mainly due to globalization (see Guillén 2001a for a review).

The nation-state

A classic topic in the globalization literature is whether increasingly free flows of people, money, goods and services erode the authority of the nation-state. Many theorists and observers have noted that technologically and financially driven globalization is not consistent with traditional political structures of a national kind. States, they argue, have become at the mercy of globalization, reducing their capacity and autonomy to act and regulate, and in general making them less relevant. The evidence in this respect is certainly powerful, as for example when countries fail to defend the value of their currency in the wake of speculation or social welfare budgets are trimmed in order to remain competitive in export markets. As Evans (1997) has argued, however, globalization is against the state because its dominant ideology is, not because states are irrelevant in the world of unhindered global markets. More nuanced analyses indicate that globalization has induced three kinds of power shifts: namely, from weak to strong states, from states to markets, and from labour markets to **financial markets**, with some power evaporating or dispersing (Strange 1996: 189). In addition, power has shifted *within* the state from social and labour ministries to economy ministries and central **banks**. In sum, states need to be seen not as passive pawns at the mercy of globalization but rather as institutions capable of adapting.

And, in the face of rising inequality, the contemporary nation-state 'may have less autonomy than earlier but it clearly has more to do' (Meyer *et al.* 1997: 157).

Global culture

One of the most sociologically relevant effects of globalization has been the creation of what has become known as the global 'culture-ideology of consumerism' (Sklair 1991: 75–81). Economic sociologists have criticized this concept on the grounds that consumers may be buying the same goods and services, but that the meaning they extract from them may be, and often is, different (Held *et al.* 1999: 374). Similarly, anthropologists have argued and shown that 'individuals and groups seek to annex the global into their own practices of the modern', and that 'consumption of the mass media worldwide provokes resistance, irony, selectivity, and, in general, *agency*' (Appadurai 1996: 4, 21). Sociologists have documented that national cultures and values are changing, in part as a result of globalization, but that the change is 'path-dependent' rather than convergent or homogenizing. Much empirical research is needed to ascertain the extent to which the rise of a global culture of consumption is taking hold, and the consequences that might emerge from it.

Towards an economic sociology of globalization

Globalization has major implications for some of the key topics studied by economic sociologists, including the social organization of production and consumption and its effects on inequality and the nation-state. Given the importance attributed to social structure, social construction and culture in the new economic sociology (Guillén *et al.* 2002), the study of the causes, processes and outcomes associated with globalization offers unique opportunities to develop and test theory. Key to this undertaking, however, will be: (1) a definition of globalization that emphasizes the reflexive aspects of mutual awareness and consciousness; (2) the development of better empirical indicators that can gauge the constructs of theoretical interest; and (3) the accumulation of more cross-national comparative evidence on how markets work and how governments, firms and individuals make decisions and adopt economic practices.

References and further reading

Albrow, M. (1997) *The Global Age*, Stanford, CA: Stanford University Press.

Appadurai, A. (1996) *Modernity at Large: Cultural Dimensions of Globalization*, Minneapolis: University of Minnesota Press.

Evans, P. (1997) 'The Eclipse of the State?' *World Politics*, 50: 62–87.

Guillén, M. F. (2001a) 'Is Globalization Civilizing, Destructive or Feeble? A Critique of Five Key Debates in the Social-Science Literature', *Annual Review of Sociology*, 27: 235–60.

—— (2001b) *The Limits of Convergence: Globalization and Organizational Change in Argentina, South Korea, and Spain*, Princeton, NJ: Princeton University Press.

Guillén, M. F., Collins, R., England, P. and Meyer, M. (2002) 'The Revival of Economic Sociology', in *The New Economic Sociology*, New York: Russell Sage Foundation, pp. 1–32.

Held, D., McGrew, A., Goldblatt, D. and Perraton, J. (1999) *Global Transformations*, Stanford, CA: Stanford University Press.

Keck, M. E. and Sikkink, K. (1998) *Activists Beyond Borders: Advocacy Networks in International Politics*, Ithaca, NY: Cornell University Press.

Meyer, J. W., Boli, J., Thomas, G. M. and Ramirez, F. O. (1997) 'World Society and the Nation-State', *American Journal of Sociology*, 103(1): 144–81.

Sklair, L. (1991) *Sociology of the Global System*, New York: Harvester Wheatsheaf.

Strange, S. (1996) *The Retreat of the State: The Diffusion of Power in the World Economy*, New York: Cambridge University Press.

Waters, M. (1995) *Globalization*, New York: Routledge.

MAURO F. GUILLÉN

GOOD GOVERNANCE

The notion of 'good governance' has multiple meanings. It is used both in a prescriptive and a descriptive or explanatory way. From the first viewpoint, the term was introduced by international economic and political actors and, through them, entered the scientific debate. In the academic debate it is mostly used in its descriptive meaning and covers many issue-areas in different disciplines. Among them are political science, urban sociology, and the sociology of development.

In the early 1990s the World Bank introduced the concept as a necessary standard that developing countries should fulfil in order to obtain financial aid. Also the International Monetary Fund was urged in 1996, by its Board of Governors, to promote good governance in all its aspects, by ensuring the rule of law, improving the efficiency and accountability of the public sector, and tackling corruption, as essential elements of a framework within which economies can prosper. In the prescriptive meaning, the concept has two main dimensions: (1) it is aimed at the introduction of new public management procedures in the public sector; (2) it shall foster market-oriented reforms in the economic sphere. Those countries that adopted such reforms were considered to be more effective in global market competition and, therefore, they were entitled to receive economic support for their development.

But the use of the concept is not limited to developing countries and it has been extended to industrialized nations. Here the term 'good governance' defines a new model of relationship between state and civil society. Multiple-level networks of social, economic and political actors shall be involved in policy-making and the implementation of socio-economic reforms. Also in the case of developed countries the role of international institutions – the European Union in particular – has been crucial for the fostering of good governance as a new way to pursue public aims. For instance, EU funding has been explicitly directed towards public and private networks of locally based actors. In both cases – in developing countries as well in industrialized nations – markets and networks, in distinction to state and hierarchy, have been at the core of the good governance discourse.

Good governance and development

The new public management promotes the introduction of private sector management methods in the public sector, along with the privatization of publicly owned industries and public services. Relevant keywords are total quality management, customer satisfaction, **incentives**, accountability, effectiveness, **efficiency** and decentralization. The promotion of market-oriented reforms in economic life is a necessary complement to it. By the 1980s, both measures gained a wide consensus among opinion leaders of public policy, in public discourse, and in the social sciences.

The new public management reforms – both through corporate management and marketization – introduce outcome and performance measuring systems for public sector organizations. This, at least, was the dominant view for the 1980s and 1990s. However, the economic results of governance-based reforms in developing countries did not fulfil the promises that the World Bank expected. By the end of the 1990s the World Bank promoted the reintroduction of state and government capacity into the general framework of good governance. In this new version of the concept multi-party competition would appear to be a constitutive element of good governance. In this way, government and politics where brought back in, but just as one actor among others, i.e. along with organized interest, associations, NGOs, lobbies and intermediate institutions of various kinds.

Good governance and state–civil society relationship

In the context of the state–civil society relationship, the term 'good governance' designates a new mode of governing. The advocated form of governance is distinct from the hierarchical control model, is potentially more cooperative and consensus-based, and puts emphasis on the cooperation of state and non-state actors who participate in mixed public/private networks. The intermixing of public/private networks can work at different levels, from the supra-national arena of international relations, to the sub-national governance of cities, regions and industrial sectors. This second level seems to have gained much attention, also for its closeness to crucial issues like the crisis of hierarchical **corporatism**, the rise of new democratic practices and **deliberation**, community participation and **social capital** building (Le Galès 2002).

Networks, as Rhodes aptly points out (2000), are the analytical heart of the notion of governance. Joel Podolny and Karen Page (1998) effectively define the 'network form' as a new mode of governing. Here a complex intermixing of motives leads social and economic exchanges among the nodes of the network. Besides purely economic reasons, social actors promote **trust** and **reciprocity** as a means of long-term collaboration. At the same time, as a rational choice approach would argue instead, networks increase one's concern for reputation and facilitate informal sanctions in case of opportunistic behaviour.

Besides market failure and state failure, networks can fail as well. For instance, social partnerships at the local level can become distributive coalitions that exclude relevant local actors and promote rent-seeking behaviour. Although there is a strong agreement in the governance debate about the importance of networks, there is much less consensus on their effectiveness and

about the mix of mechanisms through which good governance really works. Despite the multiplicity of meanings of the term and open questions regarding the mix of state, private economy and civil society, the ultimate aim of reforms associated with good governance is the creation of an effective framework beneficial to economic action and public life. In this respect – although good governance would appear to be a political science concept – the contribution of economic sociology to the understanding of good governance is crucial.

References and further reading

Le Galès, Patrick (2002) *European Cities: Social Conflicts and Governance*, Oxford: Oxford University Press.

Podolny, Joel M. and Page, Karen L. (1998) 'Network Forms of Organization', *Annual Review of Sociology*, 24: 57–76.

Rhodes, R. A. W. (2000) 'Governance and Public Administration', in Jon Pierre (ed.), *Debating Governance. Authority, Steering and Democracy*, Oxford: Oxford University Press, pp. 54–90.

FILIPPO BARBERA

GOODS/COMMODITIES

Goods, or commodities, are objects that are characterized by two aspects. First, they are socially valued. They are collectively considered as valuable or useful, to different degrees and in various forms. Second, they are fit for exchange. It is possible for them to undergo a property transfer. Those two aspects are interrelated: on the one hand, a good's value constitutes an economic value because the good may circulate and be exchanged, and, on the other hand, economic forms of exchange are based on social compromises on the values of goods. The term 'good' often refers to the valuation process and 'commodity' rather insists in the exchange process, particularly in the case of markets. But those two terms, whose use is often ambiguous, can be interchangeable.

Many sociologists and anthropologists have studied commodities as an aspect of other related topics (mass consumption, colonialism, capitalism, gift exchange, labour markets) or as a research subject as such. Among the intellectual traditions that have been most present in this area, the one originated by **Simmel**'s *Philosophy of Money* and the one inspired by **Marx**'s notion of 'fetishism of commodities' are, perhaps, the most relevant. The term 'commodification' is used to refer to both a concrete process that allows for an entity to become a commodity and to a historical extension of the domain of commodities.

Two major topics lie at the centre of the study of commodities in sociology and anthropology: the objectivity of goods, and the subjective attachment to them (Appadurai 1986; Miller 1987; Thomas 1991).

A good (or a commodity) is a thing. This does not merely mean that goods or commodities are material entities. It means that they have to undergo a process of objectification. They have to be endowed with objective properties, which allow the application of property rights and thus make them fit for a transfer of property. Things often considered as immaterial entities such as services or knowledge go through the same objectification process when they enter economic transactions. Sociological and anthropological research tries not to take this objectification process for granted: this social process of stabilization, delimitation and definition of goods is costly and complex, and does involve a wide variety of institutions (such as property law or market regulation).

But, in order to be a good, the thing must also constitute a value for someone. This means that the good must be incorporated into the world of its new owner, consumer or user. Economic sociologists and anthropologists have therefore focused consistently on the study of the various ways in which attachments between persons and things are constructed in eco-

nomic exchanges. Symbolic resources and subjective dispositions occupy a privileged position as research topics in this area.

References and further reading

Appadurai, Arjun (ed.) (1986) *The Social Life of Things: Commodities in Cultural Perspective*, Cambridge: Cambridge University Press.
Miller, Daniel (1987) *Material Culture and Mass Consumption*, Oxford: Blackwell.
Thomas, Nicholas (1991) *Entangled Objects: Exchange, Material Culture, and Colonialism in the Pacific*, Cambridge MA: Harvard University Press.

FABIAN MUNIESA

GOVERNANCE See: corporate governance; good governance

GUANXI

Central to the underlying logic and pattern of social interaction among the Chinese, *guanxi* (or kuan-hsi) refers to a dyadic, particular and sentimental tie that has potential of facilitating favour exchanges between the parties connected by the tie. In Chinese culture, any blood or marital relationship is qualified for this definition, and persons with a non-kin tie can develop *guanxi* between them if the parties repeatedly invest sentiments in the tie and, at the same time, build up obligations to each other, making the tie mutually special or particular for both parties. Although inter-group and inter-organizational connections may be characteristic of *guanxi*, the basic form of *guanxi* is interpersonal because only persons can have, express and receive sentiments. This is despite the fact that interpersonal sentiments and obligations can be used by and extended to inter-group and inter-organizational exchanges. When *guanxi* goes beyond the dyadic basis to connect more than two persons, a *guanxi* network (or *guanxiwang*) emerges.

These defining statements about *guanxi* will be controversial for a good reason. As a real-life term, that *guanxi* has a rich and complex set of cultural meanings of *mianzi* (face), *chi* (shame), *renqing* (human feeling) and *gangqing* (affection), and denotes variable behavioural expectations across localities and time, is itself a Durkheimian social fact that is difficult to define as an intellectual construct. For example, whether or not a friendship tie can be considered *guanxi* in China today is both a complicated matter and an ongoing scholarly exchange. At least, none of the literate English translations of the term (e.g. relation, relationship, connection or tie) satisfy students of Chinese society, past or present (Gold *et al.* 2002). It is, therefore, no surprise that the Chinese term *guanxi* has become a conventional usage in social science research of Chinese individuals, groups and organizations.

The term *guanxi* entered social science research through the works of Chinese scholars Liang Shumin and Fei Xiaotong. Seeing the family and kinship as the cornerstone of Chinese culture and society, these pioneering researchers consider *guanxi* as the extended familial ties that are defined by a set of ethical codes combining sentiment (*qing*) and obligation (*yî*). They argue that under these codes, Chinese individuals are relationally oriented in ways in which their normative behaviours towards others are confined to Confucian elaborations of the dyadic ties of husband and wife, father and son, older brother and younger brother, and so on. These relational codes of conduct go into village, urban and occupational communities to characterize all interpersonal relations of social significance, pushing everyone to build his/her web of 'pseudo families' with a lifelong effort. The web of 'pseudo families' is, in sociological terminology today, an ego-centric network extended from the family core to others of personal significance through strong and weak ties of sentiments and obligation. The aggregate result of these individual efforts in network building is what Fei has called the 'configuration of differentiation' (*cha xu ge ju*), or a relation-driven, rather than interest-based, social structure.

This kind of social structure persists in the communist political culture of 'principled particularism'. There, *guanxi* to authorities is instrumental for obtaining a great array of life necessities, consumer items and job opportunities that are allocated through the hierarchy of state-run organizations. While prior relationships and sentimental investments are still necessary for developing *guanxi*, instrumental reciprocity becomes the defining characteristic and the overarching goal of *guanxi*. This makes *guanxi*-building a rather deliberate and rational process under communism, eroding the traditional-ethical basis of *guanxi* as a familial and pseudo-familial tie. This tendency reached the peak during the Cultural Revolution decade (1966–76) and has continued to be alive in the reform era (after 1980) in which short-term rationality is the core of the new relational ethics shared by younger generations.

Empirical studies of *guanxi* and its significance to social and economic life in reform-era China have generated diverse and inconclusive views. Village case studies indicate that Chinese peasants normatively invest sentiments to maintain good kinship and neighbourhood ties, and that the instrumental and emotional gains are the by-product or unintended consequence of *guanxi*-building as a way of life. The studies of township and village enterprises, however, show that labour market information and economic resources flow consistently through *guanxi* networks built up within the confines of kinship, home village and home town, making China known as a model of 'network capitalism'. In urban society, Shanghai managers told an American sociologist that they had given up a *guanxi*-driven approach but instead had adopted a legal-rational management style for efficiency during the transition towards a market economy. However, *guanxi* seems

313

a persistent mechanism of occupational mobility, and *guanxi* to local government officials is the lifeblood of private businesses (see Gold *et al.* 2002).

In comparative perspective, sociologists have most recently attempted to conceptualize *guanxi* not as a unique Chinese phenomenon but as a notion belonging to the vector of social network ties. Bian (1997) has treated *guanxi* as a strong tie, rather than a weak tie, because it denotes frequent interaction, high intimacy, enduring emotional attachments or repeated resource exchanges. Lin (2001) has taken a bolder approach to define *guanxi* in the broad context of social exchange networks of asymmetric transaction, and has linked the term to the network concept of social capital. Wellman *et al.* (2002) have gone even further to suggest an analytic framework in which to examine *guanxi* and *guanxi* networks in standard terminologies of social network analysis. Various *guanxi* definitions and their empirical implications for 'social eating' are discussed in detail in Bian (2001).

References and further reading

Bian, Yanjie (1997) 'Bringing Strong Ties Back In: Indirect Connection, Bridges, and Job Search in China', *American Sociological Review*, 62: 266–85.

—— (2001) '*Guanxi* Capital and Social Eating: Theoretical Models and Empirical Analyses', in Nan Lin, Karen Cook and Ronald Burt (eds), *Social Capital: Theory and Research*, New York: Aldine de Gruyter, pp. 275–95.

Gold, Thomas, Guthrie, Doug and Wank, David (2002) *Social Connections in China: Institutions, Culture, and the Changing Nature of Guanxi*, New York: Cambridge University Press.

Lin, Nan (2001) '*Guanxi*: A Conceptual Analysis', in Alvin So, Nan Lin and Dudley Poston (eds), *The Chinese Triangle of Mainland, Taiwan, and Hong Kong: Comparative Institutional Analysis*, Westport, CT: Greenwood, pp. 153–66.

Wellman, Barry, Chen, Wenhong and Dong, Weizhen (2002) 'Networking Guanxi', in Thomas Gold, Doug Guthrie and David Wank (eds), *Social Connections in China: Institutions, Culture, and the Changing Nature of Guanxi*, New York: Cambridge University Press, pp. 221–41.

YANJIE BIAN

H

HABITS

For much of the twentieth century, the concept of habit fell out of favour in the social sciences (Camic 1986). Instead, economists prioritized rational choice and sociologists prioritized roles and norms. However, the concept of habit is enjoying a comeback, partly because of the resurgence of interest in pragmatist philosophy and instinct-habit psychology.

To acknowledge habit is to acknowledge much more than our settled ways, or repetitive human behaviour. We are all 'creatures of habit' but this is more than a mere idiosyncrasy, sluggishness or conservatism on our part. Instead, we have evolved the capacity to form habits to cope with the uncertainty, complexity and variability of circumstances that we have endured over hundreds of thousands of years. Furthermore, habituation is a social mechanism, which typically involves the imitation of others, or results from behaviour that is repeatedly constrained by others. Habits, in short, are tied up with social institutions.

What are habits?

For the pragmatist tradition, including William James, Thorstein **Veblen** and John Dewey, habit was a propensity or disposition. It did not mean behaviour as such. James (1893: 143) proclaimed: 'Habit is thus the enormous fly-wheel of society, its most precious conservative agent.' Veblen (1898: 390) wrote of 'a coherent structure of propensities and habits which seeks realisation and expression in an unfolding activity'. As Dewey (1922: 42) put it: 'The essence of habit is an acquired predisposition to *ways* or modes of response.'

The mechanisms of habit are largely unconscious, but they may press on our awareness. Habits are submerged repertoires of potential behaviour; they can be triggered or reinforced by an appropriate stimulus or context. The meaning of habit adopted by Veblen, the pragmatist philosophers and instinct-habit psychologists was of an acquired proclivity or capacity, which may or may not be actually expressed in current behaviour. Repeated behaviour is important in establishing a habit. But if we acquire a habit we do not necessarily use it all the time. It is a *propensity* to behave in a particular way in a particular class of situations.

However, with a contrasting conception of habit, Gary Becker (1992: 328) wrote: 'I define *habitual* behavior as displaying a positive relation between past and current consumption.' Becker here defines habit not as a behavioural propensity but as sequentially correlated behaviour. In contrast, the view of habit here is of a disposition, which, once acquired, is not necessarily realized in any future behaviour. Habit is a causal mechanism, not merely a set of correlated events.

One of the sources of this behaviourist definition is a reluctance to remove reason and belief from the driving seat of human action. If habits affect behaviour then it is wrongly feared that reason and belief will be dethroned. The concern is that volition would be replaced by mechanism. However, reasons and **beliefs** themselves depend upon habits of thought. Habits act as filters of experience and the foundations of intuition and interpretation. In pragmatist thought, habit is the grounding of both reflective and non-reflective behaviour. This does not make belief, reason or will any less important or real.

From the pragmatist and institutionalist perspective, habits are foundational to all thought and behaviour. All deliberations, including rational optimization, themselves rely on habits and rules (Hodgson 2004). In that habits are triggered by circumstances or stimuli, they have a conditional or rule-like structure. Even rational optimization, if and when possible, must involve rules. In turn, as suggested above, rules have to become ingrained in habits in order to be deployed by agents. Hence rational deliberation always depends on prior habits and rules as props. The view of Becker (1992) and others that rational choices can lead to the formation of habits is valid. But what is *also* being proposed here is that rational choices themselves are always and necessarily reliant on prior habits.

Habit must be distinguished from instinct. Instincts are inherited behavioural dispositions that, when triggered, take the form of reflexes, urges or emotions. They can often be suppressed or diverted. The importance of socialization does not deny the necessary role of instinct. Both instinct and habit are essential for individual development. Instinctive behaviour and socialization are not always rivals but often complements.

The human capacity to form habits has evolved as a result of highly variable environmental and other conditions. The next question is why the same capacity to form sophisticated and adaptable habits is not found to the same degree among other species, which endured similar environmental variations. The answer is in terms of the relatively more sophisticated development of social structures among early humanoids. Individual humans had to deal with a relatively complex social as well as natural environment. They evolved the capacity to create and sustain relatively complex social structures, but at the same time they had to evolve the capacities of communication and interpretation so that each individual could cope with his or her social circumstances. Habituation and sociality are linked together. The manner of this linkage is outlined in the next section.

The interplay of habits and institutions

Institutions are durable systems of established and embedded social rules that structure social interactions. Institutions also involve some shared conceptions. Language, money, law, systems of weights and measures, traffic conventions, table manners, firms (and other organizations) are all institutions. However, we need to consider why institutions are durable, how they structure social interactions, and in what senses they are established and embedded.

Generally, institutions enable ordered thought, expectation and action, by imposing form and consistency on human activities. But the hidden and most pervasive feature of institutions is their capacity to mould and change aspirations, instead of merely enabling them. By channelling our actions, institutions dispose us to change our habits or acquire new ones. The framing, shifting and constraining capacities of social institutions give rise to new perceptions and dispositions within individuals. Upon new habits of thought and behaviour, new preferences and intentions emerge.

It is a central tenet of the pragmatist philosophical and psychological perspective to regard habit and instinct as foundational to the human personality. Reason, deliberation and calculation emerge only after specific habits have been laid down; their operation depends upon such habits. In turn, the development of habits depends upon prior instincts.

The ongoing acquisition and modification of habits is central to individual human existence. For example, much deliberative thought is dependent on, as well as being coloured by, acquired habits of language. In addition, to make sense of the world we have to acquire habits of classification and habitually associated meanings. All action and deliberation depend on prior habits that we acquire during our individual development. Hence habits have temporal and ontological primacy over intention and reason.

An important implication of the idea of interaction between individuals and habits through mechanisms of habituation is that it confounds explanations of social phenomena that are exclusively unidirectional. It provides a means of avoiding both, on the one hand, the exclusively 'top down' explanations of individuals in terms of cultures, structures or institutions, and on the other hand, the exclusively 'bottom up' modes of explanation that attempt to start from individuals alone. The conceptual problems with these two alternatives have been visited elsewhere (Hodgson 2004). The approach sketched here avoids these two extremes, and instead is both interactionist and evolutionary, paying heed to both the uncertainty of the human condition and its situation in evolutionary and historical time.

References and further reading

Becker, Gary S. (1992) 'Habits, Addictions and Traditions', *Kyklos*, 45(3): 327–46.

Camic, Charles (1986) 'The Matter of Habit', *American Journal of Sociology*, 91(5), March: 1039–87.

Dewey, John (1922) *Human Nature and Conduct: An Introduction to Social Psychology*, first edition, New York: Holt.

Hodgson, Geoffrey M. (2004) *The Evolution of Institutional Economics: Agency, Structure and Darwinism in American Institutionalism*, London and New York: Routledge.

James, William (1893) *Psychology: Briefer Course*, New York: Holt.

Veblen, Thorstein B. (1898) 'Why is Economics not an Evolutionary Science?' *Quarterly Journal of Economics*, 12(3), July: 373–97. (Reprinted in Thorstein B. Veblen, *The Place of Science in Modern Civilization and Other Essays*, New York: Huebsch, 1919.)

GEOFFREY M. HODGSON

HABITUS

Habitus is an old philosophical notion, originating in the thought of Aristotle and of the medieval Scholastics, that was retrieved and reworked after the 1960s by sociologist Pierre **Bourdieu** to forge a dispositional theory of action suited to reintroducing the inventive capacity of agents within structuralist anthropology, without that falling back into the Cartesian intellectualism that skews subjectivist approaches to social conduct, from behaviourism to symbolic interactionism to **rational choice theory**. It plays a central role in Bourdieu's (1972/ 1977, 1980/1990, 2000/2004) lifelong effort to construct a 'generalized economy of practices' capable of subsuming economics by historicizing and thereby pluralizing the categories that the latter takes as invariant (such as interest, capital, market and rationality), and by specifying both the social conditions of emergence of economic actors and systems of exchange and the concrete manner in which they encounter, propel or thwart each other.

The roots of habitus are found in Aristotle's notion of *hexis*, elaborated in his doctrine of virtue, meaning an acquired yet entrenched state of moral character that orients our feelings and desires in a situation, and thence our actions. The term was translated into Latin as *habitus* (past participle of the verb *habere*, to have or hold) in the thirteenth century by Thomas

Aquinas in his *Summa Theologiae*, in which it acquired the added sense of ability for growth through activity, or durable disposition suspended midway between potency and purposeful action. It was used sparingly and descriptively by sociologists of the classical generation such as Emile **Durkheim** (in his course on *Pedagogical Evolution in France*, 1904–5), his nephew and close collaborator Marcel **Mauss** (most famously in the essay on 'Techniques of the Body', 1934), as well as Max **Weber** (in his discussion of religious asceticism in *Wirtschaft und Gesellschaft*, 1918) and Thornstein **Veblen** (who ruminates on the 'predatory mental habitus' of industrialists in *The Theory of the Leisure Class*, 1899). It resurged in phenomenology, most prominently in the writings of Edmund Husserl, who designated by habitus the mental conduit between past experiences and forthcoming actions. Husserl (1947/1973) also used as conceptual cognate the term *Habitualität*, later translated into English by his student Alfred Schutz as 'habitual knowledge' (and thence adopted by ethnomethodology), a notion that resonates with that of habit, deployed by Maurice Merleau-Ponty (1945/1962) in his analysis of the 'lived body' as the silent spring of social behaviour. Habitus also figures fleetingly in the writings of another student of Husserl, Norbert Elias, who speaks of 'the psychic habitus of "civilized" people' in his classic study *Über den Process der Civilisation* (1937).

But it is in the work of Pierre Bourdieu, who was steeped in these philosophical debates, that one finds a thorough sociological revamping of the concept designed to transcend the opposition between objectivism and subjectism: habitus is a *mediating* notion that helps us revoke the commonsense duality between the individual and the social by capturing 'the internalization of externality and the externalization of internality', that is, the way society becomes deposited in persons in the form of lasting *dispositions*, or trained capacities and structured propensities to think, feel, and act in determinate ways, which then guide them in their creative responses to the constraints and solicitations of their extant milieu.

Bourdieu first reintroduced the notion denotatively in his youthful empirical studies in the **economic anthropology** of the changing peasant society of his native Béarn in south-western France and of the Berber-speaking Kabyle communities of colonial Algeria (Bourdieu 1962; Bourdieu and Sayad 1964), and then elaborated it analytically in his *Outline of a Theory of Practice* (1972/1977). In this and subsequent writings, Bourdieu proposes that practice is neither the mechanical precipitate of structural dictates nor the result of the intentional pursuit of goals by individuals but rather

> the product of a dialectical relationship between a situation and a habitus, understood as a system of durable and transposable dispositions which, integrating all past experiences, functions at every moment as a *matrix of perceptions, appreciations, and actions*, and make it possible to accomplish infinitely differentiated tasks, thanks to the analogical transfer of schemata acquired in prior practice.
>
> (Bourdieu 1972/1977: 261)

As individual and group history sedimented in the body, social structure turned mental structure, habitus may be thought of by analogy to Noam Chomsky's 'generative grammar', which enables speakers proficient in a given language to produce proper speech acts unthinkingly according to shared rules in creative yet predictable ways. It designates a practical competency, acquired *in and for* action, that operates beneath the level of consciousness; but, unlike Chomsky's grammar, habitus (1) encapsulates not a natural but a *social* aptitude which is for this very reason variable across time, place, and most importantly across distributions of power; (2) it is *transferable* to various domains of practice, which explains the coherence that obtains, for instance, across different realms of consumption – in music, sports, food and furniture, but also in marital and political choices – within and amongst individuals of the same class and grounds their distinctive **life styles** (Bourdieu 1979/1984); (3) it is enduring but *not static or eternal*: dispositions are socially mounted and can be eroded, countered or even dismantled by exposure to novel external forces, as demonstrated by situations of migration, for example; (4) yet it is endowed with *built-in inertia*, insofar as habitus tends to produce practices patterned after the social structures that spawned them, and because each of its layers operates as a prism through which later experiences are filtered and subsequent strata of dispositions overlaid (thus the disproportionate weight of the schemata implanted in infancy); (5) it introduces a *lag*, and sometimes a hiatus, between the past determinations that produced it and the current determinations that interpellate it: as 'history made nature', habitus

> is what confers upon practices their relative autonomy with respect to the external determinations of the immediate present. This autonomy is that of the past, enacted and acting, which, functioning as accumulated capital, produces history on the basis of history and so ensures that permanence within change that makes the individual agent a world within the world.
>
> (Bourdieu 1980/1990: 56)

Against structuralism, then, the theory of habitus recognizes that agents actively make the social world by engaging embodied instruments of cognitive construction; but it also asserts, against constructivism, that these instruments were themselves made by the social world (Bourdieu 1997/2000: 175–7). Habitus supplies at once a principle of sociation and individuation: *sociation* because our categories of judgement and action, coming from society, are shared by all those who were subjected to similar

social conditions and conditionings (thus one can speak of a masculine habitus, a national habitus, a bourgeois habitus, etc.); *individuation* because each person, by having a unique trajectory and location in the world, internalizes a matchless combination of schemata. Because it is both structur*ed* (by past social milieus) and structur*ing* (of present representations and actions), habitus operates as the 'unchosen principle of all choices' guiding actions that assume the systematic character of strategies even as they are not the result of strategic intention and are objectively 'orchestrated without being the product of the organizing activity of a conductor' (Bourdieu 1980/1990: 256). For this dispositional philosophy of action, the economic actor is not the isolated, egoistic individual of neoclassical theory, a computing machine that deliberately seeks to maximize utility in pursuit of clear goals; she is instead a carnal being inhabited by historical necessity who relates to the world through an opaque relationship of 'ontological complicity' and who is necessarily tied to others through the 'implicit collusion' fostered by shared categories of perception and appreciation (Bourdieu 1997/2000: 163; 2000/2004).

Retracing the philosophical origins and initial usage of habitus by Bourdieu (2000) to account for economic rupture and social disjuncture brought by the Algerian war of national liberation allows us to clear up four recurrent misunderstandings about the concept. First, habitus is never the replica of a single social structure since it is a layered and dynamic set of dispositions that record, store and prolong the influence of the diverse environments successively encountered in one's life. It follows, second, that habitus is not necessarily coherent and unified but displays varying degrees of integration and tension, depending on the character and compatibility of the social situations that produced it over time: irregular universes tend to produce unstable systems of dispositions divided against themselves that generate irregular and sometimes incoherent lines of action. Third, the concept is no less suited to analysing crisis and change than it is cohesion and perpetuation. This is because habitus does not necessarily agree with the social world in which it evolves. Bourdieu (1980/1990: 62–3) warns that one must 'avoid unconsciously universalizing the model of the quasi-circular relation of near-perfect reproduction that is completely valid only in the case where the conditions of production of habitus are identical or homologous to its conditions of functioning'. The fact that habitus can 'misfire' and have 'critical moments of perplexity and discrepancy' (Bourdieu 1997/2000: 191) when it is incapable of generating practices conforming to the milieu constitutes a major spring of social innovation and economic change – which gives Bourdieu's notion a close affinity with neoinstitutionalist conceptions of bounded rationality and malleable preferences, as in regulation theory (Boyer 2004). Lastly, habitus is not a self-sufficient mechanism for the generation of action: it operates like a spring that needs an external trigger and thus it cannot be considered in isolation from the particular social worlds or 'fields' within which it evolves. A full analysis of practice thus requires a triple elucidation of the social genesis and structures of habitus and field, and of the dynamics of their 'dialectical confrontation' (Bourdieu 1997/2000).

Though philosophers such as Charles Taylor, Jacques Bouveresse and John Searle have discussed Bourdieu's elaboration of habitus in relation to the philosophy of mind, language and self, it must be stressed that for Bourdieu the notion is first and foremost a stenographic manner of designating a *research posture*, by pointing out a path for excavating the implicit categories through which persons ongoingly assemble their lived world, which has informed empirical inquiries into the social constitution of competent agents in the gamut of institutional venues. Thus Suaud (1976) has illumined the making and unmaking of the priestly vocation in the French Vendée by showing how the seminary acted in continuity with the closed village community during the 1930s to trigger mass callings, but lost its capacity to forge a robust religious habitus when the Church ceded symbolic pre-eminence to the school by the 1970s. Charlesworth (2000) has captured the formation and deployment of a distinctive working-class sensitivity, fostering silence and inarticulacy, born of the embodiment of the abiding experience of economic dispossession and political powerlessness in a declining small town of southern Yorkshire in England. Lehmann (2002) has traced how musical dispositions instilled by instrumental training combine with class dispositions inherited from the family to determine the professional trajectory and strategies of musicians inside the hierarchical space of the symphony orchestra. Wacquant (2000/2003) has dissected the production of the nexus of embodied skills, categories and desires that make up prize-fighting as a masculine bodily craft in the black American ghetto, revealing that the manufacturing of the pugilistic habitus entails not just the individual mastery of technique but, more crucially, the collective inscription of a heroic occupational ethic in the flesh within the microcosm of the boxing gym. These studies demonstrate that the assembly and employment of the cognitive and motivative schemata that compose habitus is accessible to methodical observation. Ultimately, the proof of the theoretical pudding of habitus must consist in its empirical eating.

References and further reading

Bourdieu, Pierre (1962) 'Célibat et condition paysanne', *Études rurales*, 5–6, April: 32–136 (Reprinted in Pierre Bourdieu, *The Ball of Bachelors*, Chicago: University of Chicago Press, forthcoming).

—— ([1972]1977) *Outline of a Theory of Practice*, Cambridge: Cambridge University Press.

—— ([1979]1984) *Distinction: A Social Critique of the Judgment of Taste*, Cambridge, MA: Harvard University Press.

—— ([1980]1990) *The Logic of Practice*, Cambridge: Polity Press.

—— ([1997]2000) *Pascalian Meditations*, Cambridge: Polity Press.

—— (2000) 'Making the Economic Habitus: Algerian Workers Revisited', *Ethnography*, 1(1), July: 17–41.

—— ([2000] 2005) *The Social Structures of the Economy*, Cambridge: Polity Press.

Bourdieu, Pierre and Sayad, Adbelmalek (1964) *Le Déracinement. La crise de l'agriculture traditionnelle en Algérie*, Paris: Editions de Minuit.

Boyer, Robert (2004) 'Pierre Bourdieu et la théorie de la régulation', *Actes de la recherche en sciences sociales*, 150, February: 65–78.

Charlesworth, Simon J. (2000) *A Phenomenology of Working-Class Experience*, Cambridge: Cambridge University Press.

Husserl, Edmund ([1947]1973) *Experience and Judgment*, London: Routledge and Kegan Paul.

Lehmann, Bernard (2002) *L'Orchestre dans tous ses états. Ethnographie des formations symphoniques*, Paris: Editions la Découverte.

Merleau-Ponty, Maurice ([1947]1962) *Phenomenology of Perception*, London: Routledge.

Suaud, Charles (1976) *La Vocation. Conversion et reconversion des prêtres ruraux*, Paris: Editions de Minuit.

Wacquant, Loïc ([2000] 2004) *Body and Soul: Notebooks of an Apprentice Boxer*, New York: Oxford University Press.

LOÏC WACQUANT

HEDONISM See: utilitarianism

HIERARCHY See: corporate governance; organization theory

HIRSCHMAN, ALBERT O.

Albert O. Hirschman, born 7 April 1915 in Berlin, is a political economist and social scientist who is a major and highly influential author in fields such as development economics (1958) the theory of the firm and other formal organizations (1970), the history of political ideas, the economics of inflation (1981: 177–208) and the epistemology of the social sciences and the sociology of knowledge (e.g. 1986: ch. 5). After fleeing his native Germany right at the beginning of the Nazi regime in 1933, he studied and worked in France, Britain and Italy before settling in the USA (1941), where he became engaged in research and teaching at Berkeley, Yale, Columbia, Harvard and Princeton universities. In 1985, he retired from his post of director of the School of Social Sciences of the Institute for Advanced Study in Princeton.

Hirschman's wide-ranging international as well as interdisciplinary academic work is significantly and self-reflectedly shaped by the author's rather unique biographical experience (cf. 1995, part II) not just as an academic (London School of Economics, 1935–6; doctorate in economics, Trieste 1938), but also as soldier (in the French and US armies, as well as in the Spanish Civil War), an underground activist in German-occupied France (1940), an employee at the US Federal Reserve Board where he was involved in the administration of the Marshall Plan (1946–52), a government advisor working for the World Bank and independent consultant (Colombia, 1952–6). His highly distinctive style of intellectual work has been described by himself and others as driven by a propensity for 'lateral' thinking, for 'self-subversion' (1995), and 'trespassing' or 'boundary-crossing' (1998), often combined with a sense of irony, a keen interest in paradoxes, unanticipated consequences (of both the 'perverse effects' and the 'blessings in disguise' variety), 'trust in doubt' and the fallibility of 'general laws'. The intellectual playfulness and elegance of much of his writings, many of which are 'non-technical' by the standards of modern economics, corresponds, with all its subtlety of imagination, to a concern for humanistic and progressive values and the role these values can play in the conduct of social and economic research.

The accomplishment of social theory is arguably its capacity for categorizing a heterogeneous variety of phenomena around by means of a few, simple and clear-cut concepts. Hirschman has become influential and famous for his innovative exploration of pairs of opposite concepts and the tensions, sequences and syntheses that occur between the respective realm of opposites. He is best known for the conceptual pair of 'exit' vs 'voice' (1970), to which he returns with revisions and elaborations in some of his later work (e.g. 1986: ch. 4). If social systems (such as states, marriages, firms, market transactions, **industrial relations**) perform disappointingly, members can leave ('exit') or 'protest', i.e. raise their 'voice' in order to seek improvement. After introducing the distinction of these two basic mechanisms of responding to failure, Hirschman proceeds to analyse the (opportunity) costs and returns that either of them yields in different situations. One idea suggested by this distinction is that 'exit' is the standard response in markets and 'voice' the standard within firms and politics. Another aspect is asymmetrical sequence of the two: after exit has been chosen, voice is no longer relevant, while the threat of exit may well increase the weight of voice, as highlighted by Hirschman in his analysis of the GDR opposition movement of summer and fall of 1989 (1995: ch. 1). That depends, among other things, on the costliness of exit, which may well be too 'cheap' to lead actors to try voice first. Yet voice, in case it is collectively and hence more effectively raised, may presuppose prior investment in and the practice of **collective action**. Following these and related lines of thought, the reader is introduced into a whole range of situations and problems of rational agency, the complexity of which defies any doctrine of some unique best way to deal with all kinds of failure and suboptimality.

This pair of concepts, as well as other related pairs such as 'interests' vs 'passions' or 'private interests' vs 'public action' (1982), or 'market dominance' vs 'pre-

capitalist forms' (1986: ch. 5) have, at least in Hirschman's own use and imaginative applications, some of the compelling simplicity, elegance and intellectual appeal that must be experienced by children who learn that their speech is structured and organized by a small set of rules of grammar of which they so far have been unaware. The interplay of these elementary forms and forces of social life yields such a virtually unlimited complexity of phenomena and situations that both prescription and prediction become matters of ill-advised ambition on the part of both social scientists and political leaders. 'After so many failed prophecies', Hirschman asks (1986: 139), 'Is it not in the interest of social science to embrace complexity, be it at some sacrifice of its claim to predictive power?' Instead of general 'laws of development', social scientists (following Hirschman's model of 'possibilism'; 1986: ch. 8) should elucidate the range of the possible, thus deconstructing both the notion of irresistible obstacles to change as well as the opposite notion of some law-like certainty of historical progress.

Hirschman ridicules in some of his writings, beginning with those on economic development, the figures of both the 'visiting expert' and the visiting revolutionary, both offering ready-made recipes or, in the case of those befallen by the doctrinaire pessimism of 'fracasomania', or 'failure complex' (1998: 87), the message that 'nothing works'. Such deterministic views, according to Hirschman, suffer from the dual liability of not only being untrue (or at best trivial), but, perhaps more importantly, of ignoring and discouraging the creativity and energy of human agents in search of improvement. Motivations of economic agents are in no way 'given', least of all by *homo economicus* assumptions, but they emerge from the specifics of a situation and the expectations it gives rise to. There is thus more than an element of hermeneutics in Hirschman's approach to **economic action**. The basic intuition of this approach is well illustrated by the famous model of the 'tunnel effect': the model is that of two lanes of traffic getting stuck in a tunnel. After a while, only the left lane traffic starts moving, inducing the hope in those still stuck in the right lane that they, too, will soon be allowed to move. After this does not happen for an amount of time, the hopes of the people in the right lane turn into frustration and anger; as a consequence, they try to squeeze themselves into the left lane, and the traffic gets stuck again.

A similar U-shaped trajectory of endogenous motivational change underlies the analysis of *Shifting Involvements* (1982). Providing an alternative to the dominant public choice models of the Prisoner's Dilemma and the Logic of Collective Action, the author provides theoretical evidence and empirical illustration of the fact that actors engaged in 'public-regarding action' do actually experience the cost of such action as a gain (or as the pleasure of acting and belonging), which would explain why the more of this action is taking place, the more resources for further action are available. Up to a point, that is, when failure to achieve intended objectives turns into frustration and eventually defection. Similarly, as Hirschman had observed much earlier (1958), an unorthodox strategy of 'unbalanced growth' can yield challenges, trigger the creativity and spontaneity of actors, and yield unanticipated upstream, downstream and intersectoral linkages and other favourable externalities, the total effect of which may be superior to what any strategy of 'balanced' growth is able to accomplish. Another example of Hirschman's interpretive approach is his account of the debates about the welfare state (1986: ch. 7) and his analysis of what he terms the 'rhetoric of reaction' (1991) where he describes how dominant interpretations of 'futility' and 'perverse effects' can inhibit the course of political and economic reform. He also shows how the false certainty concerning perverse effects can be dispelled by the reformers' insistence that the policies they advocate are called for 'on the ground that they are right and just, rather than by alleging that they are needed in order to stave off some imaginary disaster' (1993: 311).

Much of Hirschman's work on the economics of development as well as that on the rise of markets and the interaction of markets and politics has played the role of a highly influential 'instant classic' (if more so in sociology and political science than in the discipline of economics itself); this 'classical' status of the *opus* is indicated by the fact that Hirschman (by 2003) has been awarded no fewer than nineteen honorary degrees from universities in eight different countries. But studies which test, apply, elaborate, or critically confront his theoretical insights are still rare. Freeman and Medoff have used the exit/voice paradigm for an analysis of industrial relations and industrial action, and several of the contributors to his *Festschrift* (Foxley *et al.* 1986) have taken up and discussed some of his theoretical ideas. But a critical and comprehensive assessment of Hirschman's work in its entirety, including his contribution to modern political economy and the sociology of firms and other organizations, is still missing.

References and further reading

Foxley, Alejandro, McPherson, Michael S. and O'Donnell, Guillermo (eds) (1986) *Development, Democracy and the Art of Trespassing: Essays in Honor of Albert O. Hirschman*, Notre Dame, IN: University of Notre Dame Press.

Hirschman, Albert O. (1958) *The Strategy of Economic Development*, New Haven, CT: Yale University Press.

—— (1970) *Exit, Voice, and Loyalty: Responses to Decline in Firms, Organizations, and States*, Cambridge, MA: Harvard University Press.

—— (1981) *Essays in Trespassing: Economics to Politics and Beyond*, Cambridge: Cambridge University Press.

—— (1982) *Shifting Involvements: Private Interest and Public Action*, Princeton, NJ: Princeton University Press.

—— (1986) *Rival Views of Market Society and Other Recent Essays*, New York: Elisabeth Sifton Books, Viking/Penguin.

—— (1991) *The Rhetoric of Reaction: Perversity, Futility, Jeopardy*, Cambridge, MA: Harvard University Press.

—— (1993) 'The Rhetoric of Reaction – Two Years Later', *Government and Opposition*, 28(3): 292–314.

—— (1995) *A Propensity to Self-Subversion*, Cambridge, MA: Harvard University Press.

—— (1998) *Crossing Boundaries: Selected Writings*, New York: Zone Books.

CLAUS OFFE

HISTORICAL MATERIALISM

The central thesis of historical materialism is that economic conditions shape forms of social, cultural and political life, the direction of future social change, as well as our ability to critically evaluate the nature of social and political relations. This thesis is of particular importance in societies whose economies are organized on the basis of the capitalist mode of production, i.e. societies where the economic system as the dominant social value sphere influences priorities and decisions in all other social value spheres. Typically, both criteria apply in modern societies (see **modernity**).

Historical materialism commonly is identified with Karl Marx's critique of political economy and concurrent perspective on history, and regarded as synonymous with, or closely related to, economic interpretation of history, materialist interpretation of history, dialectical materialism or economic determinism. However, Marx neither employed nor introduced the concept; instead, it resulted from Friedrich Engels' efforts to systematize Marx's theory after his death in 1883 (Carver 1981, esp. ch. 7).

Historical materialism implies that in the absence of a sustained commitment to scrutinizing the nature of the relationship between concrete economic conditions ('base', 'mode of production', 'forces of production') and forms of social life

('superstructure', 'relations of production'), there is a danger to regard both as expressions of human nature, rather than as historically specific forms of mediation between 'man' and 'nature'. In Engels' view, for historical materialism to serve as a politically suggestive label it had to convey the programmatic thrust of Marx's transformative critique as a new way of theorizing economic conditions and change, in relation to social, political and cultural life in bourgeois society. By implication, historical materialism frames social science as a critical theory of modern capitalism.

Yet, while Engels appreciated that synchronizing what Marx had conceived as the most intricate, abstract and radical theory of the relationship between economics, politics and society with a programmatic label was highly problematic, most of those whose reading of Marx was influenced by the terminology Engels introduced, did not. To this day, circumscribing the meaning and relevance of historical materialism is impaired by the history of the concept being fraught with sedimented misinterpretations of Marx's theory. These misinterpretations began with regard to Marx's early writings, worsened with flawed attempts to grasp the thrust of his work as analysing how the spread of the capitalist mode of production reconfigures the perimeter and parameters of traditional societies, amplified further still with successive attempts by both proponents and critics to identify the core of his theoretical endeavours, and culminated in more or less deleterious efforts to apply his theory practically and politically. It was not until the 1980s and 1990s that opportunities emerged – first in anticipation of the impending collapse of 'actually existing socialism', and later in response to the need to scrutinize 'globalization' – for interpreters of Marx's writings to fathom the depth of the gulf between the thrust and purpose of his critical theory, and interpretations and applications of his writings that were guided by practical considerations – including, in particular, Marxism-Leninism (see Postone 1993, 1997; Sayer 1989; Murray 1988; Hazelrigg 1993).

Alongside the current revival of economic sociology, a growing number of scholars began to insist that the primary purpose of Marx's theory, as well as its greatest relevance today, relates to the challenge of preparing the possibility of forms of **collective action** that escape the fate of reproducing the most problematic features of social, political, cultural and, especially, of economic life in modern society. Accordingly, Marx's theoretical endeavours had been directed primarily at revolutionizing our understanding of the relationship between economic transformations, on the one hand, and practices, institutions and forms of organization in politics, culture and society, on the other. Thus, the project of revolutionizing bourgeois (capitalist, modern) societies – in a manner that is inspired by the prospect of the values espoused in and by political systems whose legitimacy rests on democratic validity claims, and points beyond the perpetuity of the kind of social problems that prevail in societies with capitalist economies – will become conceivable, and viable only once our ability to critically grasp the highly problematic and contradictory entwinement of priorities in the modern social sciences and the defining features of modern capitalism has reached a qualitatively higher level.

Yet, since Marx's critique of political economy was far ahead of its time, even sincere proponents of his theory and perspective on historical change tended to superimpose elements of Marx's theory on to the mode of reflection and theorizing that preceded, and was the target of, his critique. Put differently, even for Marx's most sophisticated followers, his critique was too radical for them to be able to promulgate the spirit in which he had meant it to be appropriated and applied, to pursue the objectives that inspired his writings. Even early interpretations of Marx's critique of political economy and theory of bourgeois society perpetuated, *in an inverted fashion*, the flawed theoretical presuppositions he had endeavoured to expose. Ironically, Friedrich Engels was the first prominent advocate of Marx's theory whose interpretation was fraught with flaws that channelled – and thus, impaired – attempts during the twentieth century to do justice to the *specificity* of the revolutionary thrust of Marx's inception of critical theory. In decisive regards, Engels' interpretation foreshadowed what Moishe Postone calls 'traditional Marxism'. As both a concept and the basis of critical theory, the intended referent of *historical materialism* was both more radical and more ambitious than traditional Marxist interpretations presumed, would have allowed for, and were capable of conceiving.

Postone distinguishes three predominant flaws in interpretations of Marx's theory that account for the deterioration of his critical theory into 'traditional Marxism'. As the purpose of Marx's theory was to revolutionize our understanding of the relationship between the economy and social life, proponents of his perspective did not distinguish between his concept of labour as both historically specific, and trans-historical – *and in what ways*. Marx's concept of labour can be interpreted in two different ways, with very different, mutually exclusive implications: while traditional Marxists read the critique of political economy as 'a critique of capitalism *from the standpoint of* labor', his argument pointed towards 'a critique *of* labor in capitalism' (Postone 1993: 5). Furthermore, while traditional Marxists applied Marx's theory primarily to criticize patterns and relations of distribution in capitalism, Marx was oriented towards a simultaneous critique of patterns and relations of distribution *and production*. Finally, the thrust of Marx's critical theory is directed at identifying a *new form of social domination* as endemic to capitalism:

> it has no determinate locus and, although constituted by specific forms of social practice, appears not to be social at all. The structure is such that one's own needs, rather than the threat of force or of other social sanctions, appear to be the source of such 'necessity'.

> ... The Marxian analysis includes [relations of class exploitation and domination], but goes beyond it ... [T]he forms of social mediation expressed by categories such as the commodity and capital develop into a sort of objective system, which increasingly determines the goals and means of much human activity.
>
> (Postone 1997: 62f)

Historical materialism, interpreted in the spirit of Marx's theory (rather than Engels' particular rendering), would not imply a determinist interpretation of the relationship between economy and social life, to culminate in socialism. Rather,

> [s]ocialist society, according to Marx, does not emerge as the result of a linear, evolutionary historical development. The radical transformation of the process of production ... is not an automatic consequence of the rapid increase in scientific knowledge or its application. It is, rather, a possibility that arises from a growing intrinsic social contradiction.
>
> (Postone 1993: 34)

The distinction between the 'primacy of the economy' and the 'primacy of the state' provides a useful reference point for explaining the problematic history of the concept of historical materialism. Both proponents and critics of Marx's theory – irrespective of whether they viewed it as a coherent whole or differentiated it in terms of any number of distinctions, such as between the 'early' and the 'mature' Marx – stressed that his central thesis was that in

human affairs, modes of material production and reproduction 'determine' the specific societal conditions prevalent at different stages of **economic development**. While there was a close relationship between pre-capitalist modes of production and social, political and cultural values, practices and institutions, it is only in capitalism that the economic system acquires dominance. Consequently, those who interpreted Marx's perspective in terms of historical materialism presumed that to scrutinize modern bourgeois society, a theory of the effects of the increasingly capitalist economy on all aspects of society is essential: the 'primacy of the economy' meant that the capitalist mode of production determines the nature of the relations among human beings, between humans and nature, and between individual human beings and society.

With regard to patterns of historical change during the twentieth century, especially after World War II, social scientists sympathetic to Marx's perspective and theory observed a shift from the 'primacy of the economy' to the 'primacy of the state'. In different yet still closely related ways, social theorists working in a Marxian mould 'reconstructed' historical materialism, to make the theory it purportedly implied more suitable for the analysis of advanced western societies with Keynesian economic policies and welfare states. Giddens (1995), Habermas (1976), Offe (1984) and others concluded that the more technologically developed an economy, the greater the importance of democratically elected governments in decision-making processes at the national level. Accordingly, once reconstructed, historical materialism was to provide a unique basis for tracking and analysing the shift from the primacy of the economy as the value-sphere determining priorities in policy and the trajectory of socio-economic change, to the primacy of the (democratically legitimated) political state in late twentieth-century societies.

Economic sociology thus re-emerged at a time when the latter view, implicitly or explicitly, had become widely accepted in academia. Yet precisely at that time, during the 1980s, western societies underwent a period of 'restructuring' business–labour–government relations, driven largely by developments in the United States, engendering changes that gave new relevance to the distinction between the economy and the political state as key value-spheres imbued with social power. With attention turning towards 'globalization' during the 1990s, the trend towards the increasing importance of political institutions appeared to be going into reverse. Indications kept mounting that the shift from the primacy of the economy to the 'primacy of the political' prepared the return of a much more virulent version of 'primacy of the economy' (Dahms 2000). Paradoxically, central features of globalization appear to confirm key tenets of historical materialism as conceived not only before the efforts at reinterpretation during the 1990s, but before its reconstruction during the 1970s. The evidence mounting continues to suggest that the socio-historic condition currently taking shape conforms to predictions drawn from Marx's writings as a critical theory, *as well as* from traditionalist interpretations derived from Engels' more determinist framing. 'Globalization', then, in important regards, would follow a trajectory that is intricate and crude at the same time, intimating that rather than being eclipsed by the continuing transformations of capitalism, historical materialism remains an effective means to identify and explain key features of the present.

By contrast, as terms that are linked to Engels' more practically oriented interpretation of Marx's theory, dialectical materialism, materialist interpretation of history, and economic determinism are becoming ever more problematic – and devoid of comparable heuristic acumen. Both 'economic interpretation of history'

and 'primacy of the economy' imply that we cannot causally explain any aspect of modern western societies without taking into consideration the continuing transmutations of industrialized economies, both engendering and reacting to changing conditions that result from its workings, and further transforming these conditions. Yet it is not the primacy of the economy in general that is at issue, but of the *capitalist* economy as the most important, perpetually changing system of power in modern society. Accordingly, 'primacy of the economy' does not stand for the supposition that it is sufficient to scrutinize and identify the role economic conditions play in shaping social relations, institutions and modes of organization, but that doing so is the necessary precondition for research that relates to the nature of social phenomena in modern capitalist societies.

For economic sociology, historical materialism is a reminder that it is necessary to make explicit and examine underlying, implicitly presumed orientations in, and purposes of, rigorous research. While economic sociology has been highly critical of the limitations built into neoclassical economic theory, under conditions of globalization. Yet combined with the reluctance to work towards, or adhere to, a common denominator (e.g. a common theoretical reference frame), the diversity of approaches economic sociologists put forth, presents the peril of overlooking how mainstream economists tend to frame the relationship between representations of social reality and established priorities in social-scientific research, to obscure the problematic nature of the specific reality to be discerned. Marx's theory remains an important reminder that in the interest of sustaining research agendas that are analytically pertinent and socially relevant, it is necessary to retain a critical distance from the object of study.

References and further reading

Carver, Terrell (1981) *Engels*, New York: Hill and Wang.

Dahms, Harry. F. (ed.) (2000) *Transformations of Capitalism: Economy, Society and the State in Modern Times*, New York: New York University Press.

Giddens, Anthony (1995) *A Contemporary Critique of Historical Materialism*, second edition, Stanford, CA: Stanford University Press.

Habermas, Jürgen (1976) *Zur Rekonstruktion des Historischen Materialismus*, Frankfurt/M: Suhrkamp.

Hazelrigg, Lawrence E. (1993) 'Marx and the Meter of Nature', *Rethinking Marxism*, 6(2): 104–22.

Murray, Patrick (1988) *Marx's Theory of Scientific Knowledge*, Atlantic Highlands, NJ: Humanities Press.

Offe, Claus (1984) *Contradictions of the Welfare State*, edited by John Keane, Cambridge, MA: MIT Press.

Postone, Moishe (1993) *Time, Labour and Social Domination*, Cambridge: Cambridge University Press.

—— (1997) 'Rethinking Marx (in a Post-Marxist World)', in Charles Camic (ed.), *Reclaiming the Sociological Classics. The State of the Scholarship*, Malden, MA: Blackwell, pp. 45–80.

Sayer, Derek (1989) *The Violence of Abstraction: The Analytic Foundations of Historical Materialism*, Oxford: Blackwell.

HARRY F. DAHMS

HISTORICAL SCHOOL

Representatives of the historical school analyse economic concepts, states of affairs, elements, and relations primarily with regard to their historical origination. Economic relations are then also exposed in different ways on account of the various territorial differences. As a consequence, theories purporting to be absolute and cosmopolitan, and this independent of time and space, are rejected. This could give rise to a historicism or sophistic relativism (Roscher 2002) where historical facts are merely collected and portrayed, while the varying origination of data is not adequately determined in terms of theory and epistemology. To avert the suspicion of being a mere collection of data with no theory of its own, the historical school must therefore establish epistemological points of reference to warrant a general theory on distinct territorial and temporal features. Third, the historical approach makes possible institutional, cultural, and ethical economics (Pirker and Rauchenschwandtner 1998, Shionoya 2001).

The themes of the historical school were primarily developed by German-speaking researchers in the face of German territorial characteristics (for the English-speaking historical research of Thomas Tooke, William Newmarch, Richard Jones, John K. Ingram and Thomas E. C. Leslie, cf. Brandt 1993, Vol. 2; on the reception of Wilhelm Roscher in UK and USA, cf. Senn 1995). In principle, the multifaceted streams of the historical school can be classified into an older historical school (Wilhelm Roscher, Bruno Hildebrand, Karl Knies) and a younger historical school (Gustav Schmoller, Lujo Brentano, Karl Bücher, Georg Friedrich Knapp, Werner Sombart). The historical school dates from the first third of the nineteenth century to the first third of the twentieth century. Based on its self-understanding, it needs to be distinguished from classical **political economy**, which originated with Adam Smith, from classical economy in the German countries (especially Karl Heinrich Rau), the romantic school in Germany and Austria (Adam Müller) and, in particular, from modern, neoclassical economics.

Now, if the historical avenue is the essential and distinct feature of the historical school, one needs to define what the qualifier 'historical' actually means, since classical political economy also has historical perspectives (especially with Adam Smith and Adam Ferguson). The following theoretical elements constitute the canon of the historical school: the establishment of history as a science in Germany, while political economy and historical jurisprudence

(Carl von Savigny, Carl Friedrich Eich-horn) must take into account a certain aspect of the *Volksbedürfnisse* (people's needs). The older historical school thus develops a theory of historicity for economic arguments which comprises the following elements: first, a rehabilitation of sophistry against Plato and Hegel through Roscher (Roscher 2002), the romantic valorization of Thucydides with the help of a *Kunsttrieb* (art impulse) as the ability to conceive historical occurrences, the constitution of a general law of history, which describes a theory of the economic stages of peoples in a cycle of emergence, bloom, and decline – with a clear reference to Johann Gottfried Herder – and the exposition of history's organic structure. Karl Knies recognized the weaknesses of this natural historical argumentation and adds the experiences of humans as a second factor of political economy in addition to the natural territorial differences. For Knies, culture is the link between nature and the experiences of humans.

Carl Menger, in particular, ranks among the key opponents of the historical school. In the **Methodenstreit** (Menger 1883), Menger discriminates the historical school, calling it aberrant, since it is unable to establish a theoretical and exact system of economics. Menger specifically criticizes the epistemological shortcomings of the historical school, accusing it of practising a poor sort of ontology, since the subject matter of economics for him was the analysis of typical relations (prices, subjective value theory) and not the construction of an economic subject ('people') which does business itself.

In the last third of the nineteenth century, the historical school played a vital role in the establishment of cultural studies, which in principle had the following sources: a historical approach, the axiological reformulation of Immanuel Kant's critical philosophy in the neo-Kantianism of southwestern Germany (Wilhelm Windelband,

Heinrich Rickert), the hermeneutics of Wilhelm Dilthey, and the social-science interpretation of Edmund Husserl's phenomenology. One of the leading representatives of the historical school in the first third of the twentieth century (Friedrich von Gottl-Ottlilienfeld) aspired to elaborate a principle of synthesis from these diverse theories.

In principle, the younger historical school has three streams: first, specific territorial forms of economic forces were examined (structures of agricultural production, housing issues, industrial codes), reducing the methodical and theoretical effort. The conspicuously defensive stance of Gustav Schmoller in the Methodenstreit, in particular, diminished its epistemological potency. The difference between deduction (Carl Menger) and induction (Gustav Schmoller) as a methodical approach was the only meagre result and earned Schmoller the reproach of proposing an inadequate theory. Menger's continued effort to epistemologically constitute a cognitive object in an exact system of economics was not addressed in the Methodenstreit. Second, the younger historical school stands for a further tightening of the link between economics and ethics (Shionoya 2001), which quickly earned researchers the rather unflattering designation *Kathedersozialisten* – particularly after the foundation of the Verein für Socialpolitik in 1872 – and third the epistemological orientation explaining how an economic theory of historical and particularly social facts is possible without the mere insistence on a merely inductive portrayal of historical facts. To ensure a more comprehensive in the approach to social science, epistemological reductions (the *homo economicus*) were discarded.

The historical school also had a significant bearing on public finance. In the mid nineteenth century, historically oriented state theorists (Lorenz von Stein, Albert Schäffle, Adolph Wagner) systematized the state's public economic tasks to ensure that the aggregate state organism was in a position to meet its needs. The mandate of public finance was thus the systematization of receipts and payments in order to warrant the state's civilizational and cultural developments. For Adolph Wagner this entailed an increase in the government's spending rate, since, in his opinion, the state continues to develop civilizationally and culturally.

Following the death of Gustav Schmoller (1917), and particularly after the end of World War I, the still fragile canon of the historical school became even more precarious, so that economists attempted to deny the heritage of the historical school in whose tradition they stood. However, the school continued to influence business cycle research, interdisciplinary knowledge transfer and business ethics in the 1920s (Häuser 1994). Yet after World War II, the historical school finally did come to an end. First, part of the school had been rightly discredited in a lasting way since some of its representatives had interpreted the *Volksbedürfnisse* in a racist manner and this way advocated National Socialism. Second, the mathematical modelling of individual decision-making processes supplanted the genuinely historical and social analysis of economic facts.

Recently, several theoretical concepts of the historical school have resurfaced and been discussed again in an effort to establish economics on an empirical basis. Two movements, in particular, are decisive here: on the one hand, institutional and cultural theories in economics (institutional economics, cultural economics) invoke the historical school; on the other hand, an economic policy, which takes into account various temporal and spatial developments in economies, underscores the scientific results of the historical school. The elaboration of the theory of regulation, in particular, refers to the different developments of productive forces in different economies, which had already been modelled in the historical school.

In view of the historical school, it is still disputed to what extent one can actually speak of an orthodox canon when referring to the historical school. Is the historical school a school in the strict sense, or does it not represent a uniform paradigm (Pearson 1999)? At times the defining lines blur, while idea-historical influences sometimes suggest that the historical school is a dubious construct. These questions can only be answered with the help of a general philosophy of science where the historically epistemological conditions determining the constitution of a 'school', of a 'paradigm' or an 'orthodox canon', are critically exposed. Without doubt, the historical school is necessary as a heuristic epistemological principle and regulative idea in order to critically acknowledge the achievements of an economics of space and time.

References and further reading

Brandt, Karl (1993) *Geschichte der deutschen Volkswirtschaftslehre*, vol. 2, Freiburg im Breisgau: Rudolf Haufe.

Häuser, Karl (1994) 'Das Ende der historischen Schule und die Ambiguität der deutschen Nationalökonomie in den zwanziger Jahren', in Knut Wolfgang Nörr, Bertram Schefold and Friedrich Tenbruck (eds), *Geisteswissenschaften zwischen Kaiserreich und Republik*, Stuttgart: Franz Steiner, pp. 47–74.

Menger, Carl ([1883]1985) *Investigations into the Method of the Social Sciences with Special Reference to Economics*, New York: New York University Press.

Pearson, Heath (1999) 'Was There Really a German Historical School of Economics?' *History of Political Economy*, 31: 547–62.

Pirker, Reinhard and Rauchenschwandtner, Hermann (1998) 'Sense of Community: A Fundamental Concept of Institutional Economics', *Journal of Institutional and Theoretical Economics*, 154: 406–21.

Roscher, Wilhelm (2002) *Über die Spuren der historischen Lehre bei den älteren Sophisten (1838)*, Marburg, Germany: Metropolis.

Senn, Peter R. (1995) 'Why Had Roscher So Much Influence in the USA Compared with the UK?' *Journal of Economic Studies*, 22: 53–105.

Shionoya, Yuichi (ed.) (2001) *The German Historical School. The Historical and Ethical Approach to Economics*, London: Routledge.

REINHARD PIRKER
HERMANN RAUCHENSCHWANDTNER

HOLISM See: Anti-economics; methodological individualism

HOMO ECONOMICUS See. Economics; economic action; rational choice theory; Carnegie school

HOUSEWORK

Housework is usually conceptualized as unpaid labour performed to maintain family members and their home. Other conceptual terms used to identify this activity include house and yard work; household labour, work or tasks; home chores or **production**; unpaid work; family care; and family work. Researchers rarely explicitly state a conceptual definition; instead, they detail the housework tasks measured (Shelton and John 1996). A wide range of overlapping measures have been applied but none are comprehensive. Child care often receives specific attention but is excluded in most cases. Less visible or overlapping types of work, like emotional labour and household management, are also frequently excluded.

Housework is as crucial to the existence and maintenance of social groups within society as paid work, but the latter, especially men's employment, was the focus of most early studies of work. Feeding, clothing, sheltering and caring for both children and adults were for a long time ignored or trivialized by sociologists. After 'productive' work moved away from the home, housework was increasingly characterized as 'women's work'.

Research on housework in the United States began with time-use studies initiated during the 1920s that assessed the impact of industrialization on shifting work activities.

Home economists documented the long hours that wives worked in the home while looking for ways to make housework more efficient. The US Department of Agriculture commissioned a national study in 1924–8 that set in motion a series of related state studies. Wives were asked to report how much time they usually spent per week in food preparation and clean-up, care of the house, care and construction of clothing, care of the family, management and shopping.

According to trend studies, housewives in the 1940s were devoting far more time to housework than their mothers and grandmothers had. Housewives typically reported spending about 70 hours per week despite the acquisition of 'labour-saving' devices. A comparison of time-use studies from the 1930s to the 1970s indicates that the amount of time spent on routine housework had declined but the time spent on managerial aspects, such as shopping and childrearing, increased. In the 1930s, wives typically did about 4.8 times as much housework as husbands, compared to 7.6 times as much in the 1960s. A cross-national comparison between Botswana, Denmark, Finland, Hungary, Japan, Nepal, Norway, Sweden, USA and USSR from the 1960s to the early 1980s found that wives in every nation usually performed more routine chores, home projects and child care than their husbands but the gap between spouses varied widely. The ratios decreased over time due to husbands' modest increases and wives substantial decreases in time spent on housework. Swedish husbands did the most housework, but their wives still averaged 1.8 times as much in 1984. Japanese husbands did the least amount of housework, with their wives averaging 8.9 times as much.

In the 1970s and 1980s, little change took place in the division of housework between husbands and wives despite more wives being employed and working more hours. Wives reported usually performing over 80 per cent of the daily repetitive and routine tasks, such as cooking, cleaning and child care, while husbands were more likely to mow the lawn, take out the trash, maintain the cars and play with children. Most wives did not think that their husbands should do more around the house and considered this division of labour to be fair.

In the 1990s, the total amount of time spent doing housework by household members was reported to be about equal to the time they devote to paid labour outside the home (Coltrane 2000). Also, a convergence of time spent in unpaid and paid work between men and women occurred regardless of marital and employment status. Still, women do more housework than men and are much more likely to take responsibility for these tasks. Researchers increasingly stressed the complex and shifting patterns of social relations that influence housework and took into account household structure, family interaction, and the operation of both formal and informal markets.

Explanations have focused upon relative resources, gender role attitudes and time-availability constraints. Recent developments include applying economic, socialist-feminist, morality and socialization theories; focusing on institutional constraints; and employing life-course factors. The boldest application of economic theories is by Gary Becker in *A Treatise on the Family* the 1991 enlarged edition. He infers that spouses can gain from a division of labour where one specializes in paid work and the other in housework. Besides time diaries and surveys, qualitative in-depth interviews, direct observation, discourse analysis and historical-comparative methods have been used to gather data.

The best predictors of the division of housework between spouses or partners include women's employment patterns, ideology and earnings. Women's employment hours have the strongest and most consistent effects on housework performance and on men's share of housework. Women who hold an egalitarian gender ideology and share this view with their partners report greater sharing. The more money wives earn the more equal the division. Women with more education do less housework while men with more education do more. Younger women do less housework but tend to share it more than older women. Getting married means more housework for women but less for men. Having children is associated with mothers doing more housework and sharing it less. Black men typically do more housework than white men but black women still do almost twice as much as black men. The greater the husbands' contribution to housework, the more likely wives considered the division fair. Marital satisfaction increases in relation to the amount of housework that is shared by spouses.

References and further reading

Coltrane, Scott (2000) 'Research on Household Labor: Modeling and Measuring the Social Embeddedness of Routine Family Work', *Journal of Marriage and the Family*, 62: 1208–33.

Seward, Rudy Ray, Yeatts, Dale E. and Stanley-Stevens, Leslie (1996). 'Fathers' Changing Performance of Housework: A Bigger Slice of a Smaller Pie', *Free Inquiry in Creative Sociology*, 24: 28–36.

Shelton, Beth Anne and John, Daphne (1996) 'The Division of Household Labor', *Annual Review of Sociology*, 22: 299–322.

RUDY RAY SEWARD

HUMAN RESOURCES

Human resources include abilities, dispositions, knowledge and skills that can heighten individual and social welfare. The development of human resources is shaped by education, training and welfare systems at both organizational and societal levels.

A human resources perspective on management treats human participants and their capacities as assets that can foster high organizational performance, not simply as 'labour costs' to be minimized. Human resource management practices seek to acquire, enhance and conserve human resources, marshalling them towards organizational objectives while simultaneously encouraging individuals to grow and develop. Such practices involve both structuring organizational activities and providing supportive services to organizational members.

Drawing on the work of psychologist Abraham Maslow, human resource models posit that individuals have intrinsic creative capacities and will use them responsibly and autonomously to pursue organizational goals if given the opportunity (Miles 1965). Contrasting with Taylorist presumptions that individuals will shirk unless monitored closely, these foundations imply decentralized and participatory work arrangements rather than formalized and specialized structures. Human resource conceptions assume that participation and autonomy improve organizational performance; participative management practices are not just efficient tactics for eliciting cooperation, as in some human relations models focused on improving morale.

Human resource management is rooted in personnel management, but incorporates a strategic orientation linking personnel policy to organizational performance. Among its elements are: developing human resources via training programmes, career planning and performance appraisal; overseeing staffing processes including job analysis, recruitment, selection and promotion; analysing and designing compensation practices; administering benefit programmes for health, retirement security and the work/family interface; promoting workplace health and safety; and managing employee/labour relations, including grievance/dispute resolution procedures and linkages with **trade unions**. Human resources professionals often ensure that organizations are in compliance with legislation and regulations governing equal employment opportunity and workplace health and safety. The influence of the human resource

function within an organization rises if it can successfully manage uncertainties such as labour shortages, unionization pressures or complex regulatory regimes.

Widely studied human resource structures include firm-internal labour markets (FILMs) and 'high-performance' work organization. In FILMs, external hiring is limited to entry-level positions, from which persons advance along formally defined job ladders. By offering opportunities for career progression, FILMs promote organizational commitment and the acquisition of organization-specific skills, thereby supplying trained and experienced personnel. By providing employment security, FILMs counter the reluctance of experienced employees to offer on-the-job training to younger workers.

High-performance work practices are designed to elicit discretionary effort from participants (Appelbaum *et al.* 2000). Self-directed **work teams** offer autonomy and the opportunity to participate; multi-skilling practices such as cross-training and job rotation provide the capacity to participate; and performance-related compensation arrangements supply incentives to participate. Most high-performance models maintain that these practices are most effective when adopted as a package rather than piecemeal.

Market-related sources of variety in human resource practices across organizations include competition, technological change and workforce composition. Organizations adopt high-performance practices, for instance, when product markets reward quality, customized products and consistent on-time delivery. Meeting such demands requires highly skilled and committed staff to complement advanced technology. Benefits such as child and eldercare assistance, flexitime and wellness programmes may be introduced to attract and retain qualified personnel in labour markets that are increasingly diverse in terms of sex, age and ethnic origin.

Institutional features including law, the personnel profession and trade unions also influence human resource practices. In the United States, growth in rights to due process in employment, health and safety protection, and promised employment benefits has been traced to legislative, administrative and judicial actions associated with Civil Rights and Equal Employment Opportunity law, the Occupational Safety and Health Act of 1970, and the Employment Retirement Income Security Act of 1974 (Dobbin and Sutton 1998). This occurred within an emergent cultural frame asserting that individual persons are psychologically complex and ambitious, meriting both physical and psychological protection.

Human resource professionals assert that beyond providing protection for employers, compliance with legal prescriptions can promote organizational efficiency. Unions may pressure organizations to adopt training programmes, due process protections and internal labour markets. In the absence of unions, organizations may offer these together with high-performance practices as part of a strategy of union avoidance (Kochan et al. 1986).

Systems of general and vocational education are important societal-level influences on human resource development and management practices. United States education, for example, sometimes does not ensure basic literacy, and vocational education programmes are weakly articulated with the labour market. Most training is therefore employer-provided. By contrast, vocational and adult education systems in Germanic countries are both more extensively developed and more closely linked to employers. Expanded educational systems are often elements of national or regional infrastructure programmes to promote **economic development**, as in Korea or the Emilia-Romagna district of Italy.

Numerous other national-level institutional differences also shape human resource practices. Among these are the extent of labour market regulation, union density and the design of systems of social provision. National arrangements for health services and retirement security affect the range of employer-based benefit programmes, for example.

As economic activity grows increasingly global, specialized and knowledge-based, the importance of human resources for productivity and competitive advantage likely will grow. Individuals, economic organizations and states alike will seek effective ways of developing and organizing human resources.

See also: industrial relations; institutionalism, old and new; labour markets, sociology of; law and economy; technological change.

References and further reading

Appelbaum, Eileen, Bailey, Thomas, Berg, Peter and Kalleberg, Arne L. (2000) *Manufacturing Advantage: Why High-Performance Work Systems Pay Off*, Ithaca, NY: Cornell University Press.
Dobbin, Frank and Sutton, John R. (1998) 'The Strength of a Weak State: The Rights Revolution and the Rise of Human Resources Management Divisions', *American Journal of Sociology*, 104: 441–76.
Kochan, Thomas A., Katz, Harry C. and McKersie, Robert B. (1986) *The Transformation of American Industrial Relations*, Ithaca, NY: ILR Press.
Miles, Raymond E. (1965) 'Human Relations or Human Resources?' *Harvard Business Review*, 43(4): 148–63.

PETER V. MARSDEN

HYBRIDS (INSTITUTIONAL FORMS)

Etymologically a hybrid is an entity that would have to be classified in two separate domains, or it is an entity that one finds in one domain but would expect in another. A hybrid institution is an institution that (is believed to) originate(s) from one context and is recombined with institutions from a different context. A hybrid institution has characteristics that a scholar looking at it from a certain perspective would not expect to observe in that particular context. Classifying an institution as a hybrid thus gives as much an indication of the perspective used as it does about the institution itself. One might have differing views about the extent to which they are to be desired, or even necessary. Privatization can, for instance, be perceived as an attempt to rid parts of the economic system of hybrid institutions. Systems theory implicitly or explicitly provides an important impetus for analysing hybrids, a system being perceived of as a coherent whole, where parts interact with each other to form a homogenous entity. It is the contrast with the homogenous system that allows for the classification as hybrid. Systems theory assumes boundaries between the system and the environment that are impermeable, keeping out foreign entities.

The issue revolves around the question of whether one would perceive of the economic or societal system as an open or as a closed system. A closed system is one with a finite number of entities, and a finite number of relations between them. A closed system may be a complicated system due to the fact that it includes many elements, but it will be possible – in principle – to fathom it. For the society we live in, it is impossible to determine if it is an open or a closed system. Nobel Laureate in economics Herbert Simon believes the economy to be a closed system. Another Laureate, Friedrich von Hayek, believes it is open. If the analogy with the natural environment holds, a closed system would grind to a halt, ending up in what Joseph Schumpeter has called a 'circular flow', as the equivalent to the second law of thermodynamics from chemistry would ensure entropy to increase leaving decreasing amounts of 'energy' to be put to good use. In addition, arguing that a system is closed, that it has impermeable boundaries would obviate ideas such as that of markets being embedded in broader society. It would suggest

that a market could exist that has no relations with, for instance, state or households. In reality, then, boundaries between the system and its environment are permeable.

One can think of a firm as a system. **Transaction cost economics** in a way is about determining the boundary between the firm and the market such that no foreign element enters either. For a firm to be able to sustain itself, it needs to be open to some degree for input from its environment. The necessity for a firm to allow information from its environment to enter it is a key point; the roles responsible are discussed as boundary spanners. Before being allowed into the system, information could be transformed in a way that will make it compatible to the system; gatekeepers might select out the information that would be foreign, or such information might be translated.

The relation between firms is another case in point. Such relations tend to be thought of as being either a case of competition, or one of collusion. It is now recognized, however, that both of these kinds of relations between firms might operate at the same time, giving rise to a need for hybrid institutions: 'coopetition' in networks of firms working together when innovating and establishing common standards, but at the same time competing with firms from outside the network and with firms within the network. Hybridization, thus perceived, ensures that a system is able to adapt continuously to a changing environment by allowing for or even seeking heterogeneity.

This view of hybridization as being a useful, or maybe even unavoidable, and necessary process is not generally shared. Misgivings can be seen at two levels: the societal and the theoretical. The transfer of institutions from one context to another is sometimes lamented because of the consequences it has for a particular system. An example is the use of the institution of money in spheres where it used not to be so (overtly) present (as in friendship, morality, art, religion). Similarly, the process of globalization can be though of as a process whereby institutions are introduced in a local context from outside.

A different kind of discussion is on the theoretical level: do hybrids play a useful role in the evolution of systems? Are they perhaps inescapable? One argument that is increasingly recognized as the more useful one is that in uncertain environments, a system needs to be heterogeneous, have foreign elements included in order to be able to adapt. A system that does not have 'impure' elements would not be able to survive (major) changes in its environment. There is a tendency, however, for a system that is not homogenous to increasingly become so, which requires an active role of elements within the system to (seek to) incorporate foreign elements.

References and further reading:

Biggart, N. W. and Delbridge, R. (2004) 'Systems of Exchange', *Academy of Management Review*, 29(1): 28–49.

Hodgson, G. M. (1999) *Economics and Utopia: Why the Learning Economy is not the End of History*, London: Routledge.

WILFRED DOLFSMA

I

IDEAL TYPE

The term 'ideal type' (*Idealtypus*) was introduced by Max **Weber** (1864–1920) in his paper on 'Objectivity in Social Science and Social Policy' published in 1904 (Weber 1949). Weber attempted to synthesize aspects of both positions in the **Methodenstreit** between subjectivists and positivists. He took his departure in Heinrich Rickert's distinction between the methods used in the natural sciences and, on the other side, the cultural and social sciences. Rickert argued that the characteristic method of the social sciences involves the formation of individual concepts while the method of the natural sciences involves the formation of general concepts. Weber found that many of the concepts applied in the social sciences had a conceptual status that in a particular way blended the features of individual and general concepts: they are a synthesis not of common but of significant aspects of the phenomena under examination. Weber's contribution was to describe and define these non-individual, non-general, synthetic concepts commonly applied by social scientists (Hekman 1983).

According to Weber the concepts used in abstract economic theory are a special case of this form of concept–construction that is peculiar and indispensable to the social sciences. Abstract economic theory offers us an ideal picture of the working of an exchange economy with free competition and rational conduct forming an internally consistent system. This construct is like a utopia which has been arrived at by the analytical accentuation of certain elements of reality. Ideal-typical concepts, as, for example, we find them in economic theory, serve as a heuristic device to assist grasping a diffuse empirical reality. Ideal types can be used as a yardstick for empirical studies in the social sciences, for example, by describing empirical phenomena according to their difference or their similarities with the ideal type. Ideal types are ideal in a logical sense, as pure type concepts, not in an ethical sense – the ideals may or may not be desirable. Following Max Weber an ideal type is formed by the one-sided accentuation of certain aspects of the phenomena. These aspects are arranged according to those one-sidedly emphasized viewpoints into a unified analytical construct. In its conceptual purity, this mental construct cannot be found empirically anywhere in reality.

Ideal types played a central role in Weber's vision of sociology as a science concerning itself with the interpretive understanding of social action and with a causal explanation of its course and consequences. Weber argued that for purposes of a typological analysis it is convenient to treat all irrational or affectually determined behaviour as a deviation from a conceptually pure type of rational action. In this process, the construction of a purely rational course of action serves as an ideal type which has the merit of clear understandability and lack of ambiguity. It is important to note that Weber's methodological use of rational action models did not involve a belief in the actual predominance of rational elements in human life.

Weber applied a variety of ideal types in his own work. In *The Protestant Ethic and the Spirit of Capitalism* (Weber 2002), two ideal-typical concepts, the 'Protestant ethic' and the 'spirit of modern capitalism' are formed, and the chain leading from the Protestant ethic to the spirit of capitalism is elaborated. In *Economy and Society* (Weber 1978) Weber presented a variety of ideal types, as, for example: ideal types of social action: instrumentally rational action (*zweckrational*), value-rational action (*wertrational*), affectual, and traditional action; ideal types of authority: rational, traditional and charismatic authority, and the ideal type of the bureaucratic organization.

Several of Weber's ideal types were aimed at the sociological analysis of economic action. A key notion was the ideal typical concept of 'rational economic action'. Weber made an important distinction between two radically different types of rational **economic action**. While 'budgetary management' (*Haushalten*) is oriented towards considerations of the best use of a given income, 'profit-making' (*Erwerben*) is oriented towards entrepreneurial activity aiming at acquisition of profit. These two forms of rational action may outwardly seem very similar and may only be distinguishable in terms of the difference in meaningful orientation of the corresponding economic action. Weber argued that abstract economic theory merely was focusing on the first type of rational economic action, 'budgetary management'. In his own work Weber was primarily interested in analysing the second type of rational action, profit-making.

The Austrian social scientist Alfred Schutz contributed to the further development of the concept of ideal type in *The Phenomenology of the Social World*, published in 1932 (Schutz 1967). Schutz was fascinated by Weber's methodological work on interpretive sociology and his work, especially on chapter 1 in *Economy and Society* that outlines the foundation of interpretive sociology. While Schutz agreed with Weber that the social sciences aim at understanding the subjective meaning of social action, he found that Weber failed to clearly analyse the essential characteristics of understanding and of subjective meaning. Schutz argued that ideal types, as heuristic constructs, are an indispensable part of everyday life. Social actors apprehend the action of other actors by means of typification. According to Schutz we may distinguish two types of ideal types, ideal types applied by actors in everyday life and ideal types applied by scientist in their attempt to analyse social reality.

References and further reading

Burger, Thomas (1987) *Max Weber's Theory of Concept Formation. History, Laws, and Ideal Types*, Durham, NC: Duke University Press.

Gerhardt, Uta (2001) *Idealtypus. Zur methodologischen Begründung der modernen Soziologie* [Ideal Type. On the Methodological Foundation of Modern Sociology], Frankfurt/M: Suhrkamp.

Hekman, Susan J. (1983) *Weber, the Ideal Type, and Contemporary Social Theory*, Notre Dame, IN: University of Notre Dame Press.

Schutz, Alfred (1967) *The Phenomenology of the Social World*, Evanston, IL: North Western University Press.

Weber, Max (1949) '"Objectivity" in Social Science and Social Policy', in Max Weber, *The Methodology of the Social Sciences*, New York: Free Press, pp. 49–112.

—— (1978) *Economy and Society. An Outline of Interpretative Sociology*, Berkeley, CA: University of California Press.

—— (2002) *The Protestant Ethic and the Spirit of Capitalism*, Los Angeles, CA: Roxbury Publishing.

SØREN JAGD

IDEOLOGY

Ideology is a modern concept, introduced in 1801 by the French philosopher Destutt de Tracy to affirm the possibility of an enlightened 'science of ideas' (see Head 1985). During the mid nineteenth century, as the proliferation of political parties accompanied the emergence of new social classes and strata resulting from industrialization, conservatives, liberals and radicals began to employ ideology to delegitimate the goals and strategies of competing positions and perspectives. The concept thus acquired negative connotations. Yet as Karl **Marx** demonstrated in his critique of **political economy**, the importance of the concept went beyond political conflicts and issues. Positing that ideas are not independent of socio-historical contexts, Marx's rendering of the critique of ideology stressed the need to scrutinize how political ideologies are linked to conflicting class positions and material interests, and how the modern science of economics is entwined with both (**historical materialism**). Emphasizing the economic foundations of purportedly incompatible ideas, his writings provided a framework for examining the ideological nexus between capitalist economics and forms of social, cultural and political life in modern society, and both prepared and influenced western critiques of ideology during the twentieth century (see Mannheim [1929]1936; Gramsci 1971; Berger and Luckmann 1966; and Joseph Gabel [1962]1975, 1997).

Though 'ideology' continued to serve political purposes – first in the struggle between monarchy and democracy, then in the 'age of totalitarianism', and finally in the 'Cold War' – during the closing decades of the twentieth century, representatives of newly emerging strains of critical theory (e.g. neo-Marxism, post-structuralism, feminism, post-colonialism, critical race theory) argued that in advanced western societies, elements of ideology became so submerged in the social sciences that without ongoing, rigorous and theoretically oriented critiques, it would not be possible to make visible the perpetuity of economic interests, patriarchy, imperial rule, **discrimination** according to race and ethnicity, and the reification of Enlightenment principles more generally. Some of these critics went so far as to contend that the totality of western societies is centred around a nexus between social order and ideology, fine-tuned to conceal the omnipresence of power relations rooted in economic interests whose continued prevalence is incompatible with, and perverts, Enlightenment principles of democracy and social justice. From such an angle, the distinction between ideology and science – including social science – collapses, implying the end of the modern age and the transition to postmodernity (**modernity**).

Today, the concept of ideology is relevant in the social sciences mostly as a means to scrutinize the problematic link between structures of power, and modes of presenting and representing those structures in politics, culture and society. In addition, the concept also serves to explicate how modes of framing, presenting and representing scientific objectivity have a bearing on the formulation of research questions, the design of research agendas, and the specific causal relations that define the analytical terrain of each of the social sciences. This use of ideology makes it possible to address a particular kind of tension that has been endemic to the link between social research and its social context from the start, and whose critical nature appears to have amplified in recent years. On the one hand, research interests and priorities are driven by an orientation towards discerning particular phenomena, problems and challenges, on their own terms, and independently of power relations in society – i.e. in terms of the nexus between subject matter, theoretical framing, and methodological tools at the heart of each particular discipline.

On the other hand, systems of power and structures of inequality in politics, economy and society – and corresponding forms of organization – favour research that is conducive to their continued existence and position in relation to each other. In this vein, ideology has become the concept of choice to make explicit the danger that in the name of progress and Enlightenment, and against their own interests and self-understanding, social scientists may play a role in the erosion and fragmentation of progress and Enlightenment – if the effects of the tension between research that strives to remain independent from power, and research that is a function of power, remains implicit.

Under conditions of **globalization**, as the pace of change in politics, culture and society keeps accelerating, there are indications for a growing need to deploy and apply the concept of ideology to determine whether preconceived notions – especially as they pertain to economic matters – may impair the ability of social scientists to illuminate the contradictions that infuse economic, political, social and cultural change with energy (see Dahms 2005): assuming that globalization continues to accelerate, a concept of ideology framed to track both opportunities and impediments resulting from qualitative changes in politics, economy and society is key to ensuring the practical and theoretical relevance of social research. In the absence of a concept of ideology formulated to ensure that the categories and concepts developed, employed and applied by social scientists enhance our ability to make explicit the contradictory trajectories underlying the changes currently taking place, categories and concepts are more likely to conceal and perpetuate the contradictory nature of those changes.

In relation to the research interests that are central to economic sociology, the issue of ideology is most important today with regard to potential pitfalls that are quite different from those that informed concern with ideology during most of the nineteenth and the twentieth century. Certain trends that have amplified since the 1990s suggest that the prevalence of ideologies is becoming more difficult to discern. Ideologies will be most problematic, then, in societies where systems of power are becoming less recognizable as such, acquire the air of inevitability, or appear as most beneficial to society as a whole (rather than to certain groups in society). Furthermore, both the proponents and the critics of those systems of power will be likely to relate to the actuality of forms of social, political, cultural and economic life on the basis of ideology, rather than of social science categories designed to transcend those ideologies. Indeed, under such conditions, remaining opportunities for social science to transcend ideology are likely to erode.

Due to its reliance on principles of individual self-interest, how neoclassical economic theory has begun to serve as a 'dominant ideology' grounded in social science – supporting 'capitalism' as a system of power which, due to its very nature, may be more capable of immunizing itself more effectively against scrutiny than any other known system of power – warrants particular attention. Though 'market capitalism' – as depicted in neoclassical theory – could not exist in pure form, with the spread of neo-liberal principles, the more closely configurations of business–labour–government relations approximate the pure type of neoclassical economics, the greater the likelihood that the social system affected is capable of immunizing itself against critical analysis. To the degree that modern society is defined in terms of economic imperatives, it is a social system that continually reproduces an ideology of itself as enlightened – thus amplifying impediments social scientists must overcome in the interest of grasping the nature of the social world today. Since ability to do the latter would be likely to increase the desire for qualitative and structural social changes, and opportunities to discern venues to bring about such change, modern society indeed may have evolved as a social system producing mechanisms whose purpose it is to facilitate continuous economic growth and development, while thwarting opportunities for structural change, by concealing the actual functioning of modern capitalism. Consequently, under present circumstances, successful efforts to decrease the prevalence of ideology will prepare, by default, steps towards engendering qualitative transformations in, of and between modern societies, especially with regard to constellations of business, labour and government, and the structures of inequality in which they are embedded.

References and further reading

Berger, Peter, and Luckmann, Thomas (1966) *The Social Construction of Reality: A Treatise in the Sociology of Knowledge*, Garden City, NY: Anchor Books.

Dahms, Harry F. (2005) 'Globalization or Hyper-Alienation? Critiques of Traditional Marxism as Arguments for Basic Income', in *Social Theory as Politics in Knowledge (Current Perspectives in Social Theory, vol. 23)*, Greenwich, CT: JAI Press.

Gabel, Joseph ([1962]1975) *False Consciousness. An Essay of Reification*, translated by Margaret Thompson, New York: Harper and Row.

—— (1997) *Ideologies and the Corruption of Thought*, edited by Alan Sica, New Brunswick: Transaction Books.

Gramsci, Antonio (1971) *Selections from the Prison Notebooks*, New York: International Publishers.

Head, Brian William (1985) *Ideology and Social Science: Destutt de Tracy and French Liberalism*, Hingham, MA: Kluwer.

Mannheim, Karl ([1929]1936). *Ideology and Utopia: An Introduction to the Sociology of Knowledge*, New York: Harcourt Brace Jovanovich.

HARRY F. DAHMS

IMMIGRATION See: ethnic economy

IMPERIALISM See: Marx; world systems approach

IMPOSSIBILITY THEOREM

Kenneth Arrow's *Social Choice and Individual Values*, first published in 1951, is one of the seminal works on **welfare economics**. In the opening sentence he wrote: 'In a capitalist democracy there are essentially two methods by which social choices can be made: voting, typically used to make "political" decisions, and the market mechanism, typically used to make "economic" decisions' (Arrow 1951: 1). Notice that atomistic action in decentralized markets is offered as one of two possible ways to make *social* choices.

Central to the discussion here is a social welfare function (SWF) – a decision rule (Arrow calls it a 'constitution') that indicates a functional relation which 'specifies one social ordering R for any set … of individual preference orderings – one per person' (Sen 1982: 10). Arrow advanced the idea of the *impossibility* of aggregating individual preference orderings (as given by the SWF) into a social order satisfying 'reasonable' conditions. The four conditions are: (1) collective rationality – the domain of the SWF includes all combinations of conceivable preference orderings; (2) that the constitution satisfy the weak Pareto principle – if all individuals prefer any x to any y then x is socially preferred to y; (3) no individual is a dictator – her preference ordering cannot become the social ordering; and (4) the social ranking of any pair of possible states depends on the rankings of only that pair (and no other pair) – the independence of irrelevant alternatives.

Again, the impossibility theorem is that these four 'reasonable' conditions cannot be met and hence social choice, under this description, is problematic. The ensuing literature has addressed the extent to which these conditions are indeed the correct conditions, and there has been debate as to exactly how binding is the idea of the 'impossibility' of social choice predicated on individual preferences. Those who have taken Arrow at his word tend to invoke the impossibility theorem to suggest the futility and potential inconsistency in social choices. From this nihilistic position it is easy to retreat to the 'market' as the only reliable way in which social choices can be reached – after all, markets are where volitional agents record their preferences. And since many economists see competitive markets as both necessary and sufficient for the actualization of individual preferences, markets appear as the *deus ex machina* that accomplish the otherwise 'impossible' task of reflecting (and aggregating) individual preferences into social preferences.

The problem here, and we see it in Arrow's opening proposition, is the odd idea that markets are domains over which social *choices* are effectuated. It must be noticed that no one makes a social *choice* through her participation in the market. Of course, atomistic behaviour through markets produces social *outcomes*, and those outcomes hold important social *implications*. But one cannot plausibly claim that social *choices* find voice and reasons in atomistic market processes.

References and further reading

Arrow, Kenneth J. (1951) *Social Choice and Individual Values*, New Haven, CT: Yale University Press.

Sen, Amartya (1982) *Choice, Welfare and Measurement*, Oxford: Blackwell.

DANIEL W. BROMLEY

INCENTIVES

An incentive for economic behaviour is any reward or sanction that one actor uses to induce a change in the economic behaviour of another actor. The participants in an incentive exchange relationship may be natural persons or collective actors such as teams, corporations and labour unions. An incentive's efficacy reflects its ability to satisfy some need or want of the recipient.

An effective incentive thus serves to motivate the receiver to comply with the provider's demands for a specific economic action. In economics, **rational choice theory** defines incentives primarily as monetary or non-monetary goods that maximize or satisfice an individual's subjective expected utility. The simplest example is an employer offering wage and fringe benefit incentives to a prospective employee in exchange for labour activities, which the worker accepts to satisfy a need to make a living. Some rational choice theorists posit that common interests within a group fail to induce voluntary **collective action** to attain those interests if some members can take a free ride on others' efforts (Olson 1965). Optimizing the supply of non-excludable and non-rivalrous public goods – such as clean air and water, highways, mass transit, public schooling, job training and national defence – requires *selective incentives*, individually targeted rewards or coercive penalties that motivate contributions to the collective provision of public goods and services. Examples of economic coercion include compulsory membership in labour unions and government regulations that incentivize companies to reduce pollution by imposing fines on violators.

Sociologists take much broader perspectives on incentives that emphasize how both individuals and organizations respond to a wide range of non-economic inducements that affect a variety of motivations. Non-economic incentives at both individual and organizational levels of analysis may be classified into four general categories: psychological, social, political and cultural. The following paragraphs define and exemplify these four incentive types, and review some theoretical explanations of their impacts on economic behaviour.

Psychological incentives stem from the characteristics of cognitive processing of the individual mind. Identity theory conceptualizes the support of an identity as an incentive, which is effective because the meanings attached to identities initiate mental schemas that cue behavioural responses. An example at the individual level is support of a 'breadwinner identity', which families and communities offer to heads of households to incentivize their occupational activity. Organizations also respond economically to identity incentives: for example, corporations contribute to non-profits and charities because they value the identity of 'good corporate citizen'. Another type of psychological incentive is predicated on the motive to reduce uncertainty. The planning required to meet organizational goals depends on predictability, hence organizations respond to incentives that reduce uncertainty. Resource dependence theory argues that firms try to reduce their dependency on other organizations, thereby reducing uncertainties associated with unstable resource flows. However, other organizations may offer inducements to increase inter-firm cooperation (e.g. information sharing, strategic alliances), which also satisfy organizational motives to reduce environmental uncertainty. In contrast, transaction cost theory posits that, under conditions of high complexity and uncertain information, organizations have strong incentives to internalize market transactions because organizational hierarchies can exert greater control over crucial resources.

Social incentives are rewards and sanctions offered in social networks. Kinship networks provide incentives for economic behaviour by rewarding **trust** relations and information exchange, as well as sanctions of shunning for rejecting the family business. Some examples are entrepreneurial activities of Cuban retail businesses in Miami and Korean *chaebols*, business groups dominated by members of particular families. The growth of friendship ties provides social inducements to sustain economic behaviours possibly initiated by purely economic incentives. Friendships are often symbolized and strengthened by reciprocal

gift exchanges. As institutionalism hypothesizes, professional norms reward standardized performances by certifying social status, thus incentivizing the imitation of other professionals and contributing to occupational conformity. For example, norms within the management profession shape consensus about managerial standards and practices. Institutionalists also argue that government regulations are coercive incentives that create organizational isomorphism or similarity of forms (DiMaggio and Powell 1983). Another basic social incentive in institutional theory is the **legitimacy** that organizations gain by mimicking the formal structures and practices of other members of an organizational field, especially in environments of rapid innovation and uncertain valuation. These mimetic habits may proliferate despite the absence of rational economic inducements for their persistence.

Network analysis argues that the social **embeddedness** of economic actions within interpersonal networks is vital to explaining organizational behaviour. Going beyond an 'undersocialized' perspective – seeing social institutions such as contracts as efficient solutions to economic problems such as opportunism – and beyond an 'oversocialized' perspective – relying on a generalized morality – network researchers demonstrated the importance of trust relations for discouraging organizational malfeasance (Granovetter 1985). An individual or organizational **reputation** for trustworthiness may become a valuable asset that induces others to join in a collective economic action.

Political incentives involve exchanging power and authority for economic benefits. Corporations and labour unions contribute to election campaigns in expectation of improved access to government officials and influence over the public policy decisions affecting their economic interests, such as tax breaks and collective bargaining regulations. Within organizations, resource dependence theory hypothesizes that employees accrue power and influence by demonstrating their ability to resolve crucial uncertainties: for example, research scientists who invent new products or rainmaking lawyers who attract rich clients.

Cultural incentives for economic behaviour enjoy a long tradition. Max **Weber**'s *Protestant Ethic and the Spirit of Capitalism* identified religious incentives underpinning the capitalistic activity of reinvesting profits. More recent researchers delineated incentives arising from corporate cultures: certain symbols and practices express values about intrinsic worth that are not based on rational economic calculations. For example, total quality management initiatives may fail if employees hold conflicting views about organizational goals and appropriate means. Taken a step further, market capitalism itself has become a cultural construct exulting material goods incentives as potent cultural symbols infused with high prestige and achievement.

An important theoretical question is to explain the socio-economic conditions under which alternative incentives explain economic behaviour. Rational choice perspectives maintain that actors always rationally balance costs against benefits. Researchers have investigated the extent to which decision-makers actually perform such calculations (bounded rationality), but is this the only limitation to the alleged priority of economic incentives? Further work examining the relative influences of cognitive, social network, political, and cultural processes could clarify the conditions under which particular incentives are more likely to predominate.

References and further reading

DiMaggio, Paul and Powell, Walter W. (1983) 'The Iron Cage Revisited: Institutionalized Isomorphism and Collective Rationality in Organizational Fields', *American Sociological Review*, 48: 147–60.

Granovetter, Mark (1985) 'Economic Action and Social Structure: The Problem of Embeddedness', *American Journal of Sociology*, 91: 481–510.

Olson, Mancur (1965) *The Logic of Collective Action: Public Goods and the Theory of Groups*, Cambridge, MA: Harvard University Press.

LUANNE R. JOHNSON
DAVID KNOKE

INCLUSION AND EXCLUSION

The topic of inclusion and exclusion in the economy covers a broad terrain, and refers to the hierarchical segmentation of certain groups into structural positions affording differential access to resources and opportunities. Typically these groups are demarcated by ascriptive characteristics such as sex, ethnicity, skin colour or physical disability status, but other more fluid characteristics such as immigrant status, host-country language proficiency, sexual orientation and lack of stable residence can also be included in the list of reasons individuals may be excluded from economic activity and the acquisition of private property (see **discrimination**).

Within the field of social stratification, a large body of research has documented the economic inequalities (see **wealth inequality**) between majority and minority ethnic groups and between men and women. Dual or segmented labour market theories enjoyed popularity among Marxist economists and some institutional economists from the 1950s on. The work of Peter Doeringer and Michael Piore in the early 1970s brought these theories to the attention of sociologists, and a flurry of research activity ensued. Segmented labour market theories emphasize the distinctiveness of different sectors of the labour market in terms of the prevalence of job ladders, on-the-job training and good compensation and benefit packages. Sociologists interested in stratification by sex and ethnicity explored segmented labour market theories for their potential to explain the relative exclusion of women and minorities from the capital-intensive sectors of the economy (the primary labour market) and their concentration instead in the competitive sector (the secondary labour market).

The influence of the dual labour market paradigm waned by the late 1980s as it became clear that economic sectors could be conceptualized in multiple ways, among which it was difficult to adjudicate. Empirical research on the economic segmentation of workers also proved difficult in the sense that most large-scale surveys did not include information on firms per se but rather on the industry and occupation of the individual workers. To the extent that the firm was a critical unit of analysis for studies of economic segmentation or the exclusion of certain groups of workers from the 'best' jobs, this represented a significant hurdle. Empirical work on economic segmentation was also nearly always cross-sectional. This rendered the identification of the processes and mechanisms of inclusion/exclusion problematic.

A more general line of work on inclusion and exclusion stems from **Weber**'s coinage of the concept of social closure. Weber used this term to denote the restriction of access to resources by the propertied classes and by status groups of various kinds. Exclusionary access to resources (or closure) represents domination by one group over another; as Raymond Murphy explained,

> exclusionary closure involves the exercise of power in a downward direction through a process of subordination in which one group secures its advantages by closing off the opportunities of another group beneath it that it defines as inferior and ineligible.
>
> (1984: 548)

A considerable body of theoretical work from the mid 1970s into the decade of the 1980s took closure theory as its point of departure and variously considered the uti-lity of closure theory for explicating all forms of domination, the ways in which Weberian closure theory required further elaboration and, in particular, the relations among different rules of closure including the primacy of some over others. Among the theorists most active in the debate over closure were Randall Collins, Anthony Giddens, Raymond Murphy and Frank Parkin.

Closure theory broadens the Marxist conception of exploitation, whereby the capitalist class appropriates the surplus produced by labour, to include all practices used by dominant groups to monopolize resources. While Marxist-derived theories of the labour market segmentation practices enacted by capitalists are not contradictory to closure theory, such segmentation theories can be subsumed under this broader rubric of domination and exclusion that grants theoretical importance to status groups as well as classes.

In a series of articles and a book in the 1980s, Raymond Murphy argued that Weber did not fully specify the relationship between different rules of closure. In Weber's view, **capitalism** tends to break up status group monopolies because it is in the interest of capitalists to sell to the highest bidder and to likewise obtain labour at the lowest price, without regard to status group monopolies (e.g. guilds). The same was argued to apply to the interest of members of monopolistic status groups. Yet advanced capitalism provides us with ample evidence of exclusion based on sex, race, religion and other characteristics within the context of highly developed markets. Thus, Murphy argued, it is essential to understand that the overall structure of closure in an economy is comprised of different rules of exclusion that may be related to each other in complex ways as well as to exclusion based on ownership of the means of production. In his view, 'Most societies have a tandem structure of exclusion, with derivative and contingent sets of exclusionary rules harnessed to one principal form of exclusion' (1984: 558). More recently, the work of

Aage Sørensen in the 1990s explored the concept of rent as a means of expressing the advantage of the holder of an economic **property** right over individuals without such rights. This formulation is consistent with closure theory but extends it more specifically to class analysis and to the examination of how antagonistic class interests develop.

Empirical work on inclusion and exclusion extends across a number of substantive areas in sociology beyond social stratification and **labour markets**: immigration, citizenship and assimilation; occupations and professions; race and ethnicity; housing policies and discrimination; ethnic economies (see **ethnic economy**); the **informal economy**; and welfare state studies (see **welfare state and the economy**).

References and further reading

Murphy, Raymond M. (1984) 'The Structure of Closure: A Critique and Development of the Theories of Weber, Collins, and Parkin', *British Journal of Sociology*, 35: 547–67.

Sørensen, Aage B. (2000) 'Toward a Sounder Basis for Class Analysis', *American Journal of Sociology*, 105: 1523–58.

Weber, Max (1978) *Economy and Society*, Berkeley, CA: University of California Press.

MARY C. BRINTON

INCOME SEE: class; equality; wealth

INDUSTRIAL DISTRICTS

The re-emergence of industrial districts

The contemporary re-emergence of the industrial district, as a concept, was propelled, at the end of the 1960s, by the need to understand the original paths of industrialization that were appearing, with particular evidence, in some Italian regions. The economic growth of many industrial areas was consolidating around sets of small and medium-sized firms, highly specialized and embedded in a mainly local division of labour. In the 1970s, in many of the small firms of the more rapidly developing areas, modern and specialized machinery was already in use, and labour conditions were improving. Their final products, at the core of 'Made in Italy', were winning strong positions in national and international markets. Generally, a persisting dependency upon the strategic control of big firms was not observed.

Such facts were not consistent with the traditional view of industrialization, based on the central role of big firms. The rejection of a simplistic interpretation of the vitality of such sets of small firms, as the sole result of strategies of production decentralization controlled by big manufacturing firms, paved the way for a series of studies. The empirical investigations undertaken by economists, sociologists, geographers and historians, were complemented by the search for appropriate frames of interpretation. A general if controversial foundation has been the recovery of Alfred Marshall's contribution on the so-called industrial districts, and on the concept of external economies (see Goodman *et al.* 1989).

These studies intersected soon and started to interact with new international research concerning flexible specialization or neo-artisan production (Piore and Sabel 1984) and, later on, competitive advantage of nations, new competition, new regional worlds, innovative *milieux*, regional systems of innovation, learning regions, proximity in organizations, entrepreneurial networks, new economic geography, clusters and local social capital.

The district and the cluster

At the end of the 1990s the industrial districts in developed or developing countries had gained a recognized attention in international debates on industrialization and policies of regional development (see Pyke *et al.* 1990; Unctad 1994; OECD 1996). They have become the objects of a growing literature – of course, with an accompanying cloud of definitions of what is meant as an industrial district, around the common reference to the localization of specialized firms (Porter 1998). A possible definition is supplied with the model of the so-called Marshallian industrial district (MID). The MID is a local system: that is, an area where a community of people live and work, with a great deal of persistently overlapping experiences. It is a particular type of locality. Here, a cluster of industrial and tertiary (private and public) activities is the main core of the economic and social life. These activities show some mix of horizontal (competitive), vertical (input–output) and diagonal (general services and instruments) relations at the local level; and several specialized firms, largely local, small to medium-sized, and independent, realize complementary and substitutive products and services. Some products are largely sold on external markets and define the industrial image and the economic standing of the area. Local firms, families and civic organizations are connected by way of both market mechanisms and non-market mechanisms, like trust within bilateral or team exchanges, and collective action supporting the availability of local industrial, social and environmental infrastructure.

District processes of development

A locality with the structural characters defined above is a favourable field for a compact and interlaced realization of processes of local development. They are: (1) a continuous re-articulation of the local division of labour; (2) the emergence both of industrial leaders able to pull new combinations of activities and products, and of social leaders promoting the governance of specific public goods and services; (3) the reproduction and renewal of the contextual knowledge (the 'mysteries of industry' in the words of Marshall) supporting the specialized capacities and their local contact for

productive and creative purposes; (4) the internalization, among the district agents, of common motivational tracts, and in particular of a bent towards trust in reciprocal exchanges, and attitudes towards productive and innovative entrepreneurship, participation of workers on the job, proactivity of citizens in community life; (5) social and economic mobility.

District structures and processes prosper in open economic and social spaces, in particular those characterized by international markets with a demand for diffused and variable customization and by general technological conditions of segmentation of the production and innovation processes. Here, economies partially external to the single firm's sphere of organization but internal to the district may be realized. They add up to increasing returns for the local resources and to renewal of the district structure (Becattini et al. 2003).

Industrial districts are prototypical examples of localities characterized by the economic and social vitality of a productive cluster embedded within local social relations. More generally, district processes may combine with various internal/external conditions of opportunity and challenge, contributing more or less deeply to different local paths of development (and decline). Signs of such influence have been found in rural systems shaped by agricultural–artisan–tourism clusters, cities of arts and sciences, industrial regions with high-tech clusters and large embedded firms, proto-districts in developing regions. Policies have been envisaged upon the possibility of triggering such progressive forces of specific local development.

References and further reading

Becattini, G. (2004) *Industrial Districts: A New Approach to Industrial Change*, Cheltenham, UK: Edward Elgar.
Becattini G., Bellandi M., Dei Ottati G. and Sforzi F. (2003) *From Industrial Districts to*

Local Development. An Itinerary of Research, Cheltenham, UK: Edward Elgar.

Crouch, C., Le Galés, P., Trigilia, C., and Voeltzkow, H. (2004) (eds) *Changing Governance of Local Economies. Responses of European Production Systems*, Oxford, UK: Oxford University Press.

Goodman, E., Bamford, J. with Saynor, P. (1989) (eds) *Small Firms and Industrial Districts in Italy*, London and New York: Routledge.

OECD (1996) *Networks of Enterprises and Local Development*, Paris: OECD.

Piore, M. and Sabel, C. (1984) *The Second Industrial Divide*, New York: Basic Books.

Porter, M. (1998) *On Competition*, Boston: Harvard Business School Press.

Pyke, F., Becattini G. and Sengenberger W. (eds) (1990) *Industrial Districts and Inter-Firm Cooperation in Italy*, Geneva: International Institute of Labour Studies.

Unctad and Deutches Zentrum für Entwicklungstechnologien (1994) *Technological Dynamism in Industrial Districts: An Alternative Approach to Industrialization in Developing Countries?* New York and Geneva: United Nations.

GIACOMO BECATTINI
MARCO BELLANDI

INDUSTRIAL RELATIONS

The term 'industrial relations' is used to describe the structures and practices produced by organizations representing employers and employees as they engage in conflict and/or joint regulation over the employment of labour. As such, it describes both the phenomenon itself and its academic study. By informal convention, observers and practitioners reserve the term for describing collective relations. Other terms are used to describe the practice and study of non-collective aspects of the employment relationship: in the past, 'personnel management'; since the 1980s, 'human resource management'.

Academically, industrial relations can be seen as one of the earliest fields in the revival of economic sociology from the 1970s onwards. But in English-language academic traditions the subject already existed as an autonomous field of study, which was not necessarily sociological in its approach. In German, French and other European traditions, economic sociology had a stronger foundation than in the Anglophone world (especially the UK), but did not conceptualize industrial relations as a specific field until the 1970s. More recently, as sociology has developed as a more international discipline, the two areas have developed together.

British scholars trace the study of industrial relations back to Beatrice and Sidney Webb and their work on what they called 'industrial democracy' in the early twentieth century (Webb and Webb 1919). The Webbs were typical of the British approach to sociology: determinedly empirical, concerned with 'social problems' and policy rather than with analysis. Much of this interest, including that of the Webbs themselves, was concerned with the development of what later became known as the welfare state. Strangely, however, the British have never seen industrial relations and welfare policy as constituting a combined area of Sozialpolitik or politique sociale. The term 'social policy' is used only to refer to the health, education and welfare area. Until the late twentieth century, industrial relations were seen as largely outside public policy.

British studies were placed on a more systematic basis by Hugh Clegg and Alan Flanders in their textbook *The System of Industrial Relations in Britain* in 1954 (Flanders and Clegg 1954). (Many revised editions of this work were produced by the original authors, and after them various successors, the most recent appearing in 2003 (Edwards 2003).) Although this remained empirical and problem-oriented, the authors were concerned to give the subject a conceptual basis. The main contributors to the literature that then developed were institutional economists, historians and lawyers. A particularly notable contribution was made by the jurist Otto Kahn-Freund. A former labour court judge in the Weimar republic, he was a refugee in England from the Hitler regime, and provided a theoretical framework to aid understanding and appreciation of the distinctive voluntaristic British approach.

In the late 1960s a major growth in industrial conflict and its wide political implications challenged the tendency of much British scholarship and practice to see such conflict as resolvable through managerial technique. This coincided with the rapid growth of sociology, which provided frameworks for considering industrial relations within a wider context. The study of the subject grew, attracting to it many young sociologists, several of them Marxists, but not all. Increasingly the theoretical perspectives of sociology and of political science suffused the previously rather non-disciplinary study.

A similar story can be told of the history of the field in the USA. Here too an early twentieth-century pioneer (John Commons, 1923) paved the way for a 1950s systemization – John Dunlop's Industrial Relations Systems (1958). Like Clegg and Flanders, Dunlop was a practically oriented man, close to the **trade unions**, but he was also an institutional economist and attracted to the functionalist approach to sociological theory dominant at that time. Sociology as such therefore entered industrial relations at an earlier moment than and in different circumstances from in the UK.

In continental European sociology industrial relations were part of class conflict (for Marxists) and Sozialpolitik. No specialism of industrial relations developed. Also, in the other European languages the words that are equivalent to 'industry' have retained their meaning of 'manufacturing', rather than becoming, as in English, a general word for work-related matters. Although terms like *industielle Beziehungen* and *relations industrielles* exist, they are excessively literal translations of 'industrial relations' and cause some confusion. It was, however, to the literature now emerging from the specialized field in the Anglo-phone countries that European scholars looked for analyses of the growing new conflicts – especially if they were seeking alternatives to conventional Marxism.

A key characteristic of the industrial relations focus is that it is interdisciplinary. This is important for the study of an area where economics, sociology, political science, jurisprudence, history and psychology are all clearly and fundamentally involved. But, particularly in the growing separation of social science disciplines that took place between the 1960s and 1990s, the area could not develop its theory while it remained purely interdisciplinary. Eventually it was a combination of sociologists and political scientists from Europe and the USA who developed typologies of different forms of industrial relations system, drawing from these typologies predictions of different kinds of behaviour by the parties (e.g. Crouch 1993). Jurists and historians joined in this task, but (outside the French régulationiste school (Boyer and Saillard 1995)) most economists had become so committed to elaborating their own neo-classical paradigm that they were contributing less to the shared task than in the past. Meanwhile, the sociologists had to learn how to re-engage with the study of economic phenomena – something fundamental to early sociology, but which had diminished in the post-war decades (Trigilia 1998).

By the 1990s this sociological writing was contributing to a broader and more ambitious project, emanating mainly from political science and neo-institutionalist economics: the study of different forms of capitalist economy as a whole (e.g. Hall and Soskice 2001). Work on comparative industrial relations has provided the main concepts and one of the key institutions for this task, but it is now joined by studies of the financial system, the knowledge, research and training systems, and other features of the economy. This major

349

research programme is, like industrial relations, necessarily interdisciplinary. But it needs the participating disciplines to make their own contribution. Thanks partly to its training in the study of industrial relations since the 1970s, economic sociology is now in a strong position to do this.

References and further reading

Boyer, R., and Saillard, Y. (1995) *Théorie de la régulation. L'état des savoirs*, Paris: La Découverte.

Commons, J. (1923) *Industrial Government*, New York: Macmillan.

Crouch, C. (1993) *Industrial Relations and European State Traditions*, Oxford: Clarendon Press.

Dunlop, J. T. (1958) *Industrial Relations Systems*, New York: Holt.

Edwards, P. (ed.) (2003) *Industrial Relations: Theory and Practice*, second edition, Oxford: Blackwell.

Flanders, A. and Clegg, H. A. (eds) (1954) *The System of Industrial Relations in Great Britain*, Oxford: Blackwell.

Hall, P. A. and Soskice, D. (eds) (2001) *Varieties of Capitalism*, Oxford: Oxford University Press.

Trigilia, C. (1998) *Sociologia Economica*, Bologna: Il Mulino. (English edition: *Economic Sociology*, Oxford: Blackwell, 2002.)

Webb, B. and Webb, S. (1919) *Industrial Democracy*, London: Longman.

COLIN CROUCH

INEQUALITY See: class; wealth; equality

INFLATION

There is a demand for money for various purposes, including facilitating transactions. There is also a supply of money. When the demand for it falls and/or the supply of it increases, the value of money, relative to goods, is likely to decline. Prices will rise. It takes more money to buy the same basket of goods. This decline in the value of money relative to goods is inflation.

Paper money is more convenient than coinage. By the beginning of the twentieth century, most governments had monopolized the supply of paper money within their countries. They subsequently removed the right to use paper money to redeem from the government some commodity – usually gold or silver. There was a shift to *fiat money*. It is no coincidence that the twentieth century has involved almost continuous inflation. (The Great Depression of the 1930s was an exception.) On the whole, governments have preferred to allow the money supply to grow faster than the supply of goods, though at widely varying rates in different countries at different times.

There may be some advantages to a persistent, though fairly low, rate of inflation – up to 5 per cent, say. In a competitive environment, and where there are limited possibilities of short-term increases in productivity, firms and industries confronting falling demand must either cut pay or employment. Employees seem reluctant to accept a cut in *nominal* pay, but may be less resistant to the cut in *real* pay produced by stable nominal wages within a moderately inflationary context. Persistent, low inflation, then, may reduce the likelihood of disruptive labour disputes and the unemployment caused by uneconomically high real wages.

It is harder to identify advantages to a persistent rate of inflation of greater than 5 to 10 per cent. In the 1970s and 1980s inflation rates in most OECD countries rose to about 10 per cent or above. Since the Second World War various Latin American countries have had periods of inflation of between 20 and 500 per cent per year. In the 1920s in Germany, Austria, Hungary and the Soviet Union, the rate can only be meaningfully expressed with an exponent (e.g. in Germany in 1923 it was 2×10^{12}). Rates this high are likely to have perverse distributional effects and to disrupt economic activity. As the rate of inflation rises the relative beneficiaries of contracts will shift. In general, to the extent a higher rate of inflation is *unanticipated*, creditors will lose (e.g. the old with accumulated savings in a bank) and debtors will gain. More generally, those unable to exercise

INFLATION

the bargaining power required to protect their interests will lose. Since the relative benefits to a contract are difficult to foresee, people will be less likely to enter into contracts. But contracts and their execution are the core of economic activity and prosperity in a market economy. Why, then, do governments who control the money supply allow – or provoke – higher inflation rates?

There are three main explanations: policy error, government irresponsibility, and distributional conflict. Consider these in turn.

Inspired by the Keynesian revolution in economics, after the Second World War several governments of rich capitalist countries formed the opinion that it was sensible and possible for them to moderate the business cycle and keep unemployment within a range deemed to be acceptable. From the 1950s to the 1970s, some governments chose macroeconomic policies informed by the idea of a 'Phillips curve'. The Phillips curve described a trade-off between unemployment and inflation. It suggested that governments could choose the particular combination of rates that fitted their policy preferences. Subsequent research suggested that there is sometimes a short-term fall in unemployment after an *unanticipated* increase in the rate of inflation because nominal wages lagged prices, so employers hired more labour. But, in the longer term employees build expected price increases into their contractual bargaining (e.g. through indexing wages to the cost of living). At this point there is no trade-off. Insofar as governments stimulated price rises in the belief that there was a long-term trade-off between inflation and unemployment, they erred. They pointlessly caused higher inflation. This is one example of policy error that explains some inflation in some places. There are certainly others.

A second explanation, inspired by so-called 'public choice theory', is government irresponsibility. Politicians seek to get re-elected. They help their cause by transferring income and providing services to

electors. Since tax increases are rarely popular, politicians may sometimes do both without increasing revenues. This will result in government deficits. Deficits cannot continue to rise indefinitely. To avoid the opprobrium of tax increases they sometimes choose to 'monetize' the deficit. In some contexts this has involved printing more money. But there is a variety of technical means by which governments can both increase their revenues and increase the money supply. This sort of behaviour has contributed to many of the most spectacular inflations, including those in Central Europe in the 1920s. It occurs, in part, because politicians sacrifice the long-run interests of the population in the interests of short-run political advantage.

The third explanation is the one that has been most commonly favoured by sociologists. Assume that conflict – often class conflict – is endemic in industrial and post-industrial societies. This may cause *wage-push inflation*. If powerful unions force up wages faster than productivity, employment is likely to fall. (First-in, last-out lay-off practices provide a political basis for this within unions and workplaces.) *Then* governments may respond to rising unemployment and the political pressures that it generates by stimulating the economy in ways likely to result in increased inflation. An extension of this argument claims that centralized bargaining involving government, business and organized labour may engage the latter in the collective pursuit of superior economic performance and limit the risks of a wage-push inflation.

Most empirical work on the issue by sociologists and political scientists has tested the political irresponsibility and conflict interpretations, by comparing institutions and macroeconomic outcomes across countries. Some countries (e.g. Germany) may have been sheltered from the irresponsibility of vote-seeking politicians by an independent central bank that controls monetary policy and is committed to something like price stability. There does seem to be an association between central bank independence and relative price stability, providing support for a political irresponsibility explanation of inflation where central bank autonomy is not present. In contrast, countries with centralized bargaining (a largely post-war phenomenon, it should be clear) seem not to have maintained distinctly low inflation rates. There is, however, ample historical documentation that, once an inflation has begun, distributional conflict greatly complicates the process of controlling it. Where that is so, some sort of political agreement between politically powerful groups, including organized labour, may be necessary to apportion the inevitable distributional costs of curtailing an inflationary process that is out of control.

References and further reading

Franzese, Robert J., Jr (2001) 'Institutional and Sectoral Interactions in Monetary Policy and Wage/Price-Bargaining', in Peter A. Hall and David Soskice (eds), *Varieties of Capitalism: The Institutional Foundations of Comparative Advantage*, Oxford: Oxford University Press, pp. 104–44.

Smith, Michael R. (1992) *Power, Norms, and Inflation: A Skeptical Treatment*, New York: Aldine de Gruyter.

MICHAEL R. SMITH

INFORMAL ECONOMY

The informal economy refers to economic arrangements that are either non-monetary or, if monetized, evade government regulation. The terms 'shadow economy' or 'submerged economy' are similar in use.

In rural areas, the informal economy may involve customary arrangements by which neighbours pool their work to plant or to harvest, with no individuals receiving payment but everyone receiving benefit. Informal economic arrangements may reinforce traditional or familial relationships by encouraging the employment of relatives or friends. **Barter** of goods or services is another informal arrangement. The rural informal economy is more likely than the urban informal economy to be non-monetized.

In urban areas, especially in developing countries, the informal economy may be manifest in many forms. One arrangement is casual labour, in which a worker is hired for a day or even a few hours, often to perform a specific task and without expectation of further work. (This concept may sound superficially like temporary work, but temporary work firms are careful to withhold payroll taxes, pay the minimum wage, and obey other labour laws.) A second arrangement provides for regular work, but 'off the books' so that no taxes are paid. Under such irregular or illegal employment arrangements, the worker is usually unable to benefit from protective legislation or union membership. A third type of arrangement may be for work that is itself quasi-legal or even illegal, such as smuggling, prostitution or selling contraband goods or services.

In all of these arrangements, the informal economy differs from the formal economy in its systematic evasion of legal regulation. Employers are able to evade legislation regulating minimum wage, standard hours or safety conditions. Avoiding payroll taxes is nearly always a characteristic of informal work, so that the workers cannot expect unemployment compensation, social security, health benefits or similar work-related government benefits. Moreover, because non-payment of taxes is usually a crime for the worker as well as the employer, the worker is unlikely to seek the intervention of unions or government officers for **discrimination**, harassment, unlawful termination, unpaid wages or workers' compensation for injury. This evasion of protective legislation means that informal economy workers may be exploited and mistreated without redress.

Informal arrangements persist because there is frequently a shortage of regulated, formal jobs but the workers nevertheless need an income. For the employers, formal arrangements may be too expensive to allow a profit, or the business may be so small and vulnerable that a more formal employment arrangement is beyond the employer's knowledge and means.

In both advanced and developing countries there are forces that encourage informal employment rather than formal employment. Most advanced industrial countries have a large number of regulations concerning workers and payroll, with many limitations for employers; such situations are termed rigid labour markets. Some economists believe that the rigid labour market leads to higher labour costs, which in turn make employers hesitant to create new jobs. In this setting, which describes many European countries, an informal economy may flourish alongside the formal economy. In fact, the informal economy may be more active in producing new positions for workers, albeit that these positions have little job security and tend to have lower pay than formal economy jobs.

In developing countries, especially in cities where internal migration ensures a large number of new workers every year, the informal economy may flourish because relatively few employers produce formal jobs. The formal economy may be dominated by large multinational corporations and government agencies, with jobs that are relatively highly paid but few in number. In addition, government enforcement of employment legislation is often perfunctory or lacking altogether. By contrast, small independent firms and firms with a purely local clientele may participate in the informal economy.

Because its activity is hidden, the informal economy is excluded from government statistics concerning economic growth and productivity. Data on labour force participation, on the other hand, are collected using surveys of individual workers and so might be relatively more accurate in portraying the numbers of workers in both formal and informal sectors. Finally, an active informal sector may artificially reduce the unemployment rate because workers may be able to pick up a few hours or days of casual work and thus avoid being counted as unemployed.

See also: segmentation in labour markets.

References and further reading

Portes, A. and S. Sassen-Koob (1987) 'Making It Underground: Comparative Material on the Informal Sector in Western Market Economies', *American Journal of Sociology*, 93(1): 30–61.

Tilly, C. (1996) *Half a Job: Bad and Good Part-Time Jobs in a Changing Labor Market*, Philadelphia: Temple University Press.

TERESA A. SULLIVAN

INFORMATION

From popular discussions of the 'information superhighway', one is often led to think of information as a quantitative commodity coursing through the Internet like oil flowing through a network of pipes. In this usage, knowledge seems to be basically the same stuff. Whereas information is a flow, knowledge is a stock; so when your info tank is full, you have knowledge. But this quantitative imagery, I argue, is highly misleading. The fundamental fact about information and knowledge is that they are qualitative – or *structural* – concepts.

According to the *Oxford English Dictionary*, to inform means 'to impart knowledge of some particular fact or occurrence'. This is the prevailing modern sense of the term. But in etymology and obsolete usage, the term means 'to form, shape, frame, mould, fashion'. I argue that the older meaning is the key to understanding the modern meaning. Far from being a formless liquid in a tank, knowledge is a complex structure inhering in a human cognitive

353

context, a social system, a mechanism, or even a logical structure like an optimization problem. An item of information is a kind of key that affects or changes a particular structure of knowledge in what may be complex or subtle ways (Langlois 1983). Thus information 'in-forms' knowledge.

The use of the term 'information' in neoclassical economics is an excellent illustration. The division of knowledge had been a linchpin of analysis from Adam Smith through Alfred Marshall. But with the ascendancy of the approach of Léon Walras, analysis took the form of mathematical optimization over a known and given allocation problem; and with the invention of the notion of perfect competition by theorists in the 1920s came the complementary idea of 'perfect information' or 'perfect knowledge'. After World War II, theorists began slowly reintroducing 'imperfections' of information into theory as a corrective to the economics of perfect information. But the resulting economics of imperfect information was and is only an economics of *information*, not a return to the classical concerns with knowledge.

In 1961, George Stigler argued that information is not free: it is a commodity whose scarcity must be taken into account. But what he meant by the commodity 'information' is not a flow of something homogeneous but rather a structured communication that 'in-forms' a specific optimization problem. For example, reading an advertisement or visiting a store provides a data point useful to the problem of minimizing the price I pay for a stereo. Stigler saw the economics of information as demonstrating the function of many market institutions – like **advertising** – that seem superfluous or wasteful under the assumption of perfect information.

At about the same time, Kenneth Arrow (1963) set the stage for what has become the mainstream neoclassical economics of imperfect information. Working from within the modelling tradition that gave rise to the notion of 'perfect' information in the first place, Arrow created models in which information is 'imperfect' in the limited sense that one party has differential access to some crucial datum (for example, a worker's level of effort or whether a car is a 'lemon'). Unsurprisingly, such asymmetric information can lead in theory to a 'market failure' – an undesirable equilibrium solution to the specified optimization problem. Many mainstream practitioners hold that the economics of imperfect information demonstrates the widespread failure of markets and the desirability of government intervention (Stiglitz 2002). By contrast, Stigler's Chicago School see as misleading the idealized standard of perfection against which 'market failure' is judged, and they insist that markets be compared instead to alternative feasible institutional arrangements (Demsetz 1969).

Although not treating information as a homogeneous commodity, neoclassical economics does tend to see information and knowledge as essentially the same stuff. Both are explicit or 'codified' strings of symbols. This is nowhere clearer than in a doctrine central to the 'economics of information' understood as the study of information-related goods and industries like the Internet. Also associated with the name of Arrow, this doctrine holds that markets for knowledge fail because, once created at some cost, a bit of 'knowledge' can be replicated and transmitted at zero (marginal) cost. Knowledge is a 'public good'. By contrast, students of technology, historians, sociologists and others have pointed out that knowledge is importantly tacit in the sense of the philosopher Michael **Polanyi** – it is often a structure literally embodied in human beings. This makes knowledge less of a 'public good', albeit no less a complicated one. In the science policy community, where these two traditions come together, there has arisen a rich literature – and a lively debate – about the meaning of knowledge and information and about the extent to which knowledge can be, or is becoming, increasingly codified. (See Cowan *et al.* (2000), Johnson *et al.* (2002) and Nightingale (2003).)

References and further reading

Arrow, Kenneth J. (1963) 'Uncertainty and the Welfare Economics of Medical Care', *American Economic Review*, 53: 941–73.

Cowan, Robin, David, Paul A. and Foray, Dominique (2000) 'The Explicit Economics of Knowledge Codification and Tacitness', *Industrial and Corporate Change*, 9: 211–53.

Demsetz, Harold (1969) 'Information and Efficiency: Another Viewpoint', *Journal of Law and Economics*, 12: 1–22.

Johnson, Björn, Lorenz, Edward and Lundvall, Bengt-Åke (2002) 'Why All this Fuss about Codified and Tacit Knowledge?' *Industrial and Corporate Change*, 11: 245–62.

Langlois, Richard N. (1983) 'Systems Theory, Knowledge, and the Social Sciences', in Fritz Machlup and Una Mansfield (eds), *The Study of Information: Interdisciplinary Messages*, New York: John Wiley and Sons, pp. 581–600.

Nightingale, Paul (2003) 'If Nelson and Winter are only Half Right about Tacit Knowledge, Which Half? A Searlean Critique of "Codification"', *Industrial and Corporate Change*, 12: 149–83.

Stigler, George J. (1961) 'The Economics of Information', *Journal of Political Economy*, 69: 213–25.

Stiglitz, Joseph E. (2002) 'Information and the Change in the Paradigm in Economics', *American Economic Review*, 92: 460–501.

RICHARD N. LANGLOIS

INFORMATION ECONOMICS

See: information

INHERITANCE

Changes in the ownership of property occur not only through contractual exchange of goods but also through unilateral transfers. The intergenerational transfer of property upon the death of its owner is called inheritance. The transmission of property as a gift is referred to as transfers *inter vivos*. This article focuses on the inheritance of material goods. Other uses of the term in biology or notions of cultural inheritance will not be discussed here.

Inheritance plays a role in all societies that grant individual **property** rights and do not destroy property upon the death of its owner. Since destruction of property was a religiously motivated praxis limited to a few very early social formations, inheritance is an almost universal phenomenon. Systematically speaking, inheritances are caused by the different 'life spans' of material goods and the bearers of property rights. All private property existing in a society will be bequeathed once every generation. This makes inheritance one of the most central institutions for intergenerational economic reproduction. In Germany, for instance, it is estimated that approximately 5 to 8 per cent of the country's GDP is transferred *mortis causa* annually. The testament writer can bequeath all goods for which he or she holds full property rights. In antiquity, but also in the American South during colonial times, this included a transfer in ownership of slaves. The legal regulation of the bequest of property differs widely between societies. It even frequently varies on a local level.

In addition to being an economically relevant institution, inheritance is also a prime example of an institution that effects society in almost all of its dimensions. Inheritance is related to economic welfare, to political order, to the family, to questions of social inequality, to the state and to the moral identity of a society. In this article I will discuss inheritance in the context of each of these dimensions. Although the dimensions can be separated analytically, they are, empirically, closely interwoven. Changes in the regulation of inheritance law always bring confrontation with a plethora of possible consequences in very different social realms.

The economic dimension

Economically, the bequest of property relates to the intergenerational continuity of fulfilment of economic functions. The transfer of property brings economic means of production into the hands of new owners. In economic terms it is the efficiency of these transfers that is of concern. Historically, land property has often been bequeathed to the eldest son (primogeniture) who would receive the family land in its entirety. This assured the long-term maintenance of sustainable sizes of land property by preventing its continuous subdivision. The right of primogeniture, however, not only had an economic dimension but also political and social implications. Politically, it was intended to maintain the nobility's social basis of political power. Socially, it implied that remaining children would be disadvantaged. They often had to leave the village and work as labourers, move to the cities, emigrate, live in a cloister or join the military. As a result of this practice, a real partitioning of inherited property came into law after the French Revolution. The economic consequences of primogeniture rights versus equal division is reflected in the varying levels of **wealth** in a region depending on which inheritance regime is followed. The provisions of the *Code civil*, however, were intended not so much as a means of achieving economic efficiency but to create more equal family relations and ultimately destroy the power of the old elite of the *ancien régime*.

Today, the undivided bequest of property mainly plays a role for farms and closely held family businesses. In some countries special provisions for farmland allow its undivided transfer despite intestate laws that guarantee each child and the surviving spouse a part in the inheritance (forced share). Closely held family businesses also enjoy special provisions in estate tax law that protect the heirs from being forced to sell the firm in order to pay the tax bills.

While the dissolution of accumulated property with each new generation would

clearly be economically inefficient, the prevention of dividing property can also be economically problematic. Extreme concentration of wealth undermines economic competition and can give undue political influence to the property holders. Large-scale landholding and especially entails have been criticized for giving little incentive to the owner to improve economic productivity. A general economic critique of inheritances is that they are a non-market means of capital allocation. From an economic perspective, this process results in inefficient allocation.

In today's industrialized countries the economic significance of inheritances is clearly diminished. The development of **labour markets** led to far greater independence from the need to possess means of production. The welfare state and private pension schemes have, at least in part, eliminated the need to live off revenues from land or **capital** during old age. The development of capital markets – especially the stock market – increased the divisibility of property and thereby decreased the need to prevent subdivision of production units through regulation of transfers *mortis causa*. For shareholder companies run by managers it is *relatively* insignificant whether one heir, several family members or a combination of family members and outsiders own the shares.

Nevertheless, the economic significance of inheritances still remains on an individual level. Inheriting wealth guarantees economic advantages independent of market success. If one includes transfers *inter vivos* and thereby takes into account wealth spent by parents for the education of their children, the individual economic advantages become even more pronounced.

An additional economic – but also family-related – effect of the bequest of wealth on the individual level is the possible behavioural consequences brought about by the prospect of inheritances. Children who know that they will inherit sufficient wealth and have a comfortable life without working might decide to do just that. Hence, inheritance might lead to waste in human capital. This concern has been frequently expressed by wealthy parents and motivated some of them to disinherit their children.

Effects on social inequality

A second effect of the bequest of property is that it contributes to social inequality. Wealth is distributed much less equally than income. In the USA the top 20 per cent of wealth owners possess more than 80 per cent of all private wealth. For France and Germany, the corresponding figures are 69 per cent and 63 per cent, respectively. It is disputed, however, to what extent inheritances contribute to the unequal distribution of wealth. Model-based estimations come to widely differing results. In the 1980s two economists, Kotlikoff (1988) and Modigliani (1988), debated this issue. While Kotlikoff concludes that 80 per cent of all private wealth can be traced to inheritances, Modigliani maintains that this figure is only 20 per cent. The divergence in estimates stems from different definitions of inheritance and different estimates of the current wealth effect for inheritances received in the past. Kotlikoff includes all wealth transfers received by the children after they turned 18 and calculates the accumulated interests gained from the principal. Modigliani, who only considers inheritances and large gifts, bases his calculations on the value of the property transfer. Kessler and Masson (1989) have chosen a different methodological approach. They calculated by what percentage current wealth would be reduced if inheritances would have been confiscated. Their simulation model estimates that between 35 per cent and 40 per cent of private wealth in France and the United States can be traced to inheritances. Studies based on empirical data from actual transfers have been con-

ducted in Great Britain, which has a publicly accessible probate register. Studies from the 1920s, that have been replicated later, show that most wealthy testators had been heirs to significant fortunes themselves.

Although there is considerable dispute about the contribution of inheritances to the accumulation of private wealth, it is clear that the bequest of wealth has an effect on the reproduction of social inequality. This becomes visible from empirical data on transfers *mortis causa*. In France, Germany and the United States between 55 per cent and 60 per cent of all deceased do leave an estate. However, only a small group of heirs receives the bulk of the wealth being transferred. In Germany 16 per cent of all estates represent 50 per cent of the property transferred. In France 10 per cent of the heirs inherit 51 per cent of the wealth. In the United States the top 1 per cent of heirs inherits 19 per cent of the bequeathed property.

Inheritance and the family

The relationship between inheritance and the family is the third sociologically relevant dimension. One indicator for this development is inheritance law. Changes in this law provide information on changing definitions of the family and obligations to solidarity within the kinship system. There have been some clear trends in this development over the last two hundred years. First, there is a trend towards equal treatment of sons and daughters, regardless of birth order. Although legal changes preceded actual changes in testamentary behaviour, studies that analyse last wills show a more or less equal treatment of children today. The second major trend was the improvement of the position of the surviving spouse. In the nineteenth century, spouses had only limited rights to the estate; in many countries they only had rights to the usufruct of parts of the property. Such provisions aimed at keeping the estate in the family and bear witness to the long-lasting legal legacy of feudalism. A parallel trend in inheritance law is the curtailing of inheritance rights of collateral heirs. Both developments show an increasing orientation of inheritance law towards the conjugal family. A third trend consists of the increase of inheritance rights for extra-marital kin. Children born out of wedlock previously had no inheritance rights in common law and only restricted rights to the estate of the mother in most civil law countries. This trend has been most intensely revised in the second half of the twentieth century. Today, extramarital children are legally treated as equals to their legitimate siblings in many countries.

A further family-related aspect of inheritances is not only their role in strengthening family bonds but also their being a source of severe conflicts within families. Although inheritances play a reduced economic role today, due to the development of labour markets and welfare states, they can still be important means of family **solidarity**. Transfers *inter vivos* stabilize the socio-economic situation of children. The gifts make the recipients partly independent from market generated income. This allows for higher standards of living, better education and more risky choices that might pay off later. This aspect of wealth transfers has gained attention in sociological scholarship only quite recently (Attias-Donfut 2000; Kohli 1999). The expectations of children to inherit wealth can also be used by their parents to effectively demand emotional closeness and the provision of care. This has been called the 'strategic bequest motive'. Moreover, inheritances can play an identity creating role for heirs who see themselves as taking over special obligations by inheriting goods that also have a symbolic meaning for them.

While the intra-family transfer of property can help promote closeness among family members, disputes over estates are also a significant source of family conflicts. Very often these conflicts have little to do with the distribution of material wealth but are related to the history of family dynamics.

These micro-effects of bequests on the family have at the same time a significant macro-dimension. It is also through inheritances that social stratification is intergenerationally reproduced. Since inherited wealth leaves families (partly) independent from market success, it is a protective device of social belonging. The upper **class** can be defined as the social strata that reproduces itself intergenerationally independent of its market success. Trusts are an instrument to protect family wealth from waste by individual family members. The elitist justification for such privileges stresses the service of the upper class in society by taking over important political, social or cultural roles (Aldrich 1996).

Inheritance and the state

The bequest of wealth is also connected to the state. This is true in a trivial sense, i.e. the enactment of statutory law by the state. But since antiquity, inheritances have also been seen as a source of state income. Although progressive estate or inheritance taxes were introduced only in the early twentieth century, there has been a lasting debate over the use of estates for financing social services provided by the state. Social reformers of the nineteenth and early twentieth centuries saw inheritances as a crucial resource to finance poor relief, education for the poor and emigration.

Actual state income from estate taxation has mostly been modest and rarely exceeded 2 per cent of overall tax revenues. Since it taxes only the richest part of the population it has nevertheless been seen as an important instrument for increasing progression of the overall tax burden. Estate taxation is extraordinarily controversial as can be seen from intensive parliamentary and public debates over this tax. A probable reason for this is that it affects mostly the richest part of the population, and that it doesn't interfere in a market transfer but rather a transfer *within* the family. In some countries the state has the right to escheat, i.e. it inherits the property if there is no valid last will and no surviving kin or only very distant collateral kin.

The taxation of estates, however, is not only seen as a source of state income but is also connected to the political order. The intergenerational accumulation of wealth might create centres of political power that have no democratic legitimation and might endanger democracy. In historical terms, the relationship between inheritance and political order can be seen in feudal societies. Here, the intergenerational reproduction of concentrated wealth was the social basis for the reproduction of the nobility's political power. In this context, distrust of extreme concentration of wealth has developed with the emergence of democratic ideals.

Is inheritance justified?

The last dimension of inheritance to be discussed here refers to the normative implications of the bequest of property. If we agree with **Durkheim** that social and legal norms are a part of the macro-social structure of society, they are an appropriate subject in the field of *social facts*. The bequest of property became a controversial issue once social inequality based on ascription was delegitimized. This process is generally associated with the bourgeois revolutions of the late eighteenth century. The meritocratic justification of social inequality in modern society makes inheritance a deeply problematic institution since it conserves social structures by a means characteristic of feudal and aristocratic societies. While economic and family-related arguments as well as the consequences for the state were always important issues in the debate on inheritance, its relation to the

meritocratic values of modern society was perhaps the most controversial.

This controversy is mainly played out among liberal social theorists. Socialists were, but for the early utopian socialists, surprisingly little involved in the issue. One side of the controversy maintained that private property rights must include the right to freely alienate property *mortis causa*. The restriction of the rights of the testator, either by enforcing a specific distribution within the family or through taxation, would be an undue limitation of property rights and infringe on the freedom of the testator. This position has been developed by Friedrich Hayek, among others, and in the early work of Robert Nozick.

The other side of the controversy is represented by John Stuart Mill. According to Mill, inheritance should not have a place in the legal order of modern society. In a liberal society, a distribution of wealth based on the coincidence of being born into a wealthy family has, in his opinion, no normative justification. Mill demanded to limit the wealth a person could inherit to an amount that would allow for modest living. Restrictions on inheritances should contribute to equality of opportunity. This argument and versions of it can be found throughout liberal discourse on inheritances up until the present. (Chester 1982; Erreygers 1997). It gives justification to the progressive taxation of large estates in order to achieve equal starting points in each new generation.

A significant modification of this liberal position can be seen in Rawls' *Theory of Justice* (1971). Rawls sees inheritances as permissible based on the difference principle, i.e. as long as they benefit the least fortunate and as long as they are 'compatible with liberty and fair equality of opportunity' (1971: 278). Nevertheless, inheritances should be taxed to 'gradually and continually correct the distribution of wealth and to prevent concentrations of power detrimental to fair value of political liberty and fair equality of opportunity' (ibid.: 277).

Conclusion

Inheritance is a social and economic institution of great importance. Great sums of private wealth are transferred each year to the next generation. The way these transfers are regulated has effects on the economy, political systems, the family, the social structure of society and the state. It also reflects important parts of the normative fabric of society. The different aspects of inheritance are closely interconnected. This makes inheritance a good example for the interconnection between different social spheres in institutional arrangements. The logic of economic efficiency is only one aspect in the *economic transaction* of wealth transfer *mortis causa*. It must be balanced against other societal realms affected by the bequest of property.

Despite its obvious importance, inheritance is one of the least studied fields in contemporary sociology in general and particularly in economic sociology. One can only speculate on the reasons for this. It might be caused by the 'meritocratic prejudice' of modernization theory that has been the most influential macro-theoretical approach in sociology in the second half of the twentieth century. It might also be because inheritance touches topics that are largely considered taboo for public discourse: death, wealth and internal family relations. A third possible reason is more pragmatic: quantitative data on wealth transfer *mortis causa* is rare.

References and further reading

Aldrich, Nelson W. (1996) *Old Money. The Mythology of America's Upper Class*, second edition, New York: Vintage Books.

Attias-Donfut, Claudine (2000) 'Rapports de générations. Transfers intrafamiliaux et dynamique macrosociale', *Revue Française de Sociologie*, 41: 643–84.

Beckert, Jens (1999) 'Erbschaft und Leistungsprinzip. Dilemmata liberalen Denkens', *Kursbuch*, 135: 41–63.

—— (forthcoming) 'Unearned Wealth. The Development of Inheritance Law in France, Germany, and the United States since 1800', Princeton: Princeton University Press.

Chester, Ronald (1982) *Inheritance, Wealth, and Society*, Bloomington, IN: Indiana University Press.

Clignet, Remi (1992) *Death, Deeds, and Descendents*, New York: Aldine de Gruyter.

Erreygers, Guido (1997) 'Views on Inheritance in the History of Economic Thought', in Guido Erreygers and Toon Vandervelde (eds), *Is Inheritance Legitimate? Ethical and Economic Aspects of Wealth Transfer*, Berlin and Heidelberg: Springer, pp. 16–53.

Kessler, Denis and Masson, André (1989) *Modelling the Accumulation and Distribution of Wealth*, Oxford: Clarendon Press.

Kohli, Martin (1999) 'Private and Public Transfers between Generations: Linking the Family and the State', *European Societies*, 1: 81–104.

Kotlikoff, L. J. (1988) 'Intergenerational Transfers and Saving', *Journal of Economic Perspective*, 2: 41–58.

Modigliani, Franco (1988) 'The Role of Intergenerational Transfers and Life Cycle in the Accumulation of Wealth', *Journal of Economic Perspectives*, 2: 15–40.

Rawls, John (1971) *A Theory of Justice*, Cambridge, MA: Belknap Press.

JENS BECKERT

INNOVATIONS

See: Organizational Innovation

INSTITUTIONAL ECONOMICS, OLD AND NEW

Thorstein **Veblen**, Wesley Mitchell, John Commons and others inspired the 'old' institutional economics. In the interwar period it was prominent in leading American universities and research institutes, including Columbia University, the University of Chicago, the University of Wisconsin and the National Bureau of Economic Research (Hodgson 2004). Today, the 'new institutional economics' has widespread influence. Leading names in the new institutional economics include Oliver Williamson and the Nobel Laureates Ronald Coase and Douglass North (Furubotn and Richter 1997).

There are distinguishing theoretical approaches within both the 'old' and the 'new' institutionalism. However, there are not only important theoretical and philosophical differences *between* each camp, but also *within* each camp. Furthermore, these internal differences remain significant if we turn to matters of policy. It is possible to find conservative defenders of capitalism, institutional reformers, critics of unrestrained markets, and advocates of socialism or planning that are prominent in *both* the old and the new institutional economics. The two schools are not readily distinguishable in terms of ideology.

Four sections follow. The first discusses an essential characteristic of the old institutional economics and identifies some of the problems involved. The second section briefly reviews the new institutional economics. The third examines the central theoretical project of the new institutionalism and some of the recent criticisms of its plausibility. The fourth and final section discusses some of the recent partial convergences between the old and the new institutionalism and an agenda for further enquiry.

A central theme of the 'old' institutional economics

A common theme pervades the old institutionalism, from the writings of Veblen in the 1890s to those of John Kenneth Galbraith in the post-war period. This is the notion that the individual is not given, but can be reconstituted by institutions. The 'old' institutionalism is distinguished from both mainstream economics and the 'new institutional economics' precisely for the reason that it does not assume a given individual, with given purposes or preference functions. Instead of a bedrock of given individuals, presumed by the mainstream and new institutional economics, the old institutionalism holds to the idea of interactive and partially malleable agents,

mutually entwined in a web of partially durable and self-reinforcing institutions. No other criterion demarcates so clearly the old institutional economics, on the one hand, from new institutional and mainstream economics on the other.

However, the acceptance of the institutionalized individual does not immediately rule out the possibility that institutionalism and neoclassical economics may be complementary. Some leading institutionalists searched for some rapprochement between neoclassical and institutional economics, including John R. Commons, Wesley Mitchell, John Maurice Clark and Arthur F. Burns.

The notion that individual tastes and preferences are moulded by circumstances has been criticized as leading to some kind of structural or cultural determinism. The individual, it is said, is made a puppet of social or cultural circumstances. Admittedly, some old institutionalists have promoted such a view. But it is not representative of Veblen, Commons, Mitchell or the old institutionalism as a whole. For instance, Veblen (1919: 243) argued that institutions are the outcome of individual behaviour and habituation, as well as institutions affecting individuals:

> The growth and mutations of the institutional fabric are an outcome of the conduct of the individual members of the group, since it is out of the experience of the individuals, through the habituation of individuals, that institutions arise; and it is in this same experience that these institutions act to direct and define the aims and end of conduct.

Such statements show a valid recognition of both the dependence of institutions upon individuals and the moulding of individuals by institutions. In the writings of Veblen and many other leading institutionalists there is both upward and downward causation; individuals create and change institutions, just as institutions mould and constrain individuals. Institutionalism is not necessarily confined to the 'top-down' cultural and institutional determinism with which it is sometimes associated.

A merit of the institutionalist idea that institutions shape individual behaviour is that it admits an enhanced concept of power into economic analysis. Power is not simply coercion. It is often exercised more subtly, involving the moulding of preferences and **beliefs**. Preference functions are subject to 'reconstitutive downward causation' from institutions to individuals (Hodgson 2004).

Learning typically takes place through and within social structures, and at least in this sense it is an important case of reconstitutive downward causation. In contrast, neoclassical economics treats learning as the cumulative discovery of pre-existing 'blueprint' information, as stimulus and response, or as the Bayesian updating of subjective probability estimates in the light of incoming data. However, instead of the mere input of 'facts', learning is a developmental and reconstitutive process. Learning involves adaptation to changing circumstances, and such adaptations mean the reconstitution of the individuals involved. Furthermore, institutions and cultures play a vital role in establishing the concepts and norms of the learning process (Hodgson 1988).

By adopting this approach, conceptions of social power and learning are placed at the centre of economic analysis. This means that institutionalism is more able to address questions of structural change and long-term **economic development**, including the problems of less-developed economies and the transformation processes in the former Soviet bloc countries. On the other hand, the analysis becomes much more complicated and less open to formal modelling. In normative terms, the individual is no longer taken as the best judge of his or her welfare. This opens up the

difficult question of the discernment and evaluation of human needs.

The emergence of the 'new' institutional economics

The 'new' institutional economics can in part be traced back to the work of Coase (1937). This approach was given a huge boost when Williamson coined the term 'new institutional economics' in 1975. Since then a huge and rapidly growing literature has emerged in this area.

For a long time, mainstream economists ignored matters of internal organization. The firm was treated as a 'black box' or more formally as a production function. Other institutions, including the state, were often taken as given.

Coase in 1937 was a voice in the wilderness. His article was a rare attempt to explain the existence, internal organization and boundaries of the firm. His argument was that the cost of using the market mechanism was often greater than organizing and managing human and other resources within a single institution such as the firm. Many years later, this type of explanation, now known as the 'transaction cost' approach, was developed and operationalized by Williamson (1975). Other economists, such as North (1981, 1990) have also been attracted to the idea that the nature and existence of institutions can be largely explained in terms of their potential to reduce transaction costs. However, North (1990) departs from Williamson in stressing the path-dependence and possible sub-optimality of some institutional outcomes.

Today, the transaction cost approach is the most popular among new institutional economists as a whole. There is also a large empirical literature attempting to test this approach. But within the new institutionalism there are important differences in emphasis and analysis, and alternative approaches such as those emphasizing property rights (Furubotn and Richter 1997).

The classic 'new' institutionalist project

By contrast to the 'old' institutionalism, the classic theoretical project in the 'new institutional economics' has been to explain the existence of political, legal or social, institutions by reference to a model of given, individual behaviour, tracing out its consequences in terms of human interactions. The explanatory movement is from individuals to institutions, taking individuals as primary and given. An initial institution-free 'state of nature' is typically assumed.

This approach goes back to Carl Menger's analysis of the emergence of money, originally published in German in 1871. Menger started with a **barter** economy where traders look for a convenient and frequently exchanged commodity to use in their exchanges with others. Once such usages become prominent, a circular process of institutional self-reinforcement takes place. Emerging to overcome the difficulties of barter, a prototypical money is chosen because it is a frequently used commodity, and its use becomes all the more frequent because it is chosen.

Apart from the emergence of money, other examples in this literature include driving on one side of the road and traffic conventions at road junctions (Schotter 1981; Sugden, 1986). For instance, once the convention of driving on the left of the road is established, it is clearly rational for all drivers to follow the same rule. This is because the configuration takes the form of a 'coordination game' (Schotter 1981).

This attempt to make individuals the ultimate elements in the explanation is also clearly evident in North's (1981) theory of the development of capitalism, Coase's (1937) and Williamson's (1975) transaction cost analysis of the firm, and Schotter's (1981) general game-theoretic analysis of institutions. In all these cases, the proposal is to start with given individuals and their interactions, and to move on to explain institutions.

Substantial heuristic insights about the development of institutions and conventions have been gained on the basis of the assumption of given, rational individuals. The classic new institutionalist project has yielded substantial insights by focusing on the way in which interactions between individuals can give rise to undesigned social structures or institutions.

However, Alexander Field (1979) advanced a fundamental criticism. In attempting to explain the origin of social institutions, the new institutional economics has to presume given individuals acting in a certain context. Along with the assumption of given individuals, is the assumption of given rules of behaviour governing their interaction. In the original, hypothetical, 'state of nature' from which institutions are seen to have emerged, a number of weighty rules, institutions and cultural and social norms have already been presumed.

There are other reasons why the starting point of given individuals in an institution-free 'state of nature' is generally misconceived. The reception of information by individuals in the new institutionalist explanatory project requires a paradigm or cognitive frame to process and make sense of that information (Hodgson 1988). Further, our interaction with others requires the use of language. Language itself is an institution. We cannot understand the world without concepts and we cannot communicate without some form of language. As the old institutionalists argue, the transmission of information from institution to individual is impossible without a coextensive process of enculturation, through which the individual learns the meaning and value of sensory stimuli. Up to now, new institutional economists have devoted insufficient attention to this point.

What is being contested here is the possibility of using given individuals as the institution-free starting point in the explanation. If there are institutional influences

363

on individuals and their goals, then these are worthy of explanation. In turn, the explanation of those may be in terms of other purposeful individuals. The purposes of an individual could be partly explained by relevant institutions, culture and so on. Neither individual nor institutional factors have legitimate explanatory primacy. The idea that all explanations have ultimately to be in terms of individuals (or institutions) is thus unfounded.

All theories must first build from elements which are taken as given. However, the particular problem of infinite regress identified here undermines any claim that the explanation of the emergence of institutions can start from some kind of institution-free ensemble of (rational) individuals in which there is supposedly no rule or institution to be explained. At the very minimum, the development of institutions depends upon the interpersonal communication of information. And the communication of information itself requires shared conventions, rules, routines and norms. These, in turn, have to be explained. Consequently, the new institutionalist project to explain the emergence of institutions on the basis of given individuals runs into difficulties.

This does not mean that new institutionalist research is without value, but that the main project has to be reformulated as just a part of a wider theoretical analysis of institutions. The reformulated project would stress the evolution of institutions, in part from other institutions, rather than from a hypothetical, institution-free 'state of nature'. The following section shows that to some extent that this is beginning to happen with the new institutional economics itself.

Some recent developments and convergences

The 'old' institutional economics had strong evolutionary overtones. Attempts to break the constraints of the 'comparative statics' mode of explanation with its two fixed end-points have pointed to a rehabilitation of 'evolutionary' thinking in economics. Moves with the new institutionalism toward a more evolutionary and open-ended framework of analysis have led to a degree of convergence with the evolutionary and open-ended ideas of the old institutionalists.

For example, Jack Knight (1992) criticized much of the new institutionalist literature for neglecting the importance of distributional and power considerations in the emergence and development of institutions. This amounts to a rejection of the 'institution-free' starting point. Masahiko Aoki (2001) not only takes individuals as given, but also a historically bestowed set of institutions. With these materials, he explores the evolution of further institutions, using **game theory**. He also points to a more evolutionary and open-ended framework of analysis.

However, once we take a step in the direction of a more open-ended evolutionary approach, another question is raised. If in principle every component in the system can evolve, then so too can individual preferences. Of course, most economists recognize that preferences are malleable in the real world. But they have often taken the assumption of fixed preferences as a reasonable, simplifying assumption. However, some malleability of preferences may be necessary to explain fully the evolution and stability of institutions. Institutional stability may be reinforced precisely because of the reconstitutive capacity of institutions to change preferences.

Nevertheless, it is one thing to claim that institutions affect individuals in a process of downward causation. It is another to explain in detail the causes and effects. The most satisfactory explanation of the relevant processes in the writings of the 'old' institutionalists was in the writings of Veblen (1919) who emphasized the way in which circumstances and constraints led to the formation of habits, which in turn provided the grounding for changed preferences and beliefs. Through the individual mechanism of habit, the framing, shifting and constraining capacities of social institutions give rise to new perceptions and dispositions within individuals.

Institutions are enduring systems of socially ingrained rules. They channel and constrain behaviour so that individuals form new habits as a result. At the level of the human agent, there are no mysterious 'social forces' controlling individuals, other than those affecting the actions and communications of human actors. People do not develop new preferences, wants or purposes simply because 'values' or 'social forces' control them. What does happen is that the framing, shifting and constraining capacities of social institutions give rise to new perceptions and dispositions within individuals. Upon new habits of thought and behaviour, new preferences and intentions emerge. As a result, shared habits are the constitutive material of institutions, providing them with enhanced durability, power and normative authority.

The rediscovery of the role of habit in human behaviour and the realization of the powerful role of institutional constraints, together point to the development of a research agenda focused on the reconstitutive effects of institutions on individuals, and on the degree to which institutional evolution may depend on the formation of concordant habits.

Clearly, there are many different types of institution and they can emerge and evolve in different ways. Some institutions – such as language – appear and develop with little planning or state interference. Others seem to require the support of the state. A key factor is whether the rules involve elements of coordination and are thus largely self-policing. As well as language, some legal rules have a strong self-policing element. For example, there are obvious incentives

to stop at red traffic lights and to drive on the same side of the road as others. Although infringements will occur, these particular laws can be partly enforced by motorists themselves. However, things are very different with many other laws and institutions. People frequently evade tax payments or break speed limits. These are cases that cannot be interpreted in terms of a coordination game. However, not all institutions derive from coordination games and not all rules are self-enforcing. This raises a possible role for the state.

In particular, in his analysis of contract and private property, Itai Sened (1997) has challenged the notion of property without the state. Sened's argument departs significantly from that of Robert Sugden (1986: 5) and others, who argue that legal codes 'merely formalize . . . conventions of behaviour' that have evolved out of individual interactions. Sened sees the state not as a benevolent and disinterested legislator but as an institution whose members pursue their own interests. For Sened, governments weight the benefits of granting rights against the cost of enforcement. In a world of incomplete and imperfect information, high transaction costs, asymmetrically powerful relations and agents with limited insight, powerful institutions are necessary to enforce rights.

Individual property is not mere possession; it involves socially acknowledged and enforced rights. Individual property, therefore, is not a purely individual matter. It is not simply a relation between an individual and an object. It requires a powerful, customary and legal apparatus of recognition, adjudication and enforcement. Such legal systems make their first substantial appearance within the state apparatuses of ancient civilization. Since that time, states have played a major role in the establishment, enforcement and adjudication of property rights.

But also the state has the capacity to appropriate, as well as to protect, private property. For private property to be relatively secure, a particular form of state had to emerge, countered by powerful and multiple interest groups in civil society. According to this line of argument, the emergence of a powerful institution like the state is a necessary but not a sufficient condition for the protection of property and other individual rights.

In conclusion, there is a growing overlap in areas of research and the possibility of fruitful dialogue between the two institutionalist schools. The extreme individualism of the new institutional economics in its earlier forms is being challenged from inside as well as outside that school. What emerges as 'institutional economics' in the next few decades may turn out to be very different from what was prominent in the 1980s and 1990s, and it may trace its genealogy from the old as well as the new institutionalism.

References and further reading

Aoki, Masahiko (2001) *Toward a Comparative Institutional Analysis*, Cambridge, MA: MIT Press.

Coase, Ronald H. (1937) 'The Nature of the Firm', *Economica*, 4, November: 386–405.

Field, Alexander J. (1979) 'On the Explanation of Rules Using Rational Choice Models', *Journal of Economic Issues*, 13(1), March: 49–72.

Furubotn, Eirik G. and Richter, Rudolf (1997) *Institutions in Economic Theory: The Contribution of the New Institutional Economics*, Ann Arbor: University of Michigan Press.

Hodgson, Geoffrey M. (1988) *Economics and Institutions: A Manifesto for a Modern Institutional Economics*, Cambridge and Philadelphia, PA: Polity Press and University of Pennsylvania Press.

—— (2004) *The Evolution of Institutional Economics: Agency, Structure and Darwinism in American Institutionalism*, London and New York: Routledge.

Knight, Jack (1992) *Institutions and Social Conflict*, Cambridge: Cambridge University Press.

North, Douglass C. (1981) *Structure and Change in Economic History*, New York: Norton.

—— (1990) *Institutions, Institutional Change and Economic Performance*, Cambridge: Cambridge University Press.

Schotter, Andrew R. (1981) *The Economic Theory of Social Institutions*, Cambridge: Cambridge University Press.

Sened, Itai (1997) *The Political Institution of Private Property*, Cambridge: Cambridge University Press.

Sugden, Robert (1986) *The Economics of Rights, Co-operation and Welfare*, Oxford: Blackwell.

Veblen, Thorstein B. (1919) *The Place of Science in Modern Civilisation and Other Essays*, New York: Huebsch.

Williamson, Oliver E. (1975) *Markets and Hierarchies: Analysis and Anti-Trust Implications: A Study in the Economics of Internal Organization*, New York: Free Press.

GEOFFREY M. HODGSON

INSTITUTIONALISM, OLD AND NEW

Institutions are a core analytical and theoretical focal point in economic sociology. From classical theorists such as **Weber**, **Durkheim**, **Marx** and **Simmel** to the modern writings of **Parsons**, Smelser, Merton, Selznick and Stinchcombe (considered 'old' institutionalists) to more contemporary work by Hirsch, Scott, Powell, DiMaggio, Granovetter, Nee and others, institutional analysis has proven to be a robust and dynamic area for scholarship. Institutional approaches to industries and markets have been particularly fruitful over the past couple of decades (e.g. Granovetter and Swedberg 2001; Swedberg, 2003). While new institutional analysis is best seen as an extension of the old, new institutionalist thought tends to reject oversocialized approaches to social action that were pervasive in much of mid twentieth-century institutional analysis (e.g. Granovetter 1985). In an effort to overcome this problem and develop a richer conceptualization of the structure–agency relationship, three main new institutionalisms have emerged: rational choice, relational and cultural frame (see Campbell and Pederson 2001; and Scott 2001 for a somewhat

different characterization of the new institutionalisms).

Rational choice institutional approaches
are rooted in the principle of methodological individualism and aim to explain social
phenomena by assuming the behaviour of
agents is goal-directed (Brinton and Nee
1998). They view institutions as formal and
informal rules (North 1990) that provide
constraints, external to the individual, that
affect cost–benefit assessments of different
choice options. Relational institutional
approaches alternatively conceptualize
institutions as networks of relationships that
shape actor cognition and behaviour (e.g.
Granovetter 1985). Cultural frame institutional approaches offer a theory of action
rooted in cognitive approaches to social
psychology that highlights how broader-
scale theories, models, scripts and schema
shape practices and interaction patterns of
lower-level actors (DiMaggio and Powell
1991; Scott 2001). After providing a brief
overview of the shift away from the old
institutionalism and key aspects of each of
these new institutional camps, I discuss
emergent dialogue and possibilities for
future research at the intersection of contemporary institutional perspectives.

From old to new

Old institutionalists conceptualized institutions as comprised of values and norms that
attained their power through socialization.
The research extended classic Weberian
concerns with power, domination, authority and legitimacy by focusing on how
action was situated within broader forms of
social organization. Many old institutionalists were centrally concerned with economic
life and were sympathetic to more historically oriented old institutional economists,
such as Veblen, Commons and Schumpeter, who theorized about industry and
economic change. For instance, Selznick
(1949) highlighted how organizational efforts
to reshape the environment are recursive

and explicitly enmeshed in broader political
negotiations. However, Selznick also treated organization-building as a complex
endeavour that required leaders to integrate
an organization's goals and operations with
the demands, goals and orientations of its
institutional milieu. Gouldner (1954) concentrated attention on how formal variations in work situations affected labour
relations tactics and developments within a
highly stratified industrial bureaucracy.
Stinchcombe (1959) argued that the social
organization of work into bureaucracies or
more autonomous craft occupations was
contingent upon technical features of work
processes (see Lounsbury and Ventresca
2002 for a more elaborated review of this
tradition in the context of the development
of organizational sociology).

Despite the tremendous amount of
knowledge generated by these works, this
tradition has been widely critiqued. For
instance, Powell and DiMaggio (1991)
highlighted that older institutionalists had a
limited theory of action that emphasized
socialization and the internalization of
values and norms and noted that new
developments in social psychology enable a
much richer conceptualization of institutional dynamics. Recalling Dennis Wrong's
complaint about an oversocialized conception of man in sociology, Granovetter
(1985) argued that a focus on how people
obey the dictates of consensually developed
systems of **norms and values** inhibits the
development of a more robust sociological
alternative to economic approaches to the
study of markets and organizations. There
has been a flowering of responses to such
critiques, resulting in three main perspectives that offer quite different theories of
action and conceptualizations of institutions.

Rational choice institutionalism

Inspired by new institutional economics,
rational choice institutional analysis in
sociology draws on the principle of

methodological individualism and aims to explain institutional processes by focusing on the interests of individuals. The theoretical centre of this paradigm is the idea of choice within constraints (Brinton and Nee 1998; see Ingram and Clay, 2000 for a review). Nee (1998: 8) summarizes the main assumptions of this approach:

> Institutions, defined as webs of inter-related rules and norms that govern social relationships, comprise the formal and informal social constraints that shape the choice-set of actors. Conceived as such, institutions reduce uncertainty in human relations. They specify the limits of legitimate action in the way that the rules of a game specify the structure within which players are free to pursue their strategic moves using pieces that have specific roles and status positions.

For rational choice institutionalists, institutions such as modern marriage are made stable by norms that embody the interests of a close-knit group or society. Rational choice institutionalists draw on a wide variety of theories including transaction cost theory, principal–agent theory, game theory and traditional pluralist theory (Campbell and Pederson 2001). Empirical research has examined the origins of institutions, how institutions shape choice, as well as how institutions change. As in most theories based on behavioural assumptions of rationality, however, a key weakness of this approach is its inattentiveness to the origins of interests and preferences. Even though actors may be conceptualized as boundedly rational, they are typically assumed to have exogenously given interests that propel action and provide a core analytic foundation. Ingram and Clay (2000) suggest that relational and cultural frame institutionalisms may be usefully drawn on to expand the rational choice paradigm by developing a richer and more dynamic approach to interests and rationality.

Relational institutionalism

Relational institutionalists reject over-socialized approaches to agency for a focus on how the behaviours and decisions of actors are embedded in concrete, ongoing systems of social relations (Granovetter 1985). Somers (1998: 766–7) has argued that in contrast to rational choice institutionalism, relational institutionalism 'takes the basic unit of social analysis to be neither individual entities (agent, actor, person, firm) nor structural wholes (society, order, social structure) but the relational processes of interaction between and among identities'. There are two distinct streams within the relational institutionalism – some researchers study concrete social networks with network analytic techniques while others draw on relational thinking to guide more historically oriented inquiry. Social network analysis has become a very potent methodological toolkit for sociologists and has led to a wide range of studies about the how social networks shape action. While some view relational structures more as constraints, others focus on the enabling aspects of networks as suggested by the literature on social capital.

More historically oriented researchers have drawn on relational thought to study how networks provide an important element that shapes long-term institutional processes. For example, Padgett and Ansell (1993) advance a multi-network conception of social structure and contingent social action to underscore how the distinctive patterns of fifteenth-century Florentine social, commercial and political life enabled a style of governance. Granovetter and McGuire (1998) show how social networks enabled Edison to outmanoeuvre J. P. Morgan and guarantee that central stations would be the dominant form of electricity generation. Smelser (1992: 404) suggests that the relational approach directs inquiry towards 'the question of the contextual conditions – motivational, informational, and institutional – under which maximization and rational calculation manifest themselves in "pure" form, under which they assume different forms, and under which they break down'. This more historical epistemology has much in common with cultural frame institutional approaches since it seeks to situate the notion of rationality by making it a variable.

Cultural frame institutionalism

The cultural frame institutional perspective has its roots in the work of Durkheim who highlighted the deep interpenetration of social relationships and cultural **beliefs**. Early writings in this tradition conceptualized institutions as relatively durable social structures of meanings and resources that consequently shaped the practices and behaviours of actors (Lounsbury and Ventresca 2002). While research in this tradition has informed work on globalization (e.g. Meyer *et al.* 1997), cross-national comparative studies (e.g. Dobbin 1994) and research on organizations (e.g. Scott 2001), it is widely known for its contributions to the study of diffusion. Through case studies of how particular kinds of practices become standardized and diffuse throughout organizational fields, institutionalists showed how the behaviours and structures of organizations become similar as a result of contagion and isomorphism (see Strang and Soule 1998 for a review). Initially, these ideas were directly counterposed to rational actor explanations in economics and sociology and empirical research tended to avoid contexts such as competitive markets where factors such as performance and efficiency are dominant decision-making criteria.

Beginning in the late 1980s, many cultural frame insiders began to complain that the depiction of later adopters as passive and 'a-rational' provides a very limiting conceptualization. Friedland and Alford (1991: 244) argued that the conventional institutional approach to diffusion 'assumes an institution-free conception of interest and power, and maintains the materialist–idealist dualism in which actors have objective interests, which can be understood independently of the actors' understandings'. More recent research has extended this tradition by shifting attention away from a focus on isomorphism to theorize heterogeneity and change more explicitly (e.g. Thornton and Ocasio 1999). Much of this work seeks to move beyond the false binary opposition between technical considerations and institutional pressures and conceptualizes rationality and technical demands as culturally constructed (Friedland 2002).

Further, researchers have increasingly turned their attention to the study of markets and industries. Empirical research has emphasized the importance of studying how economic institutions are embedded in wider fields of interaction that include professional and trade associations, governmental agencies, and other non-profit and for-profit actors. Schneiberg (2002), for instance, showed how the growth of mutual fire insurers in the late nineteenth and early twentieth centuries was importantly influenced by a variety of actors such as property owners and agrarian groups that enabled more decentralized and cooperative forms of **economic development**. Lounsbury *et al.* (2003) tracked how recycling activists in the 1960s and 1970s enabled the rise of a commercial recycling industry in the US solid waste management field. Even though early community recyclers had promoted non-profit forms of organizing with social justice aims, the development of curbside collection programmes in collaboration with waste haulers, the rise of Not In My Back Yard (NIMBY) social activism challenging incinerator sitings, and a new model of organized recycling politics spurred the development of a for-profit recycling industry that has largely displaced non-profit alternatives. While the cultural frame tradition is complementary to relational

369

perspectives, more recent foci on logics (Friedland and Alford 1991) and the dynamics of fields (e.g. Scott *et al.* 2000) promises a richer and more comprehensive approach to the study of institutions that is stimulating dialogue across all three new institutionalisms.

Emergent dialogue and possibilities for future research

While each of the three new institutionalisms has rejected the oversocialized conception of actors employed by old institutionalists, the different theories of agency they offer need not inhibit dialogue across camps. Despite the fact that some have engaged in particularly spirited boundary-making aimed at segregating these approaches (e.g. Brinton and Nee 1998; Scott 2001; Somers 1998), fruitful interchange has already begun to bear fruit. Going forward, the greatest possibilities for advances in knowledge will most likely come from the blending of new institutional boundaries.

For instance, building on Homans, Nee and Ingram (1998) develop a rational choice approach to social network analysis that is built on the foundations of methodological individualism. While this may not appeal to more historically oriented relational theorists, there has been a growing community of scholars interested in such microfoundations (e.g. Heckathorn 1996). The utility of this cross-fertilization can be seen in studies such as that of Heckathorn (e.g. 2002) who has developed respondent-driven sampling ideas to uncover the social structure of hidden populations such as jazz musicians and drug users. Also on the horizon are important new breakthroughs in the development of more dynamic forms of network analysis as well as agent-based and related evolutionary modelling techniques which will no doubt help to expand our ability to theorize about network mechanisms that underlie institutional change. Some of this work will be more narrowly

construed in the spirit of rational choice, but these developments are also encouraging more nuanced, relational approaches to the evolution of institutions and practices (e.g. Mische and Pattison 2000).

Even though the cultural frame institutionalism was initially developed in opposition to rationalist approaches to action, cultural approaches have increasingly focalized the study of interests and performance that could spur fruitful dialogue with rational choice institutionalists (e.g. Strang and Macy 2001). For instance, focusing on the inability of cultural frame contagion models to explain downturns in diffusion cycles related to fads, Strang and Macy (2001) argue that what looks like contagion may be plausibly explained by the assumption that organizational adoption decisions are made by intelligent, performance-oriented managers. While most cultural frame institutionalists have indeed made great strides in attending to such drivers of action, they also stress the importance of addressing the fact that what counts as performance and the conditions under which performance matters is institutionally contingent. As Fligstein (1990) showed, the goals and performance-drivers of corporations changed over the course of the twentieth century as dominant leadership backgrounds and related conceptions of control shifted from operations to sales and marketing to finance.

The notion of logic has been increasingly used to study the cultural embeddedness of technical considerations such as performance. For instance, as market logics emerged in fields such as health care (Scott *et al.* 2000) and higher education publishing (Thornton and Ocasio 1999), more narrowly construed performance criteria were invoked to guide organizational decision-making. Friedland and Alford (1991: 243) define logic as 'supraorganizational patterns of human activity by which individuals and organizations produce and reproduce their material subsistence and organize time and space'. At the level of societies, the capitalist market, bureaucratic state and the nuclear family can be conceptualized as logics that constitute the interests of actors and thereby shape cognition and action. At the level of industries, logics consist of common producer 'identities and valuation orders that structure the decision-making and the practices of the players in a product market' (Thornton and Ocasio 1999: 805). Nee (1998: 11) comments that such developments are promising because they encourage a thicker notion of rationality. This work should also facilitate a broader research agenda that develops a sociological concept of interest that restores Weber's emphasis on both material and ideal interests (Swedberg 2003).

The most consistent dialogue has occurred across the relational and cultural frame interface and shows great promise for future research. Researchers at this interface, self-described as new structuralists (see Mohr 1998), draw on a wide variety of relational methods such as multidimensional scaling, cluster analysis, network analysis and correspondence analysis to study how cultural beliefs and social relationships provide distinct yet overlapping dimensions that structure practices in fields. DiMaggio and Powell (1983) signalled the fruitfulness of this dialogue in their seminal article that emphasized the concept of organizational field. Field approaches direct attention towards the broader social context that shapes the actions of similarly situated organizations. More importantly, they aim to uncover the heterogeneity of actors and their practices as well as the multi-level processes by which fields retain coherence and become transformed (e.g. Scott *et al.* 2000). The relational underpinnings of the field idea are found in **Bourdieu**, who claims that.

> The notion of field reminds us that the true object of social science is not the individual, even though one cannot construct a field if not through individuals, since the information necessary for statis-

tical analysis is generally attached to individuals or institutions. It is the field which is primary and must be the focus of the research operations. This does not imply that individuals are mere 'illusions,' that they do not exist: they exist as agents – and not as biological individuals, actors, or subjects – who are socially constituted as active and acting in the field under consideration by the fact that they possess the necessary properties to be effective, to produce effects, in this field. And it is knowledge of the field itself in which they evolve that allows us best to grasp the roots of their singularity, their point of view or position (in a field) from which their particular vision of the world (and of the field itself) is constructed.
>
> (Bourdieu and Wacquant 1992: 107).

Some researchers have used field approaches as a way to concentrate attention on the relationship between broader societal shifts and organizational forms. For example, Haveman and Rao (1997) highlighted the co-evolutionary connection between societal level logics and organizational forms by showing how the rise of progressivism around the turn of the twentieth century facilitated the rise of new kinds of thrift organizations. At the organizational field level, Ruef (2000) tracked how changes in medical journal discourse shaped the ecological dynamics of organizational forms in the US health care field after the passage of Medicare/Medicaid Acts in 1965. Focusing on how broader field-level processes and actors shape variation in organizational practices, Lounsbury (2001) showed how an environmental social movement organization helped to instantiate ecologically committed recycling activists in bureaucratic educational organizations. In an intriguing analysis of the cultural and organizational dynamics underpinning the 1992 Brazilian impeachment of President Fernando Collor de Melo, Mische and Pattison (2000) highlighted how pro- and anti-impeachment organizational coalitions formed as a result

371

of discursive positioning in the field of Brazilian politics.

Overall, this sampling of studies highlights how dialogue across new institutionalisms can foster exciting new research directions. Even though the shift from the old to new institutionalisms has led to discrete research communities, the concept of institution continues to provide a robust and fruitful focal point for scholarship. Rational choice, relational and cultural frame approaches to institutional analysis have all yielded a great amount of insight and should continue to do so for the foreseeable future. As I have suggested here, however, it will also be valuable to pay attention to the border regions of these various new institutionalisms since a lot of interesting dialogue and work is occurring at those interstices. These are important developments because a more complete understanding of the origins, evolution and decline of institutions will be facilitated by such cross-fertilization.

References and further reading

Bourdieu, P. and Wacquant, L. J. D. (1992) *An Invitation to Reflexive Sociology*, Chicago: University of Chicago Press.

Brinton, Mary C. and Nee, Victor (1998) *The New Institutionalism in Sociology*, New York: Russell Sage Foundation.

Campbell, J. L. and Pedersen, O. K. (2001) *The Rise of Neoliberalism and Institutional Analysis*, Princeton, NJ: Princeton University Press.

DiMaggio, P. J. and Powell, W. W. (1983) 'The Iron Cage Revisited: Institutional Isomorphism and Collective Rationality in Organizational Fields', *American Sociological Review*, 48: 147–60.

—— (1991) 'Introduction', in W. W. Powell and P. J. DiMaggio (eds), *The New Institutionalism in Organizational Analysis*, Chicago: University of Chicago Press, pp. 1–40.

Dobbin, F. (1994) *Forging Industrial Policy: The United States, Britain, and France in the Railway Age*, Cambridge: Cambridge University Press.

Fligstein, N. (1990) *The Transformation of Corporate Control*, Cambridge, MA: Harvard University Press.

Friedland, R. (2002) 'Money, Sex, and God: The Erotic Logic of Religious Nationalism', *Sociological Theory*, 20: 381–425.

Friedland, R. and Alford, R. (1991) 'Bringing Society Back In: Symbols, Practices, and Institutional Contradictions' in W. W. Powell and P. J. DiMaggio (eds), *The New Institutionalism in Organizational Analysis*, Chicago: University of Chicago Press, pp. 232–63.

Gouldner, A. W. (1954) *Patterns of Industrial Bureaucracy*, New York: Free Press.

Granovetter, M. (1985) 'Economic Action and Social Structure: The Problem of Embeddedness' *American Journal of Sociology*, 91: 481–510.

Granovetter, M. and McGuire, P. (1998) 'The Making of an Industry: Electricity in the United States', in M. Callon (ed.), *The Laws of the Markets*, Oxford: Blackwell, pp. 147–73.

Granovetter, M. and Swedberg, R. (2001) *The Sociology of Economic Life*, second edition, San Francisco, CA: Westview Press.

Haveman, H. A. and Rao, H. (1997) 'Structuring a Theory of Moral Sentiments: Institutional and Organizational Coevolution in the Early Thrift Industry', *American Journal of Sociology*, 102: 1606–51.

Heckathorn, Douglas D. (1996) 'Dynamics and Dilemmas of Collective Action', *American Sociological Review*, 61: 250–77.

—— (2002) 'Respondent-Driven Sampling II: Deriving Valid Population Estimates from Chain-Referral Samples of Hidden Populations', *Social Problems*, 49: 11–34.

Ingram, Paul and Clay, Karen (2000) 'The Choice-Within-Constraints New Institutionalism and Implications for Sociology', *Annual Review of Sociology*, 26: 525–46.

Lounsbury, M. (2001) 'Institutional Sources of Practice Variation: Staffing College and University Recycling Programs', *Administrative Science Quarterly*, 46: 29–56.

Lounsbury, M. and Ventresca, M. (2002) 'Social Structure and Organizations Revisited', in *Research in the Sociology of Organizations*, vol. 19, New York: JAI/Elsevier, pp. 1–36.

Lounsbury, Michael, Venresca, Marc J. and Hirsch, Paul M. (2003) 'Social Movements, Field Frames and Industry Emergence: A Cultural-Political Perspective on US Recycling', *Socio-Economic Review*, 1: 71–104.

Meyer, John W., Boli, J., Thomas, George M. and Ramirez, Francisco O. (1997) 'World Society and the Nation State', *American Journal of Sociology*, 103(1): 144–81.

Mische, A. and Pattison, P. (2000) 'Composing a Civic Arena: Publics, Projects, and Social Settings', *Poetics*, 27: 163–94.

Mohr, J. (1998) 'Measuring Meaning Structures', *Annual Review of Sociology*, 24: 345–70.

Nee, Victor (1996) 'The Emergence of a Market Society: Changing Mechanisms of Stratification in China', *American Journal of Sociology*, 101: 908–49.

—— (1998) 'Sources of the New Institutionalism', in M. C. Brinton and V. Nee (eds), *The New Institutionalism in Sociology*, New York: Russell Sage Foundation, pp. 1–16.

Nee, Victor and Ingram, Paul (1998) 'Embeddedness and Beyond: Institutions, Exchange, and Social Structure', in M. C. Brinton and V. Nee (eds), *The New Institutionalism in Sociology*, New York: Russell Sage Foundation, pp. 19–45.

North, Douglass C. (1990) *Institutions, Institutional Change and Economic Performance*, New York: Cambridge University Press.

Padgett, J. F. and Ansell, C. K. (1993) 'Robust Action and the Rise of the Medici, 1400–1434', *American Journal of Sociology*, 98: 1259–319.

Powell, W. W. and DiMaggio, P. J. (eds) (1991) *The New Institutionalism in Organizational Analysis*, Chicago: University of Chicago Press.

Ruef, M. (2000) 'The Emergence of Organizational Forms: A Community Ecology Approach', *American Journal of Sociology*, 106: 658–714.

Schneiberg, M. (2002) 'Organizational Heterogeneity and the Production of New Forms: Politics, Social Movements and Mutual Companies in American Fire Insurance, 1900–1930', in M. Lounsbury and M. J. Ventresca (eds), *Research in the Sociology of Organizations*, vol. 19, Oxford: JAI Press, pp. 39–89.

Scott, W. R. (2001) *Institutions and Organizations*, second edition, Newbury Park, CA: Sage.

Scott, W. R., Ruef, M., Mendel, P. and Caronna, C. (2000) *Institutional Change and Organizations: Transformation of a Healthcare Field*, Chicago: University of Chicago Press.

Selznick, P. ([1949]1965) *TVA and the Grass Roots*, New York: Harper and Row.

Smelser, Neil (1992) 'The Rational Choice Perspective', *Rationality and Society*, 4: 381–410.

Somers, Margaret R. (1998) '"We're No Angels": Realism, Rational Choice and Relationality in Social Science', *American Journal of Sociology*, 104: 722–84.

Stinchcombe, A. L. (1959) 'Bureaucratic and Craft Administration of Production', *Administrative Science Quarterly*, 4: 168–87.

Strang, D. and Soule, S. A. (1998) 'Diffusion in Organizations and Social Movements: From Hybrid Corn to Poison Pills', *Annual Review of Sociology*, 24: 265–90.

Swedberg, Richard. (2003). *Principles of Economic Sociology*. Princeton, NJ: Princeton University Press.

Thornton, P. H., and Ocasio, W. (1999) 'Institutional Logics and the Historical Contingency of Power in Organizations: Executive Succession in the Higher Education Publishing Industry, 1958–1990', *American Journal of Sociology*, 105: 801–43.

MICHAEL LOUNSBURY

INSTITUTIONAL STRUCTURATION

See: Institutionalism; structuration theory

INSTITUTIONS See: institutionalism,
old and new; institutional economics, old and new

INTEGRATION See: Functional
imperatives; solidarity; systems approach to economic sociology

INTERESTS See: Hirschman; preferences;
rational choice theory

INTER-FIRM RELATIONS

Inter-firm relations have attracted much interest in the past two decades or so. Organizational scholars as well as managerial practitioners have recognized that firms have to effectively organize the relationships to other organizations in their relevant environment in order to be successful. More than ever before, the competitiveness of organizations appears to depend on firms' strategies to control their external relations efficiently.

Today, under conditions of global competition, many organizations have placed emphasis on their core businesses and decided to outsource a considerable part of their production and marketing related activities, buying in many material inputs as well as immaterial services. As a result, firms have become more vulnerable and dependent on their vertically and horizontally cooperating partners, which led to their desire to develop close, trust-based and long-term oriented external relationships. With this strategy, firms seek to compensate for increased risks and the loss of control that is a direct consequence of the organizational fragmentation of production and marketing processes.

Although in principle the quality of inter-firm relations can vary on a scale from arm's-length to very close relations, in practice there is a clear tendency today towards inter-firm relationships that are strongly based on cooperation rather than rivalry. Close forms of cooperation with strategically important partners are in fact seen as a vital precondition of maintaining and fostering organizations' competitiveness. Cooperative relations allow for pooling resources and the spreading of risk while single firms participating in a partnership can focus on their specific core competences. In vertical relationships the concept of 'preferred suppliers' has gained importance and in horizontal relationships 'strategic alliances', 'strategic partnerships', 'strategic networks', etc., have become prominent organizational arrangements reflecting these circumstances and considerations. Also, so-called 'virtual organizations', often consisting of a number of small firms that extensively use information and communication technology to organize their joint businesses, are to be mentioned in this context.

From a **transaction cost economics** (TCE) point of view, such relationships have been described as 'hybrid' forms of governance, featuring both elements of 'hierarchy' and 'market'. While most forms of close cooperation result from market-based relationships moving towards the concept of 'hierarchy', i.e. incorporate some typical characteristics of intra-organizational relationships, it is also interesting to see that some forms of close cooperation develop out of hierarchal relationships, taking on some characteristics of 'market', i.e. take on some typical characteristics of inter-organizational relationships. The latter is

relevant when large firms pursue a strategy of decentralization introducing competition among their internal units in order to increase their workforce's motivation and, in particular, to raise the level of flexibility with regard to fast-changing markets and environmental conditions.

Inter-firm relations are often, but not always, based on **contracts**. These contracts can have the form of long-term framework agreements or short-term agreements. Short-term agreements are found where simple and easy-to-assess products or services are exchanged, long-term framework agreements are specifically preferred where the products or services are complex, knowledge-intensive and strategically important. Since the knowledge-intensive industries have gained more weight in recent times, more long-term oriented and mutually beneficial contractual arrangements occur. The inclination to agree such contracts, however, is also depend on the institutional frameworks and cultural traditions that prevail in specific business systems.

A considerable part of the current literature on inter-firm relations looks at cooperative relationships across cultural boundaries. Multinational corporations (MNCs), in particular, are confronted with substantial difficulties to deal with heterogeneity stemming from diverse cultural and institutional background of their management and workforce. Recently, also small and medium-sized firms (SMEs) have been concerned with these problems in the context of relocating parts of their businesses to regions where labour is relatively cheap. In order to facilitate swift entry into foreign markets, for example in East Asia or Eastern Europe, many firms team up with local partners and collaborate on the basis of 'international joint ventures' (IJVs) – which, however, often contributes to the named problems. Cross-country diversity can also be seen as an advantage, but empirical studies report more difficulties than many firms collaborating with foreign partners had expected.

In studying the quality of inter-firm relationships, organizational research has looked at the **social mechanisms**, such as trust or power, that are important where the coordination of expectations and inter-action between two or more cooperating partners is concerned. In particular, trust has been recognized as a central precondition of the effectiveness and efficiency of inter-firm relations. It has been shown that there are different forms of trust development and some authors have suggested models of how to create trust in inter-organizational relationships. The use of power has in some views been criticized as counterproductive for the purpose of developing stable and efficient relationships between organizations. In other views, however, power appears as an inevitable ingredient in most types of relationships, sometimes even as a precondition of swiftly developing **trust** across organizational boundaries.

The dominant conceptualizations of inter-firm relations in the 1970s and early 1980s were mainly building on resource dependence theory. In this perspective the function of inter-firm relations was explained by reference to firms' needs and ambitions to secure the procurement of critical resources. Towards the end of the 1980s and in the 1990s, neo-institutional approaches gained strong momentum. In the latter perspective, aspects of routiniza-tion and legitimization were suggested to have an important influence on the nature of inter-firm relations. In more recent times, also systems theory and structuration theory are among those conceptual frame-works that are utilized by organizational researchers. Generally, all newer approaches to study the nature and quality of inter-firm relations suggest a view that is aware of the social embeddedness of rela-tionships. Also, the processual aspects of how inter-firm relationship can develop over time are important within con-temporary theories of inter-firm relations. In many ways, this stands in contrast to conventional economic perspectives which today are widely doubted to provide suffi-cient explanations where relations between organizations are under review.

References and further reading

Beamish P. W. and Killing, J. P. (eds) (1997) *Cooperative Strategies*, three volumes, San Francisco: New Lexington Press.

Oliver, C. (1990) 'Determinants of Inter-orga-nizational Relationships: Integration and Future Directions', *Academy of Management Review*, 15(2): 241–65.

Powell, W. W. (1987) 'Hybrid Organizational Arrangements', *California Management Review*, 30: 67–87.

Ring, P. S. and Ven, A. H. van de (1994) 'Developmental Processes of Cooperative Inter-organizational Relationships', *Academy of Management Review*, 19(1): 90–118.

Sydow, J. (2002) 'Inter-organizational Rela-tions', in A. Sorge (ed.), *Organization*, Lon-don: Thomson, pp. 127–44.

REINHARD BACHMANN

INTERLOCKING DIRECTORATES

A board of director interlock is a connec-tion between two firms that is created when a representative of one corporation sits on the board of directors of another. In 2002, for example, Sanford Weill, CEO of Citigroup, sat on the board of AT&T, creating a connection between these firms. The importance of these connections on politics and the economy was recognized early in the twentieth century by the Pujo Committee of the US House of Repre-sentatives, which identified interlocks as a vehicle for collusion and improper corpo-rate control, particularly by US banks. The subsequent Clayton Act prohibited inter-locks between competitors. Interlocks have been a topic of interest to sociologists since the 1970s, and academic research on the subject has focused on two main questions: why do companies establish interlocks, and what are the consequences of interlocks? Most academic work on interlocks has focused on connections among large US corporations, but there is a growing body of work on interlocks in European and East Asian countries as well.

Research on the question of why companies establish interlocks has been central in two primary approaches: the interorganizational and intraclass. The interorganizational perspective suggests that firms use their directorship ties as a means of co-opting significant sources of uncertainty, such as a major supplier or customer (Pfeffer and Salancik 1978). One version of this argument suggests that **banks**, as sources of capital, offer a continuing source of constraint for a firm and are thus the most important interlock partners (Mintz and Schwartz 1985). Consistent with this claim, banks were at the centre of most national interlock networks through the entire twentieth century, although their centrality in the USA declined sharply after 1980. Viewing the above example through this lens, AT&T may have placed Sanford Weill on its board as a means of placating his home institution, Citigroup, to which AT&T may be indebted.

The intraclass perspective suggests that interlocks represent not ties between companies, but connections between individuals, and that these ties play an important role in the maintenance of a cohesive upper class. Among the factors viewed as important within this perspective are geography, elite schooling, and social club memberships (Kono et al. 1998). In the above example, the AT&T–Citigroup tie would reflect Weill's personal relations with other AT&T board members, especially AT&T CEO Michael Armstrong, who was also on the board of Citigroup at the time. Although they were originally treated as alternative explanations, these two approaches need not be mutually exclusive. One synthesis of the two perspectives suggests that ties that are established for organizational reasons may have the consequence of creating unity among corporate elites (Mizruchi 1992).

Those who have studied the consequences of interlocks have focused primarily on their role in the diffusion of practices. A series of studies have indicated that interlocks are associated with a wide range of firm behaviours. Davis (1991), for example, showed that firms that were interlocked with companies that had recently adopted 'poison pill' takeover defence plans were likely to adopt such plans themselves. Haunschild (1993) showed that firms whose CEOs sat on the boards of firms that had recently engaged in acquisitions were likely to engage in acquisitions themselves. And Mizruchi (1992) showed that firms' political contributions and positions on political issues tended to be similar to the firms with which they were interlocked.

Research on director interlocks has not been without criticism. Most concerns about this work have focused on the lack of clarity on exactly what interlocks represent. Few researchers have had direct access to corporate boards, and this has required them to infer meaning from interlock ties, without clear evidence of the ties' content. In addition, most studies of interlocks have been cross-sectional, and the few longitudinal studies have been limited to either small samples or the very largest corporations. These criticisms point to three potentially fruitful areas of future research. First, sociological understanding of interlocks would benefit from more work that incorporated longitudinal and historical factors into the analysis of why companies establish these connections. Second, ethnographic accounts of board behaviour would deepen our understanding of what interlocks actually represent. Third, although work on interlocks outside North America has increased rapidly in recent years, the field remains heavily focused on the US. An additional research area would be to examine not only international variations, but also the role of cross-national ties. Although some researchers have begun this work, more could be done to understand the ways in which interlocks influence international diffusion processes, as well as cross-national control and business unity. The role of the international interlock network in the globalization of the world economy would also be a fruitful area of study.

References and further reading

Davis, Gerald F. (1991) 'Agents without Principles? The Spread of the Poison Pill through the Intercorporate Network', *Administrative Science Quarterly*, 36: 583–613.

Haunschild, Pamela R. (1993) 'Interorganizational Imitation: The Impact of Interlocks on Corporate Acquisition Activity', *Administrative Science Quarterly*, 38: 564–92.

Kono, Clifford, Palmer, Donald, Friedland, Roger and Zafonte, Mathew (1998) 'Lost in Space: The Geography of Corporate Interlocking Directorates', *American Journal of Sociology*, 1034: 863–911.

Mintz, Beth and Schwartz, Michael (1985) *The Power Structure in American Business*, Chicago: University of Chicago Press.

Mizruchi, Mark S. (1992) *The Structure of Corporate Political Action*, Cambridge, MA: Harvard University Press.

—— (1996) 'What Do Interlocks Do? An Analysis, Critique, and Assessment of Research on Interlocking Directorates', *Annual Review of Sociology*, 22: 271–98.

Pfeffer, Jeffrey and Salancik, Gerald R. (1978) *The External Control of Organizations: A Resource Dependence Perspective*, New York: Harper and Row.

MARK S. MIZRUCHI
CHRISTOPHER MARQUIS

INVENTIONS See: innovations

INVISIBLE HAND See: Economic action; economics, history of; Smith, Adam

J

JEVONS, WILLIAM

In the Preface to the second edition of *The Theory of Political Economy* (1879) Jevons holds that 'there must arise a science of the development of economic forms and relations'. This should be a branch of Spencer's sociology (instead of a 'congeries of miscellaneous disconnected facts'). Jevons devotes a paragraph to the life cycle of human institutions in *Methods of Social Reform*:

> A human institution has, like man, its seven ages. In its infancy, unknown and unnoticed, it excites in youth some interest and surprise. Advancing towards manhood, everyone is forward in praising its usefulness. As it grows up and becomes established, the popular tone begins to change ... It becomes the interest of certain persons to find out the weak points of the system, and turn them to their private advantage. Thus the institution reaches its critical age, which, safely surmounted, it progresses through a prosperous middle life to a venerable old age of infirmities and abuses, dying out in the form of a mere survival.
>
> (Jevons 1883: 82)

Jevons's views about institutions seem to be rather compatible with Cliffe Leslie's ideas. In the *Theory* Jevons expresses his admiration for Leslie, but at the same time he criticizes Leslie's exaggerated refutation of the deductive method.

The present chaotic state of Economics arises from the confusing together of several branches of knowledge. Subdivision is the remedy. We must distinguish the empirical element from the abstract theory, from the applied theory, and from the more detailed art of finance and administration. Thus will arise various sciences, such as commercial statistics, the mathematical theory of economics, systematic and descriptive economics, economic sociology, and fiscal science ... The manner may be theoretical, empirical, historical, or practical ... But as all the physical sciences have their basis more or less obviously in the general principles of mechanics, so all branches and divisions of economic science must be pervaded by certain general principles. It is to the investigation of such principles – to the tracing out of the mechanics of self-interest and utility – that this essay has been devoted. The establishment of such a theory is a necessary preliminary to any definitive drafting of the superstructure of the aggregate sciences.

(Jevons 1911: xvi–xviii)

Jevons therefore maintains that all economic branches must be pervaded by the general principles of the mechanics of self-interest and utility. He does not want to apply historical methods to investigate these mechanics. However, Jevons does take 'institutional considerations' into account when he tries to apply his mechanics to concrete cases, especially in his applied economic work. Here Jevons devotes much attention to important institutions such as **banks** and **trade unions**. In his work on labour relations Jevons favours heterogeneous co-operations, binding together the interests of workmen and employers, in order to overcome class antagonism.

Whereas Cliffe Leslie emphasizes that 'desires of wealth' differ widely among different (stages) of civilization(s), Jevons seems to maintain that the 'mechanics of self-interest and utility' must be present in all instances. However, the *Theory* contains some statements that indicate that Jevons's conception of economic agents does take institutional settings into account. The ability to anticipate future feelings, and thus to discount future utility, varies according to certain circumstances, as there are 'the intellectual standing of the race, or the character of the individual' (Jevons 1911: 34). The ability of foresight depends on the state of civilization: the class or race with the most foresight will work most for the future, because a powerful feeling for the future is the main incentive to industry and saving. Moreover, even the 'quality' of tastes increases with every improvement of civilization. Jevons's conception of an economic agent should therefore be altered according to the institutional setting in which the agent appears (in this case, the class or race to which the individual belongs). This conception of 'character' should be seen as an institution, as it is a collection of rules, norms and attitudes that individuals derive from their membership of a certain community at a certain stage of cultural development. Michael White (1993, 1994a, 1994b) elaborates on Jevons's use of the concepts of 'character', 'gender' and 'race'. White argues that Jevons's work was not directed to the explanation of the behaviour of specific individuals per se, unless these individuals were representative for all market participants of a certain uniform character. The theory is, however, indeterminate in cases when more infor-mation is required. For example, it is unclear whether an increase in the real wage rate, proportionate to an increase in labour productivity, results in increased or reduced hours of work. More information about the 'character' of the person is required: whereas 'learned professionals' might be expected to work more severely, 'lower class people' might prefer greater 'ease' in the case of rising real incomes. The 'average individual' of the *Theory* is linked to class and race behaviour by 'facts' expressing the 'character' of the class or race under consideration, and the Victorian middle-class is used as a yardstick for evaluation.

The characteristics of race, class and gender are simply taken as matters of fact. Especially Irish labourers are said to be responsible for the higher mortality rates in several districts, because Jevons considers the Irish to be a race that would become more easily subject to drunkenness. A similar picture emerges in Jevons's discussion of the reduction of working hours for women with young children. His ideas on this subject are gender-biased, as he regards the proper place of women as being in the home, and assumes that males make the labour supply decisions. The characters of labourers, Irish people or women are taken for granted, and are not in need of further explanation. At the same time Jevons devotes much attention to the alteration of the 'character', especially through education. This would lead to better consumption decisions, less drunkenness, enlarged savings, better forecasting of the effects of the business cycle, co-operative behaviour of employers and labourers, etc. Jevons therefore does not study the change of institutions (like habits or norms) in a theoretical sense, but rather practical ways to alter these institutions. Jevons's approach explains also why his reflections on the role of institutions are not integrated thoroughly with his theoretical writings. Institutions alter the manner in which the theory would be applied in specific cases, but they do not alter fundamentally the theory itself.

References and further reading

Jevons, W. S. (2001) *Writings on Economics*, nine volumes, Hampshire and New York: Palgrave.

White, M. V. (1993) 'The "Irish Factor" in Jevons's Statistics: A Note', *History of Economics Review*, 19: 79–85.

—— (1994a) 'Bridging the Natural and the Social: Science and Character in Jevons's Political Economy', *Economic Inquiry*, 32: 429–44.

—— (1994b) 'Following Strange Gods: Women in Jevons's Political Economy', in P. Groenewegen (ed.), *Feminism and Political Economy in Victorian England*, Aldershot, UK: Edward Elgar, pp. 46–78.

BERT MOSSELMANS

JUSTICE See: fairness, equality

JUST PRICE

There are three ways to approach the concept of *price*. The first is to invoke an argument predicated on perceptions of *morality*. The second is to invoke an argument predicated on *mechanism*. The third is to invoke an argument predicated on *pragmatism*.

In historical terms, moral arguments came first – with Aristotle, and then Thomas Aquinas, advancing moral grounds for particular prices. Aristotle had denounced traders for selling products at a price above what they had paid to acquire those products. Aquinas recognized the flaw in this argument and corrected Aristotle by insisting that traders performed useful functions and that they therefore deserved a small increment to maintain themselves and to contribute to the social good. We see here ideas of individual and social justice. That is, if traders are to be allowed to ply their trade, they must not take advantage of their customers, and the proceeds from their distasteful but necessary activities must be directed to good deeds. In the fullness of

time, a *just price* was that which would allow a trader to maintain his social position.

Classical economics was pleased to leave moral arguments behind, but it took some time to develop a satisfactory replacement. Adam Smith and John Stuart Mill agonized over the matter, but it was Alfred Marshall's marginalist transformation that proved decisive. Here, supply and demand are brought into equilibrium by a price – and that was the end of the matter. The invisible hand of millions of individual choices produced, as if by magic, the *just price*. The price thus revealed was 'just' because no single individual was able to impose her will on others. As long as there were many participants on both sides of the market (the supply side and the demand side) then the impersonal nature of this equilibration assured, *ipso facto*, the justness of the revealed price. Mechanism had replaced morality, and price had become an unimpeachable indicator of value to both buyer and seller. The very fact of a wilfully consummated transaction was decisive proof to these economists that the revealed price was *just*.

Notice the naturalistic vision in this mechanical process. What could be more natural – more human – than letting the free play of self-interest reveal what is valued by those engaged in the incessant trucking and bartering that is thought to define *homo economicus*? It is from this premise that some economists were inspired to advance the idea that markets are necessary and sufficient constituents of freedom (Friedman 1962). Other writers have found this presumption about markets and freedom to be untenable, if not wishful thinking (Macpherson 1973; Sen 1993).

Notice that there are a number of assumptions that must be met for economists to maintain their fidelity to this mechanical idea of a just price. Market participants must be rational, well (and symmetrically) informed, there must be many of them on both sides of the market, there must be no increasing or decreasing returns in production, there must be no market power on the part of producers, capital markets must work well (to facilitate forward contacting), and all other markets must be in (or close to) equilibrium. But, of course, few markets can meet these stringent requirements. And so much of applied economics is concerned with an analysis of how prices deviate from the conceptual ideal.

Moving beyond morality and mechanism brings us to the third idea about just price – an idea that traces its roots to the pragmatic philosophy of Charles Sanders Peirce, William James and John Dewey. This approach from pragmatism was developed by John R. Commons who advanced the idea of 'reasonable valuing' in his *Legal Foundations of Capitalism* (1924) and in *Institutional Economics: Its Place in Political Economy* (1934). Commons rejected the Smithian idea of markets as arenas of harmony. Instead, Commons insisted that ubiquitous scarcity preordained conflict as the sole abiding constant in the human condition. Also, unlike Smith – who saw social order emerging spontaneously out of the free play of self-interest – Commons saw order emerging from a continual need to reconcile (work out) conflicts. The Smithian vision was that social processes (and social order) are unintended but fortuitous by-products of the necessary and 'instinctual' pursuit of individual self-interest. We may think of this order as a 'gift of nature', as it were. Despite what economists say about a 'free lunch,' here was a free lunch of Herculean proportions.

Commons found this quite implausible. He insisted that the notion of *spontaneous order* (Hayek's term) was a chimera. Rather, the economy is a realm of constructed order. Markets are social constructions in that they are products of (embedded in), rather than the foundation of, this constructed order. Wage rates are not determined by some natural (magical) and harmonious process but are instead the end product of a continual need to reconcile the different perspectives and political power of management and labour. There is no automatic and *true* price for labour services – there is simply a negotiated price. The price that is negotiated becomes the 'just price' until new exigencies reveal that new negotiations are called for. To the extent that prices depict a general idea of the 'value' of something, we see the basis for Commons' emphasis on 'reasonable value.' The pragmatic origin of 'reasonable value' (or reasonable valuing) is found in the denial of mechanism.

References and further reading

Commons, John R. (1924) *Legal Foundations of Capitalism*, New York: Macmillan.
—— (1934) *Institutional Economics: Its Place in Political Economy*, New York: Macmillan.
Friedman, Milton (1962) *Capitalism and Freedom*, Chicago: University of Chicago Press.
Macpherson, C. B. (1973) *Democratic Theory: Essays in Retrieval*, Oxford: Clarendon Press.
Menand, Louis (ed.) (1997) *Pragmatism: A Reader*, New York: Random House.
Ramstad, Yngve (2001) 'John R. Commons's Reasonable Value and the Problem of Just Price', *Journal of Economic Issues*, 35: 253–77.
Sen, Amartya (1993) 'Markets and Freedoms: Achievements and Limitations of the Market Mechanism in Promoting Individual Freedoms', *Oxford Economic Papers*, 45: 519–41.

DANIEL W. BROMLEY

K

KEYNES, J. M.

Introduction: from Marx to Keynes

John Maynard Keynes (1883–1946) is famous for his contributions to the practical problems of managing the British economy in *Economic Consequences of the Peace* (1919), *A Revision of the Treaty* (1922) and *Tract on Monetary Reform* (1923). These publications were responses to policy issues arising from the German reparations and the transfer issue, the return of Britain to the gold standard, and the reform of the British currency. Although Keynes was not directly interested in theoretical issues as such, his most influential contribution to the development of economics as a science was *The General Theory of Employment Interest and Money* (1936), which can be interpreted broadly as a contribution to the analysis of the business cycle. His economic writings were characteristic of the Cambridge tradition of Alfred Marshall, Arthur Pigou and Henry Sidgwick, in which economics was a moral science. Although Keynes is recognized as an outstanding figure in the history of modern economic thought, his contributions to economic sociology have been neglected apart from the discussion of 'The Economy as a Social System' in Talcott Parsons and Neil Smelser's *Economy and Society* (1956). Keynes's economic sociology can be seen as an attempt to examine unemployment (as a social problem) that arises from the 'stickiness' of money and a psychological tendency to underconsume.

Keynes and classical political economy

We can best approach Keynes's economic sociology by exploring his relation to Karl **Marx**'s analysis of the crises of the capitalist mode of production. Both Marx and Keynes approached economic problems of **capitalism** from the perspective of macroeconomics. For Marx, these crises had to be understood in terms of the tendency of the rate of profit to decline, the competition between capitalists to reduce wages by **technological change**, and the exacerbation of the conflict between labour and capital. Keynes's approach to the business cycle was largely practical, namely to influence government policy. Both Marx and Keynes rejected the assumption of neoclassical economics that the capitalist system moved spontaneously according to market laws towards equilibrium and continuous growth. The fundamental proposition of Keynes's economic theory was that an economic equilibrium could be achieved with less than full employment and that **laissez faire** economic strategies could not insure full utilization of the factors of production. The correct anti-cyclical government policies included the creation of 'cheap money' through interest rate manipulation and the use of budget deficits.

Both Marx and Keynes rejected Say's Law, in which a given level of supply necessarily created a specific level of demand. The problem of capitalist society was for Keynes a tendency to under-consume. In mature capitalist economies, unemployment is caused by a deficiency in effective demand, because oversaving occurs as a result of the relative abundance of capital. Keynesian economics justifies income inequality as a source of capital formation. Only the rich in advanced capitalism can afford to save sufficiently to fund **economic development** through pro-ductive investment. In underdeveloped societies, the rich hoard money and devel-opment does not take place. However, the long-term historical problem is psychologi-cal: namely, the inducement to invest is always weaker than the inclination to save. The entrepreneurial spirit of creative investment is weaker than the propensity to hoard or to consume lavishly. The Key-nesian psychological puzzle of the weakness of the propensity to invest was the obverse side of Max **Weber**'s theory (1930) of the rational ethic of capitalist investment. This problem of entrepreneurship in advanced capitalism also shaped the sociological the-ories of Joseph **Schumpeter** (1942) where the rationalization of the production pro-cess undermines creative **entrepreneurship** and ushers in the socialist economy.

There are in principle several macro-economic solutions to the crises of capital-ism. These include the 'export' of surplus populations through colonialism, and the destruction of capital goods in warfare. By contrast, Keynes believed that it is possible to avoid both colonialism and the arms race by the rational management of the economy through government-induced demand. Keynes's economic analysis of investment, **consumption** and employment is the core of his **welfare economics**. The intervention of the state was necessary to promote employment during a depression, and an interventionist state would thus contribute to the continuity of capitalism. State involvement was associated with the attempt to stimulate investment that would produce higher levels of employment through the multiplier effect. These rational policies underpinned William Beveridge's post-war welfare-state strategy in reforming social security that aimed to socialize demand without the socialization of the means of production. The Beveridge Report in 1942 proposed a National Health Service, universal family allowances, full employment (or 8 per cent unemploy-ment), and central administration of the scheme which was to be financed by equal contributions from employers, employees and the state. Keynes broadly supported these proposals, although he was primarily concerned with how unemployment insurance and family allowances would fit into his scheme of business-cycle manage-ment. Beveridge's national insurance scheme came to express key components of 'social Keynesianism', namely the manage-ment of capitalism to control the business cycle in order to reduce unemployment through state expenditure on education, health, welfare and capitalist infrastructure such as roads and transport systems. While social Keynesianism provided the frame-work for state interventionism, state poli-cies to regulate the business cycle had already been attempted by President Roo-sevelt in the American New Deal, national socialism in Hitler's Germany and the social democrats in Sweden.

Keynesianism and the management of class conflict

Keynesianism has major implications for the possibilities of labour unrest and class conflict. Although Keynesian economics provided the basis for post-war British socialism, Keynes saw his work as con-tributing to the survival of advanced capit-alism. For example, Keynes argued that the working class and their trade union leaders would exhibit less political resistance to the erosion of real wages in a context of inflation and rising nominal wages than to declining nominal wages and a stable money supply. However as stagflation became the most obvious crisis of post-war Britain, both Conservative and Labour governments concentrated on incomes policies and **industrial relations** reform as a solution to industrial conflict. The Labour government's strategy *In Place of Strife* in 1969 failed to control unofficial strikes or to gain the support of the Trades Union Congress. The first (1979–83) and second (1983–7) Thatcher governments embraced monetarism (cutting personal taxation and controlling the money supply), privatization of major public utilities, adoption of welfare-for-work policies, encouragement of partnerships between voluntary and business groups to provide welfare services, and the creation of an 'enterprise culture'. Thatcherism was clearly the end of social Keynesianism. Although Thatcherism provided a solution to stagflation, it also explicitly provoked class struggle, for example in rate-capping strategies for local councils in deprived areas, in the Miners' Strike of 1984–5 and in mass protests against the Poll Tax. Conservative British governments avoided outright class warfare by limiting the political power of the trade unions (for example, through legislation that made secondary strikes illegal and compelled unions to accept liability for compensation for wild-cat strikes). The sale of council houses through the Housing Act of 1980 also contributed to the embourgeoisement of the British working class, when half a million houses and flats passed into private hands between 1979 and 1983.

Social Keynesianism was the economic counterpart to T. H. Marshall's argument (1950) that citizenship exists to include the working class in capitalism by offering them a modicum of economic security and a civilized life. These objectives cannot be enjoyed without the capacity to support individuals and households above poverty. Hence employment came to be the key feature of social citizenship. Although many democratic governments in the 1970s and 1980s abandoned formal commitments to full employment policies, unemployment remains a critical issue in domestic policy. However, with the growth of consumerism based on low interest rates, price competition, affordable personal loans, diversification of banking facilities, re-mortgaging of private properties, credit-card facilities and high personal indebtedness, advanced capitalist institutions have done much to address the Keynesian problem of the reluctance to consume.

References and further reading

Marshall, T. H. (1950) *Citizenship and Social Class and Other Essays*, Cambridge: Cambridge University Press.

Mattick, P. (1971) *Marx and Keynes*, London: Merlin Press.

Moggridge, D. E. (1992) *Keynes*, London: Macmillan.

Parsons, T. and Smelser, N. (1956) *Economy and Society. A Study in the Integration of Economic and Social Theory*, London: Routledge and Kegan Paul.

Robinson, A. and Moggridge, D. (eds) (1971–89) *The Collected Writings of John Maynard Keynes*, London: Macmillan.

Schumpeter, J. ([1942]1961) *Capitalism, Socialism and Democracy*, New York: Harper and Row.

Skidelsky, R. (2000) *John Maynard Keynes. Fighting for Britain 1937–1946*, London: Macmillan.

Weber, M. (1930) *The Protestant Ethic and the Spirit of Capitalism*: London: George Allen and Unwin.

BRYAN TURNER

KINSHIP See: economic anthropology; kula exchange; Mauss

KNOWLEDGE See: sociology of economic knowledge

KULA EXCHANGE

Kula exchange defines a distinctive system of regional exchange among peoples of the Massim island chain off the coast of Papua New Guinea. Many discussions in the long history of anthropology's fascination with systems of reciprocity and exchange as the central form of **traditional economies** have begun with a consideration of this material. Knowledge of kula exchange originates with the influential volume on this system, written by a seminal figure in establishing the modern discipline of anthropology, Bronislaw Malinowski, and based on his research in the Trobriand Islands, one group in the Massim chain, during the 1910s. Since the publication of this volume, there has appeared over the generations up to the present a large literature of new research and commentary on kula exchange.

Kula exchange operates with precise rules over long distances among peoples with different languages and local cultures. Kula participants sail for months in canoes to conduct exchanges with inhabitants of other islands. They give decorated armshells and in return get valuable necklaces. Over generations participants in kula exchange keep precise accounts of the circulation of these objects, such that they function as a kind of currency. For example, an armshell given to a kula partner continues to pass from one person to another in a counterclockwise direction. The necklace given in exchange moves in the opposite direction and comes to involve different partners than the one to whom the armshell was originally given. Thus, these armshells and necklaces circulate over great distances throughout the Massim islands in interconnected cycles.

This exchange in effect creates an integrated regional social system. It has both ceremonial and utilitarian dimensions, since during the course of these systematic voyages and contacts, much else is transacted besides the exchange of armshells and necklaces, including marriages and the exchanges of food and other utilitarian goods.

Aside from the sheer challenge to anthropologists to describe adequately the working of this system over time, the puzzle of whether kula exchange is primarily a ritual or economic system, or to what degree it is both at the same time, has preoccupied researchers. In more recent literature, the interest has been in how kula exchange creates status, power, rank, hierarchy and structured gender relations within the daily lives of participating islanders. In sum, kula exchange has for anthropologists defined one of the key prototypes of economic complexity in societies without clearly institutionalized markets or money, independent of the matrix of ritual, kinship, agriculture and fishing that defines so much of culture in traditional island societies.

References and further reading

Leach, Edmund and Leach, Jerry W. (eds) (1983) *The Kula: New Perspectives on Massim Exchange*, New York: Cambridge University Press.

Malinowski, Bronislaw (1922) *Argonauts of the Western Pacific*, London: Routledge and Kegan Paul.

Weiner, Annette B. (1976) *Women of Value, Men of Renown: New Perspectives on Trobriand Exchange*, Austin, TX: University of Texas Press.

GEORGE MARCUS

L

LABOUR MARKETS, SOCIOLOGY OF

The study of labour markets has since long been conducted as an interdisciplinary social science endeavour, and much research shares compatible if not even common concepts and terminology across disciplinary borders. Though precise questions may differ, sociologists and economists alike have come to rely on matching and related models to describe the allocation of workers to jobs, and both disciplines accept key premises of human capital models to explain the association between workers' education and the wages they earn, or in decomposing earnings gaps between men and women. Also, sociological and psychological studies often share similar concerns with respect to relating subjective well-being to individual labour market experiences.

While many topics in labour market research have thus clear interdisciplinary appeal, there have also been key strands of research that have been more exclusively pursued by sociologists, or where more explicitly sociological perspectives on the operation of labour markets have been developed. The unifying theme of these otherwise rather diverse fields of study is the explicit consideration of social, i.e. non-economic aspects in the operation of labour markets. For example, since the classics sociologists have recognized the subtle difference between labour power and actual work effort, and have emphasized the role of organization, trust and norms in overcoming the employer's **principal and agent** problem. Also, sociologists have sought to address the embeddedness of labour market processes in social relations more generally, and have stressed the importance of information flows and the structure of social networks in explaining observable patterns of worker mobility.

At the more macrosociological level, sociologists have been concerned with describing why and how labour markets differ from spot exchange markets typical for standard economic goods. One important theme in the literature has been to identify the sources of stability and predictability in individual careers or, more generally, actual mechanisms of status attainment in modern labour markets. In fact, much sociological interest in the structure of labour markets derives from the recognition that the level and structure of social inequality is closely connected to individual labour market prospects in modern economies. Related to that, the study of how labour market events and households' economic circumstances affect non-economic spheres of life – e.g. family relations, demographic behaviour or social contacts – has also always been a building block of genuinely sociological perspectives on the labour market.

Labour markets and social stratification

In fact, a concern for the impact of economic depression on social and family structures was the starting point for one of sociology's classics, Marie Jahoda's, Paul Lazarsfeld's and Hans Zeisel's Marienthal study. In that study, Jahoda, Lazarsfeld and Zeisel set out to understand the impact of the closure of the local textile company on household and social life in the small Austrian community of Marienthal. Though conducted amidst the Great Depression years, the questions posed originally by Jahoda *et al.* more than half a century ago have not yet become any less relevant, nor have their answers. The Marienthal study is a distinctively sociological study insofar as it attempted to address the impact of mass unemployment on both the (typically male) unemployed workers, their families and children, but also on the larger community life. For one thing, Jahoda *et al.* were concerned with understanding the economic responses of workers and their families, the job search efforts undertaken, their attitudes towards accepting lower pay and less favourable working conditions in new jobs, and the substitute activities undertaken to counter the experience of unemployment.

However, Jahoda *et al.* were perhaps even more interested in the *social* implications of mass unemployment in the Marienthal community. That is, they were collecting statistics on the proportion of children with an adequate packed lunch in order to demonstrate how Marienthal life had got accustomed to the fortnightly payment of unemployment compensation. Also, they were concerned with the impact of unemployment on children's performance at school, on crime levels and on changes in the nature of personal relations in the community. What the study is most renowned for, however, are its studies of time use and the meaning of time under conditions of enforced idleness. Using measures on the number of loans from the public library,

people's speed of walking and detailed time-use data, the Marienthal study arrived at the famous findings of a 'reduction of the psychological life space' in the community, especially among unemployed men. This finding of a general reduction in individual aspirations brought about by limited economic opportunities or, more generally, of spill-over effects between labour markets, family life and the social sphere has certainly stood the test of time and much subsequent empirical research.

The same notion of a close linkage between labour markets and social structures is also present in an important strand of macrosociological research on the labour market, *class analysis*. In its very essence, class analysis is interested in describing patterns of social stratification, i.e. systematic differences of standards of living and life chances across individuals and households. In empirical analyses, the traditional vehicle has been to define social **class** in terms of the occupation of the household head – with the implication that first, labour market chances are the single most important aspect of life chances more generally, and second, that households' longer-term economic prospects are best approximated by individuals' stable occupation rather than potentially fluctuating earnings at a given point in time. Like economists' use of the permanent income construct, sociologists have used occupations as an indicator of typical standards of living. Unlike economists, however, most sociologists insist on using class schemes to address potential qualitative differences in individual life chances that might not be well captured in a single quantitative metric like earnings or wages. (The additional assumption inherent in most existing class schemes that the occupation of the – usually male – household head would alone be sufficient to determine a household's socio-economic position is obviously much less defensible nowadays, however.)

Equipped with these occupation, i.e. labour market-based measures of social stratification, sociologists have addressed the processes of status attainment and intergenerational class mobility. In their landmark study *The Constant Flux*, Erikson and Goldthorpe have collected mobility tables for fifteen industrial societies, and have used these to analyse cross-national differences in the structure of class mobility from fathers to sons and daughters born between 1900 and 1950. Since the late nineteenth century, class structures in all of their sample countries have been transformed by the shift from agricultural to industrialized economies, and the ensuing sociological question of interest was on the extent to which massive industrialization was connected with more open class structures and higher levels of class mobility as claimed by liberal and modernization theories. One of the key empirical findings of the study was that the structure of class mobility has been surprisingly similar across countries that exhibit very different institutional structures and that also have experienced nationally specific patterns of economic change. Once these were statistically discounted, however, industrial societies are strikingly similar in mobility chances from a given parental class background to a specific individual class destination. Also, other than mobility chances generated by historically specific patterns of structural change, the Erikson and Goldthorpe study could obtain no evidence of any clear trend towards a greater openness of class structures in industrial societies.

Labour market processes and attainment

Sociological interest in status attainment has not been restricted to patterns of intergenerational mobility, however, and studies tracing individual status attainment over the life course constitute an equally important field of study. One of the key issues in that field has been the conversion of individual resources – notably education – into labour

market outcomes in terms of earnings, occupational status or class positions. The role of education has always assumed pivotal importance in the sociology of labour markets insofar as attainment through education has been taken to represent the ideal of meritocratic allocation, whereas evidence of continuing effects of social background factors or on the impact of ascribed characteristics associated with individual sex or race is treated as indicative of **discrimination** and persistent inequalities in status attainment.

Despite evident linkages to mainstream economic studies on earnings inequality or discrimination of minorities, most sociologists take side with institutional economics in maintaining that the standard neoclassical market model provides only a poor approximation to the real-world labour market. Rather than seeing labour market exchange in terms of spot exchanges resulting in workers being paid at their marginal productivity, sociological models describe labour markets to be segmented and structured along industrial and organizational boundaries, with often little opportunity of mobility in between. Also, sociologists typically conceive of labour markets not as simply the sum of available jobs, but more of a set of career lines where jobs are sequentially linked and hierarchically structured within and across firms. A key element in many sociological models of the labour market is the recognition that the neoclassical imagery of spot markets may at best apply to labour markets for low-qualified work that requires little training or employee effort, whereas the organization of work may involve quite different allocation mechanisms to jobs requiring high levels of skill or significant commitments on the part of the worker. Aage Sørensen's *vacancy competition model* is one example of this insofar as it juxtaposes allocation of workers and jobs in an open labour market sector where workers have little control over their work and can thus be paid at their marginal productivity with institutionally more involved allocation mechanisms in the closed sector consisting of jobs where employees exert considerable control and autonomy over their work. In the latter case, Sørensen insists, workers will not be paid at their marginal productivity, but firms will offer career jobs and considerable job security.

In addition, sociologists have also long stressed that processes of status attainment systematically deviate from pure market competition due to informational reasons. As shown by Mark Granovetter in his seminal study *Getting a Job*, a significant number of jobs are actually not found by any explicit job search efforts, but rather through personal contacts. Also, social networks of both workers and employers are obviously important in channelling **information** flows. Workers may learn through friends and relatives about available vacancies, and employers may use their own or their workers' contacts to find potentially suitable new recruits. Hence, much of labour market action does not altogether resemble the stylized market exchange for the standard goods case discussed in economics textbooks, but rather involves and is actually embedded in the existing social relations of individual actors in the market. In fact, since information in real-world **labour markets** is costly and scarce, both buyers and sellers in labour markets will rationally rely on the potentially very accurate information about workers or firms that is readily available through personal ties.

The recognition that social networks might actually be considered a valuable resource in individual status attainment has spurred a considerable research industry. Following the lead of Granovetter's strength-of-weak-ties thesis, sociologists have examined the conditions for the choice of formal or informal search channels, whether the likelihood of receiving offers is higher for informal search methods, and whether jobs found through personal contacts are actually preferable to others in terms of earnings, prestige or non-pecuniary features. Since the use of personal contacts in job search is highly endogenous in itself, however, few consistent results of any causal effect have been established so far. The most reliable evidence in favour of the importance of social networks seems to be that the use and availability of personal contacts is an asset for unemployed workers. Also, there is good evidence that the extension of personal networks – i.e. the number of ties and their spread across occupations, industries or firms – indeed constitutes a social resource in individual status attainment. Unfortunately, the number of empirical studies providing such detailed measures of individual network structure is still quite small.

Non-contractuarial antecedents of individual work effort

Naturally, social influences on labour market behaviour extend to processes beyond job search and recruitment from the external labour market. The question of individual work effort, what economists have come to call the principal–agent problem, constitutes another core area of research on labour market behaviour that has seen significant and distinctive input by sociologists. The fundamental problem, recognized already in **Marx**'s distinction between labour and labour power, is this: a market for labour comes into existence only if somebody – the prospective employer – is willing to pay someone else – the prospective worker – for conducting some task. Unlike with standard economic goods, however, the employer employing a worker is in less than full control of the worker's action on his behalf. Workers may be better informed about the skills and capacities they could utilize, they may have more accurate information about actual difficulties encountered in their work, which they may decide to conceal or exaggerate, and workers may decide to work to rule or to act proactively and diligently according to what best serves the employer's or firm's interests.

The solution offered in the new institutional economics has been principal–agent or incentive theory. Principal–agent theory casts the problem as one of optimal contract design between employers (principals) and their workers (agents), and assumes that contractual devices could be found to reduce the principal's uncertainty about the agent's performance, and hence to bring about efficient outcomes. In recognizing the informational problem, principal–agent models acknowledge spot market exchange to be insufficient in the case of human labour and often suggest devices like risk-sharing contracts or extensive monitoring of the agent's behaviour by the principal. However, the incentive literature has in fact since long come to the conclusion that any dyadic regulation between a single principal and a single agent is unlikely to yield efficient work effort outcomes under necessarily incomplete contracting. Interestingly, the new institutional economics has come to rely on explicitly social mechanisms like repeated exchange, explicit competition or promotion tournaments to enforce a solution of the principal–agent problem.

On the grounds of seeing exchange under uncertainty as ubiquitous rather than as the special case (see **risk and uncertainty**), sociologists have tended to be critical of much of the focus on individual contracts in the incentive theory literature. Rather, sociologists have regularly pointed out that the economists' focus on isolated employment relationships is fundamentally misplaced since labour market exchange typically occurs within organizational settings rather than between isolated employers and workers. In fact, a central tenet of much of the organizational sociology literature has been that it is the *social organization of work* that is critical in overcoming the principal–agent problem. Sociologists have since long pointed out that the

embeddedness of individual work in a larger organizational context activates work norms, task identification, group norms, mutual assistance and social cohesion among collaborating workers – all of which then also may be instrumental in fostering the organizations' overall goals and performance. This is exactly the gist of the 'Human Relations' movement triggered by Roethlisberger and Dickson's classic *Management and the Worker*, that originally started as a study to evaluate the effect of illumination intensity on worker productivity at the Hawthorne plant of Western Electric in the late 1920s and early 1930s, but then turned into the classic study revealing the impact of social interaction on work effort and output. From a management point of view, a potentially significant role of social factors in production may be considered quite unfortunate, however, since many of these non-pecuniary work conditions will usually be much less amenable to immediate organizational change, but will require reliability and stability in principal–agent relationships.

The notion that economic exchange between workers and employers cannot be separated from the social relationship between them as humans is one of the clearest cases of an influx of sociological ideas into economic theories of the labour market. Acknowledging the indeterminate nature of labour market exchange, economist George Akerlof has used Marcel **Mauss**' notion of the **gift** exchange to explain why firms would prefer to pay above market-clearing wages to workers even if unemployed workers might be willing to work for less. In his derivation of the **efficiency wages** model, Akerlof is quite clear about the fact that workers have expectations about fair treatment by the firm, and employers will rationally respond to this by paying wages that are clearly above the market level in order to signal their commitment. If economists are posing the long-standing problem of why wages do not fall (significantly) during a recession, it is efficiency-wage models that fare well, whereas many neoclassical models do not. Real-world employers are apparently quite aware of this fair-wage–fair-work nexus.

And on

Certainly, the above is far from representing a complete enumeration of sociological interest in the labour market, nor have any of these fields been exclusively claimed by sociologists. Rightly, research on the labour market and on individual labour market behaviour has been a genuinely inter-disciplinary field of study that requires input by different social science disciplines, and that often enforces a revision and integration of exclusive disciplinary perspectives. So far, sociologists have had significant influence in pointing out the **social mechanisms** underlying and enabling actual labour market behaviour, and have provided substantial theoretical and empirical insights on the operation of labour markets or the role of the labour market for modern societies more generally. As economists have also sought to arrive at much more realistic models of the labour market over the past decades, and have tried to incorporate sociological elements into their theories, time seems ripe for genuinely inter-disciplinary efforts on a macrosociology of real-world labour markets that heavily rely on social and institutional underpinnings.

See also: contract; fairness; institutionalism, old and new; network analysis; social ties; wealth inequality; work, sociology of.

References and further reading

Akerlof, George A. (1982) 'Labor Contracts as Partial Gift Exchange', *Quarterly Journal of Economics*, 97: 543–69.

Erikson, Robert and Goldthorpe, John H. (1992) *The Constant Flux: A Study of Class Mobility in Industrial Societies*, Oxford: Clarendon Press.

Granovetter, Mark (1974) *Getting a Job. A Study of Contacts and Careers*, Cambridge, MA: Harvard University Press.

Jahoda, Marie, Lazarsfeld, Paul F. and Zeisel, Hans ([1933]1972) *Marienthal. The Sociography of an Unemployed Community (Die Arbeitslosen von Marienthal)*, London: Tavistock.

Jones, Stephen R. G. (1990) 'Worker Interdependence and Output: The Hawthorne Studies Reevaluated', *American Sociological Review*, 55: 176–90.

Spilerman, Seymour (1978) 'Careers, Labor Market Structure and Socio-Economic Achievement', *American Journal of Sociology*, 83: 551–93.

MARKUS GANGL

LAISSEZ FAIRE

'Laissez faire' can be used in three contexts: as minimization of legal change; as a particular vision of an economy; and as legal change to bring about that particular vision. Discussion here focuses on the first.

The concept of laissez faire is simultaneously unambiguous and ambiguous. The difference turns, in part, on the issue of sentiment versus coherent substance. Both sentimentally and substantively, it stands for an economic system based upon institutions of private property, free enterprise, competition, markets, meaningful private choice, and a presumption against government activism; markets govern resource allocation. Sentimentally, it is an idealization of the western economic system, a projection of certain individualist sentiments. Compared to mercantilism and Soviet-type planning, it also has substantive meaning. While laissez faire seems an attractive solution to social problems and escapes the burden of choice, and because movement towards an idealized image is perceived as neither government nor change, problems arise in its application within a market economy.

Market economies are usefully modelled as market plus framework systems. Markets operate within frameworks of moral and legal rules structuring and operating through markets they help form. This model gives effect to (1) private choice and (2) necessary social control. Problems arise over the substance of rules, mode of determining rules, relative reliance upon moral and legal rules, and changing legal rules. The model postulates a joint process: optimizing market resource allocation, and reforming the framework.

Because the presumption against legal activism is easily rebutted, the substantive interpretation becomes ambiguous. Legal social control is necessary. The basic economic institutions are legal in character. People who believe they have problems in pragmatic, democratic regimes seek government help. Working all this out is messy. Politicians seeking re-election must attend to citizen attitudes and perceptions of problems, problems likely to be very real. For this and numerous other reasons, changing the legal rules governing property rights and other institutions happens frequently – to the dismay of believers in strict laissez faire.

Modern western economies exhibit several practical models of laissez faire. First, government is projected as an evil, to be removed from the backs of the citizens. Second, already-existing important governmental activities are taken for granted, treated as natural. In the first two models, officials' principal function is to enforce the law, and neither expand their scope nor introduce change. Third, typically inexplicit in ordinary discourse, government is the object of reform, making government do the correct things for the right people. The first model minimizes government; the second minimizes change of law and of the interests protected by government; and the third minimizes control of the agenda by the wrong people.

This practical orientation faces fundamental problems. First, conflicts exist between the three models considered as agendas for government. Second, all three are applied selectively, therefore inconsistently, with ambiguity and inconclusive-

ness the result. Third, economic policy is a function of contests among elites and between elites and non-elites to determine who are the right people to control and benefit from government. Fourth, a tension may exist between economic and social conservatives; the former want to enhance, and the latter to constrain, the range of private discretion allowed by law, generally but not necessarily in different spheres of life.

Another problem is *governance*, defined as decision-making importantly affecting other people. Official government is one institution of governance; others include other governments, international organizations, domestic and foreign corporations, non-profit organizations, organized religion, education and custom. Government has formal responsibility for the division of power within the nominally private sector and between the private and public sectors. But government is an object of a ubiquitous contest over its control. Limiting government does not limit governance.

Common to much of the above is that government 'interferes' in order to control the 'interference' by others. Freedom – freedom to manufacture and to trade – is a function of the total system of freedom and control. Legal rules both limit and enhance the individual's range of operative discretion, typically differently for different people. An historic example is the contest between labour and capital over the legal status of unions.

Private property is both what it is because of government and a check on the power of government – given suitable legislators and judges. During the period of transformation from the old to the modern **state and economy**, new forms and new meanings of property arose and old ones fell. Property was not protected because it is property; it was property because it was protected. But such did not prevent claims invoking the sacred character of property and the need to protect property against the claims of those who wanted government to protect their interests just as it had protected others, as property.

'Laissez faire' was fiction, an exercise in wishful thinking and the language of those who opposed certain proposed changes, but not their own changes. The concept has mixed sentimental and existential or substantive meaning, suffused with selectivity in application and ambiguity of meaning. Certain sentiments are effectively expressed; yet fundamentally inconclusive with respect to the issues to which they are addressed, generally represented by the question, What should government do? The question is more complicated than the phrase and its underlying sentiment might lead one to expect. Laissez faire is a simplistic and disengaging view of complex real-world problems, the dynamics of change, and the need for collective decision-making. Accordingly no country could or has practised laissez faire, though much has been done in its name and though its ostensible domestic programme has been combined with imperialism – by Great Britain in the nineteenth century and by others.

References and further reading

Fine, Sidney (1956) *Laissez-Faire and the General-Welfare State*, Ann Arbor, MI: University of Michigan Press.

Garrison, Lloyd K. and Hurst, Willard (1956) *The Legal Process*, Madison, WI: Capital Press.

Hurst, James Willard (1956) *Law and the Conditions of Freedom in the Nineteenth-Century United States*, Madison, WI: University of Wisconsin Press.

Robbins, Lionel (1952) *The Theory of Economic Policy in English Classical Political Economy*, London: Macmillan.

Samuels, Warren J. (1966) *The Classical Theory of Economic Policy*, Cleveland, OH: World.

WARREN SAMUELS

LAW AND ECONOMY

While it is clear that law plays an important role in the economy, contemporary economic sociology has largely failed to develop its own distinct analysis of this phenomenon. The situation in economic sociology can on this point be contrasted to that of economics, which has developed an immensely successful type of analysis during the last few decades. The failure of economic sociology in this respect is actually twofold: not only has it failed to develop a distinct approach of its own to the role of law in the economy, it has also produced very few individual studies on this theme.

What is nonetheless positive in the current situation is that this neglect has recently been realized, and calls have been issued for a radical change. And even if much of the hard work remains to be done, there do exist a number of ideas and studies which can be helpful in this enterprise. Some of these were produced by the classical sociologists and some by contemporary economic sociologists as well as sociologists of law. One way of summing up the situation would be to say that the classical sociologists have mainly contributed to the understanding of the following legal institutions: *the contract, property, inheritance* and *the invention of the legal personality*. Contemporary sociologists, on the other hand, have mainly paid attention to *the corporation as a legal actor, anti-trust legislation, corporate crime* and *bankruptcy*.

Several of the classical sociologists had a legal education, such as Tocqueville, **Marx** and **Weber**. Of these Weber is without doubt the person who has made the most concerted effort to develop a sociology of law. From early on Weber was also deeply interested in the relationship of law to the economy, and both of his dissertations deal with different aspects of this theme. As a professor of economics, Weber analysed, among other things, the role of legislation and self-regulation in the modern stock exchange. And as an editor of the giant *Handbook of Economics*, of which *Economy and Society* was a part, he saw to it that the role of law in the economy was assigned an important role.

But also Tocqueville, Marx and **Durkheim** made important contributions to the understanding of law in economic life. Tocqueville was a liberal and interested in the general role of law in economy and society. Marx, in contrast, mainly saw law in terms of superstructure and ideology. Durkheim, finally, encouraged the development of sociology of law as a distinct subfield in sociology. He also lectured on the evolution of the contract and respect for property.

In Durkheim's *Division of Labour* one can find a famous analysis of *the contract*. Debating Herbert Spencer's idea that society should be operated on the basis of individual contracts, Durkheim emphasized that 'everything in the contract is not contractual'. With this famous phrase he meant that you always need society to enforce contracts, to make people want to keep contracts, and to fill in various gaps in the formulation of contracts. Weber's best-known contribution to the study of contracts has to do with his distinction between contracts in pre-capitalist society, which involved the whole status of the person, and contracts in capitalist society, which are primarily economic in nature ('status contracts' vs 'purposive contracts').

While Marx assigned an enormous importance to *property* in his theory of society, he paid little attention to its legal dimension (but see e.g. Marx [1867]1906: 195). Weber, in contrast, tried to develop a distinctly sociological approach to property, drawing directly on his theory of social action. If you have a closed social relationship, whose purpose it is to appropriate something, and if you also can pass this relationship on through inheritance and sell it on the market, then you have the modern concept of property. *Economy and Society*, in addition, contains a complex typology of the many types of property and appropriation that can be found throughout history.

Insights into the nature of *inheritance* are scattered throughout the classics. Tocqueville, for example, argued that primogeniture was as necessary to aristocracy as the equal division of inheritance is to democracy. According to Durkheim, on the other hand, the whole idea of inheritance in modern society was atavistic and a leftover from earlier times. Inheritance should be eliminated since it went against the principles of modern society: 'It is obvious that inheritance, by creating inequalities amongst men from birth that are unrelated to merit or service, invalidates the whole contractual system at its roots' (Durkheim ([1950]1983): 213).

That the principle of *legal personality* is crucial to modern society as well as the modern economy has primarily been emphasized by Weber. From a legal point of view, he notes, an association or organization is created through a contract. Not until it was possible to make a sharp distinction between an organization and its individual members was it possible to develop an autonomous firm. The related idea that the individual firm can have property of its own, which is distinct from the property of its members, was also that established during the Middle Ages.

The contributions by today's sociologists to the understanding of law and economy have largely been produced while ignoring the classics. This has made them fresh, and it has also made it easier for them to be moulded to recent developments. Still, not being able to 'stand on the shoulders of giants' has perhaps also made the current contributions somewhat fragmentary in nature and also disconnected from the main tradition in economic sociology.

The most innovative contribution to the sociological understanding of the role of law in the economy is definitely the idea of *the corporation as a legal actor*. Firms, in other words, do not only follow the law or make use of it as a tool to accomplish their goals, they also can create law, just as a legislative assembly or a court. That this is the case has been suggested by several sociologists of law, especially Lauren Edelman and her co-authors. The focus of their studies have mainly been on the 1964 Civil Rights Act and related legislation. This legislation, Edelman *et al.* argue, was so vague that firms did not know how to react to it. The end result was not only that firms had to create law on their own; courts have also started to draw on this 'corporate law'.

Another area of law and the economy which has grown out of the study of the large American firms has to do with *anti-trust legislation*. The interest in this topic has not only to do with the fact that this type of law represents a unique American innovation in the nineteenth century, but also that most of the countries in the world have by now adopted anti-trust legislation. A pioneer in analysing anti-trust legislation from a sociological perspective is Neil Fligstein, who argues that the huge firms in the United States have tended to gravitate to similar strategies during certain periods – and that these strategies have often been deeply influenced by the way that anti-trust legislation has developed. When cartels, for example, were outlawed by the Sherman Act of 1890 they were soon replaced by mergers. And when some forms of mergers were outlawed, other strategies were invented so that firms could regain control over their environment.

Corporate crimes – that is, crimes that benefit the corporation but not necessarily the individuals who commit them – have increased together with the growth of corporations. Cartels are still common, even if they are outlawed in most countries, and they typically involve enormous sums of money. That networks analysis can be helpful in understanding how these cartels work has been shown in a study of the electrical industry by Wayne Baker and Robert Faulkner. A cartel involving a sim-

ple product may have a flat network structure, while one that involves a complex product may be more hierarchical in nature. Depending on their place in these networks, individuals may also be more or less easy to spot for investigators.

Finally, sociologists have also started to do research on *bankruptcy*. **Bankruptcy** is of two kinds: individuals can go bankrupt and corporations can go bankrupt. The former type of bankruptcy has skyrocketed during the last two decades in the United States, and a major reason for this has been the increase in debt of individual households. Bankruptcy for a corporation follows a very different legal procedure, and one that may differ between countries. Thanks to the cooperation between a sociologist and a legal scholar, we know today, for example, that while bankruptcy in the United States encourages the reorganization of a firm rather than its liquidation, the situation is the reverse in England.

All in all, one can say that while the classics focused on a series of basic problems in the study of law and economy, contemporary studies have mainly paid attention to current problems. One way to strengthen the economic sociology of today would no doubt be to re-establish its links to the past. Especially Weber had come close to develop a full-scale programme for what an economic sociology of law might look like. What may be even more effective than proceeding in this way, however, would simply be to set law and economy high on the agenda of economic sociology, and proceed from there.

References and further reading

Carruthers, Bruce and Halliday, Terence (1998) *Rescuing Business: The Making of Corporate Bankruptcy Law in England and the United States*, Oxford: Clarendon Press.

Durkheim, Emile ([1950]1983) *Professional Ethics and Civic Morals*, Westport, CT: Greenwood Press.

Edelman, Lauren (1992) 'Legal Ambiguity and Symbolic Structures: Organizational Mediation of Civil Rights', *American Journal of Sociology*, 97: 1531–76.

Fligstein, Neil (1990) *The Transformation of Corporate Control*, Cambridge, MA: Harvard University Press.

Marx, Karl ([1867]1906) *Capital: A Critique of Political Economy*, New York: The Modern Library.

Posner, Richard (1998) *Economic Analysis of Law*, fifth edition, Boston: Little, Brown.

Swedberg, Richard (2003) 'The Case for an Economic Sociology of Law', *Theory and Society*, 32: 1–37.

Weber, Max ([1922]1978) *Economy and Society: An Outline of Interpretive Sociology*, Berkeley, CA: University of California Press.

RICHARD SWEDBERG

LEARNING IN ECONOMY See: innovations

LEGITIMACY

Ever since the Vietnam War, 'legitimacy' in the lay press has come to mean something akin to 'winning the hearts and minds' of those involved. Indeed, in the literature of the social sciences, legitimacy means achieving the consent of the ruled. Legitimacy then is the hoped-for effect of an often difficult attempt to justify a power relationship; and, if and when it is achieved, converts power into authority.

Early in *The Social Contract,* Jean-Jacques Rousseau argued that anyone who 'believes himself the master of his fellow men, is . . . nevertheless more of a slave than they' (Rousseau [1762]1954: 2). He argued that this is so because '[t]he strongest – unless he transforms force into right and obedience into duty – is never strong enough to have his way all the time' (ibid. 6). Sociologists refer to this transformation of power into legitimated power as authority. Some sociologists even claim that when power is so transformed, authority becomes a quality of a status, something that comes with a position in a hierarchy. In such a view, however, legitimated power becomes too easily identified as a state, as a thing. This is too static a view of a process whose outcome is not determined. A liberal interpretation of Max **Weber** can help us better understand the dynamic nature of legitimacy and the process by which it is pursued.

According to Weber, *power* is 'the possibility of imposing one's own will upon the behaviour of other persons' (Weber 1968: 942), and *domination*, a special case of power. He focuses on two main kinds of domination. The first is '*domination by virtue of a constellation of interests*', sometimes called by him 'economic power', sometimes, 'monopolistic domination in the market'. This kind of domination derives its influence 'exclusively from the possession of goods or marketable skills guaranteed in some way and acting upon the conduct of those dominated, who remain, however, formally free and are motivated simply by the pursuit of their own interests' (ibid.: 941, 943). In this case, although we may talk about power, we do not talk about authority, nor do we talk about legitimacy. Here domination is simply a matter of a power holder's control over resources, and the only relationship to the power subject is defined by the subject's own appraisal of the efficacy of those resources employed to induce him or her to act.

Domination, says Weber, must be more precise, it is 'the probability that a command will be obeyed' (ibid.: 53). Thus, in his writings, the most important kind of domination is '*domination by virtue of* [a claim to] *authority*, i.e. power to command and duty to obey' (ibid.: 943). Specifically, this kind of domination refers to

> the situation in which the manifested will (*command*) of the *ruler* or rulers is meant to influence the conduct of one or more of the others (the *ruled*) and actually does influence it in such a way that their conduct to a socially relevant degree occurs as if the ruled had made the content of the command the maxim of their conduct for its very own sake.
>
> (ibid.: 946)

Kalberg prefers to call this 'rulership' rather than domination.

When Weber offers 'the authoritarian power of a patriarch or monarch with its appeal to the duty of obedience' as an example of this type of domination, the important qualifier is '*appeal*'. Elsewhere when he refers to 'claims of obedience', the important qualifier is '*claims*'. Why do the powerful make claims and appeals to authority? Because of 'the generally observable need of any power, or even of any advantage of life, to justify itself'; 'the continued exercise of every domination ... always has the strongest need of self-justification through appealing to the principle of its legitimation' (Weber 1968: 943, 953, 954).

A look at Weber's typology of social action can help us understand the role of the individual in this process of legitimation; specifically, it can show us the many possible ways an individual can react to a claim to authority (and in turn, this demonstrates how for Weber legitimacy may be considered a variable and not a constant). For Weber, conventions and rules are 'regularities induced by a belief in the[ir] existence' (ibid.: 31). It is important to remember that Weber's argument is empirical and existential and not normative. While one may obey a social order because one believes in its legitimacy, one need not obey it for that reason; belief in its existence would be sufficient. One could obey it because one believes that others accept it as legitimate (whether or not they actually do, *vide* 'The Emperor's New Clothes'), or one could obey it by calculating the consequences of its imposition. Indeed, Weber articulates many reasons for obeying a social order (be it a convention, e.g. 'don't point', or a social institution, e.g. the Health Department). The basic distinction between types of obedience is between those derived from disinterested 'purely subjective' motives and those derived 'by the expectation of specific external effects, that is, by *interest situations*'

(ibid.: 33). Self-interested motives relate to the manipulation of the external world; disinterested ones, to something internal to the actor. One may disobey an order, but if one decides to obey, then one can do so out of self-interest as does the economic man of the classical economists, or because one feels internalized emotional, value-rational or traditional reasons to do so. If one follows it for these internal reasons it is because one has concluded that the request is legitimate.

Weber doesn't simply tell us the reasons why someone may obey an order; he also tells us the reasons why someone may 'ascribe legitimacy to a social order'. He lists four reasons: tradition, emotional faith, value rational faith, and positive enactment of recognized legality. This last reason has two possibilities: because enactment has been agreed upon by all concerned (*à la* Locke) or by virtue of imposition (*à la* Hobbes). If one accepts an order as legitimate for any of these reasons, then he or she is obeying it not for self-interested reasons but for disinterested ones. The first three reasons for accepting an order as legitimate correlate one-to-one with the three disinterested reasons to obey an order. Thus if a Health Department order says 'don't smoke' and an individual holds the value that smoking is bad and should be avoided, then we have an example of shared values (almost in the Durkheimian sense of a collective conscience, shared **beliefs** and sentiments). The individual will not smoke for value-rational reasons. The fourth reason for accepting something as legitimate, positive enactment of recognized legality, is not so obvious. If one wants to smoke, but the Health Department, which one believes to have been properly established and run according to procedures one holds to be legitimate, says not to, then the individual will not smoke for value-rational reasons. But this is no longer a case of shared values. The actor followed the order because he or she thought it procedurally correct despite not believing in the rule per se. Weber even considers the Hobbesian-like case where someone can consider something legitimate if it is imposed (e.g. a person might find law and order – any law and order – better than chaos).

Weber articulated three possible ideologies that could be given to support a claim to legitimacy: (1) a legal rational appeal based on the correctness of a procedure to determine the leadership; (2) a traditional appeal based on the fact that this is the way leadership has always been determined; and (3) a charismatic appeal based on supposed special qualities of the leader. There are institutional affinities for each of these arguments: (1) for legal rational claims, direct democracy, administration by honoraries and bureaucracy are probable; (2) for traditional claims, institutionalized charisma, patriarchal, patrimonial and feudal relations are probable; and (3) for charismatic appeals, charismatic leadership is the result.

Weber wants to avoid using 'personal motives or interests' in defining empirical cases of authority domination. He asserts that 'power of command' exists when 'the authority which is claimed by somebody is actually heeded to a socially relevant degree'. And, 'we shall ascribe domination, wherever they claim, and to a socially degree find obedience to, commands given and received as such' (ibid.: 948). However, this is to view domination from either an optimistic managerial perspective or pessimistic radical perspective, both of which assume all claims to be successful. But how does one know what is happening from a power subject's perspective given that there are many ways to obey (self-interest and disinterest, and, when disinterested, many ways to consider an order as legitimate)? How can one distinguish between apparent authority and an 'authority-like distribution of resources' where people follow commands for self-interested reasons ignoring its legitimacy? Lack of clarity here can result in an under-

estimate of the potential for conflict and leaves social scientists open to what would be an untypical Weberian bias.

Weber argued that an order is most stable when considered legitimate, less so when customary and habitual, and even less so when followed for reasons of expediency; transitions between these motives 'are empirically gradual' (ibid.: 31). While this may make sense on the face of it, the inverse appears problematic: does this imply that if a social order has in fact demonstrated stability then that stability has been a result of a belief in its legitimacy? History has provided too many examples where this has not been the case.

By promoting the discussion of legitimacy, Max Weber has helped rescue sociology from an over-deterministic view of individual actors lock-stepped into socially defined patterns of activity. Weber rejected the over-individualistic picture of man of the classical economists but he did so without falling into an equally fallacious oversocialized picture of man held by many classical sociologists.

References and further reading

Kalberg, Stephen (1994) *Max Weber's Comparative-Historical Sociology*, Chicago: University of Chicago Press.

Rousseau, Jean-Jacques ([1762]1954) *The Social Contract*, Chicago: Henry Regnery.

Weber, Max (1968) *Economy and Society*, edited by Guenther Roth and Claus Wittich and based on the 1956 edition edited by Johannes Winckelmann, Berkeley, CA: University of California Press.

BARRY B. LEVINE

LEISURE

Definitions and approaches

In sociology, leisure has been defined from multiple perspectives. The most common has been as 'free time', usually understood as time separate from work and other obligated time. Leisure, then, is measured in residual hours. This approach permits cross-cultural and cross-time comparisons. Historically, industrial productivity and labour organization are identified as factors in the growth of so-called 'free time'.

This simple dichotomy has been challenged by at least three other approaches (Kelly 1987):

1. An institutional/social model defines leisure in terms of its relative freedom from institutional constraints and social obligations, including those of family and community as well as work. Pervasive, multiple and intersecting roles make leftover time difficult to locate or measure. Leisure, then, is not residual, but negotiated out of the complex social context. Further, elements of leisure may be found or constructed in the midst of other contexts including work and family.

2. A process or interactional approach locates leisure more as a dimension or theme in the constructed and dynamic social milieu. Leisure remains embedded in social contexts, but consists of action that is focused more on the experience than outcomes. Such leisure, also called 'play', can be momentary as well as defined by an event or environment. It may, then, be creative or routinized, social or solitary, physical or mental, spontaneous or organized.

3. More recent cultural approaches (Rojek 1985) take leisure to be a social construction that is made up of an infinite number of cultural themes and items. It is constantly changing in ways that reflect cultural and social diversity. It is never fixed or even definable, but may be central to attempts to negotiate personal and social identities in cultural contexts that are both fragmented and the product of the market. The countless subcultures of leisure are constructed and deconstructed as materials of the market are appropriated, reconstituted and contested amid constant change.

Running through all these metaphors is **Veblen**'s (1899) theme of the relationship of leisure to social status. His thesis of the central place of leisure in the conspicuous consumption symbolizing wealth and status has been appropriated in countless analyses of status symbolism, especially in relation to life styles and economic exploitation.

The market economy

The major shift has been from seeing leisure as an alternative or residue of economic activity to identifying the centrality of leisure in both the society and economy. Depending on what is included, leisure may be the largest single segment of a modern economy. If tourism, gambling, dining out, residential space designed for media and socializing, gardening and pleasure-oriented media are included, leisure is uncontested as a primary and growing market. The more narrowly identified leisure industries of sports, arts and entertainment, hobbies and other non-work enterprises are characterized by their variety as well as scope. Their leisure base has been highlighted by calling them the 'experience industries' (Pine and Gilmore 1999).

Leisure-based markets rise and fall in the 'product life cycles' that characterize other industries. In the 1990s, there was growth in the USA in gambling and golf. Gambling has demonstrated long-term cyclical patterns and golf is limited by accessible space. World-wide, the growth in tourism has been dampened by economic recession and various manifestations of danger and terrorism. There are no limitless 'booms'. Leisure, based on activities, is subject to cycles and fads at least as much as any other market product.

399

One reason is that leisure is different from other market products in that the consumer can always 'not do it' or substitute something else. There is, by definition, no necessity in leisure markets. Even the ubiquitous activity of shopping is subject to impacts of economic recession, distribution of income, and market controls. Further, leisure socialization varies by the familiar factors of class, status, culture, gender, race, education, age cohort, sexual orientation and everything else that shapes choices, tastes and opportunities.

Leisure is, however, no different from other market areas in being subject to variations in supply. The opening of geographical areas to legal gambling has led to increases in participation. Galbraith (1958) argued that classical economics is backward, that supply actually creates demand in an affluent society. The so-called 'sovereign consumer' is supplanted by the powerful producer. Growth is a result of market forces of production and promotion as well as socialized and constructed demand. It is no surprise, then, that growth segments are usually ones that reflect corporate interests. Gambling, of course, is the surest producer of return on investment. Capital flows towards market offerings with high prices such as upscale resorts, repeated costs such as entrance fees, and nondurable styled equipment. The market economy tends to oversupply upscale leisure and mass markets rather than the specialized narrow markets. Leisure industries produce profit by selling experience linked with commodities (Butsch 1990)

It is estimated that 97 per cent of consumer leisure spending is in the market rather than public sector. This produces an imbalance in investment towards upscale and costly offerings. Further, the public sector is underfinanced, with parks, recreation for children and low-income areas always in need of investment. Even the premier national parks in the USA have deteriorating amenities and inadequate

staffs. This imbalance is supported by an ideology that maintains that the market sector should always have priority over the public, especially in a discretionary area such as leisure.

Marketing

Market-sector leisure is like other economic segments in being connected with segmenting factors such as gender, age, education, sexual identity and income. However, even more than in markets such as durables, leisure reflects particular cultures and identities. Most obvious are the continually changing and renewing 'youth cultures' in which labelled clothing, electronics and popular culture elements of music, media stars and movies identify subcultures within schools and neighbourhoods. Sexual symbolism has become central to **advertising** directed to the coveted high-spending youth markets.

Marketing is crucial when the revised sequence of supply creating demand is recognized. Major investments are accompanied with high promotion budgets. With the prime objective of maximizing investment return, some promotional advertising stresses the experience with 'hedonic' themes and some focuses on identities that place the consumer in attractive environments or relationships. The familiar 'sun, sand, and sex' themes of tourism advertising have now been expanded from youth markets to baby boomer and retiree cohorts.

The aim is to identify leisure with the 'good life'. The sub-text, however, is that this desirable condition is identified with the ownership and control of symbolic goods that, as Veblen argued, are not necessities or even productive. 'She or he who lives with the most toys wins' (see **life styles**). Some leisure has high costs of commitment and skill acquisition, but low financial commitments. However, the market stresses financial costs rather than personal commitment.

'Cultural capital' (Bourdieu 1984) is associated with leisure in relation to the arts, education and even sports. Such capital yields social status, but must be symbolized in recognizable ways. Leisure markets can provide such symbols such as symphony guild memberships, expensive sound systems and travel, that come at a financial rather than personal price.

Critical perspectives

At least three critical approaches to the economics of leisure are fundamental:

First is the traditional Marxist and Weberian critique in which the 'iron cage' of routinized work is ameliorated and made acceptable by non-work opportunities. Leisure becomes an incentive for commitment to dehumanized work by providing a pretence of humanizing activity. It is the bait in the productivity trap. This leisure market trap is now further facilitated by the credit economy of 'play now and pay later'. Many leisure opportunities can be purchased only with the credit card.

Second is the neo-Marxist claim that leisure has become 'commodified'. The central meaning of activity is then found in the symbolic goods that are associated with the experience. The 'right' toys and togs become necessary for appearance in many leisure venues. The aim, again, is status rather than personal and social development. Further, marketing stresses style and artificially obsolete apparel and equipment.

Third is the previously mentioned 'investment bias' in market economies in which investment is directed towards return rather than towards human development, social solidarity and cultural enrichment. Even in sports the market offers symbolic identification with 'heroes' to spectators rather than accessible and affordable opportunities for engagement. Environments are exploited for current use rather than long-term conservation. To maximize profit, service employment asso-

ciated with leisure tends to be low-wage even when costs to participants are high.

References and further reading

Bourdieu, Pierre (1984) *Distinction*, London: Routledge.
Butsch, Richard (ed.) (1990) *For Fun and Profit*, Philadelphia, PA: Temple University Press.
Clarke, John and Critcher, Chas (1985) *The Devil Makes Work: Leisure in Capitalist Britain*, Urbana, IL: University of Illinois Press.
Galbraith, John (1958) *The Affluent Society*, Boston: Houghton Mifflin.
Kelly, John (1987) *Freedom to Be: A New Sociology of Leisure*, New York: Macmillan.
Pine, B. Joseph and Gilmore, James (1999) *The Experience Economy*, Boston: Harvard University Business School Press.
Rojek, Chris (1985) *Capitalism and Leisure Theory*, London: Tavistock.
Veblen, Thorstein ([1899]1953) *The Theory of the Leisure Class*, New York: New American Library.

JOHN R. KELLY

LIBERALISM

Liberalism is a political philosophy that is typically contrasted with its two main competitors, socialism and conservatism. As such, liberalism is essentially a defence of private property and laissez-faire economics. Liberal philosophy dates from the seventeenth century where it formed the basis of the constitutional settlement of 1688 and the defence of liberty and property rights. The classic text of liberal philosophy is John Locke's *Second Treatise of Government* (1690), but liberalism as a distinctive political doctrine did not, however, gain general acceptance until the 1830s. Liberal ideas are the foundation of both markets and democracy in the western tradition. The constitutive liberal ideas are: the minimal state, social contract, free markets, property rights, individual liberties and religious tolerance. The core notion is that individuals should be free from interference to pursue their desires and satisfy their needs. In social contract theory, Thomas Hobbes (1588–1679) in *Leviathan* (1651) argued that rational individuals in a state of nature come into conflict over competing interests and hence their lives are nasty, brutish and short. The state is based on a contract between rational individuals who surrender aspects of their power to a sovereign who maintains the peace in order for markets to operate freely.

Nineteenth-century liberal doctrines were associated with **utilitarianism**, in which the purpose of politics is to promote the happiness of the greatest number. Utilitarian philosophers like Jeremy Bentham (1748–1832) and J. S. Mill (1806–73) rejected natural law as a defence of the legitimacy of **social rights**, and argued that human **welfare** or **utility** is the only criterion of good government. A just society is one in which the pursuit of utility is impartially applicable to everyone. In rejecting motivation as a criterion of ethics, liberal utilitarianism is a consequentialist theory that considers actions moral if they contribute to pleasure and reduce pain. In *On Liberty* (1859), Mill defended three fundamental freedoms of the individual (belief, pursuits and association) as conditions for the cultivation of individuality. However, influenced by Alexis de Tocqueville's *Democracy in America* (1835 and 1840), Mill feared the constraint of mass society on individual conscience and parliamentary democracy, arguing that the working class required education before they could enjoy the franchise.

In the twentieth century, liberalism as the uncompromising defence of laissez-faire economics has been challenged by egalitarianism. Classical liberalism defended the rights of individuals against both state and church interference, and concluded that free markets provide the most appropriate condition of individual freedom. However, unrestrained markets typically create inequality. In particular, differences in material inheritance and genetic endow-

ments create social inequalities, for which individuals cannot be held responsible. While liberals might in principle accept welfare and taxation as constraints on individuals, welfare states have only modest success in the redistribution of income. Liberal welfare states do not address the fundamental causes of unequal wealth. The intellectual dilemma of twentieth-century egalitarian liberalism was therefore to reconcile the classical doctrine of individual freedom with economic regulation as a condition of social equality.

John Rawls (1971) noted that welfare state **capitalism** accepts significant class inequality, but attempts to reduce the resulting disparities through redistributive taxes and transfer programmes. He advocated a property-owning democracy to address underlying inequalities in property and wealth and to create greater opportunities to invest in human capital, whereby the market would create fewer initial disparities. Whereas welfare states seek to redistribute income ex post, property-owning democracies establish greater equality in the ex ante distribution of wealth. Rawls never provided a detailed description of how property-owning democracies could be created – apart from some modest proposals about inheritance – but the main difficulty is that egalitarian objectives require growing economies, which can only be protected by policies (such as low personal taxation) that are often inconsistent with these welfare objectives. These tensions have produced the 'bifurcation of liberalism' (Connolly 1984) in which either liberal principles are defended and individuals are exhorted to lower their expectations with respect to justice and freedom, or liberal principles are detached from any practical engagement with policies that might challenge the hegemony of the 'civilization of productivity'.

In the late twentieth century liberalism became increasingly associated with New Right economic doctrines. As a result 'neo-liberalism' is used interchangeably with 'neo-conservatism'. Neo-liberalism was a response to the belief that welfare bureaucracy curtailed individual freedoms and means-tested welfare payments were an assault on individual dignity. In addition, the growth of welfare states had created a 'fiscal crisis' of capitalism (Habermas 1976) that would eventually undermine the market as the ultimate buttress of civil and political liberties. Neo-liberal responses to the economic crises of the 1970s were to encourage free enterprise, reinvigorate the voluntary sector, and force individuals to take greater responsibility for their families through saving, private insurance and self-help. Neo-liberal health strategies encourage people to adopt healthy life styles, for example by exercise, diet and abstaining from smoking rather than relying on a state welfare system or, in the famous words of Margaret Thatcher, depending on the 'Nanny State'.

Neo-liberal attitudes have often merged with libertarianism as represented by Robert Nozick's *Anarchy, State, and Utopia* (1974). Nozick's entitlement theory says that if we assume that everyone is entitled to the current distribution of goods they happen to possess, then a just distribution of property is simply a distribution that emerges from current free exchanges. It is unjust for governments to tax these exchanges, and the only justification for government is to protect free exchange from fraud, theft, broken contracts and force. Nozick embraced Kant's moral theory that we should treat individuals as ends in themselves rather than as means, but he reinterpreted the Kantian imperative to mean a doctrine of self-ownership. Recognizing people as self-owners is a necessary condition for treating them as equals. Any Rawlsian redistribution would compromise self-ownership, and therefore unrestricted capitalism is the only adequate protection of dignity and equality. There are many problems with Nozick's radical defence of self-determination. For example, do parents – more specifically, mothers – own their offspring that they have produced through their own labour? Because the majority of people will need to sell their labour on the market to exist, is the wage relationship compatible with self-ownership? These examples raise the conventional criticisms against liberalism that were presented by Karl **Marx** in terms of formal and substantive liberty. Can the working class enjoy the substantive benefits of a liberal society without a fundamental transformation of property rights? Because twentieth-century liberalism did not produce a satisfactory explanation of how to combine individual freedom and substantive equality, some political philosophers have come 'to doubt the possibility of a comprehensive and coherent *modern* philosophy of liberalism' (Dunn 1993: 55).

References and further reading

Connolly, W. (1984) 'The Dilemma of Legitimacy', in W. Connolly (ed.), *Legitimacy and the State*, Oxford: Blackwell.

Dunn, J. (1993) *Western Political Theory in the Face of the Future*, Cambridge: Canto.

Habermas, J. (1976) *Legitimation Crisis*, London: Heinemann.

Hobbes, T. (1968) *Leviathan*, Harmondsworth, UK: Penguin.

Locke, J. (1960) *Two Treatises of Government*, Cambridge: Cambridge University Press.

Mill, J. S. (1982) *On Liberty*, Harmondsworth, UK: Penguin.

Nozick, R. (1974) *Anarchy, State, and Utopia*, New York: Basic Books.

Rawls, J. (1971) *A Theory of Justice*, London: Oxford University Press.

Tocqueville, A. de (2003) *Democracy in America*, London: Penguin Books.

BRYAN TURNER

LIBERTARIANISM

Libertarianism is the political ideology of voluntarism, a commitment to voluntary action in a social context, where no individual or group of individuals can initiate the use of force against others. It is not a monolithic ideological paradigm; rather, it signifies a variety of approaches that celebrate the rule of law and the free exchange of goods, services, and ideas – a laissez-faire attitude towards what philosopher Robert Nozick (1974) once called 'capitalist acts between consenting adults'.

Modern libertarians draw inspiration from writings attributed to the Chinese sage Lao Tzu, as well as the works of Aristotle, among the ancients; eighteenth- and nineteenth-century classical liberalism (e.g. John Locke, the Scottish Enlightenment, the American founders, Carl Menger, and Herbert Spencer); individualist anarchism (e.g. Benjamin Tucker and Lysander Spooner); Old Right opponents of Franklin D. Roosevelt's New Deal (e.g. Albert Jay Nock, John T. Flynn, Isabel Paterson and H. L. Mencken); modern **Austrian economics** (e.g. Ludwig von Mises, F. A. Hayek and Murray Rothbard), as well as the economics of the Chicago school (Milton Friedman) and Virginia school (James Buchanan); and the Objectivist philosopher Ayn Rand.

Classical liberalism is the most immediate predecessor of contemporary libertarianism. Locke and the American founders had an impact on those libertarians, such as Rothbard and Rand, who stress individual rights, while the Scottish Enlightenment and Spencer had a major impact on thinkers such as Hayek, who stress the evolutionary wisdom of customs and traditions in contradistinction to the 'constructivist rationalism' of state planners.

Among evolutionists, Spencer in particular made important contributions to what would become known as 'general systems theory'; some consider him to be the founder of modern sociology. Indeed, he authored *Principles of Sociology* and *The Study of Sociology*, which was the textbook used for the first sociology course offered in the United States, at Yale University. A

contemporary of Charles Darwin, he focused on social evolution – the development of societies and organizational structures from simple to compound forms. In such works as *The Man Versus the State*, he presented a conception of society as a spontaneous, integrated 'growth and not a manufacture', an organically evolving context for the development of heterogeneity and differentiation among the individuals who compose it. Just as Spencer emphasized organic social evolution, so too did he focus on the organic evolution of the state – with its mutually reinforcing reliance on bureaucracy and militarism, and how it might be overcome.

The Austrian-born Carl Menger, a founder – along with W. S. Jevons and Léon Walras – of the marginalist revolution in economics, held a similar view of social life as a dynamic, spontaneous, evolving process. Influenced by Aristotle in his methodological individualism, Menger was fervently opposed to the historical relativism of the German historicists of the **Methodenstreit**. Menger focused on the purposeful actions of individuals in generating unintended sociological consequences – a host of institutions, such as language, religion, law, the state, markets, competition and money.

In the twentieth century, the Nobel laureate Austrian economist F. A. Hayek carried on Menger's evolutionist discussion and praised it for providing outstanding guidelines for general sociology. For Hayek (1991), Menger was among the 'Darwinians before Darwin' – those evolutionists, such as the conservative Edmund Burke and the liberals of the Scottish Enlightenment, who stressed the evolution of institutions as the product of unintended consequences, rather than deliberate design. Hayek drew a direct parallel between his own concept of spontaneous order and Adam **Smith**'s notion of the 'invisible hand'. Hayek argued that, over time, there is a competition among various emergent traditions, each of which embodies rival rules of action and perception. Through a process of natural selection, those rules and institutions that are more durable than others will tend to flourish, resulting in a relative increase in population and wealth. Though he didn't argue for a theory of inevitable progress, as Spencer had, he clearly assumed that liberalism was the social system most conducive to such flourishing.

Like Karl **Marx**, Hayek criticized utopians for their desire to construct social institutions as if from an Archimedean standpoint, external to history and culture. But Hayek turned this analysis on Marx; he developed a full-fledged critique of **socialism** and central planning as utopian – requiring an unattainable 'synoptic' knowledge of all the articulated and tacit dimensions of social life. Hayek argued that market prices were indispensable to rational entrepreneurial calculation. He also focused on the sociological and psychological ramifications of the movement away from markets. He maintains in *The Road to Serfdom* (1944), for example, that there is a structural connection between social psychology and politics: to the extent that the state imposes collectivist arrangements on individuals, it is destructive of individual choice, morals and responsibility, and this destruction of individualism reinforces the spread of statism. And the more the state comes to dominate social life, says Hayek, the more state power will be the 'only power worth having' – which is 'why the worst get on top'.

The Austrian economist Ludwig von Mises was similarly opposed to statism and collectivism, and presented, in 1936, an influential book entitled *Socialism*, which was 'an economic and sociological analysis' of all forms of state intervention – from fascism to communism. Mises used the tools of praxeology, 'the science of human action', to demonstrate the calculational problems that all non-market systems face, due to their elimination of private property,

entrepreneurialism and the price system. More important, perhaps, is Mises's development of a non-Marxist, libertarian theory of **class**. Like Charles Dunoyer, Charles Comte, James Mill and other classical liberals, Mises argued that traders on the market share a mutuality of benefit that is destroyed by political intervention. For Mises, the long-term interests of market participants are not in fundamental conflict. It is only with government action that such conflict becomes possible, Mises claims, because it is only government that can create a 'caste system' based on the bestowal of special privileges.

Mises located the central 'caste conflict' in the financial sector of the economy. In such books as *The Theory of Money and Credit*, he contends that government control over money and banking led to the cycle of boom and bust. A systematic increase in the money supply creates differential effects over time, redistributing wealth to those social groups, especially **banks** and debtor industries, which are the first beneficiaries of the **inflation**.

Mises' student, Murray Rothbard, developed this theory of 'caste conflict' into a full-fledged libertarian class analysis. Rothbard views central banking as a cartelizing device that has created a powerful structure of class privilege in modern political economy. These privileges grow exponentially as government restricts market competition and free entry, thereby creating monopoly through various coercive means (e.g. compulsory cartelization, price controls, output quotas, licensing, tariffs, immigration restrictions, labour laws, conscription, patents, franchises, etc.).

Rothbard's view of the relationship between big business and government in the rise of American 'statism' draws additionally from the work of New Left historical revisionists, such as Gabriel Kolko and James Weinstein. These historians held that big business was at the forefront of the movement towards government **regulation** of the market. That movement, according to Rothbard, had both a domestic and foreign component, since it often entailed both domestic regulation and foreign imperialism to secure global markets. The creation of a 'welfare-warfare state' leads necessarily to economic inefficiencies and deep distortions in the structure of production. Like Marx, Rothbard views these 'internal contradictions' as potentially fatal to the economic system; unlike Marx, Rothbard blames these contradictions not on the free market, but on the growth of statism.

Drawing inspiration from Franz Oppenheimer's and Albert Jay Nock's distinction between state power and social power, or state and market, and from John C. Calhoun's class theory, as presented in *Disquisition on Government*, Rothbard saw society fragmenting, ultimately, into two opposing classes: taxpayers and tax-consumers. In his book *Power and Market*, Rothbard identifies bureaucrats, politicians and the net beneficiaries of government privilege as among the tax-consumers. Unlike his Austrian predecessors Hayek and Mises, however, Rothbard argues that it is only with the elimination of the state that a fully just and productive society can emerge. His 'anarcho-capitalist' ideal society would end the state's monopoly on the coercive use of force, as well as taxation and conscription, and allow for the emergence of contractual agencies for the protection of fully delineated private **property** rights (thereby resolving the problems of externalities and **public goods**) and the adjudication of disputes. His scenario had a major impact on Nozick, whose *Anarchy, State, and Utopia* was written in response to the Rothbardian anarchist challenge.

Ayn Rand, the Russian-born novelist and philosopher, author of best-selling novels *The Fountainhead* and *Atlas Shrugged*, was one of those who eschewed the libertarian label, partially because of its association with anarchism. An epistemological realist, ethical egoist and advocate of laissez-faire **capitalism**, Rand maintained that libertarians had focused too much attention on politics to the exclusion of the philosophical and cultural factors upon which it depended. But even though she saw politics as hierarchically dependent on these factors, she often stressed the reciprocal relationships among disparate elements, from politics and pedagogy to sex, economics and psychology. She sought to transcend the dualities of mind and body, reason and emotion, theory and practice, fact and value, morality and prudence, and the conventional philosophic dichotomies of materialism and idealism, rationalism and empiricism, subjectivism and classical objectivism (which she called 'intrinsicism'). Yet, despite her protestations, Rand can be placed in the libertarian tradition, given her adherence to its voluntarist political credo.

From the perspective of social theory, Rand proposed a multi-level sociological analysis of human relations under statism. Echoing the Austrian critique of state intervention in her analysis of politics and economics, Rand extended her critique to encompass epistemology, psychology, ethics and culture. She argued that statism both nourished and depended upon an irrational 'altruist' and 'collectivist' ethos that demanded the sacrifice of the individual to the group. It required and perpetuated a psychology of dependence and a group mentality that was destructive of individual authenticity, integrity, honesty and responsibility. Rand also focused on the cultural preconditions and effects of statism – since coercive social relations required fundamental alterations in the nature of language, education, pedagogy, aesthetics and ideology. Just as relations of power operate through ethical, psychological, cultural, political and economic dimensions, so too, for Rand, the struggle for freedom and individualism depends upon a certain constellation of moral, psychological, cultural and structural factors that support it. Rand advocated capitalism, 'the unknown ideal', as the only system capable of generating just social conditions, conducive to the individual's survival and flourishing.

See also: inflation; laissez faire; monopoly and oligopoly.

References and further reading

Calhoun, John C. ([1853]1953) *A Disquisition on Government and Selections from the Discourse on the Constitution and Government of the United States*, Indianapolis, IN: Bobbs-Merrill.

Hayek, F. A. (1944) *The Road to Serfdom*, Chicago: University of Chicago Press.

—— (1991) *The Collected Works of F. A. Hayek, Volume 3: The Trend of Economic Thinking: Essays on Political Economists and Economic History*, Chicago: University of Chicago Press.

Mises, Ludwig von ([1912]1981) *The Theory of Money and Credit*, Indianapolis, IN: Liberty Classics.

—— (1936) *Socialism: An Economic and Sociological Analysis*, London: Jonathan Cape.

Nozick, Robert (1974) *Anarchy, State, and Utopia*, New York: Basic Books.

Rand, Ayn (1967) *Capitalism: The Unknown Ideal*, New York: New American Library.

Rothbard, Murray ([1970]1977) *Power and Market: Government and the Economy*, Kansas City, MO: Sheed Andrews and McMeel.

—— (1978) *For a New Liberty: The Libertarian Manifesto*, revised edition, New York: Collier Books.

Sciabarra, Chris Matthew (1995) *Ayn Rand: The Russian Radical*, University Park, PA: Pennsylvania State University Press.

—— (1995) *Marx, Hayek, and Utopia*, Albany, NY: State University of New York Press.

—— (2000) *Total Freedom: Toward a Dialectical Libertarianism*, University Park, PA: Pennsylvania State University Press.

Spencer, Herbert (1873) *The Study of Sociology*, New York: D. Appleton.

—— (1882–98) *The Principles of Sociology*, three volumes, London: Williams and Norgate.

—— ([1940]1981) *The Man Versus the State, with Six Essays on Government, Society, and Freedom*, Indianapolis, IN: Liberty Classics.

CHRIS MATTHEW SCIABARRA

LIFE STYLES

Sociology and economic issues

Definitions of 'life styles' have been blurred, fuzzy and even contradictory. In some the focus has been on social characteristics that are associated with behaviour patterns. In current economic approaches, the emphasis has been on the possession of material goods and their symbolic meanings.

Sociological definitions have their foundation in the work of Max **Weber** (1968) who distinguished between social class based on economic factors and social status indexed by associations and symbols. In brief, class consists of 'life chances' and status of 'life styles'. Later **Veblen** (1899) argued that **leisure** and 'conspicuous consumption' were the defining symbols of the upper class. Most recently, cultural elements of life styles have been associated with subcultures identified by age cohort, ethnicity, geographical region, life-course period and economic level. For example, adults in the childrearing period of their lives with higher levels of financial resources may locate in suburban enclaves and gather appropriate material possessions. On the other hand, pre-teens are characterized by devotion to particular popular culture figures, music, dress and a fascination with sexuality. In both cases, social expectations and market promotion reinforce the life styles. Life styles, then, consist of possessions, location, cultural factors, activities, associations, and other material and 'cultural' capital (Bourdieu 1984).

The market economy

Traditional approaches to life style in the market economy focused on factors of place in the community and social system. These factors were believed to identify both resources and desires. In more sophisticated analyses styles were tied to habits and attachments that symbolized actual and desired social placement. Newer approaches have focused more on place in the market itself. Possessions such as cars, houses, clothing and leisure associations and goods become elements in a dynamic cultural symbol system. Symbolic self-presentations do not change only with major life-course or income-level shifts. Rather, there is an ongoing dialogue with media-depicted and market-promoted symbols of status and subcultural identification. Life styles, then, are complex and changing despite being embedded in the social and market system.

Some have argued that the traditional community system of associations and memberships has broken down. Individuals may have only limited and disposable relationships with institutions, neighbourhoods and even households Less and less are they 'investors' in their communities and commitments or 'family focused' (Kelly 1987) and more engaged in a kaleidoscopic swirl of labels and symbols. Further, the bombardment of marketing accentuates this new form of life style.

Marketing

'Taste cultures' had been identified with factors such as ethnicity and community. In this time of mass marketing, especially through the impacts of television, taste becomes something to be excited and recreated by promotion. Market segmentation is not just locating differences, but employs psychologies of motivation to create and accentuate those differences. For example, age is viewed in terms of cultural cohorts seeking symbols of identification. Display of these market-provided symbols creates markets in an ongoing dialectic in which supply creates demand. Cultural styles or 'tastes' become systems of desire and consumption (Ewan and Ewan 1982) fed by the media. Styles are, by definition, always becoming obsolete and thus creating new markets.

An endless number of marketing schemes based on life styles have been developed employing such social and cultural elements. Most are proprietary and directed towards particular industries or corporations. One older scheme is the VALS framework that developed a number of lifestyle types based not only on consumption, resource and taste patterns, but also on value orientations. It has been revised and applied to almost every kind of market from tourism to the arts. A somewhat more contemporary scheme, CLARITAS, includes family and life-course conditions, income and consumption habits, and housing type and location to formulate an 'enclave' typology that claims to incorporate everything from childrearing patterns to leisure apparel. The use of life-style frameworks in marketing has advanced traditional demographic variables into scenarios of relationships and investments as well as consumption.

The central question is how to identify critical elements in overall life styles. Clearly life-course and family conditions are central. Education level and quality are often employed to tap tastes and cultures. From a marketing perspective, emphasis is on those factors that index spending proclivities. From a sociological perspective, there tends to be more attention given to those factors that influence fundamental life decisions and patterns.

Critical approaches

Critiques of marketing stress the premise of incompleteness in possessions. There is always something more on the market that draws the consumer into purchasing. For example, luxury cars are functionally equivalent to mid-price styles. However there is always a purchase that can symbolize something about status and style. From Veblen's perspective, a high-price convertible with unusable power still has the symbolic value of conspicuous consumption. This leads the consumer into an endless round of desire in which the commodity itself rather than its use produces meaning. This desire can never be satisfied. Most recently the human body itself has been seen as a commodity with images that are always imperfect and unsatisfying. The body appearance industry now targets both genders and all ages in marketing the 'commodified body'.

In this critique the media, especially television, bombard consumers with direct and indirect images of appearance and every kind of possession so that whatever one is or has is never adequate. If consumers can be led to believe that the commodified life is the source of happiness, but that one's consumption is never enough, then markets for style-based goods are infinite. In this way, capitalist profit-seeking markets create demand with symbolic supply. When the supply can be tied to life styles that symbolize not only status but also adopted cultures, then life itself becomes endlessly commodified.

Of course, any critique must have a standpoint. The most common critical approaches are ones that stress personal development, community and social relations. A social and existential or developmental combination returns life-style emphasis to values and how one lives rather than to symbolic consumption.

References and further reading

Bourdieu, Pierre (1984) *Distinction*, London: Routledge.
Ewan, Stuart and Ewan, Elizabeth (1982) *Channels of Desire*, New York: McGraw-Hill
Kelly, John (1987) *Peoria Winter*, Lanham, MD: Lexington Books, Free Press.
Rojek, Chris (1995) *Decentring Leisure*, London: Sage.
Veblen, Thorstein ([1899]1953) *The Theory of the Leisure Class*, New York: New American Library.
Weber, Max (1968) *Economy and Society*, three volumes, New York: Bedminster Press.

JOHN R. KELLY

LOCK-IN

Lock-in is a situation wherein (groups of) individuals or organizations find that it is difficult or even impossible to change their behaviour (behavioural patterns), even if they would like to do so, prevented by structures in their environment. A situation of lock-in refers to one that is perceived to be suboptimal, by the people involved themselves, but most often by outsiders.

The term 'lock-in' is mostly associated with the example of the layout for the mechanical typewriter, as described by economist Paul David in a 1985 article in the *American Economic Review*. Here, the top-left row of letters spells QWERTY. This layout would minimize the likelihood that keys jammed, but with the use of electronic and digital devices makes little sense. Although disputed, the argument is that a different layout (specifically the so-called Dvorak layout) would allow for faster typing. The reason for the layout to persist is that it was what people have been trained to use, and that it has come to grow interdependent with other technologies or institutions. Retraining people, and generally changing a large number of institutions related to the technology that causes the lock-in, involves switching costs. An inefficient equilibrium may be the result. Other examples of extant technical (physical) structures causing lock-in phenomena are the width of railway gauges, or (technical) standards in general.

Lock-in may also be the result of 'purely' social phenomena. Existing institutions being interrelated, it may be difficult or impossible to change an institution that would itself be suboptimal because that would entail changes in related institutions. Switching costs could be steep. In addition, institutions and conventions shape people's expectations. A change in one (suboptimal) institution may entail changes in people's expectations that people are unwilling or unable to do. Changes in one person's expectations will mean that they may no longer be consistent with those of others. Organizations create channels and individuals establish habits of how to deal with information. Establishing these channels involves an investment that is irreversible to a large degree. It involves interpreting information in ways that makes information understandable, creating codes for comparing information to information that is already familiar, and it involves moulding information to disseminate it (within the organization).

The establishment of codes and mutual expectations within an organization ensures its continuity – particular individuals may leave, but others can relatively easily take their place. The reasons for social lock-in to occur are also exactly those that allow for division of labour and specialization.

The concept of lock-in allows for the study of concrete phenomena where it is believed that 'history matters'. Framing the discussion in terms of switching costs and (sunk) investments means that the concept has come to be used in mainstream neoclassical economics as well. A discussion of the possibility of the social environment to create situations of lock-in especially, however, implies a conceptualization of the individual that differs from the neoclassical utility-maximizing one who is able to process infinite amounts of objective facts. In addition, it implicitly criticizes the (New Institutionalist Economics) idea that extant institutions of necessity are optimal.

References and further reading

David, P. A. (1994) 'Why are Institutions the "Carriers of History"? Path Dependence and the Evolution of Conventions, Organizations and Institutions', *Structural Change and Economic Dynamics*, 5(2): 205–20.

Mahoney, J. (2000) 'Path Dependence in Historical Sociology', *Theory and Society*, 29: 507–48.

WILFRED DOLFSMA

LOOSE COUPLING

Relations within or between organizations are increasingly described as loosely coupled. This comes as no surprise, since in face of the increasing complexity, uncertainty and causal ambiguity of organizational environments, loose coupling of organizational and inter-organizational systems promises to increase the chances of system survival. In practice, the spread of project-based and network-like forms of organizations exemplifies this development.

The concept of loose coupling has been made popular in organization research by Karl Weick (1976), who defines loose coupling as a situation in which elements are responsive, but retain their own identity and some evidence of separateness. Although underspecified, the concept has been referred to in organizational and inter-organizational research very frequently indeed. Orton and Weick (1990) were the first to develop a more precise understanding of the concept and to develop some kind of 'loose coupling theory'. This theory does not only name causal indeterminacy and fragmented external and internal environments as the central causes of loose coupling, but persistence, buffering, adaptability and satisfaction as its major organizational outcomes. However, these outcomes do not only depend upon the level of loose coupling and its direct effects (e.g. modularity, requisite variety, behavioural discretion), but also upon measures to compensate for loose coupling (e.g. enhanced leadership, focused attention, shared values). The concept can thus be used to describe, first, the coupling on different levels of analysis: most prominently among individuals, teams, projects, other organizational subunits and organizations. Second, the concept of coupling may be used across different levels of analysis: between projects or other organizational subunits on the one hand and organizations on the other, between organizations and organizational environments, etc. Third, and perhaps most generally, the degree of coupling may be determined between ideas and activities, intentions and actions, and different hierarchical levels.

Loosely coupled relations, within as well as between organizations, seem to increase the likelihood of system survival by enabling organizational adaptation and, together with multiplexity and redundancy, by contributing to organizational adaptive capacity (Staber and Sydow 2002). In contrast to simple adaptation, organizational adaptive capacity implies balancing exploitation with exploration strategies, supporting not only single-loop learning but all kinds of learning, using rather than avoiding slack resources, and acknowledging potential organizational rigidities.

Despite the attractiveness of loose coupling, it should be noted that there is not only a strength in weak ties (Granovetter 1973) but also a 'strength of strong ties' (Krackhardt 1992). Hence, the management of organizations and inter-organizational networks (but also of national or regional innovation systems, for instance) does not only require the capacity and capability to increase or decrease the degree of coupling via respective (inter-)organizational practices – and, hence, adaptation and/or adaptive capacity – but also to analyse the contextual conditions under which a tighter or looser coupling seems to increase the chances of system survival.

References and further reading

Grabher, Gernot (1993) 'The Weakness of Strong Ties: The Lock-in of Regional Development in the Ruhr Area', in Gernot Grabher (ed.), *The Embedded Firm*, London: Routledge, pp. 253–77.

Granovetter, Mark (1973) 'The Strength of Weak Ties', *American Journal of Sociology*, 78(6): 1360–80.

Krackhardt, David (1992) 'The Strength of Strong Ties: The Importance of *Philos* in Organizations', in Nitin Nohria and Robert G. Eccles (eds), *Networks and Organizations*, Boston: Harvard Business School Press, pp. 216–39.

Orton, J. Douglas and Weick, Karl E. (1990) 'Loosely Coupled Systems: A Reconceptualization', *Academy of Management Review*, 15(2): 203–23.

Staber, Udo and Sydow, Joerg (2002) 'Organizational Adaptive Capacity: A Structuration Perspective', *Journal of Management Inquiry*, 11(4): 408–24.

Weick, Karl E. (1976) 'Educational Organizations as Loosely-Coupled Systems', *Administrative Science Quarterly*, 21: 1–19.

JOERG SYDOW

LOTTERY MARKETS

A lottery is a contract between the lottery agent and the players, whereby the latter agree to redistribute randomly the collected money and to compensate the former for organizing the whole operations. Most modern lotteries are active, pari-mutuel lotteries: players can choose their numbers, and prizes are not fixed, but vary according to the total number of winning bets. In passive lotteries players do not choose their numbers but buy a numbered ticket. They are less popular than active lotteries, and mostly played in countries with a long lottery history, such as Germany, the Netherlands or Spain.

In the Middle Ages public lotteries were occasionally launched to fund particular projects, such as the construction of public buildings or the endowment of charitable institutions. As a permanent source of fiscal revenues, however, lotteries first appeared in seventeenth-century Italian states, and rapidly spread all over Europe. In the first decades of the nineteenth century – for both economic and moral reasons – the UK and France dismantled their public lotteries, and the USA followed suit in the second half of that century. The economic downturn of the 1970s, as well as the development of new technologies that facilitated the operations of active lotteries, produced a revival of this source of public revenues.

Most of the states of the USA are now operating public lotteries, and the UK reintroduced its National Lottery in 1994. Lottery sales represent 0.5 and 0.6 per cent of GDP in the USA and Canada, respectively. They reach 1 per cent in the UK and almost 2 per cent in Spain. Currently, close to one hundred countries are running public lotteries. In Muslim countries, however, lotteries are practically non-existent.

Research on lotteries

Since the expected utility of a lottery tickets is lower than its price, lottery play challenges rationality and wealth-maximizing axioms of neoclassical economic theory. To cope with this challenge, economists have advanced different, but not mutually consistent, post hoc auxiliary assumptions that alter the marginally decreasing shape of the wealth function to make it increasing in a given section, where risk-taking is a rational course of action (McCaffery 1994). Other economists have skipped this theoretical challenge by showing that once the not-quite-rational decision to play is made, players bet rationally and with an eye to maximize returns. Applied economists, however, have jumped over this theoretical challenge (by simply adding a non-wealth factor, such as the excitement derived from participating, into the utility function of players), and focused on public policy issues, such as the fiscal impact of lotteries and earmarking policies.

Economists, as well as sociologists, have provided substantial evidence on the regressive character of lotteries. Lotteries are regressive because, compared with the relatively wealthy, the poor spend a higher proportion of their income on lottery tickets (Clotfelter and Cook 1989). Where early research on the fiscal impact of lotteries was concentrated on the collection side of lottery revenues, a second wave of research has focused on the distribution side. Most American and Canadian lotteries, as well as the British National Lottery, earmark lottery revenues for special purposes, such as education and cultural programmes. In this case, the research question is whether the earmarked programmes obtain a net increase in revenues or not, since lottery transfers can displace ordinary state spending. Research results indicate that more often than not earmarking has a negligible effect on beneficiaries. These results, however, should not be surprising, since earmarking is usually not enacted to benefit the targeted programmes, but to make lotteries more palatable or morally acceptable. Research on the fiscal impact of lotteries and earmarking is practically non-existent in continental Europe, since lotteries proceeds are usually directed to the general fund.

Even though lotteries are very popular, sociological research on this topic is scant. Also, mainstream sociology has followed the lead of economists and pictured lottery play as non-rational behaviour, as it was already exposed by classic sociologists such as Marx, Pareto, Simmel and Gramsci. In this fashion, functionalist sociologists have understood lottery play, and gambling in general, as a safety valve that helps to channel people's frustrations and, thus, to maintain social equilibrium. In a similar way, Marxist-oriented sociologists think that lotteries mesmerize the working and poor sectors of society, divert their attention from their real, objective interests, and contribute, in this way, to maintaining social inequalities. This mainstream sociological approach reproduces very closely the moral invectives of nineteenth-century clergymen and both liberal and socialist intellectuals. However, a less patronizing perspective is currently coming into the open. This new, still marginal approach takes into consideration the embedded, social dimension of lottery play, and rather than picturing players as isolated, not-quite-rational, frustration- or exploitation-driven individuals, it studies how lottery play can help to enhance social ties, and conversely, how networks of social relations can affect the decision to play the lottery.

Thus, Light (1977) showed that like other financial institutions such as rotating credit associations (see **microcredit**), a lottery can help to strengthen community ties. Also, quite often lottery winners share their prizes with relatives and make donations to charities, enhancing in this way the social fabric of their communities as well as their most significant interpersonal ties. More interesting than sharing a prize, however, is sharing a lottery ticket. Since the expected value of a ticket is exactly the same whether it is played individually or with friends, sharing a lottery ticket cannot be explained in economic terms. Quite the contrary: in strictly economic terms, sharing a lottery ticket is an irrational course of action, since it gives room to opportunistic behaviour on the side of the holder of the original ticket, who might decline to share the prize. Irrational as it might look to standard economic theory, 20 per cent of Americans, 30 per cent of British and 50 per cent of Spanish lottery players regularly share lottery tickets with friends and co-workers. By doing so, they transform a purely economic asset, such a lottery ticket, into a carrier of social ties that helps them to define their identities within and commitments to a particular network of social relations (Garvía 2004). Since syndicate players are more regular players than those who play the lottery individually, the extension and degree of institutionalization of this practice affects total lottery sales. Syndicate play, thus, illustrates a basic tenet of economic sociology: that networks of social relations affect economic outcomes.

References and further reading

Clotfelter, Charles T. and Cook, Philip J. (1989) *Selling Hope. State Lotteries in America*, Cambridge, MA: Harvard University Press.

Garvía, Roberto (2004) 'Embedded Lottery Play', paper presented at the Annual Meeting of the American Sociological Association, San Francisco, August.

Light, Ivan (1977) 'Numbers Gambling among Blacks: A Financial Institution', *American Sociological Review*, 42: 892–904.

McCaffery, Edward J. (1994) 'Why People Play Lotteries and Why It Matters', *Wisconsin Law Review*, 1994: 71–122.

ROBERTO GARVÍA

LOWE, ADOLPH

Adolph Lowe (Adolf Löwe until 1939) (Stuttgart 1893–Wolfenbüttel 1995) studied law and economics from 1911 to 1915 and received a doctorate in law in 1919. After he had been dismissed from the German army in 1915 because of a weak heart, his regiment was almost completely wiped out at Verdun, but he lived to reach the age of 102. After World War I, he became a civil servant active at the centre of political power, serving as a secretary for Reichskanzler Gustav Bauer at the signing of the Versailles Treaty and in the ministry of the economy responsible for fighting German hyperinflation in the early 1920s. From 1924 to 1926, he was head of the international branch of the German Statistical Office. In that capacity he successfully suggested the formation of an institute for business cycle research. Lowe went to Kiel in 1926 when the university there offered to build a unit for international business cycle and world economy research. In this highly successful unit, pioneering research was performed by economists like Gerhard Colm, Jakob Marschak, Hans Neisser and Wassily Leontief, all of whom Lowe was to re-encounter in exile in the United States. In 1930, he became a full professor in Kiel, taking over the chair for economics and sociology previously held by Ferdinand Tönnies. In 1931, Lowe joined the University of Frankfurt where a life-long cooperation with Karl Mannheim started. Lowe belonged to the group of 'religious socialists' around the theologian Paul Tillich and was actively involved in fighting the Nazis. When they came to power, he was one of the first persons to be dismissed from Frankfurt University, together with Horkheimer, Mannheim and Tillich. Even before that dismissal, Lowe and his family had left for England, where he held a position for economics and political philosophy at Manchester University. He became a British citizen in 1939, but could not continue working there once World War II had started. He emigrated to the United States, accepting a renewed offer by the New School for Social Research, where he was Alvin Johnson Professor of Economics from 1940 until 1963. He continued teaching far into the 1970s and wrote his best-known books – *On Economic Knowledge, The Path of Economic Growth* and *Has Freedom a Future?* – after retirement.

Lowe's main text relevant for economic sociology is his *Economics and Sociology. A Plea for Cooperation in the Social Sciences* (1935). Lowe is deeply sceptical about the usual division of labour between the social sciences. The problem starts with their self-understanding as presumedly autonomous disciplines. Lowe sets out to demonstrate that economic theory, once it reaches beyond a theory of individual utility maximizing, rests on implicit assumptions which have to be sociological in two respects. First, because markets are not a universal but a historically specific phenomenon, their social context has to be taken into account. Second, because the transition from a theory of individual utility maximizing to a theory of economic transactions involving a plurality of actors requires dealing with the social dimension of interactions.

Making explicit the linkage between the concepts of pure economic theory and the specific economic system of nineteenth-century capitalism was not Lowe's invention. Rather, he relied on a compromise found in the **Methodenstreit** between the German **historical school** and the proponents of pure economic theory. Pure theory is legitimate, but only as long as it is not mistakenly understood as universal theory. Its basic concepts inevitably reflect the specific socio–historical conditions of emerging capitalism. In particular, instrumental rationality as the dominant orientation of **economic action** is characteristic of competitive markets only and widespread competitive markets emerged only with occidental capitalism. Max Weber had taken the decisive step towards this compromise by introducing the concept of **ideal type** and considering the model of competitive markets as such an ideal type. It is simultaneously a purely theoretical construct as well as limited to typifying a historically specific structure. Lowe stressed the limited applicability of 'pure' economic theory in this Weberian manner.

However, his primary and sociologically more interesting objection against the standard self-understanding of what economic theorists do concerns the transition from a theory of individual utility maximizing to propositions about socio-economic phenomena. In his later work, Lowe laid out the problem of this transition by distinguishing between man–matter-relations and man–man-relations, the first concerning the technological core of economic activities, the latter its 'socialization' (Lowe 1965: 18). In 1935, without this distinction, Lowe argues that pure economic reasoning applies to the economic calculus of the isolated individual only and that any move beyond Robinson Crusoe relies – if only implicitly – on sociological concepts. Lowe's version of that argument (which, again, was a shared one, cf. Wieser 1914) is remarkable. He holds that the advance from the individual economic calculus to a theory of exchange, to the law of supply and demand, to the concept of general equilibrium – in short, to price determination – requires conceptual ways of restricting the individual's 'absolute freedom of choice', the latter being one of the starting postulates of pure theory.

According to Lowe, this restriction is achieved in two ways: first, by the idea of economic man, which implies that action is constrained by internalized rules of conduct; second, by the idea of perfect competition, which is used to construct constraints inherent in the situation in which economic action is taking place. Lowe finds that *homo economicus* is not a mere incarnation of instrumental rationality, relentlessly adapting means to ends. Rather, the concept expresses 'a very formal maxim of behaviour unconcerned with the ultimate ends and motives of economic actions ... because it is not related to the use of the outcome of any bargain, but to behaviour in bargaining'. This is so because pure theory 'postulates that in buying and selling we prefer the larger advantage to the smaller one, calculated not in subjective return of pleasure, but in objective quantities of goods or money' (Lowe 1935: 52f.). Thus, pure theory models consumers in exchange as quantity rather than utility maximizers. Since quantity maximizing is not simply an implication of the basic twin assumptions of rationality and utility maximizing, additional reasons have to be found for this behaviour. They can only be derived from specific social conditions. Thus, Lowe maintains that the idea of *homo economicus* brings 'an unquestionably sociological element into the pure theory of the market' (Lowe 1935: 53). 'In theory any substantial rule of bargaining conduct' would do, says Lowe, but 'whatever maxim we choose, it cannot be deduced from pure economics' (Lowe 1935: 53). Thus the need for sociology.

Lowe uses an analogous argument with respect to the idea of perfect competition as a situational constraint. It serves the same purpose as the internal constraints, namely to limit actors' freedom of choice in such ways that their behaviour realizes the 'laws' of the market as postulated by pure theory.

Again, Lowe holds that the condition of perfect competition cannot be part of the initial propositions of a pure, that is universal, economic theory. The theory relies on the idea of perfect competition to make agents behave as price-takers adjusting solely in terms of quantities, but in doing so it not only relies on a 'sociological element', but also betrays how deeply economic theory is rooted in the specific historical setting of nineteenth-century capitalism when the assumption of such markets was still realistic.

At this point, Lowe – relying on the concept of principia media developed by John Stuart Mill and taken up by Ginsberg and Mannheim – introduces what he calls 'middle principles', a precursor of the theories of the middle range later to be advocated by Robert Merton. Lowe uses his critical results in a positive manner: *homo economicus* and perfect competition are not only sociological concepts but also the 'middle principles' characteristic of nineteenth-century British capitalism. They are inadequate for understanding the contemporary constellation of economy and society, but as middle principles they can serve as an illustration for what is required today: Economists should give up the quest for universality and for the 'exact calculation of economic movements' (Lowe 1935: 147) in favour of empirical relevance. For the latter, the interdisciplinary elaboration of 'middle principles' is required, reflecting real and growing social interdependence.

'As long as economics claims to be an empirical science, the exactness of its theoretical generalizations will be judged only by their congruence with the facts. Whatever it may lose in mathematical elegance, its capacity to depict modern reality and to explain its causal concatenation will increase to the extent to which it uses the results of sociology for the constructions of its foundations' (Lowe 1935: 148).

Lowe's point is that economics as a positive science was constructed with nineteenth-century capitalism as its empirical object of reference. The niceties of the law of supply and demand and all other notions of price formation reflect social conditions which ensured stable patterns of economic activity. Only this stability and regular recurrence made economic processes accessible to standard modes of scientific reasoning. Thus, the object of economic enquiry was not simply constituted by the presumed timeless rationality of economic actors bound together by self-interest. Rather, it owed its analysability to a set of historical conditions, a unique type of competition (atomized) and specific techniques of production (high flexibility, adaptability, small units with little fixed capital). With respect to the contemporary economy of the 1930s, Lowe concedes that rational action remains dominant in the modern economic system, but that the situation in which this rationality is operative has changed drastically to monopolistic competition, big enterprises units with little flexibility and low mobility of capital, the erosion of traditional norms, etc. According to Lowe these factors lead to a destructuration of the economic system. Its mode of operation becomes more erratic, its movements are less and less predictable, the calculability underlying rational action is vanishing. So the point is not that rational action is disappearing, but rather that – despite perhaps increased efforts and capabilities to rationalize actions (more sophisticated calculations, more information-gathering, more experience) – the 'objective' conditions which form the situation in which actions take place, the context and the articulation of actions and perhaps the norms governing the selection of ends all lack the stability and regularity required to predict action outcomes successfully.

Thirty years after *Economics and Sociology*, in his *On Economic Knowledge* (1965), Lowe concluded that positive economic science is no longer possible and argued for its replacement by what he called 'instrumental analysis', using economic knowledge to realize politically set social goals. In *Economics and Sociology*, the conclusion was not quite as radical yet: Lowe hoped that interlocking economic and sociological arguments allowing for the elaboration of middle principles could generate scientifically sound and practically relevant reasoning about the socio-economic conditions of the modern age.

References and further reading

Chateauneuf, Anne (1999) 'Adolph Lowe's Contribution to a Heterodox Approach to Economic Behavior', *Creuset Document de Recherche*, 8, online. Available at www.univ-st-etienne.fr/creuset

Hagemann, Harald and Kurz, Heinz (eds) (1997) *Political Economics in Retrospect. Essays in Memory of Adolph Lowe*, Aldershot, UK: Edward Elgar.

Heilbroner, Robert L. (ed.) (1969), *Economic Means and Social Ends. Essays in Political Economics*, Englewood Cliffs, NJ: Prentice Hall.

Lowe, Adolph (1935) *Economics and Sociology: A Plea for Cooperation in the Social Sciences*, London: George Allen and Unwin.

—— (1937) *The Price of Liberty*, London: Hogarth.

—— (1965) *On Economic Knowledge: Toward a Science of Political Economics*, Armonk: M. E. Sharpe (enlarged edition 1977).

—— (1976) *The Path of Economic Growth*, Cambridge: Cambridge University Press.

—— (1987) *Essays in Political Economics, Public Control in a Democratic Society*, edited by Allan Oakley, Brighton: Wheatsheaf Books.

—— (1988) *Has Freedom a Future?* New York: Praeger.

Merton, R. K. (1968) *Social Theory and Social Structure*, New York: Free Press.

Nell, Edward (1984) 'Structure and Behavior in Classical and Neoclassical Theory', *Eastern Economic Journal*, 11(2): 139–55.

Parsons, Talcott (1937) 'Book Review: Economics and Sociology by Adolf Lowe', *American Journal of Sociology*, 43: 477–81.

Wieser, F. von (1914) 'Theorie der gesellschaftlichen Wirtschaft', in *Grundriß der Sozialökonomie I*, Tübingen: Mohr, pp. 125–444.

HEINER GANSSMANN

LUHMANN, NIKLAS

Niklas Luhmann (1927–1998) is one the most innovative and original social theorists of the late twentieth century. The conceptualization of the economy plays an important part in his work. Before discussing Luhmann's contribution to economic sociology I will briefly lay out core concepts of his general theory.

Luhmann's systems theory, i.e. his conception of 'the' society as a system with specific formal traits, follows but also substitutes great parts of the Parsonian project (see **systems approach to economic sociology**). At the same time it is based on the phenomenology of Husserl. With Parsons he shares, apart from using 'system' as fundamental concept, a strictly functional perspective on social problems and phenomena; from Husserl he takes the notion that men are living in an overcomplex world that can neither be imagined nor treated objectively. 'The world', and not only the thinking about it, always contains more possibilities than can ever be realized. To live first of all means to choose between alternatives, to decide which path to follow, i.e. to reduce complexity. Precisely this reduction of complexity is the main function of social systems.

Social systems are conceived of as pre-stabilized structures of meaning which, by excluding certain forms of action *and* (manifest) experiences, coordinate the expectations of their 'members'. It is important, however, that individuals do not belong completely to one system only. This is evident for functionally differentiated, i.e. modern, societies in which an individual is included, say, in the political system but also in the economic system. The modern individual participates in social systems as a role player via specific types of communication. Social systems might but need not be organizations (like a firm) or institutions (like the family). But also in primitive, less differentiated societies or, on the other side of the spectrum, in world society, the system does not consist of human beings as such but only of their communications. Human beings are always more than what is socially relevant: they breathe and digest, perceive and think privately. Of course, all of these activities and acts can become the subject of a conversation and thus an element of a social system, but a breath or a thought per se are not social. Communication, in Luhmann's sense of the term, is not opposed to (social) action, which sociologists generally regard as the basic social unit, but clasps and transcends it, since what is or rather what becomes an action is a social or communicative convention or decision. The criterion for distinguishing one social system from another is the form and specificity of its communications.

The subject and theme of economic communication, which must not be misunderstood as mere talk, but as a social and mostly unconscious procedure to qualify certain actions and experiences as economically relevant, is **scarcity**. By scarcity Luhmann does not simply mean natural scarcity of resources, but the fact that something that is signified as scarce is appropriated. Thus, the appropriation of a good by A reduces *his* scarcity, but at the same time increases the scarcity *for* B. Inasmuch as there are no rules of exchange – they cannot be taken for granted – this primordial economic situation resembles Parsons' **double contingency** which states that A does not know what to do since his decision to act depends on what B does, and vice versa. This is why a first solution of the paradox of scarcity presupposes the institutionalization of **property** rights. Exchange in the sense of **barter** only becomes possible on the basis of 'law'.

Nevertheless, the proto-market is the place where the logically universal, but virtual paradox of scarcity becomes actually visible. This is why means and ways have to be found and developed to pacify the exchange, i.e. to make the bystanders accept that exchange takes place and scarcity can be handled, but also that they themselves are excluded (see **inclusion and exclusion**). The mechanism or the medium which fulfils this task is money. Money as a collectively accepted, legitimate means of payment not only assures that exchange ratios can be measured exactly and realized at will, but also, and even more important, that every scarcity-increasing purchase is accompanied and compensated by a loss of general purchasing power of the buyer. It is money – not because of its technical efficiency, but because of its integration of the society as the general creditor of the means of payment – that liberates the exchange, enables markets and transforms the paradox of scarcity into a treatable problem. Economic communication is monetary exchange or simply a payment, and the economy 'is' where money is paid and received. Of course, money often buys goods or services that are consumed on the spot, and that is where the economy 'ends'. So to assure that the economy lasts, that lengthy processes of production can be organized, that firms can be founded and entertained and that investments pay, the bulk of the payments must not vanish in consumption, but have to be made in order to recover from spending. Therefore, for Luhmann, the (system of the) economy is the recursive enchainment or the autopoiesis of payments.

Luhmann's systems theory of the economy differs at least in two important points from mainstream contributions to economic sociology or economic theory respectively. On the one hand, Luhmann does not concentrate on the social (pre-) conditions and frames of **economic action**. He does not investigate the forms of **embeddedness**, but analyses a form of social communication, i.e. payments, as the constituting elements of economic action. This undermines the conventional division of labour between economists and sociolo-

gists. On the other hand, how and what Luhmann conceptualizes as the economy is not what neoclassical theory is tackling as such: neither do rational economic agents play any significant role (see **rational choice theory**), nor is **exchange** or the market one of the central notions of his theory. Both features, the presumable absence of specific sociological questions and the privilege that is given to money, as a kind of 'subject–object' of the economy, have been and still are main targets of the critique. However, the question arises, whether these are indeed the points where the theory fails.

Since, for Luhmann, money or monetary communication takes precedence over rational economic action and the market, his theory is suited to describe and understand **financial markets** much better than orthodox models. First, systems theory is in no way normative; it does not assume that economic action follows a path of optimization and that there is an equilibrium to be achieved. Second, the characteristics of money as a medium of communication which not only reduces but also preserves complexity – it combines high security of action for the money holder with high insecurity for his opponents about how he will spend it – do in part explain the development and thriving of financial markets as well as their intrinsic volatility. Financial markets are about the combination of investment and liquidity. Third, assuming that the reproduction of scarcity, which is in a fact a postponement or a *différance* (Derrida), is the basic problem of economic communication, it becomes possible and plausible to model the incessant invention and introduction of new financial products paradoxically as a simultaneous reduction and increase of money: while more (high-powered) money is bound, the amount and value of money (substitutes) rises. Therefore, **inflation** and **deflation** cannot simply be understood as an oversupply or a lack in the quantity of money, but must be interpreted as crises of trust into the purchasing power of money or, respectively, the marketability of money substitutes.

Asking for more 'traditional' sociology and/or economic orthodoxy in Luhmann's systems theory of the economy thus misses the heart of the matter. Luhmann does not intend to fill any lacunae, but to describe and analyse empirical phenomena as if the system had a logic or even a will of its own. The real deficit of economic systems theory, as it has been developed by Luhmann himself, is not that he disregards the 'real actors', but that he underrates one of the most important functional imperatives of a monetary economy, namely that it is forced to grow or to crumble. Social mechanism like competition and systemic constrains like interest are nearly absent. But it seems that these are the only forces that guarantee the autopoiesis of the system.

References and further reading

Baecker, Dirk (1988) *Information und Risiko in der Marktwirtschaft*, Frankfurt/M: Suhrkamp.

Beckert, Jens (2002) *Beyond the Market. The Social Foundations of Economic Efficiency*, Princeton, NJ: Princeton University Press.

Luhmann, Niklas (1988) *Die Wirtschaft der Gesellschaft*, Frankfurt/M: Suhrkamp.

Paul, Axel T. (2002) 'Money Makes the World Go Round. Über die Dynamik des Geldes und die Grenzen der Systemtheorie', *Berliner Journal für Soziologie*, 12: 243–62.

AXEL T. PAUL

M

McDONALDIZATION AND CONSUMPTION

The term 'McDonaldization' refers to the processes by which the principles of the fast food restaurant are coming to dominate more and more areas of American life and the rest of the world (Ritzer 2000). The theory of McDonaldization is an extension of Max Weber's argument that the modern world is becoming increasingly rationalized and disenchanted. According to George Ritzer, the fast food restaurant has replaced the modern bureaucracy as the central paradigm for understanding rationalization in contemporary life. McDonaldization refers primarily to the processes of rationalization best exemplified and most widely known through the McDonald's restaurant chain. There are four principles delineated by the concept of McDonaldization. They are efficiency, calculability, predictability, and control through non-human technology. A fifth principle, oftentimes described alongside these first four, is the irrationality of rationality. This means that attempts to increase rationality lead to unintended irrational consequences. For example, fast food restaurants are dehumanizing settings in which to work and to eat.

The shift from the bureaucracy to the fast food restaurant as the paradigm of understanding rationalization also points to the growing importance of consumption as a defining sphere of contemporary life.

When Ray Kroc established the first of McDonald's chains in 1955, he consolidated numerous rationalization processes such as scientific management, the assembly line and the franchising operation to create a model that had implications not only for the rational production of food products (Schlosser 2001), but also for the consumption of rationalized services. The fast food restaurant offered a form of consumption that was efficient, calculable, predictable and controlled through non-human technology. For example, the McDonald's restaurant provides an efficient means for people to acquire a meal so that they can immediately satisfy their hunger. Furthermore, consumers are guaranteed a predictable meal at a fast food restaurant. The hamburger that they consume, whether in their home, or across the globe, is much the same in both instances. Given this predictability, consumers are also able to calculate the amount of money that they will need to spend on a meal, the amount of food they will need to eat in order to satisfy their hunger, or the time that they will require to acquire and eat their food. This kind of calculability is important to the contemporary consumer who must increasingly plan every moment of his or her busy life. Finally, the fast food restaurant exemplifies the ways that technologies are used to control and manipulate consumer behaviour. The McDonald's restaurant is designed to get people to eat quickly and leave. Most notably, the drive-through window encourages consumers to eat their meal elsewhere, thus allowing the constant flow of consumers through the restaurant.

The processes of McDonaldization have shaped not only the way that people consume, but also people's ideas about ideal forms of consumption. In other words, McDonaldization is not only a process that facilitates consumption, but it has also become a popular symbol of consumption. Though many consumers remain ambivalent about the dangers of a McDonaldized society, in general consumers have come to expect efficient and predictable service that is also entertaining. Indeed, in this latter regard, the McDonald's restaurant demonstrates contemporary attempts to manage the irrationalities of rationality. Though McDonald's provides a rational means to obtain a meal, the lines and standardized food items can lead consumers to feel more like cattle than human beings. McDonald's' solution to this problem has been to create increasingly spectacular settings and menus so that the dehumanizing and disenchanting aspects of rationalized consumption are compensated through entertainment – play areas, movie promotions, collectibles and speciality items, among others (Ritzer 1999). In the popular imagination, then, the McDonald's restaurant is not only a place to get a quick meal, but it is also a place to have some fun. The popularity of this model, among both business owners and consumers, has led to an adoption of the model in areas quite distant from the fast food restaurant: education, health care, religion and travel (Ritzer 2002). It has now become commonplace to refer to the McUniversity, McDoctors or McJobs. Increasingly, consumption across all areas of life takes place within McDonaldized structures.

While on the one hand this McDonaldization of society offers the benefits of efficiency, predictability, calculability and control, it also threatens traditional means of consumption and the integrity of objects consumed. In recent work, Ritzer has argued that in the contemporary world there is a proliferation of social forms that are 'centrally conceived, controlled and comparatively devoid of distinctive substantive content' (Ritzer 2004: 3). Put another way, Ritzer suggests that this is a proliferation of 'nothing' at the expense of 'something'. By something, he means 'a social form that is generally indigenously conceived, controlled and comparatively rich in distinctive substantive content' (p. 7). Though not all forms of nothing are the product of McDonaldized institutions, it is clear that the kind of rationalization described here contributes to the creation of nothing. The McDonalidized institution is both an exemplar and a means of distributing nothing throughout society. For example, the McDonald's hamburger is a food product that is centrally conceived. Its preparation is carefully controlled and does not allow for individual creative impulse. It therefore lacks distinctive content. Indeed, the impulse to introduce distinctive content into the hamburger would produce variations that would threaten the principles of rationality outlined above.

While developed in America, McDonald's and the process of McDonaldization have become important features of life across the globe. To many, McDonald's is a symbol of America and in particular American consumer society. For some, McDonald's is a contemporary 'cathedral of consumption' that promises the joys of consumer society. To others, McDonald's stands as a threat to traditional forms of life and consumption. As a symbol of rationality, global imperialism and the consumer culture it has come under many forms of attack – bombings, protests and a famous libel suit. Though in recent years McDonald's has suffered economic decline it is also clear that the rational principles of McDonaldization have become central features of contemporary consumer society and will no doubt continue to structure

421

human relations well into the twenty-first century.

Further reading and references

Probyn, E. (1998) 'Mc-Identities: Food and the Familial Citizen', *Theory, Culture & Society*, 15(2): 155–73.

Ritzer, G. (1998) *The McDonaldization Thesis: Explorations and Extensions*, Thousand Oaks, CA: Sage.

—— (1999) *Enchanting a Disenchanting World: Revolutionizing the Means of Consumption*, Thousand Oaks, CA: Pine Forge Press.

—— (2000) *The McDonaldization of Society*, Thousand Oaks, CA: Pine Forge Press.

—— (2002) *McDonaldization: The Reader*, Thousand Oaks, CA: Pine Forge Press.

—— (2004) *The Globalization of Nothing*, Thousand Oaks, CA: Pine Forge Press.

Schlosser, E. (2001) *Fast Food Nation: The Dark Side of the All-American Meal*, Boston, MA: Houghton Mifflin.

GEORGE RITZER
JEFFREY STEPNISKY

MANAGEMENT

Management defines the complex set of roles and activities aimed at administrating, planning, coordinating and controlling human and physical resources within a business organization. In the abstract model of firm behaviour under perfect competition, managerial action is limited to a set of highly rigid decision rules for determining price and output. In reality, managers act in institutional contexts where market forces are only one of the key variables alongside others: the corporate organization, the larger group of organizations in which the firm is embedded, state policies and legal systems, and the strategies of both internal and external **stakeholder**s to whom managers are accountable. The managerial role is therefore a multifunctional one: decision-maker, leader-mediator between human expectations and organizational needs, custodian of institutionalized values, strategic player, and power broker between business and society. Within the enormous literature on management the contribution of eco-nomic sociology has focused on the role of managers in business organizations, managerial ideologies and styles, and the separation of ownership and control (see **managerial revolution**).

The role of managers in the firm organization

Major influences in the study of management in organization were Fayol's study on industrial administration, Weber's theory of bureaucracy, and Barnard's view of the functions of the executive. Fayol stressed forecasting, organizing, leading, coordinating and controlling as key activities. Weber laid the ground for a conception of managerial authority based on technical competence and incumbency in a legally defined office. Barnard argued that the manager's function is threefold: he must take strategic decisions through the rational evaluation of alternatives; he must assure the consensus and cooperation of all members of the business organization through shared goals and value premises; and he must achieve a satisfactory mediation between organizational needs and individual expectations. I will proceed from Barnard's view and frame it in the dominant organizational paradigms, in order to outline the key dimensions of the managerial role.

The first key dimension is that of managers as decision-makers and organization men, in the light of the organizational decision-making approach (Simon 1957). Organizations encourage decision-makers to 'satisfice' rather than maximize – that is, to settle for acceptable as opposed to optimal solutions – to cope with problems sequentially rather than simultaneously, and to utilize existing repertoires of action programmes rather than to develop novel responses for each situation. Because of the cognitive limits of individual decision-makers, organizations are needed to support rational decision-making by setting integrated subgoals and stable expectations and by subdividing responsibilities among managers and other firm members. Managers are the typical organization men of modern large-scale firms. Simon's 'bounded rationality' approach has been challenged by alternative policy-making models – such as incrementalism, garbage-can and varieties of neo-institutionalism – but is still widely accepted among managers and in management schools, and the most influential in shaping actual behaviour.

The second key dimension is that of managers as human relations-oriented leaders. The human relations perspective stresses the role of managers in exerting informal leadership, promoting worker morale, and fostering consensus and cooperation-stimulated business studies and policies aiming at increasing productivity through changes in work organization (job enlargement, job enrichment, workers' participation in decision-making). However, several decades of research demonstrated no clear relation between worker satisfaction and productivity and between participation in decision-making and worker satisfaction.

The third dimension of the managerial role – related to the institutional paradigm – is that of managers as custodians of institutionalized values and mediators between the organization and society. The manager's role is defined not in terms of his authority, but of his relation to the institutionalized culture of the organization, infused with value beyond the technical requirements of the task. Since organizations reflect and protect societal values, managers act as catalysts in this process.

These three views of the managerial role can be criticized for neglecting the dimensions of **conflict** and power, which are at the centre of the most recent studies of management in the light of what can be called the political-cultural approach. Focusing on social action in political arenas, social fields, domains, sectors or organized spaces, these studies view managers as power holders and power brokers in a conflict-ridden context.

The diversity of interests and outlooks among participants make conflict not a symptom of organizational malfunctioning, but a normal feature of organizational life. Real managerial strategies within the firm do not rationally maximize corporate ends. Instead they result from compromises within the dominant coalition as well as between the coalition and other collective actors, and adopt various mechanisms for conflict resolution, as in Cyert and March's behavioural theory of the firm (1963). The internal strategy and structure of existing firms reflect organized power and interests, and managers' ideas about appropriate corporate behaviour in light of existing conventional wisdom. Managers are the key actors in the complex relation between corporate management and control and the institutional context (made of suppliers, distributors, financial agencies, competitors, but also state laws and regulations that define what organizations can do and what the limits of legal behaviour are).

In a similar vein, business organizations are seen as the realm of dominant coalitions and negotiated orders, not as formal structures of established roles and procedures, but rather as the result of strategic power games where the freedom of the various actors playing is limited but the formal and informal rules of the organization (Crozier and Friedberg 1977). Managers can be seen as special players who have greater control over uncertain outcomes and are consequently more able to mobilize appropriate resources, like specialized competence, control of information, manipulation of norms, and control of the relations between the organization and the relevant environments.

Explicitly focused on power is Bacharach and Lawler's (1980) approach which sees managers as power holders and analyses both the power games, coalitions, alliances and conflicts organization leaders are engaged in.

Managerial cultures

The two major pioneering studies of managerial ideologies, both published in 1956, were Bendix's comparative-historical study on the similarities and differences in the ideas which aim at justifying and explaining managerial power and authority within the firm and, indirectly, the social status of the business class in the Anglo–American and Russian civilizations during the last two centuries; and Sutton *et al.*'s research on managerial ideology not as a specific device for legitimizing power in the business organization, but as a multi-functional mechanism capable of alleviating the strains to which businesspersons are inevitable subject (strains stemming from criticism of the dominant position of business in society, from the contradictory demands put on the businessperson by the different interlocutors from the conflicting demands of other social roles that managers play outside the firm).

Later studies have focused on the different managerial cultures of private and public enterprises, on the institutional arrangements and executive strategies of multinational corporations, on the spread of American or Japanese managerial values and practices, on the impact of **globalization** on the varieties of capitalism and different managerial styles (Martinelli 1994).

The impact of globalization on managerial cultures and styles shows contradictory tendencies: on the one hand, an increasingly interconnected market economy fosters the formation of a global managerial elite and the diffusion of a common cosmopolitan managerial culture among managers (although it is an open question to what extent this cosmopolitan culture is the diffusion of a single American-inspired model or the result of an hybridization of management styles and cultures). On the other hand, distinct national and corporation-specific managerial styles persist. From the studies of the varieties of capitalism literature (Crouch and Streeck 1997) we can draw the hypothesis that the different institutional regimes and cultural configurations – regulating **industrial relations**, training and recruiting, inter-company relations, and **corporate governance** – generate different micro-behaviours of managers within the firm. The most promising line of research focuses on the impact of globalization on the national varieties of capitalism and its implications for managerial roles and cultures.

References and further reading

Bacharach, S. B. and Lawler, E. J. (1980) *Power and Politics in Organizations*, San Francisco: Jossey Bass.

Bendix, R. (1956) *Work and Authority in Industry*, New York: John Wiley and Sons.

Crouch, C. and Streeck, W. (eds) (1997) *Modern Capitalism or Modern Capitalisms?* London: Sage.

Crozier, M. and Friedberg, E. (1977) *L'acteur et le système*, Paris: Seuil.

Cyert, R. M. and March, J. G. (1963) *A Behavioral Theory of the Firm*, Englewood Cliffs, NJ: Prentice Hall.

Martinelli, A. (1994) 'Entrepreneurship and Management', in N. J. Smelser and R. Swedberg (eds), *The Handbook of Economic Sociology*, Princeton, NJ: Princeton University Press.

Simon, H. (1957) *Administrative Behavior*, New York: Macmillan.

Sutton, F. X., Harris, S. E., Kaysen, C. and Tobin, J. (1956) *The American Business Creed*, Cambridge, MA: Harvard University Press.

ALBERTO MARTINELLI

MANAGERIAL REVOLUTION

The Managerial Revolution is the title of a well-known book by Burnham (1941) which popularized the thesis exposed by Berle and Means (1932) on the separation of ownership and control and linked it to the views of managers as the new ruling class through their control of the state and of the convergence between capitalism and socialism. In their empirical research on 200 American firms, Berle and Means argued that the separation of ownership and control was an organizational requirement of the modern corporation and an irreversible trend of economic life. The modern corporation is conceived as an organized social group based on the interdependence of different economic interests, i.e. those of the owners, those of the employees, those of the consumers and those of the controlling group. Conflicts of interest can arise between managers and shareholders (the former are mostly interested to reinvest most profits in order to enhance the firm's competitive power and long-term development, whereas the latter are interested in short-term economic gains), and between the managers and the employees (over wages) as well as between managers and consumers (over prices). But managers are required to take responsibility of the welfare of all those who later on will be called **stakeholder**s. The controlling group has the 'active property' of the firm – as distinct from the 'passive property' of the shareholders – and performs the entrepreneurial function. Managerial power of the controlling group is highly concentrated as religious power in the medieval Church and political power in the nation-state.

The separation of ownership and control and the rising importance of managers was viewed either as a revolutionary shift in control or as a stage in the evolution of capitalism. Both **Marx** and **Schumpeter** saw the separation of the managerial role from the ownership of capital as a sign of the crisis of capitalism. According to Marx, when this happens the capitalist can no longer legitimize his gain as a reward for a social function and he reveals his parasitic character, while **entrepreneurship** becomes a social function of the associated producers. Schumpeter predicted the progressive decay of the entrepreneurial function by virtue of the routinization of innovation in large organizations. It is the very success of the capitalist firm which undermines the system, thus rendering the entrepreneurial

function superfluous and undermining the bourgeois basis for continued dominance. And there is also the melting of key institutions like private **property** and contract. The limitation of both Marx's and Schumpeter's views in this regard is due largely to their belief that the competitive economy of the individual, innovative entrepreneur is the only brand of sustainable capitalism. Their wrong predictions of a rapid collapse of capitalism were largely imputable to the error of closely identifying capitalism with the nineteenth-century entrepreneur. In reality, capitalism has proved compatible with the existence of large, complex firms and with state intervention and control of the economy.

What Marx and Schumpeter saw as a crisis factor, other scholars viewed as a stage in capitalist development and a feature of the process of business growth. A fundamental reason for the success of the modern corporation was its ability to obtain higher productivity rates by reducing information and transaction costs, through the internalization of activities previously performed by separate autonomous business units, and by a better coordination of the flow of goods and factors of production. Coase argued that if the cost of carrying out a transaction in the market was higher than the cost of carrying out the same transaction within the firm, firms would internalize the transaction in order to lower costs (1937). **Chandler** developed the idea of the firm as an alternative allocative mechanism to the price mechanism, and of the visible hand of the managers an alternative to the invisible hand of the market (1977).

The transition from family capitalism to managerial capitalism is facilitated by the legal institution of the joint stock corporation, which comes into existence in situations where technology and expanding demand require a large amount of capital and a separation of functions between entrepreneurs and shareholders. The 'complete businessman' who was at the same time owner, entrepreneur and manager, gave place to the separation of ownership and control functions and to a plurality of specialized roles within the corporation. The advantages of corporate organization could not be fully exploited until a managerial hierarchy was created, made of managers who are rewarded, selected and promoted on the basis of their professional skills and experience and of the objectives achieved rather on the basis of their family ties and the money invested into the firm. Once formed, this managerial hierarchy becomes the source of continuity, power and growth of large firm, and it tends to assume a life of its own, independent on the individual turnover at the top.

However, the problem exists of controlling and minimizing managerial discretion and opportunism. Adopting a transaction costs perspective, Williamson argued that boards of directors act to control the information asymmetries between themselves and top managers by fostering multi-divisional forms of organization as a control mechanism and by writing contracts for top managers that bond their interests to those of the shareholders (1985). **Agency theory** has also been used in order to explain why the joint stock corporation exists, how the **principal and agent** relation between owners and managers is structured, and how the relation can go astray.

The thesis of the irreversible diffusion of managerial capitalism has been criticized on various grounds. First, it has been pointed out that family capitalism is much more resilient – mostly in small-scale firms – than the scholars of managerial control would admit, not only in continental Europe, but even in the United States.

Second, the very notion of corporate control has been challenged by studies of **interlocking directorates**, which argue that public companies with disperse ownership among many stockholders are actually controlled by financial institutions – such as national commercial **banks**, regional banks

and national insurance companies – through corporate interaction patterns, rather than by their top managers (Stokman *et al.* 1985).

Third, top managers and owners are seen as basically sharing the same interests and values, in spite of the different roles they play, due to the fact that corporate executives, while not often among the largest shareholders, receive incomes that are highly correlated with stock performance, and that a relevant part of their remuneration is in the form of stock, dividend income and capital gains (Lewellen 1971). The recent major scandals of companies like Enron, WorldCom and Parmalat show that top managers – and the related accounting firms – can violate the law in order to pursue their own gain at the expenses of the shareholders and of other stakeholders of their firms. In a similar vein, managerial capitalism is seen as a stage which has been bypassed by a further stage, that of the international business class made up of manager–entrepreneurs operating across national boundaries in transnational corporations and financial networks, with interconnected careers and sharing a common cosmopolitan culture. In today's global market, managerial capitalism is changing into international capitalism, where corporate power stems from the ability to control global production networks and financial flows.

Fourth, the idea of the firm as an alternative allocative mechanism for the price mechanism has been criticized for neglecting other important mechanisms in the regulation of economic activity, such as clans, cartels and trusts, employers' and trade associations, networks (Martinelli and Chiesi 1989).

Finally, the managerial revolution tends to obscure the basic question of the different models of corporate control (see **corporate governance**) – from control of competitors to financial control – which have been at the centre of Neil Fligstein's work (1990). There is little evidence that families, managers and states converge towards a single model of domination of ownership in various societies. Available evidence suggests that in the epoch of globalization there is, as yet, no world market for corporate control.

References and further reading

Berle, A., Jr and Means, G. C. (1932) *The Modern Corporation and Private Property*, New York: Harcourt.

Burnham, J. (1941) *The Managerial Revolution*, New York: John Day.

Chandler, A. D., Jr (1977) *The Visible Hand: the Managerial Revolution in American Business*, Cambridge, MA: Harvard University Press.

Coase, R. H. (1937) 'The Nature of the Firm: Origin, Meaning, Influence', *Economica*, 4: 386–405.

Fligstein, N. (1990) *The Transformation of Corporate Control*, Cambridge, MA: Harvard University Press.

Lewellen, W. G. (1971) *The Ownership Income of Management*, Princeton, NJ: Princeton University Press.

Martinelli, A. and Chiesi, A. (1989) 'The Representation of Business Interests as a Mechanism of Social Regulation', in P. Lange and M. Regini (eds), *State, Market and Social Regulation*, New York: Cambridge University Press.

Stokman, F. N., Ziegler, R. and Scott, J. (1985) *Networks of Corporate Power: A Comparative Analysis of Ten Countries*, Oxford: Polity Press.

Williamson, O. (1985) *The Economic Institutions of Capitalism: Firms, Markets, Relational Contracting*, New York: Free Press.

ALBERTO MARTINELLI

MARGINAL UTILITY See: utility; value; economics, history of

MARKETS, SOCIOLOGY OF

Markets are at the centre of the economy, and the focus of political controversies. Corresponding with economic liberalization and marketization, there has been an increased scientific interest in markets. This is reflected in economic sociology, which has generated a large body of knowledge on markets.

A market is *a social structure for exchange of rights, which enables people, firms and products to be evaluated and priced*. This means that at least three actors are needed for a market to exist: at least one actor, on the one side of the market, who is aware of at least two actors on the other side whose products or services can be evaluated in relation to each other. The social structure consists of roles (buyer and seller, and consumer and producer), divided on the two sides of the market interface. Different interests or goals characterize these two roles. Property rights, often embedded in **trust**, are conventional in a market, which makes market interaction peaceful. Actors take part in markets to get better off. **Exchange** implies that something, for example money, is traded for something else, such as a commodity. What is traded in a market is usually what gives it a name: for example, 'the market for used cars'.

This is a minimal definition, and in this entry several aspects of markets will be discussed. There are further aspects of real markets, but most of them are shared by other forms of social structure, such as time and size, and should not be part of a definition of markets. There are also a number of other aspects of markets that are reflected in theoretical, normative as well as empirical works by social scientists that are beyond the scope of this entry.

The first section discusses the history of ideas of markets. The following section outlines the two fundamental kinds of market structures, exchange and role markets. Finally, the most important dimensions of markets, according to the sociological literature on markets, are discussed.

The development of markets and market theories

It is not possible to identify the first real market (see Swedberg 2003 for a more extensive treatment or the topics discussed

427

in this section). Historically the market was a physical locality where people met with some regularity to **barter** goods, e.g. fish and chickens. The word is derived from the Latin *mercatus*, which refers to trade. With more advanced societies the notion took on further meanings in addition to a place of trade. It is clear that markets gradually became more sophisticated, and with the industrial revolution, consumer mass markets emerged. A change in markets occurred when money was introduced as a means for exchange; only then can one speak of actual 'buyers' and 'sellers', as Alfred Marshall argued in *Principles of Economics*, published in 1920. The introduction of the Internet means that one may speak of virtual markets, and the idea of physical markets is less important (see **electronic commerce**).

Adam **Smith** is generally seen as the economists who pulled together the dispersed knowledge of the field that existed at the time he wrote his *An Inquiry into the Nature and Causes of the Wealth of Nations* (1776). Smith, and most of his followers, saw the market, a term that is frequent in his book, as a price mechanism. In Smith's version the market is a way of generating the 'natural price'; classical economists saw price essentially as a reflection of the natural value of the product traded in the market. Later on, John Stuart Mill, David Ricardo and Karl **Marx** discussed the market, and Marx added the idea that also social relations exist between actors and the things exchanged in the market. Marx, as is well known, criticized the market logic, which he equated with exploitation.

With the marginalist revolution the market was seen as a mechanism for determination of **value**. At the same time the link between real markets and the market theory weakened. Léon Walras contributed with the market theory that is still the core of neoclassical economic theory. His theory was modelled on a single stock exchange, the Paris Bourse. Walras argued that a market is best organized as an auction,

operated by brokers and other intermediaries. Austrian economists argued that markets emerge spontaneously.

It was only with the publication, in 1933, of Edward Chamberlin's *Theory of Monopolistic Competition* that economic theory also opened up for a serious discussion of other markets than exchange markets. The development of transaction cost economics, and institutional economics more generally, with its emphasis on the role of property rights and contracts, has increased also the sociological understanding of markets. These schools put more emphasis on the structure of the market than on price, the latter being the focus of the mainstream neoclassical market model.

Economists have continued to develop the theory of the market, and Gary Becker has argued that essentially all human behaviour can be analysed with the economic approach, in which the market is key (Lie 1997: 343). Economists, of course, have raised many more aspects. Nonetheless, economists have written comparatively little on markets, and it may be due to their propensity to view the market as natural, and sometimes also as a priori good.

Max **Weber**'s outlook on markets is by and large economic, but he added the ideas of power, conflict of interests and market struggle to the analysis of markets. Many sociologists, including Weber, have studied how markets are related to the rest of society. Karl **Polanyi**, who in 1944 published his seminal *The Great Transformation*, argued that market exchange is only one of three forms of organizing the economy: the other two are redistribution and reciprocity. Pierre **Bourdieu** repeatedly mentions the market, which according to him, must be analysed in relation to the power structure of what he calls fields (Swedberg 2003: 127). Sociologists, however, did not pay much attention to markets until Harrison White, in 1981, wrote an important article, 'Where Do Markets Come From?' White's insights made ground for the fundamental distinction between exchange markets and role market, which reflect two different forms of social structure.

Exchange and role markets

In exchange markets actors do not hold permanent roles as buyers or sellers, which means that economic actors, individuals and firms, may switch roles so that one first is a buyer, and later a seller, of the same, or another, item. There are several real markets that are exchange markets, such as swap meetings, **financial markets** and stock exchange markets. People who come together to trade, barter, buy and sell, typically focused on a certain thing, such as model trains or Volkswagen Bugs, make up a swap meeting. That is, at least some of those who attend may both sell and buy, but they do not have permanent roles as buyers or sellers. The stock exchange is another example of an exchange market, but in which the commodities, stocks, are identical. Financial markets also represent exchange markets (Knorr Cetina and Bruegger 2002).

The exchange market is the archetype of the neoclassical model, and probably the type of market for which neoclassical analysis is most suited. Also sociologists have studied this form of market, and thereby shown that neoclassical theory is not necessarily the paramount tool for analysing financial and stock exchange markets (cf. Lie 1997: 344). Sociologist, however, have not presented theories of the market that seriously challenge the neoclassical analysis of these markets.

Most real markets are not exchange markets, but role markets (Aspers 2005), which means that the market identity of an actor is tied to only one side of the market (producer/seller or consumer/buyer). Thus, car manufacturers are committed to the role as producers of cars; they do not also operate as consumers of cars. They operate, however, as buyers in many busi-

ness-to-business markets, where they buy commodities, such as steel and numerous components needed for the production from other producers, typically called suppliers, who are located upstream in the production chain.

It was Harrison White, in the above-mentioned article, who initiated the sociological approach to markets. White sees the works of Marshall and Chamberlin as important contributions to a phenomenologically as well as mathematically correct theory of markets. White developed his theory to study markets characterized by few competing producers, all of whom having stable roles as producers of a certain commodity, and having identities which are relative to other producers in the same market. These producers orient themselves, not as neoclassical theory suggests, towards consumers, but towards each other. The number of producers in each market is limited, about ten to fifteen, though the number of consumers is so many that they can be treated as anonymous. White calls these markets producer markets.

A key difference between the neoclassical theory and White's theory is that the latter stresses that producers differentiate themselves by selling different products, and they also use price differentiation. This means that actors have different identities; some are known as high-quality producers and others as low-quality producers. As a result, each firm holds a niche in the producer market, which is related to the price–quality mix of its products.

White says that the market is a social structure that reproduces itself as well as its members. Firms in a market have access to essentially the same information, and they perceive the market situation in similar ways. This information is gathered through gossip and by observing the behaviour of rivals in the market, and a consequence is that only insiders know the boundaries of the market. The consumers in White's model have a less leading role; they are

429

essentially restricted to saying 'yes' or 'no' to what producers offer, but in doing this they determine what quality means in a market.

In addition to White's works on markets, Neil Fligstein's approach should be mentioned. Fligstein (2001) focuses on the market context, rather than providing a detailed theory of markets. His approach is 'political-cultural,' stressing the role of institutions, such as rules and classifications, as well as the point that markets are outcomes of political struggle. In this struggle some actors may fashion the market, which he conceptualizes as a field, for example by using the state as a means to gain benefits and a competitive edge. Fligstein stresses the role of the state in this process of stabilizing markets. Other sociologists have discussed the role of status in markets, and several studies analyse the importance of networks in the economy.

Though many economic sociological studies have addressed **labour markets**, few have produced alternative sociological theories of how they operate. One reason may be that labour markets sometimes are viewed as 'a distinct species of their own' (Swedberg 2003: 155). Moreover, both economists and sociologists have frequently used the neoclassical economic model to approach labour markets, though this theory is not developed for analyses of this type of market. Labour markets, according to the central distinction made in this section, are role markets.

Aspects of markets

This section discusses aspects that sociologists as well as others have seen as important or even essential characteristics of markets. However, the literature is divided on exactly which aspects are essential, and the minimal definition acknowledges this by not including them. Analyses of concrete markets may benefit from including one or more of these aspects.

Markets are often embedded in social structure, typically in other markets in the same production chain. The cotton market, for example, is connected downstream to the markets for fabrics, which are linked to the production market for garments, and the buyers of these products, garment retailers, face consumers in the final consumer who buys clothes in stores. This means that some markets are business-to-business markets, or wholesale markets, whereas others are consumers' markets (see **consumption**). Some markets are oriented upstream the production flow whereas others are oriented downstream, towards the consumers.

Some markets are close to the ideal market of neoclassical economics, with many small actors, each of which is a price taker, with access to essentially the same information, selling identical products, and without any formal barriers for entering the market. Other markets are monopoly markets (one seller) and monopsony markets (one buyer), or positioned in between the pure market, and the monopoly market, called oligopolistic markets. Each of these markets represents a different composition of power relations between the actors.

A market may be designed, and thus intentionally created, or an unintended consequence. The state is not a necessary condition for the existence of markets. Markets existed before states, and markets exist that defy the state, such as illegal markets. The degree of regulation differs between markets. Some have formal regulations determined by the state, whereas others are virtually self-regulating. Self-regulation can be formalized or it can consist of informal sanctions. Actors in markets try to fashion them so that they become more in line with their interests, and the state can also be seen as an arena for this kind of struggle. Actors in a market usually have some common interests, and may have an organization representing their interests, versus the rest of society.

Though the state, the law and the profound informal trust constitute the backdrop of many real markets, other dimensions for the construction of order are also important. The social structure, in terms of roles and status positions of producers and consumers, is an important element for generating order in markets where the products are not standardized, such as in art markets, or aesthetic markets (cf. Aspers 2005). Order in a market can also be constructed through product standards, for example pureness of gold (measured in the standard of carats).

Markets may be global, which means that there is just one market, which largely is the case with the foreign exchange market. Other markets, such as housing markets, are still national, both in terms of demand and supply, but also in terms of culture, legal frameworks and the like. Furthermore, most actors in markets are private entrepreneurs, but also states operate in markets. Furthermore, both private and public ownership exist of the rights that are exchanged in markets.

A market may be a demand market or a supply market. In the first case the service or product is only produced after the buyer has made a request, as is the case when one uses a hauler. A supply market exists if producers or sellers make or sell the commodities before someone has demanded them: for example, digital cameras, or a local fruit market.

Markets may be associative or disassociative. An associative market exists when it is necessary that the seller (producer) and the buyer come together. This is the case in many project-based activities, such as **advertising**, but also haircutting exemplifies this form of market relation. Disassociative markets exists when there is no need for the producer and the consumer to come together: when a shirt is made in a developing country for a retailer in a developed country, the product is made without contact with the consumer, the final buyer.

There are also future markets, where a contract is made at one point in time, and the delivery of the contract takes place in the future. In between the making of the contract and its ending, the rights may be traded in a future market. The commodity or service is also an important aspect of any market. In some markets identical products are traded, such as a given currency in a foreign exchange market. In other markets, such as markets for arts, each object is unique (see **art and economy**).

The ethical status of a commodity or service in a market may vary. Some markets are seen as highly ethical, for example fair trade markets, whereas people normally see prostitution as highly unethical (see **fairness**). Generally speaking, almost anything can be traded in a market. Furthermore, markets may be driven by profit, but other markets are driven by ethical considerations. Some of these ethical markets have the same social structure as other markets, but the logic is different.

A market is also characterized by its culture, different degrees of tradition and rationality, language, ways of interaction, meaning and so on. Furthermore, actors in a market have acquired knowledge that usually is specific to this market.

Though money sometimes is included in definitions of markets, it is not a necessary, or defining, aspect of markets. Relative evaluation (prices) of products, services or people in markets can be made without money; what is needed is some kind of ranking, and 'prices' may be expressed in real terms. Money can also be subject to trade in markets. Obviously, money facilitates this process and the operation of markets, and may be almost a necessity if one is to engage in comparison across many markets, or in studies of the interconnectedness of markets.

Real markets show great variation between each other. This suggests that it is hard to have one single theory that encompasses all markets. Sociologists have suggested that there are different kinds of markets. The definition provided here harbours empirically existing markets, and identifies what effectively makes them markets. It is clear that there are two species of markets, exchange markets and role markets, and this suggests that there should be two different theories, one for each species. Economic sociologists need to study whether markets can be seen as instances of more general forms of social structure. Another issue is the relationship between markets and capitalism.

References and further reading

Aspers, Patrik (2005) *Markets in Fashion, A Phenomenological Approach*, London: Routledge.

Fligstein, Neil (2001) *The Architecture of Markets*, Princeton, NJ: Princeton University Press.

Knorr Cetina, Karin and Bruegger, Urs (2002) 'Global Microstructures: The Virtual Societies of Financial Markets', *American Journal of Sociology*, 107: 905–50.

Lie, John (1997) 'Sociology of Markets', *Annual Review of Sociology*, 23: 241–60.

Marshall, Alfred (1920) *Principles of Economics*, London: Macmillan.

Swedberg, Richard (2003) *Principles of Economic Sociology*, Princeton, NJ: Princeton University Press.

White, Harrison (1981) 'Where Do Markets Come From?' *American Journal of Sociology*, 3: 517–47.

—— (2002) *Markets from Networks, Socioeconomic Models of Production*, Princeton, NJ: Princeton University Press.

PATRIK ASPERS

MARKET STRUCTURES See: markets, sociology of; network analysis

MARSHALL, ALFRED

Alfred Marshall (1842–1924) shaped the professional orientation of British and world economics to an extent that few other economists have equalled. His appointment to the Cambridge chair in 1885 came at a time when historicists, classicals, marginalists, Marxians and others were all struggling for the soul of the new discipline. By 1908, when he handed over to his disciple Pigou, the factions had to an unprecedented extent become united behind the banner of the canonical *Principles of Economics* (1890). Marshall's great book remains to this day the core of textbook supply and demand. Labelled 'Volume I' until the 1910 (sixth) edition, the *Principles* was never complemented by the additional volumes on macroeconomics and progress that its author had intended.

The gap is filled to some extent by Marshall's *Industry and Trade* (1919), by his *Money Credit and Commerce* (1923), by important journal articles such as 'Some Aspects of Competition' (1890), 'Mechanical and Biological Analogies in Economics' (1898), 'Social Possibilities of Economic Chivalry' (1907). Marshall gave revealing evidence to public inquiries such as the Royal Commission on the Depression of Trade and Industry (1886), the Royal Commission on the Aged Poor (1893), the Indian Currency Committee (1899). He also left unpublished lecture-notes and manuscripts, now kept in the Marshall Library, Cambridge. Of these, 'Progress: Its Economic Conditions' and 'Socialism and the Functions of Government' are among the most interesting.

Marshall was prolific and energetic. Active in university affairs, he was instrumental in 1903 in securing the introduction of the new, more specialized Tripos in Economics, as he had been in 1890 (while President of Section F of the British Association for the Advancement of Science) in encouraging the formation of the British Economic Association (now the Royal Economic Society). He was less successful in his campaign to close Cambridge degrees to women. A healthy family is essential to a healthy society, Marshall believed. That is why women's contribution to the production function of balanced and confident citizens should not be underestimated. Nor should it be undermined by higher education that would leave the next generation without an anchor in a stable home.

Marshall's Cambridge degree (in 1865) was in mathematics. He converted to the moral sciences because of a wish to do good that may have reflected his domineering father's determination that he should become a clergyman. Marshall, interested as he was in pure theory and (usually confined to footnotes and appendix) in mathematical economics, never lost sight of the teleology of a liberating science that Ruskin and Carlyle were wrong to regard as dismal. Marshall was not a strict economic determinist: he argued that ideas as well as events have a significant causal impact. Even so, he was quintessentially a maker of history-to-come: he believed economic activity to have a powerful and a valuable influence on personal development and interpersonal relationships. Marshall was not an atomistic individualist whose maximizations are a private affair, forever sealed within a *ceteris paribus* box. Marshall was a social economist who believed that economics made a difference because it upgraded the ethical content of perceived interaction and the way fellow citizens live.

Economic efficiency, allocative and dynamic, expands the choice-sets and alleviates distress. The living standards of the vanguard rich trickle down to become the conventional luxuries of the relatively deprived. The absolutely deprived are empowered to buy their way out of the slums where the only way to forget the squalor is to drink oneself into oblivion. As living standards become conspicuously more similar, so the members of one nation come to recognize one another as members of a single tribe. Economic growth promotes tolerance, respect and the common culture. Voluntary bodies such as the charity organization societies do good work in relieving the unavoidable distress of the genuine residuum, not able-bodied malingerers but the 'deserving poor' who

deserve the Good Samaritan's alms. Most of all, however, it is full employment and rising affluence that will lift up the needy and carry them along.

Just as growth enriches and includes, so it refocuses and improves. Clothing becomes aesthetic as well as protective. Leisure time is devoted to athletics and not to 'sensuous craving'. Longer schooling and economies of scale universalize the habit of reading. Better men have better wants. Better wants in turn form better men. Activities themselves have a high income elasticity: basic needs satisfied, the focus in economic endeavour shifts from passive consumption towards purposive activity, 'the aim of life', 'life itself'. Besides that, character patterns too evolve in consequence of the economic revolution. Prosperity makes men more truthful, less likely to steal a private gain or to defect from their contribution to a public good. Employers become more altruistic, more willing as well as more able to over-pay a hungry workman or to invest in on-the-job training which might become an external economy to a competitor firm. Workers become more constructive, more likely to abstain from a disruptive strike lest the consequent displacement of labour by capital put future generations out of a job, more inclined to regard their union as a 'little republic' in which informal sanctions and the status motive keep up the quality of workmanship. Marshall was aware that competition could become frenzied and divisive. Such *anomie*, he believed, would only be a social fact in the transition to a mature capitalism of solidarity and cohesion alongside entrepreneurship and change. Marshall, like Knight, Hirsch and Buchanan, was a cultural conservative. He could not imagine a market order in which trust and decency were not the background complements to exchange.

In any case, there was always the fail-safe of the state. A political economist who was never so doctrinaire as to limit authority to the constables and the law-courts, he could see a role for nationalized operation in areas such as the Post Office (where there was a natural monopoly), for a progressive income tax (since equality of subjective sacrifice presupposes inequality in absolute burdens), for a tabular standard of value (so that businesses might have information adequate to inflation-proof their contracts). It would be fully Marshallian to say even more about the constructive and leaderly role of the state. Marshall was a socially involved economist who never wanted to free the market from its duty to serve the interests of the community as a whole.

References and further reading

Groenewegen, P. (2003) 'Competition and Evolution: The Marshallian Conciliation Exercise', in R. Aréna and M. Quéré (eds), *The Economics of Alfred Marshall: Revisiting Marshall's Legacy*, Houndmills: Palgrave, pp. 113–33.

Marshall, A. ([1890]1961) *Principles of Economics*, ninth (variorum) edition, edited by C. Guillebaud, London: Macmillan.

Reisman, D. A. (1987) *Alfred Marshall: Progress and Politics*, London: Macmillan.

DAVID REISMAN

MARX, KARL

Few thinkers have had as much influence on the social sciences as the German social theorist Karl Marx (1818–83). His stress upon dialectical analysis – in which society is treated as an historically evolving and systemically interrelated whole – has had a profound impact on political science, economics and sociology. This dialectical method, which seeks to uncover the full context of historically specific social interactions in any given system, is used by Marx as a tool for understanding **class** relationships under capitalism – and as a means for altering such structures fundamentally. For Marx, immanent critique of capitalist society anticipates revolutionary change. Uniting theory and practice, Marx

declared in his 'Theses on Feuerbach': 'The philosophers have only *interpreted* the world in various ways; the point is to *change* it' (Marx 1845). How society itself might evolve and how one might change society are, therefore, questions of the utmost importance in the Marxian schema.

First and foremost, Marx's corpus is a structure of interpretive analysis that seeks to explain the historical uniqueness of capitalism. Deeply influenced by such classical political economists as Adam **Smith** and David Ricardo, Marx nonetheless criticized their representation of the capitalist mode of production and its 'bourgeois' social relations as a given. He aimed to grasp the historical origins of capitalism and its potential future development towards communism. The classical economists, in Marx's view, had reified the reciprocity of market relations – the equal exchange of value for value – while masking the fact that, under capitalism, labour produces a surplus value, upon which profits and exploitation are built.

Despite his criticisms of classical **political economy**, Marx learned much from the Scottish historical school, which included Smith, Adam Ferguson, William Robertson, and John Millar – all of whom might be considered early economic sociologists (Meek 1954). These thinkers pioneered a materialist conception of history, which fully appreciated that category of social phenomena known as 'the unintended consequences of social action'.

For Marx, however, capitalism was 'unintended consequences' writ large. He and his life-long collaborator, Frederick Engels, viewed capitalism as an outgrowth of feudalism. Their analysis of the evolution from feudalism to capitalism focused on a series of class and structural differentiations over time – the distinction of pastoral tribes from the general masses, the separation of manufacture from agriculture and of town from country, and the emergence of a class of merchants whose central function was not the production of use-values, but the facilitation of exchange in a globally expanding marketplace. These divisions of class and geography and specializations of function happen spontaneously, as it were, 'behind the backs of the producers,' as Marx explains in Volume 1 of *Capital*. Further fragmentation between purchase and sale, social production and private appropriation, state and civil society were manifestations of the deep 'contradictions' in capitalism, which propelled the system towards ever-worsening periodic crises and business cycles.

Under capitalism, the central dualism opens up between the proletarian and capitalist classes. It is this focus on class that led Marx and Engels ([1848]1968) to view '[t]he history of all hitherto existing society [as] the history of class struggle'. Though Marx was not the first thinker to propose a theory of class – Charles Comte, Charles Dunoyer, James Mill and others had offered an alternative classical liberal theory, which continues to exert influence on contemporary **libertarianism** – he was a pioneer in the use of a conflict model of social systems.

For Marx, the formation of various classes is a function of material conditions. Nevertheless, Marx was not oblivious to the political aspects of class formation. In its origins, capitalism is born of primitive accumulation, in which the mercantilist state – using outright force, political privilege and control over public debt – accelerates the accumulation of capital to crush regressive feudal social formations. But it is through the **alienation** of products from labourers, the actual producers of value, that capitalism achieves a progressive and revolutionary economic advancement. Marx presents a social stratification theory of sorts, which centres on ownership of the means of production at the core of class fragmentation and conflict. On this basis, Marx saw the propertied capitalist class as fundamentally parasitic on the propertyless proletariat, which constituted the vast majority of capitalist society. Only altering material conditions could make radical social change possible. The priority accorded to material factors in history is the essence of Marx's **historical materialism**, which locates historical movement, ultimately, in **economic development**.

In Marx's view, these material factors were tending toward communism. Though he did not provide a fully articulated blueprint for such social change, he saw the achievement of communism as an emancipatory two-stage process. In the first stage, what V. I. Lenin (1973) later called the stage of **socialism**, the proletariat takes control of the means of production and the state, which had been an instrument in the hands of the capitalist class, and uses these institutions for the benefit of the workers. This 'dictatorship of the proletariat' eventually leads to the abolition of class society in the second stage, which marks the triumph of communism. At this point, the market has been fully supplanted as the agency of circulation and the state withers away, enabling a democratized distribution of abundant goods in a post-scarcity society.

Whatever one's views of Marx's historical projections, there is much debate in the literature on the nature of historical materialism, especially Marx's view of the relationship between the material or economic 'base' and the ideological, cultural and political 'superstructure'. For example, Jeffrey Alexander, in his comprehensive work on *Theoretical Logic in Sociology*, argues that, especially in the crucial period from 1845 to 1848, Marx put forth a strict instrumentalist model of technological determinism. For Alexander, Marx banishes voluntarism from sociology. Marx's division between material life and consciousness, or base and superstructure, entails a one-way causality, in Alexander's view, since the base fully determines superstructural elements. This approach denies any autonomy to political forces and reduces human consciousness to a pure epiphenomenon of material conditions, a 'sociology' of knowledge that eliminates human agency from the social process.

Alternative nondeterminist readings are offered by such writers as Avineri (1968), Giddens (1979), Ollman (1976) and Sherman (1995). These writers emphasize the dialectical character of Marx's method as a way of combating strict determinist implications. In these readings, the base is not purely 'technological' or 'material'; it is social, consisting of conscious, reasoning, purposeful human beings who act under historically specific conditions.

Ollman (1993) argues further that Marx, whose dialectics was influenced by Joseph Dietzgen and G. W. F. Hegel, embraces a doctrine of internal relations. Externally related variables are independent: neither depends on the other for its existence or meaning. Internally related variables are reciprocally dependent on each other. In Marx's conception of society, mutual implications abound. Each unit – each structure, institution, class, etc. – is treated as an expression of capitalism, even as the totality of capitalism is comprised of the various units. Because human beings cannot cognitively digest the whole as a whole, the process of abstraction is essential to the analysis of any social problem. Marx's sociological imagination, therefore, incorporates a crucially important perspectival element. By varying his vantage points and his levels of generality, and by extending each unit of his analysis spatially and temporally, tracing its systemic relationships to other units and its dynamic relationships – especially its class relationships – across time, Marx is able to achieve a more comprehensive picture of capitalism.

It can be said that Marx and Engels lend credence to both the determinist and nondeterminist readings. For example, in *The Poverty of Philosophy*, Marx asserts that '[t]he windmill gives you society with the feudal lord; the steam mill, society with the industrial capitalist' (Marx [1847]1963). And Engels (1940) argued for a series of dialectical 'laws' – 'the transformation of quantity into quality', 'the interpenetration of opposites', 'the negation of the negation' – that, he believed, were applicable equally to the natural and social worlds. This inspired a whole generation of Soviet writers, including G. V. Plekhanov, who adopted and popularized the doctrine of 'dialectical materialism' as a Unified Science – an all-inclusive model of explanation. Many contemporary Marxists have distanced themselves from this 'scientism', which, philosopher Roy Bhaskar (1993) argues, was 'neither presupposed nor entailed' in Marx's analysis of capitalism.

Nevertheless, there is evidence that both Marx and Engels' dialectical project was far more flexible than any strict determinist model. Engels, in a series of 'revisionist' letters in the 1890s (Marx and Engels 1982), objected to the use of the materialist conception of history as an abstract formula imposed externally on the objects of study. And Marx maintained, in Volume 3 of *Capital*, that one must always take into account the 'innumerable different empirical circumstances, natural environment, racial relations, external historical influences, etc.' which are responsible, in any given society, for 'infinite variations and gradations in appearance'. The scientific study of society is immanent to its context and must be 'ascertained only by analysis of the empirically given circumstances' (Marx [1894]1967).

In the period following Marx's death, this scientific study of society became central to the discipline of sociology. As Bottomore (1983) suggests, some of the early sociologists, such as Ferdinand Tönnies, acknowledged their indebtedness to Marx, just as others – for example, Max Weber and Emile **Durkheim** – pursued their sociological work 'in critical opposition to Marxism'. Still, there have been notable Marxist contributions to sociology by Carl Grünberg, Karl Kautsky, Franz Mehring and Georges Sorel. And despite early communist governments' directives against sociology as a 'bourgeois' discipline, sociological studies were published by Russian and Austro-Marxists, as well as by 'Western Marxists' and the critical theorists of the Frankfurt School. While such writers as Georg Lukács, Karl Korsch and Antonio Gramsci developed the historical materialism of the Marxist paradigm, others, such as Louis Althusser and Nicos Poulantzas, have combined that paradigm with various insights from structuralism, functionalism and systems theory.

References and further reading

Alexander, Jeffrey C. (1982) *Theoretical Logic in Sociology, Volume Two: The Antinomies of Classical Thought: Marx and Durkheim*, Berkeley, CA: University of California Press.

Avineri, Shlomo (1968) *The Social and Political Thought of Karl Marx*, Cambridge: Cambridge University Press.

Bhaskar, Roy (1993) *Dialectic: The Pulse of Freedom*, London: Verso.

Bottomore, Tom (1975) *Marxist Sociology*, London: Macmillan.

—— (1983) 'Sociology', in Tom Bottomore, Laurence Harris, V. G. Kiernan and Ralph Miliband (eds), *A Dictionary of Marxist Thought*, Cambridge, MA: Harvard University Press, pp. 450–3.

Engels, Frederick. (1940) *Dialectics of Nature*, New York: International Publishers.

Flacks, Richard (1982) 'Marxism and Sociology', in Bertell Ollman and Edward Vernoff (eds), *The Left Academy: Marxist Scholarship on American Campuses*, New York: McGraw-Hill, pp. 9–52.

Giddens, Anthony. (1979) *Central Problems in Social Theory: Action, Structure and Contradiction in Social Analysis*, Berkeley, CA: University of California Press.

Lefebvre, Henri (1968) *The Sociology of Marx*, New York: Pantheon.

Lenin, V. I. (1973) *The State and Revolution*, Peking: Foreign Languages Press.

Marx, Karl (1845) 'Theses on Feuerbach', in Karl Marx and Frederick Engels, *Selected Works*, New York: International Publishers, 1968, pp. 28–30.

—— ([1847]1963) *The Poverty of Philosophy*, New York: International Publishers.

—— ([1867]1967) *Capital: A Critique of Political Economy, Volume 1: The Process of Capitalist Production*, New York: International Publishers.

—— ([1894]1967) *Capital: A Critique of Political Economy, Volume 3: The Process of Capitalist Production as a Whole*, New York: International Publishers.

Marx, Karl and Engels, Frederick ([1848]1968) 'Manifesto of the Communist Party', in Karl Marx and Frederick Engels, *Selected Works*, New York: International Publishers, pp. 31–63.

—— (1982) *Selected Correspondence, 1844–1895*, third revised edition, Moscow: Progress Publishers.

Meek, Ronald L. (1954) 'The Scottish Contribution to Marxist Sociology', in John Saville (ed.), *Democracy and the Labour Movement*, London: Lawrence and Wishart, pp. 84–102.

Ollman, Bertell (1976) *Alienation: Marx's Conception of Man in Capitalist Society*, second edition, Cambridge: Cambridge University Press.

—— (1993) *Dialectical Investigations*, New York: Routledge.

Sherman, Howard J. (1995) *Reinventing Marxism*, Baltimore and London: Johns Hopkins University Press.

Therborn, Goran (1976) *Science, Class and Society: On the Formation of Sociology and Historical Materialism*, London: New Left Books.

CHRIS MATTHEW SCIABARRA

MAUSS, MARCEL

Mauss (1872–1950) was the nephew and the closest collaborator of the founder of French sociology, Emile **Durkheim**. His contributions to economic sociology focused on the comparative analysis of religious practices and exchange systems in traditional societies. After Durkheim's death, he brought French sociology to its 'anthropological turn' celebrated in his famous *Essai sur le don* (*The Gift*; 1923/1924 for the French issue). Extending B. Malinowski's, F. Boas' and R. Thurnwald's fieldwork studies, *The Gift* presents the theoretical achievement of Mauss' anthropological findings. It reflects major breaks within the Durkheimian tradition and leads to four innovative theses on exchange, money, economic moral and social economy.

Mauss does not conceive the transformations of societies as linear evolutions from elementary to complex aggregates. Elementary facts such as the kula ring of Trobriand's archipelago are often more complex than those of industrial societies. As Mauss demonstrates it in *The Gift*, social facts such as things, men, messages and forms of social relations are always *total social facts*, i.e. concrete and circulating conglomerates made up of all possible aspects of daily life (physical, magical, economical, aesthetical, juridical). Mauss conceives these totalities as *symbolic systems*. Against Durkheim's normative assumption of a society regulated by **solidarity** through consensus on collective values, Mauss shows that the growth of societal complexity generates a simplification of social relations. With 'simplification', Mauss means a double process of desymbolization of societal totalities by functional specialization of economic exchanges. The division of labour reflects such a simplification. It does not reinforce organic solidarity in our society, as Durkheim believed, but weakens it.

Symbolic and economic exchanges

Symbolic exchanges are realized as gift-relationships which Mauss generally defines as the articulation of three interdependent moments: *to give, to receive* and *to return*. They provide for all systems a dynamic structure as *systems of total benefits* function on the principle of intra- and intergenerational mutual obligations that Mauss calls *total reciprocity*. As Karl **Polanyi** underlines it in *The Great Transformation* (1944), total reciprocity embedded the economy in symbolic exchanges through the social complexity of contracts. The societal value and legal validity of contracts root directly in symbolic exchanges. Therefore, economic exchange is far from being 'natural'

and prior to each possible form of societal exchanges. As to reciprocity, it could neither be reduced to the economic logic of costs and benefits (G. C. Homans), nor conceived as a universal norm (C. Lévi-Strauss, A. Gouldner). It depends on how, when and where human beings have to reciprocate in order to make social relations possible. Mauss replaces Durkheim's conception of *societal* constraints to integration in a relational dimension (coined with the concept of *collective habits*) for which symbolic exchange is the matrix-element of every human society.

Money

As far as societies analysed in *The Gift* are concerned, Mauss shows that money is attached to the personality of their owners and related to the status of clans (*vaygu'a*). As a *total social fact*, money appears in these societies mostly in the form of a talisman with magical power (*dzó*) which disseminates value to its owner. However, the owner can only stabilize the value of its money if he/she gives it away (and, further, his/her property) to someone else in the process of symbolic circulation. Money has only sense and value in these societies if it is used to stimulate the ongoing constitution of society. With the emancipation of the economic exchange from the symbolic, money gains more and more instrumental functionality. In industrial societies, it appears to be the impersonal and privileged means of economic exchange that establishes its own value exclusively within the logic of economic circulation of goods. Detached from the personality of exchangers, money progressively runs out of their control and influences immediately the circulation of merely economic exchanges.

The moral basis of the economy

Mauss indicates that symbolic gift-exchanges constitute the anthropological 'rock' of human societies and the moral basis of the economy. Although most of the time empirically visible only at the margins of our daily life, as for example when friends exchange presents, gift-relationships are nevertheless always an active principle of our daily social relations. Yet, the continuity of the gift-relationships' logic through time and space should not be taken for granted as a proof of an intrinsic and global harmony of social justice and economical progress. On the contrary, the growth of the economy uncontrolled by symbolic exchanges as a world-wide phenomenon shows the fragility of such an interlinkage. In order to reinforce it and to develop a **moral economy** in our societies, Mauss encourages its renewal in a spirit of community and association: in other words, in a gift's spirit. This is Mauss' political project, which is not a romantic or reactionary one (as for F. Tönnies' or C. Schmitt's political theories) but a progressive one that stands in the tradition of C.-H. de Saint-Simon and P. Leroux. It is directly related to corporative socialism or, to put it in the words of Célestin Bouglé, to 'socialism with a human face'.

Social economy

In his younger years, Mauss was an active corporatist close to the socialist leader Jean Jaurès. He took part in the Boulangerie corporation for primary education of French workers and also contributed to the founding of the still existing French newspaper *L'Humanité*. Mauss saw the possibility of a social economy in the collaborative work between the scientist and the politician. The scientist has to inform the politician on the state of social relations in society. The politician can then decide on the best policies to develop in order to favour the harmonious merging of the economy in society based on the cooperation of all social partners. Instead of aiming at a collective revolution, Mauss preferred

to stimulate an original vision on human relations where the economy enhances solidarity which could then in turn foster economic progress and growth.

References and further reading

Fournier, M. (1994) *Marcel Mauss*, Paris: Fayard.
James, W. and Allen, N. J. (eds) (1998) *Marcel Mauss. A Centenary Tribute*, New York and Oxford: Berghahn Books.
Tarot, C. (1999) *De Durkheim à Mauss, l'invention du symbolique. Sociologie et sciences des religions*, Paris, La Découverte/M.A.U.S.S.

ALDO HAESLER
CHRISTIAN PAPILLOUD

MAXIMIZATION

In 1932 Lionel Robbins laid down the 'nature and scope' of economics (1932). Robbins insisted that the subject concerned the allocation of scarce resources to meet unquestioned, conflicting and limitless ends. Robbins was also quite sure that the economist could draw a clear distinction between ends and means. From this effort it was not long before economics came to be one of the few disciplines to be defined by its method rather than by its subject matter. Economics came to be about 'economizing' and maximization figures prominently in this reigning view.

If one is supposed to assess allocation of scarce resources then it follows that constrained maximization is the method of choice. If one is to analyse what firms allegedly do, then maximization (of profit) is the method of choice. If one is to analyse what individuals allegedly do then maximization (of utility) is the method of choice. If one is to discuss what it means to be rational then some economists insist that rationality is the same as maximization. After all, starting with the presumption of self-interest, rationality entails maximizing what is in the interest of the individual. Others will insist that rationality entails the making of choices that are consistent with preferences. Since the nature and content of individual preferences is notoriously problematic, much of this literature is content to suggest that choices are, by definition, reflective of preferences and so rationality becomes a word applied to choices made rather than with reference to individual preferences. And of course maximization with respect to individual preferences may or may not entail maximization of individual welfare. Our preferences are not at all perfect constituents of our welfare.

Maximization figures large in all of economics. When an economic problem is first formulated the economist will inevitably write it down as a maximization problem – and from this start the first- and second-order conditions will be derived to reveal the properties of a maximum. Indeed, to those who worry that economics has become too much like physics – and too little like the other social sciences – it is precisely here that the controversy is centred.

Maximization is not limited to individual (or firm) choice. The theory of social choice and **collective action** employs similar algorithms to derive the properties of optimal social choice – an optimal choice being that which compares the aggregate valuations individuals attach to alternative social states, and declares the one most desirable (the socially preferred state) as that which produces the largest net surplus. It is from this surplus social dividend that the gainers from a social choice could (but never must) compensate the losers from that choice and still retain some of the surplus brought about by the social choice.

References and further reading

Graaff, J. de V. (1957) *Theoretical Welfare Economics*, Cambridge: Cambridge University Press.

Kreps, David M. (1990) *A Course in Microeconomic Theory*, Princeton, NJ: Princeton University Press.

Robbins, Lionel (1932) *An Essay on the Nature and Significance of Economic Science*, London: Macmillan.

DANIEL W. BROMLEY

MEANS OF CONSUMPTION/ CATHEDRALS OF CONSUMPTION

Means of consumption are those things that make it possible for people to acquire goods and services and for the same people to be controlled and exploited as consumers. More specifically, George Ritzer (1999) has described the means of consumption with the term 'cathedrals of consumption', to draw attention to the importance of the spectacular and enchanting places in which much of late and postmodern consumption occurs, such as shopping malls.

The term 'means of consumption' originates in Karl Marx's writings where it served as a complement to his better-known concept, the means of production, which refers to those things that make possible the production of commodities and the control of workers, e.g. factories. Marx's use of the term 'means of consumption' differs significantly from the way the term is used now. For Marx the means of consumption referred to the form in which commodities enter individual consumption, either as luxury or subsistence items. As such, Marx did not distinguish between commodities, and the means by which commodities are made available for consumers. In effect, Marx explained issues of consumption through theories of production, thus exhibiting a productivist bias. However, at beginning of the twenty-first century, at least in the western world, consumption has replaced production as the dominant form of social life, and as such has called for theories that explain consumption, and the means of consumption, as social processes and structures in themselves.

Michael Miller (1981), Rosalind Williams (1982) and Walter Benjamin (1999) studied the nineteenth-century precursors to our contemporary means of consumption. Both Williams and Miller take the French department store Bon Marché as exemplary of the early means of consumption. According to Williams, these department stores used décor to create enchanted 'dream worlds' which would allow consumers to live out fantasies and purchase related goods. Miller also investigated the Bon Marché, though his interest was in describing the way that the department store eventually rationalized, or disenchanted, the earlier, more fantastical incarnations described by Williams. Benjamin's massive *Arcades Project* provides a tour through the nineteenth-century Parisian arcades. The arcades developed with the invention of iron construction, after which time it was possible to cover alleyways and their shops with glass roofs. As such, the arcades became an early version of the department store, filled with the spectacle of indoor lighting, exotic commodities and new types of persons. Despite descriptions of these early department stores and shopping areas, the means of consumption did not come into their own until after World War II, as a result of growth in the American economy. As consumption replaced production at the centre of American economic life, means of consumption have proliferated and undergone significant transformations, ultimately creating a condition in which consumption, or better yet, hyperconsumption, dominates nearly all areas of life.

Despite their widespread success in the United States, and now around the world, the means of consumption face a dilemma. Cathedrals of consumption attract consumers because they satisfy the desire for fantasy, magic and dream that is generally absent from the modern, rationalized and disenchanted world described by Max Weber. In other words, the cathedrals of consumption attract consumers by re-enchanting a disenchanted world. However, in order to continue to accomplish the objectives of attracting, controlling

and exploiting consumers, the cathedrals of consumption must themselves submit to the disenchanting processes of rationalization. As the cathedrals of consumption grow larger, and offer consumers a greater number of consumables, the operators of these cathedrals must develop new techniques to ensure the efficiency, calculability, predictability and control that is necessary to maintaining large-scale profitable spectacles, but also to convincing consumers to purchase commodities that they oftentimes don't need or want. Furthermore, cathedrals of consumption are faced with the problem that as they proliferate, the fantasies that they offer become redundant, numerous instances of 'more of the same'. In turn, attempts to overcome this problem lead to a further escalation of spectacle.

Postmodern theory, and in particular the work of Jean Baudrillard, offers insight into the techniques that are used to re-enchant cathedrals of consumption. At the most general level, cathedrals of consumption are spectacles – dramatic public displays that provide consumers with exhilarating and dream-like experiences. Examples of spectacular consumption settings include Disneyland, the Mall of America, luxury cruise ships, themed restaurants and the casinos and hotels of Las Vegas. The spectacle is used to overcome the liabilities, especially the disenchantment, associated with highly rationalized structures. More specifically, spectacles are created through the techniques of simulation, implosion and the compression of time and space. Simulation achieves its spectacular effect by collapsing the distinction between the real and the imaginary. Through simulation, cathedrals of consumption can mimic, and render even more spectacular, natural environments, fictional settings and historical monuments, as is the case with the Luxor 'pyramid' hotel in Las Vegas. As a complement to the concept of simulation is the technique of theming, in which spectacle is achieved by carrying a particular motif

441

throughout all aspects of a cathedral of consumption. The theme establishes a self-contained world in which an imaginary reality provides a consistent spectacle. The term 'implosion' refers to the disappearance of boundaries so that previously differentiated entities collapse in upon one another. One example of the application of this technique is found in mega-malls that contain not only a seemingly limitless number of diverse goods and services, but also offer opportunity for entertainment (movie-going, gambling) and recreation (water-parks, mini-golf courses). The spectacle is created not only through the grandiose size of the buildings which house these imploded settings, but also in the phantasmagorical experience of abundance and seemingly limitless opportunity. Similarly, the term 'compression of time and space' describes an environment in which the limits traditionally imposed by time and space are overcome. The simulation of historical and futuristic environments, as well as the sale of 'ancient artifacts' in museum stores, fantastically implodes the boundaries between past, present and future with dizzying and exhilarating effects. In terms of space, the creation of colossal, nearly boundless spaces impresses the consumer with an awesome experience that cannot be encountered in everyday life.

Though the cathedrals of consumption emerged in response to the growth of consumption, they have subsequently had the effect of transforming the way that people consume, and society more generally. In contrast to the past, where consumption was limited to the exchange of goods, consumption is now an activity that contains elements of entertainment, recreation and the demand for spectacle. Furthermore, the ubiquity and phantasmagorical attraction of the new means of consumption have transformed consciousness to the extent that consumption is central to people's thinking, even when they are not actively consuming. In addition, the success of the cathedral 'model' has led to its increasing

adoption by institutions that have traditionally resided outside of the sphere of consumption. Athletic facilities, living communities, universities and hospitals are all examples of institutions that have recently begun to think in terms of consumers and their demand for spectacle. Finally, though the principal examples of cathedrals of consumption are large, centrally located material environments, the Internet promises to play an important role in the creation and elaboration of new means of consumption. Though the Internet does not exist in material space, its ability to simulate realities, implode differences and collapse time and space places it in an ideal position to create phantasmagorical and dreamlike environments for consumers.

References and further reading

Baudrillard, J. (1970/1998) *The Consumer Society*, London: Sage.

Benjamin, W. (1999) *The Arcades Project*, translated by R. Tiedemann, Cambridge, MA: Belknap/Harvard University Press.

Miller, M. (1981) *The Bon Marché: Bourgeois Culture and the Department Store, 1869–1920*, Princeton, NJ: Princeton University Press.

Ritzer, G. (1999) *Enchanting a Disenchanted World: Revolutionizing the Means of Consumption*, Thousand Oaks, CA: Pine Forge Press.

Williams, R. (1982) *Dream Worlds: Mass Consumption in Late Nineteenth-Century France*, Berkeley, CA: University of California Press.

GEORGE RITZER
JEFFREY STEPNISKY

MECHANISMS, SOCIAL

See: Social Mechanisms

MENTAL MODELS

Cognition is a process by which actors come to know and judge phenomena. Mental models shape what people perceive, how they process perceptions, and how they store and retrieve information. Economic actors use mental models to organize what they experience into expected relationships and to frame their understandings and responses appropriately. In complex situations, actors seek familiar patterns and expected relations, and use mental schemata to construct strategies of action. These mental models are constructed from experience and a situational understanding of what others are likely to do, what has worked in the past and, given this, what shape future market conditions are likely to take. In the following, we will relate the ways cognition and mental processes or economic mentalité have been approached in the study of markets and economic contexts.

Microeconomic theories (see **economics, history of**), **rational choice theory** and game theoretic approaches to economic settings are united in their reliance on methodological individualism: an implicit mental model of **economic action** that views individual persons as the elementary and only appropriate unit of analysis of human action(s). Likewise, individuals are also assumed to seek maximum **utility** in any given exchange. For microeconomic and classical theories of economy, social ties, norms of reciprocity, familial obligations, among other 'social forces' are typically conceived of as indirect influences on actor choice (i.e. cognitive processes) and often as distortions to the optimal exchange and distribution of goods and services. Closely aligned with neoclassical models of market mentalité, rational choice theorists also view cognition and subsequent action as rationally motivated, instrumental and calculated. Likewise, game theorists operationalize the same suppositions as those above in studying the interdependent decision-making where two or more actors perform in competitive–cooperative scenarios. As theoretical statements that outline the contours of mental processes in economic settings, microeconomic, rationalist, and game theoretic accounts also underlie a good many sociological explanations of both individuals and corporate forms in economic contexts (Hechter and Kanazawa 1997).

In contrast to these quasi-models of human cognition in economic contexts, sociological and social psychological research by a number of scholars has demonstrated that 'rationality' is both limited by the cognitive capacities of human beings as well as bounded by the context within which actors are embedded. In short, this research has found the assumptions of human behaviour operationalized under methodological individualism to be unrealistic.

Bounded rationality, as it relates to economic contexts and actor cognition, is intended to convey the idea that economic decision-making always involves incomplete information processing under a certain degree of uncertainty. This research has exposed the limited capacity of humans to make 'comprehensively' rational decisions. However, this does not presuppose irrationality; rather, actors are viewed as intendedly rational given cognitive, but also structural, cultural and network constraints. To more accurately address decision-making processes, several theorists have adopted less synoptic, bounded conceptions of mental processes captured in notions such as Lindblom's 'disjointed incrementalism', Etzioni's 'mixed scanning' and Simon's **satisficing**.

Recent developments in cognitive psychology are just beginning to find their way into economic reasoning (Kahenman and Tversky 2000). The most notable are those that have developed the importance of psychological heuristics in cognition and problem-solving. Cognitive psychologists have found that rather than abstractly weighing alternatives and deducing from a stable set of premises a course of action, actors make judgements and choices based on situational expectations using inductive logic. Working hypotheses are revised in response to feedback from others and from new observations. Called mental heuristics, they act as cognitive short-cuts or 'rules of thumb' from which actors make decisions, especially when confronted with complex circumstances. The importance of information in economic settings along with their inherent uncertainty makes understanding the heuristics economic actors employ especially relevant.

Cognitive science's concern with heuristics as the basis of mental modelling of the complex world around us has developed out of research on individual psychology, but sociological research affirms and supplements these ideas in ways that hold promise for understanding economic action (Biggart and Beamish 2003). For example, while cognitive psychologists argue that heuristics are limitations, cognitive anchor points that constrain the available options to those defined by the mental model, they fail to note, as sociologists have, that judgemental heuristics are simultaneously socially facilitating. For example, Alfred Schutz showed that people think in typifications: **ideal type**s that guide everyday life (see **phenomenology and ethnomethodology**). What is more, pragmatists such as Charles Pierce, William James, James Dewey and George H. Mead all built on the seemingly contradictory notion that limited cognition is the enabling basis of social interaction. While constraining to comprehensive choices, the boundaries intersubjectivity places on human consciousness supply the foundations for stability precisely because they limit the debilitating effects of interactional uncertainty, a prerequisite of symbolic interaction in economic settings.

Sociologists concerned with actor subjectivity have variously argued that economic settings as inherently social ones are organized social constructions and that actors impose frames of meaning on experience. These sense-making practices make meaningful economic interaction and exchange possible. At the level of interpersonal interaction, mental 'scripts' make exchange routinized and unproblematic, and at the level of industries and economies 'institutionalized' understandings and arrangements facilitate economic action by providing agreed-upon, often tacit, ways of conducting business. While not necessarily the product of conscious calculus and deductive logic, everyday economic action can be understood as inductively rational and straining towards efficiency, the result of practical reason that reflects both social setting (see **embeddedness**) and network domains, which result in specific situational logics.

What is more, sociological research has also highlighted that the content and structure of mental models vary culturally across societies and over time in any given society. Economic sociologists contend that actors are socially situated and mental models are only understandable in terms of social structure in which action takes place. Actors who ignore established arrangements and conventions, this research also tells us, risk being unintelligible to others or judged immoral or irrational.

Finally, the **Convention School**, like social interactionists, view the paralysing potential of uncertainty as a critical problem that undermines traditional economic assumptions of the 'rational actor' (see **rational choice theory**). They ask: in situations where preferences cannot be ranked, or where the interpretation of facts is debatable, is rationality possible? For the Convention School, rationality is itself an uncertainty reduction strategy that reflects the need for economic actors to 'justify' their actions to other market co-participants. Such 'justifications' become conventionalized models for action that lend acts and practices 'normality' and 'rightness'. In short, conventions theorists find economic coordination to reflect self-conceived 'rational individuals' who achieve it via obedience to shared mental models of 'what ought to be': the rules, norms, values and intersubjectively that describe the market within which they act (see **norms and values**).

References and further reading

Biggart, Nicole Woolsey and Beamish, Thomas D. (2003) 'The Economic Sociology of Conventions: Habit, Custom, Practice, and Routine in Market Order', *Annual Review of Sociology*, 29: 443–64.

Hechter, Michael and Kanazawa, Satoshi (1997) 'Sociological Rational Choice Theory', *Annual Review of Sociology*, 23: 191–214.

Kahenman, D. and Tversky, A. (2000) *Choices, Values, and Frames*, New York: Cambridge University Press.

THOMAS D. BEAMISH

MERGERS AND TAKEOVERS

Consider firms from three different perspectives: (1) firms as governance associations (a polity); (2) firms as a production coalition (team); and (3) firms as a commodity. For the most part, the focus on mergers and takeovers reflects the third of these visions – the firm as a commodity.

Mergers

Mergers reflect two (or more) firms combining ownership, governance and financial attributes into a new single going concern. Mergers can arise for a variety of reasons – to absorb a competitor, diversify against co-variant risk, acquire a promising research and development programme, acquire a particularly valuable brand name, or to blend two highly complementary commercial activities. The evidence is mixed about the long-run benefits of mergers (Hogarty 1970). It seems that somewhat less than half of all mergers turned out to be financially beneficial (Bleeke and Ernst 1993).

Takeovers

Takeovers (acquisitions) represent the second avenue to creating new combinations of firms. Some takeovers are not contested while others are bitterly resisted by the target firm. Takeovers are motivated by rea-sons similar to those for mergers. The difference is that here there is an aggressor and an unwilling target. In addition to the above reasons for takeovers, the most important reason can be traced to the idea of the firm as a commodity. If we start here, then takeovers can be understood under the concept of asymmetric information. Essentially, those who originate takeovers have different (better?) information about the target's financial performance than the stock market. This asymmetry means that the 'commodity value' of the target firm is thought by the aggressor firm to be higher than is generally recognized by others (including the current managers of the firm). If the aggressor can acquire a controlling interest in the target firm at a price below the imagined value of the commodity (firm), then profitable opportunities exist. A related dimension is that the aggressor firm often brings serious reorganization plans to the purchase of the target firm. Once the aggressor has acquired control then sweeping managerial and product changes may be imposed to reduce costs of the target firm. Indeed, many takeovers are driven by confidence on the part of the aggressor that, with adequate managerial discipline and judicious cost-cutting, the poorly managed firm can become much more valuable than it now is under its current management. As with mergers, the evidence seems strongly mixed as to the financial wisdom of most takeovers.

References and further reading

Ben-Porath, Yoram (1980) 'The F-Connection: Families, Friends, Firms and the Organization of Exchange', *Population and Development Review*, 6: 1–30.

Bleeke, J. and Ernst, D. (eds) (1993) *Collaborating to Compete: Using Strategic Alliances and Acquisitions in the Global Market Place*, New York: John Wiley and Sons.

Hogarty, Thomas F. (1970) 'The Profitability of Corporate Mergers', *The Journal of Business*, 43: 317–27.

Jensen, M. C. and Ruback, R. S. (1983) 'The Market for Corporate Control', *Journal of Financial Economics*, 11: 5–50.

Mandelker, G. (1974) 'Risk and Return: The Case of Merging Firms', *Journal of Financial Economics*, 1: 303–35.

Putterman, Louis (1988) 'The Firm as Association versus the Firm as Commodity', *Economics and Philosophy*, 4: 243–66.

DANIEL W. BROMLEY

METHODENSTREIT

The history of economics has been punctuated by two significant debates over fundamental questions of methodology. These debates consist of the first ('older') and the second ('younger') Methodenstreit ('battle of Methods').

The *first Methodenstreit* raged during the 1880s over the question of whether economics was a historically or theoretically based discipline. The main protagonists during this early debate were the Austrian Carl Menger (1840–1921) and the most influential representative of the German **historical school**, Gustav Schmoller (1838–1917). In his 1883 *Untersuchungen über die Methode der Sozialwissenschaften*, Menger defined the aim of economics as the formulation of universal laws such as those found in the natural sciences. According to this line of thought, only the purely deductive method permits the construction of a general theory of economics that is beyond time and place. The empirical-inductive research method merely offers the more or less arbitrary collection of empirical phenomena from which general conclusions cannot be drawn.

In the same year, Schmoller (1883) defended vehemently the empirical-historical method and denied the use of a purely abstract theory. According to Schmoller, those who start out with mere hypotheses end up with hypothetical conclusions, which should not to be labelled with the misleading word 'exact' as if it were 'higher science'. In Schmoller's view, economics

has to contribute to the solution of actual social problems and should, therefore, be closely linked to reality. Schmoller ceased to take part in the debate after a thorough critique of his work by Menger (1884), in effect bringing the battle between the protagonists swiftly to an end.

The *second or 'younger' Methodenstreit* saw the re-airing of aspects of the older one. The starting point of the controversy was an essay written by Max **Weber** in 1904. Weber's critique of the intermingling of objectively proven statements with personal value judgements and political bias was provoked by the focus on economic policies by the spokesman of the German historical school. Weber argued that the social sciences should not try to draw-up a blueprint for the future (*Sollensaussagen*) or make demands on the political process. According to his view it was of central importance on the part of social scientists to state clearly that value judgements could not be objectively proved and thus should be clearly identified as such.

The 'older' and the 'younger' Methodenstreit gave rise to two important conclusions: First, the equal methodological worth of the empirical-inductive and the theoretical-deductive methods was recognized, and second, the necessity of a clear distinction between objective analysis and value judgements was acknowledged.

References and further reading

Menger, Carl (1884) *Die Irrthümer des Historismus in der deutschen Nationalökonomie*, Vienna: Alfred Hödler.

Ritzel, Gerhard (1950) *Schmoller versus Menger. Eine Analyse des Methodenstreits im Hinblick auf den Historismus in der Nationalökonomie*, Offenbach: Bollwerk-Verlag.

Schmoller, Gustav von (1883) 'Zur Methodologie der Staats- und Sozialwissenschaften', *Jahrbuch für Gesetzgebung, Verwaltung und Volkswirtschaft im deutschen Reich*, 7: 974–94.

Weber, Max (1968) 'Die "Objektivität" sozialwissenschaftlicher und sozialpolitischer Erkenntnis (1904)', in Max Weber, *Gesam-*

melte Aufsätze zur Wissenschaftslehre, Tübingen: J. C. B. Mohr, pp. 146–214.

NORBERT REUTER

MICROCREDIT

Microcredit, or microfinance, refers to the practice of extending very small loans to affinity groups or small entrepreneurs who lack the necessary collateral for larger loans from **banks** or other lending institutions. Modern microcredit groups, typically of fifteen to twenty participants, are organized by employees of nongovernmental organizations (NGOs), although native microfinance groups, called rotating savings and credit associations, or 'roscas', are formed by participants.

The NGOs loan money to affinity group participants, such as fellow villagers, who must repay the funds on time in order to get further loans. Successful repayment of a small loan may lead to a more substantial loan in the future. The money in the fund, initially supplied by the NGO, 'belongs' to the group, and if there are defaults there is less money available to everyone.

Some microfinance organizations (MFOs) offer training in business development, in creating networks, nutrition and child care education, and offer other services for borrowers. In contrast to credit markets that rely on intermediation and legal tactics to collect on debts, microcredit relies on social pressure and mutual trust to guarantee high rates of repayment once the microenterprise has been established. Microenterprise refers to the model of small businesses funded by microcredit. Microcredit and microenterprise programmes can be found in a number of countries, including the United States, not only in 'developing' nations. The aim of many MFOs is specifically to alleviate rural poverty by enabling independent business schemes in order to reduce dependence on programmes such as 'food for work' or other 'welfare' programmes (Nanda 1999).

The inception of the Grameen ('Village') Bank Project is considered by most to mark the beginning of formalized microcredit lending practices. In 1976, an American-trained economics professor, Dr Muhammad Yunus, along with colleagues at the University of Chittagong, began the Grameen Bank Project as an action-research programme. The project was designed to provide credit and banking services for the rural poor in Bangladesh. In 1983, the project was transformed by government ordinance into what is now known as the Grameen Bank. The Grameen Bank claims that after 1995, it has not solicited donor funds (Grameen Bank 2003). Many microfinance organizations (MFOs) operate with the assistance of funds from governmental or nongovernmental organizations, or from development agencies, such as the World Bank or the United States Agency for International Development (USAID). The degree to which MFOs can or should be financially independent is the object of some debate (see Anderson *et al.* 2002: 103, n. 3).

Microcredit generally is touted as being a grassroots, or 'bottom-up', rather than top-down development strategy. Microcredit programmes often focus on providing credit specifically to women, aiding women to become financially independent. Women's economic well-being raises the living standard of more people because they are the primary caretakers of children. Case studies of the effectiveness of specific programmes indicate that greater financial independence may positively affect health care (Nanda 1999) and demonstrate household income growth. (e.g. Copestake *et al.*'s 2001 study of the Peri-Urban Lusaka Small Enterprise Project).

A criticism of targeting women for microcredit enterprises is that participation in these programmes may simply reinforce gender segregation in business and impose a patriarchal logic on to women's business organizations (Ehlers and Main 1998).

While the solvency of MFOs rests largely on their high repayment rates, there have been criticisms on methodological grounds of claims that MFOs are largely successful, and there have been investigations into the institutional factors that contribute to low loan repayment rates in some MFOs (Woolcock 1999).

The social conditions under which microcredit programmes are likely to succeed or fail are similar to those found in roscas or rotating savings and credit associations, which have been widely studied. Roscas are micro saving and credit institutions that develop indigenously, unlike modern microcredit institutions organized by NGOs. However, their structure and logic are much the same.

Roscas have a number of variations but typically are a group formed by participants who agree to make regular contributions to a fund which is given to each contributor in rotation. For example, if eleven participants agree to contribute $10 a month for eleven months, each would get the 'pot' once in that period, with the pot 'rotating' among each of the members in subsequent months. The amounts and rotation period can vary substantially.

Just as in modern microcredit institutions, there is no intermediation by a bank. Rather, social pressures function enforce contribution to the fund as promised. Roscas are often used for microenterprise purposes, but also for hedging against crop risk, commodity purchases and other financial needs.

Roscas, like microcredit, are found around the world in culturally, religiously and organizationally disparate societies in Asia, South America and Africa and in ethnic enclaves of developed nations. They do not exist everywhere, however, and comparative research gives evidence that this form of microcredit is only sustainable under five conditions (Biggart 2001).

First, roscas only exist where social structure is built on strong communal bases. Roscas are found in societies organized by kinship networks, clan membership and common identification with a native place or place of cohabitation, all bases for group identification and mutual control of participants. Second, roscas are found in societies where obligations, including debts, are communal. Reputation is an important source of social collateral and all members of a dishonoured family are damaged by the default of any one member. In these settings, obligations are often interpreted diffusely and are not limited by contract, either real or implied.

Third, roscas exclude people who do not demonstrate social or economic stability, however that is defined in the society. In the close communities in which roscas typically form, participants have rich, direct information both on the economic condition of actors and on their moral standing. Fourth, roscas are commonly found in settings of social or geographic isolation where members have no credit alternatives. For example, rotating savings and credit associations can be found in isolated villages where they are the only available source of money and in ethnic enclaves where members are socially excluded from participation in other credit institutions.

Finally, roscas only occur among people who share a similar social status, as more powerful members would be difficult to control through the informal means available to the other rosca members.

Under these five circumstances, affinity lending groups operate under conditions of rich information, social pressures to repay, and few if any alternative credit sources. In the absence of these conditions, intermediation and risk-pooling serve to support credit markets.

References and further reading

Anderson, C. L., Locker, L. and Nugent, R. (2002) 'Microcredit, Social Capital, and Common Pool Resources', *World Development*, 30: 95–105.

Biggart, N. W. (2001) 'Banking on Each Other: The Situational Logic of Rotating Savings and Credit Organizations', *Advances in Qualitative Organization Research*, 3: 129.

Conlin, M. (1999) 'Peer Group Micro-lending Programs in Canada and the United States', *Journal of Development Economics*, 60: 249–69.

Copestake, J., Bhalotra, S. and Johnson, S. (2001) 'Assessing the Impact of Microcredit: A Zambian Case Study', *Journal of Development Studies*, 37: 81–100.

Ehlers, T. B. and Main, K. (1998) 'Women and the False Promise of Microcredit', *Gender and Society*, 12: 424–40.

Grameen Bank (2003) *Grameen: Banking for the Poor*, online. Available at http://www.grameen-info.org/index.html (accessed 21 April 2003).

Light, I. and Gold, S. J. (2000) *Ethnic Economies*, San Diego, CA: Academic Press.

Morduch, J. (1999) 'The Microfinance Promise', *Journal of Economic Literature*, 37: 1569–614.

Nanda, P. (1999) 'Women's Participation in Rural Credit Programmes in Bangladesh and their Demand for Formal Health Care: Is There a Positive Impact?' *Health Economics*, 8: 415–28.

Snow, D. R. and Buss, T. F. (2001) 'Development and the Role of Microcredit', *Policy Studies Journal*, 29: 296–307.

Woller, G. M. and Woodworth, W. (2001) 'Microcredit and Third World Development Policy', *Policy Studies Journal*, 29: 265–6.

Woolcock, M. J. V. (1999) 'Learning from Failures in Microfinance: What Unsuccessful Cases Tell Us about How Group-Based Programs Work', *American Journal of Economics and Sociology*, 58: 17–42.

NICOLE WOOLSEY BIGGART
PENNEY ALLDREDGE

MICROSOCIOLOGY OF MARKETS

Microsociology has traditionally covered such territory as individual conduct, subjective meaning and the interaction order as accomplished in the face-to-face situation. Thus microviewpoints have traditionally been pitched at the level of *local* social forms; they have espoused an understanding of the microworld as tied to the physical setting and the social occasion, which are thought to be governed by principles and dynamics not simply continuous with or deducible from macrosociological (i.e. collective) processes and structures. A microsociology of markets cannot limit itself to the sort of reality that is focused on small spaces. By definition, markets involve transactions between many individuals and they may include distanciated spatial configurations, like those exemplified by global **financial markets**. What a microsociology of markets can offer to aggregate studies is the opening up of the processes of economic transactions across physical space. Microsociologists construct the marketworld anew by travelling inside markets, aiming at the 'molecular' level of markets' constitutive mechanisms, meanings and performative characteristics. Markets would seem to be particularly amenable to such an analysis, since they are not dominated by central authority structures but are constituted from within the performance chains of the market interface with the help of micromechanisms of coordination. A microsociological orientation can reveal processes that contradict external and macro-level concepts that have sometimes given short shrift to the actual realization of economic behaviour and to the phenomenology of real markets.

A basic conceptual shift presupposed by a microsociology of markets is the move from a focus on embodied social forms to response-presence based social forms where participants are capable of responding to one another and to market presentations in real time without being physically present in the same place. The paradigm case for response-presence based situations is that of dispersed domains linked up by information technologies, the arteries of transnational and global connectedness through which interactions flow. One task of a microsociology of markets is to reveal how technology systems enable and instantiate contemporary markets as sequentially and culturally specific actions performed at a distance. For example, contemporary financial markets embraced technology early and inhabit it more thoroughly than most other social forms do. Specific studies of such markets have revealed the presence of 'scopic' systems, that is of mechanisms of gathering up and projecting market reality comprehensively in ways that allow participants to become oriented to the reality presented rather than to individual transactions. Markets dominated by scopic systems function differently from network markets, with which electronically based markets tend to be equated. A focus on how markets are performed thus not only reveals how contemporary social forms 'inhabit' technologies, it also reveals differences between markets that determine market outcomes. A further task of a microsociology of markets is to investigate the types and patterns of structural and cultural variation that correspond to these differences and that establish multiple modes of market transactions (e.g. Smith 1993; Abolafia 1996; Preda 2004).

Modern markets are complex systems that include a variety of components, all of which, in turn, invite microsociological study. For example, market transactions normally involve payment systems and money as means and instruments of exchange. It has conventionally been assumed, as regards market transactions, that money and markets dehumanize our lives, supplanting social ties, meanings and moral values as impersonal, rationalized and instrumental principles of thinking and organization spread ever further. Yet close studies show that money and compensation are not neutral media of exchange but rather involve processes of attribution, earmarking and differentiation that restore meanings to money and associate payments with categories of social relations (Zelizer 1996). Similarly, close historical studies, rather than exposing the 'uncompromising objectivity' of money and its indifference to culture and social structure, reveal instead just how intricately connected it is to the construction of identities and its symbolic role in purveying images of collectivity and in conveying political ideology. Microstudies thus steer the analytic attention away from the assumption that modern money promotes economic calculation and rationality and is a common 'denominator for all values'. It shows instead how money cultivates various kinds of emotional attachment that affect economic and social behaviour (Helleiner 2003).

Microstudies can also disclose what lies at the root of financial crises and breakdowns. For example, MacKenzie (2003) has shown that markets develop unstable patterns of imitation among market participants who monitor and often know each other. Imitation leads to extreme price movements and to disaster when positions have to be abandoned because of an exhaustion of capital with which to ride out these price movements. Imitative practices of this sort may be a defining characteristic of 'global microstructures', patterns of relatedness and coordination that are microsocial in character and that assemble and link a global domain (Knorr Cetina and Bruegger 2002). Partially overlapping financial market positions that are interwoven with social patterns of interaction exemplify such structures. A further task of the microsociology of markets is to identify the structures of connectivity and integration that characterize the global social systems embedded in the respective economic transactions.

What we learn from a microsociology of markets may have implications for other domains, for example for that of transnational electronic services that rely on technological modes of labour integration similar to those found in financial markets. The microsocociology of markets has started to contribute to the sociology of globalization; for example, the concept of a global microstructure is applicable not only to markets but also to transnationally operating terrorist groups and to other domains that are interrelated by observation, communication and interaction patterns across space. The microsociology of markets also contributes to the understanding of the knowledge society and economy. Financial markets in particular have developed specialized roles for professional analysts and researchers who assess and define market reality for other participants, thus illustrating the working of knowledge within other societal operations.

References and further reading

Abolafia, Mitchel (1996) *Making Markets*, Cambridge, MA: Harvard University Press.

Helleiner, Eric (2003) 'One Market, One People: The Euro and Political Identities', in P. Crowley (ed.), *Before and Beyond the Euro*, London: Routledge, pp. 183–202.

Knorr Cetina, Karin (2003) 'From Pipes to Scopes: The Flow Architecture of Financial Markets', *Distinktion*, 7: 7–23.

Knorr Cetina, Karin and Bruegger, Urs (2002) 'Global Microstructures: The Virtual Societies of Financial Markets', *American Journal of Sociology*, 107(4): 905–50.

MacKenzie, Donald (2003) 'Long-Term Capital Management and the Sociology of Arbitrage', *Economy and Society*, 32(3): 349–80.

Preda, Alex (2004) 'The Investor as a Cultural Figure of Global Capitalism', in Karin Knorr Cetina and Alex Preda (eds), *The Sociology of Financial Markets*, Oxford: Oxford University Press.

Smith, Charles (1993) 'Auctions: From Walras to the Real World', in Richard Swedberg (ed.), *Explorations in Economic Sociology*, New York: Russell Sage Foundation, pp. 176–92.

Zelizer, Viviana (1996) 'Payments and Social Ties', *Sociological Forum*, 11: 481–95.

KARIN KNORR CETINA

MIMETIC PROCESSES

See: institutionalism

MODERNITY

While numerous, attempts to formulate a concept of modernity that compels most social scientists to adhere to a common reference frame remain inconclusive at the outset of the new millennium. By default, mainstream social scientific perspectives on modern society adhere strongly to the neoclassical paradigm, and reflect above all a common understanding of *modern capitalism* – rather than an understanding of society that is more expansive than the prevailing mode of production. As a result, the majority of perspectives do not facilitate a grasp of the essential differences between modern society in general, as a practical, historically specific set of social conditions, and modernity as a cultural programme articulated in and through the normative presuppositions prevalent in particular modern societies (see Eisenstadt 1996). The aim of articulating a working definition of modernity, as a cultural programme, cannot be taken up without a coincident attempt to clarify how it is distinct from the terms 'modern society' and from the process of modernization. The latter concept, in particular, is commonly submerged in dehistoricized social scientific research orientations that fail to acknowledge the context-dependency of the progress that is associated with modernization. There is also a concomitant tendency to equivocate modernization with the more contradictory and complex forms of social, political and economic organization constituting modern societies. The term 'modernization' refers to historical processes, including secularization and demystification, individuation and democratization, bureaucratization, and the rationalization of means–ends technological relations and value orientations. The concept of modern society refers to a form of social organization that is both an order and a process. It differs from static concepts and categories which are necessary tools for research, but not sufficient means to capture the complexities, contingencies and contradictions that shape the modern condition. The term thus requires more critical as well as comparatively contextualized analysis.

Indeed, only a comparative approach to the analysis of modern societies can yield perspective on the features of particular societies that are generalizable (see Hall *et al.* 1996).

The problem of distinguishing the cultural programme of modernity from 'modern society' and 'modernization' is more specifically temporal. It is not only a matter of identifying and delineating historical trends leading up to the present. Social scientists must also analyse the possible constellations of society that are being projected by the values maintained and normative orientations put forward by the constituents of modern societies, who seek ways of practically realizing their ideals in and through political institutions and economic forms of organization whose 'vanishing point' is in the future. The constellation of social and political values and economic organization that spawned the cultural programme of modernity is recognized as historically rooted in the Enlightenment within the geographical locus of Western Europe and North America. It may be regarded as a cultural product of 'bourgeois society'. It is an outgrowth of modern nation-state formation and the re-mapping of traditional sovereign power into democratic-constitutional regimes – practical political venues for reconciling Enlightenment ideals of equality and freedom, with the real structures of social inequality that are a functional precondition for, and an inescapable consequence of, economic growth and development in capitalist market economies. The end of the cultural programme of modernity is to resolve the tension between the real unequal social structure and the modern ideal of prosperity benefiting all members of society. The rationally as opposed to traditionally grounded normative ideals associated with democratic-constitutional institutions, however, will remain unattainable as long as the organization and functioning of economies adheres to capitalist market principles (see

Dahms 2005). Indeed, the inability of modern societies to practically facilitate the political expression of human agency and the actualization of democratic normative ideals within the ambit of modern bureaucratic institutions has brought into question the veracity of the Enlightenment ideals in the late twentieth century. This lacuna has yielded the suspicions contemporary postmodernists convey that the new knowledge spheres generated by the Enlightenment congeal in societal networks or regimes of power rather than opening new venues for emancipation. And these critical theoretical perspectives, in turn, have cast doubt on the cultural programme of modernity.

A comparative grasp of the distinction between non-modern, modern and postmodern orientations of social scientists also deepens our perspective on the concept of modernity. In addition, the understanding that the concept being constructed in the social sciences can also be furthered by distinguishing between the three variations in the modernist perspectives social scientists are advancing: the traditionally modernist, reflexively modernist and radically modernist perspectives. Though frequently unrecognized, differences in conceptions of modernity, particularly in specific norms modernists maintain as universally valid, lie at the heart of variations of social-scientific perspectives today. The divergent claims made by neoclassical economists and economic sociologists evince this point. Depending on whether social scientists frame research explicitly in terms of modernity and in the context of modern society, or do so implicitly, the research priorities, standards and values they espouse vary greatly. Social scientists relating their research interests explicitly to a concept of modernity situate their research in the modern age as a historically specific context. Social scientists who work with an *implicit* concept of modernity tend to presume the existence of a direct link between the methods, concepts and theories developed in the sciences and social sciences during the last two centuries, and the tools and frameworks facilitating an adequate grasp of the nature of 'reality', and any aspect thereof. Their perspective is *traditionally modern*. If social scientists include the history of science (including the social sciences) in analyses of modern society, their interest relates to a concept of modernity *explicitly*, and their perspective is *reflexively modern*. If, in addition, they emphasize that social research must guard against the danger of replicating assumptions about modern societies that are central to modern modes of legitimating structures of power and inequality – politically, economically, socially and culturally – their perspective is *radically modern*. Social scientists who work without a concept of modernity that is discernable – either to others or to themselves – tend to hypostatize the dominant features of modern societies, as they are manifest at specific points in time – without focusing on the more problematic features as warranting particular attention. Rather than scrutinizing the specificity of societal contexts, such research remains on a *nonmodern* terrain by eschewing the plurality of problematic contexts that might taint its ends. 'Nonmodern' research, as such, tends to submerge and perpetuate rather than reconcile the tensions between normative ideals espoused in modern societies. Postmodernist critiques of modernist social research paradigms, apply most boldly to 'nonmodern perspectives', in which the absence of any expressly stated set of normative orientations precludes the possibility of drawing a concept of modernity from the research. Nonmodern social research presupposes that the accumulation of 'knowledge' (in the sense of purportedly objective data) in all instances is conducive to progress, and that modernization processes constitute progress. In contrast to the nonmodernist, implicit or explicit claim that the legitimacy of its scientific insights would be compromised by such a descent

into the 'ideological' terrain, postmodernists explicitly reject assertions that normative ideals or values can influence the direction of structural change in contemporary society. Refuting the modernist position that **norms and values** can convey a universalizable ideal of humanity as a species that could be realized on a practical terrain of human plurality, postmodernists deny human agency the capacity to influence the social development of political and economic systems and the discursive spheres of scientific knowledge as structural relations of power in contemporary society. Postmodernists do not generally grant the domain of culture – in which humankind enlarges on its deliberative capacities and engages in political practice – sufficient weight to construct a conception of modernity as cultural programme. Nor do representatives of the postmodern perspective, such as Michel Foucault, maintain that the eighteenth-century Enlightenment altered the historical process of 'modernization' in a way that admitted any new emancipatory potential. By elaborating on a comparativist perspective on modernity, as distinct from the postmodern and nonmodern, we can, in short, stress the context-dependent, historically specific nature of modernity as a project being undertaken in a variety of forms.

Like nonmodernists, *traditionally modern* social scientists claim that modernization processes are conducive to progress. However, they more often maintain that such processes as secularization and individuation necessarily advance 'modernity' as well, albeit modernization theorists, structural functionalists and conflict theorists do concede the extent to which modernization can be deleterious to progress. According to the reflexive modernists Anthony Giddens and Ulrich Beck, the link between modernization processes and progress/modernity is of central concern, and the nature of the link between both an empirical question, as the challenge is to reconcile the conflicting forces that have been shaping modern societies. *Radical modernists* (e.g. Jürgen Habermas, Nancy Fraser) contend that formal modernization processes follow a logic that threatens to eviscerate the achievements of modernity. *Postmodern* approaches (e.g. Michel Foucault) emphasize that the objective of the above approaches is to produce types of knowledge oriented towards both maintaining and concealing the tension between modernity and modernization, as a configuration of power relations that continually reproduces itself. The critique formulated by postmodernists suggests that, since the 1970s, processes conducive to *modernity* as a quality of modern societies have given way to *modernization* processes which, in light of sustained efforts to interpret modernization processes as being conducive to modernity, marked the onset of the postmodern age, and the need for a radical break with modern traditions (see Kumar 1995).

The significance of modernity as a cultural programme may be further illustrated by reflecting on the extent to which neoclassical economics, on the one hand, and economic sociology, on the other, contribute to this telos. The ends of neoclassical economics can be situated at the point of intersection between traditional and nonmodern approaches (see Ruccio and Amariglio 2003). By contrast, the classics of sociology commenced with the observation that markets and capitalism are historically specific formations, and thus temporally circumscribed as economic processes, as opposed to alternative economic organizations and processes which would have the potential of being more conducive to resolving, rather than reinforcing, social, political and cultural problems (see Amin 2003). Where social scientists (including economists) acknowledge the historical specificity of the last two centuries of economic development, they generally concede that markets and capitalism are both

modern phenomena and central to modernity. However, the neoclassical paradigm continues to suspend the logic of markets and processes of capital accumulation in space and time, and thus eliminates the possibility of drawing on the reflexive perspective that took root in the classical theoretical foundations of sociology (Max **Weber**, Emile **Durkheim**, Georg **Simmel**). The paradigm of economic sociology may represent the greatest promise where its proponents embrace, and amplify, this reflexivity. In such efforts, the attempts by theoretical sociologists to move beyond postmodern dilemmas, while retaining key insights, will provide important pointers about how to proceed from here (Agger 2002; Antonio 1998; Lemert 1997).

References and further reading

Agger, Ben (2002) *Postponing the Postmodern. Sociological Practices, Selves, and Theories*, Lanham, MD: Rowman and Littlefield.

Amin, Samir (2003) *Obsolescent Capitalism. Contemporary Politics and Global Disorder*, translated by Patrick Camiller, New York. ZED Books.

Antonio, Robert J. (1998) 'Mapping Postmodern Social Theory', in Alan Sica (ed.), *What is Social Theory? The Philosophical Debates*, Malden, MA: Blackwell, pp. 22–75.

Dahms, Harry F. (2005) 'Does *Alienation* have a Future? Recapturing the Core of Critical Theory', in L. Langman and D. K. Fishman (eds), *Trauma, Promise, and the Millennium: The Evolution of Alienation*, New York: Rowman and Littlefield.

Eisenstadt, S. N. (1996) 'The Cultural Program of Modernity and Democracy: Some Tensions and Problems', in R. Kilminster and I. Varcoe (eds), *Culture, Modernity and Revolution: Essays in Honor of Zygmunt Bauman*, New York: Routledge, pp. 25–41.

Hall, Stuart, Held, David, Hubert, Dan and Thompson, Kenneth (eds) (1996) *Modernity. An Introduction to Modern Societies*, Malden, MA: Blackwell.

Kumar, Krishan (1995) *From Post-Industrial to Post-Modern Society. New Theories of the Contemporary World*, Malden, MA: Blackwell.

Lemert, Charles (1997) *Postmodernism Is Not What You Think*, Malden, MA: Blackwell.

Ruccio, David F. and Amariglio, Jack (2003) *Postmodern Moments in Modern Economics*, Princeton, NJ: Princeton University Press.

HARRY F. DAHMS
KIMBERLY P. BARTON

MONEY, SOCIOLOGY OF

Money has received less attention in recent economic sociology than other major economic institutions. A little over a decade ago, an authority could write that 'there is no systematic sociology of money' (Zelizer 1991: 1304). Progress has been made – for example, Dodd (1994), Zelizer (1994), Ingham (1996, 2004) – but it remains a relatively underdeveloped field. The relative neglect is all the more puzzling as there exists a promising sociology of money in the 'classics' – notably, in Weber and Simmel. However, modern sociology has given their work a one-sided interpretation that has focused on money's social meanings, cultural effects and its consequences for the emergence of 'modernity' (Giddens 1990). With a few notable exceptions (Carruthers and Babb 1996), the question of the actual social production of money as a social institution has received less attention. Sociology has taken money's existence for granted. Two features of the development of the social sciences account for this situation. First, money was implicitly assigned to economics in the division of intellectual labour after the **Methodenstreit** during the late nineteenth and early twentieth centuries. Eventually, the neoclassical economic explanation of money's existence was tacitly, and mistakenly, accepted. As Randall Collins remarked, it would appear that money was not 'sociological enough' (quoted in Zelizer 1994). Second, the influence of **Marx** on modern sociology has had similar consequences. His analysis of money was grounded in the narrowly economic classical labour theory of value and is largely concerned with money's

effects as an expression of human **alienation** in capitalism (Ingham 2001).

Money and the Methodenstreit

During the dispute, **Schumpeter** observed that '[t]here are only two theories of money which deserve the name . . . the commodity theory and the claim theory. From their very nature they are incompatible' (quoted in Ingham 2004: 6). All orthodox economic theories of money are based on the commodity theory. From the late nineteenth century onwards, economics sought to establish 'laws' deduced from the axioms of individual **utility** maximization and the consequential equilibrium model of the perfectly competitive market. Here, the 'economy' comprises exchange ratios between commodities (object–object relations) expressed in money prices, established by individuals' calculation of the utility of commodities (individual agent–object relations). These relations constitute what is known as the 'real' economy (for the classic description, see Schumpeter [1954]1994: 277). This is essentially a model of a (moneyless) barter economy in which agent–agent (social relations) are not analytically significant. **Barter** is held to transform myriad bilateral exchange ratios into a single market price for a uniform good. Money is introduced into the model as a commodity that functions as a medium of exchange – for example, cigarettes in prison. As a commodity, the medium of exchange can have an exchange ratio with other commodities. Or as a symbol, it can directly represent a commodity or commodities. It is in this sense that money is a 'neutral veil' that has no efficacy other than to overcome the 'inconveniences of barter' which, in the late nineteenth-century formulation, result from the likely absence of a 'double coincidence of 'wants' in bilateral trade (see Ingham 2004).

Menger's (1892) explanation of money's evolution remains the basis for subsequent neoclassical analysis (for a survey, see Klein and Selgin 2000). Money is the unintended consequence of individual economic rationality. In order to maximize their barter options, traders hold stocks of the most tradable commodities which, consequently, become media of exchange – beans, iron tools, cigarettes, etc. Coinage is explained with the conjecture that precious metals have additional advantageous properties – such as durability, divisibility, portability, etc. Metal is weighed and minted into uniform pieces and the commodity becomes money. Money is the spontaneous result of catalectic exchange (Ingham 2000). The progressive 'dematerialization' of money broke this explanatory link between individual rationality and system benefits. Why should the 'individual be ready to exchange his goods for little metal disks apparently useless as such, or for documents representing the latter?' (Menger 1892: 239–40). Modern neoclassical economics tries to resolve the problem by showing that holding (non-commodity) money reduces transaction costs for the individual (Klein and Selgin 2000). There are three major problems. First, orthodox economic method cannot distinguish money from any other commodity – that is to say, it cannot specify the 'moneyness' of money. In this regard, economics misunderstands the significance of the abstract, or nominal, money of account. Medium of exchange is taken to be the key function of money and it is assumed that the others (money of account, means of payment, store of value) follow from it. The market spontaneously produces a transactions-cost efficient medium of exchange that becomes the standard of value and subsequently the nominal money of account. For example, coins evolved from weighing pieces of precious metal that were cut from bars and, after standardization, counted.) However, there are both a priori and empirical grounds for reversing the sequence. Money of account

is logically anterior and historically prior to the market (Aglietta and Orléan 1998).

How could a measure of value (money of account) emerge from myriad bilateral barter exchange ratios based upon subjective preferences? One hundred goods could yield 4,950 exchange rates (Davis 1994: 16). What transforms discrete barter exchange ratios of, say, three chickens : one duck, or six ducks : one chicken, and so on, into a single unit of account? Economics' argument that a 'duck standard' emerges 'spontaneously' is circular. A 'duck standard' cannot be the equilibrium price of ducks established by supply and demand because, in the absence of a money of account, ducks would continue to have multiple and variable exchange values. An arbitrarily fixed, anterior abstract measurement of value (money of account) is necessary in order to produce an authentic market that can generate a single price for ducks. If the process of exchange could not have produced the abstract concept of money of account, how did it originate? Can an inter-subjective scale of value (money of account) emerge from myriad subjective preferences? The question is at heart of a problem that distinguishes economics from sociology. (For an account of the social origins of money of account, see Ingham 1996.) Second, the explanation of money in terms of transactions costs reduction also exposes the logical circularity of neoclassical economics' methodological individualism. Neoclassical economic explanations are not able to advance beyond a statement that it is 'advantageous for any given agent to mediate his transactions by money provided that all other agents do likewise' (Hahn 1987: 26 quoted in Ingham 2004). However, to state the sociologically obvious: the advantages of money for the individual presuppose the existence of money as a social institution. Third, the model of the natural barter, or 'real', economy with its 'neutral veil' of money is inappropriate for the capitalist monetary system. The financing of production by bank credit-money does not take place in the model of the 'real' economy; money exists only as a medium for gaining utility through the exchange of commodities (see Smithin 2003).

The other side in the Methodenstreit – the German **historical school** – held to one version or another of the credit, or claim, theory of money. Regardless of its specific form or substance, money is a 'token' claim – that is, credit – for goods and the discharge of debt. Credit tokens are accorded a nominal value by a money of account – pounds, shillings, dollars, cents, euros, etc. Money does not take its value from its substantive commodity content; all money, including precious metal coin is 'credit'. These theories have two sources: in the attempts to understand early capitalist credit instruments – private bank notes, bills of exchange; and in the 'state theory' of money (Knapp [1924]1973). This approach is implicitly sociological: money is not a 'thing' or commodity, but a social relation of credit and debt – most importantly, tax debt. States issue money to pay for their purchases, which the population must accept in order to meet their tax payments. 'Moneyness' is constituted by the issuers' (**banks** and states) denomination of credit in abstract value (money of account) and their promise to accept it back in payment of a debt. The promise may be backed by precious metal, or some other commodity; but this is not essential – as modern 'dematerialized' money demonstrates. Rather, money is constituted by the social relation of credit-debt; it is a promise to pay (Ingham 1996, 2004).

Influence of the 'historical school' on Simmel, Weber, Keynes

The importance of **Simmel**'s *The Philosophy of Money* ([1907]1978) for the analysis of the money's role in the cultural relativism and individual freedom of 'modernity' is well documented. For Simmel, money turns the world into an 'arithmetical problem' and 'the complete heartlessness of money is reflected in our social culture which itself is determined by money' (Simmel [1907]1978: 346). But he also extends the historical school's work on the specificity of 'moneyness' and its social production. Money is abstract – 'the value of things without the things themselves' (Simmel [1907]1978: 121); and a socially constructed 'claim'. The 'common relationship that the owner of money and the seller have to a social group – the claim of the former to a service and the trust of the latter that this claim will be honoured – provides the sociological constellation in which money transactions, as distinct from barter, are accomplished' (Simmel [1907]1978: 178; note that economic theory does not make this distinction between barter and exchange with money).

Weber's analysis of money was influenced by economic theory (von Mises) and, more importantly, by Knapp's 'magnificent book' (Weber 1978: 184). Weber endorses the economists' emphasis on money as a medium of exchange that makes possible multilateral, indirect, spatially and temporally separated exchange – that is to say, the market. But, 'these consequences are dependent on what is, in principle, the most important fact of all, the possibility of monetary calculation' (Weber 1978: 80–1): that is to say, by the use of a nominal money of account. For Weber, money is not a 'neutral' medium of exchange, but a 'weapon' in the 'struggle for economic existence' (Weber 1978: 108). The 'scarcity' and value of money is socially and politically determined by the clash of interests (Weber 1978: 79). 'The public treasury does not make its payments simply by deciding to apply the rules of the monetary system which somehow seems to it ideal, but its acts are determined by its own financial interests and those of important economic groups' (Weber 1978: 172).

Following Knapp, **Keynes** held that: 'Money of Account, namely that in which Debts and Prices and General Purchasing Power are expressed is the primary concept of a Theory of Money' (Keynes 1930: 3, 4–6, 11–15). Money of account, imposed by 'state or community', confers the quality of 'moneyness' and makes its possible to distinguish money from commodities (Keynes 1930: 5). Keynes's conception of money informs modern post-Keynesian and 'monetary circuit' heterodox economic theory (for a surveys, see Smithin 2003; Parguez and Seccareccia 2000; Ingham 2004). Again, this approach is implicitly sociological in the emphasis on the social production of money through the 'monetization' of debt by banks in their linkage to the central bank and state (Ingham 2004). In a similar way to Weber, some post-Keynesian economists hold to a social conflict model of inflation that suggests a reversal of the causal link between money and prices in the orthodox economic 'quantity' theory. That is to say, prices rise as a result of advantages gained from market power in the 'struggle for economic existence' – as in 'cost–push' wage inflation. The banking system responds to these claims by producing the necessary amount of credit-money in the form of loans (see Smithin 2003; Ingham 2004).

The Marxist theory of money

According to the labour theory of value, precious metal becomes a measure of value because the labour of mining and minting can be expressed in 'the quantity of any other commodity in which the same amount of labour-time is congealed' (Marx [1867]1976: 186). But in a departure from classical economic theory, Marx argued that money is a double 'veil'. As orthodox economics maintains, it 'veils' the 'real' relations between commodities; this also masks the underlying social relations of production appear as monetary relations.

For example, the level of money wages 'appears' to be the result of an equal economic exchange between capital and labour, but is in fact an expression on exploitative power relations. Tearing away these monetary 'veils' will demystify the alienation and capitalism will become 'visible and dazzling to our eyes' (Marx [1867]1976: 187). Marx's analysis points money's ideological naturalization of capitalist social relations – as, for example, in modern economic theory's concepts of the 'natural' rates of interest and unemployment (Smithin 2003). But, Marx follows classical economics in not granting autonomy to money (Ingham 2004); money's value cannot be separated from a material base of either its costs of production or as the embodiment of labour time. Consequently, Hilferding's later Marxist theory of 'finance capital' does not grasp that the social 'manufacture' of capitalist bank money through the act of lending involves the creation of abstract value in the social relation of debt (Ingham 2004). As expressed by post-Keynesian theory, bank loans create deposits of money *ex nihilo*.

Money in modern sociology

Parsons' early work helped to confirm the division of intellectual labour between economics and sociology. In *Economy and Society* (1956) Parsons and Smelser see money as a generalized medium of communication that facilitates the integration of the functionally differentiated parts of the social system – in an analogous way to prices in the economy. Parsons followed neoclassical economics' axiom that value is only realizable in exchange and that money is no more than a symbol of value. This tradition does not acknowledge the obvious fact that money is abstract value *sui generis* that may be appropriated (For a critique, see Ganssmann 1988). This general approach persists in the work of Habermas, **Luhmann** and Giddens (Ingham 2004). In

Giddens's *The Consequences of Modernity* money is a 'symbolic token' or 'media of interchange' (sic) that promotes 'systemic complexity' and the 'time space distanciation' of modernity (Giddens 1990). However, the explanation of the social production of money is taken no further than a reiteration of the importance of trust. Zelizer's *Social Meaning of Money* (1994) acknowledges that modern sociology has accepted economics' conception of money as a universal medium of exchange, but does not explicitly dispute the adequacy of its explanation. Rather, Zelizer argues that economic theory fails to grasp that money has multiple social meanings. Money is subjected to social 'earmarking' – for example, prostitutes carefully budget their welfare benefits, but they squander their earnings (Zelizer 1994: 3). The production of national or state money is not seen as a sociological question. Helleiner has addressed this question directly in *The Making of National Money* (2003).

Money is not merely socially produced – by mints, central banks, etc. – it is also *constituted* by the *social relation* of credit-debt (Ingham 1996, 2004). Money is essentially a promise to pay. *After* 'moneyness' has been established by the issuer's money of account and embodied in a particular form (metal, paper, electronic impulse, etc.), it then takes on the status of a 'commodity' that is exchangeable for goods (purchasing power) and other moneys in foreign exchange markets (exchange rate). In other words, once money has been produced, then economic analysis is applicable to some degree; but it is essential to understand that it cannot explain the existence of money. Furthermore, economic analysis of the exchange value of money for goods, and for another money, needs to be supplemented by sociological analysis because the *scarcity* of money is socially and politically determined. At the macro level the 'supply' of money is structured by the rules and norms governing fiscal practice (for

example, 'sound money' principles) which are the outcome of a struggle between economic interests in which economic theory plays a 'performative' role (Ingham 2004). In capitalism, the pivotal struggle between creditors and debtors is centred on forging a 'real' rate of interest (nominal rate minus inflation rate) that is politically acceptable and economically feasible. On the one hand, too high a real rate of interest will deter entrepreneurial debtors and inhibit economic dynamism. On the other hand, too low a rate or, more seriously, a negative rate of interest (inflation rate in excess of nominal interest rate) inhibits the advance of money-capital loans (Smithin 2003; Ingham 2004). On the micro level, credit-rating produces a stratification of credit risk that regulates the demand for money by differential interest rates and the refusal of loans. This has an autonomous impact on the reproduction of inequality through 'Matthew Effects': the rich receive low-interest credit and the financially excluded fall prey to 'loan sharks' (Ingham 2004). Other important areas that require a sociological analysis are the social and political construction of 'inflation expectations' by central bankers and the financial press. A promising sociology of inflation flourished in the 1970s (Hirsch and Goldthorpe 1978), but waned with the decline of its subject matter. The revitalization of economic sociology should now address this *economic* sociology of money as opposed to the narrower focus on its social and cultural effects.

References and further reading

Aglietta, M. and Orléan, A. (eds) (1998) *La Monnaie Souveraine*, Paris: Odile Jacob.
Carruthers, B. and Babb, S. (1996) 'The Colour of Money and the Nature of Value: Greenbacks and Gold in Postbellum America', *American Journal of Sociology*, 101: 1556–91.
Davies, G. (1996) *A History of Money*, Cardiff: University of Wales Press.
Dodd, N. (1994) *The Sociology of Money*, Cambridge: Polity Press.

459

Ganssmann, H. (1988) 'Money – a Symbolically Generalized Medium of Communication? On the Concept of Money in Recent Sociology', *Economy and Society*, 17: 285–315.

Giddens, A. (1990) *The Consequences of Modernity*, Cambridge: Polity Press.

Helleiner, E. (2003) *The Making of National Money: Territorial Currencies in Historical Perspective*, Ithaca, NY: Cornell University Press.

Hirsch, F. and Goldthorpe, J. H. (1978) *The Political Economy of Inflation*, London: Martin Robertson.

Ingham, G. (1996) 'Money is a Social Relation', *Review of Social Economy*, LIV, 4: 507–29.

—— (2000) 'Babylonian Madness: On the Historical and Sociological Origins of Money', in John Smithin (ed.), *What is Money?* London: Routledge, pp. 16–41.

—— (2001) 'Fundamentals of a Theory of Money: Untangling Fine, Lapavitsas and Zelizer', *Economy and Society*, 30(3): 297–309.

—— (2004) *The Nature of Money*, Cambridge: Polity Press.

Keynes, J. M. (1930) *A Treatise on Money*, London: Macmillan.

Klein, P. and Selgin, G. (2000) 'Menger's Theory of Money: Some Experimental Evidence', in John Smithin (ed.), *What is Money?* London: Routledge, pp. 217–34.

Knapp, G. F. ([1924]1973) *The State Theory of Money*, New York: Augustus M. Kelly.

Marx, K. ([1867]1976) *Capital*, vol. 1, London: Penguin Books.

Menger, K. (1892) 'On the Origins of Money', *Economic Journal*, 2(6): 239–55.

Parguez, A. and Seccareccia, M. (2000) 'The Credit Theory of Money', in John Smithin (ed.), *What is Money?* London: Routledge, pp. 101–23.

Parsons, T. and Smelser, N. (1956) *Economy and Society*, London: Routledge.

Schumpeter, J ([1954]1994) *A History of Economic Analysis*, London: Routledge.

Simmel, G. ([1907]1978) *The Philosophy of Money*, London: Routledge

Smithin, J. (2000) *What is Money?* London: Routledge.

—— (2003) *Controversies in Monetary Economics: Revised Edition*, Cheltenham, UK: Edward Elgar.

Weber, M. (1978) *Economy and Society*, Berkeley, CA: University of California Press.

Zelizer, V. (1991) 'Money', in E. F. Borgatta and M. L. Borgatta (eds), *Encyclopedia of Sociology*, New York: Macmillan, pp. 1304–10.

—— (1994) *The Social Meaning of Money*, New York: Basic Books.

GEOFFREY INGHAM

MONITORING

Monitoring is the process of acquiring information about the behaviour of individuals whose actions are inputs to a production process that yields an output or a contingent claims contract that yields a payoff. Prototypical cases of the former type that are of special interest in economic sociology include employers monitoring the actions of employees and boards of directors monitoring the actions of chief executive officers; cases of the latter type, of limited interest in economic sociology, include insurers monitoring the behaviour of insured. These are all instances of **principal and agent** relationships in which moral hazard is problematic because principals (e.g. employers and boards of directors) cannot structure incentives that will induce agents (employees and chief executives) to choose actions that optimally serve the interests of the firm. The canonical case of agents who have the ability to act in their own interest at the expense of the interest of principals arises when agents are capable of private actions that are imperfectly observable. Monitoring the action of agents is one potential remedy to this problem of imperfect information.

Monitoring emerged as a significant theoretical concept with the information revolution in economic theory that originated in the 1960s and gained momentum in the 1970s. The paradigmatic aspect of input performance that calls forth monitoring is the 'effort' of the agent. Monitoring is necessary when the payoff to the principal is increasing in effort, but effort has disutility for the agent and output alone provides imperfect information about effort because it responds to other elements of the environment (e.g. technology, economic cycles, weather, etc.) besides the actions of the agent, including other co-workers in team production. But monitoring is not just a means of determining an agent's individual contribution to output. Rather, it is a mechanism for increasing effort because it always implies some type of sanction of the agent for lack of 'effort', typically firing or dismissal.

Monitoring should be distinguished from supervision, a much broader concept. The distinction is easily eclipsed because supervision encompasses monitoring. But supervision also includes among its characteristic dimensions such responsibilities as training, coordinating, planning, problem-solving, goal-setting, and more. Yet monitoring for effort is arguably the central element of supervision. Indeed, Alchian and Demsetz (1972), in an early essay in the economics of information, trace the functional origins of the capitalist firm to the problem of detecting shirking and measuring performance in team production processes subject to the threat of free-riding (see **free rider**). They argue that when it is costly under team production to directly measure marginal outputs of cooperating input units, monitoring is an efficient means of estimating marginal productivity by observing input behaviour. As for who will monitor the monitor, Alchian and Demsetz answer that the proper incentive is established if the monitor is given title to the net output (i.e. the residual that remains after covering input costs), the size of which will depend on the monitor's success in reducing shirking by the agents. Hence, the monitor is functionally equivalent to the owner of the firm.

Insofar as many core issues in economic sociology pertain to the nature of the employment relationship and to forms of ownership in capitalist economies, they are inherently linked to the monitoring of effort and provision of incentives in environments characterized by incomplete information. Since the 1980s monitoring has figured prominently in two lines of research that have broad relevance for economic sociology. First, historical debates about the rise of the factory and the success of the industrial revolution have revolved around the relative impact of the coordination as compared to the monitoring function of supervision. In a study of British manufacturing in the early nineteenth and twentieth centuries, Clark (1994) puts the significance of monitoring in historical perspective when he asks whether '[factory] discipline triumphed because it was required for coordination or because it coerced workers into giving more effort' (p. 130). Clark finds for the coercion theory in which supervisors monitor for effort and penalize workers whose behaviour deviates from factory rules of conduct. As he puts it,

> A puzzling aspect of [early] factory discipline was that instead of rewarding workers according to their output, it used the behavior of workers as a measure of performance ... Discipline systems rewarded and penalized workers on the basis of their inputs to the production process rather than their outputs.
> (p. 132)

Second, monitoring is a core concept of efficiency wage theory (Allgulin and Ellingsen 2002), which emerged in the early 1980s as an alternative to the competitive theory of wages. Efficiency wage theory asserts that firms may pay wages above market clearing as a means of eliciting performanceenhancing behaviour in production environments in which effort levels are problematic because monitoring is by nature impossible or too costly. The shirking version of the theory proposes that firms for whom monitoring worker effort is costly could pay more than the marketclearing 'going rate', and this premium would serve as the penalty that workers would bear if they lost their job because they were caught shirking. The

gift exchange version argues that in production environments in which workers enjoy a measure of freedom over their work because monitoring is problematic, employers **exchange** the 'gift' of above-market wages for the 'gift' of work effort in excess of the minimum standard. The gift-exchange occurs because both employer and employee are subject to **fairness** norms and gain intrinsic **utility** from behaviour that conforms to such norms. Since the difference between firms that pay wages above market clearing and firms that pay wages at market clearing is precisely the difference between primary and secondary sector firms, both theories posit the existence of a dual labour market that is generated by exogenously determined variation in monitoring technology.

There are other lines of theory and research in which monitoring plays a consequential role. The traditional problem of separation of ownership and control in the modern corporation is reflected in studies of the monitoring of chief executives by boards that represent shareholders (Hermalin and Weisbach 1998; Burkart *et al.* 1997). The empirical literature on the theory of ownership forms has shown how problems of efficiently monitoring effort may shape the boundaries of the firm (Holmstrom and Roberts 1998). Finally, theories of unionization have come to increasingly recognize the efficiency-enhancing action of unions in monitoring firms for adherence to the implicit terms of labour employment agreements (Hogan 2001).

References and further reading

Alchian, A. and Demsetz, H. (1972) 'Production, Information Costs, and Economic Organization', *American Economic Review*, 62: 777–95.

Allgulin, M. and Ellingsen, T. (2002) 'Monitoring and Pay', *Journal of Labor Economics*, 20: 201–16.

Burkart, M., Gromb, D. and Panunzi, F. (1997) 'Large Shareholders, Monitoring, and the Value of the Firm', *Quarterly Journal of Economics*, 112: 693–728.

Clark, G. (1994) 'Factory Discipline', *Journal of Economic History*, 54: 128–63.

Hermalin, B. and Weisbach, M. (1998) 'Endogenously Chosen Boards of Directors and their Monitoring of the CEO', *American Economic Review*, 88: 96–118.

Hogan, C. (2001) 'Enforcement of Implicit Employment Contracts through Unionization', *Journal of Labor Economics*, 19: 171–95.

Holmstrom, B. and Roberts, J. (1998) 'The Boundaries of the Firm Revisited', *Journal of Economic Perspectives*, 12: 73–94.

CHARLES N. HALABY

MONOPOLY AND OLIGOPOLY

A monopoly is a firm that dominates a market and is able to limit entrance to the market or set the terms of competition in its favour. In sociological terms, it has achieved social closure, the power to exclude other groups from membership or resources (Weber 1978). Thus the sociological analysis of monopoly would follow the same logic as other forms of inequality in the economy such as race, ethnicity, gender and class.

The main difference between an economics and a sociological perspective on economic monopoly is the extent to which monopolies can be explained by the dynamics of markets or requires the consideration of other non-market factors. Economists see monopoly as an imperfection of markets, a breakdown in the natural ability of markets to sustain competition. In properly functioning markets, no single firm has the ability to unilaterally set prices. On one hand, economies of scale and competitive pressures shake down inefficient producers, allowing the most efficient to increase their market share. If that were the only mechanism, markets would tend towards monopolization. On the other hand, when firms secure a large enough market share to charge monopolistic prices, it creates an incentive for others to construct innovations, enter the market and undersell monopolies. Thus the equilibrium between concentration through competition and market renewal through new entrants ensures that monopolies will be rare and temporary. Monopolies should arise only under two conditions: (1) when markets break down due to government interference, social chaos, or distortions; (2) when the nature of a product precludes competition creating a natural market, such as telephones for most of the twentieth century, or cable television today.

In contrast, sociologists do not see the market as a natural mechanism. The existence of markets, the extent to which factors of production such as land, labour and capital are commodified and subject to competitive pressures, and the operation of markets are all embedded in social institutions (Polanyi 1957). Insofar as markets do operate as self-regulating systems that sustain competition and limit monopoly, they are a matter to be explained in historical terms by showing how social institutions, cultural understandings and the distribution of power foster and sustain them. Several factors are especially important from a sociological perspective.

Economic entities

The firm takes many forms defined by law and other institutional arrangements. Law and custom determine whether economic actors are individuals, partners, families or larger collectivities such as corporations. Some are better situated to attain monopoly status than others. Corporations are collective entities empowered by law to act as singular economic entities: that is, as legal individuals or artificial persons. As such they are accorded **property** rights – the rights, entitlements and responsibilities that come with ownership. Some of these are specific to the corporation, such as limited liability, which protects owners from any debts of the corporation, providing a means

by which corporations can amass resources far in excess of individuals. Thus legal and social systems that give rise to corporations and that imbue them with powers unavailable to other sorts of economic entities will be more likely to foster the rise of monopolistic power. The corporation permits the aggregation of capital from many individuals (and from other corporations) into a single large enterprise in ways not possible in other types of organization, 'socializing' capital (Roy 1997). It is no coincidence that the first great wave of incorporation in American history at the turn of the last century led to the monopolization of many of America's dominant industries. Before 1890 there were fewer than ten industrial firms listed on the American stock exchange. By 1905, there were hundreds, including virtual monopolists such as Standard Oil, American Tobacco, American Sugar Refining Co. and US Steel, America's first billion-dollar company.

Power

From a sociological perspective, monopolization is a form of power; it is a process of social closure whereby a single actor (here an organizational actor) is able to use their power to exclude others from participating in an exchange relationship by creating a different set of rules for themselves than others must conform to (Weber 1978). Power can be understood as a characteristic of a relationship between actors such that the behaviour of one actor can be explained only by reference to the other. It can either take the form of domination, by which one actor imposes his or her will on the other, or the form by which one actor sets the consequences of decisions that the other actor makes (for example, a monopolistic firm sets prices that others in the market must follow). Power is both an explanation for monopoly and a result of it. Different theories focus on different aspects of power that explain monopolization.

463

The theory of finance capital argues that the operation of **banks**, brokerage firms and other financial institutions have fundamentally transformed capitalism from an earlier era, making the growth and success of firms depend more on their relationship to capital than to product markets (Hilferding 1981). Because finance capital is concentrated in so few hands and because each finance capitalist has investments in several firms, those with controlling interests in large corporations find that their interests are better served by constraining competition. In this theory monopoly is not only a type of organization, but also a stage of capitalist development, 'monopoly capitalism'.

Charles Perrow's theory of organizational power holds that large organizations themselves, merely by their scale, can mobilize the power to dominate their industries. They gain the political clout, relationships with suppliers and customers, and social presence to prevent others from competing on the same level (Perrow 2002).

Institutions

Institutions are clusters of categories, social relationships and practices that perform a vital social task for society. Economy, polity, family, medicine, news and religion are all institutions. The degree to which a set of categories, social relationships and practices are patterned, taken-for-granted as a given, and exclusively perform a task, they can be understood as institutionalized: that is, we look at institutionalization as a process, not just a fixed state (DiMaggio and Powell 1991). The role that institutions play is one of the fundamental differences between economic and sociological perspectives on the monopolization process. Economists distinguish between markets and institutions, treating the market as a natural set of social relations and institutions as social inventions that arise only when markets fail. Sociologists tend to treat the

market as an institution that arose historically and must be affirmatively explained (Polanyi 1957). The practical difference between the two perspectives is where one's explanatory focus must lie. If markets are treated as natural, as not institutional, there is no need to explain their appearance, only their breaching.

Besides the corporation itself, the institutional factor most important in the explanation of monopoly is government (see **embeddedness**; **state and economy**). The government both created the corporate form of monopoly and regulates competition. Here again, sociologists and economists differ. Economists treat government involvement in economic life as interference, assuming that markets operate naturally. Sociologists generally echo Polanyi's argument that markets arose less from the removal of government interference than from active government involvement in creating the social conditions that make markets possible (Polanyi 1957). When governments enforce contracts or property rights, issue money, charter banks, adjudicate commercial disputes, control borders or maintain social stability, they create, reproduce and regulate markets (Campbell and Lindberg 1990). There is always discretion in how they do those things. Thus sociologists tend to see the distinction between those governmental activities that 'intervene' or 'interfere' with markets and those that let the market operate naturally to be more of an ideological than an analytical concept. Thus, sociologists examine a broad array of government activities that facilitate or discourage monopolization.

One of the legal issues that most directly affects the tendency towards monopoly is that of anti-trust laws. Anti-trust laws were first passed in the United States in the late nineteenth century in response to popular concern over the rise of monopolistic corporations that were engaging in practices of predatory competition. Early legal decisions, most notably *US vs E. C. Knight* about the 'Sugar Trust', ruled that a firm that merely controlled an entire market did not violate the law. Anti-trust laws could only prohibit specific practices such as lowering prices to drive competitors out of business or colluding with competitors to keep prices high. The immediate effect of the first anti-trust laws was paradoxically to encourage the creation of large corporations. Practices that firms had used to maintain order in unstable markets were outlawed, but domination by one or a few firms was being facilitated by the new laws of corporate ownership.

How anti-trust laws could encourage monopoly is made more understandable by the introduction of one more institutional factor: corporate governance. If we think of clusters of producers, distributors and customers around related sets of products or services as an organizational field, not just a market, we gain a richer understanding of the dynamics that affect the rise of monopolies (or other aspects of the field). The concept of market implies that the relationships among the actors only exchange transactions –buying and selling goods and services. '**Organizational fields**' implies all the kinds of social relations found in institutions: the creation of categories, sets of practices, social boundaries – that is, social relationships, not just economic exchange (Fligstein 2001). One of the most important social aspects of organizational fields is the concept of governance, a non-economic concept that describes how different actors maintain social order among themselves. A market is one way of maintaining order – many small firms make decisions that in the aggregate create incentives and constraints on other firms. But few industries work this way entirely. Other common forms of governance include trade associations, cooperative ownership, government regulations and monopoly or oligopoly. The near-monopoly status in computer-operating systems enjoyed by Microsoft was due as much to a desire of most participants in the computer industry to maintain order and avoid the chaos of competition as any technological superiority or competitive advantage.

Historical perspective

The final principle of a sociological analysis of monopoly is a historical perspective. This means that the effect of any particular variable on the propensity towards monopoly depends on the historical context in which it operates. Anti-trust laws, financial capital and modes of institutional governance can have different effects in different historical circumstances. While economists aspire to create universal models, sociologists are more inclined to qualify generalizations by scope conditions that specify where and when the generalizations apply. Thus the process of monopolization will work differently depending on the prior conditions. For example, the first major merger movement at the end of the nineteenth century was nourished by the passage of anti-trust laws, while the merger movement in the late twentieth century was fostered by relaxing anti-trust laws.

Conclusion

Sociological analyses of monopoly are much broader and historically more specific than economic analyses. Because the market is not assumed to be natural and monopoly is not assumed to be unnatural, sociological analyses imply that the conditions that give rise to monopoly are more amenable to control, especially through public policy. That is not to say that sociologists are necessarily more optimistic about the likelihood that monopolies will be contained. They give greater attention to the ways that power can be used to build monopolies and derail attempts to limit them.

See also: capitalism; corporate governance; efficiency; equilibrium; firms; inclusion and exclusion; law and economy; markets,

465

sociology of; mergers and takeovers; path-dependence; Polanyi, Karl; Weber, Max.

References and further reading

Campbell, John L. and Lindberg, Leon N. (1990) 'Property Rights and the Organization of Economic Activity by the State', *American Sociological Review*, 55: 634–47.

DiMaggio, Paul J. and Powell, Walter W. (1991) 'Introduction', in Walter W. Powell and Paul J. DiMaggio (eds), *The New Institutionalism in Organizational Analysis*, Chicago: University of Chicago Press, pp. 1–38.

Fligstein, Neil (2001) *The Architecture of Markets: An Economic Sociology of the Twenty-First-Century Capitalist Societies*, Princeton, NJ: Princeton University Press.

Hilferding, Rudolf (1981) *Finance Capital*, Boston: Routledge and Kegan Paul.

Perrow, Charles (2002) *Organizing America: Wealth, Power, and the Origins of Corporate Capitalism*, Princeton, NJ: Princeton University Press.

Polanyi, Karl (1957) *The Great Transformation: The Political and Economic Origins of Our Time*, Boston: Beacon.

Roy, William G. (1997) *Socializing Capital: The Rise of the Large Industrial Corporation in America*, Princeton, NJ: Princeton University Press.

Weber, Max (1978) *Economy and Society*, edited by Claus Wittich and Guenther Roth, Berkeley, CA: University of California Press.

WILLIAM G. ROY

MORAL ECONOMY

The concept of moral economy derives from anthropological and social-historical accounts emphasizing that human action is driven not merely by economic interests, but also by moral concerns. It often refers to traditional communities or peasant societies where forms of exchange are closely tied to social norms of **fairness**. Moral economy can be defined as collectively validated **beliefs** about just distributions and exchanges rooted in both the community and the past. These beliefs determine individual behaviour and can inspire collective action. The centrepiece of the moral economy is that all forms of social exchanges have moral attendants which convey a sense of legitimacy or illegitimacy. The moral economy frame is often used to investigate social rebellion and protest because it locates the reason for action not in objective forms of exploitation or hardship but in certain social and moral interpretations attached to them. The classic authors of the moral economy were especially concerned with the clash between traditional societies with a shared moral universe and a deep-rooted sense of obligation on the one hand, and with the market-based exchanges that are ignorant to the traditional notion of what is just on the other (Bates and Curry 1992).

Submerged economy and non-economic motives

In his path-breaking book *The Great Transformation* (1957), **Polanyi** provided the theoretical core of the moral economy approach by defining the dichotomy between non-market economies and market economies. In historical perspective he seeks to explain the transition from pre-market economies, where all forms of social exchange are submerged in social relations, to market societies that are determined by economic rationality and the spirit of calculation. Where the economy is embedded, institutions, norms and community traditions govern the forms of social exchange, not individual economic rationality. The term **embeddedness** highlights that the traditional economy is not autonomous, i.e. driven by an adjustment to the forces of supply and demand and regulated by prices, but rather subordinated to politics, religion and social relations. More precisely, market transactions are not carried out by independent and merely rent-seeking individuals, but also depend upon patterns of mutuality, reciprocity and trust. Polanyi argues against classical liberal economists such as Malthus and Ricardo that markets are not a natural outcome of the historical development, but were created and administered. Moreover, in contrast to this school of economic thought, Polanyi insists that it is mistaken to assume that a market can function regardless of certain social, political and also legal preconditions. An economy fully disembedded, as envisaged by liberal economists, would surely not be able to survive due to its destructive effect on humankind and the existence of the social world.

These ideas have widely resonated in many areas of social research because they provide a profound criticism of market society and economic reductionism. Subsequent writers have therefore asked whether theories that are based on the assumption of self-interests, maximization and relatively rigid concepts of rationality suffice to explain human action and the functioning of economic (but also social and political) institutions. For pre-modern as well as modern societies, the question was raised as to what extent economic motives can account for social action and, moreover, how non-economic motives determine human agency (Booth 1994). A moral-economic analysis can contribute to overcome some of the misleading assumptions of **rational choice theory** by encompassing the moral dimension of human action (Etzioni 1988). Along this line, modern economic sociology adheres to the thesis that the market economy is also embedded and enmeshed in non-economic institutions: rather than being self-regulated and driven by economic self-interest, economic systems are ultimately tied to the social system and its **norms and values**.

Moral assumptions

Based on this framework, many moral economists have stressed the role of moral assumptions colouring individual actions, choices and preferences. It is suggested that people often act upon collectively shared notions of justice and fairness which render certain actions as legitimate and appro-

priate. Within the community context, social exchanges are not isolated acts, but have moral attendants and meanings and thereby contribute to the maintenance of good community relationships. However, the role of communal understandings of social justice is not confined to non-market exchanges; it also applies to many forms of market or quasi-market behaviour. The idea of fair price or fair wage, for example, suggests that the market is not immune to justice demands. Moral economy argues that there are certain normative standards of behaviour that actors in the marketplace have to respect. Only then will they be considered as legitimate participants. At the community level, it is said that the dominant allocative institutions do not only operate as to maximize the total output, but also to meet key values of social justice.

The primary research area of moral economists is traditional or non-western peasant societies that are characterized by a corporate element and a strong adherence to a shared understanding of justice. Peasant societies have attracted much research attention, because they rest upon strong ideas of **social rights** and obligations. Scott (1976) argues that for the organization of the peasant life, normative concepts play a dominant role and that peasants act according to the values they share. The first fundamental value is the ethic of subsistence that conveys a right to satisfy basic needs. Because peasant communities are relatively poor and live close to the poverty line, they have a strong preference for a system of taxation and rents which provides minimum income security. Therefore, the right to subsistence determines the forms of production and exchange. The second principle is the principle of reciprocity that safeguards a specific form of exchange between the elites and the ordinary peasants. Reciprocity exchanges in such societies entail that the peasants respect their elites and make payments to them, but expect returns in the form of protection, subsistence and justice.

467

Crowd action and moral economy

The third element of moral economy literature has been inspired by research on social uprisings at the threshold between traditional societies and industrial societies. Using the notion of moral economy, authors highlight that many forms of social resistance and social protest are insufficiently understood if one focuses solely on objective, material living conditions, but that **collective action** is often inspired by perceptions of norm violations. Since traditional societies are characterized by a strong and prevailing consensus about what distinguishes legitimate from illegitimate social practices, collective action is often induced by a moral indignation about a perceived violation of social norms. A hallmark example of the understanding of the social effects of moral assumptions people shared is the work of the British historian Edward P. Thompson (1971) on the food riots of eighteenth-century England. His study departs from the 'spasmodic view' of popular uprisings in the times of dearth suggesting that they are simply 'rebellions of the belly'. Rather than assuming that such sudden social disturbances are simply responses to economic stimuli, he argues that crowd action involves some notion of legitimacy. The people of the rioting crowd were guided by the belief in defending traditional rights or customs, and since they felt that some of the fairness criteria in forms of social exchange were violated, they reacted with anger. More concretely, when millers, dealers or those farmers hoarding grain tried to profit from other people's misery by raising prices, they were confronted with popular indignation that often led to crowd action. There was the common and deeply felt conviction that 'prices *ought*, in times of dearth, to be regulated, and that the profiteer put himself outside of society' (Thompson 1971: 112).

The case of the food riots characterizes the passage from traditional and paternalis-tic forms of economic exchange to supply and demand market economies. At that time it was still considered to be 'unnatural' that market actors should profit from the necessities of others, especially in times of hardship and hunger. Hence, extraordinary prices set by farmers and dealers in accordance with profit interests were facing popular resentment. However, not an objective lack of material resources makes a certain distributional situation unacceptable, but the violation of popular conceptions of justice. When taken-for-granted assumptions about social obligations and norms are infringed, crowd action can attain some notion of legitimacy, because the action is informed by the belief that traditional rights are defended. Looking at other historical and social contexts such as the German labour movement between 1848 and 1920, Barrington Moore (1978) has fruitfully combined the question of legitimacy and collective action. He demonstrates that many political demands were not only vital to the working class in material terms, but reinforced by the existing normative framework and the workers' idea of a good society. However, moral indignation does not only explain crowd action: it also informs actions in the everyday life of the peasants. Scott's (1985) work on a Malaysian village has investigated more subtle forms of peasant resistance against those who seek to extract labour, food, taxes, rent and interest from them. Peasant politics are not confined to collective social protest, but can also take place as minor acts of resistance such as clandestinely improving the terms of exchange, desertion, false compliance or by a growing symbolic withdrawal from the elite-created social order.

The renewal of the moral economy approach

The more recent political science attempts at integrating the moral economy approach into the analysis of markets, society and political institutions mark a departure from the focus on peasant societies. It has been criticized that the traditional concept of moral economy rests too heavily on the distinction between non-market and market-based and that social goods and their attendant moral economies also characterize modern market societies. Arnold (2001), for example, looks at water supply in the American West in order to illustrate that there are also forms of moral outrage in modern market societies. He shows that water constitutes an intrinsically communal good which sets clear limits to the various forms of water transfers and allocations that, if violated, induce popular protest. It has also been stressed that the moral economy approach facilitates a better understanding of the location of the economy within the architecture of society – its institutions and values (Booth 1994). Moreover, the role of taken-for-granted beliefs about fair rewards has become prominent in the literature dealing with forms of public provision (Kohli 1987). There it has been argued that the collective welfare system represents in itself a morally impregnated arrangement that counterbalances market outcomes. The question of 'Who should get what?' within the welfare state context is closely related to commonly held ideas about fair distributions of burdens and benefits. Most recent and promising are those attempts of the institutionalist school to analyse social and political institutions in terms of the interaction between the justice conception institutions embody and the moral dimension of human action. Also, as it has been established here, moral concerns provide an important motivational reference for individual actions and preferences, and institutional settings can act as mediators and facilitators for individual moral points of view (Rothstein 1998).

References and further reading

Arnold, Thomas Clay (2001) 'Rethinking Moral Economy', *American Political Science Review*, 95: 85–95.

Bates, Robert H. (1983) *Essays on the Political Economy of Rural Africa*, Cambridge: Cambridge University Press.

Bates, Robert H. and Curry, Amy Farmer (1992) 'Community versus Market: A Note on Corporate Villages', *American Political Science Review*, 86: 457–63.

Booth, William James (1994) 'On the Idea of the Moral Economy', *American Political Science Review*, 88(3): 653–67.

Etzioni, Amitai (1988) *The Moral Dimension. Toward A New Economics*, New York: Free Press.

Kohli, Martin (1987) 'Retirement and the Moral Economy: A Historical Interpretation of the German Case', *Journal of Aging Studies*, 1(2): 125–44.

Moore, Barrington, Jr (1978) *Injustice: The Social Bases of Obedience and Revolt*, White Plains: M. E. Sharpe.

Polanyi, Karl ([1944]1957) *The Great Transformation. The Political and Economic Origins of Our Time*, Boston: Beacon Press.

Popkin, Samuel L. (1979) *The Rational Peasant. The Political Economy of Rural Society in Vietnam*, Berkeley, CA: University of California Press.

Rothstein, Bo (1998) *Just Institutions Matter. The Moral and Political Logic of the Universal Welfare State*, Cambridge: Cambridge University Press.

Scott, James C. (1976) *The Moral Economy of the Peasant: Rebellion and Subsistence in Southeast Asia*, New Haven, CT: Yale University Press.

—— (1985) *Weapons of the Weak. Everyday Forms of Peasant Resistance*, New Haven, CT: Yale University Press.

Thompson, Edward P. (1966) *The Making of the English Working Class*, New York: Vintage Books.

—— (1971) 'The Moral Economy of the English Crowd in the Eighteenth Century', *Past & Present. A Journal of Historical Studies*, 50: 79–136.

STEFFEN MAU

MORALITY See: norms and values; moral economy; socioeconomics

MOTIVATION FOR ECONOMIC ACTION

See: economic action; incentives; preferences

N

NATIONALISM

'Nationalism' as the general term refers to the entire area of human experience defined by national consciousness and identity, i.e. communities constructed on the bases of such consciousness and identity – nations, structures in which they are institutionalized in the political sphere (such as the state), political ideologies, literary traditions and educational curricula in which they are explicitly or implicitly expressed, and sentiments, positive or negative, which reflect them. Used as a specific term in this broad area of study, it is most usefully employed to denote the broad worldview, or the image of social reality, which represents the cultural framework and foundation of such experience and, the latter being distinctively modern experience, is thus the cultural framework and foundation of modernity.

Nationalism differs from images of social reality which underlie other forms of human experience and organization (such as various types of religious worldviews) in (1) that it is essentially secular – that is, focused on this, empirical, world which it endows with ultimate meaning; (2) that its representation of social relations is egalitarian; and (3) that the source of all law and values in its framework is the community. A sovereign (in this sense) community, viewed as fundamentally a community of equals, is defined as a 'nation'; the appro-priation of the word 'nation' from its ecclesiastical context (it was used in church councils to denote representatives of cultural and political authorities) and its application – in the early sixteenth-century England, which was first to develop this form of social imagination – to the population of the entire country is the source of the term 'nationalism'.

The structural effects of nationalism are enormous. In the first place, the egalitarian image of social reality that it implies dramatically changes the nature of social stratification, replacing the rigid hierarchy of legal, religiously sanctioned and in principle mutually impermeable estates by an open system of classes through which people of different backgrounds pass (as through classes in school, only both on their way up and down) on the basis of their individual achievement. Considered fundamentally equal, people in a nation become interchangeable; this makes social mobility legitimate and normal, and status, instead of being determined by nontransferable – or ascriptive – distinction (or stigma) of birth, comes to depend on acquisitions of education on wealth, which in principle everyone has the chance to gain or lose. This systemic invitation to status aggrandizement in turn changes every aspect of social life, from the relations in the family, between the sexes and between parents and children, to the nature of the characteristic passions (ambition and envy) and the emotional tenor of human association in general.

The effects of the principle of popular sovereignty (as central in nationalism's image of political reality as the fundamental equality of membership is in its image of social relations) are equally profound. The idea that sovereignty is in the deepest sense a property of the people and, therefore, can only be delegated to somebody else pre-supposes a representative: namely, imper-sonal, government. This necessitates that the government assume the form of the state (distinguished from other – i.e. patrimonial, absolutist – forms by its impersonality). The emergence of the state, in turn, changes the whole nature of the political process.

The modern economy owes to national-ism at least as much as do modern society and politics. Like the class system (the open system of stratification) and the state, in fact, the modern economy is a product of nationalism, for it is this vision of social reality which provided economic activity with the motivation which reoriented it from subsistence to sustained growth. The economic effects of nationalism are mainly the result of the egalitarian principle at its core. To begin with, the definition of the entire population, the people, as a nation – that is, as an elite (given the previous meaning of the word 'nation' in its eccle-siastical context) – symbolically elevates the lower classes and ennobles their activities. Economic activities in general, engaging the overwhelming majority of the people and traditionally denigrated in pre-national societies precisely for this reason, gain status and, with it, a hold on the talented people who, under different circumstances, reach-ing a certain level of financial indepen-dence, would choose to leave productive activity. Arguably of even greater moment is the fact that the symbolic ennoblement of the populace in nationalism makes mem-bership in the nation, i.e. nationality itself, an honourable elevated status, thereby tying one's sense of dignity and self-respect to one's national identity. This ensures one's commitment to the national community and, in particular, one's investment in the nation's collective dignity, or prestige. Prestige is a relative good: one nation's having more of it implies that another has less. Therefore, investment in national prestige necessarily gives rise to an endless international competition, for no matter how much prestige one may have gained at a certain moment, one can be outdone in the next. Unlike other types of societies, then, nations are inherently competitive. This competition goes on in all the spheres of collective endeavour: moral (the nation's record on human rights, for instance), per-taining to cultural creativity (scientific, lit-erary, musical, etc.), military, political. Any particular nation chooses those spheres of competition where it has a chance to end on, or near, the top, and disregards those in which it is likely to be shamefully out-competed. For instance, Russia has always chosen to compete in the cultural and military arenas, and has never been inter-ested in economic competition. Where economic competition is included among the areas of national engagement, however, the inherent competitiveness of nationalism gives rise to economies of sustained, end-less, growth – i.e. to what are recognized as modern economies.

The first modern economy to develop was, as is generally recognized, that of England, the birthplace of the nationalist image of social reality and the first society to be defined as a nation. National con-sciousness in England, after about a century of development, was fully rooted by 1600; by 1650, competitive at least since the Company of Merchants Adventurers called itself The Merchants Adventurers of Eng-land in 1564, the English economy was decidedly reoriented towards growth. By the end of the seventeenth century, the small country, poor in natural resources, previously dependent on outsiders for capi-tal and economic infrastructure, emerged as the greatest economic power in the world – the position it retained for quarter of a millennium, to be replaced only by the giant and naturally overabundant economy of the United States of America. In other major players in the economic sphere, France, Germany and Japan (in order of entrance into the race), the reorientation of the economy towards growth – and the 'take-off' into sustained growth – followed the development of national consciousness within a generation plus/minus a decade, depending on the historical circumstances, obstructing (as in the case of the Revolution in France) or accelerating the process (as in the case of the forcible opening of Japan to trade, as a result of which Japanese nationalism was from the start defined in economic terms). In the case of the United States, which joined the race for economic dominance at about the same time with Japan, in the last quarter of the nineteenth century, the translation of national consciousness into collective economic competitiveness was slowed, paradoxically, by the acuity of the competition within the nation and by the superabundance of its natural resources, which allowed it to disregard all economic relations with the world except on most favourable terms.

To sum up, nationalism reorients economic activity towards sustained growth, supplying – in its inherent competitiveness – the motivation without which such growth cannot happen. The so-called material or objective conditions within which this motivation arises are at best of secondary importance, for nationalism has the power to activate the previously inert resources in cases where they exist (as in Germany or the United States) and to create resources out of nothing in cases where nature fails to provide them (as in England or Japan). The existence of material conditions in the absence of the motivation is powerless to produce sustained growth, as proved by the remarkable case of the Dutch Republic. The first world economic hegemon, the dominant economy of the seventeenth century and the only one with a sophisticated developed economic infrastructure, technologically, organizationally and financially superior to any other, the Dutch economy not only stopped growing by the end of its Golden Age, but experienced an absolute decline, completely disappearing from the ranks of major players on the economic arena – and all because the Republic did not develop a national consciousness and, therefore, having all the chances to win, lacked the motivation to compete as a unit, preferring to enjoy its legendary prosperity to investing it in sustained growth.

LIAH GREENFELD

NEOCLASSICAL ECONOMICS
See: economics, history of

NEO-CORPORATISM See: corporatism

NETWORK ANALYSIS

Network analysis is both old and new. On the one hand, network analysis is based on ideas as old as sociology itself; on the other hand, network analysis is as new as the latest mathematical models imported from the cutting-edge in physics. The classic origins of network analysis are most often traced to theorist Georg **Simmel**, who thought carefully about the basic building blocks of social **structure**. In addition to the importance of the relative size of social groups that interact with each other (such as employers and labourers), Simmel considered the position of an individual actor in a group or multiple groups. One of his enduring conceptual contributions on this topic is the development of *tertius gaudens*. *Tertius* is the third who prospers from social exchange. This third individual in a triad may pit the other two against each other to his or her own benefit. Simmel's theoretical discussions of webs of affiliation are a kind of network analysis, as are contemporary computational investigations of scale-free networks where connectivity follows power-law distributions (which, rather than peak at average value like a normal distribution, start at maximum value and decrease towards infinity).

Definitions

A network, unlike a group, as Elizabeth Bott (1957: 216–17) points out, 'is a social configuration in which some, but not all, of the component external units maintain relationships with one another. The external units … are not surrounded by a common boundary.' For example, a job-seeker has a set of social relationships with friends, family and acquaintances that compose his or her network and may help in locating a job. But the set of people with whom the job-seeker maintains relationships may not know each other and do not form a bounded social group. The general applicability of network analysis is such that the units in a network may be measured at any level: individuals, organizations or nations.

Network analysis is the tool of the **embeddedness** perspective, arguably the central thesis of economic sociology. The conception of embeddedness builds on Karl **Polanyi**'s insights that the free-market mentality that emerged in the nineteenth century ignores how economies were traditionally embedded in communal life. Current economic sociology follows Mark Granovetter's argument about embeddedness, which acknowledges that social actors forming economic relationships cannot untangle them from webs of **social ties**. 'Network analysis' has most often meant a collection of quantifying tools to graph social structures in the economy, but also refers to studies of the increasingly interconnected qualities of the economy, i.e. industrial districts and firms that take on a network form of organization.

The network form of organization is a type of governance structure that relies on inter-organizational collaboration. In contrast to markets governed by spot contracts for one-shot deals, or hierarchies governed by vertical chains of command and multiple divisions, the network form is embedded in durable yet flexible ties with external units. Examples of organizations that employ the network form (sometimes called 'network organizations') abound. Older craft-based organizations such as traditional construction firms illustrate aspects of the network form, like requiring workers to use tacit knowledge and make decisions as they build. This task-based work involves a range of skills, and also the ability to cooperate with other highly skilled trades on the building project. Similarly, in the contemporary Hollywood film industry, a movie brings together actors, directors, producers and other independent contractors for a short-term project. Analyses of this labour market show that skilled participants become embedded in networks of long-term working relationships that lead to recurring ties on subsequent film projects. Other project-based organizations that often bring teams together across formal organizational boundaries can be found in **advertising**, book publishing and, of course, the high-tech industries of information technology and biotechnology.

Network analysis, then, incorporates studies that treat networks more metaphorically in investigating webs of affiliation in economic life, as well as studies with specific operationalization of network measures. In this broader definition, network analysis is both old and new; and there are both qualitative and quantitative ways of usefully analysing networks in economic sociology.

Developments in network analysis

As early as the 1920s–1930s, network analysis had been performed in firms, notably in the famous Hawthorne studies conducted in Chicago's Western Electric plant.

In the report, sociograms of relationships between workers in the bank wiring room demonstrated the informal organization by representing individuals as nodes and existing ties as lines. The strength of the visual presentation of networks is that it is a parsimonious way to easily convey a set of relationships between multiple social actors. But consider that a maximally connected set of N actors display $\frac{N(N-1)}{2}$ lines in a sociogram. For five nodes, that would be a manageable ten lines, but for a relatively small group of twenty-five, potentially drawing 300 lines describing relationships becomes more difficult. (Although note that developments in computer animation, including the ability to convey more than two dimensions on screen, have now, in the early 2000s, made dynamic visual representations of large numbers of ties possible, with software programs like Pajek). Meanwhile, the measurement of social networks awaited more practical solutions.

The 1970s brought mathematical and computational developments that laid the groundwork for quantitative network analysis. Harrison White and colleagues worked on the mathematical breakthrough of applying algebraic models to measure individuals' roles in social structure, and through this effort developed block-modelling techniques. Conceptual developments on networks were often intertwined with methodological issues. Structural equivalence, the idea that two social actors are basically interchangeable if they have the same kinds of ties to the same kinds of partners, developed with the formulation of block-modelling methods. Multidimensional scaling was another important mathematical development, one which permitted the measurement of distances in social space. As increasingly sophisticated computational resources became accessible, the character of relationships and social structural positions could be represented numerically and compared across larger and larger networks. The development of

quantitative measures of connectivity included a variety of types of centrality, or ways of determining which social actor is the most connected in a network. Some centrality measures look at the direct relationships of the focal actor, such as degree centrality – the count of each actor's total number of ties. Other measures of centrality like closeness are more global measures of connection in the network, and take into consideration how connected the focal actor's partners are. Measures that hone in on the 'groupiness' within a given network include analyses of cliques, clusters and density. A clique, for example, usually indicates a sub-group of actors within which every possible dyad is directly linked, and is not connected to other cliques in the network.

Early findings in the sociological analysis of individuals in networks focused on information flows in markets. **Coleman** and colleagues argued (in the 1960s, though their claim was later disputed by reanalyses of their data in the 1990s) that a medically innovative product diffused more quickly to physicians who were central in friendship networks with colleagues. Lee studied women in the then illegal market, pre-Roe vs Wade, for a health care provider who could perform abortions. She found that women asked over five network contacts on average before finding an abortionist. Sometimes information would come through the referral of a friend of a friend. But in searching for such sensitive information, the distance between the searcher and the abortionist remained small – usually only two intermediaries at most. Granovetter's well-known 'strength of weak ties' argument was based on a study of male white-collar job-seekers who resided in Newton, MA. Over half of his respondents found jobs not through their strong ties to family and close friends, but rather through weak ties to acquaintances. Weak ties generally provide greater access to new information, unlike strong ties.

The early network analyses of the 1970s were also concerned with the organizational level as well as individual level. Studies of interlocking directorate ties, although measured by the common membership of two individuals on a third board of directors, were used to chart the linkages between US corporations. This early period of development in network analysis was mainly based in the United States.

In the 1980s, economic sociology was reborn and network analysis of organizations and markets grew around the globe. Research on networks in economic life began to expand across social science disciplines and national borders. The rebirth of economic sociology was marked by Granovetter's renowned 1985 essay on embeddedness. His call for structural analysis of the economy in contrast to atomistic neoclassical economic models resonated with many, and brought a coherent theoretical perspective to network analysis.

Studies in the 1980s explored what networks look like around the globe, and how they relate to **economic development**. In the 'Third Italy', small artisanal firms located in regional **industrial districts** exhibited flexible specialization. Through long-estate ties, a community of independent shops, each specializing in one aspect of production, would coordinate the manufacture of a certain kind of good. In Modena, knitwear might be put together cooperatively by a series of firms that each performed one part: the weaving, the dyeing, the cutting, the stitching. The coordination occurs not through an overarching organization, but through the network ties between local producers. Because each firm relies on highly skilled employees and is not subject to a long chain of command, they can adapt production change quickly and flexibly into the process. Thus, flexible specialization within regions means networks of firms stay on the cutting edge of fashion, sharing tricks of the trade among themselves but limiting secrets to the local community. Other regional economies across Europe were found to have flourishing specialized networks of production as well – e.g. automotive parts in Baden-Württemberg, Germany, silk in Lyon, France, cutlery in Sheffield, England.

Japanese *keiretsu*, or business groups, also became the subject of network analysis in the 1980s. With the visible success of the Japanese economy, particularly in automobile production at the time, American managers were keen to learn about the Japanese model. Japanese firm practices, translated as 'total quality management' and 'just in time' production in English-speaking nations, were linked to the close relationships between employers and employees and between large companies and subcontractors. *Keiretsu* were another example of production networks, but more vertically arranged than the Italian regional networks. In Japanese business groups, one large corporation coordinates production with the input of many satellite subcontracting firms. Unlike subcontracts that go to the lowest bidder, these relationships in a business group are long-term ties characterized by shared information and mutual investment. Other Asian nations, also the subject of network analysis, displayed their own variety of business groups – e.g. *chaebol* in Korea.

Organizations exemplifying collaborative production provided the empirical ground for Walter Powell's influential essays, the first published in 1987, in which he built the theoretical argument for the network form as type of economic organization distinct from both market and hierarchy. In the network form, **trust** is a key concept. Harking back to classic concepts in sociology of ingroup and outgroup membership, trust in networks is often founded on homophily – i.e. birds of a feather flock together. The basis of trust may vary in different kinds of network organizations. *Keiretsu* firms may trust each other because of the common business group identity ('we're part of the Toyota team'), while Italian firms in a regional network trust each other because of long-estate kinship and neighbourhood ties ('I know your mother'). Nevertheless, trust sustains the durability of the collaboration.

Network analysis was never just about happy outcomes, however. The literature on interlocking directorates in the 1980s continued to investigate cronyism among the power elite, examining links between corporate boards to gauge how the inner circle coordinated the US economy. New York **banks** often showed up as central links to a variety of industries in this period, and appeared to affect corporate political contribution patterns.

Research on networks flourished during the 1990s. Many scholars contributed theoretical and empirical refinements to the analysis of networks in the economy. Ron Burt championed the concept of structural holes in networks. When two clusters in a network are unconnected, the gap between them is a structural hole. An entrepreneurial network actor who bridges that hole garners more social capital than a member of a cohesive, dense network. Managers whose networks span greater social distances receive faster promotions and higher compensation. Bourdieu's theory of **social capital** thus made its way into network analysis, defined as the benefits that accrue to network inhabitants through their social ties. Other economic sociologists, like Alejandro Portes, studied the social capital that flows through ties in ethnic enclaves and leads to **entrepreneurship** among new immigrants in both the formal and **informal economy**. Portes also described some of the downsides to networks in ethnic entrepreneurship including status levelling and obligations to make a place for sometimes lazy relatives. A darker side to networks is cast by the homophily principle. If network ties are forged on the basis of similar social backgrounds, then men who have traditionally occupied elite economic circles will exclude others, i.e. women and minorities. Herminia Ibarra and others who have studied the effects of race and gender on career networks have found that women and minorities often do better to pursue different strategies in building networks, such as finding a strong, well-connected sponsor.

At the inter-organizational level, network analysis charted the effects of networks on firms, industries, and society. Annalee Saxenian investigated how the network form used by computer firms in Silicon Valley allowed the free exchange of ideas and learning across organizational boundaries within the region. Greater innovation and economic development occurred in Silicon Valley than in Boston's Route 128 high-tech hub, where computer companies worked to buffer their secrets within vertically integrated hierarchies. European, particularly Scandinavian, studies of networks by scholars like Hakan Hakansson also demonstrated the link between networks and innovation in high-tech regional economies in Europe. Brian Uzzi found innovation and learning arising from network ties in the New York garment industry as well. The garment producers who were most successful, however, had a mix of strong, close ties and arm's-length ties. This mix provided flexibility in pursuing some trusting relationships for investing in innovative techniques and equipment, and some shorter-term contracts with lower bidders.

Banks seemed to play a less central role in interlocking directorates as other forms of financing, including international investment, became more common in the 1990s. A puzzle was that the reconstitution of broken interlock ties occurred less frequently than might be expected for ties supposedly used to coordinate the economy. Although the boards of major corporations in industrialized nations were not densely connected through direct ties, the short network path between most corporations in a given country showed that the ownership of power remains a small world. Further, interlocking directorate ties were related to the diffusion of firm strategies, such as how corporations pursue or deal with acquisitions.

The visibility of network analysis in popular culture grew during the 1990s with the *Six Degrees of Separation* play, movie and online game. In economic life, the connection between flatter, more lateral forms of network organization and successful technological innovation not only became popularized, but also may have accounted for some of the hype that peaked with the dotcom craze of 1999–2000. Meanwhile, in academic circles, network analysis played a central role in the institutionalization of economic sociology.

The early 2000s are still an exciting time in network analysis with innovation in methods and software, and with new substantive frontiers being brought together with the core focus on structural analysis in economic life. Duncan Watts and other sociologists affiliated with the Santa Fe Institute have worked to develop mathematical measures of connectivity, importing some ideas from the physical sciences and combining them with sociological insights. Growth in sophisticated software and computing capacity has greatly aided this effort. As a result, network analysis has developed the means to better understand the dynamic nature of ties over time, such as the decreasing returns to connectivity. Substantively, economic sociologists have begun to work on integrating network analysis of economic structures with other connections that are vital but have been largely missing in the literature – such as looking more closely at the family, consumerism and technology. The connection between network analysis and technology, for example, has benefited from the infusion of ideas from science and technology studies (STS). STS scholars Karin Knorr Cetina and Urs Bruegger argue that inter-

national banking is a new organizational form that takes connectivity beyond the network form with information technology. 'Platform' organizations, as they call them, provide more transparency between economic partners, as all parties have pertinent information available onscreen. International investment banks and high-energy physics collaborations provide examples where knowledge has no geographic location, but rather 'exteriority'.

Research in the 2000s also moved further toward predicting when ties and the network form of organization help or hinder outcomes of profit, innovation and equality. Mizruchi and Stearns, for example, discovered how strong ties proved detrimental to bank officers trying to make deals with corporate customers. Reliance on their strong ties to other bankers precluded more extensive search behaviour, resulting in a greater sense of security but poorer financial outcomes.

Debates and questions

A strong criticism levelled against network analysis in the late 1990s was that this stream of economic sociology assumes a politically conservative tone. This criticism that network analysis is an implicitly neo-liberalist, pro-capitalist ideology may gain strength from the fact that many of the analysts of social networks in the economy are employed in business schools, programmes out of which scholarship correspondingly has a pro-business slant. If, however, neo-liberal organizations like the IMF set out to 'destroy collective structures' (Bourdieu 1998) in order to support a pure market logic, then the study of collaborative, interconnected network forms of organization in the economy would fail to support the neo-liberal camp. On the other hand, the point that network analysis needs to spend less time 'studying up' to the elite and highly educated members of society and their successful firms is well taken. Further analysis of poverty, downward mobility and failed organizations through the study of networks at various levels is needed in economic sociology.

While the broad applicability of network analysis to both old and new questions in economic life is surely a draw, a caution for network analysis is to avoid the pitfalls of popularity. Some sociologists have contended that 'social capital' has become so overused as to almost lose meaning as a concept. Does 'network' similarly run the risk of becoming the metaphor that ate New York, so to speak, and thereby losing potency as the key tool of economic sociology?

See also: corporate governance; inter-firm relations; interlocking directorates.

References and further reading

Bott, Elizabeth (1957) *Family and Social Network*, London: Tavistock.
Bourdieu, Pierre (1998) 'The Essence of Neoliberalism', *Le Monde Diplomatique*, December, online. Available at www.mondediplo.com
Burt, Ronald S. (2000) 'The Network Structure of Social Capital', *Research in Organizational Behavior*, 22: 345–423.
Granovetter, Mark (1985) 'Economic Action, Social Structure, and Embeddedness', *American Journal of Sociology*, 91: 481–510.
Saxenian, AnnaLee (1994) *Regional Advantage: Culture and Competition in Silicon Valley and Route 128*, Cambridge, MA: Harvard University Press.
Smith-Doerr, Laurel and Powell, Walter W. (2005) 'Networks and Economic Life', in N. Smelser and R. Swedberg (eds), *Handbook of Economic Sociology*, 2nd edn, Princeton, NJ: Russell Sage Foundation and Princeton University Press.
Uzzi, Brian (1997) 'Social Structure and Competition in Interfirm Networks: The Paradox of Embeddedness', *Administrative Science Quarterly*, 42: 35–67.
Watts, Duncan J. (2003) *Six Degrees: The Science of a Connected Age*, New York: W. W. Norton.

LAUREL SMITH-DOERR

NETWORKS See: network analysis

NICHES

Developed within a scholarly tradition that lies at the intersection of human ecology (Hawley 1950) and classic structural macrosociology (Blau 1977), the niche concept features prominently in contemporary organizational sociology. The concept originated in bioecology with the work of Elton (1927) and later Hutchinson (1957) and was used to describe the environmental space (confined by parameters on multiple dimensions) in which a population of species can sustain itself. In the early 1980s, three theories of organizations adapted the concept to organizational sociology and spurred a research tradition that has greatly illuminated our understanding of the relationship between organizations and their environments. Freeman and Hannan (1983) relied on the niche concept to define organizational populations – a set of collective social actors that rely on similar resources and share the same organizational form. Broadly, the central predictions of the theory relate the adaptability and viability of a population to the distribution of resources within its *fundamental* niche. A fundamental niche is a multidimensional constrained resource space including all relevant social, economic and political dimensions in which organizations of a certain form can maintain non-negative growth in the absence of competitors (i.e. other populations with similar or overlapping resource requirements). By contrast, the term '*realized* niche' is used to describe the subset of the fundamental niche in which an organizational population operates in the presence of competitors. The distinction between a fundamental and a realized niche is important as it highlights the utility of the two concepts – the former is appropriate for analysing the population–environment relation as well as intra-population dynamics of institutionalization and competition, while the latter brings attention to the interdependence between organizations of different forms.

McPherson's (1983) network ecology framework relies on the concept of the realized niche. McPherson analysed the composition and heterogeneity of social groups by measuring the socio-demographic characteristics of their members. Shifting to the level of individual organizations' realized niches, Carroll's (1985) resource partitioning theory distinguished between generalist and specialist organizations based on their variance in resource utilization (i.e. niche width). By the logic of Carroll's model, broad niche organizations (generalists) rely on a wide array of resources, while specialists tend to focus on relatively narrow patches of resources along relevant environmental dimensions.

Subsequent research on niches tended to follow Carroll's approach and focused primarily on individual organizations. McPherson et al. (1992) studied the niche dynamics of voluntary associations by analysing the movement of individuals among them. Baum and Singh (1994) measured the fundamental niches of child day-care centres on the basis of the age ranges that they were licensed to enrol. Podolny, Stuart and Hannan (1996) investigated the niche dynamics of semiconductor companies in terms of their reliance on patent citations. Park and Podolny (2000) construed investment banks niches by looking at their activities in different industries. Sørensen (2000) measured the niches of television stations in terms of workforce characteristics. Dobrev et al. (2001, 2002, 2003) and Kim et al. (2003) conceived of the technological niches of automobile manufacturers based on the engine sizes of the cars they produced.

The three basic theories – Freeman and Hannan's population niche theory, McPherson's sociodemographic niche theory, and Carroll's resource partitioning theory – have provided fertile ground for much theory development in con-temporary organizational sociology which is briefly summarized below.

Niche and competition

An important by-product of a research focus on niches is the ability to theorize and measure the extent of *niche overlap* between organizations. A fundamental tenet of ecological theory emphasizes the diffuse nature of competition for resources among social actors that may not be directly linked or even aware of each other (Hawley 1950). The construct of niche overlap allows researchers to clearly examine the repercussions of such shared resource dependence for vital rates. Research in this direction has theorized and confirmed that niche overlap elevates the chances of failure among organizations as diverse as day-care centres (Baum and Singh 1994) and automobile manufacturers (Dobrev et al. 2001). An important qualification of this finding has been that resource overlap signifies not only competitive but also mutualistic forces. Accordingly, the effect of niche overlap has been shown to also increase survival chances (a mutualism-driven effect) in partitioned markets where resources have been divided and diffuse competition has been entirely supplanted by direct rivalries (Dobrev et al. 2002).

Niche and change

Organizational niche has been shown to impact both the likelihood of organizations to change and their ability to survive change attempts (Baum and Singh 1996; Dobrev et al. 2003; Kim et al. 2003). Broad niche organizations appear to be less likely to change but better fit to improve their fitness after undergoing transformation. At least partly, the lower change likelihood for generalists seems to hinge on the structure of the market in which they operate – in consolidated markets where unexplored resources are scarce, broad niche firms which otherwise may be more prone to change find it hard to gather the slack resources necessary to support exploration. In addition to niche width, organizations experiencing the pressure of high competition for resources are predictably more likely to change. But when niche overlap signifies mutualistic relationships developed through the common objective of building and protecting the shared resource space, organizational change is unlikely.

Niche and location

The niche concept has also been instrumental in devising research strategies to measure the location of organizations in resource space, relative to each other. Studies show that the effects of niche width and niche overlap hinge on whether an organization is located in the market centre or on the periphery. This distinction is crucial in modelling the dynamics of the resource partitioning process in which the structure of competition varies substantially between consolidated and emergent market segments. A focus on niche as a measure of location has enabled theory development related to the collective movement of organizations between resource niches (i.e. market segments) within a population over time (Dobrev 2005; Dobrev and Kim 2005).

Perhaps the greatest contribution of research on organizational niches lies in its ability to integrate existing theoretical segments within organizational ecology and between ecology and other perspectives in organizational sociology like networks, institutionalism, learning and resource dependence. No doubt, future research in this direction will make great strides in further developing these theories.

References and further reading:

Baum, Joel A. C. and Singh, Jitendra V. (1994) 'Organizational Niches and the Dynamics of Organizational Mortality', *American Journal of Sociology*, 100: 346–80.

—— (1996) 'Dynamics of Organizational Responses to Competition', *Social Forces*, 74: 1261–97.

Blau, Peter M. (1977) *Inequality and Heterogeneity*, New York: Free Press.

Carroll, Glenn R. (1985) 'Concentration and Specialization: Dynamics of Niche Width in Populations of Organizations', *American Sociological Review*, 54: 524–41.

Carroll, Glenn R. and Hannan, Michael T. (2000) *The Demography of Corporations and Industries*, Princeton, NJ: Princeton University Press.

Dobrev, Stanislav D. (2005) 'Competing in the "Looking Glass" Market: Imitation Resources and Crowding', University of Chicago GSB Working Paper.

Dobrev, Stanislav D. and Kim, Tai-Young (2005) 'Positioning among Organizations in a Population: A Model of Mutualism and Competition', University of Chicago GSB Working Paper.

Dobrev, Stanislav D., Kim, Tai-Young and Hannan, Michael T. (2001) 'Dynamics of Niche Width and Resource Partitioning', *American Journal of Sociology*, 106: 1299–337.

Dobrev, Stanislav D., Kim, Tai-Young and Carroll, Glenn R. (2002) 'The Evolution of Organizational Niches: US Automobile Manufacturers, 1885–1981', *Administrative Science Quarterly*, 47: 233–64.

Dobrev, Stanislav D., Kim, Tai-Young and Carroll, Glenn R. (2003) 'Shifting Gears, Shifting Niches: Organizational Inertia and Change in the Evolution of the US Automobile Industry, 1885–1981', *Organization Science*, 14: 264–82.

Elton, Charles (1927) *Animal Ecology*, London: Sidgwick and Jackson.

Freeman, John H. and Hannan, Michael T. (1983) 'Niche Width and the Dynamics of Organizational Populations', *American Journal of Sociology*, 88: 1116–45.

Hawley, Amos. H. (1950) *Human Ecology: A Theory of Community Structure*, New York: Ronald Press.

Hutchinson, G. Evelyn (1957) 'Concluding Remarks', *Cold Spring Harbor Symposium on Quantitative Biology*, 22: 415–27.

Kim, Tai-Young, Dobrev, Stanislav D. and Solari, Luca (2003) '*Festina Lente*: Learning and Inertia among Italian Automobile Producers, 1896–1981', *Industrial and Corporate Change*, 12: 1279–301.

McPherson, J. Miller (1983) 'An Ecology of Affiliation', *American Sociological Review*, 48: 519–35.

McPherson, J. Miller, Popielarz, Pamela A. and Drobnič, Sonja (1992) 'Social Networks and Organizational Dynamics', *American Sociological Review*, 57: 153–70.

Park, Douglas and Podolny, Joel M. (2000) 'The Competitive Dynamics of Status and Niche Width: US Investment Banking, 1920–1950', *Industrial and Corporate Change*, 9: 377–414.

Sørensen, Jesper B. (2000) 'The Ecology of Organizational Demography: Tenure Distributions and Organizational Competition', *Industrial and Corporate Change*, 8: 713–44.

STANISLAV D. DOBREV

NORMS AND VALUES

Norms are standards of behaviour and expression that serve to regulate social interaction. They help to make human behaviour predictable within certain ranges of activity, particularly within the purview of social institutions such as the economy, the family and religion. They are a moral standard against which actual or planned behaviour can be measured.

In a related vein, 'normal' behaviour falls within a range of average possibilities. Norms are culturally regulated and slow to change. While every culture has norms, the specifics of how the norms manifest themselves vary widely. As norms prescribe a range of behaviour and expression, action that does not conform to the norms is said to be 'deviant'. Because the manifestation of norms is different from one culture to the next, what is normal in one culture may be deviant in another. While it is normative in cultures throughout the world (particularly in developed societies) to exchange money for food, for example, the specifics of how this occurs may vary widely; in North American culture, the norm is to pay the marked price for groceries, while in some other cultures it is the norm to negotiate for the price of produce. The important point here is that since what is normal may vary culturally, so too does

what is deviant vary culturally. What is invariant across cultures is that they all have some norms.

When a person's behaviour is deviant in that it falls outside the purview of the normal, there typically are 'sanctions'. Sanctions are penalties, the severity of which tends to vary with the strength of the norm being violated. The sanctions may be legalistic and formal, such as penalties against murder, or they may be informal, as in being shunned or turned out of the social collective.

The first sociologist to consider norms in depth was Emile **Durkheim** (e.g. [1887] 1993, [1893]1984, [1895]1964). Thinkers in the 'functional' school of sociology, most notably Talcott **Parsons** (e.g. 1951; Parsons and Smelser 1956), built on Durkheim's work. Thus, the essay will focus primarily on these functional theorists, but will also consider other contributions – most notably from the 'new institutionalism' (e.g. DiMaggio and Powell 1991) and 'rational choice' (e.g. Coleman 1990) perspectives.

At the time Emile Durkheim was writing, a popular notion was that of the utilitarian **social contract** (as per the work of John Locke and Jean-Jacques Rousseau). According to social contract theory, individuals voluntarily gave up some of their rights in order for there to be a society in which the greater good would accrue to the maximum number of people. In such a society, people would implicitly or explicitly enter into economic and social exchange agreements. These agreements, or contracts, would be enforced by the rule of law.

Durkheim made a compelling case that, rather than the law keeping contracts in force, there was a 'pre-contractual' social solidarity, which involved a 'collective conscience' (or collective consciousness) of commonly held norms and values. Durkheim conceived of norms as prime examples of 'social facts'. He distinguished between 'material' social facts, such as the size, density and distribution of a society's population, and 'non-material' social facts, such as commonly held **beliefs** and values. A crucial set of non-material social facts were the norms serving to bind the society together.

For Durkheim, certain pre-contractual (or non-contractual) social conditions must prevail in order for any sort of economic contract to be meaningful, and thus to have a chance to be successfully discharged. In modern society, these conditions are embodied in what Durkheim termed 'organic solidarity' – a complex division of labour in which individuals feel integrated into the overall social collective and thus, to an extent, regulated by the norms. As Durkheim ([1893]1984: 160–2) writes in *The Division of Labor in Society*:

> The duties and rights of each one must be defined, not only in the light of the situation as it presents itself ... but in anticipation of circumstances that can arise and can modify it. Otherwise, at every moment there would be renewed conflicts and quarrels ... Viewed in this light, the law of contract ... is no longer a useful supplement to individual agreements, but their basic norm ... The contract is not sufficient by itself, but is only possible because of the regulation of contracts, which is of social origin.

Thus, norms are the cornerstone of social structure. Laws in a society typically reflect the norms, although this is not *necessarily* so in all cases. Laws that are not sufficiently supported by a strong normative foundation are largely unenforceable. It is not the laws that keep the norms in place, but the norms that give substance to the law.

Virtually every modern society has laws against embezzlement; and in most societies, embezzlement is a relatively rare occurrence. It is not the law that causes the rate to be low – the norm against stealing is the social fact driving *both* the law and the low embezzlement rate. In societies where the norm is not sufficiently internalized by

a critical mass of people, the embezzlement rate may tend to be higher. Recent scandals in the USA, such as the Enron debacle, for example, may in fact be indicative of the fraying of a common normative system underpinning the economy.

The question of legitimacy is important, because laws that do not have normative legitimacy ultimately become unenforceable. As a case in point, consider the 'Prohibition' against alcohol in the early part of the twentieth century in the United States. Although this law enjoyed the status of a Constitutional Amendment, it had so little legitimacy among the common citizenry that ultimately the government was forced to repeal it. In the meantime, the social effect of the law's passage was to give a tremendous windfall of business to the organized crime syndicates that were in a position to fill the substantial public demand for illegal alcohol.

Norms and the values underpinning them can change over time, but those changes tend to be very slow. It is instructive here to consider the social process that William Ogburn termed 'cultural lag'. When there is a change in some material or technological condition (such as a change from feudalism to industrial capitalism), the social norms and values typically will change as well as they adapt to those material changes – but there will be a time lag for the change to take place. The lag may be a matter of days or months, or it may be measured more in terms of years or even centuries.

Consider, for example, the norms and associated value system in modern industrial societies in its approach to **laissez faire capitalism**. Unbridled capitalism was associated with the overall level of the development of society. As such, it enjoyed a great deal of popular legitimacy. However, it also led to the concentration of wealth into relatively few hands – a condition many associated with causing the worldwide depression of the 1930s. These conditions in turn gave impetus to a reaction in which Keynesian ideas of government regulation of the economy and deficit spending, particularly as embodied in political changes associated with the rise of the 'New Deal Liberalism' of Franklin Roosevelt in the USA, were incorporated into the norms of capitalism.

Building on the work of Durkheim and others, Talcott Parsons theorized that the 'normative order' was the backbone of a functional society. Parsons emphasized the importance of the social 'role' as a key to the link between individual action and the social order in which that action takes place. There are normative behaviours and expectations to go with each of the roles in a person's life. The totality of the institutional roles in a society, together with the norms and values associated with them, formed the normative order. Examples of economic social roles include buyer, seller, employer, employee, etc. A given individual was likely to be in numerous social roles through the course of a lifetime. Each of the roles has a set of normative social expectations associated with them. What would be normal in one role (e.g. giving orders in the boss role) may be considered deviant in another role (e.g. employee).

Parsons also found that as societies modernize, the values and social norms governing them tend to become less particularistic and more universal in nature. This implies that the norms come to apply not only to one's own social collective, but to a more diverse array of social collectives. Ultimately, this 'value generalization' would be universal enough to include all others. This will be particularly important in facilitating the 'new global economy', because the people entering into exchanges in it will be dependent upon a normative system sufficiently universal to regulate the exchanges and contracts within its purview.

In focusing on the interplay between the economy and other social institutions, Talcott Parsons and Neil Smelser (1956:

109) make a case that the fabric of organizations themselves are promulgated through such exchanges and contracts. For a contract to be successful, each of the parties 'must constitute parts of a single social system [with] some kind of *integration* and some kind of *common value pattern* which they share'.

It is important to point out here that integration needs to occur on more than one level. On the micro level, individuals must be integrated into the overall institutional order, so that their actions are meaningful to one another, they are motivated by a common set of values and are constrained by a common set of norms. Yet integration on the micro level is not enough for a functional system. Aspects of 'civil society', such as voluntary associations, mediate between the individual and the overall political and economic system.

In macro terms, the advent of 'big government' parallels and largely facilitates the economy. This is the case not simply in socialist economies, but for complex capitalist ones as well. The traditional European aristocracy with its particularistic normative system was an example of a relatively undifferentiated political system. The more highly differentiated contemporary polity is able to grow synergistically with a highly differentiated capitalist economy. Likewise, the legal system, and the increasingly sophisticated sense of regulation of exchanges and contracts, grows in concert with the economy and the polity in modern society.

Growth and differentiation in one institution tends to accompany and co-facilitate growth and differentiation in institutions generally. Put in more general terms, as societies modernize, their institutions tend to become more highly differentiated. That differentiation tends to increase interdependence among the respective institutions, and is facilitated by the advent of a more universal normative system. The modern economy functions as an integral, but ultimately inseparable, part of the overall

483

social system. Thus, for Parsons and Smelser (1956: 306), 'Economic theory is a special case of the general theory of social systems and hence of the general theory of action.'

Partially in response to critiques that functional theories (such as those of Durkheim, Parsons and Smelser) tended to have an 'oversocialized' conception of social actors, a set of theories known collectively as a 'New Institutionalism' arose (see **institutionalism, old and new**). Writing in this vein, Paul DiMaggio and Walter Powell (1991) view norms in terms of interactions between thought processes of agents on the one hand, and structural constraints on behaviour, such as position in exchange networks, on the other.

DiMaggio and Powell articulate a phenomenon of 'institutional isomorphism', or the tendency of institutions to adopt a normative resemblance to one another in terms of bureaucratic structure and rationality. This similarity has not necessarily resulted in greater efficiency for any of the actors involved. Rather, DiMaggio and Powell isolate three factors that drive the process – 'coercive isomorphism', in which there are both formal and informal pressures (e.g. changes in laws or a threat of being charged with discriminatory practices) on organizations to function in common ways; 'mimetic processes', where, primarily as a response to uncertainty or ambiguous situations, an organization will follow the lead of another organization it sees as being successful – even if the modelled process has little or nothing to do with the success; and 'normative pressures'. The third process of normative pressures is largely embedded in changes such as the professionalization process (see **professions**). As DiMaggio and Powell point out, universities, professional training and trade associations are key venues through which professional and organizational norms are promulgated. Largely because of this, it is the case that 'Many professional career tracks [e.g. among Fortune 500 board members] are so closely guarded, both at the entry level and throughout the career progression, that individuals who make it to the top are virtually indistinguishable' (DiMaggio and Powell 1991: 71).

Mark Granovetter (1985) points out that strictly economic theories tend to be mis-specified largely because they are *undersocialized*. Put another way, there is virtually no such thing as a purely economic exchange – it is *always* part of a larger social system. In particular, it is important to consider that economic exchanges are 'embedded' in systems of social networks which influence the parameters of those exchanges. Rather than norms, network theory tends to emphasize the importance of the structure of the network in explaining social outcomes. For example, consider the principles of 'centrality' and 'vulnerability' from network theory. In both cases, structural asymmetries existing between the parties in an exchange constrain the actions that can occur. To add further complexity, a social system involves multiple networks, some of which are cross-cutting and some of which are embedded. While there is a network through which information flows in a corporation, for example, company actors still can obtain information about each other, potential employees or other companies, through a variety of other networks.

The functional view in general, including its view of norms and values, also has been roundly criticized by conflict-oriented theorists who hold that the social consensus associated with a normative system often tends to maintain an unjust *status quo*. Karl Mannheim (1929/1936), for example, sees norms and values that support an existing socio-economic system such as a free market, rather than a utopian alternative, as 'ideology'. This ideology tends to cloud people's thinking and makes movement towards a more just and humane society problematic. One way to counter this is for people, particularly intellectuals, to address questions of who benefits in a society from the norms as they are, and to discuss these issues openly and frankly.

Another popular alternative to the functional model of norms, particularly in the last three decades, has been the 'rational choice' model (see **rational choice theory**). This theoretical framework relies on key 'utilitarian' assumptions. Specifically, rational choice theories assume that people will seek to maximize their own gain in any situation and minimize their costs (also known as maximizing one's 'utility'), and these calculations take place on the individual, rather than collective, level.

As people attempt to maximize their individual utility, there must be some way for society to counter the **free rider** problem, in which people take more than they contribute. It is thus in the interest of societies to develop a set of norms to regulate social exchanges. People in the society are most likely to internalize these norms when there is a 'closed network' of social ties, in which information is freely exchanged about who is participating as a good citizen and who is free-riding. Free riders are sanctioned or, preferably, the norms are sufficiently strong that people self-regulate and there is no or minimal free-riding. One way social collectives optimize their chances for this is to select members based on self-sacrificing or 'altruistic' tendencies, and to try to select people with similar values, such that their costs of conformity to the norms are minimized and thus their likelihood of conformity is high. Rational choice theories also are criticized on a number of counts, including the tendency for truly 'closed' networks to exist only in theory, for the assumption that people are rational utility maximizers in the first place, and for the tendency to reduce social facts such as norms to individual exchange.

Regardless of the theoretical approach, there are some overarching themes in sociology regarding norms and values. Human interaction typically has norms governing it and values informing it. Social systems tend to have norms in order to regulate people in the society so it can function smoothly, and to keep the pursuit of individual desires from spinning out of control. Norms can change over time, but those changes tend to be slow. It is not unusual for norms to last centuries with only minor changes – far longer than the people they affect. The norms of society, particularly those of exchange and contract, are crucial ingredients of the economy.

References and further reading

Coleman, James S. (1990) *Foundations of Social Theory*, Cambridge, MA: Belknap Press of Harvard University Press.

DiMaggio, Paul J. and Powell, Walter W. (1991) 'The Iron Cage Revisited: Institutional Isomorphism and Collective Rationality in Organization Fields', in Walter W. Powell and Paul J. DiMaggio (eds), *The New Institutionalism in Organizational Analysis*, Chicago: University of Chicago Press, pp. 63–82.

Durkheim, Emile ([1887]1993) *Ethics and the Sociology of Morals*, Buffalo, NY: Prometheus Press.

—— ([1893]1984) *The Division of Labor in Society*, New York: Free Press.

—— ([1895]1964) *The Rules of Sociological Method*, New York: Free Press.

Granovetter, Mark (1985) 'Economic Action and Social Structure: The Problem of Embeddedness', *American Journal of Sociology*, 91: 481–510.

Mannheim, Karl ([1929]1936) *Ideology and Utopia*, London: Routledge and Kegan Paul.

Parsons, Talcott (1951) *The Social System*, London: Routledge and Kegan Paul.

Parsons, Talcott and Smelser, Neil J. (1956) *Economy and Society: A Study in the Integration of Economic and Social Theory*, New York: Free Press.

THOMAS J. BURNS

O

OPTIMUM

The optimum is one of the key concepts of economic theory. It assumes that someone is maximizing something with finite resources (see **maximization**). In the theory of the firm, decision-makers maximize a discounted stream of net revenue. To make revenue-generating sales, decision-makers must purchase combinations of raw materials, capital equipment and labour, making decisions on what *kinds* of each resource to purchase (e.g. more or less skilled labour) and finance the purchase of those resources at some implicit or actual rate of interest. Net revenue is maximized where total costs are minimized and the firm produces the volume of output that generates most revenue, given the demand curve it confronts. Setting the appropriate output and the *combination* of cost-minimizing inputs needed to produce that output is an optimizing problem. More generally, the economy is made up of **utility**-maximizing agents. This includes consumers. Given limited financial resources, their problem is to generate that set of purchases and savings that produces the most utility. The set that maximizes their utility, is optimal. There are optimums for the whole economy, as well as for individuals. The premise of standard **welfare economics** is that the allocation of goods and services through a competitive market is Pareto optimal, in the sense that

no reallocation would make anyone better off without making someone else worse off.

Governments are significant actors in the economy and require revenues. The premise of the *optimal taxation* literature is that governments should maximize some combination of equity and **efficiency**. Their optimizing problem is to find the set of taxes (consumption taxes, income taxes, tariffs) that simultaneously maximizes both. In making their decision they have to take into account collection costs, effects on **incentives** (e.g. the effort deployed in working hard rather than tax evasion), and distributive consequences.

There is a also a literature on optimal savings. Economic growth requires investment. Investment depends on savings, which imply a trade-off between present and future consumption. In the 1930s, **Keynes** and others were convinced that people saved too much, creating deficient aggregate demand and unemployment. In the inflationary period after the 1960s, concern shifted to the possibility that there was too little saving in some countries. Each conclusion assumes that there is some other – optimum – trade-off between the future and the present, and that economic analysis can say something useful about what it is.

Most economic sociology can be seen as an attack on the use of the concept of an optimum. Much behaviour is thought to involve a larger normative than calculative component. Where calculative behaviour is at issue, following Simon, **satisficing** is usually viewed as a more plausible model. Outcomes for individuals, firms and governments tend to be seen as the effect of a struggle for power rather than of a quest for an optimum.

References and further reading

Arrow, Kenneth J. and Hahn, Frank H. (1971) *General Competitive Analysis*, Amsterdam: North Holland.

Beckert, Jens (1996) 'What is Sociological about Economic Sociology? Uncertainty and the Embeddedness of Economic Action', *Theory and Society*, 25: 803–40.

MICHAEL R. SMITH

ORGANIZATIONAL ECOLOGY

See: organization theory

ORGANIZATIONS

See: organization theory

ORGANIZATION THEORY

Organization theory is the branch of sociology that studies organizations as distinct units in society. The organizations examined range from sole proprietorships, hospitals and community-based non-profit organizations to vast global corporations. The field's domain includes questions of how organizations are structured, how they are linked to other organizations, and how these structures and linkages change over time. Although it has roots in administrative theories, **Weber**'s theory of bureaucracy, the theory of the firm in microeconomics, and Coase's theory of firm boundaries, organization theory as a distinct domain of sociology can be traced to the late 1950s and particularly to the work of the **Carnegie School**. In addition to sociology, organization theory draws on theory in economics, political science and psychology, and the range of questions addressed reflects this disciplinary diversity. While early work focused on specific questions about organizations per se – for instance, why hierarchy is so common, or how businesses set prices – later work increasingly studied organizations and their environments, and ultimately organizations as building blocks of society. Organization theory can thus be seen as a family of mechanisms for analysing social outcomes.

Origins and early development

James March and Herbert Simon in 1958's *Organizations* identified perhaps the central puzzle of hierarchical organizations: how can structures composed of (boundedly rational) individuals, each subject to a raft of cognitive biases and limited processing capacity, manage to accomplish the magnificent? The answer was that hierarchy, long seen as simply a manifestation of a chain of command, served an information-processing function directly analogous to a computer program. Bureaucracy factored complex decision problems that were beyond the capacities of individual decision-makers into smaller parts that could be solved and aggregated back up through the hierarchy, much as computer programs factored problems into sub-routines. By framing the rationale for bureaucracy in terms of cognition (rather than power or authority), March and Simon set the tone for much subsequent work.

A second major contribution of the Carnegie School was Cyert and March's *A Behavioral Theory of the Firm* in 1963. This work was an effort to give a more plausible account of business decision-making than the stylized depiction of boundlessly rational maximizers in the economic theory of the firm. When setting prices and output quantities, or making decisions about what markets to enter and leave, the choices of top executives could often be described using relatively simple decision rules about what counted as satisfactory performance (their 'aspiration level') and where (and when) to look for solutions to shortfalls in performance ('problemistic search'). Moreover, firm outcomes in industries composed of oligopolies could be modelled using computer simulations that generated life-like results. Thus, the Carnegie School provided a robust basic model of organizations that set the agenda for almost all subsequent work.

James D. Thompson's *Organizations in Action* in 1967 completed the foundations for organization theory by synthesizing the empirical and theoretical ferment that resulted from the Carnegie School's initial statements. The focus of this work was not so much on why organizations are hierarchical, but on what they can do to achieve rationality in an uncertain world. Organizations are open systems, dependent on variable and often unknowable environments for the resources they need to survive, yet they are judged by participants and outside evaluators according to standards suited to staid bureaucracies. Their structures and actions reflect attempts to manage these conflicting pressures, and thus the 'right' structure is contingent on the sources of uncertainty and evaluation. Their designs buffer the technical core from an unruly environment with layers intended to absorb uncertainty, and when outside elements generate too much uncertainty, they are absorbed through merger or other means. Thompson catalogued an array of internal and external tactics organizations used to achieve stability, documented in substantial later empirical research.

Paradigm proliferation: organization and environment

The foundational works of the Carnegie School and Thompson suggested that a single 'theory of organizations' might suffice to hold together the diverse disciplinary sources of organization theory. But the 1970s saw a proliferation of diverse theories of organization, each focused on a somewhat different aspect of what organizations were and what they did: where they placed their boundaries, how they responded to dependence on other organizations, why they were created and disbanded at particular historical times, or how they managed perceptual or legitimacy standards of outside evaluators, among others. From a single trunk, organization theory brachiated into diverse and occasionally contradictory approaches to the study of organizations during the 1970s.

Oliver Williamson drew on Thompson and the Carnegie School to specify in more detail an answer to Coase's question: why are some exchanges done within an organization's boundaries, while others take place across boundaries (that is, on the market)? Put another way, why are there firms at all, rather than simply market transactions? The answer he gave in 1975's *Markets and Hierarchies* provided the basis for **transaction cost economics** as a theory of the firm. The frictions created by transactions are sometimes less costly in the market, and sometimes less costly within firms – particularly when the parties to the exchange have assets invested in the relationship that are less valuable elsewhere (e.g. when a supplier invests in specialized equipment that is only useful for a particular buyer, or when an employee gathers a lot of on-the-job experience tailored to their employer). The pressures of producing products or services profitably induces firms to be mindful of transaction costs and thus to implement the least-cost structure to govern them (to make an input, buy it on the market or create long-term contracts). An implication is that when transaction costs change (e.g. the Internet reduces the difficulty of communicating with suppliers), firm boundaries will change as well.

Other theorists doubted the decisive influence of market pressures on organization structure, and instead argued that organizations often looked the way they did and took particular actions in an effort to manage their environmental dependencies. Jeffrey Pfeffer and Gerald Salancik argued in *The External Control of Organiza-*

tions that exchange relations create power and dependence: a firm that relies on a particular supplier for a critical input is dependent on that supplier, and the supplier may use its power to make demands. As a result, organizations often bear the stamp of powerful outsiders: where they locate facilities, what standards they cleave to, which executives get promoted, and even what charities they support may be swayed by those in control of critical resources. Those that run organizations respond by seeking to manage their dependencies, complying when they must but also co-opting the powerful (e.g. by inviting them to serve on the supervisory board), neutralizing their power (by buying their supplier or cultivating other sources), or exiting the situation (for instance, by diversifying into a different industry). Their motivation is not profit per se, although managing the demands of investors is part of their charge. Rather, it is to maintain some autonomy by avoiding or managing exchange-based dependence. As a result, the structure of organizations and their ties to each other to some degree maps on to the flows of resource exchanges among industries, as organizations jostle to build their own power and avoid dependence.

Still other theorists contemplated the organizational world of the 1970s and saw not rampant change but remarkable stasis among the 'organizational dinosaurs' then leading the economy. Organizations may make cosmetic changes in response to their environments, but more common is inertia – continuing in the same direction as before. Several factors alluded to in prior theories make it hard for organizations to make significant changes: old organizations bear the imprint of their time and place of founding, and success with extant routines locks them into place as hallowed tradition impervious to change; large organizations that have grown using a particular business theory have difficulties rejecting that theory even when events in the world would seem to invalidate it; and top executives set up promotion procedures that reproduce themselves and their worldview. Yet in spite of this inertia at the organizational level, the world is full of different kinds of organizations with diverse structures. Thus, according to population ecologists, it is often more fruitful to study bursts of foundings and extinctions of organizational types to account for the mix of organizations in society. The research strategy implied by this stance is not to focus on the life-histories of particular firms, as in the previous approaches, but of entire populations. Much as a demographer might study the incidence of births, deaths or major life events within particular sub-populations, ecologists studied the births and deaths of organizations and linked them to environmental events (such as political revolutions or changes in legal regime) and population-level variables such as density. One regularly observed finding is that births increase and deaths decrease as a population within an industry grows larger, up to an inflection point; thereafter, greater density decreases birth rates and increases death rates. Carroll and Hannan provide an empirical and theoretical summary in *The Demography of Corporations and Industries*.

New institutional theorists such as John Meyer, Paul DiMaggio and Walter Powell argued that a shift towards a post-industrial economy and the spread of a dominant form of rationality had led to a proliferation of institutionalized myths about how to structure organizations. In contrast to the earnest organizations striving for rationality in a turbulent world described by Thompson, institutionalists described organizations judged by their rationalizations more than their rationality. Organizations often strove to meet standards imposed by external evaluators in their structures and decisions, even when these templates had little to do with getting their real work done. Schools ceremonially adopt curriculum reform and create new offices whose influence rarely reaches the classroom; non-profits adopt organization structures meant to signal their modern management to corporate funding sources even when they only exist on paper; and corporations proclaim adherence to shareholder value and create financial and organizational structures as a Potemkin Village for the **financial markets** that evaluate them. Moreover, the adoption of ceremonial structures de-coupled from the 'technical core' is not mere ceremony, but often essential for the organization's survival. Institutional theorists documented the origins and spread of these myths through a variety of channels – imitation of peers, pressure from exchange partners, demands by governments, and persuasion by executives embedded in professional networks that crossed organizations, among others. And just as population ecologists argued that the organizational population was the appropriate unit of analysis, institutionalists argued that the organizational field – the set of organizations implicated in a particular domain of social life, such as health care – was the appropriate level to make sense of social structure and why organizations come to look and act the way they do. Powell and DiMaggio's *New Institutionalism in Organizational Analysis* collects several of the seminal pieces in this approach.

And finally, network theory provided a set of tools and a framework for considering how the ties among organizations, either through exchange relations, shared directors, common geography or shared third affiliations, aggregated into an inter-organizational social structure. **Network analysis** provided a rigorous means to undergird empirical work that took seriously the injunction to study populations or fields of organizations. By considering both organizations as networks – sets of ties among constituent actors – and organizations in networks, it provided imagery and analytical tools for linking the very micro (employees) to the very macro (the larger economy of organizations).

490

Organizations as mechanisms for social explanation

While organization theory elaborated a set of perspectives oriented around topical questions – where firms place their boundaries, what strategies executives use to avoid dependence and gain power for their organizations, how organizational birth and death rates get us to the mix of organizations we have in society, when societal standards breed organizational conformity – the economic world of business continued a trajectory of globalization that challenged the kinds of organization theories that predominated in the USA in the 1970s. Trade and financial flows across borders increased dramatically after the mid 1970s, the former Soviet bloc disintegrated into separate national economies with diverse approaches to post-socialist capitalism, China mounted an aggressive 'third way' to industrialization and **economic development**, the European Union adopted a common currency and market, and different economic models rose and fell. It would be hubris to imagine that organization theory, developed in a particular time and place, would turn out to be a universal theory of organizations. Moreover, even in the USA the notion that organizations ought to be conceived as singular actors with sovereign boundaries, which dated back to the origins of the discipline, became increasingly difficult to sustain with the increased prevalence of contingent work, sub-contracting, alliances, licensing and **industrial districts**.

Developments in organization theory after the mid 1980s were increasingly oriented towards problem-driven work that developed theories of the middle range. That is, rather than seeking to develop general and trans-historical explanations of seemingly timeless phenomena such as hierarchy and density dependence in organizational birth and death rates, research increasingly focused on explaining transitions, often at the level of either the field or the national economy. This work drew on organization theory not as a falsifiable paradigm, but as a source of causal imagery (in Stinchcombe's terms), or nuts and bolts of explanation (as Elster put it). The object of explanation in such work is typically not some aspect of an organization – where it places its boundary, or how tall is its hierarchy – but a social phenomenon in which organizations play a part. For instance, stratification generally takes place through organizational processes of hiring and assignment to positions and salaries; to explain stratification requires understanding how these 'human resource practices' originate, spread and are implemented. Environmental damage and recovery is largely enacted by business and other organizations, and so to explain why a particular geographic area has the environmental quality that it does entails understanding organizational decision-making. Elections and changes in laws are largely shaped by covert or overt business influence, often mediated through still other organizations. Mapping political terrain inevitably leads one to (or through) influential organizations. And legal changes often require substantial interpretation by the organizations charged with implementing them, so organizational processes are typically the link between law and society.

Particularly engaging work drawing on organization theory during and after the 1990s examined how 'marketization', or the increasing penetration of markets into areas previously organized by other means, altered the shape and 'rules' of organizational fields such as the post-socialist economy in Hungary, health care in the USA, business groups in China, and labour markets in Japan. This work suggests that there is fruitful work to be done in asking questions at the social or civic level, while using organization theory as the set of tools for answering those questions.

See also: agency theory; corporate governance; enterprise groups; exchange theory; firms; inter-firm relations; interlocking directorates; managerial revolution.

References and further reading

Carroll, Glenn R. and Hannan, Michael T. (1999) *The Demography of Corporations and Industries*, Princeton, NJ: Princeton University Press.

Cyert, Richard M. and March, James G. ([1963]1992) *A Behavioral Theory of the Firm*, Cambridge, MA: Blackwell.

Davis, Gerald F. (2005) 'Firms and Environments', in Neil Smelser and Richard Swedberg (eds), *Handbook of Economic Sociology*, second edition, Princeton, NJ: Russell Sage/Princeton University Press.

March, James G. and Simon, Herbert A. ([1958]1993) *Organizations*, Cambridge, MA: Blackwell.

Pfeffer, Jeffrey and Salancik, Gerald R. ([1978]2003) *The External Control of Organizations: A Resource Dependence Perspective*, Stanford, CA: Stanford University Press.

Powell, Walter W. and DiMaggio, Paul J. (eds) (1991) *The New Institutionalism in Organizational Analysis*, Chicago: University of Chicago Press.

Scott, W. Richard (2002) *Organizations: Rational, Natural, and Open Systems*, fifth edition, Upper Saddle River, NJ: Prentice Hall.

Thompson, James D. ([1967]2003) *Organizations in Action: Social Science Bases of Administrative Theory*, New Brunswick, NJ: Transaction Books.

Williamson, Oliver E. (1975) *Markets and Hierarchies: Analysis and Antitrust Implications*, New York: Free Press.

GERALD DAVIS

ORGANIZATIONAL FIELDS

Organizational fields, sometimes referred to as inter-organizational or institutional fields or domains, consist of organizations that 'in the aggregate, constitute a recognized area of institutional life: key suppliers, resource and product consumers, regulatory agencies, and other organizations that produce similar services or products' (DiMaggio and Powell 1983: 148). Though similar to the concept of industry, this term emphasizes the importance of cultural norms and institutionalized practices rather than the relevance of the number of competitors and customers, the height of entry/exit barriers or other aspects of market structure (cf. Porter 1980). In addition, it highlights the role of regulatory agencies, trade and professional associations and other organizations that are likely to contribute to the regulation and institutionalization of the field.

So far, this rather broad field definition has been specified most convincingly by Leblebici *et al.* (1991), who distinguish four dimensions of organizational fields: (1) constellations of actors; (2) technologies used; (3) regulations established (by state agencies); and (4) practices characterizing the activities in the field. According to its traditional neo-institutional conception, the survival of organizations in a field is assumed to be determined by the extent to which these are capable of adhering their practices to the institutional structures of a field and, thereby, gain the legitimacy which is necessary for system survival.

An organizational field or domain forms, changes and, eventually, dissolves. The formation and 'structuration' of an organizational field is typically described in terms of

> the increase in the extent of interaction among organizations in the field; the emergence of sharply defined inter-organizational structures of domination and patterns of coalition; an increase in the information load with which organizations in a field must contend; and the development of a mutual awareness among participants in a set of organizations that they are involved in a common enterprise.
>
> (DiMaggio and Powell 1983: 148)

When it comes to organizing economic activities in or across fields, three modes of governance are obviously at hand: market, network and hierarchy (Windeler and Sydow 2001). While none of these modes

should be considered to signify a higher degree of field structuration per se, most organizational fields can be described in terms of dominance by one of these modes. With respect to the change, transformation and dissolution of fields, processes of homogenization and/or heterogenization as well as of field re-composition or re-configuration, not least in terms of the dominant mode of organizing, should be considered.

The concept of organizational fields clarifies the fact that the environment of organizations is not amorphous, but – in a 'society of organizations' (Perrow 1991) – is mainly made up of organizations and inter-organizational relationships of either a market-, a hierarchy- or a network-like character. Apart from this theoretical *Vorentscheidung*, the concept is very open to further specification. For instance, organizational fields may be issue-based (Hoffmann 1999). An organizational field may also be specified as an industry or as a region or, as in the case of media regions or the machine-building industry of Baden-Wuerttemberg, for example, as a combination of the two. In these latter cases, the boundaries of organizational fields are not only constructed functionally but also geographically (Windeler and Sydow 2001). In turn, **industrial districts**, learning regions, industry clusters or other geographical spaces may be specified as particular types of organizational fields, i.e. fields that are characterized by spatial agglomeration, intensive inter-organizational interaction and shared understandings.

The emphasis on organizations and, thus, inter-organizational relationships, however, also marks a practical limitation of the field concept: If applied to areas where, as in the case of many cultural industries, not only corporations but very small firms and, in particular, individual entrepreneurs (e.g. authors, directors and actors) are involved in the field activities, the concept literally does not pay attention to the role of these individual agents in the respective field.

Another limitation results from a fundamental neo-institutionalist assumption inherent in the original field concept, namely that organizing in the field is determined by belief systems and bundles of normative rules prevalent in the immediate organizational field and the wider society. Although emphasizing that institutional fields are an outcome of social construction processes, Sahlin-Andersson (1996), for instance, assumes that organizational identities are typically derived from organizational fields. More recent neo-institutional approaches, by contrast, highlight the role of strategic agency and power in neo-institutional theorizing in general and in organizational fields in particular: 'As a result, the focus of neo-institutional theory is now shifting from the study of fields as relatively static and predictable units of analysis to the study of fields as arenas of power dependencies and strategic interactions' (Hensmans 2003: 356). In consequence, future research will also focus on questions like how organizations shape organizational fields.

It may be added that the application of the field concept is certainly not restricted to neo-institutionalist theorizing, neither to its purist version nor to more recent political-cultural reconceptualizations. Rather, the concept may also be included in other theories of organizations and inter-organizational relationships in order to specify this highly relevant level of analysis and/or clarify this important context for organizing. For instance, a structurationist reinterpretation frees the field concept from any deterministic understanding that emphasizes coercive, normative or mimetic isomorphism (Windeler and Sydow 2001). Instead, by highlighting the strategic possibility of (groups of) individual and corporate actors to structure the institutional environment, this interpretation emphasizes the recursive interplay between organizational and inter-organizational practices on the one hand and field structures and field practices on the other. In addition, such a reconceptualization, like the political-cultural mentioned above, pays significantly more attention to the resource and, hence, power dimension of organizations and the fields they are embedded in. Thereby, the concept also overcomes its bias towards normative and cognitive **embeddedness**.

References and further reading

Beckert, Jens (1999) 'Agency, Entrepreneurs, and Institutional Change. The Role of Strategic Choice and Institutionalized Practices in Organizations', *Organization Studies*, 20(5): 777–99.

DiMaggio, Paul and Powell, Walter W. (1983) 'The Iron Cage Revisited: Institutional Isomorphism and Collective Rationalities in Organizational Fields', *American Sociological Review*, 48: 147–60.

Fligstein, Niel (2001) *The Architecture of Markets*, Princeton, NJ: Princeton University Press.

Hensmans, Manuel (2003) 'Social Movement Organizations: A Metaphor for Strategic Actors in Institutional Fields', *Organization Studies*, 24(3): 355–81.

Hoffmann, A. J. (1999) 'Institutional Evolution and Change: Environmentalism and the US Chemical Industry', *Academy of Management Journal*, 42(4): 351–71.

Leblebici, Huseyin, Salancik, Gerald R., Copay, Anne and King, Tom (1991) 'Institutional Change and the Transformation of Inter-organizational Fields: An Organizational History of the US Radio Broadcasting Industry', *Administrative Science Quarterly*, 36: 333–63.

Perrow, Charles (1991) 'A Society of Organizations', *Theory and Society*, 20: 725–62.

Phillips, Nelson, Lawrence, T. and Hardy, Cynthia (2000) 'Collaboration and the Dynamics of Institutional Fields', *Journal of Management Studies*, 37: 23–43.

Porter, Michael E. (1980) *Competitive Strategy*, New York: Free Press.

Powell, Walter W. and DiMaggio, Paul (eds) (1991) *The New Institutionalism in Organizational Analysis*, Chicago: University of Chicago Press.

Sahlin-Andersson, Kerstin (1996) 'Imitating By Editing Success: The Construction of Organizational Fields', in Barbara Czarniawska and Guje Sevón (eds), *Translating Organizational Change*, Berlin: Aldine de Gruyter, pp. 69–92.

Windeler, Arnold and Sydow, Joerg (2001) 'Project Networks and Changing Industry Practices – Collaborative Content Production in the German Television Industry', *Organization Studies*, 22(6): 1035–61.

JOERG SYDOW

ORGANIZATIONAL INNOVATION

The subject of organizational innovation has been researched within sociology since the 1960s. However, within the last several decades this topic has become increasingly important within a variety of disciplines including industrial economics, management and political science, each of which has moved this research into new arenas. Innovation is now perceived as the basis of the new economy while governments are devising policies to stimulate innovation as a solution to a range of problems and especially that of unemployment. The importance of the topic is also attested to by the variety of handbooks that have recently appeared as well as the creation of specialized education programmes in both European universities and American business schools.

Organizational innovation is defined as the adoption of an idea or behaviour that is new to the organization (Hage 1999). Economists prefer to focus only on industrial innovations that have economic significance, whereas sociologists tend to use the term innovation to include not only new programmes or services but also scientific discoveries, a new arena in innovation research. The key words in the definition are 'new to the organization'. Even the borrowing of an idea or practice from another organization, which is typical given processes of diffusion and of competition, inevitably requires some adjustments and modifications to fit the local organizational culture and its routines.

This essay considers three fundamental issues in the topic of organizational innovation. The first issue is the question of innovation types and dimensions while the second examines both sociological and management theory about the determinants of organizational innovation. Important new work in this area includes that on inter-organizational relationships and the problem of organizational learning. Finally, the concluding section reviews quite briefly the new work on the macro context as represented by the new literatures on the national systems of innovation and on the evaluation of government policies designed to stimulate organizational innovation.

A typology for organizational innovation begins with the distinction between outputs and processes for producing these outputs. The outputs are either new products or services. Generally, the focus has been on simple rather than complex products and services, such as cell phones or an AIDS treatment programme rather than the development of complex technical systems like the Internet and satellites for weather forecasting. The processes for manufacturing a product or providing a service can be either technological or administrative. Common examples are the adoption of robots or numerical control machines or the use of support groups in the provision of services. Administrative practices can vary from quality control management to changes in even the nature of the form of the organization such as halfway houses for the treatment of former prisoners and mental patients.

Generally in organizational sociology and management, the measures of outputs have been innovation rates over a specified time span. In the last ten years, the European Union has conducted surveys of industrial innovation in its member countries. In this survey the proportion of sales generated by new products that have been introduced in the previous five years is the measure of industrial innovation. As yet, the United States has not developed a systematic data collection effort for industrial innovation.

The measurement of both output and process innovations still requires considerable conceptual development and the diversity of measures may explain some of the problems in obtaining consistency in the research results, especially in the industrial economics research, which is not reviewed in this essay.

Both the outputs and the processes of innovation can be contrasted and compared with the dimensions of radical vs incremental. Generally radical means the addition of some important attribute to the product or service, a major improvement in some performance quality or a two- or threefold increase in productivity. Examples include the hybrid car, the constant improvement in microchip computing speed, or the addition of flexibility to manufacturing systems with numerical control machines. One simple way of quantifying radical is to determine whether it destroys the competencies of the firm. As can be observed, the measurement problems of radical vs incremental are even greater because the definition of what is radical varies across various literatures.

More recently Afuah and Bahram (1995) have suggested what they have called the hypercube of innovation. Essentially this has three dimensions: stability vs change in the core dimensions, stability vs change in the linkages between the core concepts and components, and whether the changes involve the supplier, customer and other innovators as well as the product and the way in which it is manufactured. The first two dimensions allow for the inclusion of architectural innovation and modular innovation as new and interesting types along with radical and incremental innovation. The last dimension considerably opens the discussion of innovation to include its impact on the supply chain and the customer.

In general, the organizational sociology and management literatures (Hage 1999) have emphasized three determinants of innovation within the organization: (1) a complex division of labour; (2) the organic structure; and (3) a high-risk strategy. As the complexity of the division of labour increases, there is more absorptive capacity about both advances in the knowledge base of the firm and problems in the competitive marketplace. A complex division of labour leads to more creative problem-solving and a greater likelihood that radical innovation will occur, whether in the process technology or in the outputs.

The organic model of organizations, which includes a decentralized decision-making structure and the absence of bureaucratic rules, also facilitates the adoption of new processes and products given complex division of labour. Centralized organizations are likely to have an organizational culture that opposed change. Finally, high-risk strategies are equally if not more important. The leaders of the firm have to decide to emphasize the development of radical process technologies and/or products or they are not likely to occur. These three determinants have been well supported in research over the past forty years and in multiple reviews (Hage 1999).

What has received much less attention and is quite important are the various mechanisms by which organizations learn internally. Here the ground-breaking work by Nonaka and Takeuchi (1995)has emphasized the problems of converting tacit knowledge into explicit knowledge. Their concrete case was the use of quality work circles, an example of a radical administrative innovation, and how they continuously improved Japanese productivity in the automobile industry incrementally. This issue of making tacit knowledge explicit is critical because frequently the problem of developing innovations is relearning and changing the routines of the organization, an issue not considered enough in the previous research on the determinants of organizational innovation. The topics of organizational learning and the importance of tacit knowledge have become critical in organizational research.

Another new and important development in the study of organizational innovation has been the movement from a focus on the organic organization with a complex division of labour to the inter-organizational network (Lundvall 1992) in which organizational learning occurs because of external relationships. Here we have an example of a radical new form of organization, an inter-organizational dyad or network. The argument is that as problems become still more complex, then it is necessary to seek technical or knowledge resources in other firms and even in other kinds of research organizations such as universities and public research laboratories as the next logical step in the development of a more complex division of labour. There has been an explosion in the number of inter-organizational relationships in the past twenty years, but not all of these are concerned with cooperation about innovation: many involve production or marketing agreements.

The studies of inter-organizational networks that focus on innovation indicate that they do increase the rates of innovation as measured by a variety of measures, although again not always output measures. Most of this research has been conducted on the supply chain where the learning is from customer to supplier or the reverse. So far, we have only case studies of some of the more interesting inter-organizational relationships such as research consortia and global alliances. These are interesting because the former involve competitors working together to develop their common knowledge base, while the latter usually involve groups of organizations that unite to compete world-wide in the development of a radical new product that can have only one standard.

More recently, Hage and Hollingsworth (2000) have further extended the need for inter-organizational networks and organizational learning by arguing that the movement from basic research to the final marketing of a new product must be seen as an idea innovation network with organizations specializing in basic research, in applied research, in proto-type development, in manufacturing research, in quality research, and finally even in research on how best to market the product. Increasingly different organizations are specializing in these different arenas creating a new problem of integration across arenas. Recent research on the paradigmatic shifts in both the telecommunications industry and in the pharmaceutical industry provides support for this movement towards specialization along the idea-innovation chain and the creation of inter-organizational networks as one of the solutions.

Throughout the forty years of research on organizational innovation, the macro context of organizations and how these might affect innovation was complete ignored by organizational sociologists and management researchers. But within the last ten years, two new literatures have emerged that can correct this omission: (1) the theoretical literature on national systems of innovation, and (2) the governmental policy literature on attempts to change their systems of innovation.

The national systems of innovation (Nelson 1993) literature focuses, as does recent work on varieties of capitalism, on why do some countries, typically the USA, have higher rates of radical innovation than Germany or Japan, which are described as having higher rates of incremental innovation. The explanations are sought in an analysis of the various institutional arrangements in the society including education, scientific research, finance, labour market and **industrial relations**, etc. One of the more important aspects of the institutional arrangements that are compared is the dominant mode of coordination that supplements the market, whether large corporations, associations, the state or inter-organizational networks. In other words, the analysis of these national systems of innovation is quite complex and attempts to discern the configuration of institutions that can explain differences in the types and rates of innovation. Unfortunately, space does not allow for a rich exposition of the various arguments that are being made.

In fact, these characterizations of the USA being better at radical innovation and Germany and Japan better at incremental innovation tend to be somewhat simplistic, because the USA has been slow to implement radical process technologies whereas Germany and Japan have done so quickly and more effectively. In addition, these two latter countries have many radical innovations within the assembled products, such as cars, which are typically ignored in these comparisons. But regardless, the question that they are posing is an important one to add to the literature on organizational innovation.

In political science, there is also a new literature that is focusing on evaluating government policies designed to change the national system of innovation. In particular, Germany has been concerned about its lack of bio-tech industry and has attempted to create one, and has been able to do so. Other governments have encouraged the development of industrial parks where a number of small firms can concentrate together, sometimes with success and sometimes without. As yet, this area of research is too new to be able to summarize any definite conclusions.

But these parallel developments about the macro context of organizational innovation contain within them several debates that are certainly will be the focus of future organizational innovation research. The first is whether the concept of the national system of innovation has any meaning in an international context of scientific research and of global alliances and international dyads. The second is whether policy chan-

ges in the institutional arrangements are possible given the national systems of innovation and the assumption of path dependency. Finally, what is absent from both organizational innovation research and research on national systems of innovation is the precise relationship between these two levels. This has yet to be carefully considered and researched.

See also: capitalism, varieties of; economic organizations.

References and further reading

Afuah, A. N. and Bahram, N. (1995) 'The Hypercube of Innovation', *Research Policy*, 24: 51–76.

Hage, J. (1999) 'Organizational Innovation and Organizational Change', *Annual Review of Sociology*, 25: 597–622

Hage, J. and Hollingsworth, J. R. (2000) 'A Strategy for Analysis of Idea Innovation Networks and Institutions', *Organizational Studies*, 21: 971–1004.

Lundvall, B. (1992) *National Systems of Innovation: Towards a Theory of Innovation and Interactive Learning*, London: Pinter.

Nelson, R. R. (ed.) (1993) *National Innovation Systems: A Comparative Study*, Oxford: Oxford University Press.

Nonaka, I. and Takeuchi, H. (1995) *The Knowledge Creating Company*, Oxford: Oxford University Press.

JERALD HAGE

OWNERSHIP AND CONTROL OF LARGE CORPORATIONS

The classic works

Scholarly interest in the ownership and control of large corporations dates back to Berle and Means' *The Modern Corporation and Private Property* (1932). Berle and Means contended that the ownership and control of large corporations had increasingly becoming separated from one another. As privately held corporations grew, their capital requirements outstripped their founders' financial capacities, and firms sold stock to private investors to fuel continued expansion. Over time, ownership became dispersed among a large number of unrelated individuals. And control passed to professional managers, who filled their boards of directors with persons who largely supported their preferred policies.

This basic line of argument was later taken up by a second generation of economists and sociologists who made sweeping claims about the implications of this 'managerial revolution'. These managerialist theorists maintained that the separation of ownership and control spelled the end of social class antagonisms, the capitalist class and even capitalism as an economic system. At the heart of these claims were two assumptions. Professional managers have different interests than their capitalist predecessors, interests in firm growth as opposed to profit maximization. Further, professional managerial interests are in accord with the interests of the broader society, interests in the expansion of products and services available for consumption (Bell 1961).

In the early 1970s, though, Zeitlin (1974) presented an alternative perspective on the ownership and control of large corporations. He presented evidence indicating that the separation of ownership and control in the United States was substantially less widespread than previously thought. Further, he contended that not only were the majority of US firms still subject to family capitalist control, but that the US economic and social order remained fundamentally capitalist. His argument was rooted in the Marxist tenet that the separation of ownership from control in the large corporation represents the abolition of private property within the context of the capitalist mode of production. According to Zeitlin, many firms that are not owned and controlled by capitalist families are owned and controlled by large financial institutions that are themselves family owned and controlled. Further, many firms that are not

owned and controlled by a capitalist family or a financial institution are run by managers who have been socialized into capitalist **norms and values**, either through early-life exposure to upper-class institutions (such as exclusive preparatory schools) or later-life exposure to upper-class institutions (e.g. upper-class clubs). As a result, Zeitlin maintained that there was little difference in the behaviour and/or performance of so-called management and capitalist-controlled firms.

The 'ownership and control debate' between managerialists and Marxists continued through the remainder of the 1970s. However, the debate petered out unceremonially as the decade drew to a close. Sociologists increasingly gravitated towards a view that ownership and control relations no longer influence corporate behaviour, while economists developed and expanded a sophisticated framework for theorizing the impact of ownership on behaviour.

Contemporary work

Most sociologists now implicitly assume that the separation of ownership and control in contemporary corporations is for all extents and purposes complete: that is, that autonomous professional managers control the large firm and that owners are dispersed and powerless. There are two sociological approaches that share this general orientation.

Proponents of the resource dependence perspective embrace the core managerialist assumption that professional managers uniformly pursue strategies that ensure their firm's stable growth as opposed to the maximization of profit. They also contend that the main engine of stable growth is the steady supply of resources needed for survival. Resource dependence theorists maintain that corporate managers can assure the stable supply of needed resources by establishing inter-organizational linkages with firms that control these resources.

Foremost among these strategies are inter-firm linkages, such as **interlocking directorates**, joint ventures, and mergers and acquisitions (Pfeffer and Salancik 1978). Thus a corporation's position in the market structure of the economy, rather than its mode of control, is the main determinant of its behaviour and performance.

Proponents of the new institutional perspective maintain that professional managers vary in their 'conception of control', by which they mean their understanding of the nature and purpose of the corporation. In particular, new institutional theorists contend that top managers, trained in the most prominent business schools and specializing in the finance function, tend to embrace the finance conception of control (also dubbed the 'firm as portfolio' view). In this cognitive schema, the firm is considered a bundle of investments and the purpose of management is to maximize this bundle's value on the stock market. Foremost among the strategies to maximize a firm's value on the stock market is the acquisition and divestment of its individual components (Fligstein 1990). Thus the educational and/or functional backgrounds of a corporation's top managers, not its mode of control, are the main determinants of its behaviour and performance.

Economists, on the other hand, implicitly adopt the view that the separation of ownership and control in the United States is incomplete and, more importantly, varies from firm to firm. Most economic analyses of ownership structure are framed by **agency theory**. According to the basic agency theory account, firms are composed of principals (owners) and agents (managers). When the two are embodied in the same individuals, as is the case in owner-managed firms, principals and owners possess the same interests, and managers pursue the classical capitalist aim of maximizing stockholder wealth and enacting behaviours that insure it. When ownership and control are separated, as is the case when stock-ownership is widely dispersed among a large number of unrelated individuals and control falls to professional managers, top managers are inclined to pursue policies that further their own parochial interests at the expense of stockholders. Specifically, managers have a tendency to pursue short-term objectives, which tend to increase their salaries, to the exclusion of long-term interests that increase stockholder value. Further, **free-rider** problems reduce dispersed owners' incentive to monitor and control managers and political problems undermine dispersed owners' capacity to monitor and control managers (Jensen and Meckling 1976).

There are, though, devices to reduce these agency costs. Managerial interests can be aligned with stockholder interests by writing employment contracts that tie managerial compensation to long-run firm profitability: in particular, by writing contracts that include stock options. The deleterious effects of conflicts between manager and stockholder interests can be mitigated by appropriate allocation of stock ownership and corporate board seats. Concentrated ownership increases stockholder incentives and power to monitor and control potentially opportunistic managers; in particular, when ownership is in the hands of financial institutions and pension funds. Corporate boards of directors can safeguard dispersed stockholder interests, in particular when board seats are occupied by independent stockholders or high-status business leaders concerned about maintaining their reputations. A substantial volume of research has demonstrated that ownership structure, CEO employment contract form and board of director composition influence corporate behaviour and performance, although the results are not always consistent with prediction (Daily *et al.* 2003).

New directions

La Porta *et al.* (1999) have conclusively demonstrated that the separation of ownership and control has not progressed very far among large firms outside the United States and has not progressed very far among small firms regardless of national origin. Indeed, over 80 per cent of *all* US firms remain family controlled. Further, Holderness *et al.* (1999) have presented evidence suggesting that ownership concentration in large US corporations has actually increased over the last sixty years, and today on average hovers around 20 per cent. Thus, it seems clear that ownership and control relations remain a potentially important determinant of corporate behaviour.

Economists, especially agency theorists, have taken note of this evidence and continued to develop their analysis of the role ownership and control relations play in corporate behaviour. Recently researchers have begun to extend the basic agency theory argument and to confront evidence that appears to contradict this argument. Some scholars have attempted to refine agency theory's analysis of the impact of outside ownership on the behaviour and performance of management controlled firms. Other scholars have attempted to refine agency theory's analysis of the impact of employment contracts containing stock options on management controlled firms. Still other scholars have attempted to extend agency theory, using it to explain the consequences of variation in ownership structure among family-controlled firms. Finally, some scholars have attempted to examine the scope conditions under which agency theory holds. The character of this research is well illustrated by a collection of papers appearing in a special issue of the *Academy of Management Journal* (2003).

Sociologists, though, have continued to neglect ownership and control issues. In fact, sociologists typically fail to even control for ownership and control relations when studying corporate behaviour. We think that sociologists' lack of attention to the ownership and control of large firms is unfortunate, because this leaves the the-orization of ownership and control relations in the hands of economists, who tend to neglect the extent to which corporate ownership and control shapes and is shaped by power relations in the larger society.

Palmer and Barber (2001) have developed a preliminary sociological conceptualization of ownership and control relations and explored how this conceptualization helps explain corporate behaviour. They contend that stock ownership, upper-class status and elite social ties should be considered jointly as indicators of a top manager's class position. Stock ownership is indicative of a manager's relation to the mode of production. And upper-class institutional affiliations and social network connections are indicative of location in the social organization of the business elite. Palmer and Barber have shown that together these three dimensions of a firm's ownership and control structure influenced a firm's propensity to pursue innovative strategies and tactics in the 1960s, in particular diversifying and often hostile corporate acquisitions. Specifically, they show that firms run by professional managers who lacked upper-class status (those who did not attend exclusive private grammar schools and who were not listed in exclusive metropolitan social registers) but who maintained extensive social network connections (those who enjoyed membership in exclusive-class social clubs) were most likely to pursue diversifying and hostile acquisitions in the 1960s.

Clearly, sociologists have a long way to go if they hope to catch up with economists in the race to theorize the ownership and control of the large firm. Because sociologists have implicitly assumed that ownership is completely separated from control in the large firm, they have neglected the theorization of ownership and control relations and their impact on corporate behaviour. And as a consequence, they have given the economists a substantial head start in the study of **corporate governance**.

References and further reading

Academy of Management Journal (2003) special issue, 46(2).

Bell, D. (1961) *The End of Ideology*, New York: Free Press.

Berle, A. A., and Means, G. C. (1932) *The Modern Corporation and Private Property*, New York: Macmillan.

Daily, C. M., Dalton, D. R. and Rajagopalan, N. (2003) 'Governance through Ownership: Centuries of Practice, Decades of Research', *Academy of Management Journal*, 46(2): 151–8.

Fligstein, N. (1990) *The Transformation of Corporate Control*, Cambridge, MA: Harvard University Press.

Holderness, C., Kroszner, R. and Sheehan, D. (1999) 'Were the Good Old Days That Good? Changes in Managerial Stock Ownership since the Great Depression', *Journal of Finance*, 54: 435–69.

Jensen, M. and Meckling, W. (1976) 'Theory of the Firm: Managerial Behavior, Agency Cost and Ownership Structure', *Journal of Financial Economics*, 3: 305–60.

La Porta, R., Lopez-de-Silanes, F. and Shleifer, A. (1999) 'Corporate Ownership around the World', *Journal of Finance*, 54: 471–517.

Palmer, D. and Barber, B. (2001) 'Challengers, Elites, and Owning Families: A Social Class Theory of Corporate Acquisitions in the 1960s', *Administrative Science Quarterly*, 46(1): 87–120.

Pfeffer, J. and Salancik, G. R. (1978) *The External Control of Organizations*, New York: Harper and Row.

Zeitlin, M. (1974) 'Corporate Ownership and Control: The Large Corporation and the Capitalist Class', *American Journal of Sociology*, 79(5): 1073–119.

DONALD PALMER
MICHAEL W. MAHER

P

PARETO, VILFREDO

The Italian Vilfredo Pareto (1842–1923) started out his career as an engineer. Later he turned to social science, and became known both as a sociologist and as an economist. He saw changes in Europe at the same time as **Weber**, **Marshall** and **Durkheim**. Among those who inspired him are Comte, Hegel and Darwin but also Nietzsche and Machiavelli. Pareto's writings span over economics, politics and sociology, but he has had the greatest influence in economics. He gradually became more cynical and sceptical about people and politics. Pareto's critique of democracy and socialism may have diminished his influence in the social sciences.

Pareto's early works are predominately economic, and the ideas that he developed render him a position in the history of economics. His ambition to lay down a natural science foundation for the discipline is one reason. The key idea in his writing, following Léon Walras, is general equilibrium theory. Pareto stressed the role of dynamics and he emphasizes the role of both economic and social undulations. His ideas of income distribution and optimality are further examples of his influence. Pareto's inclusive analysis makes him relevant in moral philosophy, and the discussion of elites is applicable to political scientists.

Pareto's contribution to sociology is mainly found in the over 2,000-page long and badly organized *Tratto*, or *Mind and Society*, which is the English title. His influence on sociology at the beginning of the second millennium is limited. In the USA his influence peaked in the 1930s when Henderson ran a seminar at Harvard, and **Parsons** gave him a central role in his theoretical work *The Structure of Social Action*, which is a good introduction and discussion of Pareto's work.

The positivistic approach, coloured with a mathematical-technical language, is evident in Pareto's writings. His analysis relies on non-observable and indirect evidence of action and derivations. An important idea outlined in *Mind and Society* is that human actions ultimately should be reduced to underlying sentiments, which are the real driving forces of society, and whose identification is the ultimate aim of his scientific analysis. To identify sentiments the researcher must know the subjective perspective of the actor. According to Pareto, most actions are subjectively logical (rational), which means that the actors have reasons for their acts. Most actions, however, lack the scientific or logical base of established relation between the means and ends of the action that is a prerequisite to speak of objective logical actions. But, to appear logical, people invent justifications for their actions, called derivations. Sentiments are not only factors that explain changes in society: they are also the subject of change, In addition to sentiments Pareto studies residues, which like sentiments are non-logical, but more tangible and easier to study empirically. His empirical work revolves around residues.

Pareto argues that over time the scientific knowledge base expands, which enables people to increase the percentage of actions that are objectively logical. People, in Pareto's view, are mainly acting non-logically, and his famous social types, such as 'Lions' and 'Foxes' and 'Rentiers' and 'Speculators', exemplify this. These types act according to certain residues but paint a varnish of logic over all their actions, though the colour of the paint differs depending on time and situation. In other words, the residues remain, or change only slowly, but the verbal expressions, derivations, reflecting the residues, fluctuate.

Actions are important in Pareto's theoretical edifice, but they play a minor role in his analysis of society, which revolves around equilibrium. Pareto speaks of partial and general equilibrium of the economy, but also of social equilibrium, which encompasses all spheres of society, including the economic. The social equilibrium is the subject field of sociology.

Pareto's contribution to economic sociology must be understood against the backdrop of his general sociology. Few have launched Pareto as an economic sociologist, and his influence on the new economic sociology is limited. Pareto's main achievement from an economic sociological perspective is the way he integrated the economy in a broader social framework. Pareto seems to say that economics deals with logical actions and sociology is defined negatively: that is, as a science dealing with non-logical actions. Logical actions are easiest to identify in the economic sphere. However, and as he is the first to admit, many **economic actions** are non-logical, and can consequently not be analysed according to the laws of economic theory. His discussion of rentiers, who are 'mistrustful of adventures', and

speculators, whom he characterizes as entrepreneurs and highly capable of adaptation, indicates his economic sociological approach. Both these types are capitalists and have profit as their overall goal; they face similar structural condition, but they also differ: One wants stability, the other turmoil.

Pareto takes the irrational forces in society seriously, and thereby touches on themes that were in the air, recognizable in the writings of, for example, Nietzsche, Freud and Le Bon. It is not wrong to view him as a forerunner of the sociology of emotions (see **emotions and the economy**). The interest for the irrational streams of human nature that Pareto shows also precedes much of the sociology of **consumption**. His sociology also shows parallels to **Schumpeter**, who also emphasized the dynamic element of the economy.

Pareto, perhaps due to his flirt with the Italian fascists, has not been very well read among sociologists since World War II. As indicated, his thoughts on irrationality are not outdated, and the general view of sociology as encompassing the economy is still highly relevant.

References and further reading:

Aspers, Patrik (2001) 'Crossing the Boundaries of Economics and Sociology: The Case of Vilfredo Pareto', *American Journal of Economics and Sociology*, 60: 519–45.

Pareto, Vilfredo ([1915–16]1935) *Mind and Society, A Treatise on General Sociology (Tratto di Sociologica generale)*, New York: Dover Publications.

Parsons, Talcott ([1937]1968) *The Structure of Social Action*, vol. I, New York: Free Press.

PATRIK ASPERS

PARSONS, TALCOTT

One of the major American theorists of twentieth-century sociology, Talcott Parsons (1902–79) was trained in and initially taught economics. Although his undergraduate degree was in biology, he became interested in economics and studied that subject first at the London School of Economics and then at Heidelberg University where he became exposed to the writings of Max **Weber**, one of the founders of modern sociology. His doctoral thesis dealt with the analysis of capitalism in then recent German social thought. Returning to the USA, in 1927 he obtained a teaching position in Harvard's economics department where the young scholar acquired knowledge of and respect for the influential neoclassical theory of the economist Alfred **Marshall** and the strong defence of the analytical method in economics propounded by Joseph **Schumpeter**. In 1931, he was appointed to the newly established department of sociology, where he remained until his retirement.

Many of his earliest journal articles dealt with issues arising in the methodology of economics and, more generally, of the social sciences (see Camic 1991). He strongly endorsed the analytical style of economic theory as practised by neoclassical writers in contrast to the more concrete approach of the institutionalists who had been critical of that style. However, like **Pareto** and Weber before him and whom he drew upon, he went on to argue that economics alone was not sufficient for the explanatory understanding of economic phenomena. In so doing, he began to formulate a general theory in which the economic aspect of human action and society were treated in relation to other aspects of social phenomena. The classical sociologist Emile **Durkheim** had stated this idea for a particularly important instance in arguing that there are non-contractual elements in any contract. So Parsons' objective was not to abandon economic theory, but to create a more general analytical framework that could address such questions as: what is the nature of such non-contractual elements? How do they relate to each other and to the economic elements?

For this purpose, in his early writings he put forth a conceptual scheme in which the key idea is that human social acts are embedded in means–ends chains. Such chains consist of ultimate means, such as the properties of the human body, and ultimate ends, such as ethical principles or religious values. But between these endpoints there are means that actors pursue as immediate ends of action, more or less remote from ultimate ends. Economic theory, he argued, was scope-restricted to an aspect of this intermediate sector, focused on rationality as a criterion of choice among alternatives of action where ultimate values are not directly involved. Sociology, by contrast, with its sensitivity to cultural variability – and here he pointed especially to the work of Weber such as the thesis that the Protestant Ethic had fostered the rise of capitalism in the West – had begun the process of building an analytical theory focused on how 'idealistic' elements (analysing the ultimate value sector of means–ends chains) were related to 'material' elements (analysing the intermediate sector). Namely, in every society, certain ultimate ends and values are given specification in normative rules that apply to economic and other modes of action. Such rules shape or direct but do not generally determine concrete actions, although the nature of that constraint can vary among societies, as Durkheim had pointed out in arguing that the collective conscience became more general and diffuse with the growing differentiation of society.

These ideas, among numerous others, were elaborated in great detail in his thesis in *The Structure of Social Action* (1937) that Weber, Durkheim, Pareto and Marshall had converged upon a general theoretical framework consisting of a variety of distinct analytical elements corresponding to the three major sectors in the structure of means–ends chains. This 'general theory of action' became the foundation conceptual structure for all of Parsons' later writings.

In writings leading up and including *The Social System* (1951), Parsons brought into the general action theory he was developing ideas from psychology, drawing especially on Freud. Through socialization processes, a human being acquires a personality structure that includes internalized values that are beyond the reach of rational choice. Thus there is an abstract symmetry: social systems are structured by institutionalized values and personality systems are structured by internalized values. The key proposition of the theory is that the stability of the social system depends upon a sufficient level of internalization of the values that are institutionalized in it. In the context of a modern economy, for instance, certain social categories of individuals are expected to enter into occupations or jobs outside the household and indeed, in normal socialization processes in modern societies, such individuals are strong motivated to 'find jobs' or 'have a career' – a matching relation between role expectation and 'need-disposition' for a long time limited to the male category but more recently extended to the female category as well.

In 1956, Parsons published his major treatise in economic sociology, *Economy and Society* (with junior author Neil Smelser). The system approach he had taken in the earlier work was now greatly elaborated and applied to the economy as one subsystem of the social system, itself a subsystem of action relating to personality systems of members as framed in the matching proposition just discussed as well as to cultural and behavioural systems. For the basic concepts pertaining to this elaborate AGIL scheme, see **economy**. The analytical scheme employs the idea that any system has four functional problems: adaptation to the environment (A), system goal-attainment (G), integration of the parts of the system (I) and maintenance of the system's institutionalized values (L). When the functional scheme is applied to a society, the economy is treated as the adaptive subsystem in a social environment consisting of other subsystems. Its function for society is to produce and allocate resources – means by which actors can realize their various ends.

Because this type of functional analysis is quite general in its formal character, it can be applied to the economy itself as a system leading to the idea that with functional differentiation – as in a complex modern society – there are four interdependent subsystems of the economy, one for each of the economy's functional problems: production (G), investment (A), organization (I) and pattern maintenance of its institutional 'givens' in terms of societal resources committed to economic production (L). This last aspect relates to a highly elaborate and complex mode of institutional analysis that employs the AGIL scheme at multiple and interrelated levels of analysis, treating individual actors, organizations, markets, subsystems and environments.

In this analysis, the fundamental economic institution is *contract,* with special cases such as the employment contract and the investment contract. The analysis has three successive levels based upon exchange analysis. At the first level, each actor in the situation is treated as a system of action with four functional problems. Here the standpoint of each party is analysed, for instance that of a person seeking employment in some organization. The second level of analysis deals with the contractual relationship as a social system, for instance the employment contract as including some terms of exchange to which the parties agree. Perhaps the most important aspect of this analysis is that it includes both instrumental and symbolic aspects of exchange relations, the latter referring to such analytical 'value' elements as prestige and social approval. Generally, the goal attainment and adaptive aspects of the contractual relation pertain to instrumental considerations, e.g. negotiating the best terms of employment, as perceived on each side of the relation. The integrative and pattern

505

maintenance aspects of contract, on the other hand, pertain to the symbolic or value elements of contract (e.g. each side agrees on the social value or prestige of the relevant occupation).

Finally, the third level of analysis pertains to markets, each an aggregate of these dyadic contractual relationships. For instance, a labour market corresponds to an aggregate of possible and actual employment contracts. The labour market, in turn, is treated as one of two 'interchange relations' between the economy and the societal pattern maintenance system. Here the analysis embeds the typical scheme of analysis employed in economic theory in which there are firms and households entering to exchange relations. In AGIL terms, firms are collectivities with economic primacy, while households are collectivities with pattern maintenance primacy and so the interchange connects the society's A and L subsystems, respectively. Socialization of members of society in the various household contexts provides the motivational basis for a supply of actors entering the labour market, and the income they earn flows back to the households. In other words, 'interchange' between systems is a mode of aggregation of contractual relations among concrete actors. There are actually two such interchanges analysed in terms of the flow of money to households for employment commitments to firms on the one hand and the flow of goods from firms to households for monetary payments on the other.

In later work, Parsons extended the notion of interchange to postulate a 'double interchange' relating each pair of functional subsystems of a societal system. This means that the analysis of the economy includes two more double interchanges, one pair relating the polity to the economy and the other relating the societal community or social integrative system to the economy. Thus, the economy is embedded in a societal system that in turn is embedded in a

wider action environment that includes cultural systems such as religious belief systems, systems of knowledge, and the like. In a paper published in the last year of his life titled 'The Symbolic Environment of Modern Economies' (reprinted in Turner 1999) Parsons treats his lifework in the area of economic sociology as having stressed economy–environment relationships, first in regard to the institutional environment of economic processes and then in regard to the interchange or 'dynamic environment', as he puts it. The paper goes on to sketch what he defines to be a third phase in which the focus is on how the modern economy relates to cultural systems in its environment, referring to these as constituting a symbolic or ideological environment. He then sets out an example of this type of cultural analysis in which particular attention is given to religion – specifically Christianity in relation to capitalism. With a focus on systems of meanings, he sets out certain parallels between core Christian **beliefs** and the Marxist theory of capitalism, e.g. the conception of heaven in the former and the conception of the communist society in the latter.

In conclusion, it should be noted that Parsons' economic sociology emphasizes a theme that subsequently became the motto of what was called 'the new economic sociology' as it emerged in the latter part of the twentieth century, namely the **embeddedness** of economic activities within a wider context of social and cultural relationships. The field emphasizes the empirical application of more recent sociological ideas such as social network and **social capital** as well as cultural analyses, with functional and systems analyses more rarely undertaken. Thus, most investigators make no attempt to coordinate their empirical data to Parsons' complex conceptual framework. Its very complexity and the intricacy – critics would say arbitrariness – of its application have deterred later analysts from making much use of it. Nevertheless, Parsons' writings relating to economic sociology are a storehouse of relevant concepts and penetrating insights about the complex interdependencies between modern economies and their environments.

References and further reading

Camic, Charles (ed.) (1991) *Talcott Parsons: The Early Essays*, Chicago: University of Chicago Press.
Holton, Robert J. and Turner, Bryan S. (1986) *Talcott Parsons on Economy and Society*, London: Routledge and Kegan Paul.
Parsons, Talcott and Smelser, Neil (1956) *Economy and Society*, New York: Free Press.
Turner, Bryan S. (ed.) (1999) *The Talcott Parsons Reader*, Oxford: Blackwell.

THOMAS J. FARARO

PATH-DEPENDENCE

Path-dependence refers to processes of social choice involving positive feedback. Positive feedback means that individual choices are mutually reinforcing: If alternative A has been preferred to alternative B once, the likelihood increases that it will be preferred again later. Since the 1980s, the concept of path-dependence has spread from economics to political science and sociology to become the dominant social science paradigm for the explanation of phenomena of structural conservatism.

Perhaps, the best known illustration of path-dependence is Paul David's case study on the adoption of the 'QWERTY' standard for (American) typewriter keyboards (David 1985). When the typewriter boom started in the 1880s, QWERTY was just one solution among many for arranging the letters on the typewriter keyboard. Its march to dominance began when a representative from the Cincinnati School of Typing won a well-publicized speed-typing contest on a QWERTY keyboard. The victory had nothing to do with QWERTY but rather the Cincinnati School's invention of the ten-finger touch-typing method. While, in principle, this method could be used with any keyboard layout, the accidental fact that it was first applied to a QWERTY design was enough to ensure that this design spread along with the typing method: The first people who learned touch-typing learned it on a QWERTY keyboard. This increased the incentive for manufacturers to supply QWERTY keyboards, which in turn made it even more attractive for users to learn touch-typing on the basis of QWERTY. Propelled by this positive feedback, QWERTY quickly drove all other designs out of the market and became the single, industry-wide standard for keyboards. It still is the dominant standard today, despite periodic attempts to replace it by allegedly superior solutions.

The QWERTY case illustrates four specific properties of path dependent processes:

- Multiple equilibria: there are a number of possible outcomes, and it is impossible to predict ex ante which one will prevail. QWERTY's rise to dominance was not structurally preordained. There are other, equally efficient ways to arrange letters on the keyboard.
- Contingency: the final outcome is determined by the particular sequence of choices at the beginning of the process. Small events during this phase can have disproportionately large consequences later because they help a particular alternative to gain an initial lead over its competitors. History matters.
- Inflexibility: once a particular solution has gained an initial lead, this lead is amplified by positive feedback and becomes increasingly difficult to reverse. The process 'locks-in' to this particular solution and 'locks-out' potential competitors.

- Non-optimality: there is no guarantee that the process will always **lock-in** to the superior alternative. If an inferior competitor gains an initial lead, it may prevail over the superior solution. Competition does not guarantee efficiency.

The concept of path-dependence emerged as a challenge to the conventional, neoclassical view of the economy (see **economics, history of**). The neoclassical view is based on the assumption of decreasing returns: utility declines as frequency inclines; the more a particular thing is done, the less attractive it becomes to do it again; the more fertilizer there is on the field, the less useful it is to add more fertilizer. Decreasing returns provide a negative feedback mechanism that steers the economy towards a unique and efficient equilibrium outcome preordained by structural conditions (factor endowments, preferences, technology). History does not matter because any departure from the equilibrium path automatically triggers corrective action. Small events and historical accidents occur but leave no lasting traces on the economy.

Since the days of Adam Smith, there had been an undercurrent in economic thought that investigated the implications of increasing returns. It was not before the 1980s, however, that this undercurrent came to the surface and merged with the economic mainstream. The credit for this feat is usually attributed to W. Brian Arthur. In a series of now famous papers, Brian Arthur used the analytical apparatus of neoclassical economics to fully model the properties of increasing returns processes, and explained, on a high level of generality, where increasing returns come from (Arthur 1994). With illustrations from the history of technology in mind (see **technological change**), he identified four sources of increasing returns in particular:

- Large set-up or fixed costs: these create an incentive to reuse available technology. Once a typist has invested time and effort to learn touch-typing on a QWERTY keyboard, it makes sense for him to stick to that keyboard. A switch to another keyboard would force him to learn touch-typing from scratch, and thus devalue his investment.
- Learning effects: proficiency often improves with repetition. Users get better at using a particular technology by using it more frequently. Typists increase their typing speed; surgeons lower the rate of mistakes. These learning-by-doing effects also put a premium on technological conservatism, and discourage experimentation.
- Coordination effects: the utility of many technical artifacts increases with the number of other artifacts connectable to it. Think of telephones, computer software or razors and razor blades as examples. These coordination – or network – externalities favour established technologies with a large installed base and handicap new technologies lacking such a base.
- Adaptive expectations: in the presence of coordination externalities, actors will base their technology choice upon expectations about future use patterns. These expectations have a self-fulfilling character: By adopting the technology that they believe to be most widespread in the future, actors contribute to actually spreading this technology.

The promise of the concept of path-dependence, and the reason why it spread so quickly across the social sciences, is to add rigour to historicist explanations. Historicist explanations, i.e. explanations that account for some event later in time by some other event earlier in time, have always been popular in the social sciences. However, they often remained case specific and ad hoc, because they were not anchored to a general theory of the conditions under which earlier events become causes for later events and the mechanisms which transmit the causal effect through time. Path-dependence provides such a theory. It has become a standard tool for explaining inflexibility, inertia and change resistance in, for example, market structures, economic geography, public policies, corporate cultures or social frames (see Pierson 2004 for a review).

References and further reading

Arthur, W. Brian (1994) *Increasing Returns and Path Dependence in the Economy*, Ann Arbor, MI: University of Michigan Press.

David, Paul A. (1985) 'Clio and the Economics of QWERTY', *American Economic Review*, 75(2): 332–7.

Pierson, Paul (2004) *Politics in Time: History, Institutions, and Social Analysis*, Princeton, NJ: Princeton University Press.

PHILIPP GENSCHEL

PERFORMANCE

Performance is a concept that is applied at various levels of socio-economic analysis. Individuals, organizations, industries, regions, nation-states, types of business systems and even the world economy are looked at in terms of performance. Human Resource Management (HRM) is concerned with the performance of individuals within organizations. Many organizations appraise their management and workforce on a regular basis, and above-average performance of individual employees may result in pay rises or promotion. Organizations as a whole often differ considerably in their productivity and, depending on whether it is high or low, are seen as high-performance or low-performance organizations. In this context it is worth noting

that the benchmark for assessing the level of organizational performance varies across sectors. What is considered an extremely well-performing organization in a mature industry may seem not very impressive if standards of a fast-growing sector are applied. The literature on so-called **industrial districts** looks at economically very successful regions, classic examples being the Silicon Valley, Baden-Württemberg or the Emilia Romagna. By contrast, regions where the average performances of firms is low, e.g. in developing countries, are researched by development studies. While the 'industrial districts' approach is interested in the institutional and cultural factors and combinations of factors that contribute to the superior performance of a specific region's industries, development studies search for ways to increase low-performance regions' potential to catch up with better-performing regions. Nation-states are researched and compared with reference to their competitive advantages and disadvantages, which are often seen as being rooted in their infrastructure of transportation systems, their cultural traditions or governance characteristics. While Germany and Japan were extremely well-performing nation-states in the post Word War II decades, in the 1990s growth rates were particularly high in the 'emerging markets' in East Asia. In the western world two socio-economic models were competing over the past decades. Continental European systems followed the model of the 'coordinated market economy' and outperformed the 'liberal market economies' in the 1970s and 1980s. Under conditions of globalization, however, the 'liberal market economies' (such as the UK or the USA) overtook the 'coordinated market economies' (such as France or Germany). Finally, the world economy seems to invariably go through cycles of higher and lower performance. While different areas of the world used to go through these cycles asynchronically, **globalization** has considerably contributed to the synchronization of the world economic cycles of boom and bust.

Performance is generally difficult to assess in empirical terms, not least because there is often no consent about the time periods which are to be looked at. Short-term returns on investment do not necessarily indicate sustainable growth and long-term success may not be reflected in short-term performance. While the latter is usually looked at in terms of fast increases of financial profits, long-term performance strategies aim to achieve competitive advantages through increasing the sustainable potential for future performance. The innovativeness of organizations or business systems is commonly seen as a strong indicator and facilitator of longer-term performance and growth potential. However, innovation is also an ill-defined concept where many contextual factors play a crucial role in creating manifest competitive advantages.

In advanced socio-economic systems it is common sense that human capital and technological knowledge are equally, if not more, important than easy access to strategically important material resources and markets in order to achieve high levels of performance. Human capital and technological knowledge are generally associated with long-term planning horizons, but under conditions of fast-changing markets they are also prone to swift invalidation. Thus, strategies to secure high performance in the long run have become increasingly difficult to formulate. The most promising strategic approach under these circumstances is therefore seen in developing procedures of continuous organizational learning and the establishment of knowledge transfer institutions to utilize universities' and other research institutions' knowledge creation for product and process innovation in the industrial and services sectors of a given regions or national socio-economic system.

In the newer socio-economic literature the concepts of **social capital** and 'organizational networks' have been closely associated with performance. This stream of research does not deny that access to relevant material resources and successful market positioning strategies are important with regard to performance. However, it is argued in this context, that these factors often do not sufficiently explain why some organizations and business systems are performing considerably better than their rivals operating under similar economic conditions. Where particularly successful cases are under review, the named literature points to 'soft factors' such as tacit knowledge, **entrepreneurship**, **trust**, corporate culture, social cohesion and organizational networking. Meanwhile, along this line of argument many case studies and descriptive work have shown how influential these factors can be. But, on the whole, there is still a lack of systematic understanding of the interrelatedness of factors and their dynamics in this important field of research.

The debate on performance assessment and measurement is also connected to the concepts of 'shareholder value' and **stakeholder** approaches. In the first perspective, it is argued that it is only the investors of financial capital who deserve to be participating in the results of firms' performance. In a 'stakeholder society' all parties that are affected by a firm's activities, e.g. workforce, investors, suppliers, customers or people living in the local community and potentially suffering from pollution, noise, increased traffic, etc., are seen to be entitled to benefit from private organizations' economic success.

References and further reading

Clark, P. (2002) 'Organizational Performance', in A. Sorge (ed.), *Organization*, London: Thomson.

Fornahl, D. and Brenner, T (eds) (2003) *Cooperation, Networks and Institutions in Regional Innovation Systems*, Cheltenham, UK: Edward Elgar.

Penrose, E. (1959) *The Theory of the Growth of the Firm*, Oxford: Blackwell.

Porter, M. E. (1985) *Competitive Advantage: Creating and Sustaining Superior Performance*, New York: Free Press.

—— (1990) *The Competitive Advantage of Nations*, London: Macmillan.

REINHARD BACHMANN

PHENOMENOLOGY AND ETHNOMETHODOLOGY

Phenomenology is a methodology of philosophical research initiated in 1900 by mathematician Edmund Husserl (1859–1938). The core of phenomenological method consists in the disciplined use of the reflective techniques of 'bracketing' and 'reduction' to disclose the essential features of intentional objects (objects perceivable or imaginable by conscious human beings). Applied to the dispositions, anticipations and intuitions of the intending subject, the same techniques disclose the 'transcendental' conditions and processes of subjectivity as such (i.e. of the rational subject of the European Enlightenment). Husserl developed first eidetic then transcendental phenomenology in an endeavour to clarify the foundations of the sciences, a project that was well under way in mathematics when he began his investigations. His realization in 1931 that '*transcendental intersubjectivity* ... constitutes the world as an *objective* world, as a *world that is identical for everyone*' (quoted in Moran 2000: 179) may be considered, at least honorifically, as the founding moment of phenomenological sociology. His most important contribution to the social sciences is the concept the lifeworld (*Lebenswelt*), the pregiven, unproblematicized, pretheoretical ground of shared language, familiar objects and tacit meanings that the intending subject inhabits 'prepredicatively'.

Ethnomethodology is a partial offshoot of phenomenological sociology with deep roots in classical social theory and socio-linguistics (Hilbert 1992). It is the descriptive study of the reporting and accounting practices ('methods') through which socially embedded actors come to attribute meaning and rationality to their own and others' behaviour. Ethnomethodologists study interactive, ad hoc sense-making at the sites where social structures are produced and reproduced through talk and coordinated action. The central claim of ethnomethodology is that '[p]henomena of order are identical with the procedures for their local endogenous production and accountability' (Garfinkel 2002: 72).

While phenomenology and ethnomethodology differ in their disciplinary orientations, research questions and levels of analysis, they share a common problematic in the constitution of objectivities. The term 'constitution' refers to the precipitation of a unified meaning from a cascading series of overlapping and synchronous perceptual, aperceptual and categorical processes, whose redundancy confirms the objectivity of the identity thus produced. What serial constitution ultimately produces is not the furniture of the universe, but the *known* structures and processes upon which human beings premise and account for their actions. When dealing with affirmed bodies of knowledge – whether in science, the professionals or everyday life – phenomenology and ethnomethodology seek to show how such knowledge is possible: they strive to retrace the steps through which articulated descriptions, definitions, axioms, concepts or formal methods have been constituted by human subjects. (The risk of not doing so, they argue, is reification, misdirection and endless controversy.) Phenomenology tackles constitutional problems epistemologically, through phenomenological psychology. Ethnomethodology tackles them sociologically, through the ethnographic description of actors' reporting and accounting practices. Neither school makes the constitution of economic knowledge

511

(either by economists or the laity) a distinct priority. Both lean heavily on the investigations of Alfred Schutz (1899–1959), a self-taught phenomenologist who considered his clarifications of the methodologies of Weberian sociology and **Austrian economics** to be the beginning of a lifelong project to disentangle the stratified, constituted meanings of the lifeworld. A group of contemporary economists considers Schutz's methodological clarifications to be essential to the rehabilitation of the Austrian paradigm (Boettke and Koppl 2001).

A student of Ludwig von Mises at the University of Vienna, Schutz was part of the intellectually vibrant *Miseskries* that met every other Friday evening during the 1920s to discuss the epistemological problems of economics and related topics. The Austrian school was known for three things: its non-mathematical version of marginal utility (which it called 'the subjective theory of value'), a strongly aprioristic position on the basic concepts and laws of economics, and uncritical adherence to the doctrine of intellectual intuition. The purpose of the biweekly seminar, as Mises saw it, was to reform the last of these commitments. This he did by synthesizing ideas from Carl Menger, founder of the Austrian school, the neo-Kantian Heinrich Rickert, and Husserl's eidetic phenomenology, while carefully studying (and ultimately rejecting) Max **Weber**'s methodological concepts of understanding (*Verstehen*) and the **ideal type**. Mises' dialogic deliberations produced a new a priori inquiry, praxeology, which derived the basic concepts and laws of marginal utility from the definition of the human person as *homo agens*.

Schutz thought that the second commitment – apriorism – had to be revisited along with the third. Dispensing with intellectual intuition, Schutz applied Husserlian phenomenology to Weber's methodological concepts, then extended the clarified concepts into the domain of the a priori. In the Schutzian view, the a priori elements of economic theory (such as *homo agens*, rationality, choice, etc.) were simply definitions constituted from processes of generalization and idealization. He thereby rescued the premises of the Austrian school from epistemological overreaching, while bridging the abyss that Mises had created between inductive and deductive social science. Schutz went on to write a number of important essays on the concepts of choice and rationality, always insisting that the products of theoretical idealization must never be confused with the reasoned choices of intentional subjects living unreflectively in the 'paramount reality' of conversant meanings.

Harold Garfinkel (b. 1917), the founder of ethnomethodology, majored in business and accounting at the University of Newark in the late 1930s. In a course called 'The Theory of Accounts', he learned to see rows and columns of numbers as indicators of a putative underlying order (Garfinkel 2002: 10). Executives refer to this underlying order – the profitability of the firm – through multiple and overlapping accounting systems, each rigorously compiled and balanced, yet never behold the object signified. Created in one location and reported to superiors in another, numbers on accounting sheets – the subject of endless talk and constant revision – nevertheless become the touchstone for all decision-making in the firm. Garfinkel generalized this lesson to the formal methods that scientists and professionals use to forge justifiable (i.e. rational, responsible, actionable) interpretations of reality. In the end, formal and technical methods amount to artful, 'shop floor' procedures of sense-making. Because they convert unseen structures and processes into signified objects of discourse, formal methods constitute the objectivities in their domain of application, but only as contingent, revisable reifications (Garfinkel 2002: 160, n. 164).

Economics would seem to provide a ripe field for ethnomethodological investigation, but only one team has taken up the challenge. R. J. Anderson, J. A. Hughes, and W. W. Sharrock analyse the methods members use to construct realities at both the theoretical and *Lebenswelt* levels. Anderson *et al.* (1988; 1989: 27–47) attend to the formal methods employed in 'Cartesian economics' (i.e. mathematized marginal utility theory) to convert actors' intuitive, qualitative valuations of everyday things into signified theoretical objects expressed as utility functions. In *Working for Profit* (1989), the team asks how closely the theorists' model of the prescient, opportunity-seizing innovator matches the observable behaviour of real-life entrepreneurs. Examining the investment decisions of the founder and top managers of a British food service company, they find that the executives' precise thresholds of risk, profitability, etc., turn into inexact rules of thumb whenever new opportunities arise. These seasoned executives cannot decide whether persistent red ink indicates a bad investment or a run of bad luck, whether opportunity A is comparable to opportunity B, or whether a new catering contract delivers a 'captive market' or just the illusion of one. To unblock one impasse, the founder ad-hoced some numbers on to a handwritten 'heuristic balance sheet' shortly before a decision had to be made. His ardent guesswork convinced the managers that the risks were manageable, the opportunity comparable enough to prior investments, and the founder's judgement as trustworthy as before. All this interpretive work is left out of the standard portrait of entrepreneurial alertness to opportunity.

Phenomenology and ethnomethodology study how elementary processes of sense-making cumulate into intricate systems of knowledge. Both trace the constitutive processes of theoretical science to their ultimate origins in the lifeworld. But how does one begin to describe a world given

'prepredicatively'? The quest for a '*Lebenswelt* economics' must either limit itself to a clarification of the constitutive processes of formal theorizing (*à la* Schutz) or replace crisp theoretical idealizations with transcriptions of actors' circuitous talk (*à la* Anderson *et al.*). Both endeavours piggy-back on existing theoretical developments. Phenomenologists and ethnomethodologists consider theory a wondrous achievement of transcendental intersubjectivity, yet decline to contribute to it themselves.

References and further reading

Anderson, R. J., Hughes, J. A. and Sharrock, W. W. (1988) 'The Methodology of Cartesian Economics: Some Thoughts on the Nature of Economic Theorizing', *Journal of Interdisciplinary Economics*, 2: 307–20.

—— (1989) *Working for Profit: The Social Organization of an Entrepreneurial Firm*, Aldershot, UK: Avebury.

Boettke, Peter and Koppl, Roger (eds) (2001) 'Special Issue on Alfred Schütz Centennial, 1899–1999', *Review of Austrian Economics*, 14: 111–213.

Garfinkel, Harold (2002) *Ethnomethodology's Program: Working Out Durkheim's Apriorism*, Lanham, MD: Rowman and Littlefield.

Hilbert, Richard A. (1992) *The Classical Roots of Ethnomethodology: Durkheim, Weber, and Garfinkel*, Chapel Hill, NC: University of North Carolina Press.

Moran, Dermot (2000) *Introduction to Phenomenology*, London: Routledge.

CHRISTOPHER PRENDERGAST

POLANYI, KARL

Karl Polanyi contributed to the development of economic sociology by emphasizing the need for an understanding of the place of economy in society, developing several important conceptual tools to pursue this understanding, and applying these tools to examine important aspects of the ethnographic record. In addition to the idealistic intellectual experience of his youth, Polanyi was influenced by the powerful historic events from his coming of age to his death – two world wars, hyperinflation, revolution, global depression, fascism and cold war. He was one of many emigrants from Central European fascism who enriched British and American intellectual development. Having observed in the uprooting of his personal life the cataclysm that a poorly instituted economy can provoke, Polanyi's central interest became the problem of lives and livelihood: the relation of individual and community life to the manner by which the community makes its living.

Polanyi was born in Vienna on 21 October 1886 and spent his childhood in Budapest. While a university student, Polanyi was a founder and first president of the Galilei Circle, a political and intellectual club from which emerged many of Hungary's influential liberal and socialist figures. Prominent scholars and artists appeared in the Circle's lecture series, including Eduard Bernstein and Georg Lukács. In 1913 Polanyi joined in the formation of a radical party to unify the dissenting elements of the intelligentsia, middle class, peasantry and non-Magyar minorities, and in June 1914 the National Citizens' Radical Party was formally chartered. In World War I, Polanyi served as a cavalry officer in the Austro-Hungarian army. Thereafter, while hospitalized in Vienna as a result of war wounds, he met Ilona Ducyznska, whom he married in 1923. Ilona was an antiwar activist and a member of the Communist Party. She had fled to Vienna in 1918 upon the collapse of the short-lived Hungarian Soviet Republic.

Polanyi worked as an economic journalist in Vienna from 1924 to 1933, when he lost the job as a result of the Great Depression and fascist censorship. Polanyi emigrated to England, making a living for the next few years lecturing there and on occasional tours to the United States. From 1940 to 1943, Polanyi lived in the USA, giving guest lectures and holding a visiting scholar's appointment at Bennington College in Vermont. He returned to England

for a short period, then returned to the USA soon after the end of the war, serving as a visiting professor at Columbia University, where he was co-director (with Conrad Arensberg) of the very influential Interdisciplinary Project on the Institutional Aspects of Economic Growth. Polanyi's final major project was the founding of *Co-Existence*, an interdisciplinary journal for the comparative study of economics and politics, dedicated to the cause of world peace through knowledge of the realities of cultural differences and the unity of the human condition. After organizing a distinguished editorial board and seeing the first issue to the printer, Polanyi died on 23 April 1964.

Economic sociology is commonly conceived as examining how people came to behave as they do. This contrasts to analysis that observes current behaviour and seeks to explain it on its own terms, without regard to its historical evolution to the present or its possible evolution in the future. The latter strategy is clearly represented by mainstream economics which adopts a methodological individualist approach based on an idealized conception of observable economic action. So-called 'economic man' is axiomatically supplied with given and fully known (to himself) preferences, capacities and opportunities, as well as the desire to reason his way to bliss in the face of scarcity. Economic sociology as commonly conceived adopts a methodologically holistic approach in which preferences, capacities, and opportunities emerge from an interactive process of social economic agents. This socially structured agency is necessarily emergent as agents, well informed or not, pursue their manifold purposes in myriad ways, in the process changing the available sets of purposes, capacities and opportunities as well as the information in these regards.

Economic sociologists, original and new institutional economists, and radical economists share this holistic approach and its common criticism of the approach that pursues explanation of observable behaviour without regard to its origin, especially methodology which bases this task on restrictive idealized assumptions about the motivation and knowledge of the individual agent. Marx criticized Smith and Ricardo for this non-evolutionary perspective, notably in the notes that decades later were published as the *Grundrisse*. Veblen joined the criticism in his celebrated 1898 essay 'Why Economics is not an Evolutionary Science', in which he notes that hedonistic economic man had neither antecedent nor consequence. This phrase aptly defines economic sociology as an approach that recognizes the social conditioning and the social effects of economic agency.

This was clearly Polanyi's view. He observed that the human element in general economic history is more or less constant; it is the institutions that vary. As human agents pursue their purposes they alter the social framework or cultural pattern which conditions their ongoing agency. Accordingly, the study of economic agency must be an institutional analysis of the motivations, capacities and opportunities that are embedded in the patterns of social interaction. The motivation for undertaking productive activity can stem from various sources, and it is the ethnocentrism of the market mentality that habitually seeks this impetus only in calculated economic advantage. Polanyi defined the economy as an instituted process for provisioning society's reproduction. Whatever degree of technical acumen and division of labour a society has achieved, its division of labour must be instituted or regularized by a pattern of socially conditioned transactions. These transactions integrate the division in a concrete sense, instructing individuals as to the place, character, tools and materials of their labour and fashioning a distribution of the real income that their coordinated activities generate. These transaction patterns take the form of reciprocity, redistribution or exchange. 'Reciprocity' refers to socially or politically mandated obligations that define one's functional duties and income privilege. 'Redistribution' refers to collection of goods at a centre for periodic function and ceremonial dispersal. 'Exchange' refers to transactions involving the swapping of goods that are supposed to be of equivalent value.

In his 1944 classic, *The Great Transformation*, Polanyi (1944) referred to this emphasis on the concrete division of labour and provisioning as the substantive approach, and contrasted it to the formalist approach that expresses the market mentality. The latter starts from the axiom that scarcity is *the* universal economic problem and focuses upon rational choice among competing individuals or groups of individuals. The axiomatic basis of the substantive view is that a human group must produce and distribute sufficient goods if it is to persist. To understand the economic activities of a human group the analyst must then examine the concrete cultural pattern within which these activities cohere. Polanyi shares with original institutional economists not just a different approach to the economy but a different conception of the economy itself. The substantive definition of economy has to do with the concrete organization of tools and materials within historical social frameworks of power and meaning, in contrast to the formalist approach which is ahistorical in its universal characterization of the economy as competitive individual activity in the face of scarcity.

Arensberg elaborates the task of institutional analysis in the influential volume that resulted from the project he and Polanyi co-directed: *Trade and Market in the Early Empires* (1957). Such an analysis must account for the origin and evolution of a cultural pattern. This accounting must be historical in that it specifies the relevant data from the ethnographic record and it must functional or holistic in that it explains the place of given institutions in the overall cultural pattern. Particular forms of instituted transactions will function quite differently in different overall societies. For example wage-labour is known to have been present in antiquity but its role was then peripheral, in sharp contrast to its importance in modern exchange economy. Hence, ultimately there must be comparative institutional analysis to establish the differences and similarities of economies in the ethnographic record.

Polanyi's accounting for the market exchange pattern is important. He emphasized that the market economy did not emerge spontaneously, as some would have it, from the natural predisposition of human beings to pursue individual interest in competitive trade. He insisted that there was no inherent tendency for the market elements such as trade, money use or prices to coalesce into a market exchange economy. Not even the mercantilist period of the early modern era would necessarily lead to a market economy. Trade at administered, treaty or traditional prices does not constitute a market economy in the modern sense. The modern market economy signifies far more than simply the existence of commercial activity because it refers to an economy in which economic integration is conducted within a system of price-making markets. The construction of such a system is a unique historical event which required conceptual guidance from the notion of self-regulating markets. The rivalrous, absolutist states of Europe encouraged commercial activity, which had the unintended consequence of the classical liberal design of the experiment with the self-regulating market economy.

Polanyi differs from the standard liberal view with regard to the receding market economy as well. Liberals tend to see the increased role of the state as the result of left-wing ideological drift but Polanyi argued that this was a spontaneous response to the dangerous experiment of reliance upon competitive markets to coordinate the application of land, labour and money. The hallmark of the market economy is innovation and rapid adjustment of resource allocation to new opportunities. The mobility and bargaining mentality that implies tends to erode social and community life. Polanyi insisted that in the face of this threat to the social fabric, a spontaneous protective response emerged to restrict and delimit the scope of the market. That this increased intervention emerged despite the dominant limited state ideology speaks to the spontaneity of the protective response.

Further support for Polanyi's spontaneous protective response is found in the welfare state, which is defined in negative terms as a mixed economy, no longer fully capitalist but not socialist either. This lack of a positive sense of the welfare state is what is to be expected from its emergence from the spontaneous protective response which arises to limit the market's reach by carving out economic space that is coordinated by reciprocal and redistributive transactions. The agency, the social or institutional person not to be confused with economic man, that is willing these protective steps has multifaceted motivation and faces multidimensional limitation of capacities. Habit, custom and routine must loom large in the behaviour of such agents, and fully conscious action is thus limited to situations of novelty or violated expectations. Even then the situation is complex, capacities are limited and consequences often turn out to be other than intended.

Like the field itself, Polanyi's contributions to economic sociology are emergent, subject to ongoing interpretation and articulation. The embeddedness issue and the protective response that arises to challenge the market exchange economy are very much on the political agenda of globalization and governance in the early twentieth century. Understanding the complex political economic dynamic involved and placing it in general economic history by means of a comparative institutional analysis is very much a work in progress. But as he similarly observed of Aristotle, Polanyi has left economic sociology with some very powerful pointers as to its scope, method and significance.

See also: economic action; embeddedness; economic sociology; exchange; institutional economics, old and new; institutionalism; markets, sociology of; Veblen.

References and further reading

Dalton, George (1981) 'Symposium: Economic Anthropology and History: The Work of Karl Polanyi', in George Dalton (ed.), *Research in Economic Anthropology 4*, London: JAI. pp. 69–94.
Mendell, Marguerite and Salee, Daniel (eds) (1991) *The Legacy of Karl Polanyi*, New York: St Martin's Press.
Polanyi-Levitt, Kari (ed.) (1990) *The Life and Work of Karl Polanyi*, Montreal: Black Rose.
Stanfield, J. R. (1986) *The Economic Thought of Karl Polanyi*, London, Macmillan.

JAMES RONALD STANFIELD
JACQUELINE BLOOM STANFIELD

POLITICAL ECONOMICS

See: political economy

POLITICAL ECONOMY

In the history of economic thought, the field of political economy is usually associated with such classics as Adam Smith and Karl Marx, and is seen as having been challenged by the marginalist revolution, which brought an increasing division of labour between the disciplines of economics, sociology and political science. Yet the relationships between politics and the economy, and more generally the effects of non-market institutions on the operation of markets, have continued to be the object of study by scholars not fully satisfied with existing neoclassical models of the economy. The most prominent contribution in this perspective was Karl **Polanyi**'s analysis

of the relationships between markets, states and social institutions. But his ideas remained long isolated. It was not until the 1970s, when inflation, stagnation and unemployment brought the long period of sustained growth of advanced economies to a stop, that a 'new political economy' was born, mainly to account comparatively for such phenomena by bringing non-market institutions back into the picture.

As several authors have noticed, however (e.g. Hall 1997), two very different views of the political economy developed, which started from different assumptions and aimed at different goals. The first view has been mainly developed by economists who sought to apply economic theories and methods outside the traditional realm of economics. Unlike most mainstream economists, these authors are interested in institutions and in examining institutional phenomena. But they hold a functionalist view of institutions, that are seen as being created to the extent that they serve economic needs (Williamson 1985). Theories of the 'political-business cycle' have been developed along these lines, as has the more sophisticated new economics of organization and, more generally, most recent attempts by economists to incorporate the role of politics into their analyses.

The second view, by contrast, sets itself in open competition with mainstream economics ability to account for economic action and performance. These are in fact seen as shaped by (or embedded in) pre-existing institutions and other non-economic factors such as political interests or ideas. In this view, institutions are often seen as the outcome of path-dependent processes of historical development and not as simply a response to functional imperatives. The general assumption of the studies that share this view of political economy is that these institutions are responsible for the overall regulatory framework of economic activities, which, by constraining or offering a range of alternative courses of action to economic actors, determines economic outcomes. Following the definition given by Lange and Regini in their book *State, Market and Social Regulation*, p. 4, by 'regulation' of the economy we mean 'the different modes by which the set of activities and/or relationships among actors, which pertain to the sphere of production and distribution of economic resources, is coordinated, the related resources allocated, and the related conflicts, whether real or potential, structured (that is, prevented or reconciled)' (1989).

It should be rather obvious why this second view of the political economy is the most interesting for (and closest to) economic sociology. In fact, several authors in this field are economic sociologists, especially in Europe, whereas in the USA political scientists, together with non-mainstream economists, have often taken the lead.

At the macro level, three major types of institutions are traditionally seen, echoing **Polanyi**, as shaping actors' economic preferences and determining aggregate economic performance: markets, the state and societal-associative institutions.

Markets incorporate exchange as the guiding principle of resource allocation. In the economists' idealized market, exchanges are based on prices determined by the interaction of supply and demand under conditions of competition; such competition is highly dispersed and is not influenced by normative linkages or the exercise of power and authority. An example of this idealized formulation is the assumption that the level of wages in an economy reflects the supply and demand for labour and the most efficient allocation of resources. As we know, however, this rarely occurs in reality. Normative factors or authority relations 'distort' the determination of prices and the destination of resources. In addition, the functioning of the free market itself is made possible by pre-existing norms that are generally ignored in the neoclassical market models.

For these reasons, political economists systematically look at the role of either state or societal institutions to understand economic outcomes and the very process through which actors form their economic preferences. The state can coordinate activities and allocate resources primarily through the exercise of its authority, which, in the last analysis, is based on its monopoly of legitimate coercion. In this case, regulative activity occurs primarily through the means of laws and administrative rulings that are binding on the actors involved. In democratic and complex societies, however, the state has found the exclusive use of authority ever less effective in the face of resistance from the individuals and groups whose activity it is seeking to regulate. In many areas, the success of its intervention depends increasingly on its ability also to use 'political' exchange and/or to call on shared values.

Shared values and collective identities, on the other hand, are the key underlying factors of communities, associations and social networks, that can be grouped together under the rubric of societal institutions. Where community institutions predominate, the coordination of activities and allocation of resources take place primarily through forms of spontaneous solidarity. This can be rooted in norms, habits or values shared by the members of the community and is based on respect and trust, or simply on identification with the community and thus its rules and hierarchy. An increasing range of economic activities, however, appear to be regulated by large interest associations rather than traditional communities. These associations often have a monopoly of representation of functional interests and a high level of disruptive power, and, as a result, are able to obtain privileged recognition from other associations and political authorities (Streeck and Schmitter 1985).

Both state and societal-associative institutions may be shown to be responsible for economic outcomes in different policy areas: e.g. the educational and vocational training system, central **banks**, industrial relations institutions, etc. Much research in the field of political economy has focused on the precise roles of each of them. Yet, in more general terms, the questions underlying most analyses are the same, as they concern the extent of change over time and variation across countries. Has there been a shift in the boundaries and balance between state, market and various social institutions in the creation and maintenance of social order? And how do the roles of these institutions in the coordination of economic activities and the management of conflicts vary cross-nationally?

Over time, different streams within the political economy literature have focused on one or the other among these sets of institutions to explain changes and variation in economic policy and performance across countries.

In the late 1960s and 1970s, the main focus was on the role of state institutions that, by adopting Keynesian policies, made for a universal expansion of welfare expenditures. Political economists proposed a rereading of the adoption of Keynesian policies and of the development of the welfare state not as two separate phenomena stemming from particular techniques of government, but as essential components of a model of economic regulation which may be termed 'concerted and centralized political regulation' (Regini 1995). From this point of view, the state decisively changed its role in the economic system when, besides the traditional functions, it came to assume two further and crucial ones. The first of them we may call 'control of the economic cycle and of crises', the aim being to stabilize the cyclical trend of economic development caused by a lack of overall coordination, thereby avoiding repetition of the disastrous crises that have marked such development and their consequences: the destruction of socially accumulated wealth and social revolt. This was the manifest objective of Keynesian doctrines and of the various public policies they inspired. The second function we may call the 'control of consensus': that is, the securing of mass consensus for the economic and political systems of the advanced capitalist democracies, mainly through the diffusion of social services and the guarantee of full employment, i.e. through the welfare state in its most fully developed form. After the Second World War, this particular compromise between state and market spread, albeit to varying extents, to almost all the western countries – not just because it was an instrument with which to coordinate the economy and to avert cyclical crises, but because the governing elites saw it as the most reliable means with which to secure the consensus of the subordinate classes. In other words, the need to stabilize the economic cycle is not enough to explain the enormous growth of public intervention in the economy after the Second World War. Keynesian policies also proved a valuable instrument – justified on the basis of economic goals – with which to satisfy a specifically political requirement of the democracies reborn or revitalized after the war: namely, that of winning mass consensus for the new regimes.

The growth of the Keynesian welfare state brought with it a number of unintended and to some extent perverse effects; effects which were responsible for the crisis in this mode of regulating the economy which started in the late 1970s and which also produced diverse attempts to cope with it. One major attempt to deal with the dramatic worsening of economic performance in advanced democracies was tripartite concertation. Within the broader field of political economy, it was now the turn of neo-corporatist literature to draw the attention of scholars and policy-makers alike to the role of interest associations in the regulation of their economies – the primary preoccupations being with such aggregate indicators as the level of inflation and unemployment. The economic crisis acted as a powerful stimulus for governments to seek the support of the large interest organizations by having them participate in economic policy-making. Two purposes were served by this strategy. First, the elites could compensate for the legitimacy they had lost as the authorities responsible for the country's economic performance with the legitimation offered them by the major social interests. Second, they could utilize these organizations as a key instrument with which to combat the economic crisis, if they were willing to direct the variables under their control (wage dynamics, investment decisions, etc.) towards this common goal or general interest.

In the 1960s, the attention of analysts had been drawn to the state's increasing intervention in the economic system; that is, to its intervention in a sphere of activities previously almost entirely dominated by the market. However, it was only towards the mid 1970s that the full importance was grasped of what was, in a certain sense, the phenomenon in reverse – the other side of the coin, so to speak: the reduction of the state and of its economic resources (public spending) to a market, to a system of exchanges among organized social groups. More generally, the realization grew that public intervention in the economy, and the partial restriction of the market's sphere of influence that this entailed, came about less through the use of the bureaucratic structures of the traditional state than through forms of exchange, of institutionalized bargaining between governments and the large interest organizations. Further developments of the original neo-corporatist theory occurred during the late 1980s, adding such other institutions as central banks and a variety of features of the organization of the political economy to the overall picture.

By the mid 1980s, the various streams of literature inspired by a political economy approach reached their peak, while at the same time showing their main shortcoming: their almost exclusive focus on the macroeconomic level of regulation, whereas adjustment to international competition was increasingly taking place at the company-level and/or at the sub-national territorial level. It was here that different post-Fordist systems of production challenged the long-recognized superiority of Fordism, with inevitable repercussions on the functioning of institutions at the macroeconomic level. A new type of political economy was slowly developed, in which the relevant institutions were less and less the national state and the peak interest associations, whereas an increasing role was played by local political institutions and even more by societal institutions based on **trust**, **social capital** and the like (Piore and Sabel 1984). The redirection of attention to the social conditions of the different patterns of production, and more generally to the logic of action of different types of firm, gave rise to a new literature on local systems of production.

However, this shift of the analytical focus towards the local level did not solve the theoretical problem of giving the different macro-outcomes a micro-foundation in the behaviour of the key economic actors. A recent and systematic attempt in this direction is the literature on the varieties of capitalism (see **capitalism, varieties of**), which has concentrated on the theoretical problem to explain cross-national differences in economic policies and performance, and which is today the most promising venue within the political economy field. The typology that best captures the aspects of divergence considered crucial to the ways in which advanced economies are regulated – and which also puts forward an embryonic theory of 'institutional complementarities' – is the one originally proposed by Soskice and later developed by Hall and Soskice (2001). They distinguished between the 'coordinated market economies' (like those of Germany or the Scandinavian countries) and the 'liberal market economies' (like the Anglo-Saxon ones). The core of the distinction goes back to differences in the capacity of employers to coordinate among themselves in order to create the conditions that can both secure wage restraint and encourage firm-based innovation and adaptation to rapidly changing markets.

This literature displays two key advantages, two sources of superiority over the neo-corporatist one, that has long dominated the political economy field. First, by focusing on the key concept and the key role of employers' coordination, it brings firms to the centre of the analysis and makes employers, rather than **trade unions** or governments, the key actors in a political economy – as they have undoubtedly become at least after the crisis of the Keynesian class compromise. Second, by conceiving of institutions as sets of rules that do not directly determine economic outcomes but rather shape the behaviour of key economic actors, it links macro- with micro-analysis. What emerges is a picture in which different institutional configurations generate firm strategies based on differences in comparative institutional advantage.

The two major missing variables in this literature, however, are culture and power. Such varieties of capitalism as the Japanese, for instance, cannot be fully understood without proper reference to the specific national culture. As to the power variable, institutional arrangements are the product of conflict and must periodically be reaffirmed or renegotiated, while the varieties of capitalism literature takes them for granted. As Thelen shows in her paper at the SASE 14th Annual Meeting, 'The Political Economy of Business and Labour in the Developed Democracies',

> the view of institutions shared by many scholars in this type of literature has a distinctly utilitarian cast, and emphasizes

how institutions solve various collective action problems in ways that redound to the benefit of all – in this case, of all firms. It is, in other words, close to the other meaning of political economy cited at the outset and developed by economists. What is obscured, however, in characterizations of institutions based on their functional or efficiency effects are the questions of power and political conflict that drove the development of these institutions in the first place, and the political settlement on which they are premised.

> (2002, pp. 27–8)

These two shortcomings may explain why two other strands of political economy literature have flourished, that pay greater attention to the role of either political interests or ideas than to the role of institutions, although this should be the key factor in any political economy studies. Interest-based approaches to political economy focus especially on 'producer group coalitions'. They call on the ways in which the material interests of producer groups, as well as coalitions among them, change, to account for economic policy processes and outcomes. Ideas-oriented approaches to political economy, on the other hand, emphasize the importance of cultural variables to economic performance. This is because ideas about 'best practices' dominant in professional communities strongly influence both firm strategies and government policies.

As has been noticed, 'some of the most exciting conceptual developments in the field [of comparative political economy] today are taking place at the boundaries of the institutional approach, where it interfaces with interest-based or ideas-oriented work' (Hall 1997). The future of the political economy perspective, and especially of a closer integration with the new economic sociology approach, may lie precisely here.

521

References and further reading

Hall, Peter (1997) 'The Role of Interests, Institutions, and Ideas in the Comparative Political Economy of the Industrialized Nations', in Mark Lichbach and Alan Zuckerman (eds) *Comparative Politics: Rationality, Culture, and Structure*, Cambridge: Cambridge University Press.

Hall, Peter and Soskice, David (eds) (2001) *Varieties of Capitalism*, Oxford: Oxford University Press.

Lange, P. and Regini, M. (1989) *State, Market and Social Regulation*, New York: Cambridge University Press.

Piore, Michael and Sabel, Charles (1984) *The Second Industrial Divide*, New York: Basic Books.

Regini, Marino (1995) *Uncertain Boundaries. The Social and Political Construction of European Economies*, Cambridge: Cambridge University Press.

Streeck, Wolfgang and Schmitter, Philippe (1985) 'Community, Market, State – and Associations? The Prospective Contribution of Interest Governance to Social Order', *European Sociological Review*, 1: 65–83.

Thelen, K. (2002) 'The Political Economy of Business and Labour in the Developed Democracies', paper presented at the SASE 14th Annual Meeting, 27–30 June, Minneapolis.

Williamson, Oliver (1985) *The Economic Institutions of Capitalism*, New York: Free Press.

MARINO REGINI

POST-INDUSTRIALISM

Mid twentieth-century sociology was substantially composed of analyses of industrial society and its emergence. Major elements were the growth of employment in manufacturing industry, urbanization and a model of family life built around the ideal of a male breadwinner. The analysis was heavily influenced by Marx, so classes and class conflict were central in the relevant theory. On one side were capitalists controlling ever larger enterprises and, on the other, male manual workers. By the second half of the century economic and social change indicated the emergence of something different. 'Post-industrialism' was conceived to characterize that emergent social form. Two main versions of the idea of post-industrialism were developed, one North American and one European.

Daniel Bell was the most important contributor to the development of the North American version. He identified five emergent trends: (1) an increase in service employment as a percentage of total employment; (2) an increase in the share of professional and technical employment; (3) a more central role for theoretical knowledge in policy formulation (of which applied Keynesian economics was an example); (4) technological forecasting and planning by firms and government; (5) the development and use in decision-making of an 'intellectual technology' built around computers and quantitative methods. Subsequently, he modified this listing. Planning was dropped and both the economic independence of women and the emergence of leisure as a problem were added. Each iteration, however, constituted a self-conscious attempt to break radically with analyses in which social classes and class conflict were the major source of change.

For Bell, increased white-collar and female employment undermined **trade unions**, while rising education levels combined with the increasing knowledge-content of jobs, increased the attractiveness of professional organizations. The bases of conflict were shifting from the ownership or non-ownership of capital, emphasized by Marxists, to the possession or lack of knowledge. One form of this conflict would be increasing scepticism with respect to private corporations, as professionals brought their expertise to bear in evaluating corporate actions. The salience of knowledge meant that the core institutions of post-industrial society were universities and research institutes. At the broader political level, the central problem was becoming the aggregation of preferences (that is at the heart of **welfare economics**) rather than the irredeemably contradictory interests of classes.

Bell's interpretation was explicitly shaped by the experience of the United States and the historical weakness of socialism within it. Another version of the theory emerged within the very different European historical context. Alain Touraine, in particular, produced a variant that was more congenial to a sociological community operating in a world where socialist parties *mattered*. Rather than reject class analysis he sought to invent one appropriate to a post-industrial world.

Touraine, acknowledged the decline in the old industrial sectors from which the working class of Marxist theory was drawn. But 'social domination', he argued, persists in different forms. Life styles (consumption, including educational choices) and the *content* of education are shaped by the needs of the system of production. Those needs, in turn, are specified and met through direct political intervention. The exercise of post-industrial domination, in other words, shifted from the numerous workplaces of an earlier period to centralized control by interlocking government agencies and large corporations. These latter make up the 'technocracy', which is the new ruling class, shaping **life styles** and the educational system. The conformism this engenders is the new form of **alienation**.

Class conflict persists in Touraine's analysis. Resistance is, above all, concentrated among those with sufficient intellectual resources to take on the technocracy, but who do not share in power. Thus, radicalism is found within research agencies, among private-sector technicians and within universities. This radicalism is directed against a broader range of targets than its industrial predecessors. No longer strictly economic, across a range of issues it resists the conformism that the technocracy seeks to impose in the pursuit of increased production. This is the origin of so-called 'new social movements'.

Subsequent work on post-industrialism has been mainly directed at two questions.

Do classes persist in post-industrial societies? Are there post-industrial imperatives that standardize outcomes across societies? Consider these questions in turn.

Inequality persists. It is related to the occupational categories that usually define classes. Evidence on trends in class-based voting is mixed. Results tend to depend on the methods used. The conclusions to be drawn from those results remains controversial. Increased employment in the service sector has not necessarily undermined trade unions. In North America, for example, the female-employing public sector (including health, education and welfare) has been about the only area of union growth. On the role of classes in post-industrial societies the jury may be said to be still out.

On the degree of homogenization associated with post-industrialism, the evidence is clearer. Across societies there remain significant differences in industrial structure, in the amount of unionization and in class-differentials in voting and attitudes. The clearest contrast is between the Scandinavian countries and the United States. In Scandinavia, public service (health, education and welfare) employment growth has been most marked, unions remain strong and centralized bargaining has tended to reinforce both unions and class allegiances. In the United States and similar countries, growth has been tilted towards private services (e.g. restaurants, retailing), union membership has collapsed, and centralized bargaining is absent.

If post-industrialism is so heterogeneous, is it a useful concept? One can equally make a case that so-called 'industrial societies' were every bit as heterogeneous as their post-industrial successors. Both 'post-industrial' and 'industrial' are labels that come with an approach that assumes that it is useful to conceive of social change in terms of consecutive stages whose core properties are embodied in ideal types. That view is common in sociology, but

523

much more controversial within the philosophy of science.

References and further reading

Bell, Daniel (1973) *The Coming of Post-Industrial Society: A Venture in Social Forecasting*, New York: Basic Books.

Clark, Terry Nichols and Seymour, Martin Lipset (2001) *The Breakdown of Class Politics: A Debate on Post-Industrial Stratification*, Washington, DC: Woodrow Wilson Center Press.

MICHAEL R. SMITH

POST KEYNESIANISM

Post Keynesianism is one of the schools of economic thought opposed to neoclassical economics. As such, post Keynesianism has been subject to the criticism that it is united around a dislike of neoclassical economics rather than around positive theoretical or methodological propositions. This criticism is unduly severe. Although there is some disagreement among post Keynesians about the defining positive characteristics of their approach, depending on the strand of post Keynesianism one belongs to, it is possible to identify some unifying ideas. Doing this has become easier over time, as most of the leading post Keynesians no longer include the group known as the neo-Ricardians among the practitioners of post Keynesianism.

Perhaps the most fundamental tenet common to all post Keynesians is the principle of effective demand. This expression has been given a few different meanings, but it is often associated with two related ideas: the determination of income by expenditure and the possibility of persistent involuntary unemployment, due to a low level of aggregate demand. Economic thought in the early twentieth century was dominated by Say's law that supply creates its own demand. This 'law' combines two ideas: production determines income; and,

for the economy as a whole, income determines expenditure or demand. This implies the absence of inherent obstacles to full employment in a market economy. With some additional assumptions, such as flexible wages and prices and the absence of destabilizing effects of disequilibrium, Say's law implies a tendency to general equilibrium and full employment. Against this, the principle of effective demand, independently developed by John Maynard Keynes and Michal Kalecki, was an important part of the birth of macroeconomics as a separate discipline, during the Great Depression of the 1930s. Kalecki's ideas never became part of mainstream economics, however, while the so-called Keynesian revolution only happened in a much milder form than intended by Keynes. Soon after the publication of Keynes's *General Theory* a process began by which some of his ideas were softened or misinterpreted and combined with the neoclassical orthodoxy that he had criticized. This resulted in a neoclassical Keynesianism, whose original variant (the neoclassical synthesis) is now known as old Keynesian economics, superseded by the more recent new Keynesian economics. In contrast with both old and new (neoclassical) Keynesian economics, post Keynesianism, a school born in the 1970s, resumes and develops the revolutionary, non-neoclassical message of Keynes and/or Kalecki, which had been kept alive by authors such as George Shackle, Joan Robinson and Sidney Weintraub. Post Keynesianism does not, therefore, refer to all that came after Keynes, or to all forms of Keynesian thought; moreover, it is not influenced only by Keynes.

Besides the principle of effective demand, another important unifying feature of post Keynesianism is the emphasis on institutions. For most post Keynesians, a crucially important institution is money. Post Keynesians have a distinctive conception of a monetary economy as one in which not only is there money but money plays a crucial role, in both the short and the long run, affecting what standard economics calls real variables, such as production (hence the reference to a monetary theory of production) and employment. Contracts, financial institutions and informal conventions are also highlighted by most post Keynesians, who, however, disagree on the need to assume the presence of large corporations. Only some post Keynesians accept the strategic usefulness of unrealistically assuming product markets with many small firms, in order to show that unemployment may occur even with flexible prices and wages, contrary to the widespread belief within neoclassical economics that unemployment is caused by price and/or wage rigidity, associated with some monopolistic power of firms or unions. Other post Keynesians deem it necessary to assume oligopolies and imperfect competition.

Closely related with the emphasis on money is an emphasis on uncertainty, in a strong or fundamental sense (see **risk and uncertainty**). Post Keynesians have developed the conception of uncertainty and clarified many of their differences with neoclassical conceptions. Money and other financial assets are important in that their liquidity gives their owners flexibility to deal with unexpected events in an unknown future.

Post Keynesianism is mainly composed of two strands: the Keynesian strand and the Kaleckian strand, particularly influenced by Keynes and Kalecki respectively, with some authors belonging to both strands. This distinction is particularly useful regarding macroeconomics, with the first strand placing more emphasis on uncertainty, money and financial institutions than the second. Regarding microeconomics, one can also refer to a Keynesian group that employs some of Keynes's Marshallian marginalist apparatus, particularly as the microfoundations of the aggregate supply and demand curves, while another group refuses to do

so, but not only under Kalecki's influence. In any case, even the first group differs from neoclassical microeconomics, by emphasizing strong uncertainty and the special role of money.

Methodologically, post Keynesians embrace some form of realism and are concerned with explanatory mechanisms, distancing themselves from the deductivism and excessive formalism of neoclassical economics. Several post Keynesians develop mathematical models, but these are not in the axiomatic, deductivist style.

Politically, post Keynesians are opposed to free-market policies. However, it is not their politics that most distinguishes them from neoclassical economics: while post Keynesians vary from moderate social democrats to more radical socialists, not all neoclassicals are free-marketers or conservative. On the other hand, post Keynesianism has some interesting points in common with **Austrian economics**, including an emphasis on strong uncertainty, against neoclassical economics; in contrast, the Austrians are generally in favour of free-market policies.

References and further reading

Arestis, P. (1996) 'Post-Keynesian Economics: Towards Coherence', *Cambridge Journal of Economics*, 20(1): 111–35.

Chick, Victoria (1995) 'Is There a Case for Post Keynesian Economics?' *Scottish Journal of Political Economy*, 42: 20–36.

Davidson, P. (1994) *Post Keynesian Macroeconomic Theory*, Aldershot, UK: Edward Elgar.

Dow, S. (1996) *The Methodology of Macroeconomic Thought*, Cheltenham, UK: Edward Elgar.

Hamouda, O. and Harcourt, G. C. (1988) 'Post-Keynesianism: From Criticism to Coherence?' *Bulletin of Economic Research*, 40(1): 1–33.

Holt, R. and Pressman, S. (eds) (2001) *A New Guide to Post Keynesian Economics*, London: Routledge.

DAVID DEQUECH

POTLATCH

The potlatch of the Northwest Coast Indians – a ceremonial gift of a chief and his followers to guests composed of other chief(s) and followers – is a central construct in **exchange theory** and anthropology. Originally a specific exchange system in a particular culture area, 'potlatch' has now acquired the general meaning of competitive feasting and the ostentatious display of wealth and is also used to describe the pig feasts in Melanesia.

Northwest Coast Indians refers to a number of societies with broad cultural similarities and coastal adaptations that stretched along the coast from southeast Alaska through northern California. Their economies were based on fishing, gathering and hunting, which provided candlefish, salmon, berries, nuts, wild plants, fowl and deer. The seasonality of the coastal climate meant that harvest seasons were short, and that foods needed to be stored for the winter months. Because their mode of production was highly intensifiable due to the prodigious annual runs of salmon, Northwest Coast Indians were able to procure surplus beyond groups' winter needs. This surplus formed the material basis for the redistributive system of the potlatch.

Cultural ecologists have argued that unpredictable fluctuations in resources, which resulted in regular scarcity and famine, made redistribution of food between different groups an adaptive strategy. In addition, it increased a chief's prestige and his following, which was critical because of frequent warfare over fishing and hunting grounds.

The potlatch covers a multitude of different exchanges, ranging from smaller distributions of food at the announcements of births and marriages to the prototypical form in which chiefs engaged in competitive feasting involving the transfer of copper shells, blankets and large quantities of food from one chief and his followers to other chiefs. Recipients had to reciprocate the gifts later

with interest to avoid being humiliated. Chiefs gained prestige, status and followers when they outdid others by giving away more.

The potlatch is a classic example of an economic institution that is embedded in a wider social structure, meaning that the exchange of gifts subsumes religious, economic, social and legal aspects that have implications for everyone in the community. This means that the analysis of exchange cannot be divorced from its social context, but also that a society can be described through an examination of transfers and obligations between its members.

The potlatch reached its most elaborate form mid nineteenth century, when goods were deliberately destroyed – due to a sudden influx of wealth and a declining population after contact with Europeans. Early twentieth century the potlatch went underground when it was outlawed by the Canadian authorities who regarded a social system based on redistribution instead of accumulation an obstacle to economic progress. In 1951, the anti-potlatch law was discarded. Today Northwest Coast Indians find renewed pride and identity in the ceremonial traditions of the potlatch.

References and further reading

Drucker, Philip and Heizer, Robert F. (1967) *To Make My Name Good: A Reexamination of the Southern Kwakiutl Potlatch*, Berkeley, CA: University of California Press.

Mauss, Marcel (1950) *The Gift: The Form and Reason for Exchange in Archaic Societies*, New York: Norton.

MARK MORITZ

POVERTY

Measurement

'Poverty' is a term that represents economic hardship. Individuals are considered poor when their economic resources fall below a pre-specified level, called the poverty line or the poverty threshold. The exact measurement of poverty is complicated and contested. The official definition of the poverty line published by the United States census bureau is considered an 'absolute' measure of poverty. This measure was established in 1963 based on the minimum amount of financial resources a family would require to meet minimum federal nutrition requirements. Poverty thresholds vary by family size, age of household members, and farm versus nonfarm residence. In 2002, the poverty threshold for a four-person household with two children under 18 was $18,244. Families who earned less than this amount were officially poor. Most sociologists focusing on poverty within the United States utilize the official measure of poverty.

Cross-national researchers, on the other hand, generally establish relative definitions of poverty, measured as 40 or 50 per cent of a nation's median income. Thus, the poverty line is unique to the income distribution in each nation. This measure accounts for variations in standards of living across nations. It represents the percentage of the population with low incomes relative to the population around them.

Research on poverty

Research on poverty falls into multiple schools. Some researchers are interested in studying why individuals fall under the poverty line. Others are concerned with aggregate poverty rates across nations and over time. In the former school, scholars have historically been divided between individualist and structuralist theories. The individualistic approach focused solely on individual characteristics and how these characteristics are valued in society. For example, these researchers have established that education and skill help individuals acquire higher incomes that allow them to escape impoverishment. Other individual-level characteristics include gender, age, race, ethnicity, nationality, occupation and

family structure. Each of these factors represents a vulnerability to impoverishment. For example, in many industrialized nations, single-parent households are at high risk of impoverishment.

Structuralists long criticized individual-level researchers for neglecting the role of structure. A purely structural model assumes that impoverishment is determined solely by the structure of society, including the distribution of occupations, industries, jobs and policies. The basic tenet of this approach is that conditions outside of individuals' control determine their economic situations. For example, if unemployment is high and jobs are unavailable then many households are unable to attain sufficient resources to remain above the poverty line.

More recently, scholars have integrated these once conflicting approaches. Researchers have established that changing individual characteristics, such as education, does not necessarily remove a person from poverty. Similarly, researchers have found that altering structural conditions, for example via welfare reform that alters the policy structure, does not necessarily help reduce impoverishment. In response to these weaknesses, researchers have established that structural and individual-level characteristics interact. Structural conditions (including industrialization, urbanization and economic downturns) may limit the opportunities available to some groups, while benefiting others. For example, researchers have found that industrialization threatens the livelihood of agricultural workers, while it enhances the opportunities of skilled workers. This integrated perspective posits that individuals and families are typically poor because they possess (or often lack) characteristics that are rewarded within the economic, social and political structures around them.

The second main school of poverty research examines aggregate trends in poverty over time and across nations. Industrialized nations vary dramatically in their poverty rates. In 2000, only 2.9 per cent of the population in Norway fell below 40 per cent of the nation's median income. Similarly, 3.8 per cent of the Swedish population was considered poor, compared to 7.3 per cent of the Italian population and 10.8 per cent of the US population (Luxembourg Income Study 2004).

Researchers have established that nations' poverty rates vary because their social, economic and political structures differ. The social **structure** is important because it represents the configuration of society. Societies with large vulnerable populations (such as a large uneducated population) are more likely to have high poverty rates than societies with relatively small vulnerable populations. The economic structure is important because certain economies are more conducive to lowering poverty than others (see **economic development**). For example, more industrialized economies generally have lower poverty rates than agricultural economies. Furthermore, poverty rates tend to increase during economic downturns when unemployment is high. Additionally, poverty rates are generally lower when workers are unionized, and when they work closely with business and the government to establish policies and wages that are mutually beneficial (see **corporatism**).

Finally, researchers have found that nations' policy structures are the most important determinants of poverty across nations. Some nations have very generous **welfare** programmes that offer state support to families universally (see **welfare state and the economy**). These nations redistribute resources from the wealthy and middle classes to the impoverished. The importance of **redistribution** is evidenced when comparing poverty rates before and after income is adjusted for taxes and welfare. For example, over the last few decades, average poverty rates in Sweden before incomes were adjusted for taxes and welfare were approximately 15 per cent. Once the Swedish government redistributed income, this percentage declined to 5 per cent (Moller *et al.* 2003). Researchers have established multiple theories to explain why some nations are more redistributive than others (see **redistribution** for a summary).

In conclusion, poverty is a widely researched topic within economic sociology. It is studied at both the micro and macro levels. Future research will continue to uncover the links between these levels by establishing how individual and structural characteristics interact to determine both individuals' risks of impoverishment and changes in poverty over time and place.

References and further reading

Brady, David (2003) 'Rethinking the Sociological Measurement of Poverty', *Social Forces*, 81: 715–52.

Danziger, Sheldon H. and Haveman, Robert H. (eds) (2001) *Understanding Poverty*, Cambridge, MA: Harvard University Press.

Edin, Kathryn and Lein, Laura (1997) *Making Ends Meet: How Single Mothers Survive Welfare and Low Wage Work*, New York: Russell Sage Foundation.

Luxembourg Income Study (LIS) (2004) 'Relative Poverty Rates for the Total Population, Children and the Elderly', accessed at *LIS Key Figures*, http://www.lisproject.org/keyfigures/povertytable.htm in December 2004.

Moller, Stephanie, Bradley, David, Huber, Evelyne, Nielsen, François and Stephens, John (2003) 'Determinants of Poverty in Advanced Capitalist Democracies', *American Sociological Review*, 68: 22–51.

STEPHANIE MOLLER

POWER See: class; democracy and economy; legitimacy, organization theory; political economy; state and the economy

PRAGMATISM

Pragmatism was founded during the last quarter of the nineteenth century by Charles Sanders Peirce (1839–1914) as a type of consensus theory of truth and knowledge. His works were the first to discuss, as their central theme, the limits and possibilities of theoretically based knowledge. For Peirce, knowledge is not the reproduction of reality but rather an instrument for dealing with it successfully. As a consequence, he rejected the notion of historical laws held by the predominant philosophies of the day. In this connection he condemned the idealistic notion of knowledge and 'Truth' and the claim to the universal validity of systems of thought. This orientation established pragmatism as one of the key sources of inspiration for the economic school of American institutionalism.

The actual birth of pragmatism, even though the term had not yet been coined, dates from Peirce's 1878 publication *How To Make Our Ideas Clear*. Peirce was not interested in constructing abstract philosophical systems, but rather in formulating techniques aimed at answering questions, solving problems and explaining terms. Central to his view was the investigation of the practical consequences of concepts, theorems and theoretical systems, the importance and validity of which the researcher was to determine in the tangible practice of life. As a consequence, supposedly hard-and-fast theories and knowledge would become mere hypotheses whose validity could be confirmed or rejected by the scientific community according to results which would be dependent on time and place. The claim of universal knowledge would, therefore, be abandoned in favour of experimental theorems about reality.

Pragmatism reached a wider audience, especially in American circles, through the lectures of that name given by William James (1842–1910) in 1907. Here he clearly defined pragmatism as a method only. For James (1907: 51) pragmatism 'means the open air and possibilities of nature, as against dogma, artificiality, and the pretence of finality in truth'. Therefore, something is 'true' only when it withstands the test of practical consequences, when

assumptions or hypotheses work satisfactorily. Correspondingly, pragmatic knowledge must be tested and achieve consensus within the scientific community through a constant dialogue with reality and, therefore, serves to develop successful plans of action.

Social relations are understood to be changeable in principle and have to be constantly reformed in the light of new knowledge and experience. Science is not only a means of knowledge but also, and above all, an instrument in the practical reform of society, in which the method of trial and error is of central importance (see **historical school**).

This preoccupation with practical issues resulted in a further emphasis on processes of democratization. With its orientation towards the concrete development of society and the economy, pragmatism gained a strong instrumentalist character. Following in the footsteps of Peirce and James, John Dewey (1859–1952) in particular, referred to the necessity of solving social problems within the scope of processes of trial and error, education and democracy.

Instrumentalism reflects Dewey's (1991) concern to render the discoveries of pragmatism into practical effect. In this context he emphasizes the role of the democratic planning of economic and societal processes. For Dewey theories are nothing but instruments for action. Both knowledge and the development of society are subject to the, in principle endless, process of trial and error. All goals are merely provisional and experimental; once attained and put to the test, goals will subject to permanent change. On this view, goals that have been achieved have a transitional character, and are part of the process – not the completion – of societal or economic development. Goals are transitory in character and have no value in themselves; rather, they must be transformed into practical steps of reform in such a way that successes and failures will become apparent. In working towards solving socio-economic problems, goals must continuously develop themselves so that they grow organically with their tasks. This excludes the possibility of fixing definite means and goals beforehand.

The doctrine of pragmatism fell on particularly fertile intellectual ground in America but failed to make much of an impression elsewhere. In America pragmatism developed into the dominant American philosophy during the first two decades of the twentieth century. It found its expression in the policy of the New Deal, in which Franklin D. Roosevelt introduced the unprecedented policy of wide-ranging government intervention in the economy, in order to combat the effects of the Great Depression. From the 1930s it was largely displaced by other systems of thought in philosophy and the social sciences. Pragmatism has remained one of the least-known currents of modern philosophy up until the present day. Initially, it was strongly criticized in Germany and was even used as proof of the philosophical backwardness of the New World because of its elevation of usefulness to the status of truth. None the less, pragmatism has now also found a home in German-language sociology and philosophy (e.g. Karl-Otto Apel, Jürgen Habermas, Hans Joas). There is also growing interest in the approach in economic sociology in the search for an alternative to the predominant rational actor theory in economics. Pragmatism offers a basis in action theory from which to understand the construction of notions of intentional rationality as a creative and intersubjective process (Beckert 2002; Joas 1996).

As noted above, pragmatism has earned particular significance as the philosophical basis of institutionalism, which developed concurrently out of the work of Thorstein B. **Veblen**, Wesley C. Mitchell and John R. Commons (Reuter 1996). Just as pragmatism stemmed from the rebellion against the predominant philosophy, so the institutionalists revolted against the reigning

school of abstract (neo-)classical economics. In the critique of the supposedly harmonious workings of market mechanics and the concept of *homo economicus*, on the one hand, and in the emphasis upon the necessity for democratic economic planning, on the other, pragmatism once again made its way to the fore.

References and further reading

Beckert, Jens (2002) *Beyond the Market. The Social Foundations of Economic Efficiency*, Princeton, NJ: Princeton University Press.

Dewey, John ([1927/1946]1991) *The Public and its Problems*, Athens, OH: Ohio University Press.

Dickstein, Morris (1998) *The Revival of Pragmatism. New Essays on Social Thought*, Durham, NC: Duke University Press.

James, William (1907) *Pragmatism. A New Name for Some Old Ways of Thinking*, London: Longmans, Green.

Joas, Hans (1993) *Pragmatism and Social Theory*, Chicago: University of Chicago Press.

—— (1996) *The Creativity of Action*, Chicago: University of Chicago Press.

Marcuse, Ludwig (1959) *Amerikanisches Philosophieren. Pragmatisten, Polytheisten, Tragiker*, Hamburg: Rowohlt.

Peirce, Charles S. (1931–58) *Collected Papers*, Princeton, NJ: Harvard University Press.

Reuter, Norbert (1996) *Der Institutionalismus. Geschichte und Theorie der evolutionären Ökonomie*, second edition, Marburg, Germany: Metropolis.

Thayer, Horace S. (ed.) (1994) *Pragmatism: The Classical Writings*, Indianapolis, IN: Hackett.

NORBERT REUTER

PRAXEOLOGY See: Austrian economics

PREFERENCES

Individual preferences (or tastes) are usually characterized by a preference relation $\succ$ such that the alternative $a \in \mathbb{R}^n$ is (strictly) preferred the alternative $b \in \mathbb{R}^n$ if $a \succ b$. Given the satisfaction of certain axioms (see **utility**), this preference relation can be represented by a utility function $u : \mathbb{R}^n \to \mathbb{R}$

where alternative *a* is (strictly) preferred to alternative *b* if $u(a) > u(b)$.

Generically conceived, preferences provide individuals with reasons for behaviour. The traditional mode of economic analysis (both normative and predictive) is one of exploring individual decision-making given a stable preference relation (i.e. a stationary utility function) and a fixed set of resources. However, it has long been recognized that individual preferences are malleable and subject to changes induced by social institutions and social interactions (see Bowles 1998).

Markets, social interactions and other economic institutions help influence the phylogeny of tastes, personality traits, goals and personal values. Preferences are acquired through genetic inheritance, learning and cultural transmission (see **evolutionary economics**; Boyd and Richerson 1985), and shaped by consumption patterns (see Becker 1996). The key element of preferences, however, is that they are *internalized* reasons for behaviour. Thus, preferences acquired under one set of circumstances become generalized reasons for behaviour in other circumstances. Therefore, the key to understanding the social formation of preferences is understanding how social interactions (broadly defined) create reasons for action that are internalized into preferences.

While there may be intentional motivations for the formation of preferences (e.g. one may seek to learn an appreciation for classical music), substantial evidence suggests that mere exposure to certain goods and activities (usually arising from interactions with others or as the unintended consequences of actions) can have a strong effect on shaping preferences. For example, the exposure to different social groups, work environments, economic institutions or cuisine can create opportunities which shape preferences. As these new experiences accrue, some of the preferences associated with these experiences are internalized by individuals (Bowles 1998). Similarly, long-lived economic and social institutions (for example, **class** and **discrimination**) have profound effects on the formation of preferences. These social structures change the way individuals perceive their opportunities and provide reasons for behaviours (Ridgeway and Walker 1995). Over time, the perceptions and reasons for behaviour created by these institutions are internalized into preferences (e.g. underclass behaviour or chronic unemployment). As a result, preferences selectively evolve through social interactions.

Analytically, this implies an evolution of the utility function such that preferences at time *t* are a function of the social interactions at time $t-1$: $u_t(a) = f(u_{t-1}(a), \theta_{t-1})$ where θ_{t-1} measures the social influences an individual was exposed to at time $t-1$. Moreover, norms of behaviour may develop and be internalized as individuals' preferences feed back on one another through repeated interactions. Empirically, evidence for this is found in 'neighbourhood effects' in which individuals' preferences within social groups (defined by either culture, race or physical proximity) tend to conform to one another more than standard theory (i.e. one based on an assumption of fixed preferences but allowing choices among locations and cultural affiliations) would predict.

Cognitive processes may also result in a modification of preferences based on social interactions and cues. According to the theory of cognitive dissonance (Festinger 1957), preferences can be formed through the process of dissonance reduction. Individuals who experience an inconsistency between their behaviour and cognitions may experience dissonance, a feeling generally described as psychological discomfort. For example, individuals may experience dissonance (i.e. an inconsistency) between their self-esteem and the social esteem they are awarded via economic and social institutions. The elimination of dissonance may involve either behavioural or cognitive change. In the case of the latter, preferences may be explicitly (but potentially unconsciously) modified. This may be manifest in various social groups abandoning mainstream norms (Montgomery 1994) or opting for adopting different values systems (Oxoby 2003). Through social interactions and contact with institutions, individuals may engage in behaviours which are inconsistent with their existing preferences. The resulting dissonance may be reduced through preference modification in which newly formed preferences provide future reasons for behaviour in support of and consistent with previous acts. Analytically, this process of cognitive adaptation implies that preferences at time t are in some respect 'chosen' via an individual's choice over means of dissonance reduction (see Oxoby 2003 for an analytic conceptualization).

See also: beliefs; habits; institutional economics; network analysis; norms and values; rational choice theory; utility.

References and further reading

Aronson, E. (1994) *The Social Animal*, New York: W. H. Freeman.

Becker, G. (1996) *Accounting for Tastes*, Cambridge, MA: Harvard University Press.

Becker, G. and Murphy, K. (2000) *Social Economics*, Cambridge, MA: Harvard University Press.

Bowles, S. (1998) 'Endogenous Preferences: The Cultural Consequences of Markets and Economic Institutions', *Journal of Economic Literature*, 36: 71–111.

Boyd, R. and Richerson, P. (1985) *Culture and the Evolutionary Process*, Chicago: University of Chicago Press.

Festinger, L. (1957) *A Theory of Cognitive Dissonance*, Stanford, CA: Stanford University Press.

Montgomery, J. (1994) 'Revisiting Tally's Corner: Mainstream Norms, Cognitive Dissonance, and Underclass Behavior', *Rationality and Society*, 6: 462–88.

Oxoby, R. J. (2003) 'Attitudes and Allocations: Status, Cognitive Dissonance and the Manipulation of Preferences', *Journal of Economic Behavior and Organization*, 52: 365–85.

Ridgeway, C. L. and Walker, H. A. (1995) 'Status Structures', in K. S. Cook, G. A. Fine and J. S. House (eds), *Sociological Perspectives on Social Psychology*, Boston: Allyn and Bacon, pp. 281–310.

Young, H. P. (1998) *Individual Strategy and Social Structure*, Princeton, NJ: Princeton University Press.

ROBERT J. OXOBY

PRICES See: markets, sociology of; value

PRIMITIVE ACCUMULATION See: Marx

PRINCIPAL AND AGENT

Agency relationship and agency problem

The terms 'principal' and 'agent' describe the poles of a bilateral relationship, whose general characteristic is, very broadly speaking, that one part, the agent, acts on behalf of another, called the principal. The participants of this relationship can be individuals or institutions (organizations). The principal engages an agent to carry out a specific task she cannot or will not carry out herself, either because the principal is unable to do the job herself or the agent can at least do it better. The relation between the principal and agent is called the agency relationship and its study **agency theory**. The interaction of principal and agent is established through a contract. A typical example is the relationship between capitalist and worker; other examples are the relation between management and owners of the firm, doctor and patient (who has the role of the principal), lawyer and client. Besides the case of 'acting on behalf', an agency relationship occurs whenever one actor, the principal, entrusts a resource to an agent, who needs it to pursue his own objectives. Examples are the relation between lender and borrower, landlord and tenant.

The reason, why the agency relationship attracts so much attention in theory and practice (scientific study and real life) is the agency problem underlying it. The latter consists in the fact that the principal cannot be certain whether the agent really acts in her interest. This uncertainty originates on the one hand in the fact that the actions of the agents are in general not observable to the principal (and if they were observable the principal may not have sufficient knowledge to judge the actions of the agent) and on the other hand in the discretion of the agent. The agent can choose between different courses of action (otherwise there would be no agency problem) and he can always choose an action that serves his instead of the principal's interests. Since the choices of the agent affect the welfare of both the agent and the principal, the main task of the principal is to motivate the agent to act in her interest.

Taken together, an agency relationship occurs when there is a necessity to delegate a task, the task the agent has to carry out being fixed in a written contract; when the interests between the participants of the relationship conflict; when the principal cannot control the agent, but her welfare is dependent on the actions chosen by the agent and the participants have not the same information – rather, the agent is being better informed than the principal. Though there are models presupposing that both the principal and the agent are fully informed, the last feature is crucial. It makes the relationship in question a prominent example for the costs and consequences of **asymmetric information**.

Though agency relationships are pervasive in economic life, not all social or economic transactions are of this kind. Pratt and Zeckhauser (1985: 2) assume that this relation is given wherever one actor is dependent on another. However, this assumption would make, for instance, family relations a case in point. Though it may be tempting to conceptualize parents as the agents of their kids, this would be a misleading perspective, since the relation between parents and children lacks the conflict of interests, an indispensable precondition for the emergence of an agency

relationship. Even the division of labour and commodity exchange is not sufficient condition for the development of agency relationships. Given these institutions, a minimum requirement for the coming into being of this type of relations is the temporal separation of the acquisition of a commodity and its payment. As already Marx has seen, this separation gives rise to the creditor–debtor relation carrying inevitably with it a serious agency problem.

Modelling the agency relationship

Given the ingredients of an agency relationship enumerated above, the solution of the agency problem seems to be straightforward. The task of the principal solely consists in designing a contract that aligns the interests of the agents perfectly with her own interests. Thus the study of the principal–agent relationship becomes a branch of the rapidly evolving economics of incentives. If the incentives are set right, the agent will choose exactly the action the principal wants him to choose. In this vein, the economic literature has reduced the study of principal–agent relationships to a problem of mechanism design. I demonstrate this problem with reference to the relation between workers and the management. This relation can be modelled as a production game (Rasmusen 1989: 140), where the task of the management consists in designing a compensation scheme that maximizes the expected utility of the firm by motivating the agent to make the objectives of the firm to his own objectives. Formally, it amounts to solving

$$\text{Max}_{w} EV[q(e^*, \theta) - w(q(e^*, \theta))] \quad (1.1)$$

subject to

$$EU[e^*, w(q(e^*, \theta))] \geq \overline{U} \quad (1.2)$$

$$e^* = \arg\max_e EU[e, w(q(e, \theta))] \quad (1.3)$$

533

The task of the principal is to propose a contract that is the solution to equation 1.1. Here E is the symbol for the expectation operator, V is the utility function of the principal, q means revenue or output, e^* the level of effort e that maximizes q, θ is a random productivity parameter (the state of the world, chosen by 'nature') and w is the wage function. Just as expected by any introductory textbook in economics, in equation 1.1 profits are the difference between revenues (output) and costs, $(q-w)$. Deviating from a standard maximization problem in a neoclassical framework, however, output depends on effort, being at the discretion of the agent (not on labour which is owned by the firm like a machine), as well as on a random productivity parameter (a state variable). Furthermore, the management maximizes the expected utility of the firm: that is, the relation between input and output is stochastic, not deterministic. Most crucially, the management has not simply to pick a number, but to choose a wage function (a compensation scheme). A minimum requirement to master this task is a training in the calculus of variation. Though Rasmusen (1989: 140) is convinced that this can be done by a 'trained ape', I doubt whether even a *trained* ape will do. Petersen (1993: 289) comes much closer to the truth, pointing to the fact that 'few managers are applied mathematicians, and even if they were, their agents would not be'.

Constraint 1.2, the participation constraint, states that maximizing the surplus is subject to the restriction that the agent will accept the contract at all. U is the utility function of the agent, and argmax (in equation 1.3) the value of the argument that maximizes the function. The expected utility of signing the contract must at least be equal to the best available alternative, $\overline{U}$. Constraint 1.3 is called the incentive compatibility constraint. It states plainly that the agent will maximize his, not the principal's, utility. 'This restriction', Macho-Stadler

and Perez-Castrillo (1997: 40) comment, reflects the moral hazard problem: 'once the contract has been accepted and since effort is not verifiable ... the agent will choose that level of effort that maximizes his objective function.' Moral hazard is that kind of private information that is typical for the agency relationship. The term stems from the insurance literature where it refers to a change of behaviour, induced by the insurance contract itself and resulting in an increased probability of exactly that risk against which the insurance contract was completed. Arrow (1985) has labelled this kind of asymmetric information 'hidden action'. A second similar prominent type of asymmetry Arrow labelled 'hidden information' (about the type of the agent). It entails the problem of adverse selection. As a particular insurance policy attracts rather the bad risks (because good risks are less inclined to take the policy), a specific job offer is accepted more by workers who know that their type is worth less than the salary.

Discussing agency theory

Though the model set up in equations 1.1–1.3 is really impressive due to its mathematical elegance and precision, it and the theory on which it is based have become the object of a severe and sometimes devastating criticism. This criticism mainly refers to the tacit, seldom explicit presuppositions it makes. To begin with, it assumes that there are no restrictions on the contracts the principal can offer (cf. Laffont and Martimort 2002: 2) This implies that the principal can write down contracts of whatever complexity. The contract the principal outlines is capable of covering all conceivable contingencies, otherwise the design of the principal's optimal contract would not reduce to a simple optimization problem (simple in theory, not in practice!). Unlike **transaction cost economics**, agency theory assumes that the principal can write complete contracts. In sharp contrast to this, Williamson has stressed again and again that all complex contracts are necessarily incomplete. In addition, agency theory assumes tacitly that devising a detailed contract will incur no costs. However, as Hart (1995: 21) has emphasized, 'one important factor missing from the principal–agent view is the recognition that writing a (good) contract is itself costly'. What is more, incomplete contracts can be revised as the future unfolds. However, the contract the principal offers is of the 'take it or leave it' kind. If the agent does not accept the offer, the game ends. Any kind of bargaining is excluded.

A further critical feature of agency theory is that it assumes 'the availability of a benevolent court of law that is able to enforce the contract and impose penalties if one of the contractual partners adopts a behavior that deviates from the one specified in the contract' (Laffont and Martimort 2002: 4). That is, agency theory totally relies on exogenous claim enforcement and disregards the necessity of endogenous claim enforcement. Unlike agency theory, Williamson (1985) emphasizes the difference between court ordering and private ordering. In agency theory there is no place for private ordering. All the principal has to do is to design an incentive scheme. If the agent agrees, there is in principle no problem of deviating behaviour or of dispute. An agent that has signed a contract is motivated exactly as the contract prescribes. If nevertheless a dispute occurs, it can always be settled by a court. In this regard, agency theory is nothing else than a variant of neoclassical economics. Like the latter, it still sticks to the idea that either contracts are obeyed without any problem or that courts will enforce them in case of non-compliance, without any costs arising for the parties of exchange from exogeneous claim enforcements.

Especially the behavioural assumptions of agency theory have come under attack.

Agency theory assumes rationality in the double meaning of an unlimited cognitive capacity and self-interested behaviour. As Sappington (1991: 61) has stressed, the actors in the principal–agent framework are omniscient in an important sense. 'Although they may have been unaware at various points in their relationship of the exact "state of nature" (θ) that prevailed, they were always aware of every state that could conceivably occur, and of the relative frequency of all states.' Similarly, the assumption that agents only pursue their private interests is open to debate. Agency theory sees no role for norms in guiding behaviour. From the sociological point of view, norm-guided behaviour is the opposite of a purely interest-driven behaviour. As Laffont and Martimort (2002: 3) admit, to investigate 'how private incentives interact with cultural norms of behavior might be the next important step of research'. Norms can generally be conceptualized as means to alleviate the agency problem. The more norms (general norms, not group norms) guide the behaviour, the less urgent the agency problem may be. Other ways to alleviate it are the reputation of the firm (at risk by an unconditional profit-seeking behaviour), selling the firm to the workers (thus conveying the risk of moral hazard to them) and, most importantly, changing the type of agent (cf. Rasmusen 1989: 170). An agent committed to the objectives of the firm does not raise an agency problem. In particular, as Simon (1991: 41) has emphasized, 'identification becomes an important means for removing or reducing ... moral hazard and opportunism'.

Apart from these theoretical objections, the empirical validity of agency theory has been jeopardized, too. As far as the firm is concerned, two objections are of particular importance. First, in the production game (equation 1.1 above) wages are dependent on output. In general, however, firms pay a fixed wage to their employees. Following Frank Knight, this can be seen as a way the firm insures worker's incomes against random fluctuations. If wages were dependent on output, as agency theory assumes, piecerate systems of remuneration should prevail. But this is not the case and there are no indications that they become more prevalent. Second, it is an empirical question to what extent moral hazard, shirking and opportunism prevail in an organizational context. The latter may vary to the extent it invites moral hazard. Therefore this type of behaviour should be treated as a variable, rather than a fixed property (cf. Perrow 1993: 232).

Concluding remarks

What makes agency theory intellectually so enticing is that it replaces the exploitation perspective (still widespread in the public discourse), where employers are blamed for exploiting their employees, with a shirking perspective. Now the agents may be blamed for a behaviour resulting in inefficiencies. But its most important merit is to have put the problem of motivation at centre-stage. The problem of bounded motivation is at least as important as Simon's problem of bounded rationality. At the core of any organization using labour stands the problem of how the proprietors can motivate the employees to work in their interest. Due to the private information agents possess, and the lack of verifiability, they indeed have the option to restrain effort. By studying the possibilities to elicit effort by setting the incentives right, agency theory joins the endeavour to overcome the neoclassical paradigm in economics and to replace it by the information paradigm (Stiglitz 2002). The future of agency theory will depend on whether it can broaden its narrow behavioural assumptions and will extend the shirking perspective to the principal, too. Principals dispose of private information as their agents do. Anticipating that the principals will use this information against the inter-ests of their agents, these are inclined to withdraw effort. Thus a downward spiral of distrust is initiated that ends up in a level of performance much lower than it would be if **trust** were to dominate the interaction of principal and agent.

References and further reading

Arrow, Kenneth (1985) 'The Economics of Agency', in John W. Pratt and Richard J. Zeckhauser (eds), *Principals and Agents: The Structure of Business*, Boston: Harvard Business School Press, pp. 36–51.

Berger, Johannes (2002) 'Normativer Konsens und das Agenturproblem der Unternehmung', in Andrea Maurer and Michael Schmid (eds), *Neuer Institutionalismus. Zur soziologischen Erklärung von Organisation, Moral und Vertrauen*, Frankfurt/M: Campus, pp. 193–217.

Hart, Oliver (1995) *Firms, Contracts and Financial Structure*, Oxford: Clarendon Press

Holmström, Bengt (1979) 'Moral Hazard and Observability', *Bell Journal of Economics*, 10: 74–91.

Laffont, Jean-Jacques and Martimort, David (2002) *The Theory of Incentives. The Principal–Agent Model*, Princeton, NJ: Princeton University Press.

Macho-Stadler, Inés J. and Pérez-Castrillo, David (1997) *An Introduction to the Economics of Information. Incentives and Contracts*, Oxford: Oxford University Press.

Milgrom, Paul and Roberts, John (1992) *Economics, Organization and Management*, Englewood Cliffs, NJ: Prentice Hall.

Perrow, Charles (1993) *Complex Organizations. A Critical Essay*, third edition, New York: McGraw-Hill.

Petersen, T. (1993) 'The Economics of Organization: The Principal–Agent Relationship', *Acta Sociologica*, 36: 277–93.

Pratt, John W. and Zeckhauser, Richard J. (1985) 'Principals and Agents. An Overview', in John W. Pratt and Richard J. Zeckhauser (eds), *Principals and Agents: The Structure of Business*, Boston: Harvard Business School Press, pp. 1–35.

Rasmusen, Eric (1989) *Games and Information. An Introduction to Game Theory*, Oxford: Blackwell.

Sappington, David E. M. (1991) 'Incentives in Principal–Agent Relationships', *Journal of Economic Perspectives*, 5: 45–66.

Simon, Herbert A. (1991) 'Organizations and Markets', *Journal of Economic Perspectives*, 5: 25–44.

Stiglitz, Joseph (1987) 'Principal and Agent', in John Eatwell (ed.), *The New Palgrave. A Dictionary of Economics*, London: Macmillan, vol. 3, pp. 966–71.

—— (2002) 'Information and the Change in the Paradigm in Economics', *American Economic Review*, 92: 460–501.

Williamson, Oliver (1985) *The Economic Institutions of Capitalism. Firms, Markets, Relational Contracting*, New York: Free Press.

JOHANNES BERGER

PRODUCTION

Production involves the creation of something new. Economic production means producing things of economic value or consequence. Production can be for a market, in which case the resulting commodity is to be sold. But significant economic production also occurs outside of markets, and so the product may not be a commodity at all (consider the domestic production of meals and clean homes by traditional housewives, who do not receive a wage for their labour, nor do they sell their product). Since market boundaries shift over time and vary across societies, the commodification of production is a variable and historical process. The distinction between domestic production and market production is drawn socially, politically and legally, and is affected by gender roles and family structure. Production may create tangible or intangible goods, with the latter becoming increasingly important as developed countries shift away from manufacturing and industry and towards service or informational economies.

Production has been a central sociological concern since Karl Marx used his labour theory of value to argue that the genesis of class exploitation lay in production. The effects of mechanization and the division of labour on industrial production was of particular interest to the founders of sociology

since it was obvious that these dramatic changes combined good features (increased productivity) with bad (dangerous and monotonous factory work). The application of 'scientific management' (e.g. Taylorism) and the development of assembly-line production ('Fordism') throughout the early twentieth century made these good and bad features even more extreme.

Production varies in terms of what is produced, who is producing and how production occurs. Production is typically accomplished through a complex set of activities involving the coordinated actions of multiple persons, in which many primary or intermediate inputs are transformed into a number of outputs, one of which is valorized as the ostensible 'product'. Production is a social activity and therefore Robinson Crusoe as a solitary producer is a fictional character not suitable for social science. The coordination of productive activity occurs administratively within firms, through formal contracts between firms, and through informal social networks both within and between firms (Uzzi 1997).

A workplace that makes furniture (or machine parts, or consulting reports) also produces tangible garbage, waste and pollution, as well as intangible outcomes likes solidarity among the workers, conflict with management, feelings of **alienation**, wage dependence, masculine identities ('working men'), social status and other forms of sociability (Perrow 2002: 12–15). Generally only one or two of these outputs is socially salient, although there may be no intrinsic reason why one outcome gets socially defined as 'product' while the other is defined as 'trash' (Thompson 1979). Consider that grappa, now an expensive Italian brandy (with a status like single-malt whisky), was until recently considered a 'garbage' beverage suitable only for poor people because it was made from the sediment and grape skins left over from the wine-making process. Grappa was redefined from secondary output to primary product.

For most of human history, production was aimed at the creation of tangible things. Now, however, intangible products have become increasingly important for post-industrial economies (e.g. software, entertainment, services, consulting reports, information). Their intangibility complicates the production process in some respects while making it much easier in others. Intangible goods often require the law (in particular, intellectual property rights like patent law, copyright or trademark law) to give them the 'thing-like' status that tangible commodities already possess as physical objects. Thus the production of intangible goods depends especially on the formal legal framework. But mass production of intangibles can be almost trivially easy. For instance, the marginal cost of producing a copy of a computer file containing pop music is close to zero (unlike the marginal cost of an additional ton of steel). Informational goods are often non-rivalrous in that if one person consumes the good it doesn't prevent others from doing so as well (Shapiro and Varian 1999).

Production for the market can be organized in several characteristic ways. Perhaps the best known is the 'Fordist' method of mass production, in which overall tasks have been broken down into simple jobs which are either performed by machinery or allocated to low-skill workers who perform them repetitively and routinely. Planning and decision-making are the responsibility of management, and workers simply follow orders. This 'assembly-line' method occurs inside a single for-profit firm, although the supply of primary or intermediary inputs can be outsourced. Factory work emerged in the early nineteenth century, most famously in the British textile industry, and replaced the older 'putting out' system. Routinization and mechanization as methods for enhancing productivity have been widely applied in manufacturing and industrial production, but more recently they have also been applied to interactive service work, albeit with mixed success (Leidner 1993). Over the twentieth century, productivity increased much more in manufacturing than in service sector industries.

A number of scholars have noted the recent emergence of 'post-Fordist' modes of production. These are characterized by smaller production runs, flexible specialization, network-based organizations, skilled workers, higher-quality goods, greater worker participation in workplace governance, and greater reliance on information technology. In some cases, 'post-Fordism' shares features of 'pre-Fordist' production arrangements like the putting-out system (Lazerson 1995). Coordination of activities occurs between firms in addition to within them, and relies on social networks as well as formal contractual agreements. Such arrangements do not happen just at the level of the firm, but are supported and reinforced by wider economic, educational and political institutions. For example, the willingness of employers to invest in the education and training of their workers depends on labour market mobility. Similarly, the willingness of workers to invest in firm-specific skills (as opposed to general skills) depends on their job security. Thus, labour market institutions complement investments in human capital (Hall and Soskice 2001). Similar complementarities exist between **corporate governance** and financial systems, and influence patterns of production.

References and further reading

Burawoy, Michael (1979) *Manufacturing Consent: Changes in the Labor Process under Monopoly Capitalism*, Chicago: University of Chicago Press.

Hall, Peter A. and Soskice, David (eds) (2001) *Varieties of Capitalism: The Institutional Foundations of Comparative Advantage*, New York: Oxford University Press.

Lazerson, Mark (1995) 'A New Phoenix? Modern Putting-Out in the Modena Knitwear Industry', *Administrative Science Quarterly*, 40: 34–59.

Leidner, Robin (1993) *Fast Food, Fast Talk: Service Work and the Routinization of Everyday Life*, Berkeley, CA: University of California Press.

Perrow, Charles (2002) *Organizing America: Wealth, Power, and the Origins of Corporate Capitalism*, Princeton, NJ: Princeton University Press.

Shapiro, Carl and Varian, Hal R. (1999) *Information Rules*, Cambridge, MA: Harvard Business School Press.

Thompson, Michael (1979) *Rubbish Theory: The Creation and Destruction of Value*, Oxford: Oxford University Press.

Uzzi, Brian (1997) 'The Sources and Consequences of Embeddedness for the Economic Performance of Organizations: The Network Effect', *American Sociological Review*, 61: 674–98.

BRUCE G. CARRUTHERS

PRODUCTION MARKETS See: markets, sociology of; network analysis

PROFESSIONS

Professions are privileged occupations. Their members enjoy, if not always, above average incomes, relative security, social esteem and cultural authority, based on their command of a specialized knowledge. Organized as corporate bodies, the most established professions govern themselves and discipline their own members. In fact, self-government and the complexity of the knowledge base distinguish learned professions like medicine and law from nursing, schoolteaching, social work and others that American sociologists have called semi-professions. Yet both types define and administer the training and the tests that are required for access to their ranks in relative independence from future employers.

While professions as a whole enjoy certain common advantages relative to other occupations, the differences among them and among their members are marked.

Derek Bok, analysing the rewards received by physicians, lawyers, college professors and teachers, among others, concedes that special inducements are necessary to fill the positions that a society values and accomplish the functions it deems important. He concludes, however, that the striking inequality of economic rewards between these occupations and within their ranks creates grave distortions in the social allocation of talent (Bok 1993).

The advantages that professions collectively enjoy are protected by *market shelters*, the effectiveness of which varies widely. This variability obviously depends on what professionals do: thus, while the demand for lawyers is conspicuously dependent on economic growth, that for physicians' services is practically untouched by economic fluctuations, although the doctor's lot, like that of the teacher, changes with demography and with the development of the welfare state.

Professionalization movements

The drives for status and control based on self-reform that sociology calls professionalization met historically with different success. It depended as much on the knowledge base of each occupation as on the kind of state and political climate to which each addressed its claims. In general terms, modern professions were either impelled to organize in the professional civil service mode by the European states, or emerged from the civil society in Anglo-Saxon countries with an associational and collegial design (Larson 1977). They acquired both new content and organizational form during the great transformation that saw the rise of a modern art of government and that of industrial capitalism. Old names and forms of 'professional' organization may have persisted and appeared to expand, but they functioned to organize new kinds of people for new tasks, contributing to the 'microphysical' order of the new regimes.

However, even if backed by administrative power, modern professions acted in the name of expertise, a different kind of authority; and they represented a different principle of allocating jobs and delivering services than the free market. The modernization of professions in the nineteenth century was not an integral part of unbridled capitalism, but the embodiment of an almost alternative principle of order. In both the European and the Anglo-American models, professionalization invoked a meritocratic creed and ideas of collective welfare, while seeking institutional shelter against the rigours of competition. For an influential sociologist of professions, they represent, like crafts and guilds, a *third logic*, an occupational principle of order in the division of labour, opposite to the market's commercial imperatives and to the commands of bureaucratic management (Freidson 2001).

Yet professions operate in markets of services or labour, while their collective discourses lend authoritative definitions of law, health, safety, efficiency, beauty and the like to a tutelary government. Professionals (the elites that speak for the field) have the right to utter authoritative statements in their area of expertise. The right is founded on their exclusive claim to specialized knowledge, guaranteed by visible credentials and the judgment of their peers, but also on the fact that professions have constituted their fields, making them into legitimate areas of research, knowledge and intervention. The professional project involves claiming such areas of expertise as work *jurisdictions*, in Andrew Abbott's terms – each a *heartland* of autonomy and control over the content of work. There, practitioners reassemble the disassembled abstract knowledge transmitted by the academy. The process of exclusion of non-professionals takes place, for Abbott, within *a system of professions* – occupations competing for jurisdiction in specific areas of the social division of labour, and subjecting them to permanent instability (Abbott 1988).

The exclusive nature of professional power rests on the mastery of complex knowledge. This complexity must seem *legitimate*, if it is to radiate cultural authority. In Eliot Freidson's view, specialized knowledge justifies the professions' claim to a *monopoly* of control over training and work (Freidson 2001). The typical development of modern professions created a structural link between training centres and the world of work – the United States providing the model of the university, France that of the *grande école*, Britain that of the qualifying association. Training is inserted into a formal and standard framework *outside the labour market*. As is particularly clear in the university's case, the hierarchical steps of the training system correspond to career thresholds.

In sum, the success of professionalization movements was historically conditioned, and it existed in a political arena. Yet these movements faced in common certain structural tasks, such as establishing a field, a knowledge base and a training system. But claiming specialized knowledge was not enough. In the Anglo-Saxon world, where professional movements typically did not arise under the aegis of a state bureaucracy, they nevertheless asked the state for some kind of institutional protection, needed to induce recruits into the new systems of training. Two schematic examples illustrate the interaction between knowledge resources, which a profession controls, and markets of labour and services, which it does not.

Two models: medicine and engineering

While the power and privileges medicine commands may be nowhere as high as in the United States, the profession everywhere appears as the archetypal profession, for the public and the media as much as for sociology. Yet its drive for monopolistic control since the middle of the nineteenth century met with variable success, showing the limits of even the most favourable market conditions. (1) The market for medical services is potentially unlimited. Yet until one sector of professional healers secures a monopolistic foothold, the pressing universal need incites competition. (2) In an extremely competitive market, all doctors, no matter how scientific their claims, could invoke traditional mechanisms of trust, such as character and social standing. Perhaps more than any other profession with a scientific base, medicine must rely on the public's ideology about health, and on its faith about treatment. (3) The secret of the consulting room gives the doctor considerable discretionary power. Despite the changes wrought by national health systems and health management organizations, medical services are still consumed by individuals and in private. Before the rise of third parties, patients could not easily organize themselves against medical power –and they still cannot. (4) Even if medicine cannot persuade the public, it can to some extent rely on the state for coercion. In principle, the grave (and political) danger of epidemics made the state willing to support the claims of that sector of the medical profession which seemed most convincing and efficient, although in the word 'seemed' lie the political vicissitudes of medical monopoly (on which see Ramsey 1984). (5) Medicine is the only 'learned' profession that has an organizational base –the hospital – different from the university. In the United States, the hospital was used effectively for professionalizing and excluding competitors (Starr 1982); the hospital, moreover, gives medicine its characteristic *dominance* over other professions. Despite these structural and cultural advantages, medical reformers were unable to negotiate a monopoly until the bacteriological revolution came from outside the profession in the 1870s. The effective scientific base could then represent

medical change as progress, whether it was indispensable in practice or not.

Engineering, on the other hand, illustrates how a subordinate labour market weakens a professional project that could rely on the unmediated control of new knowledge. (1) Engineers, and technical devisers in general, work in diverse areas of the social division of labour; they apply their knowledge to diverse needs, and their cognitive base retains to this day the dominant empirical bent of its origins. From its beginning, the exclusive competences of engineering appear as fragmented as medicine may be today by the proliferation of specialities. Despite its formal roots in mathematics and science, engineering is not one profession, but many. (2) The empirical and physically based nature of technical knowledge delays and hinders formal education. Indeed, the great majority of engineering products are *physical*, alienable, imitable and directly controllable. Even though experts set the standards, authorities can regulate the products instead of the credentials of the producers. (3) Modern engineers emerge from the factories and also from large civil projects – importantly, from war. (4) Users of engineering products are not the same as the engineers' clients, who tend to be their employers: chief among these, business corporations and the state, are organized and have power that corporate professions cannot match. (5) The common organizational base for the profession of engineering is only the training system; but we have seen that formal and theoretical education, albeit indispensable today, is less important than the divided fields of application in which professionals accumulate empirical experience.

The varieties of engineering, in sum, appear as an early incarnation of *technobureaucratic professionalism*: in the organizations that employ them, modern engineers have a double function, technical and economic. Their careers depend more strictly on the organization's own hierarchy than on the external hierarchy of professional knowledge. This weakens the collective base of autonomous power and brings engineering closer to the modern instabilities that French sociologists of work, in particular, assign to the concept of *professionalité* (qualification, or competence).

Instabilities of the professional model

In 1959, a pathbreaking article by Arthur Stinchcombe suggested a more general way to analyse skills as portable assets in a labour market (Stinchcombe 1959). In a general approach to competence, profession appears as *one* way of organizing qualifications in relatively closed labour markets. The transaction between the competence requirements of the employers and the professional achievements of the labour force is a *general* process, in which employer organizations normally have the upper hand. For J. D. Reynaud (1987), employers, workers and the state are the three players who negotiate qualifications and the impact these will have on the structure of organizational positions. Professions succeed in obtaining employers' respect for an external hierarchy of knowledge and state-sanctioned diplomas. However, a comparative research on German and French industry shows the importance of the whole system of education for the organization of *industrial* work: vocational education in Germany not only determines the technical competence of workers and foremen, but also contributes to structure work relations within firms and industrial branches (Maurice *et al.* 1982). A more general analysis of the acquisition and effects of competence also prompts researchers to generalize the problems of identity formation through work (Dubar 1995), and to extend the conflict between professional and private life projects beyond the professions' world of well-ordered careers and organized ambition.

Placing professions within the broader structure of the labour market highlights

their instability by centring attention on the *external* forces that condition the deployment of expertise. These forces do not only change the content and performance of work, as they do for Abbott, but partake of much broader trends. In the reorganization of US high-tech industry after the stock market collapse of 2000, 'offshore outsourcing' jeopardizes not low-level jobs only, but the careers of computer professionals and MBAs. In this, as in other recessions, even professional job-seekers encounter a contradictory trend: on the one hand, highly trained professionals can face rejection because they are 'over-qualified' (i.e. 'expecting too high salaries'), while those with lesser credentials often confront escalation in the formal requirements of employers. For Freidson, spreading commercialism and managerial regulation threaten professionalism, the sense of *connaisssance oblige* that justifies monopolistic control (Freidson 2001). Market restructuring, however, threatens personal and cultural expectations, weakening the structural link between superior training and work advantages that is at the heart of the professional model. Before returning to this point, the advancing European Union has recently exposed another of the model's shortcomings. Classic models of profession have logically emphasized the support of the nation-state, as the only effective agency for constituting or protecting market shelters. Monopoly, in fact, excluded foreign professionals from practice, unless bilateral agreements at the level of state organizations had established reciprocal equivalences. In front of international standards and regulations that come from Brussels and increasingly weaken national professional controls, European professions are striving to form today their own international federations. Established and less established professions are not passive in front of this special case of regulation from above, but the still uncertain outcome will in any event increase the obsolescence of the nation-based model.

Finally, the seating of professional training in the modern university introduces a structural tension between its goals and those of practitioners in 'real world' labour markets. First of all, the advancement of knowledge is equated with *research*, concentrated in the hands of professional faculties. The disciplinary emphasis on theory and abstract training increases the danger of *obsolescence* of the formal knowledge that practitioners apply on the ground, while the economic and social difficulties of continuous access to learning make the updating of knowledge one of the main problems of profession. Second, professional faculties tend to be interested in a supply of good students to help in research and teaching. To adjust the number of prospective entrants, however roughly, to the possibilities of the labour market is *not* in their interest, or in that of the host institution. The *oversupply* of credentialed professionals seldom threatens the economic status of successful professionals, but it erodes further the idea of profession as a *collectivity* with shared knowledge and interests.

Without orderly careers in a relatively stable jurisdiction, professionals have only a title and a credential. The presence of marginalized professionals weakens the link between training and work, undermining the legitimacy of professional control. In fact, the market shelter does not work against the rise of *internal* competitors. Oversupply of fully credentialed professionals (which is endemic in some LDCs, and quite visible in the 'academic proletariat' of American higher education) indicates an uncertain labour market and society's failure to serve expanding real needs. The emergence of a 'lower tier' of professional workers has deep cultural implications, for they stand in reproach to the sheltered and successful professionals, as an implicit challenge to their legitimacy and to the very notion of privileged work.

References and further reading

Abbott, Andrew (1988) *The System of Professions*, Chicago: University of Chicago Press.

Bok, Derek (1993) *The Cost of Talent*, New York: Free Press.

Dubar, Claude (1995) (ed.) *La Socialisation: Construction des identités sociales et professionnelles*, Paris: Armand Colin.

Freidson, Eliot (2001) *Professionalism: The Third Logic*, Cambridge: Polity Press.

Larson, Magali Sarfatti (1977) *The Rise of Professionalism*, Berkeley, CA: University of California Press.

Maurice, Marc, Silvestre, J. J. and Sellier, F. (1982) *Politique d'éducation et organisation industrielle en France et en Allemagne*, Paris: PUF.

Ramsey, Matthew (1984) 'The Politics of Professional Monopoly in Nineteenth Century Medicine: The French Model and its Rivals', in Gerald Geison (ed.), *Professions and the French State 1700–1900*, Philadelphia: University of Pennsylvania Press.

Reynaud, Jean Daniel (1987) 'Qualification et marché du travail', *Sociologie du Travail*, 1: 87–109.

Starr, Paul (1982) *The Social Transformation of American Medicine*, New York: Basic Books.

Stinchcombe, Arthur (1959) 'Bureaucratic and Craft Administration of Production', *Administrative Science Quarterly*, 4, September: 168–78.

MAGALI SARFATTI LARSON

PROPERTY

We all agree about consent; actions should respect the consent of others. But this 'calculus of consent' is incomplete without specifying the domain where consent is relevant, namely one's person and property. The real controversies lie in the determination of personal and property rights. Property rights have a life cycle: they are initiated, transferred and eventually terminated. Transfers by mutually voluntary contracts are not controversial; it is the initiation and termination of property rights – the 'appropriation' of assets and liabilities – where the disagreements lie.

Ronald Coase in his 1960 paper 'The Problem of Social Costs' outlined a famous argument now known as Coase's Theorem which holds that it doesn't matter for

543

efficiency purposes how rights are assigned so long as they are clear and tradeable. The logic is illustrated with an (admittedly outrageous) example. Coase was mainly concerned with pollution, but the logic has legs of its own. Person A wants to do X to person B. The act X has a monetized value to A and a monetized cost to B. If the A-value exceeds the B-cost then it is 'efficient' for X to take place, otherwise not. The Coasian logic is that it doesn't matter for the efficient outcome if B is given the right to prevent X by withholding consent (polluter pays) or A is given the right to do X without B's consent (pollutee pays).

If the B-cost exceeds the A-value, the efficient outcome is not X. If B has the right, then B would not consent to X since the maximum payment from A (the A-value) is less than the cost to B. If A had the right, then B would be willing to pay up to the B-cost to prevent X, so A would be successfully bribed not to do X.

If the A-value exceeds the B-cost, the efficient outcome is X. If B has the right, then A's payment up to the A-value exceeds the B-cost, so B would consent to the deal and X would happen. If A had the right, then B's bribe up to the B-cost would not outweigh the A-value, so A would do X anyway.

The efficient outcome is obtained no matter how the initial rights are assigned. By this efficiency logic, it doesn't matter if a person has the rights to protect their bodily integrity – or others have the rights to act at will – so long as the rights are clear and tradeable.

The Coasian logic is correct as far as it goes, but it doesn't go very far since the assignment of rights is more a matter of justice than efficiency. The basic justice principle (e.g. applied in civil and criminal trials) is to assign legal or de jure responsibility in accordance with de facto responsibility. This principle would be applicable whenever property is created or terminated by responsible human actions such as in normal pro-

ductive activities. Rights to unmade natural objects and accident liabilities are less clear topics, but even natural objects are improved upon and used up by human actions. All the people who work in an economic enterprise are jointly de facto responsible for using up the inputs (negative fruits of their labour) in the course of producing the outputs (positive fruits of their labour). Applying the justice principle to the workplace, they should have the legal responsibility for those input-liabilities (paid for as expenses) and those output-assets (sold as the revenues), i.e. they should be the legal members of the enterprise receiving the net income.

But this property appropriation does not happen in firms where workers are legally employees or 'servants' by virtue of the employment contract. Solely the employer legally appropriates all the assets and liabilities created in production by the de facto responsible actions of all who work in the enterprise – in violation of the basic justice principle often associated with John Locke in the context of property rights.

In spite of the employment contract, all employees and working employers are inextricably de facto co-responsible for the results of their joint actions. Everyone is able to recognize this when the employer and employee engage in a crime. The servant in work suddenly becomes the partner in crime. As one standard law book on the employment relationship, Francis Batt's *The Law of Master and Servant*, puts it:

> All who participate in a crime with a guilty intent are liable to punishment. A master and servant who so participate in a crime are liable criminally, not because they are master and servant, but because they jointly carried out a criminal venture and are both criminous.
>
> (1967: 612)

But the facts about de facto responsibility do not change when the venture being 'jointly carried out' is not criminous. All who work in the enterprise are still jointly responsible for the positive and negative fruits of their labour. But the trick is that the legal authorities then do not look to the facts about responsibility (e.g. as in a trial). Instead they count the obedient but inextricably co-responsible activity of the employees as 'fulfilling' the employment contract. That in turn puts the employer in the position of having paid all the expenses (including the 'labour expenses') and thus having the sole legal claim on the produced outputs which are sold to yield the net income.

Since the facts of de facto responsibility do not change when the enterprise is not criminous, the usual treatment of counting the non-criminous employee's actions as 'fulfilling' the contract amounts to a massive institutionalized fiction. The employment contract is thus inherently invalid and should be recognized as such. Then the property rights to the fruits of labour would be refounded on the justice principle of inalienable responsibility (see **democracy and economy**).

References and further reading

Batt, F. (1967) *The Law of Master and Servant*, London: Pitman.

Coase, R. (1960) 'The Problem of Social Costs', *Journal of Law and Economics*, 3: 1–44.

De Soto, Hernando (2000) *The Mystery of Capital*, New York: Basic Books.

Ellerman, David (1992) *Property and Contract in Economics: The Case for Economic Democracy*, Cambridge MA: Blackwell (full text available at: www.ellerman.org).

DAVID ELLERMAN

PROPERTY RIGHTS See: ownership, property

PROTESTANT ETHIC See: economic sociology; religion and economic life; Weber

PUBLIC BUDGET

Budgets are accounts of state revenue and expenditure flows, as well as the flows themselves. Accounts of budgets typically record a 'fiscal year' that varies in start and finish from a calendar one. According to the *Encyclopædia Britannica*, 'The word budget is derived from the Old French *bougette* ("little bag"). When the British Chancellor of the Exchequer makes his annual financial statement, he is said to 'open' his budget, or receptacle of documents and accounts.'

Budgetary institutions doubtlessly go back to various ancient imperial administrations, but are little documented until the rise of the western state in the early modern period (Mann 1991: ch. 11). In this context, they emerged as results of rising state military and ancillary (e.g. taxing) apparatuses. They also emerged as financial accounts of such administrations from the need to document state taxes and uses in accommodation disposition. This was done to accommodate economic notables and legislative assemblies who pace checks on state executive power. Thus, budgets are monetary records and indicators of state scale and focuses of state politics.

A crucial aspects of public budgets, other than as substance and sign of the scale and composition of costly state activities, is the budget as an instrument of state macroeconomic policy (Musgrave and Musgrave 1984). Here we have state investment (especially infrastructural), state debt (a drain on non-state investment) and state stimulus of consumer demand (via tax cuts, consumer stimulus and budget deficit). The waxing and waning, as well as the emergence of public budgets appears much linked to war, not only because of the frequent salience of limitary components of state budgets but also because of a tendency for states to extend entitlements – the potential benefits of new rights and entitlements to citizens – in time of war when popular allegiance is especially precious (Mann 1991). Key among the expenditure that tend to confer mass benefits are 'redistributive' social expenditures linked to social entitlements and rights, as opposed to 'distributive' expenditure linked more to the services and politics of local constituencies and patronage (Lowi 1964).

Cumulative growth in government expenditures and revenues appears closely tied to redistributive policies, which link the political interests of ruling elites to the large and mobilized constituencies of democratic electoral politics and the welfare state, in particular to left and left-centre parties and the labour movement (Hicks 1999). However, for poor states and a few relatively affluent hegemons military spending continues to loom large. Importantly, the parts played by militarism, economic development, government partisanship and labour movements in driving the expansion of state budgets has been complemented, indeed sharpened, by other social and state forces. For example, societal aging has, in interaction with the elderly's progressive entitlement to publicly insured pensions and medical care, been a force for state expansion; and the initiations and development of state spending and taxing programmes has been structured by the institutions of the state (Swank 2002).

The consequences of costly distributive and redistributive policies may hamper economic growth. In balance, expenditures and revenues apparently tend as they increase to dampen economic growth despite Keynesian theory's 'balanced budget multiplier' (Musgrave and Musgrave 1984). However, any deleterious effects of large state budgets relative to national resources (e.g. as shares of GDP) appear to be variously contingent. Distributive policies that stress infrastructural investment may accelerate economic expansion. Large budgets may provide potent leverage for fiscal policies that stimulate demand (and growth) via deficit spending when eco-

nomic capacity is underutilized, and that dampen it (and stabilize prices) when capacity is fully utilized (Musgrave and Musgrave 1984). Moreover, large budgets may be geared towards the nurture of infant industries or the invigoration of young entrants into international competition (Chang 2001). In addition, free trade may by means of comparative advantage and competitive pressures bring efficiencies that offset the economic efficacies of expensive public sectors; and interest organizations too encompassing to run rampant as rent extracting special interests may rationalize collective choice (Hicks 1999: ch. 4).

According to much economic theory and some evidence, increasing economic globalization exacerbates and leaves little room for large redistributive public sector economic inefficiency (Swank 2002). According to much empirical evidence and substantial emerging theory, globalization tends more often than not to expand states as these extend the indemnification of persons at risk of disruptions issuant upon globalization (Swank 2002).

References and further reading

Chang, H.-J. (2001) *Kicking Away the Ladder: Development Strategy in Historical Perspective*, New York: Anthem Press.

Encyclopædia Britannica Online (2004) 'Government Budget', available at http://search. eb.com/eb/article?eu=109164 (accessed 29 May).

Hicks, Alexander (1999) *Social Democracy and Welfare Capitalism*, Ithaca, NY: Cornell University Press.

Lowi, Theodore (1964) 'American Business, Case Studies, Political Theory and Public Policy', *World Politics*, July: 677–715.

Mann, Michael (1991) *Sources of Social Power*, vol. II, Cambridge: Cambridge University Press.

Musgrave, Richard A. and Musgrave, Peggy B. (1984) *Public Finance in Theory and Practice*, fourth edition, New York: McGraw-Hill.

Swank, Duane (2002) *Diminished Democracy?* New York: Cambridge University Press.

ALEXANDER HICKS

PUBLIC GOODS

The concept originates from the public finance and **welfare economics** literature. The seminal characteristic is that public or collective goods are non-depletable. That is, a public good 'is a commodity for which use of a unit of the good by one agent does not preclude its use by other agents' (Mas-Collel *et al.* 1995: 359). This property is also termed *jointness of supply*. Clean air, national defence and scientific knowledge are examples of commodities with this characteristic. In contrast, private goods are depletable: if one agent consumes a piece of bread, this reduces the amount that is available to others. Pure public goods fulfil a second criterion, which is independent of the first, namely that the *exclusion* of agents from the group of beneficiaries of the collective good is *impossible* (or prohibitively costly). In a public park, for example, exclusion may be possible, whereas it is practically impossible to exclude agents who visit Paris to have a look at the Eiffel Tower.

Public goods and suboptimality

Economics textbooks usually treat public goods as cases of *market failures*. In contrast to perfectly competitive markets for private goods, markets for public goods are inefficient. Due to free riding, the amount of public goods that is produced is *suboptimal*: Each agent has an incentive to consume the commodity provided by others while contributing insufficiently to the provision costs himself. An extreme case of a public goods situation is the Prisoner's Dilemma and its n-person variants. In these games, each player has a dominant strategy to defect. This is, however, not the unique representation of public goods situations. Sometimes, variants of the 'chicken game' are more appropriate. Then (some) agents may contribute, but still produce a suboptimal level of the good.

Sociological aspects

Mancur Olson's (1971) classic treats products of special interest organizations as public goods and points out that they are usually provided as *by-products* of private goods (selective incentives). Subsequently, further explananda have been related to collective goods: social order in a Hobbesian anarchy, certain types of social norms, common pool resources ('commons') and others. Some public goods (called *club goods*) allow for an exclusion of agents. It can be argued that religious organizations (Lawrence Iannaccone) and intentional communities (Michael Hechter) produce shared goods of this kind. In contrast to elder economists' emphasis on the necessity of state intervention in the case of public goods, cooperation is possible without external intervention. Even rational egoists contribute to the public good if they are involved in *repeated* interactions. Rational agents may under these conditions endogenously construct social institutions which contain monitoring mechanisms to enforce rules on how to optimally use the common resource (Elinor Ostrom).

References and further reading

Mas-Collel, Andreu, Whinston, Michael D. and Green, Jerry R. (1995) *Microeconomic Theory*, New York: Oxford University Press.

Mueller, Dennis C. (2003) *Public Choice III*, Cambridge: Cambridge University Press.

Olson, Mancur (1971) *The Logic of Collective Action*, second edition, Cambridge, MA: Harvard University Press.

Sandler, Todd (1992) *Collective Action*, Ann Arbor, MI: University of Michigan Press.

THOMAS VOSS

PUBLIC/SOCIAL CHOICE

Public choice theory, a theory of choices about and choices made in the context of broadly governmental or state institutions, is often traced to a classic essay by Knut

Wicksell ([1896]1958). However, it has only gained its current name and blossomed as a result of a redefinition of the discipline of economics in the second half of the last century. In place of the traditional definition in terms of the object of study (the economy), beginning in the 1950s and 1960s economics came to be defined in terms of a particular type theory (rational choice). This led to applications of the theory to new substantive domains – applications to (primarily democratic) politics came to be called public choice theory. Applications to more generally social domains beyond (if encompassing) economics are sometimes referred to as social choice theory.

Public choice theory has addressed a wide array of topics (including normative and prescriptive issues). Our focus here will be on three areas of particular interest to economic sociologists: how the institutional structure of the state determines the number of political parties and their platforms (optimal location theory), the consequences of actors lobbying the state to intervene in the market (rent-seeking), and the inability of politicians to adequately control appointed bureaucrats and the political economic consequences of their actions. However, we will also touch on a few areas beyond these three.

Models of 'optimal location' were traditionally used by economists to explain where retail outlets should be located in order to maximize customers. With the development of public choice theory, these models were applied to politics. Beginning with the assumption that politicians choose their policy platforms in order to maximize the probability of winning elections, Anthony Downs developed elegant models predicting the optimal location of political parties (the policy platform that maximizes votes) in issue spaces (continua of voters' opinions on an issue) (see Mueller 1997). In a manner analogous to Adam Smith's 'invisible hand', politicians will satisfy the preferences of the majority of voters not because they are altruistic, but because they are self-interested maximizers of votes.

The optimal location model highlights the effects of differences in political institutions. For presidential, winner-take-all systems like the United States, it yields several interesting predictions: (1) there will be only two viable political parties, and third-party bids will generally fail; (2) both parties will locate as close as possible to the middle of the ideological spectrum (they will try to attract the 'median voter'), so the differences between them will be minimal; and (3) redistributive government policies will be especially influenced by and relatively beneficial for the median voter – in public choice theories of electoral choice along redistributive dimensions a voter with roughly the median income. Such systems provide voters with little choice, but are very stable over time (both result from the fact that there is little difference between the two parties). Political systems based on proportional representation will have the opposite characteristics: they produce multiple political parties spanning the ideological spectrum, increasing the choices available to voters but decreasing the stability of the system (the latter is due to both the shorter tenure of governing coalitions and the wider swings in state policies when the ruling coalition changes).

One of the main issues addressed by public choice theorists is the dramatic growth in the size of the state over the past century (as indicated by increases in state employees and budgets). They provide two main explanations of this trend, one focusing on the nature of state policy formation and another concentrating on policy implementation. The policy formation argument concentrates on the ability of the state to intervene in the economy in ways that redistribute resources from some actors to others. The resources provided by state intervention (in the form of tax policy and economic regulation) are referred to as 'rents'. Actors can increase their wealth either by profit-seeking through the market or by 'rent-seeking' – lobbying the state to pass legislation that transfers resources to them. Profit-seeking is productive since it increases economic growth, but rent-seeking is unproductive since it simply transfers resources from some actors to others. Moreover, since politicians can gain by providing rents, rent-seeking leads to an increase in the size of the state and in the scope of state activity. Over time, fewer resources are allocated by the invisible hand of the market and more through rent-seeking deals between politicians and lobbying organizations.

The second main cause of the growth of the state is found in the implementation of state policy. There is now a fairly large literature applying public choice theory to a classic Weberian question: how can rulers (usually democratically elected officials) control the bureaucratic agencies to which they have delegated the power to implement state policies? Both Weber and public choice theorists come to the conclusion that one of the main threats to contemporary democracy is that elected politicians are unable to control their appointed bureaucrats. Public choice analyses by Niskanen and others, of agency problems in state policy implementation, typically assume that bureaucrats want to maximize the budget of the agency they control (see Mueller 1997). Bureaucrats can use the fact that they have better information than politicians (since they are specialists and politicians are forced to be generalists) to get inflated budgets for their agencies, so the state becomes larger than either politicians or voters want it to be. Generally, public choice theorists regard bureaucratic 'self-aggrandizement', like rent-seeking, as economically inefficient and thus pernicious.

Important work with implications for interest group as well as party formation and activities and, thus, for the practice and theory of rent seeking and (non-market) collective decision-making broadly construed was done by Mancur Olson (1965), among others.

Theories of policy optimization are quite relevant to economic functioning from the macroeconomic to the organizational and even divisional level. These provide models of choice under conditions of structured constraints, both cognitive schemas and social structures. More specifically, they offer one a formal, operational model of action under constraint for students of the 'agency/structure' problem salient in economic sociology to consider (Tinbergen 1952; Alt and Crystal 1983). Indeed, models of socially and culturally embedded rational action that engage market contexts and economic organizations are rife today in economics and political science, and on the increase in sociology (see Gould 2004).

References and further reading

Alt, James. E. and Crystal, Alec (1983) *Political Economics*, Berkeley, CA: University of California Press.

Gould, Roger V. (ed.) (2004) *Rational Choice Controversy in Historical Sociology*, Chicago: University of Chicago Press.

Mueller, Dennis C. (ed.) (1997) *Perspectives on Public Choice*, Cambridge: Cambridge University Press.

Olson, Mancur (1965) *The Logic of Collective Action*, Cambridge: Cambridge University Press.

Tinbergen, Jan (1952) *On the Theory of Economic Policy*, Amsterdam: North Holland.

Wicksell, Knuth ([1896]1958) 'A New Principle of Just Taxation', in Richard A. Musgrave and Alan T. Peacock (eds), *Classics in the Theory of Public Finance*, London: Macmillan, pp. 72–118.

ALEXANDER HICKS
EDGAR KISER

R

RATIONAL CHOICE THEORY

'Rational choice theory' is not a unified approach in sociology and particularly not in economic sociology. The term refers to a family of approaches that proceed from the twin assumptions that human beings pursue goals and that, being confronted with opportunities and limitations for reaching their goals, they do so in a more or less intelligent way. The term 'rational' refers to this 'more or less intelligent' way of goal seeking, and it minimally implies the anticipation of the consequences of one's action and the evaluation of these consequences for the realization of one's goal(s). For economic sociology, rational choice theories have been very important, either as tools for analysis or as a foil against which specific sociological arguments have been developed. Roughly speaking, there are two major groups of rational choice theory. First, there are the theories that assume individual rationality as given and focus on social phenomena (such as institutions and social networks) that increase collective rationality (i.e. often called 'Pareto improvement', meaning the achievement of situations in which at least one individual involved is better off than before and no other individual involved is worse off). These theories work either with the assumption of full information or of less-than-full information (the so-called bounded **rationality** belongs to the latter), as

will be explained below. Second, there are theories that assume that not just collective but also individual rationality can be (positively or negatively) affected by social phenomena. The latter approaches can be lumped together under the label of **social rationality** theories. Theories using social rationality conceptions seem to grow in the social sciences in general and in economic sociology in particular.

The place of economics

Economists since the classical times of Adam Smith assumed more or less intelligent goal-directed behaviour. However, it is only in the 1950s that economists became fully committed to *individuals* as the basic units of analysis (methodological individualism supplanting households, firms and states as basic units of analysis). At first, it was only a few economists who turned to full methodological individualism. Later, increasingly more did so, aided by the development of decision and **game theory**. This turn towards founding economics on individual behaviour brought the term 'rational choice' to prominence. With a delay of about twenty years, methodological individualism and rational choice theory also entered sociology (in the 1970s). With only a slight exaggeration one might say that economic sociology thrives to the degree that the mainstream sociology admits rational choice theory as at least one

550

legitimate way of doing sociology. In the long reign of structural functionalism, economic sociology did not do well because there was no theory integrating into one field the various phenomena that are now lumped together under the term 'economic sociology'. Rational choice theory plays an important role for developing the field, because it provides a fairly solid basis for recognizing roles of producer, trader and consumer and the ensuing relationships between them in virtually every walk of life, even as these roles and relationships are sociologically embedded in important social aspects such as network structure, power and elite structures, culture, trust, gender. For this reason, the impressive comeback of economic sociology in the 1990s can be seen as having been greatly aided by the steady growth of rational choice sociology in the 1970s and 1980s. In those two decades, rational choice analyses of economically relevant phenomena created a toolkit for economic sociology that has inspired and is likely to keep inspiring the work in economic sociology both by the use of these tools and by attempts to either refine or replace them by something better. In the next paragraph, this toolkit will be briefly described.

The basic toolkit (given full information)

Active agents

First of all, in rational choice theories, the individual is an *active agent*. This is implied by goal-directed behaviour but needed much elaboration in order to grasp the many ramifications of this assumption. In functionalist sociology, dominant after the Second World War until about the early 1980s, the individual was mainly a passive role player, subject to learning. This also holds for the only integrative treatise on sociology and economics of that time (Parsons and Smelser 1956). The individual as an active agent draws attention to search

behaviour (for example in imperfect markets), to the interest in regulating the effects of other people's behaviour ('regulatory interest'), to entrepreneurs and risk-taking behaviour, and, of course, to investment behaviour. The latter made possible theories of following education in relation to its expected returns ('human capital theory') and theories of investment in social networks (**social capital** theory). The 'active agent' of the individual eventually to led to the view of the individual as 'producer' even in daily life, which gave a completely new turn to the study of households. Finally, the active agent view made game theory relevant for the study of social situations (see 'Institutions' below).

Scarcity

The active agent is confronted with *scarcity*. Most means to achieve goals are naturally or socially scarce, so that the individual has to make choices on how to allocate these means. One concept related to scarcity among active individuals has been particularly important: substitution effects ('relative price effects') and their derivative, the law of demand. The reaction of individuals to changes in relative prices probably belongs to the most robust behavioural regularities of rational choice theory. 'Rationality' in rational choice theory is conceptually based on the individual's handling of goal achievement in the face of scarcity.

Interdependence

The social side of rational choice theory is mainly linked to various analyses of interdependencies among active agents; the problems that arise from interdependencies; and the solutions to these problems we are likely to observe under certain circumstances. Especially the analysis of groups, **collective action**, norms and institutions has received a considerable boost by the rational choice-inspired analyses of interdependencies.

There is, first of all, the prime generator of interdependencies: *positive or negative external effects* (i.e. side-effects of people's behaviour on third parties). For example, practising the trumpet creates negative external effects on neighbours; painting one's house creates positive external effects on neighbours; producing electricity with coal creates negative external effects for a large number of people in the area. Since external effects (especially negative ones) directly impact the goal realizations of third parties, they create *regulatory interests* in the third parties and, under certain conditions, pursuit of these interests will lead to devices that regulate external effects, be that the formation of groups, collective action, the formation of norms or formal institutions, or some combination of these. In the economically most interesting cases of external effects, both positive and negative externalities are combined (such as social dilemmas involving 'impure' public goods). There are few products people can produce on their own, so they often need the cooperation of others (positive externalities). However, cooperation also creates dependencies and other negative side-effects which are exacerbated by the strategic behaviour of active agents. Arrangements that foster positive and mitigate negative external effects are thus of utmost importance for economic activity. Examples are farmers, combined in a sharing group, who share irrigation facilities and their upkeep and devise rules for the maintenance of this arrangement, including arrangements to create compliance. Many social norms and the accompanying ways of sanctioning can also be explained as the result of converging regulatory interests in a group of people. Institutions, such property rights, are formal rules for the regulation of external effects. Rules for the coordination of activities (such as teamwork and driving on the right or the left side of the road) also belong to these kinds of arrangements.

The functioning of markets and market failure can be analysed in terms of these concepts, implying that markets are also a nexus of groups, norms and institutional arrangements. It is clear that the overall structure of arrangements is one of nested groups and rules with possibly conflicting requirements.

Finally, the very conception of norms and institutions based on rational choice also allows, at least conceptually, a clear criterion of the quality of an externality-regulating arrangement: Pareto optimality (sometimes simply called 'efficiency'). Arrangements which improve the well-being of at least one person in a particular system of arrangements without reducing the well-being of any other are 'better' in the sense that they produce less waste and better balance individual and social outcomes. Efficiency is thus both the result of regulatory interests and the measure of the quality of improvements through externality-reducing arrangements. However, due to the possibly conflicting nested arrangements, this Pareto criterion can often only be used in a very limited way.

The basic toolkit (given less than full information)

The analysis of interdependencies bases on rational choice made another leap forward through the explicit introduction of the twin assumptions of opportunistic behaviour and incomplete information (either through **asymmetrical information** or through inherent limitations of the information-processing capacity of human beings). Both assumptions had been made much earlier but only came to prominence in the 1970s, partly under the influence of a more open exchange between economics and sociology, fostered by Simon, Arrow, Stigler, Alchian, Akerlof, Jensen, Williamson and others.

Opportunism and limited information

Once we explicitly introduce the possibility that individuals may be differently informed, we also allow the possibility that active individuals twist the information to their own advantage. This twisting has been called 'opportunism'. Individuals may lie, distort, mislead, conceal, disguise, obfuscate, feign and confuse, and they may evade sanctions by creating or taking advantage of information asymmetries (such as shirking, cheating, stealing or getting others to do so). Opportunism creates problems of **trust** when there are information asymmetries and this opens up a whole new field of inquiry into norms and institutions that deal with problems of trust. For economic sociologists, especially, the ramifications of these problems for the analysis of markets, contracting and organizations are most important.

Markets

Given asymmetric information, certain markets may not come about unless the trust problem is solved. When it is solved in a particular way, it may create very specific markets. For example, the market for used cars uses different solutions to the trust problem than the market for medical services. In the latter case, the state may even grant quasi-monopolies through licensing. Often proxies are used as quality signals (such as educational credentials on the labour market) and may involve reputation effects and personal networks. The more (potential) trust problems there are in a market, the more likely that informal mechanisms (such a strong ties, gossip, direct monitoring) will play an important role in running the market.

Contracting

Contracting in the face of incomplete information means at least two things. First, there is a **principal and agent** problem about how a 'principal' can motivate an 'agent' to represent the principal's interest and not act opportunistically. Second, there is a problem of incompleteness of the contract because with limited information, limited capacity to predict the future and limited means of language (which includes the important problem of tacit knowledge), not all contingencies can be accounted for in advance. This causes transaction costs. Principal–agent theory thus deals with the question of how to use incentives in order to align the interests of the agent with the principal (and avoid 'moral hazard', as opportunistic behaviour is called in this theory). It also deals with the question how to use incentives to avoid attracting the wrong kind of agents for the contract ('adverse selection effects'). **Transaction costs theory** deals with both problems at the same time. They occur jointly particularly in situations in which one or both contract partners have to invest specific assets in the contractual relationship, assets which would be lost if that relationship were to break up. The situation is exacerbated when opportunistic behaviour is difficult to detect. For economic sociology, the most important aspects of both theories (but especially of transaction cost theory) is that they throw light on a socially and economically relevant class of institutions and contractual 'embeddings' that create credible commitments and provisions for dealing with contractual problems that occur ex post (i.e. in the ongoing contractual relationship).

Organizations

Both theories have greatly impacted the study of organizations. First of all, there is the question why there are organizations at all and not just markets. The answer is directly related to the trust problem. If it cannot be solved in the marketplace (because the required asset specificity is too high), it may be still solvable by the use of hierarchical relations, i.e. in organizations. It is obvious that principal–agent and transaction cost theories are directly applicable to questions of job design (how much asset specificity? What trust problems will a certain design create? How much involvement?), of recruitment (avoiding adverse selection) and of governing employment relations (aligning interests; creating credible commitments; offering **efficiency wages**; seniority rules and internal labour markets; grievance procedures). The same holds for **corporate governance**. To what degree is the organizational form and size driven by technology or by transaction costs? How is the flow of information (and thereby the chance of opportunistic behaviour) affected by centralization and decentralization? How would the function and composition of the board of directors affect the change of opportunistic behaviour? What are the consequences of compensation schemes for aligning interests, and how is this related to corporate ownership and takeover practices? What should the relation to the various stakeholders be in the light of firm-specific investments (say, in and of the community and by suppliers) and other trust-sensitive relationships (such as brand names, reputation effects and service relationships)?

In sum, rational choice theory has created a toolkit for economic sociology mainly through working out the institutional ramifications of interdependencies (creating 'externalities') among active and strategic agents and of limited information (creating opportunism and trust problems). Whether this toolkit is used in moderately modified ways (as in 'the new institutionalism') or attacked in different ways (as allowing too little room for culture, social networks and/or non-rational behaviour, see Guillén *et al.* 2002) it is difficult to imagine a blooming economic sociology without it.

References and further reading

Brinton, M. C. and Nee, V. (eds) (1998) *The New Institutionalism in Sociology*, New York: Russell Sage Foundation.

Eggertsson, T. (1990) *Economic Behaviour and Institutions*, Cambridge: Cambridge University Press.

Guillén, M., Collins, R., England, P. and Meyer, M. (eds) (2002) *The New Economic Sociology*, New York: Russell Sage Foundation.

Parsons, T. and Smelser, N. (1956) *Economy and Society*, London: Routledge and Kegan Paul.

Williamson, Oliver E. (1985), *The Economic Institutions of Capitalism*, New York: Free Press.

SIEGWART LINDENBERG

RATIONALITY

In its broadest sense, rationality may be defined as the 'disciplined use of reasoning and reasoned scrutiny' (Sen 2002; 19). The capacity for reasoned scrutiny is the ultimate 'black box' to which scientists and philosophers appeal to explain how human beings make inferences and deductions, unify facts under propositions, and justify assumptions like 'the duality of agency and structure'. In the sciences that make economic relationships their subject matter, rationality refers more narrowly to the capacity of an 'actor' or 'agent' to deliberate over ends and means, to weigh alternatives, and to select those means and methods that the chooser considers effective in practical conduct. Due to its intimate connection to human agency, some conception of rationality is implicated in the theories of action of all the social sciences, including anthropology.

One conception of rationality, however, proved to be particularly attractive in explanatory social science: reasoned scrutiny governed by the principle of **maximization**. Under this conception, it is not enough for actors to identify alternatives, to sort them into better or worse based on their understanding of how the world works, and to devise courses of action that seem to them to be feasible and/or proper under the circumstances. Rather, for decisions like picking a seed for the winter wheat, the rational actor seeks the *best* seed for her money, that is to say, the 'optimal' choice within the limits of her resources and priorities. Importantly, like rational actors generally, the seed buyer can be said to have maximized her outcomes in choice even if she wound up with the third-best seed, since the rejected options presumably were worth less to her than other uses of her resources. Theories that equate rationality with maximization are called 'rational choice theories'. Since the 1970s, attempts to supplant existing theories of practical rationality with models of maximizing agency stimulated heated controversies in economic sociology and other disciplines.

Rationality as maximizing intentionality

The development of **game theory**, decision theory, principal-agent theory and social choice theory from the a priori premise of maximizing intentionality must be considered the supreme intellectual achievement of the social sciences in the twentieth century. These disciplines have made and continue to make significant contributions to political theory, strategic studies, policy studies, social network analysis and economic sociology. Yet they also provoke increasingly urgent metatheoretical questions. What are the distinctive features, the limits and possibilities of human rationality? How does practical rationality differ from the disciplined use of reasoning that prevails in mathematics, natural science, and metatheory? Can the mathematics of extrema – a group of functions that reveal the maxima and minima of sets of points in coordinate space – be imported from the natural sciences, where they identify the paths of 'least effort' or 'efficiency' of physical processes, to the sciences of human action without fundamentally distorting the latter's subject matter?

The last question is particularly germane, since the first social science to use the mathematics of extrema to model practical rationality – neoclassical economics – borrowed its equations from kinetics, the branch of mechanics dealing with energy and motion. By making 'utility' the economic equivalent of kinetic energy, neoclassical economics modelled the rational agent as a particle of desire in a dynamic field of utility (Mirowski 1989). The new conception of *homo economicus* did not arrive uncontested. As early as the 1880s, the Austrian school of economics opposed the use of the infinitesimal calculus to measure the incremental gains in satisfaction ('utility') that consumers derived from their trades and purchases, on the grounds that utility was a discrete rather than continuous variable (see **Austrian economics**). The Austrians called marginal utility the 'subjective theory of value' and emphasized an aspect of rationality overlooked by the mathematical economists, its role in intersubjective understanding (without which no trade or purchase could be undertaken). But Austrian subjectivism lost ground during the 1920s. In his discussion of the theories of action of Alfred Marshall, Vilfredo Pareto and Max Weber, Talcott Parsons (1937) adopted what by then had become the conventional view of rationality: to be rational was to employ the laws and methods of contemporary science in the solution of practical problems. Consequently, Parsons (1937: 58) argued, the actor should be conceived as a rational being 'analogous to the scientist'. In place of the actor's own subjective reconstruction of his pre-choice deliberations, the theorist of economic phenomena would substitute a *choice function* suitable for a species of actor-scientists.

Two groups of choice function predominate in the disciplines that equate rationality with maximization: the 'utility functions' of neoclassical demand theory, which apply under conditions of certainty (where the outcomes of action are distinctly knowable and measurable), and the 'preference schedules' of expected utility theory, which apply under conditions of risk and uncertainty. Under conditions of certainty, like those pertaining to the seed buyer, the rational actor is modelled as if she formulated mental graphs of indifference curves prior to allocating her scarce resources in choice. Under conditions of risk and uncertainty, the rational actor is modelled as if he prioritized his options by assigning both outcome and probability values to them (see **risk and uncertainty**). Theorists justify these choice functions on grounds of tractability, not realism. They are easy to manipulate, even if few choosers use graphs and matrices to scrutinize their options. Moreover, they generate definite predictions about the options a maximizing agent would choose under different regimes of incentives and costs.

The use of utility functions to represent how choosers choose is extensive in rational choice theory. Here the rational peasant or voter or welfare recipient is modelled to act as if he puts the choice-relevant variables (for simplicity, x and y) into an equation like $u = f(x, y)$. Plotted on to a two-dimensional graph, the equation yields a demand curve from which the actor can read the maximand, the highest value of the function. That becomes his first choice, though constraints may compel him to accept a less-favoured option. When there are many constraints, the actor-scientist devises a more complex equation or a series of them.

Expected utility theory's representation of rationality as preference-ordering dominates **decision theory**, strategic studies and the economics of information. In this representation, the rational actor first makes a complete list of her options. She then assigns utility and probability weights to each of them, makes pair-wise comparisons of the combined utility-probability scores, and rank-orders the scores from the most preferred to the least preferred. Rationality is just the ability to carry out these tasks and to move down the preference schedule consistently. As long as the preference schedule is well ordered (i.e. complete and transitive), maximization follows automatically. So does predictiveness. Actors with similar preferences and risk tolerances acting in similar situations with similar resources at their disposal will act in similar ways, insofar as they are rational.

Critiques of rationality as maximization

There is no question about the productiveness of the rational choice paradigm or its ability to shape the research agendas and vocabularies of the social sciences. Yet many consider the conception of rationality as maximizing intentionality to be simplistic, inappropriate for everyday practical conduct, and hyperrational. Expected utility theory, in particular, has been subject to vigorous criticism by Herbert Simon, Daniel Kahneman, Amos Tversky, Jon Elster and Amartya Sen.

In thirty years of research, numerous studies on laboratory subjects document routine violations of expected utility theory's rationality and probability axioms. Subjects in these studies fail to compare and rank all the options in their feasibility set, even when making apparently simple consumer choices. When choices implicate values, subjects exhibit 'multiple equilibria' and hence cannot optimize. Subjects appear to 'regret' previous rankings and reverse preferences, establish preferences between equivalent options, allow losses to loom larger than gains when estimating risks, and allow the description (framing) of the question to affect their perception of the probabilities involved. In other studies, subjects willingly incur travel costs to save a few dollars on low-priced items but not on higher-priced ones (thus violating the principle of marginal costs), and fail to see opportunity costs as equivalent to out-of-pocket expenses. In his review of the literature, Thaler (1991) found varying percentages of subjects to be in violation of thirteen of fifteen tenets of economic rationality. As one review article concluded, 'at the individual level most of the empirical evidence is difficult to reconcile with the principle of EU [expected utility] maximization' (Schoemaker 1982: 530). Violations of the transitivity axiom (according to which, if A is preferred to B and B to C, then A is preferred to C) are particularly serious, since 'if preferences are not transitive, then rational choice theory will have little explanatory power' (Cook and Levy 1990: 7).

Theories using utility functions have been better able to deflect the judgement of predictive failure. That is because they leave so many factors affecting the choice situation exogenous to choice, and because constraints can include virtually anything, including 'self-imposed constraints' stemming from norms that condemn maximizing behaviour as selfishness. In contemporary rational choice theory, **preferences** and even ends are considered exogenous and attributed to pre-intentional 'tastes' and 'desires'. For the most part, economists grant to psychology the task of developing a theory of preference formation. An exception is Becker (1996), who argues that sociological variables such as peer pressure and parental influences can better explain the stability of preferences during a round of choice-making. Most of the critiques of utility maximization offered by economic sociologists – the social construction of tastes, the priority of institutions, the precondition of trust, etc. – fall on deaf ears. They deal with either preference formation or constraints, neither of which touches the ultimate, endogamous drama of the prioritizing individual weighing her options alone.

The use of utility functions to model the choice process becomes particularly controversial when constraints broaden to include intra-personal conditions. Under these conditions, utility maximization often becomes vacuous (content-free), tautological (true by definition) and circular (especially when preferences are read backwards from choices). Some rational choice theories, for example, consider the 'choice' of habits and addictions to be maximizing behaviour: habits economize on search costs while addictions steeply discount the future in favour of present satisfactions. Even apparently suboptimal choices, these theorists argue, will be seen as maximizing when all the unfactored cognitive costs and self-imposed constraints are included in the model (Schoemaker 1982). In response to Herbert Simon's claim that intendedly rational actors satisfice rather than optimize because of the high search costs involved in studying all the consequences of all the options in their choice sets, Beach and Mitchell (1978) argue that people make 'metadecisions' between the decision strategies in their repertoire. Like the seed buyer who husbands her resources, cognitive-effort maximizers select coin-flipping or satisficing for their lesser-valued pursuits and reserve expected utility procedures for their higher-valued ends. When theorists start adding unobservable constraints to the choice function to account for unexplained variance, or add meta-levels of rationality to explain away evidence of suboptimal behaviour, maximization becomes an irrefutable assumption that no longer generates testable predictions.

A number of efforts are underway to decouple rationality and maximization. A promising line of work seeks to develop tractable models of 'minimal' or 'quasi-rationality' (Thaler 1991). Another approach differentiates optimization from maximization, and redefines the latter as the selection of the option that is merely no worse than any other (Sen 2002). Still another develops a rule-based – normative –conception of rationality, treating maximization as a special case. All of these alternatives are compatible with economic sociology's view of rationality as collectively practised, culturally and institutionally embedded intentionality.

References and further reading

Beach, L. R. and Mitchell, T. R. (1978) 'A Contingency Model for the Selection of Decision Strategies', *Academy of Management Review*, 3: 439–49.

Becker, G. S. (1996) *Accounting for Tastes*, Cambridge, MA: Harvard University Press.

Cook, K. S. and Levi, M. (eds) (1990) *The Limits of Rationality*, Chicago: University of Chicago Press.

Mirowski, P. (1989) *More Heat than Light: Economics as Social Physics, Physics as Nature's Economics*, Cambridge: Cambridge University Press.

Parsons, T. (1937) *The Structure of Social Action*, New York: Free Press.

Schoemaker, P. J. H. (1982) 'The Expected Utility Model: Its Variants, Purposes, Evidence and Limitations,' *Journal of Economic Literature*, 20: 529–63.

Sen, Amartya (2002) *Rationality and Freedom*, Cambridge, MA: Belknap Press.

Thaler, R. H. (1991) *Quasi Rational Economics*, New York: Russell Sage Foundation.

CHRISTOPHER PRENDERGAST

RATIONALIZATION

See: rationality; Weber

RECIPROCITY

In his 1960 article '*The Norm of Reciprocity: A Preliminary Statement*', A. Gouldner claims that the norm of reciprocity is implicated in the maintenance of stable social systems because 'the more that people pay their social debts the more stable the social system' (p. 174).

Reciprocity implicitly supposes exchanges between social actors. As in all exchanges, partners must obtain economic and non-economic goods or services that they may then exchange to obtain further goods and services. Reciprocal exchanges are further characterized by mutual dependence: thus, reciprocity is exchange-based upon mutual dependence.

The greater a society's division of labour, the more important are reciprocal economic exchanges. If both partners value what they receive from the other, both will seek to supply more of their own goods or services to provide incentives for the other to increase his supply and to avoid becoming indebted to him.

An exchange is reciprocal when the counterpart received in return for the initial good or service given is subjectively perceived as equivalent by the recipient. A reciprocal exchange supposes that the nature of the exchange has been freely defined and accepted by the partners.

Intrinsically, an exchange between unequal partners cannot be reciprocal, since the more powerful partner can demand more than she offers. In such unequal exchanges, the disadvantaged partner will end the relationship as soon as he can. In the middle term, exchanges need to be based on reciprocity to be stable.

In modern societies, as Marx notes in *Capital* (Volume 1), money is a general equivalent that makes arm's-length exchange the main reciprocal economic exchange. Yet the understanding of reciprocity cannot be limited to an arm's-length exchange because it cannot explain non-economic exchanges and some particular kinds of economic exchanges.

To define reciprocity we have to distinguish between the nature of reciprocation and the temporality of reciprocation. We also need to analyse the different ways that reciprocity is enforced to understand how a norm of reciprocity can exist.

The nature and temporality of reciprocal exchange

Nature of reciprocation

In modern societies, economic exchanges are based on arm's-length relationships. That means that money is the counterpart of the good or service exchanged. Yet the counterpart can also be another good or service: this is a **barter** exchange. In both cases, reciprocal obligations are often formalized by a legal contract.

Temporality of reciprocation

Reciprocation can be instantaneous. This means that the recipient immediately reciprocates the good or service received. Conversely, reciprocation can be delayed. In this case, the recipient reciprocates but with a delay following the receipt of the initial good or service. See Figure 2.

Arm's-length, credit and barter exchanges are frequently used to explain different kinds of reciprocal economic exchanges. In addition, **Mauss** (1950) described gift exchanges, a type of exchange which, he argued, was characteristic of some non-monetary societies but which is also typical of reciprocal economic exchanges in modern societies (Ferrary 2003). Mauss' theory is thus useful for understanding how economic exchanges are embedded in non-economic exchanges in long-term reciprocal exchanges. One of the principles of gift exchange is that the gift is never free – it always incurs a counter-gift. A gift may appear 'free' because it does not lead to immediate compensation. Yet an informal accountability is always held, and if a gift is not – ultimately – reciprocated, then the exchange dynamic is interrupted. The refusal of an initial gift thus marks the refusal to begin the dynamic of reciprocal exchange. At the same time, the initial offer is an important moment in a gift exchange, since such an offer typically takes place under conditions of uncertainty regarding both the receiver's ability to reciprocate, and the time he or she will take to do so, if he/she does so at all.

Unlike many other types of exchanges, gift exchanges are informal and implicit. Thus legal means cannot be used to enforce reciprocation. This creates uncertainty about the exchange, since reciprocity is not guaranteed by a formal, binding contract.

The enforcement nature of the norm of reciprocity

Reciprocity is the basis of stable economic and non-economic exchanges. Yet a person does not exchange if he or she is not certain of obtaining an equivalent good or service. This uncertainty, which threatens the potential for exchanges of all types, is typically mediated by three different kinds of enforcement mechanisms.

Legal enforcement

Ex ante, the law ensures that the partners are free to bargain and to agree to the exchange. The exchange defined in a legal contract is supposed to be freely accepted, between equal partners. This is a prerequisite for reciprocal exchanges which must, as we have mentioned, take place within an equal power relationship.

Ex post, the law enforces the reciprocity defined in the legal contract because a person can sue his business partner if he or she does not reciprocate. The threat of legal proceedings enforces the norm of reciprocity.

Nature of reciprocation

	Monetary	Non-monetary
Instantaneous	**Arm length exchange**	**Barter exchange**
Delayed	**Credit exchange**	**Gift exchange**

(Temporality of reciprocation)

Figure 2. A classification of reciprocal exchange

Rational enforcement

Game theory (Kreps 1990) implies that in repeated exchanges, the partners have a rational interest in reciprocating the present exchange in order to ensure future exchanges: initial reciprocity reduces uncertainty about a partner's likelihood of reciprocating later. The 'Nash equilibrium' can thus be interpreted as a stable dynamic of reciprocal exchange: enforcement of reciprocity stems from the self-interested behaviour of rational actors.

Social enforcement

Ex ante, the embeddedness of the exchange gives more information about the capability and the reliability of the partner to reciprocate. Prior to the first exchange, actors typically lack information about their potential partner. Yet the other members of a social network may provide this information: the potential partner's reputation in a community or social network reinforces the possibility for an initial, reciprocal exchange.

Ex post, the social network exerts pressure to respect the norm of reciprocity. The violation of the implicit norm of reciprocity is socially punished because the other members of the social network will end economic (and often non-economic) exchanges with the contravener.

Social actors are typically embedded in multiple social roles: a person may simultaneously be an employee, a citizen, a relative, a friend, a business partner, a sports partner … The more social roles in which a given actor is embedded, the more the norm of reciprocity is enforced because the possibilities for social coercion are increased.

References and further reading

Blau, P. (1964) *Exchange and Power in Social Life*, Hoboken, NJ: John Wiley and Sons.

Ferrary, M. (2003) 'The Gift Exchange in the Social Networks of Silicon Valley', *California Management Review*, 45(4): 120–38.

Gouldner, A. W. (1960) 'The Norm of Reciprocity: A Preliminary Statement', *American Sociological Review*, 25(2): 161–78.

Kreps, D. M. (1990) *Game Theory and Economic Modelling*, New York: Oxford University Press.

Mauss, M. (1950) *Essai sur le don*, Paris: Presses Universitaires de France. (English translation: *The Gift*, New York: W. W. Norton, 1990.)

MICHEL FERRARY

REDISTRIBUTION

In economic sociology, redistribution represents the extent that economic resources, acquired in **labour markets** are reallocated across the population. Labour markets offer wages to individuals that vary by occupation and industry. These market-based wages, including wages and salary income, range tremendously. Some individuals earn meagre incomes that leave them poor while others earn millions (see **poverty**). This creates unequal income distributions. Advanced industrial democracies, however, respond to these market-based inequities by redistributing income across households. Redistribution is achieved through taxes and transfers that respectively gather money from the upper and middle segments of the income distribution and transfer it to the lower segments through **welfare** programmes.

The extent that governments redistribute income varies dramatically across nations. Some nations, including Finland and Denmark, have extensive welfare states where families are supported universally through child and family allowances. Finland's average poverty rate over the last few decades was about 17 per cent when only considering market-based income. However, after adjusting income for governmental taxes and transfers, Finland's poverty rate is substantially lower, at 3 per cent. Similarly, Denmark's average poverty rate drops from 17 per cent to 5 per cent after considering taxes and transfers (Moller *et al.* 2003). Other nations limit their involvement with the market, and as a result their levels of redistribution are much smaller. The United States is an extreme example of limited government involvement in redistribution. In the United States, taxes and transfers minimally reduce market-based poverty. Average poverty rates in the United States from the 1970s to 1990s only fall from approximately 17 per cent to 15 per cent after considering taxes and transfers.

Welfare regimes

Political economists group nations into regimes based on the size and shape of their welfare states. The social democratic regime, which includes Sweden, Finland and Denmark, is committed to reducing inequality and poverty through redistribution. This regime has a socialistic orientation with extensive welfare states and strong left parties. The Christian Democratic/Corporatist regime also values poverty reduction, but not reductions in inequality. This regime, which includes Germany and Italy emphasizes communitarian ideals, but not necessarily redistribution. The liberal regime, which includes the United States, Canada and the United Kingdom, promotes the market through limited interference. Thus, the welfare state is relatively small and minimally redistributive (Goodin *et al.* 1999).

Regime typologies are important because they represent ideologies towards redistribution which are realized in nations' policy configurations. Nations with large welfare states, and nations that devote much of their social welfare spending on child and family allowances generally have lower poverty rates. Child and family allowance programmes usually offer flat-rate benefits to families independent of income. These universal programmes protect families from the inequities of the market and help redistribute income across households.

Theories of redistribution

Researchers disagree in their conceptualizations of why nations implement redistributive policies. Pluralists focus on industrialization and citizen participation. Class theorists focus on class politics, and statist researchers emphasize governmental structures. Pluralists argue that the redistributive social policies developed from the simultaneous increase in citizen resources, citizen need and citizen demand. More broadly, the welfare state emerged out of the corresponding development of democracy and industry. Industrialization created need for governmental support. Within the working-age population, industrialization created a group of unemployed who required economic assistance. For the non-working age population, industrialization weakened families' care networks by increasing mobility and waged-labour outside of the home. This limited the ability of families to care for their dependents.

Meanwhile, democratization permitted individuals to lobby the state for support. In pluralist societies, the populace attains democratic control through the electoral process. Once leaders are elected, they face the ongoing pressures of future job security and hence must respond to citizen preferences or face the potential consequences of failure at future elections. When citizen preferences are liberal, meaning that they are more likely to support welfare programmes that redistribute income, officials are pressured to implement policies that reflect this ideology (Erikson *et al.* 1993). Researchers have found, particularly in the United States, that nations are more redistributive when the citizenry is more liberal and active.

Class theorists have also established that nations develop more extensive and redistributive welfare states when they have left political institutions, including strong unions, a strong left party, and a coordinated economy where labour, business and

561

the government work together to develop policies (see **corporatism**). These left political institutions impact poverty independently of the welfare state by altering market-based poverty. For example, unions are often effective at increasing members' wages. They also work through the welfare state to redistribute income because they help to enlarge the welfare state (Brady 2004; Moller *et al.* 2003; Huber and Stephens 2001). Indeed, scholars have found that the working class is the strongest supporter of the welfare state, and nations with a strong working class and a strong working-class party implement more redistributive policies.

Another determinant of redistribution is a country's constitutional structure. Each nation's constitution establishes the legislative process. Constitutions vary in the number of points where legislation can be blocked. When the number of points is large, small groups are better able to inhibit the passage of welfare legislation that redistributes incomes (Huber and Stephens 2001; Moller *et al.* 2003).

Redistribution is an important subject of economic sociology because it represents the extent that governments attempt to overcome inequities created in labour markets. It is a topic that is increasingly receiving sociological attention as political sociologists and economic sociologists integrate and refine their unique perspectives.

See also: political economy; structure; welfare state and the economy.

References and further reading

Brady, David (2004) 'The Politics of Poverty: Left Political Institutions, the Welfare State, and Poverty', *Social Forces*, 82: 557–88.

Erikson, Robert S., Wright, Gerald C. and McIver, John P. (1993) *Statehouse Democracy: Public Opinion and Policy in the American States*, New York: Cambridge University Press.

Goodin, Robert E., Headey, Bruce, Muffels, Ruud and Dirven, Henk-Jan (1999) *The Real Worlds of Welfare Capitalism*, New York: Cambridge University Press.

Huber, Evelyne and Stephens, John D. (2001) *Development and Crisis of the Welfare State: Parties and Policies in Global Markets*, Chicago: University of Chicago Press.

Kenworthy, Lane (2004) *Egalitarian Capitalism? Jobs, Incomes, and Equality in Affluent Countries*, New York: Russell Sage Foundation.

Korpi, Walter and Palme, Joakim (1998) 'The Paradox of Redistribution and Strategies of Equality: Welfare State Institutions, Inequality, and Poverty in Western Countries', *American Sociological Review*, 63: 661–87.

Moller, Stephanie, Bradley, David, Huber, Evelyne, Nielsen, François and Stephens, John (2003) 'Determinants of Poverty in Advanced Capitalist Democracies', *American Sociological Review*, 68: 22–51.

STEPHANIE MOLLER

REFLEXIVITY

Although the reflexive turn leads in many directions, the first step typically problematizes the relation between 'representation' and 'reality'. The problematic is not the conventional concern with the objectivity or truth of representation (Swedberg 2003). Recognizing that lay and professional representations are integral features of the institutions and activities whose workings they describe, the reflexive turn directs attention to the construction and consequences of those representations. The ways in which academic analysts and lay practitioners conceive, interpret and explain 'economic' matters (including the very characterization of a matter as 'economic') are thus examined as constituent, if not constitutive, processes of the economic order (Woolgar 1988).

The reflexive turn unsettles prevailing representational practice in several ways. First, reflexivity entails *estrangement* from conventional analytic practices and concepts in order to consider their origin, use and consequence. Second, the reflexive turn is *inclusive*: the representations of social scientists and everyday actors are equally subject to interrogation. Third, the reflexive turn is *recursive*: even efforts to describe reflexive processes may be examined for their origins and consequences. On the one hand, these features of the reflexive turn transform taken-for-granted background resources *of* analysis to substantive topics *for* analysis). On the other hand, problems, which ensue from the demands of reflexivity – such as the prospect of endless interrogation of *any* analytic resources – have led some to shun its call or discount its value.

For a reflexive economic sociology, 'representation' refers to the myriad ways of explaining; characterizing, measuring, auditing, modelling and forecasting whatever participants define as 'economic'. Included in the purview of a reflexive economic sociology are the local practices, modes of representation and bodies of knowledge employed by everyday actors whose actions comprise the 'economy'; the representational practices of the professions and professionals – economists, financial experts, accountants, analysts and bankers – comprising the economic complex; the financial media which develop and disseminate descriptions of the economic order; and, in the consummate reflexive inclusion, the analyses proffered by economic sociology itself. *Analytical* reflexivity invites the economic sociologist or economist to examine the social origins and deployment of the discourse and practices s/he uses to analyse the economic order. What are the interests, rhetorics, negotiations, critical tests and strategic choices that contribute to the emergence, content, effects and efficacy of particular methods and paradigms of analysis? *Substantive* reflexivity focuses attention upon the production, deployment and consequences of representations used by participants 'in' the economic order. How do lay and professional participants (lay and institutional investors, for example) acquire, interpret

and use 'knowledge' of the economic order in the course of **economic action**?

The reflexive turn broadens the critical and substantive horizons of economic sociology in several ways. First, the reflexive sensibility functions as intellectual vigilance against surreptitious infiltration or naive appropriation of the representations indigenous to the economic order. To the extent that economic sociology derives its analytic resources from the very discourses which comprise its focus of analysis, it risks becoming 'unintentionally complicitous with the discursive order of capital, with its attempt to establish the economy as a distinct, self-contained sphere – a sphere in whose construction the cultural, the traditional, the personal, supposedly play no part, except by their exclusion' (Mitchell 1998: 98). The conceptual estrangement of the reflexive sensibility provides the fulcrum for critical reflection *upon* prevailing discourse rather than from *within* its conceptual confines.

Second, reflexivity brings into focus the empirical processes through which representations constitute the economic order. Ever since Merton's (1957) description of the self-fulfilling prophecy, illustrated by a financially sound bank made insolvent through rumours of insolvency, sociologists have appreciated how the fates of economic institutions, markets and transactions are inextricably entwined with representation of those fates. The reflexive sensibility suggests yet more extensive and complex ways in which lay and professional findings, formulations and forecasts permeate and create aspects of the economic order. Professional economics has attained such power, for example, that it is able to orchestrate actual economic practices in accord with its models (Miller 2002). Economics is not merely descriptive: it is 'performative' (Callon 1998). The power of the models and theories of contemporary economics is not limited to organizing economic processes and practices but may include creating types of people. Tenets of neo-classical theory – the profit-maximizing *homo economicus,* for example – are incorporated in institutional design and management practices, social norms and taken-for-granted assumptions of economic activities (Ferraro *et al.* 2005). Thus, the type of actor conceived in neoclassical theory – vociferously critiqued and presumably laid to rest by sociology – is resurrected as a constructed reality.

As the preceding examples suggest, the correspondence between representations and economic reality may result from the latter being fashioned in the image of the former. Thus, a third contribution of the reflexive sensibility is awareness of the inverted processes through which formulations and formulae come to be 'true'. MacKenzie and Millo (2003) have show how the initially 'unrealistic' and inaccurate Black–Sholes–Merton theory of options pricing came to be more realistic and accurate as it was incorporated into the infrastructure of the Chicago Board Options Exchange and used by options traders themselves to guide their decisions The reflexive sensibility cautions economic sociologists against seduction by prevailing representations even when – perhaps especially when – they are apparently true.

Regardless of whether academic analysts heed the reflexive call, participants in the economic order do (Giddens 1991). The legendary investor and financier George Soros' 'theory of reflexivity' (2003) informs his own investment decisions. On a lower level of abstraction (and ethics), the fraudulent activities of accounting firms, stock market analysts and corporate executives illustrate how practitioners artfully exploit the constitutive powers of representation. In addition to expanding its critical and substantive horizon, the reflexive turn seems necessary for economic sociology to keep apace with its already reflexive subjects.

References and further reading

Callon, Michel (1998) 'The Economic Embeddedness of Economic Action', in Michel Callon (ed.), *The Laws of the Markets,* Cambridge: Blackwell.

Ferraro, Fabrizio, Pfeffer, Jeffrey and Sutton, Robert I. (2005) 'Economics Language and Assumptions: How Theories Can Become Self-Fulfilling', *Academy of Management Review,* 30(1): 8–24.

Giddens, Anthony (1991) *Modernity and Self-Identity. Self and Society in the Late Modern Age,* Cambridge: Polity Press.

MacKenzie, Donald and Millo, Yuval (2003) 'Constructing a Market, Performing Theory: The Historical Sociology of a Financial Derivatives Exchange', *American Journal of Sociology,* 109: 107–45.

Merton, Robert K. (1957) *Social Theory and Social Structure,* Glencoe, IL: Free Press.

Miller, Daniel (2002) 'Turning Callon the Right Way Up', *Economics and Society,* 31: 218–33.

Mitchell, Timothy (1998) 'Fixing the Economy', *Cultural Studies,* 12: 82–101.

Soros, George (2003) *The Alchemy of Finance: The New Paradigm,* New York: John Wiley and Sons.

Swedberg, Richard (2003) *Principles of Economic Sociology,* Princeton, NJ: Princeton University Press.

Woolgar, Steve (ed.) (1988) *Knowledge and Reflexivity: New Frontiers in the Sociology of Knowledge,* London and Beverly Hills, CA: Sage.

MELVIN POLLNER

REGULATION OF THE MARKET

The term 'market regulation' commonly refers to formal legal rules or government oversight that restricts what market participants may do. Regulation is seen to involve the imposition of external constraints on to markets, and their rigorous enforcement 'distorts' the natural operation of the market. This simple dichotomy between natural markets and artificial regulations overlooks the fact that regulation occurs even without explicit government intervention. Indeed, no matter how chaotic or disordered they may appear, all markets are regulated in some fashion. That is, markets are rule-governed in that behaviour is shaped and controlled by social rules and norms. Such rules are both constraining and enabling. Defined in this broader sense, regulation in some form is ubiquitous although it varies in scope, level and mode of enforcement; it depends on what is being regulated and who is doing the regulating; and it may involve formal legal rules or informal social norms. The most obvious, and frequently the most contentious, type of regulation is that enacted by a centralized government bureaucracy. But many implicit and informal rules act in decentralized fashion to influence the behaviour of market participants.

In the United States, federal government regulation is thought to have been instituted to curtail the excesses of gilded age laissez-faire capitalism or to resolve some of the problems of the Great Depression. In fact, public regulation occurred throughout the nineteenth century as state and local governments dealt with fire and safety hazards, public health and morality, among other issues (Novak 1996). Thus, for example, cities stipulated building codes to help reduce fire hazards and state governments licensed occupations ostensibly to ensure the quality of service. In medieval Europe, market regulation included the standardization of weights and measures by local rulers, the Church's prohibition on usury, and guild rules about prices, wages and product quality (Wood 2002).

Formal-legal regulation varies in terms of where and how it intervenes in a market. Regulations may restrict entry into a market (e.g. by imposing licensing requirements), or it may try to set prices (e.g. usury laws that put caps on interest rates for loans, or utility commissions that set the rate charged to consumers for electrical power). Regulations sometimes stipulate product quality (e.g. Food and Drug Administration rules on the safety and efficacy of pharmaceutical products) or set standards (e.g. US Department of Agri-

culture grades for fresh produce). They may set disclosure requirements (requiring corporations to file financial reports, or insist that lenders use the same metric for interest charged on a loan, e.g. APR: Annual Percentage Rate). They may also prohibit various kinds of activities (e.g. zoning laws that prevent commercial use of residential housing).

In their origins, many such regulations were instituted to protect the public interest. Occupational licensing could help ensure that service providers possessed some minimal level of qualification to perform their job. Progressive-era labour legislation helped to protect female and child workers by regulating the terms of their employment (Skocpol 1992), while New Deal era labour legislation made it easier for workers to organize into unions and so enhance their bargaining position in relation to employers (Amenta 1998: 109–10). Product standards helped consumers make informed choices in the marketplace, while product safety standards ensured that whatever was available in the market would not be harmful. Natural monopolies were regulated to protect buyers. Frequently, however, such altruistic intentions become subverted. State licences or credentialing requirements can be used to reduce occupational competition by excluding potential entrants. Price regulations curtail price competition and allow sellers to enjoy higher prices. Regulatory agencies were sometimes 'captured' by the industry they regulated, and used to serve industry interests (Stigler 1975). Such capture occurred when the industry built informal ties with the agency, or established a 'revolving door' pattern of recruitment between government and industry. This simple capture model has been modified as scholars recognized that there are multiple organized groups (e.g. consumers, political parties, etc.) with an interest in regulation, in addition to the regulated industry itself (Teske 1991). Furthermore, depending on their governance, size and funding, regulatory agencies possess variable capacity and autonomy, and so are more or less resistant to external pressures. Governments can also regulate economic activity through the less obvious route of property rights (Campbell and Lindberg 1990).

Over time, formal-legal regulation has shifted upwards from the local, to the state or provincial, and then to the national level. Now, as Braithwaite and Drahos (2000) note, the regulatory locus is increasingly international and even global. At each level, the process of regulatory competition may occur. Of all the factors of production, capital is most mobile. Other things being equal, where regulation reduces the profitability of capital, capital tends to move to those legal jurisdictions where regulation is less onerous. Regulatory competition may unleash a 'race to the bottom' where jurisdictions (cities, states, countries) compete by undercutting or weakening their own regulatory apparatus in order to attract investment. And yet under some conditions the race is to the top, so that regulations become more rigorous rather than less (Braithwaite and Drahos 2000: 522). As policy measures, sweeping regulation and deregulation often occurs as politicians respond to scandals, the pressure of interest groups, or the influence of new ideas (Derthick and Quirk 1985). Furthermore, political factors influence the implementation and enforcement of regulatory laws, as well as their passage and repeal.

Other, less visible, forms of regulation are no less important. Open-access renewable resources are vulnerable to over-exploitation (e.g. the 'tragedy of the commons'). The short-run incentive to extract as much as possible leads to long-term destruction of the resource. Clearly, regulatory laws could limit extraction and protect resources for the long-term. Historically, however, informal social institutions have regulated access and use of such resources, and helped to prevent over-

exploitation (see Neeson 1993 on the English commons, and Ostrom 1990 more generally). Moral economies helped to enforce 'fair' prices during food shortages in the early modern era (Thompson 1971).

Sometimes regulations have emerged within markets, when market participants generate and enforce their own standards. Cheit (1990) documents the large number of product standards that have been promulgated by private organizations (the American Society for Testing and Materials, for example, sets forth over 7,200 standards; see Cheit 1990: 7). Adherence to one standard rather than another often confers competitive advantage on some firms (especially in the computer industry where software compatibility is an issue), and therefore the question of which standard gets institutionalized is a contentious and consequential one (Besen and Farrell 1994).

References and further reading

Amenta, Edwin (1998) *Bold Relief: Institutional Politics and the Origins of Modern American Social Policy*, Princeton, NJ: Princeton University Press.

Besen, Stanley M. and Farrell, Joseph (1994) 'Choosing How to Compete: Strategies and Tactics in Standardization', *Journal of Economic Perspectives*, 8: 117–31.

Braithwaite, John and Drahos, Peter (2000) *Global Business Regulation*, Cambridge: Cambridge University Press.

Campbell, John L. and Lindberg, Leon N. (1990) 'Property Rights and the Organization of Economic Activity by the State', *American Sociological Review*, 55: 634–47.

Cheit, Ross E. (1990) *Setting Safety Standards: Regulation in the Public and Private Sectors*, Berkeley, CA: University of California Press.

Derthick, Martha and Quirk, Paul J. (1985) *The Politics of Deregulation*, Washington, DC: Brookings Institution Press.

Neeson, J. M. (1993) *Commoners: Common Right, Enclosure and Social Change in England, 1700–1820*, Cambridge: Cambridge University Press.

Novak, William (1996) *The People's Welfare: Law and Regulation in Nineteenth-Century America*, Chapel Hill, NC: University of North Carolina Press.

Ostrom, Elinor (1990) *Governing the Commons: The Evolution of Institutions for Collective Action*, Cambridge: Cambridge University Press.

Skocpol, Theda (1992) *Protecting Soldiers and Mothers: The Political Origins of Social Policy in the United States*, Cambridge, MA: Harvard University Press.

Stigler, George J. (1975) *The Citizen and the State: Essays on Regulation*, Chicago: University of Chicago Press.

Teske, Paul (1991) 'Interests and Institutions in State Regulation', *American Journal of Political Science*, 35: 139–54.

Thompson, E. P. (1971) 'The Moral Economy of the English Crowd in the Eighteenth Century', *Past and Present*, 50: 76–136.

Wood, Diana (2002) *Medieval Economic Thought*, Cambridge: Cambridge University Press.

BRUCE G. CARRUTHERS

RÉGULATION SCHOOL

Origins and objectives

Since the mid 1970s, the *régulation* school (this French spelling has been kept in order to distinguish the meaning of this term in *régulation* school, by opposition to the conventional regulation in English) has developed a research programme around a key issue: how do capitalist economies evolve? This question leads to the study of the transformations of social relations that create new economic and non-economic forms, organized in structures, within a given mode of production. The *régulation* school starts from an assessment of basic Marxian concepts and intuitions, and uses Kaleckian/Keynesian macroeconomic tools in order to analyse the variety of macroeconomic processes of adjustment (*régulation* modes) and growth regimes (more precisely defined as accumulation regimes). From a methodological standpoint, both long-run historical studies, in the tradition of the Annales school of economic and social history, and various comparative approaches are combined in order to exhibit the various configurations observed across time and space. In contrast to neo-classical economics that relies only on market mechanisms, the *régulation* school stresses the importance of institutional forms, defined as codifications of basic social relations. This framework delivers an interpretation of the golden age of Fordism in the 1960s, and simultaneously proposes a series of endogenous mechanisms that trigger the structural crisis of regimes. Even in the era of globalization, a large variety of capitalisms can still persist, not only in response to path dependencies but due to complementarity between institutional forms that generally derive from past social and political struggles.

Core notions

The starting point is the hypothesis that *accumulation* has a central role and is the driving force of capitalist societies. This necessitates a clarification of factors that reduce or delay the **conflict**s and disequilibria inherent in the formation of capital, and which allow for an understanding of the *possibility* of periods of sustained growth. These factors are associated with particular *regimes of accumulation*, namely the form of articulation between the dynamics of the productive system and social demand, the distribution of income between wages and profits on the one hand and on the other the division between consumption and investment. It is then useful to explain the *organizational principles* which allow for a mediation between such contradictions as the extension of productive capacity under the stimulus of competition, and downward pressure on wages which inhibits the growth of demand. The notion of *institutional form* – defined as a set of fundamental social relations – enables the transition between constraints associated with an accumulation regime and collective strategies; between economic dynamics and individual behaviour. A small number of key institutional forms, which are the result of past social struggles and the imperatives

567

of the material reproduction of society, frame and channel a multitude of partial strategies which are decentralized and limited in terms of their temporal horizon. Research on the United States and France, subsequently extended to other industrialized as well as developing countries, has introduced a series of key notions: a distinction between five institutional forms, mode of *régulation*, cyclical and structural crises.

The forms of competition describe by what mechanisms the compatibility of a set of decentralized decisions is ensured. They are competitive while the ex post adjustment of prices and quantities ensures a balance; they are monopolist if the ex ante socialization of revenue is such that production and social demand evolve together. *The type of monetary constraint* explains the interrelations between credit and money creation: credit is narrowly limited in terms of movement of reserves when money is predominantly metallic; the causality is reversed when the dynamics of credit conditions the money supply. This happens in systems where external parity represents the only constraint weighing upon the national monetary system. *The nature of institutionalized compromises* defines different configurations of relations between the state and the economy: the state-as-arbiter when only general conditions of commercial exchange are guaranteed; as the interfering state when a network of regulations and budgetary interventions codify the rights of different social groups. *Modes of insertion into the international regime* are also derived from a set of rules which organize relations between the nation-state and the rest of the world in terms of commodity exchange, capital movements and monetary settlements. History goes beyond the traditional contrast between an open and a closed economy, free trade and protectionism; it makes apparent a variety of configurations spaced out between the hegemonic economy constituting the axis of the international system, and the countries at the periphery of this system. Finally, *forms of the wage labour nexus* indicate different historical configurations of the relationship between capital and labour, i.e. the organization of the means of production, the nature of the social division of labour and work techniques, the type of employment and the system of determination of wages, and workers' way of life. If, in the first stages of industrialization, wage-earners are defined first of all as producers, during the second stage they are simultaneously producers and consumers. Hence the contrast between nineteenth-century wage labour nexus and the Fordist relations of the contemporary period.

On the basis of these forms, one can analyse the logic of the behaviour of social groups and of individuals ensuring the relative coherence and stability of the current accumulation regime. At this point appears the notion of *régulation*, as a conjunction of mechanisms and principles of adjustment associated with a configuration of wage relations, competition, state interventions and hierarchization of the international economy. Finally, a distinction between *minor and major crises* is called for. The former, which are of a rather *cyclical* nature, are the very expression of *régulation* in reaction to the recurrent imbalances of accumulation. The latter are of a *structural* nature: the very process of accumulation throws into doubt the stability of institutional forms and the *régulation* which sustains it. The partial rupture in the functioning of the system paves the way to social struggles and political alternatives.

Major results

A large number of theoretical and empirical research studies have pointed out a common and general result: institutions matter. The changing patterns of macroeconomic adjustments are the consequence of previous transformations in institutional forms.

Conversely, the diversity of contemporary economies is explained by differences in their institutional architectures. Thus, *régulation* modes and accumulation regimes vary across historical periods and space. More precisely, the *régulation* school delivers at least seven major conclusions or interpretations.

A competitive mode of regulation was operating during the nineteenth century, but it does not display the smooth and satisfactory property of a general equilibrium, since cyclical crises and modest growth rates are embedded into the related institutional architecture.

A totally different *régulation* mode has emerged from the turmoil of the post-WWII period. It operates through an ex ante adjustment of production capacity and effective demand via the Fordist wage labour nexus which indexed real wages to expected productivity increases. The diffusion of a welfare state and the wide acceptance of Keynesian principles for monetary and budgetary policy have also been part of this administered or monopolist regulation mode.

The interwar period in the USA and France gives an example of a major structural crisis that derives from the mismatch between an emerging intensive accumulation regime with the legacy of a wage labour nexus governed by competitive forces. This demonstrates that no economic force automatically warrants the dynamic stability built into a *régulation* mode. Thus the same analytical framework should explain simultaneously a stabilized regime as well as the unfolding of the disequilibria that lead to a possible economic collapse.

The so-called 'golden age', i.e. the fast and steady growth observed until the 1970s, is more than a mere catching up of lagging countries towards the technical frontier. Basically, this period was unprecedented due to the strong bargaining power of wage-earners and the central role of the Fordist capital labour compromise. This is why only a limited fraction of

nation-states could benefit from such an exceptional growth regime, in which distributive conflicts finally played a positive role on innovation and growth.

This regime came to an end not so much due to adverse shocks such as rising oil prices, high real interest rate and conservative economic policies. Paradoxically, the crisis came from the very success of the diffusion of Fordist institutional forms propagating indexation, inflation and exchange rate instability. Thus, stagflation, i.e. the coexistence of inflation and recession, was the direct consequence of a monopolist *régulation* mode. After the slow erosion of the previous institutional architecture, a still different *régulation* mode has emerged. Consequently, the stock market crisis that burst out in 2000 was not at all the repetition of the interwar depression and deflation. The institutional configuration shapes the nature and unfolding of both cyclical and structural crises.

Since most institutional forms derive from past social and political struggles, the comparative method applied to industrialized and developing countries exhibits a large spectrum of *régulation* modes and accumulation regimes. Few nation-states have been able to converge towards a Fordist growth regime. The related institutional configurations define as many 'brands' of capitalisms. Analyses of the wage labour nexus, of the welfare state organization of social systems of innovation, do converge towards a central finding. There exist at least four brands of capitalisms: market-led, meso-corporatist, state-led and social-democrat. These configurations derive from various forms of embeddedness of market relations. Here the *régulation* school converges with various approaches in economic sociology.

A direct consequence is that there is no one-best-way brand of capitalism. Even in the epoch of high internationalization of trade, investment, research and finance, the institutional architecture inherited from the past largely shapes the competitive advantage of any territory. Therefore, various *régulation* modes and growth regimes can coexist and even differentiate one from another in response to the stiffening of international competition. Nevertheless, if the financial instability propagates major negative shocks, the resilience of domestic *régulation* modes may reach clear limits. The more likely, the more diffused the benchmarking of any country with respect to a typical market-led capitalism.

Current challenges

The inner development of the theory as well as the surprises brought by the last two decades of the twentieth century now put a new agenda for research. First, the links with economic sociology become more and more apparent since the repertoire of coordinating mechanisms has been significantly enlarged: besides the market, other devices like the firm, the state, the community, associations and joint-ventures are important mechanisms in order to respond to uncertainty, to overcome social and economic conflicts, and thus share risk, income and wealth. In a sense, each institutional form is a complex mix of these elementary coordinating mechanisms. A second issue relates to the elucidation of the forces that coalesce into coherent *régulation* modes. The historical record exhibits the central role of the two world wars, as well as financial and political crises in the redesign of most of the institutional forms. Other authors invoke hazard as the implicit origin of successful institutional architectures. Still others put a strong emphasis on the selection and learning processes according which institutions, technologies and social values tend to co-evolve. Alternatively, the hypothesis of institutional complementarity may explain both the resilience and the possible brusque reversal and crisis of a given system. Last but not least, the shift of political coalitions can trigger a shift in the hierarchy of institutional forms: pro-labour in the Fordist era, pro-business and finally finance-led during the 1990s.

What could post-Fordism be? This question, frequently addressed to the *régulation* school, has not yet been given a clear answer. Successive hypotheses have proven to be partial, since a competition-led regime, a modernization of mass production, the key role of information and communication technologies or, finally, a financialization of contemporary capitalism only capture a part of the highly complex and interdependent interactions that have shifted most developed economies out of the Fordist regime and monopolist *régulation*. Some recent works argue that the next regime will be built upon education, training, leisure and health care. But there is still a more difficult issue: how to go from here to there, i.e. how do new *régulation* modes emerge? The full rationality of *homo economicus* is unable to solve the simplest coordination problems; it is not able to work out the institutionalization of new compromises. The theory suggests and the historical record confirms that the intermediation by the political process, law and jurisprudence are necessary in order to overcome structural crises. Thus the *régulation* school has now to build a joint research programme not only with economic sociologists but with political scientists too.

See also: capitalism; economic transformation in post-communist societies; economics, history of; globalization; institutionalism, old and new; markets, sociology of; political economy; regulation of the market; social construction of the economy; state and economy.

References and further reading

Aglietta, Michel (1982) *Regulation and Crisis of Capitalism*, New York: Monthly Review Press.

Baslé, Maurice, Mazier, Jacques and Vidal, Jean-François (1999) *When Economic Crises Endure*, New York: M. E. Sharpe.

Boyer, Robert and Saillard, Yves (eds) (2002) *Régulation Theory, the State of the Art*, London: Routledge.

Jessop, Bob (ed.) (2001) *Regulation Theory and the Crisis of Capitalism*, five volumes, including Volume 1, *The Parisian Regulation School*, Cheltenham, UK: Edward Elgar.

ROBERT BOYER

RELATIONAL CONTRACTS See: contract

RELIGION AND ECONOMIC LIFE

For most of the twentieth century, sociologists debated the material consequences of cultural orientations. Max Weber's 'Protestant Ethic' popularized claims of Protestant economic superiority, and tenors much of the debate in American sociology. Recently, research has once again focused on religious influences on economic factors by situating theories in individual or institutional contexts. Rather than positing grand differences in the **economic development** of nations based on religious prescriptions and proscriptions, these studies focus on how religious communities influence the development of human capital and wealth accumulation, or how religious political movements influence the operation of commerce through legal restrictions. Further, the study of religion itself is increasingly informed by economic theories, and this genre of theory and research is an important contribution to economic sociology.

Religion and macro-level economic outcomes

Weber's Protestant Ethic thesis provided an early macro-level theory linking religion to economic development and the rise of capitalism. Weber argued that a combination of otherworldly asceticism and **beliefs** in predestination combined to make

Calvinism the economic spark for capitalist accumulation, efficient production and scientific education. Weber himself pointed to school choices in Germany as indicative of Catholic aversion to scientific careers, and preferences for less economically viable humanistic studies. Merton extended Weber's thesis to specifically focus on the influence of English Puritanism and German Pietism on scientific investigation that was integral to economic development. Both Weber and Merton ignored other structural and political factors that prevented Catholics from entering science, or made studies in the humanities necessary for the priesthood, and the only option given their political exclusion from other educational opportunities.

Collins (1997) provides a more general account of the relationship between religion and the rise of capitalism by linking religious institutions to entrepreneurial activities and opposition to feudal dominion. This application is also notable since Collins (1997) uses Buddhist monasteries in Japan as his substantive example. Here, the focus turned to the **political economy** of feudalism, and how religious institutions might provide a source of opposition to feudal domination, and even a spark for capitalist enterprise.

Drawing on the works of Sombart and Gershenkron, Fernand Braudel examined how minority religious groups were pivotal for the development of banking and finance across a variety of contexts. Jews in Europe, Armenians in Persia and Russia, and Jain in India each played an important role as pariah capitalists by serving as intermediaries in trade and finance. Jews, in particular, have benefited from their ability to skirt proscriptions against usury when borrowers are non-Jews. More recently, Timur Kuran (2003) has examined how Islamic societies hindered economic development, and privileged the accumulation of capital by Christians in Jews in their own nations. Islamic proscriptions against usury hindered the development of banking and finance, and allowed non-Moslems to develop a monopoly on such activities. Theocracies in a substantial fraction of the Moslem world likely have a substantial impact on economic development, particularly with the popularization of an 'Islamic economics'. Cross-national findings are mixed regarding the influence of religion, and such studies are severely limited in their measures of religious factors across nations and over time.

Religion and status attainment

In the latter half of the twentieth century, research began to focus on the individual level relationships between religion and status attainment. Gerhard Lenski's *Religious Factor* spurred considerable research and debate regarding Catholic–Protestant differences in childrearing orientations and educational and occupational attainment. Research on the topic waned through the 1970s and 1980s for three reasons: (1) increasing awareness of sizable variation in attainment for Catholics from different ethnic origins, for Protestants from different denominations, and for any religious group across socio-historical circumstances; (2) mounting multivariate evidence suggesting that family background – rather than religious culture – created religious differences in attainment; and, (3) the irrelevance of Weberian theories for explaining differences other than those between Catholics and Protestants (Darnell and Sherkat 1997).

Contemporary research investigating the connection between religious factors and economic outcomes focuses on specific religious groups, and how they influence the development of economic human capital and status attainment processes. Secular education is often considered threatening to religious beliefs, and research shows that educational attainment reduces belief orthodoxy. Sectarian religious groups limit the joint production possibilities for this-worldly advancement and supernatural

rewards and compensators, and as a consequence members must choose between worldly gain and their status in the sect. Research shows that conservative sects in the United States inculcate fundamentalist beliefs in members that lead them to lower educational aspirations, limit educational attainment, and curb the acquisition of wealth (Darnell and Sherkat, 1997; Keister 2003). Conservative Protestants, much more Catholics and others, demand obedience from their children, enforced with harsh parenting practices, and the demand for conformity makes religious fundamentalists well suited for lower-class occupations, and less prepared for the cognitive tasks of professional and managerial occupations.

Religious fundamentalists choose educational settings and occupations that allow them to avoid contact with non-believers, and this will substantially influence their economic circumstances. Religious ties are also linked to heightened attachment to local settings, and prevent geographic migration that would open up economic opportunities. Religious commitments are also strongly associated with traditional gender roles, and this has a dramatic negative impact on women's status attainment through limiting educational attainment and forcing withdrawal from the labour market. However, not all religious traditions have a uniform negative impact on status attainment. Notably, Jews, Jain and other religious groups emphasize scholarly learning and the acquisition of skills and wealth, and collective activities in religious groups that value worldly activity can provide access to networks that may further status and wealth attainment.

Economic theory and religious markets

Once considered an avenue beyond the scope of rational discourse or explanation, religion is now theorized about and empirically examined along with other arenas of social life. Religion is a cultural industry, populated by competing firms (religious denominations), regulated by states, staffed by professionals in charge of producing religious goods (priests and other cadre workers). Religious firms produce collective goods through collective actions linked to supernatural rewards and compensators – benefits or promises of future benefits that cannot be evaluated in this world and/or cannot be attributable to worldly causes (Stark and Finke 2000). Religious firms and their agents generate valuable explanations about supernatural rewards and compensators. Individual consumers exchange rewards (time and money) for these religious benefits. Economic perspectives see religious consumers as active agents in the production of religious value, as well as consumers.

Supply-side theories of religious markets

Adam Smith produced the first economic look at religion, and recent scholarship from the 'supply side' fits firmly in this classical economic tradition (Stark and Finke 2000). Key assumptions of this perspective are that social stratification and pluralism naturally produces diverse preference for religious goods, and that preferences are stable. Religious firms have low start-up costs – requiring only social space (an empty field) and a preacher – and a limited ability to diversify production (Catholicism and Baptist faiths cannot be produced by the same firm). The natural state of religious markets should be pluralism, and monopolistic and oligopolistic markets must be produced by state regulation. State-supported religious firms do not have to conform their products to the desires of the consumers, produce high-quality goods or compete with other firms. Empirical studies generally show that religious participation is lower in places where state-supported churches dominate, or in areas where there are limited product offerings (Stark and Finke 2000). However, the relationship between pluralism and religious participation breaks down at higher levels of aggregation and in modern religious economies where high-speed travel enables a larger set of offerings (Stark and Finke 2000). Further, religious monopolies may be able to boost participation by generating normative sanctions against defection – making participation semi-involuntary (Sherkat and Ellison 1999).

Religious organizations suffer from free-rider problems just like other voluntary organizations. People can enjoy a well-constructed religious service with amenities for children, music, places to sit, reading materials, air conditioning and the like, but individual congregants are not required to donate money. Congregations with higher proportions of free-riders will have lower-quality religious services – or else they must pay higher costs and drain organizational resources. Religious organizations that do not restrict membership to the committed will therefore have less valuable religious products and will be organizationally weaker. Theory suggests that requiring sacrifice for a religious group will eliminate the free-rider problem and enable the more effective production of religious goods.

At the individual level, supply-side theorists focus on the household production of religious value, and the importance of religious human capital for driving religious behaviours. From this view, individuals with strong stocks of human capital will be able to produce copious amounts of religious value, so long as they are in a familiar religious environment. Outside of familiar venues, capital stocks may be useless, and without substantial capital, religious activity may not be worth the production effort. In line with neoclassical assumptions, human capital theory assumes that preferences are stable, and that only productive capacities change with the addition of consumption-generated capital.

Demand-side rational actor theories

Demand-side theories of religious markets resonate with economic theorizing about preference dynamics and social influences on choices. Key for demand side theories is the identification of preferences for distinctively religious goods. The narratives and ritual actions that constitute religious goods are learned through socialization processes (Sherkat and Ellison 1999). Since these explanations cannot be evaluated in the real world, religious goods are risky, and only the opinions of highly trusted others will influence religious preferences. As a consequence, family and close friends are generally the sources of religious influence, and more distal agents of socialization such as schools and the media are less effective for directing religious tastes. Religious preferences tend to be adaptive – growing stronger with repeated consumption. Religious seekers who frequently switch religious movements may be responding to preference counteradaptivity.

Religious choices are influenced by a variety of social concerns, and not simply the desire for supernatural rewards and compensators. Following Amartya Sen, sociologists of religion have identified three broad types of social influences on choices: sympathy/antipathy, example-setting and sanction. Religious choices are commonly made to enhance the well-being of others. Children attend church to please their parents and husbands frequently participate to gratify their wives or set examples for their children (Sherkat and Ellison 1999). Here, the goal of the choice is not to be spiritually fulfilled by the supernatural rewards and compensators generated by religious action, but simply to generate positive affect for a loved one. Antipathy is the opposing social motivation – when religious consumption is directed at angering those who are opposed to a particular type of religion. 'Pagan' movements in the United States are almost solely motivated by antipathetic desires to displease conservative Christians. Further, in some Eastern bloc nations individuals participated in religious activities as a foil against anti-religious communists.

Demand-side theorists recognize that individuals are often coerced or enticed into religious participation by offers of non-religious rewards or punishments. Parents, spouses and peers will positively regard behaviours that conform to their expectations, and will heap punishment on religious actions that deviate from their desired mode of conduct. Participating in religion gives one access to friendship networks, mating markets, child care, sports clubs, economic networks, political influence and social status. Failure to participate in religious organizations (or participating in the 'wrong' religion) can lead to negative social sanctions – ostracism, economic boycott, imprisonment and even death. For ethnic minorities and recent immigrants, social status and social activities may be unavailable in the broader market, and participation in religious organizations is required if one desires social status and social contact (Sherkat and Ellison 1999).

References and further reading

Collins, Randall (1997) 'An Asian Route to Capitalism: Religious Economy and the Origin of Self-Transforming Growth in Japan', *American Sociological Review*, 62: 843–65.

Darnell, Alfred and Sherkat, Darren E. (1997) 'The Impact of Fundamentalism on Educational Attainment', *American Sociological Review*, 62: 306–15.

Keister, Lisa A. (2003) 'Religion and Wealth: The Role of Religious Affiliation and Participation in Early Adult Asset Accumulation', *Social Forces*, 82: 173–205.

Kuran, Timur (2003) 'The Islamic Commercial Crisis: Institutional Roots of Economic Underdevelopment in the Middle East', *Journal of Economic History*, 63: 414–46.

Sherkat, Darren E. and Ellison, Christopher G. (1999) 'Recent Developments and Current Controversies in the Sociology of Religion', *Annual Review of Sociology*, 25: 363–94.

Stark, Rodney and Finke, Roger (2000) *Acts of Faith: Exploring the Human Side of Religion*, Berkeley, CA: University of California Press.

DARREN E. SHERKAT

REPUTATION

Colloquially, we use the term 'reputation' to refer to what is believed about a person or entity, and there are at least two different senses in which the term 'reputation' is used. In one sense, the term is highly focused; it is invariably followed by the preposition 'for', which is in turn followed by some behaviour. Thus, a market actor can have a reputation for cooperation, defection, predatory pricing, manufacturing high-quality products, and so on. In another sense, the term is diffuse; it denotes some abstract quality of character as in the statement, 'He is a man of good reputation.' In this latter sense, the term 'reputation' overlaps with notions like 'standing in the community' or concepts like 'prestige' or 'status'.

To understand the way in which 'reputation' and similar if not synonymous terms are employed in the field of economic sociology, it is helpful to bear the distinction between the focused and diffuse conceptions of reputation in mind. Both conceptions can be found in the literature. Those scholars utilizing the more focused conception tend to explore how the pattern of relations among actors affects the development and maintenance of reputations for some behaviour or how the existence of reputations for a particular behaviour impacts on an emerging pattern of relations. In effect, social structure is conceptualized in terms of networks of exchange relations; reputations are conceptualized as dispersed information regarding past demonstrations of behaviour, and the central analytical question is understanding the relationship between network structure and behaviour. As the field of economics tends to adopt the more focused conception of reputation, one can interpret this research as an attempt to provide a more contextualized or – to use Granovetter's (1985) term – 'embedded' conception of the economic notion of reputation.

Those scholars employing a more diffuse conception of reputation place less emphasis on behaviours; they understand differences in reputation as reflections of differences in network position and seek to demonstrate how these differences in network position yield distinct opportunities and rewards. Such scholars will use terms like 'status', 'prestige', 'identity' or 'legitimacy' to characterize the reputational differences among actors.

Underlying the differences between the focused and diffused views of reputation is an empirical question regarding whether reputation is grounded more in actors' behaviours or more in the underlying networks themselves. The next few paragraphs will provide a few illustrations of the focused and diffused conceptions of reputation as well as research that can be seen as integrating the two perspectives.

The focused conception of reputation

Raub and Weesie (1990) provide a good illustration of the sociological study of the more focused conception of reputation. They formally examine the behaviour of a population of actors, each of whom is engaged in a repeated Prisoner's Dilemma game with nearby partners (see **game theory**). They distinguish three types of scenarios: those in which the behaviour of actors is unembedded, perfectly embedded, and imperfectly embedded. In the unembedded scenario, an actor only has knowledge about the games in which the actor has been directly involved. An actor's reputation is highly localized; the actor has a reputation with each of his partners, and this reputation is entirely a function of the actor's tendency to cooperate or defect with that specific partner. If the actor cooperates with one partner but defects with another, the actor will have a reputation for cooperation with the first but a reputation for defection with the second. In the perfectly embedded scenario, every actor has knowledge about all the games played in the population. Reputations are thus entirely global. As the name implies, the imperfectly embedded scenario is an intermediate case; each actor has information on the games in which she and her partners have been involved. One of the main results of the Raub and Weesie (1990) paper is that embeddedness increases the propensity towards cooperation in the Prisoner's Dilemma. That is, the more fluidity with which reputations move through networks, the more that actors cooperate with one another.

While Raub and Weesie (1990) regard the pattern of ties as exogenous, Kollock (1994) designs an interesting experiment in which the pattern of ties emerging in an exchange context is an endogenous consequence of the reputational concerns that arise from uncertainty. Kollack sets up an experimental market of buyers and sellers, and he varies the uncertainty that buyers have about the quality of goods provided by the sellers. Kollock finds that the greater uncertainty there is about the quality of goods shipped by sellers, the greater the concern that market actors will have about seller reputation and the more that buyers seek out long-term relationships with a particular seller (even if another seller offers a higher price).

Nohria (1992) and Gulati (1995) undertake related empirical research. Each provides evidence that the willingness of actors to engage in cooperative relations with one another is a function of the extent to which those actors have ties to common third parties that can serve as conduits of reputational information. Though Nohria studies personal relationships in the formation of entrepreneurial ventures and Gulati studies

alliances among established firms, each finds that a pair of actors is more likely to engage in cooperative relations with one another in the presence of ties to common third-party ties.

The diffuse conception of reputation

Stuart et al. (1999) provide an illustration of the more diffuse conception of reputation in an examination of the biotechnology industry. They examine the likelihood that biotechnology start-ups go public as well as the market capitalization of those firms upon going public. They find that those start-ups with ties to prominent firms are more likely to go public and have a higher market capitalization. Though Stuart et al. (1990) use the term 'prestige' rather than 'reputation', it is clear that they are focusing on a phenomenon that is similar to that on which Raub and Weesie (1990) and Kollock (1994) focus. Raub and Weesie (1990) and Kollock (1994) are interested in situations in which market actors use information on exchanges in the past to form their **beliefs** for future exchange relations; Stuart et al. (1999) are interested in the exact same type of situations. The only difference is that Stuart et al. (1999) regard the identity of exchange partners rather than the actions of the actor as the fundamental determinant of others' beliefs. In their account, a start-up's reputation is grounded less in what the firm has done and more in the ties that the firm has.

Zuckerman (1999) offers another example of work that fits under the rubric of diffuse reputation. He argues that buyers in a market can be conceptualized as an audience, and the attention that the audience gives to a particular seller is a function of the degree to which the seller forms exchange relations that cut across the accepted cognitive categories that define the products in that market. If the seller's pattern of exchange relations does not fit within those cognitive categories, then the seller is regarded as illegitimate and does not receive attention from the buyers. So, for example, if a firm engages in acquisition activities across the cognitive categories of investment analysts or if a popular movie actor takes on film roles that cut across genres, the audience – investors, in the case of the diversified firm, and moviegoers, in the case of the lead actor – will punish such behaviour with a lack of attention. Again, while Zuckerman does not use the word 'reputation', it should be clear that he is focusing on situations in which patterns of exchange relations in the past yield information that shapes expectations around future exchange relations. Other examples of work in which an actor's pattern of exchange relations provide the foundational information for the actors' reputation are Baum and Oliver (1992) and Podolny (1993).

While both the focused and diffused conceptions of reputation emphasize the relevance of social networks to the reputations that emerge in a particular domain, the discussion of the referenced works above underscores the fact that the two conceptions differ in the way in which networks are understood. To draw on a previously elaborated metaphor (Podolny 2001), one can say that the focused conception of reputation implies an understanding of network as 'pipes' – conduits or channels – for the flow of information about actors. In contrast, under the diffuse conception of reputation, the pattern of ties are not relevant as channels through which flows the information that actors use to make inferences about future behaviour; rather, the pattern of ties are the information on which actors rely to make inferences about future behaviour. To whom an actor is (and is not) tied is the critical determinant of others' expectations of that actor. Thus, rather than networks behaving as 'pipes', they behave as 'prisms' in which the pattern of ties splits out and induces

differentiation in the expected qualities of market actors.

An integrated view of reputation?

Benjamin and Podolny (1999) design a study of reputational effects that incorporates elements of both the focused and diffused conceptions of reputation. They model the price of a bottle of wine as a function of the past quality of the winery's output and the appellation affiliations that the winery has developed over time. The first of these two variables is consistent with the focused conception of reputation in so far as it is a reflection of past behaviour; the second is consistent with the diffuse conception in so far as it is a reflection of past affiliations. Benjamin and Podolny (1999) find that both variables impact on price.

Ultimately, it seems an empirical question whether an actor's reputation is grounded more in behaviour or more in the actor's network position. Work within the sociology of science and the sociology of culture seems most concerned with trying to address this empirical question. For example, Merton (1968) and Latour (1987) offer explicit arguments that the reputation of a scientist and her work is only partially influenced by the content of the work (i.e. past behaviour) and is strongly influenced by the scientist's intellectual and institutional affiliations (i.e. position). In a comparative study of two art worlds, Greenfeld (1989) finds that when standards of quality in a genre are not well defined, artistic reputation depends more on the artist's pattern of ties to those in the artistic community; however, when standards are well defined, then reputation depends more on the artistic work itself (see **art and economy**). Greenfeld's work thus suggests a possible contingency regarding the applicability of the different conceptions of reputation: the less (greater) consensus there is on the constituent elements of quality and accordingly when some set behaviour could clearly be judged to pass a given quality threshold, the more that the diffuse (focused) conception of reputation is applicable to a particular context.

References and further reading

Baum, Joel A. C. and Oliver, Christine (1992) 'Institutional Embeddedness and the Dynamics of Organizational Populations', *American Sociological Review*, 57(4): 540–59.

Benjamin, Beth A. and Podolny, Joel M. (1999) 'Status, Quality, and Social Order in the California Wine Industry', *Administrative Science Quarterly*, 44(3): 563–89.

Granovetter, Mark S. (1985) 'Economic Action and Social Structure: The Problem of Embeddedness', *American Journal of Sociology*, 91: 481–510.

Greenfeld, Liah (1989) *Different Worlds: A Sociological Study of Taste, Choice, and Success in Art*, Cambridge: Cambridge University Press.

Gulati, Ranjay (1995) 'Social Structure and Alliance Formation Patterns: A Longitudinal Analysis', *Administrative Science Quarterly*, 40(4): 619–52.

Kollock, Peter (1994) 'The Emergence of Exchange Structures: Am Experimental Study of Uncertainty, Commitment, and Trust', *American Journal of Sociology*, 100(2): 313–45.

Latour, Bruno (1987) *Science in Action: How to Follow Scientists and Engineers through Society*, Cambridge, MA: Harvard University Press.

Merton, Robert K. (1968) 'The Matthew Effect in Science', *Science*, 159: 56–63.

Nohria, Nitin (1992) 'Information and Search in the Creation of New Business Ventures: The Case of the 128 Venture Group', in Nitin Nohria and Robert G. Eccles (eds), *Networks and Organizations: Structure, Form, and Action*, Boston, MA: Harvard Business School Press.

Podolny, Joel M. (1993) 'A Status-based Model of Market Competition', *American Journal of Sociology*, 98(4): 829–72.

—— (2001) 'Networks as the Pipes and Prisms of the Market', *American Journal of Sociology*, 107(1): 33–60.

Raub, Werner and Weesie, Jeroen (1990) 'Reputation and Efficiency in Social Interaction: An Example of Network Effects', *American Journal of Sociology*, 96(3): 626–54.

Stuart, Toby E., Hoang, Ha and Hybels, Ralph C. (1999) 'Interorganizational Endorsements and the Performance of Entrepreneurial Ventures', *Administrative Science Quarterly*, 44(2): 315–49.

Zuckerman, Ezra W. (1999) 'The Categorical Imperative: Securities Analysts and the Legitimacy Discount', *American Journal of Sociology*, 104(5): 1398–438.

JOEL M. PODOLNY

REVOLUTIONS

Revolutions are popular efforts to overthrow or transform a state entity in an irregular, extraconstitutional and often violent fashion. Successful revolutions entail not only mass mobilization and regime change, but also significant political, economic and/or cultural change. In 'great revolutions' such as those that took place in nineteenth-century France and twentieth-century Russia and China, change occurred in all three areas. Protestors sought to replace a state's leaders, sharply modify its economic structure *and* introduce a very different culture. Revolutions not only internally transform societies, they alter international relations and create new states. Even when they fail, revolutions bring new organizations and ideas into the world arena that can spark social change, even in other countries. A full understanding of them must account for structural conditions, elite and popular alignments, the processes of mobilization and leadership, the goals of revolutionary actors and the outcomes of revolutionary events.

The term 'revolution' has come to mean any major social change. Most important for economic sociology is the industrial revolution, the period of rapid industrialization around the turn of the eighteenth century centred in Britain. However, our focus here is on the main definition which concerns attempts to overthrow the state and transform society.

Theoretical approaches to the study of revolutions

Studies of revolutions undertaken in the 1960s and 1970s were usually grounded in modernization or Marxist theory. Modernization theory links revolutions to the transitions of societies characterized by fixed, inherited statuses and simple divisions of labour to 'modern' societies distinguished by social mobility and achieved status, complex divisions of labour, legally enacted rules, broader collective identifications with the nation and mass political participation. Modernization theorists such as Samuel Huntington and W. W. Rostow posited that revolutions would be most likely to occur in transitional societies undergoing very rapid – but uneven – modernization. In such situations, the rush of **economic development** is not matched by political modernization. Others such as James Davies, Vern Newton and Ted Gurr, suggested that rapid modernization raises people's sense of relative deprivation; material expectations continue to rise even when they cannot be met. Additionally, swift modernization often entails a clash between a society's traditional values and newly emergent social structure. Chalmers Johnson's and Neil Smelser's work suggested that revolutionaries sometimes offer a better-fitting set of values. Similarly, Harry Benda documented cases in which rapid modernization destroyed integrative institutions, creating a sense of anomie. Revolutionaries could replace those institutions, providing new ways for people to 'belong.'

Scholars working from a Marxist perspective also expected revolutions to occur in societies undergoing a transition: from one mode of production to another. Their emphasis was on the class struggle that emerges openly when there is a contradiction between how the means of existence are produced and how they are owned. Capitalist development increases class polarization and labour exploitation. Development of the forces of production will increase the rate of exploitation if labour productivity increases while an increased labour supply restrains wages. Terry Bos-

well and William Dixon showed that revolt is more likely in countries with high exploitation rates, especially when there is a recession. With industrialization, the proletariat becomes a potent force in class conflict, which can lead to revolution. Where class conflict garnered the franchise for the lower classes, Walter Korpi and Adam Przeworski point out that revolution abated as workers could redress their grievances through elections with less fear of repression. The French Revolution points to the irresolvable contradictions between feudal restrictions on land, labour and credit and the new capitalist activities pursued by an ascending bourgeoisie. A different situation arises in developing countries because the weak capitalist class is heavily dependent on the existing state apparatus for economic opportunities and protection and thus would not be expected to ask for democratic reforms. Instead, as expounded in the work of Leon Trotsky and Barrington Moore, workers and peasants will unite against the capitalists and the state.

A major shortcoming of modernization-based theories of revolutions is that rapid and uneven modernization certainly has not always produced revolutions. Marxists have also had their surprises. For example, in some countries socialism was seen as a development *substitute* to capitalism. And neither Marxists nor anyone else predicted the transition from state socialism to capitalism in Eastern Europe. Both modernization and Marxist theories of revolution said too little about the relationship between state structures or policies and revolutions, and about the conditions determining whether revolutionary movements will succeed. In response to these deficiencies, scholars such as Barrington Moore, Theda Skocpol, S. N. Eisenstadt, Jeffery Paige and Jeff Goodwin have shown that while economic and class grievances usually do play an important role in revolutions, the roots of revolutionary movements are in the political context in which economic institutions and class are entrenched. For example, Skocpol (1979) defines social revolutions as 'rapid, basic transformations of a society's state and class structures' that 'are accompanied and in part carried through by classbased revolts from below'. Successful revolutions generally require an additional source of state breakdown, such as a fiscal crisis or international military pressure. This line of theorizing and inquiry led to what Jack Goldstone has called the third generation of revolutionary analysis: the state-centred perspective.

A state-centred approach now dominates the study of revolutions for two main reasons. First, successful revolutions necessarily involve the breakdown or incapacitation of states. Second, strong revolutionary movements will only emerge in opposition to states that are configured and that act in certain ways. This is because people generally do not join or support revolutionary movements when they believe that the central state has little to do with their everyday problems or that doing so will increase their vulnerability to state violence. More importantly, they can obtain at least some of what they want through already institutionalized and therefore low-risk channels for political claim-making. People are more likely to conclude that revolution is the only way out of their predicament when states respond to political dissent with violent and indiscriminate repression.

Findings about the causes and processes of revolutions

Comparative historical and quantitative cross-national research has produced an increasingly consistent list of grievances that can lead to revolution:

- *income inequality* (the concentration of income and – by causal implication – income-producing capital and land, among a small elite, leading lower income groups to seek redistribution);

- *state repression* (lack of a representative voice for grievances, offering no alternative to revolt – note that extreme repression can, however, deter open revolt);
- *class exploitation* (at the societal level, this is measured as the ratio of total value added to total wages and salaries, with high levels implying situations such as intense work, low wages, or little opportunity to change jobs that generate a high return for employers and incite workers to change their conditions);
- *economic crises* (low and declining rates of economic growth, such as recessions, which encourage people to demand state action to change the economy; the effects are greatest where class exploitation is highest, creating a zero-sum conflict that is more difficult to resolve peacefully);
- *independence* (rebellion against colonialism, ethnic separatism, or liberation). Liberation refers to independence from occupation, although it is also applied to any independence revolution.

Given one or more of these circumstances, Goldstone outlines certain conditions that make a state more vulnerable to a revolution. For instance, a revolution is most likely to occur when a state's effectiveness and justice is undermined, as in the case of a defeat in war or when there is sustained population growth in excess of economic growth. A political order is also very much at risk when elite groups are divided to the point of polarization – holding very different visions of how the society should be organized. Finally, colonial regimes and personalist dictatorships are especially vulnerable to revolutions because colonial regimes insult the aspirations of native elites. Personalist dictatorships have far less justice in the eyes of elites than more broadly based authoritarian regimes such as military juntas, because they exclude all but a tiny proportion of the elites from sharing in the fruits of power.

While structural conditions set the stage for a revolution, they do not explain how revolutionary actors organize, how ideological frames are created, how individuals become vested in a revolutionary group, how a group's leaders emerge or what strategies they choose. Many critics of overarching, state-centred accounts of revolution now argue for the need to incorporate leadership, ideology and processes of identification with revolutionary movements as key elements in the production of revolution. In *Dynamics of Contention*, Doug McAdam, Sidney Tarrow and Charles Tilly (2001) contend that to understand the processes and outcomes of revolutions it is necessary to identify the relational mechanisms via which interests, identities and opportunities are created. To make their case, they compare strikingly diverse episodes of contentious politics, including but not limited to those we would define as revolutions. Their focus on mechanisms allows them to make sense of some puzzling historical paths.

Recent directions for revolutionary theory and analysis

McAdam *et al.*'s recent work is more about setting a theoretical and methodological agenda than drawing empirical conclusions. Clearly more work is needed to understand how mechanisms of contention interact with each other and with outside events. Goldstone has suggested another direction for macro-level theorists of revolution: focus on factors that keep a regime stable, and study how weakness in those factors opens the way for the thinking, identification and leadership that – in certain structural situations – creates revolutions.

A further focus of revolutionary studies is grounded in the notion that the ultimate political and economic consequences of revolution must be understood in terms of the effect they have on the world order itself. While societal revolutions are scattered throughout time and space in world history, there are modal points whose size and breadth are far greater in importance that can be called world revolutions. Terry Boswell and Christopher Chase-Dunn (2002) have argued that world revolutions – especially when coincident with a major war – are part of the process that over time shifts the character and political principles of the capitalist world-system. As scholars such as John Meyer and George Holsti have pointed out, the substance of such a shift is found not only in **collective action** or international organization, but also in innovative organizational forms that are emulated throughout the system and that institutionalize a new standardization of relations.

Advancing a world-system theory of revolution calls first for identifying world revolutions, which are clusters of revolutionary activity that qualitatively alter the world order. Their occurrence should then be examined in light of large-scale trends in the expansion of the world economy and international state system, cycles of recurring rise and decline of states with substantial economic and military superiority and cycles of consecutive periods of extended economic expansion and stagnation. Some international relations theorists suggest an alternate approach while maintaining the global perspective put forth by world-system scholars. For example, Fred Halliday (1999) makes a case for the need to study revolutions within the context of 'a unified system of states, socio-economic structures and ideologies and cultures'. The goal of this approach is to incorporate the intentions and influence of states; the interests of dominant actors and the impact of outside factors that states may seek to restrain, manage or promote, but which can also act against them. Studying revolutions from a global perspective addresses the broader issue of how to understand long-term social change – both in terms of the structural parameters within which change takes place and in terms of how people make history.

References and further reading

Boswell, T. and Chase-Dunn, C. (2002) *The Spiral of Capitalism and Socialism: Toward Global Democracy*, Boulder, CO: Lynne Rienner.

Goldstone, J. A. (2001) 'Toward a Fourth Generation of Revolutionary Theory', *Annual Review of Political Science*, 4: 139–87.

Goodwin, J. (2001) *No Other Way Out: States and Revolutionary Movements, 1945–1991*, Cambridge: Cambridge University Press.

Halliday, F. (1999) *Revolution and World Politics: The Rise and Fall of the Sixth Great Power*, London: Macmillan.

McAdam, D., Tarrow, S. and Tilly, C. (2001) *Dynamics of Contention*, Cambridge: Cambridge University Press.

Skocpol, T. (1979) *States and Social Revolutions*, New York: Cambridge University Press.

APRIL LINTON
TERRY BOSWELL

RISK AND UNCERTAINTY

Within economic sociology, as elsewhere, different objections have been raised against neoclassical economics and/or **rational choice theory**. Some of these objections have a cognitive character and others do not. Among the latter are, for example, those that concern the motivational aspect of behaviour and the multiple logics of action that people may adopt. Risk and uncertainty pertain to the former. As part of a 'cognitive turn' in the social sciences, an increasing number of economic sociologists and economists have criticized neoclassical economics and/or rational choice theory on cognitive grounds. In this debate, different conceptions of uncertainty have been used, one of which includes risk as a special case.

A taxonomy of concepts

The best-known definition of risk and uncertainty has been introduced by Frank Knight. In his *Risk, Uncertainty and Profit* (1921) Knight defined risk as referring to situations in the economy to which probabilities can be assigned. Uncertainty, by contrast, characterizes situations in which the decision-maker lacks enough information on which to base the calculation of probabilities.

Though the issue of calculation has remained in the centre of debates on risk and uncertainty in economics and economic sociology ever since, newer taxonomies allow for a more detailed understanding. Three distinctions help to identify different conceptions of uncertainty. The first distinction is that proposed by Giovanni Dosi and Massimo Egidi in their 1991 article on substantive and procedural uncertainty. Substantive uncertainty results from the lack of all the information that would be necessary to make decisions with certain outcomes. In contrast, procedural uncertainty arises from limitations on the agents' computational and cognitive capabilities to pursue their objectives in a complex environment, given the available information. In other words, it reflects the gap between the complexity of a situation and the agents' competence in handling information.

The second distinction was suggested by David Dequech in a 1997 article on strong uncertainty. In contrast to weak uncertainty, strong uncertainty is characterized by the absence of unique, additive and fully reliable probability distributions. Risk is a special case of weak uncertainty, with objective probabilities. An objective probability is an a priori probability (as in a game with a non-biased roulette) or a relative frequency. A subjective probability is a degree of belief in the occurrence of an event or in the truth of a proposition. For a staunch defender of subjective probability theory, probability is always subjective, and the idea of objective probability does not make sense. Less radical subjectivists may admit the existence of objective probabilities while claiming that the theory is applicable even to cases in which these objective probabilities are unknown to decision-makers. Although several authors associate uncertainty with the absence of numerical probabilities, subjective probability theory claims that it is possible to assign numerical probabilities to virtually any proposition or event. Weak uncertainty, then, may be based either on objective probabilities (in which case it corresponds to risk) or on subjective probabilities. In either form, weak uncertainty has been combined with the hypothesis of **utility maximization** in standard expected utility theory.

The third distinction is the one introduced by Dequech in his 2000 article on ambiguity and fundamental uncertainty, two types of strong (and substantive) uncertainty. Ambiguity is uncertainty about probability, created by missing information that is relevant and could be known. Even though the decision-maker under ambiguity does not know with full reliability the probability that each event (or state of the world) will obtain, he/she usually knows all the possible events. Even when not completely known, the list of all possible events is already predetermined or knowable ex ante. Fundamental uncertainty, in contrast, is characterized by the possibility of creativity and non-predetermined structural change. The list of possible events is not predetermined or knowable ex ante, as the future is yet to be created. This means that some relevant information cannot be known, not even in principle, at the time of making many important decisions.

Fundamental uncertainty and procedural uncertainty may be complementary rather than mutually exclusive, as a reality that is subject to non-predetermined structural change may also be complex, and people who are creative also have limited computational abilities.

Uncertainty in economics and in economic sociology

Economics is dominated by a weak notion of uncertainty. Alternative notions have been employed mainly in heterodox economics, although some of them are beginning to be incorporated into the mainstream. The precursors of alternative conceptions of uncertainty in economics are Frank Knight and John Maynard **Keynes**. After them, the expressions 'Knightian uncertainty' and 'Keynesian uncertainty' have often been used by economists. These expressions may be useful to indicate that one is not referring to weak uncertainty, but they are not clear enough to indicate which other type of uncertainty in our typology is being considered.

Procedural uncertainty, usually under a different label, has been emphasized in **behavioural economics**, influenced by Herbert Simon's pioneering work on bounded **rationality** and by psychologists Daniel Kahneman and Amos Tversky, as well as in the so-called new **institutional economics**. Mainstream economics has given increasing attention to the notion of bounded rationality, arguably in milder forms than the one originally conceived by Simon.

Strong substantive uncertainty is highlighted (sometimes together with procedural uncertainty) in **post Keynesianism**, neo-Schumpeterianism and **Austrian economics**. In these three schools, fundamental uncertainty is often exemplified by the possibility of innovations. Although less emphatically, the so-called old or original institutionalism has also embraced both procedural and fundamental uncertainty. Ambiguity, as a less strong form of strong uncertainty, is gradually becoming part of mainstream economics.

In economic sociology, when uncertainty is emphasized, it appears most often in its procedural form. This reflects the influence of Simon and his colleagues of the **Carnegie School**. Their influence is noticeable not only in research on the firm, but, more generally, in organization studies. Even more generally, Jens Beckert, in a 1996 article on uncertainty and the embeddedness of **economic action**, suggested a concept of uncertainty related to complexity as the very basis for a sociological approach to economic decision-making. This proposal is intended to apply to most or all areas of research in economic sociology. More recent work by Beckert has moved towards fundamental uncertainty, emphasizing creativity and innovations.

Uncertainty, rationality and maximization

The notion of rationality defined in terms of constrained maximization is one of the pillars of neoclassical economics. As such, it is embraced by those economic sociologists that adopt a rational choice approach. Most economic sociologists, in contrast, seem to be united by a rejection of the maximization hypothesis. The central argument used by many sociologists is that, contrary to orthodox economic theory, people behave 'irrationally'. Others, instead of criticizing standard economic theory on the grounds that people are not rational, prefer to argue that people are intentionally rational, but, as Simon put it, limitedly so: the limitations of both individual and collective actors in relation to the complexity of their decision environment prevent actors from maximizing.

There is no doubt that social reality is complex and inhabited by people with limitations, and that these important features must be dealt with by theories of human behaviour. At the same time, it is necessary to distinguish complexity and human limitations from other features of social reality that lead to cognitive challenges to rational choice theory and to neoclassical economics. In other words, as seen above, proce-

dural uncertainty is only one among a few types of uncertainty to be contrasted with weak uncertainty.

Given the opposition to the maximization hypothesis by most new economic sociologists, it is useful to discuss the relation between this hypothesis and uncertainty in order to better understand the relation between uncertainty and economic sociology. Before doing this, one should acknowledge that expected utility theory comes in three different versions: according to the descriptive (or positive) version, people do in reality deliberately maximize expected utility; the prescriptive (or normative) variety argues that people should maximize expected utility in order to be rational; in the 'as if' version, people are seen as behaving as if they were maximizing, without actually performing calculations. Also important to acknowledge is the axiomatic character of expected utility theory. Either in the standard form that still dominates neoclassical economics or in the generalized forms that are gradually becoming influential, this theory involves more than the idea that people (act so as to, should, or act 'as if' they did) maximize expected utility: it involves the satisfaction of some axioms by people's choices. Indeed, it is from these axioms that a utility function is derived. Generalized expected utility theories broaden the scope of the standard theory by relaxing some axioms.

Weak uncertainty is obviously compatible with, or even defined in the context of, the maximization of expected utility. So is uncertainty in the strong sense of ambiguity. Indeed, a very large part of the ambiguity literature is concerned with generalizing the (subjective or objective) expected utility theory. Procedural uncertainty does not necessarily imply a rejection of the standard theory, but this is a controversial issue. Several defenders of this theory claim that human limitations and complexity can be incorporated as part of the constraints on behaviour. Moreover, the 'as if' version is in principle compatible with complexity. On the other hand, Simon and other critics of the maximization hypothesis are aware of these arguments but point out what they consider to be the empirical evidence that people's behaviour does not fit expected utility theory either in its descriptive or in its 'as if' version. Still others claim, however, that the maximization hypothesis should not be criticized because it is falsified by this evidence, but because its core assumptions are not falsifiable by any evidence: in their opinion, experiments may show that people fail to maximize utility as measured by some proxy, but no one can be certain that this is the right proxy, so that people might be maximizing utility as measured by something else.

Apart from this empirical controversy, fundamental uncertainty has so far been theoretically incompatible with maximization in the particular form assumed in neoclassical economics and generalized expected utility theory. The conceptual apparatus and some axioms of the expected utility theory are not applicable to cases of fundamental uncertainty. Neither the standard nor the alternative expected utility theories developed so far (including those that deal with ambiguity) seem to have been able to overcome this problem.

To the extent that rational choice theory in sociology follows the neoclassical axiomatic treatment of maximization, it cannot deal with fundamental uncertainty. Likewise, it will remain unable to do so if it again follows what is happening in economics and starts using those less restrictive but still axiomatic generalizations of expected utility theory.

The discussion of maximization may reinforce the distinction established above between procedural and fundamental uncertainty. Fundamental uncertainty implies that an objectively defined optimal solution does not exist ex ante, since the future is not predetermined. In contrast, some versions of the notion of procedural uncertainty assume, even if implicitly, that such a solution exists in a complex situation, although complexity prevents the actor from identifying it. This is not the kind of variety of procedural uncertainty that can be combined with fundamental uncertainty.

Uncertainty, order and economic sociology

Fundamental uncertainty is a central vantage point for economic sociology because it allows for a theoretical explanation of the embeddedness of modern economies. The influence of culture and social structures on decision-making in the economy might be interpreted at first glance as irrational behaviour that leads to suboptimal outcomes. It would be expected that the embeddedness of economic action vanishes due to the forces of market competition. If, however, under conditions of fundamental uncertainty, actors are not able to identify optimal decisions ex ante, the cultural and social structural embeddedness of economic decision-making achieves a different status. It becomes a means by which actors reduce the uncertainty they confront in the decision-making process. Although actors may intend to optimize, they do not know which decision will lead them to an optimal resource allocation. At this point the embeddedness in norms and culture plays a special role. The contention is that intentionally rational economic agents do not react to uncertainty by increasing their calculative capabilities. In the case of fundamental uncertainty this would not solve the problem. Rather they rely often on *social devices* which often restrict their flexibility and create rigidity in the responses to changes in an uncertain environment. The term 'social devices' encompasses all forms of rules, social norms, conventions, institutions, social structures and power-relations

585

which limit the choice set of actors and make actions at the same time predictable.

Institutions, norms, habit, power and social structure are important features of modern economic life because they provide orientation. This contention prevailed already in the works of Frank Knight and John Maynard Keynes on uncertainty. For them hierarchical structures, role differentiation, advice and habit are mechanisms for the reduction of contingencies which arise from the indeterminacy of the situation. They reduce the choice set of actors and allow for predictable behaviour by creating expectations of alter's actions.

While the sociological critique of the rational actor model has persistently argued that economic processes are embedded in market societies, the problem of uncertainty allows one to understand *why* economic behaviour is market-driven as well as rule-driven, without necessarily assuming that actors intentionally depart from the goal of self-interest. The deregulation of exchange-relations and the constant alteration of market conditions through innovative processes in modern market economies create uncertainty for actors, which in turn leads to the reintroduction of social devices. To remain capable of decision-making, actors base their choices on these 'substitute rationalities'. The market on the one hand and social or cultural embeddedness on the other are antagonistic mechanisms of order that reinforce and negate each other but remain interdependent. This argues also counter to the assertion of economics and sociological modernization theories that economic relations become increasingly disembedded with the unfolding of capitalist market societies. Based on these theoretical considerations, to the distinctive contribution of economic sociology can be understood as the analysis of the social devices that economic actors rely on for the reduction of uncertainty in the decision-making process. Uncertainty and its reduction through social devices has become an important focus of several schools in economic sociology, most prominently for the **Convention School** and the new institutionalism (see **institutionalism, old and new**).

When emphasizing the role of social devices that reduce uncertainty, most economic sociologists, like most new institutional economists, employ a concept of procedural uncertainty. However, social devices can also be said to affect the degree of other types of uncertainty, particularly fundamental uncertainty. Moreover, if one acknowledges that social reality is marked by fundamental uncertainty, one should emphasize not only the existence of behaviour in accordance with norms, institutions or habits, but also the possibility of creative, bold, unconventional behaviour, as people may use their knowledge, including the knowledge provided by those social devices, to go against the stream. Similarly, if one does allow room for creativity, innovations and non-conformity, and views economic processes as open-ended, this is better supported by a notion of fundamental uncertainty than by that of procedural uncertainty, although both notions may and should be used together.

References and further reading

Beckert, Jens (1996) 'What is Sociological about Economic Sociology? Uncertainty and the Embeddedness of Economic Action', *Theory and Society*, 25(6): 803–40.

—— (2002) *Beyond the Market. The Social Foundations of Economic Efficiency*, Princeton, NJ: Princeton University Press.

Dequech, David (1997) 'Uncertainty in a strong sense: meaning and sources', *Economic Issues*, 2(2): 21–43.

—— (2000) 'Fundamental uncertainty and ambiguity', *Eastern Economic Journal*, 26(1): 41–60.

—— (2003) 'Uncertainty and Economic Sociology', *American Journal of Economics and Sociology*, 62(3): 509–32.

—— (2003) 'Conventional and Unconventional Behavior under Uncertainty', *Journal of Post Keynesian Economics*, 26(1): 145–68.

Dosi, G. and Egidi, M. (1991) 'Substantive and procedural uncertainty – an exploration of economic behaviour in changing environments', *Journal of Evolutionary Economics*, 1(2): 145–68.

Hodgson, G. (1988) *Economics and Institutions*, Philadelphia, PA: University of Pennsylvania Press.

Knight, F. (1921) *Risk, Uncertainty and Profit*, Boston: Houghton Mifflin.

Storper, Michael and Salais, Robert (1997) *Worlds of Production. The Action Framework of the Economy*, Cambridge, MA: Harvard University Press.

JENS BECKERT
DAVID DEQUECH

S

SACRED

In *The Elementary Forms of Religious Life,* **Durkheim** defined a religion as a 'moral community' with a 'unified system of beliefs and practices relative to sacred things, that is to say, things set apart and forbidden' ([1912]1995: 24). Religious beliefs define a category of sacred things; religious rites set out the rules by which the sacred is to be protected from the profane. Durkheim meant the concept to be quite general. In principle, anything can be sacred: 'sacred things are simply collective ideals that have fixed themselves on material objects' (1960: 335). It forms part of his argument that religion is a hypostasization of the social structure, the function of which is to represent the social group to itself, so to speak, generating social solidarity in the process. Both the ordinary business of economic life and the 'cash nexus' of the market have often been seen (in theory and practice) as profane. In the simplest case, sacred things cannot be commodities. If they can be transferred at all, it must be by some more appropriate method, such as **gift** exchange. Contact with the market is a kind of ritual pollution that defiles the sacred object and requires some form of purification.

Many critics of capitalism have argued that the market undermines individual motives, corrupts social relationships or trivializes goods by measuring them in terms of money. While they may use the language of sacred and profane, or argue that the society is undermined by the expansion of the market, they do not enter fully into the spirit of Durkheim's view. The system of **classification** that creates sacred things is an object of study from the Durkheimian point of view, not a means of argument. Cries of outrage or horror in the face of increasing commodification may be evidence that the moral order is being threatened, but from this perspective they must count as an aspect rather than an explanation of the process.

Although the details of Durkheim's theory of the sacred pose severe problems, the core notion that people make systematic efforts to keep some things 'set apart and forbidden' has proved very fruitful. Classically, sociologists examined how the sacred was protected from contact with the market. Since the late 1970s, interest has increasingly focused on the moral order of the market itself, in a way that deliberately dismantles the older contrast between economy and culture. At the level of whole societies, Durkheim's emphasis on shared systems of classification and ritual action can be found in institutionalist studies of comparative economic organization (see **institutionalism, old and new**). On a different scale, a growing body of research demonstrates that money in everyday life is subject to myriad distinctions, earmarked for special purposes, and restricted to particular circuits of exchange. Durkheim's original insight about the persistence of the sacred can be seen behind much of this work, despite its application to an area he would have seen as profane.

References and further reading

Durkheim, Emile ([1912]1995) *The Elementary Forms of Religious Life*, New York: Free Press.

—— (1960) *Emile Durkheim, 1858–1917: A Collection of Essays, with Translations and a Bibliography*, edited by Kurt Wolff, Columbus, OH: Ohio State University Press.

Zelizer, Viviana (1994) *The Social Meaning of Money*, New York: Harper Collins.

KIERAN HEALY

SATISFICING

Satisficing is the idea that decision-makers interpret outcomes as either satisfactory or unsatisfactory, with an aspiration level constituting the boundary between the two. Whereas decision-makers in neoclassical **rational choice theory** would list all possible outcomes evaluated in terms of their expected utilities, and then choose the one that is rational and maximizes utility, decision-makers in Simon's model face only two possible outcomes, and look for a satisfying solution, continuing to search only until they have found a solution which is good enough.

The idea was introduced in 1955, when Herbert Simon published a paper that provided the foundation for a behavioural perspective on human decision-making and introduced the ideas of satisficing and bounded **rationality**. The paper provided a critique of the assumption in economics of perfect information and unlimited computational capability, and replaced the assumption of global rationality with one that was more in correspondence with how humans (and other choosing organisms) made decisions, their computational limitations and how they accessed information

in their current environments (1955: 99). In Simon's illustration of the problem, the influence of his early ideas outlined in *Administrative Behavior* is clear, echoing the view that decisions are reasoned and intendedly rational, yet limited (Simon 1947). He first suggests a simple and very general model of behavioural choice which analyses choosing organisms (such as humans) in terms of basic properties to understand what is meant by rational behaviour. He introduces the simplifying assumptions (such as the choice alternatives, the payoff function, possible future states and the sub-set of choice alternatives which is considered, as well as the information about the probability that a particular outcome will lead to a particular choice; Simon 1955: 102). But immediately afterwards he turns to the simplifications of this model, stressing that upon careful examination, 'we see immediately what severe demands they make upon the choosing organism' (1955: 103). Whereas in models of rational choice, the organism must be able to 'attach definite payoffs (or at least a definite range of payoffs) to each possible outcome' (ibid.), Simon suggests that 'there is a complete lack of evidence that, in actual human choice situations of any complexity, these computations can be, or are in fact, performed' (ibid.). As a consequence of the lack of computational power, decision-makers have to simplify the structure of their decisions (and thus satisfice), one of the most important lessons of bounded rationality.

This idea later became important to the work on organizational behaviour and decision-making done by Simon and March. In addition, the idea of satisficing has been used by evolutionary and adaptive economics (such as Richard Nelson and Sidney Winter).

References and further reading

March, J. G. and Simon, H. A. (1958) *Organizations*, New York: John Wiley and Sons.

Simon, H. A. (1947) *Administrative Behavior*, New York: Free Press.

—— (1955) 'A Behavioral Model of Rational Choice', *Quarterly Journal of Economics*, 69: 99–118.

—— (1956) 'Rational Choice and the Structure of the Environment', *Psychological Review*, 63: 129–38.

MIE AUGIER

SCARCITY

Scarcity is generally defined as the limited quantity of a resource or a factor of production. The main problem in classical **political economy** was diminishing marginal returns in agriculture due to a permanent scarcity of fertile land. Neoclassical economists tend to define economics as the quest for an optimal allocation of scarce means in order to satisfy unlimited human wants. *Absolute scarcity* refers to the limited non-renewable nature of some resources such as metals and oil. *Relative scarcity* could then be seen as resulting from increasing marginal costs as compared to other locations. For instance, Jevons's *The Coal Question* (1865) argues that the British economy will be superseded by the United States, because Britain will face increasing marginal costs in coal exploitation, whereas the USA can rely on important unexploited coal reserves. Marxists tend to put other concepts, such as class and surplus value, in the core of economic theory and in doing so they challenge the economic conception of scarcity. But at the same time, Marxism can also be said to rely upon the notion of scarcity. For instance, Marx did not favour 'primitive communism', as it was simply permanent scarcity of food and other resources that forced people to work together. Scarcity should be overcome in a post-capitalist communist society, but it remains unclear how this society should be established and how it could really work in practice. So scarcity is a prerequisite that is shared by both orthodox and heterodox economic theories.

It can, however, be argued, and it has been argued by the Dutch philosopher Hans Achterhuis, that scarcity is not at all a natural condition of society. The basic argument is that people do not really have 'objective needs'. People will only desire goods if they are shown by an equal person as being desirable. When these so-called mimetical desires spread in the whole community, more and more persons and objects become involved and the image of a 'general scarcity' emerges. This scarcity does not concern objective goods, but subjectively mediated objects shown by an equal functioning as a model. In so-called primitive or traditional societies this scarcity did not exist – it could only be thought of as a limit situation, for example in cases of long-during famines. A diminution of food storage gave rise to a growing solidarity instead. Primitive societies (i.e. pre-early modern societies) used hierarchy and differentiation in order to counteract those 'mimetical desires'. People that tend to think of themselves as being unequal by nature (e.g. the slave versus the king) will not compare themselves with each other and therefore 'mimetical desires' will be tempered. Achterhuis recognizes that the concept of 'equality' did certainly exist in Greek antiquity, but he argues that the content of this concept is very different from contemporary notions. First of all, the *isonomia,* or legal equality, exists only in reference to a specific group, namely free male citizens of Athens. Women, foreigners ('barbarians') and slaves are excluded. Secondly, the *isonomia* is an artificial construction, established by humankind only because people are unequal by nature. Thirdly, the *isonomia* allows everyone to perform exceptional actions, in order to give utterance of their own specificity. Therefore, in Greek antiquity the idea of human inequality predominates; in daily social life numerous inequalities are visible;

and 'equality' is consciously seen as a social construct allowing free male citizens of Athens to emphasize their very own specificity. Marx recognizes this when he argues that Aristotle could not develop a labour theory of value in a context of prevailing slavery, as human labour was not seen as an abstract notion emerging from equal human beings. The traditional image of humankind was diametrically opposed to contemporary economic notions: humans were portrayed as having limited wants and unlimited means to satisfy them.

This changed during early modern times, when 'human equality' came to the forefront. At the beginning of modernity, the increasing 'equality' between people gives rise to an inversion of the traditional image of man. Hobbes argues that the restless desire to achieve more and more power is a neutral characteristic of man; this is radically opposed to the traditional refutation of this type of behaviour. With such an image of man, scarcity becomes a self-evident anthropological foundation of society. According to Hobbes, all men are equal; and even if they are not equal, they should be regarded as equal, otherwise no 'social contract' would be possible. After Hobbes, Locke adopts the idea of equality as being self-evident, and Rousseau, a century later, considers the contrary proposition as untenable. Traditional rules, which kept the development of scarcity within certain limits, disappear: in a slow process, everything (e.g. land) becomes expressible in money. An example of this process is Marx's famous discussion of the initial process of accumulation. The new nobility transformed agricultural land into sheepwalk, and drove the peasants from their land; the reformation gave rise to a theft of church property; and the Bill for the Enclosure of the Commons marked the end of land that was available to all members of society. Since the equality increases, mimetical violence and scarcity increase as well; how is society possible in such a constellation? Money causes scarcity, because it allows accumulation of value in exchange; but it also helps to suppress scarcity, because the equivalent of the desired good, as expressed in money, can become the object of desire. Society does not collapse because people are becoming more 'exterior' to each other. Unlike the 'vendetta' in traditional societies, the violence does not spread around the whole community because countless little wars are going on independently of each other.

It has also been argued that the idea of scarcity in political economy changed during the nineteenth century (Mosselmans 1999). Classical political economists such as Malthus and Ricardo maintained that scarcity was caused by human behaviour (e.g. poor people putting beings into existence that cannot be maintained, and landlords opposing free trade in corn). An alteration of behaviour would change, at least temporarily, this situation of scarcity. Later authors, such as Jevons, argue that scarcity results from the (mechanical) laws of economics and that an alteration of behaviour would not change the permanent condition of scarcity. This shift from 'internal' to 'external' scarcity is accompanied by a tendency to put 'scarcity' at the core of economic theory and to define 'scarcity' as the central economic problem. As a result, contemporary economists take 'scarcity' to be the 'natural' condition of society and tend to be very reluctant to consider it as a phenomenon emerging out of human interactions.

References and further reading

Achterhuis, H. (1988) *Het rijk van de schaarste. Van Thomas Hobbes tot Michel Foucault*, Baarn, Netherlands: Ambo.

Mosselmans, B. (1999) 'Reproduction and Scarcity: the Population Mechanism in Classicism and in the "Jevonian Revolution"', *European Journal of the History of Economic Thought*, 6(1): 34–57.

BERT MOSSELMANS

SCHMOLLER, GUSTAV VON

See: institutionalism, historical school

SCHUMPETER, JOSEPH A.

Of all the major economists Joseph A. Schumpeter (1883–1950) may well be the one who has shown the most interest in the idea that there can be a distinct and independent approach to economic phenomena that draws on the sociological approach and should be termed 'economic sociology'. As opposed to, say, Pareto, Schumpeter did not so much write on sociology in general as on sociological aspects of the economy. And as opposed to, say, the American institutionalists, including **Veblen**, he did not want to replace mainstream economics with a more sociological type of analysis but rather develop an alternative and complementary approach.

In *History of Economic Analysis* Schumpeter argues that the science of economics consists of several different fields: economic theory, economic history, economic sociology (*Wirtschaftssociologie*) and economic statistics. All of these approaches are needed to make a full analysis of an economic phenomenon, and each has its own tasks to fulfil. While economic theory, for example, looks at how things work in the economy, economic sociology looks at the way that economic phenomena have become what they are. Economic sociology is also concerned with economic institutions or, more precisely, with those non-economic institutions that are necessary for the economy to operate properly:

> economic analysis deals with the questions of how people behave at any time and what economic effects they produce by behaving so; economic sociology deals with the question of how they come to behave as they do. If we define human behaviour widely enough so it includes not only actions and motives and propensities, but also the social institutions

that are relevant to economic behaviour such as government, property, inheritance, contract, and so on, that phrase really tells us all we need.

> (Schumpeter 1954: 21)

The well-rounded economist, according to Schumpeter, should be trained in all of these four fields. Failure to follow what is happening in the other three fields condemns the economic theorist to being backward and narrow-minded. The same, of course, is true for the economic sociologist, the economic historian and the specialist in economic statistics. Schumpeter exemplifies this line of argument with the relationship between economists and sociologists, and he deeply bemoaned

> the fact that ever since the eighteenth century both groups have grown steadily apart until by now the modal economist and the modal sociologist know little and care less what the other does, each preferring to use, respectively, a primitive sociology and a primitive economics of his own to accepting one another's professional results.

> (Schumpeter 1954: 26)

In a formal sense it may be correct to say that Schumpeter wrote a few essays in economic sociology and nothing more. By 'formal' one would then mean those writings that Schumpeter himself considered as falling within the area of economic sociology, as opposed to the area of economics. While it is possible to proceed in this manner, there also exist good reasons to include more of Schumpeter's work in a discussion of his contribution to economic sociology. The reason for this is that in his studies in economic theory he many times argues in a way that is quite sociological. In this entry I will therefore discuss both Schumpeter's economic sociology in a narrow and in a broader sense. I shall first say something about the topics that are discussed in his three essays in economic sociology (the tax state, imperialism and social classes), and then proceed to the two areas of his economic theory where Schumpeter's approach is close to that of sociology (entrepreneurship and capitalism).

Schumpeter's first essay in economic sociology, and also the one that in my opinion has aged the best, is entitled 'The Crisis of the Tax State'. Its main focus is on the role of taxes in the economy, and it consequently falls within the area of fiscal sociology (*Finanzsoziologie*). According to Schumpeter, one can get a much more realistic picture of the state and its activities by looking at its budget rather by studying what the politicians do and say. Schumpeter also argues that the way that the state raises its resources, and has done so over the centuries, has deeply influenced the social and economic structure of a country: 'The spirit of a people, its cultural level, its social structure, the deeds its policy may prepare – all this and more is written into its fiscal history, stripped free of all phrases' ([1918]1991: 101).

According to Schumpeter, the modern state came into being as a result of the desire of the prince to capture the state so that he could use it as a tool for raising taxes. In 'The Crisis of the Tax State' Schumpeter also argues that the modern state may fall apart under certain circumstances if its tax policy is wrong. One case would be if the entrepreneurs are taxed too harshly, another if taxes are much too high. Of special interest to modern society is the following case: if people demand that the state delivers more social services than they are willing to pay for, there will be 'a crisis of the tax state'.

In 'The Sociology of Imperialisms' Schumpeter argues that imperialism is irrational to its nature and deeply alien to capitalism. 'Imperialism', as he defines it, 'is the objectless disposition on the part of the state to unlimited forcible expansion' ([1919]1991: 143). What produces imperialism is a social situation in which some

social group – typically warriors – has to expand its territory or fall apart. Since capitalism is essentially peaceful and consists of merchants, industrialists and workers – not warriors – it is alien to imperialism.

While several sociologists have noted that dictatorship and fascism may be related to the existence of strong landowning classes, Schumpeter's thesis that 'capitalism is by nature anti-imperialist' may still seem wrong. In a later work Schumpeter himself pointed to the persistence of imperialism in capitalist society and stated that analysing this issue constituted 'the deepest problem of the economic sociology of our time' (1939: 399; cf. 696).

Schumpeter's third essay in economic sociology is entitled 'Social Classes in an Ethnically Homogeneous Environment'. Economists, we here read, use the notion of class in an analytical manner, while for sociologists it reflects a piece of living reality. Schumpeter's essay on classes is also important in that it is the only place where Schumpeter directly tries to connect his economic theory to his sociology. The rise and fall of bourgeois families, he argues, is linked to the existence of entrepreneurial profit. Since one cannot inherit a talent for entrepreneurship, every successful bourgeois family is bound to decline.

One topic that Schumpeter considered as falling squarely within the field of economic theory, but where his analysis is closer to economic sociology in some respects, is that of entrepreneurship. This is so mainly for two reasons. Sometimes Schumpeter's analysis is congenial not only to economic theory but also to economic sociology. And sometimes it is simply more sociological than economic in nature.

One example of the former – where some of Schumpeter's ideas can be used also in sociology – would be Schumpeter's theory of entrepreneurship as new combinations. The essence of entrepreneurship, according to Schumpeter's well-known definition, is to rearrange already existing

593

economic resources in such a way that a new combination will appear. 'Development [or entrepreneurship] in our sense is then defined by the carrying out of new combinations' (Schumpeter 1934: 66). Schumpeter, however, does not say how and why an entrepreneur will have access to the different types of resources that he or she needs – and this is precisely where economic sociology can get into the picture.

One of the great obstacles to entrepreneurship, according to Schumpeter, is the instinctive hostility of people in his or her environment to anything that is radically new. In one of his studies Schumpeter cites the case of an entrepreneur who was strangled to death by the agitated local population. Whether this story is apocryphal or not can be discussed. The point here, however, is that Schumpeter touches on a topic that in many respects is more sociological than economic, and where such sociological concepts as custom, charisma and deviance can be useful.

Another important theme in Schumpeter which falls in economics as well as in sociology is that of capitalism. The economic mechanisms that make up capitalism are to be discussed in economic theory, according to Schumpeter, but there is nonetheless also room for 'an economic sociology of capitalism'. That this is the case can be exemplified by the analysis in *Capitalism, Socialism and Democracy*. Modern capitalism is doing perfectly fine from an economic angle, according to this work. Its institutional support, however, is giving way, and as a result of this capitalism may very well turn into socialism. 'Can capitalism survive?' Schumpeter famously asks in *Capitalism, Socialism and Democracy*, and his answer is, 'No. I do not think it can.'

As an example of how Schumpeter's economic analysis of capitalism is sometimes more sociological than economic in nature, one may cite his notion of competition. Economists discuss competitive behaviour in terms of perfect competition,

which is perfectly unrealistic according to Schumpeter. A more fruitful approach, he argues, would be to look at the struggle that takes place on a daily basis in capitalism between old and new forms of enterprises ('creative destruction').

Contemporary economic sociology has not paid much attention to Schumpeter's work, which is a pity for a number of reasons. Not only does Schumpeter's work contain one of the most suggestive theories of entrepreneurship that exists, his analysis of capitalism is also extremely insightful. To this may be added that Schumpeter made a brilliant critique of Marx's work and that he has carefully sifted through all of economic theory from Antiquity to modern times for potential contributions to economic sociology.

One reason why Schumpeter has failed to appeal to contemporary economic sociologists may be the limited role that he assigns to economic sociology. Contemporary economic sociologists often seem to follow **Durkheim**'s lead and want to replace economics with economic sociology. To Schumpeter this was just nonsense. In order to further develop economics as well as economic sociology, he argued, a clear line has to be drawn between these two types of analysis. Otherwise things might go very wrong since 'cross-fertilization might easily result in cross-sterilization' (1954: 27).

References and further reading

Schumpeter, Joseph A. ([1918]1991) 'The Crisis of the Tax State', in Joseph Schumpeter, *The Economics and Sociology of Capitalism*, edited by Richard Swedberg, Princeton, NJ: Princeton University Press, pp. 99–140.
—— ([1919]1991) 'The Sociology of Imperialisms', in Joseph Schumpeter, *The Economics and Sociology of Capitalism*, edited by Richard Swedberg, Princeton, NJ: Princeton University Press, pp. 141–219.
—— ([1927]1991) 'Social Classes in an Ethnically Homogenous Environment', in Joseph A. Schumpeter, *The Economics and Sociology of*

Capitalism, edited by Richard Swedberg, Princeton, NJ: Princeton University Press, pp. 230–83.

—— (1934) *The Theory of Economic Development*, Cambridge, MA: Harvard University Press.

—— (1939) *Business Cycles: A Theoretical, Historical and Statistical Analysis of the Capitalist Process*, New York: McGraw-Hill.

—— ([1942]1994) *Capitalism, Socialism and Democracy*, London: Routledge.

—— (1954) *History of Economic Analysis*, London: Allen and Unwin.

Swedberg, Richard (1991) *Schumpeter – A Biography*, Princeton, NJ: Princeton University Press.

RICHARD SWEDBERG

SEGMENTATION IN LABOUR MARKETS

The concept of the segmented labour market proposes that the stratification of jobs – some good, some bad – will result in a parallel stratification of the labour force into more preferred and less preferred workers. The stratification of the jobs results from the relative economic strength of the employers. Industries and firms with the strongest economic position create the best jobs. A strong economic position comes from industries that produce critical goods and services (e.g. utilities) and that have relatively low competition because only a few firms or even just one firm competes to provide the good or service. Monopoly describes a situation in which only one firm exists within an industry; oligopoly describes a situation in which only a few firms dominate most the market. Government regulations may enable or preserve the strong competitive position. Industries and firms that share this strong economic position are termed the primary (or central) sector. Primary sector firms tend to be large and well-capitalized.

Primary employers, because they are sheltered from competition, tend to have higher wages, better job security, fringe benefits and the opportunity for promotions in a career ladder within the same firm. Because of their attractive jobs, the primary employers are able to attract the best workers in the labour market. Many workers are attracted to such jobs, and so the employers in the primary market may be very selective in hiring. Workers with higher skill levels and better job experience are more likely to be successful with primary employers. By attracting the best workers in the labour market, the primary employers become even more successful.

The remaining employers constitute the secondary (or peripheral) sector. In the secondary sector the employing firms are relatively small and under-capitalized, and usually in very competitive conditions. Because of their competitive position, these firms offer lower wages and sometimes the jobs are part-time, seasonal or temporary. Benefits are likely to be minimal or non-existent. Job ladders are rare in the secondary sector, at least in part because the firms are smaller and so there are fewer opportunities for promotion. Smaller firms have fewer specialized managers, so that workplace rules and discipline are less well developed; some employers may be arbitrary in workplace discipline, so that workers are fired easily. Employers in the secondary sector are unlikely to be competitive for the best-educated and most productive workers.

Because of the segmentation of the employers in the labour market into primary and secondary sectors, with the primary sector having the most attractive jobs to offer, the workers also become segmented into primary and secondary groups. Workers in the primary segment of the market tend to be well educated or to have substantial training. Workers in the secondary segment of the labour market are less preferred for many reasons. They may be less skilled or less well educated, but other structural factors in the society may lead to a sorting of workers into primary or secondary markets. Less-preferred demographic sectors or groups that are the targets of discrimination may be more likely to be secondary market members.

Men, for example, are more likely to be in the primary segment, because they are believed to focus more of their attention on work. Women are more likely to be in the secondary market, either because they have competing demands to take care of children or because employers assume that they will have those demands. Women who raise their families and then enter the labour market may find themselves in secondary sector jobs because of their lack of recent work experience. Similarly, young people may be more likely to take secondary sector jobs because they do not yet have the work experience that would qualify them for primary sector jobs.

In a society with differential access to education or skills – for example, in a society with racial discrimination or with many immigrants – then racial minorities or immigrants may be disproportionately represented in the secondary market. In general, any group that faces discrimination or stigma will be disproportionately located in the secondary market among the less-preferred workers. Thus, workers with disabilities, former convicts, the very young or the very elderly, recent migrants, and racial, ethnic, linguistic or religious minorities may be limited to secondary-sector jobs. Workers without means of transportation may also be unable to travel to cities or regions with primary sector jobs. Eventually, some workers may be stereotyped as 'right' for certain kinds of jobs.

The segmented labour market concept also proposes that participating in the secondary labour market may eventually make a worker less attractive for primary sector jobs. Because secondary jobs are often unstable or temporary, the workers in secondary jobs may frequently experience layoff or unemployment. Also, because the secondary jobs are low paid and offer few opportunities for promotion, changing jobs may be the only way to obtain an increased wage. Either of these circumstances gives the worker a chequered work history, which may in turn make that worker appear less suitable to an employer in the primary market.

The segmented market is also called by other names, such as the dual labour market. The **informal economy** is usually populated with secondary-sector jobs. Some theorists argue that the entire world system is in effect a two-tiered global market, with the advanced industrial economies serving the role of the primary sector and the developing countries serving the role of secondary sector. There is also concern that primary employers may seek to preserve a small core of primary workers while outsourcing overflow work or less desirable work to contractors who participate only in the secondary labour market.

See also: discrimination; labour markets, sociology of.

References and further reading

Averitt, R. T. (1968) *The Dual Economy: The Dynamics of American Industrial Structure*, New York: Norton.
Beck, E. M., Horan, P. M. and Tolbert, C. M., II (1978) 'Stratification in a Dual Economy: A Sectoral Model of Earnings Determination', *American Sociological Review*, 43(5): 704–20.
Hodson, R. and Kaufman, R. L. (1982) 'Economic Dualism: A Critical Review', *American Sociological Review*, 47(6): 727–39.

TERESA A. SULLIVAN

SHOPPING See: consumption

SIMIAND, FRANÇOIS

Born in a lower middle-class family, Simiand (Gièzes 1873–Saint-Raphaël 1935) was a brilliant student who entered the Ecole Normale Supérieure; there he got the agrégation in philosophy (a highly selective exam) and was singled out by Emile Bergson as one of the brightest philosophical minds of his generation. Interested in the social sciences, Simiand joined the group of scholars that Emile **Durkheim** was organizing around the creation of his journal, *L'Année sociologie* (1897–1913 for the first series). Simiand was in charge of the section devoted to economic sociology – which was second in importance after the section on religious sociology supervised by Marcel **Mauss**. In 1904, he received a PhD with a study on wages in the coal industry (Simiand 1907).

During the war, Simiand was the head of the staff of the minister in charge of artillery and ammunitions. After the war, he came to university teaching. He became professor of work management (1919) and finally professor of political economy (1923; see Simiand 1930–1) in the Conservatoire National des Arts et Métiers. In 1932 he got a chair devoted to the history of labour in the Collège de France, the most prestigious institution in the French academic system. All through his life, he was an active member of socialist intellectual groups.

Simiand was a Durkheimian: he implemented the statistical method praised in Durkheim's *Rules of Sociological Method*, notably in his studies on wages (1907, 1932), and on price cycles (1930). Simiand was also a Durkheimian in the sense that he was a sharp critic in methodological debates whether with historians (Simiand 1906) or economists (1912 and 1932, end of Volume II; Besnard 1983). He was still a Durkheimian in his seminal essay on money (1934) since he grounded his sociological approach of monetary relations in the sociology of religion and the sociology of knowledge as Durkheim and Mauss did (Steiner 2005).

As far as methodology is concerned, Simiand's approach is in line with the points of view advocated by so-called heterodox schools such as institutionalism and historicism (Gislain and Steiner 1999; Steiner 2003). Accordingly, Simiand never accepted the rationalistic approach grounded on the economic agent supposedly able to implement rationality substantially. Instead, Simiand relentlessly advocated a sociological approach of economic phenomena based on statistics and history. However, Simiand was more a rationalist than a positivist: his economic sociology strongly relied on theoretical assumptions, such as a (class) theory of action and conflict (Simiand 1907, 1932), a theory of money involving **trust** relations and, what is more surprising in his highly rationalistic approach, relations of faith (Simiand 1934).

We can describe his research strategy with the following sequence. First, economic sociology must carefully establish the events that constitute its factual basis and thus must proceed to a critique of the sources. Second, since economic events appear in a quantitative form, these events are essentially statistical data reconstituted in series in order to permit a historical study. Third, a theoretical operation is introduced for providing a causal explanation. Simiand's central idea relies on the role of human action without which one cannot explain how socio-economic data are connected; this is the purpose of Simiand's theory of action (Gislain and Steiner 1995: ch. 3). Simiand explains that workers and bosses have a similar attitude to earnings and effort as well as on status quo and improvement, so that they rank alternatives according to the following order: increase in earnings with the same effort, increase in earnings with an increase in effort, maintenance of earning with the same effort, maintenance of earning with an increase in effort. This structure implies that the two groups are in conflict over the distribution and the production of wealth; the precise form of this conflict depending on the economic conditions that are exogenously given by price cycles (e.g. when prices rise, then nominal profits are higher, accordingly it is easier for bosses to give to workers an increased nominal wage without asking them to work harder). Price cycles are being themselves explained by variations in the supply of money (gold). Fourth, this causal structure together with the historical data provides a stylized fact that will explain wages, profits and their variations.

Simiand's works were not very influential in France, not to speak of other countries. It is likely that his statistical approach and his strong rejection of pure theory appeared too extreme to most of his colleagues, even those who were close to him – for example Gaétan Pirou, a leading professor in Paris during the inter-war period. The decline of the Durkheimian school in France is a second reason for this situation. However, Simiand's insights are still present within the Ecole de la régulation and within French economic sociology based on **Bourdieu**'s approach (Steiner 2005, ch. 5).

References and further reading

Besnard, Philippe (1983) 'The Epistemological Polemic: François Simiand', in P. Besnard (ed.), *The Sociological Domain. The Durkheimian and the Founding of French Sociology*, Cambridge: Cambridge University Press.

Gillard, Lucien and Rosier, Michel (eds) (1996) *François Simiand: sociologie-histoire-économie*, Amsterdam: Edition des archives contemporaines.

Gislain, Jean-Jacques and Steiner, Philippe (1995) *La Sociologie économique 1890–1920*, Paris: Presses Universitaires de France.

—— (1999) 'American Institutionalism and French Positive Political Economy: Some Connections', *History of Political Economy*, 31(2): 273–96.

Simiand, F. ([1906]1987) 'La Causalité en histoire', in F. Simiand, *Méthode historique et sciences sociales*, Paris: Editions des archives.

—— (1907) *Le Salaire des ouvriers des mines de charbon en France*, Paris: Cornély.

—— (1912) *La Méthode positive en sciences économiques*, Paris: Alcan.

—— (1930) *Recherches anciennes et nouvelles sur le mouvement général des prix*, Paris: Domat-Montchrestien.

—— (1930–1) *Cours d'économie politique*, Paris: Alcan.

—— (1932) *Le Salaire, l'évolution sociale et la monnaie*, Paris: Alcan.

—— (1934) 'La Monnaie, réalité sociale', *Annales sociologique*, D(1): 1–86.

Steiner, Philippe (2003) 'Durkheim's Sociology, Simiand's Positive Political Economy and the German Historical School', *European Journal of the History of Economic Thought*, 10(2): 249–78.

—— (2005) *L'ecole durkheimienne et l'économie: sociologie, religion et connaissance*, Genève: Droz.

PHILIPPE STEINER

SIMMEL, GEORG

Simmel's *œuvre* is commonly divided into an early and late philosophical and a sociological middle part. Georg Simmel (1858–1918) studied history, philosophy and Italian, but showed interest in a much broader range of subjects. He received his PhD in 1881 with a thesis on Kant and became, due to antisemitic prejudices and disciplinary egoism, an extraordinary (*außerordentlicher*) professor of sociology at the Berliner University only twenty years later. In 1914 he was appointed *Ordinarius* (chair) at the then German University of Strasburg. His early 'philosophical writings' concentrate on moral, his later ones on esthetical and ideological (or *lebensphilsophische*) problems. The 'sociological' middle period is dominated by numerous articles and essays on subjects like the poor, the nobility, the secret, the modern city or the fate of personality, papers which eventually were integrated into his *Sociology* (1908). Despite its title, however, Simmel's sociological masterpiece and main contribution to economic sociology is his *Philosophy of Money* (1900). Like none of his other monographs, the *Philosophy of Money* not only shows the inseparability but also the inner consistency and even systematic character of Simmel's work, a trait that has not been recognized for long time because of his literary style and the complexity as well as originality of his reasoning. The latest revival of Simmel and rediscovery as one of the classics of (economic) sociology, however, has led to the recognition of the richness and contemporaneousness of much of his thought, as well as the centrality of his book on money.

The *Philosophy of Money* is organized in two parts, one 'analytic', the other 'synthetic'. Far better known is the synthetic part, in which Simmel lists and scrutinizes the social, i.e. behavioural, structural and ideological consequences 'of money' or rather of a society that is used to and crucially depends on monetary exchange (see **money, sociology of**). The analytic part tackles fundamental socio-economic questions such as: What is **value**? What is **exchange**? What is money? Simmel's answers to these even (and especially) within economics only superficially settled questions, are still relevant and deserve further elaboration. However, I shall commence with giving an overview of the themes and arguments of the synthetic part.

One of the most important effects of monetary exchange or the successive monetarization of social relations and bonds is the increasing liberty of the individual. Take, for example, the medieval peasant who has to 'pay' tributes to his landlord. Inasmuch as his literally specified tributes – *in specie* being the Latin term for their objective or natural, non-monetary form – were substituted by monetary payments, the peasant became free to choose which fruits to grow and which cattle to raise, as long as he was able to pay at all. Thus, he became, with all due restrictions to using this term for medieval peasants, 'market-oriented', responding to pressures *and chances* of selling his goods and vying with others for the best bargain. Likewise, the landlord, receiving money instead of labour and goods, became in principle *free of* organizing the first and storing the latter and *free to* engage *in any kind* of business activity. Of course, the economy still had to develop and politics still had to liberate the peasants from their feudal bonds, before they could turn into agriculturalists producing for an anonymous market. But the monetarization of these social or even political bonds was instrumental for their transformation into *economic* ties.

A second characteristic of modern societies, namely the omnipresence and partial preponderance of formal organizations, is possible only on the basis of generalized monetary exchange. It is the fundamental *raison d'être* of formal organizations to reduce complexity, to rationalize procedures and to limit transaction costs. Therefore they depend on qualified labour, on disciplined and flexible personnel that sticks to its organizational tasks, even if the goals of the organization mean nothing to those who work to reach them. What has to be assured to make organizations work and survive in a changing environment is the motivation of their members who are not necessarily motivated personally. The instrument to fulfil this paradoxical task is money. Within more or less defined or negotiated boundaries, money or monetary salaries buy the obedience of organized work. Yet, money is not only the probably most important non-organizational presupposition of formal organization, but also the quintessential tool which brought it into existence historically. Forerunner of the modern organization, as a structure which may (continue to) exist independently of its individual parts, is the open trading corporation. Membership in such a corporation did not depend on character and personality but on the investment of money. Generally, inasmuch as money buys anything (including labour), money enables anyone to act.

However – and this is another significant aspect of 'monetary societies' – money does not simply depersonalize and objectify social relationships, an effect that **Marx** already termed and criticized as **alienation**. According to Simmel, it also allows its holders to develop their individuality. Alienation and the rise of individualism, far from contradicting or even excluding each other, are two sides of the same coin. Money permits and enforces social differentiation.

Social relations become mediated through money. On the one hand, we are no longer bound to and interested in the 'whole person' we are interacting with; what we expect and legitimately can demand from others is that they behave according to more or less standardized roles. On the other hand, it is only because of this liberating process, the fact that we do not belong to somebody (as, for example, the serf belongs to his landlord), that we generally interact with others only with regards to the specific functions they fulfil, that we become free to develop and assemble an individual, i.e. a specific and original character. Even if it is true, as Simmel remarks, that individuality is nothing but the intersection of different 'social circles' in one man, it is nevertheless an achievement that probably most of us consider the core of their identity. Thus, alienation is the 'price' we have to pay for unfolding our subjectivity.

Money, however, not only changes our identity; it also affects *how* we interact. Simmel makes clear that money acts as a media of communication when he shows that money contracts space, accelerates the pace of living and brings rational calculation along (see **rationality**). It contracts space, because monetary payments do not require actors to be physically present where the exchange takes place. It accelerates the pace of living since the continuous flow of payments disrupts the natural cycles of sowing and reaping and because the always precarious value of money urges its holders to spend or reinvest it. In addition, money brings rational calculation along, because money allows to homogenize, to quantify and thus to compare everything – be it goods, deeds or time. It is the necessary tool without which a 'rational way of life' of which **Weber** has shown its capitalistic importance is nothing but a pipe dream (see **religion and economic life**).

Much less known and accepted are the findings of the analytic part of the *Philoso-phy of Money*. I will limit my remarks on the analytic part on three points: on Simmel's theory of exchange, his functional theory of money, and the **legitimacy** of money.

One grave mistake of the Simmel reception was to interpret his **exchange theory** as a prototype of *rational* exchange or **rational choice theory**. That is not at all to say that exchange in Simmel's sense of the term is something irrational, but that his understanding of exchange as the fundamental form of social action is much broader than the interest-guided, self-transparent, utility-maximizing type which is meant when rational choice theorists speak of exchange. For Simmel, exchange is a concept which is nearly synonymous with 'interaction' (*Wechselwirkung*) and thus embraces all kinds of forced and voluntary exchanges like robbery and gift-giving, not only **barter**. Yet Simmel's concept does not blur substantial differences; on the contrary, Simmel outlines a genetic theory of exchange, which shows how its different forms evolved and how this evolution was shaped by the invention of money. For him, exchange is a formal concept which does not predetermine its specific forms. If there is any generic form of exchange it is **gift** exchange, as it has been described and analysed by **Mauss**. It is the gift which precedes barter and not vice versa; although – and this is stated more precisely by Simmel than by Mauss – the modern gift, i.e. the present, is as much a product of advanced civilization as is market exchange. What precedes the rational, calculated exchange and the benevolent, positively indifferent present, is the *ambivalent* gift like the sacrifice or the tribute, i.e. archaic forms of action which combine voluntary obedience and strategic manipulation. The role of money in the evolution of exchange is, that by establishing at least the idea of equivalence, a peaceful *and just* acquisition of goods becomes possible. Virtually, money transforms robbery into trade. On the other hand, it is this pacifying influence of money, the transformation of acquisitiveness into the profit motive, that alters the character of the ancient gift. It is changed from something that one had to fear as much as to take, to a present which ideally embodies nothing but the sympathy of the giver.

The second 'analytic' point I want to consider is Simmel's functional theory of money. The name of this theory – correctly – suggests that Simmel, writing in 1900, already adheres to the now widespread notion, that 'money is what money does' (Hicks). However, this should *neither* obscure the fact that Simmel was one of the first to overcome the debate between 'metalists', who insisted that, to have value, money had to be covered by gold or other precious metals, and 'chartalists', who believed in the power of the political authorities to create money *ex nihilo*. Simmel resolves this theoretical dispute historically by showing that early monies obviously had to be *perceived* by its users as actually valuable, whereas modern (paper) monies, being introduced only after the use of money had been established for centuries, are in fact without any intrinsic value to speak of. Nevertheless, there is more at stake than mere contingencies. On the one hand, money has always been a kind of credit, since there had to be trust in the value of gold, the authenticity of the coin and, last not least, the continued validity or acceptance of the money in question. On the other hand, even paper (or electronic) money is not without coverage: the state and/or the modern central **banks** (try to) guarantee that the amount of (circulating) money more or less corresponds to the (presumed) value of all available products. Nor should it be overseen that Simmel's functional theory of money does not end where the modern monetary functionalism stops to ask questions. One of the most important and economically far-reaching findings of Simmel's monetary

theory is that especially our 'worthless' money tokens, due to their universal use, newly assume value. Under normal circumstances, a certain amount of modern 'all-purpose money' has more value than a product of same 'price', for the product first needs to be sold before its purchasing power can be realized. The person who holds money is already 'liquid', while the one who owns goods only hopes to become so. Simmel terms this structural advantage of the cash holder over the wealth owner 'value extension' (*Wertplus*) of money; in substance he anticipated what **Keynes** later called the 'liquidity premium' of money. Corresponding with Keynes, Simmel conceived of the economy as always *out* of **equilibrium**, reigned by monetary impulses and inclined to speculative malinvestments. Unlike Keynes, however, Simmel did not develop his discovery of the value extension of money into a theory of interest (see **post Keynesianism**).

A third lasting 'analytic' contribution Simmel made to economic sociology is his analysis of the legitimacy of money. As indicated, all money needs coverage, and the real resource which has always covered money is trust. That the money we use is considered legitimate, is the flipside of the coin that money tends to stimulate speculative behaviour. An economy that is dynamic but also endangered by **speculation**, needs a reliable standard *and embodiment* of wealth. Without such a safe haven, the market cannot function. Countless examples for the process of disintegration of weak currencies can be found. Simmel contends that the stabilization of (the value of) money – i.e. its purchasing power and/ or its exchange rate – is a *political* task, although it is *not* at the discretion of the political authorities to decree trust in the money they emit. Thus, monetary policies have to assure something that they cannot deliver. But it is a mistake of economic liberals to assume that, due to their ever luring failure, monetary policies themselves are superfluous. Such a view underrates the symbolic nature of money; it misunderstands that money is not only a convention but an institution. What distinguishes the latter from the former is that these are not regarded as a free agreement subject to notice but as a 'natural' part of the social order. In fact, even institutions can erode and do vanish, but what protects them against too easy an attempt to become abrogated is exactly their presumed naturalness. So, besides their manifest economic function, central banks (and/or other monetary authorities) fulfil the important latent or symbolic function to *simulate* the possibility of steering the value of money, or, to abstract even more, to transform trust, which is and can only be a voluntary inner act of an individual *vis-à-vis* another, into depersonalized trust into the economy. Thus, money, and not exchange or the market, is the true denominator of our economic system.

References and further reading

Grenier, Jean-Yves *et al.* (1993) *A propos de 'Philosophie de l'argent' de Georg Simmel*, Paris: L'Harmattan.
Paul, Axel T. (2004) *Die Gesellschaft des Geldes. Entwurf einer monetären Theorie der Moderne*, Wiesbaden: Westdeutscher Verlag.
Poggi, Gianfranco (1993) *Money and the Modern Mind. Georg Simmel's 'Philosophy of Money'*, Berkeley, CA: University of California Press
Simmel, Georg (1900/1990) *The Philosophy of Money*, translated by Tom Bottomore and David Frisby, second enlarged edition, London and New York: Routledge.

AXEL T. PAUL

SMITH, ADAM

Adam Smith (1723–90) was a theorist of individual assessment and self-interested search at a time when the physiocrats were arguing that all value added came from nature-endowed land and the mercantilists were calling for wise state intervention to increase the nation's wealth. Smith took the discrete decision-maker as his unit of analysis. Factoring down in order to understand the whole, he produced theories of the self-stabilizing mechanism in which a beneficent consequentialism results from a myopic deontology as if guided by a utility-orientated invisible hand that wants to ensure humankind's maximum felt welfare on earth.

Smith was educated at the University of Glasgow. A student of philosophy, he was much influenced by the doctrine of the 'greatest happiness of the greatest number' of his teacher, Francis Hutcheson. He then spent six years at Balliol College, Oxford. Since he was a Snell Scholar, the expectation was that he would enter the Church. In fact, by the time he returned to Scotland, he seems to have moved away from revealed Christianity and transferred his allegiance to sensible nature instead. By then he had been exposed to the epistemological scepticism of David Hume. Hume had emphasized how little mere humans can know about their world. He argued nonetheless that empiricism rather than authority would give fallen beings the best-attainable purchase on unknowable reality that no great machine-maker has ever bothered to map or document.

Smith lectured on literature in Edinburgh (his *Lectures on Rhetoric and Belles Lettres* document the breadth of his interests) and then, from 1752 to 1763, was Professor of Moral Philosophy in Glasgow. Notes taken by his students have been published as *Lectures on Jurisprudence*. It was in Glasgow that he completed the first of his two major works on homeostasis in the social order. Smith's *Theory of Moral Sentiments*, appearing in 1759, is built around the axial principle of 'sympathy', of empathy, of the exchange of places in the mind that allows a conditioned agent to enter into and imagine the feelings of a fellow sentient with a degree of sensitivity that blunts the sharpness of his narrow egotism. Socialized into a given culture, people effortlessly absorb the standards of their time and place. Their conventions hold their community together. No one would approve of a social actor who repeatedly broke the rules through insufficient benevolence, inadequate justice or inappropriate prudence. Just as we would praise a social actor who showed the expected kindliness towards the needy, so we would criticize a member of our club who failed to look after himself and his family. The 'impartial spectator', fully informed and completely in touch with consensus, is the sounding-board and the baseline against which the real spectator evaluates the actions of his neighbours before he unleashes the positive and negative sanctions that keep the Hobbesian *bellum* at bay.

Smith resigned from the University of Glasgow in 1763. He spent two years accompanying the Duke of Buccleuch on his grand tour (chiefly to France, where Smith met Rousseau and other *philosophes* who were dissatisfied with the tyranny of the Bastille and the extravagance of Versailles). In 1765 he returned to his family home in Kirkcaldy and began work on a major interpretive study of how individuals create prosperity with only limited assistance from the state. *An Inquiry into the Nature and Causes of the Wealth of Nations – The Wealth of Nations* as history has come to call it – was published in 1776. Few other books have exercised so much influence from the day they came out or so perfectly captured the mood of their times. The American colonists were clamouring for self-rule. The 'industrial revolution' was giving rise to a demand for freedom of trade. The French Revolution was variations on the theme of equal rights versus the insolence of office. *The Wealth of Nations* was widely acclaimed as a book for shopkeepers and citizens who believed with Mandeville that private vices add up to public virtues. The butcher, the brewer and the baker serve us not out of benevolence but 'from a regard to their own

interest' – but they do serve us. The state does not: 'I have never known much good done by those who affected to trade for the public good.'

In 1759 the axial principle had been sympathy. In 1776 it became interest. The shift in focus only underlined the continuity of the conception. The self-equilibration and the methodological individualism had not changed. Nor, however, had the social setting within which discrete ego sets out his stall. Smith in the *Wealth of Nations* returns repeatedly to the element of conspicuous and/or prescribed consumption that makes even shopping a collective choice. He demonstrates that institutional change can be the direct consequence of producing and selling. He shows that even the factious divisiveness of monolithic religion can be vanquished by the perfect competition of multiple sects. In presenting his labour theory of value, he seems to be leaving the door open to an exploitation theory of wages such as was later to be the core of Marx on the class struggle. In treating the division of labour as an enhancement of productivity that condemns the operative, 'stupid and ignorant', to the self-denial of 'mental mutilation', he seems to be indicating that the commercial civilization has its victims as well as its successes. *Other people* throughout his book are an essential part of the theory. *The Wealth of Nations* is as much about convention, interaction and stratification as it is about the production and the exchange that make us rich.

It is also about the state. In ensuring law and order, in correcting a market failure through roads and canals, in preserving the market-distorting Usury Laws so as to keep the cost of capital low, in financing itself through the lucrative Post Office monopoly, the government is not to do the minimum. Rather, it is to intervene pragmatically, both to boost the rate of growth (the regulation of banking to prevent the contagion of failures) and to invest in social

order (the sponsorship of popular education lest the debased masses fall prey to
demagogues). The government is a social
force. Conventions in the sense of the
Moral Sentiments constrain pecuniary
advancement in the sense of *The Wealth of
Nations*. In the one case as in the other,
society is not a fiction but the organism that
allows the cells to do their best.

References and further reading

Reisman, D. A. (1976) *Adam Smith's Sociological
    Economics*, London: Croom Helm.
—— (2005) *Democracy and Exchange: Schumpeter,
    Galbraith, T. H. Marshall, Titmuss and Adam
    Smith*, Cheltenham, UK, and Northampton,
    MA: Edward Elgar.
Skinner, A. (1996) *A System of Social Science:
    Papers Relating to Adam Smith*, second edi-
    tion, Oxford: Clarendon Press.
Smith, A. ([1776]1976) *An Inquiry into the Nature
    and Causes of the Wealth of Nations*, Oxford:
    Clarendon Press.

DAVID REISMAN

SOCIAL CAPITAL

Social capital has gained currency in the
social sciences in the past decade as a paradigm to capture the contributions of social
elements in explaining a wide variety of
individual and collective behaviours. It has
been used to examine topics ranging from
status attainment and social mobility, competitive advantage in economic organizations, and political participation, to
psychological and physical well-being (see
recent reviews in Portes 1998; Lin 1999;
Lin 2001a; Burt 2000). Its research saliency
reflects the recognition by many social scientists that collective and individual actions
significantly depend on the social context
in which such actions are embedded. It also
reflects the sense that, as a type of capital,
the term shares an affinity with other forms
of capital, such as human capital and cultural capital, which have been formulated
to understand the utility of resources in

affecting life chances. It seems logical to
argue that social elements may constitute
capital as well.

However, as research expands into
numerous arenas and applications, both the
conception and operationalization of social
capital have become diverse and multidimensional. There looms an increasing
danger that the term will become a handy
catch-all, for-all and cure-all sociological
term. This danger may have emanated from
conceptual generality in its formative
development. For example, **Coleman** has
proposed conceiving social capital as 'these
social-structural resources' and consisting 'a
variety of different entities having two
characteristics in common: They all consist
of some aspect of a social structure, and
they facilitate certain actions of individuals
who are within the structure' (Coleman
1990: 302). As such, any and all elements of
the social structure are candidates, and any
of them become social capital when they
work for a particular outcome in a particular context for a particular actor – a tautological argument. When interpreted
liberally, little theory is implicated or needs
to be evoked, and falsification becomes
impossible (Portes 1998; Lin 2001a). In
order to sustain the theoretical and empirical credibility of social capital, it is critical
to clarify and consolidate its conceptual
rigor and measurement precision.

This essay will attempt to clarify the
concept of social capital and place it in a
theoretical framework. The principles
guiding this integration are threefold: (1) a
distinctive definition of social capital, independent of its possible causal or effectual
factors, should be conceived; (2) its affinity
with social relations and networks must be
affirmed and specified; and (3) its utilities or
returns must be conceptualized and specified. The first principle affirms the general
understanding that social capital contains
social elements but delineates specifications
of the 'elements' to resolve the potential
catch-all tautological fallacy mentioned

above. The second principle tightly links social capital, as a concept, with its social basis, social relations and networks, but demands that a theoretical distinction be made between the two: namely, social capital is not social relations or social networks per se. The third principle promotes a conceptual organization of types of expected returns of social capital, rather than the haphazard approaches witnessed in the literature.

Integration guided by these principles, I argue, will advance the definition of social capital and place it in a theoretical framework so that causal propositions can be formulated, better measurements devised, and systematic investigations carried out. In this conjunction, it should also help clarify how prevailing research traditions – social resources, civic engagement and trust – may be theoretically evaluated and operations refined so as to better represent social capital in empirical research.

Definition: social capital as diversity of embedded resources

A definition of social capital necessarily needs to follow some conceptualizations offered by previous efforts. The most general requirement, as offered by Coleman, is that they are elements of social structure. There is not or should not be any dispute that social capital is *rooted precisely at the juncture between individuals and their relations; and is contained in the meso-level structure or in social networks.* That is, individual actors and their relations form the basis of social capital, which have micro-consequences for the individuals as well as macro-consequences for the collectivity. A much more precise definition was offered by Lin, who argues that social capital should be defined as resources embedded in social networks (1982, 1999, 2001b) – social resources. 'They are not possessed goods of the individual. Rather, they are resources accessible through one's direct and indirect ties'

(1982: 132). He also suggests that access to and use of social resources need to be examined in research. This definition and operationalization are consistent with the notion of social capital independently offered at about the same time by **Bourdieu** (1983/1986). He defines it as 'the aggregate of the actual or potential resources which are linked to possession of a durable network of more or less institutionalized relationships of mutual acquaintance and recognition' (p. 248), and conceives it operationally as 'the sum of resources, actual or virtual, that accrue to an individual or group by virtue of possessing a durable network or more or less institutionalized relationships of mutual acquaintance and recognition'. In this conceptualization, social capital is, first of all, resources, and second, linked to relationships – that is, resources embedded in social networks. Operationally, it may be measured as a sum of resources, actual (i.e. mobilized) or virtual (e.g. perceived or accessed), embedded in enduring networks.

However, it is operationally insufficient to employ 'embedded resources' as a concept, because it would offer no precise sense of variation for analysis or testing. Again, scholars have provided several suggestions. Bourdieu suggests a simple count or quantity of resources embedded in one's networks. Lin, on the other hand, focuses on the value or quality of resources accessed or used. This 'quality', he suggests, may be reflected in the value of the resources consensually perceived in a social hierarchy (i.e. representing class, status or power). In combination, therefore, social capital can be measured by the count or quantity of resources embedded in one's social networks, weighted by their socially accepted values. An implementation of this definition and operationalization is the diversity (i.e. variation in the types of resources) of the embedded resources. Thus, we offer the formal definition of social capital as follows:

> Social capital is the extent of diversity of resources embedded in one's social networks.

It should be noted that it is not advocated here that the presence of diverse embedded resources is intrinsically 'better' than the absence of such resources. As will be seen later, it is possible to argue that less diverse embedded resources may be 'better' social capital. It simply represents a dimension that has a continuum, from diverse resources to not-so-diverse resources. The merit of a particular value along the continuum depends on the specification of their relative utility for a particular return, an issue to be addressed shortly.

This definition, I argue, captures both the 'capital' and the 'social' elements in social capital, in that embedded resources are seen as capital and distribution or diversity of such embedded resources among social ties or members in groups inevitably implicate social relations. At the same time, it dispels the usual confounding conceptions of social capital with social networks (its causing agents) or with its functions (its expected returns). It can and should be measured independent of these other notions.

Density of social networks as the exogenous factor

While it is clear in the theoretical formulations that social networks are the basis for, but are not themselves, social capital (Bourdieu 1983/1986; Lin 1982), subsequent statements have blurred the distinctions. Coleman states that 'social capital inheres in the structure of relations between persons and among persons. It is lodged neither in individuals nor in physical implements of production' (1988; 1990: 302). Putnam (2000: 19) equates social capital to features of social organization – 'such as networks, norms, and trust – that facilitate coordination and cooperation for

mutual benefit'. In his conceptual synthesis, Portes (1998) argues that social networks must be considered as the core of the concept.

A major reason for this confusion or lack of distinction is that previous statements regarding resources embedded in social networks were sufficiently vague as to pose the possibility that networks themselves constitute resources. Social networks and social capital are intimately related; however, their relationship should be propositional rather than constitutive – certain features of social networks are likely to increase or decrease diversity of embedded resources.

Just as diversity of embedded resources is seen as the constitutive element of social capital, we need to specify variation in social networks that may be conducive to producing or reducing diversity of embedded resources. As it turns out, this variation is amply discussed in the literature. The singular feature of social networks evoked in the discussion of social capital has consistently been density/closure versus openness/expansiveness of the social networks: the extent to which social ties in networks are connected to one another. The utility of dense networks has long formed the basis for sociological theorizing. Homans (1950) postulates a positive and reciprocal relationship between interaction and sentiment. Thus, Coleman (1990: 302–4) suggests that dense or reciprocal relations create norms of reciprocity, which promote a collective organization offering protection or benefit to its members. Following Coleman's lead, Putnam states,

> Social capital refers to connections among individuals – social networks and the norms of reciprocity and trustworthiness that arise from them. In that sense social capital is closely related to what some have called 'civic virtue'. The difference is that 'social capital' calls attention to the fact that civic virtue is most powerful

when embedded in a dense network of reciprocal social relations. A society of many virtuous but isolated individuals is not necessarily rich in social capital.

(Putnam 2000: 19)

Thus, density of social networks is seen as protective or beneficial to network members (Bian 1997).

On the other hand, less dense networks have also been conceived as beneficial to individuals in other conceptualizations. Granovetter (1973) suggests that weaker rather than stronger ties are more likely to create opportunities for accessing novel information. Lin brings this argument into his formulation of the social resources theory by suggesting that open or expansive networks are more likely to bring about diversity of embedded resources (1982; 2001a). Likewise, Burt (1992, 2001) argues that structural holes or bridges are not only beneficial to those at these locations but bring benefit to other members of the social group as well. Through such bridges and wider reaches, different and presumably better resources might be located and accessed, which in turn bring benefits to the actors.

As Burt (2001) summarizes, there has been substantial debate about the relative merits of density or closeness versus sparsity or openness of social networks. However, there is little argument that the dimension of social network density is probably the most relevant and important network foundation for social capital. How, then, do we resolve the seemingly contradictory postulates? In fact, the different postulats are based on the differential utility of social capital conceived. For Coleman, Putnam and others, closeness or dense social networks promote interactions and shared interests. This follows Homans, and later, Merton (Lazarsfeld and Merton 1954), who suggests that interaction and sentiment also promote shared characteristics and vice versa – the homophily principle. Stronger

ties or friends have been found to share similar characteristics and **life styles**. Thus, theoretically, it can be anticipated that closed or dense networks should be associated with homogenous embedded resources. In contrast, sparse or expansive networks are associated with heterogeneous embedded resources. We may summarize the linkages between density of networks and diversity in embedded resources as the following propositions:

> *Proposition 1a:* Less dense networks are associated with the likelihood of reaching more diverse embedded resources.

> *Proposition 1b:* Denser networks are associated with the likelihood of reaching less diverse embedded resources.

Propositions 1a and 1b can be seen as a single proposition: that density in social networks is positively associated with less diversity of embedded resources. However, at this point, they will be treated as separate propositions, since the refutation of one does not necessarily suggest the confirmation of the other. It is also necessary, as shall be seen, to pursue the parallel theoretical arguments forward in the analysis of social capital.

The next logical question, then, is why are dense networks seen as beneficial to some scholars while sparse networks to others in the analysis of social capital? Or, more appropriately here, following the deductions in Propositions 1a and 1b, why are more diverse or less diverse embedded resources better social capital?

Market competition and social solidarity as returns

The key to the question above lies in the expected returns to social capital, as different types of returns have been envisioned. For those advocating open networks and diversity in embedded resources, the returns specified tend to be competitive advantage in the marketplace. For those interested in dense networks and less diverse resources, the returns specified are geared towards benefits and advantages offered by group cohesion and identification – social **solidarity**.

Market competition represents instrumental returns expected of social capital, whereas social solidarity reflects expressive returns. For those working with the open networks and social resources, social capital is expected to yield better information (Granovetter 1973; Burt 1992), better control (Burt 1992) or more influence (Lin 1982) so as to gain relative advantages in the job market (Flap 1991; Erickson 2001), and promotions and benefits in economic organizations (see review in Burt 2000). The association between social capital and instrumental returns is clear and explicit (Lin 2001b, 1982).

For those advocating dense or closed networks for social capital, the focus is the advantage cohesive groups (Coleman 1990; Putnam 2000) bring to both individuals and the group. There has been considerable discussion about trust, support, help or reciprocal exchanges among group members. In such contexts, social capital is linked to social solidarity, and is expected to produce expressive returns.

No doubt this distinction is not entirely an either–or conceptualization. Analysis of social resources (Lin 2001b) has been extended to conjectures as to its effects on expressive returns such as mental health or well-being. Social solidarity may also bring economic or other advantages to individuals (e.g. the merchants in Cairo, or the mother who moved her family to Jerusalem, in Coleman 1990: 303). Nevertheless, it is clear that the primary returns of social capital conceived differ for the two theoretical perspectives: market competition for one and social solidarity for the other. We may offer the following propositions:

> *Proposition 2a:* More diverse embedded resources increase market competition.

> *Proposition 2b:* Less diverse embedded resources enhance social solidarity.

The parallel theoretical propositions are depicted in Figure 3. The next task is to explore whether and the extent to which research that has been carried out in social capital can be derived from these propositions. This articulation will also point to areas where further specifications or clarifications are needed.

Articulations with research traditions

In the past two decades, three principal research traditions have emerged for social capital: (1) social resources; (2) civic engagement; and (3) trust. Each is mentioned in the literature as a possible way of conceptualizing and operationalizing social capital; and each has generated an extensive research literature. Do these research traditions represent empirical derivations from

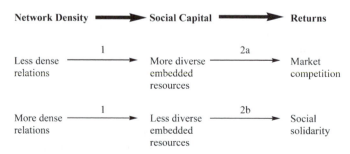

Figure 3. The parallel theoretical models and propositions of social capital

608

the two parallel theoretical developments specified earlier? I argue that while most empirical works may not capture all processes dictated by the theory, and some rely on indirect or surrogate measures rather than directly derivable measures, the conceptual intent of the empirical studies, to a great extent, does reflect the specified theory above. In the following, I will show the theoretical correspondence and empirical derivations for these research traditions, and point to areas where further clarifications and empirical work are needed.

The social resources tradition is most straightforward in its formulations as derivable from the openness-of-networks to diversity-in-embedded-resources to market-competition propositions. Research (Lin 1999; Marsden and Gorman 2001; Lin et al. 2001) focuses on the linkage between diversity of embedded resources and instrumental returns, such as socio-economic status attainment. However, the few studies exploring the relationships between open or expansive social networks and the diversity of embedded resources have yielded ambiguous results (see review in Lin 1999). Further verification for the linkage between network density and diversity in embedded resources is needed.

The research tradition of civic engagement also holds theoretical allegiance to the linkages among density of networks, social capital, and group solidarity. Putnam, its principal advocate and contributor (2000), makes clear its derivation from Coleman's arguments on closeness of networks and group cohesion. From this derivation, then, civic engagement, or its operational measures with participation in voluntary associations and groups, should be expected to be associated with less diverse embedded resources. It would require making explicit certain assumptions, largely absent so far in the discussion: (1) that voluntary associations bring together individuals who share certain interests and life styles; (2) that these entities would capture shared resources

brought in by these like-minded participants; and (3) that the participation in these entities affords access and mobilization of shared resources, and provides benefits to its members and the collectivities. If these assumptions hold true, then, we should hypothesize that shared or less diverse embedded resources in networks are linked to less diverse or more similar shared resources in associations. Greater similarity of shared resources may be indicated by the greater homophily among members. It is no surprise, therefore, that many discussions of civic engagement also link it to trust (Putnam 2000). That is, denser networks promote engagement in certain social groups and develop trust because such networks increase the likelihood for individuals of similar characteristics and life styles to engage one another. Such like-minded engagement, perhaps through reciprocal trust, affords mobilization of resources from participating individuals and the collectivity, which in turn generate certain returns to the individual members and the collectivity. These returns principally involve the preservation and promotion of the collectivity – social solidarity.

However, do voluntary associations only exist in bringing individuals with similar interests and resources and in achieving social cohesion or solidarity? Consider the flipside of the above hypothesis: *more diverse embedded resources in networks are linked to more diverse or less similar shared resources in associations*. Here, less *similarity of shared resources may be indicated by the greater heterophily among members.* That is, is it credible to speculate that certain associations bring individuals together for a shared interest, but with diverse characteristics and life styles? That such diversity affords the individuals or the collectivity to attain goals such as competition rather than cooperation?

In fact, not all associations facilitate and value trust, or merely promote cohesion and solidarity. For example, while some associations may intend to preserve existing resources (such as neighbourhood watch, environmental protection or restrictions for zoning, housing development or land use), others seek resources (ranging from petitions for more support for schools and teachers to greater health services, and seeking more information and support for scientific research). In the former cases, trust and reciprocity may be the desirable capital, since successful action may depend on unified voices and behaviours. In the latter cases, however, the association's success and utility may capitalize on diversity in memberships so as to facilitate linkage to other associations and organizations, and to find leverage in acquiring resources sought. Research on for-profit organizations (e.g. economic organizations) and markets shows that diverse inter-organizational ties and interpersonal ties accrue competitive advantage for both the organization itself and the engaging members (see review in Burt 2000). Scholars working on civic engagement have noticed the possibility that bridging may be useful. Putnam (2000), for example, mentioned that social capital may be either 'bonding' or 'bridging'. However, bridging demands open networks. Therefore, it points to the need to modify the current conceptualization of civic engagement.

Two alternatives formulations are possible. One is to argue that for most or all voluntary associations, members share certain characteristics but differ on others. Shared characteristics afford them to engage in intense and reciprocal interactions, while dissimilar characteristics afford some members to serve as bridges to others outside the association. This formulation may predict that some parts of the networks in the association is dense while other parts may be sparse. The expectation, then, is that civic engagement, undifferentiated in terms of specific groups or associations, may bring about advantages to voluntary organizations in the marketplace (competition for resources) and group solidarity (preservation of

resources). This undifferentiated view of voluntary associations suggests that each association may be bonding and bridging.

The other alternative formulation would suggest that there are different types of associations and organizations, and they differ in terms of functions or goals (expected returns). In accordance with the theory presented above, we would then expect two types of networks and embedded resources as well. In associations striving for resources, density of networks may not be important, and heterophilous memberships should be more beneficial. In associations attempting to preserve resources, density of networks and homophilous memberships should yield greater social solidarity. For the former, bridging is produced, and competition in the market is the expected return. For the latter, bonding is produced and social solidarity is the expected return.

It should then be possible to put the two alternatives, differentiated or undifferentiated associations, to empirical examinations. If civic engagement, or participation in associations, produces both instrumental (market competition) and expressive (social solidarity) returns, then the undifferentiated argument holds. If some associations tend to produce instrumental outcomes and others expressive returns, then the differentiated argument holds. Empirical verification of either of the alternative arguments may be seen as a confirmation that civic engagement is a component of social capital.

Still another theoretical possibility is that the linkage between diversity in resources embedded in social networks and different types of associations may be a causal one. *In this formulation, civic engagement is seen as a consequence of social capital rather than as its component.* Or, civic engagement is a mediating force between social capital and expected returns. Social capital enhances participation in certain types of associations, which in turn, through its mobilized resources or reciprocal trust, increase the likelihood of generating certain returns.

This theoretical possibility also deserves empirical examination.

Trust or trustworthiness is generally defined as the extent of expectation or confidence that an alter (actor) will take ego's interests into account (Misztal 1996). For many sociologists and most working on social capital, its production is seen as dependent on stable social relations and obligations. Thus, the linkage between trust to network density and homophilous embedded resources can be articulated. The homophily principle makes it a theoretical imperative that trust, interaction and homophilous resources are associated. Thus, at the micro level, trust can be seen as based on interpersonal relations and exchanges – interpersonal trust.

However, trust can also be conceived as an associative or generalized exchange. As Simmel stated (1978),

> One of the most important conditions of exchange is trust ... Without the general trust people have in each other, society itself would disintegrate, for very few relationships are based entirely upon what is known with certainty about another person, and very few relationships would endure if trust were not as strong as, or stronger than, rational proof or personal observation.
>
> (pp. 178–9)

In this context, trust, or generalized trust, or trust of others undifferentiated in the community or society, may be a public good, thus a macro-level attribute. It is the foundation of **collective action**.

But what is the connection between interpersonal trust and generalized trust? It is generally acknowledged that interpersonal trust is the foundation of generalized trust. Thus, 'seeing trust from this perspective makes it possible to show how building trust on micro level contributes to the more abstract trust on the macro-level' (Luhmann 1988: 98). For example, 'positive contact with our local doctor may gradually increase our confidence in the medical system' (Misztal 1996: 14–15). Unfortunately, much of the research on trust in the context of social capital has relied on rudimentary measures (e.g. 'Do you think others can be trusted?' Yes or No?) and provides no demonstration of its social production or underpinning.

The theoretical schema discussed earlier and presented in Figure 3 suggest the need to refine the measurement of trust or trustworthiness. First, at the micro level, interpersonal trust rather than generalized trust should be measured, since the relational foundation of trust needs to be built into the measurement. Thus, trustworthiness of others in the ego's social environment would be a good place to start. Second, it needs to be resolved as to whether interpersonal trust is a component of social capital or consequence of social capital. In either case, it should be tested that interpersonal trust is associated with network density. Then, it would be necessary to demonstrate that interpersonal trust is associated with diversity of social resources and civic engagement (or engagement in certain types of associations), the other components of social capital. Third, as expected in the theory, interpersonal trust should be associated with indicators of social solidarity. Fourth, the alternative causal models, either treating interpersonal trust as a component of social capital or its consequence (but mediating between social capital and social solidarity), should be examined. Finally, the connection between interpersonal trust and generalized trust needs to be explored – does one lead to another, or can they be conceived as indicators of a general notion, trust? These design requirements would help resolve some key issues concerning the social nature of trust in the social capital theory.

References and further reading

Bian, Yanjie (1997) 'Bringing Strong Ties Back In: Indirect Connection, Bridges, and Job

Search in China', *American Sociological Review*, 62(3), June: 366–85.

Bourdieu, Pierre (1983/1986) 'The Forms of Capital', in J. G. Richardson (ed.), *Handbook of Theory and Research for the Sociology of Education*, Westport, CT: Greenwood Press, pp. 241–58.

Burt, Ronald S. (1992) *Structural Holes: The Social Structure of Competition*, Cambridge, MA: Harvard University Press.

—— (2000) 'The Network Structure of Social Capital', in R. I. Sutton and B. M. Staw (eds), *Research in Organizational Behavior*, Greenwich, CT: JAI Press, pp. 345–423.

—— (2001) 'Structural Holes Versus Network Closure as Social Capital', in N. Lin, K. Cook and R. S. Burt (eds), *Social Capital: Theory and Research*, Hawthorn, NY: Aldine de Gruyter.

Coleman, James S. (1990) *Foundations of Social Theory*, Cambridge, MA: Harvard University Press.

Erickson, Bonnie H. (2001) 'Goods Networks and Good Jobs: The Value of Social Capital to Employers and Employees', in N. Lin, K. Cook and R. S. Burt (eds), *Social Capital: Theory and Research*, Hawthorn, NY: Aldine de Gruyter, pp. 127–58.

Flap, Henk D. (1991) 'Social Capital in the Reproduction of Inequality', *Comparative Sociology of Family, Health and Education*, 20: 6179–202.

Granovetter, Mark (1973) 'The Strength of Weak Ties', *American Journal of Sociology*, 78: 1360–80.

Homans, George C. (1950) *The Human Group*, New York: Harcourt, Brace.

Lazarsfeld, Paul F. and Merton, Robert K. (1954) 'Friendship as Social Process: A Substantive and Methodological Analysis', in Paul F. Lazarsfeld, *The Varied Sociology of Paul F. Lazarsfeld*, edited by P. L. Kendall, New York: Columbia University Press, pp. 298–348.

Lin, Nan (1982) 'Social Resources and Instrumental Action', in P. V. Marsden and N. Lin (eds), *Social Structure and Network Analysis*, Beverly Hills, CA: Sage, pp. 131–45.

—— (1999) 'Social Networks and Status Attainment', *Annual Review of Sociology*, 25: 467–87.

—— (2001a) 'Building a Network Theory of Social Capital', in N. Lin, K. Cook and R. S. Burt (eds), *Social Capital: Theory and Research*, Hawthorn, NY: Aldine de Gruyter.

—— (2001b) *Social Capital: A Theory of Structure and Action*, London and New York: Cambridge University Press.

Lin, Nan, Cook, Karen and Burt, Ronald S. (eds) (2001) *Social Capital: Theory and Research*, Hawthorn, NY: Aldine de Gruyter.

Luhmann, Niklas (1988) 'Familiarity, Confidence, Trust: Problems and Alternatives', in D. Gambetta (ed.), *Trust: Making and Breaking Cooperative Relations*, New York: Blackwell, pp. 94–107.

Marsden, Peter V. and Gorman, Elizabeth H. (2001) 'Social Networks, Job Changes, and Recruitment', in I. Berg and A. L. Kalleberg (eds), *Sourcebook on Labor Markets: Evolving Structures and Processes*, New York: Kluwer Academic/Plenum Press.

Misztal, Barbara A. (1996) *Trust in Modern Societies: The Search for the Bases of Social Order*, Cambridge: Polity Press.

Portes, Alejandro (1998) 'Social Capital: Its Origins and Applications in Modern Sociology', *Annual Review of Sociology*, 22: 1–24.

Putnam, Robert D. (2000) *Bowling Alone: The Collapse and Revival of American Community*, New York: Simon and Schuster.

Simmel, Georg (1978) *The Philosophy of Money*, London: Routledge.

NAN LIN

SOCIAL CONSTRUCTION OF THE ECONOMY

Social construction of the economy is a school of thought that seeks to explain the activities and institutions of the economy based on analyses of the facts of social life – social **beliefs**, daily practices, interpersonal networks, and institutional exchanges of people seeking to create an exchange goods within patterned manners. Rather than assuming motive, assigning intention or assuming a linear or teleological continuity of events, constructivists examine actions that generally are described and explained within the concepts of market-based behaviour by subjecting them to an empirical social 'lens', asking what people actually do and why. And how do people and firms form, interact and cooperate, toward what ends, and with effects and outcomes?

This school has its genesis in the groundbreaking work of Berger and Luckmann (1966). Reacting to the emphasis on deviant behaviour, individualism and chaos of modernity in the 1960s they argued the importance of discourse, shared experiences, common role constraints and other psychological factors within a web of social relations, in promoting the emergence of control mechanisms and institutions that channel action towards simplicity, shared interests, legitimacy and collective stability. Social constructivists were reacting to the formalism, abstraction and rationalist teleology prevalent in the mainstream academe during the 1980s and 1990s. To address these deficiencies, they elevated social motivations, agency, practices and institutions to an equal analytical footing (with psychological) as sources of informal and formal patterned activity and organization. In essence, they reintroduced the primacy of human social agency as a force in the creation, modification and institutionalization of economic structure and change, within well-defined historical and structural constraints, without succumbing to the overdeterminism of the 'hero in history' model.

Constructivists who focus on economic activity challenged technical determinism, 'rational man' and other functionalist arguments of classical, neoclassical and 'new institutional' economists who had 'depopulated' economic activities. Recognizing that disorder and destruction are endemic to economic activities, the constructivists proposed that changing social understandings and constellations of interpersonal relationships affect economic actions, altering the material reality in intentional and unintended manners. Such changes are subsequently embedded as the practices of these actors are institutionalized within and among firms, sectors and other institutional components of the economic environment. Constructivists all recognize that social and **economic actions** and developments are path-dependent. They recognize that active human agents deliberately make decisions based on their background, understandings of the array of opportunities and constraints

available within the economy, and that previous path decisions re-weigh the array and availability of future decision-making and strategic opportunities in a sequential manner. As a result, they offer historically grounded and comparative analyses, regardless of their particular subject of analysis, without reliance on technical, psychological and economic teleology.

There are two major approaches within this school. The first approach emerged in Europe (especially among British business analysts) and it sought to understand issues of 'regime change' within firms and industries. Nelson and Winter (1977), and Dosi (1982) argued that managers' cognition is central to changing institutional forms and relations within the corporate economy. They noted that corporate managers, within firms and among firms of an industry, had similar training and experience in specialized and interdependent trade associations, and had risen through similar career paths in corporations, resulting in similar perceptions and 'competencies' (skill sets and operational models). Regime changes occur when managers perceive changes of opportunity and/or constraint within their economic environment and respond by drawing upon their experiences and knowledge, and the perceived competencies and capacities (opportunities and constraints) available within their organizational structure(s) based on its composition, technology and culture. These competencies limit the array of options that a firm may pursue because firm members conceptualize, operationalize and reproduce their understandings in both ideological and institutional forms. Such codification of practice, culture and structure is roughly analogous to and anticipates what US economic sociologists would describe as **embeddedness**. Since managers can restructure and reposition their firms within the boundaries of such competencies, they can only redirect firms by creating what they call a new (or altered) 'trajectory'. Regime change advocates contend that firms seeking to change trajectories rarely hire new personnel to help change management thinking, restructure competencies or redirect trajectories, due to the resistance and resilience of the firm's existing corporate culture. Since the principal catalysts to change are managers reacting to the changing environment, and there is incremental modification in the practices and structure of firms and industries within the limits of previous knowledge, behaviour and structuration, it is fair to describe this approach as 'environmental' in impetus and as incremental or 'evolutionary' in form.

The 'regime change' approach has been widely applied to explain the changing forms of European and Asian businesses by a subsequent generation of British scholars, often ascribing efficiency as the goal of managers. Two other groups drew upon this framework but also emphasized the pursuit of socially constructed concepts of efficiency as motivating factors. Many historians of technology (cf. Hughes 1983; Bijker *et al.* 1987) utilized the framework of this approach to explain how inventors and early investors operating within specific economic environments locked in specific forms of technology. However, they strongly embraced a notion of social construction that emphasized increased technical efficiency as an almost causal factor, and thus their approach generally was much more mechanistic and essentialized an interdependent dynamic of economic and technical determinism. On the other hand, Fligstein extended the approach to US corporate culture (1990) and globally (2001), offering a nuanced theory of how managers sharing a common culture actively and through social networks transformed their corporation and sectors in a response to, and in an attempt to change state, political and legal conditions, all in pursuit of stability and control. He emphasizes the pursuit and the changing definitions of socially constructed and historically specific 'efficiency' as important factors in improved performance, limited effectiveness, corporate missteps, and market creation constitutes an important advancement for this approach.

The second major approach – the sociology of economic life – attempts to offer a more encompassing explanation of economic activity. Arguing that market and economic activity is neither natural nor 'self-regulating', advocates attempt to de-obfuscate the 'visible hand' of managers and the 'invisible hand' of markets. To render a more nuanced and encompassing theory of economic institutions and technical change, they have augmented the constructionist framework with social network theories, and more elaborate versions of path-dependence borrowed from economists.

Throughout the 1970s and 1980s, many analysts detailed the influence of identifiable social networks in areas such as employment, corporate-bank interlocks, underlying capital flow patterns, etc. Granovetter (1985) advanced this insight by wedding it with insights from social constructionism to critique the rationalist assumptions and the over-determinism of mainstream market economists, and their tendencies to over- or undersocialize human actors. He emphasized that an actor's personal understandings and their social networks arise from their specific social and historical contexts. Thus social networks are both a source of one's understandings, and resource when seeking the cooperation of like-minded individuals and/or those with similar vested interests. Networks also embody and help maintain familiarity and trust – crucial factors when seeking change within an instable and competitive environment.

Moving beyond an explanation of firms, regimes, and market trajectories, he argued that economic activities, practices and structures at all levels are permeated by socially networked relations arising from and predicated upon friendships, clubs, ethic, religious, fraternal, recreational, alumni and associational groups. Regardless of the strength, depth or breadth of such ties, social networks are essential to embedding or institutionalizing specific economic relationships, practices and institutional forms. Since social networks permeate all levels of economic organizations, they can be mobilized in multiple ways and several different levels to pursue and achieve tactical and/or technical ends. Networked individuals and organizations become increasingly interdependent and seek more permanent relationships, institutionalized practices and better control and stability in their exchanges among themselves and with other agencies and groups. These networks become institutionally embedded by the active pursuit of an agenda of control and domination by its participants, seeking both change in the external economic environment and to permanent bureaucratic forms to promote and monitor compliance to, and further enhancement of, such changes. Achieving tactical successes in pursuit of common interests and goals, they seek to shape and standardize economic transactions, and hierarchies within their own institutions. They deliberately and inadvertently transform market externalities (trade associations, the state, legal and property rights, labour, and educational institutions) by locking in institutional forms and practices that are supportive of the continuation of their specific histories, common goals and embedded relationships in specific institutional forms. Once in place, power and control processes are legitimized and promoted as 'normal', efficient, inevitable and/ or natural, rather than actively constructed.

The third component in this approach involves recognizing the influence of path-dependence on both the processes of embedding and the subsequent operations and structures of economic institutions. Path-dependent economists (David 1986; Arthur 1989) have demonstrated the origin, selection and lock-in of temporally efficient and inefficient technical and economic relationships in the emergence of several different commodities. Granovetter and others recognized that social networks and embedded relationships are actively created at specific historical points based on particular constellations of information and familiarity, limited and shared understandings, and a limited array of historically specific and sequential conditions. Path dependency allows constructivists to provide both greater specificity in their analysis and to avoid assumptions about functional prerequisites. It creates a framework that could identify perceived imperatives if they emerged but which did not assume their form, origin or influence.

The principal benefit of the integration of a continuing and sequential path dependency theory into the social constructionist and social network approach is that it can explain; what did and didn't happen (and could have), why some outcomes were encouraged and others constrained, how that happened, and with what intended and unintended effects in the immediate and longer historical context. It is constantly attentive to and capable of identifying the presence of chance, habit, accident, unintended outcomes and other irrationalities as both part of the process and the outcomes of economic life. And it has the capacity to identify why, and the extent to which, situational and institutional flexibility exists at a given historical juncture. It also permits analysts to recognize that economic relations and institutions are much more situational and fluid than has been conventionally believed. As such, it can identify and explain the shifting boundaries of firms, markets, industries and sectors, changing ownership, pricing regimes, technical preferences, and commodity form and emphases. By allowing for the existence of multiple and situational rationalities, the approach allows us to explain the uneven and different development of similar industries and commodity forms, in different settings and nations (Dobbin 1994). While acknowledging that actors and institutions seek stability, efficiency and profit (as they understand it), this approach is also capable of identifying when, how and why they also introduced chaos, technical inefficiencies (sometimes lasting decades), and economic disasters (sometimes amidst profit and stability) at various levels of economic activity.

References and further reading

Arthur, W. Brian (1989) 'Competing Technologies, Increasing Returns, and Lock-in by Historical Events', *The Economics Journal*, 99: 116–31.

Berger, Peter and Luckman, Thomas (1966) *The Social Construction of Reality: A Treatise in the Sociology of Knowledge*, New York: Anchor Books.

Bijker, Wiebe E., Hughes, Thomas P. and Pinch, Trevor J. (1987) *The Social Construction of Technological Systems: New Directions in the Sociology and History of Technology*, Cambridge, MA: MIT Press,

David, Paul (1986) 'Understanding the Economics of QWERTY; The Necessity of History', in W. N. Parker (ed.), *Economic History and the Modern Economist*, Oxford: Blackwell, pp. 30–45.

Dobbin, Frank (1994) *Forging Industrial Policy: The United States, Britain and France in the Railway Age*, Cambridge: Cambridge University Press.

Dosi, Giovanni (1982) 'Technological Paradigms and Technological Trajectories', *Research Policy*, 11: 147–62.

Fligstein, Neil (1990) *The Transformation of Corporate Control*, Cambridge, MA: Harvard University Press.

—— (2001) *The Architecture of Markets: An Economic Sociology of Twenty-First-Century Capitalist Societies*, Princeton, NJ: Princeton University Press.

Granovetter, Mark (1985) 'Economic Action and Social Structure: The Problem of Embeddedness', *American Journal of Sociology*, 91: 481–510.

Hughes, Thomas (1983) *Networks of Power: Electrification in Western Society 1880–1930*, Baltimore, MD: Johns Hopkins University Press.

Nelson, Richard and Winter, Sidney (1977) 'In Search of a Useful Theory of Innovation', *Research Policy*, 6: 36–76.

PATRICK MCGUIRE
STEVEN REVARD

SOCIAL EMBEDDEDNESS

See: embeddedness

SOCIAL MECHANISMS

A basic characteristic of all explanations is that they provide plausible accounts for why events happen, why something changes over time, or why different states or events are related to one another. Three main types of explanations can be identified in the literature:

1. Covering-law explanations.
2. Statistical explanations.
3. Mechanism explanations.

These different types of explanations differ in terms of the types of answers they consider appropriate for answering explanatory why-questions.

According to the covering-law model (e.g. Hempel 1965), a satisfactory explanation is arrived at by subsuming the event to be explained under a general law. That is, we explain the event by pointing to one or several relevant laws that make the event necessary or probable.

Statistical explanations are the norm in much of contemporary sociological research. In this tradition, an explanation is considered to be appropriate if it identifies factors that seem to make a difference for the outcome or the probability of the event one seeks to explain. While covering-law explanations are theory-based in the sense that they use established theories or law-like relationships to explain specific events through a deductive argument, statistical explanations are inductively oriented and do not necessarily require any well-specified theories (see e.g. Salmon 1971).

The core idea behind the mechanism approach is that one explains not by evoking universal laws, nor by identifying statistically relevant factors, but by specifying the mechanisms that show *how* phenomena are brought about. Philosophers and social scientists have defined the mechanism concept in numerous different ways (e.g. Bhaskar 1978; Elster 1999; Hedström and Swedberg 1998). Despite these differences, important common denominators exist. Following the lead of Machamer *et al.* (2000), mechanisms can be said to consist of *entities* (with their properties) and the *activities* that these entities engage in, either by themselves or in concert with other entities. These activities bring about change, and the type of change brought about depends upon the properties of the entities and the way in which the entities are organized spatially and temporally. A *social mechanism* is a constellation of entities and activities that are organized in such a way that a particular type of social outcome regularly is brought about. We explain an observed social phenomenon by referring to the social mechanism by which such phenomena are regularly brought about.

Most sociological theories have a nested structure, i.e. they refer to mechanisms nested within other mechanisms. In many theories individual actions are the core activities that bring about the social or macro-level phenomena that the theory seeks to explain. The way in which the actors are temporally and spatially organized defines the structure of interaction, and this is likely to influence the outcomes brought about. Nested within these 'structural' mechanisms are mechanisms that explain the actions of individual actors. Also in this case the mechanism can be described in terms of its entities (and their properties) and the way in which the entities are spatially and temporally organized. The core entities are different, however, and now refer to entities such as the **beliefs**, interests and opportunities of the actors, but the explanatory logic is the same: one explains an observed phenomenon, in this case an individual action, by referring to the mechanism (e.g. the constellation of beliefs, interests and opportunities) by which such actions are regularly brought about.

Why, then, is it important to specify the social mechanisms that are supposed to have generated observed outcomes? From the perspective of sociological theory, one important reason for insisting on a detailed specification of mechanisms is that the removal of 'black boxes' tends to produce more precise and intelligible explanations. Another important reason is that a focus on mechanisms tends to reduce theoretical fragmentation. For example, there may be numerous different theories (of markets, fashions, or whatnot), that are all based on the same set of mechanisms of action and interaction. Focusing on the mechanisms as such avoids unnecessary proliferation of theoretical concepts and may help in bringing out structural similarities between seemingly disparate processes. Finally, it is the knowledge about the social mechanism as such, i.e. that the constellation of entities and activities referred to in the explanation can be expected to regularly bring about the type of outcome one seeks to explain, that provides a reason for believing that there indeed is a genuine causal relationship between a proposed cause and its effect, and not simply a correlation.

References and further reading

Bhaskar, R. (1978) *A Realist Theory of Science*, Hassocks: Harvester Press.

Elster, J. (1999) *Alchemies of the Mind: Rationality and the Emotions*, Cambridge: Cambridge University Press.

Hedström, P. and Swedberg, R. (1998) 'Social Mechanisms: An Introductory Essay', in P. Hedström and R. Swedberg (eds), *Social Mechanisms: An Analytical Approach to Social Theory*, Cambridge: Cambridge University Press, pp. 1–31.

Hempel, C. G. (1965) *Aspects of Scientific Explanation*, New York: Free Press.

Machamer, P., Darden, L. and Craver, C. F. (2000) 'Thinking About Mechanisms', *Philosophy of Science*, 67: 1–25.

Salmon, W. C. (1971) *Statistical Explanation and Statistical Relevance*, Pittsburgh: University of Pittsburgh Press.

PETER HEDSTRÖM

SOCIAL RATIONALITY

Rational choice approaches have had an important impact on economic sociology. Among these approaches, 'social rationality' is gaining ground. It covers a number of approaches within sociology and other social sciences which share the assumptions that individuals actively and more or less intelligently pursue goals under constraints *and* that their individual rationality (i.e. the goals they pursue and the way they pursue them) is heavily influenced by social (including structural and cultural) conditions.

Traditionally, rational choice approaches have been based on the assumption that individuals are 'naturally' rational (in the sense that they by nature base their actions on calculating what course of action best serves their self-interest). Because human beings frequently don't conform to this assumption, rational choice approaches were augmented with research on 'biases' and 'anomalies'. The 'social' in these approaches is separated from rationality and is seen as the process and product of interaction among selfish individuals (involved in information transfer, coordination, conflict, negotiation, contracting and collective action). Individuals maximize their individual outcomes but this can leave the joint outcome less than it could be. The function of institutions is to get collective outcomes closer to a social optimality (in which the joint outcome is optimized).

Important as it was, this development was not satisfactory from a sociological point of view because it neglected three important aspects. First, it is likely that during the course of human evolution, rationality and social aspects co-evolved (albeit not perfectly hand-in-glove). Thus individual rationality cannot be generally juxtaposed with 'the social'. Second, social influences can affect individual rationality positively and negatively, and they can affect the criteria for rationality. Thus, contrary to the 'natural rationality' assumption, there are likely to be social arrangements directed at enhancing individual rationality, in part by prompting situationally different 'logics of action' or frames. Third, these arrangements are likely to fail to some degree in certain areas (such as conflict of interest situations and **discrimination**). Thus, it is likely that societies create social arrangements that compensate for important lapses in individual rationality. All three points emphasize that rationality and the social are interwoven rather than juxtaposed and for this reason, the variety of approaches dealing with one or more of these aspects can be grouped under the heading of 'social rationality'.

Social environments and fundamental uncertainty

Approaches of 'natural' rationality have made great strides by paying close attention to the various effects of **asymmetric information** and the ensuing problems of opportunism (see **rational choice theory**). Yet they neglect the fact that human rationality itself must have evolved to deal with opportunism and other problems arising from interaction. Thus, a useful way to start analysing rationality is to realize that it evolved in a context that was characterized by at least two important features: the environment was social and wrought with fundamental uncertainties (see Gigerenzer and Selten 2001). Under these conditions, one's own actions in the context of others, helplessness, cooperation and competition all raised questions about things that are essential to adaptive behaviour: meaning, causality, **beliefs**, intentions, trustworthiness, planning, discrimination and the like. Thus, given our ability to learn and to cognitively integrate different domains (handle symbols, create meaning), faculties to deal with problems of complexity, turbulence and uncertainty must have evolved with a strong social component, especially related to groups. A minimal list of these capabilities contains the openness to social influence (on emotions and goal-states, categorization and beliefs); the ability to feel, think and act differently as individual and as member of a group; the ability to compare oneself with others; the ability to attach oneself to others; and the underlying motivational and cognitive processes of flexible mind-sets (framing), novelty-seeking, self-categorization (identity formation), discrimination and stereotyping, self-command, the use of heuristics, and the use of groups to enhance memory. For these aspects, insights from traditional sociology become highly relevant again, albeit in a way that makes them fit into a context of goal-directed behaviour (see Forgas *et al.* 2001).

Group processes and framing

Social rationality approaches have profound consequences for what is being studied in economic sociology. Whereas 'natural rationality' approaches deal mainly with functional (i.e. task and outcome) interdependencies and externalities, social rationality approaches require additional attention to cognitive and structural interdependencies. Furthermore, since the latter two affect goals and modes of goal pursuit, they are also vital for the question under what conditions people approximate acting the way presumed in economics. Two of the most important tools for studying these interdependencies, also in economic sociology, are group processes and a focus on different frames (or mind-sets or logics of action or orientations) as well as the conditions under which they obtain (see Lindenberg 2001).

Framing

People are seemingly able to define situations in fundamentally different ways, as belonging to a certain type of goal pursuit. For example, a situation can be defined as an opportunity for gain. In that case, specific alternatives are perceived that relate to opportunities for gain, specific knowledge, schemas, scripts and rules are made cognitively more accessible while others are inhibited. A situation framed in terms of gain generates very different kinds of decision processes and criteria than a situation framed in terms of the goal 'to act appropriately', a goal that enhances other-regard, group identity and normative considerations. People pursue goals more or less intelligently in both cases, but the criteria for what is rational differ greatly. Research in or relevant to economic sociology increasingly focuses on the fact that, ironically, the creation of wealth and collectively generated value can only be produced by a partial suspension of gain-oriented behaviour on the individual level. The more complex the economy, the more this seems to hold, because complex economies seem to require much intelligent effort, intrinsic motivation, teamwork and tacit knowledge, all of which cannot be contractually enforced. Unbridled gain-oriented behaviour at the individual level ruins the cooperative relationships that are necessary for the creation of wealth. In the 'natural rationality' approach of economics, there is no room for the partial suspension of gain-oriented behaviour nor theory about the conditions (cultural, structural and social) that would bring it about and maintain it. Research in sociology focuses on ways in which this is brought about in various contexts, including the mixture of 'arm's-length ties' and 'embedded ties' between firms (Uzzi 1997) and a dynamic balance between gain and normative frames combined with relational signals between contracting partners (Mühlau and Lindenberg

619

2003). Tied to these issues are questions concerning the impact of specific ties and networks, culture (common understandings and matching frames), problems of myopic opportunism (which is not removed by interest alignment), and the generation of genuine **trust** (see DiMaggio 1994; Guillén et al. 2003).

Group processes

Fundamental uncertainty renders the interface of individual goal pursuit and group processes a vital issue, also in economic transactions. Especially the openness to social influence and the importance of comparison with others for determining one's own identity, opportunities and legitimacy, as well as the social construction of expectations, the social impact on the organization of emotions, and the impact of gender have played an important role in economic sociology. Examples are theories that link informal and formal institutions; theories of institution as devices for cognitive coordination; theories of professions; theories of markets. White (2002) is a prime example of taking social rationality seriously by linking goal-oriented behaviour, framing effects, reference group processes, identity formation, and network effects in order to explain the functioning of markets.

References and further reading

DiMaggio, P. (1994) 'Culture and economy', in N. J. Smelser and R. Swedberg (eds), *The Handbook of Economic Sociology*, Princeton, NJ: Princeton University Press, pp. 27–57.

Forgas, J. P., Williams, K. D. and Wheeler, L. (eds) (2001) *The Social Mind. Cognitive and Motivational Aspects of Interpersonal Behaviour*, Cambridge: Cambridge University Press

Gigerenzer, G. and Selten, R. (eds.) (2001) *Bounded Rationality: The Adaptive Toolbox*, Cambridge, MA.: MIT Press

Guillén, M., Collins, R., England, P. and Meyer, M. (eds) (2002) *The New Economic Sociology*, New York: Russell Sage Foundation.

Lindenberg, S. (2001) 'Social Rationality versus Rational Egoism', in J. Turner (ed.), *Handbook of Sociological Theory*, New York: Kluwer Academic/Plenum, pp. 635–68.

Mühlau, P. and Lindenberg, S. (2003) 'Efficiency Wages: Signals or Incentives? An Empirical Study of the Relationship between Wage and Commitment', *Journal of Management and Governance*, 7: 385–400.

Uzzi, B. (1997) 'Social Structure and Competition in Interfirm Networks: The Paradox of Embeddedness', *Administrative Science Quarterly*, 42(1): 35–67.

White, H. C. (2002) *Markets from Networks*, Princeton, NJ: Princeton University Press.

SIEGWART LINDENBERG

SOCIAL RESPONSIBILITY OF FIRMS

The notion 'social responsibility of firms' or 'corporate social responsibility' describes normative requirements for businesses in regard to fair business practices and commitments to improve societal problems. In a broader sense this includes ethical as well as economic and legal responsibilities (Carroll and Buchholtz 1999). In a more narrow application, it can be defined as the voluntary integration of social and environmental concerns in business practices and an 'obligation to constitute groups in society other than stockholders and beyond that prescribed by law or union contract' (Jones 1980: 59–60).

Firms can help to solve a wide range of societal problems towards more intra- and intergenerational justice (for current and future generations). 'Just' business practices can be related to issues such as fraud and corporate misconduct, **corruption**, financial misrepresentation, child labour, dangerous practices in agri-businesses and biotechnologies as well as ecological issues.

Criticism from the 'right' and the 'left' in the 1970s

In a 1970 *New York Times* article Chicago economist Milton Friedman (1970) argued that the only 'social responsibility of business is to increase its profits'. He was reacting to public discussions with respect to moral obligations of firms beyond the principle of profit maximization. Friedman suggests that (pure) business practices are themselves positive moral contributions to society. Firms and the market system – as crucial mechanisms which coordinate business activities – create economic wealth for modern societies through employment and by lowering consumer prices. Asserting social responsibility of businesses (beyond profit maximization), Friedman argues, undermines the achievement of modern societies (especially in regard to the realization of freedom). The maximization of profits through businesses is not merely a possibility or a necessity; it is a moral obligation of firms.

Social responsibility of businesses, however, has not merely been criticized by the 'right'. Left-wing critics in the 1970s have questioned the **legitimacy** of social commitment of businesses due to a lack of a genuine democratic basis. Since business activities are not the result of a democratic decision-making process but rather determined through the (financial) power of firms, it is suggested that established political structures should be followed. Just as with Friedman's liberal reasoning, they fear the undermining of modern societal structures, especially the decline of a liberal and democratic society. These two lines of arguments are still present in both the academic and the public discussion on social responsibilities of firms.

Legitimacy of business practices

Nongovernmental organizations (NGOs) are professionalized voices of civil society. With respect to economic activities of firms, one of NGOs' main goals is the mobilization of the public (and consumers) to put pressure on (multinational) corporations in order to launch concrete business practices for more social justice. A telling

example of mobilization of consumer power through NGOs is the *Brent Spar* case of Royal Dutch Shell in 1995: Shell had planned to sink an old oil platform in the North Sea. It was the first time such a form of waste disposal through an oil company was taking place and it was in accordance with international laws. Greenpeace, one of the most important NGOs on ecological issues, questioned this practice and was able to mobilize wide public attention. Although legal, Shell's plans were portrayed as illegitimate. The public reacted through a consumer boycott of Shell stations all over Europe (most notably in Holland and Germany). In the end, Shell agreed not to sink the *Brent Spar* or any other oil platforms. The company learned that moral sensitivity of the public mattered for business practices. Actions undertaken by NGOs have made firms increasingly accountable for their economic activities beyond legal concerns. One lesson is that business practices do not take place in a vacuum: they are embedded in societal contexts which include factors other than that of financial gain (see **embeddedness**).

From shareholder value to stakeholder management

In the debate on business ethics it is now widely accepted that businesses are facing claims by actors others than shareholders. This paradigmatic change is known as a shift from a shareholder value approach to a **stakeholder** one (developed by Freeman 1984). The business of business is not merely business (Friedman's position). It is, rather, to strike a balance between different claims of various stakeholder groups. Neglecting these stakes – both internal and external – would make the social responsibility of firms impossible and put any potential economic success at stake.

Why should firms take stakeholder interests into account? There are two lines of arguments for demanding socially responsible behaviour of firms: strategic and normative. From the strategic perspective it is argued that adequate social behaviour of businesses has a bottom line payoff. In the normative context, a critical moral standpoint is emphasized.

Strategic perspective

The increasing societal pressure towards just business practices causes economic costs for firms. Adequate reactions due to economic reasons are hence required. Consequently, elements of risk management to avoid 'negative attention' by stakeholder groups have been integrated in traditional management systems. In this sense the social responsibility of firms is a certain type of 'smart management' to prevent harming the corporate image and to improve the firm's **reputation**. In this way, the social responsibility of firms is related to the power of certain stakeholders and limited to the influence of stakeholders. Businesses take ethical issues into account if – and only if – 'they pay'.

With respect to the important field of internal stakeholder relations, the employees, there has been an increasing interest in coordinating organizations through values. While economic organization theories such as the **transaction costs economics**, traditionally emphasize the relevance of strict rules and incentive mechanisms ('hard facts'), it is argued that management by values such as **trust**, **fairness** and honesty ('soft facts') can be superior since they reduce transaction costs. Soft facts do not need to be supported by control mechanisms and extrinsic motivations which produce costs. They can, however, become practices through intrinsic motivations. Moreover, it has been demonstrated that hard facts can crowd out intrinsic motivations as a result of a negative atmosphere of transactions within the organization (Ghoshal and Moran 1996). The coordination through strict rules and the coordi-

nation through soft factors are also known as the compliance versus integrity approach (Paine 1994).

The creation of soft values in corporations, however, is a difficult endeavour. Soft values cannot simply be planned and implemented in organizational structures as they are strongly grounded on the history and culture of corporations. However, they can and they need to be supported by institutional arrangements. They are not solely reflected in the individual will of the members of the organization (see **corporate governance**). Institutional structures that are sensitive enough to create a valuable culture of trust, fairness and honesty are therefore required. It is important to understand that they have to be cultivated and seen as ontological values that cannot be reformulated in terms of utilities and costs. Nevertheless, seeing them as wholly original categories can lead to positive economic consequences (Wieland 2001).

Normative perspective

From a normative point of view it is argued that the negative external effects of business practices – social as well as ecological (world) problems – need to be regulated. Due to incomplete political regulations it is argued that firms have the moral obligation to avoid negative external effects of their practices. This concerns a direction of ideas that points toward intra- as well as intergenerational justice (social and ecological aspects). Ethical orientations for just business practices are formulated from various concepts of morality. The most prominent theories in business ethics are contractual, Kantian and discourse ethical approaches (see an introduction in Beauchamp and Bowie 2004).

In contrast to strategic approaches, ethical theories typically emphasize how businesses *ought* to act (moral imperatives) rather than taking into account how businesses actually do act. Ethical theories mainly develop – to borrow a Kantian term – 'categorical' rather than 'hypothetical imperatives' (Kant 1785/1956: 43). While the latter considers the economic conditions and develops possible moral practices against the background of a given economic system, the first purposefully neglects empirical circumstances. In other words, normative positions work out 'regulative ideas' of firms as (corporate) citizens rather than regarding them as pure economic actors within the economic system (Ulrich 2002).

The strengths of such a strict ethical perspective can be seen in its critical perspective. It enables a twofold criticism on the strategic stakeholder approaches: First, while the strategic stakeholder approaches on social responsibility are limited to the influence of stakeholders, the normative stakeholder approach underlines the rights of individuals or groups in a non-consequential manner. Second, an ethical perspective can enable a more general criticism of business activities since it is possible to question the ends – and not merely the means – of business practices. These two criticisms are relevant from a theoretical as well as from a practical point of view. From a theoretical perspective, they allow to conceptualize the embeddedness of firms in a broader societal context (and not merely within the economic system) and honour contributions of businesses towards a 'good society'. The normative position may therefore question core aspects of business practices. These include the ethical quality of products and services, the **production** process (including workplace issues) and the sales process. In a practical sense these normative claims may lead to an ontological basis of corporate values as a fundamental of business activities. Such corporate values may, for example, result in an explicitly formulated corporate philosophy and other institutional arrangements for just businesses practices.

Conclusion

Firms are increasingly at the centre of interest of a critical public that necessitates legitimate business practices. Strategic and normative perspectives on the relation between businesses and society have to be seen as two different approaches to social responsibility of firms. While the strategic stakeholder management seems to be more realistic since it is argued within the economic paradigm, a lack of ethical reflections within this approach has been illustrated. Conversely, normative stakeholder management has its merits in the critical reflection of the status quo. This, however, tends to lead to a position that cannot realistically be achieved. We suggest understanding these two approaches as bifocal perspectives that are both complementary and irreconcilable. They represent a tension in academic and public discourses on the social responsibility of firms. This tension can be fruitful as it has already lead to innovative measures. Different forms of ethic management systems and forms of **corporate governance** within organizations have arisen. Other examples are the 'Federal Sentencing Guidelines for Organizations' (an incentive for corporations to prevent criminal activities by their employees), social standards such as the Social Accountability 8000 or AccountAbility 1000, and the Global Compact initiative by the UN.

References and further reading

Beauchamp, Tom L. and Bowie, Norman E. (2004) *Ethical Theory and Business*, New York: Pearson Education.

Bowie, Norman E. (ed.) (2002) *The Blackwell Guide to Business Ethics*, Malden, MA: Blackwell.

Carroll, Archie B. and Buchholtz, Ann K. (1999) *Business and Society: Ethics and Stakeholder Management*, Cincinnati, OH: Southwestern Publishing.

Donaldson, Thomas and Dunfee, Thomas W. (1999) *Ties that Bind: A Social Contracts*

Approach to Business Ethics, Boston: Harvard Business School Press.

Freeman, R. Edward (1984) *Strategic Management: A Stakeholder Approach*, Marshfield, MA: Pitman Publishing.

Friedman, Milton (1970) 'The Social Responsibility of Business is to Increase its Profits', *New York Times Magazine*, 13 September: 32–3, 122–6.

Ghoshal, Sumantra and Moran, Peter (1996) 'Bad Practice. A Critique of the Transaction Cost Theory', *Academy of Management Review*, 21(1): 13–47.

Jones, Thomas M. (1980) 'Corporate Social Responsibility Revisited, Redefined', *California Management Review*, 22(3): 59–67.

Kant, Immanuel (1785/1956) *Grundlegung zur Metaphysik der Sitten. Werke in zwölf Bänden, Band 7*, Hamburg: Felix Meiner.

Koslowski, Peter (ed.) (2000) *Contemporary Economic Ethics and Business Ethics*, Berlin and New York: Springer.

Paine, L. S. (1994) 'Managing for Organizational Integrity', *Harvard Business Review*, 72(2): 106–17.

Ulrich, Peter (2002) 'Ethics and Economics', in Laszlo Zsolnai (ed.), *Ethics in the Economy. Handbook of Business Ethics*, Bern: Peter Lang, pp. 9–37.

Wieland, Josef (2001) 'The Ethics of Governance', *Business Ethics Quarterly*, 11(1): 73–87.

Zsolnai, Laszlo (ed.) (2002) *Ethics in the Economy: Handbook of Business Ethics*, Oxford, Berne and Berlin: Peter Lang Publishers.

THOMAS BESCHORNER

SOCIAL RIGHTS

Introduction: theories of rights

Individual rights are legal devices that protect persons from interference and coercion by creating a political space into which other individuals such as representatives of the state cannot enter. The concept of rights is fundamental to the key concepts of jurisprudence: **rationality**, personality, freedom and justice. Rights are necessary to protect the freedom of rational actors to obtain their goals and satisfy their needs without undue interference from others (Hart 1955). In choice or will theories of rights, the liberty of the autonomous individual are emphasized. It is customary to distinguish between negative and positive liberty (Berlin 1958). The former refers to the absence of constraint, while the latter is identified with the work of J.-J. Rousseau and the idea of human development through self-discipline and education. Negative liberty involves freedom from interference; positive liberty is freedom to develop the self fully.

Welfare rights justify some redistribution of resources in a society, either because they are essential to the satisfaction of a need, or because a person has made a contribution to society. Any analysis of rights must involve a theory of justice, which provides legitimate grounds for how people acquire or exercise their rights. There are two contending theories. Choice theories claim that rights must favour the will of the possessor over some other party, while benefit or interest theories maintain that rights serve to promote the interests of the rights holder. Benefit theories assume that human beings share a common vulnerability and that rights exist to protect human beings (Turner 1993).

Rights are divided into four categories of paired relations (Hohfeld 1919). These are (1) a liberty or privilege to some activity for which there is no necessary corresponding duty or obligation; (2) a claim on a person or institution for which there is a corresponding duty; (3) a power to bring something about, for which there is a related liability; and (4) an immunity (for example from an obligation) for which there is a corresponding disability to do something. This model serves to remind us that even the most individualistic account of rights necessarily implies a set of social relations between rights-bearers and rights-addressees. A right typically implies a duty, but there are problems with this principle of correlativity. For example, we ascribe rights to human embryos and infants, but there are no corresponding duties. Animals are said to have rights, but they do not have duties.

However, the correlativity principle provides an important criticism of human rights, because they do not appear to entail any duties. Conservative critics of 'rights talk' have defended the moral priority of duty.

Natural rights

In Roman legal theory rights were justified as natural in the sense that they are shared by human beings as rational creatures. Natural law, which derived its authority either from God or from nature, treated all men equally, but the existence of slavery showed that the natural law was imperfectly institutionalized. Natural law theory influenced the Declaration of Independence of the United States in 1776 and the Rights of Man and of Citizens of the National Assembly of France in 1791. In modern political theory, rights are regarded as social fictions rather than as facts of an ideal natural law. In accepting cultural relativism, social science has rejected the universalism of natural rights. Sociology has in particular been critical of natural law. Max **Weber** (1978: 874) thought that positive law, evolutionary thought and legal scepticism had undermined the claims of natural law. Contemporary theories, which focus on recognition and difference rather than equality and universalism, have followed G. W. F. Hegel, who showed that recognition of the rationality and freedom of other people is the precondition of ethics (Williams 1997).

Social and economic rights

Although property rights have been fundamental to liberal society, there are important tensions between rights claims and the economy. These problems are particularly evident in employee rights, workplace democracy and whistleblowing behaviour within the company. While the civil and political rights of individuals developed from the early stages of capitalist society,

economic rights have been difficult to secure and enforce. Property rights (to buy, sell and inherit property) which were well established by John Locke in the seventeenth century are constitutive of the free enterprise system. The right to work is also fundamental to independence and survival, and failure to distinguish between the worker and the product is a defining characteristic of slavery. Adam **Smith** argued that this separation was a condition of economic liberty in which labour productivity can be effectively valued. There are inevitably conflicts of interests between these individual rights (of property owners) and social rights to safety, job security and retirement benefits. The conflict is evident in whistleblowing which from the employee's perspective is covered by freedom of speech, but is often regarded in practice as disloyalty to the company, and as a breach of contract (Werhane and Radin 2004). Individual rights, for example to freedom of religious belief, do not have direct economic implications, whereas social rights such as a right to a pension typically have important economic consequences. Critics argue that rights are meaningless without appropriate social and economic supports, because they are not justiciable. Justiciability obtains when there are appropriate judicial remedies available to address violations of rights provisions. For example, Article 14 of the Universal Declaration that recognizes paid holidays as a basic human right has been frequently ridiculed on the grounds that it cannot be exercised or enforced. Universal acceptance of social and economic rights has been modest by comparison with civil and political rights.

Historically there has therefore been a tension between social and human rights. Social rights are entitlements that are enjoyed by the members of a political community or nation-state; social rights are enforceable by the state. **Social rights** are institutionalized in citizenship. By contrast, human rights are the rights (essentially claims) that are enjoyed by individuals by virtue of being human. However, the individualistic framework of the International Covenant of Civil and Political Rights (ICCPR) has been progressively supplemented and expanded by the International Covenant on Economic, Social and Cultural Rights (ICESCR) (Woodiwiss 2003). The **globalization** of rights can serve to demonstrate that human rights are not irredeemably individualistic, and there is no inevitable contradiction between individual and social rights. These developments are important because they also suggest a possible reconciliation between the individualistic western tradition and Confucian systems of rights.

References and further reading

Berlin, I. (1958) *Two Concepts of Liberty*, Oxford: Clarendon Press.

Hart, H. A. L. (1955) 'Are There Any Natural Rights?' *Philosophical Review*, 64: 175–91.

Hohfeld, W. N. (1919) *Fundamental Legal Conceptions*, New Haven, CT: Yale University Press.

Turner, B. S. (1993) 'Outline of a General Theory of Human Rights', *Sociology*, 28(3): 489–512.

Weber, M. (1978) *Economy and Society*, two volumes, Berkeley, CA: University of California Press.

Werhane, P. H. and Radin, T. J. (with Bowie, N. E.) (eds) (2004) *Employment and Employee Rights*, Oxford: Blackwell.

Williams, R. R. (1997) *Hegel's Ethics of Recognition*, Berkeley, CA: University of California Press.

Woodiwiss, A. (2003) *Making Human Rights Work Globally*, London: Glasshouse Press.

BRYAN TURNER

SOCIAL SECURITY

Social security refers to any system of compulsory and legislated social insurance programmes or pensions, meant to support the welfare of the citizens in a nation. States throughout the world provide social security programmes to support the needs of their citizens. These programmes usually include insurance to protect against old age, sickness and maternity, work injury and unemployment. In addition, many countries provide family allowances to support families with children and survivors' insurance. These programmes may form the basis of the 'welfare state,' although welfare states include a variety of other social assistance programmes. Social security systems emerged at least in part in response to worker mobilization demanding protections from the state. In Europe, labour movements developed alliances with leading political parties, or served as the impetus for paternalistic states to develop social security systems. Working-class mobilization has remained an important factor in maintaining and expanding social security programmes in most nations.

In the United States, social security is composed of a system of old age and disability pensions and unemployment insurance for workers, enacted by the 1935 Social Security Act. The Social Security Act also created Aid to Dependent Children (ADC), which later became Aid to Families with Dependent Children (AFDC) and more recently Transitional Aid to Needy Families (TANF), although this programme is generally categorized as social assistance, rather than social security. The origins of modern social insurance in the United States lay in an attempt to stabilize the economy in the aftermath of the Depression. In contrast to Europe, where organized labour was critical to the creation of social insurance programmes, the push in the United States for modern social insurance primarily came from reform movements. Business leaders generally supported the passage of the Act, particularly insofar that the provisions could only be accessed by wage earners, and did not threaten waged employment. With the passage of the Social Security Act, the United States began to provide its citizens with old age insurance (OAI), old age assurance (OAA) and unemployment insurance. However, the only federally administered component of the Social Security Act was the OAI programme, which is commonly understood to be 'social security' in the United States.

OAI was set up as a contributory programme based on the taxation of workers; OAA was noncontributory and administered at the level of the state, leading to a bifurcated system. Also, with its basis in certain types of employment, the social security system initially excluded many workers, while primarily rewarding white male workers. For example, teachers, nurses, hospital employees, librarians and social workers were not covered by OAI. Indeed, of the 22 per cent of women who were gainfully employed, 52 per cent were excluded from OAI (Quadagno 1994: 157). Similarly, agricultural and domestic workers were also excluded, which limited African Americans, Latino/as and Asians from coverage in the South, Southwest and West.

The Social Security Act has been amended numerous times, including measures providing spousal and survivors' benefits, although these benefits were for many years not available to all women; widows of some workers received coverage in 1939 while divorced women gained coverage in 1965. Disabled workers received coverage starting in 1956. It was not until 1950 that regularly employed agricultural and domestic workers were covered and not until 1983 that all federal civilian employees were covered. Most self-employed workers (except lawyers, dentists, doctors and other medical professionals) received coverage in 1954, while doctors and tip workers received coverage in 1965. Benefits were increased eight times between 1950 and 1971 primarily because of political competition; in 1972 benefits were indexed to the rate of inflation.

Currently, social security covers 150 million workers, and provides benefits to more than 45 million people. While social security has certainly dramatically decreased the poverty rate for the elderly in the United States, it also tends to reinforce inequality, in its rewards for middle-class and married workers. In recent years, the United States has decreased corporate taxes and taxes on the wealthy, even as social security taxes have been increasing. Despite significant increase in social security taxes, the social security system is currently paying out more than it takes in; potential responses to this programme include additional tax increases, limiting benefits and/or privatizing the programme.

These changes are not limited to social security in the United States. In recent years, social security systems around the globe have faced significant pressures to scale back their programmes of social insurance. There have been increased demographic pressures on social security, due to, in many countries, an aging population in need of support coupled with a lower birth rate leading to fewer workers paying into the system. At the same time, **globalization**, and in particular the ascendance of neo-liberal ideologies, have emphasized limiting the role of the state in social provision. Indeed, social security systems in many developing countries have been cut back in response to structural adjustment mandated by the World Bank and the International Monetary Fund. At the same time, wealthier countries have 'restructured' social security to limit state provision.

See also: poverty; redistribution; welfare; welfare state and the economy.

References and further reading

Esping-Andersen, Gøsta (ed.) (1996) *Welfare States in Transition: National Adaptations in Global Economies*, New York: Sage.

Hicks, Alexander (1999) *Social Democracy and Welfare Capitalism: A Century of Income Security Politics*, Ithaca, NY: Cornell University Press.

Quadagno, Jill (1994) *The Color of Welfare: How Racism Undermined the War on Poverty*, New York: Oxford University Press.

Weir, Margaret, Orloff, Ann Shola and Skocpol, Theda (eds) (1988) *The Politics of Social Policy in the United States*, Princeton, NJ: Princeton University Press.

MELISSA FUGIERO
JOYA MISRA

SOCIAL STRUCTURE

See: structure

SOCIAL TIES

Human and nonhuman beings are connected with one another and the connections are called 'ties' or 'relational ties' in social network analysis. While a physical tie such as a road, river or bridge connects two nonhuman objects, a social tie connects two human actors, whether they be individuals, groups or organizations. Social ties can take on a number of forms. They include social exchange relations (actors trading favours as equals), power relations (extracting favours by the control of valued resources), authority relations (one person conforms to another's wishes because they believe in the latter's legitimate authority) and affective relations (love, friendship, loyalty). Thus social relations range from being voluntary, particularistic and informal to being coercive, universalistic and formal. At times social ties are multiplex, e.g. a boss and his subordinate play golf together or exchange sports trivia. At minimal, two actors need to be aware of one another, communicate somehow, and thus take each other into account when interacting.

At the interpersonal level, there are many examples of social ties. Kin ties connect family members, close kin and distant kin. Non-kin ties are numerous if not endless – ties of classmates, school alumna, work colleagues, neighbourhood, home town and friendship, just to name a few. Granovetter (1973) has suggested a tripartite scheme to classify interpersonal ties into relatives, friends and acquaintances. This proves to be a useful measurement about both kinds and strengths of social ties. More significant is the theoretical insight behind the classificatory scheme: 'weak ties' of infrequent interaction or low intimacy bridge information and resources between human groups; and this insight has advanced our understanding of how macro-social structures emerge out of the micro-level processes of interpersonal and inter-group interactions. Inspired by Granovetter's original work, there is now a tremendous amount of sociological knowledge about the roles of social ties in psychological well-being, labour markets, status attainment, and economic competition (Lin 1999).

Social ties between groups are more complicated, since it is difficult to know if two groups are interacting or if the members of two groups are acting as individuals. Indeed, overlapping memberships create a link between two groups without those groups consciously interacting with or even being aware of one another. Research on inter-organizational relations has struggled with this issue because boundary spanners often use their positions as representatives of their organization to advance their own interests and agendas. Also they use their own social capital (friends and contacts) to create, nurture and sustain highly instrumental inter-organizational ties, e.g. strategic alliances. Thus it is difficult to analyse inter-group ties, because interpersonal and inter-group relations often meld into one another.

The most basic form of social ties is a pair-wise relationship in which a tie links a pair of actors in a dyad. The tie is inherently a property of the pair and not that of an individual actor, making the dyad frequently the basic unit for social network analysis. Examples of the dyadic analyses include those of marriages, friendships and relational contracts. Social ties are certainly not limited to dyadic ties. The word 'network' implies three-actor triads and, more frequently, multi-actor groups (and sub-groups) in which actors are connected with one another through direct and indirect ties. In a densely knit network, a great many actors are connected directly with one another; in a sparse network, in contrast, only some actors are connected directly and others indirectly. The existence of direct and indirect ties raises the need to consider network density, network structure and other network properties. Wasserman and Faust (1994) is an excellent text for a detailed description of social ties and other network terms.

References and further reading

Granovetter, Mark (1973) 'The Strength of Weak Ties', *American Journal of Sociology*, 78: 1360–80.

Lin, Nan (1999) 'Social Networks and Status Attainment', *Annual Review of Sociology*, available at http://www.questia.com/SM.qst

Wasserman, Stanley and Faust, Katherine (1994) *Social Networks Analysis: Methods and Applications*, New York and London: Cambridge University Press.

YANJIE BIAN
JOSEPH GALASKIEWICZ

SOCIALISM

Despite the fact that since the end of the 1980s the number of socialist countries has dramatically declined, an important part of the world population (in China, Cuba, North Korea and Vietnam) lives in a socio-economic system alternative to **capitalism**. Even in those countries where socialism fell (see **transition economies**), its heritage in the form of ideological clichés, behavioural patterns and **habitus** continue to play an important role in structuring everyday life.

Socialism should be viewed from three different perspectives: as an **ideology**, as a theoretical construction, and as a practical experience in organizing social and economic life. These aspects are closely inter-connected. Socialism has been viewed as an intermediate phase in the transition from capitalism to communism. It is characterized by the dictatorship of proletariat, the state ownership of key economic assets, and the planning of economic and social processes. As J. Kornai stated in his book *The Socialist System* (1992), ideological considerations explain the dominant position of state ownership; state ownership requires bureaucratic coordination and, consequently, planning. Bureaucratic coordination through vertical linkages implies recurrent use of coercion. 'The key to an understanding of the socialist system is to examine the structure of power' (Kornai 1992: 33). Under these conditions, two factors essentially determine **economic action**: values (derived from communist ideology) and coercion (materialized in fiats and plan targets). **Utility** and affects as other possible determinants of economic action are far less important, which limits the scope of instrumentally rational and affectual actions. Socialism favours value-rational behaviour and obedience in economic as well as in many other spheres of everyday life.

Theoretical models of socialism

In contrast to capitalism, socialism has never been established in an evolutionary way. It has always resulted from a revolution. 'Capitalism has not been built, it emerged spontaneously. Socialism as an organized system is constructed by the proletariat as an organized subject,' wrote N. Bukharin, a Soviet official and a Marxist theorist, in *Ekonomika perehodnogo perioda* (Economics of the Transition Period, 1920). Thus, theoretical debates on socialism cannot be separated from the study of its practical aspects. Revolutionary projects necessarily have a teleological nature and theoretical models of socialism have been a starting point in their realization. Marxism, market

629

socialism and anarcho-syndicalism are three of the most influential theoretical models.

K. **Marx** and F. Engels did not pay special attention to the description of socialism in their writings. First, they considered socialism as an intermediate stage on the road towards communism. Second, they were primarily interested in driving forces existing within a capitalist society and pushing it towards communism. According to them, one cannot ex ante draw a whole picture of the future society except very roughly. Several particular features of socialism in respect to communism should be mentioned. The state does not disappear during the transition period, it transforms into a mechanism of coercion in the hands of the proletariat. In other words, dictatorship has been viewed as a means to attain communist ends, including freedom in a state-less society. The second part of the communist principle of distribution, 'From everybody according to his or her forces, to everybody depending on his or her needs' becomes 'to everybody depending on his or her work' under socialism. 'Labour hours are a measure of the individual participation of a producer in common work and, consequently, they correspond to the individually consumed part of the total product,' wrote K. Marx in *Capital* (1967: vol. 1, ch. 1, §4). Labour theory of value justifies reference to work in distributing rare resources.

V. Lenin, a political and theoretical leader of the Russian revolution of 1917, adapted the Marxist vision of socialism to the socio-economic conditions of a country with a 'weakly middle' level of capitalist development (the classical Marxist writers excluded any chance of carrying out a socialist revolution in such a situation). At the beginning of the twentieth century, Russia resembled a patchwork of different socio-economic structures: traditional, early capitalist, state capitalist and socialist. Making them interact necessitated using money as a means of exchange instead of introdu-

cing more direct measures of value expressed in labour hours. This point was crucial for Marxist thought. The New Economic Policy (NEP) of the 1920s resulted from this theoretical combination of market and non-market elements. There were no further significant developments in the Marxist model of socialism following the debates of the 1920s–1930s. The official approach to socialism, the **political economy** of socialism, has progressively transformed into a dogma.

The Marxist version of socialism has generated a certain amount of criticism, as developed in liberal writings. L. von Mises refused to believe in the sustainable development of a socialist economy for two reasons: (1) a demonetized economy functioning without any reference to market price is irrational; (2) the exchange of means of production requires the existence of private property. The market exchange of consumer goods allowed during a brief period of the NEP is far from sufficient for rationalizing the exchange of means of production. To this argument, F. von Hayek added that a centralized economy excludes competition and, consequently, distorts the rational allocation of scarce resources.

The model of market socialism presents another way for shaping state ownership and market into a theoretically coherent system. The idea of market socialism is deeply rooted in the discussions of the 1930s about the plausibility and feasibility of a rational socialist economy. According to O. Lange and A. Lerner, such an economy is theoretically possible and practically workable if the planning procedure replicates the price mechanism on a perfectly competitive market. From this point of view, the Central Bureau of Planning becomes the best *commisaire-priseur* (auctioneer) that L. Walras could imagine. Instead of struggling for an equilibrium price (or quantity) through the process of trial and error in practice, the planner can calculate the equilibrium price on paper, using the information transmitted by economic agents, and then communicate the vector of equilibrium prices to them. The perfect market play paradoxically requires the existence of a central agent, planner, responsible for reaching the Walrasian **equilibrium**. The Soviet school of optimal planning further developed the idea of imitating the market during the 1960s. One of its leaders, L. Kantorovich, a joint winner of the 1975 Nobel Prize for economics, introduced the parameters related to relative scarcities of resources in the models of linear programming applied to planning.

The idea of market socialism encountered a certain amount of criticism from both neoclassical economists and orthodox Marxists. For the former, market socialism has no chance of success as a result of incentive problems: bureaucrats have no incentive to carry out the prescriptions provided by the advocates of market socialism. For the latter, planning should not imitate the market; it is derived from other processes such as communization and mobilization. The emphasis on incompleteness of information raises additional doubts about the theoretical validity of market socialism. Economic agents not only lack the incentive to disclose the true information to the planner, they are simply unable to collect and process all relevant pieces of information. Information is always imperfect and costly, especially in centralized systems. In his book *Whither Socialism?* (1994), J. Stiglitz asserts that 'the fundamental problem with the neoclassical model and the corresponding model underlying market socialism is that they fail to take into account a variety of problems that arise from the absence of perfect information and the costs of acquiring information' (Stiglitz 1994: 5).

The anarcho-syndicalist version of socialism is based on a supposedly natural human proclivity for solidarity and mutual assistance. Consequently, anarcho-syndicalists believe in a spontaneous emergence of socialism; they strongly criticize the concept of the dictatorship of proletariat as too violent and destroying natural associations. They view the Marxist reliance on the state during the transition period as a danger of submission to bureaucracy. *Statism and Anarchy*, written in 1873 by M. Bakunin, one of the founding fathers of anarchism, includes the following passage: 'The way of the anarchist social revolution, which will come from the people themselves, an elemental force sweeping away all obstacles. Later, from the depths of the popular soul, there will spontaneously emerge the new creative forms of social life' (in Bakunin 1971).

Anarcho-syndicalism became a major ideological source of the New Left movement of the 1960s. The criticism of progress in general and that of technology in particular, self-management as a key socialist practice, the romanticization of tribal peoples and ecological issues have been considered as high on the agenda of anarchists thanks to the contribution of the New Left. Another revival of theoretical interest in several problems raised by anarcho-syndicalists occurred in the second half of the 1980s in the Soviet Union and other East European socialist countries. Self-management had been considered a way of reforming centralized planning without reference either to market principles or to the procedures established by the political economy of socialism.

Practical experience of socialism

Discussions of theoretical issues are not sufficient for acquiring a comprehensive overview of socialism. The methodology of 'descending' from the abstract (theoretical models) to the concrete (everyday practices), that has been developed in the Marxist philosophy, seems pertinent in this context. It allows for the analysis of the transformations that have occurred in the course of the implementation of socialist ideas. In the wording of the **institutional economics**, institutional environment influences and changes the initial models. Socialism as an institutional system includes both formal (laws, written regulations) and informal (values, habitus) institutions. For example, the implementation of the principle of the dictatorship of the proletariat gives de facto unlimited power to bureaucrats, the representatives of the party-state. L. Trotsky was one of the first to mention the dangers related to the transformation of the communist party bureaucrats into a new ruling class (in the 1937 book *Revolution Betrayed*). The party's instructions become de facto laws. As far as informal norms are concerned, membership in a communist party ensured a series of exclusive privileges ranging from rapid advancement to travel abroad.

Let us consider the second element of the institutional structure of socialism, state ownership. Formally speaking, the nation's citizens are the sole owners of public firms. In practice, the property relations of the state-owned firm can be described as bureaucratic. High-ranked bureaucrats of ministries and public agencies have appropriated the key **property** rights: *usus* (control over the use of assets) and *usus fructus* (control of the cash flow or residual income). As a result, the initial abstract models of socialism have often transformed the everyday practices that contradict them or at least significantly differ from them.

The explanation of this transformation is still a subject of discussion. One possible way consists in inquiring into the parameters of a set of informal institutions that existed before socialist revolutions, i.e. before the implementation of abstract models. The more selective affinity and congruence a model of socialism and the set of informal institutions show, the fewer distortions appear during the transition period. A plurality of the national models of socialism is principally due to the variability of initial institutional conditions. In particular, there are Soviet, Chinese, North Korean (autarkic socialism), Yugoslavian (self-managed socialism), Hungarian (the 'goulash' socialism) and many other country-specific models.

The Soviet model of socialism has emerged as a result of the interaction between the Marxist model of socialism and the strong collectivist traditions embedded, for example in institutions such as the traditional peasant community (obshchina). There has been a surprising continuity between the obshchina-type institutions and the socialist institutions that existed during the Soviet era. The Chinese model of socialism in its current form (the Communist Party maintains political control whereas the economy is divided into two sectors − state-controlled and market) is based as well on affinities between cultural traditions and full-fledged market structures at local and regional levels. These affinities give rise to a network form of market socialism. Another form of market socialism, self-managed, existed in Yugoslavia during the 1960s to 1980s (see Vanek 1970). The regional and ethnic disparity harmful for full centralization, as well as a mild political opposition to the Soviet Union and its model of socialism, should be taken into account when explaining the emergence of the Yugoslavian model.

The informal institutions that have resulted from the interaction between the abstract models of socialism and the institutions inherited from the past ensure a relative stability of the socio-economic system. J. Kornai has pointed out that socialist economy tends to experience shortages. Shortages arise in different sectors of the socialist economy on a permanent basis. Despite this fact, the system is relatively stable, attaining a non-Walrasian equilibrium. In other words, there is a 'normal' intensity of shortages, a 'normal' level of stocks, a 'normal' length of line and so on. If economic parameters do not exceed the corresponding 'normal' values, the system as a whole returns to an equilibrium even after temporary shocks. The 'normal' values are a function of the informal institutions that determine the limits of the social acceptability of shortage and its consequences.

At first glance, the fall of socialism in Eastern Europe and the former Soviet Union at the start of the 1990s refutes the thesis concerning the existence of a non-Walrasian equilibrium. Two additional factors should be taken into consideration at this point. First, there is the intensity of external shocks. The drop in the price of oil in the 1980s heavily influenced the Soviet economy and, consequently, the other socialist economies closely linked to it. Second, J. Kornai's model ignores the existence of a parallel market. The parallel, or 'black', market has played an important role in attenuating shortages; this is equally true for both consumer and producer goods. W. Andreff, in the book *La Crise des économies socialistes* (The Crisis of Socialist Economies, 1993), showed that the parallel market has its own dynamics and can transform into a destabilizing force for the centrally planned economy as a whole. The more intensive shortage is, the more destabilizing the parallel market is in the long run.

References and further reading

Andreff, W. (1993) *La Crise des économies socialistes* [The Crisis of Socialist Economies], Grenoble: Presse Universitaire de Grenoble.

Bakunin, M. (1971) *Bakunin on Anarchy*, translated and edited by Sam Dolgoff, New York: Knopf. Relevant extracts available at http://www.marxists.org/reference/archive/bakunin/works/1873/statism-anarchy.htm

Bukharin, N. (1920) *Ekonomika perehodnogo perioda* [Economics of the Transition Period], Moscow.

Hayek, F. A. von (ed.) (1935) *Collectivist Economic Planning*, London: Routledge (especially the contributions of L. Mises and F. Hayek).

Kornai, János (1980) *Economics of Shortage*, Amsterdam: North Holland.

—— (1992) *The Socialist System*, Princeton, NJ: Princeton University Press.

Lange, Oscar (1936/1937) 'On the Economic Theory of Socialism', *Review of Economic Studies*, 4(1), October, and 4(2), February.

Marx, K. (1967) *Capital*, vol. 1, New York: International Publishers.

Oleinik, Anton (ed.)(2005) *The Institutional Economics of Russia's Transformations*, Aldershot, UK: Ashgate.

Stiglitz, J. (1994) *Whither Socialism?* Cambridge, MA: MIT Press.

Vanek, J. (1970) *The General Theory of Labor-Managed Market Economies*, Ithaca, NY: Cornell University Press.

ANTON OLEINIK

SOCIO-ECONOMICS

Socio-economics is an interstitial discipline that combines the theorems, findings and insights of economics with those of other social sciences. Hence, by definition, one or more of the independent variables in a socio-economic proposition must be psychological, sociological, historical or part of some other social science discipline other than economics. The dependent variable(s), the phenomena that are being analysed or explained, are typically going to be economic. Thus, if one seeks to explain the differences among the savings rates of people of different societies, which long have been very high in Japan and Germany compared to the United States, a socio-economic proposition would seek to establish whether the cultures of the countries under study differ in the positive moral values they associate with saving and the negative view they have of being in debt, and not just – the difference in return rates on funds deposited in various forms of saving accounts.

There are cultural differences even in the extent to which socio-economics itself is studied and followed. In the United States, neoclassical economics, which by and large excludes social variables on the theoretical level, is dominant. In other societies, various forms of socio-economics are more

633

prominent, going under such titles as humanistic economics (Lutz and Lux 1979), social economics (Catholic) (O'Boyle 1990), ecological economics (Daly 1973; Costanza 1991), institutional economics (North 1981; for a review of 'old' and 'new' institutional economics, see Hodgson 1998), **behavioural economics** (Kahneman and Tversky 2000), economic sociology (Smelser and Swedberg 1995), and socio-economics (Etzioni 1988), although their representatives are also found in the United States.

The best way to understand the essence of various forms of socio-economics is to contrast them with neoclassical economics. The latter's paradigm is centred around the individual, who is assumed to be the agent, the choice-maker, while socio-economics recognizes the individual as a member of one or more social bodies that affect the person's preferences.

To illustrate: when economics is formulated in terms of the neoclassical paradigm, it uses as a core concept the term 'consumer sovereignty', a brief examination of which will stand for many other examples that could be given. According to the thesis folded into this term, the direction of the economy *in toto* arises out of an aggregation of individual choices and transactions. This is a cardinal assumption that guides much of the work in the neoclassical approach. As a result, if neoclassical economists are asked, for instance, to recommend policies that would increase the savings rate (a goal of US public policy for several decades) they typically suggest increasing the incentives for people to save (a prescription that has led to setting up tax-deferred and tax-exempt savings accounts in the United States known as IRAs and Keoghs). For these to work, millions of people have to change their behaviour, which was assumed to be easy because a rational person would be quick to take advantage of the considerable tax benefits involved, and the aggregation of these changed choices would increase the savings rate.

In effect, it took decades and large outlays before most tax-payers even found out about these accounts. Millions still do not use them, despite the fact that there is no rational reason for them to refrain. Moreover, these accounts cost the United States Treasury many billions of dollars but have resulted in very little net new savings. (Many people who saved anyhow move their money into these accounts. Note also that the penalties on abusing them are small, and enforcement of even these, weak.) In fact, it is quite possible that the loss to the Treasury exceeded the increase in savings.

Socio-economics would lead one to consider actions by the community and state as the first step. Saving rates are best increased, accordingly, by increasing the budgetary surplus and/or paying off more of the national debt, which are much less costly and much more effective ways to boost savings than trying to affect the choices of millions of individuals. (It is true that there are macro-neoclassical economists who study national budgets, but they cannot find in their paradigm the principles and concepts that nourish analysis that is not based on aggregating individual choices.) In contrast, socio-economics studies the conditions under which communities and their moral cultures are stronger or weaker, which in turn affects their ability to affect both collective and individual economic behaviour (Putnam 2000; Etzioni 1988). There follow three core propositions of socio-economics to introduce the concept.

Self-interest and values

A core theorem of socio-economics is that individuals' decisions and behaviours, far from following one unified principle (i.e. seeking to maximize pleasure and minimize pain) reflect a conflict between two irreducible utilities. The first is our desire for pleasure: the other, our moral obligations.

Both utilities and the tension between them are reflected in a simple sentence such as 'I would *like* to go to a movie, but I *ought* to visit my friend in the hospital.' Indeed, most values serve to pull behaviour away from heeding the pleasure principle. Whether religious or secular, values urge people to fast, to give to the Church, to not engage in sex, and on and on. In other words, there are certain things one is supposed to do which are of virtue for a variety of reasons, but the common variable they share is that they are not pleasurable.

Much behaviour reflects this inevitable tension between things people would like to do and that which they believe they ought to do (Phelps 1975). Many empirical observations support this generalization. For instance, economists find it surprising that people vote; such behaviour doesn't fit the standard economic model. Individuals are expected to do things for a return, for profit, or for some other form of benefit. When one votes, one cannot reasonably expect that the vote will make a difference and hence that one will get anything in return.

For a socio-economist, this behaviour is not puzzling. The most powerful variable that explains the difference between people who vote and those who don't is the sense of civic duty. People who feel that they have an obligation to vote are much more likely to vote than those who don't have such a sense (Barry 1978). This is not to suggest that the length of lines, the weather, etc., don't make a difference; they do affect the 'costs' of voting and do affect behaviour. But the number one factor explaining the variance is the relative strength of the person's sense of civic duty.

Another case in point: if people were to act only to maximize their pleasure, those who smoke would vote against taxes on cigarettes, and those who do not would favour these taxes. The fact, though, is that there are a large number of smokers who vote *for* taxes on cigarettes because they feel

they are damaging the public and ought to do something to compensate for that. And there are a fair number of non-smokers who vote *against* these taxes because they are libertarians or they feel that the government should not interfere. Similarly, Paul Stern reports that individuals who were told that conserving energy during peak demand periods would be good for the community were likely to lower their electricity use during such periods if they felt that households as a group could make a difference (Black 1978). Alan Lewis (1982) found that whether people consider the burden of taxation to be fairly distributed and whether they believe that the funds recovered from taxes are used for legitimate purposes is an important factor in determining the level of compliance.

One last example: neoclassical economists try to explain why people – most people – with spouses who have Alzheimer's stay with them. These economists treat marriage as an economic contract, in which an exchange of services takes place for income and services. But with Alzheimer's, there is no payback because there is no reasonable hope that the person who is afflicted will recover and take care of the other person. One may say that the treating spouse does so because of the kudos he or she will receive from members of their extended family and from neighbours and friends. However, tending to an Alzheimer's patient day in and day out is so taxing that all the kudos in the world could not make up for it. And finally, economists often attribute this behaviour to the notion of psychic income. But again, socio-economists would argue that this explanation fails because the afflicted person does not respond with a warm appreciation for the service; indeed, they become ever more abusive as time goes on. So why do most spouses not walk out on their afflicted husband or wife? When one interviews these people, one repeatedly hears the statement that 'this is the right thing to do'; the same sentiment is found in Roberta Simmons' (1987) studies of kidney donations. People have a strong moral commitment, a powerful factor which outweighs the pain and losses they have to endure.

This core socio-economic theorem does not hold that values determine behaviour, but that there is a continual conflict and tension between self-interest and the plea-sure principle on one hand and powerful moral commitments on the other. Socio-economists hence take it as a starting hypothesis that people are conflicted, which helps explain why people act incon-sistently and tend to zig-zag as a result of their being subject to these two com-peting utilities.

To suggest that evidence shows that social and moral values play an important role in affecting human behaviour in gen-eral, economic behaviour included, is not to suggest that these values are given. They themselves are subject to social processes, for instance moral dialogues, that lead them to be constantly reconsidered and reformu-lated, and sometimes to break down and replaced by others. Indeed, among the factors that promote reconsideration of values are economic factors. However, even **Marx** did not claim that values simply reflect technological and economic factors or that they have no independent variance and effect of their own.

The socio-economic mind

Theories of human behaviour require a core assumption about the intellectual cap-abilities of the person. Socio-economics uses as a starting point the key observation that people are poor processors of information – just the opposite of what used to be the neoclassical economists' assumption that information flows instanta-neously and is absorbed instantaneously, all without any costs. These economists wisely retreated from these assumptions, and they now recognize that information is not

immediately absorbed and the process has costs. In this and several other contexts they refer to 'imperfect' systems. This is a tricky concept that is inadvertently misleading. The term implies that there is a speck of dust on the perfect scale. Actually, people's limits on information processing are much larger. Indeed, strong evidence shows that people start with little knowledge and that they are slow and poor learners.

A simple case in point: every day millions of people call their brokers and either ask their advice on which stock to purchase or order them to buy one, on the assumption that these individual investors could beat the market averages. (Otherwise they would buy index funds and save costs.) However, there is strong, consistent, robust data to show this is an irrational act; one cannot consistently out-perform the market averages (Malkiel 1985). Moreover, brokers have a conflict of interest with the callers; brokers benefit from high turnovers in the accounts, while investors benefit from low turnover and low transaction costs. Still, despite the fact that studies supporting the use of index funds rather than brokers have been repeatedly publicized in the popular press, in classrooms, and on television, millions persist in such untutored beha-viour. Among those who provided ample evidence along these lines are Amos Tversky, Daniel Kahneman, Richard Tha-ler, Martin Seligman, Robert Frank and Robert Schiller.

The market is a subsystem

Socio-economists consider it a grave error to treat the economy as a self-sustaining system, to view the market as separate from society (and its polity). The starting assumption of socio-economic analysis is that the economy is a subsystem of the societal system. Much of what is occurring within the economy is best explained by attributes and processes that occur outside of it. To cite just one very well-known and compelling example: Max Weber's study of the social (and religious) conditions under which capitalism arises and thrives. (To suggest that economies are nestled within societal system is not to suggest that they have no autonomy or independent power. They may well cause changes in the encompassing system. The only point made is that it is unproductive to think about the market or the economy as a self-sustaining, free-standing system. It is enough to consider the notion of private property and limited liability, both essential for a modern economy, to recognize that these are concepts rooted in the legal and cultural system of the societies in which economists are imbedded, rather than part of the economists' realm.)

To make the difference between neoclassical and socio-economics less abstract, here is a specific example: George Stigler (1968) wanted to provide an example of the governing assumption of neoclassical economics, that the market (an aggregation of the choices of all participants) ultimately set the context in which individual choices must be made. Thus, if a manager reads the market correctly in terms of what will sell at what price, then that manager's corporation will stay in business; if the manager misreads the market's signals and persists in not responding to its dictates, the firm will be soon bankrupt.

To illustrate this point, Stigler focuses on wheat farmers. Each farmer cannot decide what he or she will charge for a bushel of wheat; they can charge only what the market will bear. The market decides. The core assumption is that the market works like an anonymous box into which suppliers throw in their bids and buyers throw theirs, and out of this invisible hat the 'correct' price prints out.

Socio-economics notes that in the United States farmers are not merely 'in the market' but also in the polity; they are members of two major political lobbies. These lobbies influence Congress to enact various legislation that greatly affects the price of wheat. Indeed, for more than forty years the price of wheat (and numerous other farm products) was not determined by an autonomous machine: these prices could not fall below a certain level because the government protected the price. The price reflected the fact that the farmers lived in both the polity and the economy, and they used their lobbying citizens' hats to influence the economy.

Farming is hardly the only sector in which this occurs. Socio-economics finds many other sectors in which politics significantly affects prices (Galbraith 1971). These include textiles (through a multifibre agreement, the United States government controls how much textiles are imported from each country; the scope of these imports have an important effect on the prices because these imports come from countries in which labour is cheap); steel (whose importation was limited through various mechanisms); and cars (a 'voluntary' quota limiting the importation of cars from Japan to 1.25 million for numerous years). The same can be found in many other areas. Even small businesses, such as small restaurants and laundromats, are subject to numerous regulations that determine in which zones they can open businesses, how close they can be to one another, the hours during which they can operate, and much else, all reflecting the community's values and politics.

Socio-economics provides the concepts and measurements that allow one to study the independent variables behind the normative and political factors that affect economic behaviour rather than taking them as given.

Institutionalization

Socio-economics has been much less effectively institutionalized than neoclassical economics. Its various associational bodies, such as the Society for the Advancement of

Socio-Economics (www.sase.org), have not nearly as many members as the largely neoclassical associations, including the American Economic Association. Most of the teaching in practically all the departments of economics in the United States, as well as the teaching of economics in business schools, is provided by neoclassical economists. And the few socio-economic journals (such as *The Socio-Economic Review* and *The Journal of Socio-Economics*) have fewer subscribers and are much less often cited by academics and policy-makers than neoclassical ones.

The reasons for this low level of institutionalization of socio-economics are unclear. It is evident, though, that – as socio-economics itself points out – academic disciplines, like markets, do not function in a vacuum. Without much greater institutionalization, the future development of socio-economics will continue to be overshadowed.

References and further reading

Barry, B. (1978) *Sociologists, Economists and Democracy*, Chicago: University of Chicago Press.

Black, J. S. (1978) 'Attitudinal, Normative, and Economic Factors in Early Response to Energy-Use Field Experiment', unpublished doctoral dissertation, Department of Sociology, University of Wisconsin.

Burgenmeier, B. (1992) *Socio-Economics: An Interdisciplinary Approach*, translated by K. Cook, Boston: Kluwer Academic.

Costanza, R. (ed.) (1991) *Ecological Economics*, New York: Columbia University Press.

Coughlin, R. (ed.) (1991) *Morality, Rationality, and Efficiency: New Perspectives on Socio-Economics*, Armonk, NY: M. E. Sharpe.

—— (1996) 'Whose Morality? Which Community? What Interests? Socio-Economic and Communitarian Perspectives', *Journal of Socio-Economics*, 25: 135–55.

Daly, H. (1973) *Steady-State Economics: The Political Economy of Bio-Physical Equilibrium and Moral Growth*, San Francisco: W. H. Freeman.

Etzioni, A. (1988) *The Moral Dimension: Toward a New Economics*, New York: Free Press.

Etzioni, A. and Lawrence, P. R. (eds) (1991) *Socio-Economics: Toward a New Synthesis*, Armonk, NY: M. E. Sharpe.

Galbraith, J. K. (1971) *The New Industrial State*, second edition, Boston: Houghton Mifflin.

Hodgson, Geoffrey M. (1998) 'The Approach of Institutional Economics', *Journal of Economic Literature*, 36: 166–92.

Hollingsworth, J. R., Muller, K. H. and Hollingsworth, E. J. (2002) *Advancing Socio-Economics: An Institutionalist Perspective*, Lanham, MD: Rowman and Littlefield.

Kahneman, D. and Tversky, A. (eds) (2000) *Choices, Values, and Frames*, Cambridge: Cambridge University Press.

Lewis, A. (1982) *The Psychology of Taxations*, New York: St Martin's Press.

Lutz, M. and Lux, K. (1979) *The Challenge of Humanistic Economics*, Menlo Park, CA: Benjamin/Cummings Publishing.

Malkiel, B. G. (1985) *Random Walk Down Wall Street*, fourth edition, New York: Norton.

North, D. C. (1981) *Institutions, Institutional Change, and Economic Performance*, Cambridge: Cambridge University Press.

O'Boyle, E. J. (1990) 'Catholic Social Economics: A Response to Certain Problems, Errors, and Abuses of the Modern Age', in M. Lutz (ed.), *Social Economics: Retrospect and Prospect*, Boston: Kluwer Academic.

Phelps, E. S. (ed.) (1975) *Altruism, Morality and Economic Theory*, New York: Basic Books.

Putnam, R. D. (2000) *Bowling Alone: The Collapse and Revival of American Community*, New York: Simon and Schuster.

Simmons, R. G., Marine, S. K. and Simmons, R. L. (1987) *Gift of Life: The Effect of Organ Transplantation on Individual, Family, and Societal Dynamics*, New Brunswick, NJ: Transaction Books.

Smelser, N. J. and Swedberg, R. (1995) *The Handbook of Economic Sociology*, Princeton, NJ: Princeton University Press.

Stigler, G. (1968) 'Competition', *International Encyclopedia of Social Sciences*, vol. 3, New York: Macmillan, pp. 181–2.

AMITAI ETZIONI

SOCIOLOGY AND ANTI-ECONOMICS

The 'anti-economist' believes that economics is so wrong it is best eliminated. The mind-set is well captured by the sociologically minded Thorstein **Veblen** when he criticised accepted economic theories, not as incomplete or even wrong in specific detail, but as utterly false and deluded from beginning to end ... we should be much better off if we were to dispense with the whole question–begging rubrics with no other verdict than 'good riddance'.

(Ayers quoted in Coleman 2002: 7)

Sociologists have numbered significantly among 'anti-economists'. Expressions of anti-economics may already be found in the very germination sociology; including De Bonald, Saint Simon and Comte. The earliest book published in the United States to use the word 'sociology' in its title – *The Sociology of the South* of 1854 – was from its first page a tirade against economics. In 1896 Emile **Durkheim** recalled, 'I spent several years [studying economics] and got nothing out of it, except what can learn from a negative experience' (quoted in Steiner 1994: 137). In the 1990s sociologists in Sweden and Australia led campaigns against the status of economics in national policy-making. (See Jakee 1998, and Coleman and Hagger 2001).

Sociologists have figured large amongst anti-economists on account of the offence economics gives two precepts of sociology: 'social holism' and 'methodological collectivism'.

'Social holism' contends that it is neither possible nor desirable to decompose human affairs into an 'economy' distinct from a society.

Such a decomposition is not *possible*, according to the Comtean vision of a single universal social theory, because the economy was only a component part of single integrated social mechanism. Comte:

The avowal of the economists that their science is isolated from social philosophy in general, is itself a sufficient confirmation of my [negative] judgement; for it is a universal fact in social ... science, that all the various general aspects of the

science are scientifically one, and rationally inseparable.

(quoted in Coleman 2002: 240)

And, to the extent that this decomposition may be possible, it is not *desirable* because economic equilibrium does not coincide with social equilibrium. Consequently, the achievement of economic equilibrium will have social costs. In this vein, and with respect to the social tensions of industrialization, Comte complained that

instead of recognising in the urgent remonstrances called forth by this chasm in our social order [as] one of the most eminent and pressing occasions for the application of social science, our economists can do nothing better than repeat, with pitiless pedantry, the barren aphorism of industrial liberty.

(Comte quoted in Coleman 2002: 5)

In the twentieth century the impolicy of seeking to resolve human affairs into an 'economy' distinct a society was pressed with great acclaim by Karl **Polanyi**. In Polanyi's telling of history, markets were 'embedded' in society until the advent of the Great Transformation of the early nineteenth century, in which markets were removed from social control by political economists, with deleterious social consequences. 'The creation of a labour market was an act of vivisection performed on the body of society by such as were steeled to their task by an assurance which only science can provide', including Ricardo and Malthus, whose theory was 'essentially confused', ridden with 'perplexing pseudo-problems', and merely a 'hopeless attempt to arrive at categorical conclusions about loosely defined terms' (Polanyi quoted in Coleman 2002: 47). Polanyi has retained interest since the mid-century, and has been the intellectual figurehead of the well-publicized denunciations of the economic way of thinking by French sociologist/anthropologist Pierre **Bourdieu**.

The holistic objection to economics is accompanied by an objection to the 'methodological individualism' of economics, and its epitome in 'homo economicus'. Whereas Economic Man is self-interested, probably honest but otherwise normless, 'Sociological Man' is endowed with norms that so that other human beings are not treated only instrumentally. 'Methodological Collectivism' holds Economic Man is neither possible or desirable. He is not possible because an individual's motivations cannot be understood while abstracting from the existence of other persons. And insofar as he is possible, he is not desirable, as it is norms that make society work. Sociologists have devoted effort to a conceptual armoury to articulate their conviction that norms are critical to preserve society; from the coinages of the Saint-Simonians and Comte ('individualism' and 'altruism'), and through to the 'organic versus mechanical solidarity' of Durkheim. The concept of wealth has also been creatively varied in this frame of mind. Bonald, for example, argued that national strength was not something material, but something 'moral' (= social), and convicted economists of having mistaken the true meaning of wealth. In doing so, Bonald anticipated today's interest in 'social capital'.

Overall, the 'market society' of purely instrumental relations has left sociologists dissatisfied. Where the economist sees opportunity, the sociologist sees constraint. Whereas the economist is fascinated by the vast material improvement of the modern era, the sociologist is engrossed by those groups least integrated into economic society.

Space permits only some notes of appraisal of sociological anti-economics. The Comtean project of an integral social theory was stillborn, doomed by the very chaoticness of the collisions between the 'economic' and 'social'. Second, any doctrine as to impolicy of the autonomous market must cope with the observation that it is the most capitalist societies that seem unusually stable, while it is least marketized societies the most fractured. Finally, the advocate of 'methodological collectivism' must consider that the possibility that it is the very elevation of 'Economic Man' over 'Sociological Man' of such capitalist societies that has provided their cohesion, insofar as many of the social affects of 'Sociological Man' are hostile to social cohesion; including ethnic loyalties, religious sectarianism and class prejudice.

References and further reading

Coleman, William (2002) *Economics and Its Enemies*, New York: Palgrave Macmillan.
Coleman, William and Hagger, Alf (2001) *Exasperating Calculators: The Rage over Economic Rationalism and the Campaign against Australian Economists*, Sydney: Macleay Press.
Jakee, Keith (1998) 'Headline Economics: An Analysis of the Swedish Economic Debate', paper delivered at the International History of Economic Thought Society conference, Montreal.
Steiner, Philippe (1994) 'Durkheim, les économistes et la critique de l'économie politique', *Economies et Sociétés*, 19(4): 135–59.

WILLIAM COLEMAN

SOCIOLOGY OF ACCOUNTING
See: accounting; sociology of , rationality

SOCIOLOGY OF CONSUMPTION
See: consumption

SOCIOLOGY OF DEVELOPMENT
See: economic development

SOCIOLOGY OF LABOUR MARKETS
See: labour markets

SOCIOLOGY OF MARKETS
See: markets, sociology of

SOCIOLOGY OF WORK
See: work, sociology of

SOLIDARITY

The concept of solidarity as the underlying force that creates social order and cohesion in society was first introduced in 1893 by French sociologist Emile **Durkheim**, in his famous doctoral dissertation, *The Division of Labour in Society*. Durkheim offered an indelible contrast between the characteristics of solidarity in pre-modern societies and those of the industrialized world. In pre-modern societies, solidarity is 'mechanical'; it is constructed on the basis of shared life experiences, including common language, customs and a uniform morality. In modern societies, on the other hand, division of labour creates occupational specialization, and life experience therefore lacks the homogeneity necessary for mechanical solidarity. This has not, however, led to disintegration, because this same division of labour has made individuals less self-sufficient and thus more interdependent. This interdependence among dissimilar individuals matures into what Durkheim called 'organic' solidarity. This insight into relationship between division of labour and the two contrasting types of solidarity has become, over the past century, a fundamental component of sociological wisdom.

Durkheim offered a second – equally important, but far less honoured – insight about solidarity. Unlike earlier thinkers such as Montesquieu and Adam **Smith**, who argued for a form of direct determinism between the economic substructure and the social superstructure of society, Durkheim held a more complex view of the relationship between social integration and economic processes. Though the division of labour could be seen as the enabling legislation for organic solidarity, it was not the vehicle through which the solidarity was produced. Instead, the division of labour sets in motions a set of societal dynamics which, with no certainty as to outcome or form, may yield lasting or temporary solidarity. As a consequence, Durkheim, concluded, the organic solidarity in industrial market societies, is more subtle, more varied and more problematic than the mechanical solidarity of pre-modern societies.

Moreover, Durkheim left unanswered many of the key questions that flowed from this view: including two that have occupied recent theorists: the mechanisms that arise to enact solidarity and the degree to which organizations, particularly bureaucracies, are connected by the same mechanisms as individuals. These issues he left as part of his intellectual legacy.

Solidarity in economic sociology

Though Durkheim's faith in future analysis was vindicated, the work of his intellectual descendants served first to disconfirm a major proposition: that mechanical solidarity would recede as organic solidarity ascended. Ironically, even while Durkheim was writing *The Division of Labour in Society*, mechanical solidarity appeared in the foreground of social life as the central feature of the union movement, which was to become the centrepiece of non-elite organization for the fifty years prior to World War II. These events both challenged and vindicated the Durkheimian model. In the first instance, they validated the Marxian insight that division of labour produced vast armies of workers with situational, structural and economic similarities, thus undermining Durkheim's prediction of the demise of mechanical solidarity while validating his prediction that similarity bred solidarity (see **Marx, Karl**). More broadly, we now see that while mechanical solidarity no longer forms the glue for society-wide integration, it is an essential part of integration at the community/organizational level.

In the second instance, the episodic and situational character of union movements called for a deeper understanding of the processes that led to this united action of workers, thus confirming Durkheim's claim that economic structure does not lead directly to solidarity. It was in this realm that activists and scholars applied themselves most creatively, seeking to understand the complex dynamics that underlay the process by which a group of similar individuals abandon the deeply socialized pursuit of individual self-interest in favour of **collective action** (Fantasia 1989). Once this problematic was well established, it became the backbone of modern social movement theory, which sought to understand the same processes across the full range of mass action, and to develop a broad theory of collective mobilization.

This Durkheimian prism eventually became a cornerstone of the new economic sociology when the logic of mobilization theory was imported into the study of professions. Earlier functional analyses had sought to understand the prestige and power of professions as a mechanical reflection of their importance to the ongoing welfare of society. When this vision faltered under the onslaught of public events and scholarly dissent, professionalization theory took its place. This perspective rested on the insight that professionalization only occurred in the context of collective action organized around the same commonality of interest, experience, and socialization that Durkheim had originally identified as sources of mechanical solidarity (Collins 1979). This literature, too, emphasized the contingent nature of such solidarity, pointing to political power, class homogeneity and even racism as mediating factors that translated occupational similarity into mechanical solidarity.

Although Durkheim mistakenly predicted the demise of mechanical solidarity, he correctly understood the rise of organic solidarity in modern society, though here again his vision was drastically modified by events and further analysis. The increasing division of labour indeed created more dependency, not only among individuals,

but also among organizations. The intellectual breakthrough took place when economic sociologists placed the analysis of resource dependency at the centre of a vast literature on the conditions under which presumably independent firms became connected and acted in unison. This analysis of conditions rested, generally without attribution, Durkheim's original formulation. Resource dependency as a concept was a reformulation of Durkheim's division of labour at the organizational level; it focused on the vertical flows of economic resources – raw materials, semi-finished products, expertise and investment capital – from suppliers to customers. The perspective that developed around this concept argued that these flows also traced the structural foundation upon which inter-firm solidarity was constructed (see, for example, Pfeffer and Salancik 1978; Mintz and Schwartz 1986). The elaboration of this orientation focused on the specific social conditions under which this substructure was converted into unified action, thus fulfilling Durkheim's dictum that the underlying economic conditions were necessary by not sufficient conditions for actual solidarity. This disjunction between the resource dependency substructure and active solidarity is most visible in the vast literature on the role of **interlocking directorates** (see, for example, Mizruchi and Stearns 1988).

This logic was extended still further by the development of **embeddedness** theory (Granovetter 1985), which has become the cornerstone of the new economic sociology. Ironically, the logic of embeddedness rests on a complex synthesis of organic and mechanical solidarity. Most studies of embeddedness begin with the division of labour between or within organizations, arguing that the uncertainties of these relationships lead to sustained connections among the individuals responsible for managing them. These connections can then mature into personal relationships that facilitate mechanical solidarity among the individuals involved, not unlike the solidarity of professional organizations. This mechanical solidarity among individuals can then translate into ongoing **inter-firm relations:** that is, organic solidarity among the organizations. In embeddedness theory, therefore, resource dependency leads to structurally embedded social networks, which at least occasionally mature into both mechanical solidarity among individuals and organic solidarity among organizations. Ultimately, such concatenated solidarity is at the heart of various permanent relationships, such as *keiretsu* and **industrial districts** (Storper and Walker 1989).

This combination of Durkheim and embeddedness theory undergirds recent theorizing about capitalist **class** formation, which is based on the proposition that cross-cutting ties among the largest firms creates personal ties among the corporate leadership as a whole. These personal ties, enriched by family ties and co-participation in policy-making groups and elite social clubs, leads to the solidarity that creates a functioning capitalist class. (Zeitlin 1989). Thus, the mechanical solidarity of the business elite derives from the organic solidarity of the most important corporations.

This concatenation of various forms of solidarity is integral to neo-institutional theory, which focuses on institutional isomorphism – similar behaviours among firms in the same **organizational fields** (DiMaggio and Powell 1983). Two forms of isomorphism are particularly relevant. Normative isomorphism derives mainly from the norms developed by managers as a consequence of professional socialization, which lead them to institute similar structures and processes competitive or resource dependant firms. The diffusion of these norms through social networks among professionals and managers has been amply documented by the studies that illustrate how informal ties among individuals play a key role in the job market, with individual

job skills are often secondary concerns (Collins 1979; Granovetter 1995). In this circumstance, the mechanical solidarity of individuals animates both mechanical and organic solidarity among firms. In coercive isomorphism key actors in the field use ongoing relationships to insist on similar structures among all suppliers or customers of a particular product. In this circumstance organic solidarity based on resource dependency translates into mechanical solidarity among a set of similar organizations.

Contrary to Durkheim's prediction, mechanical solidarity neither declined nor was replaced by organic solidarity in modern society. Rather, the two forms were found in myriad complementary combinations, made even more subtle by the concatenation of personal and organizational solidarity. Findings in economic sociology have revealed not only this intricate interaction, but also their impact on the full range of dynamics in modern market societies

References and further reading

Collins, Randall (1979) *The Credential Society*, New York: Academic Press.

DiMaggio, Paul J. and Powell, Walter W. (1983). 'The Iron Cage Revisited: Institutional Isomorphism and Collective Rationality in Organizational Fields', *American Sociological Review*, 48, April: 147–60.

Durkheim, Emile (1947) *The Division of Labour in Society*, New York: Free Press.

Fantasia, Rick (1989) *Cultures of Solidarity: Consciousness, Action and Contemporary American Workers*, Berkeley, CA: University of California Press.

Granovetter, Mark (1985, second edition 1995) *Getting a Job: A Study of Contacts and Careers*, Chicago: University of Chicago Press.

Mintz, Beth and Schwartz, Michael (1986) *The Power Structure of American Business*, Chicago: University of Chicago Press.

Mizruchi, Mark S. and Stearns, Linda Brewster (1988) 'A Longitudinal Study of the Formation of Interlocking Directorates', *Administrative Science Quarterly*, 33: 194–210.

Pfeffer, Jeffery and Salancik, Gerald R. (1978) *The External Control of Organizations: A*

Resource Dependence Perspective, New York: Harper and Row.

Storper, Michael and Walker, Richard (1989) *The Capitalist Imperative: Territory, Technology and Industrial Growth*, Oxford: Blackwell.

Zeitlin, Maurice (1989) *The Large Corporation and Contemporary Classes*, New Brunswick: Rutgers University Press.

HWA JI SHIN
MICHAEL SCHWARTZ

SOMBART, WERNER

Werner Sombart (1863–1941), German economist and founding figure of sociology, was well known during his lifetime but largely forgotten after his death. Sombart is perhaps best known for his essay 'Why is there No Socialism in the United States?' (1976). To this day, political scientists, historians and labour specialists refer to the 'Sombart question' when addressing the exceptional character of the American labour movement.

His main work is *Moderner Kapitalismus*, first published in two volumes in 1902 and reissued in a much-enlarged second edition from 1916 to 1928, albeit never translated entirely into English. In this work he makes prominent the term 'capitalism' and offers a comprehensive analysis of the origins and the nature of capitalism. In contrast to the 'historical school' in economics from which he started (being a pupil of Schmoller), he aimed at an explanation based on ultimate causes. For Sombart, historical appearances build up to a social system that can be grasped by theory. Although influenced by **Marx**, Sombart did not follow the intellectual agenda of Marx's base–superstructure theorem in which productive forces are the most basic layer in society, upon which relations of production are erected and are, in turn, overlaid with an ideological sphere. In Marx, the primacy is with the former two, in Sombart with the latter – he gives definite priority to the spirit.

Among the recurring themes in Sombart's works are not only expected topics like capitalism and technology, Marxism, fashion, consumption and leisure, and methodological issues, but also race, Judaism, German-ness.

If one were to summarize Sombart's intellectual development in a nutshell, one could say that he radically changed his mind about two crucial issues: Marxism and Germany. He started out as a Marxist and ardent fighter for the cause of the socialist movement. This earned him the recognition of Friedrich Engels. In this period, Sombart did not try to reject or transcend Marx. Instead, he attempted to complete the Marxian perspective by adding a socio-psychological and sociocultural dimension to the analysis of the genesis and the nature of capitalism.

After the turn of the century, Sombart became a fervent anti-Marxist, with some anti-Semitic overtones. His relation to Germany was marked by an equal shift of valuation: in his early writings, Sombart had many reservations about his country, but around 1910 he turned into a strident nationalist. His intellectual development can also be followed through different editions of the same book, *Sozialismus und soziale Bewegung*, which first appeared in 1896. While the first nine editions were sympathetic to the socialist movement, the tenth edition (1924) revealed Sombart as a critic of Marx and socialism. This edition had the title *Proletarischer Sozialismus (Marxismus)*. In 1934, when the final edition of the book appeared, it was called *Deutscher Sozialismus* and supported the Nazi rulers. Princeton University Press published an English translation of this book under the title *A New Social Philosophy* in 1937.

Sombart and **Weber** both attempted to explain the origins of capitalism by invoking the importance of religion. While Weber saw the Protestant Spirit as root cause for the emergence of capitalism, Sombart awarded this role to the Jewish religion. While Weber and Sombart largely agreed about the role of the Jews in economic history as being traders and money-lenders, they disagreed about the Jews' role in the development of capitalism, and about the role of race. While Sombart was beset with issues of race, Weber was not. Most importantly, Sombart mixed these contested issues with ethical and moral aspects. His analysis of causes of capitalism is thus joined by a discussion about the attribution of blame. As he abhorred capitalism and free markets, he did not stop at analytical statements about the historical role of the Jews (no matter how contested they may be) with moral evaluations. The Jews are thus made responsible for the emergence of capitalism. Likewise, his discussion about the course of civilization is interspersed with arguments about 'superior' and 'inferior', 'mixed' and 'pure' races. Thus he states: 'One can be sure that the Jews have had a significant share in the genesis of capitalism. This follows from, among other things, their racial disposition' (1902: 390). He emphasizes dominance of will-power, egotism and abstract mentality in the Jewish race.

In another context, he identified two 'worldviews' in World War I. On one side were the nations of shopkeepers and merchants: on the other was the land of heroes, philosophers and soldiers, prepared to sacrifice themselves for higher ideals. England, naturally, represented the former, and Germany the latter. He did not always see it this way. In his book *Die deutsche Volkswirtschaft im Neunzehnten Jahrhundert* (published in 1903) he points to the alleged link between the national character of the German people and the spirit of capitalism. While retaining his hostility towards capitalism, he would, however, slowly develop a 'strategy' of reconciliation with '*Deutschtum*'. The distinction between two types of capitalists: entrepreneurs and traders was crucial for this move. While the entrepreneur is quick in comprehension, true in judgement, clear in thought, with a sure eye for the needful and a good memory

(Sombart 2001), the trader's 'intellectual and emotional world is directed to the money value of conditions and dealings, who therefore calculates everything in terms of money'. Sombart was to identify this role as occupied by the 'Jewish species'. The peoples less inclined to capitalism were the Celts and a few of the Germanic tribes, the Goths in particular. Wherever the Celtic element predominated capitalism made little headway.

Sombart's work on culture, consumption and luxury is still regarded as 'classic'. This field had been left almost exclusively to economists who treat consumer behaviour in an ahistorical framework of assumptions and consider it to be basically the same for all peoples at all times.

Sombart suggested a close connection between the insatiable patterns of consumption in early modern court life and the growth of capitalist production. The demand for luxury was not so much connected to a pursuit of comfort, but with social ambition and mobility. Aristocrats became especially passionate about assembling rare objects from round the world. The display of these objects, plants and animals prefigures Veblen's conspicuous consumption. Where **Veblen** would stress the point that this was wasteful consumption, Sombart sees it as a way to mark ranks where social stratification was unclear. Others have pointed out that a materialist **consumer culture** oriented around products and goods from all over the world was the 'prerequisite for the technological revolution of industrial capitalism' – not its result (Appadurai 1986).

References and further reading

Appadurai, Arjun (1986) *The Social Life of Things: Commodities in Cultural Perspective*, Cambridge: Cambridge University Press.
Grundmann, Reiner and Stehr, Nico (2001) 'Introduction', in Nico Stehr and Reiner Grundmann (eds), *Werner Sombart: Economic*

Life in the Modern Age, New Brunswick, NJ, and Oxford: Transaction Books.

Sombart, Werner (1902) *Der Moderne Kapitalismus*, Leipzig: Duncker and Humblot.

—— (1976) *Why Is There No Socialism in the United States?* New York: Macmillan.

—— (2001) 'The Origins of the Capitalist Spirit', in Nico Stehr and Reiner Grundmann (eds), *Werner Sombart: Economic Life in the Modern Age*, New Brunswick, NJ, and London: Transaction Books, pp. 33–54 (originally published 1913).

REINER GRUNDMANN
NICO STEHR

SPECULATION

Speculation consists of purchasing or selling commodities in anticipation of profitable price changes or price differences. Those who hoard, for example, buy up goods with the expectation that prices will rise and that they will be able to sell at a higher price. Hoarders do not buy for their own use. In **financial markets**, short-sellers expect prices to drop, and make money if they do. Market speculation, like speculation in the cognitive sense (e.g. 'to speculate about the future'), depends on **beliefs** about future outcomes. People often have variable and even contradictory expectations about future price movements, but sometimes a social alignment of expectations occurs and a strong consensus emerges. Such a consensus can act like a collective self-fulfilling prophecy and bring about the very circumstances it predicted. If all the participants in a market believe prices will rise in the future, then they will purchase goods and the prices will rise because of the increase in demand.

Speculators are concerned not only with their own beliefs about the future, but even more so with the beliefs of others. If everyone else thinks Ford Motor Co. stock will decline, an individual may sell that stock short even though she personally believes that Ford is in good shape. Strategic speculators who appreciate the importance of expectations can actively try to shape expectations for their own benefit. They may disseminate false information (e.g. planting a rumour of coming shortages), publicly behave in a way that will lead others to draw erroneous conclusions (e.g. making a visible purchase of Ford stock while at the same time discreetly selling off their shareholdings through intermediaries) or manipulate key market signals (e.g. two management **consultants** secretly purchased 50,000 copies of their book in order to get it on to the New York Times bestseller list, since just being on the list would further spur sales; see Bikhchandani *et al.* 1998). The importance of social learning (attending to the actions of others) can set off the herding behaviour that sometimes characterizes speculation.

The expectations and beliefs that undergird speculation are usually based on information, however imperfectly. Thus the social structuring of information affects market speculation: how information is produced, distributed and received among a group of people. This social structuring depends on whether people actively acquire information, what kind of search procedures or heuristics they use, the biases and limitations of information, and how information flows through social networks. Much decision-making in markets occurs in situations of uncertainty, where information is incomplete or inconsistent, and where it is unevenly distributed ('information asymmetries', see Stiglitz 2000). Some information may be about the objective qualities of the commodity being traded (in the case of company shares, the so-called 'fundamentals'). Some of it may be about others' expectations and beliefs about the commodity. Both types of information can encourage speculation.

Some scholars have concluded from the experience of speculative bubbles that expectations are not always rational. A bubble is characterized by a sharp increase in prices, as market actors all try to buy, followed by an even quicker drop, as they all try to sell. Such bubbles provide ample opportunity for speculation. During a market bubble (the South Sea Bubble and Tulipmania are early modern examples, the 'dotcom' bubble of the 1990s is more recent), market participants exhibit 'irrational exuberance' or collective mania ('animal spirits' is the Keynesian term, see DiMaggio 2002), and when enough of them finally 'sober up' the bubble bursts (Kindleberger 1984: 270–6). Euphoria turns to panic and the market collapses quickly. Abolafia and Kilduff (1988) argue that speculative bubbles have a well-defined social structure that drives the characteristic price dynamics of rapid inflation and sudden collapse. Others strongly take issue with the idea that large numbers of people in competitive markets could act irrationally, and so argue that so-called bubbles are in fact driven by market fundamentals (Garber 2000). Furthermore, adherents of the efficient markets hypothesis hold that market traders need pay attention only to market prices since these reflect all relevant information.

While speculation can be extremely profitable, some forms of it have long been regarded as socially illegitimate. During the Middle Ages and after, various monopolistic and speculative practices were prohibited by law (e.g. regrating, forestalling and engrossing) since they 'artificially' boosted prices above the 'fair price' (Wood 2002: 139). A merchant who purchased grain and withheld it from the market in order to take advantage of higher prices later on would be punished. Various 'producerist' ideologies (e.g. nineteenth-century populism) criticized speculation on the grounds that it was an unproductive activity that did not create economic value, and like gambling it merely redistributed value from one set of hands to another (Cowing 1965). The social definition of 'legitimate' evolves over time so that what was once sanctioned becomes taken-for-granted.

Indeed, many ordinary financial contracts (e.g. derivatives like futures and options contracts, or insurance contracts) are routinely bought and sold to deal with risks that in a previous century were considered highly speculative.

Speculative bubbles often produce public scandals and lead to legal or regulatory reform. A burst bubble creates political opportunities that can be exploited to engineer dramatic changes in the legal rules that govern markets. The South Sea Bubble of 1720 led to the Bubble Act, stock market speculation in the 1920s led to the establishment of the Securities and Exchange Commission during the New Deal, and the dotcom bubble and associated Enron/Andersen/WorldCom scandals helped to produce the Sarbanes–Oxley Act of 2002. After the rules are put into place, market actors accommodate themselves to the new rules, and often devise creative ways to evade the rules, exploit loopholes and otherwise return to the business of speculation. A co-evolutionary pattern of changing speculation and changing regulatory rules can ensue.

References and further reading

Abolafia, Mitchel Y. and Kilduff, Martin (1988) 'Enacting Market Crisis: The Social Construction of a Speculative Bubble', *Administrative Science Quarterly*, 33: 177–93.

Bikhchandani, Sushil, Hirshleifer, David and Welch, Ivo (1998) 'Learning from the Behavior of Others: Conformity, Fads, and Informational Cascades', *Journal of Economic Perspectives*, 12: 151–70.

Cowing, Cedric B. (1965) *Populists, Plungers, and Progressives: A Social History of Stock and Commodity Speculation 1890–1936*, Princeton, NJ: Princeton University Press.

DiMaggio, Paul (2002) 'Endogenizing "Animal Spirits": Toward a Sociology of Collective Response to Uncertainty and Risk', in Mauro F. Guillén, Randall Collins, Paula England and Marshall Meyer (eds), *The New Economic Sociology*, New York: Russell Sage Foundation.

Garber, Peter M. (2000) *Famous First Bubbles: The Fundamentals of Early Manias*, Cambridge, MA: MIT Press.

Kindleberger, Charles P. (1984) *A Financial History of Western Europe*, London: George Allen and Unwin.

Stiglitz, Joseph E. (2000) 'The Contributions of the Economics of Information to Twentieth Century Economics', *Quarterly Journal of Economics*, 115: 1441–78.

Wood, Diana (2002) *Medieval Economic Thought*, Cambridge: Cambridge University Press.

BRUCE G. CARRUTHERS

SPIRIT OF CAPITALISM

See: religion and economic life; Weber

STAKEHOLDER

The term 'stakeholder' was mentioned for the first time in 1963 in an internal paper of the Stanford Research Institute. Its close relationship to the word 'stockholder' is intentional. It expresses the idea that enterprises should be concerned not only with the interests of their owners – namely, their stockholders – but also all groups that are connected to them.

There are quite varying definitions of who these stakeholders are. In a narrow definition Freeman defines stakeholders as 'those groups without whose support the organisation would cease to exist' (1984; 31). Investors, the management, the employees, suppliers, customers and creditors are doubtlessly groups which are essential for a firm's survival. In a broader definition, the term is made to include all who can exercise a (more than slight) influence on an enterprise. This would include the media, the **trade unions**, state authorities and competitors. In the broadest version, anyone who feels affected by the enterprise's activities in any way is a stakeholder. The group would then be expanded to include, for example, social, Third World and environmental pressure groups. These are subsumed under the term 'public interest groups'.

The motive for concern with stakeholders may be a purely economic one. It is suggested that the firm's executives must understand stakeholder needs and concerns because the lack of such understanding might threaten the firm's survival. The economic necessity to concern oneself with the interests of groups which have the closest ties to the enterprise, e.g. its employees and customers, is quite obvious. This is not new, however. The stakeholder concept contributes to a genuine broadening of perspective only when it brings those people and groups into view that were formerly outside the field of vision, and when it goes further to include stakeholder management. This begins with a large-scale scanning of the environment to include as far as possible all the stakeholders of the enterprise. An accurate analysis of their demands follows – i.e. monitoring. In the third phase – forecasting – plausible forecasts of the direction, scope and rapidity of the development of what stakeholders want should be drawn up. Finally, an assessment is made of what stakeholders demand and, using this as the basis, decisions made regarding the strategies to be adopted in handling them. The repertoire of possible responses to stakeholder demands ranges from full acceptance through negotiations right up to rejection of these wishes and attacks on stakeholders. The strategic goal of stakeholder management is always to secure and/or improve the firm's profitability. In particular, aims could be to avert legal action, to prevent harm to the corporate image, to improve the firm's **reputation**, to dispel suspicions concerning important projects, or, quite generally, to secure the support of society for the company. Thus, in the final analysis, stakeholder management is implemented in the service of the stockholder. What has changed is the way the environment is viewed. It is seen as substantially more complex, and is expanded into an early-warning system which draws attention to future opportunities and risks.

Understood in quite a different way, concern with stakeholders is an expression of a firm's social responsibility, that is not economically but ethically motivated. The starting point is the idea that enterprises have a moral responsibility for the consequences of their actions towards all groups and persons who are impacted by their activities. In practice, management of social responsibility can operate in quite the same way as strategic stakeholder management. If one wants to take responsibility for one's actions towards those who are affected by them, one must first determine who the affected persons are and what their interests are. There is one difference, however, in the assessment phase. In making an assessment from the economic point of view, what stands to the fore is whether the stakeholders are beneficial or harmful to the enterprise. From the ethical point of view, on the other hand, what is decisive is how justified the stakeholders' interests seem to be. This kind of assessment can easily put the firm in a dilemma because different stakeholder interests might be contradictory but equally justified. For instance, should one prohibit cigarette production because parents fear for the health of their children when these smoke? Or should consideration be given to the people who owe their livelihood to tobacco consumption?

The advance of the defenders of shareholder value in the 1990s prompted an appreciable revival of concern with stakeholders as well. Concentration on the interests of shareholders to the exclusion of virtually everyone else provoked opposition. Shareholder-value management was confronted with stakeholder-value management. Stakeholder-value management too moves between two poles: on the one hand, turning stakeholder interests into a strategic tool whose actual aim is to improve shareholder value, and, on the other, an ethical orientation which requires that justified interests be taken into consideration irrespective of their economic consequences.

Especially the champions of a free-market economy reject the idea that enterprises have any ethical responsibility to their stakeholders. If the market operates perfectly, they argue, a strict orientation to profit leads to the greatest good for all. Groups which are particularly affected by an enterprise's activity can bring their interests up in contract negotiations (e.g. employees, customers, suppliers, creditors). And the enforcement of public interests is the concern of the state and the general legislative framework. The advocates of social responsibility on the part of enterprises point out that the market does not function perfectly, that, as a rule, contracts are not exhaustive, and that gaps are often found in legislation. Beyond the maximization of profits, there is plenty of scope for enterprises to act in a responsible manner.

Another controversial issue is the form in which such consideration of stakeholder interests is to be embodied. While especially the representatives of a strategic stakeholder management draw attention to the responsibility of top managers, others consider a change in **corporate governance** to be necessary. For instance, stakeholders should be allowed to send representatives to the board of directors so as to have equal rights with shareholders in shaping corporate policy. However, the selection of the entitled groups and the criteria for such selection is still an unsolved problem.

References and further reading

Carroll, Archie B. and Buchholtz, Ann K. (1999) *Business and Society: Ethics and Stakeholder Management*, Cincinnati: Southwestern Publishing.

Freeman, Edward R. (1984) *Strategic Management, A Stakeholder Approach,* Marshfield, MA: Pitman Publishing.

Janisch, Monika (1993) *Das strategische Anspruchsgruppenmanagement: Vom Shareholder Value zum Stakeholder Value* [Strategic Management of Claimants: From Shareholder Value to Stakeholder Value], Bern: Haupt.

ELISABETH GÖBEL

STANDARDS AND STANDARDIZATION

Standards are the measures by which products, processes and producers are judged. Grades are the categories used to implement the standards. Standards are ubiquitous and serve in a variety of ways to undergird industrial economies. Standards may reduce transactions costs and increase competition by making relevant information (e.g. weight and volume) about a product available to both buyer and seller. Standards may also provide consistent product quality, ensuring that each product 'meets the standard'. Standards may order production processes, requiring the use of 'good manufacturing practices'. Standards may ensure compatibility, such that products produced by different companies can be made to work together with ease. Electrical outlets and plugs are examples of compatibility standards. Finally, standards may be designed to serve broader roles that extend beyond a particular product or process, such as promoting food safety, worker health and safety, environmental protection or animal welfare.

Standards do not require standardization. The word 'standard' may mean either a leader or something established by custom. Henry Ford's assembly lines produced automobiles that were 'any colour as long as it was black'. In contrast, Alfred Sloan used standards to permit choice among a wide variety of makes, models and options, allowing General Motors to gain market share at Ford's expense.

Standards are often used by companies and nation-states as marketing strategies. For example, IBM quickly established a significant presence in the personal computer industry and made its computer the standard. In less than fifty years Japan successfully used standards to move from a nation known for producing generally shoddy goods to one with a reputation for high quality and technical excellence.

Many standards are embodied in technical artifacts. For example, pesticide residue limits on food products are unenforceable without laboratory equipment to measure those residues. Thus, in market economies, standards only become widely used when the tools needed to measure them are relatively inexpensive. In some instances, the high cost, lack of timeliness or destructive character of direct measurement leads to the use of proxies. For example, until recently oil and protein content in soybeans could not be economically measured directly. Other measures, such as test weight and foreign material, were used as proxies for the characteristics of interest. Similarly, in the initial stages of aircraft development, wind tunnels tests substitute for flight.

In recent years, there has been a significant shift from product to process standards. This paralleled the move from quality control (rejecting unsatisfactory products at the end of the line) to total quality management (ensuring that each step of the manufacturing process meets the required standards). Many large firms have found that process standards reduce rejects and thereby more than pay for themselves. For example, the food industry has widely adopted Hazard Analysis and Critical Control Points, a process-oriented management approach. Process standards are also used in instances where buyers are willing to pay a premium for adherence to the process (e.g. organic foods).

Process standards may retard innovation by reducing flexibility, requiring use of an outmoded process, and resulting in unnecessarily high prices for consumers. In contrast, product standards encourage process innovation, so as to cut costs and increase profits in manufacture. Standards usually establish technological **path-dependence** by encouraging certain types of investments over others. Thus, the establishment of Microsoft Windows as *the* standard creates disincentives to investment in other operating systems even while encouraging further development of its architecture.

Nations take diverse approaches to standards formation. The United States tends to leave most standards to the private sector, narrowly restricting the role of the National Institute of Standards and Technology. A variety of nongovernmental organizations have sprung up to fill the gap, including the American National Standards Institute and the American Society for Testing and Materials. In some instances, the US approach has proven costly, leaving some consumers with incompatible technologies, or reducing the competitiveness of US firms in foreign markets. In contrast, the German government has taken a very active role in standards creation. Its DIN (Deutsches Institut für Normung) standards encompass most manufactured goods.

With increasing globalization of trade and competition, and restructuring of economies from planned to market driven, a world-wide attempt at 'harmonization' of standards is under way. Thus, international standards bodies have increased in significance. The International Organization for Standardization (ISO) has myriad committees that design standards for tests (what shall count as an adequate test for the structural soundness of metals?) as well as for processes. The ISO 9000 standards for management and the ISO 14000 standards for the environment are now commonly used around the world.

Standards embody social and ethical values (see **norms and values**) as well as accepted practices (see **Convention School**). As a result, harmonization has generated considerable conflict across types of standards. For example, standards for maintaining forest biodiversity may be in conflict with lumber quality standards for furniture. Cosmetic quality standards for fruits that require heavy use of pesticides may conflict with worker safety and environmental standards.

While it would appear that standards set fixed limits to things and processes, in practice standards are negotiated during the processes of standard setting and enforcement. Moreover, meeting standards may be voluntary, required by law, or necessary to participate in a market. Who gets to set and enforce standards is critically important, as standards may restrict market access, either by virtue of the cost of measurement devices or by requiring additional capital investment to conform to the standard, and define the distribution and nature of social goods. Thus, standards form an important part of the **moral economy** of industrial societies, defining to a significant degree who we are, what we do, and how we do it.

References and further reading

Brouwer, Floor and Ervin, David E. (eds) (2002) *Public Concerns, Environmental Standards and Agricultural Trade*, Wallingford, UK: CABI Publishing.

Grindley, Peter (1995) *Standards Strategy and Policy: Cases and Stories*, Oxford: Oxford University Press.

Krislov, Samuel (1997) *How Nations Chose Product Standards and Standards Change Nations*, Pittsburgh, PA: University of Pittsburgh Press.

JIM BINGEN
LAWRENCE BUSCH

STATE AND ECONOMY

Since the field's revival in the 1980s, economic sociologists have insisted that economies, including contemporary market economies, are embedded within social and political structures. This approach directly challenges the tendency to conceptualize the economy as an analytically autonomous realm that is subject to its own law and logic. Most economists recognize that market economies depend on a wide variety of state actions, from maintaining law and order to educating the citizenry, but they rarely incorporate these elements into their models. The consequence is that much economics research rarely questions the Lockean narrative in which human beings, in the state of nature, spontaneously come together in trading relations that culminate in a social contract before there is any kind of state.

This Lockean story continues to be the foundation for the contemporary 'free-market' ideas popularized by Friedrich Hayek, Milton Friedman and many others. These free-market theorists claim that reducing the government's role in regulating the economy and in providing goods and services will invariably produce efficiency gains by enhancing the ability of markets to allocate resources. Implicit in their argument is the confidence that markets will spontaneously emerge and provide social order.

Economic sociologists, in contrast, tend to trace their intellectual lineage to a different seventeenth-century theorist – Thomas Hobbes. Hobbes noted that in the state of nature, human life was 'nasty, brutish, and short', and he was highly sceptical of spontaneously generated social order.

On the contrary, he argued that social order depended on a sovereign authority who could impose order. Max Weber was following Hobbes' logic when he defined the state by its legitimate monopoly over the exercise of violence. And, in his account of the rise of 'rational capitalism' in the West, Weber emphasized the ways in which **economic development** required the prior existence of states able to enforce the rule of law.

Yet there is a tension in Weber – and in the entire sociological tradition – between what can be called a weak and a strong variant of the embeddedness thesis. The weak variant acknowledges that market economies depend on certain previously existing institutional structures, but assumes that once those structures are in place, the economy will be able to operate on its own for extended periods of time. Hence, this weak variant is easily reconciled with the common assumption of economists that market economies will naturally tend towards some stable equilibrium. In contrast, in the strong variant of the embedd-

edness thesis, the economy is seen as depending upon the continuous, active and flexible exercise of state power. The argument is that if state agencies were to proceed strictly according to a fixed routine, the economy would not find an equilibrium; it would be more likely to slide into crisis.

The weak variant is usually not defended explicitly; it is more that when sociologists fail to address the issue directly, they tend to be pulled towards the conventional view that the economy is an analytically autonomous realm that will tend towards equilibrium. In Weber's case, he repeatedly drew a contrast between 'political capitalism' and the 'rational' capitalism that had emerged in Western Europe. Since the hallmark of 'political capitalism' is substantial state influence over economic activity, the implication was that rational capitalism had succeeded in keeping the state at arm's length. So Weber who had emphasized the centrality of legal institutions to the rise of capitalism simultaneously implied that those elaborate legal rules did not constitute a political structuring of economic activity.

The strong variant of the embeddedness thesis was advanced most forcefully by Karl **Polanyi** in *The Great Transformation*. It is developed most fully in his argument that land, labour and money are 'fictitious commodities' in a market society. True commodities are those things that are produced to be sold on a market. For such products, supply and demand can generally be balanced through the price mechanism. However, land, labour and the total supply of money and credit are not true commodities. Land is nature that has been subdivided, labour is provided by living, breathing human beings, and allowing the money supply to be determined only by market forces would risk either chronic deflation or chronic inflation. In all three cases, continuous action by state agencies is required to assure that the supply and demand for these fictitious, albeit indispensable, commodities reach some kind of reasonable balance. With the state managing the supply of land, labour and money, it is difficult to envision the state as somehow outside of an autonomous economic sphere.

But Polanyi adds another dimension to his argument by emphasizing the inherent instability of market competition. Instead of seeing a tendency to spontaneous order, Polanyi built on Adam Smith's understanding that economic actors have strong incentives to find ways to protect themselves from the rigors of ongoing competition. Whether through collusion, market-sharing schemes or monopolization, there is the ongoing tendency for competitive markets to be transformed into their opposite. Here again, state agencies face a continuously evolving challenge to sustain market competition itself. But if they are successful at this task, there is yet another challenge. So long as there is market competition, economic actors will have incentives to gain advantage by shifting costs on to others. The increased production of what economists call 'negative externalities', such as environmental pollution, sale of products that are dangerous for consumers, shortchanging customers, or maintaining work conditions that threaten employee health and safety is often fostered by the existence of competitive markets. Reducing these externalities requires action by the state to prohibit cost shifting and to assure that firms will be held liable for violations of the rules. Here, again, since new externalities are continually being invented or rediscovered, routine action by state agencies will not be sufficient to stabilize market economies.

A final argument along these lines has been elaborated by legal scholars who emphasize that social and technological change tends to undermine inherited legal definitions of ownership and property rights. For example, as large corporations realized that an increasing portion of their assets consisted of long strings of easily reproduced electronic code, they rushed to legislatures to demand legal changes that would protect their 'intellectual property' from unauthorized uses. Here again, without ongoing evolution in the state's legislative and regulatory activities, it is fair to assume that market economies would more frequently face circumstances where economic actors lacked the predictability required to sustain necessary levels of new investment.

But the strong variant of the embeddedness thesis does not imply a functionalist or benign view of state actions. While state action is necessary for a market economy to operate effectively, there is no guarantee that any particular state action will strengthen the economy. State actors, particularly in the absence of democratic constraints, can engage in predatory behaviour that systematically discourages new investment or new entrepreneurial initiatives. More commonly, state actors fail to respond flexibly to changing circumstances either because they are beholden to powerful economic interests who would be threatened by a shift in policy or because their view of the available policy options has been constrained by ideology. State actors also may choose to pursue policies that intensify some of the contradictory tendencies of market economies and states can also be divided against themselves, so the initiatives of one agency are offset or neutralized by those of another.

While the strong variant insists that market economies are always politically embedded, some market economies are far more successful than others in sustaining economic growth over long time periods. Explaining these different outcomes continues to be an important and fruitful area of scholarly debate. One important strand of current research analyses the 'varieties of capitalism', identifying distinct institutional patterns, and explaining the relative advantages and disadvantages of each variety. A parallel strand of research seeks to explain why some developing nations have advanced economically while others have moved backwards.

Global embeddedness

The strong embeddedness perspective also emphasizes that the choices open to nations or regions in structuring their economies are usually constrained by global political and economic institutions. These transnational institutions change over time, reflecting shifts in the global balance of political and economic power. For example, in the period from 1870 to 1914, the international gold standard, rooted in England's economic and military superiority, placed strict limits on national economic policies. And even those countries that refused to accede to the discipline of the gold standard found that their foreign economic policy options were still constrained.

The collapse of the gold standard in the early 1930s was generally seen as a cause of the global depression and World War II. The consequence was a self-conscious effort to create new institutions to stabilize and manage the global economy. When the International Monetary Fund and the World Bank were created by international agreement in the 1940s, debate over the structure and functioning of these institutions was generally limited to elite groups and policy experts. This situation did not change measurably during the relatively prosperous decades of the 1950s and 1960s – a period that has been labelled the epoch of 'embedded liberalism'. Even when international monetary arrangements were renegotiated in the early 1970s, participation in the policy debates was quite limited.

This is not surprising since the main axis of global politics during this period was the Cold War – the clash between market societies and those who had followed the Soviet model of state ownership. As a rule, the socialist societies kept their distance from the existing international economic institutions, and they created their own

rival system of trade agreements. Yet the nations that followed the Soviet model continued to be embedded in the larger world economy; it shaped their fundamental political and economic decisions, both because of the military polarization of the Cold War and because of their limited access to foreign markets and capital. Ironically, as Cold War tensions eased in the 1970s and 1980s, the growth of economic relations between the West and the socialist societies was a critical factor in generating popular discontent with the shortcomings of the socialist economies.

When the Bretton Woods system for managing exchange rates came into crisis in the early 1970s, decisions about the structure of the global economy were still made by small groups of experts and political leaders. But the changes instituted in 1971–3 ushered in a new era characterized by dramatic currency fluctuations, increased global capital mobility and sustained efforts by the United States and the global financial institutions to alter the economic policies of sovereign governments. Governments began to tell their citizens that certain policy choices had to be made because of the rules of regional or global economic institutions. As a consequence, for the first time in history, the rules and institutions governing the global economy became the focus of mass political activity in both the developed and the developing nations. Particularly by the second half of the 1990s, it was typical for meetings of the major global economic organizations to be greeted by militant street demonstrations, and a broad range of groups that formed an emergent global civil society debated the proper institutional structure for the global economy.

This new circumstance has raised hopes for a fundamental restructuring of the global economy that would emerge out of international negotiations that were influenced by a broad global political discussion and debate. But the mechanism by which this change would occur remains highly uncertain since a handful of powerful governments have been able to keep discussions of reform off the official agendas of global institutions. In this politically charged and contested environment, economic sociologists can make a major contribution by developing systematic accounts of the interrelation between global institutions and political choice within national and regional economies.

References and further reading

Block, Fred and Evans, Peter (2005) 'The State and the Economy', in R. Swedberg and N. Smelser, (eds), *Handbook of Economic Sociology*, second edition, Princeton, NJ: Princeton University Press, pp. 505–26.

Fligstein, Neil (2001) *The Architecture of Markets: An Economic Sociology of Twenty-First Century Capitalist Societies*, Princeton, NJ: Princeton University Press.

McMichael, Philip (2000) *Development and Social Change: A Global Perspective*, Thousand Oaks, CA: Sage.

Polanyi, Karl ([1944]2001) *The Great Transformation*, Boston: Beacon Press.

FRED BLOCK

STRATEGY

A significant area of theoretical and empirical research has been focused on how the social aspects of a decision environment influence individuals' strategic behaviour. As advanced by Schelling (1978) and others, the strategic choices of individuals are often profoundly influenced by the behaviour of the aggregate social group. Following these authors, research in this area has focused on how the behaviour of the social group, as an aggregate, can alter the information available for decision-making and the costs of strategic behaviours. For example, one's choice to enter an intersection on an amber light depends on the behaviour of other drivers: entering is less costly if others are doing so as well (Schelling 1978). Knowing this, there may be strategic benefits of being a 'first mover' since the chosen behaviour may influence the decisions of the social group and, where payoffs are interdependent, the welfare of the first mover.

With the development of **behavioural economics**, a new line of research has focused on the social aspects of strategic interactions as captured in the idea of 'other-regarding behaviour' (Fehr and Schmidt 1999; Rabin, 1993). 'Other-regarding behaviour' speaks to the potential that individuals account for the intentions or payoffs of others in their decision calculus. For example, individuals' choices are often made with attention to the degree to which their behaviours are deemed 'fair' by others (see **fairness**; **game theory**; **reciprocity**). Experimental research has demonstrated that in simple bargaining games individuals account for the welfare of others in their decision-making. Most noticeably, individuals pay close attention to how others construe their behaviour in terms of fairness norms. Behaviours viewed as unfair are often reciprocated with negative reciprocity: in a host of experimental games, individuals are willing to incur substantial costs in order to punish those who behaved in a manner deemed 'unfair' (Fehr and Gächter 2000). Increasingly, research is pointing to the import of social norms (which often define what is deemed as fair or appropriate behaviour) and adherence to these norms in influencing reciprocity. As such, strategic behaviour in social contexts is strongly influenced by the threat of negative reciprocity (incurring a cost to punish another) and the promise of positive reciprocity (incurring a cost to benefit another).

See also: bargaining theory; cooperation; rational choice theory.

References and further reading

Camerer, C. (2003) *Behavioral Game Theory*, New York: Princeton University Press.

Fehr, E. and Gächter, S. (2000) 'Fairness and Retaliation: The Economics of Reciprocity', *Journal of Economic Perspectives*, 14: 159–81.

Fehr, E. and Schmidt, K. (1999) 'A Theory of Fairness, Competition, and Cooperation', *Quarterly Journal of Economics*, 114: 817–68.

Rabin, M. (1993) 'Incorporating Fairness into Game Theory and Economics', *American Economic Review*, 83: 1281–302.

Schelling, T. (1960) *Strategy of Conflict*, Cambridge, MA: Harvard University Press.

—— (1978) *Micromotives and Macrobehavior*, New York: W. W. Norton.

ROBERT J. OXOBY

STRATIFICATION

See: class; labor markets

STRUCTURAL HOLES

See: network analysis

STRUCTURATION THEORY

Structuration theory is the highly influential contribution of the British sociologist Anthony Giddens to general social theory, taken up and discussed throughout the social sciences – e.g. as a sophistication of neoinstitutionalist approaches (Scott 2001), rational actor models and as a conceptualization of innovation processes in economic thinking (Beckert 2002).

Giddens (1984: 183) emphasizes the role of economic institutions. Capitalist societies are characterized by the principle of 'disembedding, yet interconnecting, of state and economic institutions. The tremendous economic power generated by the harnessing of allocative resources to a generic tendency towards technical improvement is matched by an enormous expansion in the administrative "reach" of the state.' However, he does not make these contexts a major subject of study. Giddens' theory is nevertheless fruitful for economic sociology since it entails an understanding of economic contexts that links them to social practices, that brings together **structure** and

agency (see **agency theory**), and that allows the understanding how actors are the creators of markets, organizations and inter-firm networks, yet created by them. In contrast to the rational actor model and to a structural model of the economy, Giddens accentuates the knowledgeable agent as the conceptual centre of social analysis. He places 'knowledgeability' in the context of the ongoing practices of social life. Hence, economic contexts do not appear as a phenomenon external to agency or as something based on individualized actors, but as contingently produced and reproduced (and potentially transformed) via social activity and the stretching across time and space. This approach is of particular interest for the analysis of modern societies, characterized by reflexivity, i.e. the constant examination and reformation of social practices in the light of incoming information about those very practices, thus constitutively altering their character (Giddens 1990a: 38).

From 1976 to 1984 Anthony Giddens' works focused on the critical examination of nineteenth-century European social theory and its contribution to contemporary problems in the social sciences. With the publication of *New Rules of Sociological Method* (1976) he offered a first explicit outline of his new approach to an old problem of sociological thinking, the interrelation of structure and action in micro and macro analysis. Starting from 'interpretative sociology' (especially Schutz, Garfinkel and the ethnomethodologists as well as from Gadamer and other hermeneutics) and its conceptions of 'methodological' or 'practical' consciousness, he criticizes the functionalist conceptualization of society in both **Durkheim** and **Parsons** for not giving due import to this kind of awareness. In his *Central Problems in Social Theory*, published in 1979, Giddens starts the imaginative reworking of the main concepts of structuralist thought. Following Heidegger and linking the concept of structuration to Derrida's conception of *différance*, he puts much emphasis on the time–space relations inherent in the constitution of all social interaction and social systems. His *Constitution of Society*, published in 1984, can be read as a 'summary' of this work. It offers a comprehensive outline of the core of structuration theory and an incisive overall critique of positivism and functionalism as well as of evolutionism and **historical materialism** (see Bryant and Jary 2001 for further details).

Structure, system and duality of structure: the central concepts

The core of structuration theory lies in the concepts of structure, system and duality of structure. Structures are conceived as 'rule-resource sets, implicated in the articulation of social systems' (Giddens 1984: 377) and organized as properties of social systems – allowing the binding of time and space in social systems on three institutionalized social dimensions: signification, domination and legitimation. Knowledgeable agents practically refer to discernibly similar social practices by actualizing *in situ* underlying sets of rules of signification and legitimation as well as resources of domination and thereby achieve the time–space extension of structure. Even raw materials, land, machines, etc., become resources only when incorporated within processes of structuration (ibid.: 33). This understanding of structure differs from functionalist or structuralist thinking, which conceives structure 'as some kind of "patterning" of social relations or social phenomena' (ibid.: 16) which appears "external" to human action, as a source of constraint on the free initiative of the independently constituted subject' (ibid.). In structurationist thinking, action is always accompanied by unintended consequences and agents face unacknowledged conditions of action but 'structure is not equated with constraint but is always both, constraining and

enabling' (ibid.: 25). Moreover, the 'constitution of agents and structures are not two independently given sets of phenomena, a dualism, but represent a duality' (ibid.: 25). As time–space presence, structure only exists in its instantiations in such practices and as memory traces (ibid.) and is 'in a certain sense more "internal" than exterior to their activities in a Durkheimian sense' (ibid.: 25).

'Social systems are composed of social relations and social interactions, coordinated across time and space' (Giddens 1990b: 302). Social systems 'do not have 'structures' but rather exhibit 'structural properties'' (Giddens 1984, 17). Business interactions and relations, for example, become elements of a firm through their recursive inclusion into this *social system* via their coordination through this system in time–space. Markets, organizations, inter-firm networks, etc., are predominantly identified by their different forms of coordination. Particular forms of regulation characterize their governances in contrast to modern system theory (see **Luhmann**), in which autopoiesis is the overall mechanism of (re-)production.

The *duality of structure* is always the main grounding of continuities in social reproduction across time and space, and structure has no existence independent of the knowledge agents have about what they (practically) do in their day-to-day activities. For example, economic agents communicate meanings in business affairs by utilizing interpretative schemes (like prices) as modalities of action. They make themselves (or have been made) aware of these schemes by situative demands of communication and by rules of signification. Each communication necessarily includes the exercise of power (through the use of resources like money, production utilities or business relations) and the evaluation of activities and/or events as a way of judging what happens. The powerful constitution of any economic activity or event is reflected by the fact that agents can always act otherwise, that even the less powerful exert some control over the more powerful in established power relations: dialectic of control (ibid.: 374). However, the knowledge and power of even the mightiest players are always incomplete due to unintended consequences, unacknowledged conditions of intended actions, and the omnipresence of the dialectic of control. Continuities only occur when there is continuity in what people do. Analysing the structuration of social systems, of economic processes and the (re-)production or transformation of economic institutions, therefore, means studying the patterning of social relations and social interactions in time–space involving the reproduction of situated practices and the virtual order of 'modes of structuring' on the three social dimensions recursively implicated in such (re-)production (ibid.: 17).

In the *economic sphere* economic institutions prevail and allocative resources play an inherently constitutive role in the structuration of societal totalities (ibid.: 34), whereas in the political sphere this role is occupied by authoritative resources. Political and economic institutions are thus differentiated in modern societies, yet play together in social practices at the same time (ibid.: 183) as discussions on the varieties of capitalism and the interplay of private and state governance regimes indicate. Their interlacing is therefore not seen as a deficiency, as in neoclassical thinking, but as a necessity of doing business today. Since structures of domination are only analytically separable from signification and legitimation they are seen as mutually constitutive. The dominance of allocative resources in the economic sphere means that the rules of signification as well as of legitimation and the authoritative resources are adjusted to them and may even augment these resources.

Critiques and limitations

The most fundamental critique has been articulated by Margret Archer and refers to the theorem of the 'duality of structure'. Archer (1995: 94) criticizes Giddens for 'flattening out the ontological depth of the social world by denying the existence of emergent properties' by using social practices as the basic concept of social constitution. She accuses Giddens of delineating 'mind as emergent from body' (ibid.: 102) and 'structure as emergent from social relations' (ibid.). However, I agree with Giddens (1990b: 299), who replies that 'structure and action *cannot* form a dualism … because each is constituted by and in a single "realm" – human activity' – an argument to be reiterated concerning the separation of body and mind.

One limitation of particular importance to economic sociology is that Giddens does not systematically outline the role of social systems, especially economic organizations, and of (economic) institutions in the processes of social constitution. This is astonishing since he emphasizes the importance of organizations in modern societies. Figure 4 clarifies the structurationist argument and outlines paths of further refinement: (1) *social actors* recursively refer in their actions to social practices and to other actors (and their actions and relations), be they, for example, transaction partners in business exchanges or non-present actors, e.g. executives to whom employees have to justify their actions; (2) societally embedded *social systems* and their forms of regulation of social interactions and relations are not only relevant action contexts but co-evolve as a medium and result of structuration processes; (3) actors do not only refer to these immediate contexts in their actions but – however mediated – also to 'more distant' *societal totalities* and institutions like state regulations, or cultural and societal institutions.

Social systems like organizations, inter-organizational networks or markets are recursively constituted by social actors in embedded contexts and yet are, at the same time, the very medium of this constitution.

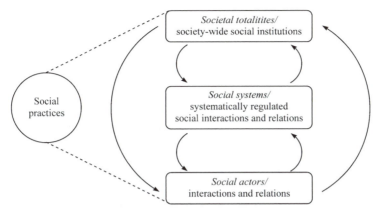

Figure 4. Constitution of social systems: the structurationist perspective
Source: Adapted from Windeler 2001: 124

Agents working for manufacturers and system suppliers respectively, for example, interact with each other referring to practices of doing business by the firm they have contracted, as well as to the economic practices and the power relations in the organizational field and more general contexts of the societal sphere. And in acting this way they (re-)produce or transform the practices, the form of system coordination, the co-evolution of the systems involved and stretch the practices and power relations in time–space.

Further paths of refining structuration theory should be related to forms of reflexive system regulation (or reflexive governances) and their mutual interrelatedness in modern societies. Especially in organizations and inter-organizational networks 'there occur processes of selective "information filtering" whereby strategically placed actors seek reflexively to regulate the overall conditions of system reproduction either to keep things as they are or to change them' (Giddens 1984: 27). These systems typically gather and use information not just as a means of surveillance, but as a way of ordering social relations across time and space (Giddens 1990b: 303). Via their reflexive regulation of practices and influence in a diversity of contexts, actors can often augment their resources and power. However, they are not the masters of developments. Collectively as human beings, however, we can exercise control to some extent. Nevertheless, social systems threaten to run out of control occasionally in unforeseeable directions (Giddens 1990a: 139).

References and further reading

Archer, Margret S. (1995) *Realist Social Theory: The Morphogenetic Approach*, Cambridge: Cambridge University Press.

Beckert, Jens (2002) *Beyond the Market: The Social Foundations of Economic Efficiency*, Princeton, NJ: Princeton University Press.

Bryant, Christopher G. A. and Jary, David (eds) (1997) *Anthony Giddens. Critical Assessments*, four volumes, London: Routledge.

—— (2001) *The Contemporary Giddens: Social Theory in a Globalizing Age*, London: Palgrave.

Cohen, Ira J. (1989) *Structuration Theory. Anthony Giddens and the Constitution of Social Life*, London: Macmillan.

Giddens, Anthony (1976) *New Rules of Sociological Method*, London: Hutchinson.

—— (1984) *The Constitution of Society. Outline of the Theory of Structuration*, Cambridge: Polity Press.

—— (1990a) *The Consequences of Modernity*, Cambridge, Polity Press.

—— (1990b) 'Structuration Theory and Sociological Analysis', in Jon Clark, Celia Modgil and Sohan Modgil (eds), *Anthony Giddens. Consensus and Controversy*, London: Falmer, pp. 297–315.

Held, David and Thompson, John B. (eds) (1989) *Social Theory of Modern Societies: Anthony Giddens and his Critics*, Cambridge: Cambridge University Press.

Scott, W. Richard (2001) *Institutions and Organizations*, second edition, London: Sage.

Windeler, Arnold (2001) *Unternehmungsnetzwerke. Konstitution und Strukturation*, Wiesbaden: Westdeutscher Verlag.

ARNOLD WINDELER

STRUCTURE

As it pertains to the economy, structure is a concept that has guided research along three broad lines. First, as used by many economists, structure pertains to the organization of economic activity, for example as distinctions among perfect competition, **monopoly and oligopoly**. Second, structure pertains to the situation of economic forms within broader types of social organization. **Embeddedness**, decoupling and **structuration** are concepts seeking to specify structure in this second sense. Third, structure pertains to the architecture, or large-scale patterning of economic relations. In this sense, for example, many market ecologies consist of 'complex and stable social structures based on repeated interactions of buyers and sellers and on the status and reputation of market participants', where the social structures comprise 'concrete social relations' as well as 'cognitive understandings' (Fligstein 2001: 7, 32).

Structure and economic organization

From Adam Smith onward, much of the history of economics consists of successive endeavours to delineate theories of economic structures, understood as patterns of organization of the economy in terms of certain attributes, notably the presence and degree of competition among agents. Zafirovski (2002: 19–165) provides a comprehensive overview. I will focus on two (related) schemes that have been particularly influential in economic sociology, those of the dual economy and dual labour market segmentation.

Robert T. Averitt, an institutional economist who published *The Dual Economy* in 1968, distinguished two sectors of the private economy: a core consisting of firms large in size and influence, with vertically integrated production processes, and a periphery populated by relatively small firms. Core firms were postulated to be monopolists or oligopolists, while the periphery was the locus of competitive, more marginal firms. Core firms were hypothesized to exploit firms in the periphery in various ways (such as demanding 'preferred' customer rebates from their suppliers). Dual economic sectors were subsequently linked to labour markets, as in a 1971 work of Peter Doeringer and Michael Piore postulating that firms at the core of the economy have internal labour markets (positions within the firm linked together in skill hierarchies and career ladders), whereas there is no barrier to movement among firms in the economy's periphery. Hodson and Kaufman (1982) provide a critical review.

Theories of the dual economy and dual labour markets were influential and controversial through the 1980s. Criticism of these theories ranged from the difficulty of finding consistently observed empirical effects of the postulated sectors, to problems of operationalizing those sectors, to a lack of emphasis on 'more sociological concerns' at the intersection of firm, industry and job characteristics. More recently economic dualism and labour market segmentation have been combined with the study of race, gender and a concern for understanding macro-level changes in the US economy, such as the increasing prevalence of flexibility in production techniques and employment. Reid and Rubin (2003) find that primary labour market jobs in the core of the economy yield the greatest rewards among 'good' jobs, and secondary labour market jobs in the core yield the greatest benefits among 'bad' jobs, and therefore that a major analytical issue is the shifts in the distribution of employment across sectors. Reid and Rubin find diminishing inequalities by race and gender, while at the same time there are persistent effects of sector, race and gender on stratification.

Economic forms and broader social organization

Karl Marx emphasized that the market consists of social relationships, and Emile Durkheim emphasized the non-contractual elements (such as kinship and the density of social interactions) upon which economic contracts often rest. In this sense, the core idea of the social embeddedness of the economy is as old as sociology itself (see Zafirovski 2002: 183 for a review). Nonetheless, Mark Granovetter's 1985 argument that personal networks are primary in generating trust and discouraging malfeasance has proven to be a crystallizing moment in the developing paradigm of the new economic sociology.

Within the so-called structural approach to economic sociology, research of Wayne Baker demonstrates that predictions of standard microeconomic theory as to market competitiveness of stock options markets are sometimes incorrect unless the analyst takes into account the distinctive structuring of the network (who trades with whom) among the traders; moreover, the patterning of the network also affects price volatility. In this way, markets may be said to be embedded within broader structures of network relations. Other research of Baker's examines the network interface between a firm and its **banks**, finding that the type of interface (whether relation-based or based on each specific transaction) has implications for how (and how much) capital is raised. Ronald Burt defines an industry's 'structural autonomy' by the extent to which it is concentrated (low

competition) and the extent to which industries with which its firms do business are competitive. Burt's focus in this respect extends to input–output tables of industrial purchases reconceptualized as networks of interaction, and he shows (for example) that structurally autonomous sectors have measurably superior profits to those of their constrained trading partners. In another example of the contributions of the structural approach to the embedding of economic behaviour, Burt shows that constraint by the consuming public, a concept inverse to autonomy, is a stronger predictor of philanthropic donations than is the tax savings predicted by the microeconomic theory of philanthropy.

Probably the most prominent writer within the structuralist approach is Harrison White (see the review in Swedberg 1994). White's concern is with production markets, which typically consist of a dozen firms that come to view each other as constituting a market and are perceived as such by buyers. Whereas embeddedness has become a primary concept for economic sociology, White emphasizes instead what he refers to as a duality of embeddedness and decoupling, two concepts that together produce distinctive markets through struggles for identity and control. As firms become embedded within sustainable markets, entailments and stable role expectations about revenue/volume matching and a host of other behaviours become fixed. A consequence is that embeddings actually suppress fluid network dynamics, decoupling embedded firms from both their suppliers and their customers. Thus, for White, production markets 'constitute an ingenious social invention that gets results by playing off ... mechanisms that decouple as they embed actions by firms into markets sited within larger networks in flows of production' (White 2002: 211).

If forms of economic activity are embedded within social networks, then within what are those networks embedded?

As seen from the work just reviewed, the structuralist approach to markets has typically understood networks to have an institutional mooring (as, for example, in White's emphasis on revenue/volume matching and a related parameter space that is generative of network identities). Beginning in the late 1980s, however, there was an increased emphasis on an adequate understanding of markets as requiring analysis of their location within larger political, cultural, historical-comparative and social-systems institutional configurations (Block 1994; Dimaggio 1994; Hamilton 1994; Swedberg 1994; Zafirovski 2002: 180–212). John Lie opposed the neoclassical economic theorization of 'placeless markets' with a conception of economic 'modes of exchange' within historically specific and specified technological, social and institutional constraints. Walter Powell and Laurel Smith-Doerr sought ways to conceptualize how actors in networks construct their worlds, implicitly invoking Anthony Giddens' concept of 'structuration' as referring to the mutual dependence of structure and agency. Neil Fligstein put forward the metaphor of 'markets as politics' as well as a social movement metaphor to stand for power struggles within and between firms and to point to the formation of markets as an aspect of state-building. Viviana Zelizer demonstrated the limits of a purely utilitarian analysis of money, showing that different 'species' of money (such as doles versus allowances) have distinctive meanings requiring cultural specification. Bruce Carruthers and Wendy Nelson Espeland put forward a view of a fundamental institution of rational economics, double-entry bookkeeping, as rooted historically as much in rhetoric and culture (such as the need to convince important audiences of the difference between the new accounting practices and usury) as in technical dimensions (such as classification systems implied by the techniques, themselves instances of cultural categorization

schemes). The developments reviewed here have to some extent led to a broadening of the structural approach, as for example in White's treatment of discourse, sociocultural constructions, and theories of action in his (2002) chapter on business cultures.

The architecture of economic relations

Several analytical approaches have been developed for the purpose of discovering an overall structure to economic transactions. Leontief's input–output analysis provides a means for specifying the interdependence of an economy's various productive sectors, detailing the dependence of each industry on the products of the others. Leontief conceptualized models of macro-structure for input–output tables. He distinguished a completely 'interdependent' economy (full connectivity among sectors) from one organized as a hierarchy (operationalized as a rearrangement of the table's categories such that all flows are discovered to be below the principal diagonal), and he distinguished both of these from a 'block triangular' macro-model that evidences 'interdependence of industries within blocks ... and hierarchical relations between blocks' (Leontief 1966: 45).

Leontief's formulation of **ideal-type** models of economic macro-structure resembles the blockmodels later formulated independently by White and collaborators for studying the large-scale patterning of social networks. This technique was used by Michael Gerlach to study the overall structure of the Japanese corporate economy on the basis of simultaneous analysis of three networks: bank borrowing, equity shareholding and director interlocks. Among Gerlach's findings was that the most appropriate model for financial centrality in the Japanese economy is not that of a fully integrated network in which central banks are tied to the economy as a whole, as exists in the USA, but of banks as coordinators of specific subsets of affiliated firms (see the review in Powell and Smith-Doerr 1994).

White's (2002) modelling of an overall architecture of production markets, introduced in the previous section, requires the analyst to account explicitly for the varied circumstances of particular industries. In his work, markets constructed among firms in networks are mapped into a space of settings with interpretable parameters that govern the ratio of demand to producers' costs; key parameters pertain to growth in volume and to variation in product quality, both of which are assessed from the point of view of producer cost and buyer need. The classical economic market occupies just one point in White's 'market plane'. White understands markets as distinctive and concrete types of social structure, comprising a self-reproducing system of niches for competing firms in a price/quality space. To illustrate with just one example: in copper-mining the quality of product actually decreases with an increase in producer cost, because the first big strikes yield ore that is both richer and less costly to mine than subsequent strikes further below ground. This illustrates the 'paradox' region of White's market plane, and a fundamental question that he pursues is the conditions under which a market schedule (a mapping of revenue on to volume) might be sustained in this (and in all the other) market regions within his overall network architecture of market niches.

See also: network analysis.

References and further reading

Block, F. (1994) 'The Role of the State in the Economy', in N. Smelser and R. Swedberg (eds), *Handbook of Economic Sociology*, Princeton, NJ: Princeton University Press, pp. 691–710.
DiMaggio, P. (1994) 'Culture and Economy', in N. Smelser and R. Swedberg (eds), *Handbook of Economic Sociology*, Princeton, NJ: Princeton University Press, pp. 27–53.

Fligstein, Neil (2001) *The Architecture of Markets*, Princeton, NJ: Princeton University Press.
Hamilton, G. (1994) 'Civilizations and the Organization of Economies', in N. Smelser and R. Swedberg (eds), *Handbook of Economic Sociology*, Princeton, NJ: Princeton University Press, pp. 183–205.
Hodson, Randy and Kaufman, Robert L. (1982) 'Economic Dualism: A Critical Review', *American Sociological Review*, 47: 727–39.
Leontief, Wassily (1966) *Input–Output Economics*, New York: Oxford University Press.
Powell, W. W. and Smith-Doerr, L. (1994) 'Networks in Economic Life', in N. Smelser and R. Swedberg (eds), *Handbook of Economic Sociology*, Princeton, NJ: Princeton University Press, pp. 368–402.
Reid, Lesley Williams and Rubin, Beth A. (2003) 'Integrating Economic Dualism and Labor Market Segmentation: The Effects of Race, Gender, and Structural Location on Earnings, 1974–2000', *Sociological Quarterly*, 44: 405–32.
Smelser, Neil J. and Swedberg, Richard (eds) (1994) *Handbook of Economic Sociology*, Princeton, NJ: Princeton University Press.
Swedberg, R. (1994) 'Markets as Social Structures', in N. Smelser and R. Swedberg (eds), *Handbook of Economic Sociology*, Princeton, NJ: Princeton University Press, pp. 255–82.
White, Harrison C. (2002) *Markets from Networks*, Princeton, NJ: Princeton University Press.
Zafirovski, Milan (2002) *A Primer on Economic Sociology*, New York: Nova Science Publishers.

RONALD L. BREIGER

SUBSISTENCE ECONOMY

A subsistence economy exists in a society whose members produce only enough to provide for their own basic needs to sustain life. Historically, this kind of economy has characterized hunting and gathering and agricultural societies without markets or developed commerce. That is, they do not produce a surplus sufficient to support the beginnings of a complex social structure of specialized, differentiated roles for specialists in religion, the arts, science or governance. In social evolutionary schemes the subsistence level of bands evolve over long periods of time into the more elaborate exchange systems of chiefdoms, and then into the market systems of empires with towns, cities and eventually states. The move from a subsistence economy, or production for use, to a commodity-based economy, dominated by production for exchange, depends ultimately on the appearance of markets, and in modern times on the demand for cash crops, like sugarcane and rice, by urban and industrial populations no longer engaged in agriculture.

The preoccupation of anthropology has been to specify, qualify, debate and define the major variants of this picture of social evolution. Still, the conception of the subsistence economy has remained the basic anchor of this scheme. For example, some anthropologists, who have worked with contemporary hunters and gatherers like the San people of South Africa and the aborigines of Australia, have tried to dispel the impression that subsistence economies mean life at the margins of existence, or a harsh, unpredictable struggle for life. Under stable ecological conditions, subsistence economies have produced viable forms of society for long periods of human history.

Only with the immense changes for agriculturalists and hunters and gatherers brought about by contact with more powerful and developed neighbours, or invaders, does the classic association of subsistence with harsh or marginal conditions of life become a reality. Much of contemporary **economic anthropology** has been the study of the changes wrought on local cultures world-wide by the spread of world capitalism through colonialism, nationalism and now **globalization**. In this world historical process, some tribal cultures have moved both out from and back into conditions of subsistence, or near-subsistence production. Subsistence economies today mostly characterize those groups that have been marginalized by global economic processes, those that are excluded from viable production for market systems. Such groups are embedded in the complex social structures of nation-states and consumer economies, in which they are unable to participate. Here the association of subsistence with poverty is merited.

References and further reading

Lee, Richard (1984) *The Dobe !Kung*, New York: Holt, Rinehart and Winston.
Service, Elman (1962) *Primitive Social Organization*, New York: Random House.
Wolf, Eric (1982) *Europe and the People Without History*, Berkeley, CA: University of California Press.

GEORGE MARCUS

SWEATSHOP LABOUR

A sweatshop is an enterprise where workers are subject to abuses, notably inadequate pay, excessive work hours, and hazardous working conditions and sometimes debt bondage, or an enterprise that uses child labour. The term originally referred to nineteenth-century US and UK textile factories, and sweatshop labour again is a cause for concern as more of the world's poor are becoming part of the international division of labour, working in industries, especially textiles, which are interconnected by extensive global subcontracting networks. Exploitative labour practices are found in other economic sectors, notably agriculture and domestic work, but textile production is distinctive owing to the subcontracting networks that allow producers flexibilities in location. Trade and investment liberalization, along with subcontracting networks, are responsible for the dramatic growth of textile operations and sweatshop conditions in developing nations, but sweatshops also exist in American metropolises with high concentrations of immigrants. The expression 'race to the bottom' refers to the ease with which producers can move from one location to another in search of low labour costs. Workers are disadvantaged in a global regime in which capital, and even production, can freely move across national boundaries but labour cannot.

The three notable sources of opposition to sweatshops are consumer boycotts, student movements and labour unions. First, groups such as No Sweat (UK) and Sweatshop Watch (US) have waged campaigns to educate the public about labour exploitation and to promote consumer boycotts. Second, students (e.g. United Students against Sweatshops) have promoted monitoring practices in factories that produce shoes and apparel purchased by universities. Third, labour unions are increasingly organized along international lines and as large confederations.

In 1998 the International Labour Organization adopted the Declaration on Fundamental Principles and Rights to Work, which enunciates the following guidelines: freedom of association and collective bargaining, elimination of forced and compulsive labour, elimination of **discrimination**, and the abolition of child labour. Although there is opposition to mandatory standards, developing nations and producers (foreign investors) are beginning to learn to work together on improving labour conditions in ways that offer benefits to producers as well as to the peoples of the host nation. The United Nations has created a larger framework ('The Global Compact') for development that includes worker rights. It is within this framework that discussions continue as to whether the World Trade Organization system should be used to design trade sanctions or monetary fines to enforce labour standards. There is growing support for such standards even though there is still ongoing debate about implementation. International financial institutions, such as the World Bank, recognize that workers' overall welfare is crucial for community and national development, as well as for the well-being of individuals and their families. Global interdependencies require more international equalities, not less, in order for the new economic order to function efficiently and fairly.

See also: fairness.

References and further reading

Moran, T. H. (2002) *Beyond Sweatshops: Foreign Direct Investment and Globalization in Developing Countries*, Washington, DC: Brookings Institution Press.

Pangalangan, R. C. (2002) 'Sweatshops and International Labour Standards', in A. Brysk (ed.), *Globalization and Human Rights*, Berkeley, CA: University of California Press, pp. 98–114.

JUDITH R. BLAU

SYSTEM See: systems approach to economic sociology; Luhmann

SYSTEMS APPROACH TO ECONOMIC SOCIOLOGY

In the perspective promoted by systems theory the economy has to be conceived of as a boundary maintaining subsystem, which fulfils a specific function for society.

According to Parsons' and Smelser's (1956) analytical approach, the economy as societal subsystem performs the function of adaptation (A) and needs an interchange of products and factors with its neighbouring subsystem of society, namely the political system performing the goal-attainment function (G); the societal community performing the function of integration (I); and the fiduciary system performing the function of latent pattern maintenance (L) (Parsons 1967; 1971). This interchange with non-economic subsystems of society is of crucial importance for the economy's achievement in performing its specific function of adaptation, which is more concretely interpreted as production of goods and services for further production and for consumption demands.

Modern capitalism is a type of economy, which has institutionalized the continuous accumulation of wealth in the unlimited production of goods and services of any kind as a goal in itself. The institutionalization and continuous working of such an economy needs, however, a number of

665

non-economic resources. There is the need of continuous *capital* input in the production process by way of credit organized by a working banking system (G). The reciprocal service of the economy is enhanced productivity. The input of *work* in the production process originates in socialization, education and vocational training in families, schools, colleges and universities and entails the commitment to work as a means of identity formation as well as technical skills (L). The corresponding service of the economy is wages that can be spent for maintaining a certain life style according to the requirements of a commonly shared value pattern. Economic production is also in need of the entrepreneurial mobilization of cooperation. This is an integrative function, which needs entrepreneurs/managers who have the necessary support from the working population at their disposal, which includes well-established employee representation, employer/trade union consultation and human relations (I). The corresponding service of the economy for the societal community is the continuous innovation of products, production and institutions through entrepreneurial activity.

The interchange between the economy and its neighbouring systems implies also a representation of their functional specialization within the institutions of the economy. As long as there is some balance in the interchange between the economy and the neighbouring subsystems there is no pressure of institutional change. However, the more imbalance is occurring, the more such pressure exists and is producing institutional change. Thus the systemic approach is not preoccupied with the analysis of institutional stability. In a reciprocal way it is also interested in the explanation of institutional change. An example of institutional change analysed by Parsons and Smelser is the differentiation between ownership and management in the modern company.

For Niklas Luhmann (1984) the establishment of systems is reducing world complexity by way of drawing a distinction between system and environment. In as much as the economy has been established as a functioning system it contributes to the reduction of complexity. Economic transactions are being freed from the complexities of any other kind of human problems; they are therefore simplified and easier to be performed. The social organization of human life is achieving a higher capacity in handling complexity with the establishment of the economy as a functionally specialized system. The function to be performed is the handling of scarcity, which entails the reduction and production of scarcity as well.

Like Parsons and Smelser, Niklas Luhmann (1988) conceives of the economy as a boundary maintaining system. The maintenance of the system's boundaries is, however, not an operation, which includes the interchange of inputs and outputs with neighbouring systems; it is instead an operation of autopoiesis. As an autopoietic system the economy draws a clear-cut distinction between system and environment, and it is reproducing itself from its own elements in a circle of self-reference. Environmental complexity is turned into an economic resource, which is processed in the system's operation of self-reproduction by way of reproducing its own elements according to its own programmes within the code of payment/non-payment. Such programmes can be the maximization of profits for firms or the maximization of utility for households. The market, which is an 'internal environment' of the economy, plays a central role of informing firms about chances of profit-maximization and households about chances of utility maximization. Prices of goods and services are formed on the market. The price of goods and services is a simplified orientation for economic production and consumption as well as for any kind of environmental event. Whatever happens in the environment of the economy can only be realized in its effect on prices of goods and services as basic criteria for the decision of paying or not paying for a good or service. In this sense economic operation proceeds in a completely self-referential manner. Operations are processes of communication. Payments/non-payments are the specific economical form of communication; they constitute the basic elements of the system. Every act of payment is reducing liquidity on the part of the giving person (buyers) and is enhancing liquidity on the part of the receiving person (seller). Economic communication is the continuous handing over of liquidity from one person to another person.

There are two evolutionary achievements that have established the autopoiesis of the modern economy, namely functional specialization with regard to the handling (reduction and production) of scarcity and money as a generalized medium of communication. Money has both a symbolic and a diabolic meaning. Its symbolic meaning is the establishment of unity in all the different types and qualities of goods and services because all of them have a price in terms of the amount of money, which has to be paid for them. Money is establishing unity in the world. However, the other side of the coin, namely its diabolic side, is the disuniting effect of money. It makes previously united people of communities independent individuals in economic exchange, whose living depends on their individual market achievement and no longer on their membership in a community. What Parsons and Smelser conceive as double interchange between the economy and neighbouring subsystems of societal organization is coined by Luhmann as structural coupling of autopoietically operating systems.

There are two basic aspects which characterize the operations of the economic system, namely tautology and paradox. In its first-order observation the system sees environmental complexity only in terms of its code, that is in terms of prices to be paid for goods and services, and it is therefore

blind for everything that cannot be expressed in the language of prices.

The economy operates in a paradoxical way insofar as it draws itself the distinction between system and environment, decides what is system and what is environment. System and environment are differences within the unity of the system. Tautology and paradox are being resolved by way of a hierarchical ordering of observations insofar as the system is able to observe on a second level its first-level distinction between system and environment. This is done according to the same distinction of the system's binary code. It is a kind of re-entry of a distinction into a distinction. Systems of **corporate governance** might serve as an example of such a re-entry, which allows for resolving tautology and paradox, however only within the same distinction.

A central problem of the economy is the paradox of scarcity. Every economic activity aims at overcoming scarcity. However, the achievement of one person or firm in this respect implies the corresponding underachievement of another person or firm. A solution to this paradox is the institutionalization of economic growth as a self-reproducing process. This is the major achievement of the capitalist economy with its orientation to profit maximization and capital accumulation.

State and households are dependent on this process. The establishment of the capitalist economy results in an autopoietic system, which operates independently of the distribution of wealth because everybody included in this system is both a capitalist and a worker at the same time. The Marxian theory of the antagonism between capital and labour is a translation of the older distinction between rich and poor, which is no longer adequate for explaining what is going on as soon as the system operates in a self-reproductive way with the inclusion of everybody as capitalist and worker at the same time. According to Luhmann's (1986) analysis in his book on

667

ecological communication, the more serious problem of the capitalist economy is the inclusion of ecological requirements in its operation by way of an ecologically adequate pricing of goods and services.

References and further reading

Luhmann, Niklas (1984) *Soziale Systeme*, Frankfurt/M: Suhrkamp.

—— (1986) *Ökologische Kommunikation*, Opladen: Westdeutscher Verlag.

—— (1988) *Die Wirtschaft der Gesellschaft*, Frankfurt/M: Suhrkamp.

Parsons, Talcott (1967) *Sociological Theory and Modern Society*, New York: Free Press.

—— (1971) *The System of Modern Societies*, Englewood Cliffs: Prentice Hall.

Parsons, Talcott and Smelser, Neil J. (1956) *Economy and Society*, London: Routledge.

RICHARD MÜNCH

T

TASTES See: preferences

TAXATION See: fiscal sociology; redistribution

TECHNOLOGICAL CHANGE

Technology, as to a simple or generic conception, is most frequently given in terms of applied knowledge. Typically, technology is defined as 'the development and application of scientific or systematic knowledge to practical tasks' (Galbraith 1973: 39). However from this relatively simple conception one engages a great complexity in analysing the impact of technology on the processes of economic growth and development and the dynamics of culture evolution. In the analysis of technological transformation and change that follows, a centre of attention will be on a combination of the economic with the social. Such an holistic and interdisciplinary analysis is accomplished by employing the seminal anthropological conception of culture offered by Edward Tylor as 'that complex whole' in an analysis of the economic process (Kroeber and Kluckhohn 1952). Culture is interdisciplinary as to conception and, consequently, by definition integrates the social with the economic.

The dynamics of culture evolution

Evolution, as to conception, relates to a sequential process of structural transformation. Consequently, an evolutionary analysis requires a stage analysis which manifests a transformation from one structure to the next. Culture, in its evolution, appears as a sequential paradigm of stages which have been described in a variety of forms. For example, one sequential pattern that could be offered characterizes a movement from a hunting and gathering stage to that of an agricultural revolution, to that of a commercial revolution, and on to that of an industrial revolution (the stage of modern economic growth).

Many reject a stage methodology vis-à-vis culture evolution in that it constitutes a unilinear or orthogenetic fallacy with teleological implications. Culture, it is argued, does not evolve along any predetermined, sui generis or teleological mandate. In addressing the unilinear fallacy, the Sahlins and Service (1960) distinction between general and specific evolution appears relevant and is of importance. General evolution, in a biological context, comprises a sequential paradigm of transformation from that of unicellular animals, to fish, to amphibians, to reptiles, and on to mammals and primates, as phylogeny. Specific evolution constitutes a process of ontogeny, wherein an evolutionary process is confined in the boundaries of a given structure such as fish. Specific evolution in terms of technology is exemplified by propeller aircraft, as a given structure, from the primitive and vintage rendition offered by the

669

Wright brothers in 1903, on to the P-38 of World War II fame.

General evolution, in terms of transportation technology, would concern the movement from the horse and buggy, to railroads, on to automobiles, propeller aircraft, jets and rockets. The paradigm of general evolution constitutes a series of 'S' growth curves that have been described by the sociologist Hornell Hart as a series of 'logistic surges' (Allen *et al.* 1957). Specific evolution ultimately takes on the form of a logistic or Gompertz growth curve. By comparison, whereas the growth curve for specific evolution is asymptotic and sigmoid in form, the growth curve for general evolution is exponential.

A stage analysis does not infer, however, that any given culture, as specific evolution and ontogeny, will necessarily evolve along any predetermined evolutionary path from one stage to the next. A specific LDC nation today need not inevitably and inexorably move towards modern economic growth; that would constitute a unilinear and teleological fallacy. Any given LDC nation may simply experience the processes of specific evolution and stagnate in the context of an agricultural society. This does not belie the fact, however, that for the whole of the earth, humankind has experienced general culture evolution in the movement from a primitive culture on to modern economic growth. It is in this sense that a stage methodology appears relevant and valid. Consequently, the question does not relate to the fact that humankind's culture, for the earth as a whole, has been transformed in a sequential paradigm of stages in the processes of general culture evolution. But rather, the question relates to an explanation of the agent of causality.

Technology and the coin of useful knowledge

Technological transformation also serves as an aid in drawing a distinction between the processes of economic growth and development (Brinkman 1995). Daniel Bell, the sociologist, has drawn attention to the 'principle of similitude' which basically states that ongoing growth is a function of structural transformation. A tepee cannot grow to the height of a 1,000-foot skyscraper. (Bell 1973: 163–74). Humankind did not achieve the growth in speed to the level of 20,000 miles/hour by adding more and more horses, but rather transformed technology to the stage of rockets. Nor could a Neolithic culture (as specific evolution) expect to achieve a level of economic growth to that of $30,000 GNP/capita.

Such an accumulative growth in the level of income is predicated on technological transformation, as the dynamic of general culture evolution, to the stage of modern economic growth. Though interrelated, the quantitative process of economic growth, as reproduction and replication of a given structure (specific evolution), is not synonymous with **economic development** that embodies a qualitative process of structural transformation (general evolution). Growth, by itself, is not synonymous with economic development. A culture may grow and yet not experience economic development – the plight of the LDC world. Consequently, it is the ongoing process of technological advance and transformation which accounts for the dynamics of economic development.

Technological advance and transformation are promoted by humankind interacting with an environment comprised of the physical world and culture in the genesis of new ideas and knowledge. Knowledge as a protean concept appears in many forms. Given the coin of knowledge, on the one side in its *application* knowledge appears as humankind's technology. And on the other side, in its *store* knowledge appears as culture, in this sense as humankind's social DNA. Therefore to change technology is to change culture in that culture is comprised of the technics of technology. The automobile to the economist constitutes material technology; to the anthropologist, the automobile constitutes material culture. The factory system and corporations constitute economic and social institutions, whereas to the anthropologist they are also relegated to the domain of nonmaterial culture.

Therefore to change technology is to change culture, in that culture is substantively comprised of material technology as well as social technology. Not all of culture, however, relates to knowledge relevant to technology, but rather it is the 'core of culture' which substantively consists of technology. Consequently, technology is endogenous to culture and accounts for the dynamics of culture evolution as process of structural transformation. By changing technology, humankind also transforms culture in that the core of culture is endogenously comprised of material and social technics contained in what might be conceptualized as an overall gestalt of technology.

A culture-conception of technology and the Veblenian dichotomy as theory

In the past, technology was primarily conceptualized as material. To conceptualize technology as comprised of both the social and the material constitutes a culture-conception of technology (Brinkman 1997). Kuznets and Myrdal and others have drawn attention to social technology in their conception of technology (Kuznets 1973; Myrdal 1969). Veblen offered an evolutionary perspective for economic analysis and theory in which the conception of culture played a dominant role. The usual interpretation of Veblen's theory of the evolution of culture resides in a dichotomy that juxtaposed the instrumental dynamic of industrial technology versus the static forces of habituation marked by the ceremonial or pecuniary role of business institutions. But, if so, why have institutional adjustments, if institutions always functioned as the static and the ceremonial?

The Veblenian dichotomy does not only focus on dissent, but can be interpreted in dynamic and positive terms. A closer read of Veblen offers a second or alternative dichotomy. This alternative dichotomy argues that social institutions do not always appear as the pecuniary but can also serve instrumental functions as industrial habits of thought, as dynamic agents of culture evolution. One of the most dynamic technics ever wrought in the crucible of culture (civilization) evolution has been of the nature of a social institution – the institution better known as science.

Whereas Veblen drew attention to a profound conception of modern economic growth as *The Place of Science in Modern Civilization* (culture), Kuznets not only gave this insight empirical and statistical buttresses, but also delved into a theory of modern economic growth (Kuznets 1968). The stage of the industrial revolution, in the context of a scientific epoch, was marked by a science-based technology and in the process nurtured an exponential advance of humankind's culture. Modern economic growth constitutes a process of applying science to both economic production and social organization (Kuznets 1966: 487).

To deny the social is to deny the solution

As a result, while material technology has advanced with a juggernaut of acceleration, a prerequisite and concomitant social organization has lagged behind. This classic cultural lag serves as conception and theory to explain the chaos and maladjustment of the current period (Brinkman and Brinkman 1997). Therefore cultural lags can be ameliorated by the origination and innovation of new techniques of social organization. There is a need to apply systematic knowledge to our social technology as we now apply it to our material technology (culture). Myrdal believed that 'the next stage in the development of cultural anthropology will necessarily be its orientation towards social technology' (Myrdal 1969: 173). Karl **Polanyi** (1944), in a framework of a double movement, forewarned of the societal collapse of the 1930s. Policy predicated on self-regulating markets, alone as the neo-liberal predilection, will not suffice as social organization. Polanyi's framework appears particularly relevant to the current globalization malaise as Polanyi déjà vu. Mainstream economics needs to experience a transformation of structure that will be permeable to incorporate a culture-conception of technology. To deny the economic connection to society is to court societal disaster.

References and further reading

Allen, F. R., Hart, H., Miller, D. C., Ogburn, W. F. and Nimkoff, M. K. (eds) (1957) *Technology and Social Change*, New York: Appleton-Century Crofts.

Bell, D. (1973) *The Coming Post-Industrial Society*, New York: Basic Books.

Brinkman, J. E. and Brinkman, R. L. (1997) 'Cultural Lag: Conception and Theory', *International Journal of Social Economics*, 24(6): 609–27.

Brinkman, R. L. (1995) 'Economic Growth versus Economic Development: Toward a Conceptual Clarification', *Journal of Economic Issues*, 29, December: 1170–88.

—— (1997) 'Toward a Culture-Conception of Technology', *Journal of Economic Issues*, 31, December: 1027–38.

Galbraith, J. K. (1973) *Economics and the Public Purpose*, Boston: Houghton Mifflin.

Kroeber, A. L. and Kluckhohn, C. (1952) *Culture: A Critical Review of Concepts and Definitions*, Cambridge, MA: Peabody Museum, Harvard University.

Kuznets, S. (1966) *Modern Economic Growth*, New Haven, CT: Yale University Press.

—— (1968) *Toward a Theory of Growth*, New York: W. W. Norton.

—— (1973) 'Modern Economic Growth: Findings and Reflections', *American Economic Review*, 63, June: 247–58.

Myrdal, Gunnar (1969) *An International Economy*, New York: Harper and Row.

Polanyi, Karl (1944) *The Great Transformation*, New York: Rinehart.

Sahlins, Marshall D. and Service, Elman R. (1960) *Evolution and Culture*, Ann Arbor, MI: University of Michigan Press.

Veblen, T. B. (1961) *The Place of Science in Modern Civilization*, New York: Russell and Russell.

RICHARD L. BRINKMAN

TRADE AND TRADE LIBERALIZATION

Trade refers to the commercial transaction of goods and services. Trade across national boundaries is subject to state policies such as tariffs, import quotas, export subsidies and other interventions in currency and investment market to protect and promote the national interest. Advocating free trade through the dissolution of these state regulations is called trade liberalization; demanding further regulations is often called protectionism.

When mercantilism was a dominant commercial policy in Europe during the sixteenth to eighteenth centuries, government interventions in trade were believed to enhance the wealth of the nation. However, as the industrial revolution advanced in Britain, the interests of rising industrial capitalists began to conflict with that of landed aristocrats. Among other regulations, the British Corn Laws maintained higher food prices by limiting grain imports, raising the real wages of factory workers and therefore making Britain's industrial products less competitive on international markets. The triumph of industrial capitalists over the aristocrats thus came with the repeal of the Corn Laws in 1846 and the Anglo-French trade treaty of 1860. Taken together, these events comprised the climax of the nineteenth-century wave of trade liberalization.

Classical economists and physiocrats advocated the notion of **laissez faire**, of which trade liberalization was a prime example. Under the doctrines set forth by

Adam Smith and David Ricardo, free trade enables trading partners to specialize in the production of particular commodities for which they have a comparative advantage; it therefore benefits the national economies of both trading partners through the realization of the most efficient international division of labour. With some elaborations by neoclassical economics, the trade theory of comparative advantage remains a standard feature in international economics textbooks.

However, free trade has only ever emerged in the most advanced countries of the world economy, and only for relatively brief periods (Bairoch 1993: chs 2 and 3). In the early nineteenth century Friedrich List argued against the classical economists, asserting that less advanced countries like Germany should rely on protectionist measures in order to develop their infant industries. Furthermore, soon after their free trade agreement with Britain, Germany and other European countries had to withdraw from the pact due to the cyclical depressions of the 1870s and 1880s, while the United States practised protectionism throughout the nineteenth century. Outside of Europe, where countries or colonies were generally not powerful enough to implement defensive measures, trade liberalization resulted in more severe consequences. For example, the unlimited export of British textiles to India resulted in the immiseration of Indian workers, prompting the Governor General of India's comment that: 'The bones of the cotton-weavers are bleaching the plains of India' (quoted in Marx [1867]1992: 406). China and Japan also experienced profound turmoil in the mid nineteenth century as a result of their forced participation in international trade with the West. Although not formally annexed by western nations, these countries were nonetheless subjected to informal control through the 'imperialism of free trade' (Gallagher and Robinson 1953).

Thus, historically, international trade has been liberalized only with the assistance of strong states and international institutions that can negotiate and enforce its rules and conditions. Within economic sociology this illustrates the central concept of **embeddedness**, or the way in which economic processes are embedded in institutional frameworks. According to Karl **Polanyi**, 'Free markets could never have come into being merely by allowing things to take their course . . . *laissez-faire* itself was enforced by the state' (Polanyi 1944: 139). From this perspective, the extension of the capitalist, self-regulating market inevitably gives rise to measures (such as trade barriers, labour laws and social welfare policies) that monitor and regulate the economy, protecting the social reproductive components of society from destructive market forces.

In the post-WWII period, the institutional foundations of the international economic system were laid by the Bretton Woods conference in 1944, where the International Monetary Fund (IMF) and the International Bank for Reconstruction and Development (World Bank) were created. The General Agreement on Tariffs and Trade (GATT), ratified in 1947, functioned as a provisional forum for multilateral negotiations to prevent the resurgence of protectionism and to promote trade liberalization. The Bretton Woods system collapsed in the international monetary crises of 1971 when US President Richard Nixon imposed a 10 per cent surcharge on all dutiable imports and suspended convertibility of the dollar into gold. Despite this recourse to protectionism, the final two GATT rounds (in Tokyo from 1973 to 1979 and in Uruguay from 1986 to 1993) continued negotiations on tariff reductions and deregulation in services and investment. Another wave of trade liberalization began in the 1990s under the 'Washington Consensus', a consensus between the IMF, World Bank and US government about market-oriented development policies

673

emphasizing deregulation in trade and investment. The World Trade Organization (WTO) was created in this context in 1995 to replace GATT and provide a permanent institutional space for trade negotiations and the resolution of trade-related disputes.

After a half-century of increasing trade liberalization – particularly with the deepening liberalization brought about by the Washington Consensus and WTO – dissenting views against this process have also intensified. In 1999, street protests severely disrupted the WTO's Fourth Ministerial Conference in Seattle, Washington; in the following year, a large number of protesters rallied in Washington, DC against IMF and World Bank policies. In 2003, the WTO's Fifth Ministerial Conference in Cancun, Mexico, was broken off prematurely after Third World and First World nations reached an impasse over protectionist agricultural policies within the First World. The persistence of such dissent underscores the degree to which it appears that international trade liberalization will remain just as much, or even more of, a critical social and economic issue in this century as it has been in the last three.

References and further reading

Bairoch, Paul (1993) *Economics and World History: Myth and Paradoxes*, Chicago: University of Chicago Press.

Gallagher, John and Robinson, Ronald (1953) 'The Imperialism of Free Trade', *Economic History Review*, Second Series, 6: 1–15.

Marx, Karl ([1867]1992) *Capital: A Critique of Political Economy*, vol. 1, New York: International Publishers.

Polanyi, Karl (1944) *The Great Transformation*, Boston: Beacon Press.

YUKIO KAWANO
BENJAMIN D. BREWER

TRADE UNIONS

Trade unions are complex and multifaceted actors, whose objectives and place in society vary over time and across countries. They were born as a defensive response to protect workers' conditions in industry, but have come to play a much wider, though often unintended, role in the transformation of their economies and societies. In several countries trade unions became powerful organizations that fully internalized the requirements and mode of operation of capitalist systems, while still appealing to a collective identity which often embodied long-term goals conflicting with these systems. They have historically led industrial conflict and social mobilization, but have crucially contributed to the integration of large masses of workers in the economic, social and political systems of industrial democracies (Hyman 2001). Today trade unions are mostly seen by companies as rent-seeking bodies, but at the same time they often play key productive functions, by providing employees' cooperation, by participating in incomes policies and by contributing to the regulation of work more generally.

Given this plurality of aspects and roles, trade unions have been a typical subject of interdisciplinary analysis for economists, political scientists and sociologists. Three main dimensions of unionism have been elucidated by cumulative research in the social sciences. First, the role of trade unions as associations that represent collective interests. Second, the problems and the opportunities faced by trade unions as organizations. Third, their role as economic and political actors.

Any trade union is an association of individual members, whose functional interests it aims to represent collectively. The difficulties with a collective representation of functional interests lie in the inevitable modification of rank-and-file demands by the association that articulates them. In fact, any trade union association must first collect and interpret employees' demands, giving voice to what are often vaguely expressed needs or grievances.

Second, the need for consistency, organizational stability and recognition prevent even highly representative associations from articulating demands that contradict their long-term strategy. Third, if it is to gain concrete benefits for its members, a trade union must make such demands negotiable, transforming any expressive behaviour into instrumental claims. Finally, to represent interests collectively, it must aggregate individual demands, that are normally dispersed and potentially contradictory. The need to go through these processes explains why, irrespective of the quality of internal democracy and of the responsiveness of its leadership, any trade union association cannot but filter and even profoundly change the demands set forth by the employees it seeks to represent. Furthermore, if it is to be considered a reliable partner by the companies or public institutions with which it reaches agreements, any trade union must control and to some extent police its members to ensure conformity of behaviour to the rules agreed upon.

This gives rise to potential 'crises of representation', that unions must learn to control if they want to survive and to keep performing their role. Neo-corporatist systems of interest representation deal with this problem by granting trade unions monopoly of representation, a high degree of centralization and privileged access to state resources. Trade unions in pluralist systems characterized by numerous and dispersed associations, on the other hand, rely on a lower modification of their members' demands, since they do not aim at aggregating interests beyond the level of individual companies, crafts, geographical areas or industries, and can therefore more easily stay in touch with, and be responsive to, their rank and file. In both systems, crises of representation may materialize in several ways, including wildcat strikes and loss of membership. In fact, the rate of unionization or 'union density', namely the percentage of union members in the

workforce, is usually considered the best indicator of a trade union ability to represent employees' interests, and indeed of its strength. As much research shows, however, its variation across countries is heavily dependent on several other factors, including the role of trade unions as providers of services – a role they play most prominently in the so-called 'Ghent systems', where they administer social security benefits (Ebbinghaus and Visser 2000). Also, union density is highly affected by the varying degree of 'coverage' of collective bargaining, which in several countries is established by the law, so that collective agreements are extended to all employees irrespective of whether or not they are members of the unions signing those agreements.

Trade unions, however, are not simply associations formed if and when employees feel a need for collective representation of their interests. After the initial constitutive period, everywhere they have become stable organizations, whose logic of action is oriented as much by the goal of maintaining and enlarging their power vis-à-vis other organizations, as it is by the original objectives of representing their members' interests. This logic of action leads trade unions to try and optimize their resources whenever they have to find solutions to the dilemmas they face.

The first such dilemma is how to define their sphere of representation, namely the boundaries of the interest group whose demands they aim to advance. Historically, the main alternative has been between 'associational' and 'class' unions. The former choose to confine their sphere of representation to the members they actually recruit, whether within a company, a trade, a geographical area, an industry or the whole economy. The latter claim to speak on behalf of all workers, whether union members or not. A second dilemma is how to define a trade union's sphere of action: will it give priority to action in the market, addressing demands to companies and negotiating with them, or in the state, targeting public institutions as the main recipients of its claims and its main partners? However they define whom they want to represent and whom they want to interact with, trade unions still have several alternatives among which to choose. One such alternative concerns the instruments for action, which can range from collective mobilization and conflict, to collective bargaining, to several forms of cooperation, joint management or partnership, to tripartite concertation. Another is about the level of action, which can be centralized at the industry or cross-industry levels, or decentralized at the company or territorial ones. Comparative research in economic sociology and **industrial relations** shows that the more a trade union has become a large-scale and stable organization, the more the solutions to these dilemmas will follow an organizational logic of optimization of its resources (Regini 1992).

Besides being associations that represent collective interests and large-scale organizations, trade unions have become important actors in several political economies. Where they have overcome an exclusively distributive function, they have come to play a wider role in **economic development**. On the one hand, in fact, they can be decisive factors of labour market rigidity and of over-generous social expenditure leading to huge public deficits. On the other, they can play positive functions for companies by organizing workforce cooperation to the new modes of production and by contributing to its skill formation. Also, they can help governments to improve economic performance by coordinating wage dynamics according to an incomes policy and by contributing to labour market and welfare reforms, as the recent experience of 'social pacts' in several European countries shows.

Whether we regard trade unions primarily as associations for interest representation, as organizations, or as economic and political actors, the importance they acquired in most advanced economies in the latter part of last century is increasingly challenged by several developments. Most important is perhaps the continuing fragmentation of employees' interests and demands brought about by such processes as the re-organization of production, the search for flexibility, the growth of the service sector and of non-manual and atypical work. It may become increasingly difficult for trade unions to build their demands around key professional figures as was the assembly-line worker in the Fordist factory. Not only has it become more difficult to aggregate demands and pinpoint 'general class interests': as individual workers identify less and less with the 'working class' as a whole – and with the plans for economic and political reform historically promoted by the labour movement – they also tend to identify more with the company or production unit they belong to. In other words, the traditional attempt by trade union organizations to impose uniform protection standards on employers is now regarded by many employees as an undue simplification of their needs and capabilities.

In conclusion, the role of trade unions in the new millennium seems to include a number of negative connotations, but also new possibilities. Among the former, we should no doubt include the reduction of the trade unions' scope for action within the economic system as a result of industrial restructuring processes and of labour markets' increased precariousness. More generally, we must recognize the disappearance of a certain type of solidarity based on homogeneous working and living conditions, ideology and ability to standardize demands. On the other hand, the new possibilities open to trade unionism seem to depend above all on the ability to interpret and mediate management's growing need to involve workers more closely in the company, by qualifying the requested co-operation/involvement and subordinating it to the attainment of workers' general interests and objectives. From this point of view, it may become very important for trade unions to develop an ability to induce companies and institutions to give up market strategies based exclusively on costs, and to adopt, instead, a competitiveness model based on product quality and a highly skilled workforce – that is, a model aimed at the full development of **human resources** rather than the development of only a few crucial segments of the workforce.

References and further reading

Ebbinghaus, Bernard and Visser, Jelle (2000) *Trade Unions in Western Europe since 1945*, London: Macmillan.

Hyman, Richard (2001) *Understanding European Trade Unionism*, London: Sage.

Regini, Marino (ed.) (1992) *The Future of Labour Movements*, London: Sage.

MARINO REGINI

TRADITIONAL ECONOMIES

Anthropologists have generally used a substantive definition of economy as a system of production, distribution and consumption of material goods and services. This definition allows for study and comparison of traditional, mercantile and capitalist economies, in which traditional economies have been described as those in which mercantile and capital integration are marginal (Earle 2002), but not necessarily entirely absent. The enormous variation in traditional economies, past and present, studied by anthropologists and archaeologists, suggests that it is more appropriate to think of a continuum of economies, in which trade and capital are more important in some economies than in others, than of different types of economies.

Traditional economies are subsistence economies in which households produce most of their wants, although exchange figures prominently because of temporary resource deficiencies as well as sociocultural reasons. Traditional economies are often classified by their primary food procurement strategy and studied as adaptive systems to the environment. Anthropologists distinguish four basic adaptive strategies: foraging, horticulture, agriculture and pastoralism. The terms 'adaptive strategies' and 'modes of production' are often used interchangeably as both concepts rest on the notion that the way people make a living has predictable consequences for a society's culture and social structure. Julian Steward (1955) was the first to outline this in a theory of cultural ecology, arguing that a society's culture core, i.e. the features closest related to subsistence activities, which include social, political and religious patterns, can be explained as adaptations to the environment.

Studies of recent and contemporary foraging populations – San in southern Africa, Inuit of northern America, and Northwest Coast Indians in northern America – have shown that the life of foragers were not as nasty, brutish, and short as once thought. On the contrary, the foraging strategy is characterized by relative abundance of food sources and efficient food procurement, meaning low work hours and energy expenditures, such that Marshall Sahlins (1972) described it as the original affluent society. Foraging societies are generally characterized by small group size, high mobility, flexibility in group composition, and a relative egalitarian social structure. However, there is a significant variation in the culture core, which is partly explained by differences in the foraging environment, e.g. seasonality of resources, availability of meat. Reciprocity is the dominant form of exchange in foraging societies, particularly in those with great variation in food sources and limited options for storage, where reciprocity functions as 'social storage'. Foraging societies with storage of surplus, on the other hand, have more hierarchical socio-political organizations and redistributive forms of exchange (e.g. the **potlatch** of the Northwest Coast Indians).

Until the domestication of plants and animals, starting 10,000 years ago, all humans lived as hunter-gatherers, as they were called before it became clear that gathering contributed the bulk of the calories and nutrients to most foraging diets. Although anthropologists do not view contemporary foragers as relics of the past, they have used ethnographic descriptions to gain more insight into the evolution of early humans. Inversely, behavioural ecologists have used an evolutionary approach to explain economic behaviour of foragers in terms of fitness (e.g. correlation between hunting and reproductive success).

Others who warn that contemporary foragers should not be studied in isolation have shown that foraging economies were incorporated in larger regional economies that included neighbouring farming and herding populations, and that foragers did not rely on hunting and gathering alone (e.g. Mbuti foragers and Bantu farmers in the Congo; San foragers and Tswana herders in southern Africa). Eric Wolf's (1982) historical study shows that many traditional economies, including those of pre-state agricultural and pastoral societies, were incorporated in world systems centuries before the European expansion, e.g. cattle hides from FulBe pastoralists in West Africa were traded via trans-Saharan caravans to the Maghreb. Similarly, 'isolated' horticulturalists in the Highlands of Papua New Guinea and the Amazon were growing new and old world crops respectively centuries before direct European contact. Traditional economies as they are studied by anthropologists are thus in part a product of the capitalist world system. The work of Structural-Marxists focused on how traditional economies articulated with capitalist modes of production (e.g. Meillassoux 1981).

Although no longer employing models of unilinear sociocultural evolution, archaeologists see important correlations between traditional economies and the emergence of complex societies. Timothy Earle (2002) argues that the type of **political economy**, i.e. the control of production, distribution, and consumption in society to extract wealth that supports ruling institutions, plays a critical role in the emergence of complex societies in what he calls Bronze Age economies, agricultural societies with chiefdoms. Earle's work demonstrates that the political economy is also a useful concept in the study of traditional economies.

Whether concepts and methods for the study of market economies can be applied to traditional economies was one of the questions that dominated economic anthropology in the 1960s and early 1970s. Formalists argued that traditional economies could be studied using the same tools, while substantivists argued that traditional economies were fundamentally different from modern capitalist economies. The substantivists showed that economic behaviour, in particular different forms of exchange, was embedded in the sociocultural structure of a society and thus had to be understood within that institutional context. One famous example is the **kula exchange** system of the Trobrianders, in which shell necklaces and armbands were exchanged between trading partners from different islands over kilometres of open sea. Bronislaw Malinowski found that the kula exchange made sense within the sociopolitical context of Trobriand society primarily because it conferred prestige on the participants. The concept of embedded economies was later adopted by social scientists studying economic behaviour in modern firms.

References and further reading

Earle, Timothy (2002) *Bronze Age Economics: The Beginnings of Political Economies*, Boulder, CO: Westview Press.

Malinowski, B. (1922) *Argonauts of the Western Pacific*, London: Routledge.

Meillassoux, Claude (1981) *Maidens, Meal, and Money: Capitalism and the Domestic Community*, Cambridge: Cambridge University Press.

Sahlins, Marshall (1972) *Stone Age Economics*, London: Routledge.

Steward, Julian (1955) *The Theory of Culture Change*, Urbana, IL: University of Illinois.

Wolf, Eric (1982) *Europe and the People without History*, Berkeley, CA: University of California Press.

MARK MORITZ

TRAJECTORIES See: path-dependence; lock-in; technological change

TRANSACTION COSTS See: transaction cost economics

TRANSACTION COST ECONOMICS

Context and contribution

Transaction cost economics (TCE), while part of the wider institutional turn in economics and social science, is distinctive because of its relation to mainstream economics. TCE does not involve a decisive methodological break from mainstream economics but instead provides a new substantive research agenda. Oliver Williamson (1975, 1985), drawing upon Coase (1937), is primarily responsible for systematizing TCE and promoting it as an internationally significant movement. The initial impetus for the development of TCE is the recognition that mainstream economics traditionally neglects transaction costs and fails to address the key institutional and organizational questions associated with their existence. TCE involves recognizing the existence of institutions and designing a suitable framework for their analysis. For TCE the analysis of institutions can be fully accommodated within a modified mainstream framework. The core contribution of TCE is not the focus upon institutions

per se. It is acknowledged that this would be far from novel. TCE addresses institutional questions while responding to the felt need to develop arguments taking a certain recognizable form. Williamson is explicitly concerned with framing explanations to institutional questions which meet certain operational standards, essentially those of mainstream economics, with the hope that eventually TCE might evolve into a fully formal science of organization capable of providing robust predictions.

Primary substantive focus and extensions

Transaction costs themselves are usefully, if ambiguously, considered as the costs associated with the coordination of economic activities. The extent and nature of these costs varies from one configuration of transactions to another. TCE acknowledges that to move from the recognition of such costs to the analysis of resulting organizational issues requires a re-examination of, and amendment to, certain assumptions of mainstream economics. TCE maintains that it is necessary to abandon, at least for the purposes of institutional analysis, the stronger forms of rationality often adopted within mainstream modelling exercises and incorporate bounded **rationality** as a guiding behavioural assumption, thereby acknowledging the inherent limitations of human foresight, cognition and calculative ability. TCE also insists that it is necessary when addressing institutional issues to drop the routine assumption of the efficacious enforcement of promises and accept the ever present possibility of opportunistic behaviour where individuals conceal and misrepresent facts, skirt rules and exploit loopholes. Even if bounded rationality and opportunism are recognized, few organizational problems arise, according to TCE, within models framed in static terms: 'Transactions conducted under certainty are relatively uninteresting except as they differ

679

in the time required to reach an equilibrium exchange configuration' (Williamson 1979: 253). The emphasis within TCE is upon an environment subject to change and uncertainty where transacting parties need to plan, monitor and continually adjust their behaviour.

The specific concern of TCE is with the match between different types of transactions and alternative organizational arrangements or governance structures. The focus of TCE is on a particular layer of social institutions; it is acknowledged that there exist other types of social institutions, customs, norms, etc., which are taken as a set of parameters for the purposes of TCE analysis:

> Transaction cost economics is mainly concerned with the governance of contractual relations. Governance does not, however, operate in isolation. The comparative efficiency of alternative modes of governance varies with the institutional environment on the one hand and the attributes of economic actors on the other. A three level schema is therefore proposed, according to which the object of analysis, governance, is bracketed by more macro features (the institutional environment) and more micro features (the individual). Feedbacks aside (which are underdeveloped in the transaction cost set up), the institutional environment is treated as the locus of shift parameters, changes in which shift the comparative costs of governance, and the individual is where the behavioral assumptions originate.
> (Williamson 1993: 112–13).

For TCE, variety at the level of organizational and contractual form is related to underlying differences in the attributes of transactions. In particular, it is argued that economizing on transaction costs is mainly responsible for the choice of one form of organization or governance structure over another. It is acknowledged that 'the argument relies in a general, background way

on the efficacy of competition to perform a sort between more and less efficient modes and to shift resources in favour of the former' (Williamson 1988: 174). Operationalizing this efficiency argument for Williamson means in essence detailing the concept of the transaction and isolating the costs and competencies associated with competing institutional arrangements sufficiently to allow the appropriate or efficient governance structure to be read off from a description of the observable circumstances surrounding the transaction.

A central task of TCE is to consider the dimensions across which transactions are likely to differ. Here, the emphasis is upon the frequency of transactions, uncertainty and the degree of asset specificity (the extent of relation specific investments). Of these critical dimensions it is asset specificity which is seen as the most important, since once physical or human capital has been specifically designed or located for a particular use or user continuity in trading relationships becomes important. According to Williamson (1989: 143), asset specificity can take at least four forms: (1) physical-asset specificity, which involves investment in equipment such as tooling or dies specifically designed to serve a particular customer; (2) site or location specificity, which occurs when a buyer or seller locates his or her facilities next to the other to economize on transportation costs, (3) human asset specificity, that arises when one or both parties develop skills or knowledge valuable only when dealing with the other; and (4) dedicated assets, which are instruments made to support exchange with a particular customer that, though not specific to that customer, would result in substantial excess capacity were the customer to discontinue purchases.

Organizational forms or governance structures, such as markets, firms and public bureaucracies, differ in terms of their relative advantages and liabilities in facilitating adaptation to changing circumstances. In elaborating upon the properties of competing governance structures Williamson (1985) draws upon Ian Macneil's distinctions between classical, neoclassical and relational contract law, suggesting that different modes of organization are supported by distinctive forms of contract law. According to Williamson classical contract law, which corresponds to market governance, operates effectively for discrete or one-off transactions characterized by a low degree of asset specificity and uncertainty, and where little or no repeat trading is envisaged. Within the classical model the contract is seen as fully expressing all future rights and obligations of the parties. Where there is an absence of relation-specific investments, opportunism can be effectively countered by the threat of exit from the relationship or by resort to the courts which, because of the low likelihood of repeat trading, does not involve the loss of significant future goodwill.

Classical contract law and market governance remain limited and not appropriate for every transaction. In conditions of uncertainty the terms of the contract can no longer specify all future contingencies. Furthermore, where parties to contracts are expected to make relation specific investments the market mechanism of exit cannot be relied upon to limit the threat of opportunism. Williamson suggests that conditions of uncertainty and asset specificity give rise at first to neoclassical contracting. Here the parties accept at the outset that the agreement is incomplete in the sense of being unable to specify their rights and obligations in all future states of the world, but nevertheless attempt to use their agreement to plan for future contingencies by other means. This takes the form of mechanisms of trilateral governance where arbitration clauses for example may be deployed as an alternative to formal litigation. With repeat trading and increasing levels of uncertainty and asset specificity the parties become yet more dependent on

each other and TCE anticipates the emergence of relational contracting. The formal contract or agreement is now of secondary importance as a reference point for dispute resolution and the continuity of the relationship itself becomes central. Neoclassical contracting is ineffective for the resolution of the disputes which arise in this situation. The generic mechanisms which it deploys are not sufficiently flexible to resolve the disputes which may arise in the course of a specific relationship. One possible institutional response to such circumstances is vertical integration, signifying the displacement of inter-firm relations by unified transactions taking place within the firm, but an alternative is complex bilateral governance between autonomous organizations.

Any issue that can be framed as a contracting problem can be addressed from a TCE perspective and numerous applications have been developed. TCE provides a new agenda for the theory of the firm and analysis of industrial organization. TCE highlights the limitations of the traditional production function portrayal of the firm in economics, depicts the firm as a distinctive governance structure and systematically relates the degree of vertical integration to the issue of asset specificity. Vertical integration represents just one governance response to be considered alongside hybrid and network arrangements, and the classification and evaluation of intermediate forms of governance represents an important development of the initial TCE framework. While the choice between competing organizational forms has been the primary focus of TCE, the perspective has been deployed in a variety of other contexts. For example, the design of firm relations has been a theme Williamson has explored, using the TCE framework to recast Chandler's account of the advent of the multidivisional corporation. The organization of work has also been examined from a TCE perspective, one argument here being that internal labour markets are

681

efficient governance solutions to the problems of bounded rationality and opportunism where jobs require workers to
develop firm specific skills. TCE carefully
draws out the ramifications for the analysis
of public policy of conceiving of the firm as
a governance structure. Business practices that
do not conform to the production function
view of the firm and various regulatory
interventions are evaluated in the broader
context provided by TCE and in particular
their potential efficiency benefits examined.

Relationship to competing institutional projects

Williamson acknowledges that certain
methodological characteristics of mainstream theory have encouraged the neglect
of social institutions. Within TCE there is
an emphasis upon the importance of
recognizing the computational limitations
of human agents, characterizing the social
world as a complex evolving process and
acknowledging the multi-layered nature of
social institutions. Other institutional projects including the resurgent old institutionalism in economics and the new
institutionalism in sociology argue that a
major methodological reorientation and
consequent shift away from the modelling
strategies of mainstream economics are
necessary if institutional issues are to be
addressed adequately. By contrast, TCE
remains confident that a modified conventional framework will suffice. Indeed,
alternative perspectives, both from within
economics and from outside, are routinely
criticized by those promoting TCE for
their lack of operational content.

To the extent that the methods characteristic of mainstream economics are
retained, or held up as a format that must be
conformed to, TCE remains restricted in
the manner in which substantive claims are
theorized. For example, the move towards
a more adequate account of rationality can
only be taken so far: given the desire to
design a framework which meets the
operational standards associated with mainstream economics, bounded rationality is
seen as an appropriate compromise between
realism and the demands of appropriate
theorizing. Variety at a substantive level has
long been recognized as a feature of the
mainstream project. Williamson, in fact,
anticipates that insights from TCE will be
'absorbed within the corpus of "extended"
neoclassical analysis' and suggests that the
'capacity of neoclassical economics to
expand its boundaries is quite remarkable in
this respect' (1989: 178). To the extent that
TCE constitutes merely a thematic turn it
does not imply an advance over mainstream
economics but one further expression of it.

See also: Chandler, Alfred Dupont; institutional economics, old and new.

References and further reading

Coase, R. H. (1937) 'The Nature of the Firm',
   Economica, N.S. 4: 386–405.
Hodgson, G. M. (1988) *Economics and Institutions*, Cambridge: Polity Press.
Williamson, O. E. (1975) *Markets and Hierarchies*,
   New York: Free Press.
—— (1979) 'Transaction Cost Economics: The
   Governance of Contractual Relations', *Journal of Law and Economics*, 22: 233–61.
—— (1985) *The Economic Institutions of Capitalism*, New York: Free Press.
—— (1988) 'The Economics and Sociology of
   Organisation: Promoting a Dialogue', in G.
   Farkus and P. England (eds), *Industries, Firms
   and Jobs*, New York: Plenum, pp. 159–85.
—— (1989) 'Transaction Cost Economics', in
   R. Schmalensee and R. D. Willig (eds),
   Handbook of Industrial Organization, Amsterdam: North Holland, pp. 136–82.
—— (1993) 'Transaction Cost Economics and
   Organization Theory', *Industrial and Corporate Change*, 2: 107–56.

STEPHEN PRATTEN

TRANSITION ECONOMIES

The collapse of communism is symbolically
marked by the fall of the Berlin Wall on 9

November 1989. This collapse posed the practical, as well as theoretical, issues of what became called the 'transition' of the formerly socialist countries. Ironically, the collapse of communism ushered in a debate over 'what should be done', the same question that occupied the early Bolsheviks. The decision to move towards a market economy posed practical and interrelated problems regarding price liberalization, exchange rates, trade and monetary policy. Failure to address any one of these issues opened up wasteful opportunities for black-market arbitrage or inflation.

To stave off these dangers, the transition economies were hospitable to loans from international financial institutions despite the often disliked conditionality. These loans signalled credibility to international markets. The conditions attached to the loans stipulated the importation of practical advice and advisers regarding macroeconomic adjustment. Even if the adjustment proved to be harder than anticipated – with all countries experiencing sharp drops in income – there were no extreme cases of a macroeconomic meltdown that characterized countries in South America and Asia during the 1990s and early 2000s, with the exception of the roller-coaster ride of the Russian economy.

Along with the advice on macroeconomic policies came also advice regarding the restructuring of state-owned enterprises. There were large differences regarding the private and state sectors. In certain countries, such as the German Democratic Republic, agricultural and industry were almost entirely state-owned. In Poland, private ownership of agriculture was very high; Hungary had already started to experiment with joint-stock companies and market reforms. Given this high heterogeneity, it is surprising in retrospect that the international financial institutions, as well as the aid agencies of many powerful countries such as the United States, advocated a homogeneous body of policies that were often poorly suited to particular country needs.

The debate around macroeconomic adjustment has often been characterized by reference to two schools of thought: 'shock therapy' advocating rapid change and 'gradualism' advocating slower changes. From the eye of history, both schools advocated rapid change. The more telling difference is 'sequencing': should political consolidation or economic restructuring take precedence? Another way to rephrase this distinction is to note the difference between the objective to make transition economies 'capitalist' or to make them 'democratic' (see **democracy and economy**). There was, in retrospect, a surprising willingness to sacrifice the democratic goal for achieving the capitalist objective.

In this respect, there are two aspects to the history of transition. The first concerns what happened in each of the countries. The second aspect of this history is the role of western advisers and academics who, often with surprising entrepreneurship, advocated policies that they felt were best. The depressing failure of communism left these countries unusually susceptible to foreign advice and a search for alternative models. The flipside of this search is the effects that transition had on the ideas of academics. Both of these aspects deserve our attention and are treated below.

Example of national debates: Poland

Though sharing a common past, the responses across Central and Eastern European countries have been very heterogeneous. Part of the explanation for this heterogeneity is that these countries differ in their domestic conditions. The outcomes in transition economies were neither structurally pre-ordained by the diffusion of powerful ideas, nor materially by pre-existing conditions.

As a consequence, each country took note of events in their neighbouring countries, but largely their evolution was directed by the struggle of competing visions. In Poland, an active debate occurred, partly because of the participation of academics, including several western ones, and also because Polish academics had unusually close ties to the West. The Polish discussion drew in Jeffrey Sachs, an economist from Harvard, Bulent Gultekin, a finance professor at the Wharton School and previously responsible for the first Turkish privatizations, Roman Frydman, an economist at NYU, and Andrej Rapaczynski, a polymath law professor at the Yale Law School; the latter two provide one of the best summaries of the debate at that time. The economist Leslek Balcerowicz – later Minister of Finance and Deputy Prime Minister – referred to the era of this debate as the 'period of unusual politics', stating an urgency to act before events could reverse the opportunity for change. This sense of urgency infused the Polish discussion, as well as that of other countries.

The privatization debate focused on two issues. The first consisted of how to distribute shares in Poland in the absence of stock markets and large domestic savings. The sale of the largest enterprises in any country causes an imbalance between the valuation of the companies and the available domestic savings; selling the companies to foreign investors (as Hungary did more than others) was politically not possible in Poland. The more subtle problem of distribution concerned the high transaction of sales: buyers would be subject to **asymmetrical information** and hence trading spreads would be large, fees for small sales would be high, the provision of information would be costly.

The second issue was **corporate governance**. If the purpose of privatization is to increase efficiency, then ultimately better corporate governance is required. One could argue that market competition for products (and for labour and managers) would be sufficient to force companies to improve. However, if this true, competition would force all companies – regardless whether state or private – to improve;

competition, not privatization, would then be the policy focus. To achieve better corporate governance, it was recognized that some form of concentrated ownership would be necessary; yet mass privatization posed the problem of dispersed owners and entrenched managers, often referred to as the Berle and Means dilemma in reference to the classic 1930s study of US large firms. Most solutions – the most articulated being that of Frydman and Rapaczynski (1994) – entailed the creation of mutual funds which would hold the shares of firms and provide monitoring; the Polish citizenry would invest in these funds. By and large, these proposals were enacted in law but not implemented. Poland was criticized for its backwardness, until it emerged as one of the brighter stars of the transition countries by the late 1990s. Later efforts to understand how Poland was able to grow despite the poor privatization record led to speculations that worker councils played a monitoring role to prevent management from theft.

This short history illustrates a few points. First, transition posed fairly technical issues regarding policy and implementation under uncertainty over their consequences. Hence, there were marked differences among countries, which even if they chose privatization, for example, still chose very different modalities that had very different outcomes. Second, the many voices in the debate contradict the blatant assumption that transition was between reformers and former communists. To the contrary, reformers were of many stripes and colours and consisted of the new professions, the old guard, academics, among many other elements in society. Third, the Polish debate surfaced immediately the importance of seizing the moment of unusual politics to lock in economic reforms. By the end of the decade, this conjecture was strongly challenged by the evidence that democratic reforms, even if permitting the return of the communist parties to power, were more successful in implementing capitalist reforms.

Differences in disciplinary perspectives

In addition to the heterogeneity among countries, there was heterogeneity within and between disciplines. This diversity is easily examined in the context of the American social science discussion, with similar discussions observed also in the context of other national academic debates. To illustrate these debates, we summarize a few of the more important articles in economics, sociology and political science.

Economics

The initial debate in economics concerned the problems of macroeconomic adjustment. However, this debate quickly moved on to the question of structural reforms regarding the content of policies (e.g. how to privatize) and the speed of change (e.g. 'shock therapy' or 'sequencing'). This debate over structural reforms is what concerns us in the following analysis.

As we saw in the discussion of the Polish debate, economists were particularly split over privatization policies. In the early 1990s, the evidence for the benefits of privatization was ambiguous, and there were no cases by which to evaluate large-scale privatization programmes (Murrell 1991). Privatization posed primarily a problem of corporate governance, and hence the main question was how governance could be exercised if shares were to be widely distributed. Others suggest that privatization was above all a 'depoliticization' of the economy (Boycko et al. 1995). This camp concluded that the primacy of removing control from the state dictated a need to provide incentives for interested stakeholders (e.g. managers and workers) to support privatization by giving them considerable shares in the newly created private companies. Privatization was a political compromise required to extricate the state from the economy. Governance was secondary. Finally, there was a sophisticated analysis that argued that too rapid economic reforms jeopardized economic reforms; hence the proper sequencing put political before economic reform (Dewatripont and Roland 1992).

The disastrous results of the reforms for many countries, such as for Russia, shifted the economic debate towards analysing better the politics of reform. The simplicity of the 'depoliticization' argument – simple, because the privatization of property transformed but did not eradicate politics – leads to an emphasis on economic motives for state capture that jeopardized the economic reforms. However, by the late 1990s, the sea change in economic thinking started to move towards the position that the problem in many countries was not incomplete economic reforms but incomplete political reform. The European Bank for Reconstruction and Development – an international financial institution founded by the World Bank to finance transition economies – endorsed the primacy of democracy in its 1999 report.

Sociology

The debate in the sociological literature was far less policy-oriented than interpretative. The American literature in sociology was strongly split between two camps regarding the fundamental nature of the transition. The first emphasized the systemic nature of the transition, that would lead, according to Michael Burawoy, to a type of 'merchant capitalism' (Burawoy and Krotov 1992). In this view, reforms would lead to an unfettered capitalism based on trading, instead of productive restructure. In other words, Russia did not evolve so much as it was 'involuted' through utilizing its networks in order to survive by **barter** relationships.

The second debate is an institutional account of the 'transformation' that stresses the importance of the past for understanding the future. A central contention of the sociology literature was to challenge the idea of transition as opposed to 'transformation'. Explaining the importance of history, David Stark and Laszlo Bruszt proposed that capitalism is 'built upon the ruins of socialism' (Stark and Bruzt 1998). The process of transformation is linked to the nature of pre-existing business and social networks in examining private sector development in post-communist countries. The sociological work on networks of firms grows out of a research tradition that examines firms and individuals as tightly embedded within broader social relations (see **network analysis**). From a network perspective, the fall of communism left agents and firms embedded in distinct sociopolitical networks: clusters of firms/ agents with strong technical and financial ties linked to particular public institutions that provided both resources and authority to these members.

A central idea in the sociology of transition is that since the past matters, there are many kinds of capitalisms and developmental trajectories. The economic literature was quick to dismiss China as irrelevant to the category of 'transition of industrial socialist economies to capitalism'. The two leading American sociologists in this area are Victor Nee and Andrew Walder, both of whom take a rational choice approach and yet differ remarkably. Their work focuses on the connections between business and society in China, and they did not directly participate in a debate into western aid and advice to post-communist countries. However, their work demonstrates the way in which events in China informed the broader sociological debate.

A key idea is that transition need not occur by top-down commands but by many small changes made by individual actors responding to altered property rights and incentives. Property rights reform in China has taken place through informal mechanisms of negotiation and compromise that often leave significant ownership control in the hands of governmental jur-

isdictions and agencies, instead of through a formal privatization programme characterized by the direct transfer of property from the state to private owners (see **property**). These changes led to the rise of new forms of social organization in China that do not match western conceptions of public and private ownership (Nee 1992; Walder 1995).

Political science

The most powerful theme developed in the political science literature is the importance of democratic *consolidation* as a precondition to economic reforms. In the economics literature, this topic was often called, as noted above, 'sequencing'. The main criticism of rapid shock therapy from political scientists is that rapid economic reform may have negative consequences for the long-term consolidation of democracy and institutions in the post-communist regime.

Claus Offe (1991) notes that the 'politics of patience' will play an important role in the long-term success of reform policies. A consideration of the consequences of initial reform on patience of individuals to support reforms over the long run needs to be considered before rapid changes in the economic system proceed without strong political restructuring. Similarly, in an early and influential formulation of the political challenges to economic reform in Eastern Europe, Przeworski (1991) proposed that transitional governments should pursue policy styles that seek to orchestrate consensus by engaging in widespread consultation with parties, unions and other organizations.

These early studies were augmented by later works that argued transitions respond to the nature of local networks and opportunities. In this change, the state plays a role in brokering deals and also in minimizing the risk that may block change (McDermott 2002). Without the state, even the introduction of money is problematic, as many actors may rely upon barter to solidify long-standing relationships as insurance against the vagaries of rapid change (Woodruff 1999).

Conclusions

By the end of the first decade, there had emerged fairly broad consensus – though hardly unanimous – that countries that preceded more slowly and succeeded in democratic political consolidation performed better than those moved too rapidly. The hasty reforms of early favourites of international organizations, such as the Czech Republic and even Russia, *created* problems of financial corruption that damaged capital market development (Kogut and Spicer 2002). The variety of national contexts required policies that took into consideration the social and political conditions of local networks. Because of this variety, no universal set of policies, e.g. privatization, could be applied to all countries.

The more subtle implications concern the learning of international organizations and academic advisers. Many of the international organizations conceded that they erred insofar that they did not consider institutional factors, such as the rule of law or corruption. Consequently, the new policies emphasized legal reforms rather than a concession to the specific nature of national, and local contexts rather than prevent universal advocacy of policies. The many policy failures led to new policy recommendations, while preserving the faith in the positive contribution of external advisers to transition economies (Stiglitz 2002).

The transition to capitalism has proven to be more complicated than many thought who imagined that the creation of markets would engender institutions. Just as there was never one socialism – each country was marked by the persistence of its history – there is neither one capitalism. The analysis of this mapping from a variety of socialisms to a variety of capitalisms is daunting. The emergence of financial industrial groups in

Russia, of autocratic rule in Uzbekistan, and of democratic capitalism implies the dependence of outcomes on initial conditions. Yet, despite this complexity, the clear theme that has emerged is that economic progress has not been an outcome of whether reformers are in power so much as whether a democratic process has been established. In the critical debate over sequencing, the retrospective evidence leans towards the primacy of political over economic reform.

References and further reading

Boycko, Maxim, Schleifer, Andrei and Vishny, Robert (1995) *Privatizing Russia*, Cambridge, MA: MIT Press.

Burawoy, Michael and Krotov, Pavel (1992) 'The Soviet Transition from Socialism to Capitalism: Worker Control and Economic Bargaining in the Wood Industry', *American Sociological Review*, 57(1): 16–38.

Dewatripont, Mathias and Roland, Gerard (1992) 'The Virtues of Gradualism and Legitimacy in the Transition to a Market Economy', *Economic Journal*, 2: 291–300.

Frydman, Roman, and Rapaczynski, Andrzej (1994) *Privatization in Eastern Europe: Is the State Withering Away?* Budapest: CEU Press.

Kogut, Bruce and Spicer, Andrew (2002) 'Capital Market Development and Mass Privatization are Logical Contradictions: Lessons from the Czech Republic and Russia', *Industrial and Corporate Change*, 11(1): 1–37.

McDermott, Gerald (2002) *Embedded Politics: Industrial Networks and Institutional Change in Post-Communism*, Ann Arbor, MI: University of Michigan Press.

Murrell, Peter (1991) 'Can Neoclassical Economics Underpin the Reform of Centrally Planned Economics?' *Journal of Economic Perspectives*, 5(4): 59–76.

Nee, Victor (1992) 'Organization Dynamics of Market Transition: Hybrid Forms, Property Rights, and Mixed Economy in China', *Administrative Science Quarterly*, 37(1): 27.

Offe, Claus (1991) 'Capitalism by Democratic Design? Democratic Theory Facing the Triple Transition in East-Central Europe', *Social Research*, 58(4): 865–92.

Przeworski, Adam (1991) *Democracy and the Market: Political and Economic Reforms in Eastern*

Europe and Latin America, Cambridge: Cambridge University Press.

Stark, David and Bruszt, Laszlo (1998) *Postsocialist Pathways: Transforming Politics and Property in East Central Europe*, New York: Cambridge University Press.

Stiglitz, Joseph (2002) *Globalization and its Discontents*, New York: W. W. Norton.

Walder, Andrew (1995) 'Local Governments as Industrial Firms: An Organizational Analysis of China's Industrial Economy', *American Journal of Sociology*, 101(2): 263–301.

Woodruff, David (1999) *Money Unmade: Barter and the Fate of Russian Capitalism*, Ithaca, NY: Cornell University.

BRUCE KOGUT
ANDREW SPICER

TRANSNATIONAL CAPITALIST CLASS

The idea of a transnational capitalist class is usually, though not always, connected with theories of the ways in which capitalism has been globalizing since the second half of the twentieth century. While the prime method of analysing capitalism itself was more or less restricted to national capitalisms and the relations between them, transnational or even globalizing aspects of capitalism were bound to receive scant attention from scholars. Therefore, though the idea of an international bourgeoisie has been part of Marxist and neo-Marxist theory for some time, the specific concept of the transnational capitalist class has had to wait for the creation of theories of capitalism as a truly global system. Theories of the international bourgeoisie tend to be conceptualized in state-centrist terms and to focus mainly on business leaders, usually big capitalists, and their corporations in rich and powerful countries exploiting capitalists, workers and peasants in poor countries. The transnational capitalist class, in contrast, transcends national class structures and, for some researchers, includes groups whose members do not directly own the means of production but, nevertheless, directly serve the interests of global capitalism.

The concept of the transnational capitalist class is anticipated by several authors, notably in Robert Cox's thesis on the emergence of a global class structure (Cox 1987) and in the work of Stephen Gill (1991) on the Trilateral Commission, where he identifies a 'developing transnational capitalist class fraction', but neither of these writers sets out to elaborate the concept fully or to establish the existence of such a class empirically. Van der Pijl, in his research on the 'Atlantic ruling class' and subsequently (1998) provides valuable conceptual indications that such a class might extend itself beyond the regional.

The transnational capitalist class (TCC) plays a central role in Sklair's theory of the capitalist global system (Sklair 1991, 1995; 2001) where it is the characteristic institutional form of political transnational practices in the global capitalist system (paralleling the role of transnational corporations in the economic sphere and consumerism in the culture-ideology sphere). In this formulation the TCC is analytically divided into four main factions:

1. those who own and control the major transnational corporations and their local affiliates (the corporate faction);
2. globalizing bureaucrats and politicians (the state faction);
3. globalizing professionals (the technical faction); and
4. merchants and media (the consumerist faction).

The transnational capitalist class may be seen as transnational in at least five senses (see Sklair 2001: ch. 2). The economic interests of its members tend to be increasingly globally linked; it seeks economic control in the workplace, political control in the domestic and international spheres, and culture-ideology control through consumerism; its members tend to hold outward-oriented rather than inward-oriented nationalist perspectives on a variety of issues, notably support for 'free trade' and neo-liberal economic and social policies; they tend to be people from many countries, more and more of whom project images of themselves as 'citizens of the world' as well as of their places of birth and/or domicile; and they tend to share similar **life styles**, particularly patterns of higher education (international business schools) and consumption of luxury goods and services. As Carroll and Carson (2002) show, there is evidence to suggest the existence of a network of global corporations and elite policy groups and that this provides important structural underpinnings for transnational capitalist class formation. Despite real geographical and sectoral conflicts the whole of the transnational capitalist class shares a fundamental interest in the continued accumulation of private profit wherever there are profits to be made.

The most radical departure from conventional theories of the capitalist class represented in this conception of the transnational capitalist class is its relocation of the role of the state. Most theories of the capitalist class either see the state as 'the executive committee of the bourgeoisie' (to use an old-fashioned though still fairly common sentiment on the left) or argue that powerful states and their big capitalists (usually in the USA) dominate the world and, latterly, the globalization process. Both Embong (2000) in his analysis of transnational class relations in the work of Cox and Sklair, and Langman (2002) in his review article, for example, criticize the inflation of the concept to include groups that are not strictly capitalist in nature, thus obscuring the role of the state. Robinson and Harris (2000) develop a related argument on the ways in which transnational state relations can be articulated with three types of neo-liberalism within the transnational capitalist class, namely free-market conservatism, neo-liberal structuralism, and neo-liberal regulationist. It can, however,

be argued that all of these critiques fail to see the state as a site of struggle between, on the one hand, globalizing bureaucrats and politicians and, on the other, nationalist bureaucrats and politicians. (Bureaucrats and politicians can, of course, be globalizing on some issues and nationalist on others.) This debate continues.

While most theory and research on class continues to be state-centrist, focusing largely on classes within specific countries, the growing influence of globalization in the social sciences appears to be encouraging more scholars to work in the global as well as the local context. In such an environment, increased interest in concepts like the transnational capitalist class is to be expected.

References and further reading

Carroll, W. and Carson, C. (2002) 'The Network of Global Corporations and Elite Policy Groups: A Structure for Transnational Capitalist Class Formation', *Global Networks*, 3(1), January: 29–58.

Cox, R. (1987) *Production, Power, and World Order: Social Forces in the Making of History*, New York: Columbia University Press.

Embong, A. R. (2000) 'Globalization and Transnational Class Relations: Some Problems of Conceptualization', *Third World Quarterly*, 21(6): 989–1000.

Gill, S. (1991) *American Hegemony and the Trilateral Commission*, Cambridge: Cambridge University Press.

Langman, L. (2002) 'Review of The Transnational Capitalist Class', *Theory and Society*, 31, August: 560–70.

Robinson, W. and Harris, J. (2000) 'Towards a Global Ruling Class? Globalization and the Transnational Capitalist Class', *Science & Society*, 64: 11–54.

Sklair, L. (1991, 1995) *Sociology of the Global System*, first and second editions, London and Baltimore: Prentice Hall and Johns Hopkins University Press.

—— (2001) *The Transnational Capitalist Class*, Boston and Oxford: Blackwell.

Van der Pijl, K. (1998) *Transnational Classes and International Relations*, London: Routledge.

LESLIE SKLAIR

TRUST

In the *Limits of Organization*, Kenneth
Arrow (1974: 23) is one of the first economists of the modern era to recognize the
economic or pragmatic value of trust.
Arrow (like **Luhmann**) views trust as an
important lubricant of a social system: 'It is
extremely efficient; it saves a lot of trouble
to have a fair degree of reliance on other
people's word.' Trust not only saves on
transaction costs but it also increases the
efficiency of a system enabling the production of more goods (or more of what a
group values) with less cost. But it cannot
be bought and sold on the open market and
it is highly unlikely that it can be simply
produced on demand. In Arrow's words,
'it is not even necessarily very easy for it
to be achieved' (1974: 36). Arrow goes on
to argue that a lack of mutual trust is one of
the properties of many of the societies that
are less developed economically, reflecting
a theme that was picked up two decades
later by Frances Fukuyama.

The lack of mutual trust makes collective
undertakings difficult, if not impossible,
since individuals cannot know if they
engage in an action to benefit another that
the action will be reciprocated. It is not
only the problem of not knowing whom to
trust, it is also the problem of having others
not know they can trust you. Arrow's discussion of trust and its economic implications is brief, but brings to the surface some
of the fundamental problems with treating
price as the main mechanism for coordinating the interests of individuals within a
society or at least the limits of price as a
governance mechanism. The lack of mutual
trust, Arrow points out, represents a distinct
loss economically as well as a loss in the
smooth running of the political system
which requires the success of collective
undertakings.

The economic value of trust in Arrow's
view thus has mainly to do with its role in
the production of public goods. Individuals

have to occasionally respond to the demands
of society even when such demands conflict with their own individual interests.
Certainly, trust has been viewed over the
decades as central in the solution of what
has come to be known as the Prisoner's
Dilemma and by extension many social
dilemmas. The two prisoners captured and
placed in separate rooms by interrogators
must trust each other enough to not turn
state's evidence on their partner in crime. If
they do, both end up with the worst possible outcomes, mutual conviction. If they
maintain mutual trust and remain silent, in
the classic version of the Prisoner's
Dilemma, they go free, obtaining the best
possible outcome. Without trust, each
defects independently, sending them both
to jail for the maximum amount of time. A
long tradition of experimental work in
social psychology and economics provides
evidence of the frequent failure of mutual
trust under such circumstances (Cook and
Cooper 2003). As Arrow (1974: 26) notes:
'the agreement to trust each other cannot
be bought.'

Trust can be defined in relational terms
as the belief that the trustee will take one's
interests to heart. In the encapsulated
interest view of trust articulated in Hardin's
(2002) book, *Trust and Trustworthiness*, A
trusts B with respect to x when A believes
that her interests are included in B's utility
function, so that B values what A desires
because B wants to maintain good relations
with A. Others define trust as the belief that
the trustee will not take advantage of one's
vulnerability. If I perceive someone as
trustworthy I am less likely to monitor her
behaviour or performance. In this way trust
reduces the cost of monitoring. It may also
reduce transaction costs in some contexts.

Arrow's brief treatment of trust foreshadowed much later discussions of the role
of trust in the economy. Perhaps the most
widely read in the 1990s was Frances
Fukuyama's (1995) major treatise, *Trust:
The Social Virtues and the Creation of Prosper-*

ity, on the economic implications of trust. This book investigates the links between social variables such as trust or reliability and various economic outcomes. He goes so far as to argue that there are major cultural differences in economic success that are based on the levels of what he terms general social trust in the societies he considers, including Japan, the United States, China, France, South Korea, Germany, Great Britain, Italy and Russia. He analyses some of the factors that support such a claim.

If, as Fukuyama argues, the ability of companies to move from large hierarchies to flexible networks of smaller firms depends on the degree of trust and **social capital** in the broader society, then understanding how trust emerges and how it varies across cultures is important in the effort to analyse what makes for economic success in different settings. Others are concerned less with economic performance and more with the social and political consequences of different levels of trust in various cultures (e.g. Japan, China, Germany, the emerging capitalist societies in the former Soviet Union, and the United States). In the United States, for example, it is sometimes argued that it is the breakdown in community and the trust it fosters that is associated with increased criminal activity, violence and anomie, all of which have consequences for economic enterprises in urban areas.

Fukuyama reasons that it is social trust that generates the conditions under which specific forms of organization emerge that facilitate competitive economic enterprise. Arrow (1974) argues that economic productivity is hampered by monitoring and sanctioning when it is required for managing relations based on distrust. Both arguments are transactions cost arguments. It is the lack of social trust that Fukuyama identifies as the reason that organizations adopt a more hierarchical form (including large networks of organizations created by contracting). The more flexible networks of smaller firms

that engage in exchange require trust. In Fukuyama's words (1995: 25):

> A 'virtual' firm can have abundant information coming through network wires about its suppliers and contractors. But if they are all crooks or frauds, dealing with them will remain a costly process involving complex contracts and time-consuming enforcement. Without trust, there will be strong incentive to bring these activities in-house and restore old hierarchies.

Traditional hierarchical forms of governance are thus viewed as inimical to modern global economic activity, resulting in lower economic performance. It is precisely the ability to be flexible and to form networks of small companies that can be responsive to change that Fukuyama identifies as central to economic growth and prosperity. Cultures that fit this motif are poised for economic success in the global economy. Ironically, he argues that it is precisely those cultures with strong and large families that have lower social trust and national prosperity. Fukuyama (1995) refers to this claim as the 'paradox of family values'.

Oliver Williamson, also an economist, views trust as having a much narrower role in the economy, treating trust as largely relevant only in the realm of personal relations and not at all in economic relations that he characterizes as laden with opportunism. His work is at odds with much that has been written on the role of trust in the economy. In some respects Williamson has a more 'romantic' view of trust, wanting to limit the term to the situation in which calculativeness is suspended. For Williamson (1993) the concept 'trust' loses its meaning if it is not restricted to apply exclusively to personal relations. In his view, personal and commercial relations are based on completely different logics involving completely distinct forms of underlying calculus. Other social scientists, such as Fukuyama, make much broader claims concerning the role of trust in society.

Bradach and Eccles in their *Annual Review of Sociology* article (1989), for example, view trust as one type of control system to be distinguished from price and authority, building upon Arrow's early treatment of governance mechanisms. Reliability and flexibility are important aspects of business relations, and Bradach and Eccles associate these characteristics with trust relations. Especially under uncertainty, trust becomes an important determinant of transactions as exchange partners seek out those who are trustworthy and likely to be reliable in continued exchange. In a related experimental literature, Yamagishi *et al.* (1998), among others, demonstrate that uncertainty leads to commitment among exchange partners as they attempt to avoid opportunism and potential exploitation or defaults. This same phenomenon is called 'relational contracting' in an older literature (cf. Macaulay 1963). The tendency to form committed relations and to 'lock-in' has some associated opportunity costs since committed exchange partners may not explore new relations that might yield better terms. It is this 'stickiness' to certain partnerships often created by trust and commitment that may have significant effects on economic outcomes, especially if there are fundamental changes in the economy such as may be created by new technologies and new or rapidly expanding markets for trade and production.

Sociologists and anthropologists who study the economy have come to conclusions similar to those of Arrow concerning the role of trust in economic endeavours. Trust, when it exists, can reduce various kinds of costs, including, but not limited to, transaction costs and the costs of monitoring and sanctioning. Granovetter (1985), for example, views economic relations as one class of social relations. In this view economic transactions are frequently embedded in social structures that are formed by the **social ties** among actors. A network of social relations thus represents a kind of 'market' in which goods are bought and sold or bartered. In addition, they set the terms of exchange, sometimes altering the mode of exchange as well as the content of the negotiations. Trust discourages malfeasance and opportunism in part, because when transactions are embedded in social relations reputations come into play. Individuals, he argues, have an incentive to be trustworthy to secure the possibility of future transactions. Continuing social relations characterized by trust have the property that they constrain opportunistic behaviour because of the value of the association. Hardin's book *Trust and Trustworthiness* (2002) portrays an encapsulated interest theory of trust, which is also based on this logic.

Walter Powell (1996) conceives trust as similar to human or moral capital operating distinctly differently than physical forms of capital. The supply of trust, he argues, increases with use rather than decreasing in value. Trust is not depleted in the same way that physical capital is over time when it is used. Powell (1996) identifies a number of types of business networks in which trust plays a role in the organization of economic activity. For example, in research and development networks such as those in Silicon Valley, trust is formed and maintained through professional memberships in relevant associations, through a high degree of information flow across the network, and by frequent shifting of employees across organizational boundaries. In another example Powell explores the role of trust in **business associations** such as the Japanese *keiretsu* and the Korean *chaebol*. In these business groups trust emerges out of a mixture of common membership in the group, perceived obligation and vigilance. Long-term repeat interactions are key to establishment of trust relations in this context as well as in most circumstances in which trust relations emerge. Repeat interactions provide the opportunity for learning, monitoring, dyadic sanctioning, and increasing mutual dependence which reinforces the basis for trust.

In a study of the garment industry Brian Uzzi (1997) also identifies the nature of the social relations that link economic actors in ways that determine economic performance. Two types of relationships seem to have been common among firms in the manufacturing business, those characterized as close relations and those characterized as arm's-length relations. Those connected by 'close' relationships were more likely to be trusting and cooperative, even though the same individuals could be self-interested and businesslike in their arm's-length relations. In the close relationships the individuals would more often engage in joint problem-solving, transfer finer-grained information to one another and generally be more trusting. In contrast, the arm's-length relationships were more typically economic relations characterized by lack of reciprocity, less continuity and a focus on narrowly economic matters. Trust developed in relations between manufacturers when extra effort was initially offered voluntarily and then reciprocated, in much the same way that Blau, in his influential book, *Exchange and Power in Social Life* (1964), suggests that trust emerges in social exchange relations. Uzzi notes that this extra effort might involve giving an exchange partner preferred treatment, offering overtime, or placing an order before it was needed to help a partner during a slow time. Trust relations involved less monitoring.

In other industries sociologists have found that trust relations can sometimes impede economic success. For example, Mizruchi and Stearns in a recent *American Sociological Review* article (2001) examined the role of trust in the closure of bank deals. Under uncertainty they discovered investment bankers turned to customers they had close ties to, involving trust relations. By engaging in deals with their close friends they were less successful in actually completing deals: thus, this practice entailed an economic cost to the banking industry. It may have been that the bankers were unwilling to exercise the same degree of authority over their friends in bringing their deals to close. The latitude one extends a friend in this context thus had a negative impact on the profitability of the **banks** involved.

Trust between partners in an alliance reduces the need for hierarchical controls (Gulati and Singh 1998). Higher levels of trust among partners to an alliance results in fewer concerns over opportunism or exploitation because the firms have greater confidence in the predictability and reliability of one another. Alliances between firms that view each other as trustworthy lower coordination costs, improving efficiency in part because the firms are more likely to be willing to learn each other's rules and standard operating procedures. Without such trust, hierarchical controls and systems of monitoring and sanctioning are more often put into place to implement the alliance and to ensure success, though frequently increasing the overall cost of the enterprise.

Portes and Sensenbrenner (1993) analyse the role of trust in economic outcomes for immigrants (see **ethnic economy**) as a means of empirically demonstrating the impact of the **embeddedness** of economic activities in social relations. In particular, trust plays a big role in the **informal economy** in which immigrants are able to **barter** and trade services apart from the formal economy with individuals they deem trustworthy in their personal networks. They also use these networks as a kind of social capital when they enter a new country to provide access to critical resources, such as educational and training opportunities, entry jobs and the provision of food and shelter, until they can become established on their own terms. The social networks provide the social capital the immigrants need to get established in a new land. Some of these network ties represent trust relations – others do not; thus, it is important to distinguish between trust and social capital. There are also downsides to the use of social networks for immigrants. Closed networks may result which lock the employees into low-wage jobs with little time to develop the human capital that would be needed to move up and out of the protective environment of their enclave.

In an interesting historical study of the US economy between 1840 and 1920 Lynne Zucker (1986) identified three basic modes of trust production in society. First, there is process-based trust that is tied to a history of past or expected exchange (e.g. **gift** exchange). Reputations work to support trust-based exchange because past exchange behaviour provides accurate information that can easily be disseminated in a network of communal relations. Process-based trust has high information requirements and works best in small societies or organizations. The second type of trust she identifies is characteristic-based trust, in which trust is tied to a particular person depending on characteristics such as family background or ethnicity. The third type of trust is institutional-based trust, which ties trustworthiness to formal societal structures that function to support cooperation. Such structures include third-party intermediaries and professional associations or other forms of certification that remove risk. Government regulation and legislation also provide the institutional background for cooperation, lowering the risk of default or opportunism. High rates of immigration, internal migration and the instability of business enterprises from the mid 1800s to the early 1900s, Zucker argues, disrupted process-based trust relations. The move to institutional bases for securing trustworthiness was historically inevitable. Interestingly, this thesis represents a direct link to studies by Greif et al. (1995) and other economic historians of the emergence of

various institutional devices for securing cooperation in long-distance trade in much earlier periods.

A number of economists and sociologists agree that trust plays a role in the economy. In Susan Shapiro's book, *Wayward Capitalists* (1984), trust is viewed as the foundation of capitalism. Building on the work of Macaulay (1963) and others, she argues that financial transactions could not easily occur without trust because most contracts are incomplete. In significant ways trust can be said to provide the social foundations for economic relations of exchange and production. Monitoring is often ineffective. Sanctioning can be costly. Transactions costs can be high. To the extent that actors are trustworthy with respect to their commitments, such costs can be reduced within organizations and in the economy more broadly. But without the institutional backing of contract law and other forms of legal protection, few societies rely strictly on the vagaries of personal relations. In economies under transition from one major form of economic organization to another, as in the transitions occurring in post-communist societies, often the reliance on personal networks and trust relations is an important step in the evolution to systems of trade that require interactions with strangers in the context of market economies. This transition, however, is not easy (Radaev 2004; Cook et al. 2004, etc.). New linkages between economics, psychology and sociology are being forged as topics such as trust take on economic significance.

References and further reading

Arrow, Kenneth J. (1974) *The Limits of Organization*, New York: W. W. Norton.

Blau, P. (1994) *Exchange and Power in Social Life*, New York: John Wiley and Sons.

Bradach, J. L. and Eccles, R. G. (1989) 'Price, Authority and Trust: From Ideal Types to Plural Forms', *Annual Review of Sociology*, 15: 97–118.

Cook, Karen S. and Cooper, Robin M. (2003) 'Experimental Studies of Cooperation, Trust and Social Exchange', in Elinor Ostrom and James Walker (eds), *Trust and Reciprocity: Interdisciplinary Lessons for Experimental Research*, New York: Russell Sage Foundation, pp. 209–44.

Cook, Karen S., Rice, Eric R. W. and Gerbasi, Alexandra (2004) 'The Emergence of Trust Networks under Uncertainty: The Case of Transitional Economies – Insights from Social Psychological Research', in Susan Rose-Ackerman, Bo Rothstein and Janos Kornai (eds), *Problems of Post Socialist Transition: Creating Social Trust*, New York: Palgrave Macmillan.

Fukuyama, Francis (1995) *Trust: The Social Virtues and the Creation of Prosperity*, New York: Free Press.

Granovetter, Mark (1985) 'Economic Institutions as Social Constructions: A Framework for Analysis', *American Journal of Sociology*, 91: 481–510.

Greif, Avner, Milgrom, Paul and Weingast, Barry R. (1995) 'Coordination, Commitment and Enforcement: The Case of the Merchant Guild', in Jack Knight and Hai Sened (eds), *Explaining Social Institutions*, Ann Arbor, MI: University of Michigan Press, pp. 27–56.

Gulati, Ranjay and Singh, Harbir (1998) 'The Architecture of Cooperation: Managing Coordination Costs and Appropriation Concerns in Strategic Alliances', *Administrative Science Quarterly*, 43: 781–814.

Hardin, R. (2002) *Trust and Trustworthiness*, New York: Russell Sage Foundation.

Macaulay, Stewart (1963) 'Non-Contractual Relations in Business: A Preliminary Study', *American Sociological Review*, 28: 55–67.

Mizruchi, M. S. and Stearns, L. B. (2001) 'Getting Deals Done: The Use of Social Networks in Bank Decision Making', *American Sociological Review*, 66: 647–71.

Portes, Alejandro and Sensenbrenner, Julia (1993) 'Embeddedness and Immigration: Notes on the Social Determinants of Economic Action', *American Journal of Sociology*, 98: 1320–50.

Powell, Walter W. (1996) 'Trust-Based Forms of Governance', in Roderick Kramer and Tom R. Tyler (eds), *Trust in Organizations: Frontiers of Theory and Research*, Thousand Oaks, CA: Sage, pp. 51–67.

Radaev, Vadim (2004) 'How Trust is Established in Economic Relationships: When Institutions and Individuals are not Trustworthy', in Susan Rose-Ackerman, Bo Rothstein and Janos Kornai (eds), *Problems of Post Socialist Transition: Creating Social Trust*, New York: Palgrave Macmillan.

Shapiro, Susan (1984) *Wayward Capitalists: Target of the Securities and Exchange Commission*, New Haven, CT: Yale University Press.

Uzzi, Brian (1997) 'Social Structure and Competition in Interfirm Networks: The Paradox of Embeddedness', *Administrative Science Quarterly*, 42: 35–67.

Williamson, Oliver E. (1993) 'Calculativeness, Trust, and Economic Organization', *Journal of Law & Economics*, 36: 453–86.

Yamagishi, Toshio, Cook, Karen S. and Watabe, M. (1998) 'Uncertainty, Trust and Commitment Formation in the United States and Japan', *American Journal of Sociology*, 104: 165–94.

Zucker, Lynn G. (1986) 'Production of Trust: Institutional Sources of Economic Structure, 1840–1920', in Barry M. Staw and L. L. Cummings (eds), *Research in Organizational Behavior*, Greenwich, CT: JAI Press, pp. 53–112.

KAREN S. COOK
ALEXANDRA GERBASI

U

UNCERTAINTY See: risk and uncertainty

UNEMPLOYMENT See: labour markets, sociology of

UNIONS See: trade unions

USURY

Usury is the charging of an illegally or immorally high interest for a loan. A usurious interest for a loan is an unjust price charged for the use of financial resources possessed by another party. Religious thought has particularly been unfavourably disposed to usury. The Bible may not be unequivocal, but Proverbs 22: 7 does seem to indicate that the practice of lending can possibly be justified, but usury certainly cannot: 'The rich ruleth over the poor, and the borrower is servant to the lender' (see **wealth inequality**). In the Islamic world charging a price (interest) to use the money of another party (loan) is illegal to date.

Since medieval times, lending for interest has become increasingly common, despite Thomas Aquinas' influential remark that it 'is to sell what does not exist, and this evidently leads to inequality which is contrary to justice' (in his *Summa Theologica*, ca. 1270). In effect, the practice of lending has become commonplace, however, even in the Islamic world. The agreement to return an amount of money to the lender that is larger than the principal constitutes a de facto interest rate.

Central to the discussion on usury is the matter of when an interest is too high. The discussion revolves around the issue of when the input (a loan) required for productive output beneficial for society is offered at a price (interest) such that it diminishes society's welfare. The mainstream concept of opportunity costs relates to this debate. Many governments have resorted to legally restricting interest rates; indeed, such restrictions are among the most pervasive forms of economic regulation.

Loans are demanded by those who find themselves in a position of a (temporary) lack of financial means to acquire a good or service that provides them with certain benefits. Actors that have sufficient financial means extend loans at an interest that is presumably equal to the benefits for the lender but higher than other uses they might have for it. This is a voluntaristic view on market transactions where it is assumed that these only take place where both parties benefit. Liberal philosophers and neoclassical economics can be associated with such a view. Jeremy Bentham's *Defence of Usury* (1787) argues, notably, that interest cannot be too high. If it were, no agreement would exist between the parties, as the marginal **utility** each derives from it would not be equal. Legal or moral restrictions on interest rates would hamper economic growth.

The use of the word 'usury' thus implies that one believes that agreements between parties can exist whereby one of these is forced by the other or by circumstances to accept conditions which actually hurt her in the longer run, for instance to stave off immediate adversity. A person's social **embeddedness** or the exertion of power in the **economy** are not acknowledged in neoclassical economics, however. Outside of this school, there is recognition for the possibility of a person accepting the conditions of an agreement (loan) even when she realizes that in the longer term her position can be hurt.

References and further reading

Glaeser, E. L. and Scheinkman, J. A. (1998) 'Neither a Borrower Nor a Lender Be: An Economic Analysis of Interest Restrictions and Usury Laws', *Journal of Law and Economics*, 41(1): 1–36.

WILFRED DOLFSMA

UTILITARIANISM

A doctrine is frequently understood in quite different ways. In the case of utilitarianism, however, this diversity of possible interpretations is somewhat astounding.

In Germany, France or Italy, until quite recently, almost nobody was interested in utilitarianism any more. It was held to be an empty and outdated doctrine. Histories of philosophy, of sociology and economics hardly mentioned it. Only sometimes they reminded their readers of the existence of a Jeremy Bentham – thought of as the father of utilitarianism and a poor philosopher as well – and of his main book, *Principles of Morals and Legislation* (1789). If they were to go into details, they added the names of his alleged precursors – the Scottish moralists Frances Hutcheson, David Hume and Adam Smith; or, on the continent, Helvetius, Maupertuis or Beccaria – and at least one important and famous heir, John Stuart

Mill, supposed to have given the utilitarian doctrine its most synthetic formulation in *Utilitarianism* (1861).

This deep lack of interest in utilitarianism is amazing if we remember that the main theoretical and political debates of the nineteenth century developed within its realm and about it. Just three examples: first, Nietzsche, when he was Paul Rhée's friend, was a utilitarian, before he became a radical anti-utilitarian, mocking and stigmatizing the calculating and utilitarian 'last man' only looking for his own happiness. Second, it was in order to oppose the utilitarian sociology of Herbert Spencer – the most popular in the occidental world around the years 1880 – that Emile **Durkheim** created the French School of Sociology and *L'Année sociologique*. Third, French nineteenth-century socialism, which culminated with Jean Jaurès, developed an ambivalent relationship to Bentham's utilitarianism. He agreed with it, based on his materialistic rationalism, but tried to surpass it by giving **altruism** a bigger importance than egoism. The same is in some sense true for Marxism as well.

Egoism? Altruism? Here we reach the puzzling core of the debate. For most economists and sociologists, utilitarianism is this doctrine which asserts: first, that actors are, or are supposed to be, mere individuals seeking nothing else but their own happiness or self-interest. Second, that this is good and legitimate, for there is no other possible rational goal. Third, that this rational goal is to be pursued rationally, i.e. through maximizing their pleasures (or their utility, or their preferences) and minimizing their pains (or their disutility). Understood in this way, utilitarianism is what one of his best connoisseurs, Elie Halévy, called '*une dogmatique de l'égoïsme*', and more than the anticipation of what is called today the 'economic model in the social sciences' (Philippe Van Parijs) or, more generally, rational-actor theory. It simply is the general theory of the *homo economicus*. This is how Talcott Parsons or Alvin Gouldner still understood utilitarianism in *The Structure of Social Action* (1937) or in *The Coming Crisis of Western Sociology* (1970). For them, as for Durkheim or Max Weber, sociology must be thought of as anti-utilitarian, i.e. a theoretical discourse recognizing the reality and the importance of interested calculations, but refusing to admit that the whole of social action could or should be reduced to instrumental rationality.

What makes things difficult, yet, is that the mainstream Anglo-Saxon moral philosophy, from J. S. Mill to John Rawls, via H. Sidgwick, G. Moore or J. C. Harsanyi, has developed in the wake of utilitarianism but in giving much less importance to the postulate of rational egoisms than to the utilitarian principle of justice formulated by Bentham: 'just' is what brings the largest amount of pleasure to the greatest number. The conclusion can be easily guessed: if I intend to be (or look) just and morally irreproachable, I may have to sacrifice my self-interest for the sake of general happiness. Utilitarianism which seemed to be a *'dogmatique de l'égoïsme'* suddenly turns into a plea for altruism. Or even for sacrifice. This is precisely the reason why John Rawls tried to formulate other principles of justice than the utilitarian ones which might prevent urging the sacrifice of individual freedom for the sake of the greatest number's interest. Did he succeed, one might ask? This is another story.

Egoism? Altruism? Is *homo economicus* necessarily self-interested? Not always, answers Gary Becker, the herald of rational-actor theory. Some individuals' satisfaction implies maximizing the satisfaction of others. They might be called altruistic egoists. Here we begin to understand that the discussion of the true nature of utilitarianism is full of enigmas and mysteries. Lacking space to explore them, I will just state five theses:

1. Utilitarianism can be defined by the paradoxical and probably impossible combination of two assertions, one positive and the other normative. The positive one (about what *is*) holds actors to be self-interested and rationally calculating individuals. The normative one (about what *ought to be*) says that it is just what permits to obtain the greatest possible happiness for the largest number.

2. Theories which advocate that the conciliation of the greatest possible happiness with individual self-interest is obtained through contract and free market can be held to be utilitarian *largo sensu*. Those, like Bentham's theory of legislation, which believe that it is possible only through the action of a rational legislator who manipulates desires through rewards and punishments – realizing what E. Halévy called an artificial harmonization of interests – can be said to be utilitarian *stricto sensu*.

3. If the word 'utilitarianism' is recent, the two basic principles of utilitarianism (about the *is* and the *ought to*), are as old as European philosophy (not to speak of the Chinese) whose history can be read as an ever renewed struggle between utilitarian and anti-utilitarian formulations.

4. Utilitarianism is a theory of practical rationality, viewed as instrumental rationality, enlarged to the whole of moral and political philosophy. Economic theory can be seen as the crystallization of the positive dimension of utilitarianism.

5. The critique of utilitarianism and of rational-actor theory can only succeed if it takes seriously the discovery by Marcel **Mauss** of the central place of **gift** in social relations.

References and further reading

Caillé, Alain, Lazzeri, Christian and Senellart, Michel (eds) (2001) *Histoire raisonnée de la philosophie morale et politique. Le bonheur et l'utile*, Paris: La Découverte.

Halévy, Elie ([1905]1995) *La Formation du radicalisme philosophique*, three volumes, Paris: PUF. (Abridged translation in English: *The Growth of Philosophic Radicalism*, translated by M. Morris, London: Faber and Faber, 1928.)

Schumpeter, Joseph (1954) *History of Economic Analysis*, London: Allen and Unwin, and Oxford University Press.

ALAIN CAILLÉ

UTILITY

The concept of 'utility' is generally associated with Jeremy Bentham's moral philosophy. It appears in several writings of classical economists from the European continent (most prominently J. B. Say), and several predecessors of 'marginalism' may be identified as well (such as Cournot, Dupuit, Von Thünen, Gossen and Von Mangoldt). Classical economists tended to use 'utility' as an objective concept, describing the inherent worth of objects. The concept of 'marginal utility' is said to have become a core theoretical concept in economics after the 'marginal revolution', but recent research suggests that the breakthrough of marginalism was really a slow and gradual process. Moreover, the so-called Jaffé thesis indicates that the three main authors of the 'marginal revolution' – William Stanley Jevons, Léon Walras and Carl Menger – had different ideas about the role of 'marginal utility'. Walras represented the economy as a set of equations that are determined simultaneously, and only introduced the notion of 'marginal utility' because he needed a maximizing mechanism. Menger was primarily interested in the subjective aspects of decision-making. Jevons used Bentham's categories as a central tool to develop his 'theory of political economy', although he altered the Benthamite conceptions to make them suitable for his mechanical economics. Jevons's use of 'utility' differs in two fundamental senses from Bentham's. First of all, Jevons's definition is much narrower. He took only four of Bentham's circumstances of 'utility' into account (intensity, duration, certainty or uncertainty, and propinquity or remoteness), whereas the other three (fecundity, purity and extent) do not 'enter into the more simple and restricted problem which we attempt to solve in Economics' (Jevons 1879: 29). A second important difference between Bentham and Jevons concerns the role of measurement. Jevons would like to measure utility indirectly by taking its quantitative effects into account (selling, buying, lending, labouring, etc.). He wanted to measure these quantitative effects in order to determine pleasures and pains. In other words, Jevons turned Bentham upside down.

It is generally said that the first generation of the marginalists used notions of cardinal utility in contrast to later notions of ordinal utility. It would perhaps be fairer to state that these authors were rather vague about this issue and only implicitly assumed cardinal notions of utility. For instance, Jevons argued that it is not only impossible, but also not required to make inter-individual comparisons of utility. However, elsewhere Jevons did compare the marginal utility of money for rich and poor people, thereby implicitly assuming a cardinal notion of utility.

Broome (1991) argues that 'utility' acquired a new technical meaning in the twentieth century, meaning 'that which represents preferences', divorced from 'usefulness'. The second meaning of 'utility', 'good', should be prohibited for causing confusion.

The concept of 'utility' attracted criticism from several authors, most notably institutional and historical economists. T. E. Cliffe Leslie (1879) is very critical regarding the use of so-called 'universal' concepts such as 'wealth' and 'desire of wealth', as these may mean different things and have different effects in different contexts and circumstances. Although Leslie sees the transition from the erroneous labour theory of value to Jevons's utility theory as an important progress, he still maintains that 'wide historical investigation must precede the construction of the true story'. **Veblen** (1909) raises similar concerns when discussing Clark's (1890/1) attempt to generalize the Ricardian theory of rent to a general theory of production in economics. According to Veblen, Clark's utility perspective necessarily leads to a doctrine about the production of values, which is a matter of valuation (throwing the 'whole excursion back into the field of distribution'). Marginal utility theory is statical and unable to take dynamic aspects into account, it is teleological and lacks an understanding of technological advance and neglects the role of institutions. The restricted hedonistic calculus is taken for granted. However, the teleological and deductive character of this calculus implies that it is justified by sufficient reason and not by efficient cause, and that explanations are not given in terms of cause and effect.

References and further reading

Broome, J. (1991) 'Utility', *Economics and Philosophy*, 7: 1–12.

Clark, J. B. (1890/1) 'Distribution as Determined by a Law of Rent', *Quarterly Journal of Economics*, 5: 289–318.

Jaffé, W. (1976) 'Menger, Jevons and Walras De-homogenized', *Economic Inquiry*, 14(4): 511–24.

Jevons, W. S. (1879) *The Theory of Political Economy. Writings on Economics Volume 2*, London: Palgrave/Macmillan.

Leslie, T. E. C. (1876) 'On the Philosophical Method of Political Economy', *Hermathena*, 2: 1–32.

Veblen, T. (1909) 'The Limitations of Marginal Utility', *Journal of Political Economy*, 17: 620–36.

BERT MOSSELMANS

V

VALUE

Value generally refers to the amount of money or other goods that must be paid to obtain something. There are nonetheless a number of very different value concepts, and in particular there is considerable difference between the ways in which economic sociology and orthodox economics treat the concept of value. In contrast, between economic sociology and heterodox economics there are significant commonalities regarding the treatment of the concept of value. The differences date back to the origins of sociology and classical economics, and persist or have perhaps become sharper between contemporary economic sociology and neoclassical economics. The commonalities between economic sociology and heterodox economics have emerged particularly since the 1980s.

In the history of sociology, value has been treated as a property of entire social systems, such as when it is associated with the concept of culture by Max **Weber**, one of the early founders of sociology: The concept of culture is a value concept. Empirical reality becomes 'culture' to us because and insofar as we relate it to value ideas (Weber 1949: 76).

On this view, our interest in reality is a function of the values which culture embodies, that is, our interest in the world is a 'value-conditioned' one. Sometimes termed the 'values approach to culture', it

has been argued that such an approach treats culture monolithically as singularly shaping 'action by supplying ultimate ends or values towards which action is directed' (Swidler 1986: 273). This perspective is to be compared with the concept of value in classical economics of Adam **Smith** and David Ricardo, where the concept concerns a set of relationships that obtain within a system in the form of commodity prices or exchange values. As Smith puts it: 'The value of any commodity ... is equal to the quantity of labour which it enables him to purchase or command. Labour ... is the real measure of the exchangeable value of all commodities' (Smith 1976: 47). Here, value is not an ultimate end towards which action is directed, but rather the effect of action involved in the work required to extract objects of consumption from nature.

Emile **Durkheim** criticized Smith's classical value theory explanation in terms of labour input by arguing that it missed the central dimension of the concept of value. Value understood in terms of labour content appears as if it were something entirely objective and impersonal. But Durkheim argued that such a conception overlooks the role of social opinion in determining value, particularly in determining notions of just value (Durkheim 1992). This same critique, it should be noted, can be extended to neoclassical value theory in that it also treats value as market price, though rather as determined by objective and impersonal forces of supply and demand. Durkheim's argument was framed primarily in terms of the value of labour, and while it might be applied to the value of consumer and other types of goods, he focused on arguing that the wage rate depends upon social standards regarding the minimum resources needed to sustain to survival, that these standards were set by public opinion, and that they changed from period to period. However, Smith, David Ricardo and even more strongly Karl **Marx** each held in varying degrees similar views regarding the social determination of the wage. And since for each of them the value of other commodities depended upon the value of labour, this implies that their values also possessed a social component.

Durkheim's critique, however, is more successful in regard to the neoclassical view of the wage as determined by the marginal productivity of labour in production and in regard to the neoclassical view of price in general as market-determined. The marginal productivity of labour is a schedule of outputs made possible by incremental increases in labour input. Its level reflects the quantity of capital employed by labour, where both labour input and the capital employed are described in natural units: hours of labour and a certain quantity of machines and equipment. While one might say that social standards and public opinion implicitly underlie these values, rarely do these considerations enter into standard analysis. Much the same can be said about the explanation of price in general in neoclassical economics. Consumers play an important role in determining market price, but consumer preferences are taken as given and unchanging (Stigler and Becker 1977), so that their social determinants may be disregarded. Even more strongly, revealed preference price theory (Samuelson 1948), which most mainstream economists now take as the standard explanation of choice, makes the very content of pre-

ferences irrelevant to consumer choice. More generally, the formalist character of much recent economics reinforces the notion that value as price lacks any social characteristics whatsoever.

In contrast, heterodox traditions in economics, particularly American institutional economics and social economics, hold views of value reminiscent of Weber's view that value is a property of entire social systems and Durkheim's conception of market values as socially influenced. American institutional economists Thorstein **Veblen**, John Commons, John Maurice Clark and others make central institutions seen as 'settled habits of thought common to the generality of men' (Veblen 1919: 239). Social economics, with origins in Simonde de Sismondi, Karl Marx, Léon Walras, Joseph **Schumpeter**, John Hobson and John Maurice Clark, see the social economy as encompassing the market economy, so that social values and worldviews permeate markets and underlie consumption, production and distribution. Other heterodox approaches, such as Marxist economics, feminist economics, some ecological economics approaches and post-Keynesian economics, are similarly holistic, historically oriented, critical of the naturalism and positivism in economics, and reject the atomistic individualism of neoclassical economics. The last is a key point of tangency between heterodox economics and economic sociology and a key difference between orthodox economics and economic sociology. Just as Georg **Simmel**, in his important early study *The Philosophy of Money* (1978), identified related types of individuals (such as the spendthrift and the miser) according to their linked positions in an economic system governed by money, radical and Marxist economists see individuals as socially connected through their membership in classes and social groups that interact within systems of power, while feminist economists see gender relationships in the economy as constitutive of individuals' economic roles and economic prospects.

Interestingly, economic sociology enjoyed a revival in the 1980s, a period in which heterodox economics was also undergoing considerable development. While crossover relationships between the two have been limited, they have nonetheless appear to have each followed certain parallel pathways that may be seen to derive from a shared critique of the assumptions of neoclassical economics. Even more interestingly, economic sociology and heterodox economics appear to share broad outlines of a view of individuals as socially embedded *à la* Karl **Polanyi**, and of individuals and society as mutually influencing. Thus, parallel to economic sociologist Mark Granovetter's influential characterization of individuals' **embeddedness** in terms of being neither undersocialized nor oversocialized (Granovetter 1985), there is critical realism, a recent heterodox research programme combining a number of different heterodox approaches, that employs a structure–agent conception of society in which individuals both influence and are influenced by social structures (Lawson 1997), and also a renewed interest in the evolutionary themes of Veblenian institutional economics, that emphasizes upward and downward causation operating between individuals and institutions (Hodgson 2004).

The 1980s also signal the beginnings of change in mainstream economics, with the emergence of a collection of new research programmes that bear limited resemblance to neoclassical economics and each other. These new research programmes have almost all originated outside economics, thus not only importing modes of thinking often quite far removed from the traditional assumptions of neoclassical economics, but also reversing a period of **economic imperialism** when the individual rationality assumptions of neoclassical economics were re-applied outside of economics. **Game theory** comes from mathematics, and challenges the notion that economic individuals are isolated from one another by examining their interaction in games. In place of value as market price, value in game theory is understood in terms of sets of alternative payoffs which depend upon how players anticipate each other's choices. Noncooperative, one-shot games bear many of the features of the neoclassical economic view of the individual, but repeated games and cooperative games introduce a variety of considerations regarding play that make social structure central. Another new research programme, **behavioural economics**, with origins in psychology, has focused on re-examination of neoclassical **rational choice theory**. Among its results, demonstrated repeatedly in experimental studies, is that economic individuals often cooperate rather than behave in a self-interested manner. Additionally, individuals' decision-making appears to reflect heuristic cognitive bias (use of rules of thumb rather than rigorous analysis) and different kinds of decision-framing effects associated with habits, 'herd mentality' and emotional attachments. For example, valuation can be influenced by strong feelings of regret individuals have regarding the loss of specially prized goods. Yet a third new research programme, **evolutionary economics**, including evolutionary game theory, with origins in Darwinian biology, has multiple currents, some overlapping with game theory and behavioural economics. Here, investigation first focused on evolutionary change in economic systems, and value is modelled as the frequency-dependent fitness of different survival strategies in populations over time. Subsequent investigation replaces this biological emphasis with the idea of cultural evolution of **beliefs** and norms, and value is modelled in terms of the 'fitness' of these beliefs and norms to promote some generally useful good. These new research programmes in mainstream economics may or may not converge on the value themes that have characterized economic sociology (and heterodox economics) in the future. While some currents in recent economics give prominence to social value concepts, others appear to be guided more by natural science and formalist ideas. On the whole, however, recent economics is a far more eclectic theoretical undertaking than neoclassical economics, particularly as reflected in the former's departures from the latter's linked postulates of value understood as market price and individuals understood as isolated beings. Thus, whereas there remain clear differences between economic sociology and neoclassical economics regarding the concept of value, whether these differences will persist between the former and economics as it emerges in the future remain to be seen.

References and further reading

Davis, John (2003) *The Theory of the Individual in Economics: Identity and Value*, London: Routledge.

Durkheim, Emile (1992) *Professional Ethics and Civic Morals*, translated by Cornelia Brookfield, London: Routledge.

Granovetter, Mark (1985) 'Economic Action and Social Structure: The Problem of Embeddedness', *American Journal of Sociology*, 91(3): 481–510.

Hodgson, Geoffrey (2004) *The Evolution of Institutional Economics*, London: Routledge.

Lawson, Tony (1997) *Economics and Reality*, London: Routledge.

Samuelson, Paul (1948) 'Consumption Theory in Terms of Revealed Preference', *Economica*, 15: 243–53.

Simmel, Georg (1978) *The Philosophy of Money*, second edition, translated by T. Bottomore and D. Frisby, Boston: Routledge and Kegan Paul.

Smith, Adam (1976) *An Inquiry into the Nature and Causes of the Wealth of Nations*, edited by R. H. Campbell and A. S. Skinner, Oxford: Oxford University Press.

Stigler, George and Becker, Gary (1977) 'De Gustibus Non Est Disputandum', *American Economic Review*, 67: 76–90.

Swidler, Ann (1986) 'Culture in Action: Symbols and Strategies', *American Sociological Review*, 51: 273–86.

Veblen, Thorstein (1919) *The Place of Science in Modern Civilization and Other Essays*, New York: Huebsch.

Weber, Max (1949) '"Objectivity" in Social Science and Social Policy', in Max Weber, *The Methodology of the Social Sciences*. New York: Free Press, pp. 49–112.

JOHN B. DAVIS

VALUES See: norms and values

VEBLEN, THORSTEIN

Thorstein Veblen (1857–1929) was a heterodox American economist who laid the intellectual foundations of American institutional economics. The son of Norwegian immigrants, Veblen studied at Carleton College, John Hopkins University, Yale University (where he received a PhD in philosophy) and Cornell University (where he did graduate work in economics). In the course of a chequered academic career, he held teaching positions at the University of Chicago (1892–1906), Stanford University (1906–9), the University of Missouri (1911–18) and the New School for Social Research (1918–26). Closely attuned to intellectual developments in a broad range of academic disciplines and national contexts, Veblen incorporated into his economic writings concepts and theories from contemporary research in psychology, ethnology and the biological sciences, as part of a determined effort to bring economics in step with the widely respected evolutionary sciences of his era.

Entering economics when the field was embroiled in controversies between so-called orthodox approaches and challenges from traditions such as the German **historical school**, Veblen sharpened and elaborated the critique of orthodox classical and neoclassical economic theory. At the same time, he upbraided exponents of the historical school for 'content[ing] themselves with an enumeration of data [and failing] to offer a theory of anything or to elaborate their results into a consistent body of knowledge' (Veblen 1898b: 375; 1901). Nevertheless, it was the 'preconceptions' of the orthodox theories that especially drew Veblen's fire, leading him to formulate a three-pronged critique which anticipates nearly all subsequent attacks on utilitarian forms of social theory (Veblen 1898b, 1899a, 1899b, 1909) (see **utilitarianism**).

According to Veblen's dissection, classical and marginal utility theories were scientifically deficient, first because their foundational premise of *homo economicus* entails a 'faulty conception of human nature', namely a 'hedonistic conception of man [as] a lightning calculator of pleasures and pains who oscillates like a homogeneous globule of desire, [yet] has neither antecedent nor consequent' (1898b: 389). Veblen deemed this conception a severely restricted basis for understanding economic action: 'such a theory can take account of conduct only in so far as it is rational conduct, guided by deliberate and exhaustively intelligent choice – wise adaptation to the demands of the main chance' (1909: 623); the theory entirely 'overlook[s] or elim inate[s] the element of valuation', or the nature and origins of actors' preferences, illegitimately rendering the 'ends' of economic conduct 'altogether a by-question' (1899b: 424, 418).

Closely related to this hedonistic, rationalistic misconception, in Veblen's view, was the second limiting feature of economic theory, its failure to embed actors in society and in the cultural-institutional environment of economic activity. Cognizant of contemporary thinking in the emerging field of sociology, Veblen objected that classical and neoclassical economic theories were 'drawn in terms of the individual simply' (1909: 609). As such, they misconstrued the economic actor as 'an isolated, definitive human datum, [s]elf-poised in elemental space', and reduced the society merely to 'the algebraic sum on the individuals' (1898b: 389; 1899b: 419). Such reductionism not only fostered the mistaken normative conviction that 'the interest of society is the sum of the interests of individual … and that, in serving his own interests … the individual serves the collective interest of the community' (1899b: 419), but it also 'shut … off [economic] inquiry at the point where modern scientific interest sets in' (1909: 627). For Veblen, this crucial point lay in what he called 'cultural' or 'institutional elements', as manifested in the modern era by property ownership, contract, the market, the price system, the business enterprise, and the vast fabric of other of socially established arrangements that constitute the context and foundation of individual economic activity. According to Veblen's attack, orthodox theory elided this institutional **embeddedness**: 'The cultural elements involved in the theoretical scheme, elements that are of the nature of institutions … are not subject to inquiry but are taken for granted as pre-existing in a finished, typical form' (1909: 623–4).

From this criticism came Veblen's third fundamental stricture. In his assessment, the classical and neoclassical tradition lacked the capacity to 'deal theoretically with the phenomena of change'; with trivial exceptions, it was a 'theory … of a wholly statical character' (1909: 620–1). This was so, argued Veblen, because economic theory tacitly universalized the social arrangements and institutions that it took for granted, thus rendering them 'immutable':

> They are part of the nature of things; so that there is no need of accounting for them or inquiring into them, as to how they have come to be such as they are, or how and why they have changed and are changing.
>
> (1909: 624)

This fatal shortcoming prevented orthodox theory from recognizing that human nature also changed over the course of history and from grasping that utility-maximizing *homo economicus* was a historically emergent phenomenon (1899c: 237–45). In this respect, Veblen's critique converged with ideas in the work of Max **Weber** that remain of fundamental importance for economic sociology.

Veblen, however, was more than a critic of orthodox economics. His critique was part and parcel of a series of ambitious studies intended to develop and exemplify the enlarged vision of economics which he held out as an alternative to the constricted mainstream view. For Veblen, the proper task of modern economic science, or **evolutionary economics** as he called it, was to furnish 'a theory of a cumulative sequence of economic institutions' (1898b: 393), 'a scientific inquiry into the nature, origin, growth, and effects of these institutions and of the mutations ... which they bring to pass in the community's scheme of life' (1909: 627). To pursue this project, Veblen, drawing from various nineteenth-century sources, divided human cultural evolution roughly into four broad stages: the peaceful savage (Neolithic) era; the predatory barbarian era (corresponding, in European history, to the Dark Ages and feudalism); the pre-modern handicraft era; and the modern industrial or machine era. In Veblen's account, these stages differ in their technological capacity (i.e. the level of their industrial arts and methods for wresting from nature the material means to support human life); in the scope that they afford to the expression of basic human instincts, such as instincts of workmanship and predation; and in the habits (of both thought and conduct) and the social institutions (economic, as well as political, religious, etc.) to which they give rise (Edgell 2001). Viewing history through this lens, Veblen noticed several striking evolutionary paradoxes, and he set himself the goal of finding the economic key that unlocked these paradoxes.

Central among these was the riddle of the 'irksomeness of labor' (Veblen 1898a). Given that cultural evolution has endowed humankind with the 'instinct of workmanship' and called forth norms of conduct that value 'efficiency and serviceability' – such that human beings 'like to see others spend their life to some purpose, and they like to reflect that their own life is of some use' – why is it, inquired Veblen, that 'people currently avow an aversion to useful effort', so much so that orthodox theory postulates this 'antipathy to work' as an eternal fact of economic life (1898a: 187–89, 196)? His first and most famous book, *The Theory of the Leisure Class* (1899c), was a detailed attempt to answer this question. Here, Veblen traced the development of the institution of the leisure class from its origins, alongside private property ownership, in the barbarian era up to its crystallization in the modern age as a differentiated social group whose vast wealth allows a permanent 'exemption from all useful employment' (1899c: 40). Rather than pursue useful labour, members of the leisure class adhere to the 'great cultural principle of conspicuous waste', which compels them, in the interest of maintaining 'the esteem of their fellowmen', to engage at once in 'a waste to time' (a quantity they squander in predatory, 'non-industrial employments' like war, politics and sports) and in 'a waste of goods' through 'conspicuous **consumption**' – unrelenting, ostentatious expenditures on luxuries, the more useless the better, as a 'means of showing [the exhibitor's] pecuniary strength' (1899c: 138, 30, 4–5, 84–5). Furthermore, these 'archaic' practices, while acting 'to lower the industrial efficiency of the community', nevertheless define 'the norm of reputability for the community' as a whole and, in this way, propagate such practices beyond the leisure class to all reaches of the social scale (1899c: 244, 84). It is due to this process of social emulation of the conduct of the leisure class, according to Veblen, that productive human labour, the basis of 'social advance', has widely acquired opprobrium as an irksome activity that 'must be shunned by self-respecting men' (1899c: 192; 1898a: 200). This attitude, in his assessment, was a 'cultural fact' for which 'there is no remedy ... short of a subversion of that cultural structure on which our canons of decency rest' (1898a: 201).

In a companion study, *The Theory of the Business Enterprise* (1904), Veblen narrowed his historical range to examine institutional developments distinctive to the modern era. Here he confronted the paradox that, although 'modern mechanical industry' makes possible a 'very high productive efficiency' that could potentially enhance the well-being of members of 'the community at large', much of this productive capacity routinely dissipates, diminishing 'the aggregate output of [beneficial] goods and services' (1904: 64–5). To explain this, Veblen distinguished modern industry itself, which he understood as an ensemble of knowledge, skill and technological innovations, from the institution of the privately owned 'business enterprise', i.e. the ownership arrangements that confer authoritative control of industry to the 'business man', whose aim is 'not industrial serviceability' but 'pecuniary gain', or 'profits from investment ... in the processes of industry' (1904: 6, 36–7, 20–2). Moreover, according to Veblen, while 'the economic welfare of the community at large is best served by [the] uninterrupted interplay' of the delicately balanced industrial system, business men 'have an interest in making the disturbances of the system large and frequent, since it is in the conjunctures of change that their gain emerges' (1904: 27–9). To the same end, business men spend wastefully on competitive **advertising** and marketing, and intrude into the workings of educational, religious and political institutions, in the latter case fomenting aggressive 'imperialist policies' (1904: 53–62, 382–96). Thus, in Veblen's view, even as the rise of monopolies and the spread of

'socialistic disaffection' among workers disciplined by the machine process and similar trends point forward to the triumph of technological advance over the system of the business enterprise, the system's wider institutional effects portend a return to the stultifying 'spiritual furniture' of the predatory, barbarian era (1904: 47–9, 348, 399). Which of these 'two divergent cultural tendencies [would] prove stronger in the long run' was a historical outcome that Veblen characteristically judged to be 'a blind guess' (1904: 400), a position he held to in his later works, where he greatly elaborated many of these same themes.

Neither in Veblen's own time nor subsequently did his ideas significantly influence the mainstream of American economics, though they did give rise to an interest in the academic study of consumption and provide a major point of departure for the diverse lines of work that eventually coalesced as institutional economics. For generations, his ideas served as well as a central pivot of many broader debates in American social thought (Tilman 1992). Expressed in the conceptual language of his day, Veblen's writings often appear foreign to the twenty-first-century reader, even as his critique of orthodox economic thought and his constructive analysis of social institutions continue to speak directly to the central concerns of economic sociology and related fields of contemporary theory and research.

References and further reading

Dorfman, Joseph (1934) *Thorstein Veblen and his America*, Clifton, NJ: Kelley.
Edgell, Stephen (2001) *Veblen in Perspective: His Life and Thought*, London: M. E. Sharpe.
Tilman, Rick (1992) *Thorstein Veblen and his Critics, 1891–1963*, Princeton, NJ: Princeton University Press.
—— (1996) *The Intellectual Legacy of Thorstein Veblen*, Westport, CT: Greenwood.
Veblen, Thorstein (1898a) 'The Instinct of Workmanship and the Irksomeness of Labor', *American Journal of Sociology*, 4: 187–201.

—— (1898b) 'Why is Economics Not an Evolutionary Science?' *Quarterly Journal of Economics*, 12: 373–97.

—— (1899a) 'The Preconceptions of Economic Science', *Quarterly Journal of Economics*, 13: 121–50.

—— (1899b) 'The Preconceptions of Economic Science', *Quarterly Journal of Economics*, 13: 396–426.

—— (1899c) *The Theory of the Leisure Class*, Harmondsworth, UK: Penguin.

—— (1901) 'Gustav Schmoller's Economics', *Quarterly Journal of Economics*, 16: 69–93.

—— (1904) *The Theory of the Business Enterprise*, New York: Charles Scribner's Sons.

—— (1909) 'The Limitations of Marginal Utility', *Journal of Political Economy*, 17: 620–36.

CHARLES CAMIC

W

WAGES See: earnings; efficiency wages; labour markets, sociology of

WEALTH INEQUALITY

Wealth is the value of the property that people own. It is *net worth* or total assets less total debts. For most families, this includes tangible assets such as the family home and vehicles. Other families also own vacation homes, other real estate and business assets. In addition, assets include financial wealth such as stocks, bonds, mutual funds, Certificates of Deposit and other financial assets. Debts or liabilities include mortgages on the family home, other mortgages, consumer debt, student loans, car loans, home equity loans and other debt to institutional lenders or informal lenders such as family members. *Financial wealth* is the value of liquid assets such as stocks and bonds, but does not include housing wealth or the value of business assets or investment real estate. Wealth is different from income. Income is a flow of money over time such as wages and salaries from work, government transfer payments, or interest or dividends earned on investments. Unlike income, wealth is not used directly to buy necessities such as food and clothing; rather, wealth is the total amount of property owned at a point in time.

Studies of inequality and the distribution of financial well-being tend to focus on income and how income changes over time. However, wealth may be an even more important indicator of well-being because it provides both direct financial benefits and other advantages. The family home, for example, provides shelter and other current services to the owner. At the same time, home ownership can be one of the most beneficial investments a family can make. Wealth also provides a financial cushion that can alleviate the impact of an emergency. For those without savings, a medical emergency, the unemployment of a primary income earner or a family break-up can be devastating. Wealth can be used to directly generate more wealth if it is invested and allowed to accumulate. It can also be used to indirectly generate more wealth if it is used as collateral for loans for further investments such as in the purchase of a home or business. Wealth can be used to purchase luxuries, and it can be used to buy physical protection and a safe and pleasant living environment. In the extreme, wealth can also buy leisure when its owner is able to decide whether to work or not. When family savings provide sufficient current income, income earned from wages and salaries is unnecessary.

Wealth ownership may also generate political and social influence. In a representative democracy, the distribution of political influence is often related to the distribution of wealth, and wealth carries with it social connections that can be used in important ways. Wealth expands educational and occupational opportunities for the current owner, and because wealth can be passed from one generation to the next, it often expands educational and occupational advantages for future generations as well. Of course, the truly rich may attract media attention, solicitations for donations, and other unwanted recognition. Wealth also invites security threats, may be socially isolating, and can dampen motivation. Yet the benefits of wealth ownership generally outweigh the disadvantages, and most agree that the rich are generally better off as a result of their asset ownership.

Wealth inequality

Owning wealth itself is not a problem; rather, wealth ownership becomes a problem with a small minority of families owning almost all the wealth. In reality, wealth inequality is extreme in nearly all countries today, and the United States is a particularly extreme example. In the USA, the majority of wealth is owned by fewer than 10 per cent of families. In recent decades, most people have not owned stocks, mutual funds, bonds or even less-risky assets such as Certificates of Deposit. Most American families own chequing and savings accounts, a vehicle or two, and have tended to keep most of their assets in owner-occupied housing. In a common scenario, many middle-class Americans first use their income to make payments on a house to take advantage of tax breaks and the combination of consuming and investing that is available in home ownership. After a mortgage payment, however, there is often little left over to save in other forms. Americans do tend to buy their homes and vehicles with credit, and they finance other expenditures with debt as well. In recent years, in fact, Americans have been willing to accumulate tremendous amounts of such debt including large amounts of mortgage debt, car loans, loans for vacations and home improvement loans. While such

liabilities may ease short-term financial woes, their long-term effect is to diminish overall wealth along with the advantages associated with wealth.

Many Americans have enjoyed remarkable and increasing prosperity, but for others, reports of sensational economic conditions in recent years bore little resemblance to their own experiences. Those in the middle and lower segments of the wealth distribution have continued to own little or no wealth, and many have watched their economic standing deteriorate. The basic facts about rising inequality have become fairly well understood. Evidence from historical records suggests that although levels of wealth inequality varied drastically during the first part of the twentieth century, inequality in wealth ownership was consistently extreme. Lampman (1962) is usually credited as being among the first to identify wealth inequality as a source of social problems. He used estate tax data to document trends in wealth ownership and inequality in the decades between 1920 and 1960. His findings indicated that between 1922 and 1953, the top 1 per cent of wealth holders owned an average of 30 per cent of total household sector wealth. While inequalities varied with macroeconomic trends during the decades Lampman studied, he provided convincing evidence that inequality was consistently extreme throughout that period.

Other historical estimates have produced similar evidence of inequality during the early twentieth century. In the early part of the century (between 1922 and the early 1950s), those in the top 1 per cent of the wealth distribution owned an average of 30 per cent of total net worth. The share of wealth owned by the top 1 per cent increased from about 29 per cent to about 32 per cent between 1922 and the 1929 stock market crash. During the 1930s and 1940s, the concentration of wealth declined, so that the top 1 per cent owned less than 30 per cent by the late 1940s.

During the 1950s, economic prosperity brought with it increased wealth inequality, and by the late 1950s, estimates suggest that the top 1 per cent of households owned nearly 35 per cent of total wealth.

Wealth data and estimates of wealth inequality began to improve in the 1960s. In 1962, the Federal Reserve Board's Survey of the Financial Characteristics of Consumers (SFCC) became the first comprehensive survey of wealth holdings in the USA. Table 1 contains estimates of wealth distribution from the SFCC and another later survey for the 1980s and 1990s. These estimates demonstrate that a very small portion of households have consistently owned the vast majority of household wealth. In 1962, the top 1 per cent of wealth owners owned 33.5 per cent of total net worth, and the top quintile owned more than 80 per cent of total net worth. Wealth inequality remained unequally distributed but relatively constant between 1962 and the mid 1970s due to an extended stock market slump and the growth of welfare programmes such as Aid to Families with Dependent Children (AFDC) and Social Security. After 1973 wealth inequality began to drop once again. Others using similar methods have found that between 1972 and 1976, the share of total wealth owned by the top 1 per cent of wealth owners declined from 29 to about 19 per cent of total wealth.

Wealth inequality began to rise considerably after 1979, a trend that continued throughout the 1980s. By 1983, wealth inequality had returned to, and indeed surpassed on some measures, 1962 levels. Indeed, the share of wealth owned by the top 1 per cent of wealth holders was 33.8 per cent in 1983 and 37.4 per cent by 1989. Real mean wealth grew at 3.4 per cent annually during this six-year period, a rate that was nearly double the rate of wealth growth between 1962 and 1983. Mean family wealth increased 23 per cent in real terms, but that median wealth grew by only 8 per cent over that period. There is also evidence that the share of the top 0.5 per cent of wealth owners rose 5 per cent during this period, from 26.2 per cent of total household sector wealth in 1983 to 31.4 per cent in 1989. The wealth of the next half per cent remained relatively constant at about 7.5 per cent of total household wealth, but the share of the next 9 per cent decreased from 34.4 per cent in 1983 to 33.4 per cent in 1989.

Most striking is evidence of the decline in the wealth of the poorest 80 per cent of households. The wealth of this group decreased by more than 2 percentage points between 1983 and 1989, leaving their share at just more than 16 per cent at the start of the 1990s. Moreover, the top 20 per cent of the distribution accumulated nearly all growth in real wealth between 1983 and 1989, and their share of total wealth grew to nearly 84 per cent. In the 1980s, wealth inequality in the United

Table 1. Growing wealth inequality: the distribution of wealth, 1962–98

	Gini coefficient	Top 1%	Top 20%	Second 20%	Third 20%	Bottom 40%
1962	0.80	33.5	81.2	13.5	5.0	0.3
1983	0.80	33.8	81.3	12.6	5.2	0.9
1989	0.85	37.4	83.6	12.3	4.8	−0.7
1992	0.85	37.2	83.9	11.4	4.5	0.2
1995	0.85	38.5	83.9	11.4	4.5	0.2
1998	0.85	38.1	83.4	11.9	45	0.2

Note:
Estimates from the Survey of Consumer Finances. Cells indicate the percentage of net worth or financial wealth held by households in each segment of the distribution.

States became severe relative to that found in European nations. Studies of wealth in the 1920s suggested that wealth in the United States was much more equally distributed than in Western European nations. Yet research suggests that by the late 1980s, household sector wealth in the USA was considerably more concentrated than in Western Europe.

While mean and median household net worth declined during the 1990s, the distribution of wealth continued to worsen. The wealth of the top 1 per cent of wealth holders increased from 37 per cent of total wealth in 1989 to nearly 39 per cent in 1995. However, between 1989 and 1998, the proportion of net worth owned by the top 1 per cent of wealth owners rose from 30 per cent to more than 34 per cent. At the same time, the proportion of net worth owned by those in the bottom 90 per cent declined from 33 per cent to just over 30 per cent. The average Forbes 400 member's wealth grew 177 per cent between 1990 and 2000. Between 1989 and 1998, the net worth of the median US household declined 8.6 per cent. In 2000, the Forbes 400 owned as much wealth as the bottom half of the US population combined. The Gini coefficient, an indicator of the degree of inequality comparable to the Gini coefficient used to measure income inequality, increased from 0.85 in 1989 and 1992 to 0.87 in 1995. The Gini coefficient ranges from 0 to 1, with 0 indicating perfect equality and 1 indicating perfect inequality. Conceptually, if a single household were to own all wealth, the Gini coefficient would equal 1. The Gini coefficient for financial wealth, that is when real assets such as the family home and other real estate are excluded, reached 0.94 in the late 1990s.

Yet another way to think about wealth inequality is to consider spread (or variance), or the difference between the wealthiest and the poorest households. Because there is a great deal of inequality in wealth ownership, the spread is naturally quite large. What is perhaps most striking, though, is the degree to which the spread in wealth inequality exceeds the spread in income inequality. In particular, it is common to compare the spread in household income to the variance in wealth ownership to demonstrate the changing nature of wealth inequality and the relative size of income inequality. Estimates such as this typically indicate that the variance in household ownership of net assets is extremely large, particularly around 1990 when wealth inequality was at historically high levels. The spread in income inequality has also been quite large, but inequality in wealth ownership surpasses inequality in income by tremendous margins. In 1990, for instance, variance in net asset ownership was more than 100 times greater than variance in income.

Racial inequality in wealth ownership is among the most extreme and persistent forms of stratification in general and wealth stratification in particular. Blacks and Hispanics, in particular, own considerably less wealth than whites. In 1992, while median black income was about 60 per cent of median white income, median net worth for blacks was only 8 per cent of median net worth for whites. In that same year, 25 per cent of white families had zero or negative assets, but more than 60 per cent of black families had no wealth. Longitudinal estimates suggest that between 1960 and 1995, whites were twice as likely as minorities to have more wealth than income and nearly three times as likely to experience wealth mobility. Minorities are also underrepresented among the very wealthy. In 1995, 95 per cent of those in the top 1 per cent of wealth holders were white, while only 1 per cent were black. The wealth position of non-black minorities has attracted less attention, but there is evidence that the wealth accumulation of whites also exceeds that of Hispanics and Asians.

What explains wealth inequality?

While basic facts about the distribution of wealth have become taken for granted, understanding of the processes that account for wealth inequality is still limited. Efforts to explain wealth inequality have typically focused on the role of aggregate influences such as market fluctuations and demographic trends. There is evidence that because the wealthy are more likely to own stocks, wealth inequality worsens when the stock market booms. Similarly, when real estate values increase, those who own houses and other land improve their position. Because those who are already well off are more likely to own appreciable land, wealth inequality tends to worsen. With rising land values, however, the middle class has historically benefited more than they do with stock booms because home ownership has been more common among middle-class families. Recent changes in portfolio behaviour – that is, the combination of assets families own – thus have important implications for wealth ownership and inequality. In fact, in recent years, because stock ownership has become more common among middle-class families, stock market booms in the late 1990s had less of an effect on wealth inequality than they would have if middle-class stock ownership had remained at previous levels.

There is a limited amount of research exploring how wealth varies by age and race. Keynesian economics, the predominant form of economics during the 1930s and 1940s, emphasized the role that individual saving played in the larger economy and proposed that current income was the primary determinant of saving. The Life Cycle Hypothesis, a reaction to the simplicity of the Keynesian approach, held that wealth increases until retirement, after which it declines. In reality, people do not behave this way because they do not know when they will die and because people want to leave an inheritance to their children and grandchildren.

Wealth ownership also varies in important ways across racial groups. Some argue that educational differences are central to explaining racial differences in wealth, while others have argued more generally that structural barriers and **discrimination** create these differences. Social scientists generally agree that discrimination in the sale of housing and lending of money to buy houses, dampened educational and occupational opportunities for minorities, and other structural constraints contribute to inequality. Others have shown that portfolio behaviour (i.e. decisions about buying stocks versus bonds versus a new car) varies systematically by race and may contribute in important ways to racial differences in well-being. The reasons that portfolio behaviour varies racially, however, are less clear, although the dominant explanation suggests that differences in willingness to postpone consumption are important. Of course, social influences on current consumption (i.e. decisions about whether to save or buy a new car) are likely quite strong, but current data restricts empirical examination of such influences.

Some also argue that family structure also plays an important role in creating and maintaining differences in wealth ownership. A relatively small percentage of the increase in poverty in the 1970s through the 1990s was accounted for by changes in family structure. Two separate studies contended that the 'feminization of poverty' between 1960 and the mid 1980s was a result of changes in relative poverty rates for various household compositions rather than changes in family structure, particularly for blacks. Yet evidence continues to mount that suggests some role for change in family structure. Few wealth researchers address issues of family structure, but both survey and simulated estimates suggest that gender and family structure affect both cross-sectional wealth ownership and longitudinal patterns of wealth mobility. These estimates suggest that at any given point in time, family structure is highly correlated with wealth ownership, net of income, education and race. In particular, there is evidence that marriage and widowhood increase wealth ownership, while family size and family dissolution through divorce or separation have the opposite effect. Researchers have also shown that family structure continues to affect poverty when it is defined in income terms.

Similarly, there is reason to suspect that wealth varies in significant ways with religious affiliation and participation both during childhood and adulthood. Religion can be among the most significant defining traits of a family, but previous research on wealth ownership has not moved beyond relatively casual references to these influences in understanding wealth accumulation and inequality. Religion is likely to affect asset accumulation *indirectly* because it shapes many of the processes that determine family wealth. A rich tradition of research demonstrates clear religious differences in childrearing, marital stability, divorce and fertility and other outcomes such as earnings, education and female employment rates. Religion is also likely to affect wealth ownership *directly* for a number of reasons. Religion shapes values and priorities, and wealth may be one of the values identified as worth pursuing. Religious **beliefs** transmitted through parents and during religious ceremonies also contribute to the set of competencies from which action is constructed, and these competencies may increase or impede wealth accumulation. In addition, religion provides social contacts that may improve opportunities to accumulate assets by providing information or assistance. Research on wealth occasionally references the potential importance of religion, but these studies focus almost exclusively on the role of income, investment behaviour, and inheritance without systematically exploring the relative importance of religion.

Related to intergenerational processes is the inheritance of wealth. We know very little about how much wealth is actually inherited because data on inheritance is quite rare, but some argue that inheritance is extreme. Indeed, between the 1970s and 1990s, as little as 20 and as much as 80 per cent of total wealth may have been inherited. Those who study inheritance typically refer to three forms of inheritance: inheritance at the death of a parent or other benefactor, inter-vivos transfers of money and other assets, and transfers of cultural capital. While we typically think of inheritance as occurring at the death of the benefactor, inter-vivos transfers account for nearly 90 per cent of intergenerational wealth transfers. Cultural capital, transferred through formal education and informal experiences, is also a vital, inherited resource. Inheritance likely explains much of the persistence of wealth inequality. Racial differences in wealth ownership, for example, are bound to be exacerbated across generations if most wealth is inherited.

References and further reading

Conley, Dalton (1999) *Being Black, Living in the Red: Race, Wealth and Social Policy in America*, Berkeley, CA: University of California Press.

Keister, Lisa A. (2000) 'Race and Wealth Inequality: The Impact of Racial Differences in Asset Ownership on the Distribution of Household Wealth', *Social Science Research*, 29: 477–502.

—— (2000) *Wealth in America*, New York: Cambridge University Press.

Keister, Lisa A. and Moller, Stephanie (2000) 'Wealth Inequality in the United States', *Annual Review of Sociology*, 26: 63–81.

Lampman, Robert J. (1962) *The Share of Top Wealth-Holders in National Wealth, 1922–56*, Princeton, NJ: Princeton University Press.

Oliver, Melvin O. and Shapiro, Thomas M. (1995) *Black Wealth/White Wealth*, New York: Routledge.

Wolff, Edward N. (1995) *Top Heavy: A Study of the Increasing Inequality of Wealth in America*, New York: Twentieth Century Fund.
—— (1998) 'Recent Trends in the Size Distribution of Household Wealth', *Journal of Economic Perspectives*, 12: 131–50.

LISA A. KEISTER

WEBER, MAX

Economic sociology was created around the turn of the twentieth century, and Max Weber (1864–1920) qualifies as one of its founders. Since Weber often wrote on economic topics throughout his career and usually applied a social perspective, one might be tempted to argue that economic sociology constitutes *the* key theme in his production. Weber's two dissertations – one on medieval trading corporations and another on Roman agriculture – would, for example, from this perspective, be of direct relevance for economic sociology. And so would his inaugural lecture in Freiburg, his lectures on economics in the 1890s, his study of rural workers east of the River Elbe, and his plentiful articles on the stock exchange that have just been republished.

While it is clear that all of these works – which were written *before* Weber started to use the term 'sociology' to describe his approach – contain many exciting and important contributions to economic sociology, in a brief entry such as this a certain priority must be given to his two major works in sociology: *Economy and Society* and *Collected Essays in the Sociology of Religion* (which includes the second edition of *The Protestant Ethic and the Spirit of Capitalism*). To this may also be added a course that Weber gave in 1919–20 and which is known in translation as *General Economic History*. The main reason for proceeding in this manner is that what is truly distinctive about economic sociology – the consistent application of sociological concepts and reasoning to economic

phenomena – comes out with the greatest clarity in these works.

In the rest of this entry I will follow the general structure that Weber himself choose to follow in *Economy and Society* for his economic sociology, namely to first present his sociological analysis of the economy itself, and then proceed to its relationship to politics (including law) and to religion. While Weber's analysis is clearly richer and more complex than what this exposition is able to give expression to, it nonetheless may serve the reader as a convenient introduction to many of Weber's main points.

The key theoretical chapter on economic sociology in *Economy and Society* was written just before Weber's death in 1920, as part of an attempt to recast his whole manuscript in a more concise and textbook-like manner. The result was a chapter the size of a small book, in which the basic concepts of economic sociology are enumerated and explicated one by one. The title of Chapter 2 is 'Sociological Categories of Economic Action', and it is generally considered to be one of the most difficult chapters in *Economy and Society*.

Just as sociology must start with social action, according to Weber, so economic sociology must begin with *economic (social) action*. An economic action is defined as behaviour invested with a meaning and aimed at utility. If it also is oriented to another actor it qualifies as being *social*. As any social action, an economic action is explained if the meaning it is invested with makes sense (adequacy on the level of meaning, in Weber's terminology) and if the behaviour of the actor is the main cause of the intended effect (adequate causality, in Weber's terminology).

If two actors orient their economic actions to each other, there will be an *economic (social) relationship*. Examples of economic relationship are competition and exchange. These relationships can be *open* and they can be *closed*. An economic relationship may also, for example, start out as open and then be closed when competition increases.

Economic relationships of some duration may lead to the emergence of an economic *order,* a term that often answers to what sociologists today mean by institution. The heart of an order consists of a series of pre-scriptions ('maxims') for how to behave that appear as exterior and obligatory to the individual actor. An order may alternatively come into being as the result of conscious action. A corporation may, for example, come into being in modern society as the result of a decision to found a firm. An economic order that has a staff to realize and enforce its goals constitutes an *economic organization* (or an *economic association*) in Weber's terms. The shareholding firm con-stitutes the most important type of eco-nomic organization in modern capitalism.

Also the market can constitute an order according to Weber: that is, a series of instructions or maxims for how to behave. What is most distinctive about Weber's view of the market, from a sociological perspective, is that it essentially consists of *two* types of social interactions. There is, on the one hand, exchange as in most theories of markets. But Weber also adds another type of interaction in the market: competi-tion to qualify as the final buyer and as the final seller. Weber argues that buyers and sellers have different but complementary interests. Though each may want to gain at the expense of the other, the end result – typically reached through negotiations – will be a compromise. Prices, according to Weber, do not so much reflect the work invested in the goods (as in classical political economy) or the subjective evaluation of the actor (as in marginal utility theory), but the power of the two actors involved in the exchange.

Weber also discusses some macro-economic or constitutional economic phe-nomena in Chapter 2 of *Economy and Society.* One example is the general economic order

of a society, be it a planned economy or a market economy. While the satisfaction of wants is essential to both of these, the mar-ket economy has the additional goal of profit-making. It may be added that Weber was personally a strong advocate of dynamic capitalism, and feared that stagna-tion and political tyranny would come with a socialist economy or with a non-dynamic type of capitalism. While the same elite typically controls both political and eco-nomic resources in socialism, this is not the case in capitalism.

In Chapter 2 of *Economy and Society* Weber also discusses different types of capitalism. As opposed to Marx, who argued that there only existed one type of capitalism, Weber argued that different types of capitalism could be found far back in history and in many different parts of the world – not just in the West. This was especially true for *political capitalism* and for small-scale forms of capitalism, related to trade and the exchange of money. A third type of capitalism, in contrast, had only developed in the West and in modern times, and this was *rational capitalism.*

By 'political capitalism' Weber means those types of profit-making where the state or the political system is crucial to the profit-making. Examples include profit-making that is successful thanks to privi-leges granted by the state or profit-making that takes place under the direct umbrella of the coercive force of the state, such as in imperialism. Modern agriculture often has elements of political capitalism and so does the defence industry.

Weber's most important type of capital-ism, however, is rational capitalism; and this concept also represents his most important contribution to the theory of capitalism more generally. As an **ideal type**, profit-making is thoroughly systematic in rational capitalism as well as independent of special favours granted by the state and the like. The key actor in this type of capitalism is the modern shareholding firm, with its sophisticated forms of accounting, reliable bureaucracy and disciplined workers. Everybody works hard and with a conscious purpose (*vocation*). In rational capitalism the state keeps in the background, and its behaviour is predictable. The legal order is similarly predictable.

In modern society the existing forms of capitalism would typically consist of a mixture of different elements, according to Weber. As elsewhere in society, one can usually find non-reflective and traditional behaviour also in the economy; and one suspects that elements of what Weber calls 'traditional capitalism' in *The Protestant Ethic* also are present in modern society. The temptation to close off a market to one's competitors with the help of state in one way or another makes it likely that there will be elements of political capitalism. There will also always be small businesses, it seems. First and foremost, however, leading sectors in modern capitalism are likely to have strong elements of rational capitalism, according to Weber.

As to the relationship of politics to economics in Weber's economic sociology, it should first of all be noted that Weber never got around to write the full-scale sociology of the state that he had planned. If he had done so, he would presumably have enlarged upon and added to the many topics relating to the interaction between economic and political forces that he had already written about. These include such phenomena as the economic policy of the state and its monetary policy.

Of Weber's many studies that do analyse the state and economics, the one that is generally considered to be the most innovative is the one devoted to domination and its legitimation. This topic is famously discussed in Chapter 3 of *Economy and Society*: that is, in one of the few chapters that Weber had time to rewrite for the new version of his work and also send off to the printer, just before his death.

Two aspects of Weber's analysis of the main types of legitimate domination (legal, traditional and charismatic domination) are of special importance in this context. The first has to do with the general impact on the economy of each of these three types of domination; and the second with the way that the state and its staff is financed. While legal domination is positive to, as well as necessary for, rational capitalism, traditional domination and charismatic domination are not. Some types of traditional domination, such as patrimonialism, are on the other hand positive to political capitalism. The ethos of feudalism (another form of traditional domination) is deeply conservative when it comes to economic matters. Charismatic domination is hostile to all forms of economic activities, until it settles down, through the process of routinization, to some kind of economic traditionalism.

While the modern rational state mainly gets its resources through taxation and pays its officials a salary as well as a pension, the charismatic ruler relies on booty or donations, which are handed out to his followers according to their needs and similar (formally) irrational criteria. In patrimonialism the property of the state is regarded as the personal property of the ruler; and the ruler decides himself what to pay his entourage. In some respects the economic situation of the feudal ruler is similar to that of the patrimonial ruler. The feudal ruler is in addition bound to his vassals through a contract; and distinct duties follow from this contract.

The legal system is part of the modern state, according to Weber, and is absolutely crucial to the operation of the capitalist economy. First of all, it helps to assure that there is some predictability in economic affairs. Since investments are so high in rational capitalism, there has to be some assurance that economic conflicts will be solved in a predictable manner. This is accomplished, among other things, by having rational laws, a rational jurisprudence and professionally trained jurists. Second, the legal system of the modern state is enabling, in the sense that it supplies the tools through which new economic relations can be constructed. The most important of these is the contract, including the contract through which a firm is created.

Weber's analysis of the relationship of the economy to religion is very celebrated, especially in the form that it took in *The Protestant Ethic*. It is also a topic to which Weber paid much attention throughout his career, as evidenced by the many studies that are included in his three-volume set *Collected Essays in the Sociology of Religion*. According to Weber's plan for this work, as announced just before his death in a famous advertisement, it was actually to be much larger in size and content.

Weber's main concern in all of his sociology of religion, to cite the advertisement just mentioned, was to address the following question: 'What is the economic and social *singularity* of the Occident based upon, how did it arise and especially, how is it connected to the religious ethos?' The well-known answer that Weber gave in *The Protestant Ethic* is that Protestantism, especially what he termed ascetic Protestantism, had infused a sense of vocation (*Beruf*), asceticism and a methodical approach more generally into the capitalist mentality or spirit. This idea was immediately criticized when it was presented, and the discussion of 'The Weber Thesis' is still going strong.

After having finished *The Protestant Ethic*, Weber wrote a small essay in which he analysed the ways in which the sect had added to the impact of ascetic Protestantism on the individual believer. This essay is also valuable for its analysis of trust in economic life and what is often referred to these days as **social capital**. A decade or so later Weber returned to the main issue he had raised in *The Protestant Ethic*, this time looking at such religions as Taoism, Confucianism, Hinduism and Buddhism. Nei-

ther of these religions contained an open endorsement of profit-making activities along the lines of acetic Protestantism, according to Weber. To this should be added a number of other reasons why rational capitalism had not emerged on its own accord outside of the West, to Weber's mind. For this you not only needed a rational capitalist mentality, but also a series of institutional prerequisites such as a rational state, rational technology, rational law and so on.

By way of summarizing Weber's work in economic sociology, one can say that it constitutes a magnificent – and still unsurpassed – achievement. Not only did he lay a solid theoretical foundation for economic sociology (in Chapter 2 of *Economy and Society*), but he also wrote voluminously on a great number of important economic topics from a sociological perspective. It should finally be emphasized that many of Weber's insights in economic sociology still remain to be located as well as properly discussed. Some beginnings in this direction do exist – but most of this work still remains to be done.

References and further reading

Chalcroft, David and Austin Harrington (eds) (2001) *The Protestant Ethic Debate: Max Weber's Replies to his Critics*, Liverpool: Liverpool University Press.

Marshall, Gordon (1982) *In Search of the Spirit of Capitalism: An Essay on Max Weber's Protestant Ethic Thesis*, London: Hutchinson.

Mommsen, Wolfgang (1974) 'The Alternative to Marx: Dynamic Capitalism instead of Bureaucratic Socialism', in Wolfgang Mommsen, *The Age of Bureaucracy*. New York: Harper and Row, pp. 47–71.

Swedberg, Richard (1998) *Max Weber and the Idea of Economic Sociology*, Princeton, NJ: Princeton University Press.

Weber, Max ([1889]2003) *The History of Commercial Partnerships in the Middle Ages*, translated by Lutz Kaelbar, London: Rowman and Littlefield.

—— ([1894–6]2000) 'Stock and Commodity Exchanges [*Die Börse* (1894)], Commerce on the Stock and Commodity Exchanges [*Die Börsenverkehr*]', *Theory and Society*, 29: 305–38, 339–71.

—— ([1898]1990) *Grundriss zu den Vorlesungen über Allgemeine ('theoretische') Nationalökonomie*, Tübingen: J. C. B. Mohr.

—— ([1904–5]1958) *The Protestant Ethic and the Spirit of Capitalism*, New York: Charles Scribner's Sons.

—— ([1922]1978) *Economy and Society: An Outline of Interpretive Sociology*, two volumes, Berkeley, CA: University of California Press.

—— ([1923]1981) *General Economic History*, New Brunswick, NJ: Transaction Books.

RICHARD SWEDBERG

WELFARE

Like the concept welfare state, the term 'welfare' is nebulous and can refer to broad sets of programmes and services designed to meet the economic, physical and social needs of persons who are unable to provide these needs themselves. Most people, however, perceive welfare more narrowly. To them, it means that some of their poor fellow citizens receive cash assistance from the state. This essay focuses on this more restrictive view of welfare, i.e. cash assistance, because it is commonly understood and drives much of the debate over state versus personal responsibility for economic security. Plainly, welfare could include non-cash assistance programmes and other means-tested social services, but then other more suitable terms exist, like 'anti-poverty programmes', 'social insurance' or 'public assistance'.

With the conspicuous exception of the United States, most industrialized countries have used welfare as the primary means to support poor people. Although control over how the poor have spent cash assistance was relinquished, governments assumed that cash assistance gave recipients more choice and flexibility. For bureaucracies as well, transferring money has been cheaper than providing and administering services. Also, for at least the middle half of the twentieth century, the politics of redistributing income from the richer to the poorer was easier because governments could argue that the recipients belonged to the deserving poor – the sick and elderly, disabled, and widowed with dependent children – who were unable to support themselves through work. Of course, spending levels and cash assistance programmes have differed across countries, but broadly speaking nations' public spending on welfare grew and kept pace with inflation until the mid to late 1970s. By the late 1970s, however, welfare recipient populations in several industrialized countries had dramatically changed from what they looked like in the 1950s, which led several countries to debate the divisive issue over acceptable benefit levels for cash assistance.

In the United States, the welfare population and the bureaucracy serving it had changed radically from what existed before the 1960s. The welfare population in America by the mid 1970s was overwhelmingly composed of divorced, separated or never married mothers with dependent children rather than widowed families, the sick and elderly, and the disabled. No longer did many Americans see their fellow citizens on welfare as the deserving poor. Instead, a new consensus emerged, rightly or wrongly, that considered the welfare population as composed of people potentially 'cheating the system' and as the able-bodied who were fit to work. By and large, the populous perceived cash assistance as subsidizing the **life styles** of the undeserving poor. Moreover, the state welfare apparatus itself had become a cumbersome ruling-making machine that was unresponsive to the needs of its recipients.

Besides public perceptions of a bloated, outmoded welfare bureaucracy and a lack of a work ethic among welfare recipients, by the 1980s a vocal group of intellectuals had coalesced to denounce the welfare system. Several well-known intellectuals, notably the sociologist Charles Murray,

719

argued that cash assistance created more problems than it solved.

Welfare, according to Murray and colleagues, created negative incentives related to work effort and child-bearing and family structure. For the former, instead of encouraging work among recipients, welfare rewarded non-work, while penalizing those who worked with high marginal tax rates. Although most detractors of welfare did not wish to see it abolished altogether, many argued that any guaranteed income floor would naturally discourage the able-bodied from working the number of hours they could work. With respect to the latter, since cash assistance could conceivably sustain a female-headed household as a viable economic unit, critics contended that welfare could encourage more single mothers to have children outside of marriage and remain unmarried rather than find husbands.

The indictments of welfare have generated much research, spurred intense political debate, and affected how industrialized countries evaluate their own welfare programmes. In an important 1992 article in the *Journal of Economic Literature*, Robert Moffitt addressed the indictments in his survey of the incentive effects of the American welfare system. He concluded from his review of the existing scientific literature that there was 'unequivocal evidence of effects on labor supply, participation in the welfare system, and on some aspects of family structure' (Moffitt 1992: 56). However, he also stated that 'the importance of these effects is limited in many respects' (Moffitt 1992: 56). For instance, estimates of the effects of welfare on family structure were too small to explain the decline in marriage rates in the United States. Likewise, the work effort effects were again too small, albeit statistically significant, to explain high rates of poverty among female-headed households. Researchers over the 1990s in the United Kingdom, Canada, Germany, the Nordic

countries, Australia and New Zealand have conducted similar reviews on the incentive effects of their own welfare programmes. Interestingly, the cross-country studies report either ambiguous findings on work effort and family structure or findings offering only tepid support for the criticisms.

Nevertheless, the change in public views about the welfare population and assertions about welfare's perverse incentives brought about draconian reforms to the American welfare system in 1996. Since then, the number of cash assistance recipients has dropped appreciably, additional income is no longer necessarily given when recipients have more children, and typically some form of work is required to receive welfare. Essentially, work requirements have replaced work incentives and temporary cash relief has replaced guaranteed cash floors. While it remains unclear whether reforms will improve the well-being of the poor, it is clear that the reforms have profound implications for the future role of the welfare state, which over the course of the twentieth century was remarkably successful at redistributing income among citizens unknown to each other without unrest or civil discord.

References and further reading

Edin, Kathryn and Lein, Laura (1997) *Making Ends Meet: How Single Mothers Survive Welfare and Low-Wage Work*, New York: Russell Sage Foundation.

Moffitt, Robert (1992) 'Incentive Effects of the US Welfare System: A Review', *Journal of Economic Literature*, 30: 1–61.

Murray, Charles (1984) *Losing Ground: American Social Policy 1950–1980*, New York: Basic Books.

PETER D. BRANDON

WELFARE ECONOMICS

Welfare economics is that branch of economics that evaluates institutional and other changes in terms of the aggregate welfare of the population. At the same time, it denies that interpersonal welfare comparisons can be scientific – this is left to politics. This stance is made possible by adoption of the criterion of Pareto-improvement – meaning that a change is desirable if at least one person is made better off and no one is worse off. This criterion has several problems. It enshrines the status quo distribution of income and rights without justification. It is difficult to actually work out all the necessary side-payments to secure agreement. This leads some economists to advocate potential Pareto-improvement (hypothetical compensation). This puts the decision in the hands of technicians rather than directly in the hands of those affected or their representatives.

Efficiency occurs when trading stops. It says nothing about the desirability of the result – nothing about equity or the substantive state of the world. It says nothing about why one party had much to trade and another had little to start with. More could be said if analysis could add up measures of output received by all individuals. But value depends on the price vector, which depends on the aggregate net output vector which in turn depends on income distribution. If people have different tastes, income distribution will change the relative demand for different goods. GNP is often used in cross-sectional and time series studies, but it suffers from the index number problem. Put another way, there is value circularity when the prices generated from one distribution of income are used to evaluate goods produced under another distribution. Efficiency is not a single thing that can be used as a reference point. There are as many efficient outcomes as there are different starting places in terms of rights and incomes. Efficiency follows logically from different distributions and cannot be a guide to choosing them.

One of the abstract concepts in welfare economics is that of consumer surplus. This is the difference between what a consumer pays for a good and the maximum they might be willing to pay. In theory, a change in policy regime could reduce one person's consumer surplus without any increase in another's welfare. The partial equilibrium character of the concept has made it contentious. The fact that a consumer did not pay their maximum bid for one good is part of the demand for another. There cannot be demand for all goods and some surplus in addition. This has led Little (1957: 184) to declare, 'The best criterion for investment decisions must, within wide limits, be determined at dynamic and administrative levels – and not at the level of static welfare theory.' Also see Boadway and Bruce (1984).

How is welfare economics related to the welfare state? The theory has been used to argue against taxes, any redistribution other than in money lump-sum transfers, a minimum wage, etc. Some economists have lent their support for tax reduction on the notion that taxes distort market outcomes and reduce consumer surplus. This gives effect to all other pre-existing taxes and other actions of government, on which existing market outcomes rest; just as in the future when a new tax is proposed, the present new tax will recede from view and be a part of the given institutional background. Taxes add to the cost of production and a reduced output. This follows only if taxes are pure tribute. If taxes pay for inputs provided by government including orderly property rights, then it is no more a distortion than payment for any input. The distribution of who pays for social overhead costs enjoyed by all is part of the question about income distribution. There is no natural market, but rather exchange structured by property rights designating whose interests are a cost to whom.

Welfare economics is the basis for benefit–cost analysis, which is another attempt to aggregate all benefits and costs regardless of their distribution. For a critique see

Schmid (1989). Welfare economics is also the basis for some normative economic analyses of law. For example, it is suggested that the liability for damages should be assigned to whomever is the cheapest avoider of the harm. But this requires a value judgement as to what is reasonable behaviour if it creates a cost for others. As Calabresi (1985: 69) argues, 'what is deemed unreasonable behavior, no less than who is the cheapest avoider of a cost, depends on the valuations put on acts, activities, and **beliefs** by the whole of our law and not on some objective or scientific notion.'

Welfare economics is often used to support public provision of high exclusion cost goods such as air quality. It can be imagined that people do not reveal their preferences (voluntarily pay) in the hope of being free riders, which results in an inefficient undersupply of the good. Is welfare enhanced by public provision via taxes? Not necessarily. Taxes eliminate the free rider and the good is produced, but there are thereby unwilling riders who were not hiding their demand, but truly did not want the good. Without a value judgement as to whose interests should count, it is not possible to say that public provision or its absence is welfare enhancing.

The Pareto criterion is akin to the unanimity rules in politics, which also needs a value judgement to justify the status quo. Buchanan and Tullock (1962) note a trade-off for the individual between being protected from unwanted change and the high cost of getting others with similar rights to make a change desired by the individual. Can there be a scientific politics that can aggregate individual preferences faithfully? Arrow's (1963) logical analysis says no. His 'impossibility theorem' states that a set of political rules can't be constructed that ensures universality, Pareto-consistency, independence and non-dictatorship. In a nutshell, if interests conflict, some people's preference will count and others' will not.

Arrow demonstrated an agenda paradox. The order in which distributive alternatives are voted on will affect which of several majority coalitions will emerge victorious.

Fligstein (2001: 177) observes, 'Sociologists tend to shy away from making claims that an organizational form is efficient in a neoclassical sense. Instead, organizational theory assumes only that organizational forms are effective; that is, they promote the survival of the organization.' These are the same thing for those economists who argue that unless firms are efficient, they will not survive. But these arguments are tautological and more apologetics than real (Samuels 1992). As some evolutionary scientists note, the only thing that survival proves is survival, not ethical or any other superiority.

Measures of aggregate welfare change depend on the stability of preferences (as well as their homogeneity). If resources can be used to meet the demands of consumers and to create these demands, it is not possible to compare two goods piles and say that welfare has increased. Aggregate measures also depend on complete commensurability of all values. Money and markets nominally reduce all values such as steel, food, art, respect, trust, honour, etc. to equivalents. But, that does not mean that the trade-offs were made consciously or consistently.

While some economists have tried to specify restrictive assumptions that get around Arrow's **impossibility theorem** and agenda paradox, they remain unreal. This has led Mishan (1968: 511) to conclude, 'it would be optimistic to expect that the continued study in welfare economics will contribute toward making the world a happier place.' Also see Mishan (1972). Feldman (1987: 894) likewise concludes, there is no logically infallible way to solve the problem of distribution.' Robinson (1962) has declared 'the end of the God Trick'. We are left with the agony of our moral judgements about interpersonal welfare, who deserves to be treated as a subject.

References and further reading

Arrow, K. J. (1963) *Social Choice and Individual Values*, New Haven, CT: Yale University Press.

Boadway, R. W. and Bruce, N. (1984) *Welfare Economics*, Oxford: Blackwell.

Buchanan, J. M. and Tullock, G. (1962) *The Calculus of Consent*, Ann Arbor, MI: University of Michigan Press.

Calabresi, G. (1985) *Ideals, Beliefs, Attitudes, and the Law: Private Law Perspectives on a Public Law Problem*, Syracuse, NY: Syracuse University Press.

Feldman, A. M. (1987) 'Welfare Economics', in J. Eatwell, M. Milgate and P. Newman (eds), *The New Palgrave Dictionary of Economics*, London: Macmillan.

Fligstein, N. (2001) *The Architecture of Markets: An Economic Sociology of Twenty-First-Century Capitalist Societies*, Princeton, NJ: Princeton University Press.

Little, I. M. D. (1957) *A Critique of Welfare Economics*, second edition, Oxford: Clarendon Press.

Mishan, E. J. (1968) 'Welfare Economics', in *International Encyclopedia of the Social Sciences*, London: Macmillan.

—— (1972) 'The Futility of Pareto-Efficient Distribution', *American Economic Review*, 62: 971–6.

Robinson, J. (1962) *Economic Philosophy*, London: C. A. Watts.

Samuels, W. J. (1992) 'Welfare Economics, Power and Property', in W. J. Samuels, *Essays on the Economic Role of Government*, vol. 1, New York: New York University Press, pp. 56–138.

Schmid, A. A. (1989) *Benefit–Cost Analysis: A Political Economy Approach*, Boulder, CO: Westview Press.

A. ALLAN SCHMID

WELFARE STATE AND THE ECONOMY

In its academic usage, 'welfare state' goes beyond anti-poverty reduction programmes like those stressed by journalistic uses of the term in the United States, to include a broad range of income security and employment policies, such as public pension and job training programmes, as well as services such as health care and child care. Spending on the welfare state has been large, typically constituting over half of national public spending in virtually all affluent democracies since the mid twentieth century (Hicks 1999). The direct and indirect economic consequences of this capacious welfare state – for equity, security and more – appear to have been correspondingly large; and battles over welfare state policies have been at the centre of the domestic politics of modern nations, affluent democracies in particular.

Writing in 1883, during a period of increased industrialization and urbanization, and when Germany's Bismarck was introducing the first welfare programmes, economist Adolf Wagner recognized the growing role of the state and its need to maintain its legitimacy by providing public programmes to offset the human costs of **economic development**. Wagner formulated the 'law of expanding state activity' ([1883]1958: 1–8), according to which, in European nations, the 'pressure for social progress' leads to a growth of the public sector. From Wagner's law various students of the welfare state derived an explanation of the growth of the public economy which asserts that citizens' demands for services and their willingness to pay taxes to finance them increase with the increase in economic wealth. In these explanations, it is economic development and the means it generates that is responsible for the development of the welfare state. However, recent authors have tended to view economic development as no more than setting the stage for, or playing accompaniment to, political action (Esping-Andersen 1990; Hicks 1999; Huber and Stephens 2001). Here, conservative efforts to cement mass loyalties in the face of developmental upheavals, including liberal and socialist challenges, figure prominently for the first social policy innovations of the late nineteenth century, while labour unions and left-centre parties, working-class parties in particular, have been seen to dominate into the third quarter of the twentieth century (Esping-Andersen 1990; Hicks 1999; Huber and Stephens 2001).

The last, foundational installations of basic income maintenance programmes were completed during the decades bordering World War II, and massive welfare state expansion continued well into the early 1980s. Income maintenance benefits constantly improved while social services soared in Scandinavian welfare states (Huber and Stephens 2001). However, by the 1980s changed demographic and economic conditions shifted the agenda to austerity, ushering in a process referred to by various authors as the 'crisis and retrenchment of the welfare state'. The first countries to cut benefits in the late 1970s and intensify them in the 1980s were the first that experienced significant increases in unemployment, which reduced the number of contributors to the welfare state and thus applied fiscal pressures to it (Korpi and Palme 2003). Not only rising unemployment but also aging populations, among other factors, increased the costs of the commitment to social insurance (Huber and Stephens 2001). However, regardless of pressures to reduce rates of entitlement and actual benefits, a general upward trend in aggregate social spending increased as the retired and unemployed ballooned (Huber and Stephens 2001). Once instituted, social policies developed support bases among those who benefit from them, in addition to those groups that supported their original enactment, thereby placing constraints on both left and right governments (Huber and Stephens 2001; Pierson 2001). Governments found it very difficult to reduce welfare benefits because net beneficiaries outnumbered net contributors, and because the elderly, having paid for others' larger benefits, were now unwilling to accept reductions in theirs (Huber and Stephens 2001). Thus, the pressures of people applying for legally entitled benefits that had driven up public spending made retrenchment difficult. Post-Thatcher Great Britain and National-Party-led New Zealand aside, cuts in welfare rights of access and benefits tended to reflect efforts to devise more robust welfare states or stymied rather than successful efforts to dismantle them (Huber and Stephens 2001).

When we survey theories of welfare states, numerous authors point to the importance of three political and three non-political factors for the development of the welfare state. Among non-political factors, increasing affluence (and fiscal capacity, despite some neo-liberal reversals), societal aging and rising long-term unemployment are the big three. Key political factors include labour union strength, centre-left party rule and neo-corporatism – the latter consisting of incorporation of large labour union confederations into macroeconomic social and labour market policy-making (Hicks 1999). Class mobilization, or the effect of group politics, appears largely mediated by nation-states and their policy legacies, in line with Skocpol's 'polity centred' view (e.g. Hicks 1999: ch. 6). Early social insurance reform was driven by state-contingent worker pressures. Increasingly, the class-linked mediation of the politics of economic interests appears to extend to business as well as labour (Swenson 2002). The role of **business associations** outside of corporatist configurations of interests may be relatively direct and large. Although the role of conservative and free-market liberal parties appears to have been generally geared towards averting or slowing down welfare state advance, that of business associations may have been relatively more accommodative with respect to welfare state extensions (Swenson 2002).

Some have argued that the era of slow-down and contraction since the early 1980s has been one of permanent budgetary austerity marked by new policy determinants

(Pierson 2001). In particular, these are seen as the pull of international economic openness and competitiveness, and unsustainable demographic and slack labour market pressures for welfare state increase, versus the push of interests deeply vested in the welfare state. However, economic growth and competitiveness *per se* appear to have been marginal factors in welfare state transformation, Britain and New Zealand and possible turns to their respective 1980s and 1990s modes of hyper-neoliberalism aside (Huber and Stephens 2001). It may be that any effective 'new politics' of these interests vested in the welfare state are principally an aspect of the old politics of social democratic parties supporting the welfare state, albeit increasingly by rendering it more robust rather than expanding it without acknowledged limit (Kenworthy 2004). Key to the new 'robust' welfare state has been a stress on supporting the expansion of the labour market and employment through active labour market and child care policies (Kenworthy 2004).

This takes us to the economic consequences of welfare state policies – for the distribution of market income, redistribution of final income through state transfer spending and taxation, economic growth and employment growth more particularly.

The distribution of pre-tax pre-transfer ('market') household income is a function of the degree of earnings inequality among employed individuals, the distribution of (full-time and part-time) employment across households, household size and structure (e.g. share of single-adult households) and marital homogamy (the tendency of high earners to be married to high earners and of low earners to be married to low earners). Generous income maintenance programmes – e.g. unemployment and sickness insurance – may raise the 'reservation wage' at which job-seekers are willing to accept a job. This puts upward pressure on wages at the low end of the distribution and may thereby reduce earn-

ings inequality among the employed. At the same time, such benefit generosity may reduce employment among the less skilled by making employers less able to afford to hire them and by making job-seekers less interested in taking a job. This may increase market inequality. Some have asserted that generous benefits can contribute to marriage avoidance, if certain types of benefits are available only to non-married adults (as with AFDC in the United States). There tends to be less pre-tax pre-transfer inequality in countries with more generous welfare states (Kenworthy 2004), but it is not clear that there is a genuine causal relationship.

The redistributive effect of welfare states is achieved via the structure and/or generosity of social-welfare programmes (Goodin *et al.* 1999; Kenworthy 2004). 'Social democratic' welfare regimes in the Nordic European countries provide benefits to most of the population, and those benefits tend to be relatively equal (flat-rate). This in itself alters the distribution of income – assuming taxes are progressive, giving every household an equal lump sum will reduce inequality. And redistribution is furthered via some targeting and inequality in benefit levels, as well as by taxing back part of the benefits paid to those who need them the least. (Social democratic welfare states also tend to offer extensive public provision of services such as health care and child care. Though it does not alter the distribution of income, this too has an equalizing effect.) 'Conservative' welfare regimes in the continental European countries rely disproportionately on social insurance programmes, in which benefit levels are determined by one's former labour market status and earnings level. This type of programme is not particularly redistributive in design, but because of some targeting and a relatively high overall level of transfers, continental welfare states nevertheless do tend to achieve a significant amount of redistribution. In the Anglo (English-

725

speaking) countries, 'liberal' welfare regimes provide minimal benefits that are narrowly targeted to the most needy (means-tested). In principle, this is the most efficient redistributive strategy; it achieves the most redistribution per amount of income transferred. But in comparative terms the level of transfers in these nations tends to be low, so relatively little redistribution is effected.

Cross-country studies have consistently found that greater welfare state generosity is linked with lower inequality and lower relative poverty via more extensive redistribution (Hicks and Kenworthy 2003; Kenworthy 2004). An important lingering limitation of these studies is the possibility that welfare state generosity might have adverse employment effects and therefore widen the distribution of market income; in this view, the welfare state reduces inequality and/or poverty that it itself caused. The few attempts to explore this possibility have found little evidence of it, but more research is needed on this question.

Debates about macroeconomic consequences of welfare states have long centred around the possibility of a trade-off between equality and economic growth (output growth). More recently, attention has focused on concern that welfare state generosity may impede employment growth. The traditional view is that welfare state generosity will reduce investment and work incentives and therefore hurt economic growth (Atkinson 1994). The wealthy are the principal source of savings and investment in a capitalist economy; if their income is reduced by progressive taxation, investment is expected to be lower. And those with limited labour market prospects may be tempted to live off government benefits rather than work.

A newer view holds that welfare state generosity may have growth-enhancing effects (Atkinson 1994). Redistribution may increase consumer demand, which can be as or more important than investment in bolstering growth. It may increase the ability of those with low earnings to invest in skill development – particularly a college education. By reducing inequality, it also may increase trust, cooperation, civic engagement and other growth-enhancing forms of social capital.

There is an extensive empirical literature on the effects of social-welfare programmes on economic growth in affluent countries, but it has yielded nothing close to a consensus. In his survey of this research, Atkinson (1995: 196) concludes that

> While popular argument often refers in a casual way to the experience of Sweden or other countries with sizeable levels of spending, the results of econometric studies are mixed, and provide no overwhelming evidence that high spending on social transfers leads to lower growth rates.

Generous benefits and high income tax rates may reduce the supply of labour by lowering its payoff relative to non-work, and high payroll tax rates may reduce the demand for labour. On the other hand, there are some elements of welfare state generosity that may have pro-employment effects. In particular, government provision or subsidization of child care may boost employment by facilitating women's labour-market participation.

Recent research on employment developments has tended to yield findings that do suggest adverse effects of certain elements of the welfare state. A variety of cross-country studies have found detrimental effects of tax rates and the level and/or duration of unemployment benefits on unemployment or employment. However, across countries these welfare state-related policies tend to be fairly closely correlated with various labour market policies and institutions, such as employment regulations, union strength and the degree of pay inequality. This makes it somewhat difficult to isolate the causal effects of particular elements of these configurations

(Kenworthy 2004). Some recent studies suggest that adverse employment effects are peculiar to the conservative welfare states of continental Europe, rather than being a product of welfare state generosity per se.

Research on the impact of policies such as public child care provision and parental leave on women's employment is inconclusive. Some cross-country research suggests no particular link between such policies and gender equality in the labour market, However, some have found that women's share of the labour force tends to be higher in countries that have more extensive social-welfare programmes, including more extensive 'family-supportive' policies (Kenworthy 2004).

Overall, within the affluent democracies, the welfare state persists as a central aspect of domestic politics with decidedly strong egalitarian effects and few or marginal adverse ones on the aggregate economy, if only because of dogged efforts by those political parties most associated with extensive welfare states to keep them economically efficient, beneficial and popular.

References and further reading

Atkinson, Anthony B. (1995) 'The Welfare State and Economic Performance', *National Tax Journal*, 48: 171–98.

Esping-Andersen, Gøsta (1990) *The Three Worlds of Welfare Capitalism*, Princeton, NJ: Princeton University Press.

Goodin, Robert E., Headey, Bruce, Muffels, Ruud and Dirven, Henk-Jan (1999) *The Real Worlds of Welfare Capitalism*, Cambridge and New York: Cambridge University Press.

Hicks, Alexander (1999) *Social Democracy and Welfare Capitalism*, Ithaca, NY: Cornell University Press.

Hicks, Alexander and Kenworthy, Lane (2003) 'Varieties of Welfare Capitalism', *Socio-Economic Review*, 1: 27–62.

Huber, Evelyne and Stephens, John (2001) *Development and Crisis of the Welfare State*, Chicago: University of Chicago Press.

Kenworthy, Lane (2004) *Egalitarian Capitalism?* New York: Russell Sage Foundation.

Korpi, Walter and Palme, Joakim (2003) 'New Politics and Class Politics in the Context of Austerity and Globalization: Welfare State Regress in 18 Countries, 1975–1995', *American Political Science Review*, 97: 425–46.

Pierson, Paul (2001) 'Coping with Permanent Austerity: Welfare State Restructuring in Affluent Democracies', in Paul Pierson (ed.), *The New Politics of the Welfare State*, New York: Oxford University Press, pp. 410–56.

Swenson, Peter (2002) *Capitalists against Markets: The Making of Labor Markets and Welfare States in the United States and Sweden*, New York: Oxford University Press.

Wagner, Adolph ([1883]1958) 'The Extracts on Public Finance', in R. A. Musgrave and A. T. Peacock (eds), *Classics in the Thery of Public Finance*, London: Macmillan.

VELINA PETROVA
LANE KENWORTHY
ALEXANDER HICKS

WINNER-TAKE-ALL ECONOMY

Although the best sopranos have always earned more than others with slightly lesser talents, the earnings gap is sharply larger now than it was in the nineteenth century. Today, top singers like Renée Fleming earn millions of dollars per year – hundreds or even thousands of times what sopranos only slightly less talented earn. Given that listeners in blind hearings often have difficulty identifying the most highly paid singers, why is this earnings differential so large?

The answer lies in a fundamental change in the way we consume most of our music. In the nineteenth century, virtually all professional musicians delivered their services in concert halls in front of live audiences. (In 1900, the state of Iowa alone had more than 1,300 concert halls!) Audiences of that day would have been delighted to listen to the world's best soprano, but no one singer could hope to perform in more than a tiny fraction of the world's concert halls. Today, in contrast, most of the music we hear comes in recorded form, which enables the best soprano to be literally everywhere at once. As soon as the master recording has been made, Renée Fleming's performance can be burned on to compact disks at the same low cost as for a slightly less talented singer's.

Tens of millions of buyers world-wide are willing to pay a few cents extra to hear the most talented performers. That knowledge leads rival recording companies to bid intensively for the best singers, assuring that these singers will earn multimillion-dollar annual salaries. Slightly less talented singers earn much less, because the recording industry simply does not need them.

The market for sopranos is an example of a winner-take-all market, one in which small differences in performance translate into large differences in pay. Such markets have long been familiar in entertainment and professional sports. But as technology has enabled the most talented individuals to serve broader markets, the winner-take-all reward structure has become an increasingly important feature of modern economic life.

For example, the tax advice industry, once a quintessentially local-practitioner market, was transformed by the emergence of tax software for the masses. Following an intense competition, critics anointed Intuit's Turbo-Tax and a small handful of other programs as the most comprehensive and user-friendly among the hundreds of rival packages. And once consumers agreed on which software was best, producers could stamp out additional copies at virtually no marginal cost. In the process, incomes shifted markedly from local accountants to the organizers of winning tax software providers.

Growth in productivity of the top performers and the more open bidding for their services have occurred for different reasons in different markets. In broad terms, however, the story has been much the same in other arenas as in the markets for sopranos and tax advice. Significant winner-take-all transformations have been identified in retailing, law, journalism, consulting, medicine, investment banking, corporate management, publishing, design, fashion, even the hallowed halls of academe.

References and further reading

Frank, Robert H. and Cook, Philip J. (1995) *The Winner-Take-All Society*, New York: Free Press.

ROBERT H. FRANK

WORK ETHIC See: Religion and Economic Life; Weber

WORK, SOCIOLOGY OF

Work is an elementary condition of human history. In its most general meaning the term refers to purposeful human activity of all types and forms, and in all material fields and social contexts: intellectual, artistical, manual, social, political work; agricultural, industrial, service, administrative and military work; household, artisanal, occupational work; forced, voluntary, paid work; male, female work. Work is an intrinsically social activity; it always implies a – however rudimentary – social division of tasks and functions which is mediated by symbolically based interaction and communication. At the same time, work is never a communicative relationship between human actors alone, but implies a tripartite relationship between the actors and some third 'material' or 'objective'.

There is a vast historical and cultural diversity of forms and settings of work which hardly could be described exhaustively even by a most encompassing social theory. Actually, sociology of work (SOW) confines itself mostly to a much more limited object: 'Work under capitalism' (Tilly and /Tilly 1998). Labour markets in modern capitalism and the labour process within and between organizations are the key fields of interest of SOW. It should be recalled that wage-labour is a historically rather new phenomenon. In most times of history, labour was not a commodity, but had the character of slave, serf, artisanal or family work; it took place either in larger organizations, like armies or farmyards, or in households, workshops, local communities. The commercialization of human labour developed at a larger social scale in Europe not earlier than in the late eighteenth and nineteenth century. It was the result of a series of social and political reforms which **Polanyi** (1944) had termed as the 'Great Transformation'. These reforms abolished the formerly very tight economic regulations of the absolutist states and extended the money nexus from finished products to land and human labour, turning them into commodities. The 'Great Transformation' has been going on since then around the globe. Even today, however, probably the largest share of all work is still being done outside labour markets.

The exchange of labour power for wages is a transaction which requires a special sociological analysis. For several reasons it does not fit into economic textbook models of 'normal' market exchange.

Although labour is treated as a commodity in capitalism, actually its commodity character is a 'fiction' (Polanyi). Workers are not born for the purpose of selling their labour power at the market. The supply of labour cannot be adapted to a rise or fall of demand in the same way as the supply of other commodities can. Falling wages as a rule will not result in a decline of the supply of labour; contrarily, the supply of labour will rise, as workers will put in extra hours or do second jobs in order to compensate the negative effect of wage declines on their income. Although the worker is personally free like any other market actor, his/her commodity in fact cannot be separated from the personality of the owner. His/her personal fate inevitably is involved into the turnover of his commodity to a much higher degree than in the case of sellers of finished goods.

A further characteristic of labour is that its use-value cannot be consumed immediately after buying. Rather, the consumption of labour is a second process taking place in a separate arena called 'organizations'. The work contract is of dual nature: on the one hand it is a market transaction; on the other hand it is a relationship of authority, as the worker has to submit to the organizational authority of the employer in order to fulfil his contractual obligations.

Moreover, the work contract is 'indeterminate', as only the terms of remuneration and certain formal aspects of work performance, such as working hours and occupational areas, are specified more or less. The details of the work process and the concrete tasks and outputs are not determined in advance, but left to the discretion of the employer. The work contract can be characterized as an agreement, which grants the employee a wage or salary for his willingness to place his time and effort at the disposal of those directing the organization (Simon 1976). The authority of the employer is limited by legal and contractual boundaries and by the incentives which the organization can offer; he cannot expect complete subordination of the worker. The fairness of the balance between performance and remuneration, the legitimate degree of entrepreneurial or managerial control are 'contested' issues (Edwards 1979). They are a continuous source for open or latent conflicts in labour relations which create a need for negotiation and settlement.

Whereas the buyer of a finished product or service expects a detailed technical description of the potential outputs of the product, the performance of workers cannot be determined in advance as precisely. Labour is a factor of production which is endowed with the capacity of learning and developing new abilities in the process of its use. The openness to variable, flexible and newly developed tasks is a key quality of labour. Employment can range from simple, routine and machine-like jobs to highly complex and variable ones. However, employees cannot simply be 'ordered' to learn by managers and supervisors. They cannot be programmed like machines, but need to qualify themselves in a process of social interaction with instructors and supervisors. Qualification is a process which always – even in the case of most simple jobs – presupposes a minimum of genuine motivation to cooperate on the side of the worker. Therefore it is important for employers to screen the motivation, the learning and development potential of applicants before hiring them. The function of screening can be fulfilled by third institutions like vocational schools or universities, or by internal procedures in the employing organization.

Although many functions of labour can be taken by machines and technical systems, there remain some unique qualities of labour which cannot be copied or replaced even by most sophisticated technologies. One of these qualities is the capacity of workers to 'safeguard' processes against unforeseen contingencies and risks. Only workers, not machines and computers, can take responsibility to finish tasks and processes successfully. A further unique quality of human workers is their capacity to cooperate. Cooperation means the willingness to coordinate action, to share knowledge and information, to give mutual help in critical situations. Obviously, cooperation is a crucial factor for the efficiency of production processes in quantitative as well as in qualitative terms. A third and perhaps even more important quality of labour is creativity. Only human beings, not machines or computers, can develop and implement ideas about new products and technical solutions. Creating new things out of 'nothing' is a unique capacity of labour which is vital for capitalist growth and development.

However, like the process of learning mentioned above, the mobilization of these capacities depends on complex social conditions. Neither responsibility, not cooperativeness, nor innovation can be enforced or commanded unilaterally by the employer.

A minimum of 'voluntary' acceptance on the side of employees and between them is always needed. Like other social systems, firms and organizations are faced with the problem of double and multiple contingency of social action. The solution of these problems cannot be left to the market, but requires particular social governance structures, whose study is the main task of SOW. Very roughly, these structures fall into four categories: formal organizations, technology, networks and institutions.

Formal organizations

Since the theories of Smith, Marx, Weber and Taylor's movement of 'scientific management', the impact of formal organizations or 'bureaucracies' on the structuration of labour processes had been a key concern of SOW. Organizations are getting formalized, as management lays down a set of rules defining positions, competencies, hierarchical levels and chains of command, procedures of qualification and promotion and other structural features. Not only structures but also processes can be formalized by dividing planning and execution, and introducing detailed 'best practice' standards for single tasks. The degree of formalization of structures and processes is variable and tends to correlate positively with the size of organizations. Mintzberg (1979) distinguishes between standardization of processes, products and qualifications. These levels of standardization correspond to three types of formal organization, which he calls the machine bureaucracy, the divisionalized form and the professional bureaucracy.

From a historical point of view, the most influential model for formal organizations were the absolutist state bureaucracies. Within the private sector, formalization developed with the rise of large-scale industrial companies and trusts in the USA and Europe since the late nineteenth century according to the logic of 'economies of scale and scope' (Chandler 1990); the spread of Taylorism since the 1920s deepened this trend. The deskilling and 'degradation' of work resulting from continuing Taylorist reorganization of work was a theme of intensive debates in industrial sociology in the decades after the Second World War (e.g. Braverman 1974).

The formalization of organization plays an important role in reducing the uncertainties of administrative decision-making. It supports the functional autonomy of the system towards the environment and enhances its capacity for strategic action. However, bureaucratic rules are set unilaterally by the management and are of an essentially impersonal character. Formal organizations tend to induce a behaviour of employees which is confined to conformity with rules and prescriptions. Although the syndrome of the 'bureaucratic personality' (Robert Merton) may be efficient under particular conditions, such as in routine functions of public administration or in industrial mass production, it is certainly not the most efficient form of organizational rationality, as Max Weber still believed. Bureaucratic forms of organization tend to fail, where firms have to adapt flexibly to individualized, complex and changing market environments. They cannot evoke those virtues of employees which are important under such conditions: commitment, cooperation and creativity. Where bureaucracies nevertheless are successful in adapting and innovating, this is often due to a silent recourse to other governance structures, networks and institutions, which will be discussed below.

A further weakness of formal organizations is that they do not provide a satisfactory solution to the problem of how to control the controllers, staffs and managers themselves. Often formalization results in a 'bureaucratic circle' (Michel Crozier), leading to an expansion of staff and managerial personnel, increasing inflexibility and mistrust between the actors, again fur-

ther bureaucratization, with the consequence of rising inefficiencies and costs. Problems of this kind were an important background of the decentralization moves in many companies and for the popularity of concepts like 'Organization Culture', 'Lean Production' or 'Business Re-engineering' since the late 1980s.

Technology

Technical systems are created, if a sequence of operations is duplicated in the form of an algorithm, which is then implemented in some 'material', whether electronic circuits, chemical reactions or mechanical machines. Employees have to supervise and control these systems, to manage the boundaries and interfaces to the environment and to fill the gaps between mechanized or automated operations. With increasing automation, functions of supervision, maintenance and boundary management tend to become more important, while process bound-functions of the latter type do not disappear, but get fewer. Many industrial sociologists view technology as a form of social control, since it seems to govern the behaviour of employees in a similar impersonal way, as formal organization does; 'Fordist' assembly lines, for example, continue the logic of formal organization with the means of technology.

Like in the case of organizational formalization, however, social control which is based on technology is anything but perfect. It can be efficient in the case of low-skilled, highly standardized jobs. Assembly lines, call centres or 'McDonaldized' service jobs are the domain of technical control. However, with the advance of modern information and communication technologies work tends to become more complex than more routinized, as many studies (e.g. Frenkel et al. 1999) have demonstrated. The high costs of capital-intensive production systems enhance the need for employee cooperation and commitment. As a rule, high-tech and capital-intensive industries are therefore characterized by high wages and benefits, cooperative **industrial relations** and elaborated internal labour markets (Tilly and Tilly 1998).

Networks

Networks are configurations of multilateral social exchange between autonomous actors. Social exchange is a form of give and take, which in difference to economic exchange is based on extended time horizons and standards of social reciprocity beyond narrow utility. Trust and personal links, but also mutual resource dependencies are vital factors (Powell 1990). Networks are less centralized than formal organizations and hierarchies, but more closed than markets, and tend to discriminate 'outsiders'. They develop in almost all spheres of work and can be found within and across firms and organizations. Informal groups at the workplace, or mutual career support networks are well known examples for intra-organizational networks. Inter-organizational networks exist in manifold forms: cooperation clusters between artisans or small firms in the craft sector, film or media industries; vertical disintegration and outsourcing practices, strategic alliances between large firms, regional industrial networks (Castells 2000). The strength of networks is their flexibility and their capability to foster cooperation and mutual commitment between the participants. Networks play a vital role in compensating the functional deficits of formal organizations and technical systems. At the other hand their capacity for coordinated strategic action is often low, and their innovative potential is limited, too, as they sometimes develop cartel-like attitudes towards outsiders.

Institutions

Institutions emerge where actors coordinate their actions by orientating themselves to a set of commonly accepted social norms. Since they are based on mutual recognition, they bind the identities of actors to a higher degree than organizations and also networks. Institutions are historical entities which are not created by fiat but are transferred from one generation to the next. Many institutions in the field of work and labour have historical roots in the pre-modern era, such as the family and family business, the institution of vocational training or the institution of employer paternalism. Other institutions emerged in the history of the modern labour movement, such as collective bargaining, labour law or the welfare state. Sometimes, seemingly modern institutions turn out to be a re-invention of older traditions, such as, for example, the Japanese system of life-long employment (Koike 1988).

Present-day labour institutions are concentrated on three areas:

1. Qualification: except in the case of 'secondary' labour markets with low-skilled, temporary or marginal jobs, individual processes of mobility and qualification usually do not follow spontaneous market forces, but are structured by institutional patterns. The build-up of human capital and the careers of employees are regulated on the one hand by vocational labour markets and education systems, on the other by internal labour markets in large firms. The relative importance of the basic three institutionalized segments of the labour market – the usual distinction is that between unskilled, vocational and internal labour markets – varies considerably between countries.

2. Collective bargaining: the institutions of collective bargaining acknowledge the position of employees and employers as collective actors and set down material standards for wages, non-wage benefits, work conditions

and rules for the procedures of negotiations. The focus of collective bargaining can be located at industrial,
sectoral or enterprise level. In the last
decades a trend towards decentralization of collective bargaining can be
observed in most countries (ILO
1997). Employees in computer, high-
tech and new media industries are,
as a rule, weakly unionized and tend
to prefer new, individualized and
'direct' forms of participation against
traditional collective bargaining.

3. Social security systems provide institutionalized rules and funds for protecting the individual employee
against the risks of worklife, such as
sickness, accident, unemployment;
they provide pensions for the old-
aged and handicapped. Like the other
institutions of work they are located
at the level of society as well as that of
the enterprise.

Modern labour institutions lay the ground
for the legitimacy of entrepreneurial action
and thus play a vital part in mobilizing
personal commitment, cooperativeness and
creativity of employees. In combination
with the other governance structures mentioned above they provide essential social
preconditions for securing economic innovation and growth.

At present, the pressure for reform and
change in the field of labour institutions is
rising in many countries. The globalization
of the economy, the spread of advanced
information and communication technologies and organizational strategies of market-
led decentralization are leading to attempts
to strengthen the element of market control
at cost of organizational and institutional
governance structures. However, these
reforms surely will not remove the basic
need of non-market coordination in the field
of labour relations. Rather, the likely result
will be a shift in the configuration of governance mechanisms; in particular, tech-

nology and networks seem to become more
important, while the influence of organizations and institutions tends to decline.

References and further reading

Braverman, H. (1974) *Labor and Monopoly Capi-
tal. The Degradation of Work in the Nineteenth
Century*, New York: Monthly Review Press.
Castells, M. (2000) *The Rise of the Network
Society*, second edition, Oxford, Blackwell.
Chandler, A. D., Jr (1990) *Scale and Scope. The
Dynamics of Industrial Capitalism*, Cambridge,
MA: Harvard University Press.
Edwards, R. (1979) *Contested Terrain*, New
York: Basic Books
Frenkel, S. J., Korczynski, M., Shire, K. A. and
Tam, M. (1999) *On the Front Line. Organi-
zation of Work in the Information Economy*,
Ithaca, NY: Cornell University Press
ILO (International Labour Office) (1997)
'Industrial Relations, Democracy and Social
Stability', *World Labour Report*, Geneva: ILO.
Koike, K. (1988) *Understanding Industrial Rela-
tions in Modern Japan*, Basingstoke, UK:
Macmillan.
Mintzberg, H. (1979) *The Structuring of Organi-
zations*, Englewood Cliffs, NJ: Prentice Hall.
Polanyi, K. (1944) *The Great Transformation*,
Boston: Beacon Press.
Powell, W. W. (1990) 'Neither Market nor
Hierarchy: Network Forms of Organiza-
tion', *Research in Organizational Behaviour*,
12: 295–336.
Simon, H. A. (1976) *Administrative Behaviour*,
third edition, New York: Macmillan.
Tilly, C. and Tilly, C. (1998) *Work under Capit-
alism*, Boulder, CO: Westview Press.

CHRISTOPH DEUTSCHMANN

WORK TEAMS

A work team is generally defined as a group
of persons organized and working together
to accomplish a specific task(s). A work
team can vary from a group of persons who
interact minimally and perform individual
tasks in a group context to a highly structured, interdependent group of persons
with a great deal of decision-making
authority related to their work (Hackman
1978). The study and development of the

work team appear to have their origin in Europe beginning with Trist and Bamforth's examination of teams that had spontaneously organized in British coal mines (1951). This coal mine research was continued in Scandinavia by Thorsrud who focused on work teams that not only took responsibility for significant technical or service tasks but also took responsibility for determining such things as how and when the work would be accomplished. Thorsrud introduced terms such as 'autonomous work group' and 'self-managed work groups' to distinguish those work teams that held a variety of decision-making responsibilities regarding their work. Meanwhile, in the 1960s in Japan, work teams were becoming an important component of efforts to improve the quality of the goods produced. The rationale used was that work teams could assist in reducing the redundancy in checking the quality of a product at each stage of its development. And, as Deming explained in *Out of the Crises* (1982), reducing the number of quality checkpoints reduced personnel and consequently saved time and money.

In the United States, work teams appear to have been first tried on a large scale by the General Electric Company in the 1960s where over a hundred teams were created in their factories. However, it was not until the 1970s that the use of work teams began to grow, spurred by international competition and reports of the advantages of work teams used in new plants by Procter and Gamble and General Foods. By the early 1980s, 'quality circles' (QCs) were being used by organizations. QCs were work teams that not only focused on working together to get specific tasks accomplished but met on a regular basis (e.g. weekly) in order to discuss ways of improving the work process and then making recommendations to their superiors based on their discussions.

By the end of the 1980s and on into the twenty-first century, the use of work teams has grown. In particular, organizations have attempted to gain the potential positive effects of allowing the members of work teams not only to focus on working together to accomplish their tasks but also to make many of the management decisions related to their work, such as the order in which various tasks are done, who will do which tasks, and addressing day-to-day work problems. As such management decisions have been turned over to the work teams, the terms 'autonomous work teams', 'self-directed work teams' and 'self-managed work teams' have become popular.

A self-managed work team (SMWT) has come to be defined as an interdependent group of employees who are responsible for managing and performing technical tasks that result in a product or service being delivered to an internal or external customer (Orsburn *et al.* 1990). Typically, the team consists of five to fifteen employees who are responsible for managing all or most aspects of the work including, for example, planning and scheduling, monitoring team performance, and staffing. Likewise, they are responsible for all the technical aspects of the work, whether it is preparing prescriptions for hospital patients or assembling a computer board to be installed in a 'smart bomb'. In addition, team members of an SMWT often are able to rotate these management and technical responsibilities among themselves periodically (Yeatts and Hyten, 1998).

The growing use of SMWTs has been the result of international competition that has forced organizations to look for better ways of competing. The growth in SMWTs is evident through national surveys that have documented the interest of corporations in teamwork and self-management (Lawler 1986), through surveys of employees who have described their job characteristics, and through an increasing number of conferences on self-managed teams.

The use of SMWTs has been found to result in higher performance at less cost (e.g. Lawler 1986; Wellins *et al.* 1994;

Yeatts and Hyten 1998). Unfortunately, social scientists have had difficulty substantiating this statistically because of the difficulty in isolating the individual effects of self-management from the many other factors operating in the workplace. Consequently, it appears that the effects of SMWTs are best determined through methodologies such as case studies rather than quantitative analyses.

Case studies have shown that under the right circumstances employees within SMWTs produce more at work than employees organized in a more hierarchical, traditional structure because they *not only* perform technical skills but management skills as well (Wellins *et al.* 1994; Orsburn *et al.* 1990). And, as Ray and Bronstein have shown in *Teaming Up* (1995), the decisions made by SMWTs are extremely effective because those making the decisions – the team members – are the most knowledgeable persons about the work. SMWTs have also been found to produce more innovation and creativity since the team members can see the whole work process.

Other performance improvements that have been attributed to SMWTs include the ability of team members to fill in for each other when a member of the team is absent, ability to help each other during times when important work has to be completed on a deadline, the ability to schedule and assign the work to match the needs and strengths of team members, and more empathy for each other's problems because the team members understand what each other is doing. Simultaneously, the number of first-line supervisors needed has been found to be less than in a more traditional work environment because the SMWT members handle a large portion of the management responsibilities (Shonk 1992). Thus, the employees within SMWTs have been found to perform at a higher level and at a lower cost than

employees within more traditional work environments.

On the other hand, the ability of SMWTs to accomplish higher performance at less cost is highly dependent on a variety of factors, including the work and interpersonal processes, numerous environmental factors such as management support and employee training, the team's design, and characteristics of the employees themselves (Hackman 1978; Yeatts and Hyten 1998). When these factors have *not* been planned and implemented to support the SMWT, studies report little or no performance improvements, little or no cost advantages, and in some cases have found that SMWTs can have negative effects.

References and further reading

Deming, W. E. (1982) *Out of the Crises*, Cambridge, MA: MASS Institute for Technology Center.

Hackman, J. R. (1978) 'The Design of Self-Managing Work Groups', in B. T. King, S. Streufert and F. E. Fiedler (eds), *Managerial Control and Organizational Democracy*, New York: John Wiley and Sons.

Lawler III, E. E. (1986) *High-Involvement Management*, San Francisco CA: Jossey-Bass.

Orsburn, J., Moran, L., Musselwhite, E., Zenger, J. H. and Perrin, C. (1990) *Self-Directed Work Teams: The New American Challenge*, Homewood, IL: Business One Irwin.

Ray, D. and Bronstein, H. (1995) *Teaming Up: Making the Transition to a Self-Directed Team Based Organization*, New York: McGraw-Hill.

Shonk, J. H. (1992) *Team-Based Organizations: Developing a Successful Team Environment*, Homewood, IL: Business One Irwin.

Trist, E. and Bamforth, K. (1951) 'Social and Psychological Consequences of the Long Wall Method of Coal Getting', *Human Relations*, 4(1): 3–38.

Wellins, R. S., Byham, W. C. and Dixon, G. (1994) *Inside Teams: How 20 World-Class Organizations are Winning through Teamwork*, San Francisco: Jossey-Bass.

Yeatts, D. E. and Hyten, C. (1998) *High-Performing Self-Managed Work Teams: A Comparison of Theory to Practice*, Thousand Oaks, CA: Sage.

DALE E. YEATTS

WORLD-SYSTEMS APPROACH TO ECONOMIC SOCIOLOGY

The world-systems approach to economic sociology focuses on whole intersocietal systems. The main insight is that important interaction networks (trade, information flows, alliances and fighting) have woven polities and cultures together since the beginning of human social evolution. Studies of the development of economic institutions need to take intersocietal systems (world-systems) as the units that evolve rather than single societies. Economic institutions have evolved over the millennia in ways that have allowed world-systems to become larger and more hierarchical.

Since the emergence of ocean-going transportation in the fifteenth century the multicentric Afroeurasian system incorporated the western hemisphere. Before the incorporation of the Americas into the Afroeurasian system there were many local and regional world-systems (intersocietal networks). Most of these became inserted into the expanding European-centred system largely by force, and their populations were mobilized to supply labour for a colonial economy that was repeatedly reorganized by the changing geopolitical and economic forces emanating from the European and (later) North American core societies.

The intellectual history of the world-systems approach has roots in classical sociology, Marxian political economy, geopolitics and theories of social evolution. But in explicit form the world-systems approach emerged only in the 1970's when Samir Amin, Andre Gunder Frank and Immanuel Wallerstein began to formulate the concepts and to narrate the analytic history of the modern world-system.

The modern world-system can be understood structurally as a stratification system composed of economically, culturally and militarily dominant core societies (themselves in competition with one another) and dependent peripheral and semiperipheral regions, a few of which have been successful in improving their positions in the larger core/periphery hierarchy, while most have simply maintained their relative positions.

This structural perspective on world history allows us to analyse the cyclical features of social change and the long-term trends of development in historical and comparative perspective. We can see the development of the modern world-system as driven primarily by capitalist accumulation and geopolitics in which businesses and states compete with one another for power and wealth. Competition among states and capitals is conditioned by the dynamics of struggle among classes and by the resistance of peripheral and semiperipheral peoples to domination and exploitation from the core. In the modern world-system the semiperiphery is composed of large and powerful countries in the Third World (e.g. Mexico, India, Brazil, China) as well as smaller countries that have intermediate levels of **economic development** (e.g. the East Asian NICs). It is not possible to understand the history of social change in the system as a whole without taking into account both the strategies of the winners and the strategies and organizational actions of those who have resisted domination and exploitation.

It is also difficult to understand why and where innovative institutional change emerges without a conceptualization of the world-system as a whole. New organizational forms that transform institutions and that lead to upward mobility most often emerge from societies in semiperipheral locations. Thus all the countries that became hegemonic core states in the modern system had formerly been semiperipheral (the Dutch, the British and the United States). This is a continuation of a long-term pattern of social evolution that Christopher Chase-Dunn and Thomas D.

Hall have called 'semiperipheral development'. Semiperipheral marcher states and semiperipheral capitalist city-states had acted as the main agents of empire formation and commercialization for millennia. This phenomenon arguably also includes organizational innovations in contemporary semiperipheral countries (e.g. Mexico, India, South Korea, Brazil) that may transform the now-global system.

This approach requires that we think structurally. We must be able to abstract from the particularities of the game of musical chairs that constitutes uneven development in the system to see the structural continuities. The core/periphery hierarchy remains, though some countries have moved up or down. The interstate system remains, though the internationalization of capital has further constrained the abilities of states to structure national economies. States have always been subjected to larger geopolitical and economic forces in the world-system, and as is still the case, some have been more successful at exploiting opportunities and protecting themselves from liabilities than others.

In this perspective many of the phenomena that have been called 'globalization' correspond to recently expanded international trade, financial flows and foreign investment by transnational corporations and **banks**. Much of the globalization discourse assumes that until recently there were separate national societies and economies, and that these have now been superseded by an expansion of international integration driven by information and transportation technologies. Rather than a wholly unique and new phenomenon, globalization is primarily international economic integration, and as such it is a feature of the world-system that has been oscillating as well as increasing for centuries. Recent research comparing the nineteenth and twentieth centuries has shown that trade globalization is both a cycle and a trend.

The great chartered companies of the seventeenth century were already playing an important role in shaping the development of world regions. Certainly the transnational corporations of the present are much more important players, but the point is that 'foreign investment' is not an institution that only became important since 1970 (nor since World War II). Giovanni Arrighi has shown that finance capital has been a central component of the commanding heights of the world-system since the fourteenth century. The current floods and ebbs of world money are typical of the late phase of very long 'systemic cycles of accumulation'.

Most world-systems scholars contend that leaving out the core/periphery dimension or treating the periphery as inert are grave mistakes, not only for reasons of completeness, but also because the ability of core capitalists and their states to exploit peripheral resources and labour has been a major factor in deciding the winners of the competition among core contenders. And the resistance to exploitation and domination mounted by peripheral peoples has played a powerful role in shaping the historical development of world orders. The comparison of the modern world-system with earlier regional systems has also revealed that all hierarchical world-systems have experienced a process of semiperipheral development in which some of the societies 'in the middle' innovate and implement new technologies of power that drive the processes of expansion and systemic transformation (see below). Thus world history cannot be properly understood without attention to the core/periphery hierarchy.

Phillip McMichael (2004) has studied the 'globalization project' – the abandoning of Keynesian models of national development and a new (or renewed) emphasis on deregulation and opening national commodity and **financial markets** to foreign trade and investment. This approach focuses on the ideological aspects of the recent wave of international economic integration. The term many prefer for this turn in global discourse is 'neo-liberalism' but it has also been called 'Reaganism/Thatcherism' and the 'Washington Consensus'. The worldwide decline of the political left predated the revolutions of 1989 and the demise of the Soviet Union, but it was certainly also accelerated by these events. The structural basis of the rise of the globalization project is the new level of integration reached by the global capitalist class. The internationalization of capital has long been an important part of the trend towards economic globalization. And there have been many claims to represent the general interests of business before. Indeed, every modern hegemon has made this claim. But the real integration of the interests of capitalists all over the world has very likely reached a level greater than at the peak of the nineteenth-century wave of globalization.

This is the part of the theory of a global stage of capitalism that must be taken most seriously, though it can certainly be overdone. The world-system has now reached a point at which both the old interstate system based on separate national capitalist classes, and new institutions representing the global interests of capital exist, and are powerful simultaneously. In this light each country can be seen to have an important ruling class fraction that is allied with the **transnational capitalist class**. The big question is whether or not this new level of transnational integration will be strong enough to prevent competition among states for world hegemony from turning into warfare, as it has always done in the past, during a period in which a hegemon (the United States) is declining.

Neo-liberalism began as the Reagan-Thatcher attack on the welfare state and labour unions. It evolved into the Structural Adjustment Policies of the International Monetary Fund and the triumphalism of the ideologues of corporate globalization

after the demise of the Soviet Union. In United States foreign policy it has found expression in a new emphasis on 'democracy promotion' in the periphery and semiperiphery. Rather than propping up military dictatorships in Latin America, the emphasis has shifted towards coordinated action between the CIA and the US National Endowment for Democracy to promote electoral institutions in Latin America and other semiperipheral and peripheral regions. William I. Robinson points out that the kind of 'low intensity democracy' that is promoted is really best understood as 'polyarchy', a regime form in which elites orchestrate a process of electoral competition and governance that legitimates state power and undercuts more radical political alternatives that might threaten their ability to maintain their wealth and power by exploiting workers and peasants. Robinson convincingly argues that polyarchy and democracy-promotion are the political forms that are most congruent with a globalized and neo-liberal world economy in which capital is given free reign to generate accumulation wherever profits are greatest.

The insight that capitalist globalization has occurred in waves, and that these waves of integration are followed by periods of globalization backlash has important implications for the future. Capitalist globalization increased both intranational and international inequalities in the nineteenth century and it has done the same thing in the late twentieth century. Those countries and groups that are left out of the 'beautiful époque' either mobilize to challenge the hegemony of the powerful or they retreat into self-reliance, or both. Globalization protests emerged in the non-core with the anti-IMF riots of the 1980s. The several transnational social movements that participated in the 1999 protest in Seattle brought globalization protest to the attention of observers in the core, and this resistance to capitalist globalization has continued and grown despite the setback that occurred in response to the terrorist attacks on New York and Washington in 2001. The recent global antiwar demonstrations against the Bush administration's threat to engage in 'preventative' war against Iraq involve many of the same movements as well as some new recruits. The several transnational social movements face difficult problems of forming alliances and cooperative action. The idea of semiperipheral development implies that support for more democratic institutions of global governance will come from democratic socialist regimes that come to power in the semiperiphery. This has already happened in Brazil, where the new labour government strongly supports the movement for global social justice.

There is an apparent tension between those who advocate deglobalization and delinking from the global capitalist economy and the building of stronger, more cooperative and self-reliant social relations in the periphery and semiperiphery, on the one hand, and those who seek to mobilize support for new, or reformed institutions of democratic global governance. But in fact these strategies are complementary, and each can benefit by supporting the other. Self-reliance by itself, though an understandable reaction to exploitation, is not likely to solve the problems of humanity in the long run. The great challenge of the twenty-first century will be the building of a democratic and collectively rational global commonwealth. The world-systems approach can be an important contributor to this effort.

References and further reading

Amin, Samir (1997) *Capitalism in the Age of Globalization*, London: Zed Press.

Arrighi, Giovanni (1994) *The Long Twentieth Century*, London: Verso.

Chase-Dunn, Christopher (1998) *Global Formation*, Lanham, MD: Rowman and Littlefield.

Chase-Dunn, Christopher and Hall, Thomas D. (1997) *Rise and Demise: Comparing World-Systems*, Boulder, CO: Westview Press.

Frank, Andre Gunder (1998) *Reorient*, Berkeley, CA: University of California Press.

McMichael, Philip (2004) *Development and Social Change: A Global Perspective*, fourth edition, Thousand Oaks, CA: Pine Forge Press.

Meyer, John W., Boli, John, Thomas, George M. and Ramirez, Francisco (1997) 'World Society and the Nation-state', *American Journal of Sociology*, 103: 144–81.

Modelski, George and Thompson, William R. (1996) *Leading Sectors and World Powers*, Columbia, SC: University of South Carolina Press.

Robinson, William I. (1994) *Promoting Polyarchy*, Cambridge: Cambridge University Press.

Shannon, Thomas R. (1996) *An Introduction to the World-Systems Perspective*, Boulder, CO: Westview Press.

Wallerstein, Immanuel (2000) *The Essential Wallerstein*, New York: New Press.

CHRISTOPHER CHASE-DUNN

X-EFFICIENCY

The term was coined by Harvey Leibenstein, who developed x-efficiency theory in a series of works beginning in 1966 and continuing into the 1990s. Economists have traditionally understood efficiency as the allocation of resources to their most productive uses. In general, the combination of utility maximization and competitive markets will produce allocative efficiency. Leibenstein, however, argued that productivity often fell short of what was possible given factor inputs and the state of technology. Consequently, an economic unit might be inefficient even with an optimal allocation of resources. Leibenstein referred to the gap between actual and potential output as 'x-inefficiency'. One source of x-inefficiency was limitation of effort by workers. Another was incomplete information search, which resulted in the neglect of opportunities for improvement. Leibenstein argued that losses from x-inefficiency might be much greater than losses from allocative inefficiency.

Leibenstein held that x-inefficiency was based in human psychology: when possible, people try to reduce stress and to maintain good social relations with their co-workers. However, x-inefficiency was not simply the result of an inherent preference for leisure: organizations could develop distinctive patterns of norms and interpersonal relations, some enhancing productivity

and others limiting it. In either case, once these patterns had been established they were not easily changed. Leibenstein suggested that there were 'inert areas' within which people had no strong preference among different effort levels. Choice of effort within the inert area would conform to custom or the general group preference. Consequently, changing prevailing effort levels was a collective action problem, not just a matter of changing individual incentives.

Leibenstein's account attracted a good deal of attention in economics, much of it directed at discovering whether x-efficiency actually existed. Critics argued that apparent cases of x-inefficiency merely reflected a failure to adequately take account of transaction costs or preferences for leisure. Although the empirical reality of x-inefficiency is now widely accepted, this development has not led to the fundamental shift in the foundations of economic theory that Leibenstein urged. Rather, x-efficiency has been incorporated into the general framework of utility maximization under imperfect information.

Sociologists generally did not need to be persuaded of the reality of x-inefficiency. However, in the sociological literature, x-inefficiency is usually lumped together with related ideas such as bounded rationality and transaction costs. There has been little effort to distinguish these concepts theoretically or empirically. Overall, x-efficiency theory has not has much impact on economic sociology. This is partly because Leibenstein presented it in an abstract fashion, making few suggestions about observable factors that might affect the degree of x-inefficiency. Moreover, since Leibenstein's account focused on individual psychology, it did not appeal to sociologists interested in structural factors. X-efficiency theory has been more important in economics, where it contributed to the development of models of the firm based on incomplete information.

References and further reading

Frantz, R. S. (1997) *X-Efficiency: Theory, Evidence and Applications*, second edition, Boston: Kluwer Academic.

Leibenstein, H. (1966) 'Allocative Efficiency vs "X-Efficiency"', *American Economic Review*, 56: 392–415.

DAVID WEAKLIEM

index

of heterodox economics, 175, 215; heterodox economics, 215, 458, 583, 590, 701, 702, 703; history, 210–16; *homo economicus*, 514–15, 530, 555, 570, 640, 697–98, 705; maximization, 439–40; modern trends, 213–15, 703; orthodoxy, 211, 212–13; pluralism, 212; professionalization, 211–12; pure theory, 414–15; rational choice theory, 550–51; risk and uncertainty, 583–84; science, 217–18; sociology and, 192–93, 197–98, 203; sociology of, 216–21; transition economies, 685; value, 701, 702–3

economics and sociology: Convention School, 112–13; economic action, 165–73; equilibrium, 250; gifts, 305

Economics and Sociology (Lowe), 414, 416

Economics and Sociology (Swedberg), 184

Economics of the Transition Period (Bukharin), 629

economics, sociology of: economic sociology and, 216–21

economies of scale, 51, 189

economies of scope, 51, 190

economy: concepts of, 175, 222–24, 677; democracy, 142–45; ecology, 161–64; economics and, 220–21; informal economy, 112, 352–53, 476, 596, 693; Marxist theories, 38, 222; real economy, 455–57; state, 651–54; trust, 694

Economy and Society (Parsons and Smelsner), 197–98, 249–50, 295, 382, 458, 505

Economy and Society (Weber), 84, 337, 394, 715–16, 717

Edelman, L.: law, 395

Edgeworth, F.: economic action, 165, 166

education, 69, 334, 523, 542, 572

effective demand, 524

efficiency: bargaining theory, 23; Chandler, 52; Coase's Theorem, 543–44; contract, 108; Convention School, 113; equilibrium, 251; rational choice theory, 552; social organization, 225–26; transaction cost theory, 680; wages, 227–28, 390–91, 461–62; welfare economics, 721; x-efficiency, 740–41

Egidi, M.: risk and uncertainty, 582

egoism, 697, 698

Ehrenhalt, A.: communitarianism, 80–81

Eisenstadt, S. N.: revolutions, 579

electronic commerce, 229–30

Elementary Forms of Religious Life (Durkheim), 11, 60, 155–56, 588

Elias, N.: habitus, 318

Elster, J.: deliberation, 140, 142

embeddedness: art, 12; concepts of, 231–33; decision theory, 135; disembeddedness, 232; duality, 661; economic action, 172–73; economic sociology, 234–35; economics, 705; enterprise groups, 241; entrepreneurship, 243–44; firms, 284–86; global, 235–36, 654–55; importance of, 203; incentives, 343; moral economy, 466; social capital, 605–6; solidarity, 642–43; states, 652; subsidiaries, 226; *see also* networks

Embong, A. R.: transnational capital class, 689

emergent properties, 264

Emerson, R. M.: exchange, 273

Emery, F. E.: environment, 89

emotions: concepts of, 236–40; homophily principle, 607; transactional needs, 295

employer associations, 33

employment: *see* labour

enclave economy, 253, 254–56

Engels, F.: 'capitalism', 35; class, 435; crisis, 132; feudalism, 434–35; historical materialism, 324–27; philosophy and, 436; revisionism, 436; socialism, 630

engineering, 541–42

England, P.: gender, 300

Enlightenment, 339, 452–53

enterprise groups, 240–41

entitlement theory, 403

entrepreneurship: Austrian economics, 16; class, 593; community, 86, 243; concepts of, 241–42; culture, 244–45; decay, 425; economic action, 165, 166; economic development, 195–96; economic sociology, 242; embeddedness, 243–44; ethnic economy, 251–57; ethnomethodology, 513; institutions, 245–46; investment, 383; Marxist theories, 244; middleman-minority, 252; obstacles to, 593–94; social capital, 476; traders, 645

environment: change, 90–91; environmental sociology, 161–62; interchange, 506; social environments, 618–19; system theory, 667

equality: earnings, 580; globalization, 308; inheritance, 357, 359; legal, 590–91; post-industrialism, 523; scarcity, 590–91; theories of, 246–48; welfare state, 402

equilibrium: concepts of, 248–49; economic knowledge, 186; economic sociology, 250; economics, 249; employment, 382; general equilibrium, 213, 214, 250, 502; history, 213; multiple equilibria, 507; Nash, 297, 298; social, 249–51, 503; socialism, 630–31

Erikson, R.: class mobility, 388

Germany: banks, 20–22; collective action, 74; inheritance, 355, 357; innovation, 497; managerial forms, 52; national character, 645; origins of capitalism, 43; private property, 143; redistribution, 561; standards, 651; varieties of capitalism, 40; welfare state, 59, 287

Getting a Job (Granovetter), 389

Giddens, A.: closure, 345; globalization, 306; historical materialism, 326; modernization, 453–54; money, 458–59; structuration theory, 656–59

Gierke, O.: contract, 144

The Gift (Mauss), 437–39

gifts: civilization, 600; potlatch, 526; reciprocity, 304, 559; symbolic, 438; theories of, 304–5

Gill, S.: transnational capital class, 688

Gingrich, D. W.: varieties of capitalism, 43

Gini coefficient, 712

Gintis, H., 11

Glass, J.: gender, 301

Glass-Steagall Act 1933, 21

globalization: causes, 306–7; convergence, 307–8; corporate governance, 124; corporatism, 127; culture, 309; decision theory, 135; definitions, 305–6; deindustrialization, 138–39; economic sociology, 309; effects, 307–9; embeddedness, 235–36, 654–55; entrepreneurship, 245; EU, 260; fiscal policy, 289; health, 45–46; ideology, 340; inequality, 308; management, 424; microsociology, 450; nation-state, 308–9; organizations, 490–91; sociology, 261–62; state expenditures, 546; transnational capital class, 688–89, 738; unemployment, 9; varieties of capitalism, 199–200; world-systems, 737–39

goal-attainment: *see* AGIL

Godbout, J. T.: gifts, 304

Goffman, E.: classification, 68

gold standard, 654

Goldin, C.: gender, 302

Goldscheid, R.: fiscal sociology, 286; taxes, 288

Goldstone, J.: revolutions, 580, 581

Goldthorpe, J. H.: class mobility, 388; corporatism, 124

good governance, 310–11

goods, 311–12

Goodwin, J.: revolutions, 579

Gouldner, A., 698; organizations, 88; reciprocity, 558

governance: accounting, 2–3; good governance, 310–11; hybrids, 374; modes of, 41; transaction cost theory, 681

'Governing Economic Life' (Miller & Rose), 3

Grameen Bank Project, 447

Gramophone (magazine), 105

Gramsci, A.: flexibilization, 290

Granovetter, M.: community, 86; constructionism, 614–15; decision theory, 135; economic action, 200, 201, 203; economic imperialism, 184; embeddedness, 234–35, 473; equality, 247; gifts, 305; knowlege, 187; networks, 475, 607, 661; new institutionalism, 367; norms, 484; relational institutionalism, 368; trust, 692

Great Depression, 102, 136, 212, 524, 530, 565

The Great Transformation (Polanyi), 232–33, 428, 438, 466, 515, 652–53, 729

Greenfeld, L.: reputation, 577

Greenfield, L.: colonialism, 78

Greif, A.: classification, 68; cultural beliefs, 299

Grief, A.: trust, 694

groups: enterprise groups, 240–41; psychology, 272; selection hypothesis, 11; social rationality, 619–20; social ties, 628; work groups, 272, 284

growth rates, 43

Grundisse (Marx), 514

Grusky, D. B.: equality, 247

guanxi, 312–14

Guetzkow, H.: organization theory, 49

Guillén, M.: corporate governance, 122

Gultekin, B.: transition economies, 684

Gurr, T.: revolutions, 579

Gutman, A.: communitarianism, 81

Habermas, J.: deliberation, 140; historical materialism, 326

habits: definitions, 315–16; institutions, 316–17, 364–65; rational choice theory, 557

habitus, 317–20

Hage, J.: innovation, 496

Hakansson, H.: networks, 476

Halévy, E.: utilitarianism, 697, 698

Hall, P. A.: deliberation, 141; varieties of capitalism, 42, 43, 123, 520–21

Hall, R.: earnings, 157

Hall, S.: consumer culture, 100

Hall, T. D.: world-systems, 736–37

Halliday, F.: revolutions, 581

Hannan, M. T.: demography, 489; niches, 479; populations, 478

Hansen, A.: institutionalism, 212

Hardin, R.: trust, 690, 692

Harris, J.: social capital, 178; transnational capital class, 689

662, 663; protection, 516; rational choice theory, 552, 553; regulation, 280–81, 518, 564–66; religion, 572; self-regulation, 232–33; social networks, 201–2; socialism, 631; socio-economics, 636–37; sociology, 427–32; structural approach, 661–62; as subsystems, 636–37; transaction costs, 13; transition economies, 206–10; trust, 433; value, 702; winner-take-all, 727–28

Markets and Hierarchies (Williamson), 234, 488

Marmot, M.: health, 44

Marshall, A.: career and influence, 211, 432–34; economic action, 166, 167; evolutionary economics, 263; industrial districts, 346–47; just price, 380; markets, 428; rationality, 555

Marshall, T. H.: citizenship, 60, 384

Martimort, D.: agency, 535

Martinez-Alier, J.: ecology, 163

Marx, K.: career and influence, 434–37

Marxist theories: alienation, 8, 435; art, 12; beliefs, 29; 'capitalism', 35; characteristics of capitalism, 36; class, 62, 64–67, 434–35; classification, 68; colonialism, 79; consumption, 440; crisis, 132–33; determinism, 435–36; division of labour, 641; economic action, 171; economic concepts, 222; economic laws, 38; entrepreneurship, 244; evolutionary economics, 263; exchange, 271; exploitation, 37, 64–67, 211; fetishism, 185; feudalism, 434–35; flexibilization, 290; historical materialism, 324–27; ideology, 339; internal relations, 436; Keynsianism, 382–83; labour, 630; law, 394; leadership, 142; leisure, 401; liberalism, 403; lottery markets, 412; management, 425; markets, 428; metabolic rift, 163; money, 458; organizations, 88; ownership and control, 498; philosophy, 436; power, 94; response to, 38–39; revolutions, 579; scarcity, 590; Schumpeter critique, 594; scientism, 436; significance of, 37; slavery, 591; socialism, 630; sociology, 436–37; Sombart, 644; taxes, 287, 288; traditional economies, 678; transnational capital class, 688–89; value, 702–3; voluntarism, 435–36; welfare capitalism, 59

mass consumption, 5–6

Masson, A.: inheritance, 357

mathematical economics, 213

M.A.U.S.S., 305

Mauss, M.: career and influence, 437–39; classification, 112; gifts, 304–5, 559, 698;

habitus, 318; money, 438; moral economy, 438–39; religious sociology, 597; social economy, 439; symbolic and economic exchange, 438

Max Weber (Swedberg), 54

maximization: behaviour, 186; concept of, 439–40; optimum, 486–87; rationality, 554–58; risk and uncertainty, 584–85

McAdam, D.: revolutions, 581

McCaffrey, D.: financial markets, 280

McCloskey, D. N.: rhetoric, 217

McDonaldization, 420–22, 731

McGuire, P.: relational institutionalism, 368

McMichael, P.: world-systems, 737–38

McPherson, J. M.: niches, 478–79

McRobbie, A., 100

Meade, J.: income estimation, 212

means-ends, 504

Means, G.: corporations, 122; management, 424–25; managerialism, 40

means of consumption, 440–42

mechanical models, 189–90

mechanism explanations, 616–17

Meckling, W.: incentives, 7

medicine as a profession, 540–41

Meillassoux, C.: economic anthropology, 175

Menger, C.: Austrian economics, 16, 17; barter, 363; economic action, 166, 168; evolutionary economics, 263; marginal utility analysis, 211; Methodenstreit, 329, 446; money, 455–56; social evolution, 404; utilitarianism, 699

mental attitude, 36

mental models, 442–44

mercantilism, 602, 672

Mercantilism (Heckscher), 216

mergers, 445, 465

Merleau-Ponty, M.: habitus, 317–20

Merton, R. K.: functional alternatives, 295; homophily principle, 607; organizations, 88; reputation, 577; science, 571; self-fulfilling prophecy, 563

Methodenstreit: Austrian economics, 17; first and second, 446; historical school, 329; ideal type, 336; money, 455–57; opponents, 404; pure economic theory, 414

methodological individualism, 16

Mexico, 220

Meyer, J.: organizations, 489; revolutions, 581

microcredit, 447–48

microeconomics, 225–26

middleman-minority, 252, 254

Middletown (Lynd), 85

organic models, 189–90

Organisation du Travail (Blanc), 35

Organization Theory (Jaffee), 91–92

organizational culture, 92

organizations: capitalism, 36; Carnegie School,
47–50; change, 479–80, 488–89, 613–14;
classification, 68; complex, 88–92; Convention
School, 114; discrimination, 149–50; ecology,
188–89; economic, 188–92; economic
sociology, 282; efficiency, 226; environment,
89–90, 488–90; fields, 491–93; human
resources, 332–34; innovation, 494–97;
inter-organizational relationships, 188–92;
location, 480; loose coupling, 410–11; Marxist
theories, 88; networks, 473; niches, 478–80;
origins, 487–88; populations, 478; proliferation
of, 488–90; rational choice theory, 553–54;
régulation school, 567; resource dependency,
642; resource partitioning theory, 479; social
capital, 69–71; social explanation, 490–91;
sociology of work, 730–31; structure, 660–61;
technology, 89; theories of, 487–91;
transaction cost theory, 681; typology, 188–92;
see also bureaucracy

Organizations and Society (journal), 1

Organizations in Action (Thompson), 90, 488

Organizations (March and Simon), 47, 49, 487

organized economies, 42, 43

The Origins of Nonliberal Capitalism (Streeck), 43

Orton, J. D.: loose coupling, 410

O'Sullivan, M.: corporate governance, 122

Out of the Crises (Deming), 734

Outline of a Theory of Practice (Bourdieu), 318

Overhead Value Analysis, 98

Overshoot (Catton), 161

ownership and control: agency, 7, 499, 500; large
corporations, 497–500; Marxist theories, 498;
profits, 707; systems, 666; theories of, 424–26

ownership patterns, 123–24

Oxford English Dictionary, 15, 78

Packard, V.: consumer culture, 100

Padgett, J. F.: relational institutionalism, 368

Page, K.: governance, 311

Paige, J.: revolutions, 579

Palmer, D.: ownership and control, 500

panics, 280–81

parallel markets, 633

Pareto-efficiency, 23, 141

Pareto-improvements, 721

Pareto, V.: career and influence, 502–3; economic
action, 172; equilibrium, 249; rationality, 555

Park, D.: niches, 479

Parkin, F.: closure, 345

Parsons, T.: AGIL, 85, 223–25, 295, 505–6,
665; career and influence, 51, 52, 503–7;
community, 85; critiques, 656; disatisfaction
with, 200–201; double contingency, 152–53;
ecological fields, 159–60; economic
imperialism, 184; economic sociology, 197–98;
equilibrium, 249–50; modernization, 198;
money, 458; norms, 481, 482; ownership
and control, 666; rationality, 555; social
action, 249, 502, 504; utilitarianism, 698

partnerships, 374

Pasmore, W.: environment, 89–90

path-dependence, 507–9, 615, 650

Pattison, P.: fields, 372

Pearson, D. E.: communitarianism, 81

peasant societies, 467–68, 599

Peirce, C. S.: pragmatism, 528–29

Perez-Castrillo, D.: agency, 534

'Perfect Equilibrium' (Rubinstein), 23

performance: concepts of, 509–10; corporate
crime, 118; logic, 370–71; monitoring, 460–
62; shareholders, 510; social conflict, 178–79;
stakeholders, 510; varieties of capitalism, 42–
43, 520

Perrow, C.: monopolies, 463–64; technology, 89

Pescosolido, B. A.: health, 46

Peters, K.: budgeting processes, 4

Petersen, T.: mathematics, 534

Peterson, R.: art, 12

Petty, W.: deindustrialization, 139; earnings, 157

Pfeffer, J.: exchange, 488–89; organizations, 92

Phelan, J. C.: health, 45

phenomenology: economic sociology, 200;
habitus, 200; ideal type, 338; theories of,
511–13

The Phenomenology of the Social World (Schutz),
337

philanthropy: health and, 46

Phillips, D.: communitarianism, 81–82

philosophy: Marxist theories, 436

Pietism, 571

Pigou, A.: economic action, 166–67

Piore, M.: flexibilization, 291; inclusion and
exclusion, 344; labour markets, 660;
organizations, 190–91

Pirenne, H.: entrepreneurship, 244

The Place of Science in Modern Civilization
(Veblen), 671

planning, 212, 522, 529, 631

Plattner, S.: art, 12

production: agency, 534; Austrian economics, 16; decision theory, 135; innovation, 42; markets, 662; means of, 440; outputs and processes, 494–95; structural approach, 661–62; theories of, 537

productivity: deindustrialization, 139; non-contractual antecedents, 389–91

professions: consultants, 97; increase, 522; mobility, 642; models, 540–43; professionalization, 539–40

profits: social responsibility, 620–21

Proletarischer Sozialismus (Sombart), 644

property: appropriation, 543–45; democracy, 142–45; entitlement theory, 403; private, 365–66; protection, 392–93; scarcity, 417–18

property rights: agency, 7; China, 686; closure, 346; Coase's Theorem, 543–44; democracy, 142; firms, 463; markets, 427, 625; socialism, 632

prospect theory: behavioural economics, 26

protectionism, 673

The Protestant Ethic (Weber), 38, 176–77, 182, 233–34, 337, 344, 571, 717, 718

Przeworski, A.: revolutions, 579; transition economies, 686

psychoanalysis: advertising, 5; mother-child dyad, 151

psychology: behavioural economics, 25–28; beliefs, 29; exchange, 268, 271, 272; groups, 272; incentives, 342–43; mental models, 442–44; organizations, 88; politics, 405; social capital, 183

public budgets, 545–46

public choice: inflation, 351; policy, 215; taxes, 288; theories of, 547–49

public finance, 286–89

public goods, 86, 547, 690, 707

public interest groups, 648

public opinion: Convention School, 113

'public-private' distinction, 142–43

Puritanism, 571

Putnam, R.: communitarianism, 81; social capital, 178, 202, 606–7, 610

Putzel, J.: social capital, 178

Puxty, A. G.: critical theory, 3

quantity theory of money, 137, 212

QWERTY, 507

R&D, 189–90, 191

race: character, 379; wealth inequality, 712, 713; *see also* ethnic economy

racism: capitalism, 644–45; historical school, 330

Radcliffe, A. R.: functional imperatives, 294

radical economics, 215

Rand, A.: libertarianism, 406–7

Rao, H.: fields, 371

Rapaczynski, A.: transition economies, 684

Rasmusen, E.: mathematics, 534

rational choice: asymmetrical information, 552–54; beliefs, 29; corporate crime, 119; economic growth, 182; economic imperialism, 184; exchange, 175; full information, 551–52; habitus, 317; incentives, 342, 344; institutions, 367–69; interdependencies, 551–52; moral economy, 467; networks, 370; norms, 484–85; outcomes, 589; preferences, 557; scarcity, 551; social rationality, 618–20; taxes, 288; theories of, 550–54; uncertainty, 582, 585

rational system theory, 91

rationality: adaptive rationality, 299; auctions, 15; bounded rationality, 27, 47, 215, 278–79, 423, 443, 682; calculation, 134; concepts of, 554–58; critiques, 556–58; decision theory, 135; definitions of, 550; economic action, 168–69; economic imperialism, 184; emotions, 237–38; entrepreneurship, 244; exchange, 271; experimental economics, 214–15; financial markets, 278–79; irrationality, 503; maximization, 554–55; maximizing intentionality, 555–56; 'natural rationality', 618; pragmatism, 530; risk and uncertainty, 584–85; scarcity, 551; social rationality, 618–20; transaction cost theory, 682; utilitarianism, 697–98

rationalization: capitalism and, 38–39; multidivisional forms, 51–52

Raub, W.: reputation, 575–76

Rawls, J.: inheritance, 359–60; justice, 698; welfare state, 402

Ray, D.: work teams, 735

Reagan, R., 39, 80

Reaganism, 738

reason: habits, 317

reciprocity: community, 84; definitions of, 515; embeddedness, 231–33; enforcement, 559–60; exchange, 272–73; game theory, 115, 560; gifts, 304, 559; integration, 193; nature of, 558–59; negative, 26; norm of, 558; strategy, 655; temporality, 558–59

redistribution: embeddedness, 231–33; poverty, 528; social expenditures, 545–46; theories of, 515, 561–62; welfare state, 560–61